THE NEW
WEBSTER'S
POCKET
DICTIONARY

THE NEW
WEBSTER'S
POCKET
DICTIONARY

THE NEW
WEBSTER'S
DICTIONARY

LEXICON PUBLICATIONS, INC.

ISBN: 0-7172-4545-4

A

A, a the first letter in the English alphabet

a *adj.* the singular indefinite article, one ‖ any, each one of a kind

aard·vark *n.* an African anteater

aard·wolf aard·wolves *n.* a carnivorous, burrowing animal of S. Africa

AB a blood group

A.B. Bachelor of Arts ‖ ablebodied seaman

a·back *adv.* with sails pressed back against the mast by head winds **taken aback** disagreeably astonished

ab·a·cus *pl.* **ab·a·ci ab·a·cus·es** *n.* a calculating instrument

abandon *v.t.* to give up ‖ to forsake ‖ to yield **a·bán·doned** *adj.* forsaken ‖ dissolute

a·ban·don·ment *n.* the act of abandoning

a·base a·bas·ing a·based *v.t.* to degrade, to humiliate **a·báse·d** *adj.* **a·báse·ment** *n.*

a·bash *v.t.* to cause embarrassment to, disconcert **a·básh·ment** *n.*

a·bate a·bat·ing a·bat·ed *v.t.* to reduce, do away with

ab·at·toir *n.* a slaughterhouse

ab·bess *n.* the superior of a nunnery or convent

ab·bey *n.* a monastery or convent

ab·bot *n.* the superior of an abbey **áb·bot·ship** *ns*

ab·bre·vi·ate ab·bre·vi·at·ing ab·bre·vi·at·ed *v.t.* to shorten

ab·bre·vi·a·tion *n.* the act or result of abbreviating a word

ABC *n.* the alphabet

ab·di·cate ab·di·cat·ing ab·di·cat·ed *v.t.* to give up

ab·di·ca·tion *n.* the renouncing of power or high office

ab·do·men *n.* part of the human body below the diaphragm ‖ *zool.* the hind part of insects, spiders etc. **ab·dom·i·nal** *adj.*

ab·duct *v.t.* to kidnap

ab·duc·tion *n.* the act of kidnapping

ab·duc·tor *n.* a person who kidnaps

a·ber·rant *adj.* straying from normal standards

ab·er·ra·tion *n.* a deviation from normal standards

a·bet a·bet·ting a·bet·ted *v.t.* to encourage, support in wrongdoing **a·bét·ment, a·bét·ter a·bét·tor** *ns*

a·bey·ance *n.* temporary suspension, usually of a custom, rule or law

ab·hor ab·hor·ring ab·horred *v.t.* to detest, regard with disgust

ab·hor·rence *n.* detestation, horror, disgust

ab·hor·rent *adj.* arousing horror or disgust

a·bid·ance *n.* (with 'by') compliance

a·bide a·bid·ing a·bode a·bid·ed *v.t.* to bear patiently, tolerate ‖ *v.i.* to continue in being, remain **a·bíd·ing** *adj.* enduring

a·bil·i·ty *pl.* **a·bil·i·ties** *n.* skill or power in sufficient quantity

ab·ject *adj.* despicable ‖ very humble ‖ servile

ab·jec·tion *n.* the state of being abject

ab·ju·ra·tion *n.* a formal renunciation

ab·jure ab·jur·ing ab·jured *v.t.* to renounce, give up solemnly, repudiate

a·blaze *pred. adj.* and *adv.* on fire ‖ lit up

a·ble *adj.* clever, competent, skilled

a·ble-bod·ied *adj.* robust and in good health

ab·ne·gate *part.* **ab·ne·gat·ing ab·ne·gat·ed** *v.t.* to renounce, give up

ab·ne·ga·tion *n.* renunciation, denial

ab·nor·mal *adj.* different from the norm **ab·nor·mal·i·ty** *pl.* **ab·nor·mal·i·ties** *n.*

ABO a classification of blood groups

a·board 1. *adj.* and *adv.* on or into a ship, plane, train etc. **2.** *prep.* on board

a·bode *n.* residence

a·bol·ish *v.t.* to do away with completely

a·bo·li·tion *n.* the act of abolishing ‖ the movement against slavery **ab·o·li·tion·ism, ab·o·li·tion·ist** *ns*

A-bomb *n.* atomic bomb

a·bom·i·na·ble *adj.* causing intense disgust

a·bom·i·nate a·bom·i·nat·ing a·bom·i·nat·ed *v.t.* to detest

a·bom·i·na·tion *n.* disgust ‖ a loathsome act

ab·o·rig·i·nal 1. *adj.* existing from the

earliest times **2.** an aborigine **ab·o·rig·i·nal·i·ty** *n.*

ab·o·rig·i·ne *n.* a native inhabitant of a country

a·bort *v.i.* to give birth to a fetus before it is viable ‖ *v.t.* to bring (a missile flight) to an end before completion of schedule

a·bor·tion *n.* the spontaneous or induced expulsion of a nonviable human fetus **a·bór·tion·ist** *n.* a person who induces abortions

a·bor·tive *adj.* of premature birth ‖ ending in failure

a·bound *v.i.* to be abundant

a·bout 1. *adv.* all around ‖ here and there ‖ in the opposite direction **2.** *prep.* concerning ‖ approximately

a·bove 1. *adj.* preceding, just mentioned **2.** *adv.* higher up, overhead ‖ earlier (in a book) **3.** *prep.* higher than ‖ beyond ‖ more than

a·brade a·brad·ing a·brad·ed *v.t.* to roughen or wear away

a·bra·sion *n.* the action of wearing by friction

a·breast *adv.* side by side

a·bridge a·bridg·ing a·bridged *v.t.* to shorten ‖ to curtail

a·bridg·ment, a·bridge·ment *n.* the act of shortening

a·broad *adv.* in a foreign land

ab·ro·gate ab·ro·gat·ing ab·ro·gat·ed *v.t.* to cancel, repeal, annul

ab·rupt *adj.* sudden, unexpected ‖ steep ‖ brusque in manner

ab·scess *n.* a localized collection of pus in the body **áb·scessed** *adj.*

ab·scond *v.i.* to flee secretly

ab·sence *n.* a being away ‖ lack

ab·sent *adj.* away, not present

ab·sent *v. refl.* to keep (oneself) away **ab·sent·tee ab·sen·tée·ism** *n.* persistent absence from work

ab·sent·ly *adv.* inattentively

ab·sent·mind·ed *adj.* preoccupied

ab·so·lute 1. *adj.* whole, complete ‖ pure **2.** *n.* something that is absolute

ab·so·lute pitch the pitch of a note ‖ the ability to identify a note sounded in

isolation

ab·so·lu·tion *n.* the forgiveness of sin

ab·so·lut·ism *n.* autocratic government

ab·solve ab·solv·ing ab·solved *v.t.* to set free from obligation, guilt or sin ‖ to acquit

ab·sorb *v.t.* to take up ‖ to take in as if by swallowing or sucking ‖ to interest profoundly

ab·sorb·en·cy *n.* the state of being absorbent

ab·sorb·ent 1. *adj.* having the ability to absorb **2.** *n.* a substance having this ability

ab·sorp·tion *n.* an absorbing

ab·stain *v.i.* (with 'from') to choose not to participate ‖ to choose not to indulge oneself

ab·sten·tion *n.* the act or practice of abstaining

ab·sti·nence *n.* refraining from food, drink or pleasure

ab·sti·nent *adj.* practicing abstinence

ab·stract 1. *adj.* considered apart from any concrete object, idealized ‖ theoretical **2.** *n.* a summary ‖ a short version of a piece of writing **3.** *v.t.* to take out, remove

ab·strac·tion *n.* abstracting ‖ formation of an idea apart from concrete things, situations etc.

ab·struse *adj.* not easy to understand

ab·surd *adj.* foolishly ‖ ridiculous

ab·surd·i·ty *pl.* **ab·surd·i·ties** *n.* something absurd

a·bun·dance *n.* richness, plenty

a·bun·dant *adj.* plentiful, copious

a·buse a·bus·ing a·bused *v.t.* to use badly or wrongly ‖ to ill-treat, injure ‖ to call (somebody) foul names

a·buse *n.* misuse ‖ ill-treatment ‖ an instance of injustice

a·bu·sive *adj.* characterized by abuse

a·but a·but·ting a·but·ted *v.i.* to border, ‖ to lean for support **a·bút·ment** *n.*

a·byss *n.* a chasm, deep gorge **a·byss·al** *adj.*

ac·a·dem·ic 1. *adj.* scholarly ‖ of theoretical interest **2.** *n.* a member of a university

ac·a·dem·i·cal *adj.* of or pertaining to a college or university

a·cad·e·my *pl.* **a·cad·e·mies** *n.* a school devoted to specialized training ‖ a society of scholars or artists

a cap·pel·la unaccompanied instrumentally

ac·cede ac·ced·ing ac·ced·ed *v.i.* to agree ‖ become invested with (an office)

ac·cel·er·ate ac·cel·er·at·ing ac·cel·er·at·ed *v.i.* to go faster

ac·cel·er·a·tion *n.* an increase of speed

ac·cel·er·a·tor *n.* a device for increasing speed

ac·cent *n.* the emphasis by stress on a word or syllable ‖ the mark used to indicate such a stress ‖ emphasis of any kind

ac·cent *v.t.* to emphasize

ac·cen·tu·al *adj.* characterized by accent

ac·cen·tu·ate ac·cen·tu·at·ing ac·cen·tu·at·ed *v.t.* to emphasize

ac·cen·tu·a·tion *n.* an accenting

ac·cept *v.t.* to take (something offered) ‖ to agree to meet (an obligation) ‖ to give an affirmative answer to

ac·cept·a·bil·i·ty *n.* the state of being acceptable

ac·cept·a·ble *adj.* agreeable, satisfactory **ac·cept·a·bly** *adv.*

ac·cept·ance *n.* approval

ac·cess *n.* way of approach ‖ right of approach

ac·ces·si·bil·i·ty *n.* the state or quality of being accessible

ac·ces·si·ble *adj.* easy to approach ‖ open **ac·ces·si·bly** *adj.*

ac·ces·so·ry, ac·ces·sa·ry 1. *n. pl.* **ac·ces·so·ries, ac·ces·sa·ries** something added for more convenience or usefulness **2.** *adj.* additional

ac·ci·dent *n.* a mishap ‖ a chance event

ac·ci·den·tal *adj.* happening by chance

ac·claim 1. *v.t.* to applaud by shouting **2.** loud applause ‖ enthusiastic praise

ac·cla·ma·tion *n.* a shouting of assent

ac·cli·mate ac·cli·mat·ing ac·cli·mat·ed *v.t.* to acclimatize **ac·cli·ma·tion** *n.*

ac·cli·ma·ti·za·tion *n.* the process by which plants and animals can live and reproduce in an environment different from their native one

ac·cli·ma·tize ac·cli·ma·tiz·ing ac·cli·ma·tized *v.i.* to become accustomed to a new climate or to new conditions

ac·co·lade *n.* any solemn recognition of merit

ac·com·mo·date ac·com·mo·dat·ing ac·com·mo·dat·ed *v.t.* to provide lodging for ‖ to oblige ‖ to adapt, adjust ‖ to settle **ac·cóm·mo·dat·ing** *adj.* obliging, willing to adapt

ac·com·mo·da·tion *n.* lodgings ‖ space, capacity to receive people ‖ a settlement or agreement

ac·com·pa·ni·ment *n.* a thing which goes naturally with something ‖ an instrumental part which supports a solo instrumentor or singer

ac·com·pa·nist *n.* someone who plays an accompaniment for a performer

ac·com·pa·ny ac·com·pa·ny·ing ac·com·pa·nied *v.t.* to escort to play an accompaniment for or to

ac·com·plice *n.* an active partner in a crime

ac·com·plish *v.t.* to bring to a successful conclusion, fulfil **ac·cóm·plished** *adj.* proficient

ac·com·plish·ment *n.* a superficial skill ‖ a feat

ac·cord *n.* an agreement ‖ harmony

ac·cor·dance *n.* agreement, conformity

ac·cor·dant *adj.* in harmony, in agreement

ac·cord·ing·ly *adv.* therefore, in consequence

ac·cor·di·on *n.* a small wind instrument **ac·cor·di·on·ist** *n.*

accordion pleats narrow pleats

ac·cost *v.t.* to approach ‖ to solicit

ac·count *v.t.* to consider, to explain, answer for ‖ to render an explanatory statement for (etc.)

account *n.* a statement of income and expenditure ‖ a statement, description, explanation **of no account** of no value, importance **on account** in part payment of a sum owed **on account of** because of **on one's own account** in one's own interest **to square accounts** to settle what is owing ‖ to redress a grievance **to take into account** to take into consideration

ac·count·a·bil·i·ty *n.* the quality or state of being accountable

ac·count·a·ble *adj.* answerable, bound to give an explanation **ac·count·a·bly** *adv.*

ac·count·ant *n.* a person skilled in keeping accounts

ac·cred·it *v.t.* to recognize (an educational institution) as meeting defined standards **ac·cred·i·ta·tion** *n.* **ac·cred·it·ed** *adj.* officially recognized

ac·cre·tion *n.* growth ‖ an adhesion of things usually separate

ac·cru·al *n.* something which has accrued

ac·crue ac·cru·ing ac·crued *v.i.* to come about as a natural consequence ‖ to accumulate

ac·cu·mu·late ac·cu·mu·lat·ing ac·cu·mu·lat·ed *v.t.* to gather together, amass

ac·cu·mu·la·tion *n.* an accumulating or being accumulated

ac·cu·ra·cy *n.* precision

ac·cu·rate *adj.* precise, exact

ac·cu·sa·tion *n.* a charge of having done wrong ‖ an indictment

ac·cuse ac·cus·ing ac·cused *v.t.* to charge with doing wrong ‖ to blame

ac·cus·tom *v.t.* to get used to **ac·cus·tomed** *adj.* usual, habitual

a·cer·bic *adj.* bitter, sour

ac·e·tate *n.* a salt or ester of acetic acid ‖ a synthetic fabric

a·ce·tic *adj.* relating to vinegar

ac·e·tone *n.* a colorless volatile inflammable liquid

a·cet·y·lene *n.* a colorless inflammable gas.

ache 1. *n.* a continuous dull pain **2.** *v.i.* **ach·ing ached** to suffer continuous dull pain

a·chiev·a·ble *adj.* able to be achieved

a·chieve a·chiev·ing a·chieved *v.t.* to carry out successfully ‖ to attain

a·chieve·ment *n.* the act of achieving

A·chil·les heel a vulnerable spot

ac·id *adj.* having a sour, sharp taste ‖ acid-producing ‖ LSD an hallucinogenic drug

a·cid·ic *adj.* acid-forming ‖ acid

a·cid·i·fy a·cid·i·fy·ing a·cid·i·fied *v.t.* to make sour

a·cid·i·ty *pl.* **a·cid·i·ties** *n.* the state or quality of being acid ‖ an acid remark

a·cid·ly *adv.* (of a manner of speaking) bitterly

ac·knowl·edge ac·knowl·edg·ing ac·knowl·edged *v.t.* to recognize as a fact, admit the truth of ‖ to report the receipt of **ac·knowl·edg·ment, ac·knowl·edge·ment** *n.*

ac·me *n.* the highest point, peak of perfection

ac·ne *n.* a skin disease

ac·o·lyte *n.* a person who assists a priest at Mass ‖ an admiring follower

a·cous·tic *adj.* pertaining to sound **a·cous·ti·cal** *adj.*

a·cous·tics *n.* the science of sound waves ‖ the study of hearing

ac·quaint *v.t.* to familiarize, inform

ac·quaint·ance *n.* someone whom one knows only slightly

ac·qui·esce ac·qui·esc·ing ac·qui·esced *v.i.* to agree, sometimes reluctantly

ac·qui·es·cence *n.* the act of acquiescing

ac·qui·es·cent *n.* submissive, compliant by nature

ac·quire ac·quir·ing ac·quired *v.t.* to gain for oneself

ac·quire·ment *n.* the act of acquiring

ac·qui·si·tion *n.* act of acquiring ‖ the thing gained or acquired

ac·quis·i·tive *adj.* very anxious to acquire

ac·quit ac·quit·ting ac·quit·ted *v.t.* to declare (a person) not guilty of an offense ‖ to settle (a debt) **ac·quit·tal** *n.*

ac·quit·tance *n.* full payment of a debt

a·cre *n.* a measure of land

a·cre·age *n.* the area of land in acres

ac·rid *adj.* bitter to the smell or taste

a·crid·i·ty *n.* the state or quality of being acrid

ac·ri·mo·ni·ous *adj.* harsh, bitter

ac·ri·mo·ny *pl.* **ac·ri·mo·nies** *n.* harshness or bitterness of temper or manner

ac·ro·bat *n.* someone who performs gymnastic feats **ac·ro·bat·ic** *adj.* **ac·ro·bat·i·cal·ly** *adv.* **ac·ro·bat·ics** *pl. n.*

ac·ro·nym *n.* a name made up of the initial letters of an official title

a·cross 1. *adv.* crosswise ‖ from side to side **2.** *prep.* on the other side of ‖ from one side to the other side of

a·cros·tic *n.* a composition, usually in verse, in which the initial, final or other prearranged letters in each line when taken together spell out a word

act *n.* a deed ‖ one of the main divisions of a play ‖ a feature in a variety show, ‖ a law passed by a legislative body

act *v.t.* to perform ‖ to play the part of ‖ *v.i.* to behave in a certain way ‖ to intervene effectively ‖ to produce an effect

act·ing 1. *adj.* doing temporary duty for someone else **2.** *n.* the art of performing in plays or films

ac·tion *n.* something done, a deed ‖ effective intervention ‖ enterprise, deeds as compared with words ‖ the series of events in a play or novel ‖ a proceeding in a court of law where someone seeks to enforce his rights ‖ goings on **ac·tion·a·ble** *adj.* **ac·tion·a·bly** *adv.*

ac·ti·vate ac·ti·vat·ing ac·ti·vat·ed *v.t.* to make particularly active

ac·ti·va·tion *n.* the act or process of activating

ac·ti·va·tor *n.* a substance which activates

ac·tive *adj.* busy, energetic ‖ (of a volcano) erupting from time to time ‖ productive, bearing interest

ac·tiv·ism *n.* a theory that calls for militant propaganda action by individuals

ac·tiv·ist *n.* someone who takes militant action in the service of a party or doctrine

ac·tiv·i·ty *pl.* **ac·tiv·i·ties** the state of being active ‖ *(pl.)* ways in which people use their energies

ac·tu·al *adj.* existing as a fact of experience, real

ac·tu·al·i·ty *pl.* **ac·tu·al·i·ties** *n.* reality

ac·tu·al·ly *adv.* in fact, really ‖ at this moment

ac·tu·ar·y *pl.* **ac·tu·ar·ies** *n.* a statistician who estimates risks, particularly in insurance

ac·tu·ate ac·tu·at·ing ac·tu·at·ed *v.t.* to put into action or motion **ac·tu·a·tion** *n.*

a·cu·i·ty *n.* shrewdness, acuteness of perception

a·cu·men *n.* keen insight or perceptiveness

a·cute *adj.* penetrating ‖ severe, sharp ‖ crucial, critical ‖ keen ‖ beginning suddenly

A.D. *ᴬᴺᴺᴼ* ᴰᴼᴹᴵᴺᴵ

ad·age *n.* an ancient piece of popular wisdom

a·da·gio 1. *adv.* and *adj.* in slow tempo **2.** a slow movement

ad·a·mant 1. *n.* a substance of utmost hardness **2.** *adj.* unyielding

a·dapt *v.t.* to put in harmony with changed circumstances ‖ to make more suitable by altering **a·dapt·a·bil·i·ty** *n.* **a·dapt·a·ble** *adj.*

ad·ap·ta·tion *n.* the act or process of adapting ‖ something adapted, sreen adaptation of a play

a·dapt·er *n.* a device for connecting two pieces of apparatus, esp. in electrical equipment

a·dap·tive *adj.* tending or able to adapt

add *v.t.* to join, unite or combine (something) with something else ‖ to add up ‖ *v.i.* to do addition

ad·den·dum *pl.* **ad·den·da** *n.* a supplementary part or appendix

ad·der *n.* a small poisonous snake

ad·dict 1. *v.t.* to habituate **2.** *n.* a person addicted to something harmful ‖ (loosely) someone inordinately fond of something not harmful

ad·dic·tion *n.* the state of being addicted

ad·dic·tive *adj.* causing addiction

ad·di·tion *n.* the process of adding **ad·di·tion·al** *adj.* extra

ad·di·tive *n.* something added to a food

product to give it color, make it keep etc.

ad·dress 1. *v.t.* to make a speech ‖ to speak or write formally to ‖ to write the destination on **2.** *n.* the place where a person lives **ad·dress·ee** *n.* the person to whom a letter is addressed

ad·e·noid ad·e·noids *pl.* a soft mass of lymphoid tissue at the back of the nose and throat

ad·ept 1. *adj.* clever **2.** *n.* an expert

ad·e·qua·cy *n.* the state of being adequate

ad·e·quate *adj.* sufficient

ad·here ad·her·ing ad·hered *v.i.* to cling, cleave, stick fast

ad·her·ence *n.* attachment

ad·her·ent 1. *adj.* clinging, sticking **2.** *n.* a follower, supporter

ad·he·sion *n.* the act or condition of adhering ‖ intermolecular attraction holding together surfaces in contact

ad·he·sive 1. *adj.* sticky **2.** *n.* a substance used to stick two surfaces together

ad hoc exclusively for some special purpose

ad·ja·cen·cy *pl.* **ad·ja·cen·cies** *n.* the condition of being adjacent

ad·ja·cent *adj.* near, nearby ‖ next, bordering

ad·jec·tive *n.* a part of speech used to qualify, define or limit a substantive

ad·join *v.t.* to lie next to, be adjacent to

ad·journ *v.t.* to suspend, defer ‖ *v.i.* to suspend **ad·journ·ment** *n.*

ad·judge ad·judg·ing ad·judged *v.t.* to judge or declare after careful consideration ‖ to find,

ad·junct *n.* something added or extra **ad·junc·tive** *adj.*

ad·ju·ra·tion *n.* earnest command, entreaty

ad·jure ad·jur·ing ad·jured *v.t.* to beseech

ad·just *v.t.* to set right, make orderly ‖ to adapt (oneself) **ad·just·er, ad·jus·tor** *n.* **ad·just·ment** *n.* a settlement

ad-lib ad-lib·bing ad-libbed *v.i.* to improvise

ad·min·is·ter *v.t.* to manage, direct ‖ to serve out, dispense ‖ to give, provide

ad·min·is·tra·tion *n.* the art or practice of carrying out a policy in government, business or public affairs ‖ management of a dead person's property

ad·min·is·tra·tive *adj.* concerned with administration

ad·mi·ra·ble *adj.* worthy of admiration ‖ excellent **ad·mi·ra·bly** *adv.*

ad·mi·ra·tion *n.* esteem, respect

ad·mire ad·mir·ing ad·mired *v.t.* to contemplate or consider with pleasure or respect ‖ to express admiration for **ad·mir·er** *n.*

ad·mis·si·ble *adj.* that may be allowed or conceded ‖ allowable as evidence or judicial proof **ad·mis·si·bly** *adv.*

ad·mis·sion *n.* the action of admitting, of giving access or entrance ‖ acknowledgment of the truth of a fact or statement

ad·mis·sive *adj.* allowing admission or inclusion

ad·mit ad·mit·ting ad·mit·ted *v.t.* to allow to enter ‖ to recognize as true ‖ to acknowledge **ad·mit·tance** *n.* the act of admitting ‖ right of entry **ad·mit·ted·ly** *adv.*

ad·mon·ish *v.t.* to reprove **ad·mon·ish·ment** *n.*

ad·mo·ni·tion *n.* warning ‖ rebuke

a·do·be *n.* sun-dried brick, not fired in a kiln

ad·o·les·cence *n.* that period of life in which the child changes into the adult

ad·o·les·cent *n.* a person who is no longer a child but is not fully adult

a·dopt *v.t.* to make one's own ‖ to become the legal parent of (a child not one's own) ‖ to accept

a·dop·tion *n.* an adopting or being adopted

a·dop·tive *adj.* of a relationship acquired by adoption

a·dor·a·ble *adj.* worthy of adoaration **a·dor·a·bly** *adv.*

ad·o·ra·tion *n.* the act of adoring, worshiping

a·dore a·dor·ing a·dored *v.t.* to worship, venerate ‖ to love **a·dor·ing** *adj.*

a·dorn *v.t.* to add beauty or splendor to

a·dorn·ment *n.*

a·dren·al·in, a·dren·a·line *n.* hormones produced by the adrenal glands

a·drift afloat without control, at the mercy of wind and sea

a·droit *adj.* dextrous, nimble

ad·sorb *v.t.* to retain by adsorption ad·sórp·tion *n.* a process by which molecules are taken up on the surface of a solid by chemical or physical action

ad·u·late ad·u·lat·ing ad·u·lat·ed *v.t.* to admire to excess

ad·u·la·tion *n.* excessive admiration

ad·u·la·tor *n.* a person who adulates

ad·u·la·to·ry *adj.* fulsomely ‖ excessively admiring

a·dult *n.* a mature, fully grown person ‖ a person who has come of age

a·dul·ter·er *n.* a man who commits adultery a·dul·ter·ess *n.* a woman who commits adultery

a·dul·ter·ous *adj.* of or characterized by adultery

a·dul·ter·y *n.* voluntary sexual intercourse of a married man with a woman other than his wife or of a married woman with a man other than her husband

ad·vance 1. *v.* ad·vanc·ing ad·vanced *v.i.* to go forward ‖ to progress ‖ to go up in rank ‖ to pay over (money) before the date when it is due 2. *n.* progress ‖ an improvement in knowledge, technique etc. ‖ a payment of money before it is due ‖ (*pl.*) attempts to make one's personal relations with someone intimate ad·vanced *adj.*

ad·van·tage *n.* something which gives benefit or profit ad·van·ta·geous *adj.*

ad·ven·ture *n.* a dangerous or exciting incident, or a hazardous enterprise ‖ a delightful experience

ad·ven·tur·er *n.* any seeker after adventure

ad·ven·tur·ess *n.* a woman out to get money or social position by guile and charm

ad·ven·tur·ous *adj.* enterprising, liable to take risks

ad·verb *n.* a part of speech which modifies or limits a verb

ad·ver·sa·ry *pl.* ad·ver·sa·ries *n.* opponent enemy

ad·verse *adj.* contrary, opposing

ad·ver·si·ty *pl.* ad·ver·si·ties *n.* misfortune, trouble, affliction ‖ a misfortune

ad·ver·tise, ad·ver·tize ad·ver·tis·ing, ad·ver·tiz·ing ad·ver·tised, ad·ver·tized *v.t.* o make known publicly ‖ to draw attention to ‖ *v.i.* to publish an advertisement ad·ver·tise·ment, ad·ver·tize·ment *n.* public notice or announcement ád·ver·tis·ing, ád·ver·tiz·ing *n.*

ad·vice *n.* a stated opinion ‖ a notification of a transaction

ad·vis·a·bil·i·ty *n.* the quality of being advisable

ad·vis·a·ble *adj.* prudent, expedient ‖ to be recommended ad·vis·a·bly *adv.*

ad·vise *pres. part.* ad·vis·ing ad·vised *v.t.* to recommend a course of action to ‖ to notify ‖ ad·vis·ed·ly *adv.* ad·vís·er, ad·ví·sor *adj.* consisting of advice

ad·vo·cate *n.* a person who speaks or writes in support of some cause, argument or proposal

aer·ate aer·at·ing aer·at·ed *v.t.* to impregnate with air ‖ aer·á·tion *n.*

aer·i·al 1. *adj.* of the air or atmosphere 2. an antenna

aer·i·al·ist *n.* an acrobat

aer·o·bics system of exercise

aer·o·dy·nam·ic *adj.* of or relating to aerodynamics

aer·o·dy·nam·ics *n.* the science of air flow

aer·o·naut·ics *n.* the science and practice of flight by aircraft

aer·o·space 1. *n.* the earth's atmosphere together with cosmis space beyond 2. *adj.* of or pertaining to the technology of flight or ballistics

aes·thete *n.* a person who professes to put beauty before other considerations

aes·thet·ic *adj.* appreciative of the beautiful aes·thet·i·cal *adj.* aes·the·tí·cian *n.* a person devoted to, or professionally occupied with, aesthetics aes·thet·i·cism *n.*

a·far *adv.* far off, at a distance

af·fa·ble *adj.* good-natured, courteous
af·fa·bly *adv.*

af·fair *n.* concern, business ‖ an incident ‖ a love affair

af·fect *v.t.* to make an impression on, move ‖ to have a hurtful effect on

affect *v.t.* to pretend, feign

af·fec·ta·tion *n.* a pretense made for effect

af·fec·tion *n.* fondness, tender feelings

af·fec·tion·ate *adj.* showing fondness, tenderness

af·fi·da·vit *n.* a written statement, sworn to be true

af·fil·i·ate 1. *v.* **af·fil·i·at·ing af·fil·i·at·ed** *v.i.* to enter into association ‖ *v.t.* to add as an associate 2. *n.* an associate

af·fil·i·a·tion *n.* an affiliating or being affiliated

af·fin·i·ty *pl.* **af·fin·i·ties** *n.* any close link or connection ‖ relationship by marriage

af·firm *v.t.* to state positively ‖ *v.i.* to make a declaration of truthfulness

af·fir·ma·tion *n.* an assertion, a positive statement ‖ a solemn declaration

af·firm·a·tive *adj.* asserting that a fact so, affirming by answering 'yes'

af·fix *n.* an appendage

af·fix *v.t.* to fasten ‖ to attach ‖ to append **ad·fix·a·tion** *n.* **af·fix·ture** *n.* the state of being affixed

af·flict *v.t.* to trouble or distress

af·flic·tion *n.* something which causes trouble or distress

af·flu·ence *n.* wealth ‖ profusion

af·flu·ent 1. *adj.* rich 2. *n.* a tributary stream

af·ford *v.t.* to be in a position (to do something) ‖ to be able to buy ‖ to give, provide

af·front 1. *v.t.* to insult, cause offense to 2. *n.* an insult, deliberate act of disrespect

a·fire *adj.* and *adv.* on fire

a·flame *adj.* and *adv.* in flames, burning

a·float *adj.* and *adv.* floating ‖ not aground ‖ free of debt, solvent

a·foot *adj.* and *adv.* walking, on foot

a·fraid *adj.* frightened ‖ apprehensive, fearful

a·fresh *adv.* anew, again

af·ter 1. *prep.* in search of, in pursuit of ‖ later than, subsequent to, following in time ‖ in spite of ‖ in imitation of, in the manner of 2. *adv.* behind in time or place, later 3. *conj.* subsequently

af·ter·birth *n.* the placenta

af·ter·burn·er *n.* device for destroying carbon wastes **af·ter·burn** *v.*

af·ter·math *n.* outcome, consequence

af·ter·noon *n.* between midday and evening

a·gain *adv.* once more ‖ furthermore, in addition

a·gainst *prep.* opposite to ‖ in contrast to ‖ in anticipation of ‖ into contact with ‖ in exchange for

a·gape *adj.* openmouthed with surprise

age 1. *n.* the length of time that a person or thing has lived ‖ a generation ‖ an epoch 2. *v.* **ag·ing, age·ing aged** *v.t.* to make older ‖ *v.i.* to become perceptibly older ‖ to mellow

a·ged *adj.* showing visible signs of old age

age·less *adj.* not affected by age or time

a·gen·cy *pl.* **a·gen·cies** *n.* an organization existing to promote the exchange of goods and services

a·gen·da *n.* things to be done ‖ a list of things to be discussed ‖ a memorandum book

a·gent *n.* someone who represents a person or a firm in business ‖ an intermediary

ag·glom·er·ate 1. *v.* **ag·glom·er·at·ing ag·glom·er·at·ed** *v.t.* to gather into a ball or mass 2. *adj.* collected into a ball or mass 3. *n.* a mass, collection **ag·glom·er·a·tion ag·glom·er·a·tive** *adj.*

ag·gran·dize **ag·gran·diz·ing ag·gran·dized** *v.t.* to make greater in power, rank, prestige or wealth **ag·gran·dize·ment** *n.*

ag·gra·vate ag·gra·vat·ing ag·gra·vat·ed *v.t.* to make more serious ‖ to irritate **ag·gra·va·tion** *n.*

ag·gre·gate 1. *v.* **ag·gre·gat·ing ag·gre·gat·ed** *v.t.* to total ‖ *v.i.* to come together 2. *adj.* total, collective ‖ made together 3. *adj.* total, collective ‖ made up of different mineral crystals 4. *n.* a total derived by addition **ag·gre·gá·tion** *n.*

ag·gres·sion *n.* a deliberate, unprovoked attack

ag·gres·sive *adj.* domineering ‖ enterprising

ag·gres·sor *n.* a person, nation etc. making a deliberate attack

ag·grieved *adj.* having a grievance

a·ghast *adj.* filled with terror or amazement or both

ag·ile *adj.* quick moving **a·gíl·i·ty** *n.*

ag·i·tate ag·i·tat·ing ag·i·tat·ed *v.t.* to shake, stir up ‖ to upset

ag·i·ta·tion *n.* a disturbance

ag·i·ta·tor *n.* a person who provokes social, political or religious disaffection

a·glow *adv.* and *adj.* in a glow

ag·nos·tic *n.* a person who thinks that nothing can be known about the existence or nature of God **ag·nos·ti·cal·ly** *adv.* **ag·nos·ti·cism** *n.*

ag·o·nize ag·o·niz·ing ag·o·nized *v.i.* to suffer intensely in mind or body, writhe with pain

ag·o·ny *pl.* **ag·o·nies** *n.* intense mental or physical suffering

a·grar·i·an *adj.* relating to land or its management

a·gree a·gree·ing a·greed *v.i.* to assent ‖ to be in harmony ‖ *v.t.* to consent

a·gree·a·bil·i·ty *n.* the state or quality of being agreeable

a·gree·a·ble *adj.* pleasant ‖ prepared **a·gree·a·bly** *adv.*

a·gree·ment *n.* a contract legally binding

ag·ri·cul·tur·al *adj.* related to or characteristic of agricultur

ag·ri·cul·tur·al·ist *n.* a person competent in farming theory

ag·ri·cul·ture *n.* the science or practice of soil cultivation

ag·ri·cul·tur·ist *n.* an agriculturalist

a·gron·o·mist *n.* someone who specializes in agronomy

a·gron·o·my *n.* the theory and practice of crop production and soil science

a·ground touching the bottom in shallow water

a·head *adj.* in front, in advance ‖ forward

aid 1. *n.* help, assistance **2.** *v.t.* and *i.* to help

AIDS, or Acquired Immune Deficiency Syndrome, a disease that attacks the body's immune system, rendering it unable to fight cancer, pneumonia, and a wide variety of other diseases.

ail *v.i.* to be slightly ill ‖ *v.t.* to trouble

ail·ment *n.* an illness of a trivial nature

aim 1. *v.i.* to direct a weapon or missile ‖ to direct efforts, purposes etc. **2.** *n.* a purpose, intention **aim·less** *adj.* without a purpose

air 1. *n.* the atmosphere, the mixture of gases surrounding the earth ‖ the space above us ‖ a melody ‖ appearance, manner **2.** *v.t.* to expose to fresh air, ventilate

air·bag *n.* plastic bag for automobile dashboard, designed to form a protective cushion

air·borne *adj.* carried by air ‖ in the air

air conditioner an air-conditioning device

air conditioning a process by which air is purified and its temperature and humidity are regulated before it enters a room or building

air·craft *sing.* and *pl.* *n.* any flying machine

air·frame *n.* the body of an aircraft without the engines

air·i·ly *adv.* in an airy manner, gaily

air·i·ness *n.* lack of concern

air·less *adj.* stuffy, oppressive

air·lift *n.* transport of goods or men by air in an emergency

air·line *n.* a regular air service for the transport of goods and passengers

air·mail *n.* letters and parcels, carried by air

air·plane *n.* a heavier-than-air flying machine

air·port *n.* buildings, hangars, workshops etc., equipped to deal with passengers, refueling and repair of aircraft etc

air raid an attack by aircraft

air·sick *adj.* nausea, vomiting etc. when flying in an aircraft

air·tight *adj.* closed tightly so that air cannot get in or out ‖ sure, certain

air·wor·thi·ness *n.* the condition of being airworthy

air·wor·thy *adj.* in suitable condition for flying

air·y *adj.* open to the air ‖ light-hearted, cheerful

aisle *n.* the passage between rows of seats in a church, theater etc.

a·jar *adj.* and *adv.* slightly open

a·kin *adj.* related by blood ‖ similar

al·a·bas·ter *n.* a translucent variety of gypsum

a·lac·ri·ty *n.* briskness ‖ eager readiness

a·larm 1. *n.* a signal warning of danger ‖ an excited anticipation of danger **2.** *v.t.* to inspire with fear

a·las *interj.* expressing grief, regret, pity, concern

al·ba·tross *pl.* **al·ba·tross·es al·ba·tross** *n.* a seabird

al·be·it even if, although

al·bi·nism *n.* the state or quality of being an albino

al·bi·no *n.* a person with a deficiency of pigment in the skin and hair ‖ any animal or plant similarly deficient in coloring pigment

al·bu·men *n.* the white of an egg ‖ albumin

al·bu·min *n.* a group of heat coagulable colloidal proteins, soluble in water, and occurring in egg white, blood plasma or serum, milk and many animal and vegetable tissues

al·bu·min·ous *adj.* having the properties of albumen or albumin

al·che·mist *n.* a person who practiced alchemy

al·che·my *pl.* **al·che·mies** *n.* a medieval chemical art to transmute base metals into gold

al·co·hol *n.* a colorless, volatile, intoxicating, inflammable liquid **al·co·hól·ic 1.** *adj.* of alcohol ‖ containing or using alcohol ‖ caused by alcohol **2.** *n.* a person who is addicted to alcohol

al·co·hol·i·cal·ly *adv.*

al·co·hol·ism *n.* dipsomania

al·cove *n.* a recess in the wall of a room

ale *n.* alcoholic beverage often stronger in alcohol and heavier in body than beer

a·lert 1. *adj.* watchful, vigilant ‖ brisk, nimble **2.** *n.* a warning, alarm **3.** *v.t.* to warn, put on guard

al·fal·fa *n.* a perennial hay crop

al·ga *pl.* **al·gae al·gas** *n.* a larger group of nonvascular plants **al·gal** *adj.*

al·ge·bra *n.* a branch of mathematics in which symbols are used to represent numbers **al·ge·bra·ic al·ge·bra·i·cal** *adjs.* **al·ge·bra·i·cal·ly** *adv.*

a·li·as *pl.* **a·li·as·es 1.** *adv.* otherwise called **2.** *n.* an assumed name

al·i·bi *pl.* **al·i·bis** *n.* the plea of having been somewhere else at the time of a crime ‖ an excuse

al·ien 1. *adj.* belonging to another country, foreign **2.** *n.* a non-naturalized foreigner ‖ intelligent extraterrestrial being come to earth

al·ien·a·ble *adj.* capable of being alienated

al·ien·ate al·ien·at·ing al·ien·at·ed *v.t.* to cause (someone) to withdraw affection ‖ to lose or give up **al·ien·á·tion** *n.*

a·light a·light·ing a·light·ed rarely **a·lit** *v.i.* to get down from a vehicle

a·lign, a·line a·lign·ing, a·lin·ing a·ligned, a·lined *v.t.* to line up ‖ to join in sympathy **a·lign·ment, a·line·ment** *n.* being in line

a·like 1. *adv.* in the same manner **2.** *adj.* similar

al·i·ment *n.* food for body or mind **al·i·men·tal** *adj.*

al·i·men·ta·ry *adj.* of or relating to nutrition

al·i·mo·ny *pl.* **al·i·mo·nies** *n.* money payable by a man to his former wife, or by a woman to her former husband, for maintenance after separation or divorce

a·live *adj.* and *adv.* living ‖ brisk, lively

al·ka·li *pl.* **al·ka·lis, al·ka·lies** *n.* a usually soluble hydroxide or carbonate of the alkali metals **al·ka·li·fy al·ka·li·fy·ing al·ka·li·fied** *v.i.* to become alkaline

al·ka·line *adj.* having the properties of an alkali

all 1. *adj.* the whole quantity of ‖ any whatever ‖ everyone of **2.** *pron.* everyone **3.** *n.* everything **4.** *adv.* entirely, completely

all-a·round *adj.* general

al·lay *v.t.* to make less, alleviate ‖ to put at rest

al·le·ga·tion *n.* an assertion yet to be proved

al·lege al·leg·ing *v.t.* to affirm without being able to prove **al·leg·ed·ly** *adv.*

al·le·giance *n.* devotion, loyalty

al·le·gor·ic *adj.* of the nature of allegory **al·le·gor·i·cal** *adj.*

al·le·go·ry *pl.* **al·le·go·ries** *n.* a work of art in which a deeper meaning underlies the superficial or literal meaning

al·le·gro 1. *adv.* and *adj.* rather fast **2.** *n.* a lively movement

al·ler·gic *adj.* caused by an allergy

al·ler·gist *n.* a doctor specializing in the treatment of allergies

al·ler·gy *pl.* **al·ler·gies** *n.* an exaggerated and specific antigen-antibody reaction

al·le·vi·ate al·le·vi·at·ing al·le·vi·at·ed *v.t.* to make lighter, mitigate, moderate **al·le·vi·a·tion** *n.* **al·le·vi·a·tive** *adj.* and *n.* **al·le·vi·a·to·ry** *adj.*

al·ley *n.* a narrow lane between buildings ‖ a wide path in a park ‖ an enclosure for bowling games

al·ley·way *n.* a narrow passage for pedestrians

al·li·ance *n.* the relationship formed by it between nations ‖ the a uniting of qualities in a perceived relationship

al·li·ga·tor *n.* large reptiles of the crocodile family

all in all *adv.* all things being considered, on the whole

al·lit·er·ate al·lit·er·at·ing al·lit·er·at·ed *v.i.* to write or speak in words beginning with the same letter **al·lit·er·a·tion** *n.* the repetition of the same initial letter in a group of words **al·lit·er·a·tive** *adj.*

al·lo·cate al·lo·cat·ing al·lo·cat·ed *v.t.* to share out ‖ to assign, earmark

al·lo·ca·tion the amount allocated ‖ something allocated

al·lo·cu·tion *n.* a formal speech of some gravity

al·lot al·lot·ting al·lot·ted *v.t.* to assign in portions ‖ to distribute by lot

al·lot·ment *n.* the share of something alloted

al·low *v.t.* to permit, let ‖ to grant ‖ (with 'for') to plan with an adequate margin **al·lów·a·ble** *adj.* **al·lów·a·bly** *adv.*

al·low·ance *n.* a regular perodical sum of money paid to a dependant ‖ permission

al·loy *v.t.* to blend (metals)

al·loy *n.* a metallic substance composed of two or more metals

al·lude al·lud·ing al·lud·ed *v.i.* to refer indirectly

al·lure 1. *v.t.* **al·lur·ing al·lured** to attract, entice **2.** **al·lure·ment** *n.*

al·lu·sion *n.* an indirect reference

al·lu·sive *adj.* containing an allusion

al·ly 1. *v.t.* **al·ly·ing al·lied** to unite in an alliance **2.** *n.* *pl.* **al·lies** a country or person allied to another

al·ma ma·ter *n.* one's school or university

al·ma·nac *n.* a calendar of the year with information about the sun, moon, stars, tides

al·might·y *adj.* all-powerful

al·mond *n.* a small, pink-flowered tree ‖ the nut obtained from the stone (fruit) of this tree

al·most *adv.* nearly, all but

alms *sing.* and *pl.* *n.* money or goods given to the poor ‖ a charitable gift

a·loft *adv.* and *adj.* high up

a·lone 1. *adj.* by oneself, unaccompanied, solitary **2.** *adv.* only, solely, exclusively

a·long 1. *prep.* from one end to the other end of **2.** *adv.* onward, forward

a·loof 1. *adv.* away, at a physical or spiritual distance **2.** *adj.* reserved, cold in manner

a·loud *adv.* in a normal voice, so as to be heard

al·pac·a *n.* a species of llama

al·pha *n.* the first letter of the greek

alphabet ‖ the brightest star in a constellation

al·pha·bet n. the letters used in writing arranged in a conventional order **al·pha·bét·i·cal** adj. **al·pha·bet·iz·ing** **al·pha·bet·ized** v.t. to arrange in alphabetical order

al·read·y adv. by this time, before a particular moment

al·so adv. as well, in addition, beside

al·tar n. any raised structure for offering sacrifices to a deity

al·ter v.t. to make different, modify, change

al·ter·a·tion n. the act or result of altering

al·ter·cate al·ter·cat·ing al·ter·cat·ed v.i. to dispute with anger or violence

al·ter·ca·tion n. a quarrel, angry dispute

al·ter e·go pl. **al·ter e·gos** second self ‖ an inseparable friend

al·ter·nate 1. adj. every other **2.** n. a substitute **3. al·ter·nat·ing al·ter·nat·ed** v.t. to interchange by turns ‖ v.i. to take turns

al·ter·na·tion n. an occurence of things by turns

al·ter·na·tive 1. adj. a choice of two things or several things **2.** n. one of two things which must be chosen

al·though conj. in spite of the fact that, though

al·tim·e·ter n. an instrument for measuring height

al·ti·tude n. height above sea level **al·ti·tú·di·nal** adj.

al·to n. the lowest female voice

al·to·geth·er adv. completely, thoroughly ‖ on the whole

al·tru·ism n. consideration for other people ‖ unselfishness **ál·tru·ist** n. **al·tru·ís·tic** adj. **al·tru·ís·ti·cal·ly** adv.

a·lu·mi·na n. aluminum oxide

a·lu·mi·num n. a light metallic element

a·lum·na pl. **a·lum·nae** n. a woman who is a former student of a school, college or university

a·lum·nus pl. **a·lum·ni** n. a man who is a former student of a school, college or university

al·ways adv. at all times, on all occasions

a.m., A.M. ANTE MERIDIEM

a·mal·gam n. an alloy of mercury

a·mal·ga·mate a·mal·ga·mat·ing a·mal·ga·mat·ed v.t. to alloy with mercury ‖ to join together, mix, unite **a·mal·ga·má·tion** n. **am·mál·ga·ma·tor** n.

a·mass v.t. to gather together, accumulate

am·a·teur n. someone who cultivates an activity as a pastime rather than as a means of making money ‖ a dabbler, dilettante **am·a·téur·ish** adj. **ám·a·teur·ism** n.

am·a·to·ry adj. dealing with or inducing love

a·maze a·maz·ing a·mazed v.t. to astonish, astound **a·máze·ment** n.

am·a·zon n. a strong, manly woman

am·bas·sa·dor n. an official of highest rank who represents his government in the another country

am·ber n. a fossilized form of resin ‖ the color of amber

am·bi·dex·ter·i·ty n. the state of being ambidextrous

am·bi·dex·trous adj. able to use both hands with equal ease ‖ two-faced

am·bi·gu·i·ty pl. **am·bi·gu·i·ties** n. the quality of having more than one meaning

am·big·u·ous adj. having more than one meaning ‖ doubtful, uncertain

am·bi·tion n. eagerness to attain success ‖ the object of a person's aspirations

am·bi·tious adj. full of ambition

am·biv·a·lence n. the state of being ambivalent

am·biv·a·lent adj. having conflicting feelings about something

am·ble 1. v.i. **am·bling am·bled** to stroll, walk in a leisurely manner **2.** n. (of horses) an easy gait

am·bu·lance n. a special vehicle for transporting sick or injured people

am·bu·la·to·ry adj. of or concerning walking, adapted to walking, movable

am·bus·cade n. an ambush, esp. by soldiers

am·bush n. hidden soldiers waiting to attack a passing enemy ‖ the place where they are hidden

ambush v.t. to attack from an ambush

ameba *AMOEBA

amebic *AMOEBIC

a·mel·io·rate **a·mel·io·rat·ing** **a·mel·io·rat·ed** v.t. to improve, make better **a·mel·io·ra·tion** n. **a·mel·io·ra·tive** adj.

a·men interj. so be it, truly it is so

a·me·na·bil·i·ty n. the state of being amenable

a·me·na·ble adj. responsive ‖ answerable, responsible **a·mé·na·bly** adv.

a·mend v.i. to change for the better

a·mend·ment n. a revision or change made in a law, bill etc. ‖ a proposed modification ‖ a correction

a·mends sing. and pl. n. to make amends to make compensation, reparation

a·men·i·ty pl. **a·men·i·ties** n. something that tends to make life more comfortable

A·mer·i·can 1. adj. of or belonging to the American continent or belonging to the U.S.A. 2. n. a citizen of the U.S.A. ‖ the English language as used in the U.S.A.

am·e·thyst n. a precious stone, purple or violet in color **am·e·thys·tine** adj.

a·mi·a·bil·i·ty n. the quality of being amiable

a·mi·a·ble adj. good-natured, friendly **á·mi·a·bly** adv.

am·i·ca·bil·i·ty n. the quality of being amicable

am·i·ca·ble adj. friendly, peaceable **am·i·ca·bly** adv.

a·mid prep. in the midst of, among

a·mid·ship adv. amidships

a·mid·ships adv. in the middle of a ship

a·midst prep. amid

a·mi·no acid a class of organic acids

a·miss 1. pred. adj. wrong 2. adv. wrongly ‖ away from the mark

am·me·ter n. an instrument for measuring electric current

am·mo·nia n. a gaseous compound of nitrogen and hydrogen

am·mo·ni·ac adj. of the nature of ammonia **am·mo·ni·a·cal** adj.

am·mu·ni·tion n. everything necessary to feed guns or small arms

am·ne·sia n. loss of memory **am·ne·sic** adj.

am·nes·ty 1. n. pl. **am·nes·ties** an act of pardon by a legislative authority 2. v.t. **am·nes·ty·ing am·nes·tied** to pardon

am·ni·on pl. **am·ni·ons, am·ni·a** n. a thin, membranous, fluid filled one enclosing the embryo

am·ni·os·co·py n. visual examination of uterine cavity of a pregnant female **amnioscope** n. instrument for examining fetus within the uterus

am·ni·ot·ic fluid the fluid in the amnion

a·moe·ba, a·me·ba pl. **a·moe·bae a·moe·bas, a·me·bae, a·me·bas,** n. a microscopic, protozoan, the simplest form of animal **a·móe·bic, a·mé·bic** adj.

a·mok, a·muck 1. n. an outbreak of violent madness 2. adv. **to run amok** to be seized with this frenzy

a·mong prep. surrounded by, in the midst of ‖ in the company of ‖ in relation to, with

a·mongst prep. among

a·mor·al adj. indifferent to morality **a·mo·ral·i·ty** n.

am·o·rous adj. much given to making love ‖ showing or betraying love

a·mor·phous adj. formless

am·or·ti·za·tion n. **am·or·tize am·or·tiz·ing am·or·tized** v.t. to provide for paying off gradually

a·mount n. the sum total ‖ a quantity

amp n. an ampere [shortening]

am·per·age n. the magnitude of an electric current expressed in amperes

am·pere n. the mks unit of electric current **am·pere-hour** n. a unit of electric charge

am·per·sand n. the sign &, symbol for 'and'

am·phib·i·an n. a class of vertebrates

am·phib·i·ous adj. able to live on land and in the water

am·phi·the·a·ter n. a round or oval arena enclosed by rising tiers of seats

am·phi·the·at·ri·cal *adj.*

am·ple *adj.* abundant, copious ‖ enough, sufficient

am·pli·fi·ca·tion *n.* an extension or enlargement

am·pli·fi·er *n.* an apparatus used to increase the volume of sound

am·pli·fy am·pli·fy·ing am·pli·fied *v.t.* to expand or enlarge ‖ *v.i.* to explain oneself in greater detail

am·pli·tude *n.* largeness, breadth, extent

am·pul·la *pl.* **am·pul·lae** *n.* an acient Roman vase

am·pu·tate am·pu·tat·ing am·pu·tat·ed *v.t.* to cut off, esp. in surgery **am·pu·tá·tion**, **ám·pu·ta·tor**, **am·pu·tée** *n.*

am·u·let *n.* an ornament or gem worn as a protection against evil spirits

a·muse a·mus·ing a·mused *v.t.* to cause to smile ‖ to divert **a·muse·ment** *n.*

an *indef. art.*

a·nach·ro·nism *n.* something which does not fit in with its context chronologically **a·nach·ro·nís·tic** *adj.*

an·a·con·da a large boa of tropical South America

an·a·gram *n.* a word or phrase made by changing the order of letters in another word or phrase

a·nal *adj.* related to, or situated near, the anus

an·al·ge·sia *n.* insensibility to pain **an·al·ge·sic 1.** *adj.* producing analgesia **2.** a drug which does this

a·nal·o·gize a·nal·o·giz·ing a·nal·o·gized *v.i.* to use analogy ‖ *v.t.* to bring into analogy

a·nal·o·gous *adj.* similar, corresponding

an·a·logue, an·a·log *n.* a thing analogous to some other thing

a·nal·o·gy *pl.* **a·nal·o·gies** *n.* the relationship between two things which are similar

analyse *ANALYZE

a·nal·y·sis *pl.* **a·nal·y·ses** *n.* the process of analyzing ‖ a document setting out the results of this process ‖ psychoanalysis

an·a·lyst *n.* someone skilled in analysis

an·a·lyt·ic *adj.* pertaining to analysis **an·a·lýt·i·cal** *adj.*

an·a·lyze an·a·lyz·ing an·a·lyzed *v.t.* to study (a problem) in detail by breaking it down into various parts ‖ to break up (a substance) into its simplest elements

an·ar·chism *n.* the political theory that all government and law is evil

an·ar·chist *n.* someone who believes in anarchism

an·ar·chy *pl.* **an·ar·chies** *n.* the absence of law and order

a·nath·e·ma *n.* the gravest ecclesiastical censure. ‖ something intensely disliked **a·náth·e·ma·tize a·nath·e·ma·tiz·ing a·nath·e·ma·tized** *v.t.*

an·a·tom·ic *adj.* pertaining to anatomy **an·a·tóm·i·cal** *adj.*

a·nat·o·mist *n.* a specialist in anatomy

a·nat·o·mize a·nat·o·miz·ing a·nat·o·mized *v.t.* to dissect

a·nat·o·my *pl.* **a·nat·o·mies** *n.* branch of morphology ‖ the science of dissection ‖ the structure of an organism

an·ces·tor *n.* a forefather ‖ an earlier type of a species

an·ces·tral *adj.* coming from one's ancestors

an·ces·tress *n.* a female ancestor

an·ces·try *pl.* **an·ces·tries** *n.* the line of descent from ancestors

an·chor *v.i.* to cast anchor

anchor *n.* a heavy iron instrument which is lowered from a ship to grip the bottom and so hold her fast

an·chor·age *n.* a place where ships may lie at anchor

an·cho·vy *pl.* **an·cho·vies** *n.* a small bony fish of the herring family

an·cient *adj.* antique, old-fashioned ‖ old, decrepit

an·cil·lar·y *adj.* subordinate, subsidiary

an·dan·te *adj.* and *adv.* at a moderate speed

an·drog·y·nous *adj.* combining characteristics of both sexes, hermaphrodite

an·ec·do·tal *adj.* relating to anecdotes

an·ec·dote *n.* a short account of an interesting event **an·ec·dot·ic**

an·ec·dót·i·cal *adjs* **án·ec·dot·ism**, **án·ec·dot·ist** *ns*

a·ne·mi·a *n.* a reduction in the amount of red cells in the blood **a·né·mic** *adj.*

a·nem·o·ne *n.* a genus of plants bearing colorful flowers

an·es·the·sia *n.* loss of the perception of pain **an·es·thet·ic** 1. *n.* a substance which produces anesthesia 2. *adj.* producing anesthesia ‖ relating to anesthesia **an·es·the·tist** *n.* someone who administers anesthetics **an·es·the·ti·za·tion** *n.* **an·es·the·tize** **an·es·the·tiz·ing an·es·the·tized** *v.t.*

an·es·the·si·ol·o·gist *n.* a specialist in anesthesiology

an·es·the·si·ol·o·gy *n.* the science of administering anesthetics

an·eu·rysm, an·eu·rism *n.* the dilation of a section of an artery

a·new *adv.* again ‖ in a new form or way

an·gel *n.* a messenger of God ‖ a person of exceptional goodness or loveliness

angel dust phencyclidine hydrochloride, a highly dangerous animal tranquilizer

an·gel·ic *adj.* of exceptional goodness or loveliness

an·ger 1. *n.* rage, displeasure 2. *v.t.* to make angry

an·gi·na *n.* inflammation of the throat

angina pec·to·ris *n.* a disease of the heart

an·gle *n.* the difference in the direction of two intersecting lines or planes ‖ a point of view

angle an·gling an·gled *v.i.* to fish with line and hook

an·gled *adj.* being at an angle

an·gler *n.* a person who fishes

An·gli·can 1. *adj.* of the Church of England 2. *n.* a member of the Church of England

An·gli·cize An·gli·ciz·ing An·gli·cized *v.* to make English in form, character or pronunciation

An·glo-Sax·on *n.* a person of English descent

an·go·ra *n.* fabric made from the hair of the angora goat or rabbit

Angora cat a variety of domestic cat

an·gri·ly *adv.* in an angry way

an·gry an·gri·er an·gri·est *adj.* feeling or showing anger

an·guish *n.* severe mental suffering

an·guished *adj.* acutely distressed, suffering

an·gu·lar *adj.* having angles or sharp corners ‖ (of people) bony, spare, scraggy

an·gu·lar·i·ty *n.* the quality of being angular

an·hy·drous *adj.* without water

an·i·mal 1. *n.* any of various organisms of the kingdom Animalia, distinguished from plants ‖ a man who behaves like a brute 2. *adj.* like or relating to animals

an·i·mate 1. *adj.* living ‖ pertaining to animal as opposed to plant life 2. *v.t.* **an·i·mat·ing an·i·mat·ed** to have a direct or inspiring influence upon, motivate **an·i·mat·ed** *adj. (of a person)* full of communicative liveliness

an·i·ma·tion *n.* the act of animating ‖ the preparation of an animated cartoon

an·i·mos·i·ty *pl.* **an·i·mos·i·ties** *n.* a feeling of hatred or ill will, strong dislike

an·i·mus *n. (sing. only)* animosity, hostility

an·ise *n.* a plant native to the Mediterranean

an·kle *n.* the joint between the foot and the leg

an·nal·is *n.* a writer of annals **an·nal·is·tic** *adj.*

an·nals *pl. n.* record of events, a chronicle

an·neal *v.t.* to improve the properties of by heating and then cooling

an·nex *n.* a building attached to a larger building ‖ an appendix or supplement to a book

an·nex *v.t.* to take possession of ‖ to append

an·nex·a·tion *n.* an annexing or being annexed

an·ni·hi·late **an·ni·hi·lat·ing an·ni·hi·lat·ed** *v.t.* to destroy completely **an·ni·hi·la·tion** *n.*

an·ni·ver·sa·ry *pl.* **an·ni·ver·sa·ries** *n.* the yearly return of the date of an event

an·no Dom·i·ni in the year specified of the

Christian era

an·no·tate an·no·tat·ing an·no·tat·ed *v.t.* to write explanatory notes **an·no·ta·tion, an·no·ta·tor** *ns*

an·nounce an·nounc·ing an·nounced *v.t.* to make known publicly ‖ to introduce (a radio or television item) **an·nounce·ment** *n.* **an·nounc·er** *n.*

an·noy *v.t.* to vex, irritate, trouble

an·noy·ance *n.* physical or mental discomfort

an·noy·ing *adj.* irritating, troublesome

an·nu·al 1. *adj.* occurring regularly once a year 2. *n.* a plant which grows from seed, comes to maturity and dies within one year

an·nu·i·ty *pl.* **an·nu·i·ties** *n.* a fixed yearly payment

an·nul an·nul·ling an·nulled *v.t.* to make null and void

an·nul·ment *n.* an annulling or being annulled

an·nun·ci·ate an·nun·ci·at·ing an·nun·ci·at·ed *v.t.* to announce

an·nun·ci·a·tion *n.* an announcement

a·noint *v.t.* to apply oil or ointment to, either medically or sacramentally **a·noint·ment** *n.*

a·nom·a·lis·tic *adj.* characterized by anomaly

a·nom·a·lous *adj.* not in conformity with what is usual or expected

a·nom·a·ly *pl.* **a·nom·a·lies** *n.* something contrary to the general rule or to what is expected

an·o·nym *n.* a person who conceals his name **an·o·nym·i·ty** *n.* the state of being anonymous

a·non·y·mous *adj.* without a known or disclosed name

an·oth·er 1. *adj.* additional ‖ different 2. *pron.* an additional one of the same kind ‖ a different one

an·swer *v.t.* to reply to ‖ to defend oneself against ‖ to correspond to ‖ *v.i* to reply in words, actions etc. ‖ to act in response answer ‖ to be judged for

answer *n.* a reply ‖ a solution

an·swer·a·ble *adj.* responsible

ant *n.* a small insect, related to bees and wasps

ant·ac·id 1. *adj.* preventing or counteracting acidity 2. *n.* an agent which does

an·tag·o·nism *n.* open opposition, hostility

an·tag·o·nist *n.* an open enemy, rival **an·tag·o·nis·tic** *adj.* **an·tag·o·nis·ti·cal·ly** *adv.*

an·tag·o·nize an·tag·o·niz·ing an·tag·o·nized *v.t.* to provoke to enmity

Ant·arc·tic 1. *adj.* South polar 2. *n.* **the Antarctic** the South polar regions

an·te·ced·ence *n.* priority in time or in a sequence of cause and effect

an·te·ced·ent *adj.* going before, preceding ‖ (*pl.*) a man's origins ‖ (*pl.*) ancestors

an·te·date an·te·dat·ing an·te·dat·ed *v.t.* to predate

an·te·di·lu·vi·anu 1. *n.* an antiquated person or thing 2. *adj.* from before the Flood

an·te·lope *pl.* **an·te·lope, an·te·lopes** *n.* a deerlike ruminant mammal

an·te·me·rid·i·an *adj.* before noon

an·te me·rid·i·em *adj.* after midnight and before noon

an·ten·na *pl.* **an·ten·nae an·ten·nas** *n.* the sensitive jointed feeler or horn of an insect or crustacean ‖ a device for converting electrical currents into electromagnetic waves, or vice versa

an·te·ri·or *adj.* nearer the front ‖ earlier in time **an·te·ri·or·i·ty** *n.*

an·them *n.* a piece of choral music sung in church ‖ a song of praise or joy

an·thol·o·gist *n.* a person who compiles an anthology

an·thol·o·gy *pl.* **an·thol·o·gies** *n.* a collection of poetry or prose

an·thra·cite *n.* a form of coal

an·thrax *pl.* **an·thra·ces** *n.* an infectious, often fatal disease in sheep and cattle

an·thro·poid *adj.* manlike in appearance

an·thro·po·log·i·cal *adj.* of or pertaining to anthropology

an·thro·pol·o·gist *n.* a specialist in anthropology

an·thro·pol·o·gy *n.* the science which

studies man both as an animal and as living in society

anti- prefix against, opposite, instead

an·ti 1. *n.* a person who opts against some action etc. **2.** *adj.* against, opposed

an·ti·bi·ot·ic *n.* a substance usually produced by a microorganism that is used therapeutically to destroy or inhibit the growth of a pathogen

an·ti·bod·y *nl.* **an·ti·bo·dies** *n.* any of a group of proteins produced by the body of higher organisms

an·tic *n.* a caper, extravagant or grotesque gesture ‖ (*pl.*) foolish, annoying or irresponsible behavior

an·ti·ci·pate   **an·ti·ci·pat·ing** **an·ti·ci·pat·ed** *v.t.* to look forward to, feel in advance ‖ to prevent by prior action ‖ to expect

an·tic·i·pa·tion *n.* an anticipating or being anticipated

an·tic·i·pa·tor *n.* one who anticipates **an·tic·i·pa·to·ry** *adj.*

an·ti·cli·max *n.* a disappointing end to what promised well

an·ti·dot·al *adj.* of or serving as an antidote

an·ti·dote *n.* a remedy counteracting a poison etc.

an·ti·his·ta·mine *n.* one of a group of synthetic drugs used in the treatment of allergic reactions

an·ti·ma·cas·sar *n.* a covering to protect the back of an upholstered chair or sofa

an·ti·mat·ter *n.* matter built up from antiparticles

an·ti·mis·sile *n.* a guided missile used for intercepting and destroying guided missiles

an·ti·pa·thet·ic *adj.* feeling antipathy **an·ti·pa·thet·i·cal** *adj.*

an·tip·a·thy *pl.* **an·tip·a·thies** *n.* a strong hostility

an·ti·pode *n.* an exact opposite

an·tip·o·des *pl. n.* that part of the earth's surface which is diametrically opposite to one's position

an·ti·quat·ed *adj.* out-of-date, obsolete, ancient

an·tique 1. *adj.* old and precious ‖ antiquated, old-fashioned **2.** *n.* an object surviving from the past

an·tiqu·ing *n.* visiting an atique shop

an·tiq·ui·ty *pl.* **an·tiq·ui·ties** the far-distant past ‖ (*pl.*) remains of ancient times and culture

an·ti·Sem·ite *n.* someone who is prejudiced against Jews **an·ti·se·mit·ic** *adj.* **an·ti-Sem·i·tism** *n.*

an·ti·sep·sis *n.* an antiseptic condition

an·ti·sep·tic 1. *adj.* counteracting the putrefying effect of bacteria **2.** *n.* something which does this **an·ti·sep·ti·cize** **an·ti·sep·ti·ciz·ing**

an·ti·so·cial *adj.* contrary to the interests of society

an·tith·e·sis *pl.* **an·tith·e·ses** *n.* a direct opposite ‖ the statement opposed to the thesis of a syllogism

an·ti·thet·ic *adj.* contrasted, containing opposite ideas **an·ti·thet·i·cal** *adj.*

an·ti·tox·in *n.* a serum which counteracts toxin

an·ti·trust *adj.* designed to prevent, the concentration of industry and commerce under the control of large combines

ant·ler *n.* the branched horn of animals of the deer family **ant·lered** *adj.*

an·to·nym *n.* a word which means the exact contrary of another

a·nus *n.* the lower opening of the rectum

an·vil *n.* the iron block on which a smith hammers metal into shape

anx·i·e·ty *pl.* **anx·i·e·ties** *n.* intense dread, apprehension

anx·ious *adj.* worried and uncertain ‖ eager

an·y 1. adj one, some ‖ every ‖ unlimited **2.** *sing.* and *pl. pron.* any person or thing **3.** *adv.* at all, to any degree

an·y·bod·y *pron.* any person

an·y·how *adv.* carelesslyer ‖ in any event

an·y·one *pron.* any person, anybody

an·y·thing *pron.* and *n.* something

an·y·way *adv.* anyhow

an·y·where *adv.* in, at or to any place

a·or·ta *n* the principal artery through which the blood leaves the heart

a·or·tal, a·or·tic *adjs*

a·part 1. *adj.* separate **2.** *adv.* in parts

a·part·heid *n.* the racial policy of the government of South Africa

a·part·ment *n.* a set of rooms on one floor of a building used as a separate residence

ape 1. *n.* an anthropoid ape **2.** *v.t.* **ap·ing aped** to copy or mimic in such a way as to make oneself ridiculous

a·pe·ri·tif *n.* a short alcoholic drink

ap·er·ture *n.* an opening, space between two things ‖ an opening in a photographic lens

a·pex *pl.* **a·pex·es, a·pi·ces** *n.* the topmost point

a·pha·sia *n.* loss of the power to speak **a·pha·sic** *n.* and *adj.*

aph·o·rism *n.* a short, neatly expressed general truth

aph·ro·dis·i·ac 1. *adj.* increasing sexual desire **2.** *n.* a drug, food etc. which does this

a·pi·ar·y *pl.* **a·pi·ar·ies** *n.* a place in which a number of beehives are kept

a·piece *adv.* to or for each one of several

a·plomb *n.* self-assurance, self-possession

ap·o·gee *n.* the farthest or highest point, climax

a·pol·o·get·ic *adj.* asking pardon **a·pol·o·get·i·cal** *adj.*

a·pol·o·gize a·pol·o·giz·ing a·pol·o·gized *v.i.* to say that one is sorry

a·pol·o·gy *pl.* **a·pol·o·gies** *n.* an excuse or defense

ap·o·plec·tic 1. *adj.* suffering from apoplexy **2.** an apoplectic person **ap·o·plec·ti·cal** *adj.*

ap·o·plex·y *n.* a sudden and total loss of movement and consciousness, 'a stroke'

a·pos·ta·sy *pl.* **a·pos·ta·sies** *n.* the public abandoning of a religious faith

a·pos·tate *n.* someone who abandons his religious faith

a·pos·ta·tize   **a·pos·ta·tiz·ing a·pos·ta·tized** *v.i.* to become an apostate

A·pos·tle *n.* one of the 12 men chosen by Christ to preach the gospel ‖ any early or prominent advocate of a belief

ap·os·tol·ic *adj.* of, like, or of the time of, the apostles **ap·os·tol·i·cal** *adj.*

a·pos·tro·phe *n.* a punctuation mark (')

a·poth·e·car·y *pl.* **a·poth·e·car·ies** *n.* druggist

ap·pal, ap·pall ap·pal·ling, ap·pall·ing ap·palled *v.t.* horrify ‖ to fill with dismay

ap·pal·ling *adj.* horrifying ‖ very bad in quality

ap·pa·ra·tus *pl.* **ap·pa·ra·tus, ap·pa·ra·tus·es** *n.* the equipment needed for a certain task

ap·par·el 1. *n.* clothing ‖ embroidery on certain church vestments **2.** *v.t.* **ap·par·el·ing ap·par·eled** to clothe, adorn

ap·par·ent *adj.* real and evident, obvious

ap·par·ent·ly *adv.* seemingly ‖ obviously

ap·pa·ri·tion *n.* an appearance from another world ‖ a ghost

ap·peal *v.t.* to call upon a higher authority to review to turn for an opinion ‖ to make an earnest request ‖ to ask for voluntary contributions ‖ to be pleasing

appeal *n.* the act of appealing

ap·peal·a·ble *adj.* (law, of a case) that can be referred to a higher court

ap·peal·ing *adj.* moving ‖ beseeching ‖ pleasing

ap·pear *v.i.* to come in sight ‖ to come on the scene, arrive ‖ to act or perform in public ‖ to be evident or probable

ap·pear·ance *n.* the act of appearing ‖ looks ‖ dress and general bearing ‖ to appear in public

ap·peas·a·ble *adj.* capable of being appeased

ap·pease ap·peas·ing ap·peased *v.t.* to calm or pacify ‖ to satisfy

ap·pease·ment *n.* the act of appeasing

ap·pel·lant 1. *adj.* appealing to a higher court **2.** *n.* someone who makes an appeal

ap·pel·late *adj.* hearing appeals

ap·pel·la·tive *n.* a common as opposed to a proper noun *adj.* relating to a common noun

ap·pend *v.t.* to attach, add, esp. as an appendix

ap·pend·age *n.* an external organ

ap·pen·dec·to·my *n.* the surgical operation of removing the appendix

ap·pen·di·ci·tis *n.* an inflammation of the appendix

ap·pen·dix *pl.* **ap·pen·dix·es ap·pen·di·ces** *n.* an addition to a document or book ‖ the vermiform part of the intestinal canal

ap·per·tain *v.i.* to belong by right or custom

ap·pe·tite *n.* a natural desire to satisfy hunger ‖ some other natural desire of the body

ap·pe·tiz·er *n.* a short drink or snack

ap·pe·tiz·ing *adj.* arousing appetite

ap·plaud *v.i.* to show approval by clapping or cheering

ap·plause *n.* approval shown by clapping or cheering ‖ praise

ap·ple *n.* a tree of the temperate regions ‖ the fruit of this tree

ap·pli·ance *n.* a mechanical or electrical device using a power supply ‖ the act of applying

ap·pli·ca·bil·i·ty *n.* the state or quality of being applicable

ap·pli·ca·ble *adj.* suitable, appropriate

ap·pli·cant *n.* someone making an application

ap·pli·ca·tion *n.* the act of applying ‖ a putting into effect of a general rule or principle ‖ a request made in person or in writing

ap·plied *adj.* turned or related to practical use

ap·pli·que *n.* a fabric decoration

ap·ply ap·ply·ing ap·plied *v.t.* to put (something on another thing) ‖ to bring into use or action ‖ to use (a word or expression) in order to name or describe ‖ to use for a particular purpose

ap·point *v.t.* to select for an office or position **ap·point·ed** *adj.* decided or determined before hand

ap·point·ment *n.* a prearranged meeting, date ‖ a selecting for an office or position

ap·por·tion *v.t.* divide into shares **ap·por·tion·ment** *n.*

ap·po·si·tion *n.* an application, addition **in apposition** in the grammatical relationship of words so used **ap·po·si·tion·al** *adj.*

ap·prais·al *n.* a judgment formed by appraising

ap·prais·ing ap·praised *v.t.* to judge the quality of ‖ to give an expert opinion on the value of

ap·prais·er someone whose profession is to estimate the market value of something

ap·pre·cia·ble *adj.* large or important enough to be taken into account or noticed **ap·pré·cia·bly** *adv.*

ap·pre·ci·ate ap·pre·ci·at·ing ap·pre·ci·at·ed *v.t.* to perceive the nature and quality of ‖ to enjoy intelligently ‖ to be grateful for

ap·pre·ci·a·tion *n.* understanding of the nature and quality of something ‖ intelligent enjoyment ‖ gratitude

ap·pre·hend *v.t.* to arrest, capture ‖ to understand ‖ to expect with anxiety **ap·pre·hen·si·ble** *adj.*

ap·pre·hen·sion *n.* anxious expectation ‖ arrest ‖ mental perception, understanding

ap·pre·hen·sive *adj.* anxious

ap·pren·tice *n.* someone learning a craft or trade ‖ a beginner **ap·pren·tic·ing ap·pren·ticed** to bind as an apprentice **ap·prén·tice·ship** *n.*

ap·prise, ap·prize ap·pris·ing, ap·priz·ing ap·prised, ap·prized *v.t.* to inform

ap·proach 1. *v.i.* to come close ‖ *v.t.* to come close to ‖ to seek a way of dealing with **2.** *n.* the act of coming close or closer ‖ a way by which one approaches ‖ a method of begining **ap·proach·a·bil·i·ty** *n.* **ap·proach·a·ble** *adj.*

ap·pro·ba·tion *n.* approval

ap·pro·pri·ate 1. *v.t.* **ap·pro·pri·at·ing ap·pro·pri·at·ed** to take for one's own property ‖ to steal **2.** *adj.* suitable

ap·pro·pri·a·tion *n.* the act of appropriating

ap·pro·pri·a·tive *adj.* relating to appropriation

ap·pro·pri·a·tor *n.* someone who appropriates

ap·prov·al *n.* favorable opinion or judgment

ap·prove ap·prov·ing ap·proved *v.i.* to give or have a favorable opinion ‖ *v.t.* to give official agreement consider to be right, good, advantageous etc.

ap·prox·i·mate 1. *v.* **ap·prox·i·mat·ing ap·prox·i·mat·ed** *v.t.* to come close to ‖ to give as roughly correct **2.** *adj.* unverified but not far from being correct **ap·prox·i·ma·tion** *n.* **ap·prox·i·ma·tive**

a·pri·cot *n.* a fruit tree ‖ its fruit

a·pron *n.* a protection for the clothes worn in front, and tied around the waist ‖ anything like an apron either in shape or in purpose ‖ the part of the stage in front of the curtain

ap·ro·pos 1. *adj.* to the point **2.** *adv.* by the way ‖ fitly, suitably **3.** *prep.* with reference to

apse *n.* aisles or transepts

apt *adj.* to the point, cleverly suited ‖ liable or likely

ap·ti·tude *n.* a natural talent ‖ ability to learn easily and quickly

a·quar·i·um *pl.* **a·quar·i·ums, a·quar·i·a** *n.* a tank (often of glass) in which fishes are kept alive

a·quat·ic 1. *adj.* living or growing in or near water ‖ (*pl.*) water sports

aq·ue·duct *n.* a channel constructed to carry water, esp. one carried on arches across a valley

a·que·ous *adj.* watery ‖ made from water

aq·ui·line *adj.* hooked like the beak of an eagle

Ar·ab *n.* one of the Semitic people inhabiting the Arabian peninsula

ar·a·besque 1. *n.* intertwining design of geometric patterns, used decoratively in early Islamic architecture ‖ a position **2.** *adj.* showing an arabesque design

Ar·a·bic 1. *adj.* of the Arabs or their language **2.** the Arabic language

Arabic numerals the figures 1, 2, 3 etc., in common use

ar·a·ble *adj.* (of land) plowed or suited to plowing **1.** arable land, plowland

ar·bi·ter *n.* someone who decides what will or should be accepted ‖ someone who controls

ar·bi·trage *n.* the buying of goods in one place in order to sell them immediately in another at a higher price

ar·bi·trar·y *adj.* resulting from personal inclination entirely ‖ decided by chance or whim ‖ absolute, despotic

ar·bi·trate ar·bi·trat·ing ar·bi·trat·ed *v.i.* to decide a dispute by arbitration ‖ to judge (a dispute) as an arbitrator

ar·bi·tra·tion *n.* the settling of a dispute by an arbitrator or arbitrators

ar·bi·tra·tor *n.* an impartial judge

ar·bor *n.* a pleasant shady spot in a garden or wood

ar·bo·re·tum *pl.* **ar·bo·re·tums, ar·bo·re·ta** *n.* a collection of trees for display

arc *n.* part of the circumference of a circle or part of any other curve ‖ an electric arc, a sustained luminous electrical discharge

ar·cade *n.* a roofed-in passage ‖ a row of arches

arch *n.* a curved construction

arch *v.t.* to span with an arch ‖ **to arch one's eyebrows** to show surprise n or disapproval by raising one's eyebrows

ar·chae·o·log·i·cal, ar·che·o·log·i·cal *adj.* of or pertaining to archaeology

ar·chae·ol·o·gist, ar·che·ol·o·gist *n.* a specialist in archaeology

ar·chae·ol·o·gy, ar·che·ol·o·gy *n.* the study of prehistory and of ancient periods of history

ar·cha·ic *adj.* belonging to ancient times ‖ fallen into disuse **ar·chá·i·cal·ly** *adv.*

arch·bish·op *n.* a bishop who has a certain limited authority over other bishops a metropolitan

arch·bish·op·ric *n.* the diocese, or office, of an archbishop

arch·er *n.* someone who shoots with a bow and arrow

ar·cher·y *n.* the sport of shooting arrows at a target

ar·che·typ·al *adj.* pertaining to an archetype

ar·che·type *n.* a prototype ‖ the perfect model which inferior examples may resemble but never equal

ar·chi·pel·a·go *pl.* **ar·chi·pel·a·goes, ar·chi·pel·a·gos** *n.* a group of islands

architect *n.* someone whose profession is to design buildings etc.

ar·chi·tec·tur·al *adj.* of or pertaining to architecture

ar·chi·tec·ture *n.* the art, science or profession of designing buildings

ar·chives *pl. n.* a place in which are kept records of interest ‖ the records themselves

arch·way *n.* a passage roofed by a vault held up by arches

Arc·tic *adj.* near or relating to the North Pole **arc·tic** intensely cold

ar·dent *adj.* passionate ‖ eager

ar·dor *n.* passion ‖ eagerness, enthusiasm

ar·du·ous *adj.* steep, hard to climb ‖ strenuous

ar·e·a *n.* the extent of a surface ‖ a district or region, vicinity ‖ a sphere of operation

a·re·na *n.* the open central area of the Roman amphitheater ‖ any large area used for sport, exhibitions, concerts etc.

ar·gon *n.* an odorless, colorless, chemically inert gaseous element

ar·got *n.* the slang of a social group

ar·gu·a·ble *adj.* for which good, if not necessarily convincing, reasons may be found ‖ open to doubt **ár·gu·a·bly** *adv.*

ar·gue ar·gu·ing ar·gued *v.i.* to dispute ‖ to wrangle

ar·gu·ment *n.* a reason put forward (for or against something) ‖ a discussion, debate ‖ a dispute ‖ a wrangling

ar·gu·men·ta·tion *n.* the mental process of constructing a chain of reasoning

ar·gu·men·ta·tive *adj.* excessively fond of arguing or raising objections

a·ri·a *n.* an air, melody, esp. in opera

ar·id *adj.* dry, barren ‖ dull, uninteresting

a·rid·i·ty *n.* the state or quality of being arid

a·rise a·ris·ing a·rose a·ris·en *v.i.* to come into being ‖ to originate from a particular source

ar·is·toc·ra·cy *pl.* **ar·is·toc·ra·cies** *n.* government by a small, privileged, hereditary class ‖ a state so governed ‖ the members of such a governing class

a·ris·to·crat *n.* a member of the ruling class in an aristocracy ‖ a noble

a·ris·to·crat·ic *adj.* of or pertaining to an aristocracy

a·rith·me·tic 1. *n.* the manipulation of numbers by addition, subtraction, multiplication, division 2. *adj.* arithmetical

a·rith·me·ti·cian *n.* someone skilled in the science or practice of arithmetic

arm *n.* the upper limb of the human body ‖ a part attached to or projecting from something ‖ a sleeve of a garment

arm (often *pl.*) a weapon ‖ (*pl.*) the heraldic devices on the shield of a family, diocese, institution, state etc.

arm *v.t.* to provide with weapons, or other means of fighting or attacking ‖ to protect or defend ‖ *v.i.* to build up armaments

ar·ma·da *n.* a fleet of warships

ar·ma·dil·lo *n.* a member of a family of edentate mammals, allied to anteaters

ar·ma·ment *n.* the weapons, with which a ship, aircraft, army, fighting vehicle etc. is equipped

arm·ful *pl.* **arm·fuls, arms** ‖ ful *n.* the amount that can be held in both arms

ar·mi·stice *n.* an agreement by which fighting is suspended while peace terms are negotiated

ar·mor *n.* protection for the body worn in battle ‖ the protective covering of an animal

ar·mor·er *n.* someone who looks after and repairs arms

ar·mor·y *n.* a place in which arms and ammunition are kept

arm·pit *n.* the hollow (axilla) under the joint of the shoulder and arm

ar·my *pl.* **ar·mies** *n.* a body of men (or women, or both) organized for war on land

a·ro·ma *n.* the characteristic odor given off by certain plants, spices etc.

ar·o·mat·ic *adj.* with a sharp, pleasant smell

a·round 1. *adv.* more or less in a circle, on all sides ‖ near, more or less in the vicinity **2.** *prep.* encircling ‖ approximately ‖ within

a·rous·al *n.* an arousing or being aroused

a·rouse *a·rous·ing a·roused v.t.* to excite, stir up ‖ to wake up

ar·raign *v.t.* to call before a court to answer a charge **ar·ráign·ment** *n.*

ar·range *ar·rang·ing ar·ranged v.t.* to put in order ‖ to dispose with taste ‖ to plan ‖ to adapt

ar·range·ment *n.* the act of arranging ‖ a settlement (of a dispute etc.) ‖ something decided in advance ‖ *(pl.)* plans, preparations

ar·ray *v.t.* to arrange in order ‖ to adress (oneself) magnificently

ar·rest *v.t.* to seize and hold by legal authority ‖ to bring to a stop, check

arrest *n.* seizure and imprisonment by legal authority ‖ a check, a stopping of forward movement or progress

ar·ri·val *n.* the act of arriving

ar·rive *ar·riv·ing ar·rived v.i.* to come to a place, reach a destination ‖ to win success, be recognized as successful

ar·ro·gance *n.* haughtiness, an overbearing manner

ar·ro·gant *adj.* haughty, showing too high an opinion of one's own position ‖ contemptuous of others

ar·ro·gate *ar·ro·gat·ing ar·ro·gat·ed v.t.* to claim for oneself improperly **ar·ro·gá·tion** *n.*

ar·row *n.* the arrow shot from a bow with a pointed head, and slender shaft ‖ a directing sign (→)

arse *ASS (buttocks)

ar·se·nal *n.* a place for the making and storing of weapons and munitions

ar·se·nic 1. *n.* a semimetallic element **2.** *adj. chem.* of a compound in which arsenic is pentavalent

ar·son *n.* the crime of maliciously burning property

art *n.* the use of the imagination to make things of aesthetic significance ‖ objects made by creative artists ‖ one of the humanities (as distinct from a science) ‖ one of the liberal arts

ar·te·ri·al *adj.* from or like an artery

ar·te·ri·o·scle·ro·sis *n.* a chronic disease of the arteries

ar·ter·y *pl.* **ar·ter·ies** *n.* one of the tubular, thick-walled, elastic vessels through which blood is pumped by the heart ‖ an important channel (road, railway, river) in a system of communication and transport

art·ful *adj.* tricky, crafty

ar·thrit·ic *adj.* of or having arthritis

ar·thri·tis *n.* inflammation of a joint or joints

ar·thro·pod *n.* a member of an animal phylum characterized by a segmented body, a chitinous exoskeleton, and jointed appendages etc. **ar·throp·o·dal ar·throp·o·dous** *adjs*

ar·ti·cle *n.* a particular thing of a distinct class ‖ a particular piece of writing in a larger work ‖ the words 'the', 'a', 'an'

ar·tic·u·late 1. *adj.* divided by joints ‖ (of speech) divided into distinct words and syllables ‖ able to speak intelligibly ‖ able to speak with fluency ‖ clearly and distinctly arranged or expressed **2.** **ar·tic·u·lat·ing ar·tic·u·lat·ed** *v.t.* to pronounce (words and syllables) clearly and distinctly ‖ to pronounce sounds distinctly

ar·tic·u·la·tion *n.* the pronouncing of distinct sounds of speech ‖ a joint

ar·ti·fi·cial *adj.* man-made ‖ synthetic ‖ insincere ‖ affected

ar·til·ler·y *n.* guns, cannon etc. ‖ the branch of the army equipped with such weapons

ar·ti·san *n.* a trained craftsman

ar·tist *n.* a person who uses deliberate skill in making things of beauty

ar·tis·tic *adj.* relating to the fine arts ‖ made or done with taste and skill, with an eye to beauty **ar·tis·ti·cal·ly** *adv.*

as 1. *conj.* because ‖ at the time when ‖ in the way in which ‖ though **2.** *prep.* in the aspect, role, function, capacity of **3.** *adv.* to the same amount or degree ‖ for example ‖ written or sent as though from

as·bes·tos 1. *n.* fibrous silicate materials, chiefly calcium magnesium silicate **2.** *adj.* made of or containing asbestos

as·cend *v.i.* to go or come up ‖ to rise ‖ to slope upwards *v.t.* to climb ‖ to mount ‖ to go up towards the source of

as·cend·ance, as·cend·ence *n.* ascendancy

as·cend·an·cy, as·cend·en·cy *pl.* **as·cen·dan·cies, as·cen·den·cies** *n.* dominating influence or control

as·cend·ant, as·cend·ent *adj.* (*astron.,* of a heavenly body) climbing towards the zenith, before beginning to set

as·cend·er *n.* the tall stroke of b,d,f,h,k,l,t

as·cend·ing *adj.* rising, mounting

as·cent *n.* the act of ascending ‖ a climbing ‖ a way up ‖ a going back in time

as·cer·tain *v.t.* to find out **as·cer·táin·a·ble** *adj.* **as·cer·táin·a·bly** *adv.* **as·cer·táin·ment** *n.*

as·cet·ic 1. *adj.* practicing self-discipline ‖ frugal, austere ‖ (of personal appearance) giving the impression of self-denial, gaunt, spare **2.** *n.* a person who lives an austere life **as·cáet·i·cal** *adj.* **as·cáet·i·cal·ly** *adv.* **as·cáet·i·cism** *n.*

as·cribe as·crib·ing as·cribed *v.t.* to assign to a cause or source ‖ to regard as belonging

as·crip·tion *n.* a document or statement which describes ‖ an ascribing

a·sep·sis *n.* freedom from bacteria

a·sep·tic 1. *adj.* free from bacterial infection ‖ sterilized **2.** *n.* a self-sterilizing substance **a·sáep·ti·cal·ly** *adv.*

a·sex·u·al *adj.* without sex, sexless **a·sex·u·ál·i·ty** *n.* **a·séx·u·al·ly** *adv.*

ash *n.* the powder left when something has been burned

ash *n.* a genus of trees ‖ the smooth-grained, springy wood of the ash

a·shamed *adj.* feeling shame, dishonor or disgust ‖ reluctant, to do something through pride or fear of ridicule

a·side *adv.* to or on one side ‖ out of the way ‖ a digression

as·i·nine *adj.* stupid **as·i·nin·i·ty** *pl.* **as·i·nin·i·ties** *n.* crass stupidity

ask *v.t.* to request ‖ to inquire ‖ to demand ‖ to invite ‖ *v.i.* to make a request ‖ to inquire

a·skance *adv.* with suspicion or disapproval

a·skew *adv.* and *adj.* crooked, out of line

ask out *v.* to withdraw

a·slant 1. *adv.* slantwise, across at an angle **2.** *prep.* obliquely across

a·sleep 1. *pred. adj.* sleeping ‖ numb **2.** *adv.* into a state of sleep

a·so·cial *adj.* tending to avoid social intercourse ‖ self-centered and indifferent

asp *n.* a small poisonous European snake

as·par·a·gus *n.* a perennial plant. Each spring the plant produces edible thick green shoots

as·pect *n.* look, outward appearance ‖ the angle from which a thing may be regarded

as·per·i·ty *pl.* **as·per·i·ties** *n.* sharpness ‖ roughness, unevenness ‖ severity

as·perse as·pers·ing as·persed *v.t.* to malign, try to hurt the reputation of

as·per·sion *n.* an oblique assault on a person's reputation ‖ a sprinkling with holy water

as·phalt 1. *n.* a bituminous derivative of petroleum **2.** *adj.* with a surface of asphalt **3.** *v.t.* to apply a surface of asphalt to

as·phyx·i·a *n.* the condition in which a person is not able to get air into his lungs **as·phýx·i·ant 1,** *adj.* causing suffocation **2.** *n.* an agent a with this property **as·phyx·i·ate as·phyx·i·at·ing as·phyx·i·rat·ed** *v.t.* to cause asphyxia in ‖ *v.i.* to be a victim of asphyxia **as·phyx·i·a·tion, as·phýx·i·rá·tor** *ns*

as·pir·ant *n.* a person anxious to win a desirable thing or position

as·pi·rate 1. *v.t.* **as·pi·rat·ing as·pi·rat·ed** to pronounce with an h sound ‖ to remove (fluid or gas) with an aspirator

2. the sound represented by the letter h

as·pi·ra·tion *n.* ambition or an ambition

as·pi·ra·tor *n.* a suction pump or similar device

as·pire as·pir·ing as·pired *v.i.* to be eager, to have an ambition

as·pi·rin *n.* acetylsalicylic acid

ass *n.* any of several mammals, the donkey ‖ a stupid person

ass *n.* the buttocks

as·sail *v.t.* to attack vigorously

as·sail·ant *n.* an attacker

as·sas·sin *n.* a person who kills, or tries to kill, another by violent means

as·sas·si·nate **as·sas·si·nat·ing** **as·sas·si·nat·ed** *v.t.* to kill as an assassin **as·sas·si·na·tion** *n.*

as·sault *n.* a vigorous attack ‖ an unlawful threat to use force

assault *v.t.* to make an assault on

as·say *n.* the determination of the proportion of a metal in an ore or alloy

as·sem·blage *n.* a number of persons or things gathered together ‖ an assembling

as·sem·ble as·sem·bling as·sem·bled *v.t.* to bring together ‖ to fit together

as·sem·bly *pl.* **as·sem·blies** *n.* a gathering of people

as·sent *n.* an acceptance as true

as·sent *v.i.* to give expressed or unexpressed mental acceptance to the truth or rightness of a doctrine, conclusion etc. ‖ to say yes

as·sert *v.t.* to state as true ‖ to maintain, insist on ‖ to make effective, use with effect ‖ to be domineering

as·ser·tion *n.* a positive statement

as·ser·tive *adj.* dominating ‖ positive

as·sess *v.t.* to fix the value or amount of ‖ to impose a charge for **as·séss·a·ble** *adj.* **as·séss·ment** *n.* the amount assessed ‖ the act of assessing ‖ an estimate

as·ses·sor *n.* a person who assesses value **as·ses·so·ri·al** *adj.*

as·set *n.* anything one owns or any quality one has that is of value or use ‖ *(pl.)* the positive items on a balance sheet

as·si·du·i·ty *n.* untiring diligence or attention

as·sid·u·ous *adj.* constant in working or attention

assign *v.t.* to give as a share, allot ‖ to nominate, appoint ‖ to give or make over ‖ to fix or determine ‖ to ascribe ‖ to give as a task

as·sig·na·tion *n.* a secret arrangement to meet ‖ an attribution of origin and esp. of date

as·sign·ee *n.* a person who has been given the right or duty of acting in place of another

as·sign·ment *n.* the act of assigning ‖ transference of property or a right ‖ the document by which this is done

as·sist *v.t.* to help ‖ *v.i.* to be of service

as·sis·tance *n.* usefulness, service

as·sis·tant 1. *n.* a helper ‖ a person holding a subordinate position **2.** *adj.* helping ‖ subordinate

as·so·ci·ate 1. *adj.* acting on equal terms **2.** *n.* a fellow worker or partner **3.** *v.* **as·so·ci·at·ing as·so·ci·at·ed** *v.t.* to connect in one's mind ‖ to join as companion etc. **as·só·ci·ate·ship** *n.* less than full membership

as·so·ci·a·tion *n.* an organized body of people with a common interest ‖ an idea identified in one's mind with some object and recalled by

as·so·nance *n.* a similarity of sound between words or syllables

as·sort *v.t.* to sort, classify *v.i.* to harmonize **as·sórt·ed** *adj.* classified

as·sort·ment *n.* a collection made up of different things, or different kinds of the same thing

as·suage as·suag·ing as·suaged *v.t.* to soothe, lessen **as·suáge·ment** *n.*

as·sume as·sum·ing as·sumed *v.t.* to suppose, (something) to be true ‖ to believe (someone) to be something ‖ to put on as a pretense ‖ to begin effectively in (office) ‖ **as·súmed** *adj.* accepted as ‖ pretended, false **as·súm·ing** *adj.* proud, arrogant

as·sump·tion *n.* something taken for granted

as·sur·ance *n.* something on which one can rely as a guarantee of truth ‖ self-confidence

as·sure as·sur·ing as·sured *v.t.* to make certain ‖ to tell as a certain fact **as·súred** *adj.* certain ‖ self-confident **as·súr·ed·ly** *adv.* emphatically yes **as·súr·ed·ness** *n.* self-confidence

as·ter·isk *n.* a mark like a star [*] which calls attention to a note

a·stern *adv.* in, at, or towards the rear

as·ter·oid *n.* one of the small planets occupying orbits mainly between those of Mars and Jupiter

asth·ma *n.* a disease which causes wheezing and difficulty in breathing

asth·mat·ic 1. *adj.* caused by asthma **2.** *n.* someone who suffers from asthma **asth·mát·i·cal** *adj.*

as·tig·mat·ic *adj.* affected by astigmatism

a·stig·ma·tism *n.* a defect of the eye, of a lens

as·ton·ish *v.t.* to strike with amazement or **as·tón·ish·ing** *adj.* amazing **as·tón·ish·ment**

as·tound *v.t.* to shock with fear ‖ to surprise greatly **as·tóund·ing** *adj.*

a·stray *adv.* on the wrong road ‖ mistaken, wrong

a·stride with one leg on each side

a·strin·gen·cy *n.* the quality of being stringent

a·strin·gent 1. *adj.* tightening ‖ causing the mouth to feel dry

as·tro·labe *n.* a circular ring or metal disk on which the heavenly sphere was projected

as·trol·o·ger *n.* a person who practices astrology

as·tro·log·i·cal *adj.* pertaining to astrology

as·trol·o·gy *n.* predicting the influence of the planets and stars on human affairs

as·tro·naut *n.* a space traveler

as·tro·nau·tics *n.* the science of travel in outer space

as·tron·o·mer *n.* a person skilled in astronomy

as·tro·nom·ic *adj.* pertaining to astronomy ‖ enormous **as·tro·nóm·i·cal** *adj.*

as·tro·nóm·i·cal·ly *adv.*

as·tron·o·my *n.* the science of the heavenly bodies

as·tute *adj.* shrewd

a·sun·der *adv.* into two or more parts, into pieces

a·sy·lum *n.* hospital for the mentally ill ‖ refuge

a·sym·met·ric *adj.* showing assymmetry **a·sym·mét·ri·cal** *adj.*

a·sym·me·try *n.* uneven disposition on each side of an (imaginary) central line or point

at *prep.* expressing position ‖ expressing place in time ‖ expressing cause or occasion of an action or state

at·e·lier *n.* an artist's studio

a·the·ism *n.* the denial of the existence of God **á·the·ist** *n.* and *adj.* **a·the·is·tic** *adj.* **a·the·ís·ti·cal·ly** *adv.*

ath·lete a person with the skill and training to be good at sports

athlete's foot a skin disease between the toes

ath·let·ic *adj.* strong, fit and agile **ath·lét·ics** *n.* the sports practiced by athletes

a·thwart *adv.* across the length of a ship or across her course **a·thwart·ships** *adv.* from side to side across a ship

at·las *n.* the first vertebra in the neck ‖ a book containing a collection of maps

at·mos·phere *n.* the gases that surround the earth

at·mos·pher·ic *adj.* **at·mos·phér·i·cal** *adj.*

atmospheric pressure the pressure exerted by the earth's atmosphere

a·toll *n.* a coral reef enclosing a lagoon

at·om *n.* the smallest portion of matter

a·tom·ic *adj.* related to atoms **a·tóm·i·cal·ly** *adv.*

atomic pile a nuclear reactor

at·om·ize at·om·iz·ing at·om·ized *v.t.* to convert a liquid into very fine particles **át·om·iz·er** *n.* a device for atomizing a liquid

a·tone a·ton·ing a·toned *v.i.* to make amends

a·tone·ment *n.* the act of atoning

a·tri·um *pl.* **a·tri·a** *n.* the central hall of a Roman house ‖ a cavity in the body

a·tro·cious *adj.* wicked ‖ of very bad quality

a·troc·i·ty *pl.* **a·troc·i·ties** *n.* shocking cruelty or wickedness ‖ extreme painfulness **1.** *n.* a wasting or withering away from lack of food or use **2.** *v.* **at·ro·phy·ing at·ro·phied** *v.t.* to cause atrophy in ‖ *v.i.* to suffer atrophy

at·tach *v.t.* to fasten, connect *v.i.* to be fastened in some specified way

at·ta·cheé a person attached to an embassy for some specific activity

at·tach·ment *n.* the act of attaching one thing to another ‖ a bond of affection or friendship

at·tack *n.* the act of attacking ‖ a bout of illness

attack *v.t.* to set upon, try to get the better of or destroy or win ‖ to make an attack

at·tain *v.t.* to arrive at, obtain **at·tain·a·bil·i·ty** *n.* **at·táin·a·ble** *adj.*

at·tain·ment *n.* the act of attaining

at·tempt 1. *v.t.* to try or make trial of ‖ to try to achieve **2.** *n.* the act of attempting, often unsuccessful

at·tend *v.t.* to be present at ‖ to visit and treat (as doctor, nurse etc.)

at·tend·ance *n.* the act of attending, being present

at·tend·ant 1. *n.* a servant, an employee in charge

at·ten·tion *n.* the giving of one's mind to something, mental concentration ‖ nursing, care, looking after ‖ the formal position of readiness on parade

at·ten·tive *adj.* paying attention ‖ thoughtful

at·test *v.t.* to bear witness to ‖ to administer an oath to ‖ *v.i.* to testify

at·test·ant 1. *adj.* attesting **2.** *n.* someone who attests

at·tes·ta·tion *n.* the act of bearing witness

at·tic *n.* a room just under the roof of a house

at·tire 1. *v.t.* **at·tir·ing at·tired** to dress grandly **2.** *n.* fine clothing

at·ti·tude *n.* posture ‖ a mental position **at·ti·tú·di·nize at·ti·tu·di·niz·ing at·ti·tu·di·nized** *v.i.* to strike an attitude

at·tor·ney *n.* a person who has legal authority to act on behalf of another

at·tract *v.t.* to draw towards itself or oneself

at·trac·tion *n.* the power or act of attracting ‖ a desirable or pleasant quality or thing

at·trac·tive *adj.* charming, good-looking

at·tri·bute 1. *n.* a quality proper to or characteristic of a person or thing **2.** *v.t.* **at·trib·ut·ing at·trib·ut·ed** to consider (something) as being proper to or belonging to a person or thing

at·tri·bu·tion *n.* the act of attributing

at·trib·u·tive 1. *adj.* preceding the word it modifies, e.g. in 'a wrong answer', 'wrong' is attributive, but in 'your answer is wrong', 'wrong' is predicative

at·tri·tion *n.* a wearing away by rubbing or friction ‖ normal reduction, e.g. by death, retirement

au·burn *adj.* reddish-brown

auc·tion 1. *n.* a public sale at which the goods are sold to the highest bidder **2.** to sell by auction

au·da·cious *adj.* daring

au·dac·i·ty *pl.* **au·dac·i·ties** *n.* boldness ‖ impudence, shamelessness

au·di·bil·i·ty *n.* the ability to be heard

au·di·ble *adj.* able to be heard **áu·di·bly** *adv.*

au·di·ence a group of persons assembled to listen to or watch something ‖ an official or formal interview

au·di·o *adj.* of or relating to sound broadcasting

au·dit 1. *n.* a full check and examination of account books **2.** *v.t.* to make such an examination

au·di·tion 1. *n.* a trial of talent in which a prospective employer assesses an actor, singer etc. **2.** *v.t.* to submit to an audition ‖ *v.i.* to compete in an audition

au·di·tor *n.* a person who makes an audit ‖ a listener, e.g. to a broadcast **au·di·to·ri·al** *adj.*

au·di·to·ri·um *n.* the part of a theater or movie theater etc. in which the audience sits

au·di·to·ry *adj.* relating to the sense of hearing

auditory meatus the channel leading from the outer ear to the eardrum

au·ger *n.* a tool, larger than a gimlet, for boring holes in wood

ought, ought *n. archaic* anything

aug·ment *v.t.* to add to ‖ *v.i.* to increase

aug·men·ta·tion *n.* an increasing or being increased

aunt *n.* a sister of one's mother or father

au·ra *n.* the atmosphere of a thing **áu·ral** *adj.*

au·re·o·la *n.* an aureole

au·re·ole *n.* the heavenly crown, often represented in art by a halo ‖ the halo of light seen around a heavenly body or bright light in misty weather

au·re·o·my·cin *n.* the antibiotic chlortetracycline

au·ri·cle *n.* the external part of the ear ‖ the chamber or either of the two chambers in the heart connecting the veins with the ventricles

au·ro·ra *n.* the redness of the sky just before sunrise

aurora aus·tra·lis *n.* a phenomenon in the southern hemisphere analogous to the aurora borealis

aurora bo·re·al·is *n.* a colored glow visible at night in high latitudes.

aus·pice *n.* the observation of the behavior of animals, so as to learn whether the gods would be pleased or displeased by a proposed action ‖ **under the auspices of** under the patronage of, by care and favor of

aus·pi·cious *adj.* giving promise of good fortune

aus·tere *adj.* stern and strict ‖ simple and without decoration

aus·ter·i·ty *pl.* **aus·ter·i·ties** *n.* the quality of being austere

au·tar·chic *adj.* of or characteristic of an autarchy **au·tár·chi·cal** *adj.*

au·tar·chy *pl.* **au·tar·chies** *n.* despotism,

the rule of an autocrat ‖ a country under such rule

au·then·tic *adj.* genuine **au·thén·ti·cal·ly** *adv.*

au·then·ti·cate au·then·ti·cat·ing au·then·ti·cat·ed *v.t.* to prove the genuineness of truth of **au·then·ti·cá·tion, au·then·ti·cá·tor** *ns*

au·then·tic·i·ty *n.* the quality of being authentic

author *n.* the writer of a book, article etc. **au·tho·ri·al** *adj.*

au·thor·i·tar·i·an 1. *adj.* favoring the theory that respect for authority is of greater importance than individual liberty ‖ domineering **2.** *n.* a person supporting this theory **au·thor·i·tár·i·an·ism** *n.*

au·thor·i·ta·tive *adj.* coming from an official source ‖ with an air of command

au·thor·i·ty *pl.* **au·thor·i·ties** *n.* the right and power to command and be obeyed ‖ (esp. *pl.*) the government, those in charge ‖ evidence, reasons for a statement

au·thor·i·za·tion *n.* an authorizing

au·thor·ize au·thor·iz·ing au·thor·ized *v.t.* to give legal power ‖ to give permission for ‖ to delegate power to **áu·thor·ized** *adj.* officially approved

au·thor·ship *n.* writing as profession ‖ the identity of the author of a literary work

au·to·bi·og·ra·pher *n.* a person who writes the story of his life

au·to·bi·o·graph·ic *adj.* relating to autobiography **au·to·bi·o·gráph·i·cal** *adj.*

au·to·bi·og·ra·phy *pl.* **au·to·bi·og·ra·phies** *n.* a written account of one's own life

au·to·bus *n.* a bus

au·toc·ra·cy *pl.* **au·toc·ra·cies** *n.* government by a single absolute ruler ‖ a state so governed

au·to·crat *n.* an absolute ruler, a despot **au·to·crát·ic, au·to·crát·i·cal** *adjs*

au·to·gi·ro, au·to·gy·ro *n.* aircraft driven by a conventional propeller but with the wings wholly or partly replaced by a freely revolving horizontal rotor

au·to·graph 1. *n.* something written in a person's own handwriting, esp. his signature **2.** *v.t.* to sign with one's name
au·to·gráph·i·cal *adjs*

autogyrou *AUTOGIRO

au·to·mat *n.* a restaurant where prepared food is served in locked glass compartments

au·to·mat·ic 1. *adj.* mechanically self-acting ‖ not controlled by the will ‖ done or said without consideration or hesitation **2.** *n.* an automatic rifle, pistol etc.
au·to·mat·i·cal·ly *adv.*

au·to·ma·tion *n.* a technique by which mechanical processes are subject to some degree of automatic control, without human intervention

au·to·mo·bile *n.* a (usually) four-wheeled vehicle driven by an engine (gasoline, diesel, electric etc.)

au·ton·o·mous *adj.* self-governing

au·ton·o·my *pl.* **au·ton·o·mies** *n.* self-government

au·top·sy *pl.* **au·top·sies** *n.* the examination of a dead body to determine the cause of death

au·to·sug·ges·tion *n.* influencing one's state of mind or body, by an idea which one keeps constantly in mind

au·tumn *n.* the third season of the year between summer and winter

au·tum·nal *adj.* of autumn

aux·il·ia·ry 1. *adj.* providing additional help when needed ‖ supplementary **2.** *n.* *pl.* **aux·il·ia·ries** a supplementary group

a·vail 1. *v.t.* be useful to ‖ to be effective **2.** *n.* use, benefit, advantage **a·vail·a·bíl·i·ty** *n.* **a·váil·a·ble** *adj.* ready or free for use

av·a·lanche *n.* a great mass of snow, ice, earth, rocks etc. which breaks away on a mountainside and pours down the slope

a·vant-garde *n.* those who experiment boldly in the arts and are in advance of their

av·a·rice *n.* greed for money

a·venge a·veng·ing a·venged *v.t.* to inflict just punishment in return for an injury

or wrong

av·e·nue *n.* a formally designed or planted approach or road ‖ a wide street

a·ver a·ver·ring a·verred *v.t.* to assert, declare firmly

av·er·age 1. *n.* the arithmetic mean **2.** *adj.* worked out as a mathematical average ‖ undistinguished, ordinary **3.** *v.* **av·er·ag·ing av·er·aged** *v.t.* to work out the average of ‖ to be on average

a·verse *adj.* opposed

a·ver·sion *n.* an active or pronounced dislike

a·vert *v.t.* to turn away ‖ to prevent, ward off

a·vi·ar·y *pl.* **a·vi·ar·ies** *n.* an enclosure or cage for breeding and rearing birds

a·vi·a·tion *n.* the science of flying aircraft

a·vi·a·tor *n.* a pilot or member of an aircraft crew

av·id *adj.* intensely eager ‖ very keen

av·o·ca·do *pl.* **av·o·ca·dos, av·o·ca·does** *n.* the alligator pear, native to tropical America

av·o·ca·tion *n.* an occupation, esp. one followed for pleasure, or one of minor importance

a·void *v.t.* to keep out of the way of ‖ to refrain from

a·void·ance *n.* *n.* measures taken in advance to avoid an unpleasantness

av·oir·du·pois *n.* a system of reckoning weight in English-speaking countries based on the pound equal to 16 ounces ‖ portliness

a·vow *v.t.* to admit to be true, openly acknowledge **a·vów·al** *n.* **a·vówed** *adj.* **a·vow·ed·ly** *adv.*

a·wait *v.t.* to wait for, look out for ‖ *v.i.* to be in store as a future experience

a·wake a·wak·ing a·woke a·wok·en a·waked a·wak·ened *v.i.* to stop sleeping ‖ (with 'to') to realize ‖ *v.t.* to wake up

awake *pred. adj.* not asleep ‖ alert

a·wak·en *v.t.* to wake up (someone) ‖ *v.i.* to awake **a·wák·en·ing** *n.* a realization of circumstances ‖ arousal of interest or activity

a·ward *n.* a prize, grant etc. won or given

award *v.t.* to give as a prize, reward, or judgment

a·ware *adj.* conscious, informed

a·wash *adj.* and *adv.* just covered by water ‖ washing about in the sea ‖ inebriated

a·way 1. *adv.* to, or at, a distance ‖ in a different direction ‖ continuously, steadily **far and away** beyond all doubt **to do away with** to get rid of, murder ‖ to do or say with impunity **to take away** to detract ‖ to subtract **2.** *adj.* absent ‖ at a distance

awe 1. *n.* a feeling of deep wonder and respect ‖ fear and respect **2.** *v.t.* **aw·ing awed** to fill with awe

aw·ful *adj.* very bad ‖ shocking, appalling ‖ very great or large **áw·ful·ly** *adv.* very

a·while *adv.* for a while, for a short time

awk·ward *adj.* not quite right ‖ inconvenient ‖ difficult to deal with ‖ obstinate, unhelpful ‖ clumsy, uncouth

awl *n.* a short pointed tool used for making holes

awn·ing *n.* a sheet of canvas, used chiefly to protect against strong sunlight or rain

A.W.O.L. absent without leave

a·wry *adv.* and *adj.* crooked, not straight

ax, axe 1. *n.* a tool used for cutting down trees, or chopping ‖ such an ax used as a battle weapon ‖ drastic cutting of expenditure **2.** *v.t.* **ax·ing** to shape with an ax ‖ to put an end to ‖ to reduce drastically

ax·i·al *adj.* of, or relating to, or like an axis

ax·i·om *n.* a self evident truth or proposition ‖ an accepted principle ‖ a maxim

ax·i·o·mat·ic *adj.* self-evident, obvious

ax·is *pl.* **ax·es** *n.* the line, real or imaginary, around which a thing rotates ‖ one of the reference lines in a coordinate system ‖ an alliance between countries to ensure solidarity of foreign policy

ax·le *n.* the bar or pin on which the hub of a wheel turns ‖ the arm joining two wheels of a vehicle

az·i·muth *n.* the horizontal arc expressed as the clockwise angle between a fixed point (such as true north) and the vertical plane through the object

az·ure 1. *adj.* sky-blue **2.** *n.* azure color

B

B, b the second letter of the English alphabet

B.A. Bachelor of Arts

bab·ble bab·bling bab·bled *v. i.* to chatter idly or continuously ‖ to murmur ‖ *v. t.* to utter confusedly or incoherently **bab·bler**

ba·boon *n.* dog-faced monkeys of Africa and Arabia

ba·bush·ka *n.* a scarf worn by a woman over her hair

ba·by 1. *pl.* **ba·bies** *n.* an infant ‖ the youngest member of a family ‖ a timorous person **2.** *adj.* **3. ba·by·ing ba·bied** *v. t.* to treat with inordinate care or indulgence

ba·by·hood *n.* the state or age of being a baby

ba·by·ish *adj.* like a baby

bac·ca·lau·re·ate *n.* the bachelor's degree

bac·cha·nal *n.* a drunken orgy **1.** *adj.* bacchanalian ‖ riotous

bach·e·lor *n.* an unmarried man ‖ a man or woman who has taken the first university degree

ba·cil·lus *pl.* **ba·cil·li** *n.* a large genus of bacteria

back 1. *n.* the hinder part of the body, or, in most animals, the upper part from the neck to the end of the spine ‖ the less important side or surface of a thing, opposite the front ‖ a defensive position in certain games **behind one's back** without one's knowledge, deceitfully or treacherously **to break one's back to** overwork **to have one's back to the wall** to be hard pressed and fighting for survival **2.** *v. t.* to give moral or material support to ‖ to cause to move backwards ‖ *v. i.* **to move backwards** ‖ to retreat **to back down** to stop asserting something **to back up** to give moral support to **3.** *adj.* to the rear ‖ remote ‖ in arrears **to take a back seat** to take a minor part in some activity **4.** *adv.* to the rear, backward, at a distance **to get back at** someone to get even with someone **to give back** to restore (something borrowed or taken) **to keep back** to

withhold ‖ to conceal (a fact etc.) **to take back** to return (something sold) ‖ to retract

back·bone *n.* the spinal column ‖ courage

back·drop *n.* a painted cloth or drop curtain at the back of the stage

back·fire 1. *n.* a premature explosion in the cylinder of an internal combustion engine, or in the breach of a gun **2.** *v. i.* **back·fir·ing back·fired** to explode in this way ‖ to go wrong

back·ground *n.* the part of a picture against which the principal figures are shown ‖ an inconspicuous position ‖ a person's past history

back·hand *n.* a backhand stroke, or the capacity to play backhand strokes **back·hand·ed** *adj.* made with the back of the hand ‖ double-edged

back·side *n.* the buttocks

back·slide back·slid·ing back·slid back·slid, back·slid·en *v. i.* to fall away or lapse from former virtuous beliefs or conduct

back·stage *n.* the stage area behind the proscenium, esp. the dressing rooms

back·ward *adj.* turned or directed to the back ‖ not progressing normally ‖ shy

back·woods *pl. n.* the remote, sparsely settled areas of a country

ba·con *n.* the flesh from a pig's back and sides, cured dry or in pickle and smoked

bac·te·ri·al *adj.* of or resulting from bacteria

bac·te·ri·ol·o·gist *n.* someone who studies bacteriology

bac·te·ri·ol·o·gy *n.* the scientific study of bacteria

bac·te·ri·um *pl.* **bac·te·ri·a** *n.* a large class of microscopic unicellular plants lacking chlorophyll and fully defined nuclei

bad 1. *adj.* **worse worst** wicked, evil ‖ defective, inadequate ‖ serious ‖ faulty ‖ disagreeable ‖ distressed, upset ‖ harmful **to go bad** to decay **2.** *n.* that which is bad ‖ misfortune **3.** *adv.* badly

badge *n.* a distinctive device worn as a sign of office

badg·er 1. *n.* a burrowing, carnivorous,

nocturnal mammal **2.** *v.t.* to nag with requests

bad·i·nage *n.* playful teasing

bad·ly worse worst *adv.* not well

baf·fle *v.t.* **baf·fling baf·fled** to puzzle, perplex

bag 1. *n.* a receptacle of leather, cloth, paper etc. often shaped like a sack **bag and baggage** (with) all one's belongings **in the bag** as good as secured **to be left holding the bag** to be left to take the blame **2.** *v.* **bag·ging bagged** *v.t.* to put into a bag or bags ‖ *v.i.* to hang loosely

bag·gage *n.* personal luggage

bag·gy bag·gi·er bag·gi·est *adj.* stretched out of shape

bag·pipe *n.* (usually *pl.*) a musical wind instrument **bag·pip·er** *n.*

bail *n.* money deposited to obtain a prisoner's freedom

bail, bale 1. *n.* a vessel used to scoop water out of a boat, a bailer **2.** *v.t.* to scoop out (water) from

bail·iff *n.* a court officer who keeps order in court

bait *v.t.* to put food on (a hook) or in (a trap) to lure a fish or animal ‖ to tease, provoke

bake bak·ing baked *v.t.* to cook (food) in dry heat, esp. in an oven ‖ to make hard by heating

bak·er *n.* a professional breadmaker

baker's dozen thirteen

bak·er·y *pl.* **bak·er·ies** *n.* a baker's shop

bal·a·lai·ka *n.* a triangular, guitar-like musical instrument popular esp. in Russia

bal·ance bal·anc·ing bal·anced *v.t.* to weigh in a balance ‖ to match, offset ‖ to keep in equilibrium ‖ *v.i.* to remain in equilibrium ‖ (of account entries) to be equal on the credit and debit sides

balance *n.* an instrument for measuring the weight of a body ‖ equilibrium ‖ mental or emotional stability ‖ the remainder

bal·co·ny *pl.* **bal·co·nies** *n.* an accessible platform projecting outwards from the window or wall of a building ‖ (theater)

a tier of seat

bald *adj.* without hair or fur

bal·der·dash *n.* nonsense, foolish talk

bale 1. *n.* a quantity of cotton, wheat, straw etc., tightly bound for ease of handling **2.** *v.t.* **bal·ing baled** to make up into bundles

bale·ful *adj.* willing evil ‖ causing evil

balk, baulk 1. *n.* a hindrance or stumbling block ‖ (baseball) a foul by a pitcher **2.** *v.t.* to hinder, thwart ‖ *v.i.* to pull up, refuse to proceed

balk·y balk·i·er balk·i·est *adj.* given to balking

ball 1. *n.* a spherical object of any size ‖ the rounded part of the foot near the base of the big toe ‖ the mound at the base of the thumb, set in the palm **2.** *v.t.* to wind up into a ball ‖ *v.i.* to form a ball **balled up** confused, muddled

ball *n.* a formal assembly for social dancing

bal·lad *n.* a narrative poem ‖ any simple song, having the same melody for each stanza

bal·last *n.* any heavy substance placed in a ship's hold, or balloon basket, to improve stability **1.** *v.t.* to stabilize

bal·le·ri·na *n.* a female ballet dancer

bal·let *n.* a performance, usually by two or more dancers, in which music, movement and mime are combined

bal·lis·tics *n.* the scientific study of projectiles

bal·loon 1. *n.* an envelope of gasproof fabric distended by the pressure of a gas less dense than air at ground level **2.** *v.i.* to go up in a balloon ‖ to swell out like a balloon

bal·lot *n.* a paper used in secret voting ‖ the total votes cast at an election

ball·room *n.* a large room for dancing

balm *n.* a genus of perennial fragrant herbs widely ‖ an aromatic and medicinal resin obtained from certain trees ‖ balsam ‖ any calming or consoling influence

balm·i·ly *adv.* in a balmy manner

balm·i·ness *n.* the state or quality of being

balmy

balm·y balm·i·er balm·i·est *adj.* fragrant, gentle, refreshing ‖ crazy, weak in the head

ba·lo·ney, bo·lo·ney *n.* bologna (sausage) ‖ nonsense, humbug

bal·sa *n.* an American tree ‖ the wood of this

bal·sam *n.* a mixture of resins in volatile oils ‖ any plant or tree yielding balsam

bal·us·ter *n.* one of the small pillars which support the railing of a staircase or balcony etc., a banister

bam·boo *n.* an arborescent grass grown in the tropics and subtropics

ban ban·ning banned *v.t.* to prohibit, forbid

ban *n.* a formal prohibition ‖ a formal interdict

ba·nal *adj.* commonplace, flat

ba·nal·i·ty *pl.* **ba·nal·i·ties** *n.* triteness

ba·nan·a *n.* the edible fruit of a genus of plants cultivated widely in tropical and subtropical areas

band *n.* a group of musicians ‖ an organized group of persons

band·age 1. *n.* a strip of cloth used to protect or bind an injured part of the body **2.** *v.t.* **band·ag·ing band·aged**

ban·dit *n.* a robber

bane *n.* a cause of misery, worry, or anxiety ‖ **bane·ful** *adj.* harmful

bang 1. *v.t.* to make a loud, sudden noise **2.** *n.* a hard knock ‖ a loud, sudden noise ‖ a thrill of pleasure

ban·ish *v.t.* to drive away from home or an accustomed place ‖ to dismiss from one's presence or thoughts **ban·ish·ment** *n.*

ban·is·ter *n.* the upright support of a stair rail

ban·jo *pl.* **ban·jos, ban·joes** *n.* a stringed musical instrument **ban·jo·ist** *n.*

bank 1. *n.* a place where money is kept and paid out, lent, borrowed, issued or exchanged ‖ a reserve supply of a thing, blood bank **2.** *v.t.* to deposit (money or valuables) at a bank **to bank on** to rely upon **bank·a·ble** *adj.*

bank *n.* the rising ground bordering a lake, river etc. ‖ an elevation of mud or sand etc. in a sea or river bed ‖ the cushion in billiards ‖ the tilting of an aircraft rounding a curve ‖ *v.i.* to tilt sideways when rounding a curve in flight

bank·er *n.* a person conducting the business of a bank

bank·ing *n.* the business of a banker

bank·rupt 1. *n.* a person who cannot pay his debts **2.** *adj.* insolvent, unable to pay one's debts **3.** *v.t.* to reduce to bankruptcy **bank·rupt·cy** *n.*

ban·ner *n.* a cloth flag on a pole used as a military standard ‖ the flag of a country

ban·quet *n.* a feast ‖ an official celebration dinner with speeches

ban·tam *n.* a small variety of domestic fowl

ban·tam·weight *n.* a boxer whose weight does not exceed 118 lbs

ban·ter 1. *n.* playful teasing **2.** *v.i.* to talk jokingly

bap·tism *n.* the religious practice of sprinkling a person with water, or immersing him in it ‖ an experience that initiates a new way of life **bap·tis·mal** *adj.*

bap·tis·try *pl.* **bap·tis·tries** *n.* the part of a church used for baptism

bap·tize bap·tiz·ing bap·tized *v.t.* to administer baptism ‖ to give a name to

bar *n.* a long piece of wood, metal etc. ‖ a barrier of any kind ‖ a metal strip on the ribbon of a medal as an additional award ‖ a vertical line across a staff dividing it into equal measures of time ‖ any tribunal ‖ the legal profession ‖ a counter over which liquor and food may be served

bar 1. *v.t.* **bar·ring barred** to fasten, secure ‖ to obstruct ‖ to prohibit **2.** *prep.* except, excluding

barb *n.* the part of an arrow, fishhook, bee's sting etc., that points backwards and hinders removal

bar·bar·i·an *n.* a savage, uncivilized person

bar·bar·ic *adj.* savage ‖ utterly lacking in taste, breeding, etc. **bar·bar·i·cal·ly** *adv.*

bar·bar·i·ty pl. **bar·bar·i·ties** n. savage cruelty

bar·bar·ous adj. uncivilized ‖ cruel ‖ uncouth

bar·be·cue 1. n. any party where food is grilled on a metal frame over charcoal ‖ the grill itself ‖ the food cooked on the grill with a highly seasoned sauce **2.** v. **bar·be·cu·ing barbe·cued** to roast over a barbecue pit or grill

barbed wire a steel wire to which pointed steel barbs are attached at close intervals

bar·ber n. a person whose business is cutting and dressing men's hair, shaving, etc.

bar·ber·shop n. a barber's premises

bar·bi·tu·rate n. one of a group of drugs derived from barbituric acid

bare 1. adj. uncovered, naked ‖ without trees or any tall growth ‖ empty ‖ scant, meager ‖ plain, unconcealed ‖ very slight **2.** v.t. **bar·ing bared** to uncover

bare·ly adv. only just, merely ‖ scantily

bar·gain n. an agreement on terms of give and take ‖ something acquired or offered cheaply

barge 1. n. a flat-bottomed freight boat without sails **2.** v.i. **barg·ing barged** to move about clumsily ‖ (with 'in', 'into') to intrude

bar·i·tone, bar·y·tone n. a male voice between tenor and bass ‖ a man having such a voice

bark n. the tissue in woody stems and roots external to the cambium

bark 1. v.i. to make the sharp, explosive, vocal noise characteristic of dogs ‖ v.t. to snap out sharply and abruptly **2.** n. the brief, explosive cry of esp. dogs and foxes ‖ any similar sound

bar·ley n. a cereal grass

bar mitz·vah n. the Jewish ceremony admitting a boy to adult membership of the Jewish community **bas mitzvah** similar ceremony for a Jewish girl

barn n. a farm building for storing grain, hay, farm implements etc. or for housing animals

bar·na·cle n. a goose of **1.** Europe ‖ a crustacean

ba·rom·e·ter n. an instrument for measuring atmospheric pressures **bar·o·met·ric bar·o·met·ri·cal** adjs. **ba·rom·e·try** n.

ba·ron a member of the lowest order of nobility

ba·roque adj. of painting and sculpture, architecture, literature and music of the late 16th and 17th cc.

bar·rack n. (esp. pl.) a large building for lodging soldiers

bar·ra·cu·da pl. **bar·ra·cu·da, bar·ra·cu·das** n. a member of fam. Sphyraenidae, predatory fishes found in warm seas

bar·rage n. a barrier, esp. of artillery shellfire, to impede enemy action

bar·rel 1. n. a flat-ended, curved cylindrical container, a cask ‖ the metal tube of a gun ‖ the case **2.** v. **bar·rel·ing, bar·rel·ling bar·reled, bar·relled** v.t. to put in barrels ‖ v.i. to travel very fast

bar·ren adj. sterile, incapable of bearing (children, fruit etc.) ‖ unprofitable, without result

bar·rette n. a hinged clip for keeping a girl's hair in place

bar·ri·cade 1. n. a defense or obstruction **2.** v.t. **bar·ri·cad·ing bar·ri·cad·ed** to block with a barricade

bar·ri·er n. an obstacle ‖ something that hinders progress ‖ a mental or emotional obstacle

bar·row n. a small wheeled handcart

bar·tend·er n. an attendant at a bar serving drinks

bar·ter 1. v.t. to exchange without using money **2.** n. trade by exchange

ba·salt n. black or dark gray rock

base 1. n. the bottom, the lowest part ‖ that on which something is mounted ‖ groundwork ‖ foundation ‖ the place from which an army starts and where its supplies are ‖ the essential ingredient of a mixture ‖ the line or area on which a figure stands ‖ wrong, mistaken **2.** v.t. **bas·ing based** to found

base·ball *n.* the national game of the U.S.A. ‖ the ball used

base·less *adj.* groundless, without foundation

base·ment *n.* the story of a building below the ground floor

bash 1. *v.t.* to strike violently ‖ 2. *n.* violent blow

bash·ful *adj.* shy, self-conscious

ba·sic *adj.* fundamental ‖ forming a basis

bas·il *n.* a genus of aromatic plants

ba·sin *n.* a hollow vessel for holding a liquid

ba·sis *pl.* **ba·ses** *n.* a foundation, base ‖ an underlying principle

bask *v.i.* to luxuriate in warmth and light

bas·ket *n.* a vessel for containing shopping, laundry, wastepaper etc. ‖ a goal in basketball

bas·ket·ry *n.* the art of making baskets

bass 1. the lowest male singing voice ‖ a singer with such a voice

bas·set hound a short-legged hunting dog

bas·so *n.* a bass voice ‖ a bass singer

bas·soon a wooden musical instrument

bas·sóon·ist *n.* a bassoon player

bas·tard 1. *n.* an illegitimate child ‖ a hybrid 2. *adj.* illegitimate ‖ not genuine, counterfeit

bas·tard·ize bas·tard·iz·ing bas·tard·ized *v.t.* to declare to be illegitimate

baste bast·ing bast·ed *v.t.* to pour hot liquids over (esp. meat) during roasting to prevent its drying out

bast·ing bast·ed *v.t.* to stitch temporarily with large loose stitches

bast·ing *n.* a temporary stitching

bas·tion *n.* part of a fortification

batch *n.* a number or quantity of things produced at one time or to be taken together as a set

bath *n.* the immersion of the body or part of it in water to clean it ‖ exposure of the body to the sun, steam etc.

ba·ton *n.* the stick with which the conductor beats time ‖ the stick carried in a relay race

bat·tal·ion *n.* a unit of infantry ‖ a large fighting or warlike force

bat·ter 1. *v.t.* to strike naviolently and often 2. *n.* a semiliquid mixture beaten before cooking

bat·ter·y *pl.* **bat·ter·ies** *n.* a battering ‖ a verbal attack ‖ a unit of artillery ‖ a grouping of cells, condensers etc., for making electricity ‖ (*baseball*) the pitcher and catcher

bat·tle *n.* a fight between armies or forces

battle bat·tling bat·tled *v.t.* to fight

bau·ble *n.* a bright, showy trinket of no value

bawd *n.* a woman who keeps a brothel

bawd·i·ly *adv.* in a bawdy way

bawd·i·ness *n.* the quality or state of being bawdy

bawd·y bawd·i·er bawd·i·est *adj.* obscene, lewd

bawl *v.t.* to shout ‖ *v.i.* to cry without restraint

bay *n.* a wide inlet of the sea

bay 1. *n.* a reddish-brown horse

bay *n.* a dog's wail ‖ **to keep** (or **hold**) **at bay** to prevent from coming in to attack ‖ to ward off

bay·o·net *n.* a dagger which can be attached to a rifle

bay·ou *n.* a marshy creek or tributary to another river

ba·zaar *n.* an Oriental marketplace ‖ a sale of goods to raise money for charity

ba·zoo·ka *n.* a portable antitank rocket launcher

be *pres.* **I am, you are, he, she, it is, we, you, they are** *past* **I was, you were, he, she, it was, we, you, they were**) *pres. part.* **be·ing** *past part.* **been** *v.i.* used as a connective verb ‖ to equal ‖ to add up to ‖ to cost ‖ to become ‖ to exist ‖ (followed by the infinitive) used to express obligation ‖ used with the present participle to form the continuous tenses

beach 1. *n.* the shore of the sea or a lake 2. *v.t.* to draw (a boat) up on to the shore

bea·con *n.* a fire or light used as a signal

bead 1. *n.* a small ball pierced for threading ‖ a small round drop ‖ *pl.* a necklace ‖   *(pl.)*   the rosary 2. *v.t.* to adorn with beading

beak *n.* the projecting jaws of a bird ‖ any beaklike projection

beak·er *n.* an antique drinking vessel

beam 1. *n.* a long, heavy piece of wood ‖ a ray of light ‖ a gleam ‖ a bright smile ‖ the bar of a balance from which the scales hang ‖ a directional radio or other electromagnetic-radiation signal **2.** *v.i.* to send forth rays of heat or light ‖ to smile broadly

bean *n.* one of the seeds from any of several climbing or erect leguminous plants ‖ any of several fruits or seeds that resemble beans

bear *n.* heavily built, thick-furred, plantigrade, carnivorous mammal

bear bear·ing bore born, borne *v.t.* to support ‖ to sustain ‖ to carry ‖ to conduct ‖ to tolerate ‖ to be suitable for ‖ to give birth to ‖ to produce ‖ to give, offer

beard *n.* the hair that grows on the lower part of men's faces ‖ the chin hair of a goat ‖ the gills of an oyster ‖ the awns of grasses,

bear·ing *n.* carriage, deportment ‖ relevancy ‖ endurance ‖ (*pl.*) position in relation to some reference point ‖ a part of a machine that bears the friction set up by a moving part

beast *n.* any four-legged animal ‖ a person with savage, brutal ways **béast·ly beast·li·er beast·li·est** *adj.* revolting to any of the senses

beat 1. *v.* **beat·ing beat beat·en** *v.t.* to strike deliberately and often ‖ to strike repeatedly so as to whip or mix ‖ to work (metal) by hammering ‖ to give the measure for (musical time) ‖ dash ‖ to throb ‖ to produce a noise by dealing blows **2.** *n.* a stroke (on a drum etc.) or the noise made ‖ a throb or pulsation ‖ the movement of a conductor's baton or hand ‖ a rhythmic pulse in music ‖ a policeman's or watchman's round **3.** *adj.* exhausted

beat·en *adj.* defeated ‖ made smooth by constant treading

beat·ing *n.* punishment by repeated striking ‖ a severe defeat

be·at·i·tude *n.* blessedness ‖ bliss

beau·ti·ful 1. *adj.* having beauty ‖ physically lovely ‖ morally or intellectually pleasing **2.** *n.* (with 'the') beauty in the abstract

beau·ti·fy beau·ti·fy·ing beau·ti·fied *v.t.* to make beautiful, adorn

beau·ty *pl.* **beau·ties** *n.* that which delights the senses or exalts the mind ‖ physical loveliness

bea·ver *pl.* **bea·ver, bea·vers** *n.* a semiaquatic rodent

be·cause *conj.* for the reason that

beck·on *v.t.* to summon ‖ to invite ‖ *v.i.* to wave, nod

be·come be·com·ing be·came be·come *v.i.* to come to be ‖ to suit ‖ to be fitting or proper in **to become of** to happen to **be·cóm·ing** *adj.* suitable, attractive

bed *n.* a piece of furniture for sleeping in ‖ a resting place for animals ‖ the firm base on which something is supported ‖ the ground at the bottom of the sea or a river etc. ‖ a piece of ground prepared for plants etc. ‖ the ballast or foundation of road or railroad ‖ a layer or stratum of rock etc.

bed bed·ding bed·ded *v.t.* to provide with a place to sleep ‖ to fix in a foundation

be·dev·il be·dev·il·ing be·dev·il·ling be·dev·iled, be·dev·illed *v.t.* to interfere with and throw into confusion ‖ to pester **be·dév·il·ment** *n.*

bed·lam *n.* a scene of uproar

be·drag·gled *adj.* with clothing, hair, fur etc. wet or hanging limply and unbecomingly

bed·rid·den *adj.* compelled to stay in bed

bed·stead *n.* the framework of a bed

bee *n.* a four-winged insect producing wax and honey

beef 1. *n.* the flesh of a bull, cow or ox **2.** *v.i.* to complain

bee·hive *n.* a hive

beer *n.* an alcoholic drink

beet *n.* a genus of fleshy roots

bee·tle 1. *n.* an insect of the order

Coleoptera‖ any of various insects resembling the beetle, e.g. the cockroach

be·fall be·fall·ing be·fell be·fall·en *v.t.* to happen to ‖ *v.i.* to come to pass

be·fit be·fit·ting be·fit·ted *v.t.* to be suitable or proper for **be·fit·ting** *adj.*

be·fore 1. *adv.* previously, already **2.** *prep.* in front of ‖ ahead of ‖ earlier than ‖ rather than **3.** *conj.* sooner in time than

be·fore·hand *adv.* and *adj.* in advance

be·friend *v.t.* to be helpful to with friendly sympathy

beg beg·ging begged *v.i.* to solicit money, clothing, food etc. ‖ to ask alms ‖ to ask earnestly ‖ *v.t.* to solicit as charity ‖ to ask for as a favor ‖ to ask earnestly

be·gin be·gin·ning be·gan be·gun *v.t.* to start ‖ to come into existence ‖ **be·gin·ner** *n.* a novice **be·gin·ning** *n.* a start ‖ the early part ‖ origin ‖ *(pl.)* early stages

be·grudge be·grudg·ing be·grudged *v.t.* to envy (someone something) **be·guile be·guil·ing be·guiled** *v.t.* to fool, deceive ‖ to charm

be·half *n.* (only in phrases) **in** (or **on**) **behalf of** in the interest of

be·have be·hav·ing be·haved *v.i.* to conduct oneself

be·hav·ior *n.* manners, deportment ‖ moral conduct **be·hav·ior·al** *adj.*

be·head *v.t.* to cut off the head of

be·hind 1. *adv.* in the rear ‖ in arrears **2.** *prep.* in back of ‖ in the past for ‖ remaining after when one has gone on ‖ in an inferior position to ‖ in support of ‖ progressing more slowly than **3.** *n.* the buttocks

be·hold be·hold·ing be·held *v.t.* to look at and consider

be·hold·en *pred. adj.* under an obligation, bound in gratitude

beige *n.* the color of natural wool

be·ing 1. *n.* existence, ‖ one who exists **2.** *adj.* (in the phrase) for the time being for the present

be·la·bor *v.t.* to thrash ‖ to abuse with words

be·lat·ed *adj.* late ‖ retarded

be·lea·guer *v.t.* to besiege

bel·fry *pl.* **bel·fries** *n.* a bell tower

be·lie be·ly·ing be·lied *v.* to give a false impression of

be·lief *n.* the conviction that something is true ‖ the conviction that something is right ‖ something accepted as true ‖ a religion or creed ‖ an opinion

be·liev·a·ble *adj.* able to be believed

be·lieve be·liev·ing be·lieved *v.t.* to accept as true ‖ to hold as one's opinion ‖ *v.i.* to have religious faith

bell 1. *n.* a hollow instrument which makes a ringing sound when struck ‖ its sound ‖ a halfhourly division of the watch ‖ something shaped like a bell **2.** *v.i.* to take the form of a bell *v.t.* to provide with a bell

bell·boy *n.* a hotel or club page boy

bel·li·cose *adj.* aggressive ‖ fond of fighting **bel·li·cos·i·ty** *n.*

bel·lig·er·ence *n.* aggressiveness

bel·lig·er·en·cy *n.* the state of being at war

bel·lig·er·ent 1. *adj.* waging a war ‖ aggressive, hostile **2.** *n.* a nation at war

bel·low *v.i.* to roar ‖ to shout very loudly ‖ *v.t.* tto shout out

bel·lows *pl.* and *sing. n.* an instrument which by expanding and collapsing, draws air in and forces it out, to give draft to a fire, cause organ pipes to sound etc. ‖ the expanding part of a folding camera

bel·ly 1. *n. pl.* **bel·lies** the abdomen ‖ anything resembling the rounded exterior of the belly ‖ the lower or undersurface of anything **2.** *v.t.* **bel·ly·ing bel·lied** *v.i.* to become swollen out

be·long *v.i.* to have a rightful place **be·long·ings** *pl. n.* possessions, property

be·loved *adj.* much loved, favored **1.** *n.* someone who is dearly loved

be·low 1. *adv.* under, in a lower place **2.** *prep.* lower than, under ‖ unworthy of, not befitting the dignity of

belt 1. *n.* a strip of fabric, leather etc., worn around the waist to support clothes or to draw them in ‖ a district characterized by certain physical or climatic conditions ‖ an endless band connecting wheels or pulleys **2.** *v.t.* to fasten with a belt ‖ (with 'out') to sing in a loud, coarse voice

be·mire be·mir·ing be·mired *v.t.* to cover with mud

be·moan *v.t.* to express deep sorrow or regret

be·mused *adj.* deep in thought ‖ dazed

bench **1.** *n.* a long wooden or stone seat for two or more people ‖ a work table ‖ a judge's seat **2.** *v.t.* to send (a player in a game) to the bench

bend **1.** *v.* **bend·ing bent** to make curved or crooked ‖ to render (something curved or crooked) straight ‖ to fold ‖ to submit ‖ to stoop **2.** *n.* a curve or turn **bend·er** *n.* a spree

be·neath **1.** *adv.* under, in a lower place **2.** *prep.* under, at, in or to a position lower than ‖ unworthy of, not befitting

ben·e·dic·tion *n.* a blessing

ben·e·fac·tion *n.* a handsome donation or gift to an organization, club etc.

ben·e·fac·tor *n.* someone who helps, esp. financially **ben·e·fac·tress** *n.* a woman benefactor

be·nef·i·cence *n.* kindness on a large scale **be·nef·i·cent** *adj.* producing good results

ben·e·fi·cial helpful, causing improvement

ben·e·fi·ci·ar·y **1.** *n. pl.* **ben·e·fi·ci·ar·ies** someone receiving a benefit

ben·e·fit **1.** *n.* help, profit ‖ advantage **2.** *v.t.* **ben·e·fit·ting, ben·e·fit·ing ben·e·fit·ted, ben·e·fit·ed** to do good to ‖ *v.i.* to receive help or benefit

be·nev·o·lence *n.* kindheartedness ‖ generous giving

be·nev·o·lent *adj.* wellwishing, friendly ‖ charitable

be·nign *adj.* kind, well-disposed ‖ not dangerous

be·nig·nant *adj.* kind, gracious

be·nig·ni·ty *n.* kindliness

bent **1.** *adj.* altered from a previous straight or even state ‖ (with 'on' or 'upon') determined, resolved **2.** *n.* a mental inclination ‖ a leaning, tendency

be·queath *v.t.* to will at one's death

be·quest *n.* something that is left under a will

be·rate be·rat·ing be·rat·ed *v.t.* to scold, chide

be·reave be·reav·ing *v.t.* **be·reaved** to leave desolate, esp. by death ‖ **be·reft** to deprive **be·reave·ment** *n.*

be·ret *n.* a soft, round, flat woolen cap

ber·i·ber·i *n.* a disease due to deficiency of vitamin B

ber·ry *n. pl.* **ber·ries** any small, juicy fruit with seeds

ber·serk frenzied

berth **1.** *n.* a bunk in a ship or train ‖ a place at a wharf where a ship can lie at anchor **2.** *v.t.* to moor (a ship) at a suitable place ‖ *v.i.* to take up moorings

be·seech be·seech·ing be·sought *v.t.* to implore **be·seech·ing** *adj.*

be·set be·set·ting be·set *v.t.* to surround, hem in **be·set·ting** *adj.* continually harassing or assailing

be·side *prep.* by the side of, close to ‖ compared with

be·sides *adv.* moreover ‖ also, in addition

be·siege be·sieg·ing be·sieged *v.t.* lay siege to ‖ to throng around ‖ to assail (with requests etc.)

be·smirch *v.t.* to cast a slur on, sully

be·speak be·speak·ing be·spoke be·spoke, be·spoken *v.t.* to order in advance ‖ to indicate, show evidence of

best **1.** *adj.* finest in quality ‖ most advantageous **2.** *n.* anything which is best ‖ greatest effort, utmost **3.** *adv.* (*superl.* of WELL) most, bears like honey best ‖ in the most excellent way, the engine runs best at night **4.** *v.t.* to do better than ‖ to get the better of

bes·tial *adj.* of or like a beast ‖ vile ‖ obscene, lustful **bes·ti·al·i·ty** *n.*

be·stow *v.t.* to confer ‖ to devote (thought, time)

bet **1.** *n.* a wager of money etc. ‖ the money etc. that is staked ‖ the thing that is wagered upon **2.** *v.* **bet·ting bet, bet·ted** *v.t.* to wager (a sum etc.) ‖ *v.i.* to lay a bet ‖ to be in the practice of laying bets

be·ta *n.* the second letter of the Greek alphabet ‖ the second brightest star in a constellation

be·tray *v.t.* to act treacherously towards ‖ to reveal treacherously ‖ to fail to justify ‖ to give evidence of **be·tray·al** *n.*

be·troth *v.t.* to affiance, promise in marriage **be·troth·al** *n.* **be·trothed** 1. *n.* the person to whom one is engaged 2. *adj.* engaged to be married

bet·ter 1. *adj.* having good qualities in a greater degree ‖ preferable ‖ improved 2. *adv.* in a more excellent manner ‖ in a higher degree ‖ (of preference) more 3. *n.* someone superior in age, rank, knowledge etc. ‖ advantage

better *v.t.* to improve ‖ to surpass

bet·ter·ment *n.* improvement

bet·tor, bet·ter *n.* a person who bets

be·tween 1. *prep.* in the intervening space of ‖ within two limits of ‖ to and from ‖ common to ‖ distinguishing ‖ linking ‖ jointly among 2. *adv.* in an intermediate space ‖ in an interval of time

bev·er·age *n.* a drink

bev·y *pl.* **bev·ies** *n.* a group or company of women, quails, larks or roes

be·ware *v.i.* to be careful, be on one's guard

be·wil·der *v.t.* to throw into mental confusion **be·wil·der·ment** *n.*

be·witch *v.t.* to fascinate or charm **be·witch·ing** *adj.*

be·yond 1. *adv.* further 2. *prep.* on the further side of ‖ later than ‖ past the comprehension of ‖ ahead of ‖ past 3. *n.* **the beyond** what lies after death

bi·as 1. *n.* a temperamental or emotional leaning to one side 2. *v.t.* **bi·as·ing** **bi·ased** to cause to be prejudiced in opinion, judgment etc.

bib *n.* a small piece of cloth placed under a child's chin at mealtimes to protect his clothes

Bi·ble *n.* the sacred writings of the Christian faith **bi·ble** the authoritative book on a subject

bib·li·cal *adj.* of or relating to the Bible

bib·li·og·ra·pher *n.* someone who writes or compiles bibliographies

bib·li·o·graph·i·cal *adj.* of or relating to bibliography

bib·li·og·ra·phy *pl.* **bib·li·og·ra·phies** *n.* a complete list of a writer's work ‖ a list of books on a particular subject ‖ a list of references at the end of a book

bi·cen·ten·ni·al *n.* a 200th anniversary or its celebration

bi·ceps *pl.* **bi·ceps, bi·ceps·es** *n.* a muscle esp. the large flexor muscle in the upper arm

bick·er 1. *v.i.* to quarrel about trifles 2. *n.* snappish quarrel

bi·cy·cle 1. *n.* a vehicle esp. for one person, consisting of two large, spoked, tandem wheels 2. *v.i.* **bi·cy·cling** **bi·cy·cled** to cycle **bi·cy·clist** *n.* a cyclist

bid 1. *v.* **bid·ding bid** *v.t.* to offer (a price), esp. at an auction sale ‖ (card games) to make (a bid) to command ‖ *v.i.* to make a bid in an auction, card games etc. 2. *n.* an offer of a price, esp. at a sale ‖ an offer to do a job etc. for a certain price **bid·der** *n.* someone who bids **bid·ding** *n.* a command or commands

bide **bid·ing bid·ed, bode bid·ed** *v.t.* (only in the phrase) **to bide one's time** to wait for the right opportunity

bi·en·ni·al 1. *adj.* lasting for two years 2. *n.* an event occurring once every two years

bier *n.* the frame on which a coffin or corpse is taken to its burial

bi·fo·cal *adj.* having two points of focus **bi·fo·cals** *pl. n.* bifocal spectacles

big 1. *adv.* **big·ger big·gest** large ‖ grown-up ‖ important ‖ boastful ‖ magnanimous 2. *adv.* boastfully

big·a·mist *n.* a person who makes a second marriage illegally while the first marriage remains valid

big·a·mous *adj.* guilty of bigamy

big·a·my *n.* illegally having two wives or husbands at the same time

big·ot *n.* someone obstinately and intolerantly devoted to his own beliefs, creed or party **big·ot·ed** *adj.* **big·ot·ry** *n.*

bike 1. *n.* a bicycle 2. *v.i.* **bik·ing**

biked to bicycle, cycle

bi·ki·ni *n.* a woman's minimal two-piece bathing suit

bi·lat·er·al *adj.* affecting each of two sides or parties

bile *n.* a bitter, greenish-yellow alkaline fluid secreted by the liver ‖ ill humor

bi·lev·el *adj.* of a two-story dwelling

bilge 1. *n.* the bottom of a ship ‖ the swelling part of a barrel ‖ foolishly mistaken ideas or remarks **2.** *v.* **bilg·ing bilged** to cause to fracture in the bilge

bil·i·ar·y *adj.* of or connected with the bile

bil·ious *adj.* of or connected with the bile ‖ ill-tempered

bilk *v.t.* to defraud (a creditor) by avoiding payment of one's debts ‖ to evade, give (someone) the slip

bill 1. *n.* an account for goods sold or services rendered ‖ the draft of a law ‖ a poster ‖ a concert or theater program ‖ a piece of paper money **2.** *v.t.* to charge (an account) for goods or services

bill *n.* a beak ‖ a narrow promontory

bill·board *n.* a wall of planks etc. for the display of advertisement

bil·let *n.* a small bar of iron or steel

billet 1. *n.* the quarters to which a soldier etc. is officially assigned **2.** *v.t.* to find or provide quarters for

bill·fold *n.* a wallet for paper money

bil·liards *n.* any of several games played on a large, cushioned, clothcovered table, ivory balls being driven by a tapering wooden cue

bil·lion *n.* NUMBER TABLE

bil·lion·aire *n.* someone whose posessions are worth a billion

bil·low 1. *n.* a large wave **2.** *v.i.* to roll along or rise and fall like a wave ‖ to bulge or swell **bil·low·y** *adj.*

bil·ly goat a male goat

bi·month·ly 1. *adj.* happening every two months ‖ happening twice a month **2.** *n. pl.* **bi·month·lies** a bimonthly publication **3.** *adv.* once in two months ‖ twice a month

bin *n.* a receptacle for storing

bi·na·ry *adj.* consisting of two

bind bind·ing bound *v.t.* to tie up ‖ to fasten together ‖ to place (someone) under an agreement or obligation

bind·er *n.* someone who binds, esp. a book binder ‖ a cover for fastening loose papers together

bind·er·y *pl.* **bind·er·ies** *n.* a factory or workshop where books are bound

bind·ing 1. *n.* the action of someone who binds ‖ a bookcover **2.** *adj.* involving moral obligation

binge 1. a drinking spree

bin·go *n.* a gambling game

bin·oc·u·lar *adj.* having or requiring the use of two eyes **bin·oc·u·lars** *pl. n.* an optical instrument

bi·og·ra·pher *n.* an author of a biography or biographies

bi·o·graph·ic *adj.* of or relating to biography **bi·o·graph·i·cal** *adj.*

bi·og·ra·phy *pl.* **bi·og·ra·phies** *n.* a written account of a person's life

bi·o·log·ic *adj.* of or relating to biology **bi·o·log·i·cal** *adj.*

bi·ol·o·gist *n.* a specialist in biology

bi·ol·o·gy *n.* the science of life and all its manifestations ‖ the plant and animal life of a given region

bi·op·sy *pl.* **bi·op·sies** *n.* the examination of tissue taken from the living body

bi·par·ti·san *adj.* of the two-party system in politics ‖ marked by the cooperation of both parties **bi·par·ti·san·ship** *n.*

bi·ped 1. *adj.* having two feet **2.** *n.* a two-footed animal, e.g. man

birch 1. *n.* a deciduous forest tree

bird *n.* a warm-blooded vertebrate covered with feathers except for the legs and having the forelimbs converted into wings

bird·ie *n.* (golf) a score of one stroke under par in playing a hole

birth *n.* the act of bringing forth young

birth·day *n.* the day of one's birth

birth·mark *n.* a mark on the skin at birth

bis·cuit *n.* a soft unsweetened roll or bun

bi·sect *v.t.* to cut or divide into two parts **bi·sec·tion** *n.* **bi·sec·tion·al** *adj.*

bi·sec·tor n. a bisecting line

bi·sex·u·al adj. having both sexes

bish·op n. a member of the highest order in the Christian Church

bish·op·ric n. the office of a bishop ‖ a diocese

bi·son pl. **bi·son, bi·sons** n. a genus of large, shaggy, bovine mammals, often called buffalo

bisque, bisk n. a rich soup made from shellfish etc.

bit n. the metal bar of a bridle ‖ the boring piece of a drill used in a brace

bit by bit gradually, piecemeal

bitch n. the female of the dog or other canine ‖ a spiteful, malicious woman **bitch·y bitch·i·er bitch·i·est** adj.

bite 1. v. **bit·ing bit bit·ten bit** v.t. to seize and grip with the teeth ‖ (of insects, snakes etc.) to sting ‖ v.i. to seize and grip something with the teeth ‖ to cause a biting sensation ‖ (of a fish) to take the bait **2.** n. the wound made by biting ‖ a snack ‖ sharp pain

bit·ter 1. adj. acrid-tasting, tart ‖ hard to bear ‖ acrimonious, showing deep resentment **2.** adv. bitingly

bit·tern n. a genus of long-legged marsh birds

bi·valve n. an animal that has a hinged double shell

biv·ou·ac 1. n. a temporary camp **2.** v.t. **biv·ou·ack·ing biv·ou·acked**

bi·zarre adj. fantastic, strange

blab 1. v. **blab·bing blabbed** v.i. to talk indiscreetly ‖ v.t. to reveal (a secret etc.) **2.** n. chatter

black 1. adj. colorless, or so dark as to appear colorless ‖ the opposite of white ‖ not hopeful ‖ sad ‖ darkskinned **2.** n. a black pigment ‖ a person whose natural skin color is black **3.** v.t. to make black

black·ber·ry pl. **black·ber·ries** n. a genus of trailing or erect bushes bearing edible berries

black·bird n. a thrush common throughout Europe

black·board n. a large piece of slate with a dark smooth surface which can be written on with chalk

black·en v.t. to make black or dark ‖ to speak ill of, defame ‖ v.i. to grow black or dark

black·guard n. a scoundrel

black·head n. a plug of grease and dirt blocking a sebaceous gland duct

black·jack n. a pirate flag ‖ a card game ‖ a small rubber club with lead in it and a flexible handle

black magic magic used in the service of evil

black·mail 1. n. an attempt to extort money by threats **2.** v.t. to extort money from (someone) by intimidation

black·out n. a preventing of lights inside a building from being seen outside ‖ a temporary loss of consciousness or memory

black·smith n. a man who works iron in a forge, shoes horses etc.

blad·der n. a sac filled with fluid or air, esp. the receptacle for urine

blade n. the cutting part of a knife, sword ‖ a long slender leaf, esp. of grass ‖ a thin flattened edge, e.g. of an oar or propeller

blam·a·ble, blame·a·ble adj. deserving blame

blame 1. v.t. **blam·ing blamed** to hold responsible **2.** n. responsibility for something wrong or unsatisfactory **blame·a·ble** adj. **blame·less** adj. free from fault or blame

blanch v.t. to make white or pale ‖ to make white by peeling away the skin of almonds, by scalding meat etc. ‖ v.i. to grow pale

bland n. mild ‖ suave ‖ soothing and nonirritating

blan·dish v.t. to coax or flatter ‖ to tempt with flattering words **blan·dish·ment** n. often pl.

blank 1. adj. not written on ‖ expressionless **2.** n. an empty space left in printed matter ‖ a void **3.** v.t. (with 'out') to blot out

blan·ket 1. n. a warm covering **2.** v.t. to stifle (noise, rumors, questions etc.) **3.** adj. applicable to all persons or in all circumstances

blare 1. *v.* **blar·ing blared** *v.i.* to make a loud, harsh sound **2.** *n.* any continuous, loud, harsh noise

blar·ney *n.* persuasive cajolery, wheedling

bla·se *adj.* satiated with pleasure and left without enthusiasm

blas·pheme blas·phem·ing blas·phemed *v.t.* to speak impiously of (God and things regarded as sacred) **blas·phe·mous** *adj.*

blas·phe·my *pl.* **blas·phe·mies** *n.* irreverent speech about God or things regarded as sacred

blast 1. *n.* a strong gust of wind ‖ a wave of highly compressed air created by an explosion **(at) full blast** at top capacity ‖ an exciting event **2.** *v.t.* to shatter ‖ to attack **3.** an expletive expressing annoyance **blast·ed** *adj.* damnable, annoying

bla·tan·cy *n.* the state or quality of being blatant

bla·tant *adj.* very obvious

bla·ther 1. *v.i.* to talk foolishly **2.** *n.* foolish talk

blaze 1. *n.* a bright fire ‖ an unintended fire ‖ full, direct light **2.** *v.i.* **blaz·ing blazed** to burn brightly

bleach 1. *v.t.* to remove the color from **2.** *n.* a chemical used in bleaching

bleak *adj.* exposed, desolate ‖ cheerless ‖ cold, bitter

blear *adj.* (of the eyes) bleary **1.** *v.t.* to blur **blear·i·ness** *n.* **blear·y blear·i·er blear·i·est** *adj.* dim, misted, filmy

bleat 1. *v.i.* (of a sheep or goat) to make its characteristic cry **2.** *n.* the cry of a sheep or goat

bleed bleed·ing bled *v.i.* to lose or emit blood ‖ (of plants) to lose sap ‖ *v.t.* to draw blood from (surgically) ‖ to extort money from **bleed·er** *n.* a hemophiliac

blem·ish 1. *v.t.* to spoil or impair **2.** *n.* a physical or moral defect or flaw

blend 1. *n.* a harmonious mixture **2.** *v.* **blend·ing blend·ed, blent** *v.t.* to mix together

bless *v.t.* **bless·ing blessed** to call down

God's favor upon ‖ to consecrate

bless·ed 1. *adj.* holy, revered ‖ beatified **2.** *n.* **the bless·ed** the souls in Heaven **bless·ed·ness** *n.* a state of happiness, esp. through the enjoyment of God's favor

bless·ing *n.* divine favor or the invocation of it

blight 1. *n.* any plant disease or injury characterized by or resulting in withering ‖ an organism which causes this **2.** *v.t.* to wither

blimp *n.* a small, nonrigid dirigible

blind *adj.* without sight ‖ undiscerning or unwilling to judge ‖ having no outlet **1.** *n.* something which prevents strong light from coming through a window **2.** *v.t.* to deprive of the faculty of sight ‖ to dazzle

blind·fold 1. *v.t.* to cover the eyes of with a cloth **2.** *n.* a cloth tied around the eyes to prevent vision

blind·ly *adv.* not being able to distinguish objects, facts etc. ‖ without resisting or questioning

blink 1. *n.* a quick shutting and opening of the eyes **2.** *v.i.* to shut and open one's eyes quickly

bliss *n.* perfect happiness **bliss·ful** *adj.*

blis·ter 1. *n.* a portion of skin raised by the pressure of fluid beneath it **2.** *v.t.* to cause blisters to form in or on ‖ *v.i.* to become covered with blisters

blithe *adj.* lightheartedly cheerful, happy

bliz·zard *n.* a blinding snowstorm

bloat *v.t.* to inflate with air or water ‖ to swell up

bloc *n.* a group of parties, governments etc. associating together to achieve (or prevent) something

block *n.* a large solid piece of stone, wood etc. ‖ an area in a city enclosed by four intersecting streets ‖ an obstruction ‖ a mental mechanism preventing a topic with unpleasant associations from being thought about

block *v.t.* to cause obstruction in, prevent the passage of ‖ to put obstacles in the way of ‖ to prevent sensation in (a nerve) by the use of a local anesthetic (sports) to obstruct (a player) ‖ v.i. to become blocked

block·ade n. an attempted starving into surrender of an enemy by preventing goods from reaching or leaving him v.t. **block·ad·ing block·ad·ed** to subject to blockade

blond, blonde adj. (of hair) yellowish in color ‖ (of the complexion) pale

blood n. a fluid circulating throughout the vertebrate body **in cold blood** deliberately, not in an excess of passion **to have blood on one's hands** to be guilty of having caused someone's death **to make one's blood boil** to make one passionately angry

blood·hound n. a powerful dog with a keen sense of smell

blood·i·ly adv. in a bloody manner

blood·i·ness n. the state or quality of being bloody

blood·shed n. violent death or injury

blood·shot adj. (of the eyes) suffused with blood

blood·y blood·i·er blood·i·est of the nature or appearance of blood ‖ stained with blood ‖ vicious, murderous

bloom 1. n. the state of flowering ‖ a flower, blossom 2. v.i. to blossom, to be or come into flower ‖ to be in, or come into, fullness of beauty

bloop·er n. a blunder

blos·som n. a flower ‖ a youthful, fresh stage of growth **blos·som·y** adj. full of blossoms ‖ resembling a blossom

blossom v.i. to open into flower ‖ to develop

blotch n. a patch of ink or color ‖ a disfiguring spot on the skin ‖ v.i. to make a blotch **blotched** adj. **blotch·y blotch·i·er blotch·i·est** adj.

blot·ter n. a piece or pad of blotting paper

blouse 1. n. a woman's shirt ‖ a loose working garment 2. v. **blous·ing bloused**

blow 1. **blow·ing blew blown** v.i. to direct air from the mouth ‖ to sound when blown into ‖ (of a fuse) to melt when

overloaded with electric current ‖ to clear (the nose) of mucus by forcing air through it **to blow away** (of the wind) to carry away ‖ **to blow up** to inflate (e.g. a balloon) ‖ to destroy by exploding ‖ to lose one's temper 2. n. a blowing of wind, esp. a gale

blow n. a sudden vigorous stroke with the hand or an instrument ‖ a stroke of bad luck

blow·er n. that which blows

blow·up n. an explosion ‖ a violent quarrel or fit of temper ‖ a big photographic enlargement

blub·ber n. fat from the whale or other marine mammal ‖ noisy weeping and complaining 1. v.t. to utter with gasping sobs **blub·ber·y** adj.

bludg·eon 1. n. a heavy stick or sticklike weapon, with one end weighted 2. v.t. to hit repeatedly with such a weapon

blue 1. adj. being the color of a cloudless sky ‖ unhappy, melancholy 2. n. a blue color, pigment a,out of the blue without any warning 3. **blue·ing, blu·ing blued**

blue·bell 1. a plant of the genus Campanula

blue·bird n. a genus of American songbirds related to the robin

blue jay a crested jay of Eastern North America

blue jeans blue work trousers of jean or denim

blue·print 1. n. a copy of an original diagram or plan 2. v.t. to make a blueprint of

blues pl. n. (with 'the') a mood of profound melancholy, depression ‖ a type of jazz

bluff 1. v.t. to mislead deliberately ‖ to intimidate by threats one cannot fulfill ‖ v.i. to use deception in these ways 2. n. a bluffer, a person who bluffs

bluff n. a steep cliff or headland with a broad, rounded front

blu·ing, blue·ing n. a product used in laundering to make clothes white

blu·ish, blue·ish adj. rather blue in color

blun·der 1. n. a crass, stupid mistake

2. *v.t.* (often with 'along', 'into', 'through') to move heavily and clumsily ‖ to make a crass mistake

blunt *adj.* having an edge or point that is not sharp ‖ (of wits) insensitive, unperceptive ‖ lacking in finesse, scorning tact

blur *n.* a confused visual impression ‖ a blemish or smudge ‖ indistinct appearance *v.* **blur·ring blurred**

blurb *n.* a publisher's commendation of one of its books, usually printed on the wrapper or in advertising notices

blur·ry blur·ri·er blur·ri·est *adj.* marked by blurs ‖ indistinct

blurt *v.t.* (with 'out') to say impulsively

blush *n.* a suffusion of the cheeks with red ‖ a rosy color **1.** *v.i.* to become red, esp. from pleasure, shame, modesty etc.

blush·er *n.* face rouge that creates a natural-seeming shining quality

blus·ter 1. *n.* a loud, gusty wind **2.** *v.i.* (of wind) to blow violently and gustily ‖ to talk with histrionic anger **blus·ter·ous, blus·ter·y** *adjs.*

boar *n.* the uncastrated male pig ‖ its flesh

board 1. *n.* a piece of sawn lumber longer than it is broad ‖ (basketball) the backboard behind the basket ‖ a council or authoritative body ‖ daily meals given in exchange for payment or services **above board** openly, without deceit **on board** aboard a ship, train etc. **2.** *v.t.* (often with up) to cover with boards or planks ‖ to provide with meals, and often with lodging ‖ to make one's way onto (a ship, train or aircraft) as a passenger

board·er *n.* a person who is given food and lodging

boast 1. *n.* a claim about oneself, or something connected with oneself made with proper pride or with inordinate pride ‖ something one is proud of **2.** *v.i.* to brag, make an exaggerated claim **boast·ful** *adj.*

boat *n.* any small open vessel propelled by oars, sail, an engine, or paddles **in the same boat** running the same risks or sharing the same misfortunes

boat·swain *n.* a ship's officer who calls

men on duty

bob 1. *v.* **bob·bing bobbed** *v.t.* to lower and quickly raise again ‖ *v.i.* to move up and down in quick jerky movements **2.** *n.* a short, bouncing or jerky movement ‖ a curtsy

bob 1. *n.* a short, straight hair style for women **2.** *v.t.* **bob·bing bobbed** to style (hair) short and straight

bob·o·link *n.* a North American migratory songbird

bob·sled 1. *n.* a long sled with independent runners at front and back **2.** *v.i.* **bob·sled·ding bob·sled·ded** to ride on a bobsled

bob·white *n.* a North American game bird

bode bod·ing bod·ed *v.t.* to portend, indicate by signs ‖ *v.i.* to be a (good or bad) omen **bode·ful** *adj.* warning of evil to come

bod·ice *n.* the top part of a woman's dress

bod·i·ly 1. *adj.* pertaining to the body **2.** *adv.* in person

bod·y *pl.* **bod·ies** *n.* the physical substance of a man or animal ‖ a corpse ‖ the main portion of an army ‖ a collective unit of people ‖ a mass of matter

bod·y·guard *n.* a man or group of men guarding the safety of another

bog 1. *n.* an area of ground saturated with water and decayed vegetation **2.** *v.* **bog·ging bogged** *v.t.* (often with down) to submerge into or as if into a bog

bo·gey *pl.* **bo·geys, bo·gies** *n.* (golf) one over par

bo·gey, bo·gy *pl.* **bo·geys, bo·gies** *n.* an imaginary source of fear

bog·gle bog·gling bog·gled *v.i.* to hesitate or hold back because one is startled or fearful

bo·gus *adj.* sham

boil 1. *v.i.* (of a liquid) to bubble at a high temperature ‖ to be very agitated ‖ *v.t.* to cook in boiling liquid **to boil away** to evaporate a, to boil down to condense **2.** *n.* the boiling point ‖ the state of boiling **to bring to a boil** to heat until the boiling point is reached

boil·er *n.* a container in which water can

be heated under pressure and converted into steam ‖ a stove which heats water for conveyance to a hot-water system

bois·ter·ous *adj.* gusty ‖ agreeably rough ‖ cheerfully loud

bold *adj.* brave ‖ daring ‖ confidently original

boll *n.* a capsule, esp. of cotton or flax

boll weevil a small gray weevil

bo·lo·gna *n.* a seasoned, boiled and smoked sausage of ground beef, pork and veal

bol·ster 1. *n.* a long cylindrical pillow stretching from one side of a bed to the other or an often wedge-shaped pillow along the back of a sofa etc. 2. *v.t.* to support, prop

bolt 1. *n.* a sliding bar for keeping a door closed ‖ the sliding piece moved in a lock by the key ‖ a thick tight roll of cloth ‖ a thunderbolt ‖ a quick dash, esp. one made so as to flee 2. *v.t.* to secure (a door or window) with a bolt ‖ to eat very quickly ‖ *v.i.* to make off at a run

bomb 1. *n.* an explosive missile dropped from an aircraft, fired from a mortar or thrown by hand ‖ (basketball) a long shot ‖ (football) a long pass ‖ (theater) a flop 2. ‖ *v.i.* to drop bombs ‖ to fail 3. *adj.* **bombed** drunk

bom·bard *v.t.* to attack with big guns, hurl shells and bombs repeatedly at ‖ to subject (a substance) to rays or the impact of small particles

bom·bar·dier *n.* that member of a bomber crew who aims the bombs at the target

bom·bard·ment *n.* a bombarding ‖ a bombarding attack

bom·bast *n.* pretentious language **bom·bás·tic** *adj.* **bom·bás·ti·cal·ly** *adv.*

bo·nan·za *n.* a very rich deposit of ore in veins of gold or silver ‖ something bringing profit

bon·bon *pl.* **bon·bons** *n.* a sweet candy

bond 1. *n.* that which unites ‖ a written legal agreement ‖ a document issued by a government or a comapany recording money borrowed and the promise to pay back with interest to the holder 2. *v.t.* to

place bricks in building (a structure) in such a way as to hold them firmly together ‖ to place (imported goods) in bond ‖ to mortgage

bond·age *n.* slavery

bond·ed *adj.* goods placed in bond ‖ under bond to pay duty on goods stored ‖ attached by adhesive to make a single product of two components

bone 1. *n.* one of the hard parts of the skeleton of a vertebrate animal 2. *v.t.* **bon·ing boned** to remove the bones from (fish, poultry)

bon·fire *n.* a fire built outdoors, for burning rubbish, for festivity or celebration

bon·net *n.* a kind of hat worn mainly by babies

bo·nus *pl.* **bo·nus·es** *n.* a grant of money as a gratuity to workers ‖ an extra dividend or gift of stock or shares from a company to its shareholders ‖ anything welcome that one receives over and above what is expected or usual

bon·y bon·i·er bon·i·est *adj.* (of persons) with large bones ‖ (of persons and animals) very thin

boo 1. *n.* a cry of contemptuous disapproval ‖ an interjection made suddenly and loudly to cause fright 2. *v.* **boo·ing booed** *v.t.* to shout contemptuous boos at

boo·by *pl.* **boo·bies** *n.* a stupid fool, a clumsy lout

booby trap a trap laid for the unwary ‖ a harmless-looking object containing an explosive charge liable to go off when disturbed

book *n.* a number of printed pages fastened together and enclosed in a cover ‖ a treatise ‖ (*pl.*) business accounts ‖ (*betting*) a record of bets made by a bookmaker at a race **to read someone like a book** to know by intuition what someone is thinking

book *v.t.* to reserve in advance ‖ to engage in advance (a speaker or performer) ‖ to record (an order)

book·bind·er *n.* someone who binds books

book·bind·ing *n*. the craft of binding books

book·ish *adj*. of or relating to books ‖ fond of reading and studying

book·keep·ing *n*. the regular recording of the essential facts about the transactions of a business

book·let *n*. a book of not very many pages

boom 1. *n*. a hollow-sounding roar, as of a distant explosion ‖ a sudden increase in prosperity 2. *v.i.* to make a hollow roar ‖ *v.t.* to cause to boom

boom *n*. a long spar, usually of wood, with one end attached to the mast, used to stretch the sail foot

boom·er·ang *n*. a curved or smoothly angular wooden missile used by Australian aborigines

boon *n*. a blessing, something that comes as a help

boor *n*. an uncouth, insensitive person **bóor·ish** *adj*.

boost 1. *n*. something that gives an impetus or encouragement 2. *v.t.* to push from below, hoist ‖ to help, assist ‖ to raise the voltage **bóost·er** *n*. a substance which increases the efficiency of an immunizing agent ‖ the first stage of a multistage rocket, used to supply the main thrust for takeoff

boot 1. *n*. an article of footwear coming to the ankle or higher ‖ a naval or marine recruit in the first stage of training ‖ dismissal 2. *v.t.* to kick

booth *pl*. **booths** *n*. a temporary structure of canvas and boards, esp. a covered stall in a fair or market

boot·leg 1. *v.t.* **boot·leg·ging boot·legged** to smuggle ‖ to sell or make (alcoholic liquor) illegally 2. *adj*. illicit **bóot·leg·ger** *n*.

boo·ty *pl*. **boo·ties** *n*. spoils taken in war, or by thieves

booze 1. *v.i.* **booz·ing boozed** to drink alcoholic liquor to excess 2. *n*. alcoholic drink

bor·der 1. *n*. an edge, an outer side ‖ a frontier, a boundary between two countries ‖ a strip (often ornamental) around the edge of a handkerchief, dress etc. 2. *v.t.* to put or be a border around ‖ *v.i.* (with 'on') to be in an adjoining position

bore 1. *n*. a deep hole made by drilling in the ground to find oil etc. ‖ the internal cylinder of a gun barrel 2. *v.* **bor·ing bored** *v.* to drill (a hole) ‖ *v.i.* to make a hole by drilling

bore·dom *n*. the state or quality of being bored, the condition of having one's interest either unaroused or extinguished

born *past part.* of BEAR (to give birth) ‖ *adj*. having a certain natural characteristic

bor·ough *n*. a municipal corporation resembling an incorporated town

bor·row *v.t.* to take (something) on the understanding that it will be returned later

bos·om 1. *n*. a human being's breast ‖ a woman's breasts 2. *adj*. intimate, beloved

boss 1. *n*. an employer ‖ a person in charge 2. *v.t.* to direct or manage

bos·sy bos·si·er bos·si·est *adj*. domineering, fond of giving orders

bo·tan·ic *adj*. botanical **bo·tán·i·cal** *adj*. of or pertaining to botany

bot·a·nist *n*. a specialist in botany

bot·a·ny *n*. the branch of biology concerned with plant life and all its manifestations

botch 1. *n*. a badly done piece of work 2. *v.t.* to bungle **bótched** *adj*.

both 1. *adj*. the two, each of two 2. *pron*. the one and the other

both·er 1. *n*. inconvenience ‖ a nuisance 2. *v.t.* to worry persistently ‖ *v.i.* (with 'about' or 'with') to take trouble ‖ (with the infinitive) to take the trouble

both·er·some *adj*. causing bother

bot·tle 1. *n*. a narrow-necked vessel without a handle 2. *v.t.* **bot·tling bot·tled** to put into bottles

bot·tle·neck *n*. a narrowing in a road, where traffic may become congested

bot·tom 1. *adj*. lowest, last 2. *n*. the lowest interior or exterior part of anything ‖ the buttocks ‖ the bed of the

bot·u·lism *n.* food poisoning

bou·doir *n.* a lady's small private room

bough *n.* a branch of a tree, esp. a main branch

bouil·la·baisse *n.* a Provençal dish containing Mediteranean fish and shellfish

bouil·lon *n.* a clear soup made esp. from beef

boul·der *n.* a large stone, or mass of rock, rounded and smoothed by water, ice or wind

boul·e·vard *n.* a broad street

bounce 1. *n.* a sudden rebound, e.g. of a rubber ball ‖ vitality **2.** *v.* **bounc·ing bounced** *v.t.* to cause to rebound ‖ *v.i.* to rebound ‖ to jump up ‖ (of a check) to be refused by a bank because there is not enough money in the account to cover it **bounc·er** *n.* an attendant employed to eject people who make themselves a nuisance in dance halls, nightclubs etc. **bounc·ing** *adj.* full of health and vitality

bound *adj.* (often with for) on the way to

bound 1. *n.* a limit of an estate etc. **2.** *v.t.* to set limits to

bound·a·ry *pl.* **bound·a·ries** *n.* the real line marking a limit

boun·ti·ful *adj.* freely giving ‖ abundant

boun·ty *pl.* **boun·ties** *n.* generosity ‖ a sum of money given as a subsidy or reward

bou·quet *n.* a bunch of flowers ‖ the distinctive perfume of a wine

bour·bon *n.* whiskey distilled from mainly corn mash

bour·geois 1. *adj.* belonging to or typical of the middle classes **2.** *n.* a member of the middle classes

bour·geoi·sie *n.* the middle classes

bout *n.* a fit (of illness) ‖ a fight, trial of strength

bou·tique *n.* a chic little store

bo·vine *adj.* of or pertaining to an ox or a cow

bow *n.* (often *pl.*) the forepart of a ship

bow 1. *n.* a weapon made of a long strip of wood, tensely arched by means of a cord stretched between the ends, used for shooting arrows ‖ a strip of wood with horsehairs stretched between the ends, used in playing string instruments ‖ a slipknot **2.** *v.* to use a bow ‖ to curve in an arch

bow 1. *n.* a bending of the head or body, in respect, greeting, assent etc. **2.** *v.i.* to submit or give in ‖ to bend the head or body in respect

bow·el *n.* the intestine, the lower end of the alimentary canal ‖ entrails ‖ the innermost part

bowl *v.* to make (something, esp. a hoop) roll along the ground ‖ to score at bowling ‖ to play lawn bowling ‖ to go bowling ‖ to move smoothly and rapidly, esp. in a vehicle **to bowl over** to knock down ‖ to overwhelm

bowl *n.* a deep, round basin or dish for holding liquids, food etc.

bow·leg·ged *adj.* with legs curved outwards

bowl·ing *n.* any of several games in which pins are bowled at

bowling alley a long wooden lane for bowling

box *n.* a container, usually lidded, made of a stiff material such as pasteboard, wood, metal etc. ‖ a small separate compartment in a theater *v.t.* to enclose in a box, or a small space

box 1. *n.* a cuff or slap **2.** *v.i.* to fight with the fists

boxcar *n.* a closed, roofed freight car

box·ing *n.* the sport of fighting with the fists

boxing gloves heavily padded, laced leather mittens

box kite a kite of paper or canvas stretched over a light frame in two boxlike sections

box office the ticket office in a theater

box spring mattress a mattress consisting of a honeycomb arrangement of spiral springs

boy *n.* a male child, till puberty or young

manhood

boy·cott 1. *v.t.* to join with others in refusing to have any dealings with (some other individual or group) ‖ to exclude (a product) from a market by united action **2.** *n.* the act of boycotting

boy·ish *adj.* characteristic of a boy

bra *n.* a brassiere

brace *n.* the tool into which a bit is inserted for boring holes ‖ (often *pl.*) a dental appliance worn to straighten crooked teeth ‖ (*pl.* a,brace) a pair, couple, esp. of pistols and of certain game birds or hunted animals

brace brac·ing braced *v.t.* to fasten tightly ‖ to prepare to take a strain or a shock

brace·let *n.* an ornamental band or chain worn on the arm

brack·et 1. *n.* a right-angled piece of metal,wood, stone etc. of which one surface bears on the upright and so allows the other surface to form a support ‖ one of a pair of punctuation marks [ ] **2.** *v.t.* to enclose within brackets

brack·ish *adj.* (of water) impure, slightly salt

brad *n.* a thin, flat, slight-headed, short nail of uniform thickness, tapering in width

brag 1. *n.* a boast ‖ a card game like poker **2.** *v.i.* **brag·ging bragged** to boast

brag·gart *n.* someone who brags, a habitual boaster

braid *n.* a plait of hair made by weaving several strands together ‖ anything plaited

braid *v.t.* to plait ‖ to edge with braid

Braille *n.* a system of representing letters and figures by raised dots, for use by the blind

brain *n.* that part of the central nervous system within the cranium that is the organ of thought, memory and emotion ‖ the intellect

brain·y brain·i·er brain·i·est *adj.* intelligent, clever above average

braise brais·ing braised *v.t.* to cook slowly in fat and very little liquid in a tightly covered pan

brake 1. *n.* a device for diminishing or preventing the motion of a body **2.** *v.* **brak·ing braked** *v.t.* to slow down ‖ *v.i.* to operate or apply a brake

bram·ble *n.* a brier, any prickly bush or vine

bram·bly bram·bli·er bram·bli·est *adj.* resembling or having brambles

bran *n.* the broken husks of grain separated from the ears by threshing

branch 1. *n.* a stem growing out from the trunk or from a bough of a tree ‖ a similar division ‖ a subunit **2.** leaving the normal sequence of instructions **3.** *v.i.* to put forth branches ‖ to subdivide

brand 1. *n.* a mark made by a hot iron ‖ a trademark ‖ an iron stamp for burning a mark ‖ a blight on leaves etc., characterized by a burnt look **2.** *v.t.* to mark (cattle etc.) with a hot iron ‖ to stigmatize morally

bran·died *adj.* preserved in brandy

branding iron an implement of iron used to brand cattle

bran·dish *v.* to wave about or flourish

bran·dy *pl.* **bran·dies** *n.* a spirit distilled from wine ‖ a liquor distilled from fermented fruit juices

brash *adj.* tiresomely self-satisfied and bragging, cocky ‖ reckless, foolhardy

brass *n.* a yellow alloy of copper and zinc ‖ impudence ‖ (*pl.*) the brass ‖ brass hats collectively **the brass** the brass wind instruments of an orchestra **to get down to brass tacks** to go to the heart of a matter

bras·siere, bras·siere *n.* a light garment which supports a woman's breasts

brass·y brass·i·er brass·i·est *adj.* of or like brass, esp. in color or sound

brat *n.* a child, esp. a bad-mannered or troublesome one

bra·va·do *n.* a bold front, a pretense of indifference to risk or misfortune

brave 1. **brav·er brav·est** *adj.* bold, courageous ‖ testifying to this quality ‖ displaying well **2.** *n.* a North American Indian warrior **3.** *v.t.* **brav·ing braved**

to face the risk of

brav·er·y *n.* courage

bra·vo *interj.* Well done!

bra·vu·ra *n.* swagger ‖ technical daring and display

brawl 1. *n.* a noisy, undignified fight **2.** *v.i.* to quarrel or fight noisily

brawn *n.* muscular strength **brawn·y brawn·i·er brawn·i·est** *adj.* muscular

bray 1. *n.* the cry of an ass **2.** *v.i.* to make the cry or noise of an ass ‖ *v.t.* (with 'out') to utter harshly and loudly

bra·zen *adj.* made of brass ‖ of a harsh yellow color like brass ‖ harsh and loud ‖ bold and shameless

bra·zier *n.* a metal holder for burning coal or coke in the open

breach 1. *n.* the breaking of a legal or moral obligation ‖ a gap made by guns **to throw oneself into the breach** to hurl oneself wholeheartedly into some emergency task **2.** *v.t.* to break through

bread 1. *n.* a food made by moistening and kneading flour or meal and baking it **2.** *v.t.* to coat with breadcrumbs

bread and butter a buttered slice or slices of bread ‖ a livelihood

breadth *n.* the linear dimension measured from side to side of a surface or volume and at right angles to its length ‖ spaciousness

break 1. *v.* **break·ing broke bro·ken** *v.t.* to cause to fall into pieces ‖ to interrupt the continuity of ‖ to shatter, destroy ‖ to disregard, violate ‖ to announce (startling or bad news) ‖ to discover or work out the secret of (a code) ‖ *v.i.* to fall suddenly into pieces ‖ to burst ‖ to distintegrate under pressure ‖ (of the voice) to change from one register to another **to break a record** to do better than the best competitive performance officially recorded **to break away** to leave suddenly ‖ (in a race) to start too soon **to break down** to go out of working condition ‖ to have an emotional, physical or nervous collapse **to break into** to enter forcibly **to break out** to start suddenly to break the bank (gambling)

to win all the dealer's money **to break up** to come to an end **to break with** to sever relations with **2.** *n.* a gap ‖ an interruption ‖ a short pause ‖ (good or bad) fortune **break·a·ble** *adj.* **break·a·bles** *pl. n.* articles easily broken **break·age** *n.*

break·er *n.* a wave breaking into foam on the shore

break·fast 1. *n.* the first meal of the day **2.** *v.t.* to eat breakfast

break·wa·ter *n.* a protective seawall built to break the force of the waves

breast 1. *n.* the upper front part of the human body between the neck and the abdomen ‖ a mammary gland **2.** *v.t.* to struggle up and over

breast·bone *n.* the sternum

breath *n.* air drawn into or expelled from the lungs ‖ a slight movement of air **a breath of fresh air** an invigorating influence **out of breath** unable to draw breath quickly enough after violent exercise again **to take one's breath away** to shock or astonish one **to waste one's breath** to talk to no avail

breathe breath·ing breathed *v.i.* to draw in air and send it out from the lungs ‖ *v.t.* to take in (air etc.) into the lungs ‖ to exhale (esp. fragrance) **not to breathe a word of** not tell anyone about

breath·er *n.* a short rest

breath·ing *n.* respiration

breech *n.* the part of a cannon behind the barrel, where the shell is inserted ‖ the back part of a rifle

breed 1. *n.* a particular group of domestic animals related by descent from common ancestors **2.** *v.* **breed·ing bred** *v.t.* to produce (young) ‖ to give rise to ‖ to mate (animals) ‖ *v.i.* to reproduce

breed·ing *n.* the propagation of plants or animals ‖ distinction of manners

breeze 1. *n.* a gentle wind **2.** *v.i.* **breez·ing breezed**

breez·y breez·i·er breez·i·est *adj.* pleasantly windy ‖ cheerful and casual

brev·i·ty *n.* shortness, esp. of time ‖ conciseness of speech or writing

brew 1. *n.* a drink made by brewing ‖ the process of brewing **2.** *v.t.* to foment ‖ to gather force

brew·er·y *pl.* **brew·er·ies** *n.* a building for brewing beer or ale

bribe 1. *n.* a secret gift (usually of money) offered to a person in a position of trust to persuade him to turn his power to the advantage of the person offering the gift ‖ any enticement meant to condition behavior **2.** *v.t.* **brib·ing bribed** to give a bribe to **brib·er·y** *n.*

brick 1. *n.* a block of fired clay and sand used in building ‖ the red color of brick **2.** *v.t.* to fill in (a space) with bricks

brid·al *adj.* relating to a bride or a wedding

bride *n.* a woman on her wedding day ‖ a newly married woman

bride·groom *n.* a man on his wedding day

brides·maid *n.* a girl or a young woman who attends the bride on her wedding day

bridge 1. *n.* a structure carrying a road, railroad or path over a road, railroad, river or ravine ‖ *(naut.)* a platform amidships for the officers on watch, from which the vessel is commanded ‖ *(dentistry)* a device for anchoring artificial to natural teeth ‖ the upper bony part of the nose **2.** *v.t.* **bridg·ing bridged** to make a bridge over

bridge *n.* a skilled card game of **1.** European origin

bri·dle 1. *n.* the headgear by which a horse is guided and controlled ‖ a check, a restraining influence **2.** *v.* **bri·dling bri·dled** *v.t.* to put a bridle on (a horse) ‖ to restrain (emotions, ambitions etc.)

brief 1. *adj.* lasting a short time ‖ concise ‖ short ‖ curt **2.** *n.* (law) a concise presentation of the facts of a client's case for counsel ‖ *(pl.)* shorts, underpants **3.** *v.t.* to instruct by brief ‖ to summarize (facts) in a brief

brig 1. a ship's prison

bri·gade 1. *n.* (mil.) one of the subdivisions of an army **2.** *v.t.* **bri·gad·ing bri·gad·ed** to form into a brigade

brig·and *n.* a member of a band of men who rob and plunder, a bandit **brig·and·age** *n.*

bright 1. *adj.* reflecting light ‖ cheerful ‖ brilliant, vivid ‖ promising success **2.** *adv.* brightly

bright·en *v.t.* to make light or cheerful ‖ *v.i.* to light up ‖ to become cheerful, lively etc.

bright·ness *n.* the quality of a source by which the light emitted varies from dim to bright

bril·liance *n.* the quality of being brilliant ‖ extreme clarity in musical performance **bril·lian·cy** *n.*

bril·liant 1. *adj.* sparkling ‖ outstanding in intelligence **2.** *n.* a cut diamond with very many facets

brim 1. *n.* the edge or lip of a cup, bowl or other hollow dish ‖ the projecting rim or edge of a hat **2.** *v.i.* **brim·ming brimmed** (with 'over') to be so full as to overflow

brim·stone *n.* sulfur ‖ hellfire

brin·dle 1. *adj.* gray or tawny with darker streaks **2.** *n.* an animal marked in this way **brin·dled** *adj.*

bring bring·ing brought *v.t.* to carry, lead, convey ‖ to persuade ‖ to cause to come ‖ to institute (proceedings) ‖ to prefer ‖ to adduce, advance (an argument) ‖ to fetch (a price) **to bring around** to win over to a new point of view ‖ to restore to consciousness **to bring forth** to give birth to ‖ to produce **to bring forward** to introduce (a topic or proposal) **to bring into play** to cause to be effective, begin using **to bring off** to achieve (something difficult or risky) **to bring to bear** to concentrate ‖ to cause to have effect **to bring up** to rear, train (a child)

brink *n.* the top or edge of a steep place

bri·quette, bri·quet *n.* a brick-shaped block, esp. of compressed coal dust

brisk *adj.* lively and quick ‖ sharply refreshing and keen ‖ (of a drink) sparkling

bris·ket *n.* the breast or lower part of the

chest of an animal, as meat for the table

bris·tle 1. *n.* a short, stiff hair on the back of an animal ‖ anything resembling this **2.** *v.i.* **bris·tling bris·tled** (of an animal's hair) to stand on end, usually through fear, anger etc. ‖ (of people) to take offense **bris·tly bris·tli·er bris·tli·est** *adj.*

brit·tle *adj.* of a solid in which the cohesion bewteen the molecules is fairly easily destroyed by a sudden stress, causing either fragmentation or cleavage along one or more planes

broach 1. *n.* a roasting spit **2.** *v.t.* ‖ to introduce (a subject) into conversation

broad *adj.* of great width ‖ (of ideas or the mind) liberal, free from prejudice ‖ general, not detailed

broad·cast 1. *adj.* transmitted by radio or television **2.** *n.* a speech or other item sent out by radio or television **3.** *v.* **broad·cast·ing broad·cast** *v.t.* to transmit by radio or television ‖ to spread (news, rumors etc.) about

broad-mind·ed *adj.* tolerant

broad·side *n.* the side of a ship from bow to quarter above the waterline ‖ all the guns on one side of a ship ‖ their simultaneous firing

bro·cade 1. *n.* a rich fabric with raised patterns woven in gold or silver thread **2.** *v.t.* **bro·cad·ing bro·cad·ed** to work (a cloth) with a raised design

broc·co·li, bro·co·li *n.* a hardy variety of cauliflower

bro·chure *n.* a pamphlet, esp. a small stitched booklet

broil *v.t.* to cook by direct exposure to a fire or other radiant heat ‖ *v.i.* to be cooked in this way **broil·er** *n.* a grill or part of a stove used for broiling ‖ a young chicken suitable for broiling

bro·ken *past part.* of BREAK ‖ *adj.* fractured ‖ interrupted ‖ uneven ‖ emotionally crushed ‖ violated, betrayed ‖ imperfectly spoken, esp. by a foreigner

bro·ken-down *adj.* reduced physically or morally to very poor condition

bro·ken·heart·ed *adj.* grieving inconsolably

bro·ker *n.* a stockbroker ‖ a professional middleman in some special market **bro·ker·age** *n.* the commission earned by a broker

bronchi *pl.* OF BRONCHUS

bron·chi·a *pl. n.* the branches of the bronchi within the lungs **bron·chi·al** *adj.* pertaining to the bronchia or the bronchi

bron·chi·tis *n.* an inflammation of the mucous membrane in the bronchial tubes

bron·chus *pl.* **bron·chi** *n.* either of the two main divisions of the trachea leading directly into the lungs

bronze 1. *n.* an alloy of copper and tin ‖ an object made of bronze ‖ the color of bronze, golden or reddish-brown **2.** *v.t.* **bronz·ing bronzed** to make the color of bronze

brooch *n.* an ornamental, sometimes jeweled clasp

brood 1. *n.* the young birds from one clutch of eggs ‖ a large family of children **2.** *v.* (of a bird) to sit on eggs and hatch them **to brood on** (or over) to think about and weigh in one's mind **brood·er** *n.* a heated device for rearing chicks artificially ‖ someone who broods

brook *n.* a small stream

broom *n.* a longhandled brush

broth *n.* a thin soup made from meat stock

broth·el *n.* a house of prostitutes

broth·er *pl.* **broth·ers,** *alt. pl.* **breth·ren** *n.* a son in his relationship to another child of the same parents ‖ a title in certain religious orders, sects

broth·er·hood *n.* the condition of being a brother ‖ a group of men living a communal life

broth·er-in-law *pl.* **broth·ers-in-law** *n.* the brother of one's husband or wife ‖ the husband of one's sister

brow *n.* the forehead ‖ the eyebrow ‖ the rounded top of a hill or projecting edge of a cliff

brow·beat brow·beat·ing brow·beat brow·beat·en *v.t.* to bully mentally and spiritually

brown 1. *n.* any color of an orange-black mixture **2.** *adj.* of the color brown **3.** *v.t.* to make brown, esp. by exposure to sun or heat ‖ *v.i.* to become brown

browse 1. *n.* the act of browsing **2.** *v.* **brows·ing browsed** *v.t.* to nibble or feed on ‖ *v.i.* to nibble, feed, on leaves, bushes etc. ‖ to graze ‖ to dip into a book, read without concentration ‖ to explore unsystematically

bruise *n.* a surface injury to the body, caused by a fall or a blow **1.** *v.* **bruis·ing bruised** *v.t.* to inflict a bruise on ‖ *v.i.* to be susceptible to bruises

bru·net, bru·nette 1. *adj.* having dark hair and complexion **2.** *n.* someone with such hair and complexion

brunt *n.* the main force or shock of a blow

brush *n.* an implement made of bristles, wire, hair, or nylon etc. set in wood, etc. ‖ a short, quick fight ‖ a controversy ‖ small trees and shrubs, land covered with thicket

brush *v.t.* to apply a brush to ‖ to apply with a brush ‖ to touch lightly in passing ‖ *v.i.* to use a brush **to brush aside** to dismiss summarily **to brush off** to dismiss curtly **to brush up** to refresh by starting to study again

brusque *adj.* abrupt, short ‖ curt, slightly hostile

bru·tal *adj.* harsh to the point of cruelty ‖ savagely violent ‖ plain and direct with no regard for feeling **bru·tal·i·ty** *pl.* **bru·tal·i·ties** *n.*

bru·tal·ize bru·tal·iz·ing bru·tal·ized *v.t.* to render brutal, inhuman, savage

brute 1. *n.* an animal ‖ a brutal person **2.** *adj.* (of actions, motives, ideas etc.) like a beast's in strength or savagery **brut·ish** *adj.*

bub·ble 1. *n.* a small volume of air or gas surrounded by a liquid, a solid or an elastic membrane such as a soap solution film ‖ something transient without substance and liable to burst **2.** *v.i.* **bub·bling bub·bled** to form bubbles ‖ to make gurgling sounds **to bubble over** to be exuberant

buck 1. *n.* the male of hares, goats, rabbits, deer, antelope, rats ‖ a dollar **to pass the buck** to dodge responsibility **2.** *v.t.* to throw by bucking ‖ to resist, oppose ‖ *v.i.* to spring up vertically clear off the ground with the back arched **buck up!**

buck·et 1. *n.* a container for holding water, milk etc., a pail **2.** *v.t.* to lift in buckets

buck·le 1. *n.* a stiff fastening attached to one end of a belt, ribbon, strap etc. **2.** *v.* **buck·ling buck·led** *v.t.* (often with 'on', 'up') to fasten with a buckle ‖ to bend sharply, kink, crumple ‖ *v.i.* to give way ‖ to bend out of shape, twist, crumple

buck·shot *n.* coarse lead shot for big-game hunting

bu·col·ic *adj.* rustic ‖ pastoral

bud 1. *n.* a much condensed, undeveloped shoot end of the axis, composed of closely crowded young leaves ‖ a half-opened flower **in bud** putting forth buds **2.** *v.* **bud·ding bud·ded bud·ding** *adj.* promising

bud·dy *pl.* **bud·dies** *n.* a pal, friend

budge budg·ing budged *v.t.* to cause (something heavy or resisting) to move slightly ‖ *v.i.* to move ‖ to yield ‖ to modify an opinion

budg·et 1. *n.* estimate of revenue and expenditure ‖ personal or household expenses **2.** *v.* to allow for in a budget ‖ *v.i.* to plan expenditure with a given amount of money **budg·et·ar·y** *adj.*

buff 1. *adj.* like buff in color, yellowish **2.** *n.* a thick, good-quality soft leather made from buffalo or oxhide ‖ an enthusiast **3.** *v.t.* to polish with a buff

buf·fa·lo 1. *n. pl.* **buf·fa·lo, buf·fa·loes, buf·fa·los** any of several wild oxen, **2.** g. the water ‖ buffalo fish **3.** *v.t.* to trick, bamboozle

buf·fet 1. *n.* a blow given by a storm, or strong waves **2.** *v.t.* to knock about

buf·fet *n.* a recessed cupboard or set of shelves for displaying china etc. ‖ in informal entertaining, a table laid with food and drink

buf·foon 1. *n.* a clownish fellow **2.** *v.i.* to act like a clown **buf·foon·er·y** *n.*

bug 1. *n.* any small insect ‖ a disease-producing organism ‖ a fault in an apparatus ‖ a concealed microphone **2.** *v.t.* **bug·ging bugged** to conceal a microphone in ‖ to pester, annoy

bug·gy *pl.* **bug·gies** *n.* a light one-horse carriage

bu·gle 1. *n.* a brass wind instrument **2.** *v.* **bu·gling bu·gled** *v.i.* to sound a bugle

build 1. *n.* shape, proportions of body **2.** *v.* **build·ing built** *v.t.* to construct **build·er 3.** *n.* someone who builds ‖ a building contractor

build·ing *n.* a permanent construction

bulb *n.* the erect underground stem of a plant ‖ a rounded part or end of a cylindrical organ ‖ that part of an electric lamp which encloses the filament

bulge 1. *n.* a curving outwards ‖ an abnormal increase in numbers **2.** *v.* **bulg·ing bulged** *v.t.* to cause to curve or swell outwards **bulg·y bulg·i·er bulg·i·est** *adj.*

bulk 1. *n.* mass ‖ food taken in to help digestion rather than for nutritional value **2.** *v.t.* (with out) to increase the size of ‖ *v.i.* to occupy space

b ulk·y bulk·i·er bulk·i·est *adj.* having bulk ‖ taking up a lot of room

bull 1. *adj.* male, esp. of large animals ‖ (stock exchange) marked by rising prices **2.** *n.* an uncastrated male of the bovine family ‖ the male of certain other large animals, **3.** *g.* whale, elephant, elk, or moose

bul·let *n.* a small, round or conical piece of lead

bul·le·tin *n.* a short official statement of news ‖ a periodical publication, e.g. of a club or society

bul·lion *n.* gold or silver in bars or ingots

bull's-eye *pl.* **bull's-eyes** *n.* the center ring of a target

bul·ly 1. *pl.* **bul·lies** *n.* someone who enjoys oppressing others weaker than himself **2.** *v.* **bul·ly·ing bul·lied** *v.t.* to persecute physically or spiritually

bul·rus *n.* a sedge of genus Scirpus

bul·wark *n.* a defensive wall, ramparts ‖ any defensive or safeguarding structure ‖ a person, institution, moral principle etc.

bum 1. *adj.* of poor quality **2.** *n.* a loafer ‖ a vagrant **3.** *v.* **bum·ming bummed** *v.t.* to get (something) by sponging ‖ *v.i.* to sponge

bum·ble·bee *n.* a genus of big, hairy, social bees

bump 1. *n.* a heavy jolt, blow or collision **2.** *v.t.* to knock or strike ‖ to preempt a place ‖ to shape (metal) into curves ‖ *v.i.* (often with into' or against') to knock or collide suddenly

bump·er *n.* a device for reducing the shock of a collision

bump·tious *adj.* self-assertive, full of noisy conceit

bump·y bump·i·er bump·i·est *adj.* having or causing jolts

bun *n.* a soft bread roll ‖ a woman's long hair done in a tight coil at the back of the head

bunch 1. *n.* a cluster of things growing or tied together ‖ a group of people **2.** *v.t.* to tie or gather together ‖ *v.i.* to gather into a close group

bun·dle 1. *n.* a number of things wrapped, rolled or tied together ‖ **2.** *v.t.* **bun·dling bun·dled** to tie up in a bundle

bun·ga·low *n.* a one-storied house

bun·gle 1. *n.* a clumsy, unsuccessful piece of work **2.** *v.* **bun·gling bun·gled** *v.t.* to botch, spoil

bun·ion *n.* an enlargement from chronic inflammation on the first joint of the big toe

bunk *n.* a narrow sleeping berth

bunk *n.* humbug, nonsense

bun·ny *pl.* **bun·nies** *n.* (child's name for) a rabbit

bunt·ing *n.* thin wool or cotten stuff used for flags and similar decorations ‖ flags

buoy 1. *n.* an anchored float marking a navigable channel **2.** *v.t.* to keep afloat ‖ to raise to the surface

buoy·an·cy *n.* the ability to float

buoy·ant *adj.* able to float or rise

bur·den 1. *n.* a heavy load ‖ a heavy moral obligation ‖ **2.** *v.t.* to put a weight on ‖ to take on a mental or moral burden **bur·den·some** a mental or moral burder

bu·reau *pl.* **bu·reaus, bu·reaux** *n.* a chest of drawers ‖ a government department or its subdivision

bu·reauc·ra·cy *pl.* **bu·reauc·ra·cies** *n.* government by officials **bu·reau·crat** *n.* **bu·reau·crat·ic** *adj.* **bu·reau·crat·i·cal·ly** *adv.*

bur·geon, bour·geon 1. *n.* a bud **2.** *v.i.* to begin to grow

bur·glar *n.* someone who commits burglary

bur·gla·ry *pl.* **bur·gla·ries** *n.* the act of breaking into houses, shops etc. to steal

bur·gle bur·gling bur·gled *v.t.* to rob by burglary

bur·i·al *n.* a burying or being buried

burl 1. *n.* a knot in wool ‖ on tree trunks **2.** *v.t.* to free (cloth) from burls

bur·lap *n.* a coarse fabric of hemp, jute or flax

bur·lesque *n.* a literary or dramatic imitation mocking its model by going to comic extremes, for fun ‖ a parody ‖ a theatrical entertainment of low comedy, esp. incorporating striptease *v.t.* **bur·les·quing bur·lesqued** to represent grotesquely, in fun

bur·ly bur·li·er bur·li·est *adj.* big and strong, heavily built

burn 1. *n.* damage or injury caused by fire, heat or acid **2.** *v.* **burn·ing burned, burnt** *v.t.* to consume or destroy by flames or heat ‖ to injure by fire or heat or acid ‖ to make by fire or heat or acid ‖ to scorch, to cause to stick to the pan ‖ to cauterize (a wound etc.) ‖ *v.i.* to flame, blaze ‖ to be destroyed by fire or heat ‖ to stick to a pan and char ‖ to suffer injury or discomfort by exposure to the sun ‖ to be passionately excited or heated with anger etc. ‖ to feel hot

burn·ing *adj.* on fire ‖ intense ‖ exciting passion

bur·nish 1. *n.* a gloss **2.** *v.t.* to polish

burr 1. *n.* a trilling pronunciation of *r* ‖ a whirring, humming sound ‖ any rough edge ‖ a coarse rock with quartz crystals used in millstones **2.** *v.i.* to speak with a burr ‖ to make a burring sound

bur·ro *n.* a small donkey

bur·row 1. *n.* a hole dug underground by some animals as a shelter **2.** *v.t.* to dig (such a hole) ‖ *v.t.* to dig a burrow ‖ to delve **to burrow into a mystery**

burst *n.* an explosion ‖ a sudden short intensive period

burst burst·ing burst *v.i.* to explode, disintegrate suddenly and violently

bur·y bur·y·ing bur·ied *v.t.* to put in the ground so as to be hidden from view ‖ to place in a grave or tomb ‖ to dismiss from the mind ‖ to cover over ‖ to hide

bus 1. *pl.* **bus·es, bus·ses** *n.* a large passenger vehicle **2.** *v.i.* **bus·sing** bussed to go by bus

bush 1. *n.* a shrub ‖ a clump of shrubs ‖ rough, shrubby, uncultivated country **2.** *v.i.* to branch out or cluster thickly

bush·el *n.* any of various measures of capacity, esp. a dry unit equal to 2150.42 cu. ins. **to hide one's light under a bushel** to keep some ability etc. secret

busi·ness *n.* one's regular employment, profession, occupation ‖ one's personal affair, concern, duty ‖ something requiring attention ‖ active selling, transactions ‖ a commercial firm or enterprise **to go about one's business** to do what concerns oneself **to have no business to** to have no right to **to mean business** to be in earnest **to mind one's own business** to refrain from interfering

bus·ing *n.* transporting students from one school area to another to promote racial integration

bust *n.* a piece of sculpture showing head, neck and something of shoulders and chest ‖ the upper front part of a woman's body

bust 1. *n.* a burst ‖ (of a person) a complete failure **2.** *v.t.* **bust·ing bust bust,**

bust·ed to burst, break ‖ to make bankrupt ‖ to demote (a soldier) ‖ to arrest

bus·tle 1. *n.* a stir ‖ brisk movement **2.** *v.* **bus·tling bus·tled** *v.i.* to move with busy or fussy purpose

bus·y bus·i·er bus·i·est *adj.* engaged in work or other occupation ‖ full of activity ‖ (of a telephone line) in use

busy bus·y·ing bus·ied *v.t.* to occupy (someone, one's hands etc.)

but 1. *adv.* only, merely ‖ just **2.** *conj.* yet, and on the other hand ‖ except (that) **3.** *prep.* except

butch·er 1. *n.* someone who sells meat that he has prepared for sale **2.** *v.t.* to slaughter ‖ to kill cruelly or in great numbers ‖ to ruin the impact of (a work) by bad reading, performing or editing **bútch·er·ly** *adj.*

but·ler *n.* the chief manservant of a house

butt *n.* the thicker or handle end, esp. of a tool or weapon ‖ the unburned end of a smoked cigarette etc. ‖ any of various flatfish, e.g. sole, turbot, plaice

butt *v.t.* to strike with the head or horns ‖ to join by making a butt joint, without overlapping ‖ *v.i.* to bump ‖ to project **to butt in** to interrupt suddenly **to butt in on** to intrude in

butte *n.* an isolated hill, with steep sides, and a flat top

but·ter 1. *n.* the fatty substance made by churning cream **2.** *v.t.* to spread with butter **to butter up** to flatter

but·ter·cup a genus of plants of Europe, Asia and North America

but·ter·fly *pl.* **but·ter·flies** *n.* an insect ‖ a frivolous person ‖ a fast swimming stroke **to have butterflies in one's stomach** to be in a state of acute nervous anticipation

but·ter·scotch *n.* a candy

but·ter·y *adj.* having the appearance or consistency of butter ‖ containing or covered with butter

but·tock *n.* one of the two rounded, muscled parts of the body on which a person sits

but·ton 1. *n.* a small disk or knob sewn on material and passed through a hole or loop to provide a loose fastening, or this used ornamentally ‖ an unopened mushroom **2.** *v.t.* (often with 'up') to fasten the buttons

but·tress 1. *n.* a support built against a wall **2.** *v.t.* to prop or support with buttresses ‖ (often with 'up') to support

buy 1. *v.t.* **buy·ing bought** to acquire by paying money, purchase **to buy off** to get rid of (a blackmailer, claimant etc.) by payment **to buy out** to pay (a person) to give up certain privileges or rights **2.** *n.* something bought, esp. a bargain

buzz 1. *n.* a humming noise, esp. of bees ‖ a muted sound of many people talking ‖ a general stir **2.** *v.i.* to make a humming sound ‖ to murmur ‖ to use a buzzer

buz·zard *n.* the turkey buzzard

by 1. *adv.* past ‖ near ‖ aside **2.** *prep.* beside ‖ close to ‖ along, over ‖ through, via ‖ past ‖ during ‖ not later than ‖ through the means of ‖ with, born of

by·gone 1. *adj.* past, of the past **2.** *n.* (*pl.*) past offenses etc. **to let bygones be bygones** to forgive and forget

by·law, bye·law *n.* a regulation or law made by a corporation, company, club

by·pass 1. *n.* an alternative road ‖ *n.* a device to direct flow around a fixture or pipe, etc ‖ a shunt **2.** *v.t.* to make a detour

by·prod·uct *n.* something produced during the manufacture of something else

by·stand·er *n.* a casual spectator

byte *n.* unit of binary digits, usually in eight bits representing two numerals or one character

by·word *n.* a word or phrase often used

C

C, c the third letter in the English alphabet

cab *n.* a car for hire ‖ the closed part of a truck or locomotive where the driver sits

ca·bal 1. *n.* an association of persons secretly united to further their interests by plotting **2.** *v.i.* **ca·bal·ling ca·balled** to plot

cab·a·ret *n.* a place serving alcoholic drinks and providing entertainment

cab·bage *n.* a plant whose leaves are eaten as a vegetable

cab·in *n.* a small wooden house ‖ a room on board ship ‖ an aircraft's compartment for passengers

cab·i·net *n.* a piece of furniture with display shelves ‖ the committee of chief ministers

ca·ble 1. *n.* a strong length of rope, wire or chain ‖ a telegraph line ‖ a message sent by this **2.** *v.* **ca·bling ca·bled**

ca·boose the rear car of a freight train used by trainmen

cache *n.* a hiding place for treasure or stores ‖ the goods in such a hiding place

cack·le 1. *n.* the harsh, clucking noise of a hen ‖ idle talk **2.** *v.* **cack·ling cack·led** *v.i.* to make such a noise ‖ to chatter or laugh shrilly

ca·coph·o·ny *pl.* **ca·coph·o·nies** *n.* a harsh discord

cac·tus *pl.* **cac·ti cac·tus·es** *n.* a genus of spiny plants

ca·dav·er *n.* a human corpse **ca·dav·er·ous** *adj.* corpse-like ‖ gaunt

cad·die, cad·dy 1. *n.* an attendant paid to carry a golfer's clubs **2.** *v.i.* **cad·dy·ing cad·died** to serve as a caddie

ca·dence *n.* the rhythmic flow of sound ‖ a beat, measure

ca·det *n.* a student at a military or naval college

ca·dre *n.* the permanent nucleus of an organization

ca·fé, ca·fe *n.* a place where coffee and occasionally food are served

caf·e·te·ri·a *n.* a self-service restaurant

caf·feine *n.* an organic compound occurring in esp. the coffee bean and tea leaf

cage 1. *n.* an airy container made with bars for keeping birds etc. in **2.** *v.t.* **cag·ing caged** to keep in a cage

cag·ey, cag·y cag·i·er cag·i·est *adj.* secretive ‖ wary **cá·gi·ly** *adv.* **cá·gi·ness** *n.*

ca·hoots *pl. n.* (only in the phrase) **in cahoots** in partnership, esp. one which involves shady dealings

ca·jole ca·jol·ing ca·joled *v.t.* to persuade or coax by flattery **ca·jóle·ment, ca·jól·er·y** ns

cake 1. *n.* a baked mixture of flour, leaven, eggs, fats, sugar and other sweet or fruity ingredients ‖ a small quantity of a substance molded into a bar **2.** **cak·ing caked** *v.i.* to become a hardened mass

cal·a·boose *n.* jail

ca·lam·i·ty *pl.* **ca·lam·i·ties** *n.* a disastrous event causing great misery

cal·ci·fi·ca·tion *n.* the deposition of insoluble calcium salts in a tissue

cal·ci·fy cal·ci·fy·ing cal·ci·fied *v.t.* to change into calcium carbonate

cal·ci·um *n.* a white divalent element of the alkaline earth group

cal·cu·late cal·cu·lat·ing cal·cu·lat·ed *v.t.* to find out or ascertain by using mathematics ‖ *v.i.* to make a calculation ‖ (with 'on') to rely **cál·cu·lat·ing** *adj.* working out mathematical processes

cal·cu·la·tion *n.* the act, process or result of using mathematical processes ‖ careful thinking

cal·cu·la·tor *n.* someone who calculates ‖ a calculating machine

cal·cu·lus *pl.* **cal·cu·li, cal·cu·lus·es** *n.* any branch of mathematics that employs symbolic computations

cal·dron, caul·dron *n.* a large deep cooking pot

cal·en·dar *n.* a table of the days, weeks and months of the year noting public holidays etc. ‖ a register or schedule

cal·en·der 1. *v.t.* to press (cloth, paper etc.) so as to produce a smooth, glossy finish **2.** *n.* a machine containing rollers to carry out this process

calf *pl.* **calves** *n.* the fleshy part of the back

of the leg below the knee

calf pl. **calves** n. the young of a cow, elephant, whale etc.

cal·i·ber, cal·i·bre n. the diameter of the bore of a gun or rifle or of a bullet or a shell ‖ the quality of a person's mind or character

cal·i·brate cal·i·brat·ing cal·i·brat·ed v.t. to indicate a scale on (a measuring instrument) ‖ to measure the internal diameter of (a tube)

cal·i·co pl. **cal·i·coes, cal·i·cos** n. inexpensive printed cotton cloth

ca·liph, ca·lif n. a successor to Mohammed as head of Islam

cal·is·then·ic adj. producing health and beauty in the body **cal·is·thén·ics**

call 1. v.i. to shout or exclaim in order to gain attention ‖ telephone ‖ (of a bird) to make its characteristic sound ‖ to pay a visit ‖ to stop (at a port) **to call for** to request **to call (someone) names** to use insulting epithets to or about (someone) **to call off** to postpone or cancel **to call on** to pay a visit **to call to order** to request (someone) to be quiet or orderly **to call up** to telephone ‖ to summon for military service **to call upon** (or **on**)to appeal to 2. n. a cry or shout to attract attention ‖ a message, esp. by telephone ‖ a short visit **on call** (of a doctor, ambulance etc.) available for duty

call·ing n. a profession or occupation ‖ a spiritual summons

cal·li·o·pe n. a musical instrument

cal·lous 1. adj. indifferent to the pain or distress of others ‖ (of the skin) hardened 2. n. a callus

cal·low adj. lacking experience of life, immature

cal·lus, cal·lous pl. **cal·lus·es, cal·lous·es** n. a thickened area of skin or plant tissue

calm 1. adj. still, without rough motion ‖ placid 2. n. a period of serenity ‖ a windless period 3. v.t. to soothe, pacify

cal·o·rie cal·o·ry n. a unit of heat energy derived by the body from food

ca·lum·ni·ate   ca·lum·ni·at·ing ca·lum·ni·at·ed v.t. to slander

ca·lum·ni·á·tion n. **ca·lúm·ni·a·tor** n. someone who slanders **ca·lúm·ni·a·to·ry** adj. slanderous **ca·lúm·ni·ous** adj.

cal·um·ny pl. **cal·um·nies** n. a slanderous accusation, made with the intention of harming another

ca·lyp·so n. a W. Indian lilting song

ca·lyx pl. **ca·lyx·es, cal·y·ces** n. an outer whorl of floral leaves

cam n. an eccentric projection of a shaft which communicates the revolution of the shaft into the linear movement of another part of a machine

cam·el n. either of two members of quadruped ruminants used in desert countries for beasts of burden **cam·el·eer** n. a camel driver

cam·e·o n. an engraved design or portrait cut in relief on hard stone or a gem

cam·er·a n. an apparatus for taking photographs **in camera** in a judge's private chamber ‖ with the public excluded

cam·ou·flage n. the hiding from observation of ships or buildings ‖ any concealment by disguise

camp 1. n. a place where forces are temporarily lodged ‖ a holiday recreational center, esp. for children **to pitch camp** to set up a camp 2. v.i. pitch tents, etc. ‖ to live in a camp 3. adj. to live elsewhere than one's home, temporarily, and in conditions involving inconvenience

cam·paign 1. n. a series of military actions in one area ‖ any organized attempt to gain public support 2. v.i. to direct, or take part in, a campaign

camp·er n. a person at a camp ‖ any vehicle fitted out with temporary living arrangements

cam·pus pl. **cam·pus·es** n. the grounds and main buildings of a school or college

can 1. n. a tinplated container in which foodstuffs are preaserved 2. v.t. **can·ning canned** to preserve by packing in an airtight can

ca·nal n. an artificial waterway ‖ a tube through which fluids are conveyed

ca·nard *n.* a piece of false information put out as a hoax

ca·nar·y *pl.* **ca·nar·ies** *n.* any of several varieties of singing birds of the finch family

ca·nas·ta *n.* a card game

can·cel *v.t.* **can·cel·ing can·celed** nullify ‖ to countermand ‖ delete ‖ to mark (postage stamps) so that they cannot be used again

can·cel·la·tion, can·cel·a·tion *n.* the act of canceling

Can·cer *n.* a northern constellation **can·cer** a malignant tumor **cán·cer·ous** *adj.*

can·de·la·brum *pl.* **can·de·la·bra** *n.* a large, branching support for a number of candles

can·did frankly truthful ‖ honest, open

can·di·da·cy *pl.* **can·di·da·cies** *n.* the position or status of being a candidate

can·di·date *n.* a person who offers himself for some post or office ‖ a person taking an examination

can·dle *n.* a cylinder of tallow or wax around a core of wick, burned to give light

can·dor *n.* frankness, even to the point of telling unwelcome truths

can·dy 1. *n. pl.* **can·dies** crystallized sugar 2. *v.* **can·dy·ing can·died** *v.t.* to preserve by coating with sugar ‖ to turn into candy

cane *n.* the long, hollow stem of plants ‖ a thin walking stick

ca·nine *adj.* of or pertaining to the family Canidae (dogs, wolves, foxes and jackals)

can·is·ter, can·nis·ter *n.* a small metal box for tea, coffee etc.

can·ker *n.* an ulceration on the inside of the mouth or lips **cán·ker·ous** *adj.*

can·na·bis *n.* hemp

can·ni·bal *n.* a human who eats human flesh **can·ni·bal·ism** *n.* **can·ni·bal·is·tic** *adj.*

can·ni·bal·ize can·ni·bal·iz·ing can·ni·bal·ized *v.t.* to repair (vehicles or aircraft) by using parts from other vehicles, instead of using spare parts

can·non *n.* (*pl.*) **can·nons** a piece of artillery

can·non·ade 1. *n.* a bombardment 2. *v.* **can·non·ad·ing can·non·ad·ed** to bombard

can·ny can·ni·er can·ni·est *adj.* cautious ‖ careful

ca·noe *n.* a light boat, propelled by paddles

can·on *n.* a church law ‖ any general principle or body of principles ‖ a member of the chapter, or administrative body, of a cathedral

can·on·i·za·tion *n.* a canonizing or being canonized

can·on·ize can·on·iz·ing can·on·ized *v.t.* to declare by authority in the Roman and Orthodox churches that a person is to be venerated as a saint

can·o·py *pl.* **can·o·pies** *n.* an ornate covering of cloth, wood etc. suspended over a bed, throne, shrine or person

cant *n.* an inclination ‖ the bevel of a sloping surface

cant 1. *n.* insincere or trite statements ‖ jargon used by members of a particular class or profession 2. *adj.* trite ‖ insincere

can·ta·loupe, can·ta·loup *n.* a variety of muskmelon

can·tan·ker·ous *adj.* bad-tempered

can·teen *n.* a shop in a military camp or barracks, selling food, liquor, etc. ‖ a water bottle

can·ter 1. *n.* the gait of a horse between a trot and a gallop 2. *v.i.* to move at a canter

can·tor *n.* the leader of a church choir **can·to·ri·al** *adj.*

can·vas, can·vass *n.* a strong, coarse cloth of unbleached hemp or flax ‖ tents or sails collectively

can·vass, can·vas 1. *v.t.* to seek votes, business orders, subscriptions, etc., from (potential supporters, clients, etc.) ‖ to ascertain (public opinion) 2. *n.* a survey of public opinion **cán·vass·er** *n.* someone who canvasses

can·yon, ca·non *n.* a deep gorge or natural cleft

cap 1. *n.* brimless head covering ‖ any caplike cover **2.** *v.t.* **cap·ping capped** to put a cap on (something) ‖ to put the finishing touch to or come as a climax to

ca·pa·bil·i·ty *pl.* **ca·pa·bil·i·ties** *n.* the quality of being capable, ability

ca·pa·ble *adj.* able, having many capacities

ca·pac·i·ty *pl.* **ca·pac·i·ties** *n.* the ability to contain or accommodate ‖ mental ability ‖ faculty

cape *n.* a sleeveless outer garment hanging from the shoulders, worn fastened at the neck

cape *n.* a piece of land jutting out into the sea

ca·per *n.* a frisky leap or jump ‖ a fantastic antic

caper *n.* a low trailing shrub with small dark-green leaves, and three-petaled white flowers

cap·il·lar·y 1. *adj.* hairlike **2.** *pl.* **cap·il·lar·ies** *n.* one of a system of minute thin-walled blood vessels

cap·i·tal *n.* the top or head of a pillar, pier or column

capital 1. involving forfeiture of life ‖ chief ‖ very great ‖ very good **2.** *n.* principal ‖ the value of this in a given instance ‖ the chief city of a country, state etc.

cap·i·tal·ism *n.* an economic system in which the means of production, distribution and exchange are privately owned and operated for private profit

cap·i·tal·ist *n.* possessing capital ‖ defending or engaging in capitalism ‖ characterized by capitalism **cap·i·tal·is·tic** *adj.*

cap·i·tal·ize cap·i·tal·iz·ing cap·i·tal·ized *v.t.* to convert into capital ‖ to provide (a business) with capital ‖ to write with an initial capital letter

cap·i·tol *n.* the building in which a state legislature meets

ca·pit·u·late **ca·pit·u·lat·ing ca·pit·u·lat·ed** *v.i.* to surrender

ca·pit·u·la·tion *n.* a surrender upon terms

ca·price *n.* a sudden and illogical fancy, a whim

ca·pri·cious *adj.* unreliable, ruled by whims

cap·size cap·siz·ing cap·sized *v.t.* to upset or cause to founder

cap·su·lar *adj.* of or like a capsule

cap·sule *n.* any closed boxlike vessel containing seeds, spores or fruits ‖ a small case of gelatin etc., enclosing a medicinal dose ‖ a sealed, pressurized cabin for high-altitude or space flight

cap·tain *n.* (navy) an officer above a commander and below a rear admiral in rank ‖ (army) an officer above a lieutenant and below a major in rank ‖ a leader, chief

cap·tion *n.* the heading of a chapter ‖ a legend to an illustration

cap·ti·vate cap·ti·vat·ing cap·ti·vat·ed *v.t.* to charm, enchant **cap·ti·va·tion** *n.*

cap·tive 1. *n.* a prisoner **2.** *adj.* imprisoned, kept in confinement

cap·tiv·i·ty *pl.* **cap·tiv·i·ties** *n.* the period of being a captive ‖ confinement

cap·ture *v.t.* to subdue, dominate or overcome and get possession of

car *n.* a wheeled vehicle, esp. an automobile ‖ any railroad carriage or wagon

ca·rafe *n.* a glass bottle for table water or wine

car·a·mel *n.* sugar melted and slightly burned ‖ a semi-hard candy ‖ a shade of light brown

car·at *n.* measure of weight used for gems

car·a·van *n.* merchants or pilgrims, traveling together for safety

car·a·vel *n.* a small sailing ship of the 15th and 16th cc.

car·bo·hy·drate *n.* one of a biologically important group of neutral organic chemicals

car·bon *n.* a tetravalent element

car·bon·ate 1. *n.* a salt of carbonic acid **2.** *v.t.* **car·bon·at·ing car·bon·at·ed** to impregnate with carbon dioxide under pressure or with carbonic acid

car·bon·a·tion *n.* a saturation with carbon dioxide

carbon dioxide a colorless, heavy gas that does not support combustion

carbon monoxide a colorless, odorless, toxic gas

car·bun·cle *n.* a painful infection of the skin **car·bún·cu·lar** *adj.* like a carbuncle

car·bu·re·tor, car·bu·ret·er *n.* an apparatus which vaporizes a liquid fuel and controls its mixing with air for combustion in an engine

car·cass *n.* a dead animal body

car·ci·no·ma *pl.* **car·ci·no·mas, car·ci·no·ma·ta** *n.* an epithelial cancer

card *n.* a piece of paper or pasteboard suitable for writing or printing on ‖ a playing card

card·board *n.* stiff pasteboard

car·di·ac *adj.* pertaining to the heart

car·di·gan *n.* a knitted jacket

car·di·nal 1. *adj.* of fundamental importance ‖ deep red **2.** *n.* one of the princes of the Catholic Church ‖ a family of small red birds

care *n.* serious attention, watchfulness, caution ‖ protection ‖ charge ‖ anxiety, concern, worry

care car·ing cared *v.t.* to feel interest in, bother about ‖ to be concerned as amuch as

ca·reer *n.* progress through life with respect to one's work ‖ a profession

care·free *adj.* free from care

care·ful *adj.* cautious ‖ painstaking ‖ done with accuracy or with caution

care·less *adj.* lighthearted, carefree ‖ casual ‖ indifferent, thoughtless ‖ negligent

ca·ress *n.* a gentle, affectionate touch or embrace

caress *v.t.* to touch gently and lovingly, fondle

care·tak·er *n.* a person employed to take charge of property etc., and see to routine matters

car·go *pl.* **car·goes, car·gos** *n.* the freight of goods or luggage carried by a ship, aircraft etc.

car·i·bou *n.* a deer related to the reindeer

car·i·ca·ture 1. *n.* ridicule (by exaggeration and distortion) of a thing or person ‖ a ludicrously poor copy or imitation **2.** *v.t.* **car·i·ca·tur·ing car·i·ca·tured** to make a caricature of **cár·i·ca·tur·ist** *n.* someone who makes caricatures

car·ies *n.* the decay of animal tissues

car·il·lon *n.* a set of bells playing either a tune or a series of notes

car·nage *n.* slaughter, esp. in battle

car·nal *adj.* pertaining to the flesh, as opposed to the spirit ‖ sexual

car·na·tion *n.* a species of pink

car·ni·val *n.* the festivities in Catholic countries just before Lent (Mardi Gras) and at mid-Lent ‖ a traveling amusement show

car·niv·o·rous *adj.* flesh-eating

car·ol 1. *n.* a Christmas hymn **2.** *v.* **car·ol·ing car·oled** *v.i.* to sing joyfully

ca·rouse 1. *v.i.* **ca·rous·ing car·oused** to take part in a drinking bout **2.** *n.* a drinking bout

carp *n.* a long-lived bony, edible, freshwater fish

carp *v.i.* to complain **to carp at** to nag, find fault with

car·pen·ter *n.* a workman in wood

car·pen·try *n.* woodwork ‖ the carpenter's trade

car·pet 1. *n.* a heavy fabric, used esp. as a covering for floors **2.** *v.t.* to cover with or as if with a carpet

car·pet·ing *n.* material used for laying as a carpet

car·riage *n.* a horse-drawn vehicle ‖ the manner of holding oneself in walking and standing

car·ri·er *n.* a person, company or corporation undertaking transport ‖ a person or animal carrying the germs of a disease

car·ri·on *n.* dead, putrefying flesh of man or beast

car·rot *n.* a biennial plant widely used as a vegetable **cár·rot·y** *adj.* yellowish red

car·rou·sel, car·ou·sel *n.* a merry-go-round

car·ry car·ry·ing car·ried *v.t.* to convey from one place to another ‖ to convey or transmit in any manner ‖ to conduct ‖ v.i. (of sound) so strong as to be heard at a distance **to carry away** to cause (someone) to be so absorbed or thrilled **to carry forward** (accounting) to transfer (a total) from one column of figures to the next ‖ to progress with **to carry on** to continue

cart 1. n. a small, shafted vehicle for moving loads by hand **2.** v.t. to drag, cause to go under compulsion ‖ v.i. to move loads by cart **cart·age** n. the act of conveying goods in a cart ‖ the charge for doing this

car·tel n. an industrial combination in which several different firms agree on some form of joint action

car·ter n. a person who transports goods for others

car·ti·lage n. a very tough, translucent, bluish-white elastic tissue **car·ti·lag·i·noid** adj. resembling cartilage

car·tog·ra·pher n. a person who makes maps

car·tog·ra·phy n. mapmaking

car·ton n. a light box made of cardboard or fiber

car·toon n. a drawing which puts a comic construction on current events or on people ‖ comic strip **car·toon·ist** n. a person who draws cartoons

car·tridge n. a cased explosive charge, also containing the missile ‖ a holder for a roll of film

carve carv·ing carved v.t. to cut (stone, wood etc.) ‖ to cut (a roast, chicken etc.) into slices or pieces

carv·ing n. the act of carving ‖ a carved work

cas·cade 1. n. a waterfall ‖ anything thought of as like a rush of water **2.** v.i. **cas·cad·ing cas·cad·ed** to fall as or like a waterfall

case 1. n. a box or crate ‖ a glass-sided box for exhibiting specimens **2.** v.t. **cas·ing cased** to enclose in a case or box, encase

case n. a set of circumstances or conditions ‖ an instance ‖ a matter for trial

case harden v.t. to harden the surface of **case·hard·ened** adj. of a person grown callous through seeing too much misery

ca·sein n. the colloidal protein in milk, caseinogen

cash 1. n. money in the form of coins or paper **2.** v.t. to give or obtain cash in exchange for (a check, money order etc.) **to cash in on** take advantage of

cash·ew n. a tropical tree

cash(d)ier n. an employee in a bank ‖ an employee in a shop, restaurant etc. who takes customers' payments

cashier v.t. (armed forces) to dismiss from the service in disgrace

cash·mere n. a very soft, fine wool

cas·ing n. a thing which encases ‖ an enclosing framework

ca·si·no n. a public room for gambling and dancing ‖ a building containing gambling rooms

cask n. a wooden barrel for liquids

cas·ket n. a small box ‖ a coffin

cas·se·role n. a covered dish in which food needing long, slow cooking is prepared ‖ food cooked in such a dish

cas·sette n. cartridge containing magnetic tape that can be inserted into a player for listening or viewing

cas·sock n. a long, close-fitting tunic

cast 1. v. **cast·ing cast** v.t. to throw ‖ to let drop, throw off ‖ to discard ‖ to shape by pouring into a mold ‖ to distribute (the parts) in a play to the actors ‖ to register (a vote) **2.** n. the act of casting ‖ the actors in a play ‖ a model made by running molten metal, plaster etc., into a mold ‖ a rigid surgical dressing

cas·ta·net n. one of a pair of wooden or ivory attached, shell-like pieces which produce a sharp, clicking sound when struck together

caste n. an inherited socioreligious rank

cast·er, cas·tor n. a small metal wheel fixed to the leg of a piece of furniture to allow it to be moved easily

cas·ti·gate cas·ti·gat·ing cas·ti·gat·ed v.t. to rebuke or criticize vehemently **cas·ti·ga·tion** n. **cas·ti·ga·tor** n.

cas·ti·ga·to·ry *adj.*

cast iron an iron-carbon alloy **cast-iron** *adj.* made of cast iron

cas·tle *n.* a fortified building ‖ (chess) a rook

cast-off *adj.* not wanted any more **cást·off** *n.* a person who has been rejected

cas·tor *n.* a substance used in medicine and perfumery

castor oil a pale yellow, thick oil, with an unpleasant taste, obtained from the seeds of the castor-oil plant

cas·trate cas·trat·ing cas·trat·ed *v.t.* to remove the testicles of (a man or male animal) **cas·tra·tion** *n.*

cas·u·al *adj.* irregular, happening by chance ‖ without formality ‖ free and easy

cas·u·al·ty *pl.* **cas·u·al·ties** *n.* an accident ‖ a soldier who is missing or has been killed in action

cat *n.* a carnivorous furry mammal ‖ any other member of fam. Felidae, e.g. a lion, tiger, leopard, wildcat etc.

cat·a·clysm *n.* any violent physical up-heaval such as a flood or an earth-quake **cat·a·clys·mal, cat·a·clys·mic** *adjs.*

cat·a·comb *n.* a series of underground galeries and chambers with recesses for burying the dead

cat·a·log, cat·a·logue 1. *n.* a complete list of articles, usually in alphabetical order, or under special headings **2.** *v.t.* **cat·a·log·ing, cat·a·log·ing cat·a·loged, cat·a·logued** to list **cat·a·log·er, cat·a·log·er** *n.*

ca·tal·y·sis *pl.* **ca·tal·y·ses** *n.* the change in the rate of chemical reaction brought about by a catalyst **cat·a·lyst** *n.* a substance that alters the rate of a chem-ical reaction and is itself unchanged by the process **cat·a·lyt·ic** *adj.* **cat·a·lyt·i·cal·ly** *adv.*

cat·a·ma·ran *n.* a boat with twin hulls connected by a frame

cat·a·pult 1. *n.* a machine for hurling stones etc. ‖ a machine for launching aircraft **2.** *v.t.* to launch (aircraft) with a catapult

cat·a·ract *n.* a waterfall ‖ any rush of water ‖ a disease of the eye

ca·tas·tro·phe *n.* a sudden and terrible event **cat·a·stroph·ic** *adj.*

catch 1. *v.* **catch·ing caught** *v.t.* to capture, ensnare ‖ to be in time for ‖ to surprise or detect ‖ to contract (an illness) ‖ to attract (attention) **to catch on** to understand, grasp an idea **2.** *n.* the act of catching ‖ the number of fish caught in a fishing expedition ‖ a fasten-ing on a door, window or gate ‖ a game

catch·er *n.* (*baseball*) the player who stands behind the batter to catch the pitched ball

catch·ing *adj.* contagious

catch·y catch·i·er catch·i·est *adj.* attrac-tive and easy to remember ‖ tricky, full of snags

cat·e·chism *n.* a set of questions and answers on religious doctrine

cat·e·gor·i·cal *adj.* unqualified, absolute ‖ of, pertaining to, or in a category

cat·e·go·ry *pl.* **cat·e·go·ries** *n.* one of the divisions in a system of classification

ca·ter *v.i.* to provide meals, refreshments etc. **cá·ter·er** *n.* a person or company supplying food for entertainment

cat·er·pil·lar *n.* the larva of a moth or butterfly

ca·thar·sis, ka·thar·sis *pl.* **ca·thar·ses, ka·thar·ses** *n.* purgation

ca·thar·tic 1. *n.* a purgative medicine **2.** *adj.* pertaining to catharsis

ca·the·dral *n.* the principal church of a diocese

cath·e·ter *n.* a tube of metal, glass or rubber passed along a mucous canal to permit the passage of fluid

Cath·o·lic 1. *adj.* any of the original Christian Church before the schism between East and West ‖ pertaining or adhering to Catholicism **2.** a member of the Roman Catholic Church

Ca·thol·i·cism *n.* the faith, practice or system of the Catholic Church

cat·nap *n.* a short doze by a human being

cat·nip *n.* an aromatic plant

cat-o'-nine-tails pl. **cat-o'-nine-tails** n. a whip of nine knotted lashes

Cat·tail n. a reedlike plant growing in marshes

cat·ti·ness n. the quality of being catty

cat·tle n. bovine animals collectively

cat·tle·man pl. **cat·tle·men** n. the owner of a cattle ranch ‖ a man who tends cattle

cat·ty cat·ti·er cat·ti·est adj. spiteful

cau·cus 1. n. a preliminary meeting of the leaders of a political party to make policy **2.** v.i. to hold a meeting of party leaders

cau·li·flow·er n. a variety of cabbage

caulk, calk v.t. to stop up and make watertight the seams of

cau·sal·i·ty pl. **cau·sal·i·ties** n. the relation of cause and effect

cause n. that which brings about a result ‖ a matter of widespread interest and concern

cause·way n. a raised roadway across wet or low-lying ground

caus·tic adj. burning, corrosive ‖ sharply biting, sarcastic **cáus·ti·cal·ly** adv.

cau·ter·ize cau·ter·iz·ing cau·ter·ized v.t. to destroy living tissue) by means of heat or a caustic agent

cau·tion 1. n. carefulness, concern for safety ‖ a warning **2.** v.t. to warn

cau·tious adj. prudent, attentive to safety

cav·al·cade n. a procession or parade

cav·a·lier 1. n. a mounted soldier **2.** adj. high-handed

cav·al·ry pl. **cav·al·ries** n. mounted soldiers ‖ (mil.) a motorized unit formerly mounted

cav·al·ry·man pl. **cav·al·ry·men** n. a member of the cavalry

cave 1. n. a natural hollow in rock **2.** v.t. **cav·ing caved** to make a hollow in to **cave in** to cause to collapse

cave·man pl. **cave·men** n. a Stone Age cave dweller

cav·ern n. a large underground chamber

cav·ern·ous adj. full of caverns

cav·i·ar, cav·i·are n. the roes of the sturgeon, salted and eaten as an appetizer

cav·il v.i. **cav·il·ing cav·iled** (with at' or aobut') to raise petty objections ‖ to find fault without reason **2.** n. a trivial, frivolous objection

cav·i·ty pl. **cav·i·ties** n. an empty space inside a solid object

ca·vort v.i. to prance about

cease ceas·ing ceased v.i. to stop, bring to an end

cease-fire n. an order to stop shooting ‖ the period during which the order holds

cease·less adj. without pause or interruption

ce·dar n. a genus of evergreen trees

cede ced·ing ced·ed v.t. to grant ‖ to surrender

ceil·ing n. the upper, inner surface of a room ‖ an imposed upper limit ‖ the cloud cover above clear air

cel·e·brate cel·e·brat·ing cel·e·brat·ed v.t. to perform (a religious ceremony) publicly ‖ to honor or observe **cél·e·brat·ed** adj. famous

ce·leb·ri·ty pl. **ce·leb·ri·ties** n. fame ‖ a famous person

ce·ler·i·ty n. rapidity, swiftness

cel·er·y n. a culinary plant

ce·les·tial adj. pertaining to the sky or heavens ‖ pertaining to a spiritual heaven, heavenly, divine

cel·i·ba·cy n. the unmarried state

cel·i·bate 1. n. a person who has vowed to remain unmarried **2.** adj. unmarried

cell n. a small enclosed space, small chamber ‖ (computer) unit of computer memory with one-word capacity ‖ the smallest structural unit of living tissue ‖ a device for producing an electric current

cel·lar n. a room, usually under a building

cel·list n. a person who plays the cello

cel·lo, 'cel·lo n. a four-stringed musical instrument

cel·lo·phane 1. n. a thin, transparent material

cel·lu·lar adj. formed of cells

cel·lu·lose n. a fibrous carbohydrate

ce·ment 1. n. a grayish powder made by heating together limestone or chalk and clay or shale, and then grinding ‖ any substance used to make materials cohere **2.** *v.t.* to join together with cement

cem·e·ter·y *pl.* **cem·e·ter·ies** *n.* a place where the dead are buried

cen·sor 1. *n.* a person empowered to suppress publications or excise any matter in them thought to be immoral, seditious or otherwise undesirable **2.** *v.t.* to examine in the capacity of a censor **cen·so·ri·al** *adj.*

cen·sor·ship *n.* the institution or practice of censoring

cen·sur·a·ble *adj.* deserving or subject to censure, blamable **cén·sur·a·bly** *adv.*

cen·sure adverse criticism, blame **censure cen·sur·ing cen·sured** *v.t.* to criticize severely

cen·sus *n.* an official counting of a country's population

cent *n.* *(symbol* [¢]*)* one hundredth of a dollar

cen·ten·ni·al *n.* a hundredth anniversary

cen·ter 1. *n.* an axis, pivot or point around which an object moves ‖ a place where activity is concentrated ‖ the part of a target which encircles the bull's-eye **2.** *v.* **cen·ter·ing cen·tered** *v.t.* to concentrate at one point ‖ to place in or bring into the middle

cen·ti·grade scale *(abbr.* C.*)* a temperature scale

cen·ti·me·ter *n.* a hundredth part of a meter

cen·tral *adj.* situated at or near the center or middle point ‖ principal, chief ‖ between extremes

cen·tral·ize cen·tral·iz·ing cen·tral·ized *v.i.* to bring under central control

cen·trif·u·gal *adj.* acting, moving or tending to move away from a center

cen·tri·fuge *n.* a machine that increases the rate of sedimentation of the suspended material

cen·tu·ry *pl.* **cen·tu·ries** *n.* a period of a hundred years

ce·ram·ic *adj.* of or having to do with pottery **ce·rám·ics** *pl. n.* the art of pottery **cer·a·mist** *n.* a potter

ce·re·al 1. *n.* any of several plants whose

seed (grain) is cultivated for food ‖ breakfast food made from grain

cer·e·bral *adj.* pertaining to the brain ‖ intellectual

cer·e·mo·ni·al 1. *n.* ritual **2.** *adj.* pertaining to ceremonies

cer·e·mo·ni·ous *adj.* observing ceremony ‖ fussily polite

cer·e·mo·ny *pl.* **cer·e·mo·nies** *n.* rites or ritual ‖ an occasion observed with ritual ‖ any formalities observed on a special occasion **without ceremony** casually

ce·rise 1. *n.* cherry red **2.** *adj.* of this color

cer·tain *adj.* sure ‖ convinced ‖ predictably reliable ‖ some, though not very much **cér·tain·ly** *adv.* definitely ‖ admittedly

cer·tif·i·cate 1. *n.* a written statement attesting some fact **2.** *v.t.* **cer·tif·i·cat·ing cer·tif·i·cat·ed** to grant a certificate to ‖ to license **cer·ti·fi·cá·tion** *n.*

cer·ti·fy cer·ti·fy·ing cer·ti·fied *v.t.* to attest formally

ces·sa·tion *n.* a ceasing

ces·sion *n.* the act of ceding or giving up

chafe 1. *v.* **chaf·ing chafed** *v.t.* to irritate or make sore by rubbing ‖ to irritate, annoy ‖ *v.i.* to rub ‖ to become worn by rubbing

chaff 1. *n.* banter **2.** *v.t.* to tease good-humoredly

chaff 1. *n.* the outer husk of grain separated by threshing ‖ useless or worthless writing **2.** *v.t.* to chop

cha·gefirin 1. *n.* disappointment, mortification **2.** *v.t.* to vex acutely because of disappointment

chain 1. *n.* a series of rings or links of metal joined one to another ‖ a series or sequence ‖ *(pl.)* bonds, bondage ‖ a number of business concerns all of one kind and owned by one person or group

chair 1. *n.* a seat with four legs and a backrest ‖ the seat and the office of a person appointed to preside over a meeting **2.** *v.t.* to preside over (a meeting) as chairman

chair·man *pl.* **chair·men** *n.* a person

appointed to preside over a meeting

cha·let n. a small wooden house in the Alps ‖ a house built in this style

chal·ice n. the cup used at the celebration of the Mass (Eucharist)

chalk 1. n. a soft, friable, earthy, whitish variety of limestone **2.** v.t. to write or mark with chalk **chálk·i·ness** n.

chalk·y chalk·i·er chalk·i·est adj. of or like chalk

chal·lenge n. a calling in question ‖ something which tests a person's qualities ‖ an objection made against someone in respect of his qualification

challenge chal·leng·ing chal·lenged v.t. to invite or summon to a match or game ‖ to dispute the truth of (a statement) ‖ to object to (a person) as voter, juryman etc. **chál·leng·er** n. someone or something that challenges

cham·ber n. a large room or hall used for the meetings of a legislative or judicial body ‖ a private room ‖ a compartment or cavity ‖ the part of a gun which holds the charge

cha·me·le·on n. an insectivorous lizard ‖ an inconstant person **cha·me·le·on·ic** adj.

cham·ois n. a horned, goatlike antelope

cham·pagne n. a sparkling white wine

cham·pi·on 1. n. a winner of a competition ‖ someone who defends another person or a cause **2.** v.t. to fight or argue on behalf of **3.** adj. first-rate **chám·pi·on·ship** n. a competition in which the title of champion is contested ‖ advocacy

chance 1. n. an occurrence that cannot be accounted for by any pattern of cause and effect ‖ an opportunity **by chance** fortuitously **to take a chance** to run a risk and trust to luck **2.** adj. unintentional, fortuitous **3.** v.i. **chanc·ing chanced** to happen by accident

chan·cel·lor n. the chief admiisrative officer of some U.S. universities **chán·cel·lor·ship** n.

chan·de·lier n. a branched holder for several candles or electric lights,

suspended from a ceiling

change n. alteration ‖ the exchange of one thing for another ‖ coins of a small denomination

change chang·ing changed v.i. to become altered ‖ to make a change or exchange ‖ v.t. to alter ‖ to take off (clothes) and put on different ones ‖ to exchange ‖ **to change hands** to pass from one owner to another

chan·nel 1. n. a natural or artificial course for running water ‖ (radio) a narrow band of frequencies ‖ the course or agency through which something passes **2.** v.t. **chan·nel·ing chan·neled** to make a channel or groove in

chant n. a simple melody ‖ singing

chant v.t. to sing ‖ to utter in a singsong voice

cha·os n. complete confusion **cha·ót·ic** adj. **cha·ót·i·cal·ly** adv.

chap n. a man or boy

chap 1. v. **chap·ping chapped** v.i. to become rough and sore **2.** n. a crack or split in the skin

chap·el n. a part of a cathedral or large church, divided off from the rest, and having a separate altar and dedication

chap·er·on, chap·er·one 1. n. someone responsible for the good behavior of young people at social gatherings **2.** v.t. **chap·er·on·ing chap·er·oned**

chap·lain n. a priest, minister or rabbi who serves a school, college, prison or hospital or attached to the armed forces **cháp·lain·cy** n.

chap·ter n. a division of a book ‖ a local section of a national club, lodge, etc.

char char·ring charred v.t. to reduce to carbon ‖ to scorch ‖ v.i. to be burned to charcoal

char·ac·ter 1. n. the total quality of a person's behavior ‖ a set of qualities or attributes distinguishing one place or country from another ‖ an imaginary person in a book or play etc. ‖ reputation ‖ a figure or sign used in writing

char·ac·ter·is·tic 1. n. a quality typical of a person, place or object **2.** adj. typical

char·ac·ter·is·ti·cal·ly *adv.*

char·ac·ter·i·za·tion *n.* the act, process or result of characterizing

char·ac·ter·ize char·ac·ter·iz·ing char·ac·ter·ized *v.t.* to describe the character of

cha·rade *n. (esp. pl.)* a party game

char·coal *n.* the amorphous form of carbon

charge *n.* the price to be paid for goods or services ‖ a duty, responsibility ‖ a legal accusation ‖ a swift concerted attack ‖ an explosive for a gun ‖ the electricity stored in a battery ‖ a financial responsibility

charge charg·ing charged *v.t.* to accuse ‖ to ask as a price ‖ to record (a debt) ‖ to give electrical energy or charge to (a battery) ‖ *v.i.* to rush forward in assault **chárge·a·ble** *adj.*

char·i·ot *n.* a two-wheeled, horse-drawn vehicle used in warfare and for racing **char·i·ot·eer** *n.*

ch a·ris·ma *pl.* **cha·ris·ma·ta** *n.* an extraordinary power in a person, group, cause etc. which takes hold of popular imagination, wins popular support etc. **cha·ris·mat·ic** *adj.*

char·i·ta·ble *adj.* generous in giving to the needy ‖ tolerant in judging other people **chár·i·ta·bly** *adv.*

char·i·ty *pl.* **char·i·ties** *n.* spiritual love for others ‖ generosity to the needy

char·la·tan *n.* a person who pretends to have knowledge or skill that he does not possess

charm *n.* a softly or gently pleasing quality ‖ an object worn to avert danger by magic ‖ a small trinket worn esp. on a bracelet

charm *v.t.* to please and attract **chárm·ing** *adj.* delightful

chart 1. *n.* an outline map giving information on a particular subject ‖ a graph showing fluctuations **2.** *v.t.* to make a map of ‖ to record on a chart or graph

char·ter 1. *n.* an official document granting rights ‖ the lease of an airplane, bus etc. to a hirer for his exclusive use **2.** *v.t.*

to grant a charter to ‖ to hire

char·treuse *n.* a liqueur first made by Carthusian monks ‖ a yellow-green color

chase *n.* a pursuit

chase chas·ing chased *v.t.* to follow at speed in order to catch ‖ to drive (someone, something) away

chas·er *n.* a short drink usually of beer or water taken after drinking neat liquor

chasm *n.* a deep cleft in the earth

chas·sis *n.* the frame of an automobile

chaste *adj.* deliberately abstaining from sexual intercourse

chas·tise chas·tis·ing chas·tised *v.t.* to punish by whipping or beating ‖ to denounce vehemently **chas·tise·ment** *n.*

chas·ti·ty *n.* total sexual abstention, continence

chat 1. *n.* light, gossipy conversation **2.** *v.i.* **chat·ting chat·ted** to talk light gossip

chat·tel *n.* a piece of property other than real estate or a freehold

chat·ter 1. *n.* light, inconsequential talk ‖ the rattling together of teeth from cold, fear etc. **2.** *v.i.* to chat

chauf·feur 1. *n.* a person employed to drive a car **2.** *v* to be or act as chauffeur to

chau·vin·ism *n.* exaggerated and aggressive patriotism **cháu·vin·ist** *n.* **chau·vin·is·tic** *adj.* **chau·vin·is·ti·cal·ly** *adv.*

cheap 1. *adj.* inexpensive ‖ easily obtained ‖ poor in quality, tawdry ‖ facile ‖ mean **2.** *adv.* inexpensively

cheap·en *v.t.* to lower or degrade ‖ *v.i.* to become cheap or cheaper

cheat 1. *v.t.* to trick or deceive **2.** *n.* a person who cheats ‖ a fraud

check 1. *n.* a restraint ‖ a control to verify information etc. ‖ a mark to show that something has abeen verified or checked ‖ a bill for a meal in a restaurant ‖ a receipt for deposit **2.** *adj.* serving to control, verify

check *n.* a pattern of crossing lines or alternating squares of colors

check *v.* to restrain ‖ to curb ‖ to verify the

correctness of (e.g. accounts)

check *n.* an order (on a specially printed form) to a bank to pay a stated sum to a named person

check·mate *n. (chess)* move or position which places the opponent's king inescapably in check

cheek *n.* the soft fleshy part of the face ‖ the side wall of the mouth **to turn the other cheek** to react with submissiveness

cheek·y cheek·i·er cheek·i·est *adj.* impudent

cheer 1. *n.* a shout of joy ‖ *(pl.)* applause 2. *v.t.* to applaud by shouts

cheer·ful *adj.* good-humored ‖ bright and attraactive

cheese *n.* a solid food of high protein content

cheese·burg·er *n.* a hamburger with cheese on top

chee·tah *n.* a small leopard

chef *n.* the head cook, esp. in a hotel or restaurant

chem·i·cal 1. *adj.* relating to the science of chemistry 2. *n.* a substance used in or obtained by a chemical process

chem·ist *n.* a person trained or engaged in chemistry

chem·is·try *n.* the study of the composition, properties and structure of substances, and of the changes they undergo

cher·ish *v.t.* to treasure ‖ to take loving care of

cher·ry 1. *pl.* **cher·ries** *n.* a genus of flowering trees bearing small fruit in color from pink to dark red ‖ the fruit 2. *adj.* bright red

cher·ub *pl.* **cher·ubs**, *(Bible)* **cher·u·bim** *n.* an order of angels ‖ a representation of such a creature **che·ru·bic** *adj.* (esp. of a child) having a round rosy face

chess *n.* an ancient, conventional, elaborate game of skill for two players, played on a chessboard

chess·man *pl.* **chess·men** *n.* one of the 16 pieces which each player of a game has on the board at the start

chest *n.* the thorax ‖ a large, strong box with a hinged lid **to get something off one's chest** to unburden oneself

chew *v.t.* to reduce (food) to a pulp in the mouth ‖ (with on' or over') to think carefully and at length about the various aspects of (a matter)

chic 1. *n.* stylishness 2. *adj.* elegant, stylish

chi·can·er·y *pl.* **chi·can·er·ies** *n.* trickery

Chi·ca·no *(masc.)* **Chi·ca·na** *(fem.)* *n.* U.S. resident of Mexican descent

chick *n.* a newly hatched chicken ‖ any very young bird

chick·en 1. *n.* the domestic fowl, or its flesh as food 2. *adj.* cowardly

chic·o·ry *n.* plant used as a coffee adulterant or substitute

chide *pres.* **chid·ing** chid, **chid·ed** chid, **chid·den** chid·ed *v.t.* to reprove, rebuke

chief 1. *n.* a leader or ruler ‖ the head of a department in an institution 2. *adj.* most important ‖ highest in rank

chief·ly *adv.* mainly, but not altogether

chief·tain *n.* the leader of a group, esp. a clan or tribe **chief·tain·cy** *n.*

chif·fon 1. *n.* a very soft, fine transparent material 2. *adj.* made of chiffon ‖ (cooking) light and fluffy in consistency

child *pl.* **chil·dren** *n.* a boy or girl at any age between infancy and adolescence ‖ a person of any age in relation to his parents **with child pregnant**

child·hood *n.* the years between infancy and adolescence

child·ish *adj.* immature ‖ puerile, not befitting an adult

child·like *adj.* possessing the good qualities of a child's character

chil·i *pl.* **chil·ies** *n.* a garden pepper

chill 1. *adj.* cold to the touch ‖ unemotional, undemonstrative ‖ unfriendly 2. *n.* an unpleasant sensation of coldness 3. *v.t.* to refrigerate but not freeze

chime 1. *n.* a set of bells ‖ the sound made by a bell or bells ‖ a musical instrument 2. **chim·ing chimed** *v.i.* to ring

chim·ney *pl.* **chim·neys** *n.* the part of a flue projecting above the roof of a house ‖ anything resembling a chimney in purpose ‖ a narrow, climbable crack in a cliff face

chim·pan·zee *n.* an African ape allied to the gorilla

chin *n.* the front part of the lower jaw

chi·na 1. *n.* a twice-fired, finegrained ceramic ware ‖ porcelain ‖ any crockery 2. *adj.* made of china

chin·chil·la *n.* South American rodent ‖ a woolen fabric with a long soft nap

chink *n.* a narrow crack or opening **a chink in someone's armor** a factor in a person's character which makes them susceptible to persuasion

chip 1. *n.* a small fragment broken or cut from wood, china, glass, stone etc. ‖ miniaturized wafer disc of silicon ‖ a counter in a gambling game 2. **chip·ping chipped** *v.i.* to become chipped

chip·munk *n.* any of several species of small, squirrel-like animals

chi·rop·o·dist *n.* a person professionally qualified to treat minor disorders of the feet **chi·rop·o·dy** *n.*

chi·ro·prac·tic *n.* the manipulation of the spinal vertebrae in an attempt to cure various ailments **chi·ro·prac·tor** *n.*

chirp *n.* a short, sharp sound made by a small bird, a cricket or grasshopper

chis·el 1. *n.* any of various steel hand tools for cutting or shaping wood, stone or metal 2. *v.t.* **chis·el·ing chis·eled** to cut or shape with a chisel ‖ to cheat or defraud **chis·eled** *adj.*

chit·chat *n.* gossip

chiv·al·rous *adj.* having the characteristics of the ideal medieval knight: courteous, honorable, ready to help those in need

chiv·al·ry *n.* honorable behavior, esp. to women

chive *n.* an Old World hardy perennial plant

chlo·rine *n.* a gaseous greenish-yellow element

chlo·ro·phyll, chlo·ro·phyl *n.* a green pigment in plant cells

choc·o·late 1. *n.* a food product made form the seeds of cacao milk 2. *adj.* flavored with chocolate ‖ of a brown color resembling that of chocolate

choice *adj.* of high quality, carefully selected

choice *n.* the act of choosing or selecting ‖ something chosen ‖ an alternative

choir *n.* a group of singers ‖ the part of a cathedral

choke 1. *v.* **chok·ing choked** *v.t.* to stop or almost stop from breathing ‖ to asphyxiate ‖ *v.i.* to be unable to breathe ‖ to be inarticulate (with emotion) ‖ to suffer strangling or suffocation 2. *n.* the act of choking ‖ the valve controlling the air intake in an internal-combustion engine

chol·er·a *n.* a highly infectious disease

chol·er·ic *adj.* inclined to be irritable

cho·les·ter·ol *n.* a fat-soluble crystalline steroid alcohol

choose choos·ing chose cho·sen *v.* to select from a number, or between alternatives ‖ to decide **choos·y, choos·ey choos·i·er choos·i·est** *adj.* hard to please

chop 1. *v.* **chop·ping chopped** *v.* to hit with a short cutting 2. *n.* a cutting stroke ‖ a cut of pork, mutton or veal ‖ (boxing) a short, downward blow

chop·py chop·pi·er chop·pi·est *adj.* (of the sea) agitated, with small tossing waves

cho·rale, cho·ral *n.* a hymn tune of simple rhythm, adapted from plainsong

chord *n.* a part of the body resembling a string

chord *n.* a simultaneous combination of notes

cho·re·og·ra·pher *n.* someone who composes choreography

cho·re·og·ra·phy *n.* the art of arranging a dance performance

chor·tle 1. *n.* a gleeful chuckle 2. *v.t.* **chor·tling chor·tled** to utter such a chuckle

cho·rus 1. *n.* a group of singers ‖ a secular choir ‖ the refrain of a song 2. *v.* to sing or speak in chorus

chow·der n. a dish of fish or clams or other foods stewed in milk with bacon, onion etc.

Christ the anointed king or Messiah ‖ the title given to Jesus by his followers

chris·ten v.t. to receive into the Christian Church by baptism ‖ to name (a child) formally, at baptism ‖ to name (a ship) at its launching

Chris·ten·dom n. the whole body of members of the Christian Church

chris·ten·ing n. the religious ceremony of baptizing

Chris·ti·an·i·ty n. the religion of those who accept Jesus Christ as God incarnate

Christ·mas n. the annual festival observed by Christians on Dec. 25, commemorating the birth of Christ

chro·mat·ic adj. colored or relating to color ‖ having notes other than those in the diatonic scale

chrome n. chromium ‖ chrome yellow

chro·mite n. an ore containing chromium

chro·mi·um n. a metallic element

chro·mo·some n. microscopic molecules which carry the hereditary material in subunits called genes

chron·ic adj. (of disease) longlasting, deep-seated ‖ constant, inveterate **chrón·i·cal·ly** adv.

chron·i·cle 1. n. a list of events in the order in which they happened 2. v.t. **chron·i·cling chron·i·cled** to record (events) in a chronicle **chrón·i·cler** n. a writer of chronicles

chron·o·log·i·cal adj. of or relating to chronology

chro·nol·o·gy pl. **chro·nol·o·gies** n. order of occurrence ‖ an arrangement (list, table, treatise etc.) in order of occurrence

chro·nom·e·ter n. an instrument measuring the passage of time with great accuracy

chrys·a·lis pl. **chrys·al·i·des** n. the pupa of butterflies and moths

chry·san·the·mum n. autumn-flowering, perennial plants

chub·bi·ness n. the state or quality of being chubby

chub·by chub·bi·er chub·bi·est nicely plump

chuck n. cut of beef or lamb ‖ a mechanical device for holding a tool in a machine (e.g. a bit in a drill)

chuck n. a playful tap under the chin ‖ (pop.) a short throw

chuck·le 1. v. **chuck·ling chuck·led** v.i. to laugh quietly with amusement, satisfaction, glee or triumph 2. n. such a laugh

chum n. a close friend **chúm·my chum·mi·er chum·mi·est** adj.

chump n. (pop.) a person who has said or done ,fiasomething silly ‖ a thick lump of wood

chunk n. a short, thick piece (of wood, bread etc.) ‖ a large amount **chúnk·y chunk·i·er chunk·i·est** adj. (of people) short and thickset

church n. a building for Christian worship

churl·ish adj. ill-mannered ‖ surly

churn 1. n. a vessel in which milk or cream is stirred to produce butter 2. v.t. to make (butter) by working a churn ‖ to agitate violently

chute n. a steep slide or trough ‖ a quick descent of water over a slope

chutz·pah or **chutz·pa** n. (Yiddish) brass, boldness, impertinence, insolence, effrontery

ci·der n. a nonalcoholic drink made from apple juice, sweet cider

ci·gar n. a roll of tobacco leaves for smoking

cig·a·rette, cig·a·ret n. finely cut tobacco rolled in very thin paper, for smoking

cil·i·a sing. **cil·i·um** pl. n. short, hairlike processes **cil·i·ar·y** adj.

cinch n. a girth for a saddle ‖ something done very easily

cinc·ture n. a girdle

cin·der n a piece of partly burned coal no longer flaming ‖ slag from a furnace ‖ (pl.) the residue of burned coal

cin·e·ma n. the art or technique of making movies

cin·na·mon *n.* a spice made from the bark of certain trees ‖ a tree yielding this

ci·pher 1. *n.* a 0, zero, naught ‖ a person or thing of no importance ‖ interwoven letters, e.g. in a monogram **2.** *v.t.* to put (a message) into cipher

cir·ca *prep. (abbr.* **c., ca.,** used with numerals) about

cir·cle 1. *n.* a plane figure with a abounding edge (circumference), all points on which are equidistant from a fixed point ‖ a group of persons with a common interest **to run around in circles** to achieve nothing because one is in a ditt ther **2.** *v.* **cir·cling cir·cled** *v.t.* to put a circle around

cir·cuit *n.* a movement around an object ‖ a geographical group of towns having courts of law, visited in turn by a judge ‖ the complete path traversed by an electric current ‖ the diagram of the connections of an electrical apparatus

cir·cu·lar 1. *adj.* having the shadpe of a circle **2.** *n.* a printed advertising leaflet, notice etc., **cir·cu·lar·i·ty** *n.* **cir·cu·lar·iz·a·tion** *n.* the act of circulizing

cir·cu·late cir·cu·lat·ing cir·cu·lat·ed *v.i.* to move around and return to a starting point ‖ *v.t.* to send or pass around

cir·cu·la·tion *n.* movement in a circuit, e.g. of water or air, ‖ the movement of blood in the blood vessels of the body ‖ distribution

cir·cum·cise cir·cum·cis·ing cir·cum·cised *v.t.* to cut off the aforeskin of (males)

cir·cum·ci·sion *n.* the act of circumcising

cir·cum·fer·ence *n.* the line bounding a circle, or its length

cir·cum·lo·cu·tion *n.* an indirect or roundabout expression **cir·cum·loc·u·to·ry** *adj.*

cir·cum·scribe cir·cum·scrib·ing cir·cum·scribed *v.t.* to draw a line around ‖ to set limits to, restrict

cir·cum·spect *adj.* cautious, discreet, prudent **cir·cum·spéc·tion** *n.*

cir·cum·stance *n.* an essential fact or detail ‖ *(pl.)* the elements of a total situation ‖ *(pl.)* the financial state of a person

cir·cum·stan·tial *adj.* giving full and precise details ‖ incidental, related but not essential **cir·cum·stan·ti·al·i·ty** *n.*

circumstantial evidence evidence made up of details tending to prove a fact by inference

cir·cum·vent *v.t.* to prevent by counterstrategy, outwit, get around **cir·cum·vén·tion** *n.*

cir·cus *n.* the entertainment made up of acts including performing animals, acrobats, clowns etc. ‖ the arena in which the show is performed

cir·rho·sis *n.* a chronic, noninfectious disease of the liver

cir·rus *pl.* **cir·ri** *n.* a fleecy cloud formation

cis·tern *n.* a tank for storing water

cit·a·del *n.* a fortress protecting or dominating a town

ci·ta·tion *n.* the act of citing ‖ a quotation ‖ a summons to appear in court

cite cit·ing cit·ed *v.t.* to give (an example), or quote (an authority) to mention in official dispatches ‖ to summon to court

cit·i·zen *n.* an inhabitant of a city or a country, native or naturalized **cit·i·zen·ship** *n.* the state of being a citizen

cit·rus *n.* trees and shrubs yielding fruits which include the orange, lemon, lime, grapefruit, shaddock, tangerine and citron

cit·y *pl.* **cit·ies** *n.* an important town ‖ a municipal corporation

civ·et *n.* any of several fierce carnivorous mammals of N. Africa and Asia

civ·ic *adj.* relating to a city, its citizens or citizenship

civ·il *adj.* relating to a community or to citizens ‖ relating to civilian as opposed to military matters

ci·vil·ian *n.* a person not a member of the armed forces

ci·vil·i·ty *pl.* **ci·vil·i·ties** *n.* conformity with normal conventions of politeness

civ·i·li·za·tion, civ·i·li·sa·tion *n.* a making

or becoming civilized‖the sum of qualities of a particular civilized society

civ·i·lize civ·i·liz·ing civ·i·lized *v.t.* to endow with law, order and the conditions favorable to the arts and sciences ‖ to refine

civil war war between the citizens of one country

claim *v.t.* to demand as a right ‖ to assert as true ‖ to profess ‖ (of things) to need, require

claim *n.* the demanding of something as a right ‖ an assertion of right to possession of a thing**cláim·ant** *n.* a person making a claim

clair·voy·ance *n.* second sight **clair·vóy·ant** *adj.* having second sight

clam 1. *n.* one of various bivalve marine or freshwater mollusks 2. *v.i.* **clam·ming clammed** to gather clams

clam·mi·ness *n.* the state or quality of being clammy

clam·my clam·mi·er clam·mi·est *adj.* damp, cold and sticky to the touch

clam·or 1. *n.* a loud confused noise ‖ a loud demanding 2. *v.i.* to make demands or complain loudly **clám·or·ous** *adj.*

clamp 1. *n.* a device for holding things together tightly 2. *v.t.* to fasten with, or place in, a clamp

clan *n.* a social group with a common ancestor ‖ a oatribe ‖ a large united family

clan·des·tine *adj.* existing or done in forced secrecy ‖ surreptitious

clang 1. *n.* a loud ringing sound, esp. of metal striking metal 2. *v.* to make such a sound

clap *n.* a sharp, loud noise

clap clap·ping clapped *v.i.* to strike the palms of the hands together

clar·et 1. *n.* red Bordeaux wine 2. *adj.* the reddish-purple color of this wine

clar·i·fi·ca·tion *n.* the act or process of clarifying

clar·i·fy clar·i·fy·ing clar·i·fied *v.t.* to make understandable, explain ‖ to make (a liquid) pure and transparent

clar·i·net *n.* a woodwind instrument

clar·i·nét·ist, clar·i·nét·tist *n.*

clar·i·ty *n.* clearness

clash 1. *v.i.* to make loud, resonant noise ‖ to skirmish ‖ to conflict (of colors) not to harmonize ‖ *v.t.* to strike together violently 2. *n.* a loud strident noise ‖ a skirmish ‖ a conflict

clasp 1. *v.t.* embrace ‖ to fasten together with a clasp 2. *n.* a fastening device ‖ a clip on a brooch etc. ‖ a firm hold, a grasp

class 1. *n.* a group of people of the same rank or status ‖ the concept or system of social divisions ‖ a group of students taught together ‖ a comprehensive group of animals or plants 2. *v.t.* to place in a class ‖ to classify ‖ *v.i.* to be classed

clas·sic 1. *adj.* received into the accepted canons of excellence ‖ conforming to Greco-Roman canons of taste 2. *n.* a great work of ancient Greek or Roman literature ‖ a writer or artists of recognized excellence, other than a contemporary

clas·si·cal 1. *adj.* of the ancient civilization of Greece and Rome ‖ (of education) humane as distinct from scientific ‖ traditional, as distinct from modern or experimental ‖ of all music other than jazz or popular music ‖ orthodox, academic

clas·si·fi·ca·tion *n.* the act or result of classifying

clas·si·fied *adj.* forbidden to be disclosed for reasons of national or military security

clas·si·fy clas·si·fy·ing clas·si·fied *v.t.* to arrange in classes ‖ to put into groups systematically

clat·ter 1. *v.* to make, or move with, the noises of impact of many hard objects 2. *n.* a confused sharp banging, rattling or clashing

clause *n.* a distinct article or proviso in a legal document ‖ a part of a sentence having a subject and predicate of its own

claus·tro·pho·bi·a *n.* a morbid dread of being in confined spaces **claus·tro·pho·bic** *adj.*

clav·i·cle n. the vertebrate bone forming part of the pectoral arch **cla·vic·u·lar** adj.

claw 1. n. the sharp, hooked nail on an animal's foot ‖ a pincer of a crustacean **2.** v.t. to scratch or tear with claws or fingernails **clawed** adj. scratched and torn by claws

clay n. a firm earthy substance **clay·ey** adj.

clean 1. adj. not dirty ‖ free from imperfections ‖ fresh, not soiled ‖ trim and definite ‖ not possessing drugs ‖ not possessing any stolen merchandise **2.** adv. completely **3.** v.i. to remove dirt

clean·li·ness n. the condition of being clean

clean·ly adv. in a clean manner

clean·ly clean·li·er clean·li·est adj. habitually kept clean

cleanse cleans·ing cleansed v.t. to make thoroughly clean ‖ to purify (from sin) **cléans·er** n. an agent which cleanses

clear 1. adj. transparent, unclouded ‖ luminous ‖ distinct to the vision ‖ untroubled ‖ (of sounds) distinct, pure ‖ easy to understand, plain **2.** n. **in the clear** innocent **3.** adv. completely **4.** v.t. to free from obstructions ‖ to free from suspicion ‖ to make as a net profit ‖ to get (a check) approved for payment ‖ to rid (land) of bushes, weeds etc.

clear·ance n. the act or process of clearing a ‖ an unobstructed space allowing passage ‖ the passing of a check through a clearinghouse

clear·ing n. a piece of land in a wood free from trees ‖ the bank process of honoring checks

clear·ly adv. in a clear manner, distinctly

clear·ness n. transparency ‖ freedom from ambiguity or confusion

cleat n. a wedge-shaped piece bolted on to a spar etc. to prevent a rope from slipping ‖ one of the studs on the sole of a shoe to prevent sliding

cleav·age n. a cleaving or being cleft ‖ cell division ‖ the breaking down of complex molecules into simpler molecules ‖ any sharp division

cleave cleav·ing clove cleaved, cleft clo·ven cleaved, cleft v.t. to split with an ax or chopper ‖ v.i. to become split in two

cleav·er n. a splitting instrument

clef n. a sign to show pitch

cleft n. an opening made by splitting, a crack, a fissure ‖ a hollow in the chin

clem·en·cy pl. **clem·en·cies** n. mercy

clem·ent adj. inclined to be merciful

clench 1. v.t. to press closely together ‖ to grasp firmly **2.** n. the act of clenching ‖ a grip

cler·gy n. ordained Christian ministers collectively **cler·gy·man** pl. **cler·gy·men** n. a member of the clergy

cler·i·cal adj. relating to the work of a clerk in an office ‖ connected with the clergy

clerk 1. an officeworker ‖ an official who acts as secretary to a council ‖ a shop assistant **2.** v.i. to work as a clerk

clev·er adj. quick to learn ‖ skillful ‖ artful

click 1. n. a slight, sharp sound ‖ a catch or detent in machinery **2.** v.t. to make a clicking sound ‖ to fit ‖ (pop., of two persons) to get along well

cli·ent n. a person who hires the services of a professional man ‖ a customer

cliff n. a high steep face of rock

cli·mate n. the sum of the prevailing weather conditions of a place over a period of time ‖ the trend of opinions and attitudes pervading a community, nation or period **cli·mat·ic** adj. **cli·mát·i·cal·ly** adv.

cli·max a culmination

climb v.t. to go up, ascend, esp. using hands and footholds ‖ v.i. to rise to a higher point ‖ to slope upward ‖ to rise in social rank or in reputation **clímb·er** n. a person who climbs mountains for sport ‖ a plant which grows vigorously up a support

clinch v.t. to settle, make conclusive ‖ to secure ‖ v.i. (boxing) to grapple as a method of making strong punches impossible **clínch·er** n. the remark or argument which settles a dispute

cling cling·ing clung *v.i.* to hold fast ‖ to keep close

clin·ic *n.* a place where hospital outpatients receive medical examination, treatment or advice **clin·i·cal** *adj.* of or concerning a clinic ‖ concerning the study of disease by observation

clip 1. *v.* **clip·ping clipped** *v.t.* to fasten together with a clip **2.** *n.* a device for fastening things together ‖ a brooch

clip 1. *v.* **clip·ping clipped** *v.t.* to cut, trim, shear ‖ *v.i.* to move swiftly **2.** *n.* the act of clipping ‖ a cuff with the hand ‖ a rapid pace

clip·ping *n.* the act of clipping ‖ a paragraph, article etc. cut from a newspaper

clique 1. *n.* (*pejorative*) a small, exclusive set of people **2.** *v.i.* to form a clique **cli·quey, cli·quish cli·quy** (*adjs.*)

cloak 1. *n.* a loose, sleeveless outer garment ‖ something which hides **2.** *v.t.* to conceal, disguise

clock 1. *n.* a device for measuring and indicating time ‖ a time clock ‖ a speedometer **2.** *v.t.* to time with a stopwatch

clod *n.* a lump of earth or mud ‖ a stupid person **clod·dish** *adj.* oafish

clog 1. *n.* a wooden shoe **2.** *v.* **clog·ging clogged** *v.t.* to choke up ‖ to encumber, make heavy ‖ to hamper ‖ *v.i.* to become choked up

clois·ter 1. *n.* a place of religious seclusion ‖ a covered walk **2.** *v.t.* to shut up in, or confine to, a convent or monastery ‖ to isolate **clois·tered** *adj.* monastic ‖ isolated from the outside world **clois·tral** *adj.*

clone *n.* the descendants produced asexually from a single animal or plant

close 1. *adj.* near ‖ intimate ‖ nearly alike ‖ nearly equal ‖ secretive ‖ mean, tight-fisted **2.** *adv.* in a close manner ‖ nearby, near ‖ tightly ‖ nearly ‖ compactly ‖ secretly

close 1. *v.* **clos·ing closed** *v.t.* to shut ‖ to bring together ‖ finish ‖ to settle (an account) finally **2.** *n.* an end, conclusion

clos·et *n.* a recess built into a room and shut off with a door, or a small room for storing things

clot 1. *n.* a lump of coagulated or thickened liquid **2.** *v.* **clot·ting clot·ted** *v.i.* to cause to form into a clot or clots

cloth 1. *pl.* **cloths** *n.* woven material or fabric ‖ the clerical profession **2.** *adj.* made of cloth

clothe cloth·ing clothed clad *v.t.* and refl. to provide with clothes ‖ to cover

clothes *pl. n.* garments, wearing apparel

cloth·ing *n.* clothes in general

cloud 1. *n.* a visible expanse of suspended droplets of water or ice particles in the air **2.** *v.t.* to overspread with clouds ‖ to darken ‖ to make opaque ‖ *v.i.* to become overcast

cloud·i·ly *adv.* in a cloudy way

cloud·i·ness *n.* the state or quality of being cloudy

cloud·y cloud·i·er cloud·i·est *adj.* overcast with clouds ‖ vague, inexact

clove a tropical tree ‖ the spice yielded by its dried flower buds

clo·ver perennial plants, having trifoliate leaves **in clover** enjoying good fortune or success

clown *n.* a buffoon in a circus **1.** *v.i.* to make people laugh by one's antics **clown·er·y** *n.* **clown·ish** *adj.*

cloy *v.t.* to glut, satiate, esp. with sweetness

club *n.* a stout stick with a thickened end, a cudgel ‖ a playing card of the suit marked with black trefoils ‖ an association of people with some common interest **2.** *v.t.* **b,club·bing b,clubbed** to beat with a club or similar weapon

clue *n.* anything serving as a guide in the solution of a mystery

clum·sy clum·si·er clum·si·est *adj.* awkward, ungainly

clus·ter 1. *n.* a number of similar things growing or gathered together **2.** *v.i.* to gather close together

clutch *n.* a tight grip ‖ the act of clutching ‖ (esp. pl.) power, control ‖ a device for connecting and disconnecting driving and driven parts smoothly

clutch *v.t.* to seize, catch hold of ‖ to hold firmly

clut·ter *n.* an untidy mess ‖ litter 1. *v.t.* make untidy

coach 1. *n.* a state carriage ‖ a railroad car for passengers ‖ a aprivate tutor ‖ a trainer in athletics 2. *v.t.* to teach privately ‖ to train (someone, e.g. in athletics)

co·ag·u·late co·ag·u·lat·ing co·ag·u·lat·ed *v.i.* to turn from a liquid to a curdlike or jellylike consistency, congeal ‖ *v.t.* to cause to congeal **co·ag·u·lá·tion, co·ág·u·la·tor** *ns*

coal *n.* a combustible deposit of vegetable matter rendered compact and hard by pressure and heat ‖ a burning ember

co·a·lesce co·a·lesc·ing co·a·lesced *v.i.* to fuse ‖ to combine in a political coalition**co·a·lés·cence** *n.* **co·a·lés·cent** *adj.*

co·a·li·tion *n.* a coalescing, union ‖ a temporary union of political parties **co·a·li·tion·ist** *n.*

coarse coars·er coars·est *adj.* rough, large-grained ‖ unrefined, rude ‖ vulgar, indecent

coars·en *v.t.* to make coarse ‖ *v.i.* to become coarse

coast 1. *n.* the seashore ‖ a ride downhill on a sled etc. ‖ a ride downhill on a bicycle without pedaling 2. *v.i.* to cycle downhill without pedaling or drive a car downhill with the engine switched off **cóast·al** *adj.*

coat 1. *n.* an overcoat ‖ a person's jacket ‖ an aanimal's protective covering 2. *v.t.* to cover with a coat

coat·ing *n.* a covering (e.g. of paint etc.)

coax *v.t.* to persuade by soft words or gentle handling ‖ *v.i.* to wheedle, cajole

co·balt *n.* a bivalent, hard, magnetic, silver-white, metallic element

cobalt blue a strong greenish-blue color

cob·ble1. *n.* a cobblestone 2. *v.t.* **cob·bling cob·bled** to pave with cobbles

cobble cob·bling cob·bled *v.t.* to mend (shoes)**cób·bler** *n.* a shoe repairer ‖ a fruit pie ‖ an iced drink

co·bra *n.* a very poisonous African and Asian snake

co·caine *n.* an alkaloid derived from coca leaves

cock 1. *n.* the male bird of the common domestic fowl ‖ a weathercock ‖ a tap ‖ the hammer in a gun ‖ an upward tilt, of a nose, hat etc. 2. *v.t.* to set aslant, tilt upwards ‖ to raise the cock of (a gun) ready to fire

cock·a·too *n.* a crested parrot

cock·le 1. *v.* **cock·ling cock·led***v.i.* (of paper etc.)to pucker, curl upr ‖ *v.t.* to cause to pucker or curl up 2. *n.* wrinkle ‖ a bivalve mollusk

cock·roach *n.* an order of insects

cock·tail *n.* a drink of liquor mixed with others or with various flavorings ‖ an appetizer

cock·y cock·i·er cock·i·est *adj.* cocksure ‖ pert

co·coa *n.* a brown powder obtained from the cacao bean ‖ a drink prepared from this powder ‖ dull reddish brown

co·co·nut, co·coa·nut *n.* the coconut palm ‖ the edible fruit (a drupe) of this palm

co·coon *n.* the silky covering which the larvae of many insects spin about themselves

cod *n.* a genus of bony fishes

cod·dle cod·dling cod·dled *v.t.* to pamper ‖ to cook slowly in water just below boiling point

code 1. *n.* a collection of statutes, rules etc. ‖ a system of signals ‖ a system in which arbitrary values are given to letters, words, numbers or symbols to ensure secrecy or brevity 2. *v.t.* **cod·ing cod·ed to put(a message) into code**

cod·i·cil *n.* a supplementary clause added to a will, revoking or modifying it

cod·i·fy cod·i·fy·ing cod·i·fied *v.t.* to draw up a code

co·ed *n.* a female student at a coeducational college

co·ed·u·ca·tion *n.* the education in a single institution of both sexes **co·ed·u·cá·tion·al** *adj.*

co·erce co·erc·ing co·erced v.t. to compel || to enforce **co·ér·ci·ble** adj.

co·er·cion n. compulsion || government by force

co·er·cive adj. compelling, intended to coerce

cof·fee n. a genus of plants || its seeds, raw, roasted or ground || a drink, made from the roasted and ground seeds || dark brown

cof·fer n. a large strongbox for storing money or valuables

cof·fin n. a box in which a corpse is placed for burial

cog n. a projection or tooth on the rim of a wheel || (carpentry) a tenon

co·gen·cy n. the state or quality of being cogent

co·gent adj. compelling, convincing

cog·i·tate cog·i·tat·ing cog·i·tat·ed v.i. to think || v.t. to plan, devise **cog·i·tá·tion** n. **cog·i·ta·tive** adj.

co·gnac n. brandy distilled in Cognac

cog·ni·zance n. awareness || the fact of being aware, knowledge **cog·nize cog·niz·ing**

co·here co·her·ing co·hered v.i. to stick together || to stay united || (of style, design, etc.) to be consistent throughout

co·her·ence n. the state or quality of being coherent

co·her·ent adj. cohering || forming a unity || consistent in sequence of thought or design

co·he·sion n. intermolecular attraction holding together particles in the mass **co·he·sive** adj.

co·hort n. a companion

coif·fure 1. n. a way of wearing the hair **2.** v.t. coif **fur·ing coif·fured** to provide (someone) with a coiffure

coil 1. v.t. to arrange in rings which lie side by side || v.i. to wind itself **2.** n. something coiled || a spiral or helix of wire used as a resistance for electromagnetic purposes

coin 1. n. a piece of metal money **2.** v.t. to mint || to invent (a new word)

coin·age n. the making of coins || money

co·in·cide co·in·cid·ing co·in·cid·ed v.i. to occur at the same time || to occupy the same space

co·in·ci·dence n. the state of coinciding

co·in·ci·dent adj. coinciding || occupying the same space || happening at the same time **co·in·ci·den·tal** adj. happening by chance

co·i·tion n. sexual intercourse

co·i·tus n. coition

coke 1. n. the hard, gray, porous residue of coal **2.** v.t. b, cok·ing b, coked to transform into coke

col·an·der n. a bowl perforated with holes, used as a strainer

cold n. low temperature, in comparison with that of the body

cold adj. unheated || feeling the cold || grown cold || unfriendly || lacking enthusieuasm || unconscious || chilling in effect

cole·slaw n. cabbage salad

col·ic n. severe pains in the bowels or abdomen

col·i·se·um n. a large building, theater, stadium etc.

col·lab·o·rate col·lab·o·rat·ing col·lab·o·rat·ed v.i. to work together || to help an enemy country **col·lab·o·rá·tion, col·láb·o·ra·tor** ns

col·lapse 1. v. **col·laps·ing col·lapsed** v.i. to fall down or apart || to fail || to suffer a breakdown || v.t. to cause to collapse **2.** n. a falling down || a breaking to pieces **col·láps·i·ble** adj. made so as to fold up when not in use

col·lar 1. n. the part of a coat, shirt, dress etc. around the neck || a ring used to limit motion or hold something in place || any structure comparable to a collar **2.** v.t. to seize

col·late col·lat·ing col·lat·ed v.t. to examine (a text) closely against another || to put (pages) in correct order

col·lat·er·al 1. adj. parallel || **2.** n. a secondary security for a loan

col·la·tion n. the act or result of collating texts

col·league n. a fellow worker

col·lect 1. *v.t.* to gather in or together ‖ to aaccumulate for pleasure ‖ to gain or recover control of (oneself) ‖ *v.i.* to take up a collection **2.** *adj.* and *adv.* to be paid for by the recipient

col·lec·tion *n.* the act of collecting ‖ things brought together by choice ‖ money taken up from members of an audience ‖ the season's models designed by a dress designer

col·lege *n.* an institution for higher education ‖ a school offering specialized professional instruction

col·le·giate *adj.* of or pertaining to a college or to college members ‖ characteristic of colleges

col·lide col·lid·ing col·lid·ed *v.i.* to come into collision ‖ to come into conflict

col·li·sion *n.* the violent coming together of a moving body with another, either moving or stationary

col·lo·qui·al *adj.* (of words, idioms, etc.) thoroughly part of living language ‖ usable in speech without being classified as slang **col·ló·qui·al·ism** *n.*

col·lu·sion *n.* a dishonest, secret agreement ‖ *(law)* a fraudulent secret agreement **col·lu·sive** *adj.*

co·logne *n.* a scented toilet water

co·lon *n.* a punctuation mark (:)

colon *n.* the major portion of the large intestine of vertebrates between the cecum and the rectum

colo·nel *n.* an officer in the U.S. army, air force or marine corps

co·lo·ni·al 1. of or pertaining to the 13 colonies which originated the United States America

col·o·nist *n.* someone who helps to establish a colony ‖ an inhabitant of a colony

col·o·ni·za·tion *n.* the act or policy of colonizing

col·on·nade *n.* an evenly spaced line of columns supporting an entablature

col·o·ny *pl.* **col·o·nies** *n.* a land or place settled by people from another country, to whose government it is in some degree subject ‖ a number of animals of the same kind living in one place ‖ a mass of organisms growing in or on a substance

col·or 1. *n.* a sensation experienced usually as a result of light of varying wavelengths reaching the eye ‖ a pigment ‖ the complexion of the face ‖ *(pl.)* **2.** *v.t.* to impart color to ‖ to make (something) seem better or worse, by selection of facts and studied emphasis, than is really the case

col·ored *adj.* having color ‖ belonging to some race other than white ‖ given deliberate bias

col·or·ful *adj.* full of color ‖ vivid, lively

col·or·ing *n.* color scheme ‖ the color of the face and hair ‖ a children's pastime of putting color on outline pictures

co·los·sal *adj.* huge

col·umn *n.* a pillar, usually with capital and base, used to support an entablature or an arch ‖ a journalist's regular feature in a newspaper **cól·umn·ist** *n.* a journalist who writes a regular newspaper feature

co·ma *n.* the state of deep unconsciousness

co·ma·tose *adj.* relating to coma

comb 1. *n.* a toothed instrument for arranging the hair ‖ the fleshy crest on a cock's head **2.** *v.t.* to arrange or clean with a comb ‖ to search through with great care

com·bat 1. *n.* a fight, struggle **2.** *v.* **com·bat·ing, com·bat·ting com·bat·ed, com·bat·ted** to fight or struggle against ‖ to oppose

com·bat·ant 1. *adj.* fighting **2.** *n.* a fighter

com·bi·na·tion *n.* a combining or being combined ‖ the single thing formed by two or more other things joining together ‖ a set of numbers or other symbols which controls the action of a combination lock

com·bine 1. *v.* **com·bin·ing com·bined** *v.i.* to join to form single unit ‖ (of substances) to join or form a different substance ‖ to join with other people in order to achieve a joint purpose **2.** *n.* a combination of people or organizations

‖ a machine which reaps and threshes as a single process

com·bus·ti·ble 1. *adj.* able to undergo combustion **2.** *n.* a substance having this property

com·bus·tion *n.* any chemical process accompanied by the emission of heat and light

come *v.* **com·ing came come** *v.i.* to approach ‖ to arrive, appear ‖ to occur to reach ‖ to result

co·me·di·an *n.* a person who tells jokes in variety shows, nightclubs etc. ‖ an actor in comedy parts

co·me·di·enne *n.* a woman who tells jokes in variety shows, nightclubs etc. ‖ a comedy actress

com·e·y *pl.* **com·e·dies** *n.* drama which seeks to please by amusing

come·ly come·li·er come·li·est *adj.* handsome appearance

com·et *n.* a heavenly body subject to the sun's force of attraction, moving in an elliptical or parabolic orbit

com·fort *n.* consolation ‖ someone or something that brings consolation ‖ well-being, contentment

comfort *v.t.* to console

com·fort·a·ble *adj.* providing comfort ‖ restful ‖ quite large

com·ic 1. *adj.* funny, amusing ‖ relating to comedy **2.** *n.* a comedian ‖ an amusing person **cóm·i·cal** *adj.* **com·i·cal·i·ty** *n.*

com·ma *n.* a punctuation mark (,)

com·mand 1. *v.t.* to control, be in authority over ‖ to dominate ‖ to order ‖ *v.i.* to be in authority **2.** *n.* an order ‖ *(computer)* a signal that sets a process in motion

com·man·deer *v.t.* to take possession of for military purposes

com·mand·er *n.* a leader

com·mand·ment *n.* an order, esp. a divine command

com·mem·o·rate com·mem·o·rat·ing com·mem·o·rat·ed *v.t.* to recall to memory

com·mem·o·ra·tion *n.* a solemn act of remembrance

com·mence com·menc·ing com·menced *v.t.* to begin

com·mence·ment *n.* the act of beginning ‖ a ceremony in some universities etc. at which diplomas and degrees are conferred

com·mend *v.t.* to recommend ‖ to praise ‖ to entrust

com·men·da·tion *n.* praise ‖ the act of commending

com·ment 1. *n.* a remark ‖ a criticism ‖ an explanatory note **2.** *v.i.* to make comments or remarks

com·men·tar·y *pl.* **com·men·tar·ies** *n.* an explanatory book ‖ a set of notes or critical remarks

com·men·ta·tor *n.* the writer of a commentary ‖ someone who is present at an event and broadcasts a description of it as it takes place

com·merce *n.* the exchange of goods

com·mer·cial 1. *adj.* concerned with commerce ‖ (of a radio program) paid for by an advertiser ‖ *n.* a broadcast advertisement

com·mis·er·ate com·mis·er·at·ing com·mis·er·at·ed *v.i.* (with 'with') to feel or express pity **com·mis·er·a·tion** *n.* **com·mis·er·a·tive** *adj.*

com·mis·sar·y *pl.* **com·mis·sar·ies** *n.* a store supplying food and equipment to army or other governmental personnel

com·mis·sion *n.* a paper or warrant conferring authority ‖ the entrusting of authority to a person ‖ a percentage paid to an aagent or employee on the business which he transacts ‖ a group of people appointed to investigate a matter

com·mit com·mit·ting com·mit·ted *v.t.* to entrust ‖ to be guilty of ‖ to consign officially to custody **com·mít·ment** *n.* a continuing obligation, esp. financial ‖ a promise, pledge **com·mit·tal** *n.* the point in the burial service at which the body is placed in the grave ‖ the sending to prison of a person

com·mit·tee *n.* a body of people appointed or elected to examine or deal with particular matters

com·mo·di·ous *adj.* roomy

com·mod·i·ty *pl.* **com·mod·i·ties** *n.* an article of trade

com·mon *adj.* belonging or relating to the public ‖ ordinary, usual, of frequent occurrence ‖ vulgar ‖ inferior

common *n.* often *pl.)* an area of grassland, usually in or near a village

common law the unwritten law of custom

com·mon·place 1. *adj.* ordinary ‖ undistinguished ‖ trite **2.** *n.* a trite saying

com·mon·wealth *n.* a free association of self-governing units in a federation

com·mo·tion *n.* a noisy disturbance caused by a number of people ‖ mental turmoil

com·mune *n.* the smallest administrative division of the country in France, Belgium, Italy, Spain ‖ a collective organization for living or working in which products and property are shared

com·mune com·mun·ing com·muned *v.i.* to be in communion ‖ to communicate, receive Communion

com·mu·ni·ca·ble *adj.* capable of being communicated

com·mu·ni·cate com·mu·ni·cat·ing com·mu·ni·cat·ed *v.t.* to make others understand one's ideas ‖ to be in touch by words or signals

com·mu·ni·ca·tion *n.* a sending, giving or exchanging (of information, ideas, etc.) ‖ exchange ‖ an item of such exchange ‖ (often *pl.*) travel and transport links between places

com·mun·ion *n.* an intimate or sublime exchange or communication of thoughts and feelings **Com·mun·ion** *eccles.*) the partaking of the consecrated bread or wine ‖ the sacrament of Holy Communion

com·mun·ism *n.* the ownership of property, or means of production by the whole of a classless society ‖ **cóm·mun·ist** *n.* a person who advocates communism

com·mu·ni·ty *pl.* **com·mu·ni·ties** *n.* a body of people living near one another and in social relationship ‖ common

ownership ‖ a sharing

com·mute com·mut·ing com·mut·ed *v.t.* to change (a punishment) into another less severe ‖ *v.i.* to travel regularly to and from a city, usually for work

com·pact *n.* an agreement between individuals or groups

com·pact 1. *adj.* densely packed ‖ closely arranged or put together ‖ (of an automobile) smaller than average **2.** *n.* a small container for face powder

com·pan·ion 1. *n.* a person who goes with or accompanies another ‖ a person or animal whose company one enjoys ‖ a thing made to match or harmonize with another

com·pa·ny *pl.* **com·pa·nies** *n.* people with whom one associates ‖ a guest or guests ‖ a firm of partners ‖ the officers and men of a ship ‖ an infantry unit ‖ companionship

com·pa·ra·ble *adj.* capable or worthy of being compared ‖ similar **cóm·pa·ra·bly** *adv.*

com·par·a·tive 1. *adj.* using or introducing comparison ‖ not absolute but existing in some a degree

com·pare *v.* **com·par·ing com·pared** *v.t.* to state a likeness of (one thing to another) ‖ to form the comparative and superlative degrees of (adjectives and adverbs) ‖ *v.i.* (*usually neg.*) to sustain comparison

com·par·i·son *n.* a comparing, an attempt to discover what is like and unlike ‖ a resemblance shown for the sake of explanation

com·part·ment *n.* one part of a space which has been divided **com·part·men·tal** *adj.*

com·pass *n.* an instrument for determining direction on the earth's surface ‖ an instrument used for making circles

com·pas·sion *n.* pity aroused by the distress of others, with the desire to help them

com·pas·sion·ate *adj.* feeling compassion

com·pat·i·ble *adj.* capable of living together harmoniously

com·pa·tri·ot *n.* someone having the same native country as another

com·pel com·pel·ling com·pelled *v.t.* to oblige ‖ to call forth and secure

com·pen·sate   com·pen·sat·ing com·pen·sat·ed *v.t.* to repay (someone) for a loss ‖ to make up for (something)

com·pen·sa·tion *n.* an act of compensating or thing which compensates

com·pete com·pet·ing com·pet·ed *v.i.* to try to win a contest

com·pe·tence *n.* sufficient ability

com·pe·tent *adj.* having the necessary qualities or skills

com·pe·ti·tion *n.* a contest in which people compete

com·pet·i·tive *adj.* based on competition

com·pet·i·tor *n.* someone who takes part in a competition ‖ a rival

com·pi·la·tion *n.* the act of compiling ‖ something compiled

com·pile com·pil·ing com·piled *v.t.* to collect (materials, facts) for a book etc. ‖ to put together

com·pla·cence *n.* complacency

com·pla·cen·cy *n.* self-satisfaction, lack of self-criticism ‖ mild contentment

com·pla·cent *adj.* self-satisfied, smug

com·plain *v.i.* to express dissatisfaction, pain or distress

com·plaint *n.* an expression of dissatisfaction

com·ple·ment *n.* that which serves to complete ‖ the full number required

com·ple·men·ta·ry *adj.* serving to complete

com·plete *adj.* with nothing missing or lacking ‖ finished ‖ absolute, entire

complete com·plet·ing com·plet·ed *v.t.* to finish ‖ round off **com·ple·tion** *n.*

com·plex *n.* a whole made up of dissimilar parts or parts in intricate relationship ‖ a fixed idea or obsession ‖ a persistent set of attitudes

complex *adj.* not simple ‖ consisting of many parts

com·plex·ion, com·plec·tion *n.* the natural color and appearance of the skin

com·plex·i·ty *pl.* **com·plex·i·ties** *n.* the state

or quality of being complex ‖ something complex

com·pli·ance *n.* willingness to follow or consent to another's wishes ‖ an instance of this quality

com·pli·ant *adj.* yielding willing to comply

com·pli·cate *v.t.* **com·pli·cat·ing com·pli·cat·ed** to make difficult or confused ‖ to make complex **cóm·pli·cat·ed** *adj.*

com·pli·ca·tion *n.* the state of being complicated ‖ an additional difficulty or accumulation of difficulties

com·plic·i·ty *pl.* **com·plic·i·ties** *n.* participation in wrongdoing

com·pli·ment *n.* a verbal expression of courteous praise ‖ an action showing praise and respect

com·pli·ment *v.t.* to praise courteously

com·pli·mén·ta·ry *adj.* of or relating to a compliment

com·ply com·ply·ing com·plied *v.i.* to act in accordance with another's wishes, or with rules and regulations

com·po·nent 1. *adj.* forming part of a whole **2.** *n.* an essential part of something

com·port *v. refl.* to behave ‖ *v.i.* to be in agreement **com·pórt·ment** *n.* one's way of behaving

com·pose com·pos·ing com·posed *v.t.* to create ‖ to arrange into good order ‖ to make calm, quiet ‖ to set up (copy) in printing types **com·pósed** *adj.* calm, in full self-possession **com·pós·er** *n.* a person who composes music

com·po·site *adj.* made up of parts

com·po·si·tion *n.* the act of creating in music or literature ‖ a work so created ‖ content with respect to constituent elements

com·po·sure *n.* a settled state of mind, calm self-possession

com·pote *n.* fruit stewed with sugar

com·pound 1. *adj.* made up of separate substances or parts ‖ **2.** *n.* something made up from things combined together ‖ a word composed of two or more other words or elements **3.** *v.t.* to combine (elements) to make a new whole ‖ to compute (interest) on the total of the principal

com·pre·hend *v.t.* to understand, grasp the meaning or significance of

com·pre·hen·sion *n.* the act of understanding ‖ the capacity to include

com·pre·hen·sive *adj.* including much ‖ all-inclusive ‖ able to understand much

com·press *n.* a soft pad of cloth, pressing on to some part of the body to relieve pain etc.

com·press *v.t.* to reduce the volume, duration etc. of, by or as if by pressure ‖ to condense **com·préssed** *adj.*

com·pres·sion *n.* a compressing **com·prés·sive** *adj.*

com·prise com·pris·ing com·prised *v.t.* to be made up of, consist of ‖ to include, contain

com·pro·mise 1. *n.* agreement in a dispute, by which each side surrenders something that it wants ‖ a course of action intermediate between extremes **2.** *v.* **com·pro·mis·ing com·pro·mised** *v.i.* to settle a dispute by a compromise

comp·trol·ler *n.* (only in official titles) a controller

com·pul·sive 1. *adj.* compelling ‖ irrationally compelling

com·pul·so·ry *adj.* that must be done or suffered

com·punc·tion *n.* the pricking of conscience

com·pu·ta·tion *n.* the act of computing

com·pute com·put·ing com·put·ed *v.t.* to calculate **com·pút·er, com·pú·tor** *n.* someone who computes ‖ a computing machine

com·rade *n.* an intimate companion who shares one's work or pleasures **cóm·rade·ship** *n.*

con- *prefix* (used before sounds other than b, p, m, l, r) with

con·cave *adj.* curving inwards

con·ceal *v.t.* to hide ‖ to keep secret **con·céal·ment** *n.*

con·cede con·ced·ing con·ced·ed *v.t.* to

grant to be true ‖ to admit having lost

con·ceit *n.* excessive satisfaction with one's character or achievements **con·céit·ed** *adj.*

con·ceiv·a·ble *adj.* capable of being thought, imagined or understood **con·céiv·a·bly** *adv.*

con·ceive con·ceiv·ing con·ceived *v.t.* to become pregnant ‖ to form (an idea)

con·cen·trate *v.* **con·cen·trat·ing con·cen·trat·ed** *v.t.* to bring together into a mass ‖ to focus ‖ *v.i.* to direct or focus one's powers or actions on some limited object **con·cen·trá·tion** *n.*

con·cept *n.* a thought or opinion, general notion or idea

con·cep·tion *n.* the act of becoming prenant ‖ the faculty of conceiving in the mind

con·cep·tu·al *adj.* pertaining to mental conception or concepts

con·cern 1. *v.t.* to have as subject ‖ (*refl.*) to take part in ‖ to implicate or involve **2.** *n.* a business, firm or organization ‖ anxiety, worry **con·cérn·ing** *prep.* about, regarding, pertaining to

con·cert 1. *v.t.* to devise, plan **2.** *n.* agreement ‖ a musical performance **con·cért·ed** *adj.*

con·ces·sion *n.* a conceding or yielding ‖ the thing yielded or conceded ‖ a grant **con·ces·sion·aire, con·ces·sion·naire** *n.* a person or company benefiting from the grant of a lease **con·ces·sion·ar·y 1.** *adj.* relating to a concession

conch *pl.* **conchs, con·ches** *n.* any of a group of large spiral-shelled marine mollusks, or the shell or animal individually

con·cil·i·ate con·cil·i·at·ing con·cil·i·at·ed *v.t.* to win (goodwill) by genial or soothing approaches ‖ to make reconcile

con·cil·i·a·tion *n.* a bringing of opponents into harmony ‖ reconcilement

con·cise *adj.* brief, condensed, expressing much in few words

con·clave *n.* the room in which cardinals meet to elect a pope ‖ the body of cardinals a ‖ a private or secret meeting

con·clude con·clud·ing con·clud·ed *v.t.* to bring to an end ‖ to decide (something) on the basis of reasoning

con·clu·sion *n.* the end or last part ‖ a reasoned judgment or inference

con·clu·sive *adj.* final, decisive

con·coct *v.t.* to prepare by mixing ingredients ‖ to make up, invent, devise

con·coc·tion *n.* something concocted ‖ a lie

con·cord *n.* a state of agreement or harmony ‖ a treaty or agreement

con·course *n.* a flocking together of people ‖ an open space where crowds may gather

con·crete 1. *n.* a hard strong substance made by mixing sand and gravel or crushed stone with cement and water **2.** *adj.* real, specific, not abstract or ideal ‖ united, compounded ‖ made of concrete **3.** *v.* **con·cret·ing con·cret·ed** *v.i.* to solidify, harden

con·cu·bine *n.* a woman who lives with a man not her husband

con·cur con·cur·ring con·curred *v.i.* to agree ‖ coincide **con·cur·rence con·cur·ren·cy** *ns.* **con·cur·rent** *adj.* running alongside, existing or happening together

con·cus·sion *n.* violent shaking ‖ impaired activity of the brain, through a blow or violent shaking

con·cus·sive *adj.* of an agitating or shaking nature

con·demn *v.t.* to censure, blame ‖ to prescribe punishment for **con·dem·na·ble** *adj.*

con·dem·na·tion *n.* a condemning or being condemned ‖ grounds for condemning

con·den·sa·tion *n.* a making more concise and brief ‖ the transition of a substance from the vapor to the liquid state

con·dense con·dens·ing con·densed *v.t.* to make more dense or compact ‖ to concentrate, increase the strength of ‖ to reduce to a liquid form ‖ *v.i.* to become more dense or compact

con·de·scend *v.i.* to behave patronizingly ‖ do something which one considers beneath one's dignity **con·de·scénd·ing** *adj.*

con·de·scen·sion *n.* a condescending

con·di·ment *n.* a seasoning, e.g. pepper, used to flavor food

con·di·tion *v.t.* to stipulate ‖ to put into the required state, make fit

condition *n.* mode or state of existence ‖ state of health ‖ a stipulation, provision ‖ a prerequisite ‖ *(pl.)* circumstances ‖ *(pl.)* terms ‖ a clause in a contract etc. that modifies, revokes or suspends a stipulation or a given contingency

con·di·tion·al 1. *adj.* dependent, made or granted on certain conditions, not absolute **2.** *n.* a conditional word, clause, mood etc. **con·diza·tion·al·i·ty** *n.*

con·dole con·dol·ing con·doled *v.i.* to express sympathetic grief, commiserate **con·dó·lence** *n.*

con·dom *n.* a contraceptive sheath

con·do·min·i·um *n.* part of a building owned usually for use by the purchaser, e.g. a single apartment in a multiple housing structure

con·do·na·tion *n.* the act of condoning

con·done con·don·ing con·doned *v.t.* to overlook ‖ to allow to continue (what ought to be stopped)

con·dor *n.* a very large vulture of the High Andes

con·duce con·duc·ing con·duced *v.i.* to lead or tend towards (a generally desirable result) **con·dú·cive** *adj.* having power to promote

con·duct 1. *v.t.* to lead, guide, escort ‖ to direct ‖ to behave (oneself) ‖ to transmit (heat, light, sound or electricity) **2.** *n.* moral behavior ‖ management

con·duc·tor *n.* someone who conducts musical performers ‖ the official in charge of passengers on a bus or streetcar ‖ a railroad official ‖ a material which can conduct heat, electricity etc.

con·duit *n.* a channel or pipe for carrying fluid ‖ a tube

cone a solid figure with circular base, tapering to a point ‖ something conical in shape **1.** *v.* **con·ing coned** *v.t.* to shape like a cone ‖ *v.i.* to bear cones

con·fec·tion 1. *n.* jam, preserves or dessert **2.** *v.t.* to prepare or make (confections) **con·féc·tion·er** *n.* a manufacturer of, or shopkeeper selling, candies, cakes etc.

con·fec·tion·er·y *n.* candy ‖ the work of a confectioner ‖ a confectioner's shop

con·fed·er·a·cy *pl.* **con·fed·er·a·cies** *n.* a league or alliance

con·fed·er·ate 1. *adj.* allied, leagued together **2.** *n.* an ally an accomplice **3.** *v.* **con·fed·er·at·ing con·fed·er·at·ed** *v.i.* to unite in a league or conspiracy

con·fed·er·a·tion *n.* an alliance of powers for some mutual benefit

con·fer con·fer·ring con·ferred *v.i.* to seek advice ‖ hold a conference ‖ *v.t.* to give or grant **con·fer·ee** *n.* someone who takes part in a conference

con·fer·ence *n.* consultation ‖ a formal meeting at which people confer **con·fer·en·tial** *adj.*

con·fess *v.* admit ‖ to acknowledge **con·féssed** *adj.* admitted, avowed

con·fes·sion *n.* an acknowledgment of a crime or fault **con·fés·sion·al** *adj.* pertaining to a confession or creed

con·fes·sion·al *n.* the enclosure in which a priest hears confession ‖ the practice of confessing sin

con·fes·sor *n.* a person confessing ‖ a priest who hears confession and grants absolution

con·fet·ti *pl. n.* small pieces of colored paper thrown for fun on festive occasions

con·fide con·fid·ing con·fid·ed *v.t.* to entrust a secret ‖ to trust ‖ *v.t.* to tell confidentially

con·fi·dence *n.* a state of trust ‖ reliance ‖ self-reliance **to take someone into one's confidence** to tell someone something private

con·fi·dent *adj.* self-assured ‖ convinced

con·fi·den·tial *adj.* spoken or written in confidence ‖ entrusted with secrets

con·fine con·fin·ing con·fined *v.t.* to limit, keep (something, oneself) within limits ‖ to shut in, imprison

con·fine·ment *n.* imprisonment ‖ inability to go out because of illness

con·firm *v.t.* to corroborate, establish the truth of ‖ to ratify

con·fir·ma·tion *n.* corroboration ‖ a proof ‖ the Christian rite by which baptized persons, at the age of discretion, are admitted to full communion

con·fis·cate con·fis·cat·ing con·fis·cat·ed *v.t.* to take away (something) from somebody under discipline

con·fis·ca·tion *n.* a confiscating or being confiscated

con·fla·gra·tion *n.* a calamitous fire

con·flict 1. *n.* armed fighting, a war ‖ a struggle between opposing principles or aims **2.** *v.i.* to be at variance, clash

con·flu·ence *n.* a flowing together of streams, roads etc.

con·form *v.i.* to comply ‖ to do as others do ‖ *v.t.* to adapt, cause to comply

con·form·ist 1. *adj.* tending to conform **2.** *n.* someone who conforms

con·form·i·ty *pl.* **con·form·i·ties** *n.* compliance ‖ likeness in form, shape or manner

con·found *v.t.* mix up, confuse ‖ to perplex deeply, utterly astonish ‖ to damn

con·front *v.t.* to face, esp. boldly or in a hostile way ‖ (with 'with') to bring face to face, force to consider something **con·fron·ta·tion** *n.*

con·fuse con·fus·ing con·fused *v.t.* to throw into disorder ‖ to perplex or muddle ‖ to abash, disconcert **con·fus·ed·ly** *adv.*

con·fu·sion *n.* lack of clarity ‖ bewilderment, perplexity ‖ embarrassment

con·fute con·fut·ing con·fut·ed *v.t.* to refute ‖ to prove (a person) mistaken

con·geal *v.i.* freeze ‖ to coagulate **con·géal·ment** *n.* a congealed mass

con·gen·ial *adj.* of the same nature, tastes ‖ suitable **con·ge·ni·al·i·ty** *n.*

con·gen·i·tal *adj.* present at birth ‖ acquired during fetal development and not hereditary

con·gest *v.t.* to pack closely, cause clogging in by overcrowding **con·gést·ed** *adj.* closely packed, crowded ‖ overpopulated ‖ overcharged with blood

con·ges·tion *n.* the state of being congested

con·glom·er·ate 1. *adj.* gathered or clustered into a ball or mass **2.** *n.* an accumulated mass of different materials ‖ corporate entity composed of several companies in a variety of industries **3.** *v.* **con·glom·er·at·ing con·glom·er·at·ed** *v.t.* to gather into a compact mass **con·glom·er·á·tion** *n.*

con·grat·u·late con·grat·u·lat·ing con·grat·u·lat·ed *v.t.* to express pleasure in the success or happiness of (another)

con·grat·u·la·tion *n.* a congratulating ‖ (*pl.*) expressions of congratulation

con·gre·gate 1. *v.* **con·gre·gat·ing con·gre·gat·ed** *v.i.* to collect into a crowd or mass **2.** *adj.* collected, assembled

con·gre·ga·tion *n.* the body of regular attenders at a particular place of worship **con·gre·gá·tion·al** *adj.*

con·gress *n.* a formal meeting **Con·gress** the federal legislature of the U.S.A.

con·gres·sion·al *adj.* of or pertaining to a congress

con·gress·man *pl.* **con·gress·men** *n.* a member of the House of Representatives

con·gru·ent *adj.* possessing congruity

con·gru·i·ty *pl.* **con·gru·i·ties** *n.* a state of agreement, harmony, correspondence

co·ni·fer *n.* a large order of gymnospermous trees and shrubs **co·nif·er·ous** *adj.*

con·jec·tur·al *adj.* doubtful, of the nature of conjecture ‖ given to, prone to conjecture

con·jec·ture *n.* guesswork, opinion or theory based on presumption or insufficient evidence

conjecture con·jec·tur·ing con·jec·tured *v.t.* to guess, infer on slight evidence

con·ju·gal *adj.* pertaining to marriage or to married persons **con·ju·gal·i·ty** *n.*

con·ju·gate 1. *v.* **con·ju·gat·ing**

con·ju·gat·ed *v.t.* to state or set out (a verb) with its various inflectional endings in order ‖ *v.i.* to join together **2.** *adj.* yoked or united, joined, connected, esp. in pairs

con·ju·ga·tion *n.* a conjugating or being conjugated **con·ju·gá·tion·al, con·ju·ga·tive** *adjs.*

con·junc·tion *n.* the apparent meeting of two or more heavenly bodies in the same part of the sky ‖ *v.i.* a word used to connect words ‖ a combination of events or circumstances **in conjunction with** together with

con·jure con·jur·ing con·jured *v.t.* to summon up by invocation ‖ to produce by sleight of hand ‖ *v.i.* to practice sleight of hand **cón·jur·er, cón·ju·ror** *n.* a magician

con·nect *v.t.* to join ‖ to establish a connection between in the mind **con·néct·ed** *adj.* joined together ‖ linked ‖ coherent

con·nec·tion *n.* a link or joint ‖ relationship of thought, plot etc. ‖ blood relationship or personal relationship ‖ economic and business relations

con·nive con·niv·ing con·nived *v.i.* to pretend ignorance of something one should condemn ‖ (with 'at') to be culpably cooperative

con·nois·seur *n.* an expert critic (of the arts) ‖ a judge in matters of taste

con·no·ta·tion *n.* the implication of a word, apart from its primary meaning

con·note con·not·ing con·not·ed *v.t.* (of a word) to suggest, imply apart from its primary meaning ‖ to involve by implication

con·quer *v.t.* to defeat in war ‖ to overcome by moral power ‖ *v.i.* to be victorious

con·quer·or *n.* a victor, a person who conquers

con·quest *n.* the act of conquering ‖ something won or acquired by physical or moral victory

con·science *n.* knowledge of one's own acts as right or wrong

con·sci·en·tious *adj.* scrupulous ‖ characterized by or done with careful attention

con·scious *adj.* recognizing the existence, truth or fact of something ‖ registered subjectively ‖ marked by the use of one's rational powers ‖ intended

con·scious·ness *n.* the state of being conscious ‖ mental activity ‖ the upper level of mental life

con·se·crate con·se·crat·ing con·se·crat·ed *v.t.* to make or declare holy ‖ to devote to a purpose, dedicate

con·se·cra·tion *n.* the act of consecrating

con·sec·u·tive *adj.* following in regular or unbroken order ‖ marked by logical consensus pl. **con·sen·sus·es** *n.* concord (of opinion, evidence, authority, testimony etc.)

con·sent *n.* permission, acquiescence, approval ‖ agreement

consent *v.i.* to give assent

con·se·quence *n.* a logical inference ‖ importance

con·se·quent *adj.* following as an effect or outcome ‖ following as a deduction, logically consistent

con·se·quent·ly 1. *adv.* accordingly, therefore **2.** *conj.* therefore, and so

con·ser·va·tion *n.* the act of keeping free from depletion, decay or injury ‖ wise management and maintaining **con·ser·vá·tion·ist** *n.* someone who is active in the conserving of natural resources

con·serv·a·tive *adj.* desiring to preserve existing institutions ‖ moderate, cautious ‖ old-fashioned ‖ considered to involve little risk

con·serv·a·to·ry con·serv·a·to·ries *n.* a greenhouse ‖ a school of music or art

con·serve *n.* fruit etc. preserved in sugar

con·serve con·serv·ing con·served *v.t.* to preserve in a sound state

con·sid·er *v.t.* to ponder, think out ‖ to assess before reaching a decision ‖ to make allowances for ‖ to believe ‖ *v.i.* to reflect or deliberate

con·sid·er·a·ble *adj.* quite large in amount, extent or degree ‖ important **con·sid·er·a·bly** *adv.*

con·sid·er·ate *adj.* careful not to hurt the feelings of others or cause inconvenience to them

con·sid·er·a·tion *n.* deliberation ‖ a point of importance ‖ a financial reward, payment

con·sid·er·ing 1. *prep.* in view of **2.** *adv.* taking all circumstances into account **3.** *conj.* seeing that

con·sign *v.t.* to send ‖ to entrust ‖ to make over formally **con·sign·ee** *n.* a person to whom goods etc. are consigned **con·sign·er** *n.*

con·sist *v.i.* (with 'of') to be made up or composed

con·sist·ence *n.* consistency **con·sist·en·cy** pl. **con·sist·en·cies** *n.* degree of solidarity ‖ firm coherence ‖ agreement, correspondence

con·sist·ent *adj.* in accordance ‖ true to principles or a policy **con·síst·ent·ly** *adv.* regularly

con·sol·a·ble *adj.* able to be consoled

con·so·la·tion *n.* the alleviation of suffering, grief, disappointment etc. by comforting

con·sole con·sol·ing con·soled *v.t.* comfort in distress

con·sole *n.* a bracket supporting a shelf or cornice ‖ the part of an organ containing the keyboard

con·sol·i·ate con·sol·i·dat·ing con·sol·i·dat·ed *v.t.* to strengthen, make firm ‖ *v.i.* to combine, merge **con·sol·i·dá·tion** *n.*

consolidation *(securities)* process of firming the market price following a substantial change in prices

con·som·mé *n.* a clear soup made from poultry or meat

con·so·nant *adj.* having consonance, consistent ‖ harmonious ‖ corresponding in sound ‖ resonant

consonant *n.* a unit of speech sound (p, t etc.) ‖ the letter representing such a unit

con·sort 1. *n.* the non-reigning wife or husband of a reigning king or queen **in consort** in harmony ‖ in company (with) **2.** *v.i.* to associate or keep company ‖ to harmonize

con·spic·u·ous *adj.* very readily perceived ‖ attracting attention

con·spir·a·cy *pl.* **con·spir·a·cies** *n.* a joining secretly with others for an evil purpose ‖ a plot

con·spir·a·tor *n.* a person taking part in a conspiracy

con·spire con·spir·ing con·spired *v.i.* to combine secretly esp. for unlawful purposes ‖ *v.t.* to devise

con·stan·cy *n.* steadfastness, fidelity ‖ fortitude, endurance ‖ stability

con·stant *adj.* continual, unceasing ‖ unremitting ‖ faithful, unwavering ‖ not subject to variation, uniform.

con·stant·ly *adv.* without stopping, continuously

con·stel·la·tion *n.* a group of fixed stars, arbitrarily considered together

con·ster·na·tion *n.* surprise and alarm, dismay

con·sti·pate con·sti·pat·ing con·sti·pat·ed *v.i.* to cause constipation ‖ *v.t.* to cause constipation in (someone)

con·sti·pa·tion *n.* infrequent passage of feces

con·stit·u·en·cy *pl.* **con·stit·u·en·cie** *n.* a body of voters represented ‖ an area or community represented thus

con·stit·u·ent 1. *adj.* forming a basic part of a whole **2.** *n.* an essential part, component ‖ a member of a constituency

con·sti·tute con·sti·tut·ing con·sti·tut·ed *v.t.* to appoint to an office or function ‖ to set up, establish

con·sti·tu·tion *n.* the total physical condition of the body ‖ the set of principles adopted by a state or society for its government **con·sti·tú·tion·al 1.** *adj.* of, due to, or inherent in one's constitution ‖ of or pertaining to a political constitution **2.** *n.* a regular walk taken for one's health

con·strain *v.t.* to persuade by pressure or force, compel **con·stráined** *adj.* ill at ease **con·strain·ed·ly** *adv.*

con·straint *n.* restricted liberty

con·struct 1. *v.t.* to put together, build ‖ to arrange mentally **con·strúct·er,**

con·strúc·tor *n.*

con·struc·tion *n.* a thing constructed ‖ the arrangement and interrelation of words in a sentence

con·struc·tive *adj.* tending to or helping to construct

con·strue con·stru·ing con·strued *v.t.* to analyze grammatically ‖ to interpret the meaning of ‖ to combine (words) grammatically ‖ *v.i.* to admit of grammatical analysis

con·sul *n.* an agent appointed by a country to look after the interests of its citizens in a foreign town

con·su·late *n.* the premises of a consul

con·sult *v.t.* to seek advice from ‖ to seek information from ‖ *v.i.* to reflect (with others)

con·sult·ant *n.* a person giving expert advice

con·sul·ta·tion *n.* the act of consulting ‖ a conference to discuss a problem

con·sume con·sum·ing con·sumed *v.t.* to eat or drink up ‖ to destroy by burning **con·súmed** *adj.* eaten up

con·sum·er *n.* someone who uses articles made by another

con·sum·mate 1. *adj.* complete, perfect, supreme **2.** *v.t.* **con·sum·mat·ing con·sum·mat·ed** to bring to completion or perfection

con·sum·ma·tion *n.* the act of completing ‖ perfection ‖ fulfillment

con·sump·tion *n.* a consuming ‖ the use of goods by consumers or producers ‖ tuberculosis of the lungs

con·tact 1. *n.* the state of touching ‖ a coming into association ‖ a person who may be helpful ‖ junction of two conductors **2.** *v.t.* to get in touch with

con·ta·gion *n.* the direct or indirect transmission of disease ‖ the spreading of an influence from person to person

con·ta·gious *adj.* (of diseases) catching, communicable ‖ easily spreading

con·tain *v.t.* to enclose ‖ to control (oneself) **con·táin·er** *n.* a carton, crate, jar, bottle

con·tam·i·nate con·tam·i·nat·ing

con·tam·i·nat·ed *v.t.* to infect with a contagious disease ‖ to pollute **con·tam·i·ná·tion** *n.*

con·tem·plate con·tem·plat·ing con·tem·plat·ed *v.t.* to consider attentively ‖ to intend, but not as part of an immediate plan ‖ *v.i.* to meditate **con·tem·plá·tion** *n.* meditation ‖ the process of considering with a view to a decision

con·tem·pla·tive *adj.* thoughtful

con·tem·po·rar·y 1. *adj.* belonging to the same time ‖ modern **2.** *n. pl.* **con·tem·po·rar·ies** a person living at the same time as another

con·tempt *n.* an attitude to something which one despises ‖ total disregard ‖ disobedience of lawful orders

con·tempt·i·ble *adj.* worthy of contempt or scorn **con·témpt·i·bly** *adv.*

con·temp·tu·ous *adj.* feeling or showing contempt

con·tend *v.i.* to struggle in rivalry ‖ to conflict ‖ to argue ‖ *v.t.* to assert, esp. against opposition

con·tent *v.t.* to make satisfied **to content oneself with** resign oneself to having only

con·tent *adj.* satisfied, not displeased

con·tent *n.* (usually *pl.*) a summary of subjects treated in a book ‖ the amount of a certain substance contained ‖ the gist of a speech

con·tent·ed *adj.* enjoying or showing contentment

con·test 1. *v.t.* to call in question ‖ *v.i.* to strive, struggle **2.** *n.* a trial of skill ‖ a competitilon

con·test·ant *n.* someone who contests, in a match

con·text *n.* the parts of a book, speech etc. which precede or follow a word or passage and affect its significance **con·tex·tu·al** *adj.*

con·ti·nent *n.* one of the seven great land masses of the world **con·ti·nen·tal** *adj.* belonging to or characteristic of a continent

con·tin·gen·cy *pl.* **con·tin·gen·cies** *n.* something likely but not certain to happen ‖ something dependent on a probable but not certain event ‖ an unforeseeable event or circumstance ‖ an incidental quality

con·tin·gent 1. *adj.* liable but not certain to happen ‖ incidental ‖ conditional, dependent ‖ a priori **2.** *n.* a quota ‖ a representative group of people

con·tin·u·al *adj.* occurring frequently, often repeated ‖ continuous, unbroken

con·tin·u·a·tion *n.* a prolonging ‖ the action of resuming after an interruption

con·tin·ue con·tin·u·ing con·tin·ued *v.t.* to go on with ‖ to prolong ‖ to resume, take up again ‖ *v.i.* to extend ‖ (of a story, speech, speaker etc.) to go on

con·tin·u·ous *adj.* connected throughout

con·tort *v.t.* to twist, force out of normal shape

con·tor·tion *n.* a twisting **con·tór·tion·ist** *n.* an acrobat who can contort his body or limbs

con·tour 1. *n.* the outline of a figure or shape **2.** *adj.* following contour lines

con·tra·band 1. *n.* illegal traffic in goods ‖ smuggled goods **2.** *adj.* prohibited

con·tra·cep·tion *n.* birth control **con·tra·cép·tive 1.** *adj.* preventing conception **2.** *n.* a contraceptive device

con·tract *v.t.* to catch (a disease etc.) ‖ to draw together ‖ to shorten ‖ *v.i.* to shrink

con·tract *n.* an agreement, a covenant ‖ an order to assault or kill a predetermined victim for a price ‖ an agreement endorsed by law

con·trac·tion *n.* a contracting (of disease, bad habits, debts etc.) ‖ a shrinking

con·trac·tor *n.* a person undertaking to do work by signing a contract ‖ a muscle which contracts

con·tra·dict *v.t.* to assert the contrary to ‖ to be inconsistent with

con·tra·dic·tion *n.* a contradicting statement ‖ opposition

con·tra·dic·to·ry *adj.* affirming the contrary ‖ inconsistent

con·tral·to *pl.* **con·tral·tos** *n.* the lowest female singing voice ‖ a singer with such a voice

con·trap·tion *n.* an odd gadget, device or contrivance

con·tra·ry 1. *adj.* opposed ‖ opposite in nature, direction etc. ‖ vexatious, perverse **con·tra·ries** the opposite **2.** *adv.* counter, contrarily

con·trast *v.t.* to display the differences between ‖ *v.i.* to show marked differences when compared

con·trast *n.* a divergence between related things, ideas etc. ‖ a relationship of difference demonstrated by juxtaposition **con·trast·y con·trast·i·er con·trast·i·est** *adj.* displaying marked contrast

con·tri·bute con·tri·but·ing con·trib·ut·ed *v.t.* to give, together with others, for a common purpose ‖ to supply (an article etc.) to a newspaper or periodical

con·tri·bu·tion *n.* something contributed

con·trite *adj.* penitent, thoroughly sorry, esp. for sin

con·tri·tion *n.* remorse, penitence

con·triv·ance *n.* mechanical appliance ‖ a dishonest device

con·trive con·triv·ing con·trived *v.t.* to devise ‖ to invent

con·trol 1. *v.t.* **con·trol·ling con·trolled** to govern, exercise control over ‖ to restrain ‖ to regulate **2.** *n.* power, authority ‖ restraint ‖ (*pl.*) the mechanisms operated by the driver's hands and feet in driving a vehicle, or those by which a pilot flies an aircraft ‖ a person who acts as a check ‖ a standard of comparison or check in an experiment

con·trol·ler *n.* a person who governs or controls **con·tról·ler·ship** *n.*

con·tro·ver·sial *adj.* disputable

con·tro·ver·sy *pl.* **con·tro·ver·sies** *n.* a disputing ‖ an argument, esp. a prolonged one ‖ a quarrel

con·tuse con·tus·ing con·tused *v.t.* to bruise, damage the subcutaneous tissue

con·tu·sion *n.* a bruise, damage to subcutaneous tissue

con·va·lesce con·va·lesc·ing

con·va·lesced *v.i.* to recover health

con·va·lés·cence *n.* **con·va·lés·cent 1.** *adj.* gradually recovering from illness **2.** *n.* a person recovering from illness

con·vene con·ven·ing con·vened *v.t.* to call together ‖ *v.i.* to assemble

con·ven·ience *n.* a convenient time or arrangement ‖ something which makes for one's comfort or for saving work

con·ven·ient *adj.* favorable to one's comfort ‖ suitable as an arrangement ‖ easy of access

con·vent *n.* a community of religious, esp. of nuns ‖ the establishment in which they live

con·ven·tion *n.* a conference, a body of delegates assembled for a common purpose ‖ an arbitrary but consistently observed usage

con·ven·tion·al *adj.* depending on or deriving from convention ‖ customary ‖ lacking originality **con·ven·tion·al·i·ty** *ns* **con·ven·tion·al·ize con·ven·tion·al·iz·ing con·ven·tion·al·ized** *v.t.* to make conventional ‖ to treat or represent conventionally

con·verge con·verg·ing con·verged *v.i.* (of two or more things having direction) to be directed towards the same point in space

con·ver·gence *n.* the act or state of converging

con·ver·gent *adj.* of things in motion or of directions or actions which converge

con·ver·sant *adj.* familiar ‖ informed about

con·ver·dsa·tion *n.* talk, esp. informal and friendly **con·ver·sá·tion·al** *adj.* pertaining to or characteristic of conversation **con·ver·sá·tion·al·ist** *n.* a practiced or gifted talker

con·verse 1. *n.* a statement which transposes the terms of another statement ‖ something which is the opposite of something else **2.** *adj.* of one statement which is the converse of another

con·verse *v.i.* **con·vers·ing con·versed** to have a conversation

con·ver·sion n. a converting or being converted, esp. to new beliefs ‖ a change in a rate of interest to a lower rate

con·vert 1. v.t. to change ‖ to bring over to a new position, faith etc. ‖ to turn to another use ‖ v.i. to undergo a conversion **2.** n. a person whose religious, philosophical or political beliefs etc. have been changed **con·vért·er** n. a device for transforming electrical voltage

con·vert·i·ble 1. adj. able to be converted ‖ interchangeable **2.** n. a car with a folding top

con·vex 1. adj. curving outwards

con·vey v.t. to carry, transport ‖ to act as a medium transmitting sound etc. ‖ to transfer by legal process **con·véy·a·ble** adj.

con·vey·ance n. the act of conveying ‖ a means of conveying, esp. a hired vehicle **con·véy·anc·ing** n. the work of drawing up deeds etc.

con·vey·or n. a conveyor belt or other device for moving articles or raw materials in a factory

con·vict v.t. to prove or find guilty after trial

con·vict n. a person convicted of crime

con·vic·tion n. a convicting ‖ firm belief

con·vince con·vinc·ing con·vinced v.t. to persuade by argument or proof

con·viv·i·al adj. festive, gay, sociable

con·vo·ca·tion n. an assembly of representatives **con·vo·cá·tion·al** adj.

con·voy n. a convoying or being escorted ‖ a group of merchant ships under aerial or naval protection

con·voy v.t. to provide military or naval escort for

con·vulse con·vuls·ing con·vulsed v.t. to throw into spasms

con·vul·sion n. (usually pl.) a violent involuntary spasm of musclesr ‖ any violent disturbance, e.g. an earthquake, tidal wave ‖ (esp. pl.) uncontrollable laughter

con·vul·sive adj. of the nature of a convulsion ‖ producing convulsions ‖ emotionally violent

cook 1. n. a person who cooks food **2.** v.t. to prepare (food) by the action of heat

cook·ie, cook·y pl. **cook·ies** n. a small, sweet cake

cool 1. adj. pleasantly cold ‖ not retaining heat, a cool dress ‖ self-possessed, calm ‖ unenthusiastic, verging on hostility ‖ excellent **2.** n. cool air ‖ a cool time ‖ a cool place ‖ coolness

cool v.i. to become cool ‖ (of temper or enthusiasm) to calm down, moderate ‖ v.t. to make cool

cool·ant n. a liquid used to lessen friction in cutting tools

cool·er n. a vessel for cooling liquids

coop 1. n. a box, cage, pen or enclosure for poultry ‖ a place of confinement **2.** v.t. to put in a coop

co-op, co·op n. (short for) a cooperative

co·op·er·ate co·op·er·at·ing co·op·er·at·ed v.i. to work jointly with others ‖ to be helpful as distinct from hostile

co·op·er·a·tion n. a cooperating, working together to a common end

co·op·er·a·tive 1. adj. of or pertaining to cooperation **2.** n. an apartament house in which the apartments are each individually owned

co·or·di·nate adj. equal in rank or order ‖ pertaining to or made up of coordinate things

co·or·di·nate co·or·di·nat·ing co·or·di·nat·ed v.t. to make coordinate ‖ to bring the parts or agents of a plan, process etc. into a common whole, to harmonize

co·or·di·na·tion n. a making or being coordinate

cop cop·ping copped v.t. to catch (something that causes death, suffering, imprisonment etc.)

cop n. a policeman

cope cop·ing coped v.i. (with 'with') to contend (with a situation, problem), esp. successfully

co·pi·ous adj. plentiful, overflowing ‖ not concise

cop·per 1. *n.* a metallic element ‖ a penny **2.** *v.t.* to sheathe with copper **3.** *adj.* made of copper

cop·per·y *adj.* mixed with copper ‖ like copper

cop·u·late cop·u·lat·ing cop·u·lat·ed *v.i.* to unite in sexual intercourse

cop·u·la·tion *n.* coition, sexual intercourse

cop·y *pl.* **cop·ies** *n.* a reproduction, not an original ‖ a duplicate ‖ material intended for printing

copy cop·y·ing cop·ied *v.t.* to make a copy of ‖ to imitate ‖ *v.i.* to cheat

cop·y·right 1. *n.* the exclusive right to reproduce literary, dramatic, artistic or musical work, given by law for a certain period to an author etc. **2.** *v.t.* to secure a copyright on

co·quet, co·quette co·quet·ting co·quet·ted *v.i.* to flirt

cor·al 1. *n.* a coelenterate of class *Anhozoa* or a colony of them. They occur as polyps only and usually are colonial, living in shallow ocean waters ‖ the hard red or white substance secreted by these animals to protect and support the polyps **2.** *adj.* of coral, or the color of red coral **cor·al·lif·er·ous** *adj.*

cord 1. *n.* a rope of small diameter or a fairly thick string ‖ a cordlike rib on textiles ‖ a ribbed fabric ‖ a cubic measure, esp. for cut wood **2.** *v.t.* to bind with cord ‖ to pile (wood) into cords **cord·age** *n.* ropes

cor·date *adj.* heart-shaped

cord·ed *adj.* bound or supplied with cords ‖ ribbed

cor·dial 1. *adj.* hearty, sincere, friendly **2.** *n.* a fortifying drink of flavored spirits **cor·dial·i·ty** *n.* friendliness, sincerity

cor·du·roy 1. *n.* a thick cotton material with a velvetlike pile on raised ribs **2.** *adj.* made of corduroy

core 1. *n.* the inner part of certain fruits containing the seeds ‖ the innermost part of anything **2.** *v.t.* **cor·ing cored** to take out the core of

cork 1. *n.* the bark of the cork oak ‖ a bottle stopper **2.** *v.t.* to furnish with cork ‖ to stop with a cork

cork·screw 1. *n.* an implement for removing corks from bottles **2.** *adj.* spiral, twisted

corn 1. *n.* maize, a tall annual American cereal grass ‖ small hard seeds of cereals, grain in general ‖ corny music, dialogue, jokes etc. ‖ corn whiskey **2.** *v.t.* to preserve with salt, *corned beef*

corn *n.* a horny hardening or thickening of the skin, esp. on the toes or feet

cor·ne·a *n.* the transparent portion of the external covering of the eyeball **cór·ne·al** *adj.*

cor·ner 1. *n.* the point or place of meeting of e.g. two converging sides ‖ the angle formed by the meeting of two streets ‖ an angular projection ‖ a position from which escape is difficult or dangerous ‖ *v.t.* to supply with corners ‖ to drive into a corner ‖ *v.i.* to form, come to or drive around a corner

cor·net *n.* a brass wind instrument of the trumpet class

cor·nice *n.* a horizontal strip of stone, wood or plaster crowning a building ‖ a molding of the wall of a room just below the ceiling

cor·nu·co·pi·a *n.* an emblem of plenty **cor·nu·có·pi·an** *adj.*

corn·y corn·i·er corn·i·est *adj.* trite, lacking in imagination

cor·ol·la·ry 1. *pl.* **cor·ol·lar·ies** *n.* a proposition which can be inferred from one already proved as self-evidently true ‖ a natural consequence or result

co·ro·na *pl.* **co·ro·nas, co·ro·nae** *n.* a luminous ring formed by reflection on a fogbank or cloud ‖ the projecting part of a cornice ‖ any of various bones etc. shaped like a crown

cor·o·nar·y *adj.* of or pertaining to a crown ‖ pertaining to either of two arteries arising from the aorta and supplying blood to the heart muscles

cor·o·na·tion *n.* the act of crowning a sovereign

cor·o·ner n. a public officer whose most usual task is to hold an inquiry into the causes of accidental or suspicious deaths **cór·o·ner·ship** n.

cor·po·ral adj. belonging or relating to the body

corporal n. a noncommissioned officer in the army

cor·po·rate adj. combined into one ‖ incorporated ‖ belonging to an incorporated body, or corporation

cor·po·ra·tion n. a body or society entitled to act as a single person

cor·po·ra·tive adj. relating to or consisting of a corporation

corps pl. **corps** n. part of an army forming a tactical unit ‖ a body of specialist troops

corpse n. the dead body of a human being

cor·pu·lence n. the state or quality of being corpulent **cór·pu·len·cy** n.

cor·pu·lent adj. having a fat body

cor·pus·cle n. any minute body

cor·pus·cu·lar adj. of or pertaining to corpuscles

cor·ral 1. n. an enclosure for cattle, horses etc. 2. v.t. **cor·ral·ling cor·ralled** to put or drive (animals) into a corral

cor·rect 1. v.t. to put right ‖ to remove faults from ‖ to admonish, reprove ‖ to adjust 2. adj. true ‖ accurate ‖ conventional

cor·rec·tion n. an emendation ‖ a punishing ‖ an allowance made for something to ensure accuracy

cor·re·late 1. n. either of two things or words implying the other, e.g. 'father' and 'son' 2. v. **cor·re·lat·ing cor·re·lat·ed** v.t. to connect systematically **cor·re·la·tion** n.

cor·re·spond v.i. to communicate, esp. by letter ‖ to be similar in function, position etc. ‖ to be in agreement or harmony **cor·re·spónd·ing** adj.

cor·re·spond·ence n. the state of having qualities in common ‖ an exchange of letters

cor·re·spond·ent 1. n. a person with whom one exchanges letters ‖ a journalist employed to send regular reports 2. adj. corresponding

cor·ri·dor n. a long passageway with doors leading off it into separate rooms

cor·rob·o·rate   cor·rob·o·rat·ing cor·rob·o·rat·ed v.t. to confirm by law ‖ to give evidence to support

cor·rob·o·ra·tion n. confirmation

cor·rode cor·rod·ing cor·rod·ed v.t. to eat away by degrees of ‖ to consume ‖ v.i. to become eaten away

cor·ro·sion n. the process of wearing away the surface of a solid

cor·ro·sive 1. adj. producing corrosion ‖ corroding the mind 2. n. a substance which corrodes

cor·ru·gate cor·ru·gat·ing cor·ru·gat·ed v.t. to form into wrinkles, folds, alternate ridges and grooves **cor·ru·gá·tion** n.

cor·rupt 1. adj. depraved ‖ changed from a sound to a putrid state ‖ dishonest, open to bribery 2. v.t. to pervert, make wicked ‖ to defile, taint ‖ to falsify ‖ to bribe ‖ v.i. to become corrupt

cor·rupt·i·bil·i·ty n. the state or quality of being corruptible

cor·rupt·i·ble adj. open to corruption, esp. to bribes **cor·rúpt·i·bly** adv.

cor·rup·tion n. a spoiling ‖ corrupt practices ‖ perversion ‖ moral decay ‖ a corrupting influence ‖ a debased form of a word

cor·sage n. the bodice of a woman's dress ‖ a spray of flowers to be worn on a dress

cor·set n. a close-fitting woman's undergarment

cos·met·ic 1. adj. designed to beautify 2. n. a preparation to enhance beauty **cos·me·ti·cian** n. a person skilled in the use of cosmetics

cos·mic adj. of or pertaining to the cosmos **cós·mi·cal·ly** adv.

cos·mo·pol·i·tan 1. adj. free from local, provincial or national prejudices ‖ composed of many nationalities, languages etc. 2. n. someone who is cosmopolitan

cos·mos n. the universe ‖ an ordered

system of ideas, self-inclusive and harmonious

cost *n.* the price paid or to be paid for something ‖ an item in the outlay of time, labor, trouble etc. on a job

cost cost·ing cost *v.t.* to require an outlay or expenditure of

cost·ly cost·li·er cost·li·est *adj.* expensive ‖ involving great loss ‖ sumptuous, luxurious

cos·tume 1. *n.* style of clothing in general ‖ a suit or dress worn at fancy-dress balls **2.** *v.t.* **cos·tum·ing cos·tumed** to supply with a costume

cot *n.* a camp bed or other small, narrow bed

co·til·lion *n.* a ballroom or country dance for couples ‖ a formal ball

cot·tage *n.* a small house, esp. in the country

cot·ton 1. *n.* a plant ‖ the soft, white fiber enclosing the seeds of the cotton plant ‖ a thread or textile of this fiber **2.** *adj.* made of cotton

cot·ton·y *adj.* of or like cotton

couch *n.* a piece of upholstered furniture

cough 1. *v.i.* to make a cough ‖ (of an engine) to fire irregularly **2.** *n.* a sudden forced expulsion of air from the lungs, and the noise made by this

could *past, conditional* and *pres. conditional* of CAN

coun·cil *n.* a consultative or advisory assembly ‖ a body elected or appointed to advise or legislate

coun·cil·lor, coun·ci·lor *n.* a member of a council **cóun·cil·lor·ship, cóun·ci·lor·ship** *n.*

coun·cil·man *pl.* **coun·cil·men** *n.* a member of a council, esp. of a city council

coun·sel *n.* advise resulting from consultation ‖ a legal adviser

counsel coun·sel·ing coun·seled *v.t.* to advise, recommend **cóun·sel·ing** *n.* a professional guidance service for individuals

coun·se·lor, coun·sel·lor *n.* an adviser, esp. a legal adviser ‖ an academic adviser ‖ a person in charge of a group of children at camp

count *n.* a European title of nobility ‖ a nobleman holding it

count *v.t.* to add up ‖ to repeat (numbers in order, up to and including a specified number) ‖ to consider (a thing or person) as belonging to a specified class ‖ *v.i.* to name or add up numbers in order ‖ to be important, have significance

coun·te·nance *n.* the expression on a face **countenance coun·te·nanc·ing coun·te·nanced** *v.t.* to show open approval of, support

coun·ter *adj.* opposite, contrary **1.** *adv.* in the opposite direction **2.** *v.i.* to answer an attack

coun·ter *n.* a flat-topped piece of shop furniture dividing sales attendants from customers ‖ a similar fitting in a bank

coun·ter *n.* a computer, device for counting

coun·ter·act *v.t.* to neutralize ‖ to act in opposition to **coun·ter·ác·tion** *n.* **coun·ter·ác·tive** *adj.*

coun·ter·feit 1. *adj.* spurious, copied or made in imitation and pretending to be genuine ‖ feigned **2.** *n.* a counterfeit object **3.** *v.t.* to imitate **cóun·ter·feit·er** *n.* a person who makes false money

coun·ter·part *n.* a person or thing complementary to, or completing, another

coun·ter·sign *v.t.* to add a ratifying signature

coun·tess *n.* the wife or widow of an earl or a count

count·less *adj.* innumerable

coun·tri·fied *adj.* characteristic of rural life

coun·try *pl.* **coun·tries** *n.* a region, district, tract of land ‖ the land in which one was born ‖ a political state ‖ regions of woods and fields, esp. as opposed to towns

coun·try·man *pl.* **coun·try·men** *n.* a compatriot

coun·ty *pl.* **coun·ties** *n.* the largest local govrenment division within a state

coup *pl*. **coups** *n*. a sudden successful stroke, blow or stratagem

coupe *n*. a closed automobile, esp. a two-seater

cou·ple *n*. a pair ‖ roughly two

couple cou·pling cou·pled *v.t.* to join, fasten ‖ to bring together, pair off ‖ *v.i.* to unite sexually **cou·pler** *n*. a device for joining two things ‖ coupling

cou·pon *n*. a detachable slip of paper giving entitlement to a payment of interest or to some service ‖ a sales promotion voucher

cour·age *n*. the capacity to meet danger without giving way to fear

cou·ra·geous *adj*. possessing or marked by courage

cour·i·er *n*. a special messenger

course 1. *n*. the direction of travel or path taken ‖ ordinary sequence ‖ a line of conduct ‖ golf links ‖ a channel in which water flows ‖ a series of lectures etc. ‖ any of the successive parts of a meal **2.** *v*. **cours·ing coursed** *v.t.* to hunt by sight and not by scent ‖ *v.i.* to move or flow quickly

court 1. *n*. an uncovered area surrounded by walls or buildings and planned as a unit ‖ an enclosed space, open or covered, marked off for certain games ‖ a palace ‖ a sovereign's family and his retinue ‖ a place or hall where justice is administered ‖ the judges, magistrates, coroners and other officials acting as a tribunal to administer justice **2.** *v.t.* to try to gain the favor or affection ‖ to seek in marriage ‖ to allure, attract, entice

cour·te·ous *adj*. polite, civil, considerate in manner

cour·te·sy *pl*. **cour·te·sies** *n*. polite, kind, considerate behavior or an instance of it

court·li·ness *n*. the quality of being courtly

court·ly court·li·er court·li·est *adj*. having or showing very polished, formal manners

court-mar·tial 1. *pl*. **courts-mar·tial, court-mar·tials** *n*. a judicial court of military or naval officers to try soldiers'

or sailors' offenses **2.** *v.t.* **court-mar·tial·ing, court-mar·tial·ling court-mar·tialed, court-mar·tialled** to try by court-martial

court·ship *n*. the wooing of a person

cous·in *n*. a first cousin ‖ a first cousin once removed, second cousin, second cousin once removed etc., or any distant relative

cou·tu·ri·er *n*. a dress designer of a high-class fashion house

cove 1. *n*. a small sheltered bay ‖ a concave molding or arch

cov·e·nant 1. *n*. an agreement, bargain ‖ a sealed contract

cov·er 1. *v.t.* to place a cover on or over ‖ to hide ‖ to keep under aim ‖ to protect financially ‖ to be enough to defray the costs of ‖ to deal with, embrace ‖ to pass over ‖ *(journalism)* to report **2.** *n*. something which extends over a thing ‖ the binding of a book ‖ a stamped envelope that has passed through the mail ‖ insurance to protect against loss

cov·ert *adj*. hidden, secret, disguised

cov·et *v.t.* to long to possess **cóv·et·ous** *adj*. strongly desiring another person's property

cow *pl*. **cows** *n*. a fully grown female animal of the ox family

cow *v.t.* to intimidate, browbeat

cow·ard *n*. a person without courage

cow·ard·ice *n*. a lack or failure of courage

cow·er *v.t.* to crouch or shrink back, esp. from fear

cowl *n*. the hood of a monk's habit ‖ part of an automobile to which are fitted the windshield and dashboard

coy *adj*. coquettishly bashful

coy·o·te *n*. a small wolf of North America

co·zi·ness, co·si·ness *n*. the state or quality of being cozy

co·zy, co·sy 1. co·zi·er, co·si·er co·zi·est, co·si·est *adj*. nicely relaxing, comfortable **2.** *n*. a cover placed over a teapot etc. to keep it warm

crab *n*. popular name for 10-legged, short-tailed crustaceans ‖ an ill-tempered person

crab crab·bing crabbed v.t. (of hawks) to scratch or pull to pieces ‖ v.i. to find fault

crab apple a wild apple with bitter fruit

crab·by crab·bi·er crab·bi·est adj. crabbed (ill-tempered, morose, peevish)

crack 1. v.t. to fracture without complete separation ‖ to make a sudden, sharp sound ‖ to fail, give way **2.** n. a sudden, sharp sound ‖ a partial breakage ‖ a narrow opening ‖ a highly potent and addictive cocaine distillate in rock form ‖ a joke **3.** adj. first-class, of the highest quality

crack·er n. a flat, dry, crisp cake ‖ a firework that explodes with a sharp crack

crack·le 1. n. a slight, sharp, cracking sound ‖ a network of surface cracks in some glazes and in some glassware **2.** v.i. **crack·ling crack·led** to make little crackling sounds

cra·dle 1. n. a small bed or cot for a baby ‖ a place where something begins or is nurtured **2.** v.t. **cra·dling cra·dled** to hold (esp. a baby) in one's arms as if in a cradle

craft n. a trade or occupation that requires skill in the use of the mind and hands ‖ cunning, deceit, guile ‖ a boat or vessel or aircraft

crafts·man pl. **crafts·men** n. a skilled worker practicing a particular craft **crafts·man·ship** n.

craft·y craft·i·er craft·i·est adj. cunning, wily, deceitful

crag n. a steep, rugged rock or cliff

crag·ged adj. craggy

crag·gy crag·gi·er crag·gi·est adj. having many crags

cram cram·ming crammed v.t. to force ‖ to stuff ‖ v.i. to eat greedily ‖ to learn hurriedly without prolonged study

cramp 1. n. a sudden painful contraction of the muscles ‖ (pl.) severe pains in the stomach **2.** v.t. to hinder, restrict **cramped** adj. restricted ‖ narrow-minded

cran·ber·ry pl. **cran·ber·ries** n. the tart, red, edible berry

crane 1. n. a family of tall, wading birds ‖ a machine for raising and lowering heavy weights **2.** v. **cran·ing craned** v.t. to raise by a crane ‖ v.i. to stretch one's neck

cra·ni·um pl. **cra·ni·ums, cra·ni·a** n. the skull of any vertebrate

crank 1. n. an arm set at right angles to a shaft or axle, used for converting reciprocal (to-and-fro) motion into circular motion ‖ an odd or eccentric person

crank·i·ness n. the state or quality of being cranky

crank·y crank·i·er crank·i·est adj. irritable, crotchety ‖ capricious ‖ crazy

crash 1. n. a sudden, violent noise ‖ a collision of vehicles ‖ the collapse of a business **2.** v.i. to make a violent noise ‖ to come into collision ‖ v.t. to attend (a party) without being invited

crass adj. gross ‖ extremely stupid

crate 1. n. a framework of wooden boards for protecting something during transport **2.** v.t. **crat·ing crat·ed**

cra·ter n. any bowl-shaped depression or cavity

cra·vat n. a trade term for any necktie

crave crav·ing craved v.t. to desire strongly, urgently and persistently

cra·ven 1. adj. cowardly, abject

crav·ing n. a strong, urgent and persistent desire

crawl 1. v.i. to move forward on hands and knees ‖ to make one's way slowly and painfully ‖ (of plants) to creep along the ground or up a wall **2.** n. a powerful overarm stroke in swimming

cray·fish pl. **cray·fish, cray·fish·es** n. any of various long-tailed, freshwater edible crustaceans

cray·on 1. n. a stick of colored chalk or chalk and wax for drawing with

craze 1. n. a great or fashionable enthusiasm for something

cra·zy cra·zi·er cra·zi·est adj. foolish ‖ insane ‖ very enthusiastic

creak 1. n. a harsh grating or squeaking

sound **2.** *v.i.* to make such a sound

cream 1. *n.* fatty part of milk ‖ a cream-like cosmetic ointment ‖ the best part of anything ‖ the color of cream, a pale yellow **2.** *v.t.* to rub a cosmetic cream into (the skin)

cream·y cream·i·er cream·i·est *adj.* having the consistency or color of cream

crease 1. *n.* a wrinkle or fold mark **2.** *v.* **creas·ing creased** *v.i.* to wrinkle ‖ to become creased

cre·ate cre·at·ing cre·at·ed *v.t.* to bring into being ‖ to produce

cre·a·tion *n.* the act of creating ‖ everything that has been created, the universe **the Creation** the creation of the world by God

cre·a·tive 1. *adj.* having the quality or power of creating ‖ imaginative

cre·a·tiv·i·ty *n.* creativeness

cre·a·tor *n.* someone who creates

crea·ture *n.* a living human or animal

cre·den·tials *pl. n.* a letter establishing the authority of the bearer

cred·i·bil·i·ty *n.* the state or quality of being credible

cred·i·ble *adj.* believable **créd·i·bly** *adv.*

cred·it 1. *n.* the power to obtain goods without immediate payment ‖ a favorable balance of an account ‖ belief ‖ an acknowledgment of merit **2.** *v.t.* to believe ‖ to trust **créd·it·a·ble** *adj.* **créd·it·a·bly** *adv.*

cred·i·tor *n.* someone to whom a debt is owing

cre·do *pl.* **cre·dos** *n.* a creed

cred·u·lous *adj.* gullible, ready to believe without proof

creed *n.* a set of beliefs or opinions

creek *n.* a small tributary river or stream

creep 1. *v.* **creep·ing crept** to move along close to the ground ‖ to move or act in a servile manner ‖ (of time etc.) to go slowly **2.** *n.* the act or pace of creeping **the creeps** a sensation of fear or horror

creep·y creep·i·er creep·i·est a physical sensation of fear or disgust

cre·mate cre·mat·ing cre·mat·ed *v.t.* to burn, incinerate **cre·ma·tion** *n.*

crepe, craepe, crape *n.* a thin fabric, usually of silk, with a wrinkled surface

cres·cent 1. *n.* the moon in its first or last quarter ‖ any crescentshaped object **2.** *adj.* crescentshaped

crest 1. *n.* the comb or tuft on the head of a bird or animal ‖ ornament on top of a helmet ‖ the top of a hill or wave ‖ *v.i.* to rise or form into a crest

cre·vasse *n.* a deep crevice

crev·ice *n.* a narrow crack or split

crew *n.* a body of men working together at a task ‖ a rowing team

crib 1. *n.* a barred wooden manger for animal fodder ‖ a bed for a small child ‖ a crèche ‖ plagiarism, a theft of other people's ideas etc. **2.** *v.* **crib·bing cribbed** *v.t.* to copy unfairly ‖ to plagiarize

crick·et *n.* insect allied to the cicada

cricket *n.* an outdoor team game

crime *n.* a violation of the law ‖ a foolish or ill-considered action

crim·i·nal 1. *adj.* relating to crime **2.** *n.* someone who has committed a crime

crimp 1. *v.t.* to pinch into waves or ridges **2.** *n.* wave or undulation **crimp·y crimp·i·er crimp·i·est** *adj.* crimped in appearance

crim·son 1. *n.* a deep red color

cringe cring·ing cringed *v.i.* to cower, shrink in fear ‖ to behave servilely

crin·kle 1. *v.* **crin·kling crin·kled** *v.i.* to wrinkle **2.** *n.* a crease, wrinkle **crin·kly** *adj.*

crip·ple 1. *n.* a badly lamed or disabled person **2.** *v.t.* **crip·pling crip·pled** to disable, lame ‖ to frustrate, hinder

cri·sis *pl.* **cri·ses** *n.* the turning point ‖ decisive moment

crisp 1. *adj.* firm and fresh ‖ concise, clear and direct

crisp·y crisp·i·er crisp·i·est *adj.* crisp

cri·te·ri·on *pl.* **cri·te·ri·a, cri·te·ri·ons** *n.* a standard or principle by which a thing is judged

crit·ic *n.* a person skilled in forming opinions and giving a judgment ‖ a professional reviewer

crit·i·cal *adj.* given to severe judgements ‖ discerning, based on thorough knowledge

crit·i·cism *n.* the art of judging merit ‖ censure, unfavorable comment

crit·i·cize crit·i·ciz·ing crit·i·cized *v.t.* to assess the merits and demerits of ‖ to censure ‖ *v.i.* to find fault

croak 1. *v.i.* to utter a deep hoarse sound ‖ to talk dismally 2. *n.* a hoarse, harsh sound **cróak·i·ly** *adv.* **cróak·y** *adj.*

cro·chet *n.* a kind of needlework

crock·er·y *n.* earthenware vessels

croc·o·dile *n.* amphibious reptile

crook 1. *n.* a crosier ‖ anything hooked or bent ‖ a thief, criminal **crook·ed** *adj.* not straight, twisted ‖ dishonest

croon 1. *v.i.* to sing or hum in an undertone 2. *n.* the sound made by crooning **cróon·er** *n.* a singer of sentimental songs

crop 1. *n.* harvested grain, fruit etc. ‖ cultivated produce while growing ‖ a group of things coming together ‖ a bird's gullet ‖ a hunting awhip 2. **crop·ping cropped** *v.t.* to cut (hair) short ‖ to cut off parts of a photograph ‖ to reap, harvest

cro·quet 1. *n.* a game

cro·quette *n.* a ball of minced meat, fish etc. coated with crumbs and fried

cross 1. *n.* a figure or mark made by placing one line across another (×, +, †) ‖ an upright wooden stake with a horizontal crossbar ‖ interbreeding ‖ the product of mixed breeding ‖ *(plumbing)* a four-way joint in the form of a cross 2. *v.t.* to go across ‖ to place crosswise ‖ (with off or out) to draw a line through (written matter) to cancel it ‖ to thwart, frustrate ‖ to meet and pass ‖ to interbreed 3. *adj.* transverse ‖ contrary, opposite ‖ peevish, annoyed

cross-ex·am·ine cross-ex·am·in·ing cross-ex·am·ined *v.t.* to question closely

cross·ing *n.* the act of crossing ‖ an intersection

crotch *n.* a fork, e.g. of a tree ‖ the bifur-cation of the human body

crouch 1. *v.i.* to stoop or bend 2. *n.* a crouching position

crou·ton *n.* a small piece of toasted or fried bread

crow *n.* a passerine bird **as the crow flies** (of distances) in a straight line **to eat crow** to admit humbly that one was wrong

crow 1. *v.i.* **crow·ing crowed** to utter the loud shrill cry of a cock ‖ to utter a cry of delight ‖ to boast 2. *n.*

crow·bar *n.* an iron bar with a wedge at the working end used as a lever

crowd 1. *n.* a large number of people ‖ a clique, set 2. *v.t.* to throng together ‖ to press forward

crown 1. *n.* a royal headdress ‖ an emblem resembling this ‖ a reward ‖ the top part of the head ‖ the crest of a road ‖ the crest of a bird ‖ the exposed part of a tooth ‖ the leafy upper part of a tree ‖ a perfecting touch, completion 2. *v.t.* to place a crown on (someone's head) ‖ to complete, perfect, put the finishing touch to

cru·cial *adj.* decisive, critical ‖ fundamental

cru·ci·ble *n.* a vessel for melting substances requiring extreme heat

cru·ci·fix *n.* a cross with the figure of Christ on it

cru·ci·fy cru·ci·fy·ing cru·ci·fied *v.t.* to put to death by nailing to a cross ‖ to torment

crude crud·er crud·est *adj.* raw ‖ unpolished, graceless ‖ blunt ‖ vulgar

cru·el *adj.* liking to inflict pain and suffering **crú·el·ty** *pl.* **cru·el·ties** *n.*

cruise 1. *v.i.* **cruis·ing cruised** to make a sea voyage for pleasure ‖ to sail about with no special destination ‖ to drive slowly about (e.g. of a taxi looking for fares) 2. *n.* a sea voyage for pleasure

cruis·er *n.* a warship

crumb 1. *n.* a small fragment

crum·ble crum·bling crum·bled *v.t.* to break into small pieces ‖ *v.i.* to fall to pieces ‖ to fail **crúm·bly crum·bli·er crum·bli·est**

adj.

crum·ple crum·pling crum·pled *v.t.* to crush into a mass of creases ‖ *v.i.* to become creased ‖ to collapse

crunch 1. *v.t.* to crush noisily with the teeth ‖ to crush underfoot with a similar noise **2.** *n.* the act of crunching ‖ high-pressure situation

cru·sade 1. *n.* any war undertaken in the name of religion ‖ any energetic movement to remove an evil or improve a situation **2.** *v.i.* **cru·sad·ing cru·sad·ed**

crush 1. *v.t.* to crease ‖ to reduce to a powder or to small pieces under pressure ‖ to squash ‖ to subdue ‖ to hug violently ‖ *v.i.* to squeeze **2.** *n.* a crushing or being crushed ‖ a large crowd of people ‖ an infatuation

crust 1. *n.* the crisp outer part of bread ‖ the pastry cover of a pie ‖ a hard outer surface or covering ‖ the light, thin mantle of the earth ‖ a scab **2.** *v.t.* to form into, or become covered with a crust

crus·ta·cean *n.* mostly aquatic arthropod

crust·i·ness *n.* the state or quality of being crusty

crust·y crust·i·er crust·i·est *adj.* having a crisp crust ‖ gruff, hard to approach

crutch *n.* support to help a lame person to walk ‖ a support, something one relies upon

cry cry·ing cried *v.i.* to call out ‖ *v.t.* to shout ‖ to announce for sale by shouting

cry *pl.* **cries** *n.* a shout or wail ‖ a fit of weeping

cry·ing *adj.* calling urgently for attention, flagrant

crypt *n.* an underground room or cell **cryp·tic** *adj.* enigmatic **crýp·ti·cal·ly** *adv.*

crys·tal 1. *n.* transparent quartz, often cut for ornamental use ‖ a very clear and transparent kind of glass **2.** *adj.* perfectly clear

crys·tal·li·za·tion *n.* the process of crystallizing

crys·tal·lize crys·tal·liz·ing crys·tal·lized *v.i.* (of ideas) to become clear and definite ‖ *v.t.* to cause to assume the form

of a crystal

cub *n.* a young bear, fox, lion, tiger, wolf etc.

cube *n.* a geometrical solid bounded by six plane faces of equal area and making right angles with one another

cube cub·ing cubed *v.t.* to cut into cubes

cu·bic *adj.* having the properties of a cube **cú·bi·cal** *adj.* cube-shaped

cuck·oo *pl.* **cuck·oos 1.** *n.* a European bird **2.** *adj.* (pop.) foolish

cu·cum·ber *n.* a genus of annual trailing vines ‖ the long green fleshy fruit

cud·dle *v.* **cud·dling cud·dled** *v.t.* to hold closely and fondly ‖ *v.i.* to curl up, nestle **cud·dle·some** *adj.* **cúd·dly** *adj.*

cudg·el 1. *n.* a short, stout stick used as a weapon **2.** *v.t.* **cudg·el·ing cudg·eled** to beat

cue 1. *n.* an agreed signal ‖ a hint meant to guide behavior etc. **2.** **cu·ing cued** *v.t.* to give a cue to

cue *n.* a long leather-tipped rod for striking the ball in billiards ‖ a queue of people **1.** **cu·ing cued** to strike with a cue

cuff *n.* the part of a sleeve which is turned back at the wrist ‖ the turned-up end of a trouser leg

cuff 1. *v.t.* to strike with the open palm or back of the hand **2.** *n.* the blow given in this way

cui·sine *n.* cooking with reference to quality or style

cu·li·nar·y *adj.* relating to cooking or the kitchen

cull 1. *v.t.* to pick, gather (flowers, facts etc.) **2.** *n.* something picked out as substandard

cul·mi·nate cul·mi·nat·ing cul·mi·nat·ed *v.i.* to reach a climax **cul·mi·ná·tion** *n.* a climax

cul·prit *n.* a guilty person ‖ a person accused of an offense, prisoner at the bar

cult *n.* a system of religious worship ‖ a creed or sect

cul·ti·vate cul·ti·vat·ing cul·ti·vat·ed *v.t.* to prepare (land) for crops ‖ to improve, refine ‖ to foster, cause to develop

cúl·ti·vat·ed *adj.* not left to grow wild ‖ (of people) cultured

cul·ti·va·tion *n.* refinement (of the mind, taste etc.)

cul·tur·al *adj.* of, or relating to, culture or a culture

cul·ture 1. *n.* the training and development of the mind ‖ the social and religious structures and intellectual and artistic manifestations etc. that characterize a society ‖ the cultivation of tissues or microorganisms in prepared media **2.** *v.t.* **cul·tur·ing cul·tured** to make a culture of

cul·vert *n.* a drain ‖ an underground channel

cum·ber *v.t.* to hinder or burden, encumber

cum·ber·some *adj.* burdensome ‖ (of objects) unwieldy

cu·mu·late cu·mu·lat·ing acu·mu·lat·ed *v.t.* to heap up, amass ‖ *v.i.* to become massed **cu·mu·la·tion** *n.* **cu·mu·la·tive** *adj.* gradually increasing by successive additions

cun·ning 1. *adj.* crafty, full of deceit ‖ skillful ‖ sweet, charming **2.** *n.* guile ‖ skill, dexterity

cup 1. *n.* a small bowl-shaped vessel ‖ an ornamental vessel offered as a sports trophy etc. ‖ a measure in cookery **2.** *v.t.* **cup·ping cupped** to form into a cup

cup·cake *n.* a small cake baked in a cup-shaped tin

cup·ful *pl.* **cup·fuls** *n.* as much as a cup will hold

cu·pid·i·ty *n.* avarice, greed, esp. for wealth

cu·po·la *n.* a rounded roof or ceiling ‖ a small dome-shaped superstructure on a roof

cup·ping *n.* the application of a cup-shaped instrument to the skin to draw the blood to the surface for bloodletting

cur *n.* a mongrel dog

cu·rate *n.* an assistant to a vicar or a rector

cu·ra·tor *n.* a person in charge of a museum **cu·ra·to·ri·al** *adj.* **cu·rá·tor·ship** *n.*

curb 1. *n.* a restraint, control ‖ a protective barrier **2.** *v.t.* to restrain

curd *n.* (esp. *pl.*) the smooth, thickened part of sour milk

cur·dle cur·dling cur·dled *v.t.* to cause to clot, congeal ‖ *v.i.* to form into curds ‖ to thicken, congeal

cure *n.* a remedy ‖ a successful treatment

cure *v.t.* **cur·ing cured** to restore to health ‖ to preserve by smoking, salting, pickling etc. ‖ *v.i.* to become cured

cur·few *n.* a fixed time after which no citizen may remain outdoors

cu·ri·o *pl.* **cu·ri·os** *n.* an interesting object

cu·ri·os·i·ty *pl.* **cu·ri·os·i·ties** *n.* eagerness to know ‖ inquisitiveness ‖ strangeness

cu·ri·ous *adj.* odd, unusual ‖ inquisitive ‖ anxious to learn

curl 1. *v.t.* to cause to form into curls ‖ *v.i.* to form into curls ‖ to move in spirals **2.** *n.* a lock of hair growing in a coiled shape, a ringlet **cúrl·er** *n.* a pin etc. for curling the hair

curl·y curl·ier curl·i·est *adj.* curling ‖ having curls

cur·rant *n.* a genus of cold-climate bush fruits ‖ a small dried grape

cur·ren·cy *pl.* **cur·ren·cies** *n.* the coins, notes or other tokens in circulation as a means of exchange

cur·rent *adj.* prevalent ‖ of the present time

current *n.* a mass of air, water or other fluid moving in a certain direction ‖ the most rapidly moving part of a river etc. ‖ electric current

cur·ric·u·lum *pl.* **cur·ric·u·lums, ocur·ric·u·la** *n.* a course of study, esp. at a school or college

cur·ry 1. *pl.* **cur·ries** *n.* a hot-tasting powder ‖ a dish flavored with this powder **2.** *v.t.* **cur·ry·ing cur·ried** to cook with curry

curry cur·ry·ing cur·ried *v.t.* to rub down and comb (a horse) **to curry favor** to seek favor by flattery

curse curs·ing cursed, curst *v.t.* utter a curse ‖ to bring harm upon ‖ to swear at ‖ *v.i.* to swear or blaspheme **curs·ed**

curst *adj.* under a curse ‖ evil, hateful

cur·so·ry *adj.* hurried, superficial

curt *adj.* short in speech ‖ abrupt, impolitely brief

cur·tail *v.t.* to cut short ‖ to cut off **cur·táil·ment** *n.*

cur·tain 1. *n.* a hanging cloth used esp. to screen or adorn windows ‖ the hanging drape dividing a theater stage from the auditorium

curve 1. *n.* a line subject to continuous deviation from the straight ‖ a thing or part shaped thus ‖ *(baseball)* a ball pitched with spin so that it curves ‖ an unfair act or statement **2.** *v.* **curv·ing curved** *v.i.* to take on the shape of a curve ‖ to move in a curved path

cush·ion 1. *n.* a cloth case stuffed with down or feathers, kapok, foam rubber etc. ‖ something that serves as a shock absorber ‖ the soft part of a horse's foot protected by the horny hoof **2.** *v.t.* to supply with cushions ‖ to shield (a person) e.g. from the full force of hostile criticism

cus·tard *n.* a sweetened mixture of eggs and milk baked or steamed

cus·to·di·an *n.* a guardian or keeper **cus·tó·di·an·ship** *n.*

cus·to·dy *n.* guardianship, care ‖ imprisonment

cus·tom 1. *n.* a generally accepted practice or habit, convention ‖ *(pl.)* duties levied on imported goods **2.** *adj.* made-to-order

cus·tom·ar·y 1. *adj.* usual, according to custom

cus·tom·er *n.* a person wishing to make a purchase from a store or firm

cut 1. *v.* **cut·ting cut** *v.t.* to make an incision in ‖ to wound ‖ to sever ‖ to separate into slices or pieces ‖ to cross, intersect ‖ to reduce ‖ to shorten ‖ to refuse to recognize (an acquaintance) ‖ to divide (a pack of playing cards) **2.** *n.* a gash, incision or wound ‖ a reduction ‖ an excision ‖ a share **3.** *adj.* having been cut ‖ reduced

cute cut·er cut·est *adj.* attractive, charming ‖ sharp-witted

cu·ti·cle *n.* the epidermis ‖ the hardened skin around the edges of fingernails and toenails

cut·ler·y *n.* knives, forks and spoons ‖ other edged instruments (shears, razors etc.)

cut·let *n.* a small chop for grilling or frying

cut-rate *adj.* offered for sale at a price below the general market price

cut·ting 1. *n.* a small shoot bearing leaf buds and used for propagation **2.** *adj.* sharp ‖ piercing ‖ sarcastic, unkind

cy·a·nide *n.* a compound of cyanogen and a metal

cy·cle 1. *n.* a series of recurring events ‖ a period of time occupied by a set of events ‖ a series of poems or songs with a central theme ‖ the period of an alternating electric current ‖ a bicycle or tricycle **2.** *v.i.* **cy·cling cy·cled** to move in cycles ‖ to ride a bicycle

cy·clic *adj.* recurring in cycles ‖ of or related to a cycle

cy·clist *n.* someone who rides a bicycle

cy·clone *n.* a region of low atmospheric pressure characterized by rotating winds

cy·clo·tron *n.* a device used to produce and focus a beam of high-energy positive ions

cyl·in·der *n.* a solid figure traced out when a rectangle rotates using one of its sides as the axis of rotation ‖ a solid or hollow body having this form ‖ the revolving part of a revolver

cy·lin·dri·cal *adj.* cylinder-shaped

cym·bal *n.* one of a pair of shallow brass plates clashed together **cým·bal·ist** *n.*

cyn·ic 1. *n.* someone who believes that self-interest is the motive of all human conduct **2.** *adj.* cynical thinking like a cynic or revealing such thoughts **cyn·i·cism** *n.* the quality of being cynical

cy·press *n.* a genus of coniferous trees ‖ the hard wood of these trees

cyst a sac containing fluid or semifluid morbid matter ‖ a nonliving membrane enclosing a cell or cells

cyst·ic *adj.* of or like a cyst

czar, tsar, tzar *n.* the emperor of Russia

czar·e·vitch, tsar·e·vitch *n.* the son of a czar

cza·ri·na, tsa·ri·na *n.* the wife of a czar

D

D, d the fourth letter of the English alphabet

dab 1. dab·bing dabbed *v.t.* to touch lightly and quickly ‖ to apply (a substance) by light strokes ‖ *v.i.* to make a weak striking movement **2.** *n.* a light, quick blow

dab·ble dab·bling dab·bled *v.t.* to splash about ‖ *v.i.* to take up a pursuit without serious and consistent effort **dáb·bler** *n.* a dilettante

daft *adj.* foolish, crazy

dag·ger *n.* a short, knifelike weapon for stabbing

dai·ly 1. *adj.* happening or recurring every day **2.** *adv.* every day

dain·ty dain·ti·er dain·ti·est *adj.* small and pretty, delicate

dair·y *pl.* **dair·ies** *n.* the part of a farm given over to milk, cream, butter, cheese etc.

da·is *pl.* **da·is·es** *n.* a raised platform in a hall

dai·sy *pl.* **dai·sies** *n.* any of several composite plants

dale *n.* a valley

dal·li·ance *n.* amorous by ‖ frivolous spending of time

dal·ly dal·ly·ing dal·lied *v.i.* to waste time ‖ to play

dam 1. *n.* a barrier constructed to hold back a flow of water **2.** *v.t.* **dam·ming dammed** to hold back (water) by constructing a dam

dam·age 1. *v.* **dam·ag·ing dam·aged** *v.t.* to injure physically ‖ *v.i.* to incur damage **2.** *n.* injury or harm **dám·age·a·ble** *adj.*

damn 1. *v.t.* to condemn ‖ to curse **2.** *adv.* damned

dam·na·ble *adj.* deserving condemnation ‖ detestable

dam·na·tion *n.* a condemning to eternal punishment

damp 1. *n.* moisture in a permeable object, esp. a fabric ‖ moisture in the air **2.** *adj.* slightly wet **3.** *v.t.* to moisten **dámp·en** *v.* to make slightly wet ‖ to depress, discourage

dance *n.* the act of dancing ‖ a series of set movements to music ‖ a party or social gathering

dance danc·ing danced *v.i.* to move rhythmically, alone or with a partner ‖ *v.t.* to dandle

danc·er *n.* a person dancing

dan·de·li·on *n.* a perennial plant

dan·druff *n.* small scales of dead skin on the scalp

dan·ger *n.* peril, exposure to harm, injury ‖ a thing or circumstance that constitutes a peril

dan·gle dan·gling dan·gled *v.i.* to be hanging loosely ‖ *v.t.* to cause to swing lightly to and fro

dank *adj.* cold and damp ‖ smelling unpleasantly

dap·per *adj.* neat and spruce in appearance

dap·ple dap·pling dap·pled *v.t.* to mark with irregular spots or patches of color

dap·pled *adj.* marked with irregular spots or patches of color

dare 1. *v.i.* **dar·ing dared** to have enough courage ‖ *v.t.* to challenge (someone) to do something as test of courage **2.** *n.* a challenge to do something as a test of courage

dar·ing 1. *n.* bravery **2.** *adj.* boldly unconventional

dark 1. *adj.* partly or totally devoid of light (of color) of a deep shade ‖ very unpromising ‖ obscure ‖ mysterious **2.** a total absence of light ‖ night **3.** *v.t.* to make dark

dar·ling 1. *n.* a beloved person **2.** *adj.* lovable

darn 1. *v.t.* to damn **2.** *interj.* damn! **darned 3.** *adj.* confounded, damnable **4.** *adv.* extremely

dart 1. *n.* a sharply-pointed light missile ‖ a feathered and pointed object thrown in the game of darts ‖ a sudden swift movement ‖ a short, tapering tuck **2.** *v.* to move swiftly and suddenly

dash *v.t.* to smash, shatter ‖ to throw violently ‖ to splash ‖ *v.i.* to go in a great hurry ‖ to discourage, disappoint *n.*

a rush, sudden movement ‖ a sprint ‖ a punctuation mark (−) ‖ a small amount ‖ verve

dash·board n. the instrument panel of a car, boat etc.

das·tard 1. n. a coward ‖ a cad 2. adj. cowardly and mean **dás·tard·ly** adj.

date 1. the day of the month and year ‖ an appointment, esp. with a person of the opposite sex ‖ a person of the opposite sex with whom an appointment is made 2. **dat·ing dat·ed** v.t. to write a date on ‖ to assign a date to ‖ to become old-fashioned **dáte·a·ble** adj. **dát·ed** adj. outmoded **dáte·less** adj. undated

daub 1. v.t. to apply a coating ‖ to coat thickly and unevenly ‖ v.i. to paint a picture unskillfully 2. n. a smear

daugh·ter n. a female human being in relation to her parents

daugh·ter-in-law pl. **daugh·ters-in-law** n. a son's wife

daugh·ter·ly adj. of, like or proper in a daughter

daunt v.t. to intimidate **dáunt·less** adj. fearless ‖ unshaken

daw·dle daw·dling daw·dled v.i. to do a job very slowly ‖ v.t. (with 'away') to waste time in idling

dawn 1. n. the first light of day, daybreak ‖ the first sign of something 2. v.i. to begin to grow light

day n. the time during which the sun is above the horizon ‖ a day as marking some event ‖ (esp.pl.) a period of time ‖ (with possessive adj.) a time when things go well

day·break n. dawn

day·dream 1. n. a reverie ‖ a wish or plan not likely to be realized 2. v.i. to indulge in such fancies

daze 1. v.t. **daz·ing dazed** to bewilder, confuse or stun 2. n. a dazed state

daz·zle v.t. **daz·zling daz·zled** to confuse the vision with bright light ‖ to impress by brilliant display **dáz·zle·ment** n.

dea·con n. a member of the clergy

dead 1. adj. inanimate, having no life ‖ having no feeling, movement or activi-

ty ‖ no longer used ‖ inert ‖ lacking resonance ‖ uncharged 2. n. **the dead** all dead persons or a dead person 3. adv. completely, thoroughly

dead-end a road closed at one end, a cul-de-sac

dead·ly 1. **dead·li·er dead·li·est** adj. causing or capable of causing death or serious injury ‖ deathlike 2. adv. intensely

deaf 1. adj. deprived of the sense of hearing ‖ unwilling to listen 2. n. **the deaf** deaf people

deaf-mute n. a person who is deaf and dumb

deal 1. **deal·ing dealt** v.t. to apportion, distribute among a number ‖ (with 'in') to engage in buying and selling some commodity ‖ (with 'with') have business relations ‖ (with 'with') to do what is necessary to meet a situation ‖ (with 'with') to treat a person, esp. to punish him 2. n. the distribution of cards, before a game ‖ treatment measured out to a person ‖ a business transaction **déal·er** n.

dean n. the head of the chapter of a cathedral or collegiate church ‖ the senior member of a body

dear 1. n. a lovable person 2. adj. a polite form of address for beginning letters ‖ precious, cherished 3. adv. at a high price ‖ very affectionately **déar·ly** adv. very affectionately

death n. the end of life ‖ an end, destruction

de·ba·cle n. a disastrous confusion

de·bar de·bar·ring de·barred v.t. to exclude from entry

de·bat·a·ble adj. questionable ‖ subject to dispute

de·bate 1. v. **de·bat·ing de·bat·ed** v.t. to discuss thoroughly ‖ to consider in one's mind ‖ v.i. to hold a formal discussion 2. n. discussion ‖ controversy

de·bauch 1. v.t. to corrupt (a person) 2. n. a bout of excessive self-indulgence in sensual pleasures

de·bauch·er·y pl. **de·bauch·er·ies**

excessive indulgence in sensual
pleasures

de·bil·i·tate de·bil·i·tat·ing de·bil·i·tat·ed
v.t. to weaken

de·bil·i·ty *pl.* **de·bil·i·ties** *n.* physical
weakness, feebleness, or an instance of
this

deb·it 1. *n.* a sum owed **2.** *v.t.* to charge
up (goods or an account)

deb·o·nair deb·o·nair *adj.* having attractive manners and vitality

de·bouch *v.i.* (of people) to emerge ‖ (of
a stream) to flow from a narrow course
into a lake, the sea etc. **de·bóuch·ment**
n.

de·bris *n.* the remnants of something
broken to pieces

debt *n.* something, esp. money, owed to
another ‖ the state of owing

debt·or *n.* a person who owes money or
service

de·but dé·but *n.* the first public appearance of someone (esp. an actor)

deb·u·tante déb·u·tante *n.* a girl making
her first appearances at formal social
functions

dec·ade *n.* a period of 10 years

dec·a·dence *n.* a falling away, decline
déc·a·dent *adj.* deteriorating ‖ falling to
lower standards

de·cal·co·ma·ni·a *n.* the process of transferring specially prepared colored
images from paper to porcelain, paper,
glass, metal etc. ‖ such an image

de·cay 1. *v.i.* (of a substance) to lose
gradually its original form, quality or
value ‖ to decrease in activity, force or
quality ‖ to fall into disrepair **2.** *n.* the
state or process of decaying

de·cease 1. *n.* (in legal or formal contexts)
death **2.** *v.i.* **de·ceas·ing de·ceased** to
die **the de·céased** *n.* the dead person

de·ceit *n.* deception ‖ a trick, fraud
de·céit·ful *adj.*

de·ceive de·ceiv·ing de·ceived *v.t.* to
mislead ‖ to break faith with

De·cem·ber (abbr. **Dec.**) *n.* the 12th and
last month of the year

de·cen·cy *pl.* **de·cen·cies** *n.* accepted stan-

dards as regards propriety in language,
behavior or modesty

de·cep·tion *n.* a tricking, deceiving ‖ the
state of being deceived ‖ a hoax

de·cep·tive *adj.* misleading

de·cide de·cid·ing de·cid·ed *v.i.* to choose
‖ to determine ‖ *v.t.* to bring to a decision **de·cíd·ed** *adj.* clearly marked,
distinct **de·cíd·ed·ly** *adv.*

dec·i·mal *adj.* relating to 10 ‖ of a number
scale based on 10

de·ci·pher *v.t.* to put (a text transmitted in
cipher) into plain writing ‖ interpret
de·cí·pher·a·ble *adj.* **de·ci·pher·ment***n.*

de·ci·sion *n.* the result of making up one's
mind ‖ resoluteness

de·ci·sive conclusive ‖ showing resoluteness

deck *n.* a floor in a ship ‖ strip of material
on which data can be recorded ‖ (Am.)
a pack of playing cards **on deck** in the
open air

deck *v.t.* to array ‖ (often with 'out') to dress
(oneself) in a fine or fancy way

dec·la·ra·tion *n.* a manifesto ‖ an
announcement or affirmation ‖ a solemn
statement

de·clare de·clar·ing de·clared *v.t.* to make
known explicitly or formally, announce
‖ to affirm or protest strongly ‖ to give
particulars of ‖ (bridge) to name (the
trump suit) ‖ *v.i.* (with 'against' or 'for')
to take sides, vote **de·cláred** *adj.* stated ‖ professed **de·clár·er** *n.*

de·cline 1. de·clin·ing de·clined *v.t.* to
refuse *v.i.* to deteriorate ‖ to refuse ‖ to fall
off ‖ to slope downwards **2.** *n.* a falling
off, loss of vigor, sinking or deterioration ‖ a downward slope ‖ a refusal

**de·com·pose de·com·pos·ing
de·com·posed** *v.i.* to disintegrate, rot ‖
v.t. to cause to break up into component
parts or elements **de·com·po·si·tion**

de·con·trol *v.t.* **de·con·trol·ling
de·con·trolled** to release from control

dec·o·rate dec·o·rat·ing dec·o·rat·ed *v.t.*
to add something ornamental to, adorn
‖ to honor (someone) with a medal, etc.

dec·o·ra·tion *n.* a decorating ‖ something

decorative ‖ a ribbon or medal etc.

dec·o·ra·tive *adj.* serving to decorate

dec·o·ra·tor *n.* someone who professionally plans interior decoration schemes

de·coy *n.* a real or imitation bird or animal used to lure other birds or animals to a place where they may be trapped or shot ‖ a person or thing used as a trap

de·crease *n.* a diminishing **on the decrease** lessening

de·crease de·creas·ing de·creased *v.i.* to grow less, diminish, dwindle

de·cree 1. *n.* an order made by a ruling body 2. **de·cree·ing de·creed** *v.t.* to appoint or order by decree

de·crep·it *adj.* made dilapidated or extremely weak by age or illness

de·cry de·cry·ing de·cried *v.t.* to disparage, attack in speech

ded·i·cate ded·i·cat·ing ded·i·cat·ed *v.t.* to devote to any serious purpose

ded·i·ca·tion *n.* the act or rite of dedicating

de·duce de·duc·ing de·duced *v.t.* to infer by reasoning from known facts

de·duct *v.t.* to subtract, take (an amount) away **de·duct·i·ble** *adj.* able to be deducted

de·duc·tion *n.* a subtracting or taking away ‖ the amount deducted ‖ reasoning in which the conclusion follows necessarily from given premises

deed 1. *n.* something done, an act ‖ a sealed written or printed agreement 2. *v.t.* to convey or transfer by deed

deem *v.t.* to consider as true in the impossibility of proving ‖ to come to believe

deep 1. *adj.* extending far down below the surface ‖ completely absorbed ‖ heartfelt ‖ well concealed ‖ thorough ‖ profound ‖ dark and intense ‖ low-pitched 2. *adv.* profoundly, deeply ‖ far down 3. *n.* a deep part of a body of water **deep·en** *v.t.* to make deep or deeper

deer *pl.* **deer deers** *n.* ruminant mammal

de·face de·fac·ing de·faced *v.t.* to disfigure, spoil the appearance of **de·face·ment** *n.*

de·fame de·fam·ing de·famed *v.t.* to attack the good reputation of (someone)

de·fault 1. *n.* a failure to carry out an obligation ‖ failure to take part in or finish a contest 2. *v.t.* to declare (someone) in default ‖ to forfeit (a contest) ‖ *v.i.* to be guilty of default

de·feat 1. *n.* an overcoming or being overcome in war, sport or argument ‖ frustration, prevention from success 2. *v.t.* to conquer ‖ to frustrate

de·fect 1. *n.* a fault, blemish 2. *v.i.* to desert

de·fec·tion *n.* a falling or breaking away

de·fec·tive *adj.* having faults ‖ incomplete

de·fec·tor *n.* someone who defects

de·fend *v.t.* to protect from danger, slander, criticism etc.

de·fend·ant 1. the accused person in a case 2. *adj.* being the accused

de·fend·er *n.* someone who protects from attack

de·fense *n.* the act of resisting attack ‖ preparation to meet attack ‖ something which defends ‖ **de·fense·less** *adj.*

de·fer de·fer·ring de·ferred *v.t.* to postpone **de·fer·a·ble** *adj.*

def·er·ence *n.* polite regard for someone else's wishes, ideas etc. ‖ respectful submission

de·fer·ment *n.* postponement

de·fi·ance *n.* a deliberate challenge (to authority) by disobedience

de·fi·ant *adj.* showing defiance

de·fi·cien·cy *pl.* **de·fi·cien·cies** *n.* a lack ‖ a shortage ‖ the quality or state of being deficient

de·fi·cient *adj.* lacking something which should be present ‖ below normal standards

def·i·cit *n.* a financial accounting loss

de·file de·fil·ing de·filed *v.t.* to desecrate, to profane ‖ to corrupt morally **de·file·ment** *n.*

de·fine de·fin·ing de·fined *v.t.* to state the precise meaning of ‖ to mark the limits of ‖ to outline clearly

def·i·nite *adj.* clear, not vague ‖ limiting ‖ **def·i·nite·ly** 1. *adv.* exactly 2. *interj.* yes, certainly

def·i·ni·tion an act of defining ‖ clearness

of detail

de·fin·i·tive *adj.* decisive, final ‖ most authoritative

de·flate de·flat·ing de·flat·ed *v.t.* to let air or gas out of ‖ to cause to shrink suddenly ‖ *v.i.* to lose shape or rigidity **de·flá·tion** *n.*

de·flect *v.t.* to bend or turn aside

de·form *v.t.* to disfigure ‖ to spoil the form

de·for·ma·tion an alteration of size or shape

de·form·i·ty *pl.* **de·form·i·ties** *n.* a misshapen part of the body

de·fraud *v.t.* to cheat (someone)

de·fray *v.t.* to pay or settle (costs or expenses) **de·fráy·al de·fráy·ment** *ns.*

de·frost *v.i.* to become free of ice or frost **de·fróst·er** *n.* a device for freeing from frost or ice

deft *adj.* quick and neat ‖ clever, quick-witted

de·funct *adj.* (of people) dead ‖ (of things) extinct

de·fuse *v.* to alleviate a tense or dangerous situation

de·fy de·fy·ing de·fied *v.t.* to challenge ‖ to disobey openly ‖ to resist

de·gen·er·ate 1. *v.i.* **de·gen·er·at·ing de·gen·er·at·ed** to decline mentally or morally ‖ to grow much worse ‖ to become enfeebled or impaired **2.** *adj.* having lost former or characteristic qualities, degraded

deg·ra·da·tion *n.* a degrading or being degraded

de·grade de·grad·ing de·grad·ed *v.t.* to lower esp. in rank or degree ‖ to debase morally **de·grád·ing** *adj.*

de·gree *n.* a step or stage in an ascending or descending series or process ‖ a measure of intensity or gravity ‖ a grade or title ‖ (symbol °) a division of a scale of measurement

de·hy·drate de·hy·drat·ing de·hy·drat·ed *v.t.* to remove water from

de·i·fy de·i·fy·ing de·i·fied *v.t.* to make a god of, treat as a god

deign *v.i.* (with 'to') to condescend

de·i·ty *pl.* **de·i·ties** *n.* a god or goddess

de·ject·ed *adj.* cast down in spirits

de·jec·tion *n.* depression, lowness of spirits

de·lay *v.t.* to cause to be late ‖ to hinder the progress of ‖ to postpone

de·lec·ta·ble *adj.* (*rhet.*) delightful to the mind or the senses

del·e·gate del·e·gat·ing del·e·gat·ed *v.t.* to appoint as a representative ‖ to give up (some degree of one's powers) to another

del·e·gate *n.* an official representative

del·e·ga·tion *n.* body of delegates

de·lete de·let·ing de·let·ed *v.t.* to cross out, erase

de·le·tion *n.* the act of deleting ‖ the thing deleted

de·lib·er·ate *adj.* made or done intentionally ‖ slow and careful

de·lib·er·ate de·lib·er·at·ing de·lib·er·at·ed *v.i.* to think out a matter with proper care

de·lib·er·a·tion *n.* careful consideration ‖ formal discussion or consultation

del·i·ca·cy *pl.* **del·i·ca·cies** *n.* fineness of quality ‖ sensitivity ‖ constitutional weakness

del·i·cate *adj.* finely made ‖ very fragile ‖ subtle ‖ exquisitely considerate ‖ of great precision ‖ (of health) ‖ precarious ‖ (of food) choice

del·i·ca·tes·sen *n.* a shop selling prepared foods ‖ the foods sold there

de·li·cious *adj.* delightful, giving pleasure esp. to the taste, smell, or sense of humor

de·light *v.t.* to please very much

delight *n.* great pleasure ‖ something which gives such pleasure

de·lin·e·ate de·lin·e·at·ing de·lin·e·at·ed *v.t.* to show by drawing, or by outlining in words **de·lin·e·á·tion de·lín·e·a·tor** *ns.*

de·lin·quen·cy *pl.* **de·lin·quen·cies** *n.* wrongdoing ‖ an action going against the law

de·lin·quent 1. *adj.* guilty of wrongdoing **2.** *n.* a delinquent person

de·lir·i·ous *adj.* raving ‖ (loosely) wildly

ex·cit·ed, in an ecstasy of joy

de·lir·i·um *pl.* **de·lir·i·ums de·lir·i·a** *n.* a temporary disorder of the mind, hallucinations ‖ wild excitement or ecstasy

de·liv·er *v.t.* to transport ‖ to convey ‖ to assist (a woman) to give birth ‖ to rescue

de·liv·er·ance *n.* a rescuing or setting free ‖ a pompous and emphatically expressed opinion

de·liv·er·y *pl.* **de·liv·er·ies** *n.* the act of giving birth ‖ the declaiming of a speech, lecture, etc. ‖ a rescuing or setting free ‖ something delivered

del·ta *n.* the fourth letter (Δ) of the Greek alphabet ‖ a low tract of alluvial land formed by the precipitation of river mud

de·lude de·lud·ing de·lud·ed *v.t.* to cause to believe wrongly

del·uge 1. *n.* an overwhelming rush of water ‖ a rush of anything (e.g. words, mail) **2.** *v.t.* **del·ug·ing del·uged** to flood

de·lu·sion *n.* a deluding or being deluded ‖ a false opinion or idea **de·lu·sion·al** *adj.*

de·lu·sive *adj.* deceptive, false **de·lu·so·ry** *adj.*

de luxe *adj.* especially lavish or elegant

delve delv·ing delved *v.i.* to search as if burrowing ‖ (of a road etc.) to dip suddenly

dem·a·gog·ic *adj.* of or like a demagogue **dem·a·góg·i·cal** *adj.*

dem·a·gogue dem·a·gog *n.* a political speaker or leader who plays upon the passions etc. of the people to win their support for himself or his party **dém·a·gogu·er·y** *pl.* **dem·a·gogu·er·ies** *n.*

de·mand *n.* a peremptory request

demand *v.t.* claim as one's due

de·mar·cate de·mar·cat·ing de·mar·cat·ed *v.t.* to mark the boundaries of

de·mean *v.t.* to behave (oneself) in a specified way

de·mean·or *n.* behavior, manner

de·ment·ed *adj.* mad, insane ‖ indicating madness

de·mer·it *n.* a quality deserving blame ‖ a fault

de·mise 1. *n.* death **2.** **de·mis·ing de·mised** *v.i.* to pass by bequest or inheritance

dem·i·tasse *n.* a small coffee cup for serving coffee ‖ a cup of this coffee

de·moc·ra·cy *pl.* **de·moc·ra·cies** *n.* government by the people ‖ a state so governed

de·mol·ish *v.t.* to destroy ‖ to reduce to nothing, overthrow

dem·o·li·tion *n.* a demolishing or being demolished

de·mon *n.* an evil spirit or devil

de·mon·ic *adj.* possessed or inspired by a demon or as if by a demon

dem·on·strate dem·on·strat·ing dem·on·trat·ed *v.t.* to show clearly and openly ‖ to prove the truth of, by logical or scientific processes

dem·on·stra·tion *n.* an expression of public feeling for or against something through meetings, marches etc. ‖ the use of practical experiments for purposes of teaching

dem·on·stra·tive *adj.* serving to point out, prove or show clearly ‖ (of persons) given to open display of feelings, esp. of affection

dem·on·stra·tor *n.* someone who demonstrates

de·mor·al·i·za·tion *n.* a demoralizing or being demoralized

de·mor·al·ize de·mor·al·iz·ing de·mor·al·ized *v.t.* undermine the confidence of ‖ to corrupt the morals of, deprave

dem·a·gogue dem·a·gog *n.* a political speaker or leader who plays upon the passions etc. of the people to win their support for himself or his party **dém·a·gogu·er·y** *pl.* **dem·a·gogu·er·ies** *n.*

de·mand *n.* a peremptory request

demand *v.t.* claim as one's due

de·mar·cate de·mar·cat·ing de·mar·cat·ed *v.t.* to mark the boundaries of

de·mean *v.t.* to behave (oneself) in a

specified way

de·mean·or *n.* behavior, manner

de·ment·ed *adj.* mad, insane || indicating madness

de·mer·it *n.* a quality deserving blame || a fault

de·mise 1. *n.* death 2. de·mis·ing de·mised *v.i.* to pass by bequest or inheritance

dem·i·tasse *n.* a small coffee cup for serving coffee || a cup of this coffee

de·moc·ra·cy *pl.* de·moc·ra·cies *n.* government by the people || a state so governed

de·mol·ish *v.t.* to destroy || to reduce to nothing, overthrow

dem·o·li·tion *n.* a demolishing or being demolished

de·mon *n.* an evil spirit or devil

de·mon·ic *adj.* possessed or inspired by a demon or as if by a demon

dem·on·strate dem·on·strat·ing dem·on·trat·ed *v.t.* to show clearly and openly || to prove the truth of, by logical or scientific processes

dem·on·stra·tion *n.* an expression of public feeling for or against something through meetings, marches etc. || the use of practical experiments for purposes of teaching

de·mon·stra·tive *adj.* serving to point out, prove or show clearly || (of persons) given to open display of feelings, esp. of affection

dem·on·stra·tor *n.* someone who demonstrates

de·mor·al·i·za·tion *n.* a demoralizing or being demoralized

de·mor·al·ize de·mor·al·iz·ing de·mor·al·ized *v.t.* undermine the confidence of || to corrupt the morals of, deprave

de·mote de·mot·ing de·mot·ed *v.t.* to reduce to a lower rank de·mo·tion *n.*

de·mur de·mur·ring de·murred to raise objections or scruples, hesitate, show reluctance

den *n.* a wild beast's lair || a snug, secluded room where a person may retire to study

de·ni·a·ble *adj.* capable of being denied

de·ni·al *n.* an assertion that something is not true || disavowal || a refusal of a request

den·im *n.* a strong, coarse, twilled cotton fabric

de·nom·i·na·tion *n.* a name, esp. one given to a class or category || one of a series of units in numbers, weights or money || a religious sect

de·nom·i·na·tion·al *adj.* pertaining to a religious sect

de·nom·i·na·tor *n.* part of a fraction. It denotes the number of equal parts into which the whole is divided

de·note de·not·ing de·not·ed *v.t.* to indicate || to signify, stand for

de·nounce de·nounc·ing de·nounced *v.t.* to inform against de·nounce·ment *n.*

dense dens·er dens·est *adj.* thick || rich in texture || slow-witted

dent *n.* a slight hollow made in a surface by pressure or a blow || *v.t.* to make a dent in

den·tal *adj.* of or relating to the teeth or dentistry

den·tist *n.* someone professionally qualified to treat ailments of the teeth den·tist·ry *n.*

den·ture *n.* a set of artificial teeth

de·nude de·nud·ing de·nud·ed *v.t.* to strip, make bare

de·nun·ci·a·tion *n.* the act of denouncing || an instance of censuring, esp. publicly

de·nun·ci·a·tor *n.* someone who denounces

de·ny de·ny·ing de·nied *v.t.* to declare to be untrue || to refuse

de·o·dor·ant *n.* an agent for neutralizing unpleasant odors, esp. of perspiration

de·o·dor·ize de·o·dor·iz·ing de·o·dor·ized *v.t.* to neutralize a bad odor in

de·part *v.i.* to go away || to deviate

de·part·ment *n.* a distinct branch of a whole de·part·men·tal *adj.*

de·pend *v.i.* to rely trustfully || to be contingent

de·pend·a·bil·i·ty *n.* the quality of being

dependable

de·pend·a·ble *adj.* reliable, trustworthy

de·pend·ant de·pend·ent *n.* someone who relies upon another for financial support

de·pend·ence de·pend·ance *n.* a depending on another for material or emotional support

de·pend·ent *adj.* (of a person) being a financial charge || (of lands or peoples) subject || contingent

de·pict *v.t.* to represent by drawing or painting || to describe verbally **de·pic·tion** *n.*

de·plete de·plet·ing de·plet·ed *v.t.* to reduce or empty by destroying or using up **de·ple·tion** *n.*

de·plor·a·ble *adj.* much to be regretted **de·plor·a·bly** *adv.*

de·plore de·plor·ing de·plored *v.t.* to regret very much || to be grieved by

de·port *v.t.* to send away from a country, exile **to deport oneself** to behave in a specified way **de·por·ta·tion** *n.* banishment

de·port·ment *n.* bearing || behavior, manners

de·pose de·pos·ing de·posed *v.t.* to remove from office || to say on oath

de·pos·it 1. *v.t.* to store for safety || to put down || to pay as a security **2.** *n.* something entrusted for safekeeping || a sum paid as a security or as a first installment || a sediment

de·pot *n.* a storage place || the place from which a bus service is run

dep·ra·va·tion *n.* a depraving or being depraved

de·prave de·prav·ing de·praved *v.t.* to corrupt, pervert

de·prav·i·ty *pl.* **de·prav·i·ties** *n.* moral corruption, perversion, wickedness

de·pre·ci·ate de·pre·ci·at·ing de·pre·ci·at·ed *v.t.* to diminish the value of || to belittle **de·pre·ci·á·tion** *n.* **de·pre·ci·a·to·ry** *adj.*

dep·re·da·tion *n.* a laying waste || (*pl.*) ravages

de·press *v.t.* dispirit || lower **de·prés·sant**

n. a sedative **de·préssed** *adj.* dispirited, miserable || substandard in economic activity

de·pres·sion *n.* a being depressed || a natural hollow || dejection

dep·ri·va·tion *n.* deprival || an instance of this

de·prive de·priv·ing de·prived *v.t.* to withhold or take away something desirable or necessary

depth *n.* deepness || an extent of deepness downwards or inwards || the quality of being profound || (of color) intensity

dep·u·ty *pl.* **dep·u·ties** *n.* someone appointed to act on behalf of another || a second-in-command

de·rail *v.i.* to run off the rails **de·ráil·ment** *n.*

de·range de·rang·ing de·ranged *v.t.* to make insane **de·ránge·ment** *n.*

der·e·lict 1. *adj.* abandoned, neglected **2.** *n.* a human wreck

der·e·lic·tion *n.* an abandoning || neglect (of duty)

de·ride de·rid·ing de·rid·ed *v.t.* to laugh at in scorn, mock

de·ri·sion *n.* mockery, ridicule

de·ri·sive *adj.* scornful, mocking || contemptible

der·i·va·tion *n.* an origin, source || the formation of a word from a root

de·riv·a·tive 1. *adj.* derived from something else **2.** *n.* something derived

de·rive de·riv·ing de·rived *v.t.* to receive, obtain || to deduce || to obtain (a compound) from another

der·ma·tol·o·gy *n.* the branch of medicine dealing with the skin and its diseases

de·rog·a·to·ry *adj.* disparaging

der·rick *n.* a hoisting apparatus

de·scend *v.i.* to go downwards || *v.t.* to go down

de·scend·ant, de·scend·ent *n.* someone or something descended

de·scent *n.* a downward slope || lineage, ancestry

de·scribe de·scrib·ing de·scribed *v.t.* to give a description of

de·scrip·tion *n.* a verbal account or

portrayal of a person, scene, event etc.

de·scrip·tive adj. serving to describe

des·e·crate **des·e·crat·ing** **des·e·crat·ed** v.t. profane **des·e·crá·tion** **dés·e·cra·tor** ns

de·seg·re·gate **de·seg·re·gat·ing** **de·seg·re·gat·ed** v.i. to abandon the practice of segregation **de·seg·re·gá·tion** n.

de·sert v.t. to abandon, forsake || v.i. to run away from service in the armed forces

des·ert n. a large area of land where there is not enough vegetation to support human life

de·sert·er n. someone who deserts

de·ser·tion n. a deserting or being deserted

de·serve **de·serv·ing** **de·served** v.t. to be worthy of, merit **de·sérved** adj. **de·serv·ed·ly** adv. **de·sérv·ing** adj.

de·sign n. a decorative pattern || the formal structure of a picture || the combination of parts in a whole || a purpose, intention

design v.t. to invent and bring into being || v.i. to make designs

des·ig·nate 1. adj. appointed to an office but not yet in possession of it **2.** v.t. **des·ig·nat·ing** **des·ig·nat·ed** to show, identify || to name, describe || to appoint to office

de·sir·a·ble adj. inspiring the wish to possess **de·sír·a·bly** adv.

de·sire n. yearning, longing || strong sexual attraction || wish

de·sist v.i. to cease (from doing something)

desk n. a piece of furniture for writing at || a lectern

des·o·late 1. v.t. **des·o·lat·ing** **des·o·lat·ed** to depopulate || to lay waste, ravage **2.** adj. lonely || forlorn || barren || uninhabited

des·o·la·tion n. a barren, neglected state or area || extreme loneliness, misery, unhappiness

de·spair 1. v.i. to lose hope **2.** n. hopelessness **de·spáir·ing** adj.

des·per·ate adj. beyond, or almost beyond, hope || frantic || reckless and violent || extremely bad

des·per·a·tion n. a state of recklessness caused by despair

des·pi·ca·ble adj. contemptible **des·pí·ca·bly** adv.

de·spise **de·spis·ing** **de·spised** v.t. feel contempt for

de·spite prep. notwithstanding

de·spoil v.t. to plunder, pillage || to ruin (land etc.) **de·spóil·ment** n.

de·spond v.i. to become very disheartened **de·spónd·ence** **de·spónd·en·cy** ns **de·spónd·ent** adj.

des·pot n. an absolute ruler, a tyrant **des·pót·ic** adj. **des·pót·i·cal·ly** adv. **dés·pot·ism** n.

des·sert n. a sweet course served at the end of a meal

des·ti·na·tion n. the place to which a person or thing is going

des·tine **des·tin·ing** **des·tined** v.t. to set apart || to foreordain

des·ti·ny pl. **des·ti·nies** n. one's predetermined lot

des·ti·tute adj. poverty-stricken

de·stroy v.t. demolish || to put an end to

de·stroy·er n. a small, fast warship || someone who destroys

de·struct·i·ble adj. capable of being destroyed

de·struc·tion n. a destroying or being destroyed || the cause of ruin, something which destroys

de·tach v.t. to separate, remove || to send on a special mission **de·tách·a·ble** **de·táched** adjs independent || separate || standing apart

de·tach·ment n. a separation || freedom from involvement

de·tail n. a small part, an item || a part of a composition or construction considered in isolation

de·tail v.t. to list || to assign to a special duty

de·tain v.t. to keep from leaving || to keep in custody

de·tect v.t. to find out, discover betraying signs of || to discover the presence of **de·téct·a·ble** adj. **de·téc·tion** n. **de·téc·tive** n. a policeman whose work is to investigate crime

dé·tente *n.* an easing of tension, esp. between nations

de·ter de·ter·ring de·terred *v.t.* to discourage from some action

de·ter·gent 1. *adj.* cleansing **2.** *n.* soap ‖ one of a large number of cleansing agents

de·te·ri·o·rate de·te·ri·o·rat·ing de·te·ri·o·rat·ed *v.t.* to make worse ‖ *v.i.* to become worse **de·te·ri·o·rá·tion** *n.*

de·té·ri·o·ra·tive *adj.*

de·ter·mi·na·tion *n.* firmness of purpose or character, resolution ‖ a coming to a decision

de·ter·mine de·ter·min·ing de·ter·mined *v.t.* to settle, fix ‖ to regulate ‖ to find out precisely ‖ *v.i.* (with 'on') to make up one's mind, resolve **de·tér·mined** *adj.* resolved, decided ‖ resolute

de·ter·rent 1. *adj.* meant to deter **2.** *n.* something which deters or is meant to deter

de·test *v.t.* to hate, abhor **de·tést·a·ble** *adj.* **de·tést·a·bly** *adv.*

de·tour *n.* a deviation from the usual route ‖ a circuitous path taken to avoid some obstacle ‖ *v.t.* to make a detour around ‖ to cause to make a detour

de·tract *v.i.* (with 'from') to lessen in value **de·trác·tion** *n.* **de·trác·tive** *adj.* **de·trác·tor** *n.*

det·ri·ment *n.* harm, damage **det·ri·mén·tal** *adj.* injurious

de·val·u·ate de·val·u·at·ing de·val·u·at·ed *v.t.* to lessen the value of **de·val·u·á·tion** *n.*

dev·as·tate dev·as·tat·ing dev·as·tat·ed *v.t.* to lay waste, ravage **dev·as·tá·tion** *n.* **dév·as·ta·tor** *ns*

de·vel·op *v.t.* to cause to grow ‖ to elaborate on ‖ to treat chemically so that the image appears ‖ *v.i.* to evolve **de·vél·op·er** *n.* a chemical reagent **de·vél·op·ment** *n.* a new factor or situation ‖ a tract of land developed as a unit

de·vi·ate 1. *v.* **de·vi·at·ing de·vi·at·ed** *v.i.* to turn aside (from a course, custom, topic etc.) **2.** *n.* someone sexually perverted

de·vi·a·tion *n.* a turning aside

de·vice *n.* a scheme, trick, stratagem ‖ something designed or adapted for a special purpose

dev·il 1. *n.* an evil spirit, a demon ‖ a cruel or vicious person ‖ someone full of spirit and daring **2.** *n.* **dev·il·ing dev·iled** *v.t.* to prepare (food) with hot seasoning

de·vi·ous *adj.* roundabout ‖ underhanded, shifty

de·vise *v.t.* **de·vis·ing de·vised** to contrive, think up ‖ to bequeath (realty) by will

de·void *adj.* (with 'of') lacking in, completely without

de·vote de·vot·ing de·vot·ed *v.t.* to give wholly, dedicate **de·vót·ed** *adj.* bound by strong affection ‖ loyal **de·vót·ed·ly** *adv.*

de·vo·tion *n.* love given with the whole heart ‖ devoutness **de·vó·tion·al** *adj.*

de·vour *v.t.* to eat up hungrily ‖ to take in eagerly with the senses ‖ to consume, destroy

de·vout *adj.* attending to religious duties ‖ earnest

dew *n.* small drops of moisture condensed from the atmosphere

dex·ter·i·ty *n.* manual skill ‖ mental adroitness

dex·ter·ous *adj.* dextrous **dex·tral** *adj.* on the right-hand side ‖ turned or moving towards the right

di·a·be·tes mel·li·tus *n.* a disease

di·a·bet·ic 1. *adj.* of diabetes ‖ suffering from diabetes **2.** *n.* a person suffering from diabetes

di·a·bol·ic *adj.* wicked, evil ‖ of or like the devil ‖ fiendish **di·a·ból·i·cal** *adj.*

di·ag·nose di·ag·nos·ing di·ag·nosed *v.t.* to determine the nature of (a disease)

di·ag·no·sis *pl.* **di·ag·no·ses** *n.* the recognition of a disease from its symptoms

di·ag·nos·tic *adj.* of diagnosis **di·ag·nós·ti·cal·ly** *adv.* **di·ag·nos·ti·cian** *n.* **di·ag·nós·tics** *n.* the art of making a diagnosis

di·ag·o·nal 1. *adj.* running from corner to corner in a slanting direction **2.** *n.* a diagonal straight line

di·a·gram n. a graph or chart **di·a·gram·mat·ic** adj. **di·a·gram·mat·i·cal·ly** adv.

di·al 1. n. a circle around or on which a scale is marked ‖ the numbered disk of an automatic telephone **2.** v.t. **di·al·ing di·aled** to compose (a desired number) with the finger on a telephone

di·a·lect n. a form of a language distinguished from other forms of the samelanguage by pronunciation, grammar or vocabulary **di·a·lec·tal** adj.

di·a·logue di·a·log n. conversation

di·am·e·ter n. a straight line passing through the center of a circle and ending at the boundary of the figure ‖ this measure through or across **di·am·e·tral** adj.

di·a·met·ric adj. diametrical **di·a·met·ri·cal** adj. of or pertaining to a diameter **di·a·met·ri·cal·ly** adv.

di·a·mond n. a very valuable precious stone ‖ a rhombus ‖ (baseball) the playing field

di·a·per 1. n. a piece of absorbent cloth or other material for catching a baby's urine and feces **2.** v.t. to put a diaper on (a baby)

di·a·phragm n. a septum or partition ‖ the midriff ‖ the physical element of an optical system that regulates the quantity of light traversing the system ‖ thin rubber cap fitted over the uterine cervix **di·a·phrag·mat·ic** adj.

di·ar·rhea n. unusually frequent passage of loose, watery stools

di·a·ry pl. **di·a·ries** n. a daily written account of events ‖ a book for keeping such an account

di·a·tribe n. a fulminating piece of invective

dice 1. n. pl. of DIE ‖ a gambling game played with these **2.** v. **dic·ing diced** v.i. to play dice ‖ v.t. to cut up (vegetables, meat etc.) into small cubes

dic·tate 1. v. **dic·tat·ing dic·tat·ed** v.t. to read or say (something) aloud that is to be written down ‖ v.i. to behave like an

autocrat **2.** n. (usually pl.) an order

dic·ta·tion n. something dictated

dic·ta·tor n. an absolute ruler

dic·ta·to·ri·al adj. autocratic ‖ of a dictator

dic·ta·tor·ship n. a form of government in which power is held by a dictator

dic·tion n. a way of speaking, enunciation

dic·tion·ar·y pl. **dic·tion·ar·ies** n. a book containing the words of a language arranged in alphabetical order, with their definitions

did past of DO

die n. (pl. **dice**) a small cube marked on its faces with 1-6 spots ‖ (pl. **dies**) any of various tools for cutting, shaping or embossing

die dy·ing died v.i. to cease to live ‖ to fade to nothing

di·et n. the food and drink normally taken by an individual or a group ‖ a prescribed course of what is to be eaten and what is not

diet v.t. to put on a diet ‖ v.i. to eat special food (for health reasons) ‖ to eat less so as to become thinner

di·e·tar·y 1. pl. **di·e·tar·ies** n. a course of diet ‖ an allowance or ration of food **2.** adj. relating to diet

di·e·tet·ic adj. relating to diet **di·e·tet·i·cal·ly** adv. **di·e·tet·ics** n. the study of the principles of nutrition

dif·fer to be different ‖ to disagree in opinion

dif·fer·ence n. a differing ‖ a distinction ‖ the result obtained by subtracting ‖ a quarrel

dif·fer·ent adj. (with 'from')dissimilar ‖ not the same ‖ unusual

dif·fi·cult adj. hard to do ‖ hard to understand ‖ obstinate **dif·fi·cul·ty** pl. **dif·fi·cul·ties** n. something which cannot easily be understood or believed ‖ (often pl.) trouble

dif·fuse 1. v. **dif·fus·ing dif·fused** v.t. to spread widely **2.** adj. widely spread, dispersed ‖ not concise **dif·fus·i·ble** adj.

dif·fu·sion n. a diffusing ‖ the transmission of light through frosted glass etc.

or the scattering caused by particles in the atmosphere

dig 1. *v.* **dig·ging dug** *v.* to break up or turn (soil) with a spade, fork, paws etc. ‖ to excavate **2.** *n.* a sarcastic remark ‖ an archaeological excavation

di·gest *n.* a synopsis of information

di·gest *v.t.* to convert (food) into a form that can be assimilated ‖ to study and master the significance of in one's mind **di·gest·i·bíl·i·ty** *n.* **di·gést·i·ble** *adj.*

di·ges·tion *n.* the conversion of food in the stomach ‖ the assimilation of ideas

dig·it *n.* a finger or a toe ‖ any of the numbers from 0 to 9

dig·it·al *adj.* pertaining to the fingers ‖ having digits ‖ *(computer)* of an instrument that accepts data and produces output in the form of characters or digits

dig·ni·fy dig·ni·fy·ing dig·ni·fied *v.t.* to confer dignity upon ‖ to add an air of distinction to

dig·ni·ty *pl.* **dig·ni·ties** *n.* worth ‖ nobility of manner ‖ the quality of commanding esteem

di·gress *v.i.* to wander from the main subject in speaking or writing

di·gres·sion *n.* a wandering from the subject ‖ a deliberate turning aside from the main track

di·gres·sive *adj.* tending to digress

dike dyke *n.* a raised bank constructed to prevent flooding ‖ a causeway **dik·ing dyk·ing diked dyked** *v.i.* to construct dikes

di·lap·i·date di·lap·i·dat·ing di·lap·i·dat·ed *v.i.* to fall into disrepair **di·láp·i·dat·ed** *adj.*

di·la·ta·tion *n.* a dilating

di·late di·lat·ing di·lat·ed *v.i.* to expand, become wider. *v.t.* to stretch (something contracted)

di·lem·ma *n.* a situation in which one is faced with a choice between unsatisfactory alternatives

dil·et·tan·te 1. *pl.* **dil·et·tan·ti dil·et·tan·tes** *n.* someone who dabbles in art, literature, music etc., without any deep knowledge or application **2.** *adj.*

superficial ‖ amateur **dil·et·tánt·ism** *n.*

dil·i·gence *n.* the quality of being diligent

dil·i·gent *adj.* hard-working, industrious

dill *n.* an annual whose seeds are used as a carminative, and also as a flavoring in pickles etc.

di·lute 1. *v.* **di·lut·ing di·lut·ed** *v.t.* to lessen the concentration of (a mixture) by adding more water ‖ to weaken, water down ‖ *v.i.* to become diluted **2.** *adj.* diluted, weakened **di·lú·tion** *n.*

dim 1. **dim·mer dim·mest** *adj.* indistinct, not clearly visible ‖ vague ‖ *(pop.)* stupid **2.** *v.* **dim·ming dimmed** *v.t.* to lower the beam of (headlights) ‖ *v.i.* to become dim

dime *n.* a coin worth 10 cents

di·men·sion *n.* a measurement in a single direction ‖ *(pl.)* size ‖ *(pl.)* extent or scope **di·mén·sion·al** *adj.*

di·min·ish *v.t.* to make less ‖ to reduce ‖ *v.i.* to become less

dim·i·nu·tion *n.* the act of diminishing ‖ a decrease

di·min·u·tive *adj.* very small ‖ expressing diminution

dim·mer *n.* a device for controlling the intensity of illumination or for lowering the beam of car headlights

dim·ple *n.* a small hollow, esp. in the cheek or chin

din *n.* a clamor of discordant, deafening noises

dine din·ing dined *v.i.* to have dinner ‖ *v.t.* to entertain to dinner **dín·er** *n.* a dining car on a train ‖ a restaurant built to resemble a dining car on a train

di·nette *n.* a small informal dining room, usually just off the kitchen

din·ghy *pl.* **din·ghies** *n.* a ship's small boat ‖ a small rowboat often fitted for sailing

din·gy din·gi·er din·gi·est *adj.* drab, dirtylooking

din·ner *n.* the main meal of the day

di·no·saur *n.* a group of fossil lizards

di·o·cese *n.* the district under a bishop's authority

dip 1. *v.* **dip·ping dipped** *v.t.* to immerse momentarily in a liquid ‖ to take up with a ladle, hand, scoop etc. ‖ to lower momentarily (a flag, sail etc.) ‖ v.i. to reach into something ‖ to sink, drop down 2. n. a quick swim ‖ a downward slope

diph·the·ri·a n. an acute infectious disease

diph·thong n. a speech sound consisting of two vowels pronounced glidingly in one syllable

di·plo·ma n. a document conferring some honor or privilege, esp. one recording successful completion of a course of academic study

di·plo·ma·cy pl. **di·plo·ma·cies** n. the science of international relations ‖ the conduct of negotiations between nations ‖ a tactful dealing with people

dip·lo·mat n. someone officially employed in international diplomacy ‖ a tactful person

dip·lo·mat·ic adj. relating to diplomacy ‖ tactful **dip·lo·mát·i·cal·ly** adv.

dire dir·er dir·est adj. dreadful, terrible ‖ most pressing

di·rect 1. v.t. to explain or point out the way ‖ to address, aim ‖ to supervise ‖ to order, instruct ‖ v.i. to give orders **2.** adj. straight, without detours ‖ straightforward, candid, blunt ‖ immediate ‖ not turned aside **3.** adv. by the direct way or in a direct manner

di·rec·tion n. the act of directing, aiming or managing ‖ a command ‖ instruction ‖ (pl.) instructions ‖ the course which something is taking or is pointed towards **di·réc·tion·al** adj.

dirt n. any unclean substance, anything that soils ‖ soil ‖ mud ‖ excrement

dirt·y 1. dirt·i·er dirt·i·est adj. soiled, not clean ‖ indecent ‖ (of color) murky **2.** dirt·y·ing dirt·ied v.t. to soil ‖ v.i. to become dirty

dis·a·bil·i·ty pl. dis·a·bil·i·ties n. a being physically or mentally disabled ‖ a cause of this

dis·a·ble dis·a·bling dis·a·bled v.t. to incapacitate physically or mentally **dis·á·ble·ment** n.

dis·ad·van·tage 1. n. an unfavorable

circumstance, drawback, handicap ‖ loss **2. dis·ad·van·tag·ing dis·ad·van·taged** v.t. to place at a disadvantage

disadvantaged adj. of economically deprived or handicapped people **disad·vantaged** n.

dis·a·gree v.i. **dis·a·gree·ing dis·a·greed** to differ in opinion ‖ to quarrel, squabble ‖ to upset the digestion

dis·a·gree·a·ble adj. unpleasant ‖ ill-natured

dis·a·gree·ment n. a disagreeing ‖ a being opposed

dis·ap·pear v.i. to vanish, cease to be visible **dis·ap·péar·ance** n.

dis·ap·point v.t. to fail to come up to the expectations of ‖ to frustrate **dis·ap·póint·ed** adj. unhappy **dis·ap·póint·ing** adj. **dis·ap·póint·ment** n. someone who or something which disappoints

dis·ap·prov·al n. moral condemnation ‖ administrative rejection

dis·ap·prove dis·ap·prov·ing dis·ap·proved v.t. to express an unfavorable opinion of ‖ to refuse to sanction ‖ v.i. to withhold approval **dis·ap·próv·ing·ly** adv.

dis·arm to deprive of weapons ‖ to turn aside the criticism of ‖ v.i. to cut down armaments, or renounce them

dis·ar·ray 1. n. a lack of order ‖ a state of confusion **2.** v.t. to throw into disorder

dis·as·ter n. a great or sudden misfortune ‖ a fiasco **dis·ás·trous** adj.

dis·a·vow v.t. to refuse to acknowledge or accept responsibility for, disclaim **dis·a·vów·al** n.

dis·band v.t. to end the existence of (an organization ‖ v.i. to disperse, break up **dis·bánd·ment** n.

dis·bar dis·bar·ring dis·barred v.t. to expel from the bar, to deprive of the status of attorney **dis·bár·ment** n.

dis·be·lieve dis·be·liev·ing dis·be·lieved v.i. (with 'in') to refuse to believe ‖ v.t. to refuse to accept as true **dis·be·líev·er** n.

dis·burse dis·burs·ing dis·bursed v.t. to

pay out **dis·búrse·ment** *n.* the money paid out

dis·card *v.t.* to get rid of

dis·cern *v.t.* to see, or make out through any of the senses **dis·cérn·i·ble** *adj.* **dis·cérn·i·bly** *adv.* **dis·cérn·ing** *adj.* discriminating, perceptive **dis·cérn·ment** *n.* discrimination, insight, perception

dis·charge 1. *v.t.* **dis·chárg·ing dis·chárged** to unload ‖ to send forth, give out ‖ to release (an arrow or bullet etc.) ‖ to rid of an electric charge ‖ to dismiss ‖ to emit (e.g. pus) 2. *n.* an unloading of a ship or cargo ‖ the firing of a gun etc. ‖ a release ‖ a dismissal ‖ *(law)* an acquittal **dis·chárg·er** *n.* an apparatus for discharging electricity

dis·ci·ple *v.t.* someone who accepts the doctrine or teachings of another ‖ one of the 12 Apostles

dis·ci·pli·nar·y *adj.* of or relating to discipline ‖ concerned with mental training

dis·ci·pline 1. *n.* the training of the mind and character ‖ a branch of learning ‖ control, order, obedience to rules 2. *v.t.* **dis·ci·plin·ing dis·ci·plined** to bring under control ‖ to punish

dis·claim *v.t.* to refuse to acknowledge (e.g. responsibility) ‖ *v.i. (law)* to make a disclaimer

dis·claim·er *n.* a renunciation, e.g. of a legal claim

dis·close dis·clos·ing dis·closed *v.t.* to reveal ‖ to expose to view **dis·clo·sure** *n.* the act of disclosing

dis·col·or *v.t.* to spoil the color of, stain ‖ *v.i.* to become changed or spoiled in color **dis·col·or·á·tion** *n.* **dis·cól·or·ment** *n.*

dis·com·fort *n.* physical or mental uneasiness

dis·con·cert *v.t.* to give a mental jolt to, confuse ‖ to upset, spoil

dis·con·nect *v.t.* to cause to be no longer connected **dis·con·néct·ed** *adj.* disjoined ‖ incoherent **dis·con·nec·tion** *n.* a disconnecting

dis·con·so·late *adj.* utterly dejected

dis·con·tent 1. *n.* dissatisfaction 2. *v.t.* to make dissatisfied **dis·con·tént·ed** *adj.* **dis·con·tént·ment** *n.*

dis·con·tin·u·ance *n.* a discontinuing

dis·con·tin·u·á·tion *n.* a discontinuing

dis·con·tin·ue dis·con·tin·u·ing dis·con·tin·ued *v.t.* to stop, give up ‖ *v.i.* to cease

dis·con·tin·u·ous *adj.* interrupted, intermittent

dis·cord *n.* disagreement ‖ a jarring combination of sounds **dis·córdance** *n.* **dis·córd·ant** *adj.*

dis·count *n.* a sum deducted from an account ‖ a reduction in price offered to the public for sales promotion

dis·count *v.t.* to refuse to accept as being wholly true ‖ to sell at a reduced price ‖ to dismiss as negligible

dis·cour·age dis·cour·ag·ing dis·cour·aged *v.* to sap ‖ to deter ‖ to lessen enthusiasm for ‖ to tend no encouragement to **dis·cóur·age·ment** *n.*

dis·cour·te·ous *adj.* unmannerly, impolite

dis·cov·er *v.t.* to find out ‖ to find by exploration ‖ to come across **dis·cóv·er·y** *pl.* **dis·cov·er·ies** *n.* the thing discovered

dis·cred·it 1. *v.t.* to destroy the trustworthiness of 2. *n.* disesteem ‖ doubt

dis·creet *adj.* circumspect in word or deed ‖ able to keep silent about matters

dis·crep·an·cy *pl.* **dis·crep·an·cies** *n.* the state of being discrepant

dis·crim·i·nate dis·crim·i·nat·ing dis·crim·i·nat·ed *v.i.* to use good judgment in making a choice ‖ to make distinctions ‖ *v.t.* to distinguish to **discriminate against** to single out for unfavorable treatment **dis·crím·i·nat·ing** *adj.* having fine judgment or taste

dis·crim·i·na·tion *n.* good taste, discernment ‖ the making of distinctions in meting out treatment, services etc.

dis·cus *pl.* **dis·cus·es dis·ci** *n. (athletics)* a heavy disk

dis·cuss *v.t.* to exchange ideas about ‖ to debate **dis·cúss·i·ble** *adj.*

dis·dain 1. *v.t.* to scorn ‖ to have contempt for **2.** *n.* contempt, scorn **dis·dáin·ful** *adj.*

dis·ease *n.* a particular malady **dis·éased** *adj.*

dis·en·chant *v.t.* to disillusion **dis·en·chánt·ment** *n.*

dis·fig·ure dis·fig·ur·ing dis·fig·ured *v.t.* to spoil the appearance of **dis·fíg·ure·ment** *n.* a disfiguring

dis·grace 1. *n.* loss of honor or esteem ‖ shame, ignominy ‖ something causing shame or discredit **2.** *v.t.* **dis·grac·ing dis·graced** to bring shame or discredit upon **dis·gráce·ful** *adj.*

dis·guise 1. *v.t.* **dis·guis·ing dis·guised** to change the normal appearance ‖ to hide **2.** *n.* an altering of appearance to conceal identity **dis·gúise·ment** *n.*

dis·gust *n.* strong aversion, loathing

dis·gust *v.t.* to fill with loathing **dis·gúst·ing** *adj.*

dish 1. *n.* a shallow vessel, typically of glass or earthenware ‖ the food served in such a dish **2.** *v.t.* to put (food) into a dish

dis·heart·en *v.t.* to discourage, dispirit **dis·héart·en·ing** *adj.* **dis·héart·en·ment** *n.*

dis·hon·est *adj.* lacking integrity ‖ insincere

dis·hon·es·ty *pl.* **dis·hon·es·ties** *n.* lack of honesty ‖ fraud

dis·hon·or *n.* disgrace ‖ something which brings disgrace

dishonor *v.t.* to treat disrespectfully ‖ to bring shame or disgrace on

dis·hon·or·a·ble *adj.* disgraceful **dis·hón·or·a·bly** *adv.*

dis·il·lu·sion 1. *v.t.* to disenchant **2.** *n.* the state of being disillusioned **dis·il·lú·sion·ment** *n.*

dis·in·fect *v.t.* to free from infection

dis·in·fect·ant *n.* an agent used to kill harmful microorganisms

dis·in·her·it *v.t.* to deprive of an inheritance

dis·in·te·grate dis·in·te·grat·ing dis·in·te·grat·ed *v.t.* to break up into

fragments ‖ *v.i.* to break up, lose unity, go to pieces **dis·in·te·grá·tion dis·in·te·gra·tor** *ns*

disk disc *n.* a flat circular plate ‖ *(computer)* magnetic coated plastic record for storing data ‖ structure in the body, esp. the gristly pads cushioned between the vertebrae

dis·like 1. *v.t.* **dis·lik·ing dis·liked** to feel an antipathy for **2.** *n.* an aversion

dis·lo·cate dis·lo·cat·ing dis·lo·cat·ed *v.t.* to put out of joint, displace **dis·lo·cá·tion** *n.*

dis·mal *adj.* gloomy, dreary ‖ depressing

dis·man·tle dis·man·tling dis·man·tled *v.t.* to take to pieces ‖ to strip of furniture and equipment

dis·may 1. *v.t.* to fill with consternation or alarm **2.** *n.* consternation, alarm

dis·mem·ber *v.t.* to divide limb from limb

dis·miss *v.t.* to send away ‖ to discharge from employment ‖ to put out of one's thoughts **dis·míss·al** *n.*

dis·o·be·di·ence *n.* failure or refusal to obey **dis·o·bé·di·ent** *adj.* failing or refusing to obey

dis·o·bey *v.t.* to refuse or fail to obey

dis·or·der *n.* confusion ‖ disarray, untidiness ‖ riot, lawlessness ‖ a disease **dis·ór·der·ly** *adj.* unruly, wild ‖ untidy

dis·or·gan·ize dis·or·gan·iz·ing dis·or·gan·ized *v.t.* to upset the planned scheme of (things)

dis·o·ri·ent *v.t.* to confuse (a person) about his bearings ‖ to make ill-adjusted

dis·own *v.t.* to deny authorship of ‖ to repudiate

dis·par·age dis·par·ag·ing dis·par·aged *v.t.* to belittle, deprecate **dis·pár·age·ment** *n.* **dis·pár·ag·ing** *adj.*

dis·par·i·ty *pl.* **dis·par·i·ties** *n.* great difference

dis·patch, des·patch 1. *v.t.* to send off ‖ to put to death, kill ‖ to put a quick end to, finish off promptly **2.** *n.* a sending off ‖ a putting to death ‖ an official report

dis·pel dis·pel·ling dis·pelled *v.t.* to

disperse

dis·pen·sa·ble *adj.* not necessary ‖ capable of being distributed

dis·pen·sa·tion *n.* the act of meting out ‖ an exemption from a rule, penalty or law

dis·pense dis·pens·ing dis·pensed *v.t.* to give out ‖ to prepare and give out (medicine) ‖ to administer ‖ to grant a dispensation to ‖ *v.i.* (with 'with') to do without **dis·pén·er** *n.* someone who dispenses or something which dispenses

dis·perse dis·pers·ing dis·persed *v.t.* to scatter, disseminate ‖ to cause to break up ‖ *v.i.* to break up, go away in different directions ‖ to become dispersed

dis·place dis·plac·ing dis·placed *v.t.* to take the place of, oust ‖ to remove from its usual place

dis·play 1. *v.t.* to exhibit ‖ to reveal, show (qualities etc.) ‖ to show ostentatiously

dis·please dis·pleas·ing dis·pleased *v.t.* to annoy, offend

dis·pleas·ure *n.* annoyance, disapproval

dis·pos·a·ble 1. *adj.* that can be disposed of, got rid of **2.** *n.* something that is to be thrown away after use

dis·pose dis·pos·ing dis·posed *v.t.* to place in position, arrange **to dispose of** to get rid of

dis·po·si·tion *n.* a being disposed ‖ a making over of property, bestowal ‖ a plan or preparatory countermeasure

dis·pos·sess *v.t.* to deprive of property ‖ to oust **dis·pos·sés·sion, dis·pos·sés·sor** ns

dis·prove dis·prov·ing dis·proved *v.t.* to prove to be false

dis·put·a·ble *adj.* questionable, open to dispute **dis·pút·a·bly** *adv.*

dis·pute 1. *v.* **dis·put·ing dis·put·ed** *v.i.* to quarrel, argue ‖ *v.t.* to question the truth of **2.** *n.* a quarrel

dis·qual·i·fi·ca·tion *n.* a disqualifying or being disqualified ‖ something which disqualifies

dis·qual·i·fy dis·qual·i·fy·ing dis·qual·i·fied *v.t.* to render unfit

dis·re·gard 1. *v.t.* to pay no heed to, ignore **2.** *n.* indifference ‖ neglect

dis·re·pair *n.* the state of needing repair

dis·re·spect *n.* lack of respect, incivility **dis·re·spéct·ful** *adj.*

dis·rupt *v.t.* to tear apart, shatter ‖ to interrupt

dis·rup·tion *n.* a disrupting or being disrupted

dis·sat·is·fac·tion *n.* a being dissatisfied

dis·sat·is·fied *adj.* not satisfied ‖ discontented

dis·sat·is·fy dis·sat·is·fy·ing dis·sat·is·fied *v.t.* to fail to satisfy ‖ to make discontented

dis·sect *v.t.* to cut up ‖ to cut open ‖ to examine in detail **dis·séc·ted** *adj.*

dis·sen·sion *n.* a difference of opinions, strife

dis·sent 1. *v.i.* to withhold assent ‖ to be in opposition **dis·sént·er** *n.* someone who dissents **2.** *n.* disagreement, difference of opinion ‖ nonconformity

dis·serv·ice *n.* a well-meant but in fact harmful attempt to be of service

dis·si·pate dis·si·pat·ing dis·si·pat·ed *v.t.* to break up, dispel ‖ to waste ‖ *v.i.* to disperse, vanish **dís·si·pat·ed** *adj.*

dis·solve dis·solv·ing dis·solved *v.t.* to cause to pass into a solution ‖ to disperse ‖ *v.i.* to pass into solution ‖ to break, melt **dis·sól·vent 1.** *adj.* capable of dissolving something **2.** *n.* a dissolving agent, a solvent

dis·so·nance *n.* (mus.) discord ‖ disagreement ‖ inconsistency

dis·suade dis·suad·ing dis·suad·ed *v.t.* to change the intention of by persuasion **dis·sua·sion** *n.* **dis·sua·sive***adj.*

dis·tance 1. *n.* an interval in space ‖ the remoter part of a view ‖ an interval of time ‖ reserve, aloofness **2.** *v.t.* **dis·tanc·ing dis·tanced** to put or maintain at a distance

dis·tant *adj.* far away ‖ far removed in relationship ‖ reserved, aloof

dis·taste *n.* dislike ‖ aversion **dis·táste·ful** *adj.*

dis·till, dis·til dis·till·ing, dis·til·ling dis·tilled *v.i.* to undergo a process of evaporation and condensation ‖ *v.t.* to extract the pure essence of (something) **dis·til·late** *n.* the product of distillation

dis·til·la·tion *n.* a distilling or being distilled

dis·till·er·y *pl.* **dis·till·er·ies** *n.* a building where spirits are manufactured by distilling

dis·tinct *adj.* clear, plain ‖ marked, definite

dis·tinc·tion *n.* the making of a difference, discrimination ‖ a difference so made ‖ a mark of honor

dis·tin·guish *v.t.* to recognize (something) as distinct from other things ‖ to tell the difference between ‖ to make out, perceive ‖ to win honor for (oneself etc.) **dis·tín·guish·a·ble** *adj.* **dis·tín·guished** *adj.*

dis·tort *v.t.* to twist out of shape ‖ to give a false significance to, misrepresent **dis·tór·tion** *n.*

dis·tract *v.t.* to divert (attention) ‖ to disturb, confuse

dis·trac·tion *n.* a distracting or being distracted ‖ a diversion, interruption

dis·traught *adj.* almost crazy with anxiety etc., frantic

dis·tress *n.* considerable mental or physical discomfort or pain ‖ acute financial hardship

distress *v.t.* to cause considerable mental or physical discomfort or pain

dis·trib·ute dis·trib·ut·ing dis·trib·ut·ed *v.t.* to deal out, divide out ‖ to spread, scatter

dis·tri·bu·tion *n.* a distributing or being distributed

dis·trib·u·tor *n.* someone who distributes ‖ a device which distributes electric power

dis·trict 1. *n.* a region ‖ a political or geographical division 2. *v.t.* to divide into districts

dis·trust 1. *n.* a lack of trust 2. *v.t.* to regard with suspicion **dis·trúst·ful**

dis·turb *v.t.* to upset the peace of, bother ‖ to worry ‖ to move out of place

dis·turb·ance *n.* public disorder, tumult

dis·u·nite dis·u·nit·ing dis·u·nit·ed *v.t.* to fall apart, separate **dis·u·ni·ty** *pl.* **dis·u·ni·ties** *n.*

ditch 1. *n.* a narrow, shallow trench 2. *v.i.* to make or repair ditches ‖ to drive (a vehicle) into a ditch ‖ to abandon, get rid of

di·ur·nal *adj.* completed once in one day ‖ daily ‖ active mainly in the daytime

di·van *n.* a long low couch

dive 1. **div·ing dived, dove dived** *v.i.* to plunge headfirst into water ‖ to go underwater ‖ to plunge down steeply through the air ‖ to dart quickly, esp. so as to hide or flee 2. *n.* a diving into water ‖ a low-class establishment for drinking, gambling etc.

div·er *n.* someone who dives

di·verge di·verg·ing di·verged *v.i.* to go in branching directions ‖ (with 'from') to turn aside ‖ to deviate from the normal, differ **di·vér·gence** *n.* **di·vér·gen·cy** *pl.* **di·vér·gen·cies** *n.* **di·vér·gent** *adj.*

di·verse *adj.* different, unlike in character or qualities ‖ various

di·ver·si·fi·ca·tion *n.* a diversifying or being diversified

di·ver·si·fy di·ver·si·fy·ing di·ver·si·fied *v.* to make varied

di·ver·sion *n.* a turning aside, deviating ‖ something which brings pleasant mental distraction **di·ver·sion·ar·y** *adj.* intended to create a diversion

di·ver·si·ty *pl.* **di·ver·si·ties** *n.* the state or quality of being diverse ‖ variety

di·vert *v.t.* to turn aside ‖ to distract ‖ to amuse, entertain **di·vért·ing** *adj.*

di·vide 1. **di·vid·ing di·vid·ed** *v.t.* to separate ‖ to deal out, share ‖ to put into separate groups ‖ *v.i.* to do mathematical division ‖ to separate, branch 2. *n.* a watershed ‖ a line of division **di·víd·ed** *adj.*

div·i·dend *n.* interest or share of profits ‖ the individual's share of a sum divided

di·vine *adj.* of God or a god ‖ having the nature of a god ‖ superlatively good or beautiful **di·vin·ing** *v.i.* to detect the presence of water or metals under

ground by means of a forked twig or
rods

di·vin·i·ty pl. **di·vin·i·ties** n. the quality
of being divine ‖ a god

di·vis·i·ble adj. capable of being divided
without a remainder **di·vís·i·bly** adv.

di·vi·sion n. a dividing or being divided
‖ a distribution ‖ a sharing ‖ something
which divides ‖ a section of a larger
group ‖ lack of harmony, disagreement
di·ví·sion·al adj.

di·vorce n. a legal dissolution of marriage
‖ any marked or total separation

di·vulge di·vulg·ing di·vulged v.t. to
make known, reveal **di·vúl·gence** ns

diz·zi·ness n. the state of being dizzy

diz·zy adj. **diz·zi·er diz·zi·est** experiencing a sensation of vertigo

do do·ing done v.t. to perform ‖ to work
at, have as occupation ‖ to deal with ‖ to
accomplish, finish ‖ to cook ‖ to render
‖ to play the part of ‖ to make a tour of
‖ to upset, ruin ‖ used as a substitute verb
to avoid repetition ‖ used as an auxiliary
verb in negation

doc·ile adj. tractable, menable, easy to
manage **do·cil·i·ty** n.

dock 1. n. an enclosure or artificial basin
in which ships may be loaded, unload-
ed, repaired etc. ‖ a pier **2.** v.t. to bring
or receive (a ship) into dock

doc·tor 1. n. a person qualified to practice
medicine ‖ the title of the holder of the
highest university degree **2.** v.t. to give
first aid to ‖ to adulterate ‖ to alter so as
to falsify **dóc·tor·al** adj. **doc·tor·ate** n.
the degree or rank of doctor **doc·to·ri·al**
adj.

doc·tri·nal adj. of or relating to doctrine

doc·trine n. the tenets of a political or
economic system, or the dogma of a
religion

doc·u·ment 1. n. an official paper that
gives information or supplies evidence
2. v.t. to support or supply with documents **doc·u·men·ta·ry 3.** adj. set down
in writing **4.** pl. **doc·u·men·ta·ries** n. a
documentary film

dodge 1. dodg·ing dodged v.i. to move

suddenly in order to avoid a blow, being
seen etc. ‖ to be evasive ‖ v.t. to avoid by
trickery ‖ to evade **2.** n. a quick evasive
movement ‖ a trick **dódg·er** n. a person
full of subterfuge

doe pl. **does, doe** n. a female deer, hare
or rabbit

doff v.t. to take off (one's hat) in salutation

dog n. a common quadruped of many
breeds ‖ a term of contempt or abuse ‖
a mechanical gripping device

dog·ged adj. obstinate, pertinacious,
persistent

dog·ma pl. **dog·mas, dog·ma·ta** n. a basic
doctrinal point in religion or philosophy

dog·mat·ic adj. of or relating to dogma,
doctrinal **dog·mát·i·cal** adj.
dog·mát·ics n.

doi·ly, doy·ley pl. **doi·lies** n. a small,
usually round, ornamental mat of lace,
paper or plastic

dole 1. n. a weekly relief payment ‖ a
charitable distribution **2. dol·ing doled**
(with 'out') to give out in small portions

doll n. a miniature human figure made as
a toy ‖ a pretty, empty-headed woman

dol·lar n. the basic monetary unit of the
U.S.A., containing 100 cents ‖ the
symbol ($) of the dollar ‖ a note of the
value of one dollar

doll·y pl. **doll·ies** n. a child's word for doll
‖ a small wheeled trolley for carrying
beams etc.

dol·or·ous adj. sad, mournful ‖ distressing

dolt n. a dull, stupid person, an oaf
dólt·ish adj.

do·main n. an estate or territory over
which authority is exerted ‖ a sphere of
action or thought

dome 1. n. a large, hemispherical structure surmounting the highest part of a
roof ‖ anything resembling the dome of
a building **2. dom·ing domed** v.t.

do·mes·tic 1. adj. belonging to the home
or house ‖ relating to family affairs ‖ tame
2. n. a household servant
do·més·ti·cal·ly adv.

do·mes·ti·cate v.t. **do·mes·ti·cat·ing**
do·mes·ti·cat·ed to tame (animals) and

teach them to live with man and under his control **do·mes·ti·cá·tion** n.

dom·i·cile 1. n. a home, dwelling place **2.** v.t. **dom·i·cil·ing dom·i·ciled** to establish in a domicile **dom·i·cíl·i·ar·y** adj.

dom·i·nance n. the quality of being dominant ‖ a dominating influence

dom·i·nant adj. controlling, ruling ‖ most noticeable ‖ commanding by position

dom·i·nate dom·i·nat·ing dom·i·nat·ed v.t. to exert authority over, control ‖ to tower above

dom·i·na·tion n. authority, control ‖ predominance

dom·i·neer v.i. to force one's wishes, opinions or commands overbearingly on others **dom·i·néer·ing** adj.

do·min·ion n. sovereignty, supreme authority

don don·ning donned v.t. to put on (robes, armor etc.)

do·nate do·nat·ing do·nat·ed v.t. to give or present (esp. money) to a society, institution etc.

do·na·tion n. a gift, esp. of money

done past. part. of DO ‖ adj. finished, completed ‖ cooked as long as thought desirable

don·key pl. **don·keys** n. the ass ‖ a stupid person

do·nor n. someone who makes a gift ‖ a person giving some of his blood for transfusion

doom 1. n. a calamitous fate ‖ ruin, destruction **2.** v.t. to destine to a fate involving death, suffering or unhappiness

door n. a solid barrier, swinging on hinges or sliding, to close the entrance of a building, a room, a cupboard etc.

dope 1. n. a narcotic ‖ a lubricant ‖ information that lets one into a secret ‖ a very stupid person **2.** v.t. **dop·ing doped** to drug

dor·mant adj. quiescent ‖ sleeping, or as if sleeping ‖ inactive, resting ‖ hibernating

dor·mer n. a projecting window built out from the slope of a roof

dor·mi·to·ry pl. **dor·mi·to·ries** a communal sleeping room with a number of beds

dor·sal adj. on or lying near the back

dos·age n. the administration of medicine in doses

dose 1. n. the amount of medicine to be taken at one time ‖ an amount of punishment or anything else one can stand in limited quantities **2.** v.t. **dos·ing dosed** to administer medicine to

dos·si·er pl. **dos·si·ers** n. a set of papers giving information about one particular subject, esp. one person's personal record

dot 1. n. a small spot or point, usually round **2.** v.t. **dot·ting dot·ted** to mark with a dot or dots **dót·ted** adj.

dot·age n. a feeblemindedness as a result of old age **in one's dotage** senile

dou·ble dou·bling dou·bled v.t. to make double, multiply by two

double 1. adj. having two parts, layers, decks, etc. ‖ forming a pair ‖ of twice the usual speed, number or quantity ‖ (of a bed or room) for two people **2.** adv. twice over, two together **3.** n. something twice as much ‖ a person or thing that resembles another extremely closely ‖ (movies) an actor who substitutes for the star, esp. in dangerous scenes

doubt n. feeling of uncertainty ‖ (esp. pl.) misgivings

doubt v.t. to disbelieve ‖ to distrust ‖ to be in doubt about ‖ v.i. to be in a state of doubt

doubt·ful adj. full of doubt

doubt·less adv. without doubt, certainly

dough n. a mass of slightly moistened flour or meal, sometimes with yeast or fat added, esp. for making bread or pastry ‖ money

dough·nut n. a ring or ball of sweetened dough fried in deep fat and often coated with sugar

dour adj. sullen, sour ‖ stern, harsh

douse, dowse dous·ing, dows·ing doused, dowsed v.t. to drench with water ‖ to immerse in water

dow·a·ger n. a widow whose title derives from her dead husband ‖ (loosely) a formidably dignified elderly lady

dow·dy dow·di·er dow·di·est adj. (of a woman and her clothes) shabby, drab and unfashionable

down n. the fluff under the feathers of birds

down 1. adv. from a higher to a lower position ‖ in a direction or place thought of as lower ‖ into a low mental or emotional state ‖ into a low physical condition ‖ less in value ‖ as an initial cash payment 2. prep. in a lower position on ‖ further along ‖ descending toward, through, into 3. adj. descending ‖ depressed v.t. to knock, throw, put, bring or drink down

down·cast adj. depressed, dispirited

down·fall n. a heavy fall of rain or snow ‖ a fall from greatness or prosperity ‖ a cause of ruin

down·grade 1. n. a downward slope 2. adj. and adv. downhill 3. v.t. down·grad·ing down·grad·ed to reduce or put in a lower category

down·heart·ed adj. depressed, dejected

down·ward adj. from a higher to a lower level

down·wards adv. downward

doze 1. v.i. doz·ing dozed to sleep lightly **to doze off** to fall lightly asleep 2. n. a catnap

doz·en pl. doz·ens, doz·en n. a group of 12 dóz·ens pl. n. a large but unspecified number

drab drab·ber drab·best adj. dull, monotonous

draft, draught 1. n. a writing, drawing, plan etc. as first put on paper and intended to be revised later ‖ the payment of money from an account held for this purpose ‖ conscription ‖ a current of air 2. adj. used for pulling loads ‖ drawn from a barrel 3. v.t. to call up for military service ‖ to make a rough, preliminary version of (a document, letter etc.)

draftee n. a conscript **dráft·i·ly** adv.

dráft·i·ness n.

draft·y draft·i·er draft·i·est adj. exposed to currents of air

drag 1. v. drag·ging dragged v.t. to pull or haul along ‖ to search the bottom of (a river, lake etc.) with a grapnel ‖ v.i. to be dragged, pulled or trailed ‖ (of time) to pass slowly 2. n. (agric.) a heavy harrow ‖ (colloq.) a boring activity ‖ (pop.) women's clothes worn by a man

drag·on n. a mythical, winged animal

drain 1. v.t. to conduct water away from (land) ‖ to remove surplus water from by sieving, standing in racks etc. ‖ to empty (a vessel) of liquid, esp. by drinking ‖ to exhaust of energy, wealth etc. 2. n. a channel for draining off water from flat land ‖ (med.) a tube or catheter for drawing off the discharge from an abscess or open wound ‖ a constant or protracted demand on wealth, energy or other resources **dráin·age** n.

dra·ma n. a play which in general is serious, not comic, but which does not rise to tragedy ‖ a slice of real life with the intensity of a play

dra·mat·ic adj. pertaining to drama ‖ (of people) inclined to give falsely heightened emphasis to ordinary events **dra·mát·i·cal·ly** adv.

dra·mat·ics pl. n. the performance of plays ‖ dramatic behavior

dram·a·tist n. a playwright

dram·a·ti·za·tion n. a turning into a play ‖ a rendering vivid by acting

dram·a·tize dram·a·tiz·ing dram·a·tized v.t. to put (a novel etc.) into the form of a play ‖ to exaggerate histrionically

drape 1. v.t. drap·ing draped to arrange (materials) in decorative folds 2. n. a draped tapestry or curtain

dras·tic adj. acting violently, having extreme effects ‖ rigorous, thoroughgoing **drás·ti·cal·ly** adv.

draw 1. v. draw·ing drew drawn v.t. to pull ‖ to attract ‖ to pull out, extract ‖ to make a picture or plan of with pencil, pen and ink, charcoal, crayon etc. ‖ to inhale ‖ to write out (a check) ‖ *v.i.* to infuse ‖ (with 'on') to obtain something from a reserve, store etc. ‖ (of smoking, with 'on') to inhale **2.** *n.* a game or match that ends without either side winning ‖ a raffle ‖ the pulling of a revolver out of its holster to shoot ‖ the choosing of a card from the pack

draw·back *n.* a disadvantage

draw·er *n.* a boxlike receptacle which slides in and out of a table, cabinet etc.

draw·ing *n.* a sketch, picture or plan in pencil, charcoal, crayon, etc. ‖ a gathering at which lots are drawn

drawl **1.** *v.i.* to speak indistinctly and slurring one word into the next ‖ *v.t.* to utter in this way **2.** *n.* this manner of speech

dread **1.** *v.t.* to be very much afraid of **2.** *n.* apprehension ‖ great fear **3.** *adj.* feared

dread·ful *adj.* inspiring dread ‖ very bad **dread·ful·ly** *adv.*

dream **1.** *n.* an idea or image present in the sleeping mind ‖ something greatly desired ‖ an extravagant fancy **2.** **dream·ing dreamt dreamed** *v.t.* to experience mentally while asleep ‖ *v.i.* to indulge in reverie or imagination, usually of a pleasant kind, esp. to daydream **dream·er** *n.* an impractical person who tends to live in a world of fantasy

drear·y drear·i·er drear·i·est dull and gloomy ‖ depressing ‖ uninteresting

dredge **1.** **dredg·ing dredged** *v.i.* to use a dredge **2.** *n.* an apparatus, such as a crane and grab, for clearing mud etc. from a riverbed or harbor

drench *v.t.* to wet thoroughly, soak

dress **1.** *v.t.* to put clothes on ‖ to arrange decoratively for display ‖ to clean and bandage (a wound) ‖ to clean and truss (poultry, game) ‖ to garnish (a dish) ‖ to style, arrange (hair) **2.** *n.* attire ‖ a woman's frock or gown

dress·er *n.* a chest of drawers

drib·ble **1.** **drib·bling drib·bled** *v.i.* to drool ‖ to flow, in a small trickle **2.** *n.* a small trickle

drift **1.** *n.* the process of being driven, usually slowly, in a certain direction by wind, water etc. in motion ‖ deviation due to current **2.** *v.i.* to be carried along by a current of water or by wind or as if by that ‖ to be piled up by wind ‖ to move aimlessly ‖ to walk slowly

drift·age *n.* material washed up on the shore **drift·er** *n.* someone who drifts, esp. rather unstable

drift·wood *n.* pieces of wood floating in the sea or cast up on the shore

drill *n.* a series of exercises in physical training ‖ a tool or machine for making holes

drill *v.t.* to train in physical or military exercises ‖ to teach by making (a pupil) repeat a set of facts etc. frequently ‖ to bore (holes)

drink *n.* a liquid to be swallowed ‖ alcoholic liquor

drink drink·ing drank drunk *v.t.* to swallow (a liquid) **drink·er** *n.*

drip **1.** **drip·ping dripped** *v.i.* (of liquid) to fall in drops **2.** *n.* the falling of liquid in drops ‖ the sound of dripping

drip·ping *n.* the act of falling in drops ‖ (also *pl.*) the fat drained off roasting meat

drive **1.** **driv·ing drove driv·en** *v.t.* to control the course of (a car, bus, truck etc., or an animal drawing a vehicle) ‖ to impel by force ‖ (of power) to activate (a piece of machinery) ‖ to cause to work very hard ‖ to force into a course of action, compel ‖ *v.i.* to travel by car or in a carriage ‖ to hit a golf ball from the tee **2.** *n.* an excursion in a car or bus ‖ the driving of animals or game ‖ a concerted effort by a numebr of people ‖ energy and willpower ‖ the part driving a piece of machinery ‖ a private road through the grounds of a house

driv·el **1.** **driv·el·ing driv·eled** *v.i.* to allow saliva to run from the mouth ‖ to talk foolishly **2.** *n.* foolish talk, nonsense

driv·er *n.* someone who drives ‖

a driving wheel ‖ (golf) a wood for driving the ball

driz·zle 1. v.i. **driz·zling driz·zled** to rain slightly **2.** n. a slight, very fine rain **dríz·zly** adj.

droll adj. amusing ‖ surprising, but humorous

drom·e·dar·y pl. **drom·e·dar·ies** n. a variety of one-humped camel

drone 1. n. the male of the honeybee ‖ a very lazy man ‖ a pilotless aircraft or boat guided by remote control ‖ low, monotonous speech, humming or singing **2.** v. **dron·ing droned** v.t. to hum or utter monotonously at a low pitch

droop v.i. to hang down ‖ to be lowered ‖ to slouch ‖ to go limp ‖ v.t. to allow to hang down, slouch etc.

drop n. a very small amount of liquid in a round or pear-shaped mass, either falling or clinging to a surface ‖ a very steep slope ‖ a sheer fall ‖ a parachute descent

drop drop·ping dropped v.t. to allow to fall, accidentally or on purpose ‖ to make (a remark, hint) casually or with studied unconcern ‖ to give up ‖ to cease to discuss (a subject) ‖ to write (a short note, postcard etc.) and mail it ‖ to lower (the voice) ‖ v.i. to fall from exhaustion ‖ to assume a lower position

drought n. a prolonged period of dry weather, a lack of rain **dróught·y** adj.

drown v. to die of suffocation by immersion in a liquid ‖ to make inaudible because of a greater sound

drowse v.i. **drows·ing drowsed** to be half-asleep, doze

drow·si·ly adv. in a drowsy way

drow·si·ness n. the state of being drowsy

drow·sy drow·si·er drow·si·est adj. half-asleep, sleepy

drudge 1. n. someone who has to work hard at uninteresting tasks **2.** v.i. **drudging drudged drudg·er·y** n.

drug 1. n. a substance used as or in a medicine ‖ a narcotic substance, esp. one which induces addiction **2. drug·ging drugged** v.t. to administer drugs to

drug·gist n. someone who dispenses or sells medical drugs, toiletries etc.

drum 1. n. percussive musical instrument ‖ a cylindrical container, or a cylinder or barrel on which cable is wound **2.** v.i. **drum·ming drummed** to make a rhythmic beating sound

drum·stick n. a stick for beating a drum ‖ the leg bone of a chicken or other fowl

drunk 1. adj. intoxicated by alcoholic drink **2.** n. a person who is drunk

drunk·ard n. a person habitually drunk

drunk·en adj. (rarely predicative) in the habit of becoming intoxicated, frequently drunk ‖ caused by or showing the effects of drunkenness

dry 1. adj. **dri·er dri·est** free from moisture ‖ not yielding milk ‖ (of wines) not sweet ‖ thirsty **2.** v. **dry·ing dried** v.

du·al adj. double

dub dub·bing dubbed v.t. to make ceremonially a knight by lightly touching his shoulder with a sword ‖ to give a nickname ‖ to fit a new sound track to (a film)

du·bi·ous adj. doubtful ‖ of questionable value or truth

duch·ess n. a duke's wife or widow ‖ a woman holding a duchy in her own right

duck n. small webfooted swimming birds

duck v.i. to bob or bend down quickly ‖ to dart off quickly in a new direction so as to avoid someone or something ‖ to plunge the head under the water and come up quickly ‖ v.t. to dodge, avoid

duct n. a tube which conveys fluid or some other substance ‖ a pipe or conduit for electric cables etc.

duc·tile adj. easily molded ‖ (of persons) easily led or influenced **duc·til·i·ty** n.

dud 1. n. a shell, bomb etc. that fails to explode ‖ a person or plan turning out a failure **2.** adj. useless

dude n. a dandy, a man of affected speech, dress and manners

due 1. adj. payable ‖ proper, fitting, adequate ‖ expected to arrive ‖ justified in expecting ‖ about (to) ‖ owing, attributable **2.** adv. directly, exactly **3.** n. (pl.) fees, charges

du·el 1. *n.* a fight, arranged and conducted according to a code of honor between two gentlemen ‖ any contest between two antagonists **2.** *v.i.* **du·el·ing du·eled** to fight a duel **dú·el·ist** *n.* someone who fights a duel

du·et *n.* a piece of music for two singers

duke *n.* (in Great Britain and some other European countries) a nobleman holding the highest hereditary title outside the royal family **dúke·dom** *n.* a territory (duchy) ruled by a duke

dul·cet *adj.* (of sounds) sweet, soothing

dull 1. *adj.* slow in understanding ‖ lacking sensitivity ‖ tedious ‖ uninteresting ‖ (of pain) not sharp ‖ (of colors and lights) dim ‖ (of sounds) muffled ‖ without vitality **2.** *v.t.* to make dull ‖ *v.i.* to become dull **dull·ard** *n.* a stupid person

dull·ness dul·ness *n.* the quality of being dull

du·ly *adv.* in a proper manner or degree ‖ at the right time

dumb *adj.* permanently unable to speak, mute *(pop.)* stupid

dumb·found dum·found *v.t.* to shock with amazement, utterly astonish

dum·my 1. *n. pl.* **dum·mies** an imitation of, or substitute for, something ‖ a puppet ‖ *(pop.)* a stupid person ‖ *(cards)* an exposed hand **2.** *adj.* sham ‖ simulating real conditions **3.** *v.i.* **dum·my·ing dum·mied**

dump 1. *v.t.* to unload ‖ to let fall with a bump ‖ to get rid of, dispose of ‖ *(commerce)* to sell in quantity at a very low price **2.** *n.* a scrap heap ‖ a shabby

house, room or place ‖ a place where military supplies are temporarily stored

dump·ling *n.* a lump of dough boiled esp. with stew ‖ a baked pudding of fruit ‖ a short, fat, dumpy person

dunce *n.* a very slow child at school ‖ a stupid person

dune *n.* a ridge of loose sand piled up by the wind

dun·ga·ree *n.* a coarse Indian calico ‖ *(pl.)* overalls or trousers of dungaree or strong cotton cloth, jeans

dun·geon *n.* *(hist.)* an underground prisoners' cell

dupe 1. *n.* someone easily deceived or tricked **2.** *v.t.* **dup·ing duped** to deceive over (a subject) ‖ to prolong **dwéll·ing** *n.* the place where one lives

dwin·dle dwin·dling dwin·dled *v.i.* to grow gradually less in size, extent, quality or importance

dye *n.* a substance capable of coloring materials ‖ a color produced by dyeing

dy·nam·ic 1. *adj.* pertaining to dynamics ‖ active, forceful, energetic **2.** *n.* a moving or driving force **dy·nám·i·cal** *adj.*

dy·na·mite 1. *n.* a powerful explosive ‖ a personality, or an element in a situation, likely to produce violent reactions **2.** *v.t.* **dy·na·mit·ing dy·na·mit·ed** to blow up or destroy with dynamite

dy·nas·ty *pl.* **dy·nas·ties** *n.* a line of rulers of the same family ‖ its period of rule

dys·en·ter·y *n.* a usually endemic disease of the colon characterized by diarrhea

E

E e the fifth letter in the English alphabet

each 1. *adj.* every one of two or more **2.** *adv.* for or to every one ‖ apiece

ea·ger *adj.* keen ‖ having a strong desire

ea·gle *n.* a large diurnal bird of prey ‖ *(golf)* a hole played in two below par

ea·glet *n.* a young eagle

ear 1. *n.* the compound spike of most cereals **2.** *v.i.* to form ears, come into ear

ear *n.* the organ of hearing ‖ the power of hearing correctly or of distinguishing and appreciating sounds

ear·drum *n.* the membrane in the ear which receives sound impulses

earl *n.* a nobleman ranking between a viscount and a marquess **éarl·dom** *n.*

ear·ly earl·i·er earl·i·est 1. *adj.* at or near the beginning of a period of time, piece of work, series etc. ‖ in the near future **2.** *adv.* at or near the beginning of a period of time, piece of work, series, etc. ‖ long ago ‖ unusually or unexpectedly soon

earn *v.t.* to get as a payment in return for work ‖ to deserve or obtain by merit or wrongdoing ‖ (of money, shares etc.) to bring in **earned** *adj.* (of income) worked for ‖ deserved

ear·nest *n.* a token or pledge

earnest *adj.* heartfelt ‖ serious and diligent ‖ emotionally intense and solemn

earn·ing *n.* (*pl.*) money earned by work or commerce

ear·ring *n.* a small ring worn on the earlobe ‖ a small ornament screwed or clipped to the lobe

ear·shot *n.* the distance within which a shout or call can be heard

earth *n.* the planet on which we live ‖ the topsoil of the earth's crust

earth·en·ware *n.* glazed or unglazed pots, plates, crockery, etc., made of clay fired at a lower temperature than that at which its particles would fuse

earth·i·ness *n.* the quality of being earthy

earth·quake *n.* a pressure wave in the earth's crust caused by a deep-seated disturbance

earth·y earth·i·er earth·i·est *adj.* of or like earth ‖ unspiritual, robust

ease 1. *n.* physical comfort and relaxation ‖ mental calm ‖ freedom from difficulty **2.** *v.* **eas·ing eased** *v.t.* to lessen the discomfort or anxiety of, relieve ‖ to make less difficult, trying, or tense ‖ *v.i.* to become less difficult, trying or tense **éase·ful** *adj.*

ea·sel *n.* an adjustable frame of wood or metal to support esp. an artist's canvas

eas·i·ly *adv.* in an easy way ‖ without strain ‖ by far

eas·i·ness *n.* freedom from difficulty ‖ the state of being comfortable or free from care

east 1. *adv.* towards the east **2.** *n.* (usually with 'the') one of the four cardinal points of the compass **3.** *adj.* facing east

East·er *n.* the chief Christian feast, which celebrates the Ressurrection of Christ

east·ern *adj.* facing or moving towards the east

east·ward *adv.* and *adj.* towards the east **éast·wards** *adv.*

eas·y eas·i·er eas·i·est 1. *adj.* not difficult ‖ free from hardship, anxiety or worry ‖ comfortable, smooth ‖ not demanding **easy on the eyes** good-looking **2.** *adv.* **easy does it!** be very careful **to take it easy** to relax ‖ not to get excited

eas·y·go·ing *adj.* not strict, very tolerant

eat eat·ing ate eat·en *v.t.* to take as food ‖ to corrode ‖ *v.i.* to have a meal **éat·a·ble 1.** *adj.* fit to eat **2.** *n.* (*pl.*) things to eat **éat·er** *n.* someone who or something which eats as specified

eaves *pl. n.* the part of a roof which projects over the top of a wall

eaves·drop eaves·drop·ping eaves·dropped *v.i.* to listen to without letting oneself be seen **éaves·drop·per éaves·drop·ing** *ns*

ebb 1. *n.* the drawing back of tidal water from the shore ‖ decline **2.** *v.i.* to decline, worsen, diminish

eb·on·y 1. *n.* the wood of many trees, blackened by a deposition of gum resin in the heartwood **2.** *adj.* black

ec·cen·tric 1. *adj.* (of circles, etc.) not having a common center ‖ not conforming to conventions, odd **2.** *n.* someone who behaves unconventionally **ec·cén·tri·cal·ly** *adv.* **ec·cen·tric·i·ty** *pl.* **ec·cen·tric·i·ties** *n.* oddness of behavior

ec·cle·si·as·tic *n.* a priest, clergyman **ec·cle·si·ás·ti·cal** *adj.* of or relating to the Christian Church or clergy **ec·cle·si·as·ti·cism** *n.* the principles that govern the organization of the Church and its well-being

ech·o 1. *n.* a second reception of sound waves, etc., when these return after reflection from a surface at some distance ‖ a repetition or close imitation **2.** *v.i.* to produce an echo ‖ *v.t.* to imitate ‖ to agree completely with (another's opinions)

é·clat *n.* (of performance) manifest brilliance

ec·lec·tic *adj.* taking from different sources ‖ not confined to one point of view **ec·léc·ti·cal·ly** *adj.* **ec·léc·ti·cism** *n.*

e·clipse 1. *n.* the total or partial cutting off of light received from a celestial body, due to another celestial body's moving into an intercepting position **2.** *v.* **e·clips·ing e·clipsed** *v.t.* to diminish the brightness, glory, etc., of, ‖ *v.i.* to be eclipsed

ec·o·log·i·cal *adj.* of or relating to ecology **e·col·o·gist** *n.* a specialist in ecology **e·col·o·gy oe·col·o·gy** *n.* the branch of biology concerned with the relation between organisms and their environment

e·co·nom·ic *adj.* relating to or concerned with economics ‖ financially sound, reasonably profitable **e·co·nóm·i·cal** *adj.* thrifty, not wasteful ‖ cheap **e·co·nóm·i·cal·ly** *adv.* **e·co·nóm·ics** *n.*

e·con·o·mist *n.* an expert in economics

e·con·o·mize e·con·o·miz·ing e·con·o·mized *v.t.* to refrain from wasting ‖ *v.i.* to reduce expenses

e·con·o·my *pl.* **e·con·o·mies** *n.* thrift ‖ a means of saving money ‖ part of a system that deals with man's material needs ‖ a system of producing and distributing the material needs of society

ec·sta·sy *pl.* **ec·sta·sies** *n.* a state in which reason yields to intense (generally delighted) feeling and one is beside oneself

ec·stat·ic 1. *adj.* feeling, or causing ecstasy **2.** *n.* someone experiencing mystical joy **ec·stát·i·cal·ly** *adv.*

ec·u·men·ic oec·u·men·ic *adj.* ecumenical **ec·u·mén·i·cal oec·u·mén·i·cal** *adj.* of or encouraging universal Christian unity ‖ worldwide **ec·u·mén·i·cal·ism oec·u·mén·i·cal·ism** *n.* the principles of the ecumenical movement **ec·u·men·i·cism oec·u·men·i·cism** *n.* **ec·u·men·i·cist oec·u·men·i·cist** *n.*

ec·ze·ma *n.* a skin disease **ec·zem·a·tous** *adj.*

ed·dy 1. *pl.* **ed·dies** *n.* a whirling movement, such as that seen when water runs out of a bath or is checked by the bank of a river ‖ a similar movement of air or of some things that float **2.** **ed·dy·ing ed·died** *v.t.* to cause to move with a circular or eddying motion ‖ *v.i.* to move in eddies

edge 1. *n.* the extreme limit, e.g., of a table, cliff, wood, sheet of paper, pond, coin ‖ the fringe ‖ the line formed by the meeting of two surfaces ‖ the sharp side or end of a cutting tool **2.** *v.* **edg·ing edged** *v.t.* to make, or serve as, an edge or border for ‖ to move gradually in a confined or awkward place

edg·ing *n.* a border

edg·y edg·i·er edg·i·est *adj.* nervous, jumpy

ed·i·bil·i·ty *n.* the quality of being edible **ed·i·ble** *adj.* wholesome to eat, eatable

e·dict *n.* an official order published by a ruler or by authority **e·dic·tal** *adj.*

ed·i·fi·ca·tion *n.* enlightening of ignorance

ed·i·fice *n.* a building, esp. an imposing one

ed·i·fy ed·i·fy·ing ed·i·fied *v.t.* to improve spiritually or morally by instruction or example

ed·it *v.t.* to prepare (literary or musical work) for publication ‖ to prepare (a film, radio or television material) in the form in which it is to be seen or heard ‖ to alter (matter for publication) so as to make it more suitable for one's purpose

e·di·tion *n.* a published literary or musical text ‖ a particular form in which a book is produced for sale ‖ one of the several issues of a daily newspaper

ed·i·tor *n.* someone who edits a manuscript, book, newspaper, periodical, film, radio or television material, etc.

ed·i·to·ri·al 1. *adj.* of or relating to an editor **2.** *n.* an article in a newspaper or periodical which gives the views of those who decide its policy **ed·i·tor·ship** *n.*

ed·u·cate ed·u·cat·ing ed·u·cat·ed *v.t.* to instruct and train ‖ to provide or obtain such training or instruction for **éd·u·cat·ed** *adj.* properly taught or trained

ed·u·ca·tion *n.* instruction or training by which people learn to develop and use their mental, moral and physical powers ‖ the art of giving such training ‖ the fruit of training or instruction **ed·u·cá·tion·al** *adj.*

eel *n.* any of several genera of teleostean fish

ee·rie ee·ry ee·ri·er ee·ri·est *adj.* mysteriously frightening, uncanny **ée·ri·ly** *adv.* **ée·ri·ness** *n.*

ef·face ef·fac·ing ef·faced *v.t.* to rub or wipe out, obliterate **ef·fáce·a·ble** *adj.* **ef·fáce·ment** *n.*

ef·fect 1. *n.* the result produced by a cause ‖ influence, power to change ‖ general meaning or purport ‖ a general appearance or impression ‖ *(pl.)* artistic contrivances **2.** *v.t.* to accomplish

ef·fec·tive *adj.* causing a desired or decisive result ‖ in use, in force or in operation

ef·fec·tu·al *adj.* capable of, or successful in, bringing about a desired effect

ef·fem·i·nate *adj.* (of men or boys) womanish or girlish, not virile

ef·fer·vesce ef·fer·vesc·ing ef·fer·vesced *v.i.* to produce a great number of bubbles ‖ to manifest high spirits **ef·fer·vés·cence ef·fer·vés·cen·cy** *ns* **ef·fer·vés·cent** *adj.*

ef·fi·ca·cious *adj.* useful or successful

ef·fi·cien·cy *n.* the degree of effectiveness with which something is done ‖ (of a machine) the ratio of the work done to the work needed to operate the machine

ef·fi·cient *adj.* competent ‖ (of a machine) producing nearly as much work as it uses (in the form of fuel, etc.)

ef·fi·gy *pl.* **ef·fi·gies** *n.* a statue, image or dummy of a person

ef·fort *n.* an expense of bodily or mental energy to achieve a desired end

ef·fort·less *adj.* making or appearing to make no effort

ef·fuse ef·fus·ing ef·fused *v.t.* to pour out or forth

ef·fu·sion *n.* a pouring out, a shedding

ef·fu·sive *adj.* unduly demonstrative, gushing

e·gal·i·tar·i·an *adj.* holding the view that all men have equal social and political rights **e·gal·i·tár·i·an·ism** *n.*

egg *n.* the female gamete, ovum ‖ an animal reproductive body consisting of an ovum with its protective coverings or membranes

egg *v.t.* (with 'on') to urge (someone) persistently

e·go *n.* the individual self ‖ the conscious personality as opposed to the unconscious

e·go·tism *n.* the frame of mind which causes a person to pay too much attention to himself, to be conceited and selfish **é·go·tist** *n.* **e·go·tís·tic e·go·tís·ti·cal** *adjs*

e·gre·gious *adj.* flagrant ‖ outstanding for some bad quality

e·gress *n.* a way out, exit ‖ the act of going out

e·gret *n.* a genus of tall, elegant, snowy white birds

eight *adj.* being one more than seven

eight·een *adj*. being one more than 17

eight·eenth 1. *adj*. being number 18 in a series

eighth 1. *adj*. being number eight in a series ‖ the eighth day of a month *adv*. in the eighth place

eight·i·eth 1. *adj*. being number 80 in a series

eight·y 1. *adj*. being ten more than 70 (*NUMBER TABLE*) **the eighties** (of temperature, a person's age, a century, etc.) the span 80-89

ei·ther 1. *adj*. each one of two ‖ one or other of two **2.** *pron*. each one of two ‖ one or other of two **3.** *conj*. used with 'or' to connect two or more alternatives

e·ject *v.t.* to turn out, force to leave ‖ *(law)* to evict

e·jec·tion *n*. an ejecting or being ejected

e·jec·tor *n*. something which ejects

e·lab·o·rate 1. *adj*. made with care and much fine detail **2.** *v.* **e·lab·o·rat·ing** **e·lab·o·rat·ed** *v.t.* to make or develop (a complicated thing) with care, to work out in detail ‖ *v.i.* to go into details about a matter **e·lab·o·ra·tion** *n*. **e·lab·o·ra·tive** *adj*. **e·láb·o·ra·tor** *n*.

e·lapse e·laps·ing e·lapsed *v.i.* (of time, or an equivalent) to pass by

e·las·tic 1. *adj*. having the ability to recover its original size or shape after deformation ‖ springy ‖ adaptable to circumstances **2.** *n*. vulcanized rubber thread ‖ a rubber band **e·lás·ti·cal·ly** *adv*. **e·las·tic·i·ty** *n*. the ability to resume the original size after deformation

e·late e·lat·ing e·lat·ed *v.t.* to fill with joy **e·lát·ed** *adj*.

e·la·tion *n*. the quality of being filled with jubilation

el·bow 1. *n*. the joint connecting the forearm and upper arm ‖ a bend or corner resembling a bent arm **2.** *v.t.* to jostle with the elbow

eld·er 1. *adj*. born at an earlier date ‖ of higher rank or other seniority **2.** (in Presbyterian Churches) a lay official

eld·er·ly *adj*. approaching old age, past middle age

eld·est *adj*. oldest

e·lect 1. *adj*. chosen, esp. chosen by God, predestined to salvation **2.** *pl. n*. **the elect** those chosen by God ‖ a group of people specially privileged in some way **3.** *v.t.* to choose by voting

e·lec·tion *n*. the act or process of electing, esp. of choosing by vote **e·lec·tion·eer** *v.i.* to try to obtain votes for a political candidate

e·lec·tive *adj*. chosen by election or voting ‖ relating to election by vote ‖ (of a course of studies) optional

e·lec·tor *n*. someone who has the right to vote ‖ a member of the electoral college

e·lec·tor·ate *n*. the whole body of those who have the right to vote in a political election

e·lec·tric *adj*. of or pertaining to electricity, containing, produced by electricity ‖ tense **e·léc·tri·cal** *adj*.

e·lec·tri·cian *n*. someone whose trade is making, installing, maintaining or repairing electrical equipment

e·lec·tric·i·ty *n*. a basic form of energy that is a property of certain fundamental particles of matter ‖ an electric current, or stream of electrons ‖ static electricity ‖ the science or study of electricity

e·lec·tri·fy e·lec·tri·fy·ing e·lec·tri·fied *v.t.* to cause to function by electric power ‖ to thrill or startle as though by an electric shock

e·lec·tro·cute *v.t.* **e·lec·tro·cut·ing e·lec·tro·cut·ed** to administer a fatal electric shock to **e·lec·tro·cú·tion** *n*.

e·lec·trode *n*. one of the two conductors (anode or cathode) by which an electric current is passed through a device such as an electrolytic cell

e·lec·trol·y·sis *n*. the passing of an electric current through an electrolyte to produce chemical changes in it ‖ depilation by means of an electric current

e·lec·tro·lyte *n*. a liquid solution or fused salt that conducts electricity **e·lec·tro·lyt·ic** *adj*.

e·lec·tron *n*. a constituent of the atom

e·lec·tron·ic *adj*. of or relating to electronics **e·lec·trón·i·cal·ly** adv. **e·lec·trón·ics** n. the branch of physics dealing with the behavior of electrons

el·e·gance n. the state or quality of being elegant

el·e·gant adj. gracefully refined ‖ showing good taste ‖ fashionable, smart ‖ very good of its kind

el·e·gize el·e·giz·ing el·e·gized v.t. to lament the death of (someone) in an elegy ‖ v.i. to write an elegy

el·e·gy pl. **el·e·gies** n. a poem which laments the death of someone

el·e·ment n. a component of a composite whole ‖ (pl.) atmospheric forces ‖ (pl.) earth, air, fire and water, formerly regarded as the basic constituents of the material universe ‖ the natural habitat of an organism ‖ the resistance coil, wire, of an electric heater, kiln, etc. **el·e·men·tal** adj. elementary

el·e·men·ta·ry adj. very simple, basic ‖ consisting of a single chemical element

el·e·phant n. the Indian or the African, the largest living land animals

el·e·phan·tine adj. of or like an elephant ‖ huge and clumsy ‖ pompous and heavy-handed

el·e·vate el·e·vat·ing el·e·vat·ed v.t. to raise to a higher level ‖ to raise in rank or dignity ‖ to encourage (hopes) or raise (spirits)

el·e·va·tion n. height above sea level ‖ loftiness, grandeur ‖ a hill or piece of rising ground

el·e·va·tor n. a machine that can raise or carry a weight from one level to another ‖ a mechanical apparatus for raising or lowering people or things from floor to floor in a building ‖ a muscle which controls the lifting of a part of the body

e·lev·en 1. adj. being one more than 10 **e·lev·enth** adj. being number 11 in a series

elf pl. **elves** n. a little creature of folklore with magic power

elf·in 1. adj. elflike ‖ fey **2.** n. an elf

elf·ish adj. of or relating to elves ‖ mischievous

e·lic·it v.t. to draw forth in response ‖ to arrive at (the truth, etc.) by questioning

el·i·gi·bil·i·ty n. the state or quality of being eligible

el·i·gi·ble adj. qualified to be chosen ‖ entitled to receive ‖ desirable, suitable

e·lim·i·nate e·lim·i·nat·ing e·lim·i·nat·ed v.t. to get rid of, excrete **e·lim·i·na·tion e·lim·i·na·tor** ns **e·lim·i·na·to·ry** adj.

e·lite n. the few who are considered socially, intellectually or professionally superior to the rest in a group

e·lix·ir n. an aromatic preparation, often sweetened and containing alcohol

elk n. the largest of the deer family

el·lipse n. a plane figure obtained when a plane intersects a cone obliquely

el·lip·tic adj. having the form of an ellipse ‖ characterized by ellipsis **el·lip·ti·cal** adj.

el·o·cu·tion n. the art of speaking or reading correctly in public **el·o·cu·tion·ar·y** adj. **el·o·cu·tion·ist** n. someone skilled in, or who teaches, the art

e·lon·gate 1. v. **e·lon·gat·ing e·lon·gat·ed** v.t. to make longer **2.** adj. (biol.) long and slender

e·lope e·lop·ing e·loped v.i. (of a pair of lovers) to run away with the intention of getting married

el·o·quence n. the skillful use of words to persuade hearers

el·o·quent adj. speaking or writing with eloquence

else 1. adv. in a different way ‖ otherwise **2.** adj. other, different

else·where adv. in, to or at another or a different place

e·lu·ci·date e·lu·ci·dat·ing e·lu·ci·dat·ed v.t. to give an explanation of **e·lu·ci·da·tion e·lu·ci·da·tor** ns

e·lude e·lud·ing e·lud·ed v.t. to slip away from, avoid capture by, dodge away from ‖ to escape the notice, understanding or memory of

e·lu·sive adj. hard to catch, find, pin down or keep hold of ‖ hard to grasp or define precisely

E·ly·sian adj. of or pertaining to Elysium ‖

(of joy, happiness) perfect

E·lys·i·um *pl.* **E·lys·i·ums E·lys·i·a** *n.* (*Gk. mythol.*) the Elysian Fields, the abode after death of the brave and good ‖ a place or state of ideal happiness

e·ma·ci·ate e·ma·ci·at·ing e·ma·ci·at·ed *v.t.* to make thin and worn, to waste **e·ma·ci·at·ed** *adj.* **e·ma·ci·a·tion** *n.*

em·a·nate em·a·nat·ing em·a·nat·ed *v.i.* to come, arise (from a source or origin)

e·man·ci·pate e·man·ci·pat·ing e·man·ci·pat·ed *v.t.* to set free from oppression **e·man·ci·pa·tor** *n.* **e·man·ci·pa·to·ry** *adj.*

e·man·ci·pa·tion *n.* a setting free or being set free, esp. from slavery

em·balm *v.t.* to preserve (a corpse) from decay **em·balm·ment** *n.*

em·bar·go *pl.* **em·bar·goes** *n.* a government order forbidding foreign ships to enter or leave its ports ‖ an order forbidding the import, export or carriage of certain commodities

em·bark *v.t.* to put on board ship ‖ *v.i.* to go on board ship ‖ to start (on something long or dangerous)

em·bar·rass *v.t.* to cause to feel self-conscious, awkward, shy or ashamed ‖ (esp. *pass.*) to involve in debt **em·bar·rass·ing** *adj.* **em·bar·rass·ment** *n.*

em·bas·sy *pl* **em·bas·sies** *n.* an official mission or delegation, esp. one which represents one country in another at the highest diplomatic level ‖ the residence or offices of the head of such a body

em·bel·lish *v.t.* to make more decorative ‖ to add made-up details to (a story) **em·bel·lish·ment** *n.*

em·ber *n.* a hot or red-hot fragment of burning coal or wood ‖ (*pl.*) the hot remains of a fire

em·bez·zle em·bez·zling em·bez·zled *v.t.* to steal or use for one's own purposes (money or other property which has been entrusted to one **em·bez·zle·ment** *n.*

em·blem *n.* an object, or the representation of an object, which serves as a recognized symbol **em·blem·át·i·cal** *adj.* **em·blem·a·tize em·blem·a·tiz·ing em·blem·a·tized** *v.t.* to symbolize, represent by an emblem or serve as an emblem of

em·boss *v.t.* to produce a raised design, pattern or lettering on a plain surface

em·brace 1. em·brac·ing em·braced *v.t.* to put one's arms lovingly around ‖ to accept gladly, seize ‖ *v.i.* hug one another **2.** *n.* a clasping or folding in the arms, a hug ‖ a tight grip

em·broi·der *v.t.* to ornament with needlework ‖ to add to (a story etc.) details that are entertaining but not true

em·broi·der·y *pl.* **em·broi·der·ies** *n.* the art or process of embroidering

em·bry·o *pl.* **em·bry·os** *n.* an animal organism during the early stages of growth and development ‖ a human individual from the time of implantation to the eighth week after conception **em·bry·on·ic** *adj.*

em·er·ald 1. *n.* a bright green precious stone

e·merge e·mer·ging e·merged *v.i.* to come out (from), to appear (from) ‖ to come out from ‖ to come to light, be discovered **e·mer·gence** *n.*

e·mer·gen·cy *pl.* **e·mer·gen·cies** *n.* a situation, often dangerous, which arises suddenly and calls for prompt action ‖ an immediate need

em·er·y *pl.* **em·er·ies** *n.* a very hard, granular corundum, used as an abrasive

em·i·grant *n.* a person emigrating or who has emigrated

em·i·grate em·i·grat·ing em·i·grat·ed *v.i.* to leave one's own country or home and settle in another **em·i·gra·tion** *n.*

em·i·nent *adj.* distinguished, widely thought of as superior in some way ‖ outstanding, conspicuous

em·is·sar·y 1. *pl.* **em·is·sar·ies** *n.* an agent sent on a mission **2.** *adj.* of, or serving as, an emissary

e·mis·sion *n.* a sending out or giving out, e.g. of light, heat, gas, smoke

e·mit e·mit·ting e·mit·ted *v.t.* to give out,

give off ‖ to put (currency etc.) in circulation

e·mote e·mot·ing e·mot·ed *v.i.* to display or affect emotion ‖ to behave histrionically

e·mo·tion *n.* a strong feeling (such as fear, wonder, love, sorrow, shame) **e·mó·tion·al** *adj.* of or relating to the emotions ‖ ruled by emotion rather than by reason **e·mó·tion·al·ism** *n.* **e·mó·tion·al·ist** *n.*

em·pa·thy *n.* the power to enter into the feeling or spirit of others **em·pa·thet·ic em·path·ic** *adjs*

em·per·or *n.* the ruler of an empire **ém·per·or·ship** *n.*

em·pha·sis *pl.* **em·pha·ses** *n.* a special stress or deliberate accent laid on a word or syllable ‖ a special vigor or deliberation given to an action ‖ a special importance given to a thing **em·pha·size em·pha·siz·ing em·pha·sized** *v.t.* to stress

em·phat·ic *adj.* expressed in words or action with emphasis ‖ strongly marked, strikingly noticeable **em·phát·i·cal·ly** *adv.*

em·phy·se·ma *n.* a condition in which the lungs and their constituent air cells are distended with air to the point of inefficiency

em·pire 1. *n.* a sovereign state whose possessions have been extended to include countries or territories originally independent of it ‖ an organization (commercial, industrial, financial) having great wealth and power **2.** *adj.*

em·pir·ic 1. *n.* someone who believes that in science and philosophy there is no truth other than that obtained by sense, observation and experiment **2.** *adj.* **em·pír·i·cal** derived from the senses and not by logical deduction **em·pír·i·cism** *n.* **em·pír·i·cist** *n.*

em·ploy 1. *v.t.* to pay (a person) to work for one ‖ to use, make use of **2.** *n.* in (someone's) **employ** working for (someone) **em·plóy·a·ble** *adj.*

em·ploy·ee *n.* someone paid to work esp. on a regular rather than a casual basis

em·ploy·er *n.* someone who pays another or others to work for him ‖ a user

em·ploy·ment *n.* the state of being employed ‖ work as livelihood

em·pow·er *v.t.* to delegate legal power to

em·press *n.* the wife of an emperor ‖ a woman ruler of an empire in her own right

emp·ti·ly *adv.* in an empty way

emp·ti·ness *n.* the state of being empty

emp·ty 1. emp·ti·er emp·ti·est *adj.* with nothing in it ‖ unoccupied ‖ (*pop.*) hungry **2. emp·ty·ing emp·tied** *v.t.* to cause to become empty, take the contents out of

em·py·re·al *adj.* of the empyrean **em·py·re·an** *n.* the vault of the sky

em·u·late em·u·lat·ing em·u·lat·ed *v.t.* to try to do as well as **em·u·lá·tion** *n.* **em·u·la·tive** *adj.*

e·mul·sion *n.* a colloidal dispersion of two incomplete miscible liquids or of a finely divided insoluble solid in a liquid

e·mul·sive *adj.* having the nature of an emulsion

en·a·ble en·a·bling en·a·bled *v.t.* to make it possible for or to allow

en·act *v.t.* to make into a law ‖ to play out, perform as though on the stage **en·ác·tive** *adj.* **en·áct·ment** *n.*

e·nam·el 1. *n.* enamel paint ‖ the hard, white, calcareous substance which coats the crown of a tooth ‖ a cosmetic applied to the nails to give a hard shiny coating **2.** *v.t.* **e·nam·el·ing e·nam·eled** to coat with enamel

e·nam·ored *adj.* in love

en·camp *v.i.* to set up a camp ‖ **en·cámp·ment** *n.* a camp

en·case in·case en·cas·ing in·cas·ing en·cased in·cased *v.t.* to enclose in an outer cover or case

en·chant *v.t.* to cast a spell on ‖ to fill with delight **en·chánt·ed** *adj.* under a spell **en·chánt·er** *n.* someone who fascinates **en·chánt·ing** *adj.* delightful ‖ fascinating **en·chánt·ment** *n.* **en·chánt·ress** *n.*

en·cir·cle en·cir·cling en·cir·cled *v.t.* to surround ‖ to move in a circular path around **en·cir·cle·ment** *n.* or being surrounded

en·close in·close en·clos·ing in·clos·ing en·closed in·closed to put (something) into an envelope or parcel with something else ‖ to surround on all sides, hem in

en·clo·sure in·clo·sure *n.* something enclosed ‖ a place shut in, fenced in ‖ a fence

en·com·pass *v.t.* to surround or hem in on every side ‖ to embrace within its scope etc.

en·core *interj.* the cry of an audience when it is pleased and wants a performer to play (or sing etc.) again **1.** *n.* the additional performance called for in this way **2.** *v.t.* **en·cor·ing en·cored**

en·coun·ter 1. *v.t.* to come upon, meet ‖ to come up against **2.** *n.* a meeting by chance ‖ a conflict, battle, or match or game between rival teams

en·cour·age en·cour·ag·ing en·cour·aged *v.t.* to give courage or confidence to ‖ to raise the hopes of **en·cour·ag·ing** *adj.* **en·cour·age·ment** *n.* a heartening or being heartened ‖ an inducement

en·croach *v.i.* (with 'on' or 'upon') to make gradual inroads **en·croach·ment** *n.*

en·cum·ber *v.t.* to hamper, impede ‖ to burden

en·cy·clo·pe·di·a en·cy·clo·pae·di·a *n.* a book or series of books giving information on all subjects or on all aspects of one subject **en·cy·clo·pé·dic en·cy·clo·pae·dic** *adj.* **en·cy·clo·pé·di·cal en·cy·clo·pae·di·cal** *adj.* **en·cy·clo·pé·dist en·cy·clo·pae·dist** *n.* someone who writes, edits or contributes to an encyclopedia

end *n.* the last part of a thing ‖ the limit beyond which a thing cannot be extended ‖ a remnant ‖ the conclusion of what has gone before ‖ a final result or ultimate state ‖ death ‖ aim or purpose

end *v.t.* to stop ‖ to conclude ‖ *v.i.* to come to an end

en·dan·ger *v.t.* to cause danger to or constitute a cause of danger to

en·dear *v.t.* to cause to be held in affection **en·déar·ment** *n.*

en·deav·or *n.* a determined effort

end·ing *n.* the action of coming or bringing to an end ‖ conclusion, finish

en·dorse in·dorse en·dors·ing in·dors·ing en·dorsed in·dorsed *v.t.* to sign or initial, or add a comment or qualification to (a document) ‖ to confirm, sanction, show approval of or agreement with (an option, action, proposal etc.) **en·dórse·ment in·dórse·ment** *n.*

en·dow *v.t.* to give money or other property for the permanent upkeep or benefit of (an institution, organization etc.) ‖ (with 'with') to provide with a natural gift, attribute etc. **en·dów·ment** *n.*

en·dur·a·ble *adj.* that can be endured

en·dur·ance *n.* the capacity to keep going or put up with pain, hardship etc. for a long time

en·dure en·dur·ing en·dured *v.t.* to bear, stand ‖ to suffer patiently ‖ to put up with, tolerate ‖ to last for a long time

en·e·my 1. *pl.* **en·e·mies** *n.* a hostile nation ‖ a person who bears another ill will and actively works or fights against him **2.** *adj.* being or pertaining to an enemy

en·er·get·ic *adj.* active, showing great physical or mental energy ‖ forceful, vigorous **en·er·gét·i·cal·ly** *adv.*

en·er·gize en·er·giz·ing en·er·gized *v.t.* to give energy to ‖ to cause electricity to flow in

en·er·gy *pl.* **en·er·gies** *n.* forcefulness and vigor in actions or words

en·er·vate en·er·vat·ing en·er·vat·ed *v.t.* to lower the vitality of **en·er·vá·tion** *n.*

en·force en·forc·ing en·forced *v.t.* to impose by force, compel **en·fórce·a·ble** *adj.* **en·fórce·ment** *n.*

en·gage en·gag·ing en·gaged *v.t.* to take into one's employment ‖ to make a promise binding on (oneself), esp. a promise of marriage ‖ *v.i.* to join battle ‖ (*mech.*, with 'with') to interlock, mesh

(with 'in') to busy oneself **en·gag·ed** *adj.*
en·gage·ment *n.* an appointment for a fixed time ‖ a battle **en·gag·ing** *adj.* attractive, charming

en·gen·der *v.t.* to give rise to

en·gine *n.* a device used to transform one form of energy into another ‖ a locomotive

en·gi·neer 1. *n.* a person qualified in any branch of engineering ‖ the driver of a locomotive ‖ someone active behind the scenes in achieving something 2. *v.t.* to carry out (a piece of engineering work) ‖ to manage, by using tact, craft or ingenuity **en·gi·neer·ing** *n.* the science of applying knowledge of the properties of matter and the natural sources of energy to the practical problems of industry

Eng·lish 1. *adj.* of, relating to or characteristic of the country, state or people of England 2. *n.* the English language **the English** (*pl.*) the people of England or its representatives

en·grain in·grain *v.t.* to instil (habits, tastes etc.) so that they become deep-rooted

en·grave en·grav·ing en·graved *v.t.* to cut a design or lettering on (a hard surface) ‖ to fix deeply in the mind, memory etc. **en·grav·er** *n.* **en·grav·ing** *n.* an impression or print taken from an engraved surface

en·gross *v.t.* to occupy (a person or his attention) to the exclusion of everything else **en·gross·ing** *adj.* holding one absorbed in interest **en·gross·ment** *n.*

en·gulf *v.t.* (of a flood, the sea etc.) to swallow up ‖ overwhelm, bury

en·hance en·hanc·ing en·hanced *v.t.* to increase, add to (a quality, price or value) **en·hanced** *adj.* heightened, intensified **en·hance·ment** *n.*

e·nig·ma *n.* something hard to define or understand fully ‖ an obscure saying, riddle

en·ig·mat·ic *adj.* puzzling, deliberately veiled in meaning **en·ig·mat·i·cal** *adj.*

en·join *v.t.* to impose as a rule ‖ to command ‖ to forbid or restrain by an injunction

en·joy *v.t.* to take pleasure or delight in ‖ to have the use, benefit or advantage of **en·joy·a·ble** *adj.* **en·joy·ment** *n.*

en·large en·larg·ing en·larged *v.t.* to make bigger ‖ to expand ‖ *v.i.* to become bigger ‖ to widen in scope **en·large·ment** *n.* **en·larg·er** *n.* an apparatus for enlarging photographs

en·light·en *v.t.* to give (someone) information about, or help him to understand, what is obscure or difficult **en·light·en·ment** *n.* an enlightening or being enlightened

en·list *v.* to join the armed forces ‖ to call in (help or support) **en·list·ment** *n.* an enlisting, or being enlisted ‖ the period for which someone enlists

en·liv·en *v.t.* to make more lively ‖ to make gayer or brighter

en·mi·ty *n.* a state or feeling of hatred or hostility

en·no·ble en·no·bling en·no·bled *v.t.* to make spiritually, intellectually or morally elevated **en·no·ble·ment** *n.*

en·nui *n.* boredom, weariness and discontent

e·nor·mi·ty *pl.* **e·nor·mi·ties** *n.* a shocking crime or offense ‖ huge size

e·nor·mous *adj.* huge, very great **e·nor·mous·ly** *adv.* to a very great degree

e·nough 1. *adj.* as much (in number, quantity or degree) as is needed 2. *adv.* sufficiently 3. *n.* a sufficient quantity 4. *interj.* stop!, no more!

en·rage en·rag·ing en·raged *v.t.* to make furiously angry

en·rich *v.t.* to make rich or richer in money or goods ‖ to improve the quality of ‖ to add fullness of flavor **en·rich·ment** *n.*

en·roll en·rol en·roll·ing en·rol·ling en·rolled *v.t.* to include (a person's name) in a list ‖ to enter (a document) in an official or legal register **en·roll·ment en·rol·ment** *n.*

en·sconce en·sconc·ing en·sconced *v.t.* to tuck (oneself) away in, install (oneself) in some snug or desirable place

en·sem·ble *n.* a chamber orchestra ‖ the whole company or cast ‖ a complete matching outfit of clothes

en·shrine en·shrin·ing en·shrined *v.t.* to place in a shrine or honored place of safety **en·shrine·ment** *n.*

en·sign *n.* a flag, standard ‖ a U.S. naval officer ranking immediately below a lieutenant junior grade

en·slave en·slav·ing en·slaved *v.t.* to make a slave of **en·slave·ment** *n.*

en·sue en·su·ing en·sued *v.i.* to happen or come afterwards or as a result

en·tail *v.t.* to bring as a necessary consequence ‖ (*law*) to settle (landed property) in such a way that it must be inherited and bequeathed in a certain way **en·tail·ment** *n.*

en·tan·gle en·tan·gling en·tan·gled *v.t.* to catch up in, seemingly inextricably ‖ to involve in difficulties **en·tan·gle·ment** *n.*

en·ter *v.t.* to go or come in or into ‖ to take up, adopt (an occupation, profession etc.) ‖ to join ‖ to make a note or record of (in the appropriate book, list, or other record) ‖ *v.i.* to go in ‖ to come in

en·ter·prise *n.* a venture, esp. one calling for initiative ‖ a commercial or industrial undertaking **en·ter·pris·ing** *adj.*

en·ter·tain *v.t.* to receive as a visitor or guest ‖ amuse ‖ to have in one's mind ‖ to give thought or consideration to ‖ *v.i.* to show hospitality **en·ter·tain·er** *n.* a person who entertains professionally **en·ter·tain·ing** *adj.* **en·ter·tain·ment** *n.*

en·thrall en·thral en·thrall·ing en·thral·ling en·thralled *v.t.* to capture the interest or attention of, delight **en·thrall·ing en·thral·ling** *adj.*

en·thu·si·asm *n.* passionate admiration or interest

en·thu·si·ast *n.* an ardent fan, supporter or admirer **en·thu·si·as·tic** *adj.* **en·thu·si·as·ti·cal·ly** *adv.*

en·tice en·tic·ing en·ticed *v.t.* to cause (a person or animal) to cease resisting and to do as one wishes **en·tice·ment** *n.*

en·tire *adj.* whole and complete, absolute and qualified ‖ intact **en·tire·ly** *adv.* wholly and completely ‖ solely

en·tire·ty *pl.* **en·tire·ties** *n.* completeness **in its entirety** as an undiminished whole

en·ti·tle en·ti·tling en·ti·tled *v.t.* to give (someone) a right ‖ to give a title to

en·ti·tle·ments *pl. n.* benefits that one may receive upon request

en·ti·ty *pl.* **en·ti·ties** *n.* something existing complete in itself, by its own right

en·tou·rage *n.* the companions or servants who attend or surround a person ‖ surroundings

en·trance *n.* a door or other opening by which one can enter a building or other place ‖ a fee paid for the right to be admitted

en·trance en·tranc·ing en·tranced *v.t.* to overcome with joy ‖ to put into a trance **en·tranc·ing** *adj.* delightful **en·trance·ment** *n.*

en·treat *v.t.* to plead with ‖ to plead for **en·treat·y** *pl.* **en·treat·ies** *n.* beseeching

en·trée en·tree *n.* freedom of entry ‖ the main course of a dinner

en·trench *v.t.* to surround or protect with a trench ‖ to settle (oneself) securely **en·trench·ment** *n.*

en·trust *v.t.* to give for safekeeping or to be looked after ‖ to give a task or duty to

en·try *pl.* **en·tries** *n.* entrance ‖ someone or something entered for a competition, race etc. ‖ the registering of something in a record, or the thing so recorded

e·nu·mer·ate e·nu·mer·at·ing e·nu·mer·at·ed *v.t.* to state or name one by one **e·nu·mer·a·tion** *n.* **e·nu·mer·a·tive** *adj.*

e·nun·ci·ate e·nun·ci·at·ing e·nun·ci·at·ed *v.t.* to articulate **e·nun·ci·a·tion** *n.* the act or way of pronouncing ‖ the stating (of a proposition, theory, doctrine etc.) **e·nun·ci·a·tive** *adj.* **e·nun·ci·a·tor** *n.*

en·vel·op *v.t.* to wrap up ‖ to cover completely, shroud **en·vel·op·ment** *adj.*

en·ve·lope *n.* a paper cover with a gummed or tuck-in flap, to hold a letter etc.

en·vi·ous *adj.* feeling, showing or prompted by envy

en·vi·ron·ment *n.* surroundings **en·vi·ron·men·tal** *adj.*

en·voy *n.* someone sent on a mission or with a message, usually official

en·vy en·vy·ing en·vied *v.t.* to feel malicious envy of or for

envy *pl.* **en·vies** *n.* a feeling of antagonism towards someone because of some good which he is enjoying but which one does not have oneself

en·zyme *n.* one of a large class of complex proteinaceous substances of high molecular weight

e·phem·er·a *pl.* **e·phem·er·as e·phem·er·ae** *n.* a mayfly ‖ something short-lived **e·phem·er·al** *adj.*

ep·ic 1. *n.* a long narrative poem, telling a story of great or heroic deeds **2.** *adj.* of or having the nature of an epic

ep·i·cure *n.* a person who cultivates and enjoys his taste for the best in food and drink

ep·i·dem·ic 1. *n.* a disease which becomes widespread **2.** *adj.* widespread, esp. of disease **ep·i·dem·i·cal** *adj.*

ep·i·der·mis *pl.* **ep·i·der·mis·es ep·i·der·mes** *n.* the protective external skin **ep·i·der·moid ep·i·der·moi·dal** *adjs* resembling epidermis

ep·i·lep·sy *n.* a chronic nervous disorder of the brain **ep·i·lep·tic** *n.* and*adj.*

ep·i·logue epi·log *n.* the concluding part of, or a final note added to, a literary work

ep·i·sode *n.* a self-contained part of a serial story ‖ an isolated event or instance, separate from the run of events **ep·i·sod·i·cal** *adj.* consisting of linked episodes ‖ spasmodic

e·pis·tle *n.* a letter ‖ a literary work (prose or poetry) cast in the form of a letter

ep·i·taph *n.* words inscribed on a gravestone or other monument in memory or in praise of a dead person or persons

e·pit·o·me *n.* a summary ‖ a person or thing typical of, or serving as a model of **e·pit·o·mist** *n.* **e·pit·o·mize e·pit·o·miz·ing e·pit·o·mized** *v.t.*

ep·och *n.* a period of time characterized by momentous events or changes **ep·och·al** *adj.*

ep·os *n.* early folk-epic poetry, either recited or written ‖ an epic of this kind

e·qua·bil·i·ty *n.* the state or quality of being equable

eq·ua·ble *adj.* steadily even, without extremes ‖ calm, not easily upset or excited **eq·ua·bly** *adv.*

equal 1. *adj.* the same in number, degree, value, rank or other standard of comparison ‖ even ‖ impartial ‖ without subservience or domination ‖ (with 'to') equivalent to **2.** *n.* someone or something equal in some point of comparison to another **3.** *v.t.* **e·qual·ing e·qualed** to be or become equal to

e·qual·i·ty *pl.* **e·qual·i·ties** *n.* the state or an instance of being equal in number, rank, meaning etc.

e·qual·ize e·qual·iz·ing e·qual·ized *v.t.* to make equal ‖ to make regular or even **e·qual·iz·er** *n.*

e·qual·ly *adv.* to the same degree ‖ in equal parts

e·qua·nim·i·ty *n.* steady calmness

e·quate e·quat·ing e·quat·ed *v.t.* to state the equality of ‖ to regard as equal in value or as mutually interdependent

e·qua·tion *n.* the act of making equal ‖ (*math.*) a statement of the equality between mathematical expressions

e·qua·tor *n.* the great circle of the earth, dividing the northern and southern hemispheres **e·qua·to·ri·al** *adj.* on or near or pertaining to the equator

e·ques·tri·an 1. *adj.* concerned with or representing horseback riding **2.** *n.* a horseback rider

e·qui·lib·ri·um *n.* a state of balance between opposing forces or effects

e·qui·nox *pl.* **e·qui·nox·es** *n.* the moment or point at which the sun crosses the equator. At the equinoxes day and night are of equal length

e·quip e·quip·ping e·quipped *v.t.* to provide with what is needed to carry out a particular purpose

e·quip·ment *n.* what is needed or is provided to carry out a particular purpose ‖ (*rail.*) rolling stock

eq·ui·ta·ble *adj.* fair and just **eq·ui·ta·bly** *adv.*

eq·ui·ty *pl.* **eq·ui·ties** *n.* fairness and justice ‖ the value of a property after deducting any charges to which it is liable

e·quiv·a·lent 1. *adj.* (with 'to') equal, having the same effect or value **2.** *n.* that which is equivalent to something else

e·quiv·o·cal *adj.* capable of being understood in more than one way ‖ suspect, of doubtful validity, honesty or sincerity

e·quiv·o·cate e·quiv·o·cat·ing e·quiv·o·cated *v.i.* to avoid a plain statement or answer and so evade the truth

e·ra *n.* a period of time in history or any relatively prolonged stage of development

e·rad·i·cate e·rad·i·cat·ing e·rad·i·cat·ed *v.t.* to stamp out or destroy utterly **e·rad·i·ca·tion** *n.* **e·rad·i·ca·tor** *n.*

e·rase e·ras·ing e·rased *v.t.* to rub out, efface **e·ras·er** *n.* something used for erasing marks

e·rect 1. *adj.* upright, without stooping or bowing ‖ (*bot.*) growing vertically **2.** *v.t.* to cause to have built or put up ‖ to put in place ‖ to set upright ‖ construct **e·rec·tion** *n.* an erecting or being erected

e·rode e·rod·ing e·rod·ed *v.t.* to eat away ‖ to wear away (land)

e·ro·sion *n.* an eroding or being eroded

e·rot·ic *adj.* of or relating to sexual love

e·rot·i·cism *n.* sexual excitement or desire

err *v.i.* to make a mistake, to be wrong

er·rand *n.* a short journey to carry out some particular task or to take a message ‖ the task itself

er·rant *adj.* erring, tending to do wrong ‖ straying

er·rat·ic 1. *adj.* not fitting into any regular pattern of events or behavior ‖ uneven in quality ‖ unstable, unbalanced **er·rat·i·cal·ly** *adv.*

er·ro·ne·ous *adj.* mistaken, wrong

er·ror *n.* departure from the truth in a statement or in a belief ‖ a mistake

er·satz *n.* a synthetic product replacing a natural one

erst·while *adj.* former

er·u·dite *adj.* learned **er·u·di·tion** *n.* scholarly learning

e·rupt to break or burst out violently from restraint, or as if from restraint ‖ *v.t.* (of a volcano or geyser, or of someone or something compared to these) to throw out violently, eject

e·rup·tion *n.* an outbreak, explosion

es·ca·late es·ca·lat·ing es·ca·lat·ed *v.t.* and *i.* to increase gradually but steadily **es·ca·la·tion** *n.*

es·ca·la·tor *n.* a moving staircase

es·ca·pade *n.* a wild, often innoacent, adventure

es·cape 1. es·cap·ing es·caped *v.i.* to get free by flight, regain one's liberty ‖ to leak, flow or otherwise issue from a container ‖ to find release or relief from worries, troubles or responsibilities **2.** *n.* the act of getting free from prison or other confinement ‖ a leak, flowing out or overflow ‖ a release or relief from misery, worries or responsibilities

es·cap·ée *n.* someone who has escaped

es·cápe·ment *n.* a device in a clock or watch

es·chew *v.t.* refrain from using, avoid **es·chéw·al** *n.*

es·cort 1. *n.* a person or group accompanying another person or group for company, to give protection ‖ a man accompanying a woman on some social occasion **under escort** accompanied by guards **2.** *v.t.* to accompany as

es·crow *n.* a formal contract or deed which does not come into effect until some specified condition has been fulfilled **in escrow** on trust as an escrow

e·soph·a·gus oe·soph·a·gus *pl.* **e·soph·a·gi** oe·soph·a·gi *n.* the tube through which food passes from the mouth to the stomach

es·o·ter·ic *adj.* with a private or secret meaning or purpose **es·o·tér·i·cal·ly** *adv.*

es·pe·cial *adj.* particular ‖ excepuational **in especial** in particular ‖ especially **es·pé·cial·ly** *adv.* exceptionally

es·pi·o·nage *n.* spying to obtain military, political, scientific, industrial etc. secrets

es·pous·al *n.* an adoption or taking up (of a cause, doctrine or line of action etc.)

es·pouse es·pous·ing es·poused *v.t.* to adopt, take up, support (a cause, doctrine, line of action etc.)

es·prit *n.* wit

es·py es·py·ing es·pied *v.t.* to catch sight of, notice

es·say *v.t.* to test, try out ‖ *v.i.* to attempt

essay *n.* a writing dealing with a particular subject **és·say·ist** *n.* a writer of essays

es·sence *n.* the most significant part of a thing's nature ‖ a concentrated extract, e.g. of vanilla **in essence** in fundamental respects

es·sen·tial 1. *adj.* necessary, such that one cannot do without it ‖ of the utmost importance ‖ containing all that is best or most important in a thing 2. *n.* something that one cannot do without ‖ (esp.pl.) the basic or fundamental part or element in a thing **es·sen·ti·al·i·ty** *n.*

es·tab·lish *v.t.* to set up, found ‖ to place on a firm basis ‖ to bring into being ‖ to achieve, secure ‖ to make clear **es·táb·lish·ment** *n.* a place of business or a residence ‖ an organization as a whole

es·tate *n.* a landed property ‖ the whole of a person's property

es·teem 1. *n.* good opinion, regard 2. *v.t.* to have a high opinion of, value

es·thet·ic *adj.* aesthetic

es·ti·ma·ble *adj.* worthy of esteem ‖ capable of being estimated **és·ti·ma·bly** *adv.*

es·ti·mate 1. *n.* a judgment of size, number, quantity, value, distance, quality etc. ‖ a stateuament of the cost or

charge which would be involved in a given piece of work 2. *v.* **es·ti·mat·ing** *v.* **es·ti·mat·ing es·ti·mat·ed** *v.t.* to make an estimate of ‖ *v.i.* to submit an estimate

es·ti·ma·tion *n.* an assessing of value ‖ an estimate

es·ti·ma·tor *n.* someone who works out cost estimates

es·trange es·trang·ing es·tranged *v.t.* to cause (a person) to become unloving or unfriendly **es·tránge·ment** *n.*

es·tro·gen oes·tro·gen *n.* one of a group of female sex hormones **es·tro·gén·ic oes·tro·gén·ic** *adj.*

es·tu·ar·y *pl.* **es·tu·ar·ies** *n.* the tidal mouth of a river

et cet·er·a *abbr.* etc.) and others, and so on **et·cet·er·as** *pl. n.* sundry items, extras

etch *v.t.* to engrave (a design etc.) on glass or a metal plate ‖ *v.i.* to practice this art **étch·ing** *n.* a print from an etched plate

e·ter·nal *adj.* never ending, lasting for ever ‖ without beginning or end in time ‖ seemingly limitless

e·ter·ni·ty *pl.* **e·ter·ni·ties** *n.* time or existence without beginning or end ‖ the endless state after death

e·ther ae·ther *n.* a volatile, inflammable colorless liquid, diethyl ether, used as an anesthetic and as a solvent ‖ the upper regions of the sky

e·the·re·al *adj.* light, airy and intangible ‖ heavenly ‖ pertaining to ether **e·the·re·al·iz·ing**

eth·ic 1. *n.* a system of ethics 2. *adj.* ethical **éth·i·cal** *adj.* dealing with ethics ‖ relating to morality of behavior **éth·i·cal·ly** *adv.* **éth·ics** *n.* moral philosophy ‖ moral principles

eth·nic *adj.* of or relating to a people whose unity rests on racial, linguistic, religious or cultural ties **éth·ni·cal** *adj.* **éth·ni·cal·ly** *adv.* according to ethnic grouping

et·i·quette *n.* the rules of behavior standard in society

é·tude *n.* a short composition

et·y·mol·o·gist *n.* a specialist in etymology

et·y·mol·o·gy *pl.* **et·y·mol·o·gies** *n.* the study of language dealing with the origin of words

eu·lo·gize eu·lo·giz·ing eu·lo·gized *v.t.* to praise highly in speech or writing

eu·lo·gy *pl.* **eu·lo·gies** *n.* a written or spoken expression of high praise

eu·nuch *n.* castrated man or boy

eu·phe·mism *n.* the use of a pleasant expression to mask harsh or infamous truths ‖ the word or phrase so used **eu·phe·mís·tic** *adj.* **eu·phe·mís·ti·cal·ly** *adv.*

eu·phon·ic *adj.* euphonious **eu·phon·i·cal·ly** *adv.*

eu·pho·ny *pl.* **eu·pho·nies** *n.* a pleasant concordance of sound

eu·pho·ri·a *n.* a feeling of well-being **eu·phor·ic** *adj.*

eu·tha·na·sia *n.* the deliberaate, painless killing of persons who suffer from a painful and incurable disease or condition

e·vac·u·ate e·vac·u·at·ing e·vac·u·at·ed *v.t.* to abandon (a town or position) ‖ to empty (a dangerous place) of troops, civilians, material etc. **e·vac·u·á·tion** *n.* **e·vac·u·ee** *n.* an evacuated person

e·vade e·vad·ing e·vad·ed *v.t.* to escape from by skill, cunning, deception, dexterity etc. ‖ dodge ‖ *v.i.* to be evasive

e·val·u·ate e·val·u·at·ing e·val·u·at·ed *v.t.* to determine or assess the value of **e·val·u·á·tion** *n.*

e·van·gel·i·cal *adj.* concerned with, or relating to, the preaching of the Christian gospel ‖ contained in, or in accordance with, the teaching of the Gospels

e·van·ge·lism *n.* the preaching of the Christian gospel

e·van·ge·list *n.* an author of one of the four Gospels ‖ a preacher of the Christian gospel **e·van·ge·lis·tic** *adj.*

e·vap·o·rate e·vap·o·rat·ing e·vap·o·rat·ed *v.i.* (of a liquid or solid) to assume the vapor state by a gradual physical change ‖ to disappear, leaving no trace ‖ *v.t.* to cause to evaporate

e·vap·o·ra·tion *n.* disappearance without trace

e·va·sion *n.* a dodging or avoiding e.g. of a question, the truth, a point under discussion etc.

e·va·sive *adj.* not candid, evading or dodging the material point ‖ not easily caught

eve *n.* the day before a day important for some event ‖ evening, dusk

e·ven *adj.* (of a surface) smooth ‖ steady, constant, uniform ‖ (of temper) equable, not easily ruffled ‖ equal ‖ exact, exactly whole, without a fraction ‖ giving a whole number when divided by two

even *adv.* exactly, precisely, just

even *v.t.* (often with 'out,' 'up,' 'off') to make even, equal or level ‖ *v.i.* (often with 'out,' 'up,' or 'off') to become even

eve·ning *n.* the later part of the day as darkness approaches ‖ the later or closing years (of a man's life, a nation's history, a civilization etc.) ‖ an entertainment taking place in the evening

e·vent *n.* an occurrence, esp. one regarded as having importance ‖ a separate item in a program of games, athletic contests, racing etc.

e·vént·less *adj.* without any notable happenings

e·vent·ful *adj.* full of important, exciting or interesting events

e·ven·tu·al *adj.* final **e·ven·tu·ál·i·ty** *pl.* **e·ven·tu·al·i·ties** *n.* something that may possibly occur **e·vén·tu·al·ly** *adv.* in the end

ev·er *adv.* at any time ‖ always **ever after ever since** for all subsequent time

every *adj.* each and all ‖ each possible or conceivable ‖ strong or well founded

e·vict *v.t.* to turn (a person) out ‖ to recover (property, a right or title) by legal proof and judgment **e·vic·tion e·víc·tor** *ns*

ev·i·dence **1.** *n.* anything that provides material or information on which a conclusion or proof may be based **2.** *v.t.* **ev·i·denc·ing ev·i·denced** to be evidence for, show

ev·i·dent *adj.* obvious **év·i·dent·ly** *adv.* clearly

e·vil 1. *adj.* wicked ‖ indicating wickedness ‖ foul, disgusting ‖ disastrous, ill-omened **2.** *n.* what is morally wrong

e·vil·do·er *n.* someone whose actions are evil

e·voke e·vok·ing e·voked *v.t.* to bring to mind, cause to be felt ‖ to summon (a spirit) by the use of magic

ev·o·lu·tion *n.* a continuous change from a simple to a more complex form ‖ gradual development ‖ the theory that all living things have changed in response to environmental conditions by the natural selection of randomly occurring mutations **ev·o·lú·tion·al ev·o·lú·tion·ar·y** *adjs*

e·volve e·volv·ing e·volved *v.i.* to change continuously from the simple to the more complex

ewe *n.* a female sheep

ew·er *n.* a widemouthed pitcher

ex·ac·er·bate ex·ac·er·bat·ing ex·ac·er·bat·ed *v.t.* to irritate or provoke (someone) to anger ‖ to make (a disease) more serious **ex·ac·er·bá·tion** *n.*

ex·act 1. *adj.* completely correct ‖ precise ‖ meticulous ‖ (of numbers, measures etc.) neither more nor less **2.** *v.t.* to demand ‖ to enforce payment of **ex·áct·a·ble** *adj.* **ex·áct·ing** *adj.* difficult to satisfy or please

ex·ag·ger·ate ex·ag·ger·at·ing ex·ag·ger·at·ed *v.t.* to lay increased emphasis upon ‖ to make larger than normal **ex·ag·ger·á·tion** *n.* **ex·ág·ger·a·tive** *adj.* **ex·ág·ger·a·tor** *n.*

ex·alt *v.t.* to raise up (in position or dignity) ‖ to praise highly, give glory to ‖ to fill with elation

ex·al·ta·tion *n.* a state of mental or spiritual elation or excitement

ex·am·i·na·tion *n.* an inspection ‖ a questioning ‖ a testing of knowledge or capabilities **ex·am·i·ná·tion·al** *adj.*

ex·am·ine ex·am·in·ing ex·am·ined *v.t.* to look carefully and closely at, inspect ‖ give careful thought to ‖ to question of

ex·am·i·nee *n.* a student who is examined **ex·ám·in·er** *n.*

ex·am·ple *n.* a specimen or instance ‖ a mode of behavior to imitate ‖ something which helps to make a meaning clearer **for example** *(abbr.* e.g.) as an instance

ex·as·per·ate ex·as·per·at·ing ex·as·per·at·ed *v.t.* to annoy or irritate beyond measure **ex·as·per·á·tion** *n.*

ex·ca·vate ex·ca·vat·ing ex·ca·vat·ed *v.t.* to expose by digging away the covering earth etc. from ‖ to hollow out by digging

ex·ca·va·tion *n.* a digging out ‖ a hole made by excavating

ex·ca·va·tor *n.* someone who excavates

ex·ceed *v.t.* to go beyond **ex·céed·ing** *adj.* very great in quality **ex·céed·ing·ly** *adv.* very

ex·cel ex·cel·ling ex·celled *v.t.* to be superior to ‖ *v.i.* to be outstandingly skilled **to excel oneself** to do outstandingly well

ex·cel·lence *n.* very great merit, quality or ability

ex·cel·lent *adj.* extremely good

ex·cel·si·or *n.* very fine wood shavings used for packing

ex·cept *v.t.* to exclude from a list, rule, statement, classification etc.

except *prep.* apart from, excluding

ex·cep·tion *n.* someone or something excepted from a general rule, class etc. ‖ an objection against a decision made by the judge **ex·cép·tion·a·ble** *adj.* open to objection **ex·cép·tion·al** *adj.* unusual, outstanding

ex·cerpt *n.* a selected passage from a written work **ex·cérp·tion** *n.*

ex·cess 1. *n.* the amount by which something is greater than what is usual or permitted etc. ‖ *(pl.)* acts which are more violent than accepted standards ‖ *(pl.)* inordinate indulgence in sensual pleasure **2.** *adj.* of something greater than what is usual or permitted

ex·ces·sive *adj.* going beyond the limit

ex·change ex·chang·ing ex·changed *v.* to give or receive (one thing in return for something else) ‖ to substitute (one for another) ‖ to change (money) from one currency to another

exchange *n.* a reciprocal giving and receiving of things of the same kind ‖ an interchange of visits, jobs etc. ‖ the conversion of the money of one country into that of another ‖ a central place of business for merchants, brokers or financiers **ex·change·a·bíl·i·ty** *n.* the state of being exchangeable **ex·chánge·a·ble** *adj.* capable of being exchanged

ex·cise 1. *n.* a tax duty levied on the manuafacture, sale or consumption within a country of ceratain commodities 2. *v.t.* **ex·cis·ing ex·cised** to lay excise duty on

ex·cise ex·cis·ing ex·cised *v.t.* to cut away by surgery **ex·ci·sion** *n.*

ex·cite ex·cit·ing ex·cit·ed *v.t.* to cause emotions to be intense ‖ to arouse ‖ to stir up **ex·cit·a·bíl·i·ty** *n.* **ex·cit·a·ble** *adj.* quickly enraged or worked up **ex·cit·ant** *n.* something which excites **ex·ci·ta·tion** *n.* **ex·ci·ta·to·ry** *adj.* stimulating **ex·cíte·ment** *n.* **ex·cít·ing** *adj.*

ex·claim *v.i.* to cry out in excitement ‖ *v.t.* to utter under the stress of sudden thought or emotion

ex·cla·ma·tion *n.* the act of exclaiming ‖ an interjection

ex·clude ex·clud·ing ex·clud·ed *v.t.* to keep out, prevent or forbid the entry of ‖ to leave out **ex·clúd·ing** *prep.* except, excepting

ex·clu·sion *n.* an excluding

ex·clu·sive *adj.* sole, not shared with any others ‖ confined to a selected few ‖ fastidiously selective

ex·com·mu·ni·cate 1. *v.t.* **ex·com·mu·ni·cat·ing ex·com·mu·ni·cat·ed** to exclude from communion with the Church 2. *adj.* excommunicated 3. **ex·com·mu·ni·cá·tion** *n.* an excommunicating or being excommunicated

ex·cor·i·ate ex·co·ri·at·ing ex·co·ri·at·ed *v.t.* to remove the skin from by tearing,

rubbing, scalding etc. ‖ to criticize savagely **ex·co·ri·á·tion** *n.*

ex·cre·ment *n.* waste matter expelled from the bowels **ex·cre·men·tal** *adj.*

ex·crete ex·cret·ing ex·cret·ed *v.t.* to eliminate (waste matter) **ex·cré·tive** *adj.* **ex·cre·to·ry** *adj.* of or for excretion

ex·cre·tion *n.* the act of excreting ‖ the matter excreted

ex·cur·sion *n.* a short pleasure trip ‖ a digression ‖ the attempting of an activity other than one's usual one **ex·cúr·sion·ist** *n.*

ex·cuse ex·cus·ing ex·cused *v.t.* to free from blame ‖ to forgive, overlook ‖ to release (someone) from an obligation, undertaking or duty ‖ to give exemption from

ex·cuse *n.* the act of excusing ‖ pretext ‖ (*pl.*) apologies

ex·e·cute ex·e·cut·ing ex·e·cut·ed *v.t.* to carry out, put into effect ‖ to perform ‖ to meet (a trade order) ‖ to put to death

ex·e·cu·tion *n.* a carrying out or fulfilling ‖ the inflicting or suffering of the death penalty **ex·e·cú·tion·er** *n.* someone who carries out the death sentence

ex·e·cu·tive 1. *adj.* concerned with the putting into effect of orders, plans or policies 2. *n.* a person holding an executive position in a business firm etc.

ex·e·cu·tor *n.* a person appointed by a testator to carry out the provisions of his will **ex·ec·u·to·ry** *adj.* administrative **ex·ec·u·trix**

ex·em·pla·ry *adj.* without fault, worthy to be copied ‖ serving as a warning example ‖ typical, serving as an example or illustration

ex·empt 1. *adj.* (with 'from') not liable to, free from 2. *v.t.* to cause to be exempt **ex·émpt·i·ble** *adj.*

ex·emp·tion *n.* immunity from some obligation

ex·er·cise 1. *n.* the use of practice of a quality, power, right ‖ training or practice to develop skill, aptitude, mental or spiritual powers, or something designed to do this ‖ (*pl.*) a program of songs, speeches etc. given at a school or college **2. ex·er·cis·ing ex·er·cised** *v.t.* to use, practice (a quality, power etc.) ‖ to carry out (duties, a function) ‖ *v.i.* to take bodily exercise

ex·ert *v.t.* to make effective use of, bring into operation **ex·er·tive** *adj.*

ex·hale ex·hal·ing ex·haled *v.i.* to breathe out

ex·haust 1 *v.t.* to use up completely, come to the end of ‖ to tire out, drain of strength **2.** *n.* the expulsion of steam or spent gases from the cylinder of a heat engine ‖ the pipe through which the spent gases are expelled **ex·haust·i·bil·i·ty** *n.* **ex·háust·i·ble** *adj.* **ex·haus·tion** *n.* **ex·háus·tive** *adj.* thorough, painstaking

ex·hib·it 1. *v.t.* to show, display **2.** *n.* a thing or collection put on show ‖ something produced as evidence in a court of law **on exhibit** out on view

ex·hi·bi·tion *n.* a display of something beautiful, valuable, salable, or of historic or other interest ‖ a performance for the pleasure of an audience ‖ a person who makes himself look ridiculous in public **ex·hi·bi·tion·ism** *n.* a form of sexual gratification **ex·hi·bí·tion·ist** *n.* and *adj.*

ex·hib·i·tor *n.* someone who exhibits at an exhibition

ex·hil·a·rate ex·hil·a·rat·ing ex·hil·a·rat·ed *v.t.* to fill with strong feelings of delight **ex·hil·a·rant** *adj.* exhilarating **ex·hil·a·rá·tion** *n.* **ex·hil·a·ra·tive** *adj.*

ex·hort *v.t.* to urge strongly, seek earnestly to persuade

ex·hor·ta·tion *n.* a persuasive sermon or speech

ex·hume ex·hum·ing ex·humed *v.t.* to disinter (a body) after burial ‖ to bring to notice again (what was long forgotten)

ex·i·gent *adj.* demanding ‖ urgent, pressing

ex·ile ex·il·ing ex·iled *v.t.* to send into exile

exile *n.* banishment or expulsion from one's home or country ‖ a person

banished from his home or country

ex·ist *v.i.* to have being ‖ to be able to maintain life

ex·ist·ence *n.* real being ‖ a way of life **ex·íst·ent** *adj.* and *n.* **ex·is·ten·tial** *adj.* relating to existence

ex·it a stage direction for an actor to go off

exit *n.* a way out

ex·o·dus *n.* a departure in great numbers

ex·on·er·ate ex·on·er·at·ing ex·on·er·at·ed *v.t.* to free from blame ‖ to release from a duty **ex·on·er·á·tion** *n.*

ex·or·bi·tant *adj.* greater than is justified, excessive

ex·or·cise ex·or·cize ex·or·cis·ing ex·or·ciz·ing ex·or·cised oex·or·cized *v.t.* to drive out (an evil spirit)

ex·or·cism *n.* the act of exorcising ‖ the words used

ex·or·cist *n.* someone who exorcises evil spirits

ex·ot·ic 1. *adj.* brought in from a foreign country ‖ very unusual, attractively strange **2.** *n.* a plant, word etc. introduced into a country from outside **ex·ót·i·cal·ly** *adv.*

ex·pand *v.t.* to make larger, swell ‖ to cause to increase ‖ to express in detail ‖ to enlarge on, treat (a topic) more fully ‖ *v.i.* to increase in scope ‖ to spread out, open out

ex·panse *n.* a wide, open stretch of earth, sky or water

ex·pan·sion *n.* an expanding **ex·pán·sion·ism** *n.* a belief in, or policy of, expansion **ex·pán·sion·ist** *n.*

ex·pan·sive *adj.* happy to communicate thoughts and feelings ‖ broad, wide **ex·pan·siv·i·ty** *n.* capacity to expand

ex·pect *v.t.* to think likely ‖ to anticipate the coming of ‖ to hope for ‖ to require (something) of somebody

ex·pect·an·cy *pl.* **ex·pect·an·cies** *n.* a state of expectation ‖ the quality of hopefulness

ex·pect·ant *adj.* expressing pleasurable hope ‖ pregnant

ex·pec·ta·tion *n.* something anticipated ‖

a looking forward with hope or pleasure ‖ a reasonable chance ‖ (pl.) prospects

ex·pe·di·en·cy pl. **ex·pe·di·en·cies** n. an expedient

ex·pe·di·ent adj. bringing a particular limited (often selfish or material) advantage, but one which is not right or just **ex·pe·di·en·tial** adj.

ex·pe·dite ex·pe·dit·ing ex·pe·dit·ed v.t. to haste ‖ to send, dispatch

ex·pe·di·tion n. a voyage to a particular place or for a particular purpose ‖ the people taking part in this ‖ promptness, quickness **ex·pe·di·tious** adj. prompt, quick and effective

ex·pel ex·pel·ling ex·pelled v.t. to deprive of membership ‖ to eject by force, force out **ex·pel·la·ble** adj. **ex·pel·lent ex·pél·lant** n. and adj.

ex·pend v.t. to spend (time, money, mental or physical effort etc.) ‖ to use up **ex·pénd·a·ble** adj. meant to be used up in the normal course of work ‖ (of a person) that can be sacrificed as of no further usefulness

ex·pend·i·ture n. the amount or amounts expended

ex·pense n. cost in terms of money ‖ (pl.) money paid out in running a business or household, doing a job etc.

ex·pen·sive adj. costly in money or damage ‖ high-priced or making a high charge

ex·pe·ri·ence 1. n. an instance of direct knowledge ‖ the skill or judgment gained by practice ‖ an interesting or remarkable event in a person's life **2.** v.t. **ex·pe·ri·enc·ing ex·pé·ri·enced** to have experience of, feel **ex·pé·ri·enced** adj. endowed with experience

ex·per·i·ment 1. n. an operation carried out under determined conditions to discover, verify or illustrate a theory, hypothesis or fact ‖ experimentation **2.** v.i. to make experiments **ex·per·i·men·tal** adj. made or designed as a trial or for use in experiment **ex·pe·ri·mén·tal·ism**

ex·per·i·mén·tal·ist   n s

ex·per·i·men·ta·tion n. the use of experiment as a method of obtaining or confirming knowledge

ex·pert 1. n. someone whose knowledge or skill is specialized and profound **2.** adj. pertaining to such knowledge or skill

ex·per·tise n. expert knowledge

ex·pi·ra·tion n. a coming to an end ‖ breathing out

ex·pire ex·pir·ing ex·pired to come to an end ‖ to die ‖ to become void at the end of a term of years ‖ to breathe out

ex·plain v.t. to make clear ‖ to give a reason that accounts for ‖ (with 'away') to show that no problem or difficulty exists ‖ v.i. to give an explanation **to explain oneself** to justify one's conduct **ex·pláin·a·ble** adj.

ex·pla·na·tion n. a making clear ‖ something which makes clear ‖ the facts put forward in justification

ex·ple·tive n. an exclamation, often an oath, expressing strong emotion ‖ a word or phrase used to pad out a sentence, line of verse etc. **ex·ple·to·ry** adj.

ex·plic·it adj. clearly and openly stated or defined ‖ direct and unambiguous

ex·plode ex·plod·ing ex·plod·ed v.i. to undergo a large sudden increase of volume resulting in destructive pressures on the surrounding materials ‖ to release emotional tension suddenly ‖ v.t. to cause to explode ‖ to destroy (a myth, theory etc.)

ex·ploit v.t. to derive unjust profit from ‖ to use for one's own selfish ends or profit ‖ to make the best use of **ex·plóit·a·ble** adj. **ex·ploi·ta·tion** n. **exploít·a·tive** adj.

ex·ploit n. a heroic or remarkable deed

ex·plore ex·plor·ing ex·plored v.t. to travel through (an unknown or little known region) in order to add to man's knowledge ‖ to investigate ‖ to consider carefully ‖ to probe or examine **ex·plór·er** n. someone who explores

ex·plo·sion n. a violent expansion accompanied by noise ‖ an outburst of violent emotion or energy

ex·plo·sive *adj.* designed to cause an explosion || liable to explode || suddenly violent

ex·po·nent *n.* someone who expounds || an index, a symbol **ex·po·nen·tial** *adj.* serving to expound, explain or interpret

ex·port 1. *v.t.* to send from one country to another in return for goods, money or services 2. *n.* the act or trade of exporting 3. *adj.* pertaining to what is exported or to exportation **ex·pórt·a·ble** *adj.*

ex·por·ta·tion *n.* the act of exporting || an export

ex·pose ex·pos·ing ex·posed *v.t.* to leave uncovered, bare, without clothing || to leave open to attack, danger etc. || to allow light to fall upon (a photographic plate or film) || to bring to light, uncover || to reveal (something secret)

ex·po·si·tion *n.* an explaining and interpreting of a theme, writing etc. || an exposing, displaying in public || an exhibition of works of art, industry, commerce etc.

ex·po·sure *n.* an exposing or being exposed (to light, heat, cold, sickness etc.) || the act of making something shameful publicly known

ex·pound *v.t.* to explain || to state with great detail

ex·press 1. *adj.* explicitly stated || specially fast 2. *n.* an express train || a fast service for transporting || the goods or money sent by express 3. *adv.* by express train || by express delivery service

express *v.t.* to state explicitly in words || to indicate by gesture or behavior || to send by express delivery **to express oneself** to communicate one's feelings **ex·préss·i·ble** *adj.*

ex·pres·sion *n.* the act of expressing something thought or felt || an idiom

ex·pres·sion·ism *n.* a mode of artistic expression in which direct communication of feeling or emotion is the main intention

ex·pres·sive *adj.* showing what a person thinks or feels

ex·pul·sion *n.* an expelling or being expelled **ex·púl·sive** *adj.* serving to expel

ex·qui·site *adj.* showing perfection in taste or workmanship || highly sensitive to quality

ex·tant *adj.* still in existence

ex·tem·po·ra·ne·ous *adj.* extempore

ex·tem·po·re 1. *adv.* without advance preparation, on the spur of the moment 2. *adj.* made or done on the spur of the moment **ex·tem·po·ri·za·tion** *n.* **ex·tém·po·rize ex·tem·po·riz·ing ex·tem·po·rized** *v.* to speak or act without advance preparation

ex·tend *v.t.* to lengthen in space or time || to make wider, greater or more inclusive || to stretch || to hold out || (with 'to') to make available | *v.i.* to reach **ex·ténd·ed** *adj.* **ex·ténd·er** *n.* a substance used to adulterate, dilute or otherwise modify a product **ex·ténd·i·ble ex·ténd·a·ble** *adj.* capable of being extended **ex·ten·si·ble** *adj.* extendible

ex·ten·sion *n.* an extending or being extended || an extra allowance of time || a telephone subconnection

ex·ten·sive *adj.* covering a wide area || great in scope

ex·tent *n.* the length to which a thing stretches or the area it covers

ex·te·ri·or 1. *adj.* outer || visible from or on the outside 2. *n.* the outside

ex·ter·mi·nate ex·ter·mi·nat·ing ex·ter·mi·nat·ed *v.t.* to destroy completely **ex·ter·mi·ná·tion** *n.* **ex·ter·mi·na·tive** *adj.* **ex·tér·mi·na·tor** *n.* **ex·ter·mi·na·to·ry** *adj.*

ex·ter·nal 1. *adj.* situated on the outside || merely superficial || (of state affairs) foreign 2. *n.* (*pl.*) outward appearances **ex·tér·nal·i·ty** *n.*

ex·tinct *adj.* (of a fire, flame etc.) put out, burnt out || (of a volcano) no longer active || (of species) died out

ex·tinc·tion *n.* an extinguishing || a making or becoming extinct || an annihilating

ex·tínc·tive *adj.* serving to extinguish

ex·tin·guish *v.t.* to put out (a fire, light etc.) ‖ to put an end to, destroy ‖ to wipe out (a debt) **ex·tín·guish·er** *n.* a fire extinguisher

ex·tol ex·toll ex·tol·ling ex·toll·ing ex·tolled *v.t.* to praise enthusiastically

ex·tort *v.t.* to obtain by force, threats, deception etc.

ex·tor·tion *n.* an extorting, esp. of money, overcharging **ex·tór·tion·ate** *adj.* using extortion **ex·tór·tion·er ex·tór·tion·ist** *ns*

ex·tra 1. *adj.* over and above what is usual ‖ of superior quality **2.** *n.* a person hired to take part in crowd scenes etc. ‖ a special (esp. a late) edition of a newspaper **3.** *adv.* more than usually, specially

extra- *prefix* outside or beyond a thing

ex·tract 1. *n.* a passage taken from a book ‖ a concentrated essence, used esp. for flavoring **2.** *v.t.* to draw, pull or otherwise take out ‖ to obtain (a substance) from the raw materials in which it is contained **ex·tráct·a·ble** *adj.* **ex·trác·tor** *n.* a device for extracting

ex·trac·tion *n.* the act of extracting, esp. the pulling out of a tooth ‖ something extracted ‖ lineage

ex·traor·di·nar·y *adj.* beyond what is normal ‖ bizarre ‖ astonishing

ex·trav·a·gance *n.* a being extravagant or an instance of this

ex·trav·a·gant *adj.* spending more money than one can afford, spending foolishly or wastefully ‖ going beyond what is reasonable

ex·trav·a·gan·za *n.* a freely imaginative or fanciful musical stage entertainment

ex·treme 1. *adj.* furthest out, furthest from the center ‖ utmost, maximum ‖ not moderate ‖ as severe and forcible as possible **2.** *n.* (esp. *pl.*) the highest or extreme degree ‖ either end of a whole range

ex·trem·i·ty *pl.* **ex·trem·i·ties** *n.* the very end, the tip ‖ (*pl.*) the most distant parts ‖ (*pl.*) the hands and feet ‖ the limit

ex·tri·cate ex·tri·cat·ing ex·tri·cat·ed *v.t.* to disentangle or free **ex·tri·cá·tion** *n.*

ex·tro·ver·sion *n.* the psychological state of an extrovert ‖ a manifestation of this

ex·tro·vert *n.* a person interested more in what happens outside him than in his own emotions

ex·u·ber·ance *n.* the state or quality of being exuberant, or an instance of it

ex·u·ber·ant *adj.* bubbling over with joy, high spirits, enthusiasm, health etc. ‖ abundant in growth

ex·ude ex·ud·ing ex·ud·ed *v.t.* to ooze with ‖ to give off, emit ‖ *v.i.* to ooze out in small drops

ex·ult *v.i.* to feel and express tremendous joy **ex·últ·an·cy** *n.* **ex·últ·ant** *adj.* **ex·ul·ta·tion** *n.*

eye 1. *n.* an organ of sight ‖ the power of seeing ‖ the power of judging and appreciating what one sees ‖ a thing like an eye in shape, e.g. the hole for the thread in a needle ‖ the low-pressure center of e.g. a hurricane ‖ an aperture allowing the entry of light, esp. the lens of a camera **2.** *v.t.* **eye·ing ey·ing eyed** to look attentively at ‖ to remove the leaf buds of (a potato)

eye·sight *n.* the power of vision ‖ range of vision

eye·sore *n.* something that offends by its ugliness

eye·tooth *pl.* **eye·teeth** *n.* one of the two upper canine teeth

eye·wit·ness *n.* a person who actually saw a crime, accident etc. take place

F

F, f the sixth letter of the English alphabet

F. Fahrenheit

fa·ble *n.* a fanciful story, usually illustrating a moral precept or ethical observation

fa·bled *adj.* celebrated in legend ‖ fictitious

fab·ric *n.* woven stuff ‖ a framework

fab·ri·cate fab·ri·cat·ing fab·ri·cat·ed *v.t.* to construct ‖ to make up, invent (nonexistent facts)

fab·ri·ca·tion *n.* a fabricating or being fabricated ‖ something fabricated ‖ a structure of falsehoods

fab·u·lous *adj.* belonging to the realm of fabel ‖ extraordinary

fa·cade, fa·çade *n.* the main front of a building ‖ an appearance intended as a pretense or mask

face 1. *n.* the front part of the head from forehead to chin ‖ the expresion of a person's countenance ‖ an outward show of self-posession ‖ the front or main side of a building, monument etc. ‖ a surface ‖ the part of a type, or other raised printing surface ‖ a dial of a clock etc. **2. faced** *v.t.* to be the opposite to ‖ to turn or have one's face towards ‖ to confront ‖ *v.i.* to be situated so as to have the fron in a specified direction

fac·et *n.* any of the small planes which constitute the surface of a crystal or cut gem ‖ any of the separate aspects of an involved problem, situation etc.

fa·ce·tious *adj.* (of a person) given to sly or pointless joking ‖ (of a remark) characterized by such joking

fa·cial 1. *adj.* of or pertaining to the face **2.** *n.* a face massage

fa·cile *adj.* of or pertaining to the face **1.** *n.* a face massage

fa·cile *adj.* performing or performed easily ‖ easily won ‖ merely superficial

fa·cil·i·tate fa·cil·i·tat·ing fa·cil·i·tat·ed *v.t.* - to make easy or easier **fa·cil·i·ta·tion** *n.*

fa·cil·i·ty *pl.* **fa·cil·i·ties** *n.* an aptitude for doing some specified thing easily ‖ (*pl.*) things that make some specified activity, task etc. easier

fac·sim·i·le *n.* an exact reproduction of a picture, document, coin, print etc.

fact *n.* a thing known to be true ‖ a statement about something which has occurred

fac·tion *n.* a small opposition group within a larger group ‖ excessive liking for political strife or troublemaking **fác·tion·al** *adj.* **fác·tion·al·ism** *n.*

fac·ti·tious *adj.* artificial, fabricated ‖ deliberately worked up, not natural

fac·tor 1. *n.* any of the facts or circumstances which, taken together, constitute a result or situation ‖ someone who acts as agent for, or is appointed to conduct the affairs of, another **2.** *v.t.* to factorize

fac·to·ry *pl.* **fac·to·ries** *n.* a building or group of buildings where goods are manufactured

fac·tu·al *adj.* concerned with facts ‖ full of facts

fac·ul·ty *pl.* **fac·ul·ties** *n.* a mental or physical power ‖ a branch of studies ‖ the teachers of school

fad *n.* a short-lived fashion or craze **fade fad·ing fad·ed** *v.i* to lose color ‖ to lose freshness or vigor ‖ (of a sound) to lose intensity gradually ‖ (of an image, memory or dream) to become gradually less and less distinct

Fah·ren·heit scale (*abbr.* **F.**) a temperature scale on which the freezing point of water is 32° and its boiling point 212°

fail *n.* (only in) **without fail** for certain

fail *v.i.* to omit or forget to do something required ‖ give out ‖ to be inadequate or deficient ‖ *v.t.* to be unsuccessful in ‖ to let (someone) down completely, to disappoint utterly **fáil·ing** the fact of failing ‖ an unsuccessful person, thing or project ‖ a financial crash **1.** *adj.* weak, feeble ‖ pale, dim, indistinct ‖ slight **2.** *n.* a sudden loss of consciousness **3.** *v.i.* to lose consciousness in a faint

fair *adj.* light-colored, blond ‖ just, equitable ‖ cloudless ‖ quite good ‖ of medium quality ‖ beautiful

fair *adv.* according to the rules ‖ squarely

fair *n.* a traveling collection of sideshows and amusements ‖ a large-scale exhibition

fair·ly *adv.* in a just and equitable manner

‖ moderately

fair·y *n. pl.* **fair·ies** a small supernatural being, capable of intervening in human affairs

faith *n.* trust, confidence ‖ complete acceptance of a truth which cannot be proved ‖ a religion based upon this **faithful 1.** *adj.* steadfast in faith ‖ loyal ‖ accurate **2.** *n.* **the faithful** conscientious adherents to a system of religious belief

faith·less *adj.* disloyal ‖ having no religious faith

fake 1. fak·ing faked *v.t.* to make a false imitation of, counterfeit ‖ to contrive ‖ *v.i.* to pretend, sham **2.** *n.* something faked **3.** *adj.* artificial, false

fal·con *n.* a diurnal bird of prey

fall 1. fall·ing fell fall·en *v.i.* drop to the ground ‖ to decrease ‖ to lose position ‖ to decline in value ‖ (of the face) to take on an expression of disappointment or dismay ‖ (of the eyes) to be suddenly lowered **2.** *n.* the act or an instance of falling ‖ a distance fallen ‖ autumn ‖ decline ‖ the taking or surrendering of a stronghold after a siege or attack ‖ the rope of a hoisting tackle

fal·la·cious *adj.* based on error ‖ misleading

fal·la·cy *pl.* **fal·la·cies** *n.* a false notion ‖ a false reasoning

fal·li·bil·i·ty *n.* the quality of being fallible

fal·li·ble *adj.* subject to the possibility of erring

fall·out *n.* the radioactive material produced by a nuclear explosion ‖ the settling of this material ‖ an unexpected byproduct of a process

fal·low 1. *adj.* plowed and harrowed **2.** *v.t.* to break up with plow and harrow, but without seeding

false 1. *adj.* untrue ‖ logically wrong ‖ incorrect ‖ artificial ‖ deceitful, lying ‖ fake ‖ *mus.)* off pitch **2.** *adv.* not honestly

false·hood *n.* a lie

fal·si·fi·ca·tion *n.* a falsifying or being falsified ‖ something falsified

fal·si·fy *v.t.* to alter with intent to defraud ‖ to misrepresent ‖ to pervert

fal·si·ty *pl.* **fal·si·ties** *n.* the quality of being false, deceitfulness ‖ an untrue assertion

fal·ter *v.i.* to stumble in movement, action or speech ‖ *v.t.* (often with 'out') to say in a hesitant or feeble way

fame *n.* the state of being widely known and esteemed or acclaimed, renown ‖ *(rhet.)* reputation

famed *adj.* renowned, celebrated

fa·mil·iar *adj.* knowing intimately ‖ accustomed ‖ much seen ‖ close and pleasantly free from formality ‖ presumptuous, impudent

fa·mil·iar·i·ty *pl.* **fa·mil·iar·i·ties** *n.* close knowledge or acquaintance ‖ an unjustified presumption of intimacy ‖ *(pl.)* unwelcome gestures of affection

fa·mil·ize fa·mil·iar·iz·ing fa·mil·iar·ized *v.t.* to cause to get to know something well

fam·i·ly *pl.* **fam·i·lies** *n.* a group of people closely related ‖ a group consisting of individuals descended from a common ancestry ‖ a household ‖ unit of a crime syndicate

fam·ine *n.* extreme scarcity of food ‖ starvation

fam·ished *adj.* hungry to the point of starvation

fa·mous *adj.* celebrated ‖ excellent **fá·mous·ly** *adv.* excellently

fan 1. *n.* a device for agitating the air ‖ the blade of a propeller **2. fan·ning fanned** *v.t.* to agitate the air ‖ (of a breeze) to blow gently upon ‖ to cause (cards etc.) to spread out like a fan ‖ to strike (a batter) out ‖ *v.i.* (with 'out') to open like a fan

fa·nat·ic 1. *adj.* overenthusiastic, zealous **2.** *n.* an inordinately zealous adherent or supporter **fa·nát·i·cal** *adj.* **fa·nat·i·cism** *n.* wild and often dangerous enthusiasm

fan·cied *adj.* favorite ‖ imagined

fan·ci·er *n.* a person specially interested in the breeding of a certain kind of animal or plant

fan·ci·ful *adj.* produced by fancy, unreal

fan·ci·ly *adv.* in a fancy way

fan·cy 1. *pl.* **fan·cies** *n.* a whim, caprice ‖ a delusion ‖ a vague intuition ‖ a liking **2.** *adj.* **fan·ci·er fan·ci·est** ornamental,

not plain ‖ (of prices) unreasonably high
the fancy enthusiastic followers of some
pastime 3. *v.t.* **fan·cy·ing fan·cied** to call
up a mental picture

fan·fare *n.* a flourish of trumpets

fang *n.* a long, pointed tooth ‖ the spike of
a tool driven into the handle or stock
fanged *adj.* having fangs

fan·tail *n.* a tail in the shape of a fan

fan·tas·tic *adj.* belonging to the realm of
fancy ‖ very pecul,iar ‖ wilfully elaborated
‖ incredible **fan·tás·ti·cal·ly** *adv.*

fan·ta·sy, phan·ta·sy *pl.* **fan·ta·sies,
phan·ta·sies** *n.* playful imagination,
fancy ‖ a daydream ‖ thinking, planning
etc. not based on sound reason or
prudence

**far far·ther, fur·ther far·thest, far·thest,
fur·thest** 1. *adv.* at a considerable
distance or to a great extent ‖ very much
2. *adj.* very distant, remote ‖ the more
distant of two

far·a·way *adj.* remote ‖ dreamy

farce *n.* a dramatic representation intended
only to amuse ‖ any event with a futile or
absurd outcome **fár·ci·cal** *adj.*

fare *n.* the cost of a journey ‖ food, diet
fare far·ing fared *v.i.* to manage, get along

fare·well 1. *interj.* goodbye 2. *n.* a
leavetaking

far·fetched *adj.* laboriously contrived, not
plausible

far-flung *adj.* of huge extent ‖ remote

farm 1. *n.* an area of land used for cultivation or animal breeding ‖ a tract of water
for cultivating fish, oysters etc. ‖ a minor-
league team attached to a major-league
team 2. *v.t.* to raise (crops, stock, poultry etc.) ‖ (often with 'out') to delegate
(work) to outside workers **fárm·er** *n.* a
person who owns or rents a farm

far-off *adj.* remote in space or time

far-sight·ed *adj.* hypermetropic ‖ prudent

fas·ci·cle *n.* a bunch, bundle, cluster ‖ a
single part of a book published in sections
fás·ci·cled *adj.* **fas·cic·u·la·tion** *n.*

fas·ci·nate fas·ci·nat·ing fas·ci·nat·ed *v.t.*
to compel delighted interest in ‖ to hold
as if under a spell **fás·ci·nat·ing** *adj.*

fas·ci·ná·tion, fás·ci·na·tor *ns*

Fas·cism *n.* the ideological outlook and its
extremist manifestations in Mussolini's
Italian dictatorship (1922-43)

Fas·cist 1. *n.* an adherent or supporter of
Fascism 2. *adj.* of or pertaining to
Fascist ideas or to the Fascist régime

fash·ion 1. *n.* way, manner ‖ the style of
clothes worn at a particular period ‖
modishness ‖ dress in its aspect of changing style 2. *v.t.* to mold shape
fásh·ion·a·ble *adj.* currently in style
fásh·ion·a·bly *adv.*

fast 1. *v.i.* to abstain from food 2. *n.* an act
of abstinence from food

fast *adj.* swift ‖ speedy ‖ lasting a short time
‖ allowing rapid progress ‖ (of a clock or
watch) in advance of the real time ‖ gay
and dissipated

fast *adv.* quickly, hurriedly ‖ fixedly ‖
soundly ‖ wildly

fas·ten *v.t.* to make secure ‖ to fix firmly,
tie, attach ‖ *v.i.* to close securely

fas·tid·i·ous *adj.* having highly developed
taste ‖ fussily particular ‖ meticulous

fast·ness *n.* fixedness, irremovability, e.g.
of dyes

fat 1. *n.* the greasy material constituting
the largest portion of the cells of adipose
tissue and occurring in other parts of
animals and in plants ‖ the best part of
something 2. *adj.* bulky ‖ thick ‖
financially rewarding ‖ (of type)
broadfaced

fa·tal *adj.* resulting in death ‖ calamitous
‖ fateful **fá·tal·ism** *n.* the belief that all
events are predetermined ‖ the mental
attitude of submission to the inevitabil-
ity of the power of fate **fá·tal·ist** *n.*
fa·tal·ís·tic *adj.* accepting one's fate with
stoicism or lethargy

fa·tal·i·ty *pl.* **fa·tal·i·ties** *n.* a disaster, esp.
one causing death ‖ a person killed in an
accident or disaster

fate *n.* a power that supposedly predeter-
mines events ‖ the history of an individual
or of a special group ‖ doom, destruction
fát·ed *adj.* predetermined, destined
fáte·ful *adj.* controlled by fate ‖ decisive

in effect

fa·ther 1. *n.* the male parent ‖ an originator ‖ a venerable person **Fa·ther** a title of reverence for a priest **the Father** the first person of the Trinity **2.** *v.t.* to be the father of

fa·ther·hood *n.* the state of being a father

fa·ther-in-law *pl.* **fa·thers-in-law** *n.* a husband's or wife's father

fath·om 1. *n.* a measure of depth of water equal to 6 ft ‖ **fáth·om·less** *adj.* too profound to understand **2.** *v.t.* to measure the depth of, to sound ‖ to comprehend

fa·tigue 1. *n.* wearness after exertion or hard work ‖ a condition of a material, esp. a metal, causing loss of elasticity and tendency to fracture after long or repeated stress **2.** *v.t.* **fa·ti·guing fa·tigued** to make weary

fat·ten *v.t.* to make fat ‖ to make (soil) fertile or rich

fat·ty fat·ti·er fat·ti·est *adj.* containing fat, adipose

fat·u·ous *adj.* foolish, empty-headed or vacuously self-satisfied

fau·cet *n.* a device for controlling the flow of a fluid from a pipe or container

fault 1. *n.* something for which one is rightly open to blame ‖ a mistake ‖ a blemish ‖ a moral failing ‖ *(geol.)* a fracture within the earth's crust **fáult·i·ly** *adv.* **fáult·less** *adj.* not to blame ‖ without blemish **fáult·y fault·i·er fault·i·est** *adj.* imperfect, defective **2.** *v.t.* imperfect, defective **3.** *v.t.* to criticize (someone) with justice

fau·na *pl.* **fau·nas, fau·nae** *n.* animal life in general, as distinguished from flora ‖ a classification of the animals of a region, environment or period **fáu·nal** *adj.*

faux pas *pl.* **faux pas** *n.* a social blunder

fa·vor *v.t.* to be to the advantage of ‖ to suit ‖ to oblige ‖ to show partiality towards ‖ to resemble in looks ‖ to be in favor of

favor *n.* approbation ‖ an act of kindness ‖ advantae ‖ unfair partiality

fa·vor·a·ble *adj.* giving or expressing approval ‖ auspicious ‖ attractive

fá·vor·a·bly *adv.*

fa·vored *adj.* granted special concessions

fa·vor·ite 1. *n.* an object or person regarded with esteem or affection above others **2.** *adj.* most or very much liked

fá·vor·it·ism *n.* the showing of a special liking by acts of partiality where impartiality is called for

fawn 1. *n.* a deer less than one year old **2.** *adj.* light yellowish-brown

fawn *v.i.* (of animals, esp. dogs) to show affection or seek attention by hand-licking, rubbing up against one etc. ‖ (of persons) to seek favor by servile and flattering behavior **fáwn·ing** *adj.*

faze faz·ing fazed *v.t.* to disconcert, daunt

fear 1. *n.* the instinctive emotion aroused by impending or seeming danger, pain or evil ‖ *(pl.)* anxiety ‖ awe **2.** *v.t.* to be afraid, feel fear **féar·ful** *adj.* frightened or showing fear **féar·ful·ly** *adv.* extremely **féar·less** *adj.* having no fear **fear·some** *adj.* causing fear ‖ daunting

fea·si·bil·i·ty *n.* the quality of being feasible

fea·si·ble *adj.* possible **féa·si·bly** *adv.*

feast 1. *n.* a fine, elaborate meal designed for celebration ‖ an abundance of anything giving enjoyment **2.** *v.t.* to provide with a feast ‖ *v.i.* to enjoy a feast

feat *n.* a deed out of the ordinary

feath·er *n.* one of the epidermal outgrowths that cover the body of a bird ‖ (usually *pl.*) plumage

feath·er·weight *n.* a boxer whose weight does not exceed 126 lbs. ‖ somebody who does not matter much ‖ something very light

fea·ture 1. *n.* a part of the face, esp. as regards appearance ‖ the distinctive part, trait or characteristic of a thing ‖ the main item in a movie program **2.** *v.t.* **fea·tur·ing fea·tured** to give promence to **féa·tured** *adj.* displayed **féa·ture·less** *adj.* lacking distinctive features

Feb. February

Feb·ru·ar·y *n.* *(abbr.* **Feb.)** the 2nd month of the year

fe·ces, fae·ces *pl.* *n.* bodily waste

fe·cund *adj.* prolific, fertile ‖ rich in inventive power

fed·er·a·cy *pl.* **fed·er·a·cies** *n.* an alliance, federation of states

fed·er·al *adj.* characterizing an agreement between states to unite, forgoing some sovereignty but remaining independent in internal affairs

fed·er·al·ism *n.* the federal principle of government ‖ the support of this principle

fed·er·al·ist *n.* a supporter of federalism

fed·er·ate 1. fed·er·at·ing fed·er·at·ed *v.t.* to organize (states) into a federation **2.** *adj.* federated

fed·er·a·tion *n.* the act of uniting with a league for common purposes, esp. in forming a sovereign power while each m;ember state retains control of internal matters

fee *n.* payment services

fee·ble *adj.* weak ‖ dim, unclear, indistinct

fee·ble-mind·ed *adj.* mentally deficient ‖ silly, foolish

feed 1. *v.* **feed·ing fed** *v.t.* to give food to ‖ to fortify ‖ to supply (material) to ‖ to supply with cue lines ‖ *v.i.* (esp. of animals) to eat **2.** *n.* food, esp. for livestock, fodder etc. ‖ a meal ‖ the process of feeding a machine with raw material etc.

feed·back *n.* the return of the input of an amplification system of part of the output in order to control amplification ‖ response following an action ‖ return to input that stimulates the proper adjustment, e.g., biofeedback

feel 1. feel·ing felt *v.t.* to perceive, learn, explore by touching ‖ to become aware of through the senses ‖ to experience (an emotion) ‖ to sense ‖ *v.i.* to have sympathy or compassion **2.** *n.* the sense of touch ‖ an instinctive understanding of **feel·er** *n.* an organ for testing by touch, e.g. the antenna of an insect **feel·ing 3.** *n.* the effect conveyed by the sense of touch ‖ sensation in general ‖ an emotion ‖ (*pl.*) susceptibilities, emotions ‖ sympathy ‖ an intuitive belief, conviction based on other grounds than reason ‖ opinion

4. *adj.* sensitive **feel·ing·ly** *adv.*

feign *v.t.* to represent by false appearance, simulate ‖ to pretend **feigned** *adj.* sham, fictitiious ‖ fraudulent

feint 1. *n.* a mock attack ‖ a deceptive movement **2.** *v.i.* to make a feint

fe·lic·i·tate fe·lic·i·tating fe·lic·i·tat·ed *v.t.* to congratulate **fe·lic·i·tá·tion** *n.*

fe·lic·i·tous *adj.* notably apt, well chosen

fe·lic·i·ty *pl.* **fe·lic·i·ties** *n.* aptness ‖ happiness

fe·line 1. *adj.* of cats ‖ catlike ‖ cunningly spiteful **2.** *n.* an animal of the cat family **fe·lin·i·ty** *n.*

fell 1. *v.t.* to cut down ‖ to knock down **2.** *n.* an amount of timber cut **fél·ler** *n.* someone who fells timber

fel·low *n.* a man of whom one speaks with familiarity or condescension ‖ (often *pl.*) a companion, associate ‖ (in combination with nouns) one of the same class ‖ an elected graduate holding endowment for a period of research

fel·low·man *pl.* **fel·low·men** *n.* another human being thought of as being like oneself

fel·low·ship *n.* the companionship and comradeship characteristic of group solidarity

fel·on *n.* someone guilty of a felony

fe·lo·ni·ous *adj.* wicked, criminal

fel·o·ny *pl.* **fel·o·nies** *n.* a grave crime

felt *n.* a fabric made by pressing and rolling (wool, hair, fur etc.) with size or lees

fe·male 1. *adj.* of the sex in animals or plants that produces or is capable of producing eggs or bearing young (symbol ♀) ‖ pertaining to women **2.** *n.* a female person, animal or plant

fem·i·nine 1. *adj.* of the female sex ‖ of women ‖ characteristic of women **2.** *n.* the feminine gender ‖ a word in this gender

fem·i·nin·i·ty *n.* the quality of being feminine

fem·i·nism *n.* the policy, practice or advocacy of political, economic and social equality for women **fém·i·nist** *n.* an advocate of feminism

fe·mur *pl.* **fe·murs, fem·o·ra** *n.* the thighbone

fen *n.* low marshy land

fence 1. *n.* a railing ‖ an artificial obstacle for a horse to jump over ‖ a person receiving stolen goods **2. fenc·ing fenced** *v.i.* to practice fencing as a sport ‖ to deal in stolen goods ‖ *v.t.* to enclose, provide or surround with a fence **fénc·er** *n.* **fénc·ing** *n.* the art of attack, defense etc. with sword or foil ‖ the art of parrying etc. in debate

fend *v.t.* (with 'off') to repel, parry ‖ *v.i.* (with 'for') to struggle to look after **fénd·er** *n.* a metal cover or guard over the wheel of a vehicle

fer·ment *v.i.* to undergo fermentation ‖ *v.t.* to cause fermentation in ‖ to inflame, excite

fer·ment *n.* any agent able to produce fermentation ‖ commotion, unrest, tumult

fer·men·ta·tion *n.* a chemical change produced by enzymes ‖ restless excitement **fer·men·ta·tive** *adj.* able to ferment or to cause to ferment

fern *n.* vascular, nonflowering plant

fe·ro·cious *adj.* savage, fierce ‖ cruel, violent

fe·roc·i·ty *pl.* **fe·roc·i·ties** *n.* an act of intense cruelty

fer·ret 1. *n.* variety of the European polecat **2.** *v.i.* to hunt with ferrets **to ferret out** to search out **fér·ret·y** *adj.* shifty, ferretlike

fer·ric *adj.* pertaining to, or containing iron

fer·ry 1. fer·ry·ing fer·ried *v.t.* to transport in a boat ‖ to transport (troops etc.) by aircraft which shuttle back and forward between two points **2.** *pl.* **fer·ries** *n.* a ferryboat

fer·ry·boat *n.* a boat working a ferry service

fer·tile *adj.* highly productive ‖ capable of breeding or reproducing ‖ productive, creative

fer·til·i·ty *pl.* **fer·til·i·ties** *n.* the state or quality of being fertile ‖ birthrate

fer·ti·lize *v.t.* **fer·ti·liz·ing fer·ti·lized** to make fertile or productive

fer·ven·cy *n.* the quality of being fervent

fer·vent *adj.* ardent, emotionally intense

fer·vid *adj.* fervent

fer·vor *n.* intensity of feeling, passion, devotion

fes·tal *adj.* gay, festive

fes·ter 1. *v.i.* to produce pus ‖ to produce bitter feelings, rankle ‖ to rot, putrefy **2.** *n.* a festering sore, pustule

fes·ti·val *n.* a joyful celebration or occasion

fes·tive *adj.* of feasts or festivals ‖ gay, a *festive party*

fes·tiv·i·ty *pl.* **fes·tiv·i·ties** *n.* merrymaking, gaiety

fetch *v.t.* to go and get, bring ‖ to obtain as its price **fétch·ing** *adj.* attractive

fete, fête 1. *n.* a festival, entertainment **2.** *v.t.* to celebrate (a success etc.)

fet·id, foet·id *adj.* having a strong offensive smell

fet·ish *n.* an object believed by certain primitive peoples to embody a spirit and exert magical powers **fáet·ish·ism** *n.* the worship of fetishes ‖ the centering of strong sexual emotion in objects **fét·ish·ist** *n.* **fet·ish·is·tic** *adj.*

fet·ter 1. *n.* a chain or shackle for the feet of a prisoner ‖ a tether for an animal **2.** *v.t.* to put fetters on ‖ to restrain, hamper

fe·tus, foe·tus *n.* a vertebrate that has passed the early stages of development

feud *n.* a long-standing quarrel between families, clans, tribes etc.

feu·dal *adj.* pertaining to feuds, fiefs or fees ‖ pertaining to the feudal system **féu·dal·ism** *n.* the feudal system **féu·dal·ist** *n.* **feu·dal·ís·tic** *adj.*

feudal system the system of economic, political and social organization which flourished in Europe (9th-14th cc.)

fe·ver *n.* human body temperature above the normal 98.6° F. or 37.0 C. ‖ a high state of excitement, agitation

fe·ver·ish *adj.* having a fever ‖ restlessly excited

few 1. *adj.* consisting of a small, indefinite number **2.** *n.* a small number of people, things etc. **the few** the minority of people

fi·an·cé n. a man in relation to the woman to whom he is engaged to be married

fi·an·cée n. a woman in relation to the man to whom she is engaged

fi·as·co pl. **fi·as·cos, fias·coes** n. an absurd or complete failure

fib 1. n. a trivial lie 2. v. i. **fib·bing fibbed** to tell such a lie

fi·ber, fi·bre n. a fine thread ‖ a threadlike structure of animal or vegetable tissue ‖ a substance, natural or man-made, that can be spun, woven, felted etc. ‖ moral strength

fiber glass name for fine glass fibers used for textile manufacture, and for material made from these

fi·brous adj. containing fibers

fic·tion n. literature consisting of invented narrative ‖ a false story or statement ‖ a pretense, invention **fic·tion·al** adj. not restricted to fact

fic·ti·tious adj. imagined, not factual ‖ imaginary, feigned

fid·dle 1. n. a violin 2. v. **fid·dled** v.i. (often contemptuous) to play the violin ‖ to make aimless, distracting movements ‖ v.t. to play (a tune) on a violin

fid·dler n. someone who plays the fiddle

fiddler crab a small crab

fi·del·i·ty pl. **fi·del·i·ties** n. the faithful performance of duty ‖ loyalty ‖ exactness

fidg·et v. to be constantly making restless little movements ‖ to be uneasy, worry **fidg·et·i·ness** n. **fidg·et·y** adj.

fi·du·ci·ar·y 1. adj. of the nature of a trust or trusteeship ‖ held or given in trust 2. pl. **fi·du·ci·ar·ies** n. someone acting in a fiduciary capacity, a trustee

field 1. n. an area of land ‖ pl. meadows or arable land ‖ a battleground ‖ a particular body of interest, study, knowledge or thought ‖ racing the competing horses ‖ all runners except the favorite ‖ all those taking part in a sport or contest out-of-doors 2. v.t. to stop or catch (the ball) ‖ to answer without previous preparation 3. adj. of or relating to a field ‖ growing in fields

fiend n. the Devil ‖ any demon or evil spirit ‖ a person actuated by intense wickedness, esp. by cruelty **fiendish** adj. devilish

fierce fierc·er fierc·est adj. savage, hostile ‖ raging, violent ‖ intense, passionate

fi·er·y fi·er·i·er fi·er·i·est adj. flaming with fire ‖ blazing red ‖ seeming to burn ‖ passionate

fif·teen adj. being one more than 14

fif·teenth 1. adj. being number 15 in a series 2. n. the person or thing next after the 14th

fifth 1. adj. being number five in a series 2. n. the person or thing next after the fourth

fif·ti·eth 1. adj. being number 50 in a series 2. n. the person or thing next after the 49th

fif·ty adj. being 10 more than 40

fif·ty-fif·ty 1. adv. equally 2. adj. equal, half-and-half

fig n. a genus of tropical trees and shrubs ‖ the fruit of the fig tree ‖ the least little bit

fight fight·ing fought v.i. to give mutual blows ‖ to take part in a war ‖ to strive, struggle ‖ to engage in a legal contest ‖ v.t. to try to stop, prevent or overcome ‖ to defend one's interests in ‖ to engage in (a boxing contest) ‖ to cause to fight

fig·ment n. a physical struggle for victory ‖ a battle 1. an effort to overcome something **fight·er** n. someone full of determination to win

fig·ment n. something made up with no basis of truth

fig·ur·a·tive adj. expressed by means of metaphor or other figure of speech

fig·ure 1. n. the written or printed symbol for a number ‖ a diagram ‖ a three-dimensional form enclosed by surfaces ‖ the human form ‖ a piece of sculpture ‖ a personage ‖ a decorative pattern or design 2. v. **fig·ur·ing fig·ured** v.t. to represent by means of a figure, diagram, picture, etc. ‖ to decorate with patterns or designs ‖ to consider ‖ v.i. to do arithmetic **fig·ured** adj. represented by a painted or sculpted figure ‖ shaped, fashioned

fig·ur·ine *n.* a small statue, carved or molded

fil·a·ment *n.* a fine threadlike body or fiber ‖ *(elec.)* a thin metallic fiber that serves as the cathode in electron tubes ‖ *(bot.)* the stalk of a stamen, bearing the anther **fil·a·men·ta·ry fil·a·men·tous** *adjs*

filch *v.t.* to steal, pilfer

file 1. *n.* a steel instrument used for smoothing, cutting through or abrading surfaces of metal etc. **2.** *v.t.* **fil·ing filed** to cut or smooth with a file

file 1. *n.* a device of various kinds for keeping papers ‖ a set of papers so kept ‖ a row of persons or things arranged one behind the other **2.** *v.* **fil·ing filed** *v.t.* to place (a document) with others so as to be available for reference ‖ (with 'off' or 'out') to cause (soldiers) to move in a file ‖ *(law)* to submit (a petition) ‖ *v.i.* to march or move in a file ‖ to apply

fil·i·al *adj.* relating to a son or daughter

fil·i·bus·ter 1. *n.* the obstruction of legislative action by delaying tactics **2.** *v.i.* to act as a filibusterer **fil·i·bus·ter·er** *n.* someone who filibusters

fil·i·gree *n.* lacy ornamental work of fine wire (gold, silver, copper etc.) ‖ any delicate or fragile openwork **fil·i·greed** *adj.*

fill *v.t.* to make full ‖ to occupy the whole space of ‖ to stock lavishly ‖ to plug up a cavity in (a tooth) ‖ to occupy (an office) ‖ to occupy (time) ‖ to satisfy, glut ‖ to dispense (a prescription etc.) ‖ *v.t.* to become full

fil·let 1. *n.* a boneless piece of meat, fish or esp of beef from the loin **2.** *v.t.* to remove the bone from (fish or meat) and divide it into long, thin slices

fil·ling *n.* the act of filling ‖ a substance used in filling a decayed tooth

fil·ly *pl.* **fil·lies** *n.* a young mare

film 1. *n.* a thin layer ‖ a growth on the yee ‖ a haze dimming the sight ‖ a sheet or strip of celluloid or other material that has been coated with a light-sensitive emulsion **2.** *v.t* to make a movie of

fil·ter 1. *n.* a device for separating solids from liquids, or suspended particles from

gases ‖ *(photog.)* a lens screen which has different absorptive powers for different wavelengths of light **2.** *v.t.* to pass (something) through a filter ‖ *v.i.* to go through or as if through a filter

filth *n.* foul matter ‖ anything that corrupts **filth·y filth·i·er filth·i·est** *adj.* extremely dirth ‖ obscene

fin *n.* one of the paired membranous limbs or unpaired dermal outgrowths used by a fish to propel and steer itself ‖ an external rib, parallel to the axis of symmetry, preserving balance and direction by dividing the airflow

fi·na·gle fi·na·gling fi·na·gled to get (something) by guile

fi·nal 1. *adj.* the last of a series ‖ coming at the end ‖ ultimate ‖ decisive, conclusive **2.** *n.* a decicing race, game, contest etc. ‖ (often *pl.*) an examination at the end of a course **fi·nal·ist** *n.* a competitor in a deciding game, competition etc. **fi·nal·ly** *adv.* lastly, in conclusion

fi·nal·e *n.* the last movement of a musical composition ‖ the last piece performed at a concert ‖ the last scene of a play ‖ the last event in a dramatic series of events

fi·nal·i·ty *pl.* **fi·nal·i·ties** *n.* the state of being final

fi·nance 1. *n.* monetary affairs ‖ the management of public or company revenue ‖ *(pl.)* monetary resources **2.** *v.t.* **fi·nanc·ing fi·nanced** to provide with money ‖ to raise the money for **fi·nan·cial** *adj.*

fin·an·cier *n.* a large-scale investor, capitalist ‖ someone skilled in financial matters

finch *n.* a small, seed-eating bird

find 1. *v.* **find·ing found** *v.t.* to discover by seeking ‖ to discover by experiment or study ‖ to discover by chance ‖ to declare (a verdict) ‖ to declare (a person) as specified (guilty, insane etc.) ‖ *v.i.* to reach and deliver a verdict **2.** *n.* something valuable that is found **find·er** *n.* someone who or something which finds

fine 1. *adj.* highly satisfactory, excellent ‖ very skilled and delicate ‖ consisting of small particles ‖ thin, sharp ‖ highly accomplished ‖ dressy ‖ refined ‖ mannered ‖ (of the weather) bright and clear 2. *adv.* very well

fine 1. *n.* a sum of money paid as an imposed penalty for an offense 2. *v.t.* **fin·ing fined** to punish by imposing a fine on **fine·a·ble** *adj.*

fin·er·y *n.* showy, elaborate clothing

fi·nesse 1. *n.* subtlety of contrivance, judgment etc. ‖ a skillful strategic maneuver 2. *v.* **fi·ness·ing fi·nessed** ‖ *v.* to make or lachieve by subtlety

fin·ger 1. *n.* a terminal digit of the hand ‖ the breadth of a finger ‖ a pointer on a dial 2. *v.t.* to touch with the fingers, handle

fin·ger·print 1. *n.* an impression of a fingertip left on a surface ‖ such an impression taken to record identification 2. *v.t.* to fingerprint

fin·ger·tip *n.* the tip of a finger

fin·ish 1. *v.t.* to arrive at the end of ‖ to complete ‖ to consume entirely ‖ to exhaust completely ‖ to put the final touches to ‖ *v.i.* to come to an end 2. *n.* conclusion, end ‖ the material used for a decorative surface ‖ surface refinement ‖ social polish **fin·ished** *adj.* concluded ‖ perfected ‖ thorough **fin·ish·er** *n.*

fi·nite *adj.* having definable bounds ‖ (of numbers) able to be counted, not infinite or infinitesimal

fink *n.* one who tells tales; a betrayer

fiord, fjord *n.* a narrow inlet of the sea

fir *n.* an evergreen tree

fire 1. *n.* a chemical change accompanied by the emission of heat and light, and often flame ‖ the discharge of a gun or guns ‖ passion 2. *v.* **fir·ing fired** *v.t.* to discharge (a gun etc.) ‖ to ask (questions) or make (remarks etc.) in rapid succession ‖ to set fire to ‖ to dismiss, discharge (an employee) ‖ to stimulate ‖ to bake (bricks, pottery etc.) ‖ to light the fuse of (an explosive) ‖ *v.i.* to shoot a gun ‖ to be affected by fire ‖ to have the compressed mixture in the cylinders ignited

fire·arm *n.* any portable weapon firing shot or bullets by gunpowder

fire·crack·er *n.* a small, cylindrical firework which goes off with a cracking noise when its fuse is lit

fire·fly *pl.* **fire·flies** *n.* any of several winged, nocturnal insects emitting light by the oxidation of luciferin

fire·man *pl.* **fire·men** *n.* a member of a fire department

fire·work *n.* a device used for entertainment by effets of colored light, smoke, noise etc. ‖ (*pl.*) a verbal display of wit or anger

firm 1. *adj.* compact, solid ‖ stable ‖ steady ‖ exercising authority with discipline ‖ not liable to cancellation 2. *adv.* firmly 3. *v.t.* to make firm ‖ *v.i.* to become firm

firm *n.* a partnership or business house ‖ stable ‖ steady ‖ exercising authority with discipline ‖ not liable to cancellation 1. *adv.* firmly 2. *v.t.* to make firm ‖ *v.i.* to become firm

fir·ma·ment *n.* the whole vault of the sky

first 1. *adj.* being number one in a series ‖ earliest in time ‖ foremost in importance, rank etc. ‖ fundamental ‖ redimentary 2. *n.* the first person or thing mentioned 3. *adv.* before any other person or thing ‖ for the first time

first aid the emergency treatment of someone wounded or taken ill

first·hand *adv.* and *adj.* from the original sources

fis·cal *adj.* of or pertaining to the public treasury or revenue ‖ financial

fish *pl.* **fish, fish·es** *n.* a class of backboned aquatic animals ‖ the flesh, whether raw or cooked

fish *v.i.* to try to catch fish ‖ to try to get something, usually by indirect methods ‖ *v.t.* to fish in

fish·er·man *pl.* **fish·er·men** *n.* someone who lives by fishing ‖ someone who fishes for pleasure

fish·er·y *fish·er·ies* *n.* the fishing industry ‖ a place where fish are bred

fis·sion *n.* the process of splitting into parts ‖ the splitting of an atomic nucleus into approximately equal parts **fis·sion·a·ble** *adj.*

fis·sure 1. *n.* a narrow opening or cleft, esp. in rock ‖ a cleaving or cleavage **2.** *v.t.* and *i.* **fis·sur·ing fis·sured** to split into fissures

fist *n.* the hand when clenched

fist·i·cuffs *pl. n.* (*old-fash.*) fighting with bare fists

fit 1. *adj.* suited to a particular end ‖ brought into a specified condition, ready ‖ in good physical condition, healthy **2. fit·ting fit·ted, fit** *v.t.* to suit ‖ to qualify ‖ to correspond with ‖ to be the right size or shape for ‖ to adjust the size or shape ‖ *v.i.* to be correct in size or shape ‖ to be in harmony or agreement **3.** *n.* the manner or degree of fitting ‖ something which fits

fit *adj.* a seizure, convulsion ‖ a short sudden attack or outburst **to have a fit** to become suddenly and violently angry or upset

fit·ful *adj.* spasmodic

fit·ness *n.* the state of being fit ‖ good health

fit·ting *n.* (esp. *pl.*) a piece of fixed equipment or furnishing ‖ a smal part for a piece of apparatus or an installation ‖ a trying-on of tailor-made clothes

five *adj.* being one more than four

fix 1. *v.t.* to fasten firmly, make fast ‖ to make as if rigid ‖ (of an object) to seize and hold (one's attention) ‖ to commit (details) to one's mind or memory ‖ to determine, establish ‖ to arrange ‖ to prepare ‖ to repair ‖ to influence by bribery etc. ‖ (*pop.*) to deal with (someone) so as to punish, reduce to silence, counter etc. ‖ *v.i.* to become fixed **2.** *n.* a difficult situation, dilemma

fix·a·tion *n.* the act of fixing ‖ the partial arrest of psychosexual development at an infantile stage with consequent immaturity of sexual or other relationships ‖ the accurate direction and focusing of the eyes, for optimum vision

fix·a·tive *n.* any of various substances used to make something more permanent

fix·ture *n.* a thing fixed permanently in position ‖ any of the fixed items bought or sold with a building ‖ someone or something thought of as invariably present

fiz·zle 1. *v.i.* **fiz·zling fiz·zled** to hiss or splutter feebly **to fizzle out** to come to nothing, esp. after a good start **2.** *n.* a complete failure, fiasco

flab·bi·ness *n.* the state or quality of being flabby

flab·by flab·bi·er flab·bi·est *adj.* lacking firmness ‖ having soft, slack flesh ‖ hanging loosely

flac·cid *adj.* limp, flabby ‖ feeble **flac·cíd·i·ty** *n.*

flag 1. *n.* a piece of cloth attached to a pole and used to denote nationality, party or ownership, to mark a position, or to exchange information ‖ the 'for hire' signal of a taxi **2.** *v.t.* **flag·ging flagged** to signal by means of flags (with 'down') to bring to a stop with motions of the hand

flag flag·ging flagged *v.i.* (e.g. of a plant) to hang down limply, droop ‖ (of a person) to show signs of exhaustion

flag·on *n.* a vessel for holding liquor ‖ a large globular glass bottle

fla·grant *adj.* conspicuously evil ‖ glaringly wrong

flair *n.* a natural ability, aptitude

flak complaints ‖ criticism difficult to handle ‖ from the exploded bullets of antiaircraft fire

flake 1. *n.* a small, thin, loose-textured fragment ‖ a thin but broad piece that scales off ‖ an eccentric person **2.** *v.* **flak·ing flaked** *v.i.* to fall as or like snow ‖ to come away in flakes ‖ to make flaky

flak·y flak·i·er flak·i·est *adj.* consisting of flakes

flam·boy·ance *n.* the quality of being flamboyant

flam·boy·ant 1. *adj.* florid, ornate, vivid in color ‖ ostentatious, overelaborate, showy

flame *n.* a body of glowing, burning gas ‖ the state of burning with a blaze ‖ intense feeling, passion ‖ (*old-fash., pop.*) a sweetheart

flame flam·ing flamed *v.i.* to burst into flame ‖ *v.t.* to pass through a flame

flam·ma·ble *adj.* liable to ignite

flank 1. *n.* the side of an animal between the ribs and thigh ‖ the side of a hill, mountain, building etc. ‖ the right or left side of an army, fleet etc. **2.** *v.t.* to attack from the flank ‖ to pass around the flank of

flap 1. *n.* the part for sealing an envelope or the cover of a coat pocket ‖ the movement made by a bird's wing or by a sail in the breeze ‖ the sound accompanying such a movement ‖ a movable airfoil on the trailing edge of an aircraft wing **2.** *v.* **flap·ping flapped** *v.i.* (of a bird's wings) to move up and down, esp. while the bird remains perched or standing ‖ to cause to move lightly one way and another with a dry, slapping sound

flare 1. *n.* a sudden emission of bright flame ‖ a device used to illuminate a position, target etc. ‖ a gradual widening **2.** *v.* **flar·ing flared** *v.i.* (of a fire) to emit flames which are bright and fierce but unsteady ‖ to become wider ‖ *v.t.* to cause to flare **to flare up** to become suddenly angry

flash 1. *v.i.* to give out a momentary, intensely bright light ‖ to give out flames or sparks ‖ to move quickly ‖ to come into the mind as quick as lightning ‖ *v.t.* to send (signals etc.) by flashes of light ‖ to allow to be seen briefly ‖ to display ostentatiously **2.** *n.* a sudden burst or gleam of light ‖ flame ‖ an instant of time ‖ a sudden, shortlived feeling ‖ a short news dispatch **3.** *adj.*

flash·back *n.* a short insertion in the plot sequence e.g. of a film or novel to relate events prior to the time of the narrative

flash·light *n.* a small, portable container fitted with an electric light bulb and dry-cell battery

flash·y flash·i·er flash·i·est *adj.* showy but worthless

flask *n.* a narrow-necked vessel ‖ a flat broad bottle for carrying liquor in one's pocket

flat 1. *adj.* (of a surface) even and level ‖ spread out ‖ completely in ruins ‖ broad, smooth and lacking thickness, e.g. like a coin ‖ without gloss ‖ outright ‖ dull, monotonous ‖ (of feet) having the instep arch fallen ‖ (of a tire) deflated ‖ lower by half a tone ‖ below the correct pitch **2.** *adv.* absolutely, precisely ‖ in a downright way **3.** *n.* level ground ‖ (*pl.*) low-lying ground over which the tide flows ‖ a punctured tire **4.** *v.* **flat·ting flat·ted**

flat *n.* an apartment (set of rooms) on one floor

flat·ten *v.t.* to make flat ‖ to knock down

flat·ter *v.t.* to praise excessively ‖ to gratify the vanity of **to flatter oneself** to delude oneself **flat·ter·y** *n.* insincere or excessive praise

flaunt 1. *v.t.* to display proudly or brazenly ‖ *v.i.* to display oneself **2.** *n.* the act of flaunting, a display

fla·vor 1. *n.* the quality belonging to food, drink etc. that is experienced through the combined senses of taste and smell **2.** *v.t.* to give flavor to **fla·vor·ing** *n.* a substance for adding flavor

flaw 1. *n.* a blemish, defect ‖ a weakness **2.** *v.* to cause a defect in **flaw·less** *adj.* perfect

flax *n.* a plant of the genus *Linum* ‖ its fibers

flax·en *adj.* like flax or of flax ‖ blond

flay *v.t.* to strip the skin or flesh from ‖ to fleece, charge (a person) extortionately

flea *n.* a small, wingless insect

fleck 1. *n.* a small mark or speck ‖ a patch of light or color **2.** *v.t.* to spot with flecks

fledg·ling, fledge·ling *n.* a bird just fledged ‖ an immature or inexperienced person

flee flee·ing fled *v.i.* to run away, esp. from danger or evil ‖ to shun

fleece 1. *n.* the coat of wool covering a sheep ‖ the amount of wool taken from sheep etc. at one shearing ‖ a thick and woolly hair or covering **2.** *v.t.* **fleec·ing fleeced** to rob by overcharging **fleec·y fleec·i·er fleec·i·est** *adj.* covered with wool

fleet *n.* a number of warships under one command ‖ any naval force ‖ a group of vehicles under one control

fleet·ing *adj.* transient, passing swiftly away

flesh 1. *n.* the muscular substance, together with the fat and connective tissues, of man and animals ‖ the pulpy part of a fruit ‖ sensual human nature **2.** *v.t.* to remove the flesh from (skin, hides etc.)

flesh·y flesh·i·er flesh·i·est *adj.* plump ‖ pulpy

flex *v.t.* to bend ‖ to move (a muscle) to bend a joint

flex·i·bil·i·ty *n.* the quality of being flexible

flex·i·ble *adj.* easily bent, not rigid ‖ pliable ‖ adaptable ‖ open to influence

flick·er 1. *v.i.* to quiver ‖ to burn fitfully **2.** *n.* a momentary stir of feeling

fli·er, fly·er *n.* a bird or insect with reference to the quality of its flight ‖ an aviator ‖ a widely distributed handbill

flight *n.* the act or mode of flying ‖ the power of flying ‖ a journey by air ‖ a flock of birds, insects etc. ‖ (of stairs) a unit block ‖ a soaring or sally

flight *n.* the act of fleeing ‖ a sudden hastening away

flim·sy flim·si·er flim·si·est *adj.* lacking substance ‖ made of poor material ‖ easily torn

flinch 1. *v.i.* to shrink or draw back ‖ to wince

fling 1. *v.t.* **fling·ing flung** to throw or hurl from the hand ‖ (with 'out') to go violently or in a temper ‖ (of a horse etc., esp. with 'out') to kick and plunge **2.** *n.* a lively, esp. Scottish, dance ‖ a period of going all out for sensual pleasure ‖ a sudden violent movement

flint *n.* a heavy and hard variety of silica which emits sparks when struck with steel ‖ a prehistoric tool of knapped flint ‖ a pebble made of flint

flip 1. *v.* **flip·ping flipped** *v.t.* to toss or flick with a quick movement of the fingers ‖ to lose control of oneself, creating either a good or bad response ‖ to move with a flick or jerk ‖ *v.i.* to make a flipping motion **2.** *n.* a light blow

flip·pan·cy *pl.* **flip·pan·cies** *n.* a flippant remark

flip·pant *adj.* treating serious matters with levity or lack of respect

flirt 1. *v.* to show amorous interest without any depth of feeling ‖ (with 'with') to take a superficial or half-serious interest **2.** *n.* someone who flirts **flir·tá·tion** *n.* the act of flirting **flir·tá·tious** *adj.* fond of amorous flirting

flit 1. *v.i.* **flit·ting flit·ted** to make sudden, brief flights from place to place ‖ to come or go swiftly **2.** *n.* the motion of flitting

float *n.* something that floats on a fluid ‖ a cork or quill on a fishing line ‖ an inflated part helping to support a fish or aircraft ‖ the hollow metal ball at the end of a lever controlling the water level in a tank, cistern etc., or a similar device ‖ a low-wheeled movable platform for displays etc. ‖ a raft

float *v.i.* to rest on or near the surface of a fluid ‖ to be held up by air, gas or fluid ‖ to move gently, drift ‖ *v.t.* (of liquid) to support ‖ to set afloat **flóat·a·ble** *adj.* capable of floating ‖ (of a river etc.) able to float rafts, logs etc.

flock 1. *n.* a number of birds living, feeding or moving together ‖ a number of goats or sheep herded together ‖ a crowd of people ‖ a church congregation **2.** *v.i.* to come together in a flock or large crowd

floe *n.* an ice floe

flog flog·ging flogged *v.t.* to beat or strike hard and repeatedly with a cane etc.

flood 1. *n.* a large quantity of water covering what is usually dry land, as the result of a river or sea's flowing over its usual limits ‖ the point of high tide **2.** *v.t.* to cover with a flood ‖ to overwhelm, e.g. with work or orders ‖ *v.i.* to be subject to submersion

floor *n.* the lower horizontal surface of a room ‖ the bottom of a sea, river, cave, mine, gallery or platform of a bridge etc. ‖ a story ‖ a level surface **to have the floor** to have the right to speak or to go on speaking in a legislative or debating assembly

flop 1. *v.t.* **flop·ping flopped** *v.i.* to move clumsily ‖ to let oneself drop (into a chair, on to a bed, to the ground etc.) ‖ to be a conspicuous failure ‖ *v.t.* (of a bird) to move (its wings) up and down with a loud flapping sound 2. *n.* a failure 3. *adv.* with a flop **flóp·py flop·pi·er flop·pi·est** *adj.* lacking firmaness

flo·ra *pl.* **flo·ras, flo·rae** *n.* plant life in general, esp. plants of a certain region, environment or period

flo·ral *adj.* of flowers ‖ of floras

flo·ret *n.* one of the small individual flowers of a composite flower

flor·id *adj.* heavily ornate

flo·rist *n.* someone who sells flowers ‖ someone who cultivates and breeds flowers

flo·til·la *n.* a small fleet ‖ a fleet of small vessels

flot·sam *n.* the wreckage of a ship or its cargo found floating on the sea

flounce 1. *n.* a brusque, self-conscious movement of the body, usually expressing petulance or high rage 2. *v.i.* **flounc·ing flounced** to go with such movements

flounce 1. *n.* a strip of cloth or lace gathered and sewn by the upper edge only 2. *v.t.* **flounc·ing flounced** to trim or adorn with a flounce or flounces

floun·der *n.* a small, edible flatfish

flounder *v.i.* to stumble about ‖ to do blunder

flour 1. *n.* finely ground and sieved wheat meal ‖ the ground meal of rye, barley or other cereals ‖ any fine, soft powder 2. *v.t.* to sprinkle with flour

flour·ish 1. *v.i.* to grow well ‖ to succeed, do well ‖ *v.t.* to display ostentatiously 2. *n.* a calculated showiness of manner ‖ an ostentatious gesture, a waving or brandishing (of a weapon) ‖ a curving, decorative stroke of the pen around a letter or word ‖ a fanfare

flout *v.* to treat with contempt ‖ *v.i.* (with 'at') to mock

flow 1. *v.i.* to move like a straem contained by banks ‖ (of blood) to circulate ‖ (of blood) to be spilled, in violence ‖ (of a stream etc.) to be full and running fast ‖ to run smoothly and effortlessly ‖ (of hair, draperies etc.) to hang with grace-

ful freedom ‖ to issue from 2. *n.* the act of flowing ‖ a steady, copious, progressive movement of goods, ideas, talk etc.

flow·er 1. *n.* a flowering plant ‖ its blossom only ‖ *(pl.)* the scum on wine etc. formed by fermentation ‖ the choicest part or specimen **in flower** blooming 2. *v.i.* to blossom ‖ *v.t.* to bring into flower **flow·er·et** *n.* a floret

flu, flue influenza

fluc·tu·ate fluc·tu·at·ing fluc·tu·at·ed *v.i.* to change constantly ‖ to show irregular variation **fluc·tu·á·tion** *n.*

flue *n.* a pipe or vent for carrying off smoke, gases, etc. to the outside air ‖ a channel for conveying a current of hot or cold air

flu·en·cy *n.* the quality of being fluent

flu·ent *adj.* having command of speaking in public, writing, using a foreign language etc.

fluff 1. *n.* any soft downy mass of feathers, fur, hair etc. ‖ a stumble in a speech or misplay in a game 2. *v.t.* to shake out into a fluffy mass ‖ to make an error ‖ *v.i.* to become fluffy **flúff·i·ness** *n.* **flúff·y fluff·i·er fluff·i·est** *adj.* of or like fluff

flu·id 1. *n.* a substance that flows and is capable of assuming the shape of its container 2. *adj.* able to flow ‖ able or likely to change

fluke 1. *n.* a stroke of luck 2. *v.* **fluk·ing fluked** *v.i.* to make a fluke ‖ *v.t.* to get by a fluke

fluk·y fluk·i·er fluk·i·est *adj.* lucky

flunk *v.t.* to fail **to flunk out** (pop.) to be dismissed, esp. from college, for failure

fluo·resce fluo·resc·ing fluo·resced *v.i.* to show fluorescence

fluo·res·cence *n.* a luminescence ‖ the property of emitting **fluo·rés·cent** *adj.*

fluorescent lamp a tubular glass electric lamp containing mercury vapor and equipped with an electron gun and anode, whose inner surface is coated with fluorescent substances

fluor·i·da·tion *n.* the addition of fluorides to (drinking water)

flur·ry 1. *pl.* **flur·ries** *n.* a sharp sudden

gust of wind ‖ a sudden gusty shower of rain or snow ‖ a fit of nervous excitement **2.** *v.i.* **flur·ry·ing flur·ried** to fluster

flush 1. *v.i.* to blush ‖ to flow and spread suddenly and freely ‖ *v.t.* to cause (water etc.) to flow ‖ to redden, inflame ‖ to make level **2.** *n.* a sudden flow (esp. of water or blood) ‖ a rush of emotion ‖ a feverish rush of heat **3.** *adj.* affluent ‖ level with adjoining surfaces **4.** *adv.* so as to be adjacent and in line

flus·ter *v.t.* to make nervous and confuse ‖ *v.i.* to be in such a state

flute 1. *n.* a woodwind instrument ‖ a long vertical rounded groove in a column, esp. in classical orders **2.** *v.* **flut·ing flut·ed** *v.* to utter in a soft, clear, high-pitched voice **flút·ing** *n.* decorative flutes on a column etc. **flút·ist** *n.* a flute player

flut·ter 1. *v.i.* to flap the wings in a short flight ‖ to flit ‖ to vibrate or beat irregularly ‖ to tremble, to be thrown into confusion ‖ *v.t.* to flap (the wings) in a short flight or without flying ‖ to throw into a state of agitation **2.** *n.* a quick irregular movement ‖ an irregular pulse or vibration ‖ an abnormal cardiac vibration

flux 1. *n.* the act of flowing ‖ the condition of continuously changing **2.** *v.t.* to make more fusible by adding a flux to ‖ *v.i.* to become fluid, melt ‖ to fuse

fly 1. *v.* **fly·ing flew flown** *v.i.* to move through the air by means of wings, jets, propellers etc. ‖ to travel by air ‖ to operate an aircraft ‖ to rush ‖ to hasten away ‖ (of time) to pass quickly ‖ to run away, flee ‖ *v.t.* to hoist (a flag) or keep (a flag) hoisted ‖ to operate (an aircraft) **2.** *pl.* **flies** *n.* the flap covering the fastening up the front of trousers ‖ a device for regulating speed in clockwork etc. ‖ a flywheel

fly *pl.* **flies** *n.* almost any dipteran insect, esp. the housefly ‖ (angling) a hook dressed with feathers, used as bait

fly·weight *n.* a professional or amateur boxer whose weight does not exceed 112 lbs

fly·wheel *n.* a solid heavy disk mounted on

a shaft, serving to offset fluctuations of the speed of the associated machinery by its inertia

foal 1. *n.* the young of a horse, donkey or other member of fam. Equidae **in (or with) foal** (of a horse etc.) pregnant **2.** *v.t.* to give birth to (a foal)

foam 1. *n.* a mass of whitish bubbles formed on liquid ‖ a lightweight cellular material, e.g. of rubber **2.** *v.i.* to rage ‖ *v.t.* to produce a lightweight cellular material by forming air bubbles in (a plastic etc.)

foam·y foam·i·er foam·i·est *adj.* consisting of foam or like foam ‖ covered with foam

fo·cus 1. *pl.* **fo·cus·es, fo·ci** *n.* a point to which waves from a distant source converge, or from which they appear to diverge, after reflection or refraction ‖ focal length ‖ adjustment for, or the condition of, distinct vision or sharpness ‖ a center of interest, importance etc. **2.** *v.* **fo·cus·ing, fo·cus·sing fo·cused, fo·cussed** *v.t.* to adjust (a mirror, lens etc.) so that waves from each point of an extended source converge to a point image ‖ to concentrate and direct (the attention etc.)

fod·der 1. *n.* dried food (hay, straw etc.) for cattle, sheep, horses etc. **2.** *v.t.* to feed with fodder

foe *n.* an enemy, adversary

fog 1. *n.* water vapor condensed on fine suspended particles, forming a dense opaque cloud at or just above the earth's surface ‖ cloudiness or opaqueness obscuring a film or print **in a fog** bewildered, mentally at a loss **2. fog·ging fogged** *v.t.* to cover or surround with fog ‖ to confuse or perplex (the mind) ‖ to cause to become cloudy

fog·gy fog·gi·er fog·gi·est *adj.* misty, thick with fog ‖ fogged ‖ muddled, indistinct

foi·ble *n.* an odd feature or mild failing in a person's character ‖ a fad

foil 1. *n.* a leaf or very thin sheet of metal, such as is used to protect packaged cigarettes or food against moisture ‖

something that sets off or enhances something else, esp. a character in a play or novel 2. *v.t.* to back or cover with foil

foil *n.* a light, thin, blunt-edged sword with a button on its point to prevent injury

foil *v.t.* to frustrate ‖ to thwart (a person) in his designs

foist *v.t.* to get rid of (something) by fraud or deception

fold 1. *n.* an enclosure to contain and protect sheep ‖ the community of those who subscribe to some organized religious or pseudoreligious system 2. *v.t.* to enclose in a fold

fold 1. *v.t.* to cause one part of (something) to lie on another ‖ to clasp around, embrace ‖ to cross and hold (the arms) close to the body ‖ to work in to a mixture gently without stirring ‖ *v.i.* to fail, collapse 2. *n.* the arrangement or crease caused by folding ‖ a little undulation in a fabric ‖ a bending back of strata

fold·er *n.* a paper or cardboard holder for loose papers ‖ a folded printed leaflet

fold·ing 1. *n.* a bending of rock strata, caused by compression of the earth's crust 2. *adj.* designed to fold away or fold into a compact shape

fo·li·age *n.* the leaves of a plant or tree ‖ sprays of leaves

folk 1. *pl.* **folk, folks** *n.* people as belonging to a class ‖ the great mass of common people ‖ (*pl., Am.* **folks**) relatives 2. *adj.* used by or springing from the mass of common people

folk·lore *n.* the stories, sayings, local customs, songs, dances etc., handed down from generation to generation among the unsophisticated members of a race or nation ‖ the science and study of these

fol·li·cle *n.* a small cavity, e.g. that in which a hair root grows **fol·lic·u·lar fol·lic·u·late, fol·lic·u·lat·ed** *adjs*

fol·low *v.* to go or come after ‖ to go in pursuit of ‖ to succeed in order of time ‖ to succeed (someone) in a position ‖ to imitate ‖ to act in accordance with ‖ to pay attention to, watch ‖ to understand ‖ to occur as a consequence ‖ as is about to be said **fol·low·er** *n.* an adherent, disciple **fol·low·ing** 1. *n.* a group of adherents or disciples 2. *adj.* succeeding, next ‖ about to be mentioned ‖ moving in the same direction 3. *prep.* immediately after

fol·ly *pl.* **fol·lies** *n.* behavior arising from stupidity ‖ a foolish act or idea ‖ a lapse from moral rectitude

fo·ment *v.t.* to treat with warm water or hot moist cloths **fo·men·ta·tion** *n.*

fond *adj.* affectionate, loving

fon·dle fon·dling fon·dled *v.t.* to handle lovingly, caress

fond·ly *adv.* affectionately ‖ credulously

font *n.* a complete set of types of a particular size and face

food *n.* any substance which a living organism can convert into fresh tissue, energy etc. ‖ a solid substance eaten for nourishment ‖ something which can be put to constructive use

fool 1. *n.* someone lacking common sense or judgment 2. *adj.* foolish, silly 3. *v.i.* to trifle, not be serious ‖ *v.t.* to deceive ‖ to cheat, trick **fool·er·y** *n.* foolish behavior

fool·har·dy fool·har·di·er fool·har·di·est *adj.* fearless but taking thoughtless, unnecessary risks

fool·ish *adj.* silly, ridiculous ‖ lacking in good sense, prudence or judgment or showing such a lack

fool·proof *adj.* absolutely safe against misinterpretation or misuse ‖ guaranteed never to go wrong

foot *pl.* **feet** *n.* the part at the end of the leg ‖ the lowest part ‖ a base ‖ the low end of a leg of a piece of furniture ‖ a unit of length equal to 12 ins ‖ a group of measured syllables constituting a metrical unit **on foot** walking (as distinct from using transportation) **foot·age** *n.* length in feet

foot·ball *n.* any of various team games played with a ball **foot·ball·er** *n.* someone who plays football

foot·hold *n.* a place to put one's foot where it will bear one's weight when climbing ‖ an initial position of advantage

foot·ing *n.* a secure place to stand on ‖ a basis of organization ‖ a social relationship

foot·note *n.* a note at the bottom of a printed page to elucidate a minor point raised in the text

foot·print *n.* a mark made by the foot

foot·step *n.* a footfall ‖ a footprint

fop *n.* a man excessively interested in his dress **fóp·per·y** *pl.* **fop·per·ies** *n.* **fóp·pish** *adj.*

for 1. on behalf of ‖ in honor of ‖ in support of ‖ with the purpose of ‖ to allow of ‖ (of feelings or capacities) towards ‖ as being ‖ in place of ‖ in spite of ‖ to set against ‖ to the amount of ‖ at the amount of ‖ to the extent or duration of ‖ in order to have, get etc. **2.** conj. because, since, seeing that

for·age 1. *n.* food for horses and cattle **2.** **for·ag·ing for·aged** *v.t.* to collect forage from ‖ to supply with forage ‖ *v.i.* to search

for·ay 1. *n.* a raid to get food, capture booty, or just pillage **2.** *v.i.* to make a raid, pillage

for·bear for·bear·ing for·bore for·borne *v.t.* to control one's patience, not give way to anger ‖ to abstain ‖ *v.i.* to refrain from **for·béar·ance** *n.*

for·bid for·bid·ding fore·bade for·bad for·bid·den *v.t.* to command (someone) not to do something ‖ to put (a place) out of bounds ‖ to make impossible, prevent **for·bíd·dance** *n.* **for·bíd·ding** *adj.* frighteningly difficult ‖ angry **for·bíd·den** *adj.*

force 1. *n.* the exertion of physical strength ‖ physical vigor ‖ mental or moral strength ‖ (*esp. pl.*) an organized body of men, troops, warships, etc. **force** by using force or by being forced **2.** *v.t.* **forc·ing forced** to compel by using physical or moral strength ‖ to produce with difficulty ‖ to drive or impel against physical resistance ‖ to hasten the growth of (plants etc.) by artificial means **forced** *adj.* compelled by force ‖ opened by force ‖ insincere

force·ful *adj.* forcible

for·ceps *pl.* **for·ceps** *n.* a two-pronged

instrument, esp. surgical and obstetrical pincers ‖ a limb shaped like a forceps

for·ci·ble *adj.* made or done by using force ‖ convincing, impressive, powerful **fór·ci·bly** *adv.*

ford 1. *n.* a place where a river is shallow and be crossed by wading **2.** *v.t.* to cross by wading

fore 1. *n.* the bows of a ship **at the fore** (*naut.*) on the foremast masthead **to the fore** (of personalities) in the public eye, conspicuous **2.** *adj.* placed in front, forward, advanced

fore- *prefix* in front, beforehand, in advance ‖ anticipatory

fore·arm *n.* to arm in advance

fore·arm *n.* the part of the arm between the elbow and the wrist

fore·bode fore·bod·ing fore·bod·ed *v.t.* to betoken, portent ‖ to have a presentiment of (disaster etc.) **fore·bód·ing** *n.* a sign of something to come

fore·cast 1. *v.t.* **fore·cast·ing fore·cast, fore·cast·ed** to predict **2.** *n.* something predicted

fore·close fore·clos·ing fore·closed *v.t.* to bar, remov e (the right of redemption) ‖ *v.i.* to take away the right to redeem a mortgage **fore·clos·ure** *n.*

fore·fath·er *n.* (esp.*pl.*) an ancestor, esp. a remote ancestor

fore·fin·ger *n.* the finger next to the thumb

fore·go·ing *adj.* mentioned above **fore·gone conclusion** a result that could be foreseen ‖ a decision reached before a matter could be properly considered

fore·ground *n.* the part of a scene nearest the viewer ‖ the most noticeable position

fore·hand *adj.* (*racket games*, of a stroke) made with the palm of the hand turned in the directio nof the stroke (opp. BACKHAND)

fore·head *n.* the front of the bertebrate head, in man above the eyebrows to where the hair begins to grow

for·eign *adj.* not of one's own country or race ‖ outside one's knowledge ‖ unrelated, extraneous

for·eign·er *n.* someone whose nationality is other than one's own

fore·man pl. **fore·men** n. someone who supervises other workmen ‖ a member of a jury who acts as leader and spokesman

fore·most 1. adj. first of several in place or time, rank or status **2.** adv. first ‖ most importantly

fore·noon n. the part of the day from dawn until midday

fo·ren·sic 1. adj. relating to law courts or to public debate **2.** n. an oral or written argumentative exercise

fore·run fore·run·ning fore·ran fore·run v.t. to be the precursor of, to come before as a token of what is to follow **fóre·run·ner** n.

fore·see fore·see·ing fore·saw fore·seen v.t. to have a vision of ‖ to arrive at a reasonable estimate of **fore·sé·a·ble** adj. of what can be anticipated

fore·sight n. prophetic capacity, prevision ‖ provident care for the future **fóre·sight·ed** adj.

fore·skin n. the fold of skin covering the end of the penis

for·est n. a large area of land covered with trees and brush growing thickly ‖ the trees on such land

fore·stall v.t. to act in anticipation of (future circumstances or poissibilities)

for·est·er n. someone in charge of a forest

for·est·ry n. the science of tending forests

fore·tell fore·tell·ing fore·told v.t. to announce (an event) before it happens

for·ev·er adv. eternally ‖ without a break

fore·word n. a preface

for·feit 1. n. a fine for breach of contract or negligence ‖ something forfeited **2.** adj. lost or taken away as a forfeit **3.** v.t. to be deprived of as a penalty for a crime, fault, error etc. lose

for·fei·ture n. the act of forfeiting

forge n. a workshop and furnace where metals are melted and refined

forge forg·ing forged v.t. to heat and hammer (metal) into shape ‖ to imitate (something) and attempt to pass it off as genuine ‖ v.i. to commit forgery

forge forg·ing forged v.i. to move forward

with effort ‖ (with 'ahead') to make rapid progress

for·ger·y pl. **for·ger·ies** n. the acto or art of forging or falsifying ‖ something counterfeit

for·get for·get·ting for·got for·got·ten, for·got v.t. to fail to keep in the memory ‖ to stop thinking about **for·gét·ful** adj. apt to forget

for·giv·a·ble, for·give·a·ble adj. that may be forgiven or pardoned **for·gív·a·ble** adj. **for·gív·a·bly** adv.

for·give for·giv·ing for·gave for·giv·en v.t. to excuse ‖ to pardon ‖ v.i. to show or grant foregiveness or pardon **for·gív·a·ble** adj. **for·gíve·ness** n. **for·giv·ing** adj. willing to forgive

for·go, fore·go for·go·ing, fore·go·ing for·went, fore·went for·gone, fore·gone v.t. to go without, renounce for oneself

fork 1. n. an agricultural implement ‖ a pronged instrument for handling food, in cooking, serving or eating ‖ the place where something divides ‖ a tuning fork **2.** v.i. to divide or develop into branches ‖ v.t. to form into the shape of a fork ‖ to pick up or pitch with a fork ‖ with 'out', 'over' or 'up') to pay **forked** adj. Y-shaped, cleft

for·lorn adj. hopeless·**deserted, forsaken** ‖ wretched-looking, pitiful

form n. shape ‖ outward appearance ‖ pattern ‖ a document with blank spaces for information to be weitten in ‖ a mold ‖ state of performance or training (physical or mental) ‖ behavior according to rule, custom, convention or etiquette ‖ a formula ‖ a body of type secured in a chase

form v.t. to make, shape ‖ to put together ‖ to mold by instruction or discipline ‖ to develop ‖ to conceive ‖ to organize ‖ to constitute

for·mal 1. adj. of or pertaining to form, rule or ceremonial ‖ perfunctory ‖ explicit **2.** n. a social event for which one has to wear formal dress

for·mal·ism n. strict adherence to prescribed forms **for·mal·iís·tic** adj.

for·mal·i·ty pl. **for·mal·i·ties** n. conformity or attention to rule, custom or etiquette ‖ a merely formal act

for·mal·ize **for·mal·ix·ing** **for·mal·ized** v.t. to put on a legal, official or regular basis ‖ v.i. to act with formality

for·mat 1. n. the general typographical style and physical characteristics of a publication ‖ the general characteristics of organization of something 2. v. to produce in a special plan, size, shape, or proportion

for·ma·tion n. a forming or being formed ‖ that which has been formed ‖ the form in which something is arranged

for·mer adj. earlier ‖ of the first or first mentioned of two **fór·mer·ly** adv. at a time in the past

for·mi·da·ble adj. likely to prove hard ‖ to be feared ‖ impressive **fór·mi·da·bly** adv.

form·less adj. without shape, amorphous

for·mu·la pl. **for·mu·las**, **for·mu·lae** n. (chem.) a symbolic representation of the composition of a substance ‖ (logic, math) a statement expressed in symbols ‖ a form of words defining a doctrine, principle etc. **for·mu·lar·i·zá·tion** n. **for·mu·lar·ize** **for·mul·iz·ing** **for·mu·lar·ized** v.t.

for·mu·late **for·mu·lat·ing** **for·mu·lat·ed** v.t. to express in a clear or systematic way **for·mu·lá·tion** n.

for·ni·cate **for·ni·cat·ing** **for·ni·cat·ed** n. to commit fornication

for·ni·ca·tion n. voluntary sexual intercourse between an unmarried man and an unmarried woman

for·sake **for·saking** **for·sook** **for·sak·en** v.t. to desert, abandon **for·sak·en** adj. deserted

fort n. a fortified place

forth adv. out from concealment **and so forth** and so on, et cetera

forth·com·ing adj. approaching ‖ shortly to appear

forth·right adj. direct, frank, decisive

forth·with adv. at once, immediately

for·ti·eth 1. adj. being number 40 in a series 2. the person or thing next after the 39th

for·ti·fi·ca·tion n a fortifying or being fortified

for·ti·fy **for·ti·fy·ing** **for·ti·fied** v.t. to strengthen ‖ encourage ‖ to add nutritive value to ‖ v.i. to build fortifications

for·ti·tude n. endurance or courage in the face of pain or adversity ‖ moral strength

fort·night n. a continuous period of two weeks

for·tress n. a fortified place, military stronghold

for·tu·i·ous adj. happening by chance or accident **for·tú·i·ties** n.

for·tu·nate adj. owing to good luck or receiving good luck, luck ‖ favorable

for·tune n. chance ‖ personal wealth ‖ a large sum of money ‖ success ‖ destiny

forty adj. being ten more than 30

fo·rum pl. **fo·rums**, **fo·ra** n. (Rom. hist.) the marketplace ‖ any place or institution where questions of public concern can be discussed or decided

for·ward 1. adj. toward the front ‖ precociously developed ‖ radical ‖ onward, advancing ‖ eager, prompt 2. adv. towards the front, ahead ‖ towards improvement or progress ‖ onward in time 3. n. (football, hockey etc) one of the players positioned near or towards the opponents goal 4. v.t. to convey ‖ dispatch **forward·er** n. someone who forwards

for·wards adv. (of a direction or movement) forwards

fos·sil n. the recognizable remains, or an impression left by them, of a plant or animal of the remote, geological past, preserved in the earth's crust ‖ someone or something out of date **fós·sil·ize** **fos·sil·iz·ing** **fos·sil·ized** v.i. to become a fossil

fos·ter v.t. to rear ‖ to encourage, promote

foul v. to pollute ‖ to bring dishonor on ‖ jam ‖ tangle ‖ collide ‖ (sports) to commit a foul

foul 1. adj. extremely offensive to the senses, dirty, disgusting, stinking ‖ polluted ‖ entangled ‖ indecent or profane ‖ obnoxious ‖ (sports) contrary to the rules of the game ‖ (of weather) stormy **2.** *n.* a collision esp. of boats ‖ an entanglement ‖ (sports) an act forbidden by the rules

found *v.t.* to originate ‖ to establish by endowment ‖ (with 'on' or 'upon') to base

foun·da·tion *n.* a founding or being founded ‖ the solid base on which a building is raised ‖ the lowest courses of a wall, building etc. ‖ the establishment and endowment of an institution ‖ an underlying principle ‖ a foundation garment ‖ a liquid or cream cosmetic used as the base for makeup

found·er *n.* someone who founded or helped to found an institution

founder *v.i.* (of a building etc.) to fall down, collapse ‖ to go lame, stumble ‖ to sink ‖ to fail, esp. financially ‖ (of a ship) to sink ‖ *v.t.* to cause to founder

found·ling *n.* an abandoned infant

found·ry *pl.* **found·ries** *n.* a building where metal or glass is founded ‖ the art or process of casting metals

fount *n.* a source, spring or fountain

foun·tain *n.* a water spring ‖ a contrived ornamental jet of water ‖ a jet of drinking water ‖ a soda fountain

four *adj.* being one more than three (NUMBER TABLE) **on all fours** with hands and knees on the ground

four-di·men·sion·al *adj.* having four dimensions

four·score *adj.* eighty

four·some *n.* (golf) a game between two pairs of players ‖ a group of four persons

four·teen *adj.* being one more than 13

four·teenth *adj.* being number 14 in a series

fourth *adj.* being number four in a series

fowl *pl.* **fowl, fowls** *n.* a domestic cock, hen, duck or turkey

fox 1. *pl.* **fox·es, fox** *n.* a mammal of fam. Canidae **2.** *v.* to trick, baffle

fox terrier a small, lively wirehaired or smooth-haired breed of dog

fox·y fox·i·er fox·i·est *adj.* foxlike, full of guile ‖ sexy, as describing a woman

fra·cas *pl.* **fra·cas·es** *n.* a noisy disturbance, brawl

frac·tion 1. *n.* a very small proportion ‖ an amount less than the whole, a part **2.** *v.t.* to separate into fractions **frác·tion·al** *adj.* pertaining to fractions ‖ of that which is a fraction **frac·tion·ate frac·tion·at·ing frac·tion·at·ed** *v.t.* to separate (a mixture or substance) into smaller portions **frac·tion·á·tion** *n.* **frác·tion·ize frac·tion·iz·ing frac·tion·ized** *v.t.* to divide into fractions

frac·tious *adj.* with frequent outbreaks of temper, unruly

frac·ture 1. *n.* a break in a bone or cartilage **2.** *v.* **frac·tur·ing frac·tured** *v.t.* to break ‖ *v.i.* to become broken

frag·ile *adj.* easily broken ‖ delicate **fra·gil·i·ty** *n.*

frag·ment *n.* a piece broken off from the whole ‖ the existing part of something unfinished **frag·men·tal** *adj.* fragmentary **frag·men·tar·y** *adj.* composed of broken parts ‖ broken up **frag·men·tá·tion** *n.* a breaking into fragments

fra·grance *n.* sweetness of scent ‖ a sweet scent

fra·grant *adj.* having a delicious smell

frail *adj.* easily broken, fragile ‖ feeble **frail·ty** *pl.* **frail·ties** *n.* moral weakness ‖ a shortcoming

frame 1. *n.* an arrangement of parts fitted together, holding something in place or keeping the form of something unchanged ‖ the build of a person ‖ a border of wood or other material put around a picture or mirror ‖ (pool, snooker) a triangular form used in setting up the balls **2.** *v.t.* **fram·ing framed** to surround with a frame ‖ to assemble (ideas etc.) in an orderly way ‖ (pop.) to place (someone) in an incriminating position by falsifying the evidence

frame·work *n.* a basic structure which supports and gives shape, or a broad outline plan

fran·chise *n.* (with 'the') the right to vote ‖ a privilege or right usually granted to a person or company, to exercise an exclusive service or office, or to form a company to do this ‖ the jurisdiction over which a franchise extends

frank *adj.* without guile ‖ stating unwelcome facts without trying to soften their impact ‖ undisguised

frank 1. *v.t.* to send (mail) free of charge **2.** *n.* a sign indicating that mail is to be sent free ‖ a letter sent free

frank·furt·er, frank·fort·er *n.* a smoked beef, or beef and pork, sausage

fran·tic *adj.* nearly mad with anger, pain, grief, fear etc. **frán·ti·cal·ly** *adv.*

fra·ter·nal *adj.* brotherly ‖ designating twins from two ova **fra·tér·nal·ism** *n.*

fra·ter·ni·ty *pl.* **fra·ter·ni·ties** *n.* brotherliness ‖ (in U.S. colleges) a private, usually residential, social club of male students

frat·er·ni·za·tion *n.* a fraternizing

frat·er·nize frat·er·niz·ing frat·er·nized *v.i.* to be friendly ‖ (of occupying troops) to be intimate with civilians of the country occupied

fraud *n.* the use of deception for unlawful gain ‖ someone who is not what he pretends he is

fraud·u·lence *n.* the quality of being fraudulent

fraud·u·lent *adj.* characterized by fraud

fraught *adj.* (with 'with') filled with

fray *n.* a fight, brawl

fray *v.t.* to break threads by hard wear ‖ to strain (the nerves, temper etc.) almost to breaking point ‖ *v.i.* to become frayed

freak *n.* a person or animal malformed in a way which makes him or it an object of curiosity ‖ an eccentric person ‖ an inexplicable act or happening **fréak·ish** *adj.*

freck·le 1. *n.* a small brownish fleck in the skin **2.** *v.* **freck·ling freck·led** to become covered or marked with freckles **fréck·ly** *adj.*

free 1. *adj.* not subject to external constraints ‖ not captive ‖ loose ‖ not having to be paid for ‖ (with 'from') clear of ‖ not reserved ‖ not being used ‖ able to act and choose for oneself ‖ spontaneous, voluntary ‖ generous, profuse ‖ not

literal ‖ open to all without restrictions ‖ unimpeded ‖ not fastened **2.** *adv.* without expense ‖ without penalty **3.** *v.t.* set free ‖ to disengage ‖ to relieve

free·dom *n.* enjoyment of personal liberty, of not being a slave nor a prisoner ‖ the enjoyment of civil rights (freedom of speech, freedom of assembly etc.) ‖ liberty in acting and choosing ‖ ability to move with ease ‖ unrestricted use ‖ (with 'from') an absence of

free-for-all *n.* a fight without rules

freeze 1. *v.* **freez·ing froze fro·zen** *v.i.* to change from a liquid to a solid by heat loss ‖ to be cold enough to turn water into ice ‖ to suffer intense cold ‖ to die by frost ‖ to become rigid as a result of shock or fright ‖ *v.t.* to form ice in or on ‖ to preserve (meat, fruit, vegetables, fish etc.) by refrigeration below freezing point ‖ to anesthetize by artificial freezing ‖ to fix (a price, wage etc.) **2.** *n.* a freezing ‖ a cessation of changes, usu. in economic factors **fréez·er** *n.* the part of a refrigerator in which the temperature is below freezing point

freight 1. *n.* the hire of a ship for transporting goods ‖ the transporting of goods by ship, or by other means of transport ‖ a train carrying goods **2.** *adj.* carrying goods rather than passengers *v.t.* to load (a ship) with cargo ‖ to transport by freight **fréight·age** *n.* the charge for the transportation of goods ‖ cargo

freight·er *n.* a ship which carries cargo ‖ anyone concerned in the transportation of goods by freight

fre·net·ic, phre·net·ic *adj.* frenzied, frantic

fren·zy *pl.* **fren·zies** *n.* a state of mental disturbance close to madness ‖ intense activity

fre·quen·cy *pl.* **fre·quen·cies** *n.* the quality or condition of occurring repeatedly ‖ the number of times a periodic phenomenon or process occurs in a unit of time (cycles)

fre·quent *adj.* occurring often ‖ habitual

fre·quent *v.t.* to resort habitually to **fre·quen·tá·tion** *n.*

fres·co *pl.* **fres·coes, fres·cos** *n.* a method of painting pictures on plaster by laying on the color before the plaster is dry ‖ a picture painted by this method

fresh 1. *adj.* just picked, gathered, made etc. ‖ not stale ‖ brisk and cold, refreshing ‖ not tired ‖ not soiled ‖ new, different ‖ healthy-looking ‖ too familiar, impertinent **2.** *adv.* freshly, quite recently **3.** *n.* a stream of fresh water, a freshet **fresh·en** *v.* to make fresh ‖ *v.i.* to become fresh ‖ (with 'up') to freshen oneself up

fresh·man *pl.* **fresh·men** *n.* a student in his first year at a university or college

fret 1. *v.* **fret·ting fret·ted** *v.i.* to be in a state of anxiety, vexation or discontent ‖ *v.t.* to cause to be in a state of anxiety, vexation or discontent **2.** *n.* a state of anxiety, vexation or discontent **fret·ful** *adj.* inclined to fret, e.g. from vexation or illness

fri·a·bil·i·ty *n.* the state or quality of being friable

fri·a·ble *adj.* (of soil etc.) easily crumbled

fric·as·see 1. *n.* a dish of meat, poultry or game cooked in a sauce **2.** *v.t.* to cook in this way

fric·tion *n.* (mech.) the force which opposes the movement of one surface sliding or rolling over another with which it is in contact ‖ discord between individuals **fric·tion·al** *adj.*

Fri·day *n.* the sixth day of the week

friend *n.* someone on terms of affection and regard for another who is neither relative nor lover ‖ an acquaintance ‖ an **friend·ly 1.** *adj.* **friend·li·er friend·li·est** showing interest and good will, amiable ‖ manifesting kindness ‖ sympathetic ‖ not hostile **2.** *adv.* amicably

friend·ship *n.* a relationship of mutual affection and good will ‖ harmonious cooperation

frieze *n.* an ornamental band of sculpture ‖ the decorative border of a wallpaper below the ceiling or cornice

fright *n.* a sudden shock of fear or alarm **fright·en** *v.t.* to cause to feel fear **fright·ful** *adj.* causing horror

fright·ful·ly *adv.* in a frightful way ‖ very, extremely

frig·id *adj.* extremely cold ‖ forbidding ‖ of a person not being able to achieve orgasm in sexual intercourse

fri·gid·i·ty *n.* the quality or state of being frigid

frill 1. *n.* an ornamental edging ‖ (*pl.*) superficial embellishments **2.** *v.t.* to ornament with a frill **fril·ly fril·li·er fril·li·est** *adj.* adorned with frills ‖ like a frill

fringe 1. *n.* an ornamental border of loose or twisted threads ‖ a border of hair on an animal or plant ‖ an outer margin ‖ a marginal group of any society **2.** *v.t.* **fring·ing fringed** to form a border for ‖ to put a fringe on **3.** *adj.* at the limit or border

frisk 1. *v.i.* to scamper and jump about playfully ‖ *v.t.* to search (a person) for weapons or stolen goods, by quickly feeling over his clothing ‖ to steal in this manner **2.** *n.* a frolic, gambol ‖ a quick search of a person

frisk·y frisk·i·er frisk·i·est *adj.* lively and playful

frit·ter *n.* a small lump of batter fried in deep fat

fritter *v.t.* (with 'away') to waste (time, money etc.)

fri·vol·i·ty *pl.* **fri·vol·i·ties** *n.* the quality of being frivolous ‖ a frivolous piece of behavior

friv·o·lous *adj.* lighthearted in pursuit of trivial pleasures ‖ lacking in seriousness ‖ without importance

frog *n.* a small, coldblooded, tailless, leaping animal living both on land and in water

frog *n.* a coat-fastening consisting of a loop and a spindle-shaped button

frol·ic 1. *v.i.* **frol·ick·ing frol·icked** to frisk, gambol **2.** *n.* an outburst of high spirits **frol·ic·some** *adj.*

from *prep.* indicating outward movement or distance in relation to a point in space or time ‖ indicating a point of departure ‖ indicating a place of origin ‖ indicating cause ‖ indicating source or derivation ‖ (with 'to') indicating limits ‖ sent or given by

frond the leaf of a palm ‖ the leaf of a fern, often bearing spores

front 1. *n.* the most forward part or surface of anything ‖ (in static warfare) the most advanced battle line ‖ a grouping of separate bodies of people for some common objective ‖ a face of a building ‖ outward demeanor ‖ a person used to cover up some illegal activity ‖ the auditorium of a theater and all that is in front of the curtain **2.** *adj.* of the, or in the, more or most forward position **3.** *adv.* at or to the front

front *v.t.* to face toward ‖ to supply a front or face to ‖ to confront ‖ *v.i.* to serve as a front

front·age *n.* the front of a plot of land ‖ the front of a building

fron·tal *adj.* relating to the forward part ‖ pertaining to the forehead ‖ relating to a meteorological front

fron·tier 1. *n.* the border separating one country from another ‖ (esp. *pl.*) an area of mental activity where much remains to be done **2.** *adj.* at a frontier

fron·tiers·man *pl.* **fron·tiers·men** *n.* someone living in a frontier territory

frost 1. *n.* the crystallization of water ‖ the ice thus formed ‖ temperature below freezing point **2.** *v.t.* to cover with ice crystals ‖ to coat with frosting

frost·bite 1. *n.* an injury caused by exposure to freezing cold **2.** *v.t.* **frost·bit·ing frost·bit frost·bit·ten frost·bit** to injure by exposure to freezing cold

frost·ing *n.* a mixture of fine sugar, white of egg etc. used to coat a cake ‖ an unglossed finish on metal or glass

froth 1. *n.* bubbles ‖ foam ‖ spume ‖ frivolous or trivial talk **2.** *v.t.* to cause to form froth ‖ *v.i.* to foam ‖ to cover with something insubstantial **fróth·i·ly** *adv.* **fróth·i·ness** *n.* **fróth·y froth·i·er froth·i·est** *adj.* light as froth ‖ superficial

fro·ward *adj.* stubbornly self-willed

frown 1. *v.i.* to wrinkle the brow ‖ (with 'on', 'upon', 'at') to be disapproving in attitude **2.** *n.* a wrinkling or drawing together of the brows

frowz·y frowz·i·er frowz·i·est *adj.* (of people or things) unkempt, slovenly ‖ (of the atmosphere) stale

fru·gal *adj.* scanty ‖ economical **fru·gal·i·ty** *n.*

fruit 1. *n.* fruit with an edible pulp commonly eaten as dessert ‖ dessert fruits collectively ‖ the result of effort, esp. success **2.** *v.i.* to bear fruit ‖ *v.t.* to cause to bear fruit

fruit·ful *adj.* fertile, productive in abundance ‖ producing beneficial results

fru·i·tion *n.* (of plans etc.) a coming to fulfillment

fruit·less *adj.* yielding no fruit ‖ unprofitable, useless

fruit·y fruit·i·er fruit·i·est *adj.* like fruit in taste or smell ‖ (of the voice) thickly sweet

frus·trate frus·trat·ing frus·trat·ed *v.t.* to prevent (someone) from achieving an object, often by foiling ‖ having some fundamental need unsatisfied

frus·tra·tion *n.* a frustrating or being frustrated ‖ something which frustrates

fry 1. *n. pl.* **fries** a dish of fried food ‖ an outdoor social gathering at which the main dish is fried **2.** *v.* **fry·ing fried** *v.t.* to cook in hot fat or oil in a shallow open pan

fuch·sia *n.* perennial shrubs

fudge 1. *n.* a soft candy ‖ nonsense **2.** *v.* **fudg·ing fudged** *v.i.* to talk nonsense ‖ *v.t.* to make or do in a makeshift or blurry way

fu·el 1. combustible material used as a source of heat or energy ‖ anything that makes strong feelings **2.** *v.* **fu·el·ing fu·eled** *v.t.* *v.i.* to take in fuel

fu·ga·cious *adj.* evanescent, fleeting **fu·gac·i·ty** *n.*

fu·gi·tive 1. *n.* someone fleeing **2.** *adj.* in flight, running away ‖ ephemeral

ful·crum *pl.* **ful·crums, ful·cra** *n.* the point about which a lever turns or on which it is supported ‖ a supporting organ

ful·fill, ful·fil ful·fil·ling ful·filled *v.t.* to carry out ‖ to obey ‖ to satisfy ‖ accomplish ‖ to comply with ‖ to prove true ‖ to realize **to fulfill oneself** to realize all one's potentialities as a person **ful·fill·ment, ful·fíl·ment** *n.*

full 1. completely filled ‖ crowded ‖ well filled with food ‖ ample ‖ (of sounds) having depth or volume ‖ (of light, color) strong ‖ (of materials) arranged in gathers or folds ‖ (with 'of') having an abundance **2.** *n.* (with 'the') the highest point **3.** *adv.* exactly ‖ perfectly, entirely ‖ *v.i.* (of the moon) to become full

full-fledged *adj.* (of birds) having all their feathers ‖ completely qualified

full·ness, ful·ness *n.* the quality or state of being full

ful·ly *adv.* entirely, completely ‖ at least

ful·mi·nate *v.* **ful·mi·nat·ing ful·mi·nated** *v.i.* to flash like lightning or to explode like thunder ‖ *v.t.* to thunder forth (threats or commands)

ful·dome *adj.* excessively or offensively exaggerated

fum·ble 1. *v.* **fum·bling fum·bled** *v.t.* to deal with clumsily ‖ *v.i.* to grope awkwardly **2.** *n.* a clumsy or groping use of the hands ‖ a bungling of an action

fume 1. *n.* (esp. *pl.*) pungent, often noxious, vapor or smoke **2.** *v.* **fum·ing fumed** to give off fumes ‖ to be angry in a pent-up way

fu·mi·gate fu·mi·gat·ing fu·mi·gat·ed *v.t.* to subject to smoke or fumes, esp. in order to disinfect, kill insects, etc. **fu·mi·gá·tion, fú·mi·ga·tor** *ns* a device for fumigating ‖ someone who fumigates

fum·y fum·i·er fum·i·est *adj.* full of fumes

fun 1. *n.* pleasure and amusement ‖ gaiety, playfulness **2.** *adj.* characterized by or providing fun

func·tion 1. *n.* a characteristic activity ‖ purpose ‖ an official duty ‖ a ceremony or social gathering of some formality **2.** *v.i.* to act, perform a function ‖ to be in working order **func·tion·al** *adj.* pertaining to function·**designed in accordance with**

criteria determined by use

fund 1. *n.* an available store of immaterial resources ‖ an accumulation of money, esp. one set aside for a certain purpose ‖ *(pl.)* financial resources **2.** *v.t.* to put in a fund

fun·da·ment *n.* the anus ‖ the buttocks

fun·da·men·tal 1. *adj.* basic, essential ‖ affecting the foundations of something **2.** *n.* something fundamental

fu·ner·al *n.* the ceremony of burial or cremation of a dead person ‖ the burial service

fu·ne·re·al *adj.* mournful, gloomy

fungi *pl.* of FUNGUS

fun·nel 1. *n.* a cone-shaped vessel ending in a tube at the base, used for pouring liquids ‖ a smokestack **2.** **fun·nel·ing fun·neled** *v.t.* to cause to pass through a funnel ‖ *v.i.* to take the shape of a funnel

fun·nies *pl. n.* comic strips

fun·ny fun·ni·er fun·ni·est *adj.* that makes one laugh ‖ puzzling ‖ ill

fur 1. *n.* the dressed pelt of certain animals ‖ the soft, fine, thick hair that covers many animals ‖ *(pl.)* the skins of animals with the fur attached **2.** *adj.* made of, or pertaining to, fur **3.** *v.* **fur·ring furred** to provide, cover, trim or clothe with fur ‖ to make (a floor or ceiling) level by inserting strips of wood

fur·bish *v.t.* to polish ‖ (with 'up') to renovate

fu·ri·ous *adj.* passionately angry ‖ violent, frantic

furl 1. *v.t.* to roll up (a sail) ‖ to fold up, close (a flag, umbrella, fan etc.) ‖ *v.i.* to become furled **2.** *n.* a roll of something furled

fur·long *n.* a unit of distance equaling one eighth of a statute mile or 220 yds

fur·lough 1. *n.* leave of absence **2.** *v.t.* to grant a furlough to ‖ *v.i.* to spend a furlough

fur·nace *n.* an apparatus in chamber form for the production of intense heat

fur·nish *v.t.* to supply, equip ‖ to provide **fúr·nish·ings** *pl. n.* furniture and fittings for a house etc. ‖ haberdashery

fur·ni·ture *n.* movable articles ‖ accessories or equipment

fu·ror *n.* a furore

fu·rore *n.* intense ‖ mass rage, uproar

fur·ri·er *n.* a dealer in furs ‖ someone who makes fur garments **fur·ri·er·y** the craft of a furrier

fur·row 1. *n.* a trench in the earth made by a plow ‖ any track, channel or groove ‖ a deep wrinkle **2.** *v.t.* to make a furrow, channel or groove in ‖ to wrinkle deeply

fur·ry fur·ri·er fur·ri·est *adj.* covered with or clothed in fur

fur·ther alt. *comp.* of FAR ‖ *adj.* additional ‖ more remote in time ‖ more distant

further *v.t.* to advance, promote **fúr·ther·ance** *n.*

fur·ther·more *adv.* moreover, besides

fur·thest alt. *superl.* of FAR ‖ **1.** *adj.* most distant **2.** *adv.* to the greatest distance or degree

fur·tive *adj.* stealthy ‖ done so as not to be noticed

fu·ry *pl.* **bu·ries** *n.* violent rage ‖ a fit of rage

fuse 1. fus·ing fused *v.t.* ‖ to join by melting together **2.** *n.* a short length of wire or metal of low melting point inserted in an electric circuit and melting (thus breaking the circuit) if the current flow heats it above its melting point

fuse, fuze 1. *n.* a combustible or detonating tube, piece of cord, metal etc. which ignites or detonates an explosive **2.** *v.t.* **fus·ing, fuz·ing fused, fuzed** to furnish with a fuse

fu·se·lage *n.* a melting together into a fused mass ‖ the union of light atomic nuclei to form heavier ones under extreme conditions of temperature and pressure resulting in great energy release ‖ a coalition **fú·sion·ist** *n.* someone joining in a coalition

fuss 1. *n.* unnecessary excitement ‖ worry about trifles **2.** *v.* to be in a state of restless commotion ‖ to worry unduly or about trifles

fuss·y fuss·i·er fuss·i·est *adj.* given to fussing ‖ fastidious, exacting ‖ bustling

fus·ty fus·ti·er fus·ti·est *adj.* musty, moldy ‖ out-of-date

fu·tile *adj.* unavailing ‖ pointless, trifling and wearisome **fu·til·i·ty** *pl.* **fu·til·i·ties** *n.* something futile

fu·ture 1. *adj.* of or in time to come ‖ destined to be **2.** *n.* time yet to come ‖ prospects

fuzz 1. *n.* a fluffy mass or coating of fine particles or fibers etc. ‖ a blurred effect **2.** *v.t.* to blur ‖ *v.i.* to become covered with fuzz

fuzz·y fuzz·i·er fuzz·i·est *adj.* like fuzz, covered with fuzz, downy etc. ‖ indistinct, blurred, not clear

G

G, g the seventh letter of the English alphabet

ga·ble *n.* the triangular upper part of a wall closing the end of a ridged roof ‖ a triangular architectural decoration **gá·bled** adj.

gad *v.i.* **gad·ding gad·ded** to gad about to be constantly going out in search of pleasure

gad·a·bout *n.* someone constantly moving around

gad·fly *pl.* **gad·flies** *n.* any of various flies that bite cattle ‖ an irritating person

gadg·et *n.* a clever but trivial device that is hardly more than a knickknack

gaff *n.* a barbed fishing spear ‖ an iron hook for lifting heavy fish into a boat

gag 1. *v.* **gag·ging gagged** *v.t.* to stop up the mouth with a gag ‖ to restrict the freedom of speech of ‖ *v.i.* to retch or choke ‖ to interpolate jokes into a script **2.** *n.* something crammed into the mouth to prevent sound ‖ a joke

gai·e·ty, gay·e·ty *pl.* **gai·e·ties, gay·e·ties** *n.* being or looking gay ‖ merrymaking, entertainment

gai·ly, gay·ly *adv.* in a gay fashion

gain *n.* financial profit ‖ (*pl.*) winnings ‖ the acquiring of wealth ‖ advantage

gain *v.t.* to acquire, obtain ‖ to obtain as a profit ‖ to earn ‖ to win ‖ to reach ‖ *v.i.* to improve, advance **gáin·ful** *adj.* profitable **gáin·ings** *pl. n.* earnings

gait *n.* a manner of walking, running etc. ‖ (of horses) a manner of moving the feet

ga·la 1. *n.* a grand social occasion **2.** *adj.* festive

gal·ax·y *pl.* **gal·ax·ies** *n.* one of the vast number of systems containing stars and interstellar matter that make up the universe ‖ a brilliant company

gale *n.* a strong wind

gall 1. *n.* an injury caused by achronic chafing ‖ a cause of intense irritation ‖ impertinence ‖ bile ‖ the gallbladder **2.** *v.t.* to chafe ‖ *v.i.* to become sore through chafing

gall *n.* a growth on the tissues of plants, caused by plant or animal parasites

gal·lant *adj.* showing noble courage ‖ showily attentive to women

gal·lant·ry *pl.* **gal·lant·ries** *n.* dashing bravery ‖ showily attentive behavior to women

gal·ler·y *pl.* **gal·ler·ies** *n.* the highest balcony ‖ a room or series of rooms used for exhibiting works of art ‖ an underground passage made by animals ‖ a working drift or level ‖ an underground passage

gal·ley *n.* an ancient Greek or Roman warship with one or several banks of oars ‖ the kitchen of a ship

galley proof a printer's proof taken before the type is made up in pages

gal·li·vant *v.i.* to gad about

gal·lon *n.* (abbr. gal.) a liquid measure

gal·lop 1. *n.* the fastest pace of horses **at a gallop, at full gallop** at full speed **2.** *v.t.* to make (a horse) gallop ‖ *v.i.* to progress quickly

gal·lows *pl. n.* (often treated as sing.) a wooden structure for execution by hanging

ga·losh *n.* a waterproof boot worn over the shoe

gal·va·ni·za·tion *n.* a galvanizing

gal·va·nize gal·va·niz·ing gal·va·nized *v.t.* to stimulate by electric currents ‖ to coat (iron or steel) with zinc ‖ to rouse to sudden action

gam·bit *n.* an opening move in chess to secure an advantageous position ‖ any purposeful opening to a contest etc.

gam·ble 1. *v.* **gam·bling gam·bled** *v.i.* to play a game for money ‖ to take risks in the hope of getting better results than by some safer means **2.** *n.* a risky undertaking **gam·bler** *n.*

gam·bol 1. *n.* a frisking, playful leaping **2.** *v.i.* **gam·bol·ing gam·boled** to frisk, leap about

game 1. *n.* any playful activity for amusement or diversion ‖ a scheme, plan or intrigue against others ‖ wild animals or birds hunted for sport or food **2.** *adj.* pertaining to game (animals) **3.** *v.i.* **gam·ing gamed** to gamble, play for money

game *adj.* (of a limb) chronically stiff and painful

game *adj.* ready and willing to perform any challenging action

ga·mut *n.* the entire range or scope of something

gan·der *n.* the male goose ‖ a look, glance

gang 1. *n.* a team of workmen working together ‖ a number of men or boys banding together, esp. lawlessly **2.** *v.i.* (often with 'up') to band together

gan·gling *adj.* lanky and awkward

gang·plank *n.* a long, narrow movable bridge or plank for going between quay and boat

gan·grene 1. *n.* the necrosis of part of a living body **2.** *v.* **gan·gren·ing gan·grened** *v.i.* to become affected with gangrene **gan·gre·nous** *adj.*

gang·ster *n.* a member of a gang of criminals or gunmen

gap *n.* an opening or breach ‖ a pass through hills, a defile ‖ a break in continuity, a pause

gape 1. *v.i.* **gap·ing gaped** to open the

mouth wide ‖ to be wide open ‖ to stare in wonder or surprise 2. *n.* an open-mouthed stare

ga·rage 1. *n.* a building in which cars etc. are kept ‖ enterprise for the repair of motor vehicles 2. *v.t.* **ga·rag·ing ga·raged** to put (a vehicle) in a garage

garb *n.* manner of dress or the clothes themselves

gar·bage *n.* refuse, kitchen waste, rubbish ‖ (computer) inaccurate or unsuitable data

gar·ble gar·bling gar·bled *v.t.* to give a confused version of (a message, facts)

gar·den 1. *n.* a piece of ground where flowers, fruit and vegetables are grown, usually near a house 2. *v.i.* to work in a garden

gar·gan·tu·an *adj.* huge, enormous

gar·gle *v.* **gar·gling gar·gled** *v.i.* to wash the throat with esp. anatiseptic liquid ‖ to make gargling noises ‖ *v.t.* to wash (the throat) by gargling

gar·ish *adj.* harsh, glaring and gaudy in color

gar·land *n.* a circlet of flowers ‖ a laurel or other wreath as a festive sign of victory

gar·lic *n.* any of several plants of the genus Allium much used for flavoring **gár·lick·y** *adj.*

gar·ment *n.* any article of clothing ‖ (*pl.*) clothes

gar·ner 1. *n.* a granary, storehouse 2. *v.t.* to collect or gather in or as if in a granary

gar·net *n.* a hard, brittle, deep red gem

gar·nish 1. *v.t.* to decorate 2. *n.* a savory or decorative addition, esp. to a dish at table **gár·nish·ment** *n.*

gar·ri·son 1. *n.* the troops stationed in a fort or town 2. *v.t.* to occupy as a garrison ‖ to put on garrison duty

gar·ru·lous *adj.* given to constant idle, tedious talking

gar·ter *n.* a band of elastic used to keep up one's stocking ‖ an elastic device with a fastener for keeping a sock up

gas 1. *n. pl.* **gas·es, gas·ses** a substance or mixture of substances in a gaseous state used to produce light and heat (e.g. natural gas), anesthesia (e.g. laughing gas), or a poisonous or irritant atmosphere (e.g. tear gas) ‖ gasoline 2. *v.* **gas·sing gassed** *v.i.* to give off gas ‖ *v.t.* to harm or kill (someone) by poison gas

gas·e·ous *adj.* in the form of a gas ‖ of or pertaining to gas

gash 1. *n.* a deep long cut or slash 2. *v.t.* to make a gash in

gas·ket *n.* a thin sheet of rubber, leather or metal placed between two flat surfaces to seal the joint ‖ a rope used to secure a furled sail to a yard

gas·o·line, gas·o·lene *n.* a refined mixture of the hydrocarbon series, esp. hexane, heptane and octane

gasp 1. *v.i.* to catch the breath suddenly in astonishment ‖ to pant ‖ *v.t.* to utter breathlessly 2. *n.* a convulsive struggle to draw breath

gas·tric *adj.* of or relating to the stomach

gas·tron·o·my *n.* good eating as an art or science

gate 1. *n.* a wooden or metal barrier capable of being opened and shut, and filling the opening in a wall or fence ‖ any means of entrance or exit ‖ the number of people paying to see an athletic contest etc., or the amount of money collected from them 2. *v.t.* **gat·ing gat·ed**

gath·er 1. *v.t.* to collect as harvest ‖ to amass ‖ to summon up (one's thoughts, strength) for an effort ‖ pucker ‖ to deduce ‖ *v.i.* to assemble ‖ to accumulate 2. *n.* (usually *pl.*) part of a dress, cloth in **gáth·er·ing** *n.* an assembly of people

gauche *adj.* awkward ‖ lacking in social graces

gaud·y gaud·i·er gaud·i·est *adj.* showy and cheap

gauge, gage 1. *n.* a standard measure ‖ an instrument for measuring quantity of rainfall, force of wind etc. ‖ means of estimating, criterion 2. *v.t.* **gaug·ing, gag·ing gauged, gaged** to measure with a gauge ‖ to estimate, appraise **gáuge·a·ble** *adj.* **gáug·er, gág·er** *n.* someone who measures the capacity of casks etc.

gaunt *adj.* haggard, emaciated, esp. from illness

gaunt·let *n.* a strong glove with a covering for the wrist ‖ a steel glove of mail or plate worn with armor from the 14th c.

gaunt·let, gant·let *n.* (in phrase) **to run the gauntlet** to be forced as punishment to run between rows of men and be struck by them

gauze *n.* a thin, open-woven fabric of silk, cotton or linen ‖ a thin haze **gáuz·i·ness** *n.* **gáuz·y gauz·i·er gauz·i·est** *adj.*

gav·el *n.* the hammer with which e.g. the chairman of a meeting calls for attention or silence

gawk 1. *n.* a stupid and awkward person **2.** *v.i.* to stare stupidly **gáwk·i·ly** *adv.* in a gawky way **gáwk·i·ness** *n.* **gáwk·y gawk·i·er gawk·i·est** *adj.* clumsy, ungainly

gay *adj.* merry, cheerful, lighthearted ‖ bright in color, brilliant ‖ a homosexual, usu. male

gaze 1. *n.* a long, intent look **2.** *v.t.* **gaz·ing gazed** to look intently

ga·zelle *n.* a genus of small, swift antelopes

ga·zette *n.* a periodical news sheet

gaz·et·teer *n.* a geographical dictionary

gear 1. *n.* tools, materials ‖ personal belongings ‖ a combination of moving parts with a specified mechanical function **2.** *v.t.* to put into gear ‖ to adjust according to need ‖ *v.i.* to be in gear ‖ (with 'into') to fit exactly

gel·a·tin, gel·a·tine *n.* a transparent, tasteless colloidal protein ‖ blasting gelatin **ge·lat·i·nate ge·lat·i·nat·ing ge·lat·i·nat·ed** *v.t.* and i. to gelatinize **ge·lát·i·nize ge·lat·i·niz·ing ge·lat·i·nized** *v.t.* to make gelatinous ‖ *v.i.* to become gelatinous

ge·lat·i·nous *adj.* jellylike ‖ of or containing gelatin

geld geld·ing geld·ed, gelt *v.t.* to castrate (an animal) ‖ to spay

geld·ing *n.* a gelded animal, esp. a gelded horse

gem *n.* a precious stone, esp. when cut and polished ‖ a work of art that is small and exquisite

gen·der *n.* the classification of words according to the sex of the referent ‖ sex (male or female)

gene *n.* a portion of a chromosome

ge·ne·al·o·gy *pl.* **ge·ne·al·o·gies** *n.* the descent of a person or family from an ancestor, generation by generation ‖ a pedigree

gen·er·al 1. *adj.* pertaining to a whole, not particular, not local ‖ prevalent, widespread ‖ usual ‖ concerned with main features and not with details ‖ not specialized **2.** *n.* an army officer

gen·er·al·i·ty *pl.* **gen·er·al·i·ties** *n.* a vague statement

gen·er·al·i·za·tion *n.* a general statement derived from particular instances

gen·er·al·ize gen·er·al·iz·ing gen·er·al·ized *v.i.* to draw a general rule or statement from particular instances ‖ to use generalities ‖ to popularize

gen·er·al·ly *adv.* usually, for the most part ‖ widely

gen·er·ate gen·er·at·ing gen·er·at·ed *v.t.* to cause to be, produce ‖ to procreate

gen·er·a·tion *n.* a producing ‖ procreation ‖ the body of persons thought of as being born about the same time ‖ a period of time, about 25 or 30 years

gen·er·a·tive *adj.* able to produce

gen·er·a·tor *n.* an apparatus for converting mechanical energy into electricity, a dynamo

ge·ner·ic *adj.* of or pertaining to a genus or class ‖ not specific **ge·nér·i·cal·ly** *adv.*

gen·er·os·i·ty *pl.* **gen·er·os·i·ties** *n.* the quality of being generous ‖ an instance of this

gen·er·ous *adj.* giving freely, liberal, not stingy ‖ noble-minded, magnanimous ‖ plentiful, copious

Gen·e·sis the first book of the Old Testament

gen·e·sis *pl.* **gen·e·ses** *n.* origin ‖ mode of generation

ge·net·ic *adj.* relating to the origin or development of something **ge·nét·i·cal·ly**

adv. **ge·net·i·cist** *n.* **ge·nét·ics** *n.* the branch of biology concerned with the heredity and variation of organisms

gen·ial *adj.* pleasant, cheerful, kindly

gen·i·tal *adj.* pertaining to the reproductive organs

gen·i·tals *pl. n.* the organs of reproduction

gen·ius *pl.* **gen·ius·es, gen·i·i** *n.* extraordinary power of intellect, imagination or invention ‖ a person gifted with this ‖ (*pl.* **genii**) a guardian spirit of a person, place or institution

gen·o·cide *n.* the deliberate extermination of a race of people

gen·teel *adj.* excessively refined ‖ of or relating to the upper class

gen·tile *adj.* not Jewish, esp. Christian

gen·til·i·ty *n.* refinement in conduct and manners

gen·tle *adj.* mild, sensitively light ‖ moderate, not strong or violent ‖ docile

gen·tle·man *pl.* **gen·tle·men** *n.* a man of high principles, honorable and courteous (regardless of social position)

gen·tly *adv.* in a gentle manner

gen·try *n.* people of good family

gen·u·ine *adj.* real ‖ authentic ‖ frank, honest, sincere

ge·nus *pl.* **gen·e·ra, ge·nus·es** *n.* a group of animals or plants within a family, closely connected by common characteristics

ge·og·ra·pher *n.* a specialist in geography

ge·o·graph·ic *adj.* of geography **ge·o·gráph·i·cal** *adj.*

ge·og·ra·phy *pl.* **ge·og·ra·phies** *n.* the science of the earth

ge·o·log·ic *adj.* pertaining to geology **ge·o·lóg·i·cal** *adj.*

ge·ol·o·gist *n.* a specialist in geology

ge·ol·o·gy *pl.* **ge·ol·o·gies** *n.* the scientific study of the nature, formation, origin and development of the earth

ge·o·met·ric *adj.* of or pertaining to geometry **ge·o·mét·ri·cal** *adj.*

ge·om·e·try *pl.* **ge·om·e·tries** *n.* the mathematical study of the properties of, and relations between, points, lines, angles, surfaces and solids in space

ge·o·phys·i·cal *adj.* of or pertaining to geophysics

ge·o·phys·ics *n.* the application of the methods of physics to the study of the earth and its atmosphere

ge·ra·ni·um *n.* a plant having brightly colored flowers and pungent-smelling leaves

ger·i·at·ric *adj.* of or relating to aging or the aged **ger·i·át·rics** *n.* the branch of medicine dealing with old age and its diseases

germ *n.* a microorganism, often pathogenic ‖ a seed or embryo

ger·mane *adj.* relevant

ger·mi·nate ger·mi·nat·ing ger·mi·nat·ed *v.i.* to begin to grow, develop ‖ *v.t.* to cause to sprout

ger·mi·na·tion *n.* the beginning of growth

ger·und *n.* a verbal noun ending in 'ing' **ge·run·di·al** *adj.*

ges·ta·tion *n.* the inter-uterine period in the development of the mammalian embryo

ges·tic·u·late ges·tic·u·lat·ing ges·tic·u·lat·ed *v.t.* to express by gestures **ges·tic·u·lá·tion** *n.* **ges·tic·u·la·tive** *adj.* **ges·tic·u·la·tor** *n.* **ges·tic·u·la·tor·ry** *adj.*

ges·ture 1. *n.* a movement of the hand or body to express an emotion or intention **2.** *v.i.* **ges·tur·ing ges·tured** to make gestures, gesticulate

get get·ting got got, got·ten *v.t.* to acquire ‖ to procure ‖ to fetch ‖ to buy ‖ to receive ‖ to earn ‖ to catch ‖ understand ‖ to induce, persuade ‖ *v.i.* (with 'across', 'over', 'here', 'there' etc.) to succeed in moving, arriving etc. ‖ to become ‖ clear out!, go away!

gey·ser *n.* a spring which throws up jets of hot water and steam from time to time

ghast·ly *adj.* **ghast·li·er ghast·li·est** horrifying, gruesome ‖ deathlike, ghostlike ‖ very unpleasant

gher·kin *n.* an immature cucumber selected for pickling

ghet·to *pl.* **ghet·tos, ghet·toes** *n.* a quarter where members of a minority reside as a result of social or economic pressure

ghost 1. *n.* an apparition ‖ a slight trace, a

glimmer ‖ a secondary image or bright spot caused by a defect in the lens of an instrument 2. *v.t.* to be the ghost-writer of (a book) ‖ *v.i.* to act as ghost-writer

ghost·ly ghost·li·er ghost·li·est *adj.* like a ghost ‖ eerie, preternatural

ghoul *n.* (in Oriental stories) a spirit which robs graves and devours corpses ‖ a person of weird or macabre appearance or habit **ghóul·ish** *adj.*

G.I. 1. *n.* an American serviceman, esp. an enlisted man **2.** *adj.* of, characteristic of or belonging to the U.S. Army [GOVERNMENT ISSUE]

gi·ant 1. *n.* a mythical person of superhuman size ‖ an abnormally tall person ‖ anything large of its kind ‖ someone of exceptional ability **2.** *adj.* exceptionally big **gi·ant·ess** *n.*

gib·ber·ish *n.* rapid inarticulate chatter

gib·bon *n.* an anthropoid ape

gib·bous *adj.* rounded out, convex ‖ humpbacked, having a hump

gibe, jibe 1. *v.* **gib·ing, jib·ing gibed, jibed** *v.t.* to jeer, scoff ‖ *v.t.* to mock **2.** *n.* a taunt, sneer

gib·lets *pl. n.* the gizzard and edible innards of a fowl

gid·di·ness *n.* the quality or state of being giddy

gid·dy gid·di·er gid·di·est *adj.* dizzy ‖ frivolous

gift 1. *n.* a thing given ‖ a natural talent **2.** *v.t.* to endow with a natural talent ‖ to give as a gift

gi·gan·tic *adj.* very large **gi·gán·ti·cal·ly** *adv.*

gig·gle 1. *v.* **gig·gling gig·gled** to laugh foolishly or nervously **2.** *n.* foolish, nervous or half-suppressed laughter **the giggles** a fit of such laughter **gig·gly** *adj.*

gig·o·lo *pl.* **gig·o·los** *n.* a man kept by a woman ‖ a professional paid escort

gild gild·ing gild·ed, gilt *v.t.* to cover with a fine layer of gold or gold leaf ‖ to give a speciously attractive appearance to

gill *n.* the vascular respiratory organ in water-breathing animals

gilt 1. *n.* gilding ‖ superficial glitter **2.** *adj.* gilded

gim·mick *n.* a gadget ‖ any clever scheme ‖ any deceptive trick or device

gin *n.* a strong liquor distilled from grain ‖ gin rummy

gin 1. *n.* a snare ‖ a machine for removing seeds etc. from fiber, esp. cotton **2.** *v.t.* **gin·ning ginned** to trap ‖ to remove seeds from (cotton) with a gin

gin·ger 1. *n.* a perennial cultivated for its aromatic rhizome ‖ a sandy reddish color **2.** *adj.* of a sandy, reddish color

gin·ger·bread *n.* cake made with molasses and ginger ‖ cheap, gaudy ornamentation

gin·ger·ly *adv.* very cautiously or warily

ging·ham *n.* an inexpensive cotton fabric, usually checked or striped

gi·raffe *n.* an African ruminant quadruped

gir·an·dole *n.* branched candle holder ‖ a rotating firework ‖ a rotating water jet

gird *v.i.* (with 'at') to jeer, gibe, scoff

gird gird·ing gird·ed, girt *v.t.* to encircle (the waist) with a belt ‖ (refl., rhet.) to clothe oneself, equip oneself **gírd·er** *n.* one of the main joist-supporting, horizontal members

gir·dle 1. *n.* a belt or sash encircling the waist ‖ anything which encircles like a girdle ‖ a bony arch to support a limb **2.** *v.t.* **gir·dling gir·dled** to bind with a girdle ‖ to encircle, enclose

girl *n.* a female child ‖ a girlfriend, sweetheart

girl·ish *adj.* of, like or suitable to a girl

girth *n.* the band which fastens around the body of a horse or other animal to secure the saddle ‖ the circumference of a thing

gist *n.* the main point, the heart of the matter

give 1. giv·ing gave giv·en *v.t.* to offer as a present ‖ to hand over ‖ to pay as price ‖ to supply ‖ to produce, yield ‖ to show ‖ to confer ownership of ‖ to pledge ‖ to allow, permit ‖ to concede ‖ to deliver ‖ to bestow ‖ to perform before an audience ‖ to name for a toast ‖ to sacrifice ‖ *v.i.* to make a gift ‖ to yield to pressure **2.** *n.*

elasticity, springiness

giv·en past part of GIVE ‖ *adj.* agreed, fixed

gla·cial *adj.* icy, frozen ‖ (geol.) of or pertaining to glaciers

gla·cier *n.* a river of ice

glad glad·der glad·dest *adj.* joyful ‖ happy about some specific circumstance, pleased **glad·den** *v.t.* to make glad

glade *n.* a clear, open space in a forest

glad·i·a·tor *n.* a fighter with a sword or other weapon at a Roman circus **glad·i·a·tor·i·al** *adj.*

glad·i·o·lus *pl.* **glad·i·o·li** *n.* a plant of genus Gladiolus

glad·ly *adv.* with gladness ‖ willingly

glam·or·ous *adj.* having glamour

glam·our, glam·or *n.* dazzling charm

glance 1. glanc·ing glanced *v.i.* to look briefly ‖ to flash, gleam **2.** *n.* a brief look ‖ a sudden gleam of light

gland *n.* a single structure of cells, which takes certain substances from the blood and secretes them in a form which the body can use or eliminate

glan·du·lar *adj.* of, like, consisting of, or containing a gland or gland cells

glare 1. glar·ing glared *v.i.* to shine brightly and fiercely ‖ to stare fiercely **2.** *n.* a strong, fierce light ‖ a fierce, intense look **glár·ing** *adj.* bright and dazzling

glass 1. *pl.* **glass·es** *n.* a hard, brittle, transparent or translucent solid ‖ a drinking vessel made of glass ‖ its contents ‖ (*pl.*) spectacles ‖ (*pl.*) binoculars **2.** *v.t.* to fit with, cover with, or encase in glass **3.** *adj.* made of glass, pertaining to glass

glass·y glass·i·er glass·i·est *adj.* like glass ‖ dull, lifeless ‖ smooth, calm

glau·co·ma *n.* a disease of the eye **glau·có·ma·tous** *adj.*

glaze 1. glaz·ing glazed *v.t.* to give a smooth, glossy coating to ‖ to polish ‖ *v.i.* to become glassy **to glaze in** to enclose with glass panels **2.** *n.* the glassy compound fired on pottery etc. to make it watertight or to please the eye ‖ a brightness, sheen ‖ a stretch of icy ground

gla·zier *n.* someone who cuts and sets glass in windows professionally

glá·zier·y *n.*

gleam 1. *n.* a glint ‖ a faint light, or something compared to this **2.** *v.i.* to glow, to shine dimly

glean *v.* to gather leavings of grain after the reaping ‖ to collect little by little **gléan·ing** *n.* (usually *pl.*) something gathered by gleaning

glee *n.* effervescent, demonstrative mirth ‖ laughing satisfaction at the misfortunes of others

glee·ful *adj.* filled with glee

glen *n.* a narrow valley

glib glib·ber glib·best *adj.* too pat ‖ shallow and facile

glide 1. glid·ing glid·ed *v.i.* to move smoothly forward without apparent effort **2.** *n.* the act of gliding **glíd·er** *n.* an engineless aircraft

glim·mer 1. *v.i.* to shine feebly or intermittently **2.** *n.* a feeble or intermittent light ‖ a glimpse **glím·mer·ing** *n.*

glimpse 1. *v.t.* **glimps·ing glimpsed** to catch sight of briefly or fleeingly **2.** *n.* a brief view

glint 1. *v.i.* to flash, sparkle ‖ *v.t.* (of the eyes) to express (an emotion) by flashing **2.** *n.* a flash, gleam

glis·ten 1. *v.i.* to sparkle, glitter **2.** *n.* a glitter

glitch a misfunction in machinery

glit·ter 1. *v.i.* to sparkle very brightly **2.** *n.* brilliance **glít·ter·y** *adj.*

gloat *v.i.* to look at or think about something with malicious, greedy or lustful pleasure

glo·bal *adj.* spherical ‖ involving the whole world ‖ comprehensive, total

globe *n.* a sphere ‖ a spherical model of the earth ‖ the earth

glob·ule *n.* a small round particle or drop

gloom *n.* semidarkness ‖ heavy shadow ‖ melancholy, dejectedness

gloom·y gloom·i·er gloom·i·est *adj.* dark, obscure ‖ melancholy ‖ dismal, depressing

glo·ri·fi·ca·tion *n.* a glorifying or being glorified

glo·ri·fy glo·ri·fy·ing glo·ri·fied v.t. praise ‖ to make radiantly beautiful ‖ to swell pompgaously the importance of

glo·ri·ous adj. illustrious ‖ splendid, thrilling ‖ immensely enjoyable

glo·ry 1. pl. **glo·ries** n. praise, adoration ‖ great renown ‖ magnificence ‖ sublime beauty ‖ the splendor of heaven, beatitude **2.** v.i. **glo·ry·ing glo·ried** to exult, rejoice ‖ to take pride (in)

gloss 1. n. an explanatory interlinear or marginal insertion in the text of a book ‖ a verbal interpretation or paraphrase **2.** v.t. to insert glosses in or provide a glossary for (a text)

gloss 1. n. sheen ‖ deceitful appearance **2.** v.t. to give a gloss to

glos·sa·ry pl. **glos·sa·ries** n. a list of difficult, old, technical or foreign words with explanations, usually at the end of a text

gloss·y adj. **gloss·i·er gloss·i·est** shiny, smooth, highly polished

glot·tis n. the opening between the vocal cords

glove n. one of a pair of coverings for the hands

glow 1. v.i. to emit light without the smoke or flame of rapid combustion ‖ to be radiant ‖ to have a bright, warm color **2.** n. the emission of light without smoke or flame ‖ warmth of emotion or passion

glow·er 1. v.i. to stare with sullen anger **2.** n. a look of sullen anger

glue 1. n. a substance obtained from crude gelatin and used as an adhesive when softened by heating ‖ any similar adhesive **2.** glu·ing glued v.t. to attach with glue or as if with glue ‖ v.i. to become glued

glum glum·mer glum·mest adj. morose

glut 1. v.t. **glut·ting glut·ted** to fill to excess, oversupply ‖ to overfeed, gorge **2.** n. oversupply

glut·ton n. someone who eats excessively **glút·ton·ous** adj.

glut·ton·y n. excessive eating and drinking

gnash v.t. to grind (the teeth) together, in anger etc.

gnat n. any of various very small, two-winged flies

gnaw gnaw·ing gnawed gnawed, gnawn v.t. (of hunger, worry etc.) to be a continuous inner torment to ‖ v.i. to bite on something continuously **gnáw·ing** n. a persistent fretting discomfort, pain or anxiety

gnome n. a goblin or dwarf

gnu pl. **gnu, gnus** n. one of several southern African antelopes

go v.i. **go·ing went gone** v.i. to be in motion ‖ to leave ‖ to disappear ‖ (of time) to pass ‖ to remain ‖ to share ‖ to die ‖ to become worn ‖ to commit oneself to action or expense ‖ to have recourse ‖ to fit, be contained ‖ to belong ‖ (of colors) to harmonize, be compatible ‖ to be sold ‖ to be applied ‖ v.t. to travel on ‖ to follow (a way, road etc.)

goad 1. n. a pointed stick for driving beasts **2.** v.t. to urge on by continually irritating

goal n. the pair of posts between which the ball has to be sent to score point ‖ an aim or objective

goat n. a wild or domesticated horned ruminant ‖ a lecher

goat·ee n. a small, pointed or tufted beard

gob·ble 1. v.i. **gob·bling gob·bled** (of a turkeycock) to make its characteristic guttural sound **2.** n. this sound

gob·let n. a wineglass with a foot and a stem

gob·lin n. a mischievous, ugly spirit

god n. a being to whom worship is ascribed ‖ an image of such a deity ‖ an idolized person or thing **God** (in monotheistic religions) the supreme being

god·dess n. a female deity

god·fa·ther n. a man who sponsors a child at baptism ‖ chief-of-chiefs in the Mafia

god·ly god·li·er god·li·est adj. pious, devout

god·moth·er n. a woman who sponsors a child at baptism

god·par·ent n. a godfather or a godmother

god·send n. something received unexpectedly just when needed

gog·gle gog·gling gog·gled *v.i.* to stare with eyes protruding or rolling ‖ *v.t.* to roll (the eyes)

go·ing 1. *n.* departure ‖ rate of progress **2.** *adj.* in operation ‖ available ‖ viable ‖ current

goi·ter, goi·tre *n.* an enlargement of the thyroid gland

gold 1. *n.* a yellow, malleable, ductile metallic elemen ‖ coins minted from this metal ‖ the color of gold, a deep yellow **2.** *adj.* made of gold, or having the color of gold

gold·en *adj.* having the color of gold ‖ made of gold ‖ eminently favorable ‖ having the qualities associated with gold ‖ (of a jubilee) fiftieth

golf 1. *n.* an outdoor game, originating in Scotland **2.** *v.i.* to play golf

go·nad *n.* a primary sexual gland, the testicle or ovary

gon·do·la *n.* a graceful narrow flat-bottomed boat propelled by a single oar at the stern ‖ a car suspended from a dirigible or balloon ‖ an open railroad car

gon·do·lier *n.* the rower of a gondola

gong *n.* a metal disk with its rim turned back, when struck gives a muffled, resonant note

gon·or·rhe·a, gon·or·rhoe·a *n.* a venereal disease

good 1. bet·ter best *adj.* having desired qualities ‖ morally excellent, virtuous ‖ kind ‖ beneficial ‖ thorough ‖ considerable ‖ efficient,competent ‖ reliable ‖ orthodox and devout ‖ valid **2.** *n.* that which is morally right ‖ profit, benefit, advantage **for good** forever **3.** *adv.* very **4.** *interj.* an exclamation of satisfaction or pleasure

good-bye, good-by 1. farewell **2.** *n.* a farewell

good-heart·ed *adj.* kind, quick to offer help

good·ly good·li·er good·li·est *adj.* sizable

good·ness 1. *n.* the quality or state of being good ‖ the good element of something **2.** *interj.* used as a euphemism for 'God' in mild expletives

goose *pl.* **geese** *n.* a waterfowl ‖ the flesh

of the goose as food ‖ a silly person ‖ (*pl.* **goos·es**) a tailor's iron **to cook someone's goose** to destroy someone's chances

gore gor·ing gored *v.t.* to pierce or wound with horns or tusks

gore *n.* blood, esp. blood that has been shed

gore 1. *n.* a triangular piece of material used to give a flare to a skirt etc. **2.** *v.t.* **gor·ing gored** to vary width with a gore

gorge *n.* a narrow ravine between hills ‖ a choking mass **to make oone's gorge rise** to give one a feeling of revulsion

gorge gorg·ing gorged *v.i.* to eat greedily ‖ *v.t.* to fill (oneself) with food ‖ choke, stuff

gor·geous *adj.* splendid, sumptuous, maginificent

gosh *interj.* used to express mild surprise

gos·ling *n.* a young goose

Gos·pel *n.* one of the first four books of the New Testament ‖ the content of Christian preaching ‖ anything that is to be firmly believed ‖ a principle that one acts upon

gós·pel·er *n.* the reader of the gospel at High Mass

gos·sa·mer 1. *n.* a light film of spiders' threads ‖ one single such thread ‖ exceedingly light, gauzy material **2.** *adj.* as light and delicate as gossamer

gos·sip 1. *n.* easy, fluent, trivial talk ‖ talk about people behind their backs ‖ a person who indulges in gossip **2.** *v.i.* to talk idly **gós·sip·y** *adj.*

gouge 1. *n.* a chisel with a concavo-convex across section for cutting grooves **2.** *v.t.* **goug·ing gouged** to cut out with a gouge

gou·lash *n.* a stew of beef or veal and vegetables

gourd *n.* a small, ornamental, hard-rinded, inedible variety of pumpkin

gour·mand *n.* someone who appreciates good food but without refinement of taste

gour·met *n.* someone who is an expert judge of good food and wine

gout *n.* an intensely painful form of arthritis

gov·ern *v.t.* to control and direct, rule ‖ to be dominant in, determine ‖ to restrain ‖

v.i. to rule **gov·ern·a·ble** *adj.*

gov·ern·ess *n.* a woman employed to teach children in their own homes

gov·ern·ment *n.* a governing, nationwide rule, authoritative control ‖ a system of governing ‖ the ministers who govern a country **gov·ern·men·tal** *adj.*

gov·er·nor *n.* the chief executive of each state of the U.S.A. ‖ a device for keeping the speed of rotation of a driven shaft constant

gown *n.* a woman's dress ‖ a loose robe, esp. worn as official dress by judges etc.

grab 1. *v.* **grab·bing grabbed** *v.t.* to seize suddenly, snatch ‖ to capture ‖ to hold excited attention **2.** *n.* the act of grabbing ‖ a forcible or unscrupulous seizure

grace 1. *n.* charm, elegance, attractiveness ‖ courtesy ‖ delay conceded as a favor ‖ an attractive feature ‖ a social accomplishment ‖ favor ‖ God's loving mercy ‖ a short prayer ‖ a title used in referring to or addressing a duke, duchess or archbishop **to be in someone's good graces** to enjoy someone's favor **2.** *v.t.* **grac·ing graced** to honor, do credit to

grace·ful *adj.* elegant in proportions or movement, slender or lithe ‖ pleasing, attractive

gra·cious 1. *adj.* showing grace in character, manners or appearance ‖ courteous ‖ having qualities associated with good breeding and refinement of taste **2.** *interj.* an exclamation of surprise etc.

gra·da·tion *n.* a grading or being graded ‖ the gradual passing of one color into another

grade 1. *n.* a degree or step in rank, quality or value ‖ a yearly stage in a child's school career ‖ the pupils in such a stage **on the upgrade (downgrade)** rising, improving (falling, worsening) **to make the grade** to achieve the required standard **2.** **grad·ing grad·ed** *v.t.* to arrange in grades ‖ to gradate, blend ‖ to award a grade or mark to

grad·u·al *adj.* proceeding or taking place slowly

grad·u·ate 1. *n.* someone who has completed a set course of study at school or college and received a diploma **2.** *v.* **grad·u·at·ing grad·u·at·ed** *v.i.* to become a graduate ‖ *v.t.* to grant a degree or diploma to ‖ to attach a scale of numbers to (a measuring instrument), or to mark (it) at fixed places of measurement

grad·u·a·tion *n.* the ceremony of conferring academic degrees etc. ‖ a mark on a vessel, gauge etc. to indicate measurement

graf·fi·to *pl.* **graf·fi·ti** *n.* a rude scribbling on a wall

graft 1. *n.* a shoot or bud from one plant inserted in a slit or groove cut in another plant ‖ a piece of transplanted living tissue ‖ the process of grafting ‖ the dishonest use of public office for private gain **2.** *v.t.* to insert as a graft ‖ *v.i.* to become joined in a graft ‖ to make a graft

Grail *n.* the cup used by Christ at the Last Supper

grain 1. *n.* the seed of a cereal grass ‖ harvested cereals in general ‖ a minute, hard particle ‖ the smallest unit of weight ‖ the direction and pattern in which wood fibers grow **against the grain** against one's natural tendency or inclination **2.** *v.t.* to give a granular surface to ‖ *v.i.* to become granulated

gram *n.* (abbr. gm) the unit of mass in the metric system

gram·mar *n.* the science dealing with the systematic rules of a language, its forms, inflections and syntax

gram·mat·i·cal *adj.* of or pertaining to grammar ‖ in accordance with the rules of grammar **gram·mat·i·cal·ly** *adv.*

gran·a·ry *pl.* **gran·a·ries** *n.* a storehouse for threshed grain

grand *adj.* accompanied by pomp and display, splendid ‖ imposing ‖ self-important ‖ highest, or very high in rank ‖ main, principal ‖ noble, dignified, lofty ‖ very enjoyable

grand·child *pl.* **grand·chil·dren** *n.* a child of one's son or daughter

grand·daugh·ter *n.* the daughter of one's

child

grand·fa·ther *n.* the father of either of one's parents

gran·dil·o·quence *n.* the quality of being grandiloquent

gran·dil·o·quent *adj.* overeloquent in style

gran·di·ose *adj.* impressive, imposing

grand jury a jury which investigates certain indictments in private session and decides whether or not there is sufficient evidence to warrant a trial

grand·moth·er *n.* the mother of either of one's parents

grand·par·ent *n.* a grandfather or grandmother

grand·stand *n.* a roofed-over stand with tiered seats

grange *n.* a country house, esp. with associated farm buildings

gra·nite *n.* a very hard igneous rock valuable for building **gra·nít·ic** *adj.*

grant 1. *v.t.* to agree to fulfill ‖ to allow to have, give ‖ to admit, concede **to take for granted** to assume ‖ to accept (someone) thoughtlessly **2.** *n.* something granted, esp. money ‖ the formal bestowal of property **gran·tée** *n.* someone who receives a grant

gran·u·lar *adj.* consisting of grains

gran·u·late gran·u·lat·ing gran·u·lat·ed *v.t.* to form into grains ‖ *v.i.* to become granular **gran·u·lá·tion** *n.*

gran·ule *n.* a small grain

grape *n.* a green or purple berry growing in bunches on a vine

grape·fruit *n.* a small tree native to the West Indies ‖ the large yellow citrus fruit which it yields

graph 1. *n.* a diagram showing the relation of one variable quantity to another **2.** *v.t.* to denote by a graph

graph·ic *adj.* (of descriptive writing, drawing etc.) conjuring up a clear picture in the mind, vivid ‖ having to do with graphs or diagrams **gráph·i·cal** *adj.* **gráph·i·cal·ly** *adv.*

graph·ite *n.* a naturally occurring form of carbon

grap·nel *n.* a small, clawed anchor or other hooked instrument, used e.g. in dragging

grap·ple 1. *n.* a grip, grasp **2.** *v.* **grap·pling grap·pled** *v.i.* to fight at close quarters or hand to hand ‖ to try hard to find a solution

grasp 1. *v.t.* to seize hold of firmly with the hand ‖ to comprehend ‖ *v.i.* to reach out eagerly **2.** *n.* a tight hold, grip ‖ control ‖ understanding **within (beyond) one's grasp** within (out of) reach **grasp·ing** *adj.*

grass 1. *n.* the low green herbage of pastureland and lawns ‖ pasture, grazing ‖ marijuana **2.** *v.t.* to feed on grass pasture

grass·hop·per *n.* any of several leaping plant-eating insects, allied to locusts

grass·y grass·i·er grass·i·est *adj.* planted with grass

grate *n.* a frame of metal bars ‖ the fireplace ‖ a grating, grill

grate grat·ing grat·ed *v.t.* to reduce to small pieces by rubbing against a sharp or rough surface, making a harsh noise ‖ *v.i.* to make a harsh sound ‖ to have an irritating effect

grate·ful *adj.* feeling or showing gratitude

grat·i·fi·ca·tion *n.* a gratifying ‖ a source of satisfaction

grid 1. *n.* a frame of spaced parallel bars, a grating ‖ a lattice or spiral electrode positioned between two others in an electron tube ‖ a frame of numbered squares superimposed on a map so that exact reference may be made to any point on the map **2.** *v.t.* **grid·ding grid·ded** to furnish with a grid

grid·dle *n.* a circular plate, usually of iron, for cooking pancakes etc. on

grid·i·ron *n.* a framework of metal bars with legs or a handle, used for broiling ‖ (football) the playing field, so called from its network of marked lines

grief *n.* deep sorrow **to come to grief** to meet with disaster ‖ to fail

griev·ance *n.* a wrong, hardship, or cause of complaint

grieve griev·ing grieved *v.t.* to cause deep sorrow to ‖ *v.i.* to feel grief, mourn

griev·ous *adj.* bringing great suffering and trouble ‖ pitiful ‖ serious, heinous

grif·fin, grif·fon, gryph·on *n.* a fabulous creature

grill 1. *v.t.* to broil on a gridiron or under the broiling apparatus of a gas or electric stove ‖ to interrogate closely, torment by severe questioning **2.** *n.* a device on stoves for radiating an intense direct red heat for cooking meat, making toast etc. ‖ the act of grilling

grim grim·mer grim·mest *adj.* stern, severe ‖ unrelenting ‖ sinister ‖ mirthless

gri·mace 1. *n.* a twisted expression of the face caused by slight pain, or to convey disgust, distaste etc. **2.** *v.i.* **gri·mac·ing gri·maced** to make a grimace

grime 1. *n.* ingrained dirt or soot **2.** *v.t.* **grim·ing grimed** to cover with dirt, soil **grim·y grim·i·er grim·i·est** *adj.* covered with grime

grin 1. *v.* **grin·ning grinned** to smile broadly **to grin and bear it** to suffer without complaining **2.** *n.* a broad or distorted smile

grind 1. *v.* **grind·ing ground** to crush to powder or tiny pieces by friction ‖ (with 'down') to crush with harsh rule or misery, treat cruelly ‖ to sharpen, smooth, file down or shape by friction ‖ to cause to grate ‖ to work by turning a handle ‖ (with 'out') to force out ‖ (of a vehicle) to move laboriously ‖ to work or study hard ‖ to grate **2.** *n.* a period of unbroken hard work or study ‖ a long, steady gradient or the effort needed to climb it

grind·stone *n.* a thick stone disk revolving on an axle and used for grinding, sharpening and smoothing **to keep one's nose to the grindstone** to keep steadily at a task by an effort of the will

grip 1. *n.* a tight hold, strong grasp ‖ hold, power ‖ mental grasp ‖ the power to hold attention ‖ the part of a racket etc. that one holds ‖ a traveling bag **to come to grips** to fight in close struggle **to lose one's grip** to lose control **2.** *v.* **grip·ping gripped**

gripe *v.* **grip·ing griped** *v.i.* to complain continually

gris·ly gris·li·er gris·li·est *adj.* horrifying, terrifying ‖ ghastly

grist *n.* grain for grinding ‖ malt crushed for brewing

gris·tle *n.* cartilage **gris·tli·ness** *n.* **gris·tly** *adj.*

grit 1. *n.* tiny particles of stone or sand ‖ pluck and tenacity **2.** *v.* **grit·ting grit·ted** *v.t.* to grate or grind ‖ *v.i.* to emit a grating sound

grits *pl. n.* oats with the husk removed, but not ground ‖ coarse oatmeal ‖ loose gravel for road-surfacing

grit·ty grit·ti·er grit·ti·est *adj.* like grit ‖ plucky, brave

griz·zle griz·zling griz·zled *v.i.* to become gray or gray-haired **griz·zled** *adj.* gray-haired

griz·zly 1. griz·zli·er griz·zli·est *adj.* gray-haired or turning gray **2.** *pl.* **griz·zlies** *n.* a grizzly bear

groan 1. *v.i.* to make a deep moaning sound through pain, grief or distress ‖ *v.t.* to utter with a groan **2.** *n.* a deep moaning sound

gro·cer·y *pl.* **gro·cer·ies** *n.* the grocer's trade ‖ *(pl.)* goods bought at the grocer's ‖ a grocer's store

groin *n.* the fold or depression between belly and thighs

groom 1. *n.* a bridegroom ‖ a man or boy who looks after horses **2.** *v.t.* to look after (horses) ‖ to smarten (oneself) up ‖ to prepare, train

groove 1. *n.* a channel or rut ‖ a routine which makes for dullness **2.** *v.t.* **groov·ing grooved** to make a groove or grooves in

grope grop·ing groped *v.i.* to feel about, search blindly ‖ to feel or search mentally

gross 1. *adj.* repulsively fat ‖ glaring ‖ vulgar ‖ total, all-inclusive **2.** *n.* sum total **in gross, in the gross** in bulk, wholesale **3.** *v.t.* to gain as gross profit

gro·tesque *adj.* strangely fanciful, bizarre ‖ ludicrously incongruous, absurd ‖ unnaturally distorted ‖ ridiculously bad

grot·to *pl.* **grot·toes, grot·tos** *n.* a picturesque cave

grouch 1. *n.* a bad-tempered, grumbling person **2.** *v.i.* to complain ‖ to be bad-tempered **gróuch·i·ly** *adv.* **gróuch·i·ness** *n.* **gróuch·y grouch·i·er grouch·i·est** *adj.*

ground 1. *n.* the surface of the earth ‖ the upper soil ‖ (often *pl.*) a basis for action or belief, motive, sound reason ‖ a basic surface or foundation ‖ (elec.) an electrical conductor enabling electricity to pass into the earth **on grounds of** because of **to break ground** to begin work on a building site **to cut the ground from under someone's feet** to anticipate someone's arguments or ideas and dispose of them before they are put forward **to keep one's (or both) feet on the ground** to be realistic and not idealistic **to lose ground** to fall behind **2.** *adj.* of, at or near the ground **3.** *v.t.* to run (a ship) aground ‖ to base or establish ‖ to connect with a ground ‖ *v.i.* to touch bottom

ground·hog *n.* a woodchuck

ground·work *n.* a foundation, basis ‖ basic labor

group 1. *n.* a number of people or things gathered closely together ‖ a number of persons or things classed together ‖ a blood group **2.** *v.t.* to put into groups ‖ to arrange artistically ‖ to classify ‖ *v.i.* to form a group

grouse *v.i.* **grous·ing groused** to grumble

grouse *pl.* **grouse** *n.* any of several game birds

grove *n.* a group of trees without undergrowth ‖ (of certain trees) an orchard

grov·el grov·el·ing grov·eled *v.i.* to crawl at someone's feet as if begging for mercy ‖ to abase oneself abjectly ‖ to wallow **gróv·el·ing** *adj.* abject ‖ obsequious

grow grow·ing grew grown *v.i.* to develop ‖ to be cultivated ‖ to increase in size ‖ to become larger ‖ *v.t.* to cultivate **to grow into** to become **to grow out of** to become too big for **to grow up** to reach adulthood

growl 1. *v.i.* to make the characteristic threatening guttural sound of a dog **2.** *n.* the sound made in growling

grown-up 1. *adj.* adult, past adolescence **2.** *n.* an adult

growth *n.* the process of growing or developing ‖ increase in size ‖ origin, cultivation ‖ something growing ‖ a morbid formation such as a cancer or tumor

grub grub·bing grubbed *v.i.* to dig in the ground ‖ to search laboriously

grub·by grub·bi·er grub·bi·est *adj.* dirty, unwashed

grudge 1. *v.t.* **grudg·ing grudged** to be reluctant to grant (something) through envy, spite or meanness **2.** *n.* a feeling of resentment **grudg·ing** *adj.* reluctant

gru·el·ing 1. *adj.* exhausting **2.** *n.* a harsh testing

grue·some *adj.* ghastly, sickening, revolting

gruff *adj.* (of the voice) hoarse, harsh ‖ blunt, surly

grum·ble 1. *v.* **grum·bling grum·bled** *v.i.* to complain in a persistent, bad-tempered way ‖ to make a low growling sound, rumble ‖ *v.t.* to mutter surlily **2.** *n.* something said in a nagging, complaining way ‖ a low growling sound **grúm·bler** *n.*

grump·y grump·i·er grump·i·est *adj.* bad-tempered

grunt 1. *v.i.* to make a low, gruff, snorting sound ‖ *v.t.* to utter as if with grunts **2.** *n.* a low gruff sound made by hogs

guar·an·tee 1. *n.* a pledge given by the makers of an article that they will repair or replace it free if it is unsatisfactory or develops defects within a stated time from the date of purchase ‖ the person who gives such a guarantee ‖ a thing given as a security for payment of a loan or fulfillment of a duty ‖ a firm promise, assurance **2.** *v.t.* **guar·an·tee·ing guar·an·teed** to accept responsibility ‖ to secure ‖ to promise, assure someone of (something)

guar·an·ty *pl.* **guar·an·ties** *n.* a guarantee

guard *v.t.* to keep watch over so as to protect from danger, defend ‖ to control ‖ to provide with a guard, protective device etc. ‖ *v.i.* to take precautions

guard·i·an *n.* a protector, keeper,

custodian

gu·ber·na·to·ri·al *adj.* pertaining to a governor

gudg·eon *n.* a pivot at the end of a beam or axle ‖ a ring on a gate which drops over a hook on the gatepost ‖ the socket in which a rudder turns

guer·ril·la, gue·ril·la *n.* someone engaged in harassing, raiding or sabotage operations carried out by small bands of irregulars acting independently

guess 1. *v.* to hazard an opinion about without full knowledge or detailed reasoning ‖ to conjecture correctly ‖ to think likely, suppose ‖ *v.i.* to conjecture **2.** *n.* a rough estimate

guest *n.* someone who receives hospitality

guf·faw 1. *n.* a loud, coarse laugh **2.** *v.i.* to make such a laugh ‖ *v.t.* to utter with such a laugh

guid·ance *n.* direction, advice ‖ leadership

guide guid·ing guid·ed *v.t.* to direct the course of, steer ‖ to direct, influence ‖ *v.i.* to act as a guide

guide *n.* a person who shows the way ‖ a book of information ‖ an adviser ‖ the principle governing behavior or choice

guild, gild a medieval association of merchants or craftsmen

guile *n.* deceiving trickery, low cunning ‖ wiliness **guile·ful, guile·less** *adjs*

guil·lo·tine 1. *n.* a machine for beheading people **2.** *v.t.* **guil·lo·tin·ing guil·lo·tined** to use the guillotine on

guilt *n.* the fact of having committed a legal offense ‖ a feeling of culpability

guilt·y guilt·i·er guilt·i·est *adj.* having committed an offense ‖ feeling guilt

guin·ea pig a small, tailless, short-eared rodent kept as pet, also widely used in medical and biological research

guise *n.* outward appearance, esp. assumed to conceal the truth

gui·tar *n.* a musical instrument, normally with six strings. These are plucked **gui·tár·ist** *n.*

gulch *n.* a short, steepsided ravine

gulf *n.* an area of sea partly surrounded by coast ‖ a huge gap

gull *n.* a genus of web-footed, long-winged seabirds

gul·let *n.* the esophagus ‖ the throat ‖ a channel for water ‖ a gully

gul·li·ble *adj.* easily deceived or cheated

gul·ly 1. *pl.* **gul·lies** *n.* a small steep valley made by water **2.** *v.t.* **gul·ly·ing gul·lied** to make channels in

gulp 1. *v.t.* (often with 'down') to swallow (usually a drink) quickly or greedily ‖ *v.t.* to swallow food or drink quickly or greedily ‖ to gasp, pant **2.** *n.* the act of gulping ‖ a large mouthful

gum 1. *n.* a sticky liquid used as an adhesive or thickening agent in making emulsions, cosmetics and food preparations, and in calico aprinting ‖ a substance resembling this ‖ a candy made from gelatin or from some other gumlike substance ‖ chewing gum **2. gum·ming gummed** *v.t.* to stick with gum ‖ to smear with gum ‖ *v.i.* to become gummy **to gum up the works** to cause great delay or bring things to a halt in confusion

gum *n.* the flesh by which the teeth are partly surrounded ‖ (often *pl.*) the alveolar part of the jaw

gum·bo *n.* the okra plant or its pods ‖ a soup thickened with gummy okra pods and containing vegetables and meat or seafood

gun 1. *n.* any weapon, e.g. a revolver, rifle, machine gun, cannon or piece of artillery, having a metal tube along which a bullet or shell is propelled by explosive force ‖ a tool etc. like a gun in that it ejects some object, substance etc. **to stick to one's guns** to defend doggedly one's position **2.** *v.* **gun·ning gunned** *v.t.* (esp witth 'down') to shoot ‖ to accelerate (a motor, engine etc.)

gun·ny *n.* coarse cloth, usually made from jute

gun·pow·der *n.* an explosive still used in fireworks

gun·smith *n.* someone who makes and repairs small firearms

gun·wale, gun·nel *n.* the upper edge of the side of a ship or boat

gup·py *pl.* **gup·pies** *n.* a small freshwater fish

gur·gle 1. *v.* **gur·gling gur·gled** *v.i.* to make a bubbling sound ‖ *v.t.* to utter with such a bubbling sound **2.** *n.* the sound made in gurgling

gush 1. *v.i.* to flow or pour out in torrents ‖ to behave or speak with excess of feeling ‖ to produce a copious flow ‖ *v.t.* to emit suddenly **2.** *n.* an outpour ‖ exaggerated display of feeling **gúsh·er** *n.* an oil well in which the oil spurts from the ground without pumping **gúsh·i·ly** *adv.* in a gushy manner **gúsh·i·ness** *n.* the quality of being gushy **gúsh·y gush·i·er gush·i·est** *adj.* fulsomely effusive

gust *n.* a strong burst of wind

gus·ta·to·ry *adj.* pertaining to tasting or sense of taste

gut 1. *n.* *(pl.)* entrails ‖ *(pl.)* pluck and determination ‖ the alimentary canal or its lower part ‖ a piece of animal intestine used for the strings of musical instruments, fishing lines, tennis rackets and surgical stitching **2.** *v.t.* **gut·ting gut·ted** to remove the entrails of ‖ to destroy all but the framework of **3.** *adj.* intuitive

gut·ter 1. *n.* a metal trough along the edge of a roof to catch and carry away rainwater ‖ a channel in a road for draining off rainwater ‖ slum environment **2.** *v.t.* to make channels in ‖ *v.i.* (of water) to flow in channels

gut·tur·al *adj.* of the throat ‖ (of speech sounds) produced in the throat ‖ throaty,

harsh, grating

guy *n.* a rope or chain to keep something steady

guy *n.* a man, fellow

guz·zle guz·zling guz·zled *v.t.* and *i.* to drink or eat greedily and rapidly

gym *n.* a gymnasium ‖ gymnastics

gym·na·si·um *pl.* **gym·na·si·a, gym·na·si·ums** *n.* a room or building for physical exercise

gym·nast *n.* a person skilled in gymnastics

gym·nas·tic *adj.* having to do with gymnastics **gym·nás·tics** *n.* exercises to teach body control and agility and strengthen the muscles

gy·ne·col·o·gist, gy·nae·col·o·gist *n.* a specialist in gynecology

gy·ne·col·o·gy, gy·nae·col·o·gy *n.* the study of women's diseases

gyp 1. *n.* a cheat, swindle ‖ a swindler **2.** *v.i.* and *t.* **gyp·ping gypped** to swindle, cheat

gyp·sum *n.* a mineral, hydrated calcium sulfate

gyp·sy, gip·sy *pl.* **gyp·sies, gip·sies 1.** *n.* a member of a swarthy Caucasoid people believed to have originated in India **2.** *adj.* of or relating to a gypsy

gy·rate 1. *v.i.* **gy·rat·ing gy·rat·ed** to whirl, revolve **2.** *adj.* having convolutions **gy·rá·tion** *n.* **gy·ra·to·ry** *adj.*

gy·ro·scope *n.* a rapidly spinning wheel mounted in such a way that its plane of rotation can vary **gy·ro·scop·ic** *adj.*

H

H h the eighth letter of the English alphabet

hab·it *n.* a tendency to repeat an act again and again ‖ a behavior pattern that has a degree of automatism ‖ a monk's or nun's robe

hab·it·a·ble *adj.* able to be lived in

hab·i·tat *n.* a place or region inhabited by an animal or plant in the natural state

hab·i·ta·tion *n.* a place or building lived in

ha·bit·u·al *adj.* performed as the result of a habit ‖ having a fixed habit, confirmed ‖ usual, accustomed

ha·bit·u·ate ha·bit·u·at·ing ha·bit·u·at·ed *v.t.* to make familiar by repetition **ha·bit·u·á·tion** *n.*

ha·bit·u·é *n.* someone who assiduously

frequents a place

hack 1. *n.* a horse let out for hire ‖ a writer employed to write matter of no great literary merit ‖ a taxi **2.** *v.i.* to ride on a hired horse ‖ to do the work of a hack writer ‖ to drive a taxi **3.** *adj.* to write matter of no originality

hack 1. *v.t.* to cut by using a sharp blow ‖ to cut unskillfully ‖ *v.i.* to cough raspingly **2.** *n.* a rough cut made by a sharp blow ‖ a tool used for hacking ‖ a harsh, dry cough

hack·ney 1. *pl.* **hack·neys** *n.* a horse of compact, strong build **2.** *adj.* (of a cab) let out for hire

hack·neyed *adj.* made tedious by frequent repetition

had past and past part. of HAVE

hag *n.* an ugly old woman ‖ a hagfish

hag·gard *adj.* looking worn out by suffering

hag·gle *v.i.* **hag·gling hag·gled** to argue about the price of an article or about the conditions attached to an agreement etc.

hail 1. *n.* pieces of ice varying in size from a pea to a small ball ‖ a thick shower of anything **2.** *v.i.* to fall like hail

hail 1. *v.t.* to call out to ‖ to welcome ‖ *v.i.* (with 'from') to be a native of a named place **2.** *n.* a call made to attract attention ‖ a salute

hail·stone *n.* a single piece of hail

hail·storm *n.* a violent storm during which hail falls

hair (heir)*n.* a threadlike tube of horny, fibrous substance rooted in the skin and growing freely outwards ‖ the covering of these on the human head or an animal body **to get in someone's hair** to get on someone's nerves **to let one's hair down** to discard formality and restraint and give free expression to one's feelings **to make one's hair stand on end** to horrify or terrify one **to split hairs** to draw unimportant distinctions in an argument

hair·breadth 1. *n.* a very small margin **2.** *adj.* extremely narrow

hair·y hair·i·er hair·i·est *adj.* covered with hair ‖ like hair

hale *adj.* physically sound and well

hale hal·ing haled *v.t.* to force to go

half 1. *pl.* **halves** *n.* one of two equal parts **2.** *adj.* being one half of something **3.** *adv.* to the extent of a half

half-heart·ed *adj.* lacking enthusiasm

half-way 1. *adj.* equally distant between two points **2.** *adj.* half the distance

halfway house sheltered residence designed to help adjustment of institutionalized persons in the process of release

half-wit *n.* someone of subnormal intelligence **hálf-wit·ted** *adj.*

hal·i·but *pl.* **hal·i·but hal·i·buts** *n.* a food fish

hal·i·to·sis *n.* bad-smelling breath

hall *n.* a connecting passage or corridor between rooms ‖ a large room used for meetings or social occasions

hal·le·lu·jah *n.* alleluia [Heb. praise Jehovah]

hal·low *v.t.* to make sacred ‖ to revere as holy

hal·lu·ci·nant *n.* cause of hallucinants **hallucinate** *v.* to see what does not exist **hallucinogenic** *n.* a causative drug

hal·lu·ci·nate hal·lu·ci·nat·ing hal·lu·ci·nat·ed *v.t.* to cause to suffer from hallucinations ‖ *v.i.* to experience hallucinations **hal·lu·ci·na·tion** *n.* perception unaccompanied by reality ‖ an object of such perception **hal·lu·ci·na·to·ry** *adj.*

hal·lu·cin·o·gen *n.* a drug which induces hallucinations **hal·lu·cin·o·gén·ic** *adj.*

hall·way *n.* an entrance hall ‖ a passage connecting two or more rooms

ha·lo *pl.* **ha·loes ha·los** *n.* a disk of diffused light ‖ a bright ring painted above the head of a holy person as a symbol of glory

halt 1. *n.* a cessation of movement or action **2.** *v.i.* to stop suddenly ‖ *v.t.* to cause to come to a halt

halt·er 1. *n.* a rope or strap used to lead an animal or to tie it to a firm support ‖ the rope used to hang a criminal ‖ a woman's garment **2.** *v.t.* to put a halter on (an animal)

halt·ing *adj.* (of steps) slow ‖ (of rhythm) uneven ‖ marked by hesitance or awkwardness

halve halv·ing halved *v.t.* to divide into two equal portions ‖ to share equally ‖ to lessen by half

ham 1. *n.* a whole thigh of a hog, salted and smoke-dried ‖ a ham actor or performer ‖ a licensed amateur operator of a radio station **2.** *adj.* of an actor or performer who plays his part with overemphasis **3. ham·ming hammed** *v.i.* to behave like a ham actor

ham·burg·er *n.* chopped beef ‖ a hamburg steak ‖ a bun containing fried or grilled chopped steak

ham·let *n.* a small group of dwellings in a rural district

ham·mer 1. *n.* a tool ‖ the part of the mechanism of a firearm which strikes the cap of the cartridge ‖ the malleus **to come under the hammer** to be put up for sale by auction **2.** *v.t.* to hit with a hammer blow ‖ to shape

ham·mock *n.* a rectangle of canvas or strong net suspended from firm supports by thin ropes

ham·per *v.t.* to make (action or progress) difficult

hamper *n.* a large rectangular basket usually of coarse wickerwork, with a lid

ham·ster *n.* a genus of thick-bodied rodents

hand 1. *n.* the part of the human body from the wrist to the fingertips ‖ a pointer on a dial ‖ applause ‖ four inches as a unit of measurement for the height of a horse ‖ an employee on a farm or in a factory **a free hand** unrestricted powers of decision and action **at first** (second etc.) **hand** directly **at hand** near and available **by hand** with the hands as distinct from by machinery **from hand to hand** from person to person **hands down** (of winning) by an easy victory **hands off!** don't touch! **out of hand** beyond control **the upper hand to lend** (or give) **a hand** to assist **2.** *v.t.* to give with the hand ‖ to assist or guide with the hand **to hand out** to distribute **3.** *adj.* of or pertaining to the hand ‖ created by hand

hand·bag *n.* a woman's bag

hand·ball *n.* a game for two or four players, something like squash ‖ the ball used

hand·book *n.* a guidebook

hand·cuff 1. *n.* a steel band which can be clamped around the wrist and locked **2.** *v.t.* to fasten handcuffs on (a person)

hand·ful *pl.* **hand·fuls** *n.* a small number

hand·i·cap 1. *n.* a disadvantage ‖ an allowance to the weaker competitors ‖ the allowance given or disadvantage imposed **2.** *v.t.* **han·di·cap·ping hand·i·capped** to allot a handicap to (a competitor) ‖ to put at a disadvantage **hand·i·cap·per** *n.* an official who decides what handicap to allot

hand·i·craft *n.* a craft (trade or occupation)

hand·i·ly *adv.* in a handy way ‖ conveniently ‖ easily

hand·i·work *n.* the product of handwork

hand·ker·chief *n.* a usually square piece of fabric used for blowing the nose

han·dle *n.* the part of a tool, utensil, weapon etc. designed for the hand or fingers to grasp **to fly off the handle** to become suddenly very angry

handle han·dling han·dled *v.t.* to touch or take in the hands ‖ to deal with ‖ to treat ‖ *v.i.* to respond to control

hand·ler *n.* someone who professionally exhibits dogs etc. in shows ‖ someone who helps in the training of a boxer

hand·out *n.* an item of clothing or food given to a beggar, or anything given for nothing

hand·some *adj.* good-looking ‖ ample, generously large ‖ gracious, highly praising ‖ impressive

hand·y hand·i·er han·di·est *adj.* conveniently near ‖ able to do useful small manual jobs ‖ dexterous

hand·y·man *pl.* **hand·y·men** *n.* a man employed to do a variety of jobs

hang 1. *v.* **hang·ing hung** *v.i.* to be suspended ‖ to await a decision ‖ (of flowers) to droop **hang·ing hanged** to suffer death by being suspended by the neck ‖ *v.t.* to suspend (something) ‖ to attach ‖ to display (a picture) on a wall ‖ **hang·ing hanged)** to kill by suspending by the neck **to hang about** (or **around**) to linger or loiter in a place or near a person **to hang on to** to hold firmly to **2.** *n.* the manner in which something hangs ‖ a very small bit **to get the hang of** to grasp the meaning or way of working of

han·gar *n.* a very large shed used to house aircraft

hang·er *n.* a coat hanger

hang·er on *pl.* **hang·ers on** *n.* someone attaching himself to an influential person or group

hang·ing 1. *n.* the act of suspending ‖ execution or killing by suspending by the neck ‖ (*pl.*) curtains or draperies **2.** *adj.*

han·ker *v.i.* (with 'after' or 'for', or the infinitive) to have a continual nagging desire **hán·ker·ing** *n.*

hap·haz·ard 1. *adj.* of events occurring by chance **2.** *adv.* according to no set plan or system

hap·less *adj.* unlucky

hap·pen *v.i.* to occur, take place ‖ to occur spontaneously ‖ to chance

hap·pen·ing *.n* a special or unusual staged event

hap·pen·stance *n.* a chance circumstance

hap·pi·ness *n.* feelings of joy and pleasure

hap·py hap·pi·er hap·pi·est *adj.* experiencing joy and pleasure ‖ apt

ha·rangue 1. *n.* a long and forceful speech **2.** *v.t.* **ha·rangu·ing ha·rangued**

har·ass *v.t.* to subject (someone) to continuous vexatious attacks or other unpleasantness **hár·ass·ment** *n.*

har·bor *n.* a bay or inlet of quiet water protected from stormy waves ‖ a place of refuge

harbor *v.t.* to shelter ‖ to cherish secretly ‖ *v.i.* to take refuge or anchor in a harbor

hard 1. *adj.* difficult to cut, crack or crush ‖ not easy ‖ oppressive ‖ unfeeling ‖ tough ‖ energetic and persistent ‖ unfavorable ‖ (of liquor) having a high percentage of alcohol **2.** *adv.* strongly **hard up** acutely short of money **hard up for (something)** lacking

hard-core *adj.* **1.** of persons whose status is not easily changed **2.** of pornography, explicit

hard·en *v.i.* to become hard ‖ to become callous or intolerant ‖ *v.t.* to make (something) hard or harder **hárd·en·er** *n.* a substance added to give a paint or varnish a harder finish

hard·head·ed *adj.* realistic and practical

hard·heart·ed *adj.* callous, unfeeling

hard·ly *adv.* not to any great degree, scarcely ‖ only just, barely ‖ severely, harshly

hard·ness *n.* the quality of being hard ‖ difficulty ‖ unfeelingness ‖ harshness ‖ physical toughness

hard·ship *n.* suffering or privation difficult to bear

hard·ware *n.* metal goods ‖ equipment used in computing

har·dy hard·i·er hard·i·est *adj.* strong, robust

hare *pl.* **hares hare** *n.* a herbivorous lagomorph

har·em *n.* the women's apartments in a Moslem household ‖ the wives and servants of the master

hark *v.i.* to listen closely ‖ *v.t.* to listen to

Har·le·quin *n.* a character in commedia dell'arte. He survives as a buffoon in European and American pantomime **har·le·quin** *adj.* of variegated, bright colors

har·lot *n.* a prostitute **hár·lot·ry** *n.* prostitution

harm 1. *n.* injury, hurt ‖ moral wrong **2.** *v.t.* to injure, hurt

harm·ful *adj.* injurious, hurtful

harm·less *adj.* not likely to cause trouble

har·mon·i·ca *n.* a small rectangular wind instrument

har·mo·ni·ous *adj.* pleasing to the ear, tuneful ‖ free from jarring differences

har·mo·nize har·mo·niz·ing har·mo·nized *v.i.* to be, sing or play in harmony ‖ to be in agreement ‖ *v.t.* to provide (a melody) with harmonies

har·mo·ny *pl.* **har·mo·nies** *n.* a pleasing combination of musical sounds ‖ agreement ‖ pleasing relationship

har·ness 1. *n.* the complete set of leather belts and straps with their metal fittings worn by a draft animal ‖ reins for children learning to walk ‖ the armor and accessories of a knight or man-at-arms **in harness** at work **to die in harness** to die before retiring from work **2.** *v.t.* to put a harness on (an animal) ‖ to control and utilize

harp *n.* a musical instrument

harp *v.i.* to play on a harp ‖ (with 'on') to make frequent, boring or annoying reference

harp·ist *n.* someone who plays the harp

har·poon 1. *n.* a barbed spear with an attached line, fired from a gun to bury itself in the flesh of a whale **2.** *v.t.* to spear with a harpoon

har·row 1. *n.* an iron frame with spikes used after plowing to break up clods of soil into a fine tilth **2.** *v.t.* to work over (a field) with a harrow ‖ to lacerate (the feelings) **hár·row·ing** *adj.*

har·ry har·ry·ing har·ried *v.t.* to harass ‖ to make repeated attacks on ‖ to lay waste, ravage

harsh *adj.* without mercy ‖ oppressive ‖ displeasing ‖ stark

har·vest 1. *n.* the gathering in of ripe crops or fodder ‖ crops with respect to their yield ‖ the result of action or behavior **2.** *v.t.* to gather in

har·ves·ter *n.* a machine used in harvesting ‖ a harvest worker

has *3rd pers. sing. pres. tense* of HAVE

hash 1. *n.* meat chopped with potatoes and baked or fried **to make a hash of** to make a lamentable failure of **2.** *v.t.* to cut (esp. meat) into small pieces **to hash over** to talk about in detail

hasp 1. *n.* a bar used as a fastening for a door, window, lid etc. **2.** *v.t.* to fasten by means of a hasp

has·sle 1. *n.* a wrangle, dispute **2.** *v.* **has·sling has·sled** *v.i.* to bicker ‖ *v.t.* to bother, annoy

has·sock *n.* a small, firm, stuffed cushion

haste *n.* deliberate speediness **in haste** hastily **to make haste** to hurry **has·ten** *v.* to move with hurry ‖ to treat as urgent

hast·i·ly *adv.* in a hurry ‖ in too great a hurry

hast·i·ness *n.* the state or quality of being hasty

hast·y hast·i·er hast·i·est *adj.* impetuous, precipitate ‖ made or done with haste

hat *n.* an article designed to protect or adorn the head **something under one's hat** to keep something a secret **to take one's hat off** to affirm one's admiration for

hatch *v.i.* to emerge from an egg ‖ *v.t.* to produce (young) from eggs by incubation ‖ (often with 'up') to produce as a result of scheming

hatch *n.* an aperture, fitted with a door or lid ‖ a covering for a ship's hold or stairway ‖ a hatchway

hatch·er·y *pl.* **hatch·er·ies** *n.* a device where eggs (e.g. of trout) are hatched under care

hatch·way *n.* a large opening in the deck of a ship giving access to the hold ‖ any opening that may be shut by a hatch

hate 1. *n.* intensely hostile aversion, compounded of anger and fear **2.** *v.t.* **hat·ing hat·ed** to experience the sensation of hate ‖ to dislike strongly **háte·ful** *adj.* unkind, mean

ha·tred *n.* the passion of hate

haugh·ti·ly *adv.* in a haughty manner

haugh·ti·ness *n.* the state of being haughty

haugh·ty haugh·ti·er haugh·ti·est *adj.* displaying overbearing pride

haul 1. *v.t.* to pull with an effort ‖ to transport by road, railroad etc. ‖ *v.i.* to give a long, steady pull **to haul down the flag** to surrender **2.** *n.* a strong steady pull ‖ the quantity of fish taken in a net or in a catch ‖ the valuables stolen by a thief on one job **hául·er** *n.* someone who transports goods by road

haunch *n.* the lateral part of the body between the ribs and the thigh

haunt 1. *v.t.* to pay frequent visits to ‖ to follow (someone) about in an unwelcome way ‖ to be always present as a nagging anxiety in the mind of **to be haunted** to be frequented by ghosts, spirits etc. **2.** *n.* a place which one frequents ‖ a den or feeding place of an animal

haut·bois haut·boy *pl.* **haut·bois haut·boys** *n.* the former name for an oboe

haute cou·ture *n.* the art and industry of the leading women's fashion houses

hau·teur *n.* haughtiness

have (h;aev) **have has have hav·ing had** *v.t.* to own, possess ‖ to be in a specified personal relationship to ‖ to contain ‖ to take ‖ to experience ‖ to be afflicted with ‖ to cause to do ‖ to be under an obligation **to have done with** to have finished with **to have it coming** to observe what one gets, esp. punishment or bad luck **to have it out** quarrel etc. **to have nothing on** to have no information to the discredit of **to let someone have it** to hurt someone physically or with words etc.

ha·ven *n.* a small natural bay or inlet providing shelter and anchorage for ships ‖ a refuge

hav·er·sack *n.* a bag slung over the shoulder by a strap and used to carry food etc.

hav·oc *n.* destruction on a wide and intense scale

hawk 1. *n.* a diurnal bird of prey ‖ a person who advocates a military or bellicose solution to a disagreement 2. *v.i.* to hunt with hawks

hawk *v.t.* to peddle (goods) in the street ‖ *v.t.* to be a hawker

hawk·er *n.* someone who peddles goods esp. from a cart

haw·ser *n.* a cable, often of steel, used in mooring or warping a ship

hay 1. *n.* grasses as a crop that is cut and dried for fodder 2. *v.t.* to cut and dry (grasses) **to make hay while the sun shines** to profit from favorable circumstances

hay·ride *n.* a ride in an open truck or wagon with some hay in it, esp. at night, by a group, for fun

hay·stack *n.* a quantity of hay built up outdoors into a compressed mass, with a thatched, ridged or conical top to drain off the rain

hay·wire 1. *n.* a wire used to bind bales of hay 2. *adj. (pop.)* mixed up, out of order ‖ crazy

haz·ard *v.t.* to place (something) in a dangerous or risky situation ‖ to attempt (an answer, guess etc.)

hazard *n.* a risk or chance danger ‖ *(golf)* a ground obstacle **haz·ard·ous** *adj.* risky

haze *n.* a cloudy, misty appearance of the air ‖ a cloudy appearance in a liquid or on a solid surface ‖ obscurity of mental vision

haze haz·ing hazed *v.t.* to place (someone, esp. an initiate into a fraternity) in an embarrassing or humiliating situation

ha·zel 1. *n.* a genus of hairy-leaved shrubs 2. *adj.* (esp. of eyes) having the reddish-brown color of hazelnuts

ha·zel·nut *n.* the fruit of the hazel

ha·zy ha·zi·er ha·zi·est *adj.* characterized by haze ‖ indistinct ‖ not clear

he *pron. 3rd person sing. nominative case* a male person, animal or personified thing already mentioned

head 1. *n.* the top part of the human or foremost part of an animal's body ‖ the leading person in a community, institution etc. ‖ the foremost, most effective part of a tool ‖ the froth on beer etc. ‖ a critical stage ‖ a headland ‖ the height or length of a head ‖ (also *pl.*) the obverse side of a coin **head and shoulders** by far **head over heels** deeply, overwhelmingly **to act** (or go) **over someone's head** to act without someone's knowledge or consent **to be weak in the head** to be of subnormal intelligence **to keep one's head** to remain calm **to keep one's head above water** to remain solvent or otherwise manage to cope **to lose one's head** to lose one's self-control **to talk someone's head off** to talk at great length to someone 2. *adj.* chief in authority 3. *v.i.* to move in a certain direction ‖ *v.t.* to lead ‖ to be at the top of ‖ to cause (something) to move in a certain direction

head·ache *n.* a usually persistent pain in the head ‖ a vexing problem

head·ing *n.* the title of a piece of writing

head lamp a headlight

head·land *n.* a point of land projecting into the sea

head·less *adj.* lacking prudence or proper thought

head·light *n.* a powerful light fitted on the

front of a motor vehicle

head·line 1. *n.* the title of a news item in a newspaper ‖ a news summary given at the beginning of a news broadcast **2.** *v.t.* **head·lin·ing head·lined** to be performing as the headliner in **héad·lin·er** *n.* a starring performer

head·long 1. *adv.* headfirst ‖ full tilt ‖ impetuously **2.** *adj.* done or proceeding with the head foremost ‖ impetuous

head·most *adj.* leading, foremost

head-on *adj.* with the head, or foremost part moving toward or facing another person or thing

head·phone *n.* a set of receivers for both ears attached to a headband

head·quar·ters *n.* a center from which operations are directed

head·room *n.* the clear space above a person's head e.g. in a doorway or an automobile

head·stone *n.* a stone erected at the head of a grave

head·strong *adj.* willful and obstinate

head·way *n.* progress ‖ the rate of progression

head·y head·i·er head·i·est *adj.* likely to intoxicate ‖ intended to incite or inflame

heal *v.i.* to become well or whole again ‖ *v.t.* to restore to health ‖ to cause (painful emotions) to be no longer grievous **to heal a breach** to bring about a reconciliation

health *n.* the state of fitness of the body or of the mind

health·ful *adj.* promoting good health

health·i·ness *n.* the state or quality of being healthy

health·y health·i·er health·i·est *adj.* normally having good physical and mental health ‖ conducive to good health ‖ likely to be for one's good ‖

heap 1. *n.* any material gathered or thrown together into a pile ‖ a large number or quantity **heaps of** plenty of

hear hear·ing heard *v.t.* to experience or be aware of (sounds) ‖ to listen to so as to consider ‖ to conduct the trial of (a case) ‖ *v.i.* (with 'of' or 'from') to receive information or news ‖ to be informed **not**

to hear of not to permit **to hear out** to listen to to the end

hear·er *n.* someone who hears, esp. one of several

hear·ing *n.* the act of apprehending or the ability to apprehend sounds aurally ‖ the listening to evidence and pleas in a law court **hard of hearing** a little deaf

heark·en hark·en *v.i.* to listen, pay attention (to what is said)

hear·say *n.* that which one has been told but has not directly experienced

hearse *n.* a vehicle used for conveying a corpse in its coffin to the place of burial etc.

heart *n.* the hollow muscular organ which forces the blood through the circulatory system of vertebrates ‖ the central part of something ‖ the most important part of something ‖ (*pl. cards*) a suit marked with a representation of one or more red hearts (♡) **have a heart!** be merciful! **not to have the heart to** to be unwilling to **to break one's heart** to be acutely distressed in one's affections or sensitivity **to give (or lose) one's heart to** to give all one's affection to **to have something at heart** to have great interest in or sympathy for **to learn (or known) something by heart** to memorize **take to heart** to heed with seriousness

heart·ache *n.* persistent mental suffering

heart·beat *n.* one of the rhythmical muscular movements of the heart

heart·break *n.* overwhelming sorrow **héart·break·ing** *adj.* tending to crush the spirits **heart·bro·ken** *adj.* suffering overwhelming sorrow

heart·burn *n.* a burning sensation felt in the stomach (near the heart) caused by indigestion

heart·en *v.t.* to inspire with fresh determination

heart·felt *adj.* deeply and sincerely felt

hearth *n.* the floor of a fireplace or the area immediately in front of a fireplace

heart·i·ly *adv.* very warmly ‖ with a good appetite ‖ enthusiastically ‖ thoroughly

heart·i·ness *n.* the quality of being hearty

heart·less *adj.* devoid of all feelings of

affection || cruel, pitiless

heart·rend·ing adj. causing grief and pity

heart·sick adj. depressed and weak with yearning, or marked by such depression

hearty heart·i·er heart·i·est adj. very warm || vigorous || abundant || exuberant, genial

heat n. high temperature || intensity of emotional feeling || (with 'in') a period of intense sexual excitement in a female || a preliminary race or other contest

heat v.t. to supply heat to, make hot or hotter

heat·ed adj. subjected to heat || emotionally violent

heat·er n. a device that gives off heat

heath n. a plant, usually found growing in open, barren, poorly drained soil

hea·then 1. pl. **hea·thens hea·then** n. a person who does not worship the God of the Christians, Jews or Moslems **2.** adj. of or relating to heathens, their beliefs and practices

heave 1. heav·ing heaved hove v.t. to raise with much effort || to throw || to emit (a long-drawn-out sigh) || v.i. to rise and fall rhythmically **to heave to** to bring a ship to a standstill heading into the wind **2.** n. the act of heaving

heav·en n. the upper regions, regarded in many religions as the abode of the deity or deities, and of the blessed || perfect happiness **to move heaven and earth** to do one's utmost

heav·en·ly adj. pertaining to heaven or the heavens || very delightful

heav·i·ly adv. in a heavy manner

heav·i·ness n. the state or quality of being heavy

heav·y heav·i·er heav·i·est adj. of considerable weight || oppressive || joyless || clumsy in conception or execution || (of soil) clayey || lacking in grace || steep **1.** pl. **heav·ies** n. the actor who plays the part of the villain

heavy adv. heavily

heav·y-hand·ed adj. domineering || clumsy

heav·y-heart·ed adj. worried and sad

heck·le heck·ling heck·led v.t. to harass by interrupting

hec·tare n. a metric unit of area equal to 10,000 sq. meters, or 2.471 acres

hec·tic adj. exciting, wildly agitated

hedge 1. n. a continuous line of shrubs planted around the edge of a field, garden etc. || a protective line **2. hedg·ing hedged** v.t. to enclose, protect or obstruct with a hedge || to reduce (a risk) by making opposing speculations || v.i. to avoid giving a direct answer or statement

he·don·ism n. the doctrine that pleasure is the highest good and that moral duty is fulfilled through the pursuit of pleasure **hé·don·ist** n. **he·do·nís·tic** adj. **he·do·nís·ti·cal·ly** adv.

heed 1. n. careful attention and consideration **2.** v.t. to take into consideration **héed·ful** adj. attentive **héed·ful·ly** adv. **héed·ful·ness** n. **héed·less** adj. negligent **héed·less·ly** adv. **héed·less·ness** n.

heel 1. n. the rounded hind part of the human foot || the corresponding part of an animal's hind limb || the back part of the base of a shoe || something shaped or positioned like a heel || (pop.) a cad **to be at one's heels** to be close behind one **to turn on one's heel** to turn away sharply **2.** v.i. (in a dance step) to touch the ground with the heel || (of a dog) to follow along at the heels of an owner or trainer

heel v.i. (of a ship) to list || v.t. to make (a ship) list

heft 1. n. heaviness **2.** v.t. to hoist

heft·y heft·i·er heft·i·est adj. heavily built and strong

heif·er n. a young cow that has not borne any young

heigh interj. used to hail someone or to remonstrate with him

height n. (of an object, person etc.) the distance or measurement from the base or foot to the top || distance above the earth, altitude

height·en v.t. to increase the height of || v.i. to increase in amount or degree || to become more intense

hei·nous adj. (of a crime or conduct) very wicked

heir n. a person who will become or who has become the owner of all or part of another's property or titles on that other's death

her·ess *n.* a female who is or will become an heir

hcir·loom *n.* a piece of valuable personal property that has been handed down within a family for a considerable period of time

hel·i·cop·ter *n.* a small aircraft supported in the air solely by propellers rotating in a horizontal plane

he·li·um *n.* a light, colorless, odorless, chemically inert gaseous element

he·lix *pl.* **he·li·ces, he·lix·es** *n.* a spiral ornament ‖ the outer rim of the external ear

hell *n.* traditionally the abode of Satan and his fallen angels and a place of physical anguish for impenitent souls after death

hell·ish *adj.* relating to hell ‖ like or worthy of hell

hel·lo 1. *interj.* an informal greeting expressing pleasure or surprise or both ‖ a call to attract or ensure attention **2.** *pl.* **hel·los** *n.*

helm *n.* a device (e.g. a tillzer or wheel) attached to the rudder for steering a vessel

hel·met *n.* a protective covering for the head

helms·man *pl.* **helms·men** *n.* the person at the helm who steers the ship

help *n.* the act of helping or an instance of this ‖ someone who or something which helps ‖ a domestic servant, farmhand ‖ employees

help *v.t.* to join (someone) and contribute to the performance or completion of a task ‖ used as a cry of distress ‖ to make easier, likelier or more probable ‖ to prevent oneself from ‖ to serve (food) at a meal **to help oneself** to steal, misappropriate ‖ to serve oneself without putting others to the trouble of serving one ‖ *v.i.* to supply help **help·er** *n.*

help·ful *adj.* giving or offering help

help·ing *n.* a serving of food

help·less *adj.* unable to tend one's own needs

hem 1. *n.* the edge of a garment, handker-

chief etc. folded back and stitched in place **2.** *v.* **hem·ming hemmed** *v.t.* to make a hem around **to hem in** to surround and keep tight in

hem·i·sphere *n.* the half of a sphere ‖ one half of the roughly spherical surface of the earth ‖ either of the two chief parts of the brain **hem·i·spher·ic hem·i·sphér·i·cal** *adjs*

hem·lock *n.* any of several poisonous flower-bearing plants ‖ hemlock spruce

hem·or·rhage 1. *n.* a heavy bleeding from the blood vessels **2.** **hem·or·rhag·ing hem·or·rhaged** *v.i.* to suffer this heavy bleeding

hem·or·rhoids *pl. n.* groups of distended veins at the anus

hemp *n.* a genus of widely cultivated annuals ‖ this plant's fiber used for ropes and coarse fabrics ‖ a narcotic made from hemp, e.g. hashish, marijuana, bhang

hen *n.* a female bird, esp. of the domestic chicken

hence *adv.* at a time in the future measured from now ‖ therefore

hence·forth *adv.* from now on

hence·for·ward *adv.* henceforth

hench·man *pl.* **hench·men** *n.* a reliable underling

hep·a·ti·tis *n.* inflammation of the liver

her *possessiveadj.* of, pertaining to or belonging to a female person or animal

her *pron.* , objective case of SHE

her·ald *v.t.* to announce as imminent

herald *n.* the official messenger ‖ a state officer who superintends state ceremonies **he·ral·dic** *adj.* pertaining to the office or duties of a herald ‖ pertaining to heraldry **her·ald·ry** *n.* coats of arms

herb *n.* a plant valued for flavoring food, for medicinal purposes, or for its fragrance

her·ba·ceous *adj.* of, or like, herbs

herb·age *n.* the edible parts of herbaceous plants

her·biv·ore *n.* an animal feeding chiefly on plant food **her·biv·o·rous** *adj.*

Her·cu·le·an *adj.* exceptionally strong ‖ demanding exceptional effort

herd 1. *n.* a number of animals of one kind

feeding or gathered together ‖ the common run of people, the masses **2.** *v.t.* to tend (a herd) ‖ *v.i.* to form a herd or crowd

herds·man *pl.* **herds·men** *n.* a man who tends herds

here 1. *adv.* in this place ‖ at this or at that moment in time, action, thought etc. **neither here nor there** irrelevant ‖ of no importance **2.** *n.* this place

here·af·ter 1. *adv.* from now on ‖ in the future **2.** *n.* a life after death

he·red·i·tar·y *adj.* of physical or psychological qualities transmitted by heredity

he·red·i·ty *n.* the transmission of qualities from parent to offspring

here·in *adv.* (esp. legal contexts)in this

her·e·sy *pl.* **her·e·sies** *n.* religious or ideological belief opposed to orthodoxy ‖ an instance of this

her·e·tic *n.* someone advocates a heresy

he·ret·i·cal *adj.* of or relating to a heresy

here·to·fore *adv.* until now ‖ formerly

her·it·age *n.* what has been, or can be, inherited

her·met·ic *adj.* impervious to air or airtight

her·mit *n.* someone who lives in solitude

her·mit·age *n.* the abode of a hermit

her·ni·a *pl.* **her·ni·as, her·ni·ae** *n.* the protrusion of a bodily organ from the cavity in which it is normally contained

he·ro *pl.* **heroes** *n.* a man of exceptional quality ‖ the male character of a play, novel etc.

he·ro·ic *adj.* of or relating to a hero or heroine ‖ of or relating to the acts of a hero or heroine ‖ larger than life-size **he·ró·i·cal·ly** *adv.*

her·o·in *n.* a white, crystalline narcotic

her·o·ine *n.* a female hero

her·o·ism *n.* extreme courage ‖ an instance of this

he·ron *n.* migratory wadings bird **her·on·ry** *pl.* **her·on·ries** *n.* a breeding place of herons

hers possessive*pron.* that or those things belonging to a female person or animal or something personified as female

her·self *pron.* refl. form of SHE

hes·i·tance *n.* hesitancy

hes·i·tan·cy *pl.* **hes·i·tan·cies** *n.* the quality of being hesitant or an instance of this

hes·i·tant *adj.* (of speech) marked by pauses ‖ having doubts about taking an action or a decision

hes·i·tate hes·i·tat·ing hes·i·tat·ed *v.i.* to pause before acting ‖ to be indecisive ‖ to pause repeatedly when speaking **hes·i·ta·tion** *n.* the act of hesitating

het·er·o·ge·ne·ous *adj.* dissimilar in character ‖ composed of different or disparate elements

hew hew·ing hewed hewn *v.t.* to cut by blows with an ax or other sharp-edged instrument ‖ *v.i.* to make blows with an ax or other sharp-edged instrument **héw·er** *n.* a person who hews

hex·a·gon *n.* a figure with six sides and six angles **hex·ag·on·al** *adj.* having six sides

hey *interj.* used to hail someone

hey·day *n.* a time of greatest prosperity and vigor

hi·a·tus *pl.* **hi·a·tus·es, hi·a·tus** *n.* a break or pause in the continuity of action, speech, writing etc.

hi·ber·nate hi·ber·nat·ing hi·ber·nat·ed *v.i.* to spend the winter in a torpid state **hi·ber·ná·tion** *n.*

hic·cup, hic·cough 1. *n.* a sudden, spasmodic contraction of the diaphragm and audible closing of the glottis ‖ an attack of this **2.** *v.i.* **hic·cup·ing, hic·cup·ping, hic·cough·ing hic·cuped, hic·cupped, hic·coughed** to make the sound of a hiccup

hide *v.* **hid·ing hid hid·den, hid** to put or keep out of sight ‖ to keep from the knowledge of others

hide *n.* the raw or dressed skin of an animal

hid·e·ous *adj.* so ugly as to be repulsive ‖ fearful

hie *v.i.* to go off with haste

hi·er·ar·chy *pl.* **hi·er·ar·chies** *n.* the group of persons in any organization vested with power and authority ‖ any arrangement of principles, things etc. in an ascending or descending order

hi·er·o·glyph *n.* a character used in hieroglyphics

hi·er·o·glyph·ic 1. *adj.* of or written in hieroglyphs **2.** *n.* (*pl.*) a method of writing in which a symbol, usually pictorial, represents a word, syllable or sound ‖ such a symbol

high 1. *adj.* being at, or reaching to, a position at a relatively large distance above some plane of reference ‖ great in degree ‖ (of sounds) produced by a relatively large number of vibrations ‖ (of latitude) far from the equator ‖ occupying an important position ‖ noble ‖ intense ‖ elated ‖ at the zenith ‖ intoxicated ‖ a state of exhilaration **high and dry** (pop.) stranded **it is high time** it is quite certainly time without more delay **2.** *adv.* in or to an elevated degree, price, station etc. **3.** *n.* an area having a high barometric pressure ‖ top gear

high·fa·lu·tin *adj.* pretentious, high-flown

high·fa·lu·ting *adj.* highfalutin

high-hat 1. *adj.* affecting superiority, supercilious **2.** *v.i.* **high-hat·ting high-hat·ted** to snub

high·light 1. *n.* the part of a surface that catches most light ‖ an event of special importance **2.** *v.t.* to draw special attention to ‖ to render the light-catching surfaces of (in painting or etching)

high-ten·sion *adj.* having a high voltage

high·way *n.* a public road

hi·jack, high-jack *v.t.* to steal (something) while it is in transit

hike 1. *v.i.* **hik·ing hiked** to walk a long way ‖ to raise (prices) **2.** *n.* a long walk ‖ a price increase

hi·lar·i·ous *adj.* farcical or highly comic

hi·lar·i·ty *n.* the state or condition of being hilarious

hill *n.* an elevation of the earth's surface that typically has a rounded top

hill·ock *n.* a small hill or mound

hilt *n.* the handle of a sword or dagger

him *pron.* , objective case of HE

him·self *pron.* , refl. form of HE ‖ emphatic form of HE, he did it himself

hind *adj.* at the back, the hind legs of a horse

hind *pl.* **hinds, hind** *n.* a female deer

hin·der *v.t.* to impede, slow down, or hold up ‖ *v.i.* to be a hindrance

hind·er *adj.* located at the back or rear

hind·most *adj.* furthest back

hin·drance *n.* a hindering ‖ that which hinders

hind·sight *n.* the understanding that is brought to bear on an event thanks to the passage of time

hinge 1. *n.* an attachment connecting two solid objects which enables one object to rotate in relation to the other **2.** *v.* **hing·ing hinged** *v.i.* (witth 'on' or 'upon') to depend upon ‖ *v.t.* to connect by a hinge

hint 1. *n.* an aid in guessing or in drawing a conclusion ‖ an indirect mention ‖ a slight suggestion **2.** *v.t.* to suggest ‖ *v.i.* (with 'at') to make an oblique reference to or suggestion of

hip *n.* the flesh-covered, lateral extension of the pelvis and the upper thighbone

hip·po·pot·a·mus *pl.* **hip·po·pot·a·mus·es, hip·po·pot·a·mi** *n.* a genus of four-toed, ungulate Old World mammals

hire *n.* a payment for temporary use of something

hire hir·ing hired *v.t.* to obtain the use of (something) temporarily for an agreed payment ‖ to obtain the services of (someone) for an agreed wage

hire·ling *n.* a mercenary

hir·sute *adj.* hairy, esp. having shaggy hair

his 1. possessive*pron.* that or those things belonging to him **2.** possessive*adj.* of, pertaining to or belonging to him

hiss 1. *v.i.* to make the sound of a prolonged 's' ‖ *v.t.* to show disapproval **2.** *n.* the sound itself

his·to·ri·an *n.* someone who specializes in history

his·tor·ic *adj.* of or relating to the past

his·tor·i·cal *adj.* of or relating to history ‖ authenticated in history, not legendary

his·tór·i·cal·ly *adv.*

his·to·ry *pl.* **his·to·ries** *n.* a record of past events ‖ the study and writing of such records ‖ a narrative

his·tri·on·ic *adj.* excessively theatrical

his·tri·on·i·cal·ly *adv.* **his·tri·on·ics** *pl. n.* theatrical behavior off the stage

hit 1. *v.* **hit·ting hit** *v.t.* to strike with a blow ‖ to strike by throwing an object or sending a missile ‖ to strike against with a sudden impact ‖ to hurt emotionally or financially ‖ to criticize adversely ‖ *v.i.* to make a blow, strike etc. **to be hard hit** to be the victim of very adverse circumstances **to hit below the belt** to take an unfair advantage **to hit the road** to start traveling to **hit the spot** to be exactly what is wanted at the moment **2.** *n.* a popular success ‖ (underworld slang) a murder committed under a "contract"

hitch 1. *v.t.* to fasten temporarily or loosely ‖ *v.i.* to move slowly and jerkily **to hitch up** to pull up with a little tug ‖ to harness (a draft animal) **2.** *n.* an obstacle, impediment

hitch·hike hitch·hik·ing hitch·hiked *v.i.* to travel by begging free rides

hith·er 1. *adv.* to this place **2.** *adv.* nearer

hith·er·to *adv.* up till this time

hive *n.* a man-made shelter for honeybees to live in ‖ a swarm of bees in such a shelter

hives *pl. n.* a temporary skin condition of allergic origin

hoard *v.t.* to collect, keep and store away

hoard *n.* a quantity of material, esp. money or valuables, put together in a safe, usually secret place ‖ a body of ideas stored up for future use

hoard·ing *n.* a temporary board wall placed around construction work

hoarse *adj.* (of a voice) rough, scratchy or husky **hóars·en** *v.t.* to make hoarse ‖ *v.i.* to become hoarse

hoax 1. *v.t.* to deceive, esp. in fun **2.** *n.* a deception

hob·ble 1. *v.* **hob·bling hob·bled** *v.i.* to walk with short, unsteady steps ‖ *v.t.* to join the legs of (a horse, camel etc.) by a short rope so that it will not stray far **2.** *n.* a hobbling gait

hob·by *pl.* **hob·bies** *n.* a spare time interest or occupation, esp. one taken up just for pleasure

hob·nob hob·nob·bing hob·nobbed *v.i.* (with 'with') to be on familiar terms

ho·bo *pl.* **ho·boes, ho·bos** *n.* a tramp

hock *n.* a joint of the hind leg in some quadrupeds

hock 1. *n.* in debt **2.** *v.t.* to pawn

hock·ey *n.* ice hockey ‖ field hockey

hod *n.* a trough used for carrying bricks, mortar etc. up and down scaffolding ‖ a coal scuttle

hodge·podge *n.* an ill-assorted mixture, medley

hoe 1. *n.* a hand tool used for breaking up clods of earth etc. **2. hoe·ing hoed** *v.i.* to use a hoe

hog 1. *pl.* **hogs, hog** *n.* omnivorous mammals ‖ (pop.) a greedy person **2.** *v.t.* **hog·ging hogged** to take more than one's share of

hoi pol·loi *n.* the common people

hoist *adj.* carried off

hold 1. *v.* **hold·ing held** *v.t.* to have in one's hand ‖ to support ‖ to detain ‖ to contain ‖ to retain ‖ to consider, regard as having a specified value ‖ to keep in a certain position or condition ‖ to force (someone) to abide by a promise etc. ‖ to preside over ‖ *v.i.* to remain whole under pressure ‖ to remain valid **to hold back** to be reticent **to hold down** to keep under restraint **to hold off** to keep at a distance **to hold one's breath** to be in a state of sympathetic anxiety **to hold one's ground (or one's own)** to keep one's position in fighting or argument **to hold one's head high** to face the world confidently **to hold one's tongue** to refrain from speaking out **to put on hold** to ask a telephone caller to wait **to hold water** to be valid **2.** *n.* something providing a grip ‖ in a missile-launching countdown, an order to stop **to take hold** (of ideas etc) to begin to become established

hold·er *n.* someone who holds ‖ something which holds

hold·ing *n.* land, shares etc. owned

hole *n.* a small space or cavity partly or wholly surrounded by matter ‖ a situation that is embarrassing or from which there is apparently no escape

hol·i·day *n.* a day on which one does not go to work

ho·li·ness *n.* the quality of being holy

hol·ler 1. *v.i.* and t. to shout or cry out **2.** *n.* a yell

hol·low *n.* a little hole ‖ a saucer-shaped piece of ground

hol·ly *pl.* **hol·lies** *n.* evergreen shrubs and trees

hol·o·caust *n.* a large-scale sacrifice or destruction esp. of life, esp. by fire

hol·ster *n.* a pistol case

ho·ly ho·li·er ho·li·est *adj.* of God, his works, dwelling place, attributes etc. ‖ sacred

hom·age *n.* a mark of respect or veneration **to do homage** to express homeage by word or gesture

home 1. *n.* the private living quarters of a person or family ‖ the place, city etc. where a person lives ‖ a building where orphans, old people etc. are housed and cared for **to be at home with** to be familiar with, or used to **2.** *adj.* of or associated with a home, one's home or native country **3.** *adv.* to or into one's home **nothing to write home about** (pop.) not very good

home·li·ness *n.* the quality of being homely

home·ly home·li·er home·li·est *adj.* simple, plain ‖ plain-featured, not attractive

home·made *adj.* made at home

home plate (baseball) a piece of rubber set into the ground beside which the batter stands

home run (baseball) a hit which enables the batter to run all the bases and score a run

home·sick *adj.* longing for home

home·spun 1. *n.* cloth woven from yarn spun at home **2.** *adj.* of such cloth ‖ plain, unsophisticated

home·ward 1. *adv.* towards home **2.** *adj.* going in the direction of home

home·y, hom·y hom·i·er hom·i·est *adj.* cozy and unpretentious ‖ lacking a sense of style

hom·i·ci·dal *adj.* pertaining to homicide

hom·i·cide *n.* the killing of a human being by another

hom·i·ly *pl.* **hom·i·lies** *n.* a sermon in which spiritual values are discussed ‖ a moralizing lecture

hom·i·ny *n.* hulled corn kernels eaten boiled or fried

ho·mo·ge·ne·ous *adj.* similar in character ‖ having at all points the same composition and properties

ho·mog·e·nize ho·mog·e·niz·ing ho·mog·e·nized *v.t.* to make homogeneous

hom·o·nym *n.* a word having the same sound as another which has a different meaning, e.g. 'bare' and 'bear'

ho·mo·sex·u·al 1. *adj.* characterized by sexual attraction felt by a person for another person of the same sex **2.** *n.* a person so attracted **ho·mo·sex·u·al·i·ty** *n.*

hone 1. *n.* a piece of stone with a fine abrasive surface, used to grind a cutting tool to a sharp edge **2.** *v.t.* **hon·ing honed** to sharpen

hon·est *adj.* never deceiving ‖ sincere, truthful **hón·est·ly** *adv.* with honesty

hon·es·ty *n.* the act or condition of being honest

hon·ey 1. *pl.* **hon·eys** *n.* a sweet viscous fluid made by honeybees ‖ (pop.) a term of endearment **2. hon·ey·ing hon·eyed hon·ied** *v.t.* (often with 'up') to blandish (someone)

hon·ey·comb *n.* an aggregate of hexagonal wax cells, made by bees for their eggs, larvae and store of honey

hon·ey·moon 1. *n.* a holiday taken by a newly married couple **2.** *v.i.* to spend a honeymoon

hon·ey·suck·le *n.* a member of *Lonicera*, fam. *Caprifoliaceae*, esp. the woodbine

honk 1. *n.* the call of the wild goose ‖ a similar sound, e.g. of a car horn **2.** *v.i.* to make such a sound

hon·or *n.* moral integrity ‖ the esteem accorded to virtue or talent ‖ an award or distinction ‖ (pl.) the honors program **Honor** (with possessive) a title of respect used esp. for judges **to do the honors** to do what is expected of the host

honor *v.t.* to confer honor on ‖ to treat as valid

hon·or·a·ble *adj.* showing great respect or self-respect ‖ worthy of respect **Honorable** a U.S. courtesy title of certain government officials

hon·or·ar·y *adj.* of an unpaid office or the person holding it ‖ of duties which are merely nominal

hood 1. *n.* a loose bonnetlike covering for the head and neck ‖ the cover over the engine of a car **2.** *v.t.* to cover, or furnish, with a hood

hood·lum *n.* a gangster

hood·wink *v.t.* to deceive by trickery

hoof 1. *pl.* **hooves hoofs** *n.* the sheath of horn covering the forepart of the foot in a horse, cow, sheep, pig etc. **2.** *v.t.* to dance

hook 1. *n.* a piece of metal, curved or bent sharply and able to support a considerable strain ‖ a fishhook ‖ a short swinging blow **by hook or by crook** by fair means or foul **hook line and sinker** completely **2.** *v.t.* to use a hook to catch, fasten or suspend (something) ‖ *(golf cricket)* to hit (the ball) with a hook ‖ *(boxing)* to hit with a hook ‖ *(baseball)* to pitch (the ball) so that it curves ‖ to trap (someone) into doing something

hoop *n.* a strip of metal, wood etc. bent to form the circumference of a circle, used in binding the staves of a cask ‖ a child's toy

hoot 1. *n.* an aspirated, loud sound of derision or laughter ‖ the call of an owl **not to care** (or **give**) **a hoot** not to care at all **2.** *v.i.* to make derisive hoots at (someone) **hóot·er** *n.*

hop 1. hop·ping hopped *v.i.* (of persons) to jump from the ground using only one foot ‖ to make a short flight or a quick short journey ‖ *v.t.* to jump over **2.** *n.* an instance of hopping

hope hop·ing hoped *v.i.* to have hope ‖ *v.t.* to wish and expect

hope *n.* a confident expectation that a desire will be fulfilled ‖ wishful trust

hope·ful *adj.* being full of hope

hope·less *adj.* without hope

hop·per *n.* something that hops ‖ a container, usually narrow at the bottom and wide at the top, which delivers its contents to something below it

horde *n.* a vast number of people

ho·ri·zon *n.* the apparent line of junction of earth or sea with sky

hor·i·zon·tal 1. *adj.* at right angles to a radius of the earth **2.** *n.* a line, plane etc. that is horizontal

hor·mone *n.* a group of substances of variable composition which are produced in most living systems

horn 1. *n.* a hard, pointed, permanent outgrowth of epidermis ‖ *(mus.)* any of various wind instruments ‖ an instrument for making loud warning noises, e.g. a foghorn **2.** *v.t.* to pierce with a horn ‖ *v.i.* **to horn in** to intrude

hor·net *n.* strong members of *Vespidae* , a family of wasps **to stir up a hornets' nest** to arouse fierce anger

ho·rol·o·gy *n.* the science of measuring time ‖ the art of making timepieces

hor·o·scope *n.* a diagram representing the configuration of the stars and planets at any given time **ho·ros·co·py** *n.*

hor·ren·dous *adj.* dreadful

hor·ri·ble *adj.* giving rise to horror ‖ extremely unpleasant **hór·ri·bly** *adv.*

hor·rid *adj.* very unkind ‖ horrible

hor·ri·fy hor·ri·fy·ing hor·ri·fied *v.t.* to cause horror to ‖ to shock

hor·ror *n.* intense fear joined with repulsion ‖ *(pop.)* someone who behaves in a horrid way

hors d'oeu·vre *pl.* **hors d'oeu·vres** *n.* various dishes served as appetizers

horse 1. *n.* a large, herbivorous animal ‖ a vaulting horse **a horse of a different color** quite a different matter **from the horse's mouth** from the source **hold your horses!** don't be impatient **2. hors·ing horsed** *v.i.* **to horse around** *(pop.)* to fool around

horse·rad·ish *n.* a perennial plant cultivated for its fleshy white root ‖ a pungent condiment made from this root

horse-shoe *n.* a curved bar of iron, shaped to fit the rim of a horse's hoof, to which it is nailed for protection

hor·ti·cul·ture *n.* the art of growing

flowers, fruit and vegetables **hor·ti·cúl·tur·ist** n.

ho·san·na n. a cry of praise and worship

hose 1. n. a flexible tube used for conveying water ‖ stockings **2.** v.t. **hós·ing hosed** to spray with a hose

hosier n. someone who deals in stockings, socks **hó·sier·y** n. the goods dealt in by a hosier

hos·pice n. a building, usually kept by a religious order, where travelers can obtain rest and food

hos·pi·ta·ble adj. gladly and generously receiving guests **hos·pít·a·bly** adv.

hos·pi·tal n. an institution equipped and staffed to provide medical and surgical care

hos·pi·tal·i·ty pl. **hos·pi·tal·i·ties** n. the receiving of a guest

hos·pi·tal·i·za·tion n. a hospitalizing or being hospitalized

hos·pi·tal·ize **hos·pi·tal·iz·ing** **hos·pi·tal·ized** v.t. to place as a patient in a hospital

host n. someone who provides hospitality ‖ (biol.) any organism in which a parasite spends part or the whole of its existence

host n. a great number

hos·tage n. a person held as a pledge that certain conditions will be fulfilled

hos·tile adj. antagonistic ‖ warlike ‖ of or relating to an enemy

hot adj. at a high temperature, above normal ‖ causing a sensation of body heat ‖ controversial ‖ following or pressing closely ‖ electrically charged ‖ radioactive ‖ (pop.) stolen ‖ (jazz) characterized by exciting rhythm and tonality and by improvisation

hot-blood·ed adj. passionate ‖ rash, impetuous

hot dog a hot, freshly cooked sausage (esp. a frankfurter)

ho·tel n. a large building with a resident staff, providing accommodation and often meals

hot·house pl. **hot·hous·es** n. a greenhouse

hound 1. n. a dog used in hunting or tracking **2.** v.t. to pursue relentlessly

hour n. a 24th part of the mean solar day ‖ a fixed period of time ‖ time of day ‖ (pl.) times for habitual activities

hour hand the shorter hand of a watch or clock

hour·ly 1. adj. done, or occurring, every hour **2.** adv. every hour

house hous·ing housed v.t. to provide or be a home or shelter

house pl. **hous·es** n. a building for a person or family to live in ‖ the place where a legislature meets or the legislative body itself ‖ (astrology) one of the 12 equal parts into which the celestial sphere is divided **like a house afire** with great success **on the house** paid for by the management, not by the customer **to keep house** to manage the domestic arrangements of another person

hov·el n. a small, squalid dwelling

hov·er v.i. to remain in the same place in the air for a short time as though suspended

how adv. in what way or manner ‖ in or to what degree, amount, number **how about** used to introduce a suggestion **how do you do?** how are you?

how·ev·er 1. adv. in whatever way or manner **2.** conj. nevertheless, but

howl 1. v.i. to make a prolonged, hollow, wailing call ‖ to laugh very loudly and unrestrainedly **2.** n.

how·so·ev·er adv. in whatever way ‖ to whatever extent

hub n. the central part of a wheel ‖ the point of greatest interest and importance

hub·bub n. a tumult or uproar

hu·bris n. a scornful, overweening pride

huck·ster n. a peddler or market vendor

hud·dle 1. hud·dling hud·dled v.t. (with 'up') to draw (oneself) in ‖ v.t. to gather together very close **2.** n. a group of people or animals gathered very close together **to go into a huddle** to get together in order to discuss something privately

hue n. that quality of a color which allows it to be classed

huff v.t. to cause (someone) to be offended **húff·i·ly** adv. **húff·i·ness** n. **húff·y** **huff·i·er huff·i·est** adj.

hug 1. *n.* an affectionate embrace **2.
hug·ging hugged** *v.t.* to clasp tightly between one's arms ‖ to keep close to (something)

huge *adj.* extremely large

hulk *n.* the body, or hull, of a ship no longer seaworthy ‖ a big clumsy man
húlk·ing *adj.* big and clumsy

hull *n.* the body framework of a ship

hull *n.* the pod, shell etc. of a seed or fruit

hum 1. hum·ming hummed *v.i.* to make a continuous sound in the throat, with the mouth closed ‖ (of bees, moving machine parts etc.) to make a similar sound **2.** *n.* the sound or act of humming

hu·man 1. *adj.* of or characteristic of man ‖ **2.** *n.* (*pop.*) a person

hu·mane *adj.* showing kindness, consideration etc. ‖ of or relating to the humanities

hu·man·ism *n.* any of several movements purporting to advocate the universally human

hu·man·i·tar·i·an 1. *n.* someone who actively promotes the welfare of the human race **2.** *adj.* characteristic of a humanitarian **hu·man·i·tár·i·an·ism** *n.*

hu·man·i·ty *pl.* **hu·man·i·ties** *n.* mankind ‖ kindness to other people, or to animals ‖ (*pl.*) studies emphasizing the cultural aspects of civilization

hum·ble 1. hum·bler hum·blest *adj.* possessing or marked by the virtue of humility ‖ of lowly condition or rank **2.** *v.t.* **hum·bling hum·bled** to cause to feel humble **to humble oneself** to perform an act of submission

hum·bug 1. insincere talk or writing ‖ a person behaving insincerely **2. hum·bug·ging hum·bugged** *v.t.* to mislead (someone) by a sham

hum·drum *adj.* uninspired, flat

hu·mid *adj.* containing a high percentage of water vapor ‖ damp, moist **hu·mid·i·fy hu·mid·i·fy·ing hu·mid·i·fied** *v.t.* to make humid

hu·mid·i·fi·er *n.* a device for humidifying a room or building

hu·mid·i·ty *n.* the state of being humid

hu·mil·i·ate hu·mil·i·at·ing hu·mil·i·at·ed *v.t.* to make (a person) suffer by lessening his dignity or self-esteem

hu·mil·i·a·tion *n.* a humiliating or being humiliated

hu·mil·i·ty *n.* the quality of being without pride

hu·mor 1. *n.* the capacity for recognizing, reacting to, or expressing something which is amusing, funny etc. ‖ a mood, frame of mind **out of humor** cross **2.** *v.t.* to keep (someone) in a good temper

hu·mor·ist *n.* someone who expresses humor in his writing, conversation etc. **hu·mor·ís·tic** *adj.*

hu·mor·ous *adj.* having, or giving rise to, humor

hump 1. *n.* a rounded, raised protrusion **2.** *v.t.* to make (something) hump-shaped

hu·mus *n.* the organic part of soil

hunch 1. *n.* a hump on a person's back ‖ an intuitive feeling about a situation or a coming event **2.** *v.t.* to bend into a hump

hunch·back *n.* a humpback **húnch·backed** *adj.*

hun·dred 1. *pl.* **hun·dred hun·dreds** *n.* ten times ten **2.** *adj.* being ten more than 90

hun·ger 1. *n.* a desire or craving for food ‖ a strong desire for anything **2.** *v.i.* to feel hunger for food or other objects of desire

hun·gry hun·gri·er hun·gri·est *adj.* feeling hunger ‖ having a strong desire for

hunk *n.* a large, thick piece of something

hunt 1. *v.t.* to pursue with the intention of capturing or killing ‖ *v.i.* to participate in a hunt ‖ to search **2.** *n.* the act of hunting ‖ the district hunted over **húnt·er** *n.* someone who hunts, esp. for game ‖ a horse bred and trained to be ridden for hunting

hur·dle 1. *n.* obstacle to be jumped over by horses ‖ an open frame to be cleared by athletes in a race ‖ an obstacle to a course of action **2. hur·dling hur·dled** *v.t.* to surround with hurdles ‖ to jump (a hurdle) **húr·dler** *n.*

hurl *v.t.* to throw violently ‖ to utter (threats, abuse etc.) with vehemence

hur·rah hoo·rah 1. *interj.* used to express

triumph, appreciation etc. **2.** *n.* this cry

hur·ri·cane *n.* a cyclone with wind velocities exceeding 73 and often reaching over 100

hur·ry 1. *n.* the performing of an action quickly and without delay **in a hurry** quickly ‖ soon **2. hur·ry·ing hur·ried** *v.i.* to be quick, waste no time ‖ *v.t.* to make (someone or something) act, move etc. more quickly

hurt hurt·ing hurt *v.i.* to cause or feel pain

hurt *n.* something which causes pain

hur·tle hur·tling hur·tled *v.i.* to move with great force and noise ‖ *v.t.* to make (something) move with great force and noise

hus·band *n.* the male partner in a marriage

hus·band·ry *n.* farming

hush 1. *v.i.* to stop making noise ‖ *v.t.* to cause (someone or something) to cease to make a noise **2.** *n.* silence

husk 1. *n.* a dry, outer covering of some seeds and fruits **2.** *v.t.* to remove the husk from

husk·y *pl.* **hus·kies** *n.* an Eskimo dog

husk·y husk·i·er husk·i·est *adj.* (of speech, or a voice) having a dry, rough sound of lower pitch than normal ‖ tough, strong and heavily built

hus·sy *pl.* **hus·sies** *n.* a shamelessly immoral woman

hus·tle 1. hus·tling hus·tled *v.t.* to shove, jostle rudely ‖ to push quickly forward, off, out etc. ‖ *v.i.* to push one's way quickly **2.** *n.* a hurry **hús·tler** *n.*

hut *n.* a small, roughly-built single-story and usually one-room building used as a dwelling or shelter

hutch *n.* a box used to house small animals ‖ a trough for washing ore ‖ a low cupboard

hy·brid *n.* an offspring resulting from crossbreeding

hy·brid·ism *n.* the production of hybrids

hy·drant *n.* a pipe, fitted with tap and nozzle, by which water may be drawn from a supply main

hy·drau·lic *adj.* of fluids, esp. awater, in motion ‖ of the pressure exerted by water when conveyed through pipes ‖ of substances, machinery etc. affected by or

operated by fluids in motion **hy·dráu·li·cal·ly** *adv.*

hy·dro·e·lec·tric *adj.* of the production of electricity by water power

hy·dro·gen *n.* a nonmetallic, monovalent element

hydrogen bomb (*abbr.* H-bomb) a bomb releasing enormous energy by the fusion at extremely high temperature and pressure of nuclei of isotopes of hydrogen to form helium

hy·dro·pho·bi·a *n.* aversion to water ‖ rabies **hy·dro·phó·bic** *adj.*

hy·dro·phone *n.* an instrument for detecting sound transmitted through water

hy·dro·plane *n.* a light motorboat which, by means of hydrofoils, can rise partially or completely out of the water at high speed

hy·drous *adj.* containing water

hy·e·na hy·ae·na *n.* a carnivorous Old World quadruped

hy·giene *n.* the science of health **hy·gi·en·ic hy·gi·én·i·cal** *adjs* **hy·gíen·ics** *n.* **hy·gien·ist** *n.*

hy·men *n.* the thin fold of mucous membrane at the entrance to the vagina

hymn 1. *n.* a song in praise, adoration or supplication of God

hym·nal *n.* a book containing a collection of hymns

hyper- *prefix* excessive, overmuch, above

hy·per·ten·sion *n.* abnormally high blood pressure

hy·phen *n.* a punctuation mark (-) used to join two words or two elements of a word

hy·phen·ate hy·phen·at·ing hy·phen·at·ed *v.t.* to join or divide by a hyphen **hy·phen·a·tion** *n.*

hyp·no·sis *pl.* **hyp·no·ses** *n.* an artificially induced state, resembling sleep, but characterized by continued responsiveness to the voice of the hypnotist

hy·po·chon·dri·a *n.* a state of mental depression often accompanying hypochondriasis

hy·po·chon·dri·a·sis *n.* excessive preoccupation with real or fancied ailments

hy·poc·ri·sy *pl.* **hy·poc·ri·sies** *n.* pretense of virtue, benevolence or religious devotion

hy·po·crite n. someone guilty of hypocrisy

hy·po·der·ma n. a layer of supporting tissue just under the epidermis **hy·po·dér·mal** adj. being beneath the epidermis **hy·po·dér·mic 1.** adj. of the area just beneath the skin **2.** n. a hypodermic syringe ‖ a hypodermic injection **hy·po·dér·mi·cal·ly** adv.

hy·po·der·mis n. the hypoderma

hy·pos·ta·sis pl. **hy·pos·ta·ses** n. (philos.) the substantial essence of things as distinguished from their attributes

hy·pos·ta·tize **hy·pos·ta·tiz·ing** **hy·pos·ta·tized** v.t. to attribute personality or substantial essence to

hy·pot·e·nuse n. the side opposite the right angle of a right-angled triangle

hy·poth·e·sis pl. **hy·poth·e·ses** n. an idea formed and used to provide the foundation or primary assumption of an argument **hy·poth·e·size** **hy·poth·e·siz·ing** **hy·poth·e·sized** v.t. to assume

hy·po·thet·ic adj. involving a hypothesis ‖ of or based on a hypothesis **hy·po·thét·i·cal** adj.

hys·ter·ec·to·my pl. **hys·ter·ec·to·mies** n. surgical removal of the womb

hys·ter·i·a n. a condition characterized by excessive excitability and anxiety

hys·ter·ic 1. adj. of or characterized by hysteria **2.** n. a hysterical person **hys·tér·i·cal** adj.

I

I, i the ninth letter of the English alphabet

I pron. 1st person sing., nominative case oneself

i·bex pl. **i·bex·es, i·bex** n. wild mountain goats

i·bi·dem in the same already specified book, chapter etc.

i·bis pl. **i·bis·es, i·bis** n. wading birds allied to the storks

ice 1. n. water solidified by freezing ‖ the frozen surface of water ‖ a dessert of frozen **2.** v. **ic·ing iced** v.t. to cover with ice ‖ to cover with icing

ice·berg n. a large, floating mass of ice

ice cream a frozen dessert made of cream, eggs and sugar, and flavored with syrups, fresh fruit etc.

i·ci·cle n. a hanging, tapering piece of ice

ic·ing n. sweet coating for cakes etc., esp. frosting

i·con, i·kon n. a painting, mosaic or enamel of Christ, the Virgin Mary or a saint

i·con·o·clasm n. the practice or beliefs of an iconoclast

i·con·o·clast n. a person who destroys religious images ‖ a person who seeks to destroy the established order **i·con·o·clás·tic** adj. **i·con·o·clás·ti·cal·ly** adv.

i·cy i·ci·er i·ci·est adj. covered with ice ‖ very cold in manner

i·de·a n. a mental image, conception ‖ an opinion ‖ hunch ‖ appraisal, estimate

i·de·al 1. n. a model of perfection or beauty **2.** adj. desirable ‖ existing only in thought

i·de·al·ism n. the attitude which consists in conceiving ideals and trying to realize them

i·de·al·ist n. a person who accepts and adheres to the concepts of idealism **i·de·al·is·tic** adj. **i·de·al·is·ti·cal·ly** adv.

i·de·al·i·za·tion n. an idealizing ‖ something idealized

i·de·al·ize i·de·al·iz·ing i·de·al·ized v.t. to attribute ideal perfection to ‖ to show something in its ideal form

i·de·al·ly adv. perfectly ‖ theoretically

i·den·ti·cal adj. the same in all respects ‖

designating twins produced from one zygote ‖ the very same

i·den·ti·fi·ca·tion *n.* an identifying or being identified

i·den·ti·fy i·den·ti·fy·ing i·den·ti·fied *v.t.* to recognize the identity of ‖ to establish or demonstrate the identity of ‖ to consider as being the same ‖ *v.i.* to think of oneself as being one with another person or thing

i·den·ti·ty *pl.* **i·den·ti·ties** *n.* the fact of being the same in all respects ‖ who a person is, or what a thing is

i·de·ol·o·gy *pl.* **i·de·ol·o·gies** *n.* the science of ideas, esp. those springing from sensory stimulation

ides *pl. n.* (in the ancient Roman calendar) the 15th day of March, May, July and October and the 13th day of all other months

id·i·om *n.* the language peculiar to a people ‖ the structure of the usual patterns of expression of a language ‖ a writer's characteristic use of words

id·i·o·mat·ic *adj.* peculiar to the patterns of expression of a particular language **id·i·o·mát·i·cal·ly** *adv.*

id·i·o·syn·cra·sy *pl.* **id·i·o·syn·cra·sies** *n.* a personal peculiarity **id·i·o·syn·crat·ic** *adj.* **id·i·o·syn·crát·i·cal·ly** *adv.*

id·i·ot *n.* a person afflicted by idiocy, having a mental age of two years or less ‖ a dolt **id·i·ot·ic** *adj.*

id·i·ot·i·cal·ly *adv.* in an idiotic manner

i·dle 1. *adj.* not working **2. i·dling i·dled** *v.i.* to waste time ‖ (of an engine) to consume fuel without being connected with moving parts **íd·ler** *n.* someone who is idle

i·dly *adv.* in an idle manner

i·dol *n.* an image of a god constructed of wood, stone etc. and worshipped as if it were the god it represents ‖ a person of intense admiration or love

i·dol·a·ter *n.* someone who worships idols **i·dól·a·tress** *n.* a female idolater

i·dol·a·trous *adj.* practicing idolatry

i·dol·a·try *n.* the worship of an idol or of idols

i·dol·ize i·dol·iz·ing i·dol·ized *v.t.* to treat as an idol, esp. to love with inordinate affection

if *conj.* in case, in the event that ‖ on the assumption that ‖ granting that ‖ on condition that ‖ although ‖ whether

ig·loo, ig·lu *n.* an Eskimo dwelling

ig·nite ig·nit·ing ig·nit·ed *v.t.* to set on fire ‖ *v.i.* to begin to burn

ig·ni·tion *n.* the method or process of igniting a fuel mixture, e.g. in an internal-combustion engine

ig·no·ble *adj.* unworthy or degraded in character

ig·no·min·i·ous *adj.* disgraceful ‖ humiliating

ig·no·min·y *n.* public disgrace

ig·no·ra·mus *n.* someone who has little knowledge

ig·no·rance *n.* the state of not knowing ‖ a lack of education

ig·no·rant *adj.* not knowing ‖ lacking education

ig·nore ig·nor·ing ig·nored *v.t.* refuse to consider

i·gua·na *n.* a family of edible, herbivorous, usually arboreal, tropical American lizards

ilk *n.* (esp. in the phrase) **of that ilk** of that sort

ill 1. *adj.* **worse worst** in bad health, not well, sick **ill at ease** uneasy **2.** *n.* anything causing evil, harm, pain, trouble etc. **3.** *adv.* **worse worst** adversely, badly

ill ad·vised *adj.* not judicious

il·le·gal *adj.* violating the law **il·le·gál·i·ty** *pl.* **il·le·gal·i·ties** *n.* an illegal act

il·leg·i·bil·i·ty *n.* the quality of being illegible

il·leg·i·ble *adj.* not legible **il·lég·i·bly** *adv.*

il·le·git·i·ma·cy *n.* the state or quality of being illegitimate

il·le·git·i·mate *adj.* born out of wedlock ‖ contrary to law

il·lic·it *adj.* not permitted by law

il·lit·er·a·cy *n.* the quality or state of being illiterate

il·lit·er·ate 1. *adj.* unable to read or write ‖ having little or no knowledge of a specified subject **2.** *n.* a person who is illiterate

ill·ness *n.* the state of being ill (in health) ‖ a

particular disease

il·log·i·cal adj. contrary to the laws of logic

il·lu·mi·nate **il·lu·mi·nat·ing** **il·lu·mi·nat·ed** v.t. to give light to ‖ to decorate with bright or colored lamps ‖ to decorate (a manuscript) by means of colored initials etc. ‖ to enlighten (someone)

il·lu·mi·na·tion n. the act of illuminating ‖ the decoration of streets or buildings by bright or colored lights ‖ the decoration of a manuscript

il·lu·sion n. a delusion ‖ a false interpretation by the mind of a sense perception **il·lú·sion·ar·y** adj. **il·lú·sion·ist** n. a conjurer

il·lu·so·ry adj. illusive

il·lus·trate **il·lus·trat·ing** **il·lus·trat·ed** v.t. to ornament (a book, periodical etc.) with pictures or designs ‖ to make clear by means of examples ‖ v.i. to make something clear with pictures, designs or examples **il·lus·tra·tive** adj. **il·lus·tra·tor** n.

il·lus·tra·tion n. the act of illustrating ‖ a picture, ornament etc. used to illustrate a book or paper

il·lus·tri·ous held in or conferring the highest public esteem

im·age 1. n. a carved, painted or drawn effigy of a person or thing ‖ a mental picture or concept **2.** v.t. **im·ag·ing** **im·aged** to form an image of

im·ag·i·na·ble adj. capable of being conceived by the imagination

im·ag·i·nar·y adj. existing only in the imagination

im·ag·i·na·tion n. the power to form mental images of objects not perceived or not wholly perceived by the senses ‖ the power to form new ideas by a synthesis of separate elements of experience ‖ intuitive understanding

im·ag·i·na·tive adj. having intuitive understanding

im·ag·ine **im·ag·in·ing** **im·ag·ined** v.i. to use the imagination viably ‖ v.t. to picture in the imagination ‖ to conceive of

im·bal·ance n. lack of balance

im·be·cile 1. n. a mentally deficient person

‖ a dolt **2.** adj. of or relating to an imbecile ‖ stupid

im·be·cil·i·ty n. mental deficiency

im·bibe **im·bib·ing** **im·bibed** v.t. to take in (liquid, moisture etc.)

im·bro·glio n. a very involved, confused situation

im·bue **im·bu·ing** **im·bued** v.t. to fill, esp. with moisture or color ‖ to fill, e.g. with an emotion

im·i·tate **im·i·tat·ing** **im·i·tat·ed** v.t. to mimic, ape

im·i·ta·tion 1. n. the act of imitating ‖ a copy produced by imitating **2.** adj. made so as to be mistakable for what is genuine

im·mac·u·late adj. impeccably clean ‖ having no fault

im·ma·nent adj. inherent, intrinsic

im·ma·te·ri·al adj. having no importance or relevance **im·ma·te·ri·ál·i·ty** n.

im·ma·ture adj. not mature **im·ma·tú·ri·ty** n.

im·meas·ur·a·ble adj. incapable of being measured **im·méas·ur·a·bly** adv.

im·me·di·a·cy n. the state or quality of being immediate

im·me·di·ate adj. without interval, instant ‖ direct

im·me·di·ate·ly 1. adv. at once ‖ directly ‖ closely **2.** conj. as soon as, directly

in·me·mo·ri·al adj. so old as to have its origin beyond the recall of memory

im·mense adj. tremendously large

im·men·si·ty pl. **im·men·si·ties** n. the state or quality of being immense ‖ something immense

im·merse **im·mers·ing** **im·mersed** v.t. to put in below the surface level of a liquid or gas

im·mer·sion n. an immersing or being immersed

im·mi·grant n. someone who immigrates

im·mi·grate **im·mi·grat·ing** **im·mi·grat·ed** v.i. to enter a country of which one is not a native, in order to live in it permanently **im·mi·grá·tion** n.

im·mi·nent adj. about to happen

im·mo·bile adj. not in motion ‖ immovable

im·mo·bil·i·ty n. the quality or state of being immobile

im·mod·er·ate *adj.* going beyond the proper limits

im·mo·dest *adj.* violating conventional standards of decency ‖ lacking humility

im·mor·al *adj.* violating accepted standards of moral (esp. sexual) behavior

im·mo·ral·i·ty *pl.* **im·mo·ral·i·ties** *n.* the aquality or state of being immoral ‖ an immoral act

im·mor·tal *adj.* everlasting ‖ never to be forgotten

im·mor·tal·i·ty *n.* the quality or state of being immortal

im·mov·a·ble *adj.* not subject to being moved ‖ unyielding in attitude, purpose etc.

im·mune *adj.* having immunity ‖ protected or safe from a danger etc.

im·mu·ni·ty *pl.* **im·mu·ni·ties** *n.* the state of being temporarily or permanently able to resist an infection ‖ exemption from a tax, duty or jurisdiction ‖ freedom from danger of penalty

im·mu·nize im·mu·niz·ing im·mu·nized *v.t.* to render immune

im·mu·ta·ble *adj.* incapable of being changed **im·mu·ta·bly** *adv.*

imp *n.* a mischievous sprite

im·pact 1. *n.* a clash or collision ‖ the impression made by a person, thing or idea **2.** *v.t.* to press together **im·pact·ed** *adj.*

im·pair *v.t.* to lessen in quality or strength, damage **im·pair·ment** *n.*

im·part *v.t.* to give a share of (something) ‖ to make known, communicate

im·par·tial *adj.* without prejudgment ‖ not favoring one side more than the other **im·par·ti·al·i·ty** *n.*

im·pas·sioned *adj.* full of passionate emotion

im·pas·sive *adj.* not feeling pain, sensation or emotion **im·pas·siv·i·ty** *n.*

im·pa·tience *n.* the state or quality of being impatient

im·pa·tient *adj.* eagerly desiring and restive at delay

im·peach *v.t.* to charge with a crime, esp. to accuse (a state official) of treason or corruption before a special tribunal

im·peach·a·ble *adj.* **im·peach·ment** *n.*

im·pec·ca·ble *adj.* without fault or flaw **im·péc·ca·bly** *adv.*

im·pede im·ped·ing im·ped·ed *v.t.* to hamper, obstruct or hold back

im·ped·i·ment *n.* something which impedes

im·pel im·pel·ling im·pelled *v.t.* to drive forward ‖ to urge

im·pend *v.i.* to be on the verge of happening

im·per·a·tive 1. *adj.* which must at all costs be obeyed ‖ necessary ‖ of the mood that expresses command **2.** *n.* an order ‖ the imperative mood

im·per·fect 1. *adj.* not perfect ‖ not complete ‖ expressing continuous but unfinished action or state **2.** *n.* the imperfect tense ‖ a verb form in this tense

im·per·fec·tion *n.* a defect

im·pe·ri·al *adj.* pertaining to an emperor or an empire ‖ majestic

im·per·il im·per·il·ing im·per·iled *v.t.* to expose to danger

im·pe·ri·ous *adj.* overbearing ‖ imperative

im·per·ish·a·bil·i·ty *n.* the quality or state of being imperishable

im·per·ish·a·ble *adj.* of that which will not perish, decay or be destroyed **im·pér·ish·a·bly** *adv.*

im·per·ma·nence *n.* the quality or state of being impermanent **im·pér·ma·nen·cy** *n.*

im·per·ma·nent *adj.* not permanent

im·per·me·a·ble *adj.* not permeable **im·pér·me·a·bly** *adv.*

im·per·son·al *adj.* without personal content, reference or quality

im·per·son·ate im·per·son·at·ing im·per·son·at·ed *v.t.* to pretend to be (someone else) ‖ to imitate or mimic in order to entertain **im·per·son·á·tion** *n.* **im·pér·son·a·tor** *n.*

im·per·ti·nence *n.* the quality or state of being impertinent **im·pér·ti·nen·cy** *pl.* **im·per·ti·nen·cies** *n.*

im·per·ti·nent *adj.* showing an offensive lack of respect

im·per·vi·ous *adj.* impenetrable ‖ not open

im·pe·ti·go *n.* a contagious pustular skin disease

im·pet·u·ous *adj.* showing or acting with

impulsiveness ‖ rushing violently

im·pe·tus *n.* the force which causes a given motion or activity ‖ a stimulus resulting in increased activity ‖ incentive, driving force

im·pinge im·ping·ing im·pinged *v.i.* to come into sharp contact ‖ to make an impression ‖ to encroach

im·pi·ous *adj.* lacking piety ‖ wicked

imp·ish *adj.* mischievous

im·plac·a·ble *adj.* deaf to all appeals ‖ inexorable **im·plác·a·bly** *adv.*

im·plant 1. *v.t.* to plant deeply or firmly ‖ to insert beneath the skin ‖ to instill firmly in the mind **2.** *n.* the tissue, drug etc. used in implanting

im·plan·ta·tion *n.* an implanting or being implanted

im·plau·si·ble *adj.* lacking the appearance of truth **im·pláu·si·bly** *adv.*

im·ple·ment 1. *n.* a tool **2.** *v.t.* to carry into effect **im·ple·men·tal** *adj.* helpful **im·ple·men·tá·tion** *n.*

im·pli·cate im·pli·cat·ing im·pli·cat·ed *v.t.* to involve, often in an unpleasant, incriminating manner

im·pli·ca·tion *n.* an implying or being implied

im·plic·it *adj.* understood though not stated ‖ unquestioning, absolute

im·plied *adj.* suggested without being stated, involved without being specified

im·plode im·plod·ing im·plod·ed *v.i.* to burst inward

im·plore im·plor·ing im·plored *v.t.* to beseech with great intensity of feeling ‖ to beg for

im·plo·sion *n.* a bursting inwards **im·plo·sive** *adj.*

im·ply im·ply·ing im·plied *v.t.* to suggest

im·po·lite *adj.* having or showing bad manners

im·pol·i·tic *adj.* lacking in tact or prudence

im·pon·der·a·bil·i·ty *n.* the state or quality of being imponderable

im·pon·der·a·ble 1. *adj.* having an importance impossible to estimate **2.** *n.* a factor in a situation whose importance is unknowable

im·port 1. *v.t.* to bring in (goods) from abroad ‖ to mean, imply **2.** *n.* something imported ‖ meaning

im·por·tance *n.* the quality of being important

im·por·tant *adj.* having great influence or significance

im·por·tune im·por·tun·ing im·por·tuned *v.t.* to vex (someone) by demanding too often or too vehemently or unreasonably

im·pose im·pos·ing im·posed *v.t.* to place (a tax, fine etc.) as a burden ‖ to use superior strength or authority to secure submission to (one's will etc.) ‖ *v.i.* (with 'on') to take unfair advantage ‖ (with 'on') to use deception **im·pós·ing** *adj.* impressive

im·po·si·tion *n.* the taking of an unfair advantage

im·pos·si·ble *adj.* incapable of occurring **im·pós·si·bly** *adv.*

im·pos·tor, im·pos·ter *n.* a person pretending to be someone he is not

im·po·tence *n.* state of being impotent **ím·po·ten·cy** *n.*

im·po·tent *adj.* having no power or force ‖ unable to perform the sexual act

im·pound *v.t.* to take into temporary protective legal custody ‖ to confine (stray animals) in a pound

im·pov·er·ish *v.t.* to make poor ‖ to exhaust the strength or productivity of **im·póv·er·ish·ment** *n.*

im·prac·ti·ca·ble *adj.* (of an idea or plan) not feasible ‖ not usable **im·prác·ti·ca·bly** *adv.*

im·prac·ti·cal *adj.* not practical

im·pre·cate im·pre·cat·ing im·pre·cat·ed *v.t.* to invoke (evil) ‖ to curse

im·pre·ca·tion *n.* cursing ‖ a curse

im·pre·cise *adj.* not precise, vague

im·preg·na·ble *adj.* capable of being impregnated

im·preg·nate *v.t.* **im·preg·nat·ing im·preg·nat·ed** to make pregnant ‖ saturate ‖ to imbue **im·preg·ná·tion** *n.*

im·pre·sa·ri·o *n.* someone who promotes, manages or organizes concerts

im·pre·scrip·ti·ble *adj.* of that which cannot be taken away **im·pre·scrip·ti·bly**

adv.

im·press 1. *v.t.* to make a mark on using pressure ‖ to have an effect on ‖ *v.i.* to arouse admiration **2.** *n.* an imprint ‖ an effect on the mind, character etc.

im·pres·sion *n.* an impressing or being impressed ‖ a mark made by impressing ‖ an effect produced on the feelings or senses ‖ a vague notion or belief

im·pri·ma·tur *n.* official license to print or publish ‖ any sanction, approval

im·print *n.* a mark or design produced by pressure

im·pris·on *v.t.* to confine in a prison

im·prob·a·ble *adj.* not probable ‖ hard to believe **im·prób·a·bly** *adv.*

im·promp·tu 1. *adj.* without preparation

im·prop·er *adj.* offending against accepted standards

im·pro·pri·e·ty *pl.* **im·pro·pri·e·ties** *n.* an improper action ‖ an improper use of language

im·prove im·prov·ing im·proved *v.t.* to make better ‖ *v.i.* to become better

im·prove·ment *n.* an improving or being improved ‖ an instance of this

im·prov·i·dent *adj.* not provident

im·prov·i·sa·tion *n.* something improvised

im·prov·i·sa·tor *n.* someone who improvises

im·pro·vise im·pro·vis·ing im·pro·vised *v.t.* to perform or say extemporaneously ‖ to select, make or provide (a substitute for something not available)

im·pru·dent *adj.* lacking or showing a lack of prudence

im·pu·dence *n.* the quality of being impudent ‖ impudent behavior

im·pu·dent *adj.* bold and shameless

im·pugn *v.t.* to challenge the integrity, veracity etc. of

im·pulse *n.* motion produced by a suddenly applied force ‖ a sudden desire to do something

im·pu·ni·ty *n.* exemption from punishment

im·pure *adj.* not pure ‖ not chaste ‖ lewd ‖ of mixed style

im·pu·ri·ty *pl.* **im·pu·ri·ties** *n.* the quality or state of being impure

im·pute im·put·ing im·put·ed *v.t.* to attribute

in- *prefix* in, into, on, upon, towards, against

in- *prefix* not, non-, un-

in 1. *prep.* contained by, placed physically so as to be surrounded by ‖ into ‖ within ‖ having as a condition or state ‖ with regard to ‖ under the influence of ‖ working for or as part of ‖ at **in that** because **2.** *adv.* from the outside to the inside ‖ so as to agree **3.** *adj.* at home ‖ currently popular among important people

in. inch

in·a·bil·i·ty *n.* the state or quality of being unable

in ab·sen·tia being tried or sentenced, or of someone being given an award in his or her absence

in·ac·ces·si·ble *adj.* which cannot be reached

in·ac·cu·ra·cy *pl.* **in·ac·cu·ra·cies** *n.* the quality of being inaccurate ‖ an instance of this

in·ac·cu·rate *adj.* making or containing errors

in·ac·tive *adj.* not active ‖ making no effort

in·ad·e·quate *adj.* not enough ‖ not capable

in·ad·mis·si·ble *adj.* not admissible **in·ad·mís·si·bly** *adv.*

in·ad·vert·ent *adj.* not intended, accidental

in·ad·vis·a·ble *adj.* not advisable, not prudent

in·a·lien·a·ble *adj.* of that which cannot be given or taken away **in·ál·ien·a·bly** *adv.*

in·ane *adj.* having no meaning or sense

in·an·i·mate *adj.* showing no sign of having life ‖ lacking liveliness

in·ap·pre·ci·a·ble *adj.* too small or unimportant to be taken into account **in·ap·pré·ci·a·bly** *adv.*

in·ap·pro·pri·ate *adj.* not appropriate

in·ar·tic·u·late *adj.* unable to speak intelligibly

in·as·much *adv.* insofar as ‖ since, because

in·au·gu·rate in·au·gu·rat·ing in·au·gu·rat·ed *v.t.* to install in office with ceremony

in·au·gu·ra·tion *n.* an inaugurating or being inaugurated ‖ a formal beginning

in·aus·pi·cious *adj.* unfavorable

in·born *adj.* inherent

in·cal·cu·la·ble *adj.* not able to be reckoned ‖ unpredictable **in·cál·cu·la·bly** *adv.*

in·can·desce in·can·desc·ing in·can·desced *v.i.* to be or become incandescent

in·can·des·cence *n.* the quality or state of being incandescent

in·can·des·cent *adj.* (of bodies heated to a high temperature) emitting a white or bright red alight

in·ca·pa·bil·i·ty *n.* the quality or state of being incapable

in·ca·pa·ble *adj.* not capable ‖ incompetent **in·cá·pa·bly** *adv.*

in·ca·pac·i·tate in·ca·pac·i·tat·ing in·ca·pac·i·tat·ed *v.t.* to make incapable **in·ca·pac·i·tá·tion** *n.*

in·car·cer·ate in·car·cer·at·ing in·car·cer·at·ed *v.t.* to imprison **in·car·cer·á·tion** *n.*

in·car·nate 1. *adj.* embodied **2. in·car·nat·ing in·car·nat·ed** *v.t.* to embody, esp. in human form ‖ to be the embodiment of

in·car·na·tion *n.* an embodiment

in·cen·di·ar·y 1. *adj.* pertaining to the malicious burning of property ‖ causing fires to start ‖ arousing or tending to arouse rebellion, conflict etc.

in·cense 1. *n.* a mixture of gums, spices etc. which when burned emit perfumed vapor **2. in·cens·ing in·censed** *v.t.* to make fragrant with incense

in·cense in·cens·ing in·censed *v.t.* to make angry

in·cen·tive *n.* something that serves as a stimulus to action by appealing to self-interest

in·cep·tion *n.* a beginning, originating

in·ces·sant *adj.* never ceasing ‖ continuous

in·cest *n.* sexual intercourse between persons so closely related that marriage is forbidden by law

in·ces·tu·ous *adj.* of or having the nature of incest

inch 1. *n.* a unit of length equal to the twelfth part of a foot **2.** *v.t.* and *i.* to move very gradually

in·cho·ate *adj.* in its first stage of develop-

ment, just begun

in·ci·dence *n.* the rate or extent to which something occurs

in·ci·dent 1. *n.* an episode ‖ a limited occurrence of trouble **2.** *adj.* of that which falls upon a surface etc.

in·ci·den·tal *adj.* occurring by chance ‖ of secondary importance ‖ arising out of something else **in·ci·dén·tal·ly** *adv.* used to introduce a remark made parenthetically

in·cin·er·ate in·cin·er·at·ing in·cin·er·at·ed *v.t.* and *i.* to burn to ashes **in·cin·er·á·tion** *n.* **in·cín·er·a·tor** *n.* a device constructed for burning refuse etc. in

in·cip·i·ent *adj.* beginning, at an early stage

in·ci·sion *n.* a cut ‖ the quality of being incisive

in·ci·sive *adj.* keen and penetrating

in·ci·sor *n.* a tooth adapted for cutting

in·cite in·cit·ing in·cit·ed *v.t.* to stir (someone) to action ‖ to cause by encouraging **in·cite·ment** *n.*

in·cle·ment *adj.* severe, rough, stormy

in·cli·na·tion *n.* liking ‖ a physical tendency ‖ an incline ‖ dip

in·cline 1. *v.* **in·clin·ing in·clined** *v.i.* to deviate from the vertical or horizontal, to slant or slope ‖ to tend **2.** *n.* an inclined plane, a slope **in·clined** *adj.* mentally disposed ‖ at an angle, sloping, slanting

inclined plane a plane surface at an oblique angle to the plane of the horizon

in·clude in·clud·ing in·clud·ed *v.t.* to contain as part of a whole **in·clúd·ed** *adj.* comprised or contained

in·clu·sion *n.* an including or being included

in·clu·sive *adj.* including everything, comprehensive

in·cog·ni·to 1. *adj.* being under an assumed name or character

in·co·her·ent *adj.* not in any logical order, disjointed and unintelligible

in·come *n.* whatever is received as gain

in·com·pa·ra·ble *adj.* of a thing or quality so superior that no other can be compared with it **in·cóm·pa·ra·bly** *adv.*

in·com·pat·i·bil·i·ty *n.* the state or

quality of being incompatible

in·com·pat·i·ble 1. *adj.* not compatible

in·com·pe·tence *n.* the state or quality of being incompetent

in·com·pe·tent 1. *adj.* not competent

in·com·plete *adj.* not complete

in·com·pre·hen·si·ble *adj.* that which cannot be understood **in·com·pre·hén·si·bly** *adv.*

in·con·ceiv·a·ble *adj.* not imaginable ‖ not believable **in·con·céiv·a·bly** *adv.*

in·con·clu·sive *adj.* failing to lead to or result in a conclusion

in·con·gru·ous *adj.* not in harmony or agreement

in·con·se·quence *n.* lack of logical sequence or of relevance

in·con·se·quent *adj.* not derived logically from a premise, illogical ‖ irrelevant ‖ unimportant

in·con·se·quen·tial *adj.* of no importance ‖ irrelevant

in·con·sid·er·ate *adj.* lacking, or showing a lack of, regard for the feelings or well-being of someone else

in·con·sist·ent *adj.* in contradiction, not in harmony

in·con·spic·u·ous *adj.* not attracting attention

in·con·ti·nent *adj.* lacking self-restraint ‖ unable to control the evacuation of the bladder or bowels

In·con·ven·ience 1. *n.* something which causes difficulty or annoyance 2. *v.t.* **in·con·ven·ienc·ing in·con·ven·ienced** to cause to suffer inconvenience

in·con·ven·ient *adj.* not convenient

in·cor·po·rate 1. **in·cor·po·rat·ing in·cor·po·rat·ed** *v.t.* to unite into a whole ‖ *v.i.* to form a legal corporation 2. *adj.* formed or united in a whole ‖ formed into a corporation

in·cor·po·ra·tion *n.* an incorporating or being incorporated

in·cor·rect *adj.* not true, in error ‖ improper

in·cor·ri·gi·ble *adj.* bad beyond hope of reform **in·cór·ri·gi·bly** *adv.*

in·crease 1. *v.* **in·creas·ing in·creased** *v.i.* to become greater in size, amount, number, value, degree etc. **in·créas·ing·ly**

adv. to a continually increasing degree

in·cred·i·bil·i·ty *n.* the quality or state of being incredible

in·cred·i·ble *adj.* impossible to believe **in·créd·i·bly** *adv.*

in·cre·du·li·ty *n.* the quality or state of being incredulous

in·cred·u·lous *adj.* not believing, skeptical

in·cre·ment *n.* an increase or growth ‖ the amount by which something increases **in·cre·men·tal** *adj.*

in·crim·i·nate in·crim·i·nat·ing in·crim·i·nat·ed *v.t.* to involve in a charge of crime **in·crim·i·na·to·ry** *adj.*

in·cu·ba·tor *n.* an apparatus for keeping eggs warm until they hatch ‖ an apparatus for surrounding premature babies with a controlled environment

in·cul·cate in·cul·cat·ing in·cul·cat·ed *v.t.* to teach by constant repetition **in·cul·cá·tion** *n.* **in·cúl·ca·tor** *n.*

in·cum·bent *adj.* resting as an obligation or duty ‖ lying or pressing (upon something)

incumbent *n.* the holder of any office

in·cur in·cur·ring in·curred *v.t.* bring upon oneself ‖ to meet with (esp. something undesirable)

in·cur·a·ble *adj.* incapable of being cured **in·cúr·a·bly** *adv.*

in·debt·ed *adj.* owing money ‖ owing gratitude

in·de·cen·cy *pl.* **in·de·cen·cies** *n.* the quality or state of being indecent ‖ an instance of this

in·de·cent *adj.* offensive ‖ lacking modesty ‖ indecorous

in·de·ci·sion *n.* the state or quality of being indecisive

in·deed *adv.* admittedly, in fact, certainly 1. an expression denoting surprise, disbelief etc.

in·de·fat·i·ga·ble *adj.* impossible to tire out **in·de·fát·i·ga·bly** *adv.*

in·de·fen·si·ble *adj.* not possible to justify or condone

in·def·i·nite *adj.* not clearly stated, vague ‖ not limited

in·del·i·ble *adj.* not possible to rub out or delete **in·dél·i·bly** *adv.*

in·del·i·cate *adj.* coarse, mildly indecent

in·dem·ni·fy **in·dem·ni·fy·ing** **in·dem·ni·fied** *v.t.* to secure against harm or loss ‖ to compensate for loss or injury

in·dem·ni·ty *pl.* **in·dem·ni·ties** *n.* insurance or protection against loss or injury

in·dent 1. *v.t.* to notch, made jagged ‖ *v.i.* to set written or printed matter in from a margin 2. (indent)*n.* an indentation ‖ an indenture

in·de·pend·ence *n.* the quality or state of being independent

in·de·pend·ent *adj.* free from the authority, control or influence of others, self-governing ‖ self-supporting ‖ not committed to an organized political party 1. *n.* an independent person or thing

in·de·scrib·a·ble *adj.* not possible to describe ‖ surpassing description **in·de·scrib·a·bly** *adv.*

in·de·struct·i·ble *adj.* impossible to destroy **in·de·strúct·i·bly** *adv.*

in·dex 1. *pl.* **in·dex·es** **in·di·ces** *n.* the forefinger ‖ an alphabetical list of names, subjects, titles etc. 2. *v.t.* to make an index for

in·di·cate **in·di·cat·ing** **in·di·cat·ed** *v.t.* to direct attention to ‖ to point out, show

in·di·ca·tion *n.* something that indicates

in·dic·a·tive 1. *adj.* showing, giving an indication 2. *n.* the indicative mood

in·di·ca·tor *n.* something which points out or gives information

in·dict *v.t.* to accuse formally of an offense **in·dict·a·ble** *adj.* liable to be indicted

in·dict·ment *n.* a formal written statement accusing a person of a crime

in·dif·fer·ence *n.* lack of interest or feeling

in·dif·fer·ent *adj.* not interested ‖ having no preference, impartial

in·di·gence *n.* the quality or state of being indigent

in·dig·e·nous *adj.* of or relating to natives ‖ innate, inborn

in·di·gent *adj.* needy, poor

in·di·ges·tion *n.* difficulty in digesting food

in·dig·nant *adj.* angered by unwarranted accusation, injustice, meanness etc.

in·dig·na·tion *n.* anger aroused by injustice, unkindness, unwarranted accusation, meanness etc.

in·dig·ni·ty *pl.* **in·dig·ni·ties** *n.* treatment that makes one feel humiliated ‖ an insult or outrage

in·di·rect *adj.* roundabout ‖ not immediate

in·dis·creet *adj.* lacking or showing a lack of prudence, good judgment or tact

in·dis·cre·tion *n.* lack of prudence, tact etc.

in·dis·crim·i·nate *adj.* making no distinctions, random

in·dis·pen·sa·ble *adj.* absolutely necessary, impossible to do without **in·dis·pén·sa·bly** *adv.*

in·dis·pose **in·dis·pos·ing** **in·dis·posed** *v.t.* to upset somewhat the state of mind or health of **in·dis·pósed** *adj.* slightly unwell ‖ unwilling, averse

in·dis·po·si·tion *n.* a slight illness ‖ a disinclination

in·dis·tinct *adj.* confused, vague

in·dis·tinc·tive *adj.* having nothing to distinguish it from others

in·di·vid·u·al 1. *adj.* of, relating to, used by or intended for only one person or thing ‖ distinctive 2. *n.* one person

in·di·vid·u·al·i·ty *n.* the quality or characteristics that make one person or thing different from others

in·di·vis·i·ble *adj.* impossible to divide into parts

in·doc·tri·nate **in·doc·tri·nat·ing** **in·doc·tri·nat·ed** *v.t.* to instill certain ideas or beliefs into **in·doc·tri·ná·tion** *n.*

in·do·lence *n.* the state or quality of being indolent

in·do·lent *adj.* disliking exertion, lazy

in·dom·i·ta·ble *adj.* unconquerable, not to be subdued **in·dóm·i·ta·bly** *adv.*

In·du·bi·ta·ble *adj.* unquestionable **in·dú·bi·ta·bly** *adv.*

in·duce **in·duc·ing** **in·duced** *v.t.* to persuade ‖ cause ‖ to infer **in·dúce·ment** *n.* **in·dúc·i·ble** *adj.*

in·duct *v.t.* to install formally in office ‖ to bring into the armed forces **in·duc·tée** *n.*

in·duc·tile *adj.* not ductile **in·duc·til·i·ty** *n.*

in·duc·tive *adj.* based on, or pertaining to, induction

in·dulge **in·dulg·ing** **in·dulged** *v.t.* pamper ‖ humor ‖ to give way to

in·dul·gence *n.* an indulging or being indulged ‖ granted as a favor

in·dul·gent *adj.* having or showing indulgence

in·du·rate in·du·rat·ing in·du·rat·ed *v.t.* and *i.* to harden physically or morally

in·dus·tri·al *adj.* of, connected with or characterized by industry

in·dus·tri·ous *adj.* hardworking

in·dus·try *pl.* **in·dus·tries** *n.* the section of an economy concerned with manufacturing ‖ diligence, application

in·e·bri·ate 1. *v.t.* **in·e·bri·at·ing in·e·bri·at·ed** to intoxicate **2.** *adj.* drunk **3.** *n.* a habitual drunkard **in·é·bri·at·ed** *adj.* **in·e·bri·á·tion** *n.*

in·ef·fa·ble *adj.* incapable of being expressed or adequately described **in·éf·fa·bly** *adv.*

in·ef·fec·tive *adj.* not producing the desired effect ‖ incompetent

in·ef·fec·tu·al *adj.* not effectual

in·el·i·gi·bil·i·ty *n.* the quality or state of being ineligible

in·el·i·gi·ble 1. *adj.* not eligible **2.** *n.* someone not eligible

in·ept *adj.* out of place, not apt ‖ incompetent

in·ept·i·tude *n.* the quality or state of being inept ‖ something inept

in·ert *adj.* incapable of moving, acting, or resisting an opposing force ‖ devoid of mental energy

in·er·tia *n.* the property of matter that causes its velocity to be constant in the absence of external forces ‖ the quality or state of being inert **in·ér·tial** *adj.*

in·es·cap·a·ble *adj.* impossible to escape or avoid

in·es·ti·ma·ble *adj.* too great to be assessed

in·ev·i·ta·ble *adj.* unavoidable ‖ certain to happen **in·év·i·ta·bly** *adv.*

in·ex·o·ra·ble *adj.* impossible to move or influence by entreating **in·éx·o·ra·bly** *adv.*

in·ex·pe·di·en·cy *n.* the quality of being inexpedient

in·ex·pe·di·ent *adj.* not expedient

in·ex·pen·sive *adj.* not expensive

in·ex·pe·ri·ence *n.* lack of skill resulting from experience

in·ex·pert *adj.* lacking or showing a lack of skill

in·ex·pli·ca·ble *adj.* not capable of being explained **in·éx·pli·ca·bly** *adv.*

in·ex·tri·ca·ble *adj.* from which one cannot extricate oneself **in·éx·tri·ca·bly** *adv.*

in·fal·li·bil·i·ty *n.* the quality of being infallible

in·fal·li·ble *adj.* incapable of error ‖ never failing **in·fál·li·bly** *adv.*

in·fa·mous *adj.* of foul reputation ‖ arousing horror

in·fa·my *pl.* **in·fa·mies** *n.* the quality of being infamous ‖ an infamous action ‖ disgrace

in·fan·cy *pl.* **in·fan·cies** *n.* the period of being an infant

in·fant *n.* a very young child

in·fan·tile *adj.* of or pertaining to infants ‖ childish

in·fan·try *pl.* **in·fan·tries** *n.* a branch of an army consisting of soldiers trained to fight on foot

in·fat·u·ate in·fat·u·at·ing in·fat·u·at·ed *v.t.* to inspire with excessive passion **in·fat·u·á·tion** *n.*

in·fect *v.t.* to transfer a disease to ‖ to affect (another) with one's own emotion, belief etc.

in·fec·tion *n.* a disease etc. produced by infecting ‖ something which infects

in·fec·tious *adj.* able to cause infection ‖ caused by infection ‖ easily communicated

in·fer in·fer·ring in·ferred *v.t.* to deduce ‖ to hint, imply **in·fér·a·ble in·fér·i·ble** *adj.*

in·fer·ence *n.* something inferred **in·fer·en·tial** *adj.*

in·fe·ri·or 1. *adj.* of poor quality ‖ of low or lower rank, status etc. **2.** *n.* a person of lower rank **in·fe·ri·or·i·ty** *pl.* **in·fe·ri·or·i·ties** *n.*

inferiority complex a neurotic condition

in·fer·nal *adj.* of hell or the underworld ‖ fiendish

in·fer·tile *adj.* not fertile, barren **in·fer·til·i·ty** *n.*

in·fest *v.t.* to overrun or swarm

in·fes·ta·tion *n.* an infesting or being infested

in·fi·del 1. *n.* someone having no religious faith, an atheist **2.** *adj.* pertaining to an infidel

in·fi·del·i·ty *pl.* **in·fi·del·i·ties** *n.* failure in loyalty ‖ adultery ‖ lack of religious belief

in·fil·trate 1. *v.* **in·fil·trat·ing in·fil·trat·ed** to penetrate ‖ to permeate or pass through a substance, by or as if by filtering **2.** *n.* something that infiltrates **in·fil·tra·tion** *n.*

in·fi·nite 1. *adj.* absolutely without limits, endless **2.** *n.* something infinite

in·fin·i·tes·i·mal *adj.* too small to be measured

in·fin·i·tive 1. *adj.* of an uninflected verb form **2.** *n.* such a verb form

in·fin·i·ty *pl.* **in·fin·i·ties** *n.* the quality of being infinite ‖ an indefinitely large amount or number

in·firm *adj.* physically weak ‖ morally weak

in·fir·ma·ry *pl.* **in·fir·ma·ries** *n.* a place where the sick are cared for in a school or other institution

in·fir·mi·ty *pl.* **in·fir·mi·ties** *n.* the quality or state of being infirm ‖ an instance of this

in·flame in·flam·ing in·flamed *v.t.* to excite passion in, arouse ‖ to redden with or as if with flames ‖ to cause inflammation in

in·flam·ma·bil·i·ty *n.* the state of being inflammable

in·flam·ma·ble *adj.* easily set on fire ‖ easily excited or angered **in·flám·ma·bly** *adv.*

in·flam·ma·tion *n.* the response of body tissue to infection or to many kinds of injury ‖ the state of being inflamed ‖ the stirring up of passion, esp. anger

in·flate in·flat·ing in·flat·ed *v.t.* to cause to swell out with air or gas ‖ to cause to swell with pride, vanity etc. ‖ to raise (prices) artificially **in·flát·ed** *adj.*

in·fla·tion *n.* a general rise in prices ‖ a sharp increase in the amount of paper money put into circulation **in·flá·tion·ar·y** *adj.*

in·flect *v.t.* to treat (word forms) with inflection ‖ to modulate (the voice)

in·flec·tion *n.* a turning or bending ‖ a change in tone or pitch of voice ‖ a change of word forms and endings to indicate change of case, tense etc. **in·fléc·tion·al** *adj.*

in·flex·i·ble *adj.* unchangeable ‖ rigid, unadaptable **in·fléx·i·bly** *adv.*

in·flict *v.t.* to cause or give (wounds, pain etc.) by or as if by striking ‖ to impose (a penalty etc.)

in·flic·tion *n.* the act of inflicting ‖ that which is inflicted

in·flic·tive *adj.* tending to inflict

in·flu·ence 1. *n.* a person's indirect power over men, events or things, e.g. through wisdom, wealth, force of character etc. ‖ such power used to sway authority **2.** *v.t.* **in·flu·enc·ing in·flu·enced** to exert influence on

in·flu·en·tial *adj.* possessing or exerting influencee

in·flu·en·za *n.* an acute, infectious disease

in·flux *n.* a flowing in ‖ the place where a river joins another body of water

in·form *v.t.* to communicate information to ‖ *v.i.* to give information ‖ (with 'against') to denounce someone

in·for·mal *adj.* free of conventional forms or restrictions ‖ relaxed, casual **in·for·mál·i·ty** *pl.* **in·for·mal·i·ties** *n.*

in·form·ant *n.* someone who communicates information

in·for·ma·tion *n.* the communication of news, knowledge etc. ‖ knowledge obtained by search, study etc. **in·for·má·tion·al** *adj.*

in·form·a·tive *adj.* giving information, instructive

in·form·er *n.* someone who informs

infra- *prefix* below

in·fra·red 1. *adj.* relating to infrared radiation **2.** *n.* such radiation

in·fre·quent *adj.* happening rarely

in·fringe in·fring·ing in·fringed *v.t.* violate ‖ *v.i.* to encroach **in·fringe·ment** *n.*

in·fu·ri·ate in·fu·ri·at·ing in·fu·ri·at·ed *v.t.* to fill with fury, enrage

in·fuse in·fus·ing in·fused *v.t.* to inspire ‖ to instill

in·fu·sion *n.* something blended or mixed

in
in·gen·ious *adj.* cleverly invented, contrived

in·gé·nue in·ge·nue *n.* a naive, unsophisticated girl

in·ge·nu·i·ty *n.* cleverness in contriving or inventing

in·gest *v.t.* to take (food) into the digestive system

in·got *n.* a lump of metal, esp. of gold, silver or steel, cast in convenient form

in·grained *adj.* thoroughly imbued ‖ inveterate

in·gra·ti·ate in·gra·ti·at·ing in·gra·ti·at·ed *v.t.* to get (oneself) into the good graces of another

in·grat·i·tude *n.* lack of gratitude ‖ an instance of this

in·gre·di·ent *n.* an element in a mixture, constituent

in·gress *n.* a going in

in·grown *adj.* grown inward ‖ innate

in·hab·it *v.t.* to live in

in·hab·it·a·ble *adj.* fit to be inhabited

in·hab·it·ant *n.* a permanent resident in a place

in·hale in·hal·ing in·haled *v.* to breathe in

in·hál·er *n.* an apparatus which facilitates the inhalation of medicines

in·her·ent *adj.* existing in someone or something as a permanent characteristic or quality

in·her·it *v.t.* to receive by legacy ‖ to receive by heredity ‖ *v.i.* to come into an inheritance

in·her·it·ance *n.* the act of inheriting ‖ something inherited

in·hib·it *v.t.* to hold in check, restrain ‖ to obstruct, hinder

in·hi·bi·tion *n.* an inhibiting or being inhibited

in·hos·pi·ta·ble *adj.* not offering hospitality ‖ not affording sustenance, barren **in·hós·pi·ta·bly** *adv.*

in·hos·pi·tal·i·ty *n.* lack of hospitality

in·hu·man *adj.* machinelike, lacking or showing a lack of human warmth ‖ not belonging to or suggestive of the human race

in·im·i·ta·ble *adj.* too good to be success-

fully imitated **in·ím·i·ta·bly** *adv.*

in·iq·ui·ty *pl.* **in·iq·ui·ties** *n.* great wickedness or injustice

in·i·tial 1. *adj.* of or occurring at the very beginning **2.** *n.* (esp. *pl.*) the first letter of a personal name ‖ a large decorative letter **3.** *v.t.* **in·i·tial·ing in·i·tialed** to sign or mark with an initial or initials

in·i·ti·ate *v.t.* **in·i·ti·at·ing in·i·ti·at·ed** to instruct in the fundamentals of a subject ‖ to introduce ceremonially into a society etc.

in·i·ti·a·tion *n.* an initiating or being initiated ‖ the rite of introduction into a society etc.

in·i·ti·a·tive *n.* personal capacity for thinking up and initiating action

in·i·ti·a·tor *n.* a person who or thing that initiates

in·ject *v.t.* to force (a fluid) into a body esp. by means of a hypodermic syringe ‖ to introduce (a new or different quality) into

in·jec·tion *n.* the act of injecting ‖ a substance that is injected

in·ju·di·cious *adj.* lacking good judgment

in·junc·tion *n.* an authoritative command

in·jure in·jur·ing in·jured *v.t.* to inflict physical hurt upon ‖ to cause intangible detriment or hurt to

in·ju·ri·ous *adj.* causing or likely to cause injury ‖ (of language) offensive, insulting

in·ju·ry *pl.* **in·ju·ries** *n.* physical impairment ‖ unjust treatment ‖ an instance of physical or moral hurt ‖ an actionable wrong

in·jus·tice *n.* violation of justice, unfairness

ink 1. *n.* a colored fluid used for writing or printing **2.** *v.t.* to cover or mark with ink

ink·ling *n.* the slightest notion ‖ a faint suggestion

in·land 1. *n.* the interior of a country **2.** *adj.* away from the coast **3.** *adv.* in or toward the interior

in-law *n.* a relative by marriage

in·lay 1. *v.t.* **in·lay·ing in·laid** to set (a material or pattern) into another material or object **2.** *n.* a design made by inlaying

in·let *n.* a narrow arm of the sea or of a river ‖ a passage between islands into a lagoon

|| entrance

in·mate *n.* a person living in an institution

inn *n.* a hotel || a tavern

in·nards *pl. n.* viscera, entrails

in·nate *adj.* belonging to a person's nature || inherent in a thing

in·ner *adj.* located within || not obvious, hidden

in·ner·vate in·ner·vat·ing in·ner·vat·ed *v.t.* to stimulate to activity **in·ner·va·tion** *n.*

in·no·cence *n.* the quality or state of being innocent

in·no·cent *adj.* free from guilt || knowing nothing of evil || naive, simple-minded || benign

in·noc·u·ous *adj.* not actively harmful || calculated to give no offense || lacking in force

in·no·vate in·no·vat·ing in·no·vat·ed *v.i.* to make changes, introduce new practices etc.

in·no·va·tion *n.* something newly introduced

in·no·va·tor *n.* someone who innovates

in·nu·en·do *pl.* **in·nu·en·does** *n.* an oblique referring or insinuating || an instance of such hinting

in·nu·mer·a·ble *adj.* too many to be counted || very many **in·nú·mer·a·bly** *adv.*

in·oc·u·late in·oc·u·lat·ing in·oc·u·lat·ed *v.t.* to introduce a disease into (an organism) to protect against subsequent infection || to introduce particular ideas into (a person's mind) so as to imbue him with them

in·oc·u·la·tion *n.* the act of inoculating

in·oc·u·la·tor *n.* a person who inoculates

in·op·er·a·ble *adj.* not able to be treated by operation

in·op·por·tune *adj.* not opportune

in·or·gan·ic *adj.* (*chem.*) not composed of plant or animal material || artificial **in·or·gán·i·cal·ly** *adv.*

in·pa·tient *n.* a person who is lodged, fed and treated in a hospital

in·put *n.* something put in, esp. power or energy supplied to a machine or storage system || effort put into any project || data fed into a computer

in·quest *n.* a judicial or official inquiry || the jury engaged in such an inquiry || a minute and semi-accusing investigation

in·quire en·quire in·quir·ing en·quir·ing in·quired en·quired *v.t.* to seek (information) by asking || *v.i.* to ask questions || (with 'after') to ask about the health or welfare of

in·quir·y en·quir·y *pl.* **in·quir·ies en·quir·ies** *n.* the act of inquiring || a question || an investigation

in·qui·si·tion *n.* an investigation by close interrogation || a judicial inquiry **in·qui·si·tion·al** *adj.*

in·quis·i·tive *adj.* wanting to ferret out the private concerns of other people || asking a lot of questions

in·quis·i·tor *n.* a cruel, severe questioner

in·road *n.* (usually *pl.*) a heavy encroachment

in·sane *adj.* afflicted with a mental illness || highly reckless or foolish

in·san·i·ty *pl.* **in·san·i·ties** *n.* the state of being insane || a foolish act

in·sa·tia·ble *adj.* incapable of being satisfied || continually craving **in·sá·tia·bly** *adv.*

in·scribe in·scrib·ing in·scribed *v.t.* to write or engrave || to dedicate informally

in·scrip·tion *n.* an inscribed text || an informal dedication, e.g. in a book **in·scríp·tion·al** *adj.*

in·scru·ta·ble *adj.* of such a kind that the meaning or intention cannot be perceived **in·scrú·ta·bly** *adv.*

in·sect *n.* a member of the class *Insecta*, phylum *Arthropoda*, with external skeleton and jointed legs

in·se·cure *adj.* not safe, liable to collapse

in·sen·sate *adj.* lacking moral or emotional perception, insensitive || foolish

in·sen·si·ble *adj.* indifferent || not aware || not feeling **in·sén·si·bly** *adv.*

in·sen·si·tive *adj.* not sensitive

in·sep·a·ra·ble *adj.* incapable of being separated || utterly devoted in friendship **in·sép·a·ra·bly** *adv.*

in·sert 1. *v.t.* to put inside **2.** *n.* an extra page set within a newspaper, magazine or book **in·sért·ed** *adj.*

in·ser·tion *n.* something inserted

in·side 1. *n.* the inner portion or side of something ‖ (*pl.*) the stomach and intestines **2.** *adj.* situated in the inner portion or on the inner surface **3.** *adv.* in or into the inner part of something

in·sid·er *n.* a member of a group, organization etc. who has special information, rights, privileges etc.

in·sid·i·ous *adj.* working or acting maliciously

in·sight *n.* the imaginative power to see into and understand immediately (a person, situation etc.)

in·sig·ni·a *pl. n.* symbols of authority or importance ‖ emblems used as distinguishing marks or signs

in·sig·nif·i·cance *n.* the quality of being insignificant

in·sig·nif·i·cant *adj.* having no importance ‖ meaningless ‖ small

in·sin·cere *adj.* not sincere **in·sin·cer·i·ty** *n.*

in·sin·u·ate in·sin·u·at·ing in·sin·u·at·ed *v.t.* to suggest or hint indirectly, imply slyly, esp. maliciously

in·sin·u·a·tion *n.* the act of insinuating

in·sip·id *adj.* tasteless ‖ uninteresting **in·si·pid·i·ty** *pl.* **in·si·pid·i·ties** *n.*

in·sist *v.t.* to assert emphatically ‖ *v.i.* to repeat a request with persistence ‖ to make a demand authoritatively **in·sist·ence** *n.* **in·sist·en·cy** *n.*

in·sist·ent *adj.* persistent **in·sist·ent·ly** *adv.*

in·so·lence *n.* the quality of being insolent

in·so·lent *adj.* rudely disrespectful

in·sol·u·ble *adj.* not soluble ‖ unable to be solved **in·sol·u·bly** *adv.*

in·sol·vent *adj.* unable to pay one's debts

in·som·ni·a *n.* persistent inability to sleep **in·som·ni·ac** *n.* a person suffering from this inability

in·spect *v.t.* to look closely at, scrutinize

in·spec·tion *n.* the process of inspecting

in·spec·tor *n.* someone appointed to make inspections and report to an authority **in·spec·tor·ate** *n.* the office of an inspector **in·spec·to·ri·al** *adj.*

in·spi·ra·tion *n.* the creative impulse of an artist ‖ a person who inspires ‖ inhaling

in·spi·ra·tion·al *adj.*

in·spire in·spir·ing in·spired *v.t.* to stimulate ‖ to affect ‖ be the motivating power behind

in·spis·sate in·spis·sat·ing in·spis·sat·ed *v.t.* and *i.* to thicken, condense

in·sta·bil·i·ty *pl.* **in·sta·bil·i·ties** *n.* lack of stability

in·stall *v.t.* to place in a position of power or dignity ‖ to set in position for use ‖ to settle

in·stal·la·tion *n.* an apparatus set in position for use ‖ a military establishment

in·stall·ment in·stal·ment *n.* one of the parts of a serial ‖ part of the sum paid at regular intervals

in·stance *n.* an example **for instance** as an illustration **in the first instance** initially, at the first stage

in·stant 1. *adj.* urgent ‖ immediate **2.** *n.* a short space of time

in·stan·ta·ne·ous *adj.* happening in an instant ‖ done immediately

in·stead *adv.* in place of, rather than

in·step *n.* the arching area of the middle of the human foot

in·sti·gate in·sti·gat·ing in·sti·gat·ed *v.t.* to incite

in·sti·ga·tion *n.* an instigating ‖ a stimulus

in·sti·ga·tor *n.* someone who instigates

in·still in·stil in·still·ing in·stil·ling in·stilled *v.t.* to cause to absorb gradually ‖ to put in drop by drop

in·stil·la·tion *n.* the act of instilling ‖ something instilled

in·stinct 1. *n.* a specific, complex pattern of responses by an organism, supposedly inherited, which is quite independent of any thought processes ‖ any drive or impulse **2. in·stinc·tive in·stinc·tual** *adjs*

in·sti·tute *n.* an institution for study or research

institute in·sti·tut·ing in·sti·tut·ed *v.t.* to set up, found

in·sti·tu·tion *n.* an organization whose purpose is to further public welfare, learning etc. ‖ an established law or custom ‖ a person who is a familiar sight in a locality **in·sti·tu·tion·al** *adj.*

in·struct *v.t.* to teach ‖ to order ‖ to advise,

inform

in·struc·tion *n.* the act of instructing ‖ *(pl.)* a direction for procedure **in·strúc·tion·al** *adj.*

in·struc·tive *adj.* serving to instruct

in·struc·tor *n.* someone who instructs, a teacher

in·stru·ment 1. *n.* any object used for making, achieving something, an implement ‖ a means ‖ a device for producing music **2.** *v.t.* to orchestrate (a score)

in·stru·men·tal *adj.* serving as an instrument, helping to bring something about **in·stru·men·tál·i·ty** *n.* agency or means

in·suf·fer·a·ble *adj.* very hard to endure ‖ not to be tolerated **in·súf·fer·a·bly** *adv.*

in·suf·fi·cien·cy *pl.* **in·suf·fi·cien·cies** *n.* the state of being insufficient ‖ failure of an organ to perform its normal function

in·suf·fi·cient *adj.* not sufficient

in·su·late in·su·lat·ing in·su·lat·ed *v.t.* to place in an isolated situation, to segregate **in·su·lá·tion** *n.* **ín·su·la·tor** *n.* a material or device that serves to insulate

in·su·lin *n.* a hormone that maintains the level of sugar in the blood

in·sult *n.* a remark calculated to offend someone

in·sult *v.t.* to abuse in speech or action in such a way as to show contempt

in·sur·ance *n.* the practice by which an individual secures financial compensation for a specified loss or damage

in·sure in·sur·ing in·sured *v.t.* to take out insurance for ‖ to issue an insurance policy for ‖ *v.t.* to take out insurance **in·súr·er** *n.* a person or company issuing an insurance policy

in·sur·gen·cy *n.* the state or quality of being insurgent

in·sur·gent 1. *n.* a rebel against a lawful government or civil authority **2.** *adj.* rebelling

in·sur·rec·tion *n.* organized opposition to authority ‖ a revolt **in·sur·réc·tion·al** *adj.* **in·sur·réc·tion·ar·y** *adj.* of, involving or producing insurrection

in·tact *adj.* left in its complete state, undamaged

in·tan·gi·ble 1. *adj.* not readily defined, vague **2.** *n.* something that is not tangible **in·tán·gi·bly** *adv.*

in·te·ger *n.* a whole number ‖ an entity

in·te·gral 1. *adj.* necessary to complete an entity, essentially part of some whole ‖ whole and complete **2.** *n.* the integral whole **in·te·grál·i·ty** *n.*

in·te·grate in·te·grat·ing in·te·grat·ed *v.t.* to absorb into an existing whole ‖ *v.i.* to become racially integrated

in·te·gra·tion *n.* the giving of full civil or membership rights to those deprived of them on racial grounds **in·te·grá·tion·ist** *n.* someone in favor of integration

in·teg·ri·ty *n.* moral soundness, probity ‖ the quality of being unimpaired

in·teg·u·ment *n.* an outer covering **in·teg·u·men·ta·ry** *adj.*

in·tel·lect *n.* mental power, intelligence

in·tel·lec·tu·al 1. *adj.* relating to, using or performed by the intellect **in·tel·léc·tu·al·ism** *n.*

in·tel·li·gence *n.* the ability to perceive logical relationships and use one's knowledge to solve problems

in·tel·li·gent *adj.* having a high degree of intelligence ‖ capable of reasoning

in·tel·li·gi·ble *adj.* that can be understood **in·tél·li·gi·bly** *adv.*

in·tem·per·ance *n.* lack of moderation

in·tend *v.t.* to have as intention

in·tend·ed *adj.* planned ‖ deliberate

in·tense *adj.* very great, extreme

in·ten·si·fy in·ten·si·fy·ing in·ten·si·fied *v.t.* to render more intense ‖ *v.i.* to become more intense

in·ten·si·ty *pl.* **in·ten·si·ties** *n.* the quality or state of being intense

in·ten·sive *adj.* concentrated

in·tent *adj.* having a firm intention ‖ having one's attention concentrated ‖ searching

in·ten·tion *n.* purpose ‖ meaning, significance

in·ten·tion·al *adj.* done on purpose

in·ter in·ter·ring in·terred *v.t.* to put in the ground

inter- *prefix* between, within ‖ reciprocal

in·ter·act *v.i.* to act upon each other **in·ter·ac·tion** *n.* **in·ter·ác·tive** *adj.*

in·ter·breed in·ter·breed·ing in·ter·bred

v.t. to cross-breed

in·ter·cede in·ter·ced·ing in·ter·ced·ed *v.i.* to intervene on behalf of another

in·ter·cept 1. *v.t.* to seize (something) before it can reach its destination **2. in·ter·cep·tion** *n.* **in·ter·cep·tive** *adj.* **in·ter·cep·tor** *n.* someone who or something that intercepts

in·ter·ces·sion *n.* the act of interceding

in·ter·change *n.* a substitution for one another of two things ‖ mutual exchange ‖ a junction on separate levels of two or more highways

in·ter·change   in·ter·chang·ing in·ter·changed *v.t.* to substitute ‖ to exchange ‖ *v.i.* to change places

in·ter·change·a·ble *adj.* capable of being mutually substituted **in·ter·change·a·bly** *adv.*

in·ter·con·ti·nen·tal *adj.* between or among continents

in·ter·cos·tal *adj.* between the ribs

in·ter·course *n.* reciprocal dealings between individuals or nations ‖ sexual union between two people

in·ter·est 1. *n.* curiosity about something ‖ something on which these feelings are fixed ‖ concern for one's own advantage or profit ‖ a premium paid for the use of capital ‖ the money so paid **2.** *v.t.* to arouse the attention or curiosity of **in·ter·est·ed** *adj.* feeling or showing attention or curiosity ‖ having a share or concern in something **in·ter·est·ing** *adj.*

in·ter·face *n.* a surface forming the common boundary of two bodies or two spaces **in·ter·fa·cial** *adj.*

in·ter·fere in·ter·fer·ing in·ter·fered *v.i.* to conflict in such a way as to hinder something   **in·ter·fer·ence** *n.* **in·ter·fe·ren·tial** *adj.*

in·ter·im 1. *n.* an interval between two actions **in the interim** meanwhile **2.** *adj.* provisional, temporary

in·te·ri·or 1. *adj.* of, relating to or placed at the inner part of something ‖ having to do with the domestic affairs of a country ‖ in or towards the part of a country away from the coast or frontier **2.** *n.* the inner part of something

in·ter·ject *v.t.* to interpose abruptly

in·ter·jec·tion *n.* an exclamation expressing emotion (e.g. 'ouch!') ‖ an interjected   remark   **in·ter·jec·tion·al in·ter·jec·to·ry** *adjs*

in·ter·lock *v.t.* to engage locking parts of so that they are held rigidly together ‖ *v.i.* to be connected in this way

in·ter·lope in·ter·lop·ing in·ter·loped *v.i.* to meddle in the affairs of others **in·ter·lop·er** *n.* someone who intrudes

in·ter·mar·riage *n.* marriage between different racial, religious or tribal groups ‖ marriage between close relations

in·ter·me·di·ate 1. *adj.* being between two things, events, extremes etc. **2.** *n.* someone through whom two other parties communicate

in·ter·ment *n.* a burial

in·ter·mi·na·ble   *adj.*   endless **in·ter·mi·na·bly** *adv.*

in·ter·mis·sion *n.* an interval coming between periods of activity

in·ter·mit·tent *adj.* stopping from time to time

in·tern 1. *n.* (also **in·terne**) a newly qualified doctor serving in a hospital to complete his training **2.** *v.i.* to serve in a hospital to complete one's training ‖ *v.t.* to detain

in·ter·nal *adj.* of or on the inside ‖ inside the body ‖ intrinsic

in·ter·na·tion·al *adj.* common to, involving or used by two or more nations **in·ter·na·tion·al·ize in·ter·na·tion·al·iz·ing in·ter·na·tion·al·ized** *v.t.* to bring (a territory) under the combined control of several nations

in·tern·ist *n.* a specialist in internal medicine

in·tern·ship *n.* the position of an intern in a hospital

in·ter·plan·e·tar·y *adj.* situated between the planets

in·ter·play 1. *n.* an acting upon each other with reciprocal effect **2.** *v.i.* to act upon each other

in·ter·po·late   in·ter·po·lat·ing in·ter·po·lat·ed *v.t.* to put (new words, passages etc.) into a text ‖ to enter with (a remark) into a conversation between others

in·ter·po·la·tion *n.* an interpolating

in·ter·pose in·ter·pos·ing in·ter·posed *v.t.* to introduce (a remark etc.) into a conversation ‖ to introduce as an insertion ‖ *v.i.* to interrupt ‖ to intervene

in·ter·po·si·tion *n.* something interposed

in·ter·pret *v.t.* to explain the meaning of ‖ to attribute a specified meaning to ‖ *v.i.* to act as a linguistic interpreter

in·ter·pre·ta·tion *n.* an explanation produced by interpreting

in·ter·pret·er *n.* someone who interprets

in·ter·ro·gate in·ter·ro·gat·ing in·ter·ro·gat·ed *v.* to ask questions of, esp. formally

in·ter·ro·ga·tion *n.* the act of interrogating

in·ter·rupt *v.t.* to stop abruptly ‖ to make a break in the continuity of ‖ *v.i.* to interfere in some action **in·ter·rúpt·er in·ter·rúp·tor** *n.* someone who or something that interrupts

in·ter·rup·tion *n.* something that interrupts

in·ter·sect *v.t.* to divide by passing through or across ‖ *v.i.* to meet and cross each other

in·ter·sec·tion *n.* a place where two roads cross each other **in·ter·séc·tion·al** *adj.*

in·ter·sperse in·ter·spers·ing in·ter·spersed *v.t.* to put here and there ‖ to diversify **in·ter·sper·sion** *n.*

in·ter·state *adj.* between two or more states

in·ter·val *n.* a period of time between two actions ‖ a space between two points **at intervals** now and then

in·ter·vene in·ter·ven·ing in·ter·vened *v.i.* to happen unexpectedly to prevent some event etc. ‖ to happen between points of time, events etc.

in·ter·ven·tion *n.* interference in the affairs of others

in·ter·view 1. *n.* a meeting of persons face to face esp. for formal discussion **2.** *v.t.* to meet with (someone) to examine his qualifications or to get information etc. from him

in·tes·tate 1. *adj.* not having made any valid will **2.** *n.* a person who dies without having made a valid will

in·tes·ti·nal *adj.* relating to or in the intestines

in·tes·tine *n.* the portion of the alimentary canal in vertebrates between the stomach and the anus

in·ti·ma·cy *pl.* **in·ti·ma·cies** *n.* an intimate act

in·ti·mate 1. *adj.* being on familiar, esp. affectionate, personal terms ‖ very private and personal **2.** *n.* a familiar friend **3. in·ti·mat·ing in·ti·mat·ed** to hint, give someone to understand

in·ti·ma·tion *n.* something that gives an insight

in·tim·i·date in·tim·i·dat·ing in·tim·i·dat·ed *v.t.* to frighten, esp. to influence by threats **in·tim·i·dá·tion in·tím·i·da·tor** *ns*

in·to *prep.* from the outside to the inside of ‖ up against

in·tol·er·a·ble *adj.* that cannot be tolerated **in·tól·er·a·bly** *adv.*

in·tol·er·ance *n.* the state of being intolerant

in·tol·er·ant *adj.* not tolerating beliefs etc. that differ from one's own ‖ unfriendly or hostile towards persons of another racial or religious group

in·to·nate in·to·nat·ing in·to·nat·ed *v.t.* to intone **in·to·ná·tion** *n.* the modulation of the voice ‖ the producing of musical sounds, with regard to accuracy of pitch

in to·to *adv.* as a whole, completely, altogether

in·tox·i·cate in·tox·i·cat·ing in·tox·i·cat·ed *v.t.* (of an alcoholic drink, drug etc.) to cause to lose physical or mental control ‖ to exhilarate ‖ to poison **in·tox·i·cá·tion** *n.*

in·trac·ta·ble *adj.* not docile **in·trác·ta·bly** *adv.*

in·tra·mu·ral *adj.* occurring within the limits of specific groups

in·tran·si·gence *n.* the quality or state of being intransigent **in·trán·si·gen·cy** *n.*

in·tran·si·gent *adj.* refusing to compromise

in·tran·si·tive *adj.* (*gram.*, of verbs) not governing a direct object

in·tra·per·son·al *adj.* occurring within a person's mind

in·tra·state *adj.* within a state

in·tra·u·ter·ine device plastic or steel coil or loop, etc., placed within the uterus to prevent conception

in·tra·ve·nous *adj.* in or into a vein

in·trep·id *adj.* fearlessly **in·tre·pid·i·ty** *n.*

in·tri·ca·cy *pl.* **in·tri·ca·cies** *n.* the quality or state of being intricate

in·tri·cate *adj.* complicated

in·tri·gant in·tri·guant *n.* someone who engages in intrigue **in·tri·gante in·tri·guante** *n.* a woman who does this

in·trigue *n.* secret plotting, scheming ‖ a plot

in·trigue in·tri·guing in·trigued *v.i.* plot secretly ‖ *v.t.* to arouse the interest or curiosity of

in·trin·sic *adj.* inherent, essential **in·trín·si·cal·ly** *adv.*

in·tro·duce in·tro·duc·ing in·tro·duced *v.t.* to make acquainted ‖ to bring into use or practice ‖ to add as a feature ‖ to insert ‖ to bring (a bill etc.) before a legislative body

in·tro·duc·tion *n.* something that introduces ‖ an introducing or being introduced ‖ something introduced

in·tro·spect *v.i.* to examine one's own thoughts and feelings **in·tro·spéc·tion** *n.* **in·tro·spéc·tive** *adj.*

in·tro·ver·sion *n.* an introverting or being introverted **in·tro·vér·sive** *adj.*

in·tro·vert 1. *v.t.* to direct (one's mind, thoughts) upon oneself **2.** *n.* (psychol.) someone who is more interested in himself and his own mental or emotional processes than in outside events etc.

in·trude in·trud·ing in·trud·ed *v.* to thrust or force in an unwelcome way

in·tru·sion *n.* wrongful entry upon someone else's property

in·tu·i·tion *n.* a perception of truth in the absence of conscious rational processes **in·tu·í·tion·al** *adj.*

in·tu·i·tive *adj.* having, perceived by, or relating to intuition

in·ure in·ur·ing in·ured *v.t.* cause by habituation to be less sensitive ‖ *v.i.* take effect

in·úre·ment *n.*

in·vade in·vad·ing in·vad·ed *v.t.* to enter by armed force ‖ to encroach on ‖ *v.i.* to make an invasion

in·val·id *adj.* not valid, having no legal force

in·va·lid 1. *adj.* chronically ill or disabled ‖ suitable for a sick person **2.** *n.* an invalid person **3.** *v.t.* to make ill, disable

in·val·u·a·ble *adj.* very valuable **in·vál·u·a·bly** *adv.*

in·var·i·a·ble 1. *adj.* never changing, constant **2.** *n.* something constant **in·vár·i·a·bly** *adv.*

in·va·sion *n.* an invading or being invaded

in·vent *v.t.* to devise, originate ‖ to think up

in·ven·tion *n.* the act of inventing ‖ something invented ‖ ingenuity

in·ven·to·ry *pl.* **in·ven·to·ries** *n.* an itemized list, esp. of property ‖ stocktaking

in·verse 1. *adj.* reversed **2.** *n.* a direct opposite

in·ver·sion *n.* an inverting or being inverted ‖ something inverted

in·vert *v.t.* to turn upside down ‖ to reverse the order or position of

in·ver·te·brate 1. *adj.* having no backbone **2.** *n.* an animal having no internal skeleton or backbone

in·vest *v.t.* to put (money) to a use expected to yield a profit ‖ to confer the insignia of office or rank upon ‖ to envelop

in·ves·ti·gate in·ves·ti·gat·ing in·ves·ti·gat·ed *v.t.* to seek information about ‖ *v.i.* to make an investigation

in·ves·ti·ga·tion *n.* an examination for the purpose of discovering information about something

in·ves·ti·ga·tor *n.* someone who investigates

in·ves·ti·ture *n.* the act of investing someone with an honor or office

in·vest·ment *n.* the act of investing, esp. of money ‖ something invested, esp. money

in·ves·tor *n.* someone who invests

in·vet·er·ate *adj.* deep-rooted, firmly established

in·vid·i·ous *adj.* causing envy or ill-feeling

in·vig·o·rate   in·vig·o·rat·ing
in·vig·o·rat·ed   *v.t.*   enliven
in·vig·o·rá·tion *n.*

in·vin·ci·ble *adj.* that cannot be conquered
or overcome in·vín·ci·bly *adv.*

in·vi·o·la·ble *adj.* that cannot be violated
‖ that must not be violated in·ví·o·la·bly
adv.

in·vis·i·ble *adj.* that cannot be seen

in·vite in·vit·ing in·vit·ed *v.t.* to ask
hospitably to come somewhere or to do
or participate in something ‖ to ask for
in·vít·ing *adj.* tempting, attractive

in·voice 1. *n.* an itemized list of goods
dispatched or delivered to a buyer, with
prices and charges 2. *v.t.* in·voic·ing
in·voiced to make an invoice of

in·voke in·vok·ing in·voked *v.t.* to appeal
to in prayer etc.

in·vol·un·tar·i·ly *adv.* in an involuntary
manner

in·vol·un·tar·y *adj.* not intended

in·volve in·volv·ing in·volved *v.t.* to
include, concern ‖ to entail in·vólved *adj.*
complicated in·vólve·ment *n.*

in·vul·ner·a·ble *adj.* not susceptible to
injury ‖ able to resist any attack
in·vúl·ner·a·bly *adv.*

in·ward *adj.* toward the inside ‖ relating to
the mind

in·ward·ly *adv.* internally ‖ in mind or spirit

in·wards *adv.* inward

i·o·dine *n.* a nonmetallic element

i·on *n.* an atom which is electrically
charged

i·o·ta *n.* a very small amount

i·rate *adj.* angry or showing anger

ire *n.* anger íre·ful *adj.*

ir·i·des·cent *adj.* having shifting rain-
bowlike colors

i·ris *pl.* i·ris·es i·rid·es *n.* the broad colored
muscular ring surrounding the pupil of
the eye ‖ *(pl.)* also i·ris) a genus of perennial plants

irk *v.t.* to irritate, annoy irk·some *adj.*

i·ron 1. *n.* a widely occurring and widely
used metallic element ‖ an implement to
press garments etc. **to have other (or
many) irons in the fire** to have other
projects in hand 2. *v.t.* to press with an
iron ‖ to cover or furnish with iron

i·ron·clad *adj.* protected with iron plates
‖ (e.g. of contracts or agreements) hard
to break

i·ron·ic *adj.* of, using, or said in irony
i·rón·i·cal *adj.*

i·ro·ny *pl.* i·ro·nies *n.* a manner of speaking in which the meaning literally
expressed is the opposite of the meaning
intended

ir·ra·di·ate ir·ra·di·at·ing ir·ra·di·at·ed
v.t. to treat by exposure to infrared,
ultraviolet, X rays or other rays

ir·ra·di·a·tion *n.* treatment by exposure to
radiation

ir·ra·tion·al *adj.* unreasonable

ir·rec·on·cil·a·ble *adj* incapable of being
won over ‖ incompatible, inconsistent
ir·réc·on·cil·a·bly *adv.*

ir·re·deem·a·ble *adj.* that cannot be
reclaimed or reformed ‖ not redeemable
ir·re·déem·a·bly *adv.*

ir·re·duc·i·ble *adj.* that cannot be reduced
or made smaller ir·re·dúc·i·bly *adv.*

ir·ref·u·ta·ble *adj.* that cannot be refuted
ir·réf·u·ta·bly *adv.*

ir·reg·u·lar 1. *adj.* asymmetrical ‖ not in
accordance with normal practice ‖ not
belonging to the standing army of a country 2. *n. (pl.)* irregular troops

ir·reg·u·lar·i·ty *pl.* ir·reg·u·lar·i·ties *n.* the
quality or state of being irregular ‖ something irregular

ir·rel·e·vance *n.* the quality or state of being
irrelevant ‖ ir·rél·e·van·cy *pl.*
ir·rel·e·van·cies *n.*

ir·rel·e·vant *adj.* not applicable, not related
to whatever is being considered,
discussed etc.

ir·re·me·di·a·ble *adj.* that cannot be remedied or corrected ir·re·mé·di·a·bly *adv.*

ir·re·mis·si·ble *adj.* unpardonable
ir·re·mis·si·bly *adv.*

ir·rep·a·ra·ble *adj.* that cannot be repaired,
remedied, retrieved etc. ir·rép·a·ra·bly
adv.

ir·re·place·a·ble *adj.* for whom or for
which there is no substitute

ir·re·pres·si·ble *adj.* that cannot be
controlled or repressed ir·re·prés·si·bly

adv.

ir·re·proach·a·ble *adj.* not subject to reproach, having no faults or flaws **ir·re·próach·a·bly** *adv.*

ir·re·sist·i·ble *adj.* too powerful, tempting, charming etc. to be resisted **ir·re·sist·i·bly** *adv.*

ir·res·o·lute *adj.* hesitant, undecided

ir·re·spec·tive *adv.* without regard to

ir·re·spon·si·ble *adj.* having or showing no sense of responsibility **ir·re·spón·si·bly** *adv.*

ir·rev·er·ence the quality or state of being irreverent

ir·rev·er·ent lacking respect

ir·rev·o·ca·ble *adj.* that cannot be revoked or altered **ir·rév·o·ca·bly** *adv.*

ir·ri·gate ir·ri·gat·ing ir·ri·gat·ed *v.t.* to provide (land) with water by artificial flooding, spraying etc. ‖ to wash with a constant flow of liquid

ir·ri·ga·tion *n.* the artificial increase of water supply to assist the growing of crops ‖ washing with a flow of water for cleansing **ir·ri·gá·tion·al** *adj.*

ir·ri·ta·ble *adj.* easily annoyed, apt to become impatient or exasperated ‖ over-sensitive, apt to become sore, inflamed etc. ‖ very sensitive to stimuli **ir·ri·ta·bly** *adv.*

ir·ri·tate ir·ri·tat·ing ir·ri·tat·ed *v.t.* to cause to be impatiently angry, annoy

ir·ri·ta·tion *n.* being irritated ‖ something that irritates

is·land *n.* a piece of land entirely surrounded by water **is·land·er** *n.* someone who lives or was born on an island

is·let *n.* a small island

i·so·late i·so·lat·ing i·so·lat·ed *v.t.* to place apart and alone ‖ to obtain (a substance) from one of its compounds

i·so·la·tion *n.* an isolating or being isolated

i·sos·ce·les *adj.* (of a triangle) having two sides equal

is·sue 1. *n.* a flowing, going or passing out ‖ something published or given out ‖ a

question, point etc. under dispute ‖ offspring **2.** *v.* **is·su·ing is·sued** *v.i.* to come or flow forth ‖ to be derived, result ‖ to be descended ‖ to be put into circulation

isth·mus *n.* a narrow strip of land joining two larger tracts

it *pron. 3rd person sing. nominative* and *objective cases* an inanimate object, infant, animal, group or collection, unidentified person, idea ‖ the subject of an impersonal verb

I·tal·ic 1. *adj.* of or relating to ancient Italy **i·tal·ic** of, relating to or printed in a type slanting to the upper right **2.** *n.* the Italic languages collectively **i·tal·ics** *pl. n.* italic letters

i·tal·i·cize i·tal·i·ciz·ing i·tal·i·cized *v.t.* to print in italics ‖ *v.i.* to use italics

itch *n.* an irritation or tickle in the skin ‖ a restless longing

itch *v.i.* to feel an irritating or tickling sensation ‖ to have a restless longing

itch·y itch·i·er itch·i·est *adj.* feeling or causing an itch

i·tem *adv. n.* a single article, unit, feature or particular in a list ‖ a piece of news

i·tem·ize i·tem·iz·ing i·tem·ized

it·er·ate it·er·at·ing it·er·at·ed *v.t.* to say again, repeat

i·tin·er·ant *adj.* traveling from place to place

i·tin·er·ar·y *pl.* **i·tin·er·ar·ies** *n.* a route taken or planned ‖ a record or account of a journey

its *possessive adj.* of, pertaining to or belonging to it

it·self *pron. refl.* form of IT ‖ emphatic form of IT

i·vo·ry *pl.* **i·vo·ries** *n.* the hard creamy-white dentine forming the tusks of the elephant, hippopotamus, narwhal and walrus ‖ the color of ivory

i·vy *n.* an evergreen woody climbing or creeping plant

j

J, j the tenth letter of the English alphabet

jab 1. *v.t.* **jab·bing jabbed** to thrust ‖ to poke sharply ‖ to give a short straight blow with the fist to **2.** *n.* a quick poke or stab

jab·ber 1. *v.i.* to talk rapidly ‖ to make unintelligible sounds resembling speech **2.** *n.* this kind of speech or noise

jack 1. *n.* a device for raising an automobile or other heavy load ‖ a small flag ‖ a playing card ‖ the male of various animals **2.** *v.t.* (with 'up') to lift with a jack ‖ (with 'up') to raise or increase

jack·ass *n.* the male ass ‖ a stupid person

jack·et 1. *n.* a short coat ‖ a detachable paper cover of a book ‖ the metal casing of a projectile **2.** *v.t.* to surround with a jacket

jack·knife *pl.* **jack·knives** *n.* a large pocketknife ‖ a dive **1.** *v.i.* **jack·knif·ing jack·knifed** to perform a jackknife dive

jack·pot *n.* the accumulated kitty **to hit the jackpot** to win all there is to win ‖ to be suddenly very successful

jade *n.* a hard stone that is either jadeite or nephrite, used in jewelry, ornaments etc.

jad·ed *adj.* dulled by satiety ‖ tired

jag·uar *pl.* **jag·uars jag·uar** *n.* a large carnivore found in the American tropics

jai a·lai *pl.* **jai a·lais** *n.* a game of Basque origin

jail 1. *n.* a civil prison **2.** *v.t.* to put in prison

jail·bird *n.* someone who is, or who is often, in jail

ja·lop·y *pl.* **ja·lop·ies** *n.* an old dilapidated model, esp. an automobile

jal·ou·sie *n.* a shutter or blind consisting of horizontal, often adjustable, overlapping slats

jam *n.* a sweet thick mixture made by simmering fruit with sugar at the boiling point

jam jam·ming jammed *v.t.* to force (a body) to enter a confined or small space ‖ to bruise by crushing between two solid objects ‖ to block or impede the movement of by crowding etc. ‖ *v.i.* to become immovably fixed or wedged ‖ to crowd tightly together

jamb *n.* one of the vertical sides of a doorframe

jam·bo·ree *n.* an international scouts' camp ‖ a festive gathering ‖ a spree

jan·gle 1. *n.* an unpleasant combination of clanging or ringing sounds **2.** **jan·gling jan·gled** *v.i.* to produce this sound

jan·i·tor *n.* a caretaker of a building, set of offices etc. ‖ a doorkeeper **ján·i·tress** *n.* a woman janitor

Jan·u·ar·y *n.* the 1st month of the year

jar *n.* a container of earthenware, glass or stone, with a short wide neck (or none) and wide mouth

jar 1. jar·ring jarred *v.i.* to vibrate in an irregular way ‖ (of colors, shapes, styles etc., or of a sound, or of opinions or interests) to be discordant ‖ (with 'on' or 'upon') to have an unpleasant effect on the sympathies **2.** *n.* a discordant sound

jar·di·niere jar·di·niere *n.* a large ornamental receptacle for a potted plant

jar·gon *n.* the vocabulary of a specialized field

jaun·dice 1. *n.* a yellowish coloring of the skin, whites of the eyes and various body tissues. It results from excessive bile in the bloodstream due to damage to or malfunction of the liver or bile ducts **2.** to **jáun·diced** *adj.* afflicted with jaundice ‖ hostile, embittered

jaunt 1. *n.* a short journey made purely for pleasure **2.** *v.i.* to make such a journey

jaun·ty jaun·ti·er jaun·ti·est *adj.* gay and perky, spirited

jave·lin *n.* a lightweight spear

jaw 1. *n.* either of two bony or cartilaginous structures of vertebrates forming part of the mouth ‖ (*pl.*) the parts of a tool between which things are gripped or crushed **2.** *v.i.* to talk at great length, esp. in reproach ‖ to chat

jazz 1. *n.* syncopated music played over strong dance rhythm **2.** *v.i.* to play or dance jazz ‖ (with 'up') to make more lively **jázz·y jazz·i·er jazz·i·est** *adj.* excessively vivid or ostentatious

jeal·ous *adj.* racked by jealousy

jeal·ous·y *pl.* **jeal·ous·ies** *n.* a state of fear, suspicion or envy caused by a real or imagined threat or challenge to one's possessive instincts

jeans *pl. n.* pants made from a heavy durable cotton cloth in a twill weave

jeep *n.* a small, strong motor vehicle with four-wheel drive

jeer *v.i.* to speak in mockery or derision ‖ (with 'at') to scoff or laugh with contempt ‖ *v.t.* to pour scorn on

Je·ho·vah *n.* an Old Testament name for God

je·june *adj.* lacking nourishment, interest or substance ‖ juvenile, immature

jel·ly 1. *pl.* **jel·lies** *n.* a semitransparent, soft food preparation **2. jel·ly·ing jel·lied** *v.i.* to become jelly ‖ *v.t.* to make into jelly

jel·ly·fish *n.* any of several marine coelenterates ‖ someone lacking in self-reliance and firmness of will

jeop·ard·ize jeop·ard·iz·ing jeop·ard·ized *v.t.* to put in jeopardy

jeop·ard·y *n.* the state of being exposed to danger

jerk 1. *n.* a sudden, abrupt movement or change of motion ‖ an involuntary muscular spasm **2.** *v.t.* to move (a body) by applying a short, sudden force ‖ to utter in short, abrupt phrases

jerk *v.t.* to cure (meat, esp. beef) by drying long thin strips of it in the sun

jerk·y jerk·i·er jerk·i·est *adj.* moving in jerks ‖ characterized by jerks

jer·sey *n.* a machine-knitted cloth of wool, cotton, silk etc.

jest 1. *n.* a word or deed designed to evoke laughter ‖ a taunting remark or action **2.** *v.i.* to speak frivolously or jokingly ‖ to speak tauntingly **jést·er** *n.*

Je·sus a Jewish religious leader whom Christians worship as the Son of God and Savior of Mankind

jet 1. *n.* a stream of vapor, gas or liquid coming out fast from a narrow orifice ‖ an airplane having a jet engine **2. jet·ting jet·ted** *v.i.* to emit a jet of

jet lag fatigue, irritability, and other symptoms resulting from travel through several times zones

jet·sam *n.* the cargo, gear etc. thrown overboard from a ship in distress to lighten the load

jet stream a narrow current of high-velocity westerly winds, close to the tropopause

jet·ti·son *v.t.* to discard (part of any load) which has become an encumbrance

jet·ty *pl.* **jet·ties** *n.* a structure built out into the water to shelter a harbor or to break waves or currents ‖ a small landing wharf

Jew *n.* a member of the worldwide Semitic group whose religion is Judaism

jew·el *n.* a precious stone ‖ a person whose qualities one is praising **jéw·eled jéw·elled** *adj.* set with jewels

jew·el·er jew·el·ler *n.* someone who trades in or makes jewelry

jew·el·ry *n.* personal ornaments made of precious metals, and precious stones

jib *n.* a triangular sail stretching from the masthead to the bowsprit ‖ the long arm of a crane ‖ the boom of a derrick

jig 1. *n.* a rapid, gay, springy dance ‖ a device which maintains the proper positional relationship between a material and the machine that is working on it **2. jig·ging jigged** *v.t.* to use a jig on ‖ *v.i.* to dance a jig ‖ to move with rapid up-and-down motions

jig·gle jig·gling jig·gled *v.i.* to move in quick little successive motions

jig·saw *n.* a mechanical saw with a vertical blade used to cut along irregular or curved lines

jilt *v.t.* to break with (a lover) in a callously light hearted way

jim·my 1. *pl.* **jim·mies** *n.* a thick bar of iron with one end flattened as a chisel edge **2.** *v.t.* **jim·my·ing jim·mied** to pry open

jin·gle 1. jin·gling jin·gled *v.* to produce a jingle **2.** *n.* a pleasing sound composed of a number of high-pitched percussion notes in continuous but unrhythmical combination **jin·gly** *adj.*

jinx 1. *n.* a person or thing bringing bad luck **2.** *v.t.* to cause (someone) bad luck

jit·ter 1. *v.i.* to tremble with anxiety **2.** *n.* (esp. *pl.*) a fit of acute anxiety **jít·ter·y** *adj.*

job 1. *n.* a piece of work ‖ an occupation as a steady source of livelihood **2.** *v.t.*

job·bing jobbed to buy and sell (goods) as a middleman ‖ to buy and sell (stocks and shares) **jób·ber** n. a middleman

job lot a collection of miscellaneous articles, usually of small value, offered for sale as a single lot

jock·ey 1. n. a professional rider in horse racing **2.** v.t. to edge (a person, thing, situation) by tact in the direction one wishes to impose

jo·cose adj. given to joking, full of jokes

joc·u·lar adj. joking **joc·u·lar·i·ty** n.

joc·und adj. cheerful **joc·ún·di·ty** n.

jodh·purs pl. n. pants for horseback riding

jog jog·ging jogged v.t. to give (something) a slight push ‖ v.i. (with 'on' or 'along') to move along at a regular pace without hurrying ‖ to exercise using such a pace **jogging** slow running

join v.t. to bring together to make a single unit ‖ to fasten (one thing to another) ‖ to become a member of (an organization or group) ‖ v.i. to be contiguous

joint 1. n. the place where two or more things or parts of things are joined together ‖ a place where two or more bones come together ‖ any establishment, esp. a low-class place of entertainment **2.** v.t. to fit (something) together by means of a joint

joint adj. owned, made or done in common with one or more persons, groups, governments etc.

joist n. one of a number of parallel wood or steel beams which support floorboards or ceiling

joke 1. n. an action, saying, event or circumstance which causes or is intended to cause amusement or laughter **2.** v.t. **jok·ing joked** to make jokes **jók·er** n. someone who makes jokes ‖ a 53rd card usually depicting a jester **jók·ing·ly** adv.

jol·ly jol·li·er jol·li·est adj. full of good humor and fun

jolt 1. v.t. to cause (something) to move or shake by a sudden jerk **2.** n. a rough jerk ‖ a sudden shock to one's feelings

josh v.t. to tease

jos·tle jos·tling jos·tled v.i. to push and shove ‖ to struggle with someone for something

jot 1. n. a very small amount **2.** v.t. **jot·ting jot·ted** (with 'down') to make a quick written note

jour·nal n. a record of events, personal experiences and thoughts etc. ‖ a daily record of business transactions ‖ a newspaper or magazine ‖ a logbook

jour·nal·ism n. the profession of collecting news for, writing for, editing or managing a newspaper or other periodical ‖ journalistic writing

jour·nal·ist n. a professional writer for or editor of a newspaper or other periodical **jour·nal·is·tic** adj.

jour·ney 1. pl. **jour·neys** n. a movement over a considerable distance from one place to another **2.** v.i. to make a journey

jour·ney·man pl. **jour·ney·men** n. a craftsman who has completed his training and works for an employer

jo·vi·al adj. good-humored **jo·vi·ál·i·ty** n.

jowl n. a jawbone, esp. the lower jaw ‖ a cheek

joy n. intense happiness or great delight

joy·ful adj. filled with, causing or showing joy

joy·ous adj. full of joy ‖ expressing joy

ju·bi·lant adj. rejoicing

ju·bi·late ju·bi·lat·ing ju·bi·lat·ed v.i. to be jubilant

ju·bi·la·tion n. a jubilating ‖ an instance of this

ju·bi·lee n. a 50th anniversary ‖ an anniversary other than the 50th, silver jubilee (25th), diamond jubilee (60th) ‖ celebration of such anniversaries

Ju·da·ism n. the religion of the Jews

judge judg·ing judged v.t. to hear (a case) and pronounce sentence ‖ to examine and determine the relative merits of ‖ to estimate ‖ v.i. to arrive at an opinion

judge n. a title for any of several law officers who may try cases in courts ‖ any person appointed to settle a dispute

judg·ment judge·ment n. the process of judging in law ‖ a legal decision or sentence ‖ an opinion ‖ the process of assessing

ju·di·cial adj. of the administration of

justice or of acts, places, persons or powers associated with it

ju·di·ci·ar·y *pl.* **ju·di·ci·ar·ies** *n.* the judicial branch of government

ju·di·cious *adj.* governed by or arising from sound judgment ‖ using sound judgment

ju·do *n.* a modern form of jujitsu

jug *n.* a vessel for holding and pouring liquids

jug·ger·naut *n.* an irresistible destructive force

jug·gle 1. jug·gling jug·gled *v.* to perform tricks of dexterity ‖ (with 'with') to make complex, confusing play ‖ to alter (facts or figures) with the intention of deceiving **2.** *n.* an act of juggling ‖ a fraud

jug·gler *n.* someone who juggles

jug·u·lar 1. *adj.* of or located in the neck or throat **2.** *n.* a vulnerable point

jugular vein a vein, running through the neck

juice *n.* the fluid contained in or extracted from fruits and vegetables or from the animal body

juic·y juic·i·er juic·i·est *adj.* rich in juice ‖ profitable ‖ sexy, racy

ju·jit·su ju·ju·tsu *n.* a Japanese method of self-defense

Ju·ly *n.* the seventh month of the year

jum·ble 1. *n.* a disorderly or confused group of things, persons etc. **2.** *v.t.* **jum·bling jum·bled** (with 'up' or 'together') to mix (things) in a jumble

jum·bo *adj.* very large

jump 1. *v.i.* to rise momentarily into the air ‖ to leap from one place to another ‖ to shift quickly from one state, topic etc. to another ‖ (of prices, wages etc.) to rise quickly ‖ *v.t.* to pass over (something) by jumping ‖ to cause to jump ‖ to attack (someone) esp. with malicious intent **to jump ship** (of a sailor etc.) to leave the ship while legally obliged to remain **to jump the gun** to start too soon **to jump to conclusions** to make an unjustified assumption **2.** *n.* the act of jumping ‖ a sudden startled movement ‖ a gap in an otherwise continuous process

jump·er *n.* a sleeveless dress worn over a blouse

jumper *n.* someone or something that jumps

jump·y jump·i·er jump·i·est *adj.* marked by jumps ‖ in a nervous or apprehensive state

junc·tion *n.* the place where things join ‖ a joining or being joined

junc·ture *n.* a joining or being joined ‖ a point in time

June *n.* the sixth month of the year

jun·gle *n.* an area of land overgrown with tangled shrubs, vines, trees, roots and tall vegetation, found in the Tropics ‖ this dense growth ‖ an intermingled number of things difficult to analyze or sort out

jun·ior *n.* a younger person or person of lower status ‖ a high school or college student in the third year of studies

ju·ni·per *n.* a genus of evergreen shrubs and trees

junk *n.* a sailing vessel used in the Orient

junk *n.* objects having neither value nor further use ‖ rubbish

jun·ket 1. *n.* a food prepared from milk ‖ a pleasure trip made at public expense **2.** *v.i.* to go on a junket

jun·ta *n.* a junto

jun·to *pl.* *n.* a political or other group of persons united by a common purpose

ju·ris·dic·tion *n.* the legal power to administer and enforce the law ‖ the region within which this power is valid or in which a person has authority ‖ authority **ju·ris·dic·tion·al** *adj.*

ju·ris·pru·dence *n.* the science or philosophy of law ‖ a legal system or body of laws

ju·rist *n.* a lawyer or judge ‖ a scholar of jurisprudence **ju·ris·tic ju·ris·ti·cal** *adj.*

ju·ror *n.* a member of a jury

ju·ry *pl.* **ju·ries** *n.* a body of (usually 12) responsible, impartial citizens summoned to hear evidence in a court of law and bound under oath to give an honest answer ‖ a body of persons appointed to judge a contest etc.

just 1. *adj.* legally valid ‖ deserved, merited ‖ well founded ‖ accurate **2.** *adv.* exactly, precisely ‖ very recently

jus·tice *n.* behavior to oneself or to another which is strictly in accord with currently accepted ethical law or as decreed by legal authority ‖ rectitude of the soul enlivened by grace ‖ the process of law ‖ a judge or magistrate

jus·ti·fi·a·ble *adj.* able to be justified

jus·ti·fi·ca·tion *n.* a justifying or being justified ‖ that which justifies ‖ *(printing)* the arranging of a line of type so that it evenly fills the measure

jus·ti·fy jus·ti·fy·ing jus·ti·fied *v.t.* to show or prove to be just or right

jut jut·ting jut·ted *v.i.* to protrude from, stick out

jute *n.* a fiber made from the bark of plants native to tropical Asia ‖ these plants

ju·ve·nile 1. *adj.* relating to youth or young people ‖ immature **2.** *n.* a child or young person

jux·ta·pose jux·ta·pos·ing jux·ta·posed *v.t.* to place (things, facts etc.) side by side

jux·ta·po·si·tion *n.* a juxtaposing or being juxtaposed

K

K k the 11th letter of the English alphabet

ka·lei·do·scope *n.* a tubular viewing device containing two plane mirrors set at an angle of 60 degrees to one another and multiple fragments of colored glass or paper etc. These produce symmetrical patterns, which shift when the instrument is rotated

kan·ga·roo *pl.* **kan·ga·roos kan·ga·roo** *n.* a member of a family of herbivorous, marsupial mammals

kar·at *n.* a measure of the purity of gold

ka·ra·te *n.* a Japanese system of self-defense

kay·ak *n.* an Eskimo canoe made of sealskins

keel *n.* the curved base of the framework of a ship

keen *adj.* sharp ‖ (of a sensual stimulus) strong ‖ (of a mental process) acute, incisive ‖ (of feelings) intense ‖ enthusiastic

keep keep·ing kept to own and manage ‖ to fulfill (a promise etc.) ‖ to maintain ‖ to raise (livestock) ‖ to refrain from disclosing ‖ to continue, to stay ‖ to remain in good condition, not be spoiled, over a period of time **kéep·er** *n.* someone, esp. a gamekeeper, who keeps, manages, guards etc. ‖ a contrivance for maintaining something in position, e.g. a latch

kéep·ing *n.* care, charge ‖ the action of one who keeps

keg *n.* a small cask or barrel

kelp *n.* any of various large brown seaweeds

ken·nel *n. (pl.)* a place where dogs are kept, bred, trained etc.

ker·chief *n.* a cloth, usually folded to a triangular shape, worn by a woman over her head

ker·nel *n.* the soft, usually edible, innermost part of a seed ‖ the whole grain of a cereal ‖ the center, or essential part, of an argument etc.

ker·o·sene ker·o·sine *n.* mixtures of hydrocarbons used as fuels and solvents

ket·tle *n.* a large metal cooking utensil

ket·tle·drum *n.* a large drum having a hemispherical brass or copper shell and a parchment drumhead

key *n.* a reef or low island, esp. a coral island

key 1. *pl.* **keys** *n.* an instrument for locking and unlocking a lock ‖ something which enables someone to explain, solve or decipher a problem, dilemma, code etc. ‖ a series or system of notes, related in frequency to that of a particular note ‖ the disk which actuates a printing lever, e.g. in a typewriter ‖ a tone or style of writing or expression **2.** *adj.* of critical importance

key *v.t.* **key·ing keyed** to furnish with a key or keys ‖ to attune **to key up** to make nervously tense

key·board 1. *n.* the keys of a piano, organ, typewriter etc. **2.** *v.t.* to set (copy) ‖ *(computer)* to use the keyboard to record data

key·note *n.* the tone to which the other tones of a musical key are related ‖ the basic idea or principle informing a speech, policy etc.

key·stone *n.* the central stone in an arch

khak·i *pl.* **khak·is** *n.* a light yellowish-brown color ‖ the cloth of this color

kick 1. *v.t.* to hit with the foot voluntarily or involuntarily ‖ to move (something) by hitting it with the foot ‖ (of a firearm) to recoil ‖ *(pop.)* to protest or complain **2.** *n.* the act of kicking or an instance of this ‖ a jolt from a firearm recoil ‖ a pleasant stimulus or thrill of pleasure

kick·back *n.* a percentage of the sale price given secretly to the middleman or the purchaser by the seller

kick·off *n.* the act of beginning something

kid kid·ding kid·ded *v.t.* to deceive ‖ to tease

kid 1. *n.* a young goat ‖ kidskin ‖ the young of various other animals, e.g. an antelope ‖ a child **2.** *adj.* made of kidskin ‖ younger, *a kid brother*

kid·nap kid·nap·ping kid·nap·ing kid·napped kid·naped *v.t.* to take away and hold (a person) by force

kid·ney *pl.* **kid·neys** *n.* one of a pair of abdominal organs in all vertebrates

kill 1. *v.t.* to cause life to cease in ‖ to deprive of further existence or effectiveness ‖ to defeat or veto (legislation) ‖ *v.i.* to destroy life **dressed to kill** dressed to make a stunning impression **2.** *n.* the act of killing

kiln *n.* a chamber of brick etc., with a fire, used to burn, bake or dry ceramics

kil·o·cy·cle *n.* a unit of frequency equal to 1,000 cycles per second

kil·o·gram kil·o·gramme *n.* the standard metric unit of mass

kil·o·hertz *n.* a radio-frequency unit

kil·o·me·ter *n.* 1,000 meters

kil·o·watt *n.* a unit of power equal to 1,000 watts

kilt *n.* a heavily pleated knee-length tartan skirt worn esp. by the Highlanders of Scotland

ki·mo·no *pl.* **ki·mo·nos** *n.* a long, loose Japanese robe ‖ a dressing gown

kin *n.* ancestral family ‖ relatives

kind *n.* a group or division of persons or things having one or more characteristics, qualities, interests etc. in common **nothing of the kind** *(emphatic)* quite different

kind *adj.* sympathetic, helpful, friendly ‖ thoughtful and gentle ‖ well-disposed

kin·der·gar·ten *n.* a school in which very young children are encouraged to develop their skills

kind·heart·ed *adj.* having a kind nature

kin·dle kin·dling kin·dled *v.t.* to cause (a fire) to begin to burn ‖ to cause (an emotion) to be felt or intensified

kind·ling *n.* dry twigs, pieces of wood etc. used to start a fire

kind·ly *adj.* in a kind way **to take kindly to** to like

kind·ness *n.* the quality of being kind

kin·dred 1. *n.* kin **2.** *adj.* having kinship ‖ being in many ways similar

ki·net·ic *adj.* relating to motion ‖ producing motion

king *n.* a male monarch ‖ a card representing a king ‖ *(chess)* the piece in whose defense the game is played

king·dom *n.* the territory over which a king or queen has authority ‖ a state having a monarchal form of government

kink *n.* a sharp twist or loop in a wire, rope, hair etc. ‖ a sharp muscle pain ‖ an odd trait of character or mental quirk

kink·y kink·i·er kink·i·est *adj.* having kinks ‖ of peculiar tastes in sexual satisfaction

kin·ship *n.* the condition of being related

ki·osk *n.* a small outdoor structure, e.g. a newsstand

kiss *n.* an instance of kissing

kiss *v.t.* to press or touch with the lips as

an expression of passion, affection or respect || *v.i.* to join lips

kit *n.* a collection of tools usually contained in a bag, box etc.

kitch·en *n.* the part of a house where food is prepared

kite *n.* small hawk || a light, usually wooden framework covered with paper or material and flown on the wind at the end of a long string

kit·ten 1. *n.* a young cat **2.** *v.i.* to bring forth kittens **kit·ten·ish** *adj.* playful and winning

kit·ty *pl.* **kit·ties** *n.* *(card games)* a pool into which each player puts a stake

kitty *pl.* **kitties** *n.* cat, kitten

klep·to·ma·ni·a *n.* a compulsive, neurotic desire to steal **klep·to·má·ni·ac** *n.*

knack *n.* a special deftness learned by practice

knap·sack *n.* a canvas bag worn strapped to the back

knave *n.* a cheat, a rogue

knead *v.t.* to work (dough, clay) into a homogeneous mass with the hands

knee 1. *n.* the knee joint in man || something resembling a bent knee **to go on one's knees to** to beg humbly of **2.** *v.t.* to strike (someone) with the knee

kneel kneel·ing knelt kneeled *v.i.* to rest or fall on one or both knees

knell 1. *n.* the sonorous, doleful sound of a single bell tolled as a token of mourning **2.** *v.i.* to toll a bell

knick-knack *n.* any trivial small ornamental article

knife 1. *pl.* **knives** *n.* a hand tool, culinary utensil or weapon used for cutting **2.** *v.t.* knifing knifed to cut or stab with a knife

knight 1. *n.* a man given knighthood by the British monarch || a man of noble birth who was given an honorable military rank || *(chess)* a piece shaped like a horse's head **2.** *v.t.* to make a knight of

knight·hood *n.* the rank of a knight

knit knit·ting knit·ted knit *v.t.* to fashion (a garment, fabric etc.) by working yarn on knitting needles || to cause to join as if grown together or interwoven || *v.i.* (esp. of a broken bone) to unite **knít·ting** *n.* the

act of someone who knits || work being knitted

knob *n.* a rounded handle || a rounded hill

knock 1. *v.t.* to make a sudden impact on || (with 'down') to demolish || to find fault with || *v.i.* to rap on a door || to come together with a sudden impact || to find fault **to knock off** to do (a piece of work) esp. quickly and shoddily || to cease (work) || to deduct from **to knock together** to construct in a rough and ready way **to knock up** to make (a woman) pregnant **2.** *n.* the impact or sound made by knocking

knock·out *n.* (abbr. K.O.) a blow in boxing which makes a boxer unable to get up before he is counted out || someone or something superlatively attractive

knoll *n.* a small rounded hill

knot 1. *n.* a place in a thread, string etc. where the thread passes through a loop in its own length and is pulled tight || a constriction in a muscle || a protrusion of growing plant tissues || a cluster of persons or things || a difficulty, a problem hard to solve || a unit of speed **2.** *v.* **knot·ting knot·ted** *v.t.* to tie in or with a knot || *v.i.* to become tied in knots

knot·ty knot·ti·er knot·ti·est *adj.* having knots || hard to solve

know 1. *v.* **know·ing knew known** *v.t.* to apprehend with the conscious mind || to be acquainted with by experience || to have acquired skill in || to realize **to know of** to be aware of **to make oneself known** to introduce oneself **2.** *n.* (only in) **in the know** having inside information or sharing a secret

know·ing *adj.* shrewd **knów·ing·ly** *adv.* deliberately

knowl·edge *n.* cognition || understanding || that which is known **knowl·edge·a·ble** *adj.* well-informed

knuck·le 1. *n.* a joint in the finger, esp. one at the base of each finger || the middle joint of the tarsus of an animal **2.** *v.* **knuck·ling knuck·led** *v.t.* to hit with the knuckles || *v.i.* **to knuckle under** to submit

ko·a·la *n.* a sturdy marsupial of E. Australia

kook *n.* an eccentric **kooky** *adj.*

kook·a·bur·ra *n*. a large Australian kingfisher

Ko·ran *n*. the holy scripture of Islam

ko·sher *adj*. (of food) conforming to the requirements of the Jewish dietary laws ‖ legitimate

kum·quat, cum·quat *n*. a genus of Asiatic citrus trees ‖ a fruit of any of these trees

L

L, l the 12th letter of the English alphabet

la·bel 1. *n*. a piece of paper, card, metal etc. to be attached to an article with the name, ownership, destination, description etc. of the article **2.** *v.t.* **la·bel·ing labeled** to attach a label to ‖ to classify

la·bi·al *adj*. of the lips or labia **la·bi·al·i·zá·tion** *n*.

la·bor *n*. prolonged hard work ‖ a task demanding great effort ‖ the muscular uterine contractions preceding childbirth ‖ work as a production factor ‖ workers as an economic or political force

labor *v.i.* to work hard ‖ to make slow, painful progress ‖ *v.t.* to express in unnecessary detail

lab·o·ra·to·ry *pl.* **lab·o·ra·to·ries** *n*. aplace equipped for experimental study, research, analysis, testing

la·bored *adj*. done with difficulty

la·bor·er *n*. a wage earner who does unskilled work

la·bo·ri·ous *adj*. involving prolonged, hard work

lab·y·rinth *n*. a maze **lab·y·rín·thine** *adj*.

lace 1. *n*. a patterned fabric of open texture ‖ a cord or thin strip of leather, used to draw together the opposite edges of a shoe

lace lac·ing laced *v.t.* to draw together using a lace ‖ to attach ornamental lace to ‖ to add liquor to (coffee etc.) ‖ to lash, beat ‖ *v.i.* to be fastened by a lace

lac·er·ate lac·er·at·ing lac·er·at·ed *v.t.* to rend (the flesh) with a tearing movement **lác·er·at·ed** *adj*. mangled, torn **lac·er·á·tion** *n*.

lac·ing *n*. laces used for fastening ‖ ornamental trimming ‖ a beating, lashing

lack 1. *n*. want, need ‖ that which is missing or needed **2.** *v.i.* to be wanting

lack·a·dai·si·cal *adj*. lacking in seriousness, energy etc.

lack·ey *pl.* **lack·eys** *n*. a liveried manservant ‖ a servile and obsequious person

lack·ing *prep*. short of, without

lack·lus·ter *adj*. lacking in vitality or brilliance

la·con·ic *adj*. using terse, unemotional language **la·cón·i·cal·ly** *adv*.

lac·quer 1. *n*. a hard, glossy varnish ‖ a hair spray **2.** *v.t.* to coat with lacquer

la·crosse *n*. a field game of North American Indian origin

lac·tic *adj*. of or pertaining to milk

la·cy la·ci·er la·ci·est *adj*. of or resembling lace

lad *n*. a boy or youth

lad·der *n*. a device consisting of two long wood or metal uprights joined at short intervals by crosspieces (rungs) which serve as footrests, for climbing

lade lad·ing lad·ed lad·en *v.t.* to put goods on board (a ship) **lád·en** *adj*. loaded

la·dle 1. *n*. a spoon with a long handle and a large, cuplike bowl **2.** *v.t.* **la·dling la·dled** (often with 'out') to transfer with a ladle

la·dy *pl.* **la·dies** *n*. a woman of the wealthy, leisured class ‖ (in polite and conventional usage) a woman **La·dy** a British title of rank

lag 1. *v.i.* **lag·ging lagged** to go slowly ‖ (with 'behind') to fail to keep up with others **2.** *n.* the distance or time between one thing and another

lag·gard 1. *adj.* lagging **2.** *n.* a person who is slow

la·gniappe, la·gnappe *n.* a small gift presented by a storekeeper

la·goon *n.* a shallow stretch of water partly separated from the sea by a strip of sand or an atoll

la·ic 1. *adj.* lay **2.** *n.* a layman **la·i·cal** *adj.*

lair *n.* a place in which a wild animal rests

la·i·ty *n.* laymen

lake *n.* a large expanse of water surrounded by land

lamb *n.* a young sheep ‖ the flesh of this as food ‖ a meek, mild, innocent person

lam·baste lam·bast·ing lam·bast·ed *v.t.* to give a hard whipping to ‖ to scold

lame 1. *adj.* unable to walk normally because of a defect of a foot or leg ‖ stiff and sore ‖ having no force or effectiveness **2.** *v.t.* **lam·ing lamed** to make lame

la·mé *n.* a fabric woven from metal thread mixed with silk or other fiber

la·ment *v.* to mourn for

lament *n.* an expression of mourning or grieving

lam·en·ta·ble *adj.* giving cause for adverse comment **lám·en·ta·bly** *adv.*

lam·en·ta·tion *n.* the act of lamenting

lam·i·na *pl.* **lam·i·nae, lam·i·nas** *n.* any thin plate or scale ‖ the blade of a leaf or petal **lám·i·na** *adj.*

lam·i·nate lam·i·nat·ing lam·i·nat·ed *v.t.* to split into thin layers ‖ to make by uniting layer upon layer

lam·i·na·tion *n.* a laminating or being laminated

lamp *n.* a device for giving off light

lam·poon 1. *n.* a piece of satirical verse designed to ridicule someone **2.** *v.t.* to attack in this way

lam·prey *n.* an order of marine or freshwater vertebrates

lance *n.* a long shaft with a pointed steel end

lance lanc·ing lanced *v.t.* to pierce with a lance

lan·cet *n.* a sharp-pointed, two-edged surgical instrument

land 1. *n.* the solid surface of the earth ‖ a particular area of this, distinguished from other areas by political, geographical, economic or other considerations **the land** the country, esp. agricultural areas, as distinct from the city **2.** *v.i.* to step onto land from a ship ‖ to arrive ‖ (of an aircraft) to come to rest on the ground ‖ *v.t.* to put on shore from a ship ‖ to deliver (a blow)

land·ing *n.* a disembarking ‖ an alighting of an aircraft ‖ a place where goods or persons are taken aboard ‖ a level place at the top of a flight of stairs

land·la·dy *pl.* **land·la·dies** *n.* a woman who takes in lodgers

land·locked *adj.* (of water) almost or completely surrounded by land ‖ (of a country) without a seacoast

land·lord *n.* a man who leases property to another

land·mark *n.* a prominent feature on land ‖ any monument of historic interest

land·scape 1. *n.* a painting or photograph of a piece of inland scenery ‖ such a piece of scenery **2.** **land·scap·ing land·scaped** *v.t.* to beautify by enhancing the natural scenery

land·slide *n.* the slipping down from a hillside or cliff of masses of earth and rock ‖ an overwhelming electoral victory

lane *n.* a narrow country road ‖ a prescribed channel for sea or air traffic ‖ one of a series of parallel marked sections of road ‖ a wooden bowling alley

lan·guage *n.* the organized system of speech used by human beings as a means of communication among themselves ‖ a manner of expressing oneself ‖ use of words

lan·guish *v.i.* to become languid ‖ to live under dispiriting conditions ‖ to pine ‖ to wane

lan·guor *n.* a state of languishing **lan·guor·ous** *adj.*

lank *adj.* extremely slim

lank·i·ness *n.* the state or quality of being lanky

lank·y lank·i·er lank·i·est *adj.* tall, thin and ungainly

lan·o·lin *n.* a waxy substance obtained from wool grease

lan·tern *n.* a portable case with transparent sides containing a source of light and protecting this from wind and rain

lap *n.* the crook of the body between waist and knees of someone sitting down

lap lap·ping lapped *v.t.* to drink by taking it up with the tongue || *v.i.* to make a soft slapping sound **to lap up** to absorb or accept eagerly and quickly

lap 1. lap·ping lapped *v.* (with 'over') to fold, esp. on itself || to overlap || to make a circuit of (a racecourse) **2.** *n.* a section that overlaps || a circuit of a racecourse

la·pel *n.* the part of the front of a coat or dress folded back along the neckline

lap·i·dar·y 1. *pl.* **lap·i·dar·ies** *n.* someone who cuts, polishes or engraves gems **2.** *adj.* pertaining to precious stones

lapse 1. *n.* a passing away || a slip or minor mistake || a falling into disuse **2.** *v.t.* **laps·ing lapsed** to cease to be || to become void through lack of attention || (of time) to pass

lar·ce·nous *adj.* guilty of larceny

lar·ce·ny *pl.* **lar·ce·nies** *n.* the illegal taking and removal of another's personal property

lard *n.* the rendered fat of pigs used in cooking

lard *v.t.* to cover with lard

lar·der *n.* a cool room in which meat and other foods are stored until ready for use

large *adj.* extensive in area or scope || of greater size, capacity or number than average for its kind

large·ly *adv.* in large measure, mostly

lar·gess, lar·gesse *n.* generosity on a big scale

lar·i·at *n.* a lasso || a long rope or leather line

lark *n.* any of several songbirds esp. the skylark

lark *n.* something done for fun or mild adventure

lar·va *pl.* **lar·vae, lar·vas** *n.* the free-living, immature state in many insects **lár·val** *adj.*

la·ryn·ge·al *adj.* of or pertaining to the larynx

lar·yn·gi·tis *n.* inflammation of the larynx

lar·ynx *pl.* **la·ryn·ges, lar·ynx·es** *n.* an organ of the respiratory system

las·civ·i·ous *adj.* sexual lust || stimulating sexual lust

la·ser *n.* a maser operating at optimal frequencies to produce a high-energy monochromatic beam of light or infrared radiation (Light Amplification by Stimulated Emission of Radiation)

lash *v.t.* to fasten or bind with a rope etc. **lásh·ing** *n.* a rope, wire etc. so used

lass *n.* a girl or young woman

las·si·tude *n.* weariness of spirit

las·so 1. *pl.* **las·sos, las·soes** *n.* a long leather thong or rope with a running noose, used by cowboys for catching cattle or horses **2.** *v.t.* to catch with a lasso

last *n.* a wood or iron form shaped like the human foot used in shoemaking

last *v.i.* to go on existing for a period of time || to continue without being used up || *v.t.* to go on meeting the need of

last 1. *adj.* nearest to the present time || which will not, or cannot, be followed by any other person or thing of the same kind **the last (or latest) thing** the newest fashion **2.** *n.* someone or something which comes or is last || the end **3.** *adv.* finally || most recently

last·ing *adj.* existing for a long period of time

last·ly *adv.* in the last place || in conclusion

latch 1. *n.* a fastening for a door or window, a catch **2.** *v.t.* to fasten by means of a latch

late *adj.* coming or happening after the usual, expected or proper time || belonging to a recent time in the past || recently in existence but now over || recently deceased

late *adv.* after the usual, expected or proper time || recently

late·ly *adv.* recently, in recent years

la·ten·cy *n.* the quality or state of being latent

la·tent *adj.* hidden, dormant

lat·er·al 1. *adj.* of, to or from a side || located to one side of the central axis of the body **2.** *n.* something located at the side

la·tex *pl.* **lat·i·ces, la·tex·es** *n.* a milky fluid obtained from various trees and plants, e.g. rubber plants

lath 1. *pl.* **laths** a thin, narrow strip of wood, used for supporting slates **2.** *v.t.* to provide with laths

lathe 1. *n.* a machine used to shape or cut wood, metal etc. **2.** *v.i.* **lath·ing lathed** to shape or cut on a lathe

lath·er 1. *n.* the foamy froth produced when soap is agitated in water ‖ foamy froth from excessive sweat, esp. on a horse **2.** *v.i.* to form lather ‖ *v.t.* to cover with lather **láth·er·y** *adj.*

lath·ing *n.* laths collectively

lat·i·tude *n.* the angular distance of a place on the earth's surface from the equator measured in degrees ‖ the possibility of acting as one pleases ‖ (esp. pl.) a region in relation to average distance from the equator **lat·i·tú·di·nal** *adj.*

la·trine *n.* a toilet in any army camp, factory etc.

lat·ter *adj.* of the second of two

lat·ter·ly *adv.* recently, of late

lat·tice 1. *n.* a framework of wooden or metal laths crossing one another at regular intervals, leaving spaces between them **2.** *v.t.* **lat·tic·ing lat·ticed** to furnish with a lattice

laud·a·bil·i·ty *n.* the quality of being laudable

laud·a·ble *adj.* worthy of praise **láud·a·bly** *adv.*

laud·a·to·ry *adj.* praising, complimentary

laugh 1. *v.i.* to express amusement by explosive sounds, usually accompanied by convulsive muscular movements, esp. of the face ‖ *v.t.* to utter with a laugh **to laugh in someone's face** to treat someone with mocking defiance to his face **2.** *n.* an instance of laughing **láugh·a·ble** *adj.* such as to cause contempt **láugh·a·bly** *adv.*

laugh·ing *adj.* causing amusement **no laughing matter** something likely to have serious consequences

laugh·ter *n.* the act of laughing

launch 1. *v.t.* to cause to move from land into water ‖ to cause to become airborne ‖ to cause to be propelled **2.** *n.* the act of launching

launch *n.* a fast, small, power-driven boat

laun·der *v.t.* to wash and iron ‖ *v.i.* to do laundry ‖ to legitimatize illegally obtained funds

laun·der·ette *n.* a laundromat

laun·dress *n.* a woman whose job is laundering clothes

laun·dro·mat *n.* premises where customers can use washing machines and usually dryers for a fee

laun·dry *pl.* **laun·dries** *n.* a place equipped for laundering clothes etc. ‖ a batch of clothes etc. to be laundered

lau·rel *n.* any of various evergreen trees or shrubs **to rest on one's laurels** to be content with past achievement and make no more effort

la·va *n.* molten rock which issues from a volcano

lav·a·liere *n.* a pendant worn on a chain around the neck

lav·a·to·ry *pl.* **lav·a·to·ries** *n.* a room with a toilet and a washbasin ‖ a room with a washbasin

lav·en·der *n.* a small European shrub ‖ the color of the flowers ‖ the dried flowers used in sachets etc.

lav·ish 1. *adj.* given with great generosity and abundance **2.** *v.t.* to bestow with large generosity

law *n.* a custom or practice recognized as binding by a community, esp. as a result of having been so decreed by the governing authority ‖ the whole body of such customs or practices ‖ obedience to such customs or practices ‖ the profession of interpreting and enforcing such customs or practices ‖ a relationship between cause and effect ‖ a practice accepted as correct **to take the law into one's own hands** to act, esp. to punish, outside the sanction of the law

law·a·bid·ing *adj.* obedient to the law

law·ful *adj.* allowed by law ‖ legitimate ‖ valid

law·less *adj.* without law ‖ illegal ‖ disorderly

lawn *n.* a stretch of grass-covered land kept closely cut

law·suit *n.* a claim brought for judgment

before a court

law·yer *n.* someone qualified to practice law

lax *adj.* free from tension, slack ‖ not strict ‖ careless, negligent

lax·a·tive 1. *adj.* loosening the bowels and relieving constipation **2.** *n.* a laxative medicine

lax·i·ty *n.* the quality or condition of being lax

lay 1. *v.* **lay·ing laid** *v.t.* to place in a horizontal position ‖ to do this ceremonially ‖ to bring forth (an egg) ‖ to stake as a bet or wager ‖ to get (the table) ready for a meal ‖ to impute ‖ *v.i.* to bring forth eggs **to lay bare** to uncover **to lay hands on** to seize **to lay off** to discharge from employment **to lay on the line** to put up (money) in full **to lay out** to spend (money) in a planned way ‖ to prepare for burial **to lay over** to stop for a usually short period during a journey **2.** *n.* the manner, position or direction in which something lies **the lay of the land** the main aspects of a situation as one discerns it

lay·er 1. *n.* one thickness, coating etc. of one or more substances lying upon or under one or more other substances ‖ a laying hen **2.** *v.i.* to form in layers, strata etc.

lay·ette *n.* the outfit of clothing, furniture, linen etc. for a newborn child

lay·man *pl.* **lay·men** *n.* a person who is not a priest or cleric ‖ a person without recognized status or expert knowledge, in contrast to a professional man

lay·out *n.* the way in which things are placed in relation to one another ‖ a mock-up for such display

laz·i·ly *adv.* in a lazy manner

laz·i·ness *n.* the quality or state of being lazy

la·zy la·zi·er la·zi·est *adj.* with little will to work, idle ‖ slow-moving

lead 1. *v.* **lead·ing led** *v.t.* to show (someone) the way to go ‖ to take (someone) to a place ‖ to persuade to do something ‖ to cause to believe something ‖ to conduct (an orchestra, chorus etc.) ‖ to hold first

place in ‖ to cause to follow one's example ‖ *v.i.* to be at the head of a group in motion ‖ to show the way ‖ to bring about a specified result ‖ to hold the foremost position **to lead up to** to prepare the way for **2.** *n.* a showing of the way ‖ the principal or guiding part in a group action ‖ the foremost or front position ‖ leadership ‖ example ‖ (acting) the most important role

lead 1. *n.* a malleable metallic element **2.** *v.t.* to cover or frame with lead

lead·en *adj.* made of lead ‖ of a dull gray color ‖ very heavy, hard to lift ‖ oppressive ‖ sluggish, lacking animation

lead·er *n.* someone who acts as a guide ‖ someone who or something that leads ‖ someone or something that holds first place ‖ a conductor of a musical group ‖ the front horse in a harnessed team

léad·er·ship *n.* the position of a leader ‖ the quality displayed by a leader

lead·ing *adj.* coming firstn ‖ prominent, influential

lead·ing *n.* (printing) lead (thin strip of metal) or the spacing between lines achieved by such leads

leaf 1. *pl.* **leaves** *n.* a thin expanded outgrowth of a plant, usually green and consisting of a broad blade and a stalk ‖ a single sheet of folded paper ‖ the movable section of a table top ‖ leaves of tea, tobacco etc. **to turn over a new leaf** to make a fresh start **2.** *v.i.* to produce leaves ‖ (with 'through') to turn over the pages of (a book etc.)

leaf·let *n.* a small printed sheet of paper

leaf·y leaf·i·er leaf·i·est *adj.* full of leaves ‖ like a leaf

league 1. *n.* an association of persons, cities etc. formed to assist one another ‖ an association of football, baseball or other athletic clubs **2.** *v.i.* and *t.* **lea·guing leagued** to unite in a league

league *n.* a measure of distance, about three miles

leak *n.* a small hole, crack etc. through which e.g. fluid or light escapes or penetrates ‖ that which leaks or is leaked

leak *v.i.* (e.g. of a fluid or light, with 'in'

or 'out') to pass through a small hole or crack ‖ (of secret or restricted information) to become known to people not intended to have the information **leak·age** *n.* the act of leaking or an instance of this

leak·y leak·i·er leak·i·est *adj.* allowing fluids etc. to leak in or out

lean 1. *v.* **lean·ing leaned** *v.i.* to stand not quite upright ‖ (with 'on' or 'upon') to depend for support or encouragement ‖ *v.t.* to cause to lean **to lean over backward** to spare no effort in trying **2.** *n.* the act of leaning

lean 1. *adj.* having little fat ‖ thin **2.** *n.* that part of meat which has little fat

lean·ing *n.* tendency, inclination

leap *n.* the act of leaping ‖ something to be leaped ‖ an abrupt change **by leaps and bounds** very fast

leap leap·ing leaped, leapt *v.i.* to project the body through the air with a sudden movement ‖ *v.t.* to pass over by leaping

learn learn·ing learned, learnt *v.t.* to acquire knowledge of or skill in by study, instruction, practice or experience ‖ to be aware of ‖ *v.i.* (with 'of') to become aware, to be told **learn·ed** *adj.* having a great deal of knowledge

lease *n.* a legal contract between lessor and lessee putting property of the former at the disposal of the latter ‖ the document itself

lease leas·ing leased *v.t.* to put (land, buildings etc.) at the disposal of a lessee under a lease

leash 1. *n.* a strap, cord or chain fastened to the collar of an animal for control **2.** *v.t.* to put a leash on

least 1. *adj.* (superl. of LITTLE) smallest in size, amount, quality, importance etc. **2.** *n.* the smallest amount **at least** as the bare minimum **least of all** with the smallest justification **3.** *adv.* in the smallest degree

leath·er 1. *n.* the skin of an animal, cleaned and made flexible and durable by tanning **2.** *adj.* pertaining to, or made of, leather

leath·er·y *adj.* like leather in consistency or appearance ‖ tough

leave *n.* permission, esp. to be absent from duty ‖ the period of such absence **to take one's leave** to say goodbye and go

leave *v.* **leav·ing left** *v.i.* to depart, go away ‖ to cease to serve an employer ‖ *v.t.* to allow to remain by oversight ‖ to be survived by ‖ to bequeath **to leave alone** to stop interfering with **to leave behind** to go away without **to leave out** to omit

leave leav·ing leaved *v.i.* to put out leaves

leav·en 1. *n.* a substance added to dough which makes the dough rise and become porous **2.** *v.t.* to cause (dough) to ferment by adding leaven

lech *v.* to lust **lech** *n.* one who leches

lech·er *n.* a man given to lechery

lech·er·ous *adj.* characterized by or encouraging lechery

lech·er·y *n.* gross indulgence in carnal pleasure

lec·tern *n.* a stand with a sloping top for holding a reader's or lecturer's book, papers etc.

lec·ture 1. *n.* a prepared disquisition made to an audience, class, etc., designed to instruct ‖ a tedious reprimand **2.** **lec·tur·ing lec·tured** *v.i.* to deliver a lecture ‖ *v.t.* to instruct ‖ to reprimand **léc·tur·er** *n.* someone who lectures

ledge *n.* a narrow horizontal projection in a vertical or steep surface ‖ a ridge of rock, esp. under water

ledg·er *n.* a large book in which are recorded the credits and debits of commercial transactions

lee 1. *n.* the sheltered side, opposite to that against which the wind blows **2.** *adj.* of the sheltered side

leech *n.* a class of segmented, chiefly aquatic, suctorial annelids, which cling hard to the skin of an animal while sucking blood ‖ a human parasite

leek *n.* an edible vegetable allied to the onion

leer 1. *v.t.* to cast a knowing sidelong look that travesties a smile, and may indicate lust, malicious triumph or stupidity **2.** *n.* such a look

leer·y *adj.* suspicious, wary

lee·way *n.* a margin of freedom of action

left 1. *adj.* of or on the side of the body

where the heart is situated ‖ or on to this side as perceived by an observer ‖ (of a river bank) on this side of an observer facing downstream **2.** *adv.* in or to a left direction or side **3.** *n.* the left side or direction

leg 1. *n.* one of the limbs supporting a human or animal body and used in moving it from place to place ‖ a support for an object raised above the ground ‖ a side of a triangle other than the base or hypotenuse ‖ one section or stage of a journey, a relay race etc. **2.** *v.i.* **leg·ging legged** (with 'it') to walk in a hurry or run

leg·a·cy *pl.* **leg·a·cies** *n.* money or property bequeathed in a will

le·gal *adj.* of or pertaining to law ‖ in agreement with, or as prescribed by, the law

le·gal·i·ty *pl.* **le·gal·i·ties** *n.* accordance with the law ‖ (*pl.*) the requirements and procedure of the law

le·gal·ize leg·al·iz·ing le·gal·ized *v.t.* to make legal

le·ga·tion *n.* the official residence and office of a diplomatic representative ‖ a diplomatic mission

leg·end *n.* a story, handed down from the past, popularly accepted as true ‖ an inscription, esp. on a coin or medal ‖ an explanation beneath a photograph in a newspaper **leg·end·ar·y** *adj.* told of in legends

leg·er·de·main *n.* deception of the eye by quickness of the hand

leg·gings *pl. n.* a sturdy outer covering for the legs

leg·gy *adj.* having long legs

leg·i·bil·i·ty *n.* the quality of being legible

leg·i·ble *adj.* able to be read **lég·i·bly** *adv.*

le·gion *n.* a division of the Roman army ‖ a great number

le·gion·naire *n.* a member of a legion

leg·is·late leg·is·lat·ing leg·is·lat·ed *v.* to make laws

leg·is·la·tion *n.* a law enacted ‖ a law under consideration by a legislative body

leg·is·la·tive 1. *adj.* empowered to legislate ‖ of or effected by legislation **2.** *n.* a legislature

leg·is·la·tor *n.* someone who makes laws

leg·is·la·ture *n.* the body empowered to make, amend or repeal laws for a nation or unit of a nation

le·git·i·ma·cy *n.* the quality of being legitimate

le·git·i·mate 1. *adj.* born of a legally recognized marriage ‖ in accord with the provisions of law **2.** *v.t.* **le·git·i·mat·ing le·git·i·mat·ed** to make legitimate ‖ to justify **le·git·i·ma·tize le·git·i·ma·tiz·ing le·git·i·ma·tized** *v.t.* to legitimate

le·git·i·mize le·git·i·miz·ing le ‖ git·i·mized *v.t.* to make legitimate

lei·sure 1. *n.* time when one is free from the need to do any work **at one's leisure** when convenient and without any compulsion to hurry **2.** *adj.* free from work

lei·sure·ly 1. *adj.* unhurried **2.** *adv.* in an unhurried manner

lem·on *n.* a tree ‖ its yellow oval fruit ‖ the color of the ripe fruit

lem·on·ade *n.* a drink made by mixing lemon juice and sugar with water

lend lend·ing lent *v.t.* to place in the temporary possession of another ‖ to loan ‖ *v.i.* to make a loan **to lend a hand** to assist

length *n.* linear extent in space from end to end ‖ extent in time from beginning to end **to go to great length (or lengths)** to set hardly any limits on what one is prepared to do **to keep at arm's length** to avoid too intimate a contact with

length·en *v.i.* to become longer ‖ *v.t.* to cause (something) to become longer

length·wise 1. *adv.* in the direction of the length **2.** *adj.* going in the direction of the length

length·y length·i·er length·i·est *adj.* excessively long

le·ni·ence *n.* the quality of being lenient

le·ni·en·cy *n.* lenience

le·ni·ent *adj.* tolerant ‖ (of punishment) mild

lens *pl.* **lens·es** *n.* a piece of glass, or other transparent refracting substance, with two opposite regular surfaces, of which at least one is curved, used in optical systems to converge or diverge light rays to form an image ‖ a transparent, almost spherical body behind the pupil of the eye

leop·ard *n.* a large, fierce, carnivorous mammal native to Africa and S. Asia

lep·er *n.* a person suffering from leprosy ‖ outcast

lep·ro·sy *n.* a chronic infective disease

Les·bi·an 1. *adj.* pertaining to Lesbos ‖ relating to homosexuality in women **2.** *n.* a woman homosexual **Lésbianism** *n.*

le·sion *n.* a change in the structure of a tissue ‖ injury

less alt. comp. of LITTLE, c.f. LESSER ‖ **1.** *adj.* smaller in size, degree, extent etc. ‖ not so much ‖ lower in rank **2.** prep. made smaller by **3.** *adv.* in or to a smaller degree or extent **4.** *n.* the smaller amount

les·see *n.* someone who is granted a lease

less·en *v.i.* to become less

less·er alt. comp. of LITTLE ‖ *adj.* smaller in size, amount, quality, importance etc.

les·son *n.* something to be learned ‖ *(pl.)* a series of sessions of instruction ‖ one unit in a series of sessions of instruction

les·sor *n.* someone who grants a lease

lest conj. in order that…not

let **let·ting** *v.t.* to permit to ‖ (often with 'out') to assign (a contract) **let alone** without mentioning **to let down** to cause (someone) disappointment by failing to do what was expected **to let on** to reveal a secret

let *n.* (law, only in) **without let or hindrance** without impediment ‖ (lawn tennis, rackets etc.) an obstruction of the ball, esp. contact with the top of the tennis net

-let suffix added to nouns to express smallness or minor importance

let·down *n.* a disappointment ‖ a relaxation or lowering of standards

le·thal *adj.* causing or able to cause death

le·thar·gic *adj.* of, marked by or causing lethargy **le·thár·gi·cal·ly** *adv.*

leth·ar·gy *n.* the state of lacking energy and interest

let·ter 1. *n.* one of the printed or written symbols of an alphabet ‖ a written, printed or typed personal communication ‖ *(pl.)* literature ‖ *(pl.)* scholarly study or knowl-

edge **to the letter** precisely and completely **2.** *v.t.* to inscribe

let·tered *adj.* marked with letters ‖ cultured ‖ learned

let·ter·head *n.* the heading printed at the top of writing paper ‖ a piece of paper so printed

let·ter·ing *n.* the act of marking with letters, esp. as used in calligraphy

lettuce *n.* a crisp leaved, annual plant

leu·ke·mi·a, leu·cae·mi·a *n.* an acute or chronic disease of unknown origin

lev·ee *n.* an embankment

lev·el 1. *n.* an instrument for testing whether something is horizontal ‖ a horizontal line, plane or surface ‖ a horizontal condition ‖ a degree of attainment **on the level** honest, truthful **2.** *adj.* horizontal, having no part higher than another ‖ unflustered ‖ steady and direct **3.** **lev·el·ing leveled** *v.t.* to make level ‖ to aim, direct ‖ *v.i.* to become level **to level off** to make level, smooth

lev·el·er *n.* someone or something which brings things or people to the same level

lev·el-head·ed *adj.* showing balanced judgment and good sense

lev·er 1. *n.* a rigid bar turning about a fixed point, used to modify or transmit a force or motion applied at a second point so that it acts at a third point **2.** **lév·er·age** *n.* the action or effect of a lever

lev·i·tate lev·i·tat·ing lev·i·tat·ed *v.i.* to rise or float in the air as if weightless **le·vi·tá·tion** *n.*

lev·i·ty *pl.* **lev·i·ties** *n.* lighthearted and frivolous behavior

lev·y 1. *pl.* **lev·ies** *n.* the imposition by a state or organization of a tax, duty, fine etc. **2.** **lev·y·ing lev·ied** *v.t.* to impose (a tax, fine etc.) ‖ *v.i.* to make a levy

lewd *adj.* offending modesty, indecent ‖ lascivious

lex·i·cal *adj.* of or pertaining to a lexicon or lexicography

lex·i·cog·ra·pher *n.* someone who compiles or writes a dictionary **lex·i·co·graph·i·cal** *adj.* **lex·i·cóg·ra·phy** *n.* the process of compiling or writing a dictionary

lex·i·con n. a dictionary

li·a·bil·i·ty pl. **li·a·bil·i·ties** n. thequality or condition of being liable ‖ (pl.) debts

li·a·ble adj. legally bound or responsible ‖ subject ‖ having a tendency, apt ‖ likely

li·ai·son n. a love affair outside marriage ‖ the establishment of harmonious cooperation between separate units of an armed force

li·ar n. someone who tells a lie or habitually tells lies

li·ba·tion n. the act of pouring wine or oil upon the ground as a sacrifice ‖ the wine or oil so sacrificed

li·bel 1. n. a published statement, photograph etc. which without due cause has the result of bringing its subject into disrepute ‖ any false and insulting statement **2.** v.t. **li·bel·ing li·beled** to publish a libel about ‖ make false and malicious statements about **li·bel·ous** adj.

lib·er·al 1. adj. giving freely ‖ generously large ‖ not subject to the common prejudices or conventions ‖ favorable to individual liberty, social reform and the removal of economic restraints **2.** n. a person who holds liberal views

lib·er·al·ism n. the quality or state of being liberal

lib·er·al·ize lib·er·al·iz·ing lib·er·al·ized v.t. to make liberal ‖ v.i. to become liberal

lib·er·ate lib·er·at·ing lib·er·at·ed v.t. to set free, release

lib·er·a·tion n. a liberating or being liberated

lib·er·a·tor n. someone who liberates

lib·er·ty pl. **lib·er·ties** n. the condition of being free to choose ‖ the right to do as one pleases ‖ a short period of leave ‖ free will **at liberty** free ‖ unemployed, not busy ‖ authorized **to take the liberty** to presume

li·bi·do n. the sexual urge

li·brar·i·an n. a person in charge of a library

li·brar·y pl. **li·brar·ies** n. a room or building housing a collection of books ‖ such a collection of books

li·bret·to pl. **li·bret·tos, li·bret·ti** n. the words of an opera, oratorio etc.

li·cense, li·cence 1. n. a right formally granted in writing by an authority ‖ the official certificate of this right ‖ a degree of freedom ‖ licentious behavior **2.** v.t. **li·cens·ing, li·cenc·ing li·censed, li·cenced** to grant a license to (someone) or for (something) **li·cen·see** n. someone to whom a license is granted **li·cens·er** n. someone who grants a license

li·cen·tious adj. disregarding the laws of morality

lick 1. v.t. to draw the tongue over ‖ (of waves, fire, flames etc.) to play lightly over the surface of ‖ to get the better of ‖ (pop.) to thrash, beat **2.** n. the act of licking or an instance of this

lic·o·rice, liq·uo·rice n. a black extract used as a demulcent and expectorant, in confectionery, and for flavoring

lid n. a cover closing the top of a receptacle fitting inside or outside its walls ‖ an eyelid

lie v.i. **ly·ing lay lain** to have the body more or less horizontal upon a surface ‖ (usually with 'down') to assume such a position ‖ to be in the grave **to take lying down** to accept without protest

lie ly·ing lied v.i. to tell a lie ‖ to deceive by making a false impression

lie n. an intentionally false statement or impression

lie detector a device which registers the physical changes in the body (e.g. respiration, blood pressure) of someone under questioning

lien n. the right to hold another's goods or property until a claim is met

lieu n. **in lieu** instead **in lieu of** as a substitute for

lieu·ten·ant n. someone acting for a superior in rank ‖ an officer

life pl. **lives** n. the state of an organism characterized by certain processes or abilities that include metabolism, growth, reproduction and response ‖ the period of time from birth to death ‖ a specified period or aspect of one's existence ‖ a way or manner or existence ‖ a human being ‖ the gay, animating presence **a matter of life and death** a very critical matter **from life**

(art) from the living model **to have the time of one's life** to enjoy oneself very much **to take life** to kill

life·guard *n.* an expert swimmer employed to prevent casualties at a swimming pool etc.

life·less *adj.* without life ‖ providing no stimulus

life·long *adj.* for the period of a lifetime

life·size *adj.* (of a portrait, sculpture etc.) of the same size as the subject **life-sized** *adj.*

life·time *n.* the duration of the life of a person, thing, institution etc. ‖ a very long time

lift 1. *v.t.* to raise, hoist ‖ to steal ‖ to plagiarize ‖ to remove ‖ *v.i.* to move upwards, disperse **2.** *n.* the act of lifting or an instance of this ‖ a mechanical hoist ‖ an emotional bolstering up ‖ a free ride in a vehicle ‖ an airlift

lift-off *n.* the action of a rocket leaving its launch pad or of a helicopter etc. becoming airborne

lig·a·ment *n.* a short fibrous band which connects one bone with another or supports an organ **lig·a·men·tal, lig·a·men·tar·y, lig·a·men·tous** *adjs*

lig·a·ture 1. *n.* something used to bind or unite ‖ a piece of nylon, wire etc. used as a surgical suture ‖ the action of binding with such a suture **2. lig·a·tur·ing lig·a·tured** to bind with a ligature

light *n.* the wave band of electromagnetic radiation to which the retina of the eye is sensitive and which the brain interprets ‖ a brightness ‖ someone who is a luminary ‖ the aspect in which something is seen ‖ daylight ‖ daytime ‖ a flame or spark used to ignite something, or the thing providing this flame or spark ‖ (pl., theater) illuminated letters outside a theater **to bring (or come) to light** to make (or become) known

light *adj.* of little weight, not heavy ‖ having less than the correct weight ‖ having, because of its texture, small mass in relation to volume ‖ quick-moving, nimble ‖ not strenuous, easy to do ‖ easy to bear ‖ designed merely to amuse and give pleasure ‖ dizzy ‖ easy to digest ‖ having a relatively small alcoholic content **to travel light** to travel with little luggage **with a light heart** cheerfully

light *adj.* having considerable light, not dark ‖ pale

light light·ing lit, light·ed *v.t.* to cause to emit light or burn ‖ to show the way to by carrying a light ‖ *v.i.* to become lit

light·en *v.t.* to reduce the load of ‖ mitigate ‖ to make more amusing ‖ *v.i.* to become lighter

lighten *v.t.* to make (a dark place) (a color etc.) lighter ‖ *v.t.* to become brighter

light·er *n.* a device for lighting a cigarette, a blunt etc.

lighter *n.* a large, usually flat-bottomed, boat

light-head·ed *adj.* not quite in control of one's words or behavior ‖ frivolous, silly

light·heart·ed *adj.* free from worries, cheerful

light heavyweight a professional boxer whose weight does not exceed 175 lbs

light·ly *adv.* in a manner devoid of heaviness

light·ness *n.* the quality of an object that depends on its ability to reflect or transmit light ‖ degree of illumination

light·ning *n.* an electric discharge

lightning rod an earthed metal rod attached to a building to divert lightning from it

light·weight *n.* a professional boxer whose weight does not exceed 135 lbs

light-year *n.* an astronomical unit of distance: the distance traveled by light in one terrestrial year

lig·nite *n.* coal intermediate between peat and bituminous coal and containing much volatile matter

lik·a·ble, like·a·ble *adj.* amiable

like 1. *adj.* identical, equal or almost equal ‖ faithful to the original ‖ resembling **2.** *prep.* characteristic of ‖ indicative of ‖ to compare with ‖ identical or almost so **3.** *adv.* **as like as not** probably **4.** *conj.* as, in the same way as ‖ similar to **5.** *n.* counterpart, equal

like 1. *v.t.* **lik·ing liked** to find pleasing,

agreeable or attractive ‖ to be fond of ‖ (in conditional constructions) to wish 2. *n. (pl.)* preferences

like·li·hood *n.* probability

like·ly 1. *adj.* **like·li·er like·li·est** probable ‖ plausible, credible ‖ suitable 2. *adv.* probably **likely as not** quite possibly

lik·en *v.t.* to represent as similar

like·ness *n.* a similarity, resemblance

like·wise 1. *adv.* similarly 2. *conj.* also, moreover

li·lac 1. *n.* a small deciduous tree ‖ flowers of these trees ‖ pinkish-mauve color 2. *adj.* of this color

lilt *n.* a gentle, pleasing, rising and falling rhythm in songs, voices, etc. ‖ a light swaying or sprightly movement **lilt·ing** *adj.*

lil·y *pl.* **lil·ies** *n.* a genus of bulbous, perennial plants ‖ a flower ‖ something compared to a lily in purity, delicacy, whiteness etc. ‖ (heraldry) the fleur-de-lis

limb *n.* one of the projecting paired appendages (e.g. arm, leg, wing, fin, parapodium) of an animal body ‖ a large bough of a tree

lim·ber 1. *adj.* bending easily, flexible 2. *v.t.* (with 'up') to make supple

lime 1. *n.* a caustic and highly infusible solid consisting essentially of calcium oxide 2. *v.t.* **lim·ing limed** to spread lime over

lime *n.* a citrus tree native to the East Indies

lime·light *n.* an intense white light ‖ the flood of publicity accorded to a public figure

lim·er·ick *n.* a five-lined nonsense verse

lime·stone *n.* a hard rock that consists mainly of calcium carbonate

lim·it 1. *n.* the furthest extent, amount etc. ‖ (often pl.) boundary, confines ‖ an established highest or lowest amount, quantity, size etc. **within limits** within moderation 2. *v.t.* to restrict ‖ to serve as a limit to

lim·i·ta·tion *n.* a limiting or being limited ‖ something that limits ‖ a limit of capability

lim·ou·sine *n.* a car with a closed body and a partitioned seat for the driver ‖ a luxurious car

limp 1. *v.i.* to walk awkwardly or painfully because of some deformity or injury to one leg ‖ (of verse) to have a halting rhythm 2. *n.* a lame or crippled walk

limp *adj.* floppy ‖ weak, feeble

lim·pid *adj.* clear, transparent **lim·pid·i·ty** *n.*

lim·y lim·i·er lim·i·est *adj.* like, made of, containing or covered with lime

line 1. *n.* a length of rope ‖ a length of cord, thread etc. with a hook for catching fish ‖ a clothesline ‖ a telephone wire or cable, or this route of communication ‖ a pipe through which liquids, gases etc. may be transported ‖ a long thin stroke marked on a surface ‖ an outline, contour ‖ the style or cut of a garment ‖ a wrinkle or crease in the skin ‖ a row of written, typed or printed words ‖ a brief letter ‖ *(pl.)* the words of an actor's part ‖ a number of things, persons or events ‖ lineage, family ‖ route ‖ a rail route, or part of a rail system ‖ a course of conduct, direction of thought, or mode of procedure ‖ a branch of business or activity ‖ a stock of a certain kind of goods **to drop a line** to write a brief letter or note **to fall into line with** to adjust oneself **to get a line on** to obtain information on **to read between the lines** to understand what is being implied 2. **lin·ing lined** *v.t.* to mark or cover with lines ‖ to stand or be in a line along ‖ to set or arrange in a line ‖ *v.i.* (with 'up') to form a line

line lin·ing lined *v.t.* to provide with an inner layer

lin·e·age *n.* a line of descent, ancestry

lin·e·al *adj.* in the direct line of descent ‖ of or in lines

lin·e·ar *adj.* of or in lines ‖ (of a unit of measure) involving one dimension only ‖ able to be shown as a straight line on a graph

lin·en 1. *n.* cloth made from flax fiber ‖ yarn or thread made from flax ‖ (collect.) articles made of this cloth 2. *adj.* made of flax or linen

line·up *n.* a row of people made to assemble for identification of suspected criminals ‖ (football, baseball) a list of players and their respective playing positions

lin·ger *v. i.* to dawdle ‖ to loiter ‖ to be slow in dying

lin·ge·rie *n.* women's underclothing

lain·go *pl.* **lin·goes, lin·gos** *n.* jargon ‖ an unusual vocabulary

lin·gual *adj.* of, like or near the tongue ‖ articulated esp. with the tongue ‖ linguistic

lin·guist *n.* someone who is proficient in several foreign languages **lin·guis·tic** *adj.*

lin·guis·tics *n.* the scientific study of language

lin·i·ment *n.* a liquid medicinal preparation for rubbing into the skin to relieve pain and muscular stiffness

lin·ing *n.* the material which lines an inner surface

link 1. *n.* a ring or loop of a chain ‖ someone or something that joins other people or things ‖ (computer) portion of a program or equipment that directs information from one part to another 2. *v.t.* to join ‖ to entwine

link·age *n.* a linking or being linked

links *pl. n.* a golf course

link·up *n.* a connection or contact

li·no·le·um *n.* a floor covering

lin·seed *n.* the seed of flax

lint *n.* a material used for dressing wounds ‖ bits of loose thread, fluff etc.

li·on *n.* a large carnivorous mammal **the lion's share** the largest share

li·on·ess *n.* the female lion

li·on·ize **li·on·iz·ing** **li·on·ized** *v.t.* to treat as a celebrity and make a great fuss over

lip 1. *n.* one of the two fleshy, muscular, highly sensitive folds bordering the mouth ‖ the edge of a cavity, opening, vessel, wound etc. ‖ impudent talk, answering back etc. **to hang on someone's lips** to listen to someone with complete attention **to keep a stiff upper lip** show fortitude **to lick (or smack) one's lips** to show eager anticipation 2. *adj.* labial

lip·read·er *n.* someone who does lipreading

lip·read·ing *n.* a method of understanding speech by observing the movements of the speaker's lips

lip·stick *n.* a stick of cosmetic, usually in a retractable holder, for coloring the lips

liq·ue·fi·er *n.* an apparatus in which gases are liquefied

liq·ue·fy **liq·ue·fy·ing** **liq·ue·fied** *v.t.* to make liquid

li·queur *n.* a strongly flavored and highly fortified alcoholic liquor

liq·uid 1. *adj.* of or being a fluid substance ‖ readily changeable for cash 2. *n.* a liquid substance

liq·ui·date **liq·ui·dat·ing** **liq·ui·dat·ed** *v.i.* to pay or settle (a debt) ‖ to wind up (a company or business) ‖ to convert into cash ‖ *v.i.* to become liquidated **liq·ui·dá·tion** *n.* a liquidating **líq·ui·da·tor** *n.* someone appointed to supervise the liquidation

liq·uor *n.* drink of high alcoholic content ‖ a solution of a specified drug in water

lisp 1. *v.* to mispronounce 's' or 'z' as 'th' 2. *n.* a lisping pronunciation

lis·some, lis·som *adj.* lithe, slim and supple

list 1. *n.* a number of names of persons or things ‖ a catalog 2. *v.t.* to make a list of ‖ to register

list 1. *n.* a lean to one side 2. *v.i.* to lean to one side

lis·ten *v.i.* to hear ‖ to pay attention ‖ to be influenced by

list·less *adj.* lacking energy ‖ uninterested

li·ter, li·tre *n.* a metric unit of capacity

lit·er·a·cy *n.* the condition or quality of being literate

lit·er·al *adj.* true in the usual sense of the words used ‖ prosaic, matter-of-fact

lit·er·ar·i·ly *adv.* in a literary way or manner

lit·er·ar·y *adj.* of literature ‖ well versed in literature ‖ characteristic of a written as distinct from a spoken style

lit·er·ate 1. *adj.* able to read and write 2. *n.* someone who can read and write

lit·er·a·ture *n.* written compositions in prose or verse ‖ writings produced in a certain country or during a certain period ‖ books or treatises on a particular subject

lithe *adj.* slim, sinewy and supple

lith·o·graph 1. *v.t.* to print by the process

of lithography 2. *n.* an impression or print so made **li·thog·ra·pher** *n.* someone skilled in lithography

lith·o·graph·ic *adj.* produced by lithography

li·thog·ra·phy *n.* the process of printing

lith·o·log·i·cal *adj.* of or relating to lithology

li·thol·o·gy *n.* the study of stones and rocks

lit·i·gate lit·i·gat·ing lit·i·gat·ed *v.i.* to carry on a lawsuit ‖ *v.t.* to contest at law **lit·i·gá·tion** *n.*

lit·ter 1. *n.* rubbish ‖ the young brought forth at one birth by e.g. a sow or bitch ‖ a stretcher **2.** *v.t.* to throw down as litter ‖ *v.i.* (of an animal) to bring forth young

lit·ter·bug *n.* someone who drops litter on a street

lit·tle 1. *adj.* **less less·er lit·tler least lit·tlest** small in size, amount, number, degree etc. ‖ (of children) young ‖ short ‖ (of distance or duration) brief ‖ trivial petty, mean **2.** *adv.* **less least** not much, very slightly **3.** *n.* a small amount **little by little** gradually

lit·ur·gy *pl.* **lit·ur·gies** *n.* the public rites and services of the Christian Church

liv·a·ble, live·a·ble *adj.* good for living in

live liv·ing lived *v.i.* to have life as an animal or plant ‖ to subsist, maintain life ‖ to flourish, remain in people's memory ‖ to reside, dwell ‖ *v.t.* to pass, spend **to live and let live** to be tolerant of others' views, weaknesses etc.

live *adj.* living, not dead ‖ existing, not fictional ‖ energetic, lively ‖ unexploded ‖ direct, not recorded ‖ carrying electric current

live·li·hood *n.* means of subsistence

live·ly live·li·er live·li·est 1. *adj.* brisk, vigorous ‖ vivid ‖ active **2.** *adv.* in a lively way

liv·en *v.t.* to enliven ‖ *v.i.* to become more active

liv·er *n.* a large, vascular, glandular organ of vertebrates ‖ the liver eaten as food

live·stock *n.* animals, esp. cattle, kept on a farm

liv·id *adj.* bluish-gray in color ‖ discolored as if by bruising ‖ (pop.) exceedingly

angry **li·víd·i·ty** *n.*

liv·ing 1. *n.* the condition of having life ‖ livelihood **2.** *adj.* endowed with life ‖ now existing ‖ of or pertaining to life ‖ sufficient for life

living room the room in a house where the family spends most of the day when at home

liz·ard *n.* a suborder of reptiles

lla·ma *pl.* **lla·mas, lla·ma** *n.* any of several South American ruminant mammals, closely allied to the camel but humpless

lo *interj.* esp. in the phrase **lo and behold!** by a curious chance

load 1. *n.* something which is supported by or carried in something ‖ an amount of work expected to be done ‖ the quantity of electrical power used by a machine, circuit etc. **2.** *v.t.* to put a load on or in ‖ to be a load or weight on ‖ to make heavier ‖ to add a weight to (dice) so that they fall as one wants them to ‖ to insert the charge, cartridge or shell in (a firearm or gun) ‖ to insert (film) in a camera ‖ to burden ‖ *v.i.* to take on a load

load·er *n.* someone or something that loads

loaf *pl.* **loaves** *n.* bread, meat or other food done up in a shaped piece ‖ a sugar loaf

loaf *v.* to pass (time) in idleness **lóaf·er** *n.* a lazy person

loaf·er *n.* a type of leather walking shoe

loam *n.* a loose rich soil of clay and sand **lóam·y loam·i·er loam·i·est** *adj.*

loan 1. *n.* something lent, usually money, on condition that it is returned **2.** *v.t.* to grant a loan of

loan·word *n.* a word adopted from a foreign language and freely used

loath, loth unwilling, reluctant

loathe loath·ing loathed *v.t.* to regard with disgust or abhorrence **lóath·ing** *n.* abhorrence **loath·some** *adj.* repulsive

lob 1. *v.t.* **lob·bing lobbed** (tennis) to hit (the ball) in a high parabola, usually to the back of the opponent's court **2.** *n.* a ball tossed in this manner

lob·by 1. *pl.* **lob·bies** *n.* a corridor or room used as an entrance hall, vestibule, waiting room, anteroom etc. ‖ a group of people trying to bring pressure to bear on legislators to pursue policies favorable to their interests **2. lob·by·ing lob·bied** *v.t.* to try to influence (legislators) in favor of a certain policy ‖ *v.i.* to influence legislators in this way **lób·by·ist** *n.* a person who lobbies

lobe *n.* the soft rounded lower end of the human ear **lobed** *adj.* having a lobe or lobes

lob·ster *pl.* **lob·sters, lob·ster** *n.* a family of marine crustaceans

lo·cal 1. *adj.* of, relating to or restricted to a particular place or area **2.** *n.* someone who lives or works in a particular neighborhood or area ‖ a local train, bus etc. ‖ the local branch of a large organization

lo·cale *n.* a place or location, a setting

lo·cal·i·ty *pl.* **lo·cal·i·ties** *n.* a particular district or neighborhood

lo·cate lo·cat·ing lo·cat·ed *v.t.* to look for and discover ‖ to situate ‖ *v.i.* to take up residence

lo·ca·tion *n.* a geographical situation ‖ (movies) a site chosen outside the studio for purposes of filming

lock *n.* a curl, tress or tuft of hair

lock 1. *n.* a fastening device for doors, lids, drawers etc. ‖ a device for preventing movement in a wheel ‖ any of several holds in wrestling ‖ a part of a canal or river enclosed between gates **2.** *v.t.* to fasten (a door etc.) with a lock ‖ to join tightly ‖ *v.i.* to become fastened with a lock

lock·er *n.* a small cupboard usually with a lock ‖ a storeroom or compartment in a ship

lock·et *n.* a small metal case worn around the neck on a chain, containing a portrait or lock of hair

lock·jaw *n.* an early symptom of tetanus

lo·co·mo·tive *n.* a self-propelled vehicle running on rails

lo·cust *n.* a family of grasshoppers ‖ a cicada ‖ a locust tree

lo·cu·tion *n.* a turn of speech, phrase or idiom

lode *n.* a deposit of ore as a vein in a rock

lode·stone, load·stone *n.* a naturally occurring magnetic iron ore

lodge *n.* a small house on the grounds of a large country house, usually occupied by an employee ‖ the meeting hall of a branch of a Masonic or similar body ‖ the den of a beaver or otter

lodge lodg·ing lodged *v.i.* to live in someone else's house, paying for accommodation ‖ to deposit ‖ to put in a place for safety ‖ to make formal statement of **lódg·er** *n.* someone who occupies a rented room

lódg·ing *n.* temporary accommodation

lo·ess, loss *pl.* **lo·ess, löss·es** *n.* a deposit of fine yellowish soil transported by the wind

loft 1. *n.* an attic ‖ a room over a stable for hay ‖ the upper story of a warehouse or factory ‖ a gallery in a church or hall **2.** *v.t.* (esp. golf) to hit in a high arc above the ground

loft·y loft·i·er loft·i·est *adj.* towering ‖ proud, haughty

log 1. *n.* a long and heavy piece of the trunk or a branch of a tree ‖ a shorter segment of unshaped timber used for fuel ‖ a logbook or the record entered in it **2.** *v.* **log·ging logged** *v.t.* to enter in a logbook

log·a·rithm *n.* the power to which a selected number b (the base) must be raised in order to be equal to the number a under consideration: if a ;eq b;xn, n is the logarithm of a to base **log·a·ríth·mic** *adj.* **log·a·ríth·mi·cal·ly** *adv.*

log·book *n.* a book containing a record of the progress of a ship and all events of the voyage kept daily

loge *n.* a box in a theater or opera house

log·ger *n.* someone who earns his living by logging

log·ic *n.* the science of pure reasoning ‖ compelling power

log·i·cal *adj.* related to logic ‖ consistent with correct reasoning ‖ inevitably following from the application of reason

lo·gi·cian *n.* a specialist in logic

lo·gis·tic *adj.* of or pertaining to logistics

lo·gis·tics *n.* the branch of military science concerned with troop movements and supplies ‖ symbolic logic

log·o·gram *n.* an arbitrary symbol

loin *n.* the cut of meat taken from the hindquarters of an animal ‖ (esp. pl.) the area in a man or quadaruped between the hipbone and ribs

loi·ter *v.i.* to hang around, stay or wander about near some spot apparently aimlessly ‖ *v.t.* (with 'away') to waste in idleness

loll *v.i.* to hang in a loosely relaxed, drooping way ‖ (of the tongue) to hang out ‖ *v.t.* to allow to dangle

lone *adj.* single, alone, not one of a pack or group ‖ isolated **lóne·li·ness** *n.* **lóne·ly lone·li·er lone·li·est** *adj.* **lóne·some** *adj.* (of people) lonely and sad

long long·er long·est *adj.* measuring a more than usual distance from one end to the other in space or duration ‖ of specified length or duration ‖ extending to relatively remote time, far back or forward ‖ (of betting odds) in which a bettor stands to win a large multiple of his stake ‖ served in a tall glass **in the long run** eventually

long long·er long·est *adv.* for a long time ‖ throughout a specified period **so long** goodbye

long *v.i.* to desire earnestly and intensely

lon·gev·i·ty *n.* long life or unusually long life

long·ing *n.* intense desire for what is not attainable

lon·gi·tude *n.* the angular distance between the meridian passing through a given point on the earth's surface and the poles, and the standard meridian at Greenwich, England

lon·gi·tu·di·nal *adj.* of longitude ‖ lengthwise

long·shore·man *pl.* **long·shore·men** *n.* a stevedore

long-suf·fer·ing *adj.* patient, not easily provoked

look *v.i.* to use the faculty of sight, make an effort to see ‖ to direct the eyes in a particular direction ‖ to appear ‖ *v.t.* to examine, regard intensely ‖ to find out, come to know through seeing **1.** *n.* a glance, a regard ‖ appearance

look·out *n.* a keeping awatch ‖ an observation post for this purpose ‖ someone stationed to keep a watch

loom 1. *v.i.* to appear indistinctly, e.g. through a mist ‖ to figure a future threat **2.** *n.* the indistinct and somewhat menacing appearance of something

loom *n.* a machine for weaving cloth

loon *n.* an order of large, aquatic, diving birds

loon *n.* someone extremely silly

loon·y loon·i·er loon·i·est *adj.* crazy

loop 1. *n.* a closed figure with a curved outline and central aperture ‖ the running noose of a lasso ‖ a closed circuit **to knock (or throw) for a loop** to throw into a totally unexpected state of surprise, bewilderment or inactivity **2.** *v.t.* to form into a loop ‖ to fasten with a loop ‖ *v.t.* to move in a loop ‖ to form a loop

loop·hole *n.* a narrow vertical slit in a wall to admit light and air ‖ a way of evading rule, law etc.

loose 1. *adj.* not fitting tightly ‖ not bound together ‖ not fastened, not firmly fixed ‖ unconfined ‖ slack ‖ careless, vague ‖ free, not literal ‖ lacking moral restraint ‖ not under strict control **2.** *adv.* in a loose way **to cut loose** to free oneself from ties **3.** *n.* **on the loose** freed from control or restrictions **4.** **loos·ing loosed** *v.t.* to set free ‖ to unfasten, release ‖ to untie

loos·en *v.t.* to make less tight ‖ to unfasten ‖ to relax ‖ *v.i.* to become loose

loot 1. *n.* booty ‖ goods come by illicitly **2.** *v.t.* to pillage, esp. after a calamity ‖ *v.i.* to steal by pillaging

lop *v.t.* **lop·ping lopped** to trim (branches) from a tree ‖ to cut off

lop lop·ping lopped *v.i.* to droop, e.g. of a spaniel's ears ‖ (of a rabbit) to go with short bounds

lope 1. *v.i.* **lop·ing loped** (esp. of animals) to move with a long effortless stride

lope *n.* (esp. in animals) a loping stride

lop·sid·ed *adj.* drooping at one side ‖ unevenly balanced

lo·qua·cious *adj.* talkative

lord *n.* a nobleman or person entitled to use 'Lord' before his name ‖ a master, ruler, sovereign **to live like a lord** to live in great luxury

lord·ly lord·li·er lord·li·est *adj.* befitting

a lord ‖ haughty

lore *n.* the knowledge and stock of beliefs relating to a certain subject place, person etc.

lose los·ing lost *v.t.* to become unable to find ‖ to cease to have, fail to keep ‖ to be deprived of ‖ to get rid of ‖ to waste ‖ to fail to win ‖ to miss ‖ to fail to keep in sight ‖ to decrease in ‖ *v.i.* to fail to win, be defeated ‖ to suffer loss

loss *n.* a losing ‖ defeat ‖ excess of cost over selling price ‖ the financial detriment suffered by an insured person as a result of damage to property, theft etc. ‖ energy wasted in a machine ‖ decrease in quality or degree

lost *adj.* unable to find the way ‖ wasted ‖ missed ‖ ruined ‖ (of persons) killed ‖ bewildered ‖ helpless ‖ engrossed

lot 1. *n.* one's fate or destiny in life ‖ a plot or area of land having established limits ‖ a studio and the surrounding land belonging to it **to draw lots** to decide by using some method of random choice **a lot, lots** a large number or amount 2. *adv.* **a lot** much, considerably

lo·tion *n.* a liquid preparation applied to the skin

lot·ter·y *pl.* **lot·ter·ies** *n.* a method of raising money by the sale of a large number of tickets and the subsequent chance selection of certain ones entitling the bearers of these to a prize

lot·to *n.* a form of bingo

loud *adj.* producing a powerful stimulus on the ear ‖ clamoring, noisy ‖ vulgar, unrefined

loud *adv.* in a loud manner

loud·speak·er *n.* a device that converts electrical impulses into sounds

lounge 1. *v.* **loung·ing lounged** *v.i.* to loll ‖ *v.t.* (with 'away') to pass (time) in idleness or loafing 2. *n.* a room in a hotel, club etc. ‖ a long sofa with a headrest at one end

louse *pl.* **lice** *n.* orders of small wingless parasitic insects ‖ (*pl.* **louses**) a person for whom one feels contempt **lous·y lous·i·er lous·i·est** infested with lice ‖ rotten, disgusting, bad in quality

lout *n.* a rough, clumsy, stupid fellow

lou·ver, lou·vre *n.* an arrangement of overlapping boards or slats with gaps between them so that air is admitted but rain excluded **lóu·vered, lóu·vred** ,*adj.*

lov·a·ble, love·a·ble *adj.* for whom people instinctively feel warm affection **lóv·a·bly, lóve·a·bly** *adv.*

love *n.* a powerful emotion felt for another person manifesting itself in deep affection, devotion or sexual desire ‖ the object of this emotion ‖ a great liking, fondness

love lov·ing loved *v.t.* to feel the passion of love for ‖ to be fond of ‖ to enjoy ‖ *v.i.* to be in love

love·li·ness *n.* the state or quality of being lovely

love·ly love·li·er love·li·est *adj.* beautiful ‖ delightful

lov·er *n.* a man in relation to his mistress ‖ (*pl.*) two people in love with one another ‖ someone who greatly enjoys something specified

lov·ing *adj.* devoted, affectionate

low 1. *adj.* being at a relatively small distance above some plane of reference ‖ at or near the bottom of some scale of moral or social values or ranking ‖ mean, contemptible ‖ obscene ‖ depressed ‖ unfavorable ‖ quiet, soft 2. *adv.* in or to a low position ‖ softly 3. *n.* low gear ‖ an area of low barometric pressure

low·down *n.* the real facts of a situation as known to someone with inside information

low·er 1. *adj.* relatively little advanced in biological evolution 2. *v.t.* to let down ‖ to reduce ‖ to make less loud ‖ to degrade ‖ *v.i.* to decrease

low·li·ness *n.* the quality or state of being lowly

low·ly 1. *adj.* **low·li·er low·li·est** humble, modest ‖ far down in a hierarchy 2. *adv.* in a lowly manner

loy·al *adj.* faithful to ‖ displaying fidelity **lóy·al·ist** *n.* someone who is loyal

loy·al·ty *pl.* **loy·al·ties** *n.* the quality of being loyal

loz·enge *n.* a small medicinal candy ‖

diamond-shaped

lub·ber *n.* a clumsy unskilled sailor

lu·bri·cant 1. *n.* a substance (e.g. grease, oil, soap) that reduces friction and its effects 2. *adj.* lubricating

lu·bri·cate lu·bri·cat·ing lu·bri·cat·ed *v.t.* to make smooth or slippery ‖ to diminish friction by applying a lubricant to **lu·bri·ca·tion, lú·bri·ca·tor** *ns*

lu·cid *adj.* clear, easily understood ‖ sane **lu·cíd·i·ty** *n.*

luck *n.* chance ‖ good fortune ‖ success due to chance **to be down on one's luck** to be going through a time of bad luck **to be in (out of) luck** to be fortunate (unfortunate) **to try one's luck** to take a chance

luck·i·ly *adv.* in a lucky manner, fortunately

luck·i·ness *n.* the state or quality of being lucky

luck·y luck·i·er luck·i·est *adj.* having good luck ‖ bringing good luck ‖ successful due to chance

lu·cra·tive *adj.* very profitable

lu·di·crous *adj.* absurd, ridiculous

lug lug·ging lugged *v.t.* to haul clumsily, with great expenditure of effort, half pulling and half carrying ‖ *v.i.* to tug

lug·gage *n.* suitcases, bags and trunks full of a traveler's belongings ‖ empty suitcases, trunks etc.

lu·gu·bri·ous *adj.* dismal, mournful

luke·warm *adj.* tepid ‖ halfhearted

lull 1. *v.t.* to calm, soothe ‖ to quiet, esp. by guile 2. *n.* a temporary period of peace and quiet

lull·a·by *pl.* **lull·a·bies** *n.* a soothing song to put a baby to sleep

lum·ber 1. *n.* wood suitable for, or prepared for, use in construction 2. *v.t.* to fell and saw timber into logs and remove it from (an area)

lumber *v.i.* to move clumsily, heavily and noisily

lu·mi·nar·y *pl.* **lu·mi·nar·ies** *n.* a body giving light ‖ a person of outstanding intellectual, spiritual or moral quality

lu·mi·nes·cence *n.* the emission of electromagnetic radiation

lu·mi·nes·cent *adj.* of, relating to or exhibiting luminescence

lu·mi·nos·i·ty *pl.* **lu·mi·nos·i·ties** *n.* the state or quality of being luminous ‖ the amount of radiation emitted by a star or other heavenly body

lu·mi·nous *adj.* emitting a steady, diffused light ‖ shining, bright ‖ lucid, enlightening and inspiring

lump 1. *n.* a firm irregular mass ‖ a large amount or quantity ‖ a dull, heavy awkward person ‖ a swelling 2. *v.t.* to put together in a lump ‖ to treat alike without discrimination ‖ *v.i.* to move heavily

lump·y lump·i·er lump·i·est *adj.* full of or covered with lumps ‖ (of water) choppy

lu·na·cy *n.* the state of being a lunatic ‖ insanity ‖ incredible foolishness

lu·nar *adj.* to do with the moon

lu·na·tic 1. *adj.* mad, insane ‖ exceptionally foolish or irresponsible ‖ wildly frivolous 2. *n.* a person who is insane ‖ a wildly foolish or eccentric person

lunch 1. *n.* the midday meal 2. *v.i.* to eat lunch

lunch·eon *n.* the midday meal, lunch

lung *n.* one of the pair of spongy saclike organs that oxygenate the blood in air-breathing vertebrates and remove carbon dioxide from it

lunge 1. *n.* a sudden thrust ‖ a sudden, forward plunging movement 2. **lung·ing lunged** *v.i.* to make a lunge ‖ to start off suddenly

lure 1. *n.* some quality or thing that entices or attracts ‖ a device to attract animals 2. *v.t.* **lur·ing lured** to entice, tempt

lu·rid *adj.* gaudy, sensational ‖ repulsive ‖ reddish and menacing ‖ ashen, pallid

lurk *v.i.* to lie hidden waiting to attack ‖ to prowl

lus·cious *adj.* rich, full and delicious in flavor or smell ‖ voluptuously attractive

lush *adj.* growing thickly and richly, luxuriant

lust 1. *n.* strong sexual desire ‖ any passionate desire

lus·ter 1. *n.* a surface sheen or gloss ‖ the quality of having such a gloss ‖ radiance, brightness ‖ splendor, renown, distinction ‖ a chandelier 2. *v.t.* **lus·ter·ing, lus·tring**

lus·tred to add luster to

lust·ful *adj.* full of lust ‖ characterized by lust

lust·i·ness *n.* the state or quality of being lusty

lus·trous *adj.* shining, having a luster

lust·y lust·i·er lust·i·est *adj.* vigorous, sturdy

Lu·ther·an 1. *adj.* of or relating to Martin Luther ‖ of the Protestant denomination **2.** *n.* a member of the Lutheran Church

Lú·ther·an·ism *n.* a Protestant faith

lux·u·ri·ance *n.* the state or quality of being luxuriant

lux·u·ri·ant *adj.* abundant ‖ prolific, richly varied

lux·u·ri·ous *adj.* opulent, sumptuous ‖ sensually delightful

lux·u·ry *pl.* **lux·u·ries** *n.* habitual indulgence in expensive food, clothes, comforts etc. ‖ something voluptuously enjoyed ‖ abundance of rich comforts

lymph *n.* a colorless, plasmalike fluid that bathes many of the tissues of vertebrates

lym·phat·ic *adj.* relating to, produced by or conveying lymph

lynch *v.t.* (of a mob) to take the law into its own hands and kill (someone) in punishment for a real or presumed crime

lynx *pl.* **lynx, lynx·es** *n.* a genus of wildcats native to the northern hemisphere

lyr·ic 1. *adj.* (of poetry) expressing the poet's intense personal emotions ‖ (of a poet) writing such poetry **2.** *n.* a lyric poem ‖ (*pl.*) the words of a popular song

lyr·i·cal *adj.* lyric ‖ written or expressed in language appropriate to lyric poetry ‖ passionately enthusiastic, esp. in praising

lyr·i·cist *n.* someone who writes the words for popular songs

M

M, m the 13th letter of the English alphabet

ma·ca·bre *adj.* suggestive of the terrifying aspect of death

mac·ad·am *n.* small broken stones which fit closely together when pressed by a heavy roller and so constitute an even and durable road surface ‖ a road having such a surface **mac·ád·am·ize mac·ad·am·iz·ing mac·ad·am·ized** *v.t.* to construct (a road surface) of layers of macadam

mac·a·ro·ni *pl.* **mac·a·ro·nies** *n.* a pasta made of semolina, usually rolled into long thin tubes

ma·caw *n.* any of several large, bright-feathered parrots

mace a club with a heavy, spiked metal head, used as a weapon ‖ an ornamented staff of office

mace *n.* a spice

Mace tradename of a temporarily incapacitating liquid nerve irritant in aerosol form **mace** *v.t.* to use mace

mac·er·ate mac·er·at·ing mac·er·at·ed *v.i.* to become softened or separated by soaking ‖ to waste away, esp. by fasting **mac·er·á·tion** *n.*

ma·chet·e *n.* a long, heavy, broad-bladed knife

mach·i·nate mach·i·nat·ing mach·i·nat·ed *v.i.* to form a plot or intrigue, esp. in order to work harm

mach·i·na·tion *n.* the act of machinating ‖ a plot

ma·chine 1. *n.* an apparatus, made of organized, interacting parts, which takes in some form of energy, modifies it, and delivers it in a more suitable form for a desired function ‖ an organization whose members collaborate for some purpose **2.** *v.t.* **ma·chin·ing ma·chined** to make or operate on by machinery

ma·chin·er·y *n.* machines in general ‖ the assembled parts of a machine

ma·chin·ist *n.* someone who repairs or operates machines

ma·chis·mo *n.* exaggerated masculinity; manly assurance **macho** *adj.*

mack·i·naw *n.* a heavy woolen blanket originally distributed by the U.S. government to North American Indians

mac·ro·cosm *n.* the universe as contrasted with a microcosm **mac·ro·cós·mic** *adj.*

mac·ro·or·gan·ism *n.* an organism visible to the naked eye

mac·ro·scop·ic *adj.* visible to the unaided eye

mad mad·der mad·dest *adj.* insane ‖ utterly foolish ‖ angry ‖ wildly enthusiastic about ‖ rabid **like mad** frantically

mad·am *n. (pl.)* **mes·dames** a polite title used in addressing a woman ‖ *(pl.)* **mad·ams** a woman in charge of a brothel

madm·cap 1. *n.* lacking prudence **2.** *adj.* foolishly impulsive

mad·den *v.t.* to make mad

mad·e·moi·selle *n.* a courtesy title for an unmarried French girl or woman (the equivalent of 'Miss')

mad·house *pl.* **mad·hous·es** *n.* a mental hospital ‖ a scene of uproar or confusion

mad·man *pl.* **mad·men** *n.* a man who is insane or acts as if he were

ma·don·na *n.* a statue or picture of the Virgin Mary

mad·ri·gal *n. (mus.)* a contrapuntal secular composition for several voices

mael·strom *n.* a large and dangerous whirlpool ‖ a turbulent situation

maes·tro *pl.* **maes·tros, ma·es·tri** *n.* a great musical conductor, composer or teacher ‖ a master in any art

ma·ga·zine *n.* a paperback periodical publication ‖ a storage place for arms, ammunition and explosives ‖ a receptacle for cartridges

ma·gen·ta 1. *n.* a brilliant, bluish-red aniline dye ‖ the color of this dye **2.** *adj.* having this color

mag·got *n.* an insect larva **mág·got·y** *adj.*

mag·ic *n.* the art which claims to control and manipulate the secret forces of nature by occult and ritualistic methods ‖ the art or practice of producing illusions etc. by sleight of hand

magic *adj.* of, relating to, used in or produced by magic **mág·i·cal** *adj.*

ma·gi·cian *n.* a person who practices magic

mag·is·trate *n.* a civil legislative or executive officer

mag·nan·i·mous *adj.* generously and benevolently overlooking faults

mag·nate *n.* a person of great prominence and wealth

mag·ne·sia *n.* a white low-melting solid oxide of magnesium **mag·né·sian** *adj.*

mag·ne·sium *n.* a light divalent silvery metallic element

mag·net *n.* a piece of steel, iron, cobalt, nickel or alloy exhibiting ferromagnetism ‖ the magnetized needle of a compass ‖ something or someone exerting a powerful attraction

mag·net·ic *adj.* of or relating to a magnet or to magnetism ‖ strongly attractive **mag·nét·i·cal·ly** *adv.*

mag·net·ism *n.* the study of the behavior and effects of magnetic fields ‖ the ability to attract by personal charm

mag·net·ize mag·net·iz·ing mag·net·ized *v.t.* to make (something) magnetic ‖ to exert an irresistible influence upon

mag·ni·fi·ca·tion *n.* the act or process of apparently changing the dimensions of an object by optical methods ‖ a celebrating with praise

mag·nif·i·cence *n.* the quality of being magnificent

mag·nif·i·cent *adj.* splendid, lavish, beautiful

mag·ni·fy mag·ni·fy·ing mag·ni·fied *v.t.* to make (something) appear larger or more important than it is ‖ to celebrate with praise, laud

mag·ni·tude *n.* size ‖ largeness in size or number ‖ importance ‖ a number designating the relative brightness of a star

mag·nol·ia *n.* a genus of trees and shrubs

ma·hog·a·ny *pl.* **ma·hog·a·nies 1.** *n.* the wood of any of several trees, esp. the reddish brown wood of the West Indian Swietonia mahogani ‖ the color of the wood **2.** *adj.* of, pertaining to or made of mahogany ‖ of the dark-reddish-brown color of mahogany

maid *n.* a female domestic servant ‖ a girl

maid·en 1. *n.* a girl ‖ a virgin **2.** *adj.* unmarried ‖ of a horse that has not won a race

mail 1. *n.* the public organization dealing with the collection and delivery of correspondence and other postal matter ‖ the letters and parcels sent by this organization **2.** *v.t.* to send by this organization

mail·box *n.* a box into which people drop their letters for dispatch ‖ a box into which letters etc. delivered to an address are placed

mail·man *pl.* **mail·men** *n.* a man employed to collect and deliver mail

maim *v.t.* to deprive of the full or partial use of a limb or limbs by inflicting an injury

main 1. *n.* a principal pipe system, duct etc. for gas, water etc. **2.** *adj.* most important, chief, principal

main·land *n.* a continuous land mass as compared with an island

main·ly *adv.* chiefly, principally

main·spring *n.* the chief spring in a mechanism

main·tain *v.t.* to cause to remain unaltered ‖ to declare to be true, valid etc. ‖ to provide for the needs of

main·te·nance *n.* a maintaining or being maintained ‖ the provisions, money etc. needed for subsistence

maize *n.* corn

ma·jes·tic *adj.* having majesty
ma·jés·ti·cal *adj.*

maj·es·ty *pl.* **maj·es·ties** *n.* royal stateliness, splendor etc. ‖ sovereign power

ma·jor *n.* an army officer ranking below a lieutenant colonel and above a captain

ma·jor·i·ty *pl.* **ma·jor·i·ties** *n.* the greater number or part, more than half the total

make 1. *v.* **mak·ing made** *v.t.* to bring into being, cause to exist ‖ to contrive ‖ to arrive at ‖ to cause to acquire some specified quality ‖ to compel ‖ to utter (a remark,

a statement) ‖ to deliver (a speech) ‖ to arrange ‖ to establish, frame ‖ to draw up (e.g. a contract) ‖ to add up to, be the equivalent of ‖ to gain (money etc.) ‖ to shuffle ‖ *v.i.* (with an adjective) to cause oneself to become as specified **to make out** to understand ‖ to decipher ‖ to succeed, get along satisfactorily ‖ to neck **to make up** to invent (a story) ‖ to put an end to (a quarrel) by being reconciled ‖ to apply cosmetics **2.** *n.* provenance of manufacture ‖ style or quality of making

mak·er *n.* someone who makes, usually in compounds indicating the thing made **Mak·er** God

make·shift *n.* something used temporarily as a substitute

make·up *n.* the way in which the parts of something are put together ‖ cosmetics ‖ a special examination taken to make up for one missed

mal·ad·just·ed *adj.* psychologically unable to adjust

mal·ad·just·ment *n.* the quality or state of being maladjusted ‖ an instance of this

mal·a·dy *pl.* **mal·a·dies** *n.* a physical, mental or moral disorder

ma·laise *n.* a feeling of general discomfort

mal·a·prop·ism *n.* a ludicrous misuse of a word

mal·ap·ro·pos 1. *adv.* at an unsuitable time, or in an inappropriate manner **2.** *adj.* inopportune

ma·lar·i·a *n.* an infectious, chiefly tropical disease

mal·con·tent *n.* someone who is discontented

male 1. *adj.* of the sex in animals or plants that fertilizes in order to reproduce ‖ of, pertaining to or characteristic of men ‖ manly **2.** *n.* a male person, animal or plant

mal·e·dic·tion *n.* a curse called down upon someone

mal·e·fac·tion *n.* an evil deed, crime

mal·e·fac·tor *n.* someone who does evil

ma·lev·o·lence *n.* the quality of being malevolent

ma·lev·o·lent *adj.* having a desire to do harm

mal·fea·sance n. the committing of illegal acts by a public official **mal·féa·sant** adj. and n.

mal·for·ma·tion n. something malformed **mal·fórmed** adj. abnormal in structure

mal·func·tion 1. v.i. to function improperly **2.** n. malfunctioning

ma·lice n. the will to do harm to another

ma·li·cious adj. having or showing malice

ma·lign adj. having an evil effect, doing harm

malign v.t. to make false or misleading statements about (someone) so as to injure him

ma·lig·nan·cy pl. **ma·lig·nan·cies** n. the quality or state of being malignant ‖ a malignant tumor

ma·lig·nant adj. feeling, showing or acting with extreme ill will ‖ tending to be fatal without treatment

ma·lin·ger v.i. to pretend to be ill in order to avoid one's work or responsibility

mall n. a usually public, tree-lined walk

mal·lard pl. **mal·lard, mal·lards** n. the common wild duck

mal·le·a·bil·i·ty n. the quality or state of being malleable

mal·le·a·ble adj. able to have its shape changed permanently through the applying of stress, e.g. by hammering ‖ easily affected or formed by external influences

mal·let n. a hammer, usually of wood

mal·nu·tri·tion n. poor nutrition

mal·o·dor·ous adj. having a foul smell

mal·prac·tice n. the improper treatment of a patient by a doctor

malt 1. n. grain, esp. barley, used in brewing and distilling **2.** v.t. to convert (grain) into malt

mam·ma, ma·ma n. (a child's word for) mother

mam·mal n. a member of Mammalia, the highest class of vertebrates, including man **mam·ma·li·an** adj.

mam·moth 1. n. any of several extinct elephants **2.** adj. of very great size

man pl. **men** n. the human race in general ‖ an adult human male ‖ a husband (only in 'man and wife') **as one man** in unison, unanimously

man man·ning manned v.t. to supply (a post, vessel, field gun etc.) with the man or men needed

man·a·cle 1. n. a steel clasp, heavy chain or handcuff **2.** v.t. **man·a·cling man·a·cled** to fasten manacles on ‖ to restrict the freedom of action

man·age man·ag·ing man·aged v.t. to exercise control over ‖ to handle, manipulate ‖ to influence ‖ v.i. to be able to cope with a situation **man·age·a·bil·i·ty** n. **mán·age·a·ble** adj. **mán·age·a·bly** adv.

man·age·ment n. a managing or being managed ‖ the body of those in positions of administrative authority

man·ag·er n. someone who manages **man·ag·er·ess** n. a female manager **man·a·ge·ri·al** adj.

man·date 1. n. an instruction or authorization given or conferred **2.** v.t. **man·dat·ing man·dat·ed** to assign

man·da·to·ry adj. of, relating to or having the force of a mandate

man·di·ble n. the lower jaw, formed either of a single bone or of fused bones **man·dib·u·lar** adj.

man·drill n. a large, ferocious baboon of W. Africa

mane n. the long hair growing on the top or sides of the neck of some animals

ma·nege, ma·nege n. a riding academy

ma·neu·ver n. a tactical movement of military troops, naval vessels etc. ‖ (usually pl.) training exercises involving such movement ‖ a cleverly thought-out or dextrous movement, action or plan

maneuver ma·neu·ver·ing ma·neu·vered v.t. to move, manage or guide cleverly and dextrously ‖ to cause by clever contriving ‖ v.i. to engage in a maneuver **ma·neu·ver·a·bil·i·ty** n. **ma·néu·ver·a·ble** adj.

man·ga·nese n. a grayish-white, polyvalent metallic element

mange n. any of several contagious skin diseases of domestic animals and sometimes man

man·ger n. a trough from which horses and cattle feed

man·gle man·gling man·gled *v.t.* to hack or cut or crush ‖ to ruin by bad pronunciation, etc.

man·gle 1. *n.* a machine having heated rollers between which damp linen is pressed smooth **2.** *v.t.* **man·gling man·gled** to press in a mangle

man·go *pl.* **man·goes, man·gos** *n.* a large Indian tree ‖ the fruit of this tree

man·gy man·gi·er man·gi·est *adj.* infected with mange ‖ shabby, poorly kept-up

man·han·dle man·han·dling man·han·dled *v.t.* to handle roughly, beat up

man·hole *n.* a hole in a floor, street, etc. allowing access to a sewer, pipe etc.

man·hood *n.* the state of being an adult male ‖ men collectively

man-hour *n.* the amount of work done by one man in one hour

ma·ni·a *n.* a form of mental disorder ‖ an irrational and prolonged desire or enthusiasm

ma·ni·ac 1. *adj* of, relating to or typical of mania **2.** *n.* a person affected with mania **ma·ni·a·cal** *adj*

man·ic *adj.* pertaining to or resembling mania

man·i·cure 1. *n.* a beauty treatment for the hands, esp. the nails **2.** *v.t.* **man·i·cur·ing man·i·cured** to give a manicure to **man·i·cur·ist** *n.* a person who gives manicures

man·i·fest *n.* a detailed list of a ship's cargo

manifest *v.t.* to show plainly

manifest *adj.* immediately evident

man·i·fes·ta·tion *n.* a public demonstration ‖ something that makes manifest

man·i·fes·to *pl.* **man·i·fes·tos, man·i·fes·toes** *n.* a public statement of opinions or intentions

man·i·fold 1. *adj.* having many different parts, applications, forms etc. **2.** *n.* a pipe with several lateral outlets

man·i·kin, man·ni·kin *n.* an anatomical model of the human body ‖ a mannequin

ma·nip·u·late ma·nip·u·lat·ing ma·nip·u·lat·ed *v.t.* to handle, esp. with skill ‖ to cause by clever maneuvering to act as one wishes

ma·nip·u·la·tion *n.* a manipulating or being manipulated

ma·nip·u·la·tor *n.* someone who or something that manipulates

man·kind *n.* the human race

man·li·ness *n.* the state or quality of being manly

man·ly man·li·er man·li·est *adj.* having qualities regarded as proper in a man

man·na *n.* (Bible) food miraculously supplied to the Israelites in the wilderness ‖ any food for the mind or spirit that is felt as something miraculously given

man·ne·quin *n.* a model (person who demonstrates clothes) ‖ a dummy

man·ner *n.* a way of doing something ‖ *(pl.)* social behavior with respect to standards **mán·nered** *adj.*

man·ner·ism *n.* an affected gesture, habit, manner of speaking

man·ner·li·ness *n.* the quality of being mannerly

man·ner·ly *adj.* having or showing good manners

man·or *n.* a landed estate

man·pow·er *n.* the persons available for some purpose, regarded as one of the resources of a nation, industry etc.

man·sion *n.* a very large, imposing house

man·slaugh·ter *n.* the unlawful killing of a human being without malicious intent

man·tel *n.* an ornamental structure above and around a fireplace

man·tle 1. *n.* a loose outer garment or sleeveless cloak ‖ anything that covers or conceals **2.** **man·tling man·tled** *v.t.* to cover with or as if with a mantle

man·u·al 1. *adj.* relating to, done with or operated by the hands **2.** *n.* a book containing information set out briefly

man·u·fac·ture 1. *n.* the making of things on a large scale, by hand or machine or both **2.** *v.t.* **man·u·fac·tur·ing man·u·fac·tured** to make (goods) in this way ‖ to make up, fabricate **man·u·fac·tur·er** *n.*

ma·nure *n.* matter, esp. dung, added to soil for fertilizing

man·u·script *n.* a document or book written by hand ‖ an author's written or typ written copy of his work

man·y 1. *adj.* **more most** consisting of a large but indefinite number **2.** *pron.* a large, indefinite number of people or things

map 1. *n.* a representation in scale, usually on a flat surface, of part or the whole of the earth's surface **2.** *v.t.* **map·ping mapped** to represent on a map

ma·ple *n.* a large genus of hardwood trees and shrubs ‖ their hard, light-colored, close-grained wood, used for furniture etc.

maple syrup a syrup consisting of the concentrated sap of the sugar maple

mar mar·ring marred *v.t.* to lessen the perfection of

ma·ra·ca *n.* a dried gourd containing pebbles, used as a musical percussion instrument

ma·ras·ca *n.* a small, black, bitter Dalmatian cherry

mar·a·schi·no *n.* a liqueur distilled from the marasca

mar·a·thon *n.* a long-distance race over 26 miles 385 yards ‖ any contest testing endurance

ma·raud *v.t.* (esp. pass) to raid

mar·ble 1. *n.* naturally occurring calcium carbonate which has been crystallized from limestone ‖ a small ball made of something resembling this material, used as a toy **2.** *v.t.* **mar·bling mar·bled** to treat (something) so as to give it the mottled or veined appearance of marble **3.** *adj.* of, pertaining to, or like marble

March *n.* the 3rd month of the year

march *n.* the act of marching ‖ a piece of music to accompany marching

mare *n.* a female horse

mar·ga·rine *n.* a substitute for butter prepared from milk and certain vegetable fats

mar·gin *n.* an outer limiting edge ‖ an extra supply of something forming a reserve in case of need ‖ the difference between net sales and costs ‖ the least profit at which a transaction is economically sound ‖ cash or collateral paid to a broker as security

mar·gin·al *adj.* close to the limit of accept-

ability ‖ at or close to an edge

mar·i·gold *n.* an annual composite garden plant

mar·i·jua·na *n.* the dried leaves and top of the common hemp, often smoked as a narcotic

ma·rim·ba *n.* a musical instrument resembling a xylophone

ma·ri·na *n.* a boat basin that rents moorings and provides other services for small craft

mar·i·nade *n.* a combination of wine or vinegar with oil, herbs and spices

mar·i·nate mar·i·nat·ing mar·i·nat·ed *v.t.* to season by steeping in a marinade

ma·rine 1. *adj.* of, relating to, found in or produced by the sea **2.** *n.* a member of a class of soldiers specially trained in combined operations with the navy ‖ seagoing ships collectively

mar·i·ner *n.* a sailor

mar·i·on·ette *n.* a puppet moved by strings

mar·i·tal *adj.* of or relating to marriage

mar·i·time *adj.* of, connected with, or bordering on the sea

mar·jo·ram *n.* any of several aromatic plants used in cookery

mark *n.* a spot, stain, scratch etc. breaking the uniform appearance of a solid surface ‖ any distinguishing characteristic ‖ an object whose position is known, used as a fixed reference point or guide ‖ a letter, numeral etc. put on something to indicate quality, provenance, ownership etc. ‖ something aimed at

mark *v.t.* to make a mark on ‖ to disfigure ‖ to be a distinguishing trait of ‖ to indicate ‖ to assess the merit of (a piece of work) by a letter, numeral etc. ‖ to show the position of ‖ to heed, pay attention to

mark *n.* a deutsche mark ‖ a coin representing this value

marked *adj.* bearing a mark or marks ‖ noticeable **mark·ed·ly** *adv.*

mark·er *n.* a device for marking

mar·ket 1. *n.* a place where many sellers display and sell their goods ‖ the demand for a commodity ‖ a region or outlet for successful trading ‖ the class of persons to whom a particular commodity can readily be sold **2.** *v.t.* to sell (goods) in a market ‖ *v.i.* to go shopping for provisions **már·ket·a·ble** *adj.*

mark·ing *n.* the making of a mark ‖ the awarding of a mark ‖ a mark

mar·lin *n.* a genus of big-game sea fish

mar·ma·lade *n.* a preserve made by boiling shredded oranges, or other citrus fruits, with sugar

ma·roon *v.t.* to land (someone) on a desolate shore

ma·roon *n.* a dark brownish-red color

mar·quee *n.* a permanent rooflike projection over the entrance to a theater, moviehouse etc.

mar·quis *n.* a European and English title of nobility

mar·riage *n.* the institution under which a man and a woman become legally united ‖ the act of entering into this institution ‖ an intimate linking together **mar·riage·a·ble** *adj.* fit for marriage

mar·row *n.* a soft tissue filling up the cavities in most bones ‖ the pith of certain plants ‖ the essential part of something

mar·ry mar·ry·ing mar·ried *v.t.* to join (two people) in marriage ‖ to take in marriage ‖ to join closely or match ‖ *v.i.* to enter into marriage

marsh *n.* a tract of low-lying land, usually wet

mar·shal 1. *n.* a military commander of the highest rank ‖ someone who regulates ceremonies and directs processions ‖ a U.S. civil officer **2.** *v.t.* **mar·shal·ing mar·shaled** to arrange in correct order

marsh·mal·low *n.* a soft white confection made from glucose, sugar, albumen and gelatin

mar·su·pi·al 1. *n.* a member of Marsupialia, the lowest order of mammals incl. the kangaroo, opossum etc. **2.** *adj.* of, relating to or being a marsupial

mar·tial *adj.* of, relating to, suited to or suggestive of war

martial art any of several Oriental techniques of self-defense, e.g., karate, judo, tai-chi

mar·tyr *n.* someone who suffers death rather than renounce his faith ‖ someone

who suffers greatly for some cause or principle

mar·tyr·dom *n.* great suffering

mar·vel *n.* something that causes astonishment and admiration

mas·ca·ra *n.* a cosmetic for darkening the eyelashes

mas·cot *n.* an object, animal or person whose presence is supposed to bring good luck

mas·cu·line 1. *adj.* of the male sex ‖ relating to or characteristic of men **2.** *n.* the masculine gender ‖ a word having this gender

mas·cu·lin·i·ty *n.* the quality or state of being masculine

mash 1. *n.* a mixture of things crushed together into a pulp **2.** *v.t.* to cause to become a mash, by grinding, crushing etc.

mask 1. *n.* any of several coverings for the face, worn as a disguise, as protection, or to filter air breathed in or out ‖ a likeness, esp. a cast of a face ‖ (photog.) a screen used to modify the size or shape of an image **2.** *v.t.* to cover with a mask ‖ to conceal with some disguise

mas·o·chism *n.* a condition in which the subject delights in being hurt or humiliated **más·o·chist** *n.* **mas·o·chís·tic** *adj.*

ma·son *n.* a craftsman who builds with stone, brick etc.

ma·son·ry *n.* that which is built by a mason ‖ the mason's craft

mas·quer·ade 1. *n.* a ball at which masks are worn ‖ a false show for pretense or concealment of the truth **2.** *v.i.* **mas·quer·ad·ing mas·quer·ad·ed** to wear a disguise **mas·quer·ád·er** *n.*

mass *n.* a property of matter ‖ an aggregation of a quantity of matter ‖ a large amount or number ‖ massiveness ‖ an expanse **the masses** the ordinary working people

mas·sa·cre *n.* a ruthless, indiscriminate killing of many people or animals

massacre mas·sa·cring mas·sa·cred *v.t.* to kill (many) ruthlessly and indiscriminately

mas·sage 1. *n.* treatment of the muscles

etc. by rubbing or kneading **2.** *v.t.* **mas·sag·ing mas·saged** to apply this treatment to

mas·seur *n.* a man who professionally gives massage **mas·seuse** *n.* a female masseur

mas·sif *n.* an elevated mass with a number of peaks rising from it

mass-pro·duce mass-pro·duc·ing mass-pro·duced *v.t.* to manufacture (goods) by mass production **máss-pro·dúced** *adj.*

mass production production of one article or type of goods in large numbers by a standardized mechanical process

mast *n.* a long pole of wood or metal set up on a ship's keel or deck to carry sails or other rigging ‖ an upright pole

mas·ter 1. *n.* a man in control or authority ‖ a spiritual leader or guide ‖ a person of consummate skill, in an art, technique etc. ‖ a skilled workman ‖ a person with a degree between a bachelor's and a doctor's ‖ the owner of a pet animal ‖ the male head of a household ‖ the head of a college, guild, masonic lodge etc. **2.** *v.t.* to gain control over, overcome ‖ to become completely skilled in **3.** *adj.* clearly outstanding in some profession, occupation etc. ‖ controlling the operation of a number of individually controlled devices

mas·ter·ful *adj.* domineering, wanting to dictate to others ‖ having or showing the ability to command

mas·ter·piece *n.* a work of art etc. made with consummate skill

mas·ter·y *n.* command, control

mas·ti·cate mas·ti·cat·ing mas·ti·cat·ed *v.t.* to chew ‖ to grind **mas·ti·cá·tion, más·ti·ca·tor** ns

mas·tiff *n.* big, powerful, short-haired dog

mas·to·don *n.* any of several extinct mamamals related to modern elephants

mas·toid *adj.* shaped like a breast or nipple

mas·tur·bate mas·tur·bat·ing mas·tur·bat·ed *v.i.* to produce orgasm in oneself by manipulation of the genitals, erotic fantasies etc., exclusive of sexual intercourse **mas·tur·bá·tion** *n.*

mat mat·ting mat·ted *v.t.* to render dull ‖ to frost (glass)

mat 1. *n.* a mount (for pictures) **2.** *adj.* without luster or shine

ma·ta·dor *n.* (bullfighting) the man whose role is to kill the bull with his sword

match 1. *n.* one of two persons or things exactly alike ‖ a person or thing harmonizing well with another ‖ a marriage ‖ a game or contest between two teams or persons **2.** *v.t.* to bring into competition ‖ to equal ‖ to be in harmony with ‖ *v.i.* to have the same color, shape etc. as what is taken for comparison

match *n.* a small, thin piece of wood covered at one end with material of low ignition point which will burn when heated by the friction of striking it on a rough surface

mate 1. *n.* the male or female of a couple ‖ one of a pair ‖ a deck officer on a ship ‖ any assistant **2.** **mat·ing mat·ed** *v.t.* to pair (birds, animals) for breeding

ma·te·ri·al 1. *adj.* of or consisting of matter ‖ worldly, not spiritual ‖ connected or concerned with bodily comfort ‖ substantially important **2.** *n.* the stuff from which a thing is made ‖ cloth ‖ *(pl.)* necessary tools, equipment etc.

ma·te·ri·al·ism *n.* the theory that matter is the basic reality of the universe

ma·te·ri·al·ist *n.* someone who values material things more than spiritual ones **ma·te·ri·al·ís·tic** *adj.* **ma·te·ri·al·ís·ti·cal·ly** *adv.*

ma·te·ri·al·i·za·tion *n.* a materializing or being materialized ‖ an apparition of a spirit

ma·te·ri·al·ize ma·te·ri·al·iz·ing ma·te·ri·al·ized *v.i.* to become tangible ‖ (of spirits) to appear in bodily form

ma·te·ri·al·ly *adv.* substantially ‖ with regard to matter or material things

ma·ter·nal *adj.* of or pertaining to a mother ‖ motherly

ma·ter·ni·ty 1. *n.* the state of being a mother **2.** *adj.* of or pertaining to the time when a woman is pregnant

math·e·mat·i·cal *adj.* of, pertaining to or using mathematics ‖ used in mathematics ‖ very precise

math·e·ma·ti·cian *n.* a specialist in mathematics

math·e·mat·ics *n.* the science of expressing and studying the relationships between quantities and magnitudes as represented by numbers and symbols

mat·i·nee, mat·i·née *n.* an afternoon performance at a moviehouse or theater

ma·tri·arch *n.* a woman who rules a group ‖ a venerable old woman **ma·tri·ár·chal** *adj.* **má·tri·ar·chate** *n.* a community etc. ruled by a matriarch **má·tri·ar·chy** *pl.* **ma·tri·ar·chies** *n.* government by women

ma·tric·u·late   ma·tric·u·lat·ing ma·tric·u·lat·ed *v.t.* to enroll in a university or college **ma·tric·u·lá·tion** *n.*

mat·ri·mo·ni·al *adj.* pertaining to marriage or married life

mat·ri·mo·ny *pl.* **mat·ri·mo·nies** *n.* the state of being married ‖ marriage as a Christian sacrament

ma·trix *pl.* **mat·ri·ces ma·trix·es** *n.* a mold in which type or other matter in relief is shaped or cast ‖ (computer) a table of variables

ma·tron *n.* a married woman or a widow, usually having children and no longer young ‖ a female attendant or guard in a public institution **má·tron·li·ness** *n.* **má·tron·ly** *adj.*

mat·ter 1. *n.* that which any physical thing is composed of ‖ that which occupies space and possesses inertia ‖ a substance serving a specified purpose ‖ importance ‖ a circumstance, issue, topic etc. ‖ trouble, difficulty **2.** *v.i.* to be of importance

mat·ting *n.* woven material, esp. of hemp, grass, bast etc., used for floor covering etc.

mat·tress *n.* a flat case of some strong fabric, stuffed with sponge rubber etc., put on a bedstead or serving as a bed

ma·ture *adj.* having reached a state of full natural development ‖ ripe ‖ (of a bond etc.) due

ma·tu·ri·ty *n.* the quality or state of being mature

ma·tu·ti·nal *adj.* of or occurring in the morning

mat·zo, mat·zoh *pl.* **mat·zoth mat·zos** *n.*

an unleavened bread eaten by Jews at Passover

maud·lin *adj.* weakly and tearfully sentimental

maul 1. *n.* (also **mall**) any of several kinds of heavy hammer, usually wooden, for driving in stakes **2.** *v.t.* (also **mall**) to attack savagely and injure

maun·der *v.i.* to talk ramblingly, with no obvious purpose ‖ to move or act aimlessly and slowly

mau·so·le·um *pl.* **mau·so·le·ums, mau·so·le·a** *n.* a large and elaborate tomb

mauve 1. *n.* a pale purple dye obtained from crude aniline ‖ the color of this dye **2.** *adj.* having this color

mav·er·ick *n.* a person who refuses to conform and acts independently

max·il·la *pl.* **max·il·lae, max·il·las** *n.* the upper jaw **max·il·lar·y** *adj.* of, pertaining to, or in the region of the maxilla

max·im *n.* a succinct general truth, moral reflection or rule of conduct

max·i·mal *adj.* to the greatest possible degree

max·i·mum 1. *pl.* **max·i·mums, max·i·ma** *n.* the greatest possible amount, number or degree **2.** *adj.* greatest in amount, number or degree

May *n.* the fifth month of the year

may *infin.* and *parts.* lacking, *neg.* **may not, mayn't** *3rd pers. sing.* **may** *past* **might** (or, by suppletion, 'was', 'were able to') *auxiliary v.* to be permitted to ‖ expressing possibility

may·be *adv.* perhaps, possibly but not certainly

may·hem *n.* the malicious, permanent maiming or mutilating of a person

may·on·naise *n.* a thick creamy dressing of egg yolks beaten with oil, vinegar and seasoning

may·or *n.* the head of a municipal corporation of a city, town etc. **máy·or·al** *adj.*

may·or·al·ty *pl.* **may·or·al·ties** *n.* the office, or term of office, of a mayor

maze *n.* a contrived layout of paths, often hedged ‖ something intricately complicated or confusing

me *pron.*, objective case of "*I*"

mead·ow n. a piece of grassland

mea·ger adj. low in quantity or quality

meal n. the edible part of coarsely ground grain

meal n. food eaten to satisfy hunger

meal·y meal·i·er meal·i·est adj. powdery and dry ‖ sallow, unhealthy looking ‖ covered with meal or powder

mean adj. midway between two extremes in number, quantity, degree, kind, value etc.

mean adj. stingy ‖ small-minded, petty ‖ unkind ‖ bad-tempered ‖ squalid

mean mean·ing meant v.t. to intend

me·an·der 1. n. a rambling stroll ‖ an ornamental linear pattern **2.** v.i. to wander aimlessly

mean·ing 1. n. that which is intended or meant **2.** adj. expressive, conveying emotion etc. **méan·ing·ful, méan·ing·less** adjs

mean·time adv. during the intervening time

mea·sles n. a contagious disease caused by a virus

meas·ur·a·bil·i·ty n. being measurable

meas·ur·a·ble adj. that can be measured **méas·ur·a·bly** adv.

meas·ure n. the magnitude of something as determined by measuring ‖ an instrument used to determine magnitude ‖ a unit of length, volume etc. as a standard for measuring ‖ amount, extent or degree ‖ a legislation bill or statute ‖ rhythm in verse or music

measure meas·ur·ing meas·ured v.t. to determine the magnitude, extent, degree, quality or nature of in terms of some standard **méas·ured** adj. accurately determined ‖ (of speech etc.) calculated **méas·ure·less** adj. vast **méas·ure·ment** n.

meat n. the flesh of animals used for food ‖ the edible part of an animal ‖ the substance or essence of something

meat·y meat·i·er meat·i·est adj. of, like or consisting of meat

me·chan·ic n. a workman skilled in making, using or repairing machinery

me·chan·i·cal adj. pertaining to or involving machines

me·chan·ics n. a branch of physics that deals with energy and force in their relation to material bodies

mech·a·nism n. a structure of interacting parts working mechanically ‖ any system, process etc. composed of parts which, working together, reasemble the workings of a machine

mech·a·ni·za·tion n. a mechanizing or being mechanized

mech·a·nize mech·a·niz·ing mech·a·nized v.t. to make mechanical ‖ to introduce the use of machines in

med·al n. a small, flat piece of metal, cast with an inscription or design, that is awarded in recognition for distinguished service

me·dal·lion n. a large medal ‖ a license to operate a taxicab

med·dle med·dling med·dled v.i. to concern or busy oneself impudently or interferingly **méd·dle·some** adj. given to meddling

me·di·an 1. adj. designating a plane dividing a body or part into symmetrical halves **2.** n. something situated in the middle

me·di·ate me·di·at·ing me·di·at·ed v.t. to bring about (a settlement) ‖ to act as agent in ‖ v.i. to intervene in order to bring about a reconciliation

me·di·a·tion n. a mediating or being mediated

me·di·a·tor n. someone who mediates **me·di·a·to·ri·al mé·di·a·to·ry** adjs

med·ic n. a physician or surgeon, or a student or military corpsman doing medical work

Med·i·caid n. government-administered program in U.S. to provide medical services to the poor

med·i·cal adj. of, concerned with or realating to the practice of medicine

Med·i·care, med·i·care n. a U.S. government insurance program that provides medical care for old people

med·i·cate med·i·cat·ing med·i·cat·ed v.t. to saturate with a medical preparation **med·i·cá·tion** n. the act of medicating ‖ a substance used in medicating

med·i·ca·tive *adj.*

me·dic·i·nal *adj.* relating to medicine **me·dic·i·nal·ly** *adv.*

med·i·cine *n.* any preparation or substance used in the treatment of disease ‖ the science of the prevention and cure of disease

med·i·e·val *adj.* of, relating to or characteristic of the Middle Ages

me·di·o·cre *adj.* neither good nor bad, without distinction ‖ of distinctly poor quality

me·di·oc·ri·ty *n.* the state or quality of being mediocre

med·i·tate med·i·tat·ing med·i·tat·ed *v.i.* to reflect deeply ‖ *v.t.* to contemplate

med·i·ta·tion *n.* deep, serious thought

me·di·um 1. *pl.* **me·di·ums, me·di·a** *n.* a middle quality or degree ‖ something through which a force is transmitted ‖ the material that an artist works with ‖ *(pl.)* **me·di·a** environment ‖ *(pl.)* **me·di·ums** a person credited with special powers for communicating between the living and the dead **2.** *adj.* average

med·ley *pl.* **med·leys** *n.* a confused mixture ‖ a miscellaneous musical or literary collection

me·dul·la *pl.* **me·dul·las, me·dul·lae** *n.* the central part of an organ

me·dul·la ob·lon·ga·ta *pl.* **me·dul·la ob·lon·ga·tas, me·dul·lae ob·lon·ga·tae** *n.* that part of the brainstem continuous posteriorly with the spinal cord

meek *adj.* humbly submissive ‖ too mild, lacking spirit

meet 1. meet·ing met *v.t.* to come face-to-face with ‖ to be present at the arrival of ‖ to make the acquaintance of ‖ to keep an appointment with ‖ to satisfy ‖ to deal with **2.** *n.* a gathering for a sporting event **meet·ing** *n.* a coming together of people or things

meg·a·phone *n.* a trumpet-shaped instrument used to magnify or direct the voice

meg·a·ton *n.* an explosive power equal to that of a million tons of TNT

mel·an·cho·li·a *n.* a form of mental disorder

mel·an·chol·ic *adj.* having a tendency

towards melancholy ‖ in a melancholy mood

mel·an·chol·y 1. *n.* depression, low spirits **2.** *adj.* sad, depressed

mé·lange, me·lange *n.* a heterogeneous mixture

meld *v.t.* to declare (a card or cards) for scoring

me·lee, me·lée *n.* a confused struggle

mel·lif·lu·ous *adj.* sweet to listen to

mel·low 1. *adj.* full and rich, not harsh ‖ warmly human, genial ‖ (of fruit) soft, ripe and sweet **2.** *v.t.* to make mellow ‖ *v.i.* to become mellow

me·lod·ic *adj.* of, pertaining to or containing melody **me·lód·i·cal·ly** *adv.*

me·lo·di·ous *adj.* (of sound) pleasing to the ear

mel·o·dra·ma *n.* a play with a sensational plot and violent emotional appeal **mel·o·dra·mat·ic** *adj.* **mel·o·dra·mát·i·cal·ly** *adv.*

mel·o·dy *pl.* **mel·o·dies** *n.* the principal part in a piece of harmonized music ‖ sweet, pleasing music

mel·on *n.* the edible fruit of either the muskmelon or the watermelon ‖ either of these plants

melt 1. melt·ing melt·ed, mol·ten *v.i.* to become liquefied ‖ to dissolve ‖ to blend **2.** *n.* something molten ‖ an amount of some substance melted in one operation

melt·down *n.* the melting of the protective cases surrounding a nuclear reactor

mem·ber *n.* a person who belongs to a group or organization ‖ a part of the body, esp. a limb

mem·ber·ship *n.* the state of being a member ‖ the total number of members

mem·brane *n.* a very thin, strong, pliable tissue which covers, lines or connects parts of an animal or vegetable body

me·men·to *pl.* **me·men·toes, me·men·tos** *n.* an object kept as a reminder of a person, event etc.

me·men·to mo·ri *n.* something that serves as a reminder of death

mem·o *pl.* **mem·os** *n.* a memorandum

mem·oir *n.* a record of events ‖ an autobiography

mem·o·ra·bil·i·a *pl. n.* memorable things or events

mem·o·ra·ble *adj.* outstanding, worthy of being remembered **mém·o·ra·bly** *adv.*

mem·o·ran·dum *pl.* **mem·o·ran·dums, mem·o·ran·da** *n.* a brief record of an event or analysis of a situation ‖ an informal letter, usually unsigned

me·mo·ri·al 1. *adj.* commemorative **2.** *n.* a monument commemorating a person or event

me·mo·ri·al·ize me·mo·ri·al·iz·ing me·mo·ri·al·ized *v.t.* to commemorate

mem·o·rize mem·o·riz·ing mem·o·rized *v.t.* to commit to memory

mem·o·ry *pl.* **mem·o·ries** *n.* the faculty by which sense impressions and information are retained in the mind and subsequently recalled ‖ a person's capacity to remember ‖ the total store of mentally retained impressions and knowledge

men·ace *n.* a threat

menace men·ac·ing men·aced to threaten

me·nag·er·ie *n.* a collection of animals exhibited in cages

mend *v.t.* to repair ‖ to cause to become better ‖ *v.i.* to improve, esp. to recover from an illness

me·ni·al 1. *adj.* lowly **2.** *n.* a domestic servant

men·o·pause *n.* the time when the menstrual cycle ceases

men·ses *pl. n.* the discharge of the mucous lining of the womb occurring in the menstrual cycle

men·stru·al *adj.* of or pertaining to the menses

menstrual cycle the cycle of changes in the reproductive organs of women and female higher anthropoids

men·stru·ate men·stru·at·ing men·stru·at·ed *v.i.* to discharge the menses **men·stru·á·tion** *n.*

men·tal *adj.* of or pertaining to the mind

men·tal·i·ty *pl.* **men·tal·i·ties** *n.* the attitude toward life, society etc. ‖ intellectual capacity

men·thol *n.* a white crystalline substance with a strong smell of peppermint **men·tho·lat·ed** *adj.* containing menthol

men·tion *n.* a mentioning or being mentioned

mention *v.t.* to refer to, esp. casually ‖ to cite the name of (a person) as official recognition of merit

men·tor *n.* an experienced and trusted adviser

men·u *n.* a restaurant's list of the dishes available

mer·can·tile *adj.* pertaining to or engaged in trade or commerce **mér·can·til·ism** *n.* trade and commerce

mer·ce·nar·i·ness *n.* the quality of being mercenary

mer·ce·nar·y 1. *adj.* inspired merely by a desire for gain **2.** *pl.* **mer·ce·nar·ies** *n.* a hired soldier serving a country other than his own

mer·cer·ize mer·cer·iz·ing mer·cer·ized *v.t.* to treat (cotton thread) to strengthen it and make it slightly glossy

mer·chan·dise 1. *n.* goods bought and sold **2.** *v.* **mer·chan·dis·ing mer·chan·dised** *v.i.* to practice the buying and selling of goods

mer·chant 1. *n.* a person who directs large-scale trade ‖ a retailer **2.** *adj.* of or pertaining to a merchant

mer·ci·ful *adj.* showing or feeling mercy

mer·ci·less *adj.* showing no mercy

mer·cu·ri·al *adj.* quick-wittedness, eloquence, changeability ‖ pertaining to or containing mercury

mer·cu·ry *n.* a silverwhite, poisonous, metallic element

mer·cy *pl.* **mer·cies** *n.* compassionate rather than severe behavior towards someone in one's power

mere *adj.* being no more or better than

mere·ly *adv.* in no way more than as specified

merge merg·ing merged *v.t.* to unite or blend **mérg·er** *n.* the combination of two companies

me·rid·i·an *n.* a great circle of the celestial sphere, passing through its poles and the zenith of a given point ‖ the highest point of success or greatness

me·ringue *n.* a light, fluffy baked mixture of sugar and beaten egg whites used as topping on cakes etc.

mer·it *n.* excellence, deserving praise ‖ the intrinsic goodness or badness

merit *v.t.* to be worthy of

mer·i·to·ri·ous *adj.* deserving praise or reward

mer·maid *n.* a mythical sea creature with the tail of a fish and the head, arms and trunk of a woman

mer·ri·ment *n.* laughter and gaiety

mer·ry mer·ri·er mer·ri·est *adj.* gay, cheerful

mer·ry-go-round *n.* a machine in a fair with a circular, revolving platform and models of horses etc. as seats on which children ride around to music

mesh 1. *n.* the strands of a net ‖ *(pl.)* something which captures and holds fast ‖ a network or net **2.** *v.i.* (of cogwheels etc.) to become interlocked

mes·mer·ism *n.* hypnotism **més·mer·ist** *n.* **més·mer·ize mes·mer·iz·ing mes·mer·ized** *v.t.* to induce the state of being hypnotized in (someone)

mes·quite, mes·quit *n.* a North American tree Its sugary pods are used as food and fodder

mess 1. *n.* a state of untidiness or disorder ‖ *(mil.)* a number of men or women, usually of the same rank, who have meals together ‖ the place where they eat **2.** *v.t.* to make a mess of

mes·sage *n.* a written or spoken communication ‖ an inspired revelation

mes·sen·ger *n.* a person employed to do errands ‖ a courier

mes·sy mess·i·er mess·i·est *adj.* untidy or disordered ‖ disagreeably confused

met·a·bol·ic *adj.* of or caused by metabolism

me·tab·o·lism *n.* the sum total of the chemical processes of living organisms **me·táb·o·lize me·tab·o·liz·ing me·tab3·o·lized** *v.t.* and *i.* to change by metabolism

met·al 1. *n.* an element ‖ a compound or alloy of such an element **2.** *v.t.* **met·al·ing met·aled** to supply or cover with metal

me·tal·lic *adj.* made of, like metal **me·tál·li·cal·ly** *adv.*

met·al·lur·gic *adj.* metallurgical

met·al·lúr·gi·cal *adj.* of or pertaining to metallurgy

met·al·lur·gist *n.* a specialist in metallurgy

met·al·lur·gy *n.* the science of extracting metals from their ores, of studying their physical and chemical suitability for particular uses etc.

met·a·mor·phic *adj.* resulting from metamorphosis

met·a·mor·pho·sis *pl.* **met·a·mor·pho·ses** *n.* transformation of one structure into another, e.g. stamens into petals

met·a·phor *n.* a figure of speech **met·a·phor·ic met·a·phór·i·cal** *adjs*

me·ta·phys·ics *n.* the branch of philosophy dealing with the first principles of things

me·tas·ta·sis *pl.* **me·tas·ta·ses** *n.* the spreading of disease from one part of the body to another ‖ an instance of this **me·tás·ta·size me·tas·ta·siz·ing me·tas·ta·sized** *v.i.* to spread by metastasis

mete met·ing met·ed *v.t.* to distribute

me·te·or *n.* a solid body from outer space, which glows as it enters the earth's atmosphere

me·te·or·ic *adj.* of or pertaining to meteors ‖ brilliant and rapid **me·te·ór·i·cal·ly** *adv.*

me·te·or·ite *n.* a meteor which reaches the surface of the earth either in one piece or in fragments

me·te·or·o·log·ic *adj.* **me·te·or·o·lóg·i·cal** of or pertaining to meteorology

me·te·or·ol·o·gist *n.* a specialist in meteorology

me·te·or·ol·o·gy *n.* the study of conditions in the earth's atmosphere

me·ter *n.* an instrument for measuring and recording the amount of duration of use of something

me·ter *n.* *(abbr.* m.) the fundamental unit of length in the metric system

me·ter *n.* the rhythmic recurrence of patterns within a line of poetry or in lines of poetry ‖ musical rhythm

meth·a·done *n.* a synthetic narcotic

meth·ane *n.* an odorless, colorless, inflammable hydrocarbon

meth·od *n.* a way of doing something ‖ orderliness in doing ‖ an orderly arrangement or system **me·thód·di·cal** adj.

me·tic·u·lous adj. paying scrupulous attention to detail

met·ric adj. pertaining to the meter (unit of length)

met·ri·cal adj. pertaining to or composed in meter

metric system a decimal system of measurement of length (incl. area and volume) and mass (incl. weight)

met·ro·nome n. a clockwork device used esp. to mark musical time **met·ro·nom·ic** adj.

me·trop·o·lis n. the chief city of a country or region

met·ro·pol·i·tan adj. of, pertaining to or characteristic of a metropolis

met·tle n. spirit, courage or fortitude **mét·tle·some** adj. spirited

mez·za·nine n. a low-ceilinged extra story between two main ones ‖ the first balcony in some theaters

mez·zo for·te adv. moderately loud

mi·ca n. any of several transparent silicates which can be split into very thin, pliable sheets

micro- prefix. (esp. in scientific terms) small, minute

mi·crobe n. a microorganism, esp. one which causes disease **mi·cró·bi·al, mi·cró·bic** adjs

mi·cro·bi·ol·o·gy n. the branch of biology concerned with microorganisms

mi·cro·cosm n. the universe in miniature **mi·cro·cós·mic** adj.

mi·cro·film 1. n. a very small photographic film **2.** v.t. to reproduce on microfilm

mi·crom·e·ter n. an instrument fitted with scale and vernier for measuring very small objects and distances

mi·cro·phone n. an instrument for amplifying or transmitting sound **mi·cro·phon·ic** adj.

mi·cro·pho·to·graph n. a very small photograph

mi·cro·scope n. an optical instrument used to examine minute objects by giving an enlarged, well resolved image of them

mi·cro·scop·ic adj. too small to be visible to the naked eye **mi·cro·scóp·i·cal** adj.

mi·cro·scóp·i·cal·ly adv.

mi·cro·wave n. an electromagnetic wave of wavelength less than 10 m. in the radio-frequency range

microwave oven an oven that utilizes electromagnetic energy for rapid food preparation

mid adj. in the middle of

mid·day n. the middle of the day

mid·dle 1. adj. central ‖ intermediate ‖ medium in size, quality, status etc. **2.** n. a place or moment or thing occupying a middle position ‖ the waist

mid·dle·man pl. **mid·dle·men** n. anyone who buys from the aproducer and sells to the retailer or consumer

midg·et 1. n. a very small person ‖ anything much smaller than others of its kind **2.** adj. very small

mid·night 1. n. 12 o'clock at night **2.** adj. of or happening at this time

mid·riff n. the part of the body including the lower ribs and the top of the abdominal cavity

mid·ship·man pl. **mid·ship·men** n. a student training for the rank of ensign in the U.S. Navy

midst n. (only in phrases) **in our midst** among us **in the midst of** in the middle of

mid·way 1. n. the part of a fair etc. where sideshows and amusements are located **2.** adv. halfway

mid·wife pl. **mid·wives** n. a woman who assists in the delivery of babies **mid·wife·ry** n. obstetrics

mien bearing, demeanor or appearance

miff (pop.) to offend

might n. strength, power

might past of MAY ‖ used as an auxiliary verb to express a degree of possibility less than that expressed by 'may'

might·i·ly adv. with great might ‖ extremely

might·y 1. might·i·er might·i·est adj. large and strong, esp. in physique ‖ powerful **2.** adv. very

mi·graine n. a severe, periodically recurring headache, often accompanied by nausea, vertigo etc.

mi·grant 1. adj. making a periodical migration **2.** n. an animal that migrates

‖ a person who migrates

mi·grate **mi·grat·ing** **mi·grat·ed** *v.i.* to change habitat, esp. at certain seasons ‖ (of people) to leave one country or region to settle or work for a period in another

mi·gra·tion *n.* the act of miagrating

mi·gra·to·ry *adj.* relating to migration ‖ wandering

mi·ka·do *n.* a title of the emperor of Japan

mil *n.* a unit of measurement equivalent to 1/1000 in.

mild *adj.* gentle and moderate, not severe or extreme ‖ (of weather) fairly warm and windless

mil·dew 1. *n.* a whitish, fuzzy growth produced on the surface of various forms of organic matter and living plants by certain fungi 2. *v.i.* to become covered with mildew **míl·dew·y** *adj.*

mile *n.* a unit of linear measurement equaling 1,760 yds (1,609.35 m.) ‖ a nautical mile **míle·age, míl·age** *n.* a number of miles traveled

mile·stone *n.* an event of significance in the history of a nation, person etc.

mi·lieu *n.* environment

mil·i·tan·cy *n.* the quality or state of being militant

mil·i·tant *adj.* engaged in fighting ‖ aggressive

mil·i·ta·rism *n.* the policy of constantly building up armaments and the armed forces ‖ the tendency in a society to encourage an excessively military spirit

mil·i·ta·rist *n.* a person who encourages militarism **mil·i·ta·rís·tic** *adj.* **mil·i·ta·rís·ti·cal·ly** *adv.*

mil·i·ta·rize **mil·i·ta·riz·ing** **mil·i·ta·rized** to build up the military strength of ‖ to imbue with military spirit

mil·i·ta·ry *adj.* pertaining the armed forces or the military the army

mi·li·tia *n.* a reserve body of citizens enrolled for military duties **mi·li·tia·man** *pl.* **mi·li·tia·men** *n.* a member of the militia

milk *n.* a white or yellowish liquid secreted by the mammary glands for the nutrition of the newborn ‖ such a secretion drawn from a cow, goat etc. for use as human food

milk *v.t.* to extract (milk) from an animal ‖ to extract (money etc.) to one's advantage from someone or something, esp. over a period of time ‖ to draw the venom from (a snake)

milk·er *n.* a person who milks

milk·sop *n.* a man or boy who lacks proper spirit

milk·y **milk·i·or** **milk·i·ost** *adj.* like milk ‖ cloudy

mill 1. *n.* a building containing machinery which grinds grain into flour ‖ a machine that grinds grain ‖ a building containing machinery used in some kinds of manufacture 2. *v.t.* to grind (grain, beans etc.) ‖ to cut grooves across the rim edge of (a coin) ‖ *v.i.* to move about in a confused mass

mil·len·ni·um *pl.* **mil·len·ni·ums, mil·len·ni·a** *n.* a period of 1,000 years

milli- *prefix* (esp. in terms of the metric system) one thousandth

mil·li·me·ter *n.* one thousandth of a meter

mil·li·ner *n.* someone who makes, trims or sells women's hats **mil·li·ner·y** *pl.* **mil·li·ner·ies** *n.* the hats made or sold by a milliner

mil·lion 1. *n.* a thousand thousands

mil·lion·aire *n.* a person whose possessions are worth a million or more dollars

mil·lionth 1. *adj.* being number 1,000,000 in a series

mill·stone *n.* one of two large circular channeled slabs of stone, between which grain is ground **a millstone around one's neck** some burden

mime 1. *n.* a form of entertainment in which story and emotion are conveyed by gesture only, without words ‖ an actor in this kind of entertainment 2. *v.* **mim·ing** **mimed** *v.t.* to mimic ‖ *v.i.* to enact a story without words

mim·e·o·graph 1. *n.* a machine for making many copies of a document ‖ a copy made on such a machine 2. *v.t.* to copy with a mimeograph

mim·ic *n.* someone who imitates others, often satirically *v.t.* **mim·ick·ing** **mim·icked** to imitate, esp. in order to ridicule of **mim·ic·ry** *pl.* **mim·ic·ries** *n.* the superficial resemblance that an organism may show to some other animate or inanimate structure, and which serves as a means of concealment

mi·mo·sa *n.* a genus of trees, shrubs and low-growing plants of tropical and warm regions

min·a·ret *n.* a tall slender tower of a mosque from which Moslems are summoned to prayer

min·a·to·ry *adj.* menacing

mince 1. *v.* **minc·ing minced** *v.t.* to cut up (meat etc.) into very small pieces ‖ to utter (words etc.) with affected refinement ‖ *v.i.* to walk with showy steps

mince·meat *n.* a chopped mixture of apples, dried fruits etc., often with suet, used as a filling in pies

mind 1. *n.* the seat of consciousness, thought, feeling and will ‖ the intellect ‖ opinion ‖ sanity ‖ mentality **2.** *v.t.* to have charge of, take care of ‖ to pay attention to, heed ‖ *v.i.* to worry ‖ to have an objection **never mind** do not worry

mind·ful *adj.* giving thought or heed to

mine *possessive pron.* that or those belong to me

mine *n.* an excavation in the earth from which minerals are extracted ‖ a rich source ‖ an explosive charge in a container

mine min·ing mined *v.i.* to dig a mine ‖ to put explosive mines on or under the earth or in the water ‖ to dig (ores etc.) from the earth

mine·field *n.* an area on land or in the sea where mines have been laid

mine·lay·er *n.* a ship used to lay underwater mines

min·er *n.* a man who works in a mine

min·er·al 1. *n.* a solid, homogeneous crystalline chemical element or compound, formed by natural processes and usually extracted from the earth ‖ any inorganic substance **2.** *adj.* of, containing or consisting of minerals ‖ inorganic

min·er·al·o·gy *n.* the science of minerals

min·gle min·gling min·gled *v.t.* to mix, blend ‖ to bring together ‖ *v.i.* to become part of a group etc.

min·i·a·ture 1. *n.* a small painting on vellum, ivory etc. ‖ a small model **2.** *adj.* on a small scale **min·i·a·tur·ist** *n.* an artist specializing in miniatures

min·i·mal *adj.* pertaining to the least possible

min·i·mize min·i·miz·ing min·i·mized *v.t.* to reduce to the smallest possible degree ‖ to underestimate

min·i·mum 1. *pl.* **min·i·ma min·i·mums** *n.* the least possible amount, number or degree **2.** *adj.* least in amount, number or degree

min·ing *n.* the act or process of extracting coal, ore etc. from a mine or mines ‖ the laying of explosive mines

min·is·ter *n.* a person in charge of some high office of state ‖ a diplomat raking below an ambassador ‖ in a Christian church, esp. *(Am.)* any Protestant clergyman

minister *v.i.* to give aid or service ‖ to serve as a minister of religion

min·is·try *pl.* **min·is·tries** *n.* a ministerial department of a government ‖ a governing body of ministers ‖ the building occupied by a ministerial department ‖ the office and duties of a minister of religion ‖ the period during which a minister serves a congregation

mink *pl.* **mink, minks** *n.* the highly valued fur of one of several small semiaquatic carnivorous mammals closely related to the weasel ‖ one of these animals

min·now *n.* a small freshwater fish about 3 ins long

mi·nor 1. *adj.* less in importance, size etc. than something else ‖ not having reached the full legal age **2.** *n.* a person under full legal age **3.** *v.i.* to study a specified minor subject

mi·nor·i·ty *pl.* **mi·nor·i·ties** *n.* less than half of a total ‖ group distinguished by its religious, political, racial or other characteristics from a larger society of which it forms a part

min·strel *n.* a medieval musician who sang, recited, and accompanied himself on an instrument

mint *n.* any of various aromatic plants

mint 1. *n.* a place where official coins are made **2.** *adj.* not marred or soiled, as if new **3.** *v.t.* to coin (money) **mint·age** *n.* the act or process of minting money

mi·nus 1. *prep.* reduced by ‖ deficient in, lacking **2.** *adj.* indicating subtraction ‖ negative **3.** *n.* a minus sign ‖ a minus quantity

min·ute 1. *n.* a unit of time equal to a sixtieth of an hour ‖ an undefined short time ‖ a written record of a decision etc. made at a meeting

mi·nute *adj.* tiny ‖ trivial ‖ precise and detailed

mir·a·cle *n.* a supernatural event regarded as due to divine action ‖ an unexpected piece of luck

mi·rac·u·lous *adj.* of, like, involving, or having the nature of a miracle

mi·rage *n.* an optical illusion ‖ something illusory

mire 1. *n.* an area of swampy land ‖ deep soft mud **2.** *v.t.* **mir·ing mired** to cause to be stuck fast in mire

mir·ror 1. *n.* a polished surface, esp. of glass which reflects light, and on which images can therefore be seen ‖ a true portrayal or representation **2.** *v.t.* to reflect in a mirror

mirth *n.* merriment **mirth·ful, mirth·less** *adjs*

mis- *prefix* (in combination with verbs) badly or incorrectly ‖ (in combination with nouns) bad, wrong

mis·ad·ven·ture *n.* an unlucky accident

mis·an·thrope *n.* a person who hates or distrusts all mankind **mis·an·throp·ic** *adj.* **mis·an·throp·i·cal·ly** *adv.* **mis·an·thro·pist mis·án·thro·py** *ns*

mis·ap·pli·ca·tion *n.* a misapplying or being misapplied

mis·ap·ply mis·ap·ply·ing mis·ap·plied *v.t.* to use badly or mistakenly

mis·ap·pre·hend *v.t.* to misunderstand **mis·ap·pre·hen·sion** *n.*

mis·be·have mis·be·hav·ing mis·be·haved *v.i.* to behave badly **mis·be·hav·ior** *n.*

mis·cal·cu·late mis·cal·cu·lat·ing mis·cal·cu·lat·ed *v.t.* and *i.* to calculate wrongly **mis·cal·cu·lá·tion** *n.*

mis·car·riage *n.* the expulsion of a human fetus from the womb before it is viable ‖ mismanagement

mis·car·ry mis·car·ry·ing mis·car·ried *v.i.* (of a plan) to go wrong ‖ to undergo a miscarriage of a fetus

mis·ce·ge·na·tion *n.* interbreeding or marriage between members of different races

mis·cel·la·ne·ous *adj.* formed of things of several kinds

mis·chance *n.* bad luck ‖ an instance of this

mis·chief *n.* annoying but not seriously harmful behavior ‖ playful teasing ‖ harm

mis·chie·vous *adj.* inclined toward or characterized by playful teasing

mis·con·ceive mis·con·ceiv·ing mis·con·ceived *v.t.* to misunderstand, interpret mistakenly

mis·con·cep·tion *n.* the act of misconceiving

mis·con·duct 1. *n.* bad management **2.** *v.t.* to mismanage ‖ to conduct (oneself) improperly

mis·con·strue mis·con·stru·ing mis·con·strued *v.t.* to interpret mistakenly

mis·cre·ant 1. *adj.* evil **2.** *n.* a criminal or villain

mis·deal 1. *n.* (cards) a mistake made in dealing **2.** *v.t.* and *i.* (cards) to deal incorrectly

mis·deed *n.* an evil or criminal action

mis·de·mean·or *n.* an offense technically less than a felony ‖ a misdeed

mi·ser *n.* an avaricious person, esp. one who lives in discomfort or squalor in order to hoard his wealth

mis·er·a·ble *adj.* extremely unhappy ‖ causing misery ‖ extremely inadequate, worthless **mís·er·a·bly** *adv.*

mi·ser·ly *adj.* characteristic of or relating to a miser

mis·er·y *pl.* **mis·er·ies** *n.* extreme wretchedness due to poverty, squalor etc.

mis·fea·sance *n.* the illegal or improper performance of an action in itself lawful **mis·féa·sor** *n.*

mis·fire 1. *v.i.* **mis·fir·ing mis·fired** to fail to ignite properly or at the right time ‖ (of a plan, joke etc.) to fail to have the effect intended

mis·fit *n.* a person who is unable to adjust himself to society ‖ a garment etc. that does not fit

mis·for·tune *n.* mischance, bad luck

mis·give mis·giv·ing mis·gave mis·giv·en *v.t.* **mis·giv·ing** *n.* distrust, apprehension, or anticipation of failure

mis·guide mid·guid·ing mis·guid·ed *v.t.* to misdirect **mis·gúid·ed** *adj.* mistaken because of poor advice

mis·hap *n.* an unlucky accident

mis·in·form *v.t.* to give wrong or misleading information to **mis·in·for·ma·tion** *n.*

mis·judge mis·judg·ing mis·judged *v.t.* to judge wrongly **mis·júdg·ment, mis·júdge·ment** *n.*

mis·lay mis·lay·ing mis·laid *v.t.* to lose (something) temporarily by forgetting where one has put it

mis·lead mis·lead·ing mis·led *v.t.* to deceive ‖ to lead in a wrong direction **mis·léad·ing** *adj.*

mis·no·mer *n.* a wrong name

mi·sog·a·my *n.* hatred of marriage

mi·sog·y·nist *n.* a man who hates women **mi·sóg·y·nous** *adj.* **mi·sóg·y·ny** *n.*

mis·print 1. *v.t.* to print inaccurately **2.** *n.* a mistake in printing

mis·rep·re·sent *v.t.* to give a false impression or account of **mis·rep·re·sen·tá·tion** *n.*

miss 1. *v.t.* to fail to hit, reach, meet or make contact with ‖ to allow (an opportunity etc.) to pass by ‖ to fail to perceive ‖ to notice the loss or absence of ‖ to void ‖ to be unable to attend **2.** *n.* a failure to hit or catch

mis·sal *n.* (*Roman Catholicism*) a book containing everything said or sung at Mass for the entire year

mis·sile 1. *n.* a weapon or object that is thrown or fired or designed for this

miss·ing *adj.* lost or absent

missing link a hypothetical organism intermediate between two known types, esp. between the apes and man

mis·sion *n.* a group of people sent esp. abroad by a religious organization to make conversions ‖ the buildings acting as its center ‖ a body of representatives sent abroad for special diplomatic discussions etc. ‖ the work they are sent to do ‖ a permanent diplomatic delegation abroad ‖ an aim in life, arising from a conviction

mis·sion·ar·y *n. pl.* **mis·sion·ar·ies** a person who undertakes the work of a religious mission

mis·sive *n.* a formal or official letter

mis·spell mis·spell·ing mis·spelled, mis·spelt *v.t.* to spell incorrectly **mis·spéll·ing** *n.* an instance of incorrect spelling

mis·step *n.* a step taken in a wrong way ‖ an error

mist *n.* a mass of minute particles of water, precipitated in particles finer than raindrops ‖ a film or haze before the eyes

mist *v.i.* to become misty ‖ *v.t.* to make misty

mis·tak·a·ble *adj.* be mistaken or misunderstood

mis·take 1. *v.t.* **mis·tak·ing mis·took mis·tak·en** to misunderstand ‖ to have a wrong opinion of ‖ (someone) **2.** *n.* a misunderstanding **mis·ták·en** *adj.* involving error in judgment or behavior

Mis·ter *n.* (*abbr.* Mr.) a courtesy title for any male adult

mis·tle·toe *n.* evergreen shrub. It bears a white viscous berry

mis·treat *v.t.* to treat wrongly or badly, abuse

mis·tress *n.* a woman in relation to a man not her husband with whom she frequently has sexual relations ‖ a woman in relation to her servants or pets

mis·tri·al *n.* a trial declared void because of an error in proceedings ‖ a trial in which the jury cannot agree upon a verdict

mis·trust 1. *v.t.* to regard with suspicion ‖ to feel no confidence in **2.** *n.* suspicion ‖ lack of confidence **mis·trúst·ful** *adj.*

mist·y mist·i·er mist·i·est *adj.* blurred, indistinct

mis·un·der·stand mis·un·der·stand·ing mis·un·der·stood *v.t.* to interpret incorrectly **mis·un·der·stánd·ing** *n.* a misin-

terpretation ‖ a disagreement
mis·un·der·stóod *adj*. wrongly interpreted
mis·use 1. *n*. improper or incorrect use **2.**
v.t. **mis·us·ing mis·used** to use improperly ‖ to treat abusively
mite *n*. any of several widely distributed,
minute, sometimes microscopic
arachnids
mite *n*. a very small thing, quantity
mi·ter *n*. a tall ornamented liturgical
headdress
miter 1. *n*. a miter joint **2.** *v.t.* **mi·ter·ing
mi·tered** to fit together in a miter joint
mit·i·ga·ble *adj*. capable of being mitigated
mit·i·gate mit·i·gat·ing mit·i·gat·ed *v.t.* to
make less severe, alleviate **mit·i·gá·tion**
n. **mit·i·ga·tive** *adj*. **mít·i·ga·tor** *n*.
mit·i·ga·to·ry *adj*.
mitt *n*. a glove which leaves the fingers and
thumb bare ‖ *(baseball)* a padded glove
used to catch the ball
mit·ten *n*. a glove which has a single
section for the four fingers and a separate
division for the thumb
mix 1. *v.t.* to combine ‖ to bring together
into a single uniform mass ‖ to cause to
associate ‖ to crossbreed ‖ *v.i.* to become
mixed ‖ to be capable of being mixed **2.**
n. a mixture **mixed** *adj*. blended ‖ including persons of both sexes
mixed-up *adj*. confused, esp. emotionally
mix·ture *n*. something made by mixing ‖
a substance made up of two or more
components not in fixed proportion
mix·up *n*. a state of confusion ‖ an instance
of this
mne·mon·ic 1. *adj*. meant to help the
memory **2.** *n*. **mne·món·ics** *n*. a technique or system used to train the memory
moan 1. *n*. a low, long sound expressing
pain or grief **2.** *v.t.* to lament about,
bewail ‖ *v.i.* to utter a moan ‖ to
complolain or lament
moat *n*. a deep, wide trench around a fortification filled with water **móat·ed** *adj*.
surrounded by a moat
mob 1. *n*. a large, esp. rough and disorderly crowd ‖ a gang of criminals **2.** *v.*
mob·bing mobbed *v.t.* to crowd into ‖ *v.i.*

to form a mob
mo·bile 1. *adj*. moving or moved with ease
2. *n*. a sculpture kept constantly moving
in various planes by air currents
mo·bil·i·ty *n*. the state or quality of being
mobile
mo·bi·li·za·tion *n*. a mobilizing or being
mobilized
mo·bi·lize mo·bi·liz·ing mo·bi·lized *v.t.* to
assemble (troops) in readiness for active
service
moc·ca·sin *n*. a soft heelless shoe of deer-
skin ‖ a North American poisonous snake
mock 1. *v.t.* to imitate, esp. in order to ridicule ‖ *v.i.* to express ridicule **2.** *adj*. false,
sham
mock·er·y *pl*. **mock·er·ies** *n*. derision ‖ a
travesty
mode *n*. a way or manner of doing, being
etc. ‖ a fashion (esp. style of clothes) ‖ the
value of the variable occurring most often
in a series of data ‖ mood **the mode**
common prevailing style or fashion in
behavior, speech etc.
mod·el 1. *n*. a three-dimensional representation, usually in miniature, of a thing to
be constructed, sculptured etc. ‖ a design
intended for mass production ‖ a person
or thing considered as an object for imitation ‖ a person who poses for an artist ‖
a person who demonstrates clothes **2.**
adj. suitable to be a model **3.** *v.*
mod·el·ing mod·eled, mod·elled *v.t.* to
work (clay or other plastic material) ‖ to
form ‖ to wear (clothes) in demonstrations
‖ *v.i.* to act as a mannequin
mod·er·ate 1. *adj*. between extremes in
size, quality, degree etc. ‖ reasonable ‖
limited ‖ not severe or violent ‖ not
extremist **2.** *n*. a politically moderate
person **3.** *v.* **mod·er·at·ing mod·er·at·ed**
v.t. to make less violent, severe etc. ‖ to
preside over ‖ *v.i.* to become less extreme
mod·er·a·tion *n*. the quality of being
moderate
mod·er·a·tor *n*. a mediator ‖ someone who
presides at a meeting
mod·ern 1. *adj*. of the present day ‖ up-to-
date **2.** *n*. a person holding progressive
opinions in conflict with earlier ideas

mo·dern·i·za·tion *n.* a modernizing

mod·ern·ize mod·ern·iz·ing mod·ern·ized *v.t.* to change, in order to bring into harmony with modern taste

mod·est *adj.* aware of one's limitations ‖ avoiding pretension ‖ limited but not negligible ‖ shunning indecency **mód·es·ty** *n.*

mod·i·fi·a·ble *adj.* capable of being modified

mod·i·fi·ca·tion *n.* a partial change

mo·di·fi·er *n.* someone who or something that modifies

mod·i·fy mod·i·fy·ing mod·i·fied *v.t.* to change to some extent but not completely ‖ to make less extreme

mod·u·lar *adj.* of, relating to or based upon a module

mo·du·late mod·u·lat·ing mod·u·lat·ed *v.t.* to regulate by a standard measure, esp. to vary the pitch of (a voice or other sound) ‖ *v.i.* to lead out of one key into another

mod·u·la·tion *n.* a modulating or being modulated ‖ a variation produced by modulating

mod·ule *n.* a unit used as a standard of measurement ‖ a spacecraft unit that is self-contained ‖ an independent unit containing electronic components, esp. one that can be incorporated in a computer system

mo·dus o·pe·ran·di *n.* a manner of working

modus vi·ven·di *n.* an agreement establishing a temporary compromise between two groups in conflict

Mo·gul *n.* someone with influence

mo·hair *n.* the hair of the Angora goat ‖ a fabric made from this

moist *adj.* slightly wet ‖ humid **mois·ten** *v.t.* to make moist ‖ *v.i.* to become moist

mois·ture *n.* diffused or condensed liquid

mo·lar *n.* one of the posterior teeth in mammals, adapted for grinding

mo·las·ses *n.* the uncrystallized syrup produced in the process of refining sugar

mold 1. *n.* a hollow container into which fluid or plastic material is put and allowed to harden, so that the material takes on the container's interior shape ‖ the shape

created in this way **2.** *v.t.* to form into a certain shape ‖ to modify the shape or character of

mold *n.* a woolly or fluffy growth produced by various fungi ‖ a fungus that produces mold

mold·ing *n.* a continuous band on the cornice of a building, on ceilings of rooms etc. ‖ an ornamental edging

mold·y mold·i·er mold·i·est *adj.* covered with mold

mole *n.* any of several small burrowing insectivorous mammals, with dark velvety fur

mole *n.* a congenital mark on the skin

mole *n.* a wall of masonry constructed in the sea to form a breakwater ‖ a harbor formed by such a wall

mole *n.* an intelligence agent

mo·lec·u·lar *adj.* pertaining to molecules

mol·e·cule *n.* the smallest amount of a chemical element retaining the characteristic properties of the substance

mo·lest *v.t.* to meddle with (someone) in such a way as to harm or annoy him

mo·les·ta·tion *n.* a molesting or being molested

moll *n.* a gangster's girl

mol·li·fi·ca·tion *n.* a mollifying or being mollified

mol·li·fy mol·li·fy·ing mol·li·fied *v.t.* to lessen the anger of ‖ to soften the effect of

mol·lusk, mol·lusc *n.* unsegmented, generally shelled and bilaterally symmetrical invertebrates

molt 1. *v.i.* to shed feathers, fur, skin etc., which are later replaced by new growth ‖ *v.t.* to shed in this way **2.** *n.* the act of molting

mol·ten *adj.* melted, esp. by extremely high heat

mo·ment *n.* a small, indefinite period of time

mo·men·tar·i·ly *adv.* for a moment

mo·men·tar·y *adj.* lasting only for a moment

mo·men·tous *adj.* having great importance

mo·men·tum *pl.* **mo·men·ta, mo·men·tums** *n.* the force built up by a moving body

mon·arch *n.* a person ruling over a kingdom or people ‖ a large orange and black American butterfly **mo·nar·chal** *adj.*

mo·nar·chic *adj.* having the characteristics of a monarchy or monarch **mo·nár·chi·cal** *adj.*

mon·ar·chism *n.* the monarchical system of government ‖ belief in monarchical principles of government **món·ar·chist** *n.*

mon·ar·chy *pl.* **mon·ar·chies** *n.* a state ruled by a monarch ‖ rule by a monarch

mon·as·ter·y *pl.* **mon·as·ter·ies** *n.* the group of buildings housing a community of monks

mo·nas·tic *adj.* pertaining to monks or to a monastery

Mon·day *n.* the second day in the week

mon·e·tar·i·ly *adv.* with regard to money

mon·e·tar·y *adj.* pertaining to money, esp. to coinage

mon·ey *pl.* **mon·eys, mon·ies** *n.* anything that serves as a medium of exchange for goods and services, in the form of tokens ‖ personal wealth

mon·grel 1. *n.* something (esp. a dog) of mixed breed 2. *adj.* of mixed breed

mon·i·tor 1. *n.* a pupil appointed to assist in keeping discipline etc. ‖ an instrument that monitors a broadcast ‖ *(computer)* diagnostic program used to respond to questions about a computer program 2. *v.t.* to check (radio, television or telephonic communication) for quality of transmission **mon·i·to·ri·al** *adj.* **món·i·tor·ship** *n.*

monk *n.* a member of a religious community of men, bound by vows of obedience to the rules of the order

mon·key 1. *pl.* **mon·keys** *n.* any of certain primates, generally smaller than the anthropoid apes, often arboreal and usually having prehensile hands and feet ‖ a playful, mischievous child 2. *v.i.* to tamper ‖ to act playfully

mono- *prefix* alone, single

mo·nog·a·mist *n.* someone who practices or believes in monogamy

mo·nog·a·mous *adj.* practicing monogamy

mo·nog·a·my *n.* marriage to only one husband or wife at a time ‖ having only one mate

mon·o·gram *n.* a character composed of two or more interwoven letters, esp. a person's initials

mon·o·graph *n.* a treatise about a single subject **mo·nog·ra·pher** *n.* **mon·o·graph·ic** *adj.* **mon·o·gráph·i·cal·ly** *adv.*

mon·o·lith *n.* a very large single block of stone **mon·o·líth·ic** *adj.* massive, solid

mon·o·logue, mon·o·log *n.* a dramatic speech by one actor ‖ a writing in the form of a soliloquy

mo·nop·o·li·za·tion *n.* a monopolizing

mo·nop·o·lize **mo·nop·o·liz·ing** **mo·nop·o·lized** *v.t.* to make a monopoly of ‖ to assume exclusive control of

mo·nop·o·ly *pl.* **mo·nop·o·lies** *n.* exclusive control of a product or service in a particular market ‖ a commodity under exclusive control

mon·o·rail *n.* a railway consisting of a single rail on which the wheels run ‖ this rail

mon·o·syl·la·ble *n.* a word of one syllable

mon·o·the·ism *n.* belief in only one God **món·o·the·ist** *n.* **mon·o·the·ís·tic, mon·o·the·ís·ti·cal** *adjs*

mon·o·tone *n.* a succession of sounds of the same pitch

mo·not·o·nous *adj.* repetitious, lacking variety

mo·not·o·ny *n.* sameness of tone or pitch

Mon·sieur *pl.* **Mes·sieurs** *n.* the French equivalent of 'Mr'

Mon·si·gnor *pl.* **Mon·si·gno·ri Mon·si·gnors** *n.* (abbr. Msgr) a title given to certain dignitaries of the Roman Catholic Church

mon·soon *n.* a wind system in the rainy summer season (Apr.–Sept.) in S.E. Asia

mon·ster 1. *n.* a deformed animal or plant ‖ an imaginary beast ‖ a person who is horrifyingly cruel, abrutal, selfish etc. ‖ something of extraordinarily great size

mon·strance *n.* (Roman Catholicism) a vessel of gold or silver in which the consecrated Host is exposed to the congregation for veneration

mon·stros·i·ty *pl.* **mon·stros·i·ties** *n.* something monstrous ‖ the quality or state of being monstrous

mon·strous *adj.* having the qualities of a monster

mon·tage *n.* the making of a single picture from several others or pieces of others ‖ *(movies)* a medley of shots built up into a single unified effect

month *n.* one of 12 periods into which the year is divided in the Gregorian calendar

month·ly 1. *adj.* occurring once each month **2.** *adv.* once a month

mon·u·ment *n.* something erected in memory of a person or event

mon·u·men·tal *adj.* like a monument ‖ large, massive

mooch *v.i.* to sponge

mood *n.* an emotional state

mood·y mood·i·er mood·i·est *adj.* characterized by sudden changes of mood ‖ gloomy, depressed

moon 1. *n.* the only natural satellite of the earth ‖ any planetary satellite **2.** *v.i.* to behave in a dreamy abstracted manner

moon·beam *n.* a beam of light from the moon

moon·light 1. *n.* light received by reflection from the moon **2.** *v.i.* to engage in moonlighting

moonlighting working at a job in addition to one's regular one —**moonlight** *v.* —**moonlighter** *n.*

moon·lit *adj.* illuminated by moonlight

moor *n.* a tract of open uncultivated ground

moor *v.t.* to secure (a vessel) to the land or buoys by means of ropes, chains etc. **móor·age** *n.* a place for mooring

moor·ing *n.* the cables, ropes etc. by which a vessel is moored ‖ the place where a vessel is moored

moose *pl.* **moose** *n.* a North American deer closely related to the European elk

moot *v.t.* to put up (an idea etc.) for discussion

moot 1. *n.* a discussion of fictitious cases arranged for practice among law students **2.** *adj.* open to argument, uncertain

mop 1. *n.* an implement for washing or polishing floors etc. ‖ something resem-

bling this, e.g. thick, unruly hair **2.** *v.t.* **mop·ping mopped** to wipe clean with a mop

mope 1. *v.* **mop·ing moped** *v.i.* to be listless and gloomy **2.** *n.* (esp. *pl.*) a fit of low spirits **móp·ish** *adj.*

mor·al 1. *adj.* concerned with right and wrong and the distinctions between them ‖ virtuous, good ‖ relating to the mind or will, *moral support* **2.** *n.* the moral teaching contained in a fable, story, experience etc. ‖ *(pl.)* principles of conduct

mo·rale *n.* psychological state with regard to dependability, confidence, strength of purpose etc.

mor·al·ist *n.* a person who moralizes ‖ a teacher of morals **mor·al·is·tic** *adj.*

mo·ral·i·ty *pl.* **mo·ral·i·ties** *n.* ethics ‖ upright conduct

mor·al·ize mor·al·iz·ing mor·al·ized *v.i.* to talk or write on moral themes etc. ‖ *v.t.* to draw a moral from

mo·rass *n.* a marsh, swamp

mor·a·to·ri·um *pl.* **mor·a·to·ri·ums, mor·a·to·ri·a** *n.* a legally authorized period of delay before debts have to be paid ‖ the authorization for this

mor·bid *adj.* unwholesome ‖ given to gruesome thoughts or feelings ‖ relating to disease **mor·bíd·i·ty** *n.* the quality or state of being morbid

mor·dant 1. *adj.* incisive and caustic ‖ corrosive **2.** *n.* a corroding substance

more most 1. *adj.* greater in quantity, amount, number or degree ‖ additional, further **2.** *n.* greater number ‖ a greater quantity

more·o·ver *adv.* further, besides

mo·res *pl. n.* fixed or traditional customs

morgue *n.* a place where dead bodies are laid out ‖ a place where photographs, clippings, back numbers etc. are kept for reference by a newspaper or magazine

mor·i·bund *adj.* near death ‖ about to collapse

morn·ing *n.* the early part of the day between midnight and noon ‖ dawn

mo·ron *n.* a mentally deficient person **mo·rón·ic** *adj.*

mo·rose *adj.* glum, sour-tempered and

unsocial

mor·phine *n.* the principal alkaloid of opium, a habit-forming narcotic **mór·phin·ism** *n.* addiction to morphine

mor·sel *n.* a small bite or mouthful of food ‖ a small piece, esp. a choice one

mor·tal 1. *adj.* subject to death ‖ fatal ‖ relating to or accompanying death ‖ tedious **2.** *n.* a human being

mor·tal·i·ty *pl.* **mor·tal·i·ties** *n.* the human race ‖ the number of deaths in a given period or place ‖ the death rate

mor·tar *n.* a bowl in which substances are pounded and ground to powder with a pestle ‖ a short cannon ‖ a mixture of lime (or cement), sand and water, used for binding stones, bricks etc.

mort·gage 1. *n.* a conditional conveyance of land, a house etc. as security for a loan ‖ the documents making this agreement ‖ the state of property thus conveyed **2.** *v.t.* **mort·gag·ing mort·gaged** to make over, grant as security for debt **mort·ga·gee** *n.* a creditor who receives a mortgage **mort·ga·gor, mort·gag·er** *n.* the debtor who gives his property in a mortgage

mor·ti·cian *n.* an undertaker

mor·ti·fy mor·ti·fy·ing mor·ti·fied *v.t.* to subdue (passions, bodily desires etc.) by discipline ‖ to humiliate

mor·tu·ar·y *pl.* **mor·tu·ar·ies** *n.* a place where dead bodies are kept before burial or cremation

mo·sa·ic 1. *n.* a form of surface decoration made by inlaying small pieces of colored glass, stone etc. **2.** *adj.* resembling mosaic in pattern or structure

mo·sey *v.i.* to move in a leisurely, sauntering way

mosque *n.* a Moslem place of worship

mos·qui·to *pl.* **mos·qui·toes, mos·qui·tos** *n.* any of many two-winged flies distributed throughout the world

moss *n.* a class of primitive, green land plants

most *adj.* (*superl.* of MUCH, MANY) greatest in number, quantity, amount, extent or degree **to make the most of** to use to the best advantage **1.** *adv.* to very

-most *suffix* indicating a superlative

most·ly *adv.* in most cases, chiefly ‖ usually

mote *n.* a small particle, e.g. of dust

mo·tel a roadside hotel for motorists

moth *pl.* **moths** *n.* any of several lepidopterous insects

moth·er 1. *n.* a female parent ‖ something regarded as a source **2.** *adj.* of, relating to or being a mother **3.** *v.t.* to take care of as a mother does

moth·er·hood *n.* the state of being a mother

moth·er-in-law *pl.* **moth·ers-in-law** *n.* a husband's or wife's mother

moth·er·ly *adj.* of or characteristic of a mother

mo·tif *n.* a feature or theme, esp. one dominant or recurring in a work of art, music or drama

mo·tile *adj.* showing, or capable of, spontaneous movement **mo·til·i·ty** *n.*

mo·tion 1. *n.* the act or process of passing through space or changing position ‖ an act or instance of moving the body or part of the body ‖ a formal proposal ‖ an application to a judge or court **in motion** moving **2.** *v.t.* to direct by sign or gesture ‖ *v.i.* to make a meaningful gesture **mó·tion·less** *adj.* perfectly still

mo·ti·vate mo·ti·vat·ing mo·ti·vacat·ed *v.t.* to be the motive of ‖ to supply a motive to **mo·ti·vá·tion** *n.*

mo·tive 1. *n.* the sense of need, desire, fear etc. that prompts an individual to act

mot·ley 1. *adj.* miscellaneous, varied in character, type etc. **2.** *n.* an incongruous mixture, e.g. of colors

mo·tor 1. *n.* that which imparts motion ‖ an internal-combustion engine ‖ a machine transforming electrical into mechanical energy **2.** *adj.* of any form of movement **3.** *v.i.* to travel by automobile

mo·tor·cy·cle *n.* a two-wheeled, gasoline-driven vehicle larger and heavier than a bicycle

mo·tor·ist *n.* a person who drives an automobile

mot·tle 1. *n.* a colored spot or blotch **2.** *v.t.* **mot·tling mot·tled** to mark with blotches **mót·tled** *adj.*

mot·to *pl.* **mot·toes, mot·tos** *n.* a sentence

or phrase used as a watchword, maxim or guiding principle

mound 1. *n.* a bank of earth ‖ a heap ‖ (*baseball*) a slight rise in the ground where the pitcher stands when pitching **2.** *v.t.* to heap up into a mound

mount *n. (abbr.* Mt) a mountain (used esp. before a mountain's name) ‖ a high hill

mount 1. *v.t.* to climb ‖ to place oneself in riding position on (a horse, bicycle etc.) ‖ to put in a fixed position ‖ to put (a picture etc.) inside a raised border ‖ to prepare or set up for view ‖ to fit into a setting ‖ to put (a play, opera etc.) on the stage **2.** *n.* the act of mounting ‖ something mounted ‖ a gun carriage for a cannon etc. ‖ a ground or raised border used in mounting a drawing etc. ‖ a setting of precious metal for jewels

moun·tain *n.* a conspicuously elevated, steep part of the earth's surface ‖ a great quantity

moun·tain·eer 1. *n.* a person skilled in mountain climbing **2.** *v.i.* to climb mountains

moun·tain·ous *adj.* containing mountains ‖ huge

moun·te·bank *n.* a man who uses show-manship to exploit public credulity unscrupulously

mourn *v.i.* to express or feel grief esp. because of a death ‖ *v.t.* to express or feel grief for

mourn·er *n.* a person who mourns ‖ a person attending a funeral

mourn·ful *adj.* feeling or showing sadness ‖ doleful, causing sadness

mourn·ing *n.* grieving, lamentation ‖ the customary period during which a dead person is mourned

mouse 1. *pl.* **mice** *n.* any of a large number of rodents resembling rats but smaller ‖ a timid or retiring person **2.** *v.i.* **mous·ing moused** to hunt and catch mice

mous·tache, mus·tache *n.* the hair on the upper lip ‖ bristles or hair around an animal's mouth

mouth 1. *pl.* **mouths** *n.* the external open-ing of the lips as a facial feature ‖ the open-ing in an animal's body through which

food is taken in ‖ the part of a river where it empties into the sea **2.** *v.t.* to shape (words) with the lips without saying them

móuth·ful *n.* the amount of food etc. that will go into the mouth easily **to say a mouthful** to say something strikingly apt or true

mouth·piece *n.* part of a wind instrument ‖ something placed at the mouth ‖ the part of a tobacco pipe which is placed in the mouth ‖ the part of a telephone into which one speaks ‖ a spokesman

mov·a·bil·i·ty, move·a·bil·i·ty *n.* the state or quality of being movable

mov·a·ble, move·a·ble 1. *adj.* capable of being moved **2.** *n.* an article, esp. of furniture, that can be moved from a house

move 1. *v.* **mov·ing moved** *v.t.* to change the location or position of ‖ to become active, stir ‖ to arouse the feelings of ‖ to influence, impel ‖ to cause (the bowels) to eject feces ‖ to propose formally in an assembly ‖ to depart **as the spirit moves one** when one feels inclined **to move out (in)** to remove one's belonging from a resi-dence **to move up** to advance **2.** *n.* a calculated maneuver made to gain some advantage ‖ a change of place or residence

move·ment *n.* the act or process of moving ‖ the rhythmic quality of a poem ‖ the moving parts of a mechanism ‖ usually self-contained structural division of a symphony, sonata etc. ‖ a series of acts and events planned towards a definite end by a body of people ‖ an emptying of the bowels ‖ a change or trend in the price of some commodity or stock

mov·er *n.* someone who professionally moves people's belongings from one resi-dence to another

mo·vie *n.* a sequence of pictures project-ed on a screen

mov·ing *adj.* changing place, posture etc. ‖ causing movement or action ‖ affecting the feelings

moving picture a movie (sequence of pictures)

mow mowed mown *v.t.* to cut (grass etc.) ‖ (with 'down') to cause to fall in great numbers

much more most 1. *adj.* great in quantity, extent or degree **2.** *n.* a great quantity, extent or degree ‖ something great, important, admirable **3.** *adv.* almost

mu·ci·lage *n.* a solution of gum etc. prepared as an adhesive **mu·ci·lag·i·nous** *adj.* sticky

muck 1. *n.* moist farmyard manure ‖ dark, moist, fertile soil ‖ dirt, filth ‖ mud **2.** *v.t.* to make dirty

mu·co·sa *pl.* **mu·co·sae mu·co·sa, mu·co·sas** *n.* a mucous membrane

mu·cous *adj.* containing or secreting mucus

mu·cus *n.* a slippery, slimy substance covering and lubricating the inner surfaces of the respiratory, alimentary and genitourinary tracts etc.

mud *n.* a sticky mixture of water and earth or dust ‖ malicious abuse

mud·dle 1. *v.* **mud·dling mud·dled** *v.t.* to mix (things) in a confused manner ‖ to make (speech, words) unclear **2.** *n.* a state of disorder ‖ a state of mental confusion

mud·dy 1. *adj.* **mud·di·er mud·di·est** covered with mud ‖ like mud in color or texture **2.** *v.t.* **mud·dy·ing mud·died** to make muddy ‖ *v.i.* to become muddy

muff *n.* a covering of fur etc. for protecting the hands from cold, shaped like a tube with open ends

muff 1. *v.t.* to miss ‖ to bungle ‖ a bungling performance

muf·fin *n.* a quick bread baked in a cup-shaped mold

muf·fle muf·fling muf·fled *v.t.* to cover up for protection against cold ‖ to wrap or pad ‖ to deaden (sound) **muf·fler** *n.* a scarf for protecting the throat from cold ‖ a device to deaden or muffle noise

mug 1. *n.* a drinking vessel ‖ the face or mouth **2.** *v.* **mug·ging mugged** *v.t.* strike or assault in order to commit robbery **múg·ger** *n.* someone who assaults a person in order to rob him

mug·gy mug·gi·er mug·gi·est *adj.* warm and damp, oppressive

mug·wump *n.* someone who is neutral or undecided, esp. in politics

mul·ber·ry *pl.* **mul·ber·ries** a worldwide genus of trees cultivated for their delicious multiple fruit

mulch 1. *n.* a layer of wet straw, compost etc. spread over the roots of plants to protect from frost etc. **2.** *v.t.* to apply mulch to

mulct *v.t.* to punish by means of a fine ‖ to get hold of money by swindling or extortion

mulct *n.* a fine ‖ a penalty ‖ a compulsory payment

mule *n.* a slipper made without a back

mule *n.* a sterile hybrid produced by crossing a male ass and a mare ‖ a stubborn or obstinate person

mul·ish *adj.* obstinate, stubborn

mull *v.t.* (with 'over') to ponder

multi- *prefix* having, containing or consisting of much or many

mul·ti·far·i·ous *adj.* having great variety or diversity

mul·ti·ple 1. *adj.* having many parts, sections or components ‖ manifold **2.** *n.* a quantity or number which contains another an exact number of times without a remainder

mul·ti·pli·a·ble *adj.* capable of being multiplied

mul·ti·plic·a·ble *adj.* multipliable

mul·ti·pli·ca·tion *n.* a multiplying or being multiplied

mul·ti·plic·i·ty *n.* a great number

mul·ti·ply mul·ti·ply·ing mul·ti·plied *v.t.* to increase in number or quantity ‖ to breed

mul·ti·tude *n.* a great number ‖ a crowd

mul·ti·tu·di·nous *adj.* existing in great numbers

mum·ble 1. *v.* **mum·bling mum·bled** *v.i.* to speak in a low indistinct way **2.** *n.* a low indistinct utterance

mum·mi·fy mum·mi·fy·ing mum·mi·fied *v.t.* to embalm

mum·my *pl.* **mum·mies** *n.* a dead body embalmed for burial by the ancient Egyptians so as to abe preserved from decay ‖ any dead body that has been naturally well preserved

mumps *n.* an acute, contagious, virus

disease

mun·dane *adj.* down-to-earth, matter-of-fact

mu·nic·i·pal *adj.* of, relating to or carried on by local self-government (esp. of a town, city etc.)

mu·nic·i·pal·i·ty *pl.* **mu·nic·i·pal·i·ties** *n.* a town, city or district having powers of local self-government

mu·nif·i·cence *n.* the quality or state of being munificent ‖ an instance of this

mu·nif·i·cent *adj.* lavish in giving

mu·ni·tion *n.* (*pl.*) ammunition and weapons

mu·ral *n.* a fresco or painting made directly on a wall

mur·der 1. *n.* the unlawful killing of a human being with malice aforethought ‖ an instance of this ‖ circumstances of great danger or hardship 2. *v.t.* to kill unlawfully with malice aforethought ‖ to spoil or ruin by bad performance or interpretation

mur·der·er *n.* a person guilty of murder

múr·der·ess *n.* a woman guilty of murder

mur·der·ous *adj.* relating to, like, involving, or having the nature of murder

murk, mirk *n.* thick darkness, intense gloom

murk·i·ly, mirk·i·ly *adv.* in a murky way or manner

murk·y, mirk·y murk·i·er, mirk·i·er murk·i·est, mirk·i·est *adj.* thickly dark, intensely gloomy ‖ heavy with mist, smoke etc.

mur·mur *v.t.* to utter in a soft, low, indistinct voice

murmur *n.* soft, low and indistinct speech ‖ a continuous low, soft sound ‖ a half-suppressed complaint or objection ‖ (*med.*) an abnormal sound of the heart

mus·cle 1. *n.* a bundle of fibers (in human and animal bodies) which have the property of contracting and relaxing and which produce motion ‖ muscular strength 2. *v.i.* **to muscle in** to push one's way in

mus·cu·lar *adj.* having well-developed muscles

muse the source of a poet's or artist's inspiration

muse mus·ing mused *v.i.* to meditate

mu·se·um *n.* a building used for exhibition of objects illustrating human or natural history

mush *n.* any soft pulpy mass ‖ cornmeal boiled in water ‖ mawkish sentimentality

mush·room 1. *n.* the exposed fleshy fruiting body of some fungi 2. *adj.* like a mushroom in shape or in rapidity of growth and decay 3. *v.i.* to grow with sudden rapidity

mush·y mush·i·er mush·i·est *adj.* soft and pulpy, like mush ‖ mawkishly sentimental

mu·sic *n.* the art of giving structural form and rhythmic pattern to combinations of sounds produced instrumentally or vocally ‖ the written score of a composition of such sounds ‖ any series or combination of pleasant sounds ‖ the quality of being harmonious and pleasant to the ear

mu·si·cal 1. *adj.* of, relating to or having the nature of music ‖ talented or skilled in music ‖ fond of music 2. *n.* a musical comedy

mu·si·cian *n.* a person skilled in music

musk *n.* a reddish-brown substance with a pungent, lasting odor, used as a basis for perfumes

musk deer a small, sturdy deer of central Asia

musk·rat *n.* a brown aquatic rodent of North America

mus·lin *n.* a woven cotton material

mus·sel *n.* any of several bivalve marine or freshwater mollusks

must 1. *v.*, *neg.* **must not, mustn't** to be obliged or required or compelled to 2. *n.* something that should be done, seen, read etc. without fail

mus·tang *n.* a small, tough, half-wild horse

mus·tard *n.* any of certain plants, having linear beaked pods and yellow flowers ‖ the condiment made from the powdered seeds ‖ the color of the ground seed, a dark yellow

mus·ter *v.i.* to assemble or gather together

must·y must·i·er must·i·est *adj.* smelling or tasting moldy, stale

mu·ta·ble *adj.* liable to change or capable

of being changed

mu·tate mu·tat·ing mu·tat·ed *v.i.* to undergo mutation ‖ *v.t.* to cause mutation in

mu·ta·tion *n.* a changing or being changed ‖ the hypothetical occurrence of new forms, arising through change in gene construction of the nucleus and differing sufficiently from the parent forms to constitute new varieties ‖ umlaut

mute 1. *adj.* not speaking, not uttering a sound ‖ permanently unable to utter meaningful speech **2.** *n.* a person who cannot speak ‖ a clip clamped on the bridge of a stringed instrument to deaden the resonance of the strings **3.** *v.t.* **mut·ing mut·ed** to deaden or soften the sound of

mu·ti·late mu·ti·lat·ing mu·ti·lat·ed *v.t.* to hack or tear off a limb or other important part of (a person or animal) ‖ to damage (something) seriously

mu·ti·la·tion *n.* a mutilating or being mutilated

mu·ti·ny 1. *pl.* **mu·ti·nies** *n.* open revolt aagainst lawful authority **2.** *v.i.* **mu·ti·ny·ing mu·ti·nied** to revolt against lawful authority

mutt a mongrel dog

mut·ter *v.i.* to speak in a low, indistinct voice ‖ to murmur in annoyance or complaint

mut·ton *n.* the flesh of a full-grown sheep as food

mu·tu·al *adj.* done, shared or experienced in common by all members of a group

muz·zle 1. *n.* the projecting jaws and nose in certain animals ‖ a cagelike contrivance aof wires or straps put over this part of an animal (esp. a dog) to prevent it from biting ‖ the mouth of a gun **2.** *v.t.* **muz·zling muz·zled** to put a muzzle on ‖ to prevent (criticism etc.) from being expressed

my *possessive adj.* belonging to or relating to me

my·o·pi·a *n.* the inability to see distant objects **my·op·ic** *adj.*

myr·i·ad 1. *n.* a very large number **2.** *adj.* countless, very many

myrrh *n.* a gum resin with a sweet smell and a bitter taste, obtained from the bark of trees

myr·tle *n.* a genus of fragrant evergreen plants

my·self *pron.* refl. form of 'I' ‖ emphatic form of 'I'

mys·te·ri·ous *adj.* of, relating to or characterized by mystery, suggestive of hidden secrets

mys·ter·y *pl.* **mys·ter·ies** *n.* something that cannot be or has not been explained or understood ‖ a detective story

mys·tic 1. *adj.* of or relating to mystics or mysticism ‖ having a hidden, secret, esoteric meaning **2.** *n.* a person who believes in mysticism **mys·ti·cal** *adj.*

mys·ti·cism *n.* the doctrine or belief that direct spiritual apprehension of truth or union with God may beobtained through contemplation or insight in ways inaccessible to the senses or reason

mys·ti·fy mys·ti·fy·ing mys·ti·fied *v.t.* to puzzle, bewilder, baffle

mys·tique *n.* a quasi-mystical set of attitudes adopted towards some idea, person, art or skill, investing it with an esoteric significance

myth *n.* an old traditional story or legend ‖ any fictitious story or account or unfounded belief

myth·ic *adj.* mythical **myth·i·cal** *adj.* of, desginating, relating to or existing in myth ‖ imaginary, nonexistent

my·thol·o·gy *pl.* **myl·thol·o·gies** *n.* myths collectively ‖ the study of myths

N

N, n the 14th letter of the English alphabet

nab nab·bing nabbed *v.t.* to arrest

na·dir *n.* the lowest point ‖ the point of the celestial sphere diametrically opposite to the zenith

nag 1. *v.* **nag·ging nagged** *v.t.* to scold or find fault with repeatedly ‖ *v.i.* to cause persistent discomfort **2.** *n.* a person who nags

nag *n.* an inferior or aged horse

nail *n.* the hard thin covering on the upper surface of the ends of the fingers or toes ‖ a thin, usually metal, spike, driven into an object to join it to another **hard as nails** hardhearted

nail *v.t.* to fix with a nail ‖ to secure ‖ to prove (a lie) to be false ‖ to catch

na·ive *adj.* lacking worldly experience or guile

na·ive·té *n.* simplicity, artlessness **na·ive·ty** *n.*

na·ked *adj.* without clothes ‖ uncovered ‖ without decoration **with the naked eye** without the aid of an optical instrument **ná·ked·ness** *n.*

name 1. *n.* a word or words by which a person, place or thing is known ‖ a reputation **in name, in name only** by mere designation but not in reality **2.** *v.t.* **nam·ing named** to give a name to ‖ to identify by name ‖ to appoint **3.** *adj.* well-known, renowned **náme·a·ble, nám·a·ble** *adj.*

name·less *adj.* not known by name

name·ly *adv.* that is to say

nap 1. *v.i.* **nap·ping napped** to sleep for a short time **2.** *n.* a short sleep, esp. by day

nap *n.* the soft, fuzzy surface on cloth

na·palm *n.* a fuel, made from jellied gasoline

nape *n.* the back of the neck

nap·kin *n.* a cloth used at meals for wiping the fingers and lips ‖ a sanitary towel

nar·cis·sism *n.* a tendency to erotic self-love **nár·cis·ist** *n.* **nar·cis·sís·tic** *adj.*

nar·co·sis *n.* a state of unconsciousness induced by narcotics

nar·cot·ic 1. *n.* a drug which dulls sensibility, relieves pain and induces sleepi-

ness **2.** *adj.* pertaining to or having the effects of narcotics **nar·co·tism** *n.* narcosis ‖ addiction to narcotics

nar·rate nar·rat·ing nar·rat·ed *v.t.* to tell or write (a story) ‖ to give an account of (events)

nar·ra·tion *n.* an account or story

nar·ra·tive 1. *n.* an orderly description of events ‖ the act or art of narrating **2.** *adj.* of, relating to or having the form of a narrative

nar·ra·tor, nar·ra·ter *n.* a person who narrates

nar·row 1. *adj.* small in width ‖ restricted in scope ‖ marginal **2.** *n.* (esp. pl.) a narrow passage in mountains or between two bodies of water **3.** *v.t.* to make narrower ‖ limit further

nar·row-mind·ed *adj.* lacking tolerance

na·sal *adj.* of or pertaining to the nose

nas·ty nas·ti·er nas·ti·est *adj.* very unpleasant, repugnant ‖ morally dirty ‖ mean ‖ offensive ‖ awkward to deal with

na·tal *adj.* of or connected with birth

na·tion *n.* a body of people recognized as an entity by virtue of their historical, linguistic or ethnic links

na·tion·al 1. *adj.* of or relating to a nation **2.** *n.* a member of a nation

na·tion·al·ism *n.* devotion to one's nation

na·tion·al·ist 1. *n.* a person who believes in or supports nationalism **2.** *adj.* of nationalism or nationalists **na·tion·al·ís·tic** *adj.* **na·tion·al·ís·ti·cal·ly** *adv.*

na·tion·al·i·ty *pl.* **na·tion·al·i·ties** *n.* membership of a nation ‖ a nation or ethnic group

na·tive 1. *n.* a person born in a given place, country etc. ‖ one of the original inhabitants of a country ‖ a plant or animal which originated in a district or area **2.** *adj.* belonging to a person or thing by nature, inherent ‖ of or relating to the natives of a place ‖ (of plant or animal life) not introduced

Na·tiv·i·ty *n.* the birth of Jesus Christ

nat·ti·ly *adv.* in a natty way

nat·ti·ness *n.* the state or quality of being natty

nat·ty nat·ti·er nat·ti·est *adj.* very neat and tidy

nat·u·ral 1. *adj.* pertaining to, existing in, or produced by nature ‖ not artificial ‖ in accordance with normal human nature ‖ free from self-consciousness ‖ of food containing no chemical additives **2.** *n.* a person who takes naturally to an activity

nat·u·ral·i·za·tion *n.* a naturalizing or being naturalized

nat·u·ral·ize **nat·u·ral·iz·ing** **nat·u·ral·ized** *v.t.* to grant citizenship to ‖ to introduce (a plant or animal) into a new habitat where it flourishes

nat·u·ral·ly *adv.* in a natural or normal way ‖ as one would expect, of course ‖ in accordance with the laws of nature

na·ture *n.* the physical universe and the laws and forces which govern changes within it ‖ the essential character of something ‖ (of a substance) the permanent property or properties ‖ (of persons) inborn character, disposition

naught *n.* nothing ‖ a zero

naugh·ti·ly *adv.* in a naughty way

naugh·ti·ness *n.* the state or quality of being naughty

naugh·ty naugh·ti·er naugh·ti·est *adj.* bad, disobedient ‖ mildly indecent

nau·se·a *n.* a feeling of sickness with a desire to vomit ‖ strong disgust

nau·se·ate nau·se·at·ing nau·se·at·ed *v.t.* to cause a feeling of nausea in

nau·seous *adj.* causing nausea

nau·ti·cal *adj.* of ships, seamen or navigation

na·val *adj.* pertaining to or characteristic of a navy

nave *n.* the central part of a church

nave *n.* the central block or hub of a wheel

na·vel *n.* a small hollow in the middle of the belly, marking the point of attachment of the umbilical cord

nav·i·ga·ble *adj.* allowing the passage of ships ‖ able to be steered or sailed

nav·i·gate nav·i·gat·ing nav·i·gat·ed *v.i.* to direct the course of a ship, aircraft or car

nav·i·ga·tion *n.* the act or practice of navigating ‖ maritime traffic

nav·i·ga·tor *n.* a person who navigates

na·vy *pl.* **na·vies** *n.* a state's ships of war ‖ navy blue

navy blue a deep, dark blue

nay 1. *adv.* (archaic) no **2.** *n.* a negative vote ‖ denial

neap *n.* a neap tide

neap tide a tide at the first and third quarters of the moon, in which the high water is lower than at any other time

near 1. *adv.* at or within a short distance **2.** *prep.* within a short distance of ‖ within a short time of **3.** *adj.* not far distant in space ‖ not far distant in time ‖ not far distant in relationship ‖ almost correct ‖ direct **4.** *v.t.* to approach ‖ *v.i.* to come closer in time

near·by 1. *adj.* near at hand **2.** *adv.* not far away

near·ly *adv.* almost, closely

near-sight·ed *adj.* myopic

neat *adj.* clean and tidy, orderly ‖ undiluted

neb·bish *n.* a meek, ineffectual person

neb·u·la *pl.* **neb·u·lae** *n.* a diffuse, cloudlike mass of usually luminous gas **néb·u·lar** *adj.*

neb·u·lous *adj.* vague, formless ‖ of or like a nebula

nec·es·sar·y 1. *adj.* that is required, that must be ‖ that cannot be done without **2.** **néc·es·sar·ies** *pl. n.* essentials

ne·ces·si·tate ne·ces·si·tat·ing ne·ces·si·tat·ed *v.t.* to make necessary

neck 1. *n.* that part which joins the head to the body ‖ the narrowest part of an object, e.g. of a bottle ‖ a narrow stretch of land **to break one's neck** to go out of one's way **to risk one's neck** to put one's life in danger **2.** *v.i.* to hug and kiss

nec·tar *n.* the drink of the gods ‖ a sweet substance collected by bees to make honey

nec·ta·rine *n.* a smooth-skinned variety of peach

need *n.* a condition necessitating supply or relief ‖ poverty ‖ obligation **if need be** if necessary

need *v.i.* to be in want ‖ *v.t.* to require

nee·dle 1. *n.* a slender pointed piece of steel, bone etc., used in sewing, darning etc. ‖ a surgical instrument ‖ an obelisk ‖ a leaf, e.g. of the pine ‖ the pointer of a compass or gauge **a needle in a haystack** something almost impossible to find **2.** *v.t.* **nee·dling nee·dled** to tease or goad

need·less *adj.* unnecessary

need·y need·i·er need·i·est *adj.* poverty-stricken

ne·far·i·ous *adj.* wicked, iniquitous

ne·gate ne·gat·ing ne·gat·ed *v.t.* to render null and void

ne·ga·tion *n.* denial, contradiction

neg·a·tive 1. *adj.* having the effect of saying 'no', esp. to a question or request ‖ lacking in positive character ‖ not constructive ‖ (elec., of a charge) carried by electrons **2.** *n.* a reply which has the effect of saying 'no' ‖ a quantity less than zero ‖ a developed negative image

neg·a·tiv·ism *n.* an attitude of resistance to other people's suggestions **nég·a·tiv·ist** *n.* and *adj.*

ne·glect 1. *v.t.* to fail to perform, esp. through carelessness ‖ to fail to attend to, disregard **2.** *n.* negligence **ne·glect·ful** *adj.*

neg·li·gee, nég·li·gée *n.* a woman's light dressing gown, usually loose and flowing

neg·li·gence *n.* want of care **nég·li·gent** *adj.*

neg·li·gi·ble *adj.* so small that it may be neglected

ne·go·tia·ble *adj.* which can be negotiated

ne·go·ti·ate ne·go·ti·at·ing ne·go·ti·at·ed *v.i.* to discuss in order to reach an agreement ‖ *v.t.* to transfer or cash (a check, securities etc.) ‖ to succeed in accomplishing, crossing, climbing etc.

ne·go·ti·a·tion *n.* discussion to bring about some result

ne·go·ti·a·tor *n.* a person who negotiates

ne·gri·tude *n.* **1.** the state and pride of being black **2.** pride in the cultural heritage of black people **negritudinous** *adj.*

neigh 1. *v.i.* to make the cry of a horse **2.** *n.* this cry

neigh·bor 1. *n.* a person living close to another **2.** *v.t.* to be situated near to, adjoin ‖ *v.i.* to abut

neigh·bor·hood *n.* a district ‖ the people in a district **in the neighborhood** of close

to ‖ approximately

neigh·bor·ing *adj.* situated in the neighborhood

neigh·bor·ly *adj.* friendly, sociable

nei·ther 1. *adj.* not either of two **2.** *pron.* not either of two (usually with a singular verb) **3.** *conj.* nor yet **neither here nor there** irrelevant

nem·a·tode *n.* unsegmented worms

nem·e·sis *pl.* **nem·e·ses** *n.* retribution and punishment ‖ an act of retributive justice

neo- *prefix* now, recent ‖ a later revival of

ne·o·lith *n.* a polished stone implement of the last period of the Stone Age

ne·on *n.* an inert gaseous element

neph·ew *n.* a son of a person's brother or sister

nep·o·tism *n.* favoritism shown in the advancement of relatives **nép·o·tist** *n.*

nerve 1. *n.* any of the cordlike fibers or bundles of fibers of neural tissue that connect the nervous system with other organs of the body for the purpose of conducting nervous impulses to or away from these organs ‖ nervous fiber ‖ courage ‖ impudence **2.** *v.t.* **nerv·ing nerved** to give courage to

ner·vous *adj.* of or relating to the nerves or the nervous system ‖ apprehensive ‖ excitable ‖ without confidence

nerv·y nerv·i·er nerv·i·est *adj.* impudent, brazen

nest 1. *n.* the structure built or place chosen and prepared by a bird for holding its eggs ‖ a place built or prepared by certain mammals, and by certain fish, reptiles, crustaceans and insects to rear their young in ‖ a place of retreat ‖ a collection of similar objects, esp. ones that fit into one another **2.** *v.i.* to build and occupy a nest ‖ to stack compactly together

nes·tle nes·tling nes·tled *v.i.* to settle oneself down comfortably ‖ to press snugly (against) ‖ to lie protected ‖ *v.t.* to settle protectively

net 1. *n.* an open-meshed fabric used for catching fish, birds, insects or animals ‖ a snare, trap ‖ a network **2. net·ting net·ted** *v.t.* to catch with a net ‖ to cover with a network pattern ‖ *v. i.* to make nets or netting

net 1. *adj.* clear of all charges and deductions **2.** *v.t.* **net·ting, net·ting net·ted, nett·ed** to gain as a clear profit **3.** *n.* clear profit

net·ting *n.* the process of making nets ‖ the act of fishing with a net ‖ netted string ‖ a piece of such material

net·tle 1. *n.* a plant with stinging hairs on the leaves **2.** *v.t.* **net·tling net·tled** to irritate or provoke

net·work *n.* a fabric of crossed threads knotted at the intersections ‖ an interconnected system ‖ a chain of radio or television stations

neu·ral·gia *n.* a severe intermittent pain in a nerve or nerves **neu·rál·gic** *adj.*

neu·ri·tis *n.* a nerve inflammation

neu·dro·sis *pl.* **neu·ro·ses** *n.* a nervous disorder often with the symptoms of hysteria, anxiety, obsessions and compulsions **neu·rot·ic 1.** *adj.* relating to the nerves **2.** *n.* a person suffering from a neurosis **neu·rót·i·cism** *n.*

neu·ter 1. *adj.* neither masculine nor feminine ‖ sexless **2.** *n.* a word or form of neuter gender ‖ a castrated animal

neu·tral 1. *adj.* assisting or siding with neither of two opposing sides in a war, dispute, controversy etc. ‖ having no distinctive color or other quality ‖ uncharged **2.** *n.* someone who, or something which, is neutral ‖ a disengaged position of gears

neu·tral·i·ty *n.* the state of being neutral ‖ the status of any nation which remains neutral while hostilities between other nations are going on

neu·tral·i·za·tion *n.* a neutralizing or being neutralized

neu·tral·ize neu·tral·iz·ing neu·tral·ized *v.t.* to render ineffective by counterbalancing

neu·tron *n.* a constituent of all atomic nuclei except that of the lightest hydrogen isotope

nev·er *adv.* not at any time, not on any occasion

nev·er·he·less *adj.* in spite of that

new *adj.* made, discovered, known, heard or seen for the first time ‖ recently made ‖ replacing the former ‖ different ‖ freshly attempted ‖ regenerated ‖ never before used

new·el *n.* the central pillar of a winding staircase ‖ the top or bottom post of a handrail on a staircase

new·fan·gled *adj.* (*contemptuous*) modern and inferior

new·ly *adv.* in a new way ‖ recently

new·ly·wed *n.* a person recently amarried

news *n.* recent information ‖ recent events, esp. as reported in newspapers, on the radio or on television

next 1. *adj.* nearest in space ‖ following in time without anything similar intervening **2.** *adv.* in the place, time or order immediately following **3.** *prep.* closest to

nib·ble 1. nib·bling nib·bled *v.t.* to take small, quick bites of ‖ *v.i.* to show signs of interest **2.** *n.* a small bite

nice *adj.* (used as a loose term of general approval) pleasant, kind, attractive, delightful, fine ‖ delicate, precise

ni·ce·ty *pl.* **ni·ce·ties** *n.* delicacy and precision

niche 1. *n.* a recess in a wall ‖ a place precisely suited to a person's talents **2.** *v.t.* **nich·ing niched** to place in a niche

nick 1. *n.* a shallow cut or chip **in the nick of time** just before it is too late **2.** *v.t.* to make a nick in

nick·el 1. *n.* a metallic element which is hard and rust-resisting ‖ a five-cent coin in the U.S.A. and Canada **2.** *v.t.* **nick·el·ing nick·eled** to plate with nickel

nick·name 1. *n.* a name by which a person is called familiarly, other than his real name **2.** *v.t.* **nick·nam·ing nick·named** to dub with a nickname

nic·o·tine *n.* a very poisonous volatile alkaloid. It is the most active constituent of tobacco

niece *n.* a daughter of a person's brother or sister

nig·gard *n.* a stingy person

nig·gard·ly 1. *adj.* stingy **2.** *adv.* in a stingy way

nigh *adv.* near **nigh on** (archaic) almost

night *n.* the time during which the sun is below the horizon ‖ darkness ‖ mental or moral darkness **a night off** a night or evening taken off from work **a night out** a night or evening spent in entertainment outside the home **night and day** continually **to make a night of it** to spend a night or evening in festivity

night·in·gale *n.* any of several European thrushes

night·ly 1. *adj.* happening every night or every evening **2.** *adv.* every night

night·mare *n.* a terrifying dream ‖ a frightening experience or persistent fear **night·mar·ish** *adj.*

night·time *n.* the period between dusk and dawn

nil *n.* nothing

nim·ble *adj.* light and quick in motion, agile ‖ alert, quick-witted **ním·bly** *adv.*

nine *adj.* being one more than eight **dressed to (or up to) the nines** very elaborately dressed in an eye-catching way

nine·teen *adj.* being one more than 18 **to talk nineteen to the dozen** to talk continually

nine·teenth *adj.* being number 19 in a series

nine·ti·eth *adj.* being number 90 in a series

nine·ty 1. *adj.* being ten more than 80 **the Nineties** the last decade of the 19th c.

nin·ny *pl.* **nin·nies** *n.* a person who behaves stupidly

ninth *adj.* being number nine in a series

nip *n.* a small measure or drink of liquor

nip 1. nip·ping nipped *v.t.* to pinch ‖ (with 'off') remove by pinching **to nip in the bud** to stop (something) before it has time to develop **2.** *n.* a sharp pinch ‖ a mildly stinging coldness

nip·per *n.* (*pl.*) small pincers, e.g. forceps, pliers etc. ‖ the claw of a crustacean

nip·ple *n.* a protuberance marking the opening of the mammary duct in mammals, e.g. of a woman's breast ‖ a teat on an infant's feeding bottle ‖ a protuberance shaped like this

ni·tro·gen *n.* a colorless, tasteless, gaseous element

ni·tro·glyc·er·in, ni·tro·glyc·er·ine *n.* glyceryl trinitrate, an unstable oily liquid used in making dynamite and other explosives and as a vasodilator in certain heart ailments

nit·ty-grit·ty *n.* the essential point **nitty-gritty** *adj.*

nit·wit *n.* an ignorant, stupid person

no 1. *adv.* negation, refusal, denial etc. ‖ not at all ‖ surely not **2.** *pl.* **noes, nos** *n.* the word 'no' ‖ (*pl.*) those who vote against a motion

no·bil·i·ty *n.* the quality or state of being noble

no·ble *adj.* illustrious by rank or birth ‖ of high character, lofty

no·ble·man *pl.* **no·ble·men** *n.* a man of noble rank

no·ble·wom·an *pl.* **no·ble·wom·en** *n.* a woman of noble rank

no·bly *adv.* in a noble way ‖ of noble ancestry

no·bod·y 1. *pron.* not anybody **2.** *pl.* **no·bod·ies** *n.* a person of no importance

noc·tur·nal *adj.* happening at night ‖ active at night

nod 1. nod·ding nod·ded *v.t.* to bow the head forward quickly in greeting, agreement ‖ to bow the head involuntarily because of sleepiness ‖ *v.t.* to indicate (assent, agreement etc.) by bowing the head **2.** *n.* a quick forward nodding movement of the head

nod·u·lar *adj.* of, pertaining to or having nodules

nod·ule *n.* a small rounded mass ‖ a small protuberance **nod·u·lose nod·u·lous** *adjs*

no-fault insurance *n.* legal provision in some states that motorists be reimbursed for medical expenses by their own insurance companies, no matter which party is at fault in an accident

noise 1. *n.* any sound which causes discomfort to the hearer ‖ irrelevant background sounds **2.** *v.t.* **nois·ing noised** to make noise **nóise·less** *adj.* silent

nois·i·ly *adv.* in a noisy way

nois·y nois·i·er nois·i·est *adj.* full of noise ‖ loud

no·mad *n.* a member of a people without

a fixed location, wandering from place to place ‖ a person who chooses to roam **no·mád·ic** *adj.* **nó·mad·ism** *n.*

no-man's-land *n.* an unowned area ‖ a belt of debated ground between entrenched enemies

nom de plume *pl.* **nom de plumes** *n.* a pen name

no·men·cla·ture *n.* names which classify things ‖ systematic naming

nom·i·nal *adj.* existing only in name or form, not real or actual ‖ very small, hardly worth the name

nom·i·nate nom·i·nat·ing nom·i·nat·ed *v.t.* to name as a candidate ‖ to appoint to office

nom·i·na·tion *n.* a nominating or being nominated

nom·i·na·tive 1. *n.* the case of the subject of a verb, or of a word in agreement with it ‖ a word in this case **2.** *adj.* describing or pertaining to the nominative ‖ chosen or appointed by nomination

nom·i·na·tor *n.* a person who nominates

nom·i·nee *n.* a person nominated for office

non·cha·lance *n.* the quality of being nonchalant

non·cha·lant *adj.* casual ‖ offhand ‖ unperturbed

non·com·bat·ant 1. *n.* a person in the armed forces whose duties do not include fighting ‖ a civilian **2.** *adj.* not involving combats

non·com·mit·tal *adj.* not committing the speaker to either side in a dispute

non·con·form·ist 1. *n.* a person who does not conform to rule or convention **2.** *adj.* of or relating to a nonconformist

non·con·form·i·ty *n.* the beliefs or practices of nonconformists

non·de·script *adj.* not easily classified or described

none 1. *pron.* not any, not one ‖ no part, nothing **2.** *adv.* not at all, to no extent, by no amount

non·en·ti·ty *pl.* **non·en·ti·ties** *n.* a person or thing of no importance or distinction ‖ nonexistence

non·fea·sance *n.* failure to do something

non·ob·jec·tive *adj.* of a work of art which

does not represent recognizable objects or natural appearances

non·pa·reil 1. *n.* a person or thing of matchless excellence **2.** *adj.* matchless

non·par·ti·san 1. *adj.* not involved in political party ties ‖ objective **2.** *n.* someone who is nonpartisan

non·plus non·plus·ing non·plused *v.t.* to perplex, baffle

non·prof·it *adj.* not maintained or organized for profit

non·sense *n.* senseless talk or ideas ‖ behavior that is foolish

non·sen·si·cal *adj.* foolish, full of nonsense

non se·qui·tur *n.* a conclusion that does not follow from the stated premise

non·vi·o·lence *n.* the policy of refusing to use violence

noo·dle *n.* a strip of pasta, served in quantity

nook *n.* a hidden or quiet corner ‖ a recess

noon *n.* 12 o'clock in the daytime

noon·time *n.* midday

noose 1. *n.* a loop in a rope etc. with a running knot which draws tighter as the rope is pulled ‖ a snare **2.** *v.t.* **noos·ing noosed** to entrap by a noose

nor *conj.* and not

norm *n.* standard of attainment ‖ that which is normal

nor·mal 1. *adj.* conforming to a norm, standard, regular ‖ mentally or emotionally sound **2.** *n.* the usual or average state, level etc. **nor·mal·i·ty** *n.* the state of being normal

nor·mal·ly *adv.* in a normal way

north 1. *adv.* towards the north **2.** *n.* one of the four cardinal points of the compass ‖ the direction to the left of a person facing east **3.** *adj.* of, belonging to or situated towards the north

north·ern *adj.* facing or moving towards the north

northern lights the aurora borealis

north·ward 1. *adv.* and *adj.* towards the north

nose 1. *n.* the facial prominence above the mouth of man and other mammals, containing the nostrils and the nasal cavity ‖ a sense of smell ‖ an ability to detect what is hidden ‖ a forward or projecting part **to follow one's nose** to go straight on ‖ to do as instinct suggests **to look down one's nose at** to show disdain for **to pay through the nose** to pay an exorbitant price **to turn up one's nose at** to scorn **2.** *v.* **nos·ing nosed** *v.t.* (with 'out') to detect by or as if by smelling ‖ to work (one's way) forward

nos·tal·gia a longing to experience again some real or imagined former pleasure **nos·tál·gic** *adj.*

nos·tril *n.* one of the external apertures of the nose

nos·y, nos·ey nos·i·er nos·i·est *adj.* inquisitive

not *adv.* (with auxiliary verbs and 'to be') used to express a negative ‖ used as an emphatic denial ‖ used to emphasize the opposite

no·ta·ble 1. *adj.* worthy of note **2.** *n.* a prominent person **nó·ta·bly** *adv.* particularly

no·ta·rize no·ta·riz·ing no·ta·rized *v.t.* to validate

no·ta·tion *n.* the representation of numbers, quantities or other things by a set or scale of symbols

notch 1. *n.* a V-shaped cut or indentation ‖ a narrow pass or gap between mountains **2.** *v.t.* to cut notches in

note 1. *n.* a brief written record made to assist the memory ‖ a brief, informal, written communication ‖ a sound of definite pitch ‖ a symbol **2.** *v.t.* **not·ing not·ed** to fix in the mind ‖ to pay special attention to

note·wor·thy *adj.* worthy of being noted, remarkable

noth·ing 1. *n.* no thing, not anything at all ‖ naught, zero **2.** *adv.* not in any way **nóth·ing·ness** *n.* the state of nonexistence ‖ the absence of any thing whatsoever

no·tice 1. *n.* mental awareness, attention ‖ a printed or written announcement ‖ a review in a newspaper etc. ‖ a warning **2.** *v.t.* **no·tic·ing no·ticed** to be or become aware of **nó·tice·a·ble** *adj.* conspicuous **nó·tice·a·bly** *adv.*

no·ti·fi·ca·tion *n.* a communication which gives notice

no·ti·fy *v.t.* to inform (someone) of a fact

no·tion *n.* a conception, idea ‖ an understanding ‖ a whim or fancy ‖ *(pl.)* inexpensive small useful articles

no·to·ri·e·ty *pl.* **no·to·ri·e·ties** *n.* the quality or state of being notorious ‖ a notorious person

no·to·ri·ous *adj.* widely known to someone's discredit

not·with·stand·ing 1. prep. in spite of **2.** *adv.* nevertheless **3.** conj. although

nou·gat *n.* a confection of sugar, with almonds or other nuts or candied fruit or honey

nought naught

noun *n.* a word used to name a person, place, thing, state or quality

nour·ish *v.t.* to supply or sustain with food ‖ to foster or keep alive in the mind **nóur·ish·ment** *n.* food

nou·veau riche *pl.* **nou·veaux riches** *n.* someone newly rich who lacks social standing, culture etc.

nov·el *n.* an imaginative prose narrative of some length

nov·el·ist *n.* a person who writes novels

nov·el·ty *pl.* **nov·el·ties** *n.* a novel thing or event ‖ the quality or state of being novel ‖ a small manufactured article

No·vem·ber *n.* the 11th month of the year

nov·ice *n.* a beginner ‖ a person received on probation into a religious order

now 1. *adv.* at the present time ‖ without delay ‖ at a certain time under consideration ‖ reckoning to the present moment **2.** conj. because **3.** *n.* the present time

no·where 1. *adv.* not anywhere ‖ to make no progress towards being successful **2.** *n.* a state of not existing ‖ a place that does not exist

nox·ious *adj.* harmful ‖ corrupting

noz·zle *n.* a projecting aperture at the end of a tube

nu·ance *n.* a slight difference in color, tone, meaning, emotion etc.

nu·bile *adj.* (of women) of an age to marry **nu·bíl·i·ty** *n.*

nu·cle·ar *adj.* pertaining to a nucleus ‖ of or relating to atomic energy

nu·cle·us *pl.* **nu·cle·i** *n.* the central part of a whole ‖ a center of activity, influence etc. ‖ the positively charged dense mass at the center of an atom

nude 1. *adj.* naked ‖ undraped **2.** *n.* an undraped figure in painting, sculpture etc.

nudge 1. *v.t.* **nudg·ing nudged** to push gently **2.** *n.* such push

nud·ism *n.* the belief in, and practice of, living naked, as being physically and psychologically beneficial

nud·ist 1. *n.* a person who practices nudism **2.** *adj.* of or pertaining to nudism or nudists

nu·di·ty *n.* the state or quality of being nude

nug·get *n.* a small lump of precious metal, esp. gold

nui·sance *n.* a person or thing causing annoyance or trouble

null having no force in law ‖ zero

nul·li·fy nul·li·fy·ing nul·li·fied *v.t.* to make null

numb 1. *adj.* lacking sensation ‖ lacking the ability to feel any emotion ‖ to be incapable of action **2.** *v.t.* to make numb

num·ber *n.* a word or symbol used to express how many or what place in a sequence ‖ a figure used to denote one thing in particular ‖ a total ‖ the property of being countable ‖ an item performed on the stage, television etc. ‖ *(pl.)* a large collection of persons or things **number one** the first of a series ‖ the best of many

number *v.t.* to denote by a number

num·ber·less *adj.* too many to be counted

nu·mer·al 1. *n.* the symbol of a number **2.** *adj.* pertaining to, having or denoting number

nu·mer·a·tor *n.* that part of a fraction, written above the denominator and separated from it by a horizontal or oblique line

nu·mer·i·cal *adj.* pertaining to or denoting number

nu·mer·ous *adj.* of large number

nu·mis·mat·ic *adj.* of or relating to the study of coins or currency **nu·mis·mát·ics, nu·mis·ma·tist nu·mis·ma·tol·o·gy** *n.*

num·skull, numb·skull *n.* a stupid person

nun *n.* a woman belonging to a religious order

nun·ner·y *pl.* **nun·ner·ies** *n.* a communal residence of nuns

nup·tial 1. *adj.* pertaining to marriage **2.** *n.* (pl.) a wedding

nurse *n.* a person trained to care for the sick or the infirm ‖ a woman employed to look after young children

nurse nurs·ing nursed *v.t.* to take care of, be a nurse to ‖ to suckle (an infant) ‖ to take special care of in order to promote growth ‖ to try to cure ‖ to keep (a feeling etc.) alive in one's mind ‖ *v.i.* to be a nurse ‖ to suckle a child ‖ to feed at the breast

nurs·er·y *pl.* **nurs·er·ies** *n.* a room set apart for children in a house ‖ a nursery school ‖ a place where young plants or trees are grown for subsequent transplanting

nur·ture 1. *n.* food, or whatever nourishes figuratively ‖ upbringing, training **2.** *v.t.* **nur·tur·ing nur·tured** to provide for

nut *n.* a dry, one-celled fruit or seed consisting of a fleshy kernel (often edible) enclosed in a hard or tough shell ‖ a piece of metal whose central hole has a screw thread which engages on a screw or bolt, to hold one thing to another ‖ a person behaving in a crazy way

nut·meg *n.* a hard seed, used as a spice obtained from an evergreen tropical tree ‖ the tree itself

nu·tri·ent 1. *n.* a substance serving as food, esp. for plants **2.** *adj.* nourishing

nu·tri·tion *n.* a nourishing or being nourished

nu·tri·tious *adj.* nourishing

nut·ty nut·ti·er nut·ti·est *adj.* tasting like nuts ‖ silly

nuz·zle nuz·zling nuz·zled *v.t.* to make pushing movements with the nose against, or into ‖ *v.i.* to snuggle

ny·lon *n.* any of several polymeric thermoplastic amides ‖ *(pl.)* stockings made of this

nymph *n.* (Gk and Rom. mythol.) one of the lesser goddesses, portrayed as beautiful girls ‖ an insect in the stage between larva and imago

nym·pho·ma·ni·a *n.* excessive sexual desire in a woman **nym·pho·ma·ni·ac** *n.*

O

O, o the 15th letter of the English alphabet

oaf pl. **oafs, oaves** n. a stupid lout **óaf·ish** adj.

oak n. tree and shrub native to the northern hemisphere ‖ Oaks yield some tannin and hard, durable wood

oak·en adj. made of oak

oar 1. n. a long, usually wooden shaft with a flattened blade at one end, used as a lever in propelling a boat **2.** v.t. and i. to row

oar·lock n. a device to hold the oar and provide leverage for its action

oars·man pl. **oars·men** n. a rower

o·a·sis pl. **o·a·ses** n. an area in a desert made fertile by the presence of water ‖ a quiet, peaceful place

oat n. (usually p.) a genus of wild and cultivated grasses ‖ (pl.) the crop or its yield

oath pl. **oaths** n. the invoking of God as witness of the truth of a statement or the binding nature of a promise ‖ a profane use of a sacred name or phrase

ob·du·rate adj. unyielding

o·be·di·ence n. submission of one's own will to the will of another **in obedience to** according to the instructions or ruling of

o·be·di·ent adj. submitting one's will ‖ not resisting

o·bei·sance n. (rhet.) a curtsy, salaam etc., expressing great respect for someone **to do obeisance to** (rhet.) to perform an act of homage to

o·bese adj. (of a person) very fat

o·bes·i·ty n. the state of being obese

o·bey v.t. to be obedient to ‖ v.i. to be obedient

o·bit·u·ar·y 1. adj. relating to the death of someone **2.** pl. **o·bit·u·ar·ies** n. a notice announcing a person's death

ob·ject n. a perceptible body or thing ‖ an aim or purpose

ob·ject v.i. to be opposed ‖ v.t. to present or put forth as an objection to a statement, proposal etc.

ob·jec·tion n. an act of objecting ‖ a feeling of opposition ‖ a reason for objecting **ob·jéc·tion·a·ble** adj. unpleasant ‖ open to objection **ob·jéc·tion·a·bly** adv.

ob·jec·tive 1. adj. of or pertaining to an object ‖ having a real, substantial existence ‖ pertaining to an external event quite independent of the observer's emotions or imagination ‖ unbiased **2.** n. an aim or goal

ob·jec·tiv·i·ty n. the state of being objective

ob·jur·gate ob·jur·gat·ing ob·jur·gat·ed v.t. to reprove strongly **ob·jur·gá·tion** n. **ob·jur·ga·to·ry** adj.

ob·li·gate v.t. **ob·li·gat·ing ob·li·gat·ed** v.t. to place under a moral or legal obligation

ob·li·ga·tion n. an obligating ‖ a binding legal agreement or a moral responsibility ‖ something which a person is bound to do or not do

ob·lig·a·to·ry adj. which must be done, as required by by authority ‖ of or being an obligation

o·blige o·blig·ing o·bliged v.t. to cause (someone) by physical or moral means to do something ‖ to render a service or favor to ‖ to bind (someone) by contract or promise

o·blig·ing adj. helpful and accommodating to others

ob·lique adj. slanting, diverging ‖ implied but not specified

ob·lit·er·ate ob·lit·er·at·oing ob·lit·er·at·ed v.t. to remove all trace of, destroy ‖ to blot out from memory, knowledge etc. **ob·lit·er·á·tion** n.

ob·liv·i·on n. the state of being completely forgotten ‖ utter forgetfulness ‖ unconsciousness

ob·liv·i·ous adj. totally unaware

ob·long adj. of a figure with greater length than breadth

ob·nox·ious adj. unpleasant, offensive

o·boe n. a woodwind instrument with a long, thin double reed **o·bo·ist** n. someone who plays the oboe

ob·scene adj. of that which depraves, esp. of sexual matters ‖ offensive, revolting

ob·scen·i·ty pl. **ob·scen·i·ties** n. an obscene utterance

ob·scure ob·scur·er ob·scur·est adj. dim, insufficiently lit ‖ difficult to see ‖ difficult to understand ‖ (of places) remote ‖ indistinctly heard

ob·scure ob·scur·ing ob·scured *v.t.* to make obscure ‖ to hide from view

ob·scu·ri·ty *pl.* **ob·scu·ri·ties** *n.* the state of being obscure

ob·se·qui·ous *adj.* self-abasing

ob·serv·ance *n.* the act of obeying a law, rule etc. ‖ the keeping of a custom ‖ *(pl.)* the ceremonies or rites performed in keeping a religious feast, custom etc.

ob·serv·an·cy *n.* the quality of being observant

ob·serv·ant *adj.* giving careful attention

ob·ser·va·tion *n.* an observing the faculty of observing something ‖ an expression of an opinion

ob·serv·a·to·ry *pl.* **ob·serv·a·to·ries** *n.* a room or building sheltering instruments (telescopes, chronometers etc.) used by observers studying heavenly bodies

ob·serve ob·serv·ing ob·served *v.t.* to look at with attention ‖ to comply with ‖ to celebrate ceremonially ‖ to perceive, notice ‖ to comment ‖ *v.i.* to note attentively

ob·sess *v.t.* to occupy or engage the mind of (someone) to an inordinate degree

ob·ses·sion *n.* the state of being obsessed **ob·sés·sion·al, ob·sés·sive** *adjs* causing an obsession

ob·so·les·cence *n.* the state of being virtually obsolete or the process of becoming obsolete

ob·so·les·cent *adj.* becoming obsolete

ob·so·lete *adj.* no longer in use, out-of-date

ob·sta·cle *n.* an obstruction

ob·stet·rics *n.* the branch of medical practice which is concerned with the care of mothers before, during and immediately after childbirth

ob·sti·na·cy *n.* the quality or state of being obstinate

ob·sti·nate *adj.* (of people) stubborn

ob·strep·er·ous *adj.* noisily resisting control or

ob·struct *v.t.* to prevent (something) by placing an obstacle in its path ‖ to block from sight ‖ *v.i.* to hinder, impede

ob·struc·tion *n.* an obstructing ‖ something which obstructs **ob·strúc·tion·ism, ob·strúc·tion·ist** *ns*

ob·struc·tive *adj.* of, being or producing an obstruction

ob·tain *v.t.* to become the possessor of, secure for oneself or another **ob·táin·a·ble** *adj.*

ob·tuse *adj.* of an angle greater athan 90° but less than 180° ‖ not keenly perceptive or sensitive

ob·verse 1. *adj.* turned towards the spectator ‖ having a base narrower than the apex **2.** *n.* the principal surface of a coin, medal etc. ‖ the other side of a question or statement

ob·vi·ate ob·vi·at·ing ob·vi·at·ed *v.t.* to remove, get rid of

ob·vi·ous *adj.* self-evident ‖ easily seen

oc·ca·sion 1. *n.* set of circumstances viewed as having special importance **2.** *v.t.* to cause, directly or indirectly **oc·cá·sion·al** *adj.* occurring at irregular intervals of some length ‖ designed for, and used, only on particular occasions

oc·ca·sion·al·ly *adv.* at irregular intervals of some length

oc·clude oc·clud·ing oc·clud·ed *v.t.* to close up (a passage) ‖ to keep (something) from passing through a passage ‖ to adsorb and retain (esp. gases)

oc·clu·sion *n.* an occluding or being occluded

oc·cult 1. *adj.* beyond the range of normal perception ‖ secret, mysterious, esoteric ‖ dealing with magic, alchemy, astrology etc. **2.** *n.* (with 'the') the supernatural

oc·cult·ism *n.* occult beliefs or practices

oc·cu·pan·cy *pl.* **oc·cu·pan·cies** *n.* a residing or being resided in ‖ the act of becoming an occupant

oc·cu·pant *n.* someone who occupies a particular space, position

oc·cu·pa·tion *n.* an occupying or being occupied, esp. by a military force ‖ an activity by which one earns one's living or fills one's time **oc·cu·pá·tion·al** *adj.* arising from or pertaining to one's occupation or an occupation

oc·cu·py oc·cu·py·ing oc·cu·pied *v.t.* to take, or have, possession of ‖ to reside in ‖ to take or retain possession of by military force ‖ (of someone) to fill (a position) ‖ to keep (one's mind) busy ‖ to keep employed

oc·cur oc·cur·ring oc·curred *v.i.* to happen ‖ to be found at a place or within a region ‖ to come into the conscious mind

oc·cur·rence *n.* the fact, act or process of occurring ‖ something which occurs

o·cean *n.* the part (seven tenths) of the earth's surface which consists of salt water

o·ce·an·ic *adj.* of, relating to or found in the ocean

o·cher, o·chre *n.* a yellow or red form of hydrated ferric oxide ‖ the color of yellow ocher

oc·ta·gon *n.* a figure having eight sides

oc·tave 1. *n.* (*mus.*) the note having twice or one half the frequency of a given note **2.** *adj.* consisting of eight parts

oc·ta·vo (*abbr.* 8vo) *n.* the size of a book leaf formed by folding a sheet three times, giving eight leaves or 16 pages

oc·tet, oc·tette *n.* a musical composition written for eight players or singers ‖ a group of eight lines of verse

Oc·to·ber *n.* the tenth month of the year

oc·to·pus *pl.* **oc·to·pus·es, oc·to·pi** *n.* a marine cephalopod mollusk. Octopuses have eight arms equipped with suckers

oc·u·lar 1. *adj.* of, by, with or pertaining to the eye **2.** *n.* the eyepiece of an optical instrument

odd *adj.* of a number which is not a multiple of 2 ‖ lacking a mate to make a pair ‖ unusual, not fitting in to the accepted pattern ‖ random ‖ occasional

odd·i·ty *pl.* **odd·i·ties** *n.* something which or someone who does not conform to the accepted standard of normality

odds *pl. n.* the chances of success or failure ‖ probability ‖ the ratio supposed to exist between the chances of winning or losing a wager and which is used as a basis for reckoning bets

o·di·ous *adj.* offensive, hateful

o·di·um *n.* hatred or condemnation of the community ‖ the hatefulness of some act or stigma involved in some situation

o·dom·e·ter *n.* an instrument used to measure distance traveled

o·dor *n.* the characteristic smell of something

o·dor·if·er·ous *adj.* diffusing an odor pleasant or obnoxious

o·dor·ous *adj.* odoriferous

of *prep.* from ‖ during ‖ expressing cause ‖ produced by ‖ constituted by ‖ with respect to a ‖ indicating simple apposition

off 1. *adv.* at a distance in time or space ‖ to be separated in some way ‖ to deviate from a course ‖ to be no longer in operation etc. ‖ to be smaller, fewer etc. ‖ away from one's usual activity etc. ‖ into a state of unconsciousness **2.** *prep.* at a distance from ‖ in a direction diverging from ‖ so as to be separated from in some way ‖ not up to a usual standard etc. in, (*pop.*) abstaining from **3.** *adj.* far, further away ‖ in error ‖ not functioning ‖ canceled ‖ less, fewer ‖ remote ‖ wrong

off·beat 1. *adj.* of or having a style which departs from the ordinary or conventional **2.** *n.* (*mus.*) the unaccented beat in a measure

of·fend *v.t.* to affront, hurt the feelings of ‖ *v.i.* to act contrary to law, moral principle etc. ‖ to cause resentment or disgust **of·fend·er** *n.*

of·fense, of·fence *n.* an act against the law ‖ the act of offending someone ‖ something which causes someone to be offended ‖ the act of attacking

of·fen·sive 1. *adj.* insulting ‖ revolting to the senses ‖ aggressive **2.** *n.* a large-scale attack

of·fer *n.* something offered for consideration ‖ an expression of willingness to give or do something ‖ a sum named by a would be purchaser in bargaining

offer *v.t.* to put forward for acceptance, rejection or consideration ‖ to present for sale ‖ to bid, propose as a price ‖ to make available

of·fer·ing *n.* the act of offering ‖ something offered

off·hand 1. *adv.* without preparation or reference **2.** *adj.* done without preparation **óff·hánd·ed** *adj.*

of·fice *n.* a room or premises for transacting business ‖ a doctor's consulting room ‖ a position of authority in administration

of·fi·cer *n.* a person holding a public

appointment ‖ a policeman ‖ a person holding a position of responsibility and trust ‖ a person holding a commission to command others

of·fi·cial *n.* a person who holds a public office or is employed on authorized duties

official *adj.* of or relating to an office or the administering of an office **of·fi·cial·dom** *n.*

of·fi·cious *adj.* too zealously exercising authority ‖ offering unwanted services or advice

off·set 1. *n.* an offshoot ‖ a compensation or counterbalance ‖ a bend made in a pipe to circumvent an obstacle ‖ a method of printing **2.** *v.t.* **off·set·ting off·set** to balance (one thing) against another, to compensate for **3.** *adj.* of or printed by offset

off·shoot *n.* a shoot, or branch from a main stem ‖ a subsidiary activity, by-product

off·spring *n.* a child or children, progeny

of·ten *adv.* frequently, repeatedly ‖ in a number of instances

o·gle 1. *v.* **o·gling o·gled** *v.t.* to try to attract by giving enticing looks **2.** *n.* an amorous or provocative glance

o·gre *n.* a fairy-tale monster or giant who eats humans ‖ a hideous or cruel man **ó·gre·ish, o·grish** *adjs*

oil 1. *n.* one of a large group of substances which are typically viscous liquids. They are insoluble in water, and may have animal, vegetable, mineral or synthetic origin ‖ petroleum ‖ a painting worked in oil colors **2.** *v.t.* to lubricate ‖ *v.i.* to become oily

oil·y oil·i·er oil·i·est *adj.* containing, saturated with, or covered with oil ‖ having the characteristics of oil ‖ (of human behavior) heavily ingratiating, using suave hypocrisy

oint·ment *n.* an unguent

OK, o·kay 1. *adj.* all right, agreed **2.** *v.t.* **OK'ing, o·kay·ing OK'd, o·kayed** to approve, endorse **3.** *pl.* **OK's, o·kays** *n.* an endorsement or authorization

old 1. *adj.* advanced in years ‖ having a specified age or duration ‖ no longer new ‖ stale ‖ inveterate ‖ former ‖ antique ‖

familiar ‖ accustomed ‖ out-of-date

old·en *adj.* (only in the phrases) **in olden days, in olden times** belonging to a time long past

old-fash·ioned *adj.* of or belonging to former times ‖ out-of-date

old fo·gy, old fo·gey *pl.* **old fo·gies, old fo·geys** *n.* a bore with old-fashioned, ridiculously conservative ideas

o·le·o *n.* margarine

o·live 1. *n.* a small evergreen tree native to the Mediterranean region ‖ its small, oval, edible fruit **2.** *adj.* of the color olive

om·buds·man *pl.* **om·buds·men** *n.* a person appointed by a legislative body to receive, investigate and report on complaints by private individuals

om·e·let, om·e·lette *n.* eggs beaten lightly together and cooked in a frying pan

o·men 1. *n.* a phenomenon or occurrence interpreted as a sign of good or evil to come **2.** *v.t.* to portend

om·i·nous *adj.* threatening, foreboding

o·mis·sion *n.* something which is left undone or left out

o·mit o·mit·ting o·mit·ted *v.t.* to neglect or fail (to do something)

om·ni·bus *pl.* **om·ni·bus·es** *n.* a book collecting together several different but related works ‖ a bus

om·nip·o·tence *n.* the state or quality of being omnipotent

om·nip·o·tent 1. *adj.* all-powerful, having unlimited authority **2.** *n.* **the Om·nip·o·tent** God

om·nis·cience *n.* infinite knowledge or wisdom

om·nis·cient *adj.* all-knowing, infinitely wise

om·ni·vore *n.* an animal adapted to eat a wide variety of food, both animal and vegetable

om·ni·vor·ous *adj.* feeding on animal and vegetable substances ‖ taking in everything, not selective

on 1. *prep.* supported or suspended by ‖ occupying part of and supported by ‖ attached to ‖ located at ‖ in a condition or state of ‖ deriving from, yielded by ‖ at the expense of ‖ added to **2.** *adv.* expressing forward movement or progress in space ‖ in a situation of covering or contacting ‖ by way of clothing ‖ as a planned activity **3.** *adj.* functioning, in action

once 1. *adv.* on one occasion only ‖ a single time **once in a while** occasionally **2.** *conj.* whenever ‖ if ever **3.** *n.* one time **at once** immediately ‖ simultaneously **for once** on this particular occasion

on·com·ing *adj.* approaching

one 1. *adj.* being a single unit ‖ on an unspecified (occasion) ‖ a certain (person) **one and the same** exactly the same **one or two** a few **the one** the only ‖ the (person, thing etc.) above all others **2.** *pron.* a certain person or thing ‖ some ‖ a blow **all in one** combined **for one** at least **one after another** successively **3.** *n.* the lowest of the cardinal numbers, denoting unity and represented by the figure 1 or the letter I ‖ a single unit ‖ one o'clock

on·er·ous *adj.* burdensome, troublesome

one·self *pron.* refl. form of ONE ‖ emphatic form of ONE **by oneself** unaided ‖ alone

one-sid·ed *adj.* limited to one side ‖ partial, unfair

one·time *adj.* former ‖ occurring only once

one-track *adj.* obsessed by or dwelling boringly on one thing only

on·ion *n.* a Middle Eastern plant widely cultivated for its edible bulb

on·look·er *n.* a passive spectator

on·ly *adj.* single, sole ‖ belonging to a unique class

only 1. *adv.* solely ‖ merely, just ‖ as little as **2.** *conj.* but, except that

on·set *n.* an attack ‖ the beginning of something

on·slaught *n.* a fierce attack

on·to *prep.* to a position on or upon

o·nus *n.* responsibility, burden

on·ward 1. *adj.* advancing, directed forward **2.** *adv.* further forward, towards the front **on·wards** *adv.*

ooze 1. *n.* an oozing or that which oozes **2.** **ooz·ing oozed** *v.i.* to flow slowly and viscously ‖ to exude moisture etc. ‖ to escape or leak out gradually ‖ *v.t.* to exude (moisture etc.)

ooze *n.* mud saturated with water **óoz·y ooz·i·er ooz·i·est** *adj.* containing, consisting of or like ooze

o·pac·i·ty *pl.* **o·pac·i·ties** the quality or state of being opaque ‖ obscurity of meaning

o·pal *n.* an amorphous form of hydrous silica cut and used as a gem

o·paque *adj.* of a medium whose molecular aggregation is such that light cannot pass through it ‖ obscure ‖ obtuse ‖ dull

o·pen not shut ‖ expanded, unfolded, outspread ‖ free and unoccupied ‖ allowing passage, unblocked ‖ exposed, unfenced, unobstructed ‖ receptive ‖ available ‖ not definite, decided or concluded ‖ frank ‖ widely spaced ‖ (of water) free from ice or other water hazards ‖ (of an account) still operative

open *v.t.* to make open ‖ to unwrap, unfasten ‖ to unfold ‖ to begin, start (something) ‖ to unblock, to make clear or passable ‖ to loosen ‖ to enlighten ‖ to cut into ‖ to start (a card game) by bidding or betting first ‖ *v.i.* to become open ‖ to expand, unfold ‖ to break open, come apart ‖ to begin ‖ to become receptive to ideas

o·pen·er *n.* someone or something that opens ‖ the first game in a series

o·pen-hand·ed *adj.* generous

o·pen·ing 1. *n.* a making or becoming open or an instance of this ‖ a gap, an aperture ‖ a beginning ‖ a vacancy ‖ *(chess)* a recognized series of moves at the beginning of a game ‖ a forest clearing **2.** *adj.* first, introductory

o·pen·ly *adv.* frankly ‖ without concealment, publicly

o·pen-mind·ed *adj.* unprejudiced

op·er·a *n.* a stage drama with orchestral accompaniment

op·er·a·ble *adj.* admitting of a surgical operation ‖ capable of being operated

op·er·ate op·er·at·ing op·er·at·ed *v.i.* to be in action, function ‖ to take effect ‖ to perform an operation ‖ (of a stockbroker) to buy and sell ‖ *v.t.* to put into action, cause to work ‖ to manage, run

op·er·at·ic *adj.* of, relating to, or resembling opera **op·er·át·i·cal·ly** *adv.*

op·er·a·tion *n.* the act of operating, or an

instance of this ‖ the way in which a thing works ‖ (pl.) work, activity ‖ an instance of the work done by a surgeon ‖ a financial transaction ‖ a military action on a large scale **op·er·a·tion·al** adj. of or connected with an operation

op·er·a·tive 1. adj. working, in operation ‖ effective **2.** n. a hand (workman), e.g. in a factory ‖ a private detective

op·er·a·tor n. someone who operates a machine or instrument ‖ someone habitually engaged in large financial dealings ‖ a shrewd individual capable of evading legal restrictions

o·pi·ate 1. n. a drug containing opium

o·pin·ion n. a formal expression by an expert of what he judges to be the case or the right course of action

o·pin·ion·at·ed adj. stubbornly affirming one's own opinions

o·pi·um n. a habit-forming, narcotic drug

o·pos·sum pl. **o·pos·sums, o·pos·sum** n. an American family of nocturnal, largely arboreal marsupial mammals

op·po·nent n. a person who or group that opposes another in a fight, game, debate, contest etc.

op·por·tune adj. suitable, well chosen ‖ timely **op·por·tun·ism** n. **op·por·tun·ist 1.** n. **2.** adj. characterized by opportunism **op·por·tu·nis·tic** adj.

op·por·tu·ni·ty pl. **op·por·tu·ni·ties** n. a set of circumstances providing a chance or possibility

op·pose op·pos·ing op·posed v.t. to cause (something or someone) to be or act against something or someone

op·po·site 1. adj. to be looking, going etc. directly away from someone ‖ utterly different ‖ (of leaves) placed in pairs, one on either side of the stem **2.** n. something opposite **3.** adv. on opposite sides

op·po·si·tion n. disagreement, hostility or resistance ‖ any group opposing authority, or those opposing some proposal etc. **op·po·si·tion·al** adj.

op·press v.t. to treat with unjust harshness, esp. to rule over tyrannically ‖ to cause to feel mentally or spiritually burdened

op·pres·sion n. an oppressing or being oppressed ‖ something that oppresses

op·pres·sive adj. burdensome, unjustly harsh ‖ heavy

op·pres·sor n. someone who oppresses

opt v.i. to make a choice

op·tic 1. adj. relating to the eye or to vision **2.** n. an optical system or part of one (lens, mirror etc.) **óp·ti·cal** adj.

op·ti·cian n. a person who makes or sells optical instruments, esp. glasses to correct vision

op·tics n. the science of the nature and laws of light

op·ti·mal adj. most favorable, best

op·ti·mism n. the inclination to take a hopeful view **óp·ti·mist** n. **op·ti·mís·tic** adj. **op·ti·mís·ti·cal·ly** adv.

op·ti·mum pl. **op·ti·mums, op·ti·ma** n. the most favorable or best quality, number etc.

op·tion n. a choosing ‖ that which is chosen ‖ freedom of choice **óp·tion·al** adj. not compulsory

op·tom·e·ter n. an instrument for measuring the refractive power of the eye **op·tóm·e·trist** n. someone who specializes in optometry **op·tóm·e·try** n. the profession of examining people's eyes for faults

op·u·lence n. wealth, riches ‖ profuse abundance

op·u·lent adj. extremely rich ‖ profuse, luxuriant

or conj. introducing an alternative a synonym for the preceding ‖ indicating vagueness or uncertainty

or·a·cle n. the place where the ancient Greeks and Romans went to ask the advice of their gods about the future ‖ a person regarded as infallibly wise

o·ral adj. using speech rather than writing, spoken ‖ of or relating to the mouth

or·ange 1. n. the reddish-yellow fruit of any of certain trees of genus Citrus ‖ the color of the fruit **2.** adj. having the color orange

o·rang·u·tan n. a large heavy reddish-brown anthropoid ape

o·rate o·rat·ing o·rat·ed v.i. to hold forth in a bombastic style

o·ra·tion *n.* a formal speech or discourse

or·a·tor *n.* a person who speaks in public

or·a·tor·i·cal *adj.* given to using oratory

or·a·to·ry *n.* the art of public speaking

orb 1. *n.* a sphere ‖ a heavenly body **2.** *v.t.* to form into a circle or sphere ‖ *v.i.* to move in an orbit

or·bit 1. *n.* the closed path, usually elliptical, in which a planet moves around the sun, or a satellite around the parent body ‖ a sphere of influence ‖ the bony socket of the eye **2.** *v.i.* to move in an orbit

or·bit·al *adj.* of, relating to or describing an orbit

or·chard *n.* a stretch of land with cultivated fruit trees ‖ the trees collectively

or·ches·tra *n.* a group of musicians ‖ the orchestra pit in a theater ‖ the main floor of a theater **or·ches·tral** *adj.*

or·chid *n.* a family of perennial monocotyledonous terrestrial plants, epiphytes or saprophytes ‖ *(pl.)* compliments, praise

or·dain *v.t.* to consecrate (someone) ‖ to appoint, decree, establish

or·deal *n.* a severe or exacting experience that tests character or powers of endurance

or·der *n.* a sequence, arrangement, the way one thing follows another ‖ the rules, laws and structures which constitute a society ‖ the natural, moral or spiritual system governing things in the universe ‖ an authoritative instruction, command ‖ something ordered, e.g. in a restaurant ‖ brotherhood ‖ social purposes ‖ (pl.) ordination ‖ a prescribed form of service ‖ (in plant and animal classification) a category of closely allied organisms ‖ commands ‖ a decision by a court ‖ a written direction to pay money or surrender goods

order *v.t.* to put in order ‖ to give authoritative instruction to (someone) to do something or for (something) to be done ‖ to request (goods etc.) to be supplied

or·der·li·ness *n.* the quality or state of being orderly

or·der·ly 1. *adj.* in good order, well arranged ‖ disciplined and peaceable **2.**

pl. **or·der·lies** *n.* a soldier attendant on an officer ‖ an attendant in charge of cleaning etc. in a hospital

or·di·nance *n.* a decree or authoritative order

or·di·nar·i·ly *adv.* generally, in the usual course of events

or·di·nar·y *adj.* usual ‖ not exceptional or unusual, undistinguished

ord·nance *n.* heavy guns, artillery ‖ military stores and materials

ore *n.* a naturally occurring metallic compound from which the metal can be extracted

or·gan *n.* a musical wind instrument ‖ a structure of an animal or of a plant adapted for some specific and usually essential function ‖ a means or instrument of action ‖ a publication attached to some group, party etc.

or·gan·ic *adj.* of or relating to an organ of the body ‖ having the physical structure characteristic of living organisms ‖ of or relating to the compounds of carbon ‖ inherent, structural **or·gán·i·cal·ly** *adv.*

or·gan·ism *n.* any living being or its material structure

or·gan·ist *n.* a person who plays the organ

or·gan·i·za·tion *n.* an organizing or being organized ‖ an association or society of people working together to some end **or·gan·i·zá·tion·al** *adj.*

or·gan·ize or·gan·iz·ing or·gan·ized *v.t.* to give an orderly or organic structure to ‖ to make arrangements for, prepare ‖ to unionize ‖ *v.i.* to become organic or systematized **ór·gan·iz·er** *n.* someone who or something that organizes

or·gy pl. **or·gies** *n.* a bout of debauchery ‖ a display of excessive indulgence

or·i·ent *v.t.* to determine the position of (someone or something) ‖ to adjust (someone or something) to the surroundings or a situation

Ori·en·tal 1. *adj.* of, relating to, characteristic of or coming from the Orient **2.** *n.* a native or inhabitant of the Orient, esp. of the Far East

or·i·en·tate or·i·en·tat·ing or·i·en·tat·ed *v.t.* to orient

o·ri·en·ta·tion *n.* position with relation to the points of the compass ‖ situation of a church on an east-west axis so that the altar is at the east end

or·i·fice *n.* a mouthlike opening

or·i·ga·mi *n.* the art or process of folding paper into representational or decorative forms

or·i·gin *n.* the point in time or space at which a thing first arises ‖ parentage or ancestry

o·rig·i·nal 1. *adj.* firsthand, not copied or derivative ‖ inventive, creative **2.** *n.* a model or archetype that has been copied, translated etc.

o·rig·i·nal·i·ty *n.* the quality or state of being original, esp. creative or novel

o·rig·i·nate o·rig·i·nat·ing o·rig·i·nat·ed *v.i.* (with 'in', 'from', 'with') to have its source or beginning **o·rig·i·ná·tion** *n.* origin

or·na·ment 1. *n.* an object, detail etc. meant to add beauty to something to which it is attached or applied or of which it is a part ‖ such objects, details etc. collectively **2.** *v.t.* to add or apply an ornament or ornaments to **or·na·men·tal** *adj.* **or·na·men·ta·tion** *n.*

or·nate *adj.* elaborately adorned

or·ner·y *adj.* inclined to be stubborn

or·ni·tho·log·i·cal *adj.* of or pertaining to ornithology

or·ni·thol·o·gist *n.* a specialist in ornithology

or·ni·thol·o·gy *n.* the branch of zoology which deals with birds

or·phan 1. *n.* a child whose parents are dead **ór·phan·age** *n.* an institution for the care and education of orphans

or·tho·don·tia *n.* orthodonatics **or·tho·dón·tic** *adj.* of or pertaining to orthodontics **or·tho·dón·tics** *n.* the branch of dentistry concerned awith the prevention and correction of displacement or overcrowding of the teeth **or·tho·dón·tist** *n.*

or·tho·dox *adj.* of, conforming to or holding the official, accepted or standard opinions

or·tho·dox·y *pl.* **or·tho·dox·ies** *n.* the qual-

ity or state of being orthodox

or·tho·pe·dic, or·tho·pae·dic *adj.* of, relating to or used in orthopedics

or·tho·pe·dics, or·tho·pae·dics *n.* the prevention or curing of deformities of bones **or·tho·pé·dist, or·tho·páe·dist** *n.*

os·cil·late os·cil·lat·ing os·cil·lat·ed *v.i.* to swing to and fro ‖ to vibrate ‖ vacillate

os·cil·la·tion *n.* an oscillating **ós·cil·la·tor** *n.* a device for the production of oscillations

os·cil·la·to·ry *adj.* characterized by oscillation

os·cu·la·tion *n.* the act of kissing

os·mo·sis *n.* the passage of a solvent, but not its solute, through a semipermeable membrane into a more concentrated solution **os·mót·ic** *adj.*

os·si·fi·ca·tion *n.* the process of becoming bone or an instance of this process

os·si·fy os·si·fy·ing os·si·fied *v.i.* to change into bone ‖ (of ideas, behavior etc.) to make or become hardened, set or rigid

os·ten·si·ble *adj.* apparent, pretended, avowed **os·tén·si·bly** *adv.*

os·ten·ta·tion *n.* unnecessary show or display of wealth etc. **os·ten·tá·tious** *adj.* showy ‖ intended to attract attention

os·te·op·a·thy *n.* a form of medical treatment by manipulation of the joints of the body

os·tra·cism *n.* an ostracizing or being ostracized

os·tra·cize os·tra·ciz·ing os·tra·cized *v.t.* to refrain deliberately and ostentatiously from having any sociable dealings at all with, esp. in order to punish by humiliating

os·trich *n.* a flightless bird inhabiting the sandy plains of Africa

oth·er 1. *adj.* different, not the same ‖ further or additional ‖ former **every other the other world** life after death **2.** *n.* or *pron.* other person or thing **someone or other**some unknown person **3.** *adv.* **other than** in any other way ‖ besides

oth·er·wise 1. *adv.* in another or different way ‖ in other respects **2.** *adj.* different

o·ti·ose *adj.* idle, lazy ‖ superfluous

ot·to·man *n.* an upholstered or cushioned

seat, stool or sofa without a back

ought *auxiliary v.* expressing duty or obligation ‖ expressing necessity or expedience ‖ expressing strong likelihood

oui·ja *n.* a board marked with the alphabet and various signs used to obtain messages in spiritualist practice

ounce *n. (abbr.* oz.) a unit of weight equal to 1/16 of a pound avoirdupois ‖ a very little

our *possessive adj.* of, pertaining to or belonging to us ‖ experienced, done or made by us

ours *possessive pron.* that or those belonging to us

our·self *pl.* **our·selves** *pron.* refl. form of WE ‖ emphatic form of WE

oust to dispossess ‖ eject

oust·er *n.* an illegal or wrongful dispossession from property or an inheritance

out 1. *adv.* away from a place, situation etc. ‖ on the outside ‖ away from home, place of work etc. ‖ expressing finality ‖ in or into public knowledge ‖ openly ‖ into or in disuse ‖ into or in a state of unconsciousness **all out** with one's whole effort **out and away** by far 2. *adj.* (baseball) failing to get on a base or complete a successful play 3. prep. forth from, jump out the window 4. *n.* a way out, an excuse 5. *interj.* get out! go away!

out- prefix beyond ‖ in excess of ‖ excelling

out·break *n.* a sudden, violent bursting out ‖ an epidemic ‖ a revolt

out·burst *n.* emotional fit ‖ an eruption

out·cast 1. *adj.* cast out from home, friends etc. or by society 2. *n.* someone who has been so treated

out·class *v.t.* to surpass by so much as to seem to belong to a higher class

out·come *n.* a result or consequence

out·cry *pl.* **out·cries** *n.* a public expression of anger or disapproval

out·date **out·dat·ing** **out·dat·ed** *v.t.* to make obsolete

out·dis·tance **out·dis·tanc·ing** **out·dis·tanced** *v.t.* to leave far behind

out·do **out·do·ing** **out·did** **out·done** *v.t.* to do better than, surpass

out·doors *adj.* in the open air

out·er *adj.* farther out or outside ‖ away

from the center ‖ external

out·er·most *adj.* furthest out from the center

out·face **out·fac·ing** **out·faced** *v.t.* to stare down ‖ to resist by bravery

out·fit 1. *n.* articles or instruments required to equip or fit out ‖ clothing etc. for a special purpose ‖ persons making up an organization, institution, regiment etc. 2. *v.t.* **out·fit·ting** **out·fit·ted** to furnish, supply **óut·fit·ter** *n.*

out·flank *v.t.* to extend one's own flank beyond the flank of (the enemy) ‖ to circumvent

out·flow *n.* a flowing out ‖ the amount of such a flowing out

out·go 1. *pl.* **out·goes** *n.* outflow ‖ expenditure (opp. INCOME) 2. **out·go·ing** **out·went** **out·gone** *v.t.* to go one better than, with an advantage over

out·go·ing 1. *adj.* leaving ‖ retiring ‖ willing to be sociable

out·grow **out·grow·ing** **out·grew** **out·grown** *v.t.* to grow too big for ‖ become too old for ‖ to grow faster than

out·growth *n.* a result, product or by-product

out·ing *n.* a pleasure trip or excursion

out·land·ish *adj.* bizarre-looking ‖ uncouth

out·last *v.t.* to last longer than, outlive

out·law *n.* a person deprived of the protection of the law

outlaw *v.t.* to deprive of the benefit of the law ‖ to cause to be no longer tolerated

out·lay *n.* expenditure ‖ an instance of this

out·let *n.* an opening which provides a way to the outside ‖ a means of channeling ‖ a market for goods ‖ a pair of terminals in an electric wiring system

out·line 1. *n.* a line or lines bounding the outer limits of a figure ‖ a sketch ‖ a rough draft of a plan, scheme of work etc. ‖ a short summary ‖ (*pl.*) general principles or chief elements of a subject 2. *v.t.* **out·lin·ing** **out·lined** to draw or mark the outline of ‖ to give the main points of

out·live **out·liv·ing** **out·lived** *v.t.* to live longer than, survive

out·look *n.* a prospect or view

out·mod·ed *adj.* no longer widely accepted

out·num·ber *v.t.* to be greater than in number

out-of-date *adj.* old-fashioned ‖ not current

out·post *n.* a position held by a detachment in front of the main body of troops

out·put *n.* the total product of a factory, mill etc. ‖ the creative work of an artist

out·rage 1. *n.* a violent attack ‖ a flagrant offense ‖ a feeling of angry resentment **2.** *v.t.* **out·rag·ing out·raged** to subject to an outrage

out·ra·geous *adj.* extravagant, outré

out·rank *v.t.* to have a higher rank

out·right 1. *adv.* not by installments or degrees, once for all ‖ openly, straightforwardly **2.** *adj.* thorough, downright ‖ complete

out·set *n.* the first stage, the beginning

out·shine out·shin·ing out·shone, out·shined *v.t.* to surpass

out·side 1. *n.* the surface, exterior, outer parts ‖ external appearance ‖ superficial aspect **at the outside** at the most **2.** *adj.* on, of or nearer the outside ‖ from a source other than some specified or understood group ‖ just within the limit of possibility **3.** *adv.* on or to the outside ‖ out-of-doors **4.** *prep.* on or to the outer side of

out·sid·er *n.* a person not included in some particular group, party, clique etc.

out·skirts *pl. n.* outlying parts remote from the center

out·smart *v.t.* to outwit

out·spo·ken *adj.* said without fear of the consequences

out·stand·ing *adj.* conspicuous ‖ remarkable ‖ not yet settled or completed

out·strip out·strip·ping out·stripped *v.t.* to go at a quicker rate than and leave behind

out·ward 1. *adj.* moving or directed toward the outside ‖ exterior **2.** *adv.* towards the outside and away from the inside

out·ward·ly *adv.* externally ‖ on the surface

out·wards *adv.* outward

out·wear out·wear·ing out·wore out·worn *v.t.* to last longer in use than

out·wit out·wit·ting out·wit·ted *v.t.* to defeat by cleverness or cunning

o·val 1. *adj.* having the form of an ellipse ‖ egg-shaped **2.** *n.* an oval figure or shape

o·va·ry *pl.* **o·va·ries** *n.* one of a pair of female reproductive organs

o·va·tion *n.* an enthusiastic public welcome

ov·en *n.* an enclosed cavity of stone, brick, metal etc. for baking, roasting, heating or drying

o·ver 1. *prep.* above ‖ so as to cover ‖ in excess of ‖ along ‖ by means of ‖ through out ‖ during ‖ more than ‖ up to and including ‖ in preference to ‖ against and across the top of **2.** *adv.* across ‖ expressing upward and outward motion from a container ‖ so as to turn the upper surface forward and down ‖ from one side to the other ‖ to one's or someone's house ‖ afresh **3.** *adj.* in excess

o·ver·age *adj.* beyond a specified or usual age

o·ver·all *n.* (*pl.*) loose trousers of durable material, with apron and shoulder straps

overall *adj.* including everything, total

o·ver·bear o·ver·bear·ing o·ver·bore o·ver·borne *v.t.* to bear down by greater force, weight, determination etc. **o·ver·béar·ing** *adj.* aggressively masterful

o·ver·blown *adj.* (of flowers) just past full bloom

overblown *adj.* blowzy ‖ (of style) pretentious, windy

o·ver·board *adv.* over the side of a ship etc., to go to extremes

o·ver·cast 1. *v.t.* **o·ver·cast·ing o·ver·cast** to stitch to prevent unraveling **2.** *adj.* cloudy

o·ver·charge 1. o·ver·charg·ing o·ver·charged *v.t.* to charge (someone) too high a price ‖ to load too highly with electricity, explosive etc. ‖ *v.i.* to charge excessively **2.** *n.* an excessive charge

o·ver·coat *n.* a warm coat

o·ver·come o·ver·com·ing o·ver·came o·ver·come *v.t.* to conquer ‖ to overpower or overwhelm (a person) physically or emotionally

o·ver·do o·ver·do·ing o·ver·did o·ver·done *v.t.* to exaggerate, carry too far ‖ to cook too long

o·ver·dose 1. *v.t.* **o·ver·dos·ing o·ver·dosed** to give an excessive dose to **2.** *n.* an excessive dose

o·ver·due *adj.* not paid by the time it was due ‖ behind the scheduled time of arrival ‖ more than ready

o·ver·es·ti·mate 1. o·ver·es·ti·mat·ing o·ver·es·ti·mat·ed *v.t.* to put the value, amount etc. of (something) too high **2.** *n.* an estimate that is too high

o·ver·flow *v.t.* (of liquids) to flow over the brim of ‖ to flood ‖ to be abundant

o·ver·flow *n.* a flowing over ‖ something which flows over ‖ an outlet or receptacle for excess fluids

o·ver·grown *adj.* grown over with rank weeds etc. ‖ grown to an excessive size

o·ver·growth *n.* excessive growth ‖ dense vegetation

o·ver·haul 1. *v.t.* to examine thoroughly and repair or correct defects in **2.** *n.* repairs, renovations etc.

o·ver·head 1. *adj.* located, working etc. above one's head **2.** *n.* expenses which are a general charge to a business **3.** *adv.* above one's head

o·ver·hear o·ver·hear·ing o·ver·heard *v.t.* to hear accidentally or by eavesdropping

o·ver·joyed *adj.* exceedingly delighted

o·ver·kill 1. *n.* national capacity in nuclear armament over and above what would be needed to destroy an enemy **2.** *v.* to exert more force than necessary

o·ver·lap 1. o·ver·lap·ping o·ver·lapped *v.t.* to cover partly ‖ *v.i.* to coincide partly **2.** *n.* an instance or place of overlapping

o·ver·lie o·ver·ly·ing o·ver·lay o·ver·lain *v.t.* to lie over or on

o·ver·look *v.t.* to look over from above ‖ to fail to notice **o·ver·look·er** *n.* an overseer

o·ver·ly *adv.* excessively

o·ver·night 1. *adv.* during or for the night **2.** *adj.* lasting or staying one night ‖ happening etc. in the space of one night

o·ver·pass *n.* a raised crossing, e.g. of a road over a railroad

o·ver·pow·er *v.t.* to overcome physically

o·ver·print 1. *v.t.* (printing) to print (matter) on top of something already

printed ‖ to print too many copies of **2.** *n.* a word, device, figure etc. printed across the surface of a stamp to alter its value or use

o·ver·rate o·ver·rat·ing o·ver·rat·ed *v.t.* to value or prize too highly

o·ver·ride o·ver·rid·ing o·ver·rode o·ver·rid·den *v.t.* to decide to disregard or go against ‖ to dominate

o·ver·rule o·ver·rul·ing o·ver·ruled *v.t.* to give a legal decision or ruling about something which goes against (the decision or ruling of a lower authority)

o·ver·run 1. o·ver·run·ning o·ver·ran o·ver·run (esp. mil.) to attack and obtain complete mastery over ‖ to infest **2.** *n.* an overrunning ‖ the amount of this

o·ver·seas 1. *adv.* beyond the sea **2.** *adj.* of or pertaining to countries or people or things beyond the sea

o·ver·see o·ver·see·ing o·ver·saw o·ver·seen *v.t.* to supervise, direct **o·ver·se·er** *n.*

o·ver·sha·dow *v.t.* to cast a shade over ‖ to cause to seem to have less than full merit, because of detrimental comparisons

o·ver·sight *n.* failure to notice something or an instance of this ‖ supervision

o·ver·sleep o·ver·sleep·ing o·ver·slept *v.i.* to sleep beyond the time for getting up

o·ver·state o·ver·stat·ing o·ver·stat·ed *v.t.* to express in stronger terms than the truth warrants **o·ver·state·ment** *n.*

o·ver·step o·ver·step·ping o·ver·stepped *v.t.* to go beyond (what is prudent or acceptable)

o·vert *adj.* unconcealed, public

o·ver·take o·ver·tak·ing o·ver·took o·ver·tak·en *v.t.* to come upon suddenly ‖ to catch up with and do better than (in competition)

o·ver·tax *v.t.* to strain by making excessive demands on ‖ to tax excessively

o·ver·throw 1. *v.t.* **o·ver·throw·ing o·ver·threw o·ver·thrown** to cause to fall from power ‖ (games) to throw (a ball) beyond the point intended ‖ to upset, overturn **2.** *n.* an overthrowing

o·ver·time 1. *n.* extra time worked ‖ money paid for such work **2.** *adv.* beyond the

usual hours ‖ beyond the usual playing time
1. *adj.* for overtime

o·ver·ture *n.* a preliminary proposal or a formal offer ‖ an orchestral piece preceding the rise of the curtain in an opera

o·ver·turn 1. *v.* to turn over, upset ‖ to overthrow **2.** *n.* an overturning

o·ver·view *n.* a general survey

o·ver·weight 1. *n.* weight over that usual or required ‖ weight that is higher than is compatible with good health **2.** *adj.* suffering from overweight **3.** *v.t.* to overburden

o·ver·whelm *v.t.* to overpower

o·ver·work 1. *v.t.* to work excessively ‖ *v.i.* to work too hard **2.** *n.* work in such quantity that mental or physical health is endangered or affected

o·ver·wrought *adj.* worked up ‖ much too elaborate

o·vi·form *adj.* ovoid

o·void 1. *adj.* egg-shaped **2.** *n.* an egg-shaped body

o·vu·late o·vu·lat·ing o·vu·lat·ed *v.i.* to produce an egg or eggs, or to discharge them from the ovary

o·vum *pl.* **o·va** *n.* a mature egg or egg cell, esp. of mammals, fish or insects

owe ow·ing owed *v.t.* to have an obligation to pay or repay (money etc.) ‖ to be or feel obliged ‖ *v.i.* to be in debt

owl *n.* a large cosmopolitan family of nocturnal birds of prey

owl·ish *adj.* (of a person, or his appearance) having characteristics suggestive of those of an owl

own 1. *adj.* belonging to oneself or itself **2.** *n.* that which belongs to one

own *v.t.* to have, possess, be the proprietor of ‖ *v.i.* (with 'to') to make an admission **to own up** to confess, admit guilt **own·er, own·er·ship** ns

ox *pl.* **ox·en** *n.* the adult castrated male of Bos taurus ‖ any of several animals of Bos and related genera, e.g. the bison, buffalo, yak

ox·y·gen *n.* a colorless, tasteless, gaseous element

oys·ter *n.* an edible marine bivalve ‖ a color between light gray and white

o·zone *n.* an allotropic form of oxygen **o·zon·ic** *adj.* **o·zo·nif·er·ous** *adj.* **o·zon·ize o·zon·iz·ing o·zon·ized** *v.t.* to convert into ozone **o·zon·iz·er** *n.* an apparatus that converts oxygen into ozone

P

P, p the 16th letter of the English alphabet

pab·u·lum nourishment

pace 1. *n.* rate of traveling or progressing ‖ manner of walking or running ‖ a step made in walking **2.** *v.* **pac·ing paced** *v.i.* to walk with regular steps

pace·mak·er *n.* a person who sets the pace ‖ a part of the body serving to maintain a rhythmic activity ‖ a device for stimulating the heart to resume a steady beat

pac·er *n.* a horse with a pacing gait, used esp. in harness racing

pach·y·derm *n.* any of certain thick-skinned, hoofed mammals, esp. the rhinoceros and elephant **pach·y·der·ma·tous** *adj.*

pa·cif·ic *adj.* peaceful ‖ unaggressive in disposition **Pa·cif·ic** of the Pacific Ocean **pa·cif·i·cal·ly** *adv.*

pac·i·fism *n.* the belief that war is morally wrong and that disputes should be settled by negotiation **pac·i·fist** *n.* a person who subscribes to this

pac·i·fy pac·i·fy·ing pac·i·fied *v.t.* to cause to be calm, or no longer angry ‖ to establish peace

pack 1. *n.* a bundle or parcel ‖ a company of animals, esp. of wolves or hounds ‖ a company or gang of people ‖ a packet or container **2.** *v.t.* to put in a container ‖ to fill tightly, cram ‖ *v.i.* to put things together for a trip ‖ to assemble, crowd together

pack *v.t.* to select members of (a committee etc.) so as to secure an unfair advantage

pack·age 1. *n.* a parcel or wrapped bundle **2.** *v.t.* **pack·ag·ing pack·aged** to make into a parcel

pack·et *n.* a small package or parcel

packet boat a boat sailing a regular route, carrying passengers, mail and packages

pact *n.* an agreement, a treaty between states

pad 1. *n.* a flat cushion or ‖ a piece of soft material used to fill or distend ‖ *(sports)* a protective guard worn on the front of the legs etc. ‖ a person's apartment or residence ‖ graft for a group **2.** *v.t.* **pad·ding pad·ded** to fill or line with soft material ‖ to lengthen by adding superfluous material

pad·ding *n.* the material used to pad something

pad·dle 1. *v.i.* **pad·dling pad·dled** to wade in shallow water ‖ to toddle **2.** *n.* the act of paddling

paddle 1. *n.* a wooden pole with a broad blade at one end, used singly without an oarlock to propel and guide a canoe or other small craft ‖ the act of using an oar in this way ‖ one of the projecting boards of a paddle wheel ‖ a seal's flipper **2.** *v.* **pad·dling pad·dled** *v.t.* to propel by using a paddle ‖ to spank ‖ *v.i.* to row gently

pad·dock *n.* a small grassy enclosed area in which a horse can graze and exercise ‖ a racecourse enclosure in which the horse are saddled and unsaddled

pad·lock 1. *n.* a small, portable lock **2.** *v.t.* to fasten

pa·dre *n.* *(armed services, pop.)* a chaplain

pa·gan 1. *n.* a heathen **2.** *adj.* characteristic of a pagan

pa·gan·ism *n.* pagan beliefs and practices

page 1. *n.* one side of a piece of paper or leaf of a book **2.** *v.t.* **pag·ing paged** to make up (printed matter) into pages

page 1. *n.* a boy employed in a hotel to carry messages ‖ a boy attendant in a legislative body, esp. Congress **2.** *v.* **pag·ing paged** to attend as a page ‖ to summon (a person) by calling his name repeatedly

pag·eant *n.* a colorful spectacle

pág·eant·ry *n.* spectacular, colorful display

pag·i·nate pag·i·nat·ing pag·i·nat·ed *v.t.* to divide (a printed text) into pages ‖ to number pages **pag·i·ná·tion** *n.* the numbers etc. distinguishing the pages

pa·go·da *n.* an elaborately decorated Far Eastern sacred building

pail *n.* an open container having an arched handle at the top and used for carrying liquids

pain 1. *n.* an unpleasant sensation caused by the stimulation of certain nerves, esp. as a result of injury or sickness ‖ a distressing emotion ‖ *(pl.)* specially concentrated effort **2.** *v.t.* to inflict esp. mental pain upon

pain·ful *adj.* causing pain ‖ requiring laborious care

pain·less *adj.* not causing pain ‖ not requiring trouble

pains·tak·ing *adj.* showing ‖ using great care and effort

paint *u* **1.** *v.t.* to create (a picture, design etc.) on a surface, using paint ‖ to make a vivid written or spoken description of ‖ to apply cosmetics to ‖ *v.i.* to practice the art of creating pictures with paint **2.** *n.* a liquid or paste consisting of a suspension of a pigment in oil or water etc.

paint·er *n.* an artist who paints pictures ‖ an artisan

paint·ing *n.* a picture ‖ the act or art of making such pictures

pair 1. *pl.* **pairs, pair** *n.* a set of two things of the same kind **2.** *v.t.* to divide or arrange into groups of two ‖ *v.i.* to form a pair

pa·ja·mas *pl.* *n.* a loose-fitting sleeping garment consisting of jacket and trousers

pal·ace *n.* a large, often ornate residence of an emperor, king, pope etc. ‖ a large mansion

pal·at·a·bil·i·ty *n.* the quality of being palatable

pal·at·a·ble *adj.* pleasant to taste **pál·at·a·bly** *adv.*

pal·ate *n.* the roof of the mouth ‖ the sense of taste

pa·la·tial *adj.* having the magnificence etc. of a palace

pa·lav·er 1. *n.* any wordy discussion ‖ flowery, ingratiating language **2.** *v.i.* to engage in palaver

pale *n.* a length of wood driven into the ground, with a pointed upper end, used with others in a fence

pale *adj.* lacking intensity of color ‖ a whitish color

pale pal·ing paled *v.i.* to become pale ‖ to lose importance, esp. by contrast ‖ *v.t.* to make pale

pa·le·on·to·log·ic, pa·lae·on·to·log·ic *adj.* pertaining to paleontology **pá·le·on·to·lóg·i·cal, pá·lae·on·to·lóg·i·cal**

pa·le·on·tol·o·gist *n.* a specialist in paleontology

pa·le·on·tol·o·gy *n.* the study of the fossil remains of animal and plant life of past geological periods

pal·ette *n.* a small board on which a painter mixes his colors ‖ the range of colors used by a particular artist or for a particular picture

pal·i·sade 1. *n.* a fence of wooden or iron pales *v.t.* **pal·i·sad·ing pal·i·sad·ed** to enclose or fortify with palisades

pall *v.i.* to cease to be interesting or attractive

pall·bear·er *n.* one of the little group of men who carry the coffin at a funeral

pal·let *n.* a hard bed ‖ a mattress stuffed with straw

pal·li·ate pal·li·at·ing pal·li·at·ed *v.t.* to disguise the gravity of (a fault) with excuses etc. ‖ to relieve but not cure

pal·lid *adj.* abnormally pale ‖ lacking color

pal·lor *n.* unusual paleness of the skin

palm 1. *n.* the inner part of the hand, between wrist and fingers **2.** *v.t.* to conceal in the palm, esp. for the purpose of cheating

palm *n.* a family of monocotyledonous, largely tropical trees and shrubs, generally having a tall trunk with no branches and a crown of large leaves

palm·ist *n.* a person who practices palmistry

palm·is·try *n.* the practice of foretelling a person's future by interpreting the crease lines in the palm of his hand

pal·o·mi·no *pl.* **pal·o·mi·nos** *n.* a horse of a light tan or golden color with a whitish mane and tail

pal·pa·bil·i·ty *n.* the quality of being palpable

pal·pa·ble *adj.* tangible, perceptible to the touch ‖ obvious **pál·pa·bly** *adv.*

pal·pate pal·pat·ing pal·pat·ed *v.t.* to examine by feeling, esp. in medical examination **pal·pá·tion** *n.*

pal·pi·tate pal·pi·tat·ing pal·pi·tat·ed *v.i.* to tremble ‖ (of the heart) to throb rapidly and strongly

pal·pi·ta·tion *n.* an irregular and violent heartbeat ‖ a trembling

pal·sy *pl.* **pal·sies** *n.* paralysis, sometimes with shaking tremors

pal·tri·ness *n.* the quality of being paltry

pal·try pal·tri·er pal·tri·est *adj.* trivial, petty

pam·pas *pl. n.* treeless plains in South America

pam·per *v.t.* to overindulge (someone), coddle

pam·phlet *n.* a small printed publication, often just a folder, containing informative literature **pam·phlet·eer** *n.* a person who writes controversial pamphlets

pan 1. *n.* metal containers of different shapes, used in cooking and baking ‖ any shallow, open receptacle ‖ a vessel in which gold etc. is separated from gravel by washing ‖ a salt pan **2.** *v.* **pan·ning panned** *v.t.* to wash (gravel or sand bearing gold etc.) in a pan ‖ to criticize harshly

pan pan·ning panned *v.i.* to move a cinema or television camera to get a panoramic effect or to follow a moving object ‖ *v.t.* to move (the camera) in this way

pan- *prefix* all ‖ completely

pan·a·ce·a *n.* a cure for all ills, a universal remedy

pa·nache *n.* bravura, swagger

pan·a·ma *n.* a hat of fine material plaited from the dried young leaves of the jipijapa

pan·cake *n.* a thin, flat cake made of batter cooked on a griddle, or in a pan

pan·chro·mat·ic *adj.* sensitive to all the wavelengths of the visible spectrum

pan·cre·as *n.* a large gland. It consists of two portions, one secreting digestive, the other secreting insulin **pan·cre·at·ic** *adj.*

pan·dem·ic *adj.* (of a disease) affecting a whole country, or the whole world

pan·de·mo·ni·um *n.* a state of confusion and uproar

pan·der *n.* a procurer for prostitutes

pane *n.* a single sheet of glass in a window

pan·e·gyr·ic 1. *n.* a speech eulogizing someone 2. *adj.* having the nature of a panegyric **pan·e·gyr·i·cal** *adj.* **pan·e·gyr·ist** *n.*

pan·el 1. *n.* a flat, rectangular piece of wood etc. forming part of a wall, door etc. but distinguished from the rest by being recessed, framed etc. ‖ a board etc. in which the controls or instruments of a machine etc. are set ‖ a group of persons, usually experts, required to judge or give an answer 2. *v.t.* **pan·el·ing pan·eled** to furnish with panels ‖ to empanel **pan·el·ing** *n.* panels of wood applied to a wall or ceiling **pan·el·ist** *n.* a member of a panel

pang *n.* a brief, keen spasm of pain ‖ a sudden mental or emotional pain

pan·han·dle 1. *n.* a narrow, protruding strip of land 2. *v.* **pan·han·dling pan·han·dled** *v.i.* to beg

pan·ic 1. *n.* intense, contagious irrational fear 2. **pan·ick·ing pan·icked** *v.i.* to lose rational control of one's behavior ‖ *v.t.* to affect with panic 3. *adj.* relating to panic

pan·o·ram·a *n.* a wide uninterrupted view over a scene

pan·o·ram·ic *adj.* **pan·o·ram·i·cal·ly** *adv.*

pan·sy *pl.* **pan·sies** *n.* a wild or cultivated plant with variously colored flowers ‖ an effeminate man

pant 1. *v.i.* to breathe quickly and in spasms ‖ to yearn ‖ (of the heart) to throb

rapidly ‖ to utter gaspingly 2. *n.* labored breathing

pan·ther *n.* a leopard ‖ a cougar ‖ a jaguar

pant·ie, pant·y *pl.* **pant·ies** *n.* (esp. *pl.*) underpants for a woman or a child

pan·to·mime 1. *n.* a form of entertainment in which story and emotion are conveyed by gesture only, without words 2. **pan·to·mim·ing pan·to·mimed** *v.t.* to represent by pantomime ‖ *v.i.* to express oneself by pantomime

pan·try *pl.* **pan·tries** *n.* a larder ‖ a room where the silver, glass etc. are kept

pants *pl. n.* trousers

pan·ty·hose or **pan·ti·hose** *n.* a woman's garment consisting of panties and stockings as a single unit

pap *n.* soft, mashed food for babies or invalids ‖ political patronage ‖ vapid literature etc.

pa·pa *n.* (a child's word for) father

pa·pa·cy *pl.* **pa·pa·cies** *n.* the office of the pope

pa·pal *adj.* of the pope, his office, jurisdiction, acts etc.

pa·per 1. *n.* thin sheet of compactly interlaced fibers of cellulose etc. and used for writing, printing or drawing on, wrapping parcels, covering the walls of a room etc. ‖ an essay, esp. on a scholarly subject ‖ an official document ‖ a newspaper ‖ (*pl.*) documents carried to prove identity 2. *adj.* made of paper 3. *v.t.* to cover (a wall etc.) with paper

pa·per·back *n.* a book bound in paper

pa·pier-ma·che, pa·per-ma·che *n.* a light, tough material made of paper pulp mixed with a liquid adhesive, shaped or molded, and allowed to dry

pa·poose *n.* a North American Indian baby

pap·ri·ka *n.* a mildly pungent, red spice ground from the dried ripe fruit of sweet pepper ‖ the fruit itself

Pap smear or **Papanicolaou smear** diagnostic test to detect uterine or cervical cancer

pa·py·rus *pl.* **pa·py·ri, pa·py·rus·es** *n.* an aquatic plant indigenous to the Nile Valley. The pith, shredded and pressed into sheets, was used to write on

par 1. *n.* equality of value ‖ average or normal state ‖ nominal value **2.** *adj.* at par ‖ average, normal

par·a·ble *n.* a story designed to teach a moral

par·a·chute 1. *n.* contrivance used esp. in aeronautics **2. par·a·chut·ing par·a·chut·ed** *v.i.* to descend by parachute

par·a·chut·ist *n.* a person who makes descents from aircraft by parachute

pa·rade 1. *n.* a ceremonial procession, esp. of troops ‖ a passing in review for appraisal **2. pa·rad·ing pa·rad·ed** *v.t.* to cause (soldiers) to be drawn up for inspection or drill ‖ *v.i.* to take part in, a parade ‖ to stroll, promenade

par·a·digm *n.* an example serving as a pattern **par·a·dig·mat·ic** *adj.* **par·a·dig·mat·i·cal·ly** *adv.*

par·a·dise *n.* a place in which spiritual bliss is enjoyed after death, heaven ‖ any place of or offering perfect happiness **Par·a·dise** the garden of Eden

par·a·dox *n.* a statement which, though true, seems false and self-contradictory ‖ a statement which is self-contradictory and false, though it may seem true or clever **par·a·dox·i·cal** *adj.*

par·a·gon *n.* a model or pattern of something good

par·a·graph 1. *n.* a distinct unit of writing ‖ a brief article or item in a newspaper or magazine **2.** *v.t.* to divide or arrange into paragraphs

par·a·le·gal *n.* a paraprofessional legal assistant; one trained to assist an attorney **par·a·le·gal** *adj.*

par·al·lel 1. *adj.* (of lines, curves, or planes) equidistant from each other at all points **2.** *n.* a line, curve or plane which is parallel to another ‖ similarity between situations etc. ‖ a comparison **3.** *v.t.* **par·al·lel·ing par·al·leled** to be parallel to

pa·ral·y·sis *pl.* **pa·ral·y·ses** *n.* inability to move a muscle or group of muscles ‖ inability to act or move

par·a·lyt·ic 1. *adj.* of, affected with paralysis **2.** *n.* a person affected with paralysis **par·a·lyt·i·cal·ly** *adv.*

par·a·lyze, par·a·lyse par·a·lyz·ing, par·a·lys·ing par·a·lyzed, par·a·lysed *v.t.* to affect with paralysis

par·a·med·ic *n.* **1.** trained medical worker **2.** member of the medical corps **paramedical** *adj.*

pa·ram·e·ter *n.* a variable which is kept constant while others are being investigated **par·a·met·ric** *adj.*

par·a·mount *adj.* supreme in rank, importance etc.

par·a·mour *n.* a married man's mistress or married woman's lover

par·a·noi·a *n.* a mental disorder in which the sufferer believes that other people persecute him or in which the sufferer has delusions **par·a·noid** *n.* and *adj.*

par·a·pet *n.* a low wall at the edge of a bridge, flat roof, balcony etc. to prevent people from falling off

par·a·pher·na·lia *pl. n.* miscellaneous personal belongings or equipment

par·a·phrase *n.* a restatement in different words of a text

paraphrase par·a·phras·ing par·a·phrased *v.t.* to make a paraphrase

par·a·site *n.* an organism living in or on another living organism and deriving its nutriment partly or wholly from it

par·a·sit·ic *adj.* of, relating to, having the nature of or characteristic of a parasite **par·a·sit·i·cal** *adj.*

par·a·sol *n.* an umbrella to give shade from the sun

par·boil *v.t.* to boil until partially cooked

par·cel 1. *n.* one or more things secured by a string or wrapping ‖ a portion, esp. of land forming part of a property **2.** *v.t.* **par·cel·ing par·celed** to distribute in portions ‖ to make a parcel of **par·cel·ing** *n.* the act of making a parcel

parch *v.t.* to make dry by heating ‖ to make very thirsty ‖ *v.i.* to become hot and dry

parch·ment *n.* the skin of a calf, kid or sheep prepared for writing on ‖ paper made to resemble this

par·don *n.* a pardoning ‖ an official release from a penalty

pardon *v.t.* to choose to let (a person) be unpunished for wrongful acts ‖ to excuse or forgive

par·don·a·ble *adj.* capable of being pardoned

pare par·ing pared *v.t.* to cut the skin from something

par·e·gor·ic *n.* tincture of opium, used to relieve diarrhea

par·ent *n.* someone who gives birth to offspring ‖ an organism which is the source of a new one

pa·ren·tal *adj.* characteristic of, or like a parent

pa·ren·the·sis *pl.* **pa·ren·the·ses** *n.* a word, phrase or sentence inserted into a sentence and marked off from it by punctuation ‖ either of the punctuation marks (or) used to contain such a word, phrase etc. **pa·ren·the·size pa·ren·the·siz·ing pa·ren·the·sized** *v.t.* to place parentheses around (a written word etc.)

pa·ri·ah *n.* a social outcast

par·i·mu·tu·el *n.* a betting system by which all bets are recorded and the total sum wagered is divided, in proportion to the stake, among those who placed bets on the winner

par·ish *n.* an administrative district of a diocese in the charge of a priest or minister ‖ the members of the congregation of a Protestant church

pa·rish·ion·er *n.* someone who belongs to a parish

par·i·ty *n.* equality in status, values etc.

park 1. *n.* a very large area of land accessible to the public ‖ an enclosed area that is used for games or sports **2.** *v.t.* to leave (a vehicle) temporarily

par·ka *n.* a long fur jacket with an attached hood ‖ a similar garment of windproof fabric

park·way *n.* a broad highway lined with trees and grass, sometimes landscaped

par·lay *v.t.* to lay (a former bet and its winnings) on a later race, contest etc. ‖ to make use of (some asset) to gain some greater advantage

par·ley 1. *v.i.* to confer, esp. to talk peace terms with an enemy **2.** *pl.* **par·leys** *n.* an official conference

par·lia·ment *n.* the supreme legislative

body of certain countries

par·lia·men·tar·i·an *n.* a person well versed in parliamentary procedure

par·lia·men·tar·i·an·ism *n.* the doctrine of government by a parliament

par·lia·men·ta·ry *adj.* of or relating to parliament ‖ in accordance with the uses and practices of parliament

par·lor *n.* reception room, living room ‖ business establishment equipped to perform some specified service

pa·ro·chi·al *adj.* relating to a parish ‖ narrow, provincial **pa·ro·chi·al·ism** *n.* narrowness of opinions

par·o·dy *pl.* **par·o·dies** *n.* an imitation of a literary, artistic or musical work, designed to ridicule ‖ a poor imitation, travesty

pa·role 1. *n.* a promise ‖ the conditional release of a prisoner ‖ liberation gained by parole **2.** *v.t.* **pa·rol·ing pa·roled** to release on parole

par·ox·ysm *n.* a sudden and violent muscular contraction and relaxation ‖ a sudden explosive burst of laughter, rage etc. **par·ox·ys·mal** *adj.*

par·quet 1. *n.* flooring consisting of pieces of wood arranged in a pattern **2.** *v.t.* to make (a floor) of parquet

par·quet·ry *n.* woodwork arranged in geometric patterns, used for flooring etc.

par·ra·keet, par·a·keet *n.* any of various small parrots

par·ri·cid·al *adj.* of, relating to or guilty of parricide

par·ri·cide *n.* someone who murders his father ‖ someone who murders his mother ‖ any of these crimes

par·rot 1. *n.* any of a great number of tropical birds with brilliant plumage ‖ someone who repeats words mechanically without using the intelligence **2.** *v.t.* to repeat mechanically

par·ry 1. par·ry·ing par·ried *v.t.* to avert by interposing something ‖ *v.i.* to ward off a blow **2.** *pl.* **par·ries** *n.* the act of parrying esp. in boxing, fencing etc.

par·si·mo·ni·ous *adj.* scanty, meager

pars·ley *n.* aromatic herb

pars·nip *n.* a European biennial plant. Its

long whitish taproot is used as a vegetable ‖ the root itself

par·son *n.* a Protestant clergyman

par·son·age *n.* the house of a parish parson

part 1. *n.* that which is less than all ‖ the lines and actions assigned to a performer ‖ one of the parties in a transaction ‖ an individual thing that constitutes an essential element in something ‖ one of the units of a serial publication ‖ a dividing line formed where the hair is combed in opposite directions ‖ *(pl.)* regions ‖ *(pl.)* abilities **2.** *adv.* partly

part *v.t.* to divide into parts ‖ to separate ‖ to comb (the hair) so as to make a part ‖ *v.i.* to go away, ‖ to let go of something ‖ to separate into two or more pieces

par·take par·tak·ing par·took par·tak·en *v.i.* to take or receive a share in ‖ to eat (a meal)

par·tial *adj.* involving only a part ‖ showing a bias ‖ fond of

par·ti·al·i·ty *n.* bias

par·tic·i·pant 1. *n.* someone who participates **2.** *adj.* participating

par·tic·i·pate *v.i.* **par·tic·i·pat·ing par·tic·i·pat·ed** to be active or have a share in some activity

par·tic·i·pa·tion *n.* the act of participating

par·ti·ci·ple *n.* a derivative of a verb as an adjective

par·ti·cle *n.* a small portion

par·tic·u·lar 1. *adj.* relating to one thing singled out among many ‖ unusual, special ‖ concerned with details, minute ‖ fussy, fastid **2.** *n. (pl.)* details of information

par·tic·u·lar·i·ty *pl.* **par·tic·u·lar·i·ties** *n.* the state of being particular ‖ a particular feature or detail

par·tic·u·lar·ly *adv.* in particular

part·ing *n.* separation or division

par·ti·san, par·ti·zan 1. *n.* someone who engages in guerrilla warfare **2.** *adj.* of a partisan ‖ one-sided, biased **par·ti·san·ship, par·ti·zan·ship** *n.*

par·ti·tion 1. *n.* a dividing into parts ‖ a thin wall **2.** *v.i.* to divide into parts ‖ to separate by erecting a partition

part·ly *adv.* in part, not completely

part·ner 1. *n.* someone associated with another in a common undertaking **2.** *v.t.* to be the partner of

part·ner·ship *n.* the relationship between partners ‖ an association of persons who share risks and profits in joint venture

par·tridge *n.* plump game bird ‖ any of several somewhat similar game birds e.g. the bobwhite, the ruffed grouse

part time *adj.* working, operating etc. for less than a full number of hours

par·tu·ri·ent *adj.* giving birth or about to give birth ‖ of or relating to parturition

par·tu·ri·tion *n.* the act of giving birth

par·ty *pl.* **par·ties** *n.* a group of people united for some common purpose ‖ a group of people united in support of a national political organization ‖ a gathering to which guests are invited to enjoy one another's company ‖ one of the persons engaged in a legal action

par·ve·nu *n.* a person who has suddenly risen from comparative poverty or obscurity to wealth, power etc.

pass *v.i.* to move along, proceed ‖ to go by something ‖ to go from one place, quality, state etc. to another ‖ to cease ‖ to occur ‖ (of time) to be spent, elapse ‖ to be judged satisfactory ‖ to be approved by a legislative body ‖ (ball games) to throw, kick etc. the ball to a teammate ‖ (cards) to decline one's turn to play, bid, take cards etc. ‖ *v.t.* to go by, beyond, over, through etc. and leave behind ‖ to spend (time etc.) ‖ to approve (a motion, bill etc.) ‖ to convey, esp. by handing ‖ to pronounce (a sentence or judgment) ‖ to expel from the body

pass *n.* a document which gives the holder a special privilege ‖ a free ticket ‖ (baseball) a walk

pass *n.* a narrow way by which one can cross over or between mountains

pas·sage *n.* a corridor in a building ‖ a moving along, progressing ‖ the passing of a measure by a legislative body ‖ the right or opportunity to pass ‖ a journey by sea or air ‖ brief extract from a literary or musical work

pas·sé *adj.* no longer in style, out-of-date

pas·sen·ger *n.* a person who travels in a

vehicle but is not the driver

pass·ing 1. *adj.* going past ‖ transitory ‖ incidental **2.** *n.* death

pas·sion *n.* intense emotion, esp. sexual desire or love ‖ intense anger

pas·sion·ate *adj.* easily moved to strong emotion ‖ intense

pas·sion·less *adj.* without passion

pas·sive 1. *adj.* not reacting to an external influence, inert ‖ offering no resistance ‖ (of a person) lacking initiative or drive **2.** *n.* the passive voice

Pass·o·ver *n.* a Jewish feast commemorating the release of the Israelites from slavery

pass·port *n.* a document certifying nationality

pass·word *n.* a word or phrase used to show that one is authorized to enter, pass a barrier etc.

past 1. *adj.* (of a period of time) just ended ‖ relating to an earlier time ‖ of or designating a tense that expresses an action or state in time that has gone by **2.** *n.* time that has gone by ‖ the earlier part of a person's life ‖ the past tense **3.** *prep.* beyond or further than ‖ beyond the scope, capacities or limit of **4.** *adv.* in such a way as to pass by

pas·ta *n.* an alimentary paste of wheat flour used in processed form or as fresh dough

paste 1. *n.* a soft, creamy foodstuff made by pounding, grinding etc. ‖ dampened clay used in making earthenware or porcelain ‖ an adhesive **2.** *v.t.* **past·ing pasted** to make stick, using paste

paste·board 1. *n.* a stiff material made by pasting together two or more sheets of paper **2.** *adj.* made of pasteboard

pas·tel *n.* small, colored sticks for drawing ‖ the art of drawing with such sticks ‖ a drawing made with these ‖ (of color) light in tone

pas·teur·i·za·tion *n.* a process which renders milk free of disease-producing bacteria

pas·teur·ize pas·teur·iz·ing pas·teur·ized *v.t.* to sterilize by pasteurization

past·ies *n.* adhesive covering for a woman's nipples

pas·tille *n.* a flavored or medicated lozenge

pas·time *n.* anything that serves as recreation

pas·tor *n.* a priest or minister

pas·to·ral 1. *adj.* (of land) used for grazing ‖ dealing with idealized country life ‖ relating to the office and work of a minister **2.** *n.* a circular letter sent by a bishop

pas·try *pl.* **pas·tries** *n.* dough used baked as piecrust etc. ‖ baked goods consisting of this ‖ an individual tart, pie etc.

pas·ture *n.* grass or other vegetation that provides food for cattle etc. ‖ land which produces such vegetation

pasture pas·tur·ing pas·tured *v.i.* to feed on pasture

past·y past·i·er past·i·est *adj.* pale, flabby, or unhealthy in appearance

pat 1. *n.* a gentle stroke or blow made with something flat (esp. with the hand) ‖ the sound of a gentle blow ‖ a small, neat piece of some soft substance, esp. butter **2.** *v.t.* **pat·ting pat·ted** to give a pat to ‖ to shape with blows of the hands or of some flat implement

pat 1. *adv.* in exactly the right way or at exactly the right time **2.** *adj.* glib

patch 1. *n.* a piece of material sewed on something to mend it ‖ any of the bits of cloth which, when sewn together, form patchwork ‖ a small piece of ground ‖ a piece of cloth worn over an injured eye **2.** *v.t.* to mend by putting a patch on or over

patch·y patch·i·er patch·i·est *adj.* consisting of or containing patches ‖ uneven in quality

pate *n.* the head

pa·teu *n.* an edible paste of finely minced meat or fish

pat·ent 1. *n.* an official paper guaranteeing an inventor and his heirs exclusive rights over an invention, process etc. for a given length of time ‖ this invention or process **2.** *adj.* protected by a patent ‖ of or relating to the granting of patents ‖ original and individual as if protected by a patent ‖ evident, obvious **3.** *v.t.* to obtain a patent for **pat·ent·ee** *n.* the person to whom a patent has been granted

pat·ent·ly *adv.* obviously, evidently

pa·ter·nal *adj.* of or relating to a father
pa·ter·nal·is·tic *adj.*
pa·ter·nal·is·ti·cal·ly *adv.*

pa·ter·ni·ty *n.* descent from a father, male parentage ‖ authorship or origin

path *pl.* **paths** *n.* a narrow way or trail ‖ (computer) the proper sequence for executing a routine

pa·thet·ic *adj.* arousing pity or sympathetic sorrow ‖ arousing pitying contempt
pa·thet·i·cal·ly *adv.*

path·o·log·ic *adj.* pertaining to pathology
path·o·log·i·cal *adj.* involving or resulting from disease ‖ morbid

pa·thol·o·gist *n.* a specialist in pathology

pa·thol·o·gy *n.* the study of disease and all its manifestations

pa·thos *n.* a quality which arouses profound feelings of compassion or sorrow

pa·tience *n.* the ability to wait or persevere without losing heart or becoming bored

pa·tient **1.** *adj.* showing or having patience **2.** *n.* a client of a doctor, dentist etc., whether sick or not

pat·i·na *n.* a surface formed on metal by long exposure to the air, or produced artificially by an acid

pa·ti·o *pl.* **pa·ti·os** *n.* an open courtyard enclosed by the walls of a house ‖ an area, adjoining a house, used esp. for outdoor cooking or dining

pat·ois *n.* the speech or dialect peculiar to one part of a country

pa·tri·arch *n.* the father or head of a family or tribe

pa·tri·ar·chy *pl.* **pa·tri·ar·chies** *n.* a social system in which the chief authority is the father or eldest male member of the family or clan

pa·tri·cian **1.** *n.* a member of one of the privileged families of ancient Rome **2.** *adj.* noble, aristocratic

pat·ri·mo·ny *pl.* **pat·ri·mo·nies** *n.* property, money etc. inherited from one's father or an ancestor

pa·tri·ot *n.* a person who loves his native country and will do all he can for it

pa·tri·ot·ic *adj.* inspired by, showing or aimed at arousing love of one's country

pa·tri·ot·i·cal·ly *adv.*

pa·tri·ot·ism *n.* zealous love of one's country

pa·trol pa·trol·ling pa·trolled *v.i.* to go the rounds of a place in order to guard it etc.

patrol *n.* a patrolling

pa·tron *n.* a person or institution that gives financial support to a cause ‖ a customer, esp. a regular one, in a shop, restaurant etc.

pat·ter **1.** *n.* the quick talk or chatter of a comedian or entertainer, salesman etc. ‖ mechanically repeated words **2.** *v.t.* to repeat mechanically without considering the meaning

patter **1.** *v.t.* to make a series of short, light, rapid taps **2.** *n.* the noise made

pat·tern **1.** *n.* an orderly sequence consisting of a number of repeated or complementary elements ‖ a style of design ‖ a model ‖ a sample **2.** *v.t.* to make or form in imitation of another person or thing

pat·ty *pl.* **pat·ties** *n.* a little pie ‖ a small, flat, cake of minced meat etc.

pau·ci·ty *n.* smallness, insufficiency

paunch *n.* a fat, protruding belly

pau·per *n.* a completely destitute person
páu·per·ism, pau·per·i·zá·tion *ns*
páu·per·ize pau·per·iz·ing pau·per·ized *v.t.* to reduce to the condition of a pauper

pause *n.* a short period of time when sound, motion or activity stops before starting again

pause paus·ing paused *v.i.* to make a pause ‖ to hesitate, stop to reflect

pave pav·ing paved *v.t.* to cover (a road, path etc.) with a surface

pave·ment *n.* any paved surface

pa·vil·ion *n.* a large tent ‖ a light building or shelter in a park etc. ‖ one of several buildings into which a large institution, is sometimes divided

paw **1.** *n.* the foot of a four-footed animal having claws ‖ a hand, esp. a clumsy or dirty one **2.** *v.t.* to strike, scrape or scratch with the paw

pawn **1.** *n.* something pawned **2.** *v.t.* to hand over as a pledge or security for a loan of money

pawn *n.* (chess) one of the men of least size and value ‖ a person whom others use for their own ends

pawn·bro·ker *n.* a person licensed to lend money on articles pawned

pay 1. pay·ing paid *v.t.* to give (someone) money in return for goods, work or services ‖ to give (someone) money owed or due ‖ to discharge ‖ *v.i.* to be profitable **2.** *adj.* (of earth) yielding oil or valuable metals ‖ made available for use by the insertion of a coin or coins in a slot

pay *n.* money received as wages or salary for work or services

pay·a·ble *adj.* that must, can, should or may be paid

pay·ment *n.* the money etc. paid for work or services ‖ something given in return, or as a reward, punishment or revenge

peace *n.* the condition that exists when nations or other groups are not fighting ‖ the ending of a state of war ‖ freedom from noise, worries, troubles, fears etc.

peace·a·ble *adj.* not given to fighting or quarreling ‖ in a state of peace **péace·a·bly** *adv.*

peace·ful *adj.* calm, quiet, untroubled ‖ not warlike or violent

peach 1. *n.* a small tree of the temperate zone. The fruit is sweet, juicy, yellow or white ‖ any particularly excellent person or thing ‖ soft, pale, yellowish red **2.** *adj.* of the color peach

pea·cock *n.* a male member of a genus of large birds

pea jacket a short, double-breasted black or navy blue overcoat worn esp. by seamen

peak *n.* a pointed top or projection ‖ the pointed top of a mountain ‖ the highest point, maximum

peaked *adj.* having a peak or point ‖ looking sickly and thin

peal 1. *n.* a loud ringing of a bell or bells ‖ a sudden burst of noise **2.** *v.i.* (of bells, thunder, laughter etc.) to ring out, burst into sudden noise

pea·nut *n.* a branched, trailing annual plant ‖ its nutlike seed

pear *n.* a tree native to W. Asia and E.

Europe ‖ its fruit

pearl *n.* a secretion, chiefly of calcium carbonate, produced by some mollusks ‖ a hard, lustrous, usually white, almost spherical deposit of this around a small solid irritant ‖ a very pale gray color with bluish overtones

pearl·y pearl·i·er pearl·i·est *adj.* of or like a pearl or mother-of-pearl

peas·ant *n.* a hired farm laborer or the owner or tenant of a small farm **péas·ant·ry** *n.*

peat *n.* a dense accumulation of water-saturated, partially decayed vegetable tissue

peat·y peat·i·er peat·i·est *adj.* of, like or consisting of peat

peb·ble 1. *n.* a small stone **2.** *v.t.* **peb·bling peb·bled** to pave or cover with pebbles **péb·bly** *adj.*

pe·can *n.* an edible, smooth-shelled, olive-shaped nut

pec·ca·dil·lo *pl.* **pec·ca·dil·los, pec·ca·dil·loes** *n.* a trifling fault or transgression

pec·cant *adj.* sinful ‖ diseased or causing disease

peck 1. *v.t.* (of a bird) to strike or make holes in with the beak ‖ to make (a hole) by striking with a rapid movement **2.** *n.* an instance of pecking ‖ a quick perfunctory kiss

pec·tin *n.* any of a group of polysaccharides occurring in plant tissues esp. in fruits

pec·to·ral 1. *adj.* of or relating to the chest or breast **2.** *n.* a pectoral muscle or fin

pec·u·late pec·u·lat·ing pec·u·lat·ed *v.t.* to embezzle **pec·u·la·tion, péc·u·la·tor** *ns*

pe·cu·liar *adj.* odd, unusual, strange **pe·cu·li·ar·i·ty** *pl.* **pe·cu·li·ar·i·ties** *n.* a distinctive characteristic ‖ an odd, unusual characteristic

pe·cu·ni·ar·y *adj.* of or relating to money

ped·a·gog·ic *adj.* having to do with teaching **ped·a·góg·i·cal** *adj.* **ped·a·góg·ics** *n.* the science of teaching

ped·a·gogue, ped·a·gog *n.* a teacher

ped·al 1. *n.* a lever operated by the foot **2.** **ped·al·ing ped·aled** *v.t.* to operate by a pedal or pedals

ped·al *adj.* of or relating to a foot

ped·ant *n.* an overprecise person who is unimaginative about using rules or knowledge **pe·dan·tic** *adj.* **pe·dan·ti·cal·ly** *adv.*

ped·ant·ry *pl.* **ped·ant·ries** *n.* the pedantic show or use of learning or knowledge

ped·dle ped·dling ped·dled *v.i.* to travel around with goods to sell **ped·dler** *n.* someone who travels about peddling goods

ped·es·tal *n.* a separate base supporting a column, statue, large vase etc.

pe·des·tri·an 1. *n.* a person going about on foot 2. *adj.* dull, commonplace, lacking imagination

pe·di·at·ric, pae·di·at·ric *adj.* of or relating to the medical care of children **pe·di·a·tri·cian, pae·di·a·tri·cian** *n.* a specialist in peadiatrics **pe·di·at·rics, pae·di·at·rics** *n.* the branch of medicine concerned with the health and illnesses of children

ped·i·cure *n.* chiropody ‖ a cleaning, cutting and polishing of the toenails

ped·i·gree *n.* a genealogical or family tree ‖ a table of descent of purebred animals ‖ ancestry **péd·i·greed** *adj.*

pe·dom·e·ter *n.* an instrument which counts the number of steps taken by a person walking and measures the approximate distance covered

peek 1. *v.i.* to peep, look, esp. in such a way as not to be seen 2. *n.* a quick or furtive look

peel 1. *v.t.* to remove the outer covering, skin, rind etc. from ‖ *v.i.* to shed an outer covering or skin 2. *n.* the rind or outer skin

peen 1. *n.* the thin end of the head of a hammer 2. *v.t.* to strike or work with a peen

peep 1. *v.i.* to take a quick look ‖ *v.t.* (with 'out') to cause to protrude a bit 2. *n.* a surreptitious, furtive glance

peep 1. *n.* the high, weak noise made by very young birds 2. *v.* to utter in a high, weak voice

peep·er *n.* a person who looks furtively

peer *n.* a member of one of the British degrees of nobility ‖ someone having the same status in rank, age, ability etc. as another **péer·age** *n.* **péer·less** *adj.* so excellent as to have no equal

peeve 1. *v.t.* **peev·ing peeved** to make peevish 2. *n.* a peevish mood

peev·ish *adj.* irritable, apt to complain

peg 1. *n.* a small piece of wood, metal, plastic etc., used to secure a joint, bung a hole, hang things on, mark the score in cribbage or darts, fasten ropes to etc. ‖ a step or degree 2. **peg·ging pegged** *v.t.* to fasten, secure or attach with a peg or pegs

peign·oir *n.* a negligee

pel·i·can *n.* a genus of large, web-footed, birds

pel·let *n.* a little ball ‖ a small piece of shot

pell-mell 1. *adv.* in great haste and confusion 2. *adj.* confused, disorderly 3. *n.* hurry and confusion

pelt 1. *v.t.* to throw (objects) continuously ‖ *v.i.* (e.g. of rain) to pour or beat down continually with force 2. *n.* a hard blow

pelt *n.* the skin of an animal with the hair or wool on

pel·vic *adj.* related to or situated at or near the pelvis

pel·vis *pl.* **pel·vis·es, pel·ves** *n.* a bony cavity in vertebrates, formed in man by the pelvic girdle together with the coccyx and sacrum

pen 1. *n.* an instrument for writing in ink 2. *v.t.* **pen·ning penned** to write

pen pen·ning penned (with 'in', 'up')*v.t.* to shut up in a confined space

pe·nal *adj.* concerned with esp. legal punishment of crime ‖ legally punishable **pé·nal·ize pe·nal·iz·ing pe·nal·ized** *v.t.* to inflict a penalty upon **pe·nal·i·zá·tion** *n.*

pen·al·ty *pl.* **pen·al·ties** *n.* a punishment for committing an offense ‖ a disagreeable consequence ‖ (games) a disadvantage imposed as punishment for breaking the rules

pen·ance *n.* punishment or suffering undergone voluntarily to atone for sin or wrongdoing

pen·chant *n.* an inclination towards, a liking for

pen·cil 1. *n.* an instrument for writing or drawing with core of graphite or black lead ‖ a long, converging, narrow beam of light **2.** *v.t.* **pen·cil·ing pen·ciled** to write, draw or mark in pencil

pen·dant 1. *n.* something suspended ‖ a piece of jewelry hanging from a chain ‖ a companion piece **2.** *adj.* pendent

pen·dent *adj.* hanging ‖ overhanging ‖ undetermined, pending

pend·ing 1. *adj.* in process of being decided, settled, arranged etc. ‖ about to happen **2.** prep. until

pen·du·lum *n.* a body suspended from a pivot and able to swing to and fro

pen·e·tra·ble *adj.* capable of being penetrated **pén·e·tra·bly** *adv.*

pen·e·trate pen·e·trat·ing pen·e·trat·ed *v.* to spread through ‖ to discern ‖ to make or force a way ‖ to discern the truth or meaning of something obscure **pén·e·trat·ing** *adj.*

pen·e·tra·tion *n.* the act of penetrating ‖ keenness of mind, insight

pen·e·tra·tive *adj.* penetrating

pen·guin *n.* aquatic, flightless bird of Antarctic regions

pen·i·cil·lin *n.* a mixture of antibiotic substances produced by molds

pen·in·su·la *n.* a piece of land that is almost an island with the sea on three sides **pen·ín·su·lar** *adj.*

pe·nis *pl.* **pe·nes pe·nis·es** *n.* the male organ of copulation in mammals

pen·i·tence *n.* the quality or state of being penitent

pen·i·tent 1. *adj.* feeling or showing sorrow for having sinned or done wrong **2.** *n.* a penitent person

pen·i·ten·tia·ry *pl.* **pen·i·ten·tia·ries** *n.* a prison

pen·nant *n.* a long, narrow, tapering flag

pen·ni·less *adj.* having no money or virtually none

pen·ny *pl.* **pen·nies** *n.* a U.S. or Canadian coin worth one cent

pe·nol·o·gist *n.* a specialist in penology

pe·nol·o·gy *n.* the study of how to treat criminals and of how prisons or other establishments for their reform should be organized

pen·sion *n.* a sum of money paid regularly to a person who no longer works because of age, disablement etc., or to his widow or dependent children, by the state, by his former employers, or from funds to which he and his employers have both contributed **pén·sion·a·ble** *adj.* entitled to a pension

pen·sion·er *n.* a person who receives a pension

pen·sive *adj.* deep in serious thought

pent *adj.* shut in, confined

pen·ta·gon *n.* a plane figure with five angles and five sides **pen·tag·o·nal** *adj.*

pen·tath·lon *n.* an athletic competition in which each competitor has to take part in five events

pent·house *pl.* **pent·hous·es** *n.* a rooftop apartment or other structure

pe·num·bra *pl.* **pe·num·bras, pe·num·brae** *n.* the partial shadow cast by a body where light from a given source is not wholly excluded, e.g. in an eclipse **pe·núm·bral** *adj.*

pe·nu·ri·ous *adj.* poor or showing extreme poverty

pen·u·ry *n.* poverty ‖ lack, scarcity

pe·on *n.* a laborer, esp. formerly one compelled to work for a master in order to work off a debt ‖ any laborer **pe·on·age** *n.* servitude of any kind

pe·o·ny *pl.* **pe·o·nies** *n.* a genus of usually herbaceous plants native to Europe and Asia

peo·ple 1. *pl. n.* human beings ‖ other persons in general ‖ a collective group of persons **2.** *v.t.* **peo·pling peo·pled** to populate ‖ to fill as if with people

pep 1. *n.* energy, liveliness **2.** *v.t.* **pep·ping pepped** to put new life into

pep·per 1. *n.* a product consisting of the dried, usually ground fruit of a plant native to the East Indies used universally as a seasoning ‖ this plant **2.** *v.t.* to season with

pep·per·mint *n.* a small, perennial, aromatic plant

pep·tic *adj.* relating to digestion or to gastric juice

per- prefix through, throughout ‖ thoroughly, completely

per prep. for each ‖ by means of

per·am·bu·late per·am·bu·lat·ing per·am·bu·lat·ed v.t. to walk through

per·am·bu·la·tor n. (Br.) a baby carriage

per an·num adv. (abbr. per an.) yearly

per·cale n. a closely woven cotton material

per cap·i·ta adv. and adj. (abbr. per cap.) per head of population for each person

per·ceive per·ceiv·ing per·ceived v.t. to become aware of

per·cent (abbr. p.c., pct, per ct. symbol %) **1.** adv. in a hundred, for each hundred **2.** pl. **per·cent, per·cents** n. a hundredth part **per·cent·age** n. rate or proportion per hundred ‖ a proportion

per·cept n. a recognizable mental impression

per·cep·ti·ble adj. capable of being perceived **per·cép·ti·bly** adv.

per·cep·tion n. the act of perceiving ‖ the ability to perceive, esp. to understand **per·cép·tion·al** adj.

per·cep·tive adj. having or showing keen understanding or insight **per·cep·tiv·i·ty** n.

perch n. a small, edible freshwater fish

perch n. anything on which a bird alights or rests ‖ any resting place, esp. an elevated or temporary one

perch v.i. (of a bird) to alight or sit ‖ to sit or settle on or as if on a perch

per·chance adv. perhaps, maybe

per·co·late per·co·lat·ing per·co·lat·ed v.i. to seep through a porous substance ‖ to become diffused ‖ (of coffee) to be brewed in a percolator

per·co·la·tor n. a machine for preparing coffee as a drink

per·cus·sion n. the act of causing one body to make a sudden impact on another ‖ percussion instruments collectively

per di·em 1. adv. daily, by the day **2.** adj. daily, a per diem allowance

per·di·tion n. damnation, eternal death

per·emp·to·ry adj. imperious, curtly authoritative ‖ final, absolute

per·en·ni·al 1. adj. perpetual, long-lasting ‖ living more than two years **2.** n. perennial plant

per·fect 1. adj. complete or correct in every way ‖ utter, absolute **2.** n. the perfect tense **3.** v.t. to put the finishing touches to

per·fec·tion n. the quality or state of being perfect **per·féc·tion·ist** n. a person who is not content with anything less than the very best

per·fi·dy pl. **per·fi·dies** n. treachery, faithlessness

per·fo·rate per·fo·rat·ing per·fo·rat·ed v.t. to pierce ‖ to make a row of holes through (paper etc.)

per·fo·ra·tion n. a perforating or being perforated ‖ a small hole cut or punched into something ‖ a series of holes made in paper etc. to facilitate division

per·fo·ra·tor n. a machine for making perforations

per·force adv. through necessity

per·form v.t. to do, fulfill, carry out, accomplish ‖ to render, execute ‖ v.i. to execute a stage role, play, piece of music etc. **per·fór·mance** n.

per·form·ance n. what is accomplished

per·fume n. a sweet smell ‖ a sweet-smelling liquid for personal use

per·fume per·fum·ing per·fumed v.t. to give a sweet smell to ‖ to apply perfume to **per·fúm·er·y** pl. **per·fum·er·ies** n. a place where perfumes are manufactured

per·func·to·ry adj. behaving or performing in an offhand manner

per·haps adv. possibly, maybe

per·i·gee n. the point in the orbit of the moon when it is nearest to the earth

per·i·he·li·on pl. **per·i·he·li·a** n. the point of a comet's or planet's orbit when it is nearest to the sun

per·il n. risk of serious injury, destruction, disaster, etc.

per·il·ous adj. involving or exposing one to peril

per·im·e·ter n. the line bounding a closed plane figure or an area on the ground ‖ the length of this line **per·i·met·ric** adj.

pe·ri·od 1. n. a portion of time forming a division in a development, life, chronology, timetable ‖ the symbol (.) ‖ a single menstruation ‖ a division of geological time, part of an era **2.** *adj.* having the characteristics of a particular historical period

pe·ri·od·ic *adj.* recurring intermittently **pe·ri·ód·i·cal 1.** *adj.* periodic ‖ (of a magazine etc.) published at regular intervals **2.** *n.* a periodical publication

per·i·pa·tet·ic *adj.* moving about from place to place **per·i·pa·tét·i·cal·ly** *adv.*

pe·riph·er·y *pl.* **pe·riph·er·ies** *n.* the line bounding a figure ‖ the outermost part of something ‖ the boundary or outer surface of a space or body

per·i·scope *n.* a tubular optical device used in submarines etc.

per·ish *v.i.* to suffer utter ruin or destruction **pér·ish·a·ble** *adj.* liable to decay or deterioration **pér·ish·a·bles** *pl. n.* perishable goods **pér·ish·ing** *adj.* (of cold, pain etc.) extreme

per·i·to·ne·um, per·i·to·nae·um *pl.* **per·i·to·ne·a, per·i·to·nae·a** *n.* the membrane lining the abdominal viscera

per·jure per·jur·ing per·jured *v. refl.* to make (oneself) guilty of perjury **per·jur·er** *n.* a person guilty of perjury

per·ju·ry *pl.* **per·ju·ries** *n.* telling a lie when under oath to tell the truth ‖ failure to do what one has sworn on oath to do

perk *v.t.* (with 'up') to restore good spirits or courage to

per·ma·nent 1. *adj.* continuing and enduring without change **2.** *n.* a permanent wave

per·me·a·ble *adj.* able to be permeated

per·me·ate per·me·at·ing per·me·at·ed *v.t.* to pervade, soak through **per·me·á·tion** *n.*

per·mis·si·ble *adj.* that may be permitted **per·mís·si·bly** *adv.*

per·mis·sion *n.* freedom, power, privilege etc. which one person or authority grants to another

permit 1. *v.* **per·mit·ting per·mit·ted** *v.t.* to give voluntarily or officially some right, opportunity, power etc. ‖ to accept or agree to (something) **2.** *n.* a license

per·mu·ta·tion *n.* a change or the process of changing

per·mute per·mut·ing per·mut·ed *v.t.* to change

per·ni·cious *adj.* destructive, extremely injurious, or deadly

per·o·ra·tion *n.* the concluding portion of a speech

per·pen·dic·u·lar 1. *adj.* at right angles to the horizontal

per·pe·trate per·pe·trat·ing per·pe·trat·ed *v.t.* to commit, perform (something bad) **per·pe·trá·tion, pér·pe·tra·tor** *ns*

per·pet·u·al 1. *adj.* eternal, everlasting ‖ constant, continual

per·pet·u·ate per·pet·u·at·ing per·pet·u·at·ed *v.t.* to cause to continue ‖ to save from oblivion **per·pet·u·á·tion, per·pét·u·a·tor** *ns*

per·plex *v.t.* to make (someone) uncertain about something difficult to understand ‖ to complicate

per·qui·site *n.* an extra profit or item received over and above one's agreed wage ‖ a tip, gratuity

per se *adv.* intrinsically, considered independently of other things

per·se·cute per·se·cut·ing per·se·cut·ed *v.t.* to vex, harass

per·se·cu·tion *n.* a persecuting or being persecuted

per·se·ver·ance *n.* the quality of being persistent and persevering ‖ the act of persevering

per·se·vere per·se·ver·ing per·se·vered *v.i.* to try hard and continuously in spite of obstacles and difficulties

per·si·flage *n.* light and bantering speech, writing etc.

per·sist *v.i.* to continue, esp. in spite of opposition or difficulties ‖ to continue to exist

per·sist·ence *n.* the quality or state of being persistent

per·sist·ent *adj.* continuing in spite of opposition ‖ enduring ‖ (of a disorder) not readily cured

per·snick·et·y *adj.* fastidious, finicky, fussy ‖ complex

person *n.* a man, woman or child, regarded as having a distinct individuality or personality, or as distinguished from an animal or thing **in person** being physically present

per·son·a·ble *adj.* good-looking

per·son·al 1. *adj.* belonging or particular to one person, private ‖ done by oneself, in person **2.** *n.* (esp. *pl.*) newspaper paragraphs about individual persons, or containing paid personal messages to individuals

per·son·al·i·ty *pl.* **per·son·al·i·ties** *n.* the total of the characteristics that make up the individual, esp. as others see him ‖ an eminent or famous person ‖ pronounced individuality

per·son·al·ly *adv.* in a personal way ‖ in person, not using an agent ‖ for one's part

per·son·i·fi·ca·tion *n.* the treating of an abstract quality or thing as if it had human qualities a ‖ a person regarded as the embodiment of a quality

per·son·i·fy per·son·i·fy·ing per·son·i·fied *v.t.* to treat (an abstraction, thing or inanimate object) as a person

per·son·nel *n.* the body of employees in a business

per·spec·tive *n.* the appearance of objects with reference to distance, relative position etc. ‖ relative importance ‖ evaluation of events according to a particular way of looking at them

per·spi·ca·cious *adj.* having clear insight

per·spic·u·ous *adj.* clearly expressed so as to be easily understood

per·spi·ra·tion *n.* sweat ‖ the act of sweating

per·spire per·spir·ing per·spired *v.i.* and *t.* to sweat

per·suade per·suad·ing per·suad·ed *v.t.* to cause (someone) to do or to believe something by reasoning etc.

per·sua·sion *n.* a persuading or being persuaded ‖ a strongly held conviction

pert *adj.* jaunty ‖ in good spirits, lively

per·tain *v.i.* to be a natural part ‖ to be suitable ‖ to have reference

per·ti·nent *adj.* referring centrally to the matter being discussed or considered

per·turb *v.t.* to cause to be anxious

pe·ruse pe·rus·ing pe·rused *v.t.* to read through carefully or critically

per·vade per·vad·ing per·vad·ed *v.t.* to spread throughout and into every part of

per·va·sion *n.* **per·va·sive** *adj.* pervading or tending to pervade

per·verse *adj.* obstinate, intractable

per·ver·sion *n.* a deviation from usual esp. sexual behavior

per·vert 1. *v.t.* to cause to be misused, falsified, wrongly understood etc. **2.** *n.* a person who is perverted, esp. someone given to homosexuality or other abnormal sexual practices

per·vi·ous *adj.* capable of being permeated ‖ (with 'to') willing to be influenced

pes·ky pes·ki·er pes·ki·est *adj.* annoyingly troublesome

pes·si·mism *n.* the tendency to expect the worst or to stress the worst aspect of things

pés·si·mist **pes·si·mís·tic** *adj.* **pes·si·mís·ti·cal·ly** *adv.*

pest *n.* an animal which is destructive to crops ‖ a tiresome, annoying person ‖ the plague

pes·ter *v.t.* to annoy

pest·i·cide *n.* a susbtance, e.g. an insecticide, used for destroying pests

pes·ti·lence *n.* a deadly epidemic disease ‖ something morally or socially pernicious

pes·tle *n.* any of several instruments used for pounding or stamping

pet 1. *n.* a tame animal kept as a companion ‖ someone who is treated as a favorite **2.** *adj.* kept as a pet ‖ favorite **3. pet·ting pet·ted** *v.t.* to pat or caress ‖ to pamper

pet·al *n.* one of the colored, modified leaves forming part of the corolla of a flower

pe·tite *adj.* (of a person) small and neat in figure

pe·ti·tion 1. *n.* a formal request **2.** *v.t.* to make a petition to (someone) for something

pe·tri·fy pet·ri·fy·ing pet·ri·fied *v.t.* to turn (an organic structure) into stone, or a substance hard as stone ‖ to render (a person) rigid or numb with fear or horror

pe·trog·ra·phy *n.* the scientific classification of rocks

pe·tro·le·um *n.* an oily liquid mixture of complex hydrocarbons, natural gas

pet·ti·coat *n.* an undergarment

pet·ty pet·ti·er pet·ti·est *adj.* minor, trivial

pet·u·lance *n.* the quality or state of being petulant

pet·u·lant *adj.* discontented and irritable over trifles

pew *n.* a long bench with a back used as church furniture

pew·ter *n.* any of several gray alloys of tin, usually with lead

pe·yo·te *n.* any of several cacti growing in the southwest U.S.A. and Mexico, esp. mescal ‖ a stimulant from mescal buttons

phal·lic *adj.* of or relating to a phallus

phal·lus *pl.* **phal·li** *n.* a symbol of the penis

phan·tasm *n.* an illusion ‖ a ghostly apparition

phan·tom 1. *n.* something that appears to be seen but that has no real physical existence **2.** *adj.* illusory

phar·aoh *n.* the title of ancient Egyptian kings **phar·a·on·ic** *adj.*

phar·ma·ceu·tic *adj.* of or relating to pharmacy **phar·ma·céu·ti·cal** *adj.* **phar·ma·céu·tics** *n.* the science of the preparation and use of medicines

phar·ma·cist *n.* a person skilled in pharmacy

phar·ma·col·o·gy *n.* the study of the preparation, properties, use and effects of drugs

phar·ma·cy *pl.* **phar·ma·cies** *n.* the art or profession of dispensing drugs ‖ a drugstore

phase *n.* **1.** each of the successive aspects or stages in any course of change or development **2.** *v.t.* **phas·ing phased** to cause to be in phase **phá·sic** *adj.*

pheas·ant *n.* long-tailed gallinaceous game birds

phe·no·bar·bi·tal *n.* phenylethylbarbituric acid, used medicinally as a hypnotic and sedative

phe·nom·e·nal *adj.* extraordinary, unusual

phe·nom·e·non *pl.* **phe·nom·e·na** *n.* any fact or event which can be described and explained in scientific terms ‖ an extraordinary or remarkable event, thing, person etc.

phi·lan·der *v.i.* (of a man) to have many but casual love affairs **phi·lan·der·er** *n.*

phil·an·throp·ic *adj.* doing good works, benevolent **phil·an·thróp·i·cal** *adj.*

phil·an·thro·pist *n.* a humanitarian

phil·an·thro·py *pl.* **phil·an·thro·pies** *n.* generous help or benevolence toward one's fellow men

phil·a·tel·ic *adj.* relating to philately

phi·lat·el·ist *n.* an expert in philately ‖ a stamp collector

phi·lat·e·ly *n.* the collection and study of postage stamps, etc., usually as a hobby

phil·har·mon·ic *adj.* loving music

phi·lol·o·gist *n.* a specialist in philology

phi·lol·o·gy *n.* the study of language from the written texts by which it is known

phi·los·o·pher *n.* a person who engages in the study of philosophy

phil·o·soph·ic *adj.* of or relating to philosophy **phil·o·sóph·i·cal** *adj.*

phi·los·o·phize phi·los·o·phiz·ing phi·los·o·phized *v.i.* to theorize ‖ to moralize

phi·los·o·phy *pl.* **phi·los·o·phies** *n.* the love or pursuit of wisdom ‖ systematized principles of any subject or branch of knowledge ‖ an attitude towards life ‖ calm resignation

phlegm *n.* mucus ‖ self-possession

phleg·mat·ic *adj.* imperturbable **phleg·mát·i·cal** *adj.*

pho·bia *n.* morbid and often irrational dread of some specific thing

phoe·nix, phe·nix *n.* (*Egypt. mythol.*) a bird sacred to the sun, reborn from the ashes of the funeral pyre which it made for itself

pho·net·ic *adj.* of or relating to vocal sounds and speech **pho·nét·i·cal·ly** *adv.*

pho·ne·ti·cian *n.* a specialist in phonetics **pho·nét·ics** *n.* the branch of language study concerned with the production of speech sounds

phon·ics *n.* the use of sound-symbol (phoneme-grapheme) relationships in the teaching of reading

pho·no·graph *n.* a machine for reproducing sounds recorded on a disk or cylinder **pho·no·gráph·ic** *adj.* **pho·no·gráph·i·cal·ly** *adv.*

pho·nog·ra·phy *n.* a phonetic spelling or writing

pho·ny, pho·ney pho·ni·er pho·ni·est 1. *adj.* not genuine, counterfeit **2.** *pl.* **pho·nies** *n.* a person who is not what he pretends to be

phos·pho·res·cence *n.* a luminescence

phos·pho·res·cent *adj.* exhibiting phosphorescence

pho·to·cop·y 1. *pl.* **pho·to·cop·ies** *n.* a photographic reproduction of a document, illustration, etc. **2.** *v.t.* **pho·to·cop·y·ing pho·to·cop·ied** to make a photocopy of

pho·to·e·lec·tric *adj.* of any of the factors involved in the effect of electromagnetic radiation on the electrical behavior of matter

pho·to·en·grav·ing *n.* a process by which a printing block is made from a photograph

photo finish the finish of a race so close that a photograph at the finish line is required to identify the winner

pho·to·gen·ic *adj.* photographing to advantage ‖ causing or producing light

pho·to·graph 1. *n.* a reproduction made by photography **2.** *v.t.* to take a picture of by photography **pho·tog·ra·pher** *n.* a person who practices photography

pho·to·graph·ic *adj.* pertaining to photography **pho·to·gráph·i·cal·ly** *adv.*

pho·tog·ra·phy *n.* the art, process of producing photographs

pho·to·sen·si·tive *adj.* affected by the incidence of light **pho·to·sen·si·tív·i·ty** *n.*

pho·to·stat 1. *n.* a machine used to make photographs of documents etc. ‖ a photograph thus made **2.** *v.t.* **pho·to·stat·ing pho·to·stat·ed** to make a photostatic copy of **pho·to·stát·ic** *adj.*

pho·to·syn·the·sis *n.* the synthesis of chemical substances with the aid of light

phrase 1. *n.* a sequence of words expressing a single idea ‖ an expression that is pithy or idiomatic **2.** *v.t.* **phras·ing phrased** to express in words

phra·se·ol·o·gy *n.* manner of using and arranging words

phy·lum *pl.* **phy·la** *n.* the primary division of classification in the plant or animal kingdom

phys·i·cal *adj.* of or pertaining to matter or nature ‖ pertaining to the body (in contrast to the mind)

phy·si·cian *n.* a doctor of medicine

phys·i·cist *n.* a specialist in physics

phys·ics *n.* the science of matter and energy

phys·i·og·no·my *pl.* **phys·i·og·no·mies** *n.* the facial features as indicative of character

phys·i·ol·o·gy *n.* the branch of biology concerned with the functions of living organisms

phy·sique *n.* the form, structure, organization or constitution of a person's body

pi·a·nis·si·mo *(abbr. app.)* **1.** *adj.* very soft **2.** *adv.* very softly

pi·an·ist *n.* a person who plays the piano

pi·a·no 1. *adv.* softly **2.** *adj.* soft **3.** *pl.* **pi·a·ni pi·a·nos** *n.* a passage rendered softly

pi·an·o *pl.* **pi·an·os** *n.* a musical stringed percussion instrument

pi·ca *n.* (printing) a size of type

pic·a·yune 1. *n.* anything of little value **2.** *adj.* of very small value **pic·a·yún·ish** *adj.* trivial

pic·ca·lil·li *pl.* **pic·ca·lil·lis** *n.* a relish of chopped vegetables and pungent spices

pic·co·lo *pl.* **pic·co·los** *n.* a small flute

pick 1. *v.t.* to gather ‖ to choose or select ‖ to probe or scratch with an instrument or with one's fingers ‖ to steal from ‖ to pluck (the strings of a banjo, guitar etc.) ‖ to open (a lock) with a wire etc. instead of with a key ‖ to find an opportunity or pretext for, and begin (a quarrel, fight etc.) ‖ *v.i.* to work with a pick ‖ to eat sparingly or with small bites **2.** *n.* the act of selecting ‖ the right or privilege of selecting ‖ the person or thing selected ‖ someone or something selected as the best

pick *n.* a pickaxe ‖ any of several tools used for picking, e.g. an ice pick ‖ a plectrum

pick·et 1. *n.* a group of workers posted to dissuade other workers or clients from entering their place of work during a strike ‖ a member of such a group ‖ a pointed stake **2.** *v.t.* to act as a picket at ‖ to post (men) as a picket

pick·le 1. *n.* a liquid in which food is

preserved || food or a piece of food (e.g. a cucumber) so preserved || an awkward situation, sorry plight 2. *v.t.* **pick·ling pick·led** to preserve in, or treat with, a pickle

pick·pock·et *n.* a person who picks people's pockets

pick·up *n.* recovery || a person whose acquaintance one makes casually || acceleration, esp. of a car || a light truck used esp. for deliveries

pick·y pick·i·er pick·i·est *adj.* choosy

pic·nic 1. *n.* an outing in which the people involved eat a meal outdoors || something easy or pleasant to do or experience **2.** *v.i.* **pic·nick·ing pic·nicked** to have or participate in a picnic **pic·nick·er** *n.*

pic·to·ri·al *adj.* of, containing, expressing or illustrating by pictures

pic·ture 1. *n.* a representation or image on a surface, e.g. a painting, drawing, print or photograph || a perfect likeness || a type, symbol || a mental image, idea || a film, movie || a picturesque sight **2.** *v.t.* **pic·tur·ing pic·tured** to imagine || to depict

pic·tur·esque *adj.* (of scenery, landscapes etc.) full of charm || (of language etc.) strikingly vivid

pid·dle pid·dling pid·dled *v.i.* to trifle, waste time || to urinate || *v.t.* (with 'away') to pass (time etc.) wastefully **píd·dling** *adj.* trivial

pie *n.* a dish of fruit, meat etc., baked with a crust

pie·bald *adj.* marked in patches of two different colors

piece 1. *n.* a distinct part, separated or broken off from a whole || a single unit || belonging to a set || a coin of a specified kind || a musical or literary composition || not broken **2.** *v.t.* **piec·ing pieced** to mend or patch by adding a piece || (with 'together') to join (things) so that they make a whole

piece de ré·sis·tance *n.* the choice item in a collection or series

piece·meal *adj.* done bit by bit

piece·work *n.* work paid for by the amount done

pied *adj.* parti-colored

pier *n.* a breakwater of masonry || a structure built to extend for some distance into the sea used to give passengers access to vessels

pierce pierc·ing pierced *v.t.* to make a hole in or through || to make a way into or through **pierc·ing** *adj.* penetrating sharply or deeply

pi·e·ty *pl.* **pi·e·ties** *n.* devotion and reverence for God || an act which shows this quality

pig *n.* a young hog || a greedy, dirty or selfish person **a pig in a poke** something which one buys or accepts without seeing it first **to make a pig of oneself** to eat too much

pi·geon *n.* a large family of birds of worldwide distribution

pi·geon·hole 1. *n.* a recess in a desk, cabinet etc. for keeping letters, papers etc. **2.** *v.t.* **pi·geon·hol·ing pi·geon·holed** to put away for future attention or indefinitely

pi·geon-toed *adj.* having the toes turned inwards

pig·gy·back 1. *adj.* of a transport system by which road-haulage loads in their vehicles are carried by rail **2.** *adv.* on the back and shoulders **3.** *n.* a ride made piggyback

pig·head·ed *adj.* stupidly obstinate

pig iron the impure iron

pig·ment *n.* coloring matter

pig·men·ta·tion *n.* coloring or discoloring, esp. in tissues, as a result of pigment

pig·skin *n.* leather made from a hog's skin || a football

pig·tail *n.* a braid of hair

pike *pl.* **pike, pikes** *n.* a genus of voracious freshwater fishes

pike *n.* a gate or bar across a road where a toll is paid || a road, esp. one on which a toll is levied || a toll

pi·laf, pi·laff, pi·lau *n.* an Oriental dish of rice boiled with fish, meat or chicken and spices

pile 1. *n.* a stout beam driven vertically into unfirm ground as a support for a superstructure **2.** *v.t.* **pil·ing piled** to support with piles

pile 1. *n.* a number of things lying one

upon another ‖ a large amount of **2. pil·ing piled** *v.i.* to crowd together ‖ (esp. with 'up') to come together in or as if in a pile

pile *n.* soft down, fur, hair or wool

pile driver a machine used to drive piles into the ground

piles *pl. n.* hemorrhoids

pil·fer *v.t.* to steal in small quantities

pil·grim *n.* a person who makes a journey to some sacred place as an act of religious devotion

pill *n.* a pellet of medicine ‖ (with 'the') an oral contraceptive ‖ a disagreeable person

pil·lage 1. *n.* the act of taking goods by force **2. pil·lag·ing pil·laged** *v.t.* to plunder

pil·lar 1. *n.* a vertical structure of masonry, metal etc., of much greater height than thickness ‖ a chief supporter of a cause or institution **2.** *n.* to support or ornament with pillars

pil·lo·ry 1. *pl.* **pil·lo·ries** *n.* a wooden framework with three holes into which the head and hands of an offender were locked, exposing him to public abuse and ridicule **2.** *v.t.* **pil·lo·ry·ing pil·lo·ried** to set in a pillory ‖ to expose to public scorn

pil·low *n.* a rest and support for the neck or head of a recumbent person ‖ a block, e.g. of wood, used as a cushioning support

pil·low·case *n.* a loose, removable cover of cotton or linen for a pillow

pi·lot 1. *n.* a person qualified to direct a vessel on its course ‖ a person qualified to operate an aircraft ‖ a machine part which guides another part in its movement **2.** *adj.* serving as an experimental model for others to follow

pilot *v.t.* to act as the pilot of ‖ to guide

pi·men·to *pl.* **pi·men·tos** *n.* allspice ‖ the pimientoe

pi·mien·to *pl.* **pi·mien·tos** *n.* any of certain red sweet peppers, a source of paprika etc.

pimp 1. *n.* a male procurer of clients for a prostitute **2.** *v.i.* to act as a pimp

pim·ple *n.* a small, rounded, raised area on the skin, caused by inflammation etc. **pim·pled, pim·ply** adjs

pin 1. *n.* a short, thin, sharp-pointed length of metal, with a small, flat head at one end, used to fasten textiles, paper etc. ‖ any of several fastening devices, e.g. a hairpin or safety pin, or a wooden peg used in carpentry ‖ a brooch **2.** *v.t.* **pin·ning pinned** to fasten a pin

pin·a·fore *n.* a sleeveless, apronlike garment

pin·ball *n.* a game played on a pinball machine

pinball machine a glass-covered slot machine

pin·cers *pl. n.* a tool consisting of two arms used to crush, extract nails, grip etc. ‖ the chela of certain crustaceans

pinch 1. *v.t.* to grip between the forefinger and thumb with strong pressure ‖ to squeeze ‖ to steal ‖ to arrest ‖ *v.i.* to exert painful pressure by squeezing ‖ be stingy **2.** *n.* an amount which can be taken up between the forefinger and thumb **in a pinch** if absolutely necessary

pinch-hit pinch-hit·ting pinch-hit *v.i.* to act as substitute

pinch hitter (baseball) a player who hits for another ‖ someone who acts as a substitute

pine *n.* a genus of coniferous trees with needlelike evergreen leaves ‖ the wood of any of these trees

pine pin·ing pined *v.i.* to lose vitality gradually through hunger, unhappiness etc. ‖ to long for

pine·ap·ple *n.* a perennial tropical plant widely cultivated for its fruit

ping *n.* a sharp ringing sound

pin·hole *n.* a hole made by a pin

pin·ion *n.* the smallest toothed of two gear wheels

pinion 1. *n.* a flight feather of a bird's wing **2.** *v.t.* to cut off or bind the wings of (a bird) to prevent flight ‖ to make (someone) powerless by binding his arms

pink 1. *n.* a genus of plants cultivated for their fragrant, white, pale red or crimson flowers ‖ a pale, bluish-red color **2.** *adj.* having the color pink

pink·eye *n.* a highly contagious form of conjunctivitise

pin·na·cle 1. *n.* a slender peak of rock ‖ the highest point, climax **2.** *v.t.* **pin·na·cling pin·na·cled** to place on a pinnacle ‖ to be the pinnacle of

pin·point 1. *n.* the pointed end of a pin **2.** *v.t.* to locate precisely ‖ to direct (an attack) with great accuracy **3.** *adj.* requiring extreme accuracy of aim

pint *n.* liquid or dry units of capacity

pin·to *pl.* **pin·tos** *n.* a pony or horse that is mottled ‖ a pinto bean

pi·o·neer 1. *n.* a person who plays a leading part in the early development of something ‖ an early settler **2.** *v.t.* to explore and be among the first to develop (a region etc.)

pi·ous *adj.* devout or showing religious devotion

pipe pip·ing piped *v.t.* to convey through pipes ‖ to play (a tune) on a pipe ‖ *v.i.* to play a pipe, esp. the bagpipes

pipe *n.* a long hollow cylinder, used chiefly to convey fluids, gas etc. ‖ a musical wind instrument ‖ a tubular organ, vessel etc. in the body ‖ a device for smoking ‖ a boatswain's whistle or the sounding of it ‖ (*pl.*) bagpipes

pipe·line *n.* a long line of pipes used to convey liquids or gases ‖ a channel of communication or transport

pi·quant *adj.* sharply stimulating the sense of taste ‖ stimulating the curiosity or interest

pique piqu·ing piqued *v.t.* to cause resentment in ‖ to stimulate, arouse

pique *n.* resentment caused by injured self-esteem

pi·qué *n.* stiff fabric of esp. cotton with a ribbed surface

pi·ra·cy *pl.* **pi·ra·cies** *n.* robbery of ships at sea ‖ unauthorized use of a patented or copyrighted work

pi·rate 1. *n.* someone who commits piracy **2.** *v.* **pi·rat·ing pi·rat·ed** *v.t.* to use (another's copyright material) without permission **pi·rat·ic pi·rát·i·cal** *adjs*

pi·rogue *n.* a dugout canoe

pir·ou·ette 1. *n.* a rapid spin or whirl of the body on the point of the toe esp. in ballet **2.** *v.i.* **pir·ou·et·ting pir·ou·et·ted** to execute a pirouette

pis·ta·chi·o *pl.* **pis·ta·chi·os** *n.* a small tree. Its fruit contains an edible seed, the pistachio nut ‖ the yellowish-green color of the nut

pis·til *n.* the female seedbearing organ of a flower **pis·til·late** *adj.* having or bearing a pistil

pis·tol *n.* a small firearm held and fired with one hand

pis·ton *n.* a disk fitted closely inside a hollow cylinder, within which it can be driven up and down by fluid pressure

pit 1. *n.* a deep hole in the ground ‖ a coal mine ‖ the space, often depressed, in front of the stage in a theater, where the orchestra sits **2.** **pit·ting pit·ted** *v.t.* (with 'against') to match (one's strength, courage, willpower) against another's ‖ to make a pit in (the skin etc.)

pit 1. *n.* the stone of a peach, cherry, plum etc. **2.** *v.t.* **pit·ting pit·ted** to remove the pit from

pitch 1. *n.* a dark-colored, sticky, substance which is a residue from distillation of tars, turpentine or fatty oils etc. **2.** *v.t.* to coat or smear with pitch

pitch 1. *v.t.* to fix and set up ‖ (baseball, cricket) to throw or deliver (the ball) to the batter or batsman ‖ *v.i.* to encamp ‖ to dip, slope **2.** *n.* the act of pitching ‖ the quality of a sound with respect to the frequency of vibration of the sound waves ‖ the degree of slope of something ‖ the pitching motion of a ship ‖ a line of talk

pitch·er *n.* a jug for holding liquids

pitcher *n.* a person who pitches, esp. (baseball) ‖ (golf) an iron used for short approach shots to the green

pitch·fork *n.* a longhandled fork for lifting and turning hay, straw etc.

pit·e·ous *adj.* arousing pity

pit·fall *n.* a hidden danger or difficulty

pith *n.* the central region of parenchymatous cells in the stem of a vascular plant ‖ the substance or gist of a matter ‖ forceful relevance

pith·y pith·i·er pith·i·est *adj.* forcefully concise, terse

pit·i·a·ble *adj.* arousing or deserving pity

‖ arousing or deserving pitying contempt
pit·i·a·bly *adv.*

pit·i·ful *adj.* calling forth compassion ‖
contemptible

pit·i·less *adj.* showing or feeling no pity

pit·tance *n.* a very small allowance

pi·tu·i·tar·y gland a small vascular endocrine gland located at the base of the brain

pit·y 1. *pl.* **pit·ies** *n.* a feeling of sympathy for the sufferings or privations of others ‖ compassion **2.** *v.t.* **pit·y·ing pit·ied** to feel pity for

piv·ot *n.* a fixed shaft or pin having a pointed end which acts as the point of balance upon which a plate or bar can turn or oscillate ‖ a person, thing or fact on which a set of circumstances etc. depends

pivot *v.t.* to balance on a pivot ‖ *v.i.* to turn on a pivot

pix·ie, pix·y *pl.* **pix·ies** *n.* a small, mischievous fairy

pix·i·lat·ed, pix·il·lat·ed slightly crazy

pi·zazz *n.* a provocative vitality

piz·za *n.* a flat, breadlike crust spread with tomatoes, cheese and sometimes other ingredients and baked

piz·zi·ca·to *adj.* plucking the strings with the finger

plac·a·ble *adj.* easily placated ‖ showing tolerance or forgiveness

plac·ard 1. *n.* a notice for advertising **2.** *v.t.* to advertise by such means ‖ to display as a placard

pla·cate pla·cat·ing pla·cat·ed *v.t.* to pacify, esp. by making concessions **pla·ca·tion. pla·ca·to·ry** *adj.*

place 1. *n.* a particular part of space ‖ a particular spot or area ‖ a particular city, town, village etc. ‖ position in space ‖ proper function that goes with status ‖ a building or area appointed for a specified purpose ‖ home, dwelling ‖ (racing) a position among the winners, esp. second or third **in place of** as a substitute for, rather than **out of place** inappropriate, unsuitable **to go places** to achieve worldly success or distinction **to take place** to occur, happen **2. plac·ing placed** *v.t.* to put in a particular place ‖ to identify ‖ to give (an order for goods etc.) ‖ *v.i.* to be

among the first three contestants to finish, esp. to finish second in a horse or dog race

pla·ce·bo *pl.* **pla·ce·bos, pla·ce·boes** *n.* an an inactive but harmless preparation given to humor a patient

pla·cen·ta *pl.* **pla·cen·tas, pla·cen·tae** *n.* the organ which joins the fetus to the maternal uterus and acts as the site of metabolic exchange between them

plac·er *n.* a deposit of sand or gravel where gold or other valuable minerals can be obtained in particles

plac·id *adj.* not easily roused **pla·cid·i·ty** *n.*

pla·gia·rism *n.* the act of plagiarizing **pla·gia·rist** *n.* someone who plagiarizes

pla·gia·rize pla·gia·riz·ing pla·gia·rized *v.t.* to use and pass off (someone else's ideas, inventions, writings etc.) as one's own

pla·gia·ry *pl.* **pla·gia·ries** *n.* plagiarism ‖ a plagiarist

plague 1. *n.* an epidemic, often fatal disease occurring in various forms ‖ a nuisance, annoyance **2.** *v.t.* **pla·guing plagued** to pester or harass **plá·guey, plá·guy** *adj.* annoying, bothersome

plaid 1. *n.* woolen cloth of tartan pattern **2.** *adj.* having a tartan pattern **pláid·ed** *adj.* made of or wearing plaid

plain 1. *adj.* easy to see ‖ simple, not embellished ‖ absolute ‖ unelaborate ‖ bluntly frank ‖ unsophisticated ‖ lacking physical beauty, but not ugly **2.** *n.* a large expanse of level, open country **3.** *adv.* clearly

plain·tiff *n.* a person who brings a lawsuit against another

plain·tive *adj.* quietly mournful

plait 1. *n.* a length of hair, straw, ribbon etc. consisting of at least three interlaced strands **2.** *v.t.* to form a plait ‖ to make (a basket, mat etc.)

plan 1. *n.* a design for a construction, layout, system etc. ‖ a scheme ‖ a proposed course of action **2. plan·ning planned** *v.t.* to make a design for (a building, garden, city etc.) ‖ *v.i.* to make plans

plane 1. *n.* a carpenter's tool used for producing a smooth surface on wood **2.** *v.* **plan·ing planed** to work with this tool

plane 1. *adj.* flat, level **2.** *n.* a level surface ‖ a level of development, existence, accomplishment, thought, value etc. ‖ an aircraft ‖ one of the natural faces of a crystal

plane plan·ing planed *v.t.* to glide

plan·et *n.* one of the bodies in space which revolve around the sun ‖ any similar body revolving about a star

plan·e·tar·i·um *pl.* **plan·e·tar·i·ums, plan·e·tar·i·a** *n.* a complex system of optical projectors by means of which the positions and relative motions of the planets and visible stars are displayed on the inner surface of a large dome ‖ the building containing this

plan·e·tar·y *adj.* of a planet ‖ moving like a planet

plan·et·oid *n.* an asteroid

plank 1. *n.* a long, heavy board, usually at least 2 ins thick ‖ idea, principle etc. in an argument, political program etc. **2.** *v.t.* to cover or provide with planks ‖ (esp. with 'down') to put (something) on a counter, table etc. with force **plánk·ing** *n.* planks collectively

plank·ton *n.* minute plants and animals which float near the surface of fresh or salt water **plank·ton·ic** *adj.*

plant *v.t.* to put the roots of (a plant) in the ground to enable it to grow ‖ to stock with plants ‖ to instill (ideas) in the mind ‖ to put firmly in position

plant *n.* any organism belonging to the kingdom Plantae, characterized usually by lack of independent locomotion, cell walls composed of cellulose, and a nutritive system based on photosynthesis ‖ the assemblage of buildings used to manufacture some kind of goods or power ‖ a carefully planned swindle ‖ a carefully planned trap laid to catch a wrongdoer

plan·tain *n.* a species of banana plant ‖ its fruit

plan·ta·tion *n.* an estate on which a crop such as sugarcane, cotton, tea etc. is cultivated ‖ settlement

plant·er *n.* a person who plants ‖ a machine used to plant ‖ a container for potted or unpotted house plants

plaque *n.* a flat piece of metal etc. attached to a wall to record a fact of historical interest ‖ in a culture, an area destroyed by a virus

plas·ma *n.* the viscous living matter of a cell surrounding the nucleus **plas·mat·ic, plás·mic** *adjs*

plas·ter *n.* a mixture of slaked lime, sand and water applied wet to an interior wall or ceiling and hardening to a smooth surface when dry

plaster *v.t.* to cover with wet plaster ‖ to apply a medicinal plaster to ‖ to shell heavily

plas·ter·board *n.* a board made by compressing sheets of fiber separated by a layer of partly set plaster of paris

plaster of paris a white or pinkish powder obtained by calcining gypsum. With water it forms a quick-setting paste, drying to form a tough, hard solid. It is used for casts and molds and building materials

plas·tic 1. *adj.* of material which changes shape when pressure is applied and retains its new shape when the pressure is removed ‖ (art) characterized by three-dimensional movement, form and space ‖ pliable ‖ synthetic ‖ so changeable as to be phony **2.** *n.* a plastic material **plás·ti·cal·ly** *adv.*

plate 1. *n.* a flat, shallow dish from which food is eaten ‖ the food served on such a dish ‖ a thin flat piece of metal for engraving on or bearing an inscription ‖ a thin coating of precious metal put on base metal by electrolysis ‖ a set of false teeth **2.** *v.t.* **plat·ing plat·ed** to cover with a thin layer of metal

pla·teau *pl.* **pla·teaus, pla·teaux** *n.* a level, horizontal region above sea level or surrounding regions ‖ a level section in a graph

plat·form *n.* a raised structure of planks ‖ a raised structure next to the track ‖ the open area at the end of a railroad passenger car ‖ a ledge, e.g. on a cliff face

‖ a flat, esp. raised, piece of ground ‖ a statement of aims and policies in the program of a person or party seeking electoral support

plat·ing n. the covering with a thin layer of metal

plat·i·num n. a very heavy, ductile, malleable, silvery white metallic element

plat·i·tude n. a commonplace statement uttered as if it were informative and important ‖ the quality of being dull or commonplace **plat·i·tu·di·nize plat·i·tu·di·niz·ing plat·i·tu·di·nized** v.i. to utter platitudes **plat·i·tu·di·nous** adj.

pla·ton·ic adj. of or designating love that is free of carnal desire **pla·tón·i·cal·ly** adv.

pla·toon n. a tactical infantry unit

plat·ter n. a shallow, usually oval serving dish

plat·y·pus n. a primitive aquatic mammal. It has a flat bill like a duck. It lays eggs, but nurses its young

plau·dits pl. n. praise or approval

plau·si·ble adj. apparently true **pláu·si·bly** adv.

play n. activity or exercise performed for amusement ‖ freedom of movement, scope ‖ manner of playing ‖ a dramatic stage performance ‖ gambling

play v.t. to take part in a game of ‖ to make music ‖ to perform ‖ to act in a theatrical performance ‖ to move, (a card) in a game ‖ to place a bet ‖ to imitate or pretend to be, for fun ‖ v.i. to trifle, toy ‖ to frolic, gambol ‖ to gamble ‖ (of a play, film etc.) to be performed

play·back n. a playing back of a recording ‖ part of tape recorder which serves to play back transcriptions

play·bill n. a poster or handbill advertising a theatrical performance ‖ a theater program

play·boy n. a rich young man who cares chiefly about having a good time

play·er n. a person who plays ‖ a person who performs a musical instrument ‖ an actor

play·ful adj. liking to play ‖ humorous

play·ground n. a piece of ground set apart

for children to play on ‖ a district for recreation

play·house pl. **play·hous·es** n. a theater ‖ a little house for children to play in

play·mate n. a child's friend with whom he plays

play-off n. (games) a match played to decide a tie

play·thing n. something designed to be played with

play·wright n. a writer of theatrical plays

pla·za n. a public square in a town or city

plea n. an appeal ‖ a request ‖ an argument used to excuse

plea bargaining negotiation between defense attorney in a criminal action and the prosecutor for a reduced charge in exchange for a plea of guilty

plead plead·ing plead·ed, pled v.i. to beg with emotion and at length, implore ‖ to state a plea ‖ to argue in court **to plead (not) guilty** to admit (deny) guilt, as a method of procedure

pleas·ant adj. agreeable, pleasing

pleas·ant·ry pl. **pleas·ant·ries** n. pleasant, goodhumored joking back and forth

please pleas·ing pleased v.t. to gratify, satisfy, give pleasure to ‖ v.i. to make oneself pleasant, agreeable **if you please** if you wish **pléased, pléas·ing** adjs

pleas·ur·a·ble adj. giving pleasure **pléas·ur·a·bly** adv.

pleas·ure n. a general feeling of enjoyment ‖ something which causes this feeling ‖ self-gratification

pleat 1. n. a fold, esp. one made by doubling cloth etc. upon itself 2. v.t. to make a pleat in

ple·bei·an, ple·bi·an 1. n. a member of the common people 2. adj. uncultured, vulgar

pleb·i·scite n. a vote of the entire electorate on a national issue (e.g. constitutional change

pledge 1. n. something of value left as security for a loan ‖ a solemn promise 2. v.t. **pledg·ing pledged** to hand over as security for a loan ‖ to prom

ple·na·ry adj. complete ‖ attended by all members

plen·i·po·ten·ti·ar·y 1. *adj.* invested with unlimited power **2.** *pl.* **plen·i·po·ten·ti·ar·ies** *n.* an ambassador or envoy with full powers of action

plen·i·tude *n.* completeness ‖ abundance

plen·te·ous *adj.* plentiful

plen·ti·ful *adj.* abundant

plen·ty 1. *n.* abundance ‖ more than enough ‖ a great quantity **2.** *adj.* abundant **3.** *adv.* more than adequately

ple·num *pl.* **ple·nums, ple·na** *n.* the entirety of a space regarded as being filled with matter ‖ a full assembly

ple·o·nasm *n.* the using of more words than necessary, redundancy **ple·o·nas·tic** *adj.* **ple·o·nás·ti·cal·ly** *adv.*

pleth·o·ra *n.* a great quantity ‖ an unhealthy physical condition caused by an excess of blood **pleth·or·ic** *adj.* pretentious ‖ having an excess of blood

pleu·ra *pl.* **pleu·rae, pleu·ras** *n.* a thin membrane lining the chest cavity and surrounding each lung

pleu·ri·sy *n.* inflammation of the pleura

plex·us *n.* a network of intertwining nerves or blood vessels

pli·a·ble *adj.* readily bent, pliant ‖ readily influenced **plái·a·bly** *adv.*

pli·ant *adj.* pliable ‖ readily yielding to influence

pli·ers *pl.* *n.* small pincers used for handling small objects, for bending or cutting wire etc.

plight *n.* a state of distress, predicament

plod 1. *v.i.* **plod·ding plod·ded** to walk heavily and slowly ‖ to make slow progress when working **2.** *n.* a laborious tread **plód·der** *n.* someone who learns by hard work rather than by natural aptitude

plop 1. *n.* the sound made when an object or body drops into a liquid **2.** *v.i.* **plop·ping plopped** to fall with a plop

plot 1. *n.* a small piece of ground ‖ a secret plan or conspiracy ‖ the plan of events in a novel, play etc. **2.** **plot·ting plot·ted** *v.t.* to plan secretly ‖ to make a plan ‖ to mark on a chart ‖ to construct the plan of (events in a novel, play etc.) ‖ *v.i.* to conspire

plow 1. *n.* an agricultural implement used for cutting through and turning over soil **2.** *v.t.* to turn over, break up etc. (soil) with a plow ‖ to furrow ‖ (of ships) to cut through the surface of (water) ‖ *v.i.* to work with a plow ‖ to proceed slowly and laboriously

plow·share *n.* the cutting and turning blade of a plow

ploy *n.* a cunning tactic or gambit

pluck 1. *v.t.* to pull the feathers from ‖ to pull quickly at ‖ to pick **2.** *n.* courage **plúck·i·ly** *adv.* **plúck·y pluck·i·er pluck·i·est** *adj.* courageous

plug 1. *n.* a piece of wood etc. used to fill a gap or hole ‖ any electrical connection ‖ the favorable mention of a product **2.** *v.t.* **plug·ging plugged** *v.t.* to insert a plug in ‖ to publicize (something) ‖ *v.i.* (with 'up') to become obstructed **to plug in** to connect to an outlet

plum *n.* a small tree ‖ the edible fleshy fruit of the tree ‖ the bluish-red color of this fruit

plum·age *n.* the feathers of a bird

plumb 1. *n.* a small, heavy piece of metal, usually lead, attached to a line and used to indicate the vertical **2.** *adj.* vertical **3.** *adv.* vertically **4.** *v.t.* to do the work of a plumber

plumb·er *n.* a skilled worker who fits, repairs and maintains pipes, bathroom fixtures, cisterns, drains etc.

plumb·ing *n.* the craft of a plumber ‖ the entire water-supply and drainage system of a building

plume *n.* a large feather ‖ visible emission from a chimney flue or volcano

plum·met 1. *n.* the weight attached to a plumb line ‖ a clock weight **2.** *v.i.* to drop vertically downwards

plump 1. *v.i.* to fall heavily ‖ *v.t.* to drop, place, put down etc. heavily **2.** *adv.* suddenly and heavily downwards **3.** *n.* the act of falling heavily or the sound of this

plump 1. *adj.* pleasantly rounded, without being fat ‖ (of animals) fleshy **2.** *v.* (with 'up') to knead (a pillow etc.) so as to shake up the feathers in it

plun·der 1. *v.t.* to strip of goods by force ‖ *v.i.* to commit robbery **2.** *n.* the act of plundering

plunge 1. *v.* **plung·ing plunged** *v.t.* to thrust (something) forcefully into something else ‖ *v.i.* to throw oneself into water, (esp. of a ship) to pitch **2.** *n.* the act of plunging ‖ a leap into **plúng·er** *n.* a moving machine part, a piston ‖ a rubber suction cup

plunk 1. *n.* the dull, short sound made by the forceful impact of inelastic bodies ‖ a twang **2.** *v.t.* to put down suddenly and heavily ‖ to pluck the strings of **3.** *adv.* with the sound of a plunk

plu·ral 1. *adj.* of or including more than one **2.** *n.* a word in the plural form

plu·ral·i·ty *pl.* **plu·ral·i·ties** *n.* the state of being plural ‖ (in a political election involving three or more candidates) a number of votes obtained by one candidate exceeding that of any other candidate but not constituting an absolute majority

plus 1. *prep.* added to ‖ in addition to **2.** *adj.* positive ‖ credit **3.** *pl.* **plus·es, plus·ses** *n.* an additional quantity

plush 1. *n.* a fabric resembling velvet **2.** *adj.* luxurious

plu·toc·ra·cy *pl.* **plu·toc·ra·cies** *n.* rule by the rich ‖ a ruling class of rich people **plu·to·crat** *n.* a member of a plutocracy **plu·to·crát·ic** *adj.*

plu·to·ni·um *n.* an artificial metallic element

ply ply·ing plied *v.t.* to use with vigor and diligence ‖ to work busily at ‖ to supply persistently ‖ to keep at constantly

ply *pl.* **plies** *n.* one of the thin wooden layers in plywood

ply·wood *n.* a material composed of thin layers of wood glued or cemented together

pneu·mat·ic *adj.* of, pertaining to, or using air, wind or gas ‖ operated by pressure of air ‖ filled with air **pneu·mát·i·cal·ly** *adv.*

pneu·mát·ics *n.* the branch of physics dealing with gases, esp. air, and certain elastic fluids

pneu·mo·nia *n.* inflammation of the lungs **pneu·mon·ic** *adj.*

poach *v.t.* to cook in a liquid that is never allowed to boil ‖ to drop (an egg removed from its shell) into simmering water and let it cook until the white coagulates

poach *v.t.* to take (game or fish) illegally from another person's property ‖ to soften or make holes in (ground) by trampling ‖ *v.i.* to trespass ‖ to take game or fish illegally **póach·er** *n.* someone who trespasses in order to steal or kill game

pock·et 1. *n.* a small, baglike receptacle ‖ a hollow place in which something could collect **2.** *v.t.* to take (money etc.) dishonestly ‖ to accept submissively **3.** *adj.* suitable for or adapted for carrying in a pocket

pock·et·book *n.* a woman's purse or handbag

pock·et·knife *pl.* **pock·et·knives** *n.* a small knife having blades folding into the handle

pock·mark *n.* the pitlike scar left in the skin by smallpox **póck·marked** *adj.* having pockmarks

pod 1. *n.* protective envelope **2.** *v.t.* to split and empty the pods of (peas etc.)

po·di·a·trist *n.* a chiropodist

po·di·a·try *n.* chiropody

po·di·um *pl.* **po·di·a po·di·ums** *n.* a dais, e.g. for an orchestra conductor

po·em *n.* a piece of poetry

po·et *n.* a person who writes poetry

po·et·ic *adj.* pertaining poets or poetry ‖ composed in verse

po·et·i·cal *adj.* poetic

po·et·ry *n.* a type of discourse which achieves its effects by rhythm, sound patterns and imagery ‖ poems

po·grom *n.* an organized massacre, esp. of Jews

poign·an·cy *n.* the quality or state of being poignant

poign·ant *adj.* causing or marked by feelings of sadness ‖ deeply felt ‖ stimulating

point *n.* a specific place having a definite position in space but no definite size or shape ‖ a definite, often decisive, moment in time ‖ (of something spoken or written) the most prominent or important idea ‖ the climax of a joke ‖ a particular item in a speech, argument, exposition etc. ‖ purpoe ‖ the sharp end of something ‖ *(games)* a unit of counting in scoring ‖

a unit of academic credit ‖ *(printing)* a unit for measuring size of type ‖ a useful suggestion

point *v.t.* to give a point to ‖ to cause (something) to be turned in a particular direction ‖ *v.i.* to indicate position with a finger ‖ to be turned in a particular direction ‖ to explain

point-blank 1. *adv.* with level aim ‖ directly **2.** *adj.* fired at a very close target ‖ direct

point·ed *adj.* having a sharp point ‖ sharply, though obliquely, critical ‖ made deliberately obvious

point·er *n.* a person or thing that points ‖ a rod used for pointing ‖ a gundog ‖ a useful indication or suggestion

poise *n.* balance ‖ carriage, bearing ‖ emotional stability

poise pois·ing poised *v.t.* to balance ‖ to hold suspended for a moment ‖ to put in a state of readiness ‖ *v.i.* to be balanced

poi·son 1. *n.* a substance which can seriously injure an organism or destroy life ‖ anything having a pernicious effect on the mind of an individual **2.** *adj.* poisonous

poison *v.t.* to injure or destroy by using a poison ‖ to make poisonous ‖ to exert a pernicious influence

poi·son·ing *n.* the condition produced by the application or absorption of a poison

poi·son·ous *adj.* having the properties of a poison ‖ containing poison ‖ hateful

poke 1. *v.* **pok·ing poked** *v.t.* to stir up with a poker ‖ to hit with a short, jabbing blow of the fist ‖ *v.i.* to make little digs or thrusts with a stick, finger etc. ‖ to go slowly, dawdle **to poke fun at** to make the object of ridicule **2.** *n.* a short, jabbing blow with the fist ‖ a slow-moving person, slow coach

po·ker *n.* a gambling game

poker *n.* a heavy, usually iron, rod used to poke a fire

po·lar 1. *adj.* of the regions located near the poles ‖ pertaining to the pole of a magnet ‖ opposite in nature, character etc.

po·lar·i·ty *n.* the state of having one or other of two opposite polar conditions

po·lar·i·za·tion *n.* the act of polarizing ‖ the state of being polarized

po·lar·ize po·lar·iz·ing po·lar·ized *v.t.* to produce polarization in or give polarity to ‖ *v.i.* to become concentrated around two opposites or extremes ‖ to serve as a point around which concentration takes place

pole *n.* either of two differentiated areas that lie at opposite ends of an axis ‖ one of two extremes ‖ a point of attraction **Pole** either end of the axis of a sphere, e.g. the North Pole or South Pole of the earth or the celestial sphere

pole 1. *n.* a long, usually rounded piece of wood or other material ‖ a unit of length ‖ a mast **2.** *v.t.* **pol·ing poled** to propel by using a pole

po·lem·ic 1. *adj.* of or pertaining to controversy **2.** *n.* a disputation **po·lém·i·cal** *adj.* **po·lém·i·cist** *n.* a person who engages in polemics

po·lém·ics *n.* the practice of theological disputation

po·lice *pl.* **po·lice** *n.* a department of government responsible for the preservation of public order, detection of crime and enforcement of civil law ‖ the police force

police po·lic·ing policed *v.t.* to control, or maintain law and order in ‖ to provide with police

pol·i·cy *pl.* **pol·i·cies** *n.* a selected, planned line of conduct ‖ shrewdness in support of an aim

policy *pl.* **policies** *n.* a document containing the contract made between an individual and an insurance company

po·lio·o·my·e·li·tis *n. (abbr.* polio) a serious infectious virus disease characterized by fever, motor paralysis and muscular atrophy, often resulting in permanent deformity

pol·ish 1. *v.t.* to make smooth and lustrous by rubbing ‖ to cause (a person) to become more refined ‖ to bring nearer perfection ‖ *v.i.* **to polish up** to make brighter by rubbing ‖ to revise and improve **2.** *n.* a preparation used in polishing ‖ personal refinement

po·lite *adj.* having good social manners ‖ characterized by refinement

pol·i·tic *adj.* shrewdly judicious in support of an aim

po·lit·i·cal *adj.* of or pertaining to politics

pol·i·ti·cian *n.* a person engaged in politics and in the techniques of civil government

pol·i·tics *n.* the art and science of the government of a state ‖ the opinions, principles or policies by which a person orders his participation in such affairs

pol·ka 1. *n.* a lively dance for couples ‖ the music for this type of dance 2. *v.i.* to dance the polka

poll 1. *n.* the number of votes cast in an election ‖ the casting of votes ‖ the place where votes are cast ‖ a canvassing of persons chosen at random in order to discover trends of public opinion 2. *v.t.* to record the votes of ‖ to canvass (people) ‖ *v.i.* to cast a vote

pol·len *n.* the male reproductive cells of a seed plant

pol·lute pol·lut·ing pol·lut·ed *v.t.* to make unhealthily impure ‖ to corrupt

pol·lu·tion *n.* a polluting or being polluted

po·lo *n.* a game played on horseback by two teams

po·lo·ni·um *n.* a radioactive element

pol·y·chrome *adj.* painted or printed in many colors

po·lyg·a·mist *n.* a person who practices polygamy

po·lyg·a·mous *adj.* having more than one wife or husband at the same time

po·lyg·a·my *n.* the practice of being polygamous

pol·y·gon *n.* a plane figure enclosed by five or more straight lines **po·lyg·o·nal** *adj.*

polygraph LIE DETECTOR

pol·y·he·dron *pl.* **pol·y·he·dra, pol·y·he·drons** *n.* a figure or solid formed usually by seven or more plane faces

pol·y·no·mi·al 1. *adj.* having two or more terms 2. *n.* an expression of this kind

pol·yp *n.* any of various coelenterates having tubular, hollow bodies and an anterior mouth surrounded by tentacles ‖ a projecting growth of hypertrophied mucous membrane

pol·y·syl·lab·ic *adj.* having more than three syllables **pol·y·syl·láb·i·cal** *adj.*

pol·y·tech·nic 1. *adj.* of or pertaining to instruction in a number of technical subjects 2. *n.* a school giving instruction of this kind **pol·y·téch·ni·cal** *adj.* **pol·y·tech·ní·cian** *n.*

pol·y·the·ism *n.* belief in or worship of more than one god **pól·y·the·ist** *n.* **pol·y·the·is·tic** *adj.*

pom·ace *n.* a mass of apple pulp

pome·gran·ate *n.* a small shrubby tree ‖ its edible, orange-sized fruit

pom·mel 1. *n.* a knob on a sword hilt ‖ a knoblike projection on the front of a saddle 2. *v.t.* **pom·mel·ing pom·meled** to pummel

pomp *n.* splendor in display

pom·pa·dour *n.* a woman's hairstyle ‖ a man's hairstyle

pom·pon *n.* a small, brightly colored ball usually of yarn used for ornamenting ‖ any of several varieties of chrysanthemum

pom·pos·i·ty *pl.* **pom·pos·i·ties** *n.* the quality of being full of self-importance

pom·pous *adj.* full of self-importance ‖ pretentious

pon·cho *pl.* **pon·chos** *n.* a Spanish-American cloak like a blanket with a central slit for the head

pond *n.* a small area of still water

pon·der *v.i.* to meditate ‖ *v.t.* to consider carefully

pon·der·a·bil·i·ty *n.* the state of being ponderable

pon·der·a·ble *adj.* able to be weighed

pon·der·ous *adj.* lacking ease and a light touch ‖ slow, lumbering ‖ very heavy

pon·tiff *n.* the pope ‖ a bishop

pon·tif·i·cal *adj.* of or relating to a pontiff ‖ absurdly dogmatic or pretentious

pon·toon *n.* a flat-bottomed boat or a metal cylinder used in quantity to support a temporary bridge

po·ny *pl.* **po·nies** *n.* a small horse of any of several breeds

pool *n.* a small body of fresh water

pool 1. *n.* (gambling) the total of sums staked, all to be taken by the winner, or divided among several winners ‖ pocket billiards ‖ a fund common to various undertakings on a basis of shared profits and liabilities **2.** *v.t.* to contribute to a common fund

poop 1. *n.* a deck at the stern of a ship ‖ the stern of a ship **2.** *v.t.* (of a wave) to break over the stern

poor 1. *adj.* having little money, few possessions ‖ relating to poverty ‖ inferior **2.** *n.* **the poor** poor people collectively

poor·ly 1. *adv.* inadequately **2.** *adj.* not in good health

pop 1. *n.* a small, sharp, explosive sound ‖ an effervescent nonalcoholic drink **2.** **pop·ping popped** *v.t.* to cause to make a sharp explosive sound ‖ to cause to burst open ‖ *v.i.* to move, come, enter etc., suddenly or unexpectedly or for a short time ‖ to protrude **3.** *adv.* with a pop ‖ like a pop

pop·corn *n.* a variety of corn, the kernels of which pop when heated in butter or oil ‖ these popped kernels

pope *n.* the head of the Roman Catholic Church

pop·eyed *adj.* having protruding eyes

pop·lin *n.* a tightly woven fabric, frequently of mercerized cotton, used for shirts, pajamas etc.

pop·o·ver *n.* a puffy, light muffin having a hollow center

pop·py pl. **pop·pies** *n.* plants usually containing white latex ‖ an extract made from poppy juice, used in pharmacy

pop·py·cock *n.* nonsense, foolish talk

pop·u·lace *n.* the common people, the masses

pop·u·lar *adj.* liked ‖ adapted to the tastes, understanding or needs of people in general ‖ cheap ‖ of people in general ‖ prevalent

pop·u·lar·i·ty *n.* the quality of being popular

pop·u·lar·ize **pop·u·lar·iz·ing** **pop·u·lar·ized** *v.t.* to cause to become widely known and adopted ‖ to present in a form easily understood by people in general

pop·u·late pop·u·lat·ing pop·u·lat·ed *v.t.* to provide with inhabitants

pop·u·la·tion *n.* the inhabitants of a country, town etc.

pop·u·lous *adj.* densely populated

por·ce·lain 1. *n.* fine, translucent nonporous ceramic ware used esp. for tableware **2.** *adj.* made of porcelain

porch *n.* the covered entrance of a building ‖ an open, roofed gallery extending along a side of a house

por·cine *adj.* of, relating to, or resembling a pig

por·cu·pine *n.* any of several vegetarian rodents having the body covered with brown or black barbed spines intermixed with stiff hairs

pore **por·ing pored** *v.i.* to study intently ‖ to think deeply about

pore *n.* a minute opening esp. in mammalian skin

pork *n.* hog's flesh (fresh or cured) as food

por·nog·ra·pher *n.* a person who writes pornography

por·no·graph·ic *adj.* relating to pornography

por·nog·ra·phy *n.* obscene literature, photographs, paintings etc.

po·rous *adj.* full of pores, permeable

por·poise *n.* a genus of toothed whales

por·ridge *n.* a soft food made by boiling cereal

port *n.* a harbor

port *n.* the side of a ship that is on the left of someone aboard facing the bow

port *n.* a sweet, rich red wine from Portugal

port·a·bil·i·ty *n.* the quality of being portable

port·a·ble 1. *adj.* easily carried or transported **2.** *n.* anything easily carried

por·tage 1. *n.* the carrying of boats or goods by land from one river etc. to another **2.** *v.t.* **por·tag·ing por·taged** to carry (boats or goods)

por·tal *n.* a door, gateway or other entrance, esp. when large and imposing

por·tend *v.t.* to give signs of (impending evil)

por·tent *n.* an omen, esp. as an evil omen

por·ten·tous *adj.* highly significant

por·ter *n.* a person employed to carry baggage or other loads ‖ a man who cleans or does errands

port·fo·li·o *pl.* **port·fo·li·os** *n.* a case for carrying state documents ‖ the securities etc. held by a bank, investment trust etc.

port·hole *n.* an opening in a ship's side to admit light and air ‖ an opening in a tank to shoot through

por·ti·co *pl.* **por·ti·coes, por·ti·cos** *n.* a colonnade or covered passageway in classical architecture

por·tion 1. *n.* part of a whole ‖ a helping of food ‖ a share

portion *v.t.* to divide into portions ‖ to share

port·li·ness *n.* the state or quality of being portly

port·ly **port·li·er** **port·li·est** *adj.* stout, corpulent

por·trait *n.* a painting, photograph, drawing etc. of a person ‖ a vivid verbal description **pór·trait·ist** *n.* a person who makes portraits

por·tray *v.* to paint etc. a portrait of ‖ to describe vividly in words **por·tráy·al** *n.*

pose *n.* a way of standing or sitting, esp. the position held by a model etc. in posing ‖ manner of behavior assumed for its effect on others

pose **pos·ing** **posed** *v.t.* to place (an artist's model) in a certain position for artistic effect ‖ to state or present (a problem etc.) ‖ *v.i.* to assume a certain position ‖ to represent oneself falsely

po·seur *n.* a person who pretends to be what he is not

posh *adj.* very smart ‖ high-class

po·si·tion 1. *n.* the place occupied by a person in relation to another person ‖ a way of looking at things ‖ a person's standing in the social or business world ‖ financial circumstances ‖ employment ‖ physical posture **2.** *v.t.* to place in position **po·sí·tion·al** *adj.*

pos·i·tive 1. *adj.* leaving no doubt or question ‖ indicating affirmation ‖ constructive as opposed to skeptical ‖ showing the presence of a specific condition, disease etc. ‖ greater than zero ‖ of a magnetic pole attracted towards the magnetic north **2.** *n.* that which is positive ‖ a positive print or transparency

pos·se *n.* a force of men having legal authority

pos·sess *v.t.* to have as property, own ‖ to have as a faculty, quality etc. ‖ to get control over **pos·séssed** *adj.* crazy ‖ controlled by an evil spirit

pos·ses·sion *n.* a possessing ‖ that which is possessed ‖ *(pl.)* property

pos·ses·sive 1. *adj.* tending to want to concentrate all another's affections on oneself ‖ jealously assertive of one's rights over something **2.** *n.* a possessive case or form

pos·ses·sor *n.* a person who owns or controls

pos·si·bil·i·ty *pl.* **pos·si·bil·i·ties** *n.* the fact or state of being possible ‖ something that is possible

pos·si·ble *adj.* that may exist, happen, be done etc. ‖ potential ‖ reasonable **pós·si·bly** *adv.* perhaps

post 1. *n.* a strong piece of wood, metal etc., fixed in an upright position, and serving as a support ‖ (horse racing) a pole marking the starting point or finishing point **2.** *v.t.* to affix (a public notice, placard etc.) to a post, wall etc. ‖ to put (a list of names etc.) on a bulletin board etc. ‖ to advertise by poster

post 1. *n.* the position a soldier occupies, or the area he patrols when he is on duty ‖ the place at which a soldier or body of troops is stationed ‖ a position to which a person is appointed ‖ a trading post **2.** *v.t.* to station in a specific place

post- prefix after ‖ behind

post·age *n.* the charge for conveying a letter by mail

post·date **post·dat·ing** **post·dat·ed** *v.t.* to assign a later than actual date to

post·er *n.* a placard displayed in public

pos·te·ri·or 1. *adj.* located behind ‖ later in time **2.** *n.* the buttocks

pos·ter·i·ty *n.* generations not yet born

pos·tern 1. *n.* a back or side door or gate **2.** *adj.* at the back or side

post·grad·u·ate 1. *adj.* of or relating to studies that go beyond the first degree **2.** *n.* a student who continues his studies beyond a first degree

post·haste adj. with the greatest possible speed

post·hu·mous adj. published after the death of the author‖occurring after death **póst·hu·mous·ly** adv.

post·mark 1. n. an official post-office mark serving to cancel the stamp **2.** v.i. to stamp with a postmark

post me·rid·i·em adv. (abbr. p.m., P.M.) after noon and before midnight

post·mor·tem 1. adj. of or relating to the period after death **2.** n. a postmortem examination

post·na·tal adj. after birth

post·pone post·pon·ing post·poned v.t. to put off, defer **post·póne·ment** n.

post·script n. (abbr. P.S.) a brief afterthought added to a letter below the signature at the end of a book

pos·tu·late n. an assumption‖a hypothesis **pos·tu·late pos·tu·lat·ing pos·tu·lat·ed** v.t. to demand, to require as an essential condition‖to assume without need to prove **pos·tu·lá·tion** n. **pós·tu·la·tor** n.

pos·ture 1. n. the way a person holds himself‖the position held by a model in posing **2.** v.i. **pos·tur·ing pos·tured** to assume a physical posture, esp. for effect

post·war adj. of or relating to the period after a war

po·sy pl. **po·sies** n. a flower

pot 1. n. a container of earthenware, glass, metal etc. used for cooking, boiling etc. ‖(card games, esp. poker) the total of bets ‖marijuana **to go to pot** to go to ruin **2. pot·ting pot·ted** v.t. to set (e.g. a plant) in a flowerpot‖to preserve (meat, fish etc.)

po·ta·ble adj. suitable for drinking

po·tas·si·um n. a silver-white univalent metallic element

po·ta·to pl. **po·ta·toes** n. a starchy tuber eaten cooked as a vegetable

pot·bel·ly pl. **pot·bel·lies** n. a protuberant belly

po·ten·cy pl. **po·ten·cies** n. capability

po·tent adj. strong, powerful‖convincing ‖(of a male) able to perform the act of sexual intercourse

po·ten·tate n. a powerful monarch, ruler

po·ten·tial 1. adj. existing but not fully developed‖having the capacity to be‖ expressing possibility **2.** n. potential **po·tén·tial·ize po·ten·tial·iz·ing po·ten·tial·ized** v.t.

po·tion n. a dose of medicine in liquid form

pot·luck n. a meal for an unexpected guest or guests

pot·pour·ri n. dried flower petals and flavoring herbs displayed in bowls to scent a room‖medley‖anthology

pot·tage n. a thick soup

pot·ter n. a person who makes pottery

pot·ter·y pl. **pot·ter·ies** n. clay vessels, esp. earthenware‖the potter's craft‖the workshop of a potter

pouch 1. n. a small bag‖an abdominal receptacle for the young of a marsupial ‖a bag equipped with a lock for holding diplomatic papers **2.** v.t. to put into a pouch‖v.i. to form a pouch

poul·tice 1. n. a warm, soft, moistened mass, applied to a sore or inflamed part of the body to draw pus **2.** v.t. **poul·tic·ing poul·ticed** to apply a poultice to

poul·try n. domesticated birds raised for food

pounce 1. n. the swooping, grabbing or springing motion made in pouncing **2.** v.i. **pounc·ing pounced** to make a sudden swoop, spring or grasp

pound n. an enclosure where stray or unlicensed animals are kept until they are claimed or disposed of‖a place where personal property is held until redeemed

pound 1. v.t. to thump with repeated blows ‖v.i. to strike heavy, thumping blows‖(of a ship) to hit the water heavily and repeatedly‖to throb violently **2.** n. a thud or blow

pound pl. **pounds, pound** n. (abbr. lb.) the unit of mass equal to 16 oz.‖the pound sterling, the British monetary

pour 1. v.t. to send out in a stream‖to discharge profusely‖v.i. to flow in copious streams‖to rain heavily **2.** n. a downpour

pout 1. v.i. to express displeasure, bad humor etc.‖to sulk‖v.t. to utter with a pout 2. *n.* a sulky thrusting out of the lips

pov·er·ty *n.* the condition of being poor ‖ deficiency in something

pow·der 1. *n.* a dry substance composed of fine particles ‖ a medicine in powdered form ‖ a scented cosmetic for the face or body ‖ gunpowder 2. *v.t.* to cover with powder ‖ to convert to powder ‖ to apply cosmetic powder ‖ *v.i.* to become powder

pow·der·y *adj.* resembling powder

pow·er 1. *n.* physical strength ‖ control ‖ military strength ‖ controlling influence ‖ authority, authorization ‖ mechanical or electrical energy **in power** in authority or control 2. *v.t.* to supply with a source of power

pow·er·ful *adj.* having great power ‖ strong ‖ potent

pow·er·less *adj.* without power ‖ unable

pox *n.* any of various specified diseases characterized by pustules, e.g. chicken pox

prac·ti·ca·bil·i·ty *n.* the or condition of being practicable

prac·ti·ca·ble *adj.* feasible ‖ capable of being used

prac·ti·cal *adj.* obtained through practice ‖ that can be put into practice ‖ able to apply theory **prac·ti·cál·i·ty** *n.*

prac·ti·cal·ly *adv.* in a practical way ‖ virtually

prac·tice 1. *v.* **prac·tic·ing prac·ticed** *v.t.* to make a practice of ‖ to work at as a profession ‖ to study, exercise ‖ to drill 2. *n.* customary code of behavior ‖ systematic exercise ‖ the exercise of a profession, esp. law or medicine **prác·ticed, prác·tised** *adj.* expert through long experience

prac·ti·tion·er *n.* a person who practices a profession

prag·mat·ic *adj.* dealing with events in the light of practical lessons or applications **prag·mát·i·cal***adj.*

prag·ma·tism *n.* a doctrine which tests truth by its practical consequences

prai·rie *n.* a wide tract of treeless grassland

praise 1. *v.t.* **prais·ing praised** to speak of with approval ‖ to glorify 2. *n.* a praising

pra·line *n.* a confection of almonds or other nuts browned in boiling sugar

prance pranc·ing pranced *v.i.* (of a horse) to leap up on the hind legs ‖ (of a person) to move in a gleeful way

prank *v.t.* to deck, adorn

prank *n.* a piece of mischief **pránk·ish** *adj.*

prate 1. *v.i.* **prat·ing prat·ed** to babble idly 2. *n.* foolish talk

prat·tle 1. *v.* **prat·tling prat·tled** *v.i.* to talk incessantly ‖ to chatter ‖ *v.t.* to babble 2. *n.* chatter

prawn *n.* any of several crustaceans related to the shrimp and the lobster

pray *v.i.* to implore God or an object of worship

prayer *n.* a humble communication in thought or speech to God or to an object of worship expressing supplication, thanksgiving, praise, confession etc.

pre- prefix earlier than, preceding ‖ beforehand

preach *v.i.* to deliver a religious address publicly ‖ to advocate (a course or principle) **préach·er** *n.*

pre·am·ble *n.* an introductory part of a speech or piece of writing

pre·car·i·ous *adj.* uncertain ‖ dangerous

pre·cau·tion *n.* care with respect to the foreseeable future **pre·cáu·tion·ar·y, pre·cáu·tious** adjs

pre·cede pre·ced·ing pre·ced·ed *v.t.* to go before in rank, importance etc. ‖ to come before in time

prec·e·dence *n.* the act, fact, right or privilege of preceding another or others

prec·e·dent 1. *n.* a previous instance or case that may serve to justify a subsequent act, procedure etc. of a similar kind 2. *adj.* coming before in order, time etc. **préc·e·dent·ed** *adj.*

pre·cept *n.* a commandment or instruction intended as a rule of action or conduct

pre·cep·tor *n.* a teacher

pre·cinct *n.* a subdivision of a county, city or city ward for police and election purposes

pre·ci·os·i·ty *n.* excessive refinement

pre·cious 1. *adj.* of great value ‖ beloved ‖ complete 2. *adv.* extremely

prec·i·pice *n.* the very steep or overhanging part of the face of a cliff

pre·cip·i·tant *adj.* precipitate

pre·cip·i·tate 1. pre·cip·i·tat·ing pre·cip·i·tat·ed *v.t.* to hasten ‖ *v.i.* to condense from a vapor and fall as rain, snow etc. **2.** *adj.* sudden, hasty ‖ rushing violently ‖ rash, head strong

pre·cip·i·ta·tion *n.* excessive or reckless haste ‖ a deposit of water in either liquid or solid form, e.g. rain, snow ‖ the quantity deposited

pre·cip·i·tous *adj.* resembling a precipice ‖ hasty

pre·cise *adj.* accurate in every detail ‖ exact ‖ punctilious **pre·cise·ly** *adv.*

pre·ci·sion *n.* the quality of being precise

pre·clude pre·clud·ing pre·clud·ed *v.t.* to prevent ‖ to make practically impossible

pre·clu·sion *n.* a precluding or being precluded

pre·clu·sive *adj.* tending to preclude

pre·co·cious *adj.* displaying highly developed mental or physical characteristics at an early age

pre·coc·i·ty *n.* the condition or quality of being precocious

pre·con·ceive pre·con·ceiv·ing pre·con·ceived *v.t.* to form (an idea or opinion) beforehand

pre·cur·sor *n.* someone who prepares the way for another or who precedes him in office

pred·a·tor *n.* a predatory animal

pred·a·to·ry *adj.* (of persons) given to preying upon others

pre·de·cease pre·de·ceas·ing pre·de·ceased *v.t.* to die before (another person)

pred·e·ces·sor *n.* a person preceding another in an office, position etc.

pre·des·ti·nate 1. *v.t.* **pre·des·ti·nat·ing pre·des·ti·nat·ed** to predestine **2.** *adj.* determined beforehand

pre·des·ti·na·tion *n.* the act of predestinating ‖ the doctrine that everything was determined by God from the beginning

pre·de·ter·mi·na·tion *n.* a predetermining or being predetermined

pre·de·ter·mine pre·de·ter·min·ing

pre·de·ter·mined *v.t.* to calculate or determine in advance

pre·dic·a·ment *n.* a situation involving a hard or unpleasant choice

pred·i·cate *v.* **pred·i·cat·ing pred·i·cat·ed** *v.t.* to state as an assumed attribute, quality or property ‖ to imply, connote ‖ to affirm or deny ‖ *v.i.* to make a statement

pred·i·ca·tion *n.* a predicating or being predicated

pre·dict *v.t.* to foretell **pre·dict·a·ble** *adj.*

pre·dic·tion *n.* the action of predicting ‖ that which is predicted

pre·di·lec·tion *n.* a special taste or liking

pre·dis·pose pre·dis·pos·ing pre·dis·posed *v.i.* to make (someone) tend to act, feel, suffer etc. in a particular way or be prone

pre·dis·po·si·tion *n.* a tendency, susceptibility

pre·dom·i·nance *n.* the quality or state of being predominant

pre·dom·i·nant *adj.* most frequent, prevailing

pre·dom·i·nate pre·dom·i·nat·ing pre·dom·i·nat·ed *v.i.* to be most frequent, or lead in quality

pre·em·i·nence *n.* the quality or state of being preeminent

pre·em·i·nent *adj.* superior to others

pre·empt *v.t.* to purchase before others have the opportunity to purchase ‖ to acquire beforehand

pre·emp·tion *n.* the act or right of purachasing before others have a chance to purchase ‖ (Am. hist.) the preempting of public land ‖ a taking possession before others

pre·emp·tive *adj.* occurring before, and in anticipation of, a situation developing

preen *v.t.* (of a bird) to trim (the feathers) with the beak ‖ (of a person) to make (oneself) trim in appearance ‖ to congratulate (oneself) mildly

pre·fab·ri·cate pre·fab·ri·cat·ing pre·fab·ri·cat·ed *v.t.* to construct sections of (e.g. a house) in a factory for assembly on a site elsewhere **pre·fab·ri·ca·tion** *n.*

pref·ace 1. *n.* introduction ‖ a leading up

tp something **2.** *v.t.* **pref·ac·ing pref·aced** to introduce ‖ to lead up to

pre·fer pre·fer·ring pre·ferred *v.t.* to like better ‖ to choose rather **pref·er·a·ble** *adj.* **préf·er·a·bly** *adv.*

pref·er·ence *n.* the right to choose ‖ priority

pref·er·en·tial *adj.* relating to, or constituting preference

pre·fix 1. *v.t.* to place or put (a syllable, group of syllables or word) in front of a word to modify its meaning or form a new word **2.** *n.* that which is placed in front in this way, e.g. 'un' in 'unable'

preg·nan·cy *pl.* **preg·nan·cies** *n.* the condition of being pregnant

preg·nant *adj.* carrying an unborn child or unborn young within the body ‖ deeply significant or full of implication ‖ full of ideas, imaginative

pre·hen·sile *adj.* able to grasp and hold **pre·hen·sil·i·ty** *n.*

pre·his·tor·ic *adj.* of or relating to the period before recorded history **pre·his·tór·i·cal·ly** *adv.*

pre·his·to·ry *n.* the period of history before there were written records

prej·u·dice prej·u·dic·ing prej·u·diced *v.t.* to cause (someone) to have a prejudice

prejudice *n.* a preconceived opinion, usually unfavorable ‖ an unjustified and unreasonable bias

prej·u·di·cial *adj.* injuring, or likely to injure

prel·ate *n.* a high-ranking Church diginitary

pre·lim·i·nar·y *adj.* introductory or preparatory

prel·ude 1. *n.* something serving to introduce, or set the mood for, some event, performance, action etc. to follow **2.** *v.t.* **prel·ud·ing prel·ud·ed** to serve as a prelude to

pre·ma·ture *adj.* occurring, done, existing etc. before the proper time **pre·ma·túre·ly** *adv.*

pre·med·i·tate pre·med·i·tat·ing pre·med·i·tat·ed to think about and plan beforehand

pre·mier 1. *adj.* first in position, importance etc. **2.** *n.* prime minister

premiere, pre·miere *n.* the first public performance of a play or showing of a film

prem·ise, prem·iss 1. *n.* a fact, statement or assumption on which an argument is based or from which conclusions are drawn ‖ *(pl.)* a piece of land and the house and buildings on it **2.** **prem·ise** *v.t.* **prem·is·ing prem·ised** to state or assume as a premise

premium *n.* a prize or reward ‖ a sum paid for an insurance contract ‖ very hard to get and therefore valuable

pre·mo·ni·tion *n.* a forewarning ‖ a presentiment

pre·na·tal *adj.* occurring or existing before birth

pre·oc·cu·pa·tion *n.* being preoccupied

pre·oc·cu·pied *adj.* completely engrossed, esp. in thought

pre·oc·cu·py pre·oc·cu·py·ing pre·oc·cu·pied *v.t.* to engage the attention or interest of (someone) almost completely

prep·a·ra·tion *n.* a preparing or being prepared ‖ that which is prepaired ‖ *(pl.)* preparatory measures

pre·par·a·to·ry *adj.* of that which prepares or introduces

pre·pare pre·par·ing pre·pared to get ready ‖ to get (someone) ready ‖ to put (someone) in a receptive state of mind ‖ to make preparation ‖ *v.i.* to take necessary previous measures **to be prepared to** to be willing to **pre·par·ed·ly** *adv.* **pre·pár·ed·ness** *n.*

pre·pay pre·pay·ing pre·paid *v.t.* to pay for in advance **pre·páy·ment** *n.*

pre·pon·der·ance *n.* the condition of being preponderant

pre·pon·der·ant *adj.* superior in weight, number, influence, power, importance

prep·o·si·tion *n.* a word (in some languages) expressing the relationship between a noun, pronoun or noun phrase ‖ a compound construction which functions as a preposition **prep·o·sí·tion·al** *adj.*

pre·pos·ter·ous *adj.* ridiculous ‖ unreasonable

pre·puce *n.* the foreskin

pre·req·ui·site 1. *adj.* requisite in an antecedent condition **2.** *n.* that which is prerequisite

pre·rog·a·tive *n.* an exclusive right or privilege

pres·age 1. *n.* that which foretells a future event **2.** *v.t.* **pres·ag·ing pres·aged** to foretell

pre·scribe pre·scrib·ing pre·scribed *v.t.* to order ‖ to order the use of ‖ *v.i.* to lay down a rule

pre·scrip·tion *n.* the act of prescribing ‖ that which is prescribed

pres·ence *n.* the state or fact of being in a certain place ‖ distinction of bearing and demeanor

pres·ent *n.* a gift

present 1. *adj.* being in a specified place ‖ existing, being done, or occurring at this time ‖ of or designating a tense that expresses action now **2.** *n.* this time ‖ the present tense

pre·sent 1. *v.t.* to bring (someone) to the notice of or into the presence of someone else ‖ to offer as a gift ‖ (with 'with') to cause to face ‖ to submit for consideration or action ‖ *v.i.* (of a fetus) to be directed towards the opening of the womb **2. pre·sent·a·bíl·i·ty** *n.* the condition or quality of being presentable **pre·sént·a·ble** *adj.* fit to be presented, shown, or offered **pre·sént·a·bly** *adv.*

pres·en·ta·tion *n.* a presenting or being presented ‖ that which is presented ‖ a formal introduction **pres·en·tá·tion·al** *adj.*

pres·ent·ly *adv.* in a short time

pre·serv·a·tive 1. *adj.* having the ability to preserve **2.** *n.* a substance added to preserve

pre·serve 1. pre·serv·ing pre·served *v.t.* to prepare (fruit, vegetables, meat or fish) by boiling, salting, pickling etc. and packing into containers for future use ‖ to prevent from ruin or decay ‖ to keep from decomposition ‖ to retain (e.g. a quality) ‖ *v.i.* to make preserves **2.** *n.* a large area of land or body of water where game or fish is protected ‖ (esp. *pl.*) jam

pre·side pre·sid·ing pre·sid·ed *v.i.* to be in a position of control or authority

pres·i·den·cy *pl.* **pres·i·den·cies** *n.* the office or function of president ‖ the term of office of a president

pres·i·dent *n.* the elected head of government in the U.S.A. and many other republics ‖ the chief officer of a bank, company, corporation etc.

press *v.t.* to exert a steady force upon by applying pressure ‖ to make flat by exerting such pressure ‖ to try to force or persuade ‖ to put foward (a claim) with energy ‖ to squeeze (fruit etc.) in order to extract juice ‖ *v.i.* to throng about someone or something ‖ to force one's way ‖ (of time) to suffice barely for what must be done

press *n.* an instrument or machine by which a substance or material is shaped, smoothed, stamped, compressed etc. by the force of pressure ‖ newspapers and periodicals collectively ‖ journalists collectively **off the press** just printed **to go to press** to print off the edition of a newspaper etc.

press·ing *adj.* requiring immediate attention

pres·sure 1. *n.* the action of pressing ‖ the force acting per unit area ‖ electromotive force ‖ interference with someone's freedom in making a decision ‖ a burden **2. pres·sur·ing pres·sured** to influence or force by using psychological pressure

pres·sur·ize pres·sur·iz·ing pres·sur·ized *v.t.* to cause the air preasure within (an aircraft cabin etc.) to remain equal to atmospheric pressure at ground level whatever the external air pressure may actually be

pres·ti·dig·i·ta·tion *n.* sleight of hand

pres·ti·dig·i·ta·tor *n.* someone skilled in sleight of hand

pres·tige *n.* widely acknowledged high reputation

pres·tig·ious *adj.* held in high esteem

pre·sum·a·ble *adj.* that may be presumed **pre·súm·a·bly** *adv.*

pre·sume pre·sum·ing pre·sumed *v.t.* to assume as true

pre·sump·tion *n.* a supposition ‖ a too

high opinion of oneself ‖ a deduction made from known facts but lacking direct evidence

pre·sump·tu·ous *adj.* displaying excessive self-confidence and taking liberties

pre·tend *v.t.* to allege falsely ‖ to claim

pre·tend·er *n.* a claimant to a throne without just title ‖ someone who pretends

pre·tense *n.* the deliberate creating of a false impression ‖ something pretended

pre·ten·sion *n.* a claim, whether true or false

pre·ten·tious *adj.* claiming to possess superior qualities or great importance

pre·text *n.* a false reason

pret·ty **pret·ti·er** **pret·ti·est** 1. *adj.* pleasing to see or hear ‖ excellent, fine, good (used ironically) 2. *adv.* rather

pret·zel *n.* a cracker shaped like an open knot, glazed and salted

pre·vail *v.i.* to be victorious ‖ to be widespread or current **pre·vail·ing** *adj.*

prev·a·lent *adj.* widespread, generally used

pre·var·i·cate **pre·var·i·cat·ing** **pre·var·i·cat·ed** *v.i.* hiding the truth

pre·vent *v.t.* to cause not to do something ‖ to cause not to happen, or not to be made or done

pre·vent·a·ble, pre·vent·i·ble *adj.* capable of being prevented

pre·ven·tion *n.* the act of preventing

pre·ven·tive 1. *adj.* preventing or intended to prevent something 2. *n.* something that prevents or is intended to prevent something

pre·view *n.* a presentation of a film, book etc. to critics before it is presented to the general public ‖ (also **prevue**)

pre·vi·ous 1. *adj.* occurring or done earlier ‖ before the right time 2. *adv.* (with 'to') before

prey *n.* an animal seized as food ‖ a victim

prey *v.i.* to seek for or seize prey ‖ to make raids in order to take booty

price *n.* that which is given or demanded in return for a thing, service etc. offered for sale or for barter ‖ that which must be done, sacrificed, suffered etc. in return for something

price **pric·ing** **priced** *v.t.* to state or ascertain the price or market value of

price·less *adj.* too valuable to carry any price ‖ very valuable ‖ very funny, ridiculous

prick *v.t.* to make (a hole) in something with a sharp point ‖ to wound by piercing with a sharp implement ‖ to pain mentally, esp. to goad as if with spurs ‖ (with 'up') to cause (esp. the ears) to point upward or forward as a sign of sudden attention or interest

prick the act or an instance of pricking ‖ a small puncture made by pricking ‖ the pain caused by pricking

prick·le 1. *n.* a pointed process arising from epidermal tissue ‖ a tingling or prickling sensation 2. *v.* **prick·ling** **prick·led** *v.i.* to feel a tingling or prickling sensation

prick·ly **prick·li·er** **prick·li·est** *adj.* feeling as if pricked by prickles ‖ quick to take offense, very touchy

pride 1. *n.* excessive self-esteem ‖ behavior that shows this ‖ a sense of satisfaction with one's achievements etc. ‖ the best ‖ (of lions) a group, often a family, in the wild state **prid·ing**

priest *n.* an ordained person ‖ any member of the clergy

prig *n.* a narrow-minded person who makes an annoying parade of being morally or culturally superior to others **prig·gish** *adj.*

prim 1. *adj.* **prim·mer** **prim·mest** stiff and formal 2. *v.t.* **prim·ming** **primmed** to shape (the face or lips) into a prim expression

pri·ma·cy *n.* the state of being first in rank, importance etc. ‖ the office or dignity of a primate

pri·ma don·na *pl.* **pri·ma don·nas** *n.* the chief woman singer in an opera

pri·ma fa·cie *adj.* having every appearance of proving a fact though it may not constitute certain proof

pri·mal *adj.* primitive or earliest in history ‖ first in importance

pri·ma·ri·ly *adv.* principally ‖ originally

pri·ma·ry 1. *adj.* first in time of origin

of order of development ‖ basic, fundamental ‖ first in a succession or series ‖ first in importance 2. *pl.* **pri·ma·ries** *n.* something which is primary ‖ (esp *pl*) a primary election

pri·mate *n.* a bishop having authority over other bishops ‖ the highest order of mammals, including man, apes etc.

prime 1. *adj.* first in time, importance, quality or rank ‖ fundamental **2.** *n.* the fundamental note in a harmonic series

prime prim·ing primed *v.t.* to fill (a pump) with water to initiate action ‖ to fill pores of (wood etc.) with a first coat of paint etc. ‖ to provide (someone) with information etc. beforehand

prime meridian the meridian at 0° longitude, passing through Greenwich, England

prim·er *n.* something that primes ‖ a cap, cylinder etc. containing an explosive compound

pri·me·val, pri·mae·val *adj.* belonging to the earliest era of life on the earth

prim·i·tive 1. *adj.* having the characteristics of the earliest stages of civilization ‖ roughly constructed, crude and simple a ‖ without civilized accretions ‖ of or pertaining to an early stage of development ‖ showing little change from an early ancestral type **2.** *n.* a primitive person ‖ a primitive work of art or artist

prim·i·tiv·ism *n.* primitivity ‖ primitive practices, customs etc. ‖ the style of a primitive (deliberately unsophisticated) artist **prim·i·tiv·i·ty** *n.* the quality or state of being primitive

pri·mor·di·al *adj.* existing from the beaginning ‖ fundamental, underived

primp *v.i.* to busy oneself fussily about one's dress or appearance

prince *n.* any male member in certain royal families ‖ the ruler of a principality ‖ a cardinal

prince·ly pince·li·er prince·li·est *adj.* worthy of a prince, splendid

prin·ci·pal 1. *adj.* first in importance **2.** *n.* a person employing another as his agent ‖ the sum of money on which interest is earned ‖ someone who is primarily liable

prin·ci·ple *n.* a law of nature as formulated and accepted by the mind ‖ an essential truth ‖ the acceptance of moral law as a guide to behavior ‖ a fundamental implication **in principle** as regards essentials, principles one accepts

print 1. *n.* a picture or design made by an inked impression of a block, engraved plate etc. ‖ a photograph made from a negative ‖ printed matter ‖ a textile made with an applied colored or black and white pattern ‖ a dress made of this

print *v.t.* to make an impression on the surface of (paper, fabric etc.) by pressing inked blocks etc. on it ‖ to reproduce (a text, news etc.) by this process ‖ to make (a photograph) from a negative ‖ to fix firmly (a memory, idea etc.) on the mind ‖ *v. i.* to practice the art of making inked impressions on paper etc. ‖ to write in characters resembling type forms **print·er** *n.* someone who prints, esp. as a profession

print·ing *n.* the art or business of a printer ‖ the total number of printed copies of a book etc. made at one time

print·out *n.* the printed record of the solution to the program or of the contents of the computer memory **print out** *v.*

pri·or 1. *adj.* earlier **2.** *adv.* earlier than

pri·or·i·ty *pl.* **pri·or·i·ties** *n.* the quality or state of coming first in time or in importance ‖ the right or privilege of precedence over others

prism *n.* a device used to disperse light or change its direction, consisting of a transparent solid with two nonparallel plane faces

pris·on *n.* a building used to confine offenders or suspects awaiting trial ‖ imprisonment

pris·on·er *n.* a person who is in custody or under restraint

pris·sy pris·si·er pris·si·est *adj.* primly precise ‖ prudish

pris·tine *adj.* unspoiled, still in an uncorrupted state

pri·va·cy *n.* freedom from undesirable intrusions

pri·vate 1. *adj.* not holding public office

|| secret, hidden from others 2. *n*. a soldier in the U.S. army **in private** not openly, without witnesses

pri·va·tion *n*. complete or serious lack of the usual necessities of life || an instance of this

priv·i·lege *n*. a benefit or advantage || any of the fundamental rights common under a modern constitutional government

priv·i·leged *adj*. enjoying a privilege

priv·y 1. *adj*. (in the phrase) **privy to** having private knowledge of 2. *pl*. **priv·ies** *n*. an outdoor toilet

prize 1. *n*. something of value or satisfaction received in recognition of distinction || something of value or satisfaction that is gained or worth gaining 2. *adj*. awarded or worthy of receiving a prize || award as a prize

prize priz·ing prized *v.t*. to value highly

prize *n*. (also **prise**) leverage || a vessel or property captured at sea in war time

pro *n*. a professional, esp. a professional athlete or coach

pro- prefix favoring or advocating || taking the place of || forward, to the front of || before, in advance

pro and con *adv*. for and against **pros and cons** *pl. n*. the arguments for and against

prob·a·bil·i·ty *pl*. **prob·a·bil·i·ties** *n*. the state or quality of being probable || something regarded as probable, based on the experience that of two or more possible effects one tends to predominate **in all probability** quite probably

prob·a·ble *adj*. likely though not certain

prob·a·bly *adv*. very likely, with probability

pro·bate 1. *n*. the official establishing of the legal validity of a will 2. *v.t*. **pro·bat·ing pro·bat·ed** to prove (a will)

pro·ba·tion *n*. a critical testing, esp. to discover a person's suitability for a job || the suspension of the sentence of a convicted offender, allowing him his freedom subject to regular supervision **pro·ba·tion·ar·y** *adj*. of or relating to probation **pro·ba·tion·er** *n*. a person undergoing probation

probe 1. *n*. a blunt surgical instrument

used to explore wounds or cavities in the body || a device used for scientific exploration || an investigation 2. **prob·ing probed** *v.t*. to investigate thoroughly || *v.i*. to make an examination with a surgical probe

pro·bi·ty *n*. scrupulous honesty

prob·lem *n*. a question whose answer is doubtful or difficult to find || a matter that causes worry

prob·lem·at·ic *adj*. constituting a problem || open to question **prob·lem·át·i·cal** *adj*.

pro·bos·cis *pl*. **pro·bos·cis·es, pro·bos·ci·des** *n*. a trunklike process of the head e.g. in many insects and in elephants

pro·ce·dure *n*. a prescribed way of doing something

pro·ceed *v.i*. to move forward || to continue || to come forth, arise || (with 'against') to begin action or take legal measures **pro·céed·ing** *n*. a course of action || *(pl.)* transactions or negotiations || *(pl.)* legal measures **pro·ceeds** *pl. n*. the sum yielded by a sale

proc·ess 1. *n*. a method of manufacturing something || a moving foraward || an outgrowth or extension of an organ or an organism || legal proceedings, or the writ or summons beginning them 2. *v.t*. to submit (something) to a treatment, preparation or process

pro·ces·sion *n*. an orderly line of persons moving together in the same direction

pro·claim *v.t*. to announce publicly || to declare

proc·la·ma·tion *n*. a proclaiming || an announcement

pro·cliv·i·ty *pl*. **pro·cliv·i·ties** *n*. a tendency or inclination towards some habit, attitude of mind etc.

pro·cras·ti·nate pro·cras·ti·nat·ing pro·cras·ti·nat·ed *v.i*. to keep delaying **pro·crás·ti·na·tor** *n*.

pro·cras·ti·na·tion *n*. the act or habit of procrastinating

pro·cre·ate pro·cre·at·ing pro·cre·at·ed *v.t*. to produce || *v.i*. to bear offspring **pró·cre·a·tive** *adj*.

pro·cre·a·tion *n*. a procreating or being

procreated

proc·tor 1. *n.* someone who supervises **2.** *v.t.* to supervise students **proc·to·ri·al** *adj.*

proc·u·ra·tor *n.* someone who manages another's legal affairs ‖ a proctor in a court of civil or canon law **proc·u·ra·tó·ri·al** *adj.*

pro·cure pro·cur·ing pro·cured *v.t.* to obtain ‖ *v.i.* to obtain women for prostitution **pro·cúre·ment** *n.*

pro·cur·er *n.* someone who procures

prod 1. prod·ding prod·ded *v.t.* to goad ‖ *v.i.* (with 'at') to poke **2.** *n.* a poke or sharp dig ‖ an urge to activity

prod·i·gal 1. *adj.* wasteful ‖ lavishly generous **2.** *n.* a spendthrift

pro·di·gious *adj.* amazing

prod·i·gy *pl.* **prod·i·gies** *n.* a person, esp. a child, with extraordinary talents

pro·duce 1. pro·duc·ing pro·duced *v.t.* to bring forward ‖ to bring forth ‖ to create, write ‖ to bear, yield ‖ to give birth to ‖ to manufacture ‖ to bring (a play) before the public ‖ to assume overall responsibility for the making of (a film) ‖ *v.i.* to yield or manufacture products **2.** *n.* agricultural or horticultural products **pro·dúc·er** *n.* a person who produces

prod·uct *n.* something produced ‖ an outcome, result ‖ the number obtained by multiplying numbers together

pro·duc·tion *n.* something produced, esp. an artistic work

pro·duc·tive *adj.* producing in abundance ‖ yielding results ‖ producing goods **pro·duc·tiv·i·ty** *n.* ability to produce

pro·fane *adj.* blasphemous, irreverent ‖ heathen **profane pro·fan·ing pro·faned** *v.t.* to treat with irreverence, desecrate ‖ to treat disrespectfully

pro·fan·i·ty *pl.* **pro·fan·i·ties** *n.* an irreverent utterance

pro·fess *v.t.* to claim or declare ‖ *v.i.* to make a profession, esp. of religious vows **pro·féssed** *adj.* openly declared ‖ having taken religious vows **pro·fess·ed·ly** *adv.* according to a person's own claims

pro·fes·sion *n.* any vocation or occupation ‖ open declaration, avowal ‖ a declaration of religious belief ‖ a taking of religious vows **pro·fés·sion·al 1.** *adj.* of or relating to a profession ‖ showing a sound workman's command ‖ of or done by professionals **2.** *n.* someone who engages in an activity, esp. a sport, to earn money **pro·fés·sion·al·ism** *n.*

pro·fes·sor *n.* a university teacher of the highest rank in a faculty **pro·fés·sor·ate** *n.* the office or term of office of a professor **pro·fes·so·ri·al** *adj.* **pro·fes·só·ri·ate** *n.* a body of professors **pro·fés·sor·ship** *n.*

prof·fer *n.* an offer

proffer *v.t.* to offer, tender

pro·fi·cien·cy *n.* the state or quality of being proficient

pro·fi·cient *adj.* having effective command in an art

pro·file 1. *n.* the shape of something, esp. the face, as seen from a side view ‖ a concise biographical description **2.** *v.t.* **pro·fil·ing pro·filed** to draw or write a profile of

prof·it *n.* advantage, benefit ‖ financial gain ‖ an excess of income over expenditure ‖ net income

profit *v.i.* to obtain financial gain or other benefit

prof·it·a·ble *adj.* yielding profit **prof·it·a·bly** *adv.*

prof·li·ga·cy *n.* the state or quality of being profligate

prof·li·gate *adj.* dissolute ‖ wildly extravagant

pro·found *adj.* searching into the deepest problems or truths ‖ requiring deep thought ‖ intense ‖ coming as if from a great depth

pro·fun·di·ty *pl.* **pro·fun·di·ties** *n.* depth, intensity

pro·fuse *adj.* lavish, generous ‖ abundant

pro·fu·sion *n.* the state of being profuse ‖ great abundance

pro·gen·i·tor *n.* an ancestor

prog·e·ny *pl.* **prog·e·nies** *n.* offspring

prog·no·sis *pl.* **prog·no·ses** *n.* a doctor's assessment of the probable course of an illness ‖ a forecast

prog·nos·ti·cate prog·nos·ti·cat·ing

prog·nos·ti·cat·ed *v.t.* to foretell ‖ *v.i.* to make a prediction

pro·gram 1. *n.* a sequence of things to be done ‖ a list of items planned to constitute a concert, dramatic performance ‖ the performance itself ‖ a plan of the operations to be executed by a computer **2.** *v.t.* **pro·gram·ing pro·grammed** to work out a plan of the operations to be executed by (a computer) **pro·gram·mer** *n.* someone who programs a computer

prog·ress 1. *n.* forward movement ‖ a forward course of development ‖ improvement, advancement **in progress** going on now **2. pro·gress** *v.i.* to go forward or onward ‖ to develop

pro·gres·sive 1. *adj.* moving forward ‖ increasing ‖ having to do with political and social progress **2.** *n.* someone who is progressive

pro·hib·it *v.t.* to forbid with authority ‖ to prevent

pro·hi·bi·tion *n.* a prohibiting by authority **pro·hi·bi·tion·ist** *n.* an advocate of prohibition of the sale of liquor

pro·hib·i·tive *adj.* serving to prohibit

proj·ect *n.* a systematic planned undertaking ‖ a set task for a class of schoolchildren

pro·ject *v.t.* to throw by mechanical means ‖ to cause (light, an image etc.) to fall on a certain surface ‖ to cause (oneself) to enter imaginatively ‖ *v.i.* to stick out, protrude

pro·jec·tile 1. *n.* a body projected, esp. a missile **2.** *adj.* suddenly thrusting forward

pro·jec·tion *n.* a projecting or being projected ‖ a system by which lines of longitude and latitude are translated onto a plane surface so as to represent the curved surface of the earth or the celestial sphere

pro·jec·tor *n.* an instrument for projecting or for throwing an image onto a screen

pro·le·tar·i·an 1. *n.* a member of the proletariat **2.** *adj.* of or relating to the proletariat

pro·le·tar·i·at *n.* the lowest class in a modern society

pro·lif·er·ate **pro·lif·er·at·ing**

pro·lif·er·at·ed *v.i.* to grow or reproduce rapidly ‖ *v.t.* to cause to increase greatly in number

pro·lif·er·a·tion *n.* a proliferating

pro·lif·er·ous *adj.* reproducing by budding

pro·lif·ic *adj.* reproducing rapidly ‖ abundant ‖ very productive **pro·lif·i·ca·cy** *n.* **pro·lif·i·cal·ly** *adv.*

pro·logue, pro·log *n.* an introduction or preface

pro·long *v.t.* to make longer, extend, draw out

prom·e·nade 1. *n.* a slow walk ‖ a place suitable for this, esp. a paved walk along the seafront at a resort ‖ a series of walking steps in a square dance **2. prom·e·nad·ing prom·e·nad·ed** *v.i.* to take a stroll ‖ to perform a promenade in a dance

prom·i·nence *n.* the state or quality of being prominent ‖ a hill, elevation etc. **próm·i·nen·cy** *n.*

prom·i·nent *adj.* conspicuous ‖ jutting out ‖ eminent

prom·is·cu·i·ty pl. **prom·is·cu·i·ties** *n.* the fact or an instance of being promiscuous

pro·mis·cu·ous *adj.* having sexual relations with many

prom·ise 1. *n.* an assurance ‖ a firm prospect **2. prom·is·ing prom·ised** *v.t.* to make a promise ‖ to assure

prom·is·ing *adj.* likely to turn out well

prom·is·so·ry *adj.* containing a promise

prom·on·to·ry pl. **prom·on·to·ries** *n.* a point of high land jutting out into an area of water

pro·mote pro·mot·ing pro·mot·ed *v.t.* to raise in rank ‖ to help forward, further ‖ to push the sales of by intensive advertising etc. ‖ to encourage

pro·mo·tion *n.* a being promoted ‖ advancement to higher status ‖ a striving to secure greater sales by intensive advertising etc. **pro·mó·tion·al, pro·mó·tive** *adjs*

prompt *adj.* quick to respond and act without delay ‖ immediate, instant

prompt *v.t.* to rouse to action ‖ to inspire ‖ to whisper to (an actor) words which he has forgotten **prómpt·er** *n.*

prom·ul·gate **prom·ul·gat·ing**

prom·ul·gat·ed *v.t.* to proclaim
prom·ul·ga·tion, próm·ul·ga·tor *ns*
prone *adj.* prostrate ‖ inclined, disposed
prong 1. *n.* a tine of a fork ‖ a fork for lift-ing hay etc. ‖ any thin pointed object, e.g. the point of an antler **2.** *v.t.* to pierce or lift
pro·noun *n.* a word used to replace noun
pro·nounce pro·nounc·ing pro·nounced *v.t.* articulate ‖ to utter or declare formally ‖ *v.i.* to produce speech sounds ‖ to give one's authoritative opinion **pro·nóunced** *adj.* very noticeable **pro·nóunce·ment** *n.* an official anouncement
proof 1. *n.* convincing evidence ‖ the alco-holic content of a beverage compared with the standard for proof spirit ‖ an impres-sion of composed type to verify correct-ness **2.** *adj.* (with 'against') able to resist ‖ (in compounds) impenetrable by, bullet-proof ‖ of a standard alcoholic strength
proof·read proof·read·ing proof·read *v.* to read and correct (a printer's proof)
prop *n.* (theater) a property
prop *n.* a propeller
prop 1. *n.* a support **2.** *v.t.* **prop·ping propped** (often with 'up') to support with, keep upright
prop·a·gan·da *n.* information and opinions (esp. prejudiced ones) spread to influence people **prop·a·gán·dist** *n.* someone who spreads propaganda **prop·a·gán·dize prop·a·gan·diz·ing prop·a·gan·dized** *v.t.* to spread (ideas etc.) through propaganda
prop·a·gate prop·a·gat·ing prop·a·gat·ed *v.t.* to transmit from one generation to another ‖ to make widely known ‖ to trans-mit ‖ *v.i.* to multiply by natural reproduction
prop·a·ga·tion *n.* a propagating or being propagated
pro·pel pro·pel·ling pro·pelled *v.t.* to push or drive forward or onward **pro·pél·lant, pro·pél·lent 1.** *adj.* able to propel **2.** *n.* a propelling agent **pro·pél·ler** *n.* something that propels
pro·pen·si·ty pl. **pro·pen·si·ties** *n.* dispo-sition, tendency
prop·er *adj.* decent, seemly ‖ fitting, suita-ble ‖ accurate
prop·er·ty pl. **prop·er·ties** *n.* a thing or

things owned ‖ a piece of real estate ‖ abun-dant wealth ‖ ownership ‖ an attribute, characteristic ‖ any piece of furniture or accessory used on the stage or set
proph·e·cy pl. **proph·e·cies** *n.* a prediction
proph·e·sy proph·e·sy·ing proph·e·sied *v.t.* to foretell ‖ to predict
proph·et *n.* a person who, by divine inspi-ration, declares to the world the divine will, judgments etc. ‖ a leader, founder or spokesman of a cause **próph·et·ess** *n.* a woman prophet
pro·phy·lac·tic 1. *adj.* preventive **2.** *n.* anything which guards against disease
pro·phy·lax·is pl. **pro·phy·lax·es** *n.* meas-ures aiming to prevent disease ‖ the prevention of disease
pro·pin·qui·ty pl. **pro·pin·qui·ties** *n.* near-ness in place or time ‖ nearness of kinship
pro·pi·ti·ate pro·pi·ti·at·ing pro·pi·ti·at·ed *v.t.* to gain the favor of by appeasement or conciliation
pro·pi·tious *adj.* favorable, giving prom-ise of success
pro·po·nent *n.* a person who advocates a proposal
pro·por·tion *n.* a part, share ‖ ratio, comparative relation ‖ balance ‖ (*pl.*) dimensions
pro·por·tion·al *adj.* in proportion **pro·por·tion·ál·i·ty** *n.*
pro·por·tion·ate 1. *adj.* being in propor-tion **2.** *v.t.* **pro·por·tion·at·ing pro·por·tion·at·ed** to proportion
pro·pos·al *n.* a course of action put forward for consideration ‖ an offer of marriage ‖ the act of proposing
pro·pose pro·pos·ing pro·posed *v.t.* to offer for consideration ‖ to intend ‖ to put forward for approval ‖ *v.i.* to offer marriage
prop·o·si·tion 1. *n.* a proposal ‖ a statement of which the subject can be affirmed or denied ‖ a scheme, offer, usually commer-cial ‖ an invitation to sexual intercourse **2.** *v.t.* to make a business proposal to ‖ to suggest sexual intercourse to **prop·o·sí·tion·al** *adj.*
pro·pound *v.t.* to set forth for consideration
pro·pri·e·tar·y 1. *adj.* relating to owner-ship **2.** pl. **pro·pri·e·tar·ies** *n.* a body of

owners ‖ right of ownership

pro·pri·e·tor *n.* a person who has legal rights of possession, an owner **pro·pri·e** ‖ **tress** *n.* a woman proprietor

pro·pri·e·ty pl. **pro·pri·e·ties** *n.* suitability, correctness

pro·pul·sion *n.* a propelling ‖ a driving force

pro ra·ta *adv.* at a proportionate rate

pro·sa·ic *adj.* commonplace ‖ dull **pro·sa·i·cal·ly** *adv.*

pro·scribe pro·scrib·ing pro·scribed *v.t.* to outlaw (a person) ‖ to condemn or forbid (a practice)

prose 1. *n.* the language of ordinary speech ‖ dull, commonplace discourse or writing **2.** *v.i.* **pros·ing prosed** to talk or write tediously

pros·e·cute pros·e·cut·ing pros·e·cut·ed *v.t.* to start legal proceedings against ‖ *v.i.* to act as a prosecutor

pros·e·cu·tion *n.* a prosecuting ‖ the bringing of formal criminal charges against an offender in court

pros·e·cu·tor *n.* a prosecuting attorney

pros·pect 1. *n.* a wide or distant scenic view ‖ the assumed course of the future ‖ reasonable expectation ‖ a potential client or customer ‖ mineral extracted from a test sample **2.** *v.* to explore a region in search of oil, gold, minerals etc.

pro·spec·tive *adj.* destined or expected to be

pros·pec·tor *n.* someone who prospects etc.

pro·spec·tus *n.* a circular containing information

pros·per *v.i.* to thrive ‖ to achieve financial success

pros·per·i·ty *n.* the condition of being prosperous

pros·per·ous *adj.* financially successful

pros·tate 1. *adj.* of the partially muscular gland at the neck of the bladder **2.** *n.* this gland **pro·stat·ic** *adj.*

pros·the·sis pl. **pros·the·ses** *n.* an artificial device to replace a missing part of the body

pros·thet·ic *adj.* relating to prosthesis **pros·thét·ics** *n.* branch of surgery which

deals with artificial limbs

pros·ti·tute 1. *n.* a woman who has sexual intercourse for payment ‖ a person who degrades his talents for money **2.** *v.t.* **pros·ti·tut·ing pros·ti·tut·ed** to degrade

pros·ti·tu·tion *n.* the profession of offering the body for sexual relations for money ‖ degradation for money

pros·trate 1. pros·trat·ing pros·trat·ed to cast to the ground face downwards ‖ to abase (oneself) in submission, worship etc. ‖ to exhaust bodily ‖ to overcome with shock, grief etc. **2.** *adj.* lying full-length face downwards ‖ physically exhausted ‖ utterly defeated

pro·te·an *adj.* versatile ‖ able to take on different shapes

pro·tect *v.t.* to shield or defend against danger, injury etc.

pro·tec·tion *n.* a protecting ‖ a person who protects

pro·tec·tive *adj.* giving or intended to give protection

pro·tec·tor *n.* a person who or thing which protects **pro·téc·tor·al** *adj.* **pro·téc·tor·ate** *n.* government by a protector ‖ authority assumed by a strong state over a weak one for the defense of the latter

pro·té·gé *n.* someone who is under the patronage or guidance of another, esp. for help in his career

pro·tein *n.* any of a class of amino acids which are essential constituents of all living cells **pro·tein·á·ceous, pro·téin·ic, pro·téin·ous** *adjs*

pro tem·po·re *adv.* and *adj.* (*abbr.* pro tem.) for the time being

pro·test *n.* a strong dissent from or disapproval of something done or some policy adopted ‖ (in diplomacy etc.) a solemn declaration of disapproval **to do (something) under protest** to do (something) having first stated one's disapproval

pro·test *v.i.* to express strong objection ‖ *v.t.* to affirm emphatically ‖ to make a protest against

Prot·es·tant *n.* a member of any Christian body which separated from the Roman Catholic Church at the Reformation

prot·es·tant 1. *n.* someone who protests **2.** *adj.* protesting

pro·to·col 1. *n.* a code of correct procedure in diplomatic exchange and state ceremonies ‖ a preliminary draft of a diplomatic document **2. pro·to·col·ling, pro·to·col·ing pro·to·colled, pro·to·coled** *v.t.* to record in a protocol ‖ *v.i.* to draw up a protocol

pro·ton *n.* positive particle

pro·to·plasm *n.* a viscous, translucent, colloidal substance constituting all living cells

pro·to·type *n.* an original model ‖ an ancestral form or archetype **pro·to·typ·i·cal** *adj.*

pro·to·zo·an *n.* microscopic single-celled organisms **pro·to·zó·ic** *adj.*

pro·tract *v.t.* to draw out in time, prolong **pro·tráct·ed·ly** *adv.* **pro·trac·tile** *adj.* capable of being extended

pro·trac·tor *n.* an instrument for measuring angles on a flat surface ‖ a muscle whose function extends a limb

pro·trude pro·trud·ing pro·trud·ed *v.t.* to thrust forward or outward ‖ *v.i.* to stick out or project

pro·tru·sion *n.* something which protrudes

pro·tu·ber·ance *n.* something that is protuberant

pro·tu·ber·ant *adj.* bulging, swelling out

proud *adj.* manifesting inordinate self-esteem ‖ feeling proper satisfaction ‖ splendid, glorious

prove prov·ing proved, prov·en *v.t.* to establish the truth of by evidence ‖ to show to be true by reasoning ‖ to test ‖ to establish the authenticity of ‖ to proof, take proofs of ‖ *v.i.* (sometimes with 'to be') to be shown by later knowledge to be

pro·verb *n.* a brief familiar maxim of folk wisdom

pro·vide pro·vid·ing pro·vid·ed *v.t.* to supply ‖ to equip ‖ *v.i.* to ensure a supply of the necessities of life **pro·vid·ed** *conj.* on condition that

prov·i·dence *n.* forethought ‖ thrift **Prov·i·dence** divine care and guidance

prov·ince *n.* an administrative division of certain countries ‖ proper scope of profes-

sional or business action ‖ (*pl.*, with 'the') the parts of a country beyond the capital

pro·vin·cial 1. *adj.* of or relating to a provaince ‖ taking or characterized by a limited view **2. pro·vin·cial·ism** *n.* the narrow attitude of mind or the unpolished behavior held to be characteristic of the provinces ‖ love of one's own region not enlarged into patriotism **pro·vin·ci·al·i·ty** *n.*

pro·vi·sion 1. *n.* a providing or being provided ‖ preparation ‖ a clause in a legal document, esp. a proviso ‖ (*pl.*) food supplies **2.** *v.t.* to supply **pro·ví·sion·al** *adj.* temporary ‖ requiring later confirmation

prov·o·ca·tion *n.* a provoking or being provoked ‖ something which provokes

pro·voc·a·tive *adj.* tending to provoke ‖ arousing annoyance deliberately

pro·voke pro·vok·ing pro·voked *v.t.* to rouse to anger ‖ to incite, instigate ‖ to excite

prow *n.* the forepart of a boat or ship, the bow

prow·ess *n.* dexterity and daring ‖ great ability

prowl *v.* to roam stealthily in search of prey, or as if in search of prey

prowl·er *n.* someone who prowls, esp. a sneak thief

prox·i·mate *adj.* nearest, next

prox·im·i·ty *n.* being near in space, time or kinship

prox·y 1. *pl.* **prox·ies** *n.* authority given by one person to another to act for him ‖ the person thus authorized **2.** *adj.* of an act done by a proxy

prude *n.* a person who affects an excessively rigid attitude in matters of personal modesty and conduct

pru·dence *n.* foresight leading a person to avoid error or danger ‖ practical discretion

pru·dent *adj.* guided by prudence

prune *n.* a plum that has been dried

prune prun·ing pruned *v.t.* to cut off from (a tree or bush) branches ‖ to reduce, cut down

pru·ri·ent *adj.* excessively interested in or curious about sexuality

pry pry·ing pried *v.i.* to look closely into something which is not one's own concern

pry *v.t.* **pry·ing pried** to force open or lift with or as if with a lever ‖ to extract with difficulty

Psalm *n.* any of the sacred songs in the Book of Psalms **psalm** a song to God

pseudo- prefix sham ‖ spurious ‖ unreal

pseu·do·nym *n.* a name other than one's own, assumed for some purpose **pseu·do·nym·i·ty** *n.*

pshaw *interj.* used as a mild expression of irritation, disbelief etc.

psy·che *n.* the soul ‖ the mind, both conscious and unconscious

psych·e·del·ic *adj.* of a mental condition induced by certain drugs and characterized by hallucinations ‖ of a drug inducing this state

psy·chi·a·trist *n.* a doctor who specializes in psychiatry

psy·chi·a·try *n.* the branch of medicine concerned with the treatment and study of mental disorders

psy·chic 1. *adj.* nonphysical ‖ of or pertaining to the mind or spirit ‖ apparently able to respond to nonphysical influences **2.** *n.* a person able to act as a medium **psy·chi·cal** *adj.*

psy·cho·a·nal·y·sis *n.* a technique of psychotherapy **psy·cho·an·a·lyst** *n.* a person who practices psychoanalysis **psy·cho·an·a·lyt·ic, psy·cho·an·a·lyt·i·cal** *adj* **psy·cho·an··a·lyt·i·cal·ly** *adv.* **psy·cho·an·a·lyze, psy·cho·an·a·lyse psy·cho·an·a·lyz·ing, psy·cho·an·a·lys·ing psy·cho·an·a·lyzed, psy·cho·an·a·lysed** *v.t.* to subject (someone) to psychoanalytic treatment

psy·cho·gen·ic *adj.* originating in the mind, mental

psy·cho·log·i·cal *adj.* of or relating to the mind

psy·chol·o·gy *n.* the scientific study of human or animal behavior

psy·cho·path *n.* a person suffering from a mental disorder

psy·cho·sis *pl.* **psy·cho·ses** *n.* serious mental derangement

psy·cho·so·mat·ic *adj.* of, pertaining to or resulting from the interaction between mind and body

psy·cho·ther·a·pist *n.* a person who practices psychotherapy

psy·cho·ther·a·py *n.* the treatment of mental illness by psychological methods

ptomaine any food poisoning

pu·ber·ty *n.* the period of life when the reproductive glands begin to function **pu·bes·cence** *n.* the reaching of puberty ‖ a downy or hairy covering **pu·bés·cent** *adj.*

pu·bic *adj.* of or pertaining to the pubis

pu·bis *pl.* **pu·bès** *n.* the foremost of the three sections of the hipbone

pub·lic 1. *adj.* of or pertaining to the community as a whole ‖ that is or can be known by all members of the community **2.** *n.* (usually with 'the') the members of a community in general **in public** in the state of being visible or accessible to the public

pub·li·ca·tion *n.* a printed and published book, magazine, pamphlet etc.

pub·lic·i·ty *n.* the disseminating of advertising or informative matter ‖ the condition of being exposed to the knowledge of the general public, esp. through newspaper reports

pub·li·cize pub·li·ciz·ing pub·li·cized *v.t.* to bring to public notice

pub·lish *v.t.* to arrange the printing and distribution of (books, newspapers etc.) for sale to the public ‖ to announce publicly **púb·lish·er** *n.*

puck *n.* a hard rubber disk used in ice hockey

puck·er 1. *v.t.* (often with 'up') to gather into narrow folds or wrinkles **2.** *n.* a narrow fold or wrinkle

pud·ding *n.* a sweet dessert, thick and soft

pud·dle *n.* a small pool of liquid **púd·dly** *adj.* having many puddles

pudge *n.* a short, fat person **púdg·i·ness** *n.* the quality of being pudgy **púdg·y pudg·i·er pudg·i·est** *adj.* short and fat

pueb·lo 1. *pl.* **pueb·los** *n.* a type of Indian village built as communal dwelling houses of adobe **2. Pueb·lo** *adj.* of the Pueblo Indians or their culture

pu·er·ile adj. childish **pu·er·il·i·ty** n.

puff 1. v.i. to breathe quickly ‖ to emit steam, smoke etc. in a series of whiffs ‖ to blow in rapid gusts ‖ (with 'up') become inflated ‖ (with 'out') to extinguish **2.** n. a short, light gust of air, steam, smoke etc. ‖ a small cloud ‖ a draw on a cigarette etc. ‖ a shell of soft light pastry etc. ‖ a fluffy mass ‖ publisher's blurb

pug n. a dog of a small, short-haired breed

pu·gil·ism n. boxing **pú·gil·ist** n. a boxer **pu·gil·ís·tic** adj.

pug·na·cious adj. fond of fighting, aggressive

puke 1. puk·ing puked v.i. to vomit **2.** n. vomit

pul·chri·tude n. physical beauty

pull 1. v.t. to apply a force to (something) in order to make it move towards the person or thing applying the force ‖ to extract ‖ to strain (a muscle etc.) ‖ to draw out (a knife, gun etc.) ready for use ‖ to accomplish with daring ‖ to assert (superiority) in order to obtain an advantage over someone **to pull a fast one** to play an unfair trick **to pull down** to demolish ‖ to weaken in health **to pull for** to encourage **to pull one's punches** to abstain from hitting as hard as one can ‖ to criticize or accuse less forcibly than would be justifiable **to pull through** to survive illness, danger etc. **2.** n. the act of pulling ‖ an instance of this ‖ a force which pulls or attracts ‖ a draw on a cigarette, drink etc. ‖ influence exerted to obtain a privilege or advantage ‖ a knob, handle etc. by which a drawer, bell etc. may be pulled ‖ (printing) a proof

pul·let n. a hen before the first moult

pul·ley pl. **pul·leys** n. a wheel on a fixed shaft used to transmit power by means of a belt, chain etc. passing over its circumference

pul·mo·nar·y adj. of, like or affecting the lungs ‖ pulmonate

pulp 1. n. a soft, moist mass of animal or vegetable matter ‖ such a part of a fruit or of an animal body ‖ a mixture, made by mechanical or chemical treatment of wood used as the raw material in paper-making **2.** v.t. to make into a pulp ‖ v.i. to become a pulp **púlp·i·ness** n.

pul·pit n. a small stone or wooden structure from which a preacher preaches

pul·sate pul·sat·ing pul·sat·ed v.i. to move rhythmically to and fro ‖ to be as if throbbing or vibrating

pulse 1. n. the regular expansion and contraction of the arteries due to the rhythmical action of the heart in forcing blood through them ‖ the frequency with which the resultant throbs occur ‖ a generalized group sentiment divined rather than known by direct experience **2.** puls·ing pulsed v.i. to pulsate

pul·ver·ize pul·ver·iz·ing pul·ver·ized v.t. to reduce to a fine powder ‖ to defeat with devastating effect **púl·ver·iz·er** n. someone who or something which pulverizes

pu·ma pl. **pu·mas, pu·ma** n. a cougar

pum·ice 1. n. a light, porous volcanic stone used as an abrasive in cleaning, smoothing and polishing ‖ a piece of this **2.** v.t. **pum·ic·ing pum·iced** to clean, smooth or polish with pumice

pump 1. n. a device for raising or moving a liquid or gas **2.** v.t. to raise, move or eject by using a pump or as if with a pump ‖ to supply with air by means of a pump ‖ to inflate ‖ to extract information from (a person) by subtle questions ‖ to invest heavily in a business, industry etc. ‖ v.i. to work a pump

pump n. light shoe fitting without laces or other fastening

pum·per·nick·el n. a very dark, close-textured bread

pump·kin n. a genus of vines bearing a large, edible, globular fruit ‖ the fruit of such a plant

pun n. a witticism involving the playful use of a word

punch 1. v.t. to indent or make a hole in ‖ to strike with the closed fist ‖ to herd (cattle) **2.** n. a blow with the closed fist ‖ forcefulness

punch n. a tool used to emboss or make holes in metal, paper etc.

punch n. a drink composed of sugar, spice and fruit, usually mixed with wine or liquor

punc·til·i·ous *adj.* paying scrupulous attention to points of detail in behavior, ceremony

punc·tu·al *adj.* occurring, arriving etc. at the agreed, right or stated time **punc·tu·al·i·ty** *n.*

punc·tu·ate punc·tu·at·ing punc·tu·at·ed *v.t.* to mark the divisions of (written matter) by inserting punctuation marks ‖ *v.i.* to use punctuation

punc·tu·a·tion *n.* the act, practice or system of inserting the correct marks to punctuate written matter

punc·ture 1. *n.* the act of making a hole in something by pricking ‖ a small hole made thus **2. punc·tur·ing punc·tured** *v.t.* to make (a hole, perforation etc.) by pricking ‖ to sustain a puncture in ‖ to destroy as if by pricking and deflating

pun·gent *adj.* pricking or stinging ‖ sharply biting ‖ forthright and very much to the point

pun·ish *v.t.* to prescribe a form of suffering in penalty for (an offense) ‖ to treat harshly ‖ *v.i.* to inflict punishment **pún·ish·a·ble** *adj.* deserving or capable of being, or liable to be, punished **pún·ish·ment** *n.* a punishing or being punished ‖ the suffering given or received

punk 1. *n.* a person, esp. a young one, regarded as inferior **2.** *adj.* worthless, of poor quality

punt *n.* a long, shallow, square-ended, flat-bottomed boat

pu·ny pu·ni·er pu·ni·est *adj.* much below normal in development, size or strength

pup *n.* a puppy ‖ a young seal

pu·pa *pl.* **pu·pae, pu·pas** *n.* the stage in the metamorphosis of an insect between the larva and the imago ‖ an insect in this stage **pú·pal** *adj.* **pu·pate pu·pat·ing pu·pat·ed** *v.i.* to pass into or through the pupal stage **pu·pá·tion** *n.*

pu·pil *n.* a person, esp. a child, receiving tuition

pupil *n.* the aperture in the iris of the eye

pup·pet *n.* a small model of a human being or an animal with mobile limbs controlled by strings or wires, or made in the form of a glove and operated by a hand inserted in it ‖ a person whose actions are controlled by the will of another **pup·pet·eer** *n.* a person who operates puppets **púp·pet·ry** *n.* the art of making or operating puppets

pur·chase 1. *v.t.* **pur·chas·ing pur·chased** to acquire by paying money **2.** *n.* the act of purchasing ‖ a thing purchased

pure pur·er pur·est *adj.* free from the presence of any other substance ‖ free from contamination or admixture ‖ free from moral guilt ‖ unalloyed ‖ chaste ‖ a priori

pu·rée 1. *n.* a thick liquid prepared by forcing cooked fruit or vegetables through a sieve **2.** *v.i.* to make a purée of

pur·ga·tive 1. *adj.* having the quality of purging **2.** *n.* a medicine which has this quality

pur·ga·to·ry *pl.* **pur·ga·to·ries** *n.* a condition or place of purification ‖ a condition of suffering

purge 1. purg·ing purged *v.t.* to cause (the bowels) to be evacuated ‖ to remove undesirable elements from ‖ to make expiation for ‖ to clear (oneself or another) of a charge or suspicion **2.** *n.* a purging or being purged ‖ a purgative

pu·ri·fy pu·ri·fy·ing pu·ri·fied *v.t.* to make pure by removing impurities ‖ to free from guilt or sin

pur·ism *n.* strict emphasis on purity

pur·ist *n.* a person, who will admit no departures from some chosen method, technique or ideal of perfection

Pu·ri·tan *n.* a member of a Protestant movement in England (16th and 17th cc.) **pu·ri·tan 1.** *n.* a person who seeks to regulate his own way of life and that of the community by a narrow moral code **2.** *adj.* of or relating to the Puritans **pu·ri·tán·ic, pu·ri·tán·i·cal** *adjs* **Pú·ri·tan·ism, pú·ri·tan·ism** *ns*

pu·ri·ty *n.* the state or quality of being pure

purl 1. *n.* a stitch in knitting **2.** *v.t.* to invert (stitches) in knitting

purl *v.i.* to flow in eddies, making pleasing soft sounds

pur·loin *v.t.* to steal

pur·ple 1. *n.* a composite deep color of

red and blue 2. *adj.* of the color purple

pur·port 1. *v.t.* to have as meaning or purpose ‖ to be meant to appear 2. *n.* the meaning of a document, speech etc.

pur·pose *n.* a result which it is desired to obtain ‖ willpower **on purpose** deliberately, intentionally **to the purpose** relevant **púr·pose·ful** *adj.* serving or having a purpose **púr·pose·less** *adj.* **púr·pose·ly** *adv.* on purpose

purr 1. *n.* the soft, intermittent vibratory sound made by a contented cat ‖ a similar sound 2. *v.i.* to make this sound

purse 1. *n.* a small container for coins etc. ‖ a handbag ‖ a sum of money offered or prize **to hold the purse strings** to control the money in a household etc. 2. *v.t.* **purs·ing pursed** to pucker

purs·er *n.* a ship's officer

pur·su·ant 1. *adj.* pursuing 2. *adv.* in accordance with

pur·sue pur·su·ing pur·sued *v.t.* to follow ‖ to harass persistently ‖ to continue with ‖ to go on talking about ‖ *v.i.* to go in pursuit ‖ to resume an argument after interruption

pur·suit *n.* the act of pursuing ‖ the act of proceeding with or towards an aim ‖ an occupation

pu·ru·lent *adj.* consisting of, or exuding pus

pur·vey *v.t.* to supply ‖ to provide

pur·view *n.* the extent of the meaning of a document ‖ the extent of the knowledge, authority or responsibility

pus *n.* yellowish-white fluid matter, produced by infected body tissue

push 1. *v.t.* to apply a force to (something) in order to make it move ‖ to cause to move by exerting pressure ‖ to exert influence upon (someone) so that he acts in a desired way ‖ *v.i.* to make a steady effort towards some end ‖ to advance, esp. with persistence or energy **to push one's luck** to act rashly, take a dangerous risk 2. *n.* the act of pushing ‖ an instance of this ‖ influence ‖ self-assertion, aggressive drive

push·o·ver *n.* a person easily persuaded, tricked etc.

pu·sil·lan·i·mous *adj.* showing a lack of

moral courage

puss·y *pl.* **puss·ies** *n.* (pet name for) a cat

puss·y·foot *v.i.* to avoid committing oneself

pus·tule *n.* a tiny abscess on the skin surface

put 1. **put·ting put** *v.t.* to cause to be in a specified place, position etc. ‖ to cause to be in a specified condition, situation, relationship etc. ‖ to submit for attention or consideration ‖ to impose ‖ to apply, bring to bear ‖ to lay ‖ to invest ‖ to gamble (money) ‖ to fix ‖ *v.i.* (of a ship) to take a specified course **to put away** to place (something) where it should be when not in use ‖ to have (an animal) killed painlessly **to put forward** to submit (a proposal etc.) for attention or consideration **to put in** to present (a claim) **to put it over on** (someone) to deceive (someone) **to put off** to postpone **to put out** to extinguish **to put through** to cause to undergo ‖ to negotiate (a business deal) **to put together** to assemble **to put upon** to impose on **to put up with** to endure 2. *n.* a throw of the weight or shot 3. *adj.* (in the phrase) **to stay put** to remain in the same position, condition, situation etc.

pu·ta·tive *adj.* commonly thought to be, reputed

pu·tre·fac·tion *n.* the chemical decomposition of animal or vegetable tissue

pu·tre·fy pu·tre·fy·ing pu·tre·fied *v.i.* to become putrid ‖ *v.t.* to cause to become putrid

pu·trid *adj.* rotten, decayed

putt 1. *v.t.* (*golf*) to strike (the ball) gently so that it rolls across the green towards the hole 2. *n.* (*golf*) a stroke made in this way

putt·er *n.* (*golf*) a short-shafted wood or iron with an almost vertical face, used for putting

put·ter *v.i.* to loiter, dawdle

put·ty 1. *n.* powdered chalk mixed with linseed used e.g. to hold window glass in its frame 2. *v.t.* **put·ty·ing put·tied** to fix, fill or cover with putty

puz·zle 1. **puz·zling puz·zled** *v.t.* to perplex (someone) ‖ *v.i.* to make a great mental effort to find a solution or meaning 2. *n.* a question or device which sets a problem to be worked out by ingenuity

pyg·my, pig·my 1. *pl.* **pyg·mies, pig·mies** *n.* a person of very small stature **Pyg·my, Pig·my** *pl.* **Pyg·mies, Pig·mies** a member of a Negrillo people of equatorial Africa **2.** *adj.* of or relating to a person of very small stature

py·lon *n.* a lofty structure used esp. to carry electric cables etc. over a long span ‖ a large monumental gateway

py·or·rhe·a, py·or·rhoe·a *n.* a discharge of pus, esp. from the gums

pyr·a·mid *n.* a solid figure of which the base is a polygon and the other faces are triangles with a common vertex ‖ any of the very large square-based stone monuments of this form, constructed by the ancient Egyptians and by the Aztecs and Mayas

pyre *n.* a heaped mass of material for the burning of a corpse

py·ro·ma·ni·a *n.* an irrational compulsion to destroy by fire **py·ro·ma·ni·ac** *n.* **py·ro·ma·ni·a·cal** *adj.*

py·rom·e·ter *n.* an instrument used to measure temperatures too high for ordinary thermometers **py·ro·met·ric**, **py·ro·met·ri·cal** *adjs* **py·rom·e·try** *n.*

py·ro·tech·nics *n.* the art of making or displaying fireworks ‖ (*pl.*) a brilliant or witty display **py·ro·tech·nist**, **py·ro·tech·ny** ns

py·thon *n.* a genus of nonvenomous snakes which kill their prey by constriction

Q

Q, q the seventeenth letter of the English alphabet

quack 1. *n.* a person who pretends to have medical knowledge ‖ a fraudulent person **2.** *adj.* fraudulent, bogus **quack·er·y** *n.*

quad·ran·gle *n.* a plane figure with four sides, esp. a square or rectangle **quad·ran·gu·lar** *adj.*

quad·rant *n.* a quarter of a circle's circumference ‖ an instrument for measuring angles

quad·ri·lat·er·al 1. *n.* a plane figure enclosed by four straight lines **2.** *adj.* having four straight sides

quad·ru·ped 1. *n.* a four-footed animal **2.** *adj.* four-footed **quad·ru·pe·dal** *adj.*

quad·ru·ple *adj.* four times as much or as many

quadruple quad·ru·pling quad·ru·pled *v.t.* to multiply by four

quad·ru·plet *n.* one of four offspring of a single birth

quaff 1. *v.i.* to take copious drinks **2.** *n.* a hearty drink

quag·mire *n.* shaky, muddy ground ‖ a situation which threatens to become inextricable

quail *pl.* **quail, quails** *n.* a migratory game bird

quail *v.i.* to flinch, to lose courage

quaint *adj.* old and picturesque

quake 1. *v.i.* **quak·ing quaked** to shake **2.** *n.* a trembling or quaking ‖ an earthquake

qual·i·fi·ca·tion *n.* a limiting, narrowing down, reservation ‖ a skill ‖ a requirement which has to be met **qual·i·fi·ca·to·ry** *adj.*

qual·i·fy qual·i·fy·ing qual·i·fied *v.t.* to render fit or competent, to entitle ‖ to modify, restrict ‖ mitigate ‖ *v.i.* to be or become qualified

qual·i·ty *pl.* **qual·i·ties** *n.* grade, degree of excellence ‖ trait, characteristic, attribute etc. ‖ timbre

qualm *n.* a scruple ‖ a sensation of nausea

quan·da·ry *pl.* **quan·da·ries** *n.* a dilemma, perplexity

quan·ti·ty *pl.* **quan·ti·ties** *n.* an amount

quan·tum *pl.* **quan·ta** *n.* amount, quantity ‖ share

quar·an·tine 1. *n.* a period of isolation imposed to lessen the risk of spreading an infectious or contagious disease **2.** *v.t.* **quar·an·tin·ing quar·an·tined** to put in quarantine, to isolate

quark *n.* a hypothetical basic subatomic nuclear particle

quar·rel quar·rel·ing quar·reled *v.i.* to wrangle, to dispute anygrily ‖ to find fault

quarrel *n.* an angry dispute, altercation ‖ disagreement **quár·rel·some** *adj.* quick to quarrel

quar·ry *pl.* **quar·ries** *n.* prey

quarry 1. *pl.* **quar·ries** *n.* an open cavity where stone or slate is extracted **2.** *v.t.* **quar·ry·ing quar·ried** to take from a quarry ‖ to extract (information) from books, records etc. ‖ *v.i.* to search for information **quar·ry·man** *pl.* **quar·ry·men** *n.* a person who works in a quarry

quart *n.* any of various units of liquid or dry capacity

quar·ter 1. *n.* one of four equal parts, a fourth part ‖ a district in a town ‖ any point or direction of the compass, esp. a cardinal point or division ‖ a source of information, help etc. ‖ mercy granted to an enemy or opponent in a contest ‖ 25 cents ‖ a coin of this value ‖ the lateral part of a horse's hoof between the heel and the toe ‖ lodging **at close quarters** very near by **2.** *v.t.* to divide into four equal parts ‖ to lodge, assign accommodation to **3.** *adj.* consisting of or equal to a quarter

quar·ter·back *n.* (football) the player whose position is behind the line of scrimmage and who generally calls the signals for the plays

quar·ter·ly 1. *adj.* occurring every quarter of a year **2.** *adv.* once every quarter **3.** *pl.* **quar·ter·lies** *n.* a publication issued once every quarter

quar·tet, quar·tette *n.* a musical composition for four voices or instruments ‖ a group of performers of such compositions

quartz *n.* a common and widely distributed form of silicon dioxide

qua·sar *n.* any of several very intense celestial radio sources

quash *v.t.* to annul ‖ to put down

qua·si- 1. *adj.* seeming **2.** prefix seeming, almost real, apparent ‖ semi-, more or less

qua·ver 1. *v.i.* (of the voice) to shake, tremble **2.** *n.* a tremulous unsteadiness in speech

quay *n.* an artificially constructed wharf for loading and unloading ships

queen 1. *n.* the wife of a king ‖ a female monarch ‖ a woman, creature or thing thought of as the foremost of its kind ‖ the fertile female of social insects ‖ a playing card ‖ *(chess)* the most mobile piece **2.** *v.t.* *(chess)* to convert (a pawn) into a queen

queen·ly queen·li·er queen·li·est *adj.* befitting a queen ‖ of or like a queen

queer 1. *adj.* strange, peculiar ‖ eccentric, odd ‖ homosexual **2.** *v.t.* to spoil, ruin **3.** *n.* a homosexual

quell *v.t.* to subdue ‖ to crush, to suppress

quench *v.t.* to put out, extinguish ‖ to slake (thirst)

quer·u·lous *adj.* complaining, peevish

que·ry 1. *pl.* **que·ries** *n.* a doubt or objection **2.** *v.t.* **que·ry·ing que·ried** to pose as a question ‖ to question (someone)

quest *n.* a pursuit, search **in quest of** in search of

ques·tion *n.* a word, phrase or sentence asking about a particular point, fact etc. ‖ doubt ‖ a topic, esp. one involving a difficulty ‖ a questioning, interrogation **beyond question, beyond all question** without doubt, certainly **in question** in doubt ‖ under consideration **out of the question** impossible, not to be thought of

question *v.t.* to ask, to interrogate ‖ to dispute **qués·tion·a·ble** *adj.* open to doubt **qués·tion·a·bly** *adv.*

question mark a punctuation mark (?) after a question

ques·tion·naire *n.* a set of questions drawn up for answering usually to provide statistical information

queue *n.* the line-up of messages waiting to be processed, transmitted, or stored ‖ a plait of hair

quib·ble 1. *n.* a piddling piece of faultfinding **2.** *v.i.* **quib·bling quib·bled** to use a quibble or quibbles

quiche *n.* a pastry shell filled with egg custard into which bits of ham and grated cheese have been added

quick 1. *adj.* fast-moving, rapid ‖ prompt ‖ hasty, impulsive **2.** *n.* the sensitive living flesh, esp. the part under the nail **3.** *adv.* quickly

quick·en *v.t.* accelerate ‖ to stimulate, rouse ‖ *v.i.* to become faster

quick·sand *n.* a mass of unstable sand saturated with water, tending to suck down into it anyone or anything that comes on to it ‖ such sand

quick·sil·ver *n.* mercury

quick-tem·pered *adj.* having a temper that flares up easily

quick-wit·ted *adj.* quick to understand

quid pro quo *n.* something said or done in return for something else, esp. by way of retaliation

qui·es·cence *n.* the state or quality of being quiescent

qui·es·cent *adj.* at rest, dormant, inactive

qui·et *n.* silence, stillness ‖ repose

quiet *adj.* peaceful, calm and undisturbed ‖ noiseless ‖ free from anguish, worry etc. ‖ (of people) having a gentle, reserved manner ‖ (of colors) soft, unobtrusive ‖ tranquil, free from social pressures ‖ informal

quiet *v.t.* to soothe ‖ *v.i.* to become quiet

qui·e·tude *n.* stillness, calm

qui·e·tus *n.* death, final dissolution

quill 1. *n.* a long feather of a bird's wing or tail ‖ a pen made from the hard stem of a bird's feather ‖ the hollow spine of a porcupine ‖ a spindle or bobbin **2.** *v.t.* to wind onto a spindle or bobbin

quilt 1. *n.* a bedcover made of feathers, flock or other padding **2.** *v.t.* to stitch like a quilt ‖ *v.i.* to make a quilt **quilt·ing** *n.* padded material used for making quilts

quince *n.* a small tree. It bears pear-shaped, astringent yellow fruits, used cooked or preserved ‖ its fruit

qui·nine *n.* an alkaloid used esp. as a febrifuge in antimalarial treatment

quin·tes·sence *n.* the chief part of anything ‖ something perfectly exemplifying a quality **quin·tes·sen·tial** *adj.*

quin·tet, quin·tette *n.* a composition for five performers ‖ a group of five instrumentalists or singers

quin·tu·ple 1. *adj.* five times as many ‖ having five parts **2.** *n.* a quantity five times as large as another **3. quin·tu·pling quin·tu·pled** *v.t.* to multiply by five ‖ *v.i.* to become five times as much or as many

quin·tu·plet *n.* one of five children born at a single birth

quip 1. *n.* a drily witty or sarcastic remark **2.** *v.t.* **quip·ping quipped** to make (such a remark)

quirk *n.* a peculiar trait of character

quit quit·ting quit, quit·ted *v.t.* to leave ‖ to resign ‖ to discontinue

quite *adv.* completely, entirely ‖ very much

quiv·er 1. *v.* to tremble, to shake **2.** *n.* a quivering ‖ a tremulous sound

quiver *n.* a case to hold arrows

quix·ot·ic *adj.* striving for lofty ideals in a way that is totally unrealistic ‖ rashly altruistic **quix·ot·i·cal·ly** *adv.*

quiz 1. *pl.* **quiz·zes** *n.* a short test **2.** *v.t.* **quiz·zing quizzed** to test (someone) by asking a series of questions

quiz·zi·cal *adj.* interrogative, indicating a state of puzzlement ‖ mildly eccentric or odd

quo·rum *n.* a number of people that must be present to make valid the proceedings of a committee

quo·ta *n.* an allotted share

quo·ta·ble *adj.* which may be publicly repeated

quo·ta·tion *n.* a passage or phrase quoted ‖ the amount declared as the current price for a commodity etc. ‖ a contractor's estimate

quotation marks (" ") punctuation marks signalizing direct speech, a quoted passage or phrase etc.

quote 1. quot·ing quot·ed *v.t.* to repeat in speech or writing a passage from ‖ to refer to (a person, work etc.) in support of a statement ‖ to state (the price) of ‖ *v.i.* to make a quotation **2.** *n.* a quotation

quo·tid·i·an 1. *adj.* daily, occurring each day **2.** *n.* a quotidian fever

quo·tient *n.* the result obtained after dividing one number by another

R

R, r the eighteenth letter of the English alphabet

rab·bi *n.* an ordained leader of a Jewish congregation

rab·bit *pl.* **rab·bits, rab·bit** *n.* gray-brown, extremely prolific, herbivorous animal ‖ the fur a rabbit

rab·ble *n.* a large, disorderly mob of people

rab·id *adj.* affected with rabies ‖ violent, unreasoning **ra·bid·i·ty** *n.*

ra·bies *n.* an acute virus disease transmitted with infected saliva through the bite of a rabid animal

race *n.* a distinct group of people which share certain inherited physical characteristics ‖ a subdivision of a species ‖ a particular breed

race 1. *n.* a contest of speed ‖ a strong, swift current ‖ a slipstream **2.** *v.i.* **rac·ing raced** to take part in a contest of speed ‖ to go swiftly

rac·er *n.* a person or animal who races ‖ a car, bicycle etc. made and used for racing ‖ any of several snakes

ra·cial *adj.* pertaining to the distinction between races

rac·ism *n.* the assumption that one race is biologically superior to another ‖ a social system based on these assumptions **rác·ist** *n.* and *adj.*

rack *n.* a framework of wooden or metal bars, pegs etc., for holding objects ‖ *(pool games)* a triangular frame for setting up the balls at the beginning of a game

rack 1. *v.t.* to torture by stretching on a rack **rack one's brains** to think very hard ‖ to try very hard to remember **2.** *n.* an instrument of torture

rack·et, rac·quet *n.* a bat formed by a long-handled oval wooden frame across which a mesh of catgut or nylon is stretched

racket *n.* a clattering noise ‖ a fraudulent means of gaining money ‖ an easy way of making money which is lawful but not praiseworthy

rack·et·eer *n.* a person who is engaged in fraudulent business

rac·on·teur *n.* a person who tells anecdotes well

rac·y rac·i·er rac·i·est *adj.* spirited ‖ wittily indecent

ra·dar *n.* a radio system which detects the presence, position and speed of such objects as ships, aircraft, vehicles etc. [*RA*dio *D*etection *A*nd *R*anging]

ra·di·al 1. *adj.* pertaining to a radius ‖ having radiating lines ‖ moving along a radial nerve or artery

ra·di·ance *n.* the state of being radiant **rá·di·an·cy** *n.*

ra·di·ant *adj.* emitting energy in the form of electromagnetic waves ‖ shining ‖ bright with great joy

ra·di·ate ra·di·at·ing ra·di·at·ed *v.t.* to emit (something) in all directions from a central point ‖ *v.i.* to lose energy by emission

ra·di·a·tion *n.* the act or process of radiating ‖ energy radiated in the form of waves or particles

ra·di·a·tor *n.* any of various heating or cooling devices which work by radiating heat

rad·i·cal 1. *adj.* relating to fundamentals ‖ relating to the root of a number ‖ the rhizome, or rootlike stem ‖ seeking to make drastic reforms in society as it is **2.** *n.* a number ‖ the base or root of a word from which other words can be formed ‖ a person of radical views or sympathies

rad·i·cal·ism *n.* the quality of being radical ‖ the doctrines of radicals, esp. political radicals

ra·di·o 1. *n.* the transmission and reception of messages by electromagnetic waves ‖ broadcasting ‖ a radio receiving set **2.** *adj.* operated by electromagnetic waves ‖ of or relating to radio **3.** *v.i.* to communicate by radio

ra·di·o·ac·tive *adj.* having radioactivity **ra·di·o·ac·tiv·i·ty** *n.* the property possessed by some natural elements and many synthetic elements of spontaneously undergoing nuclear decay

ra·di·ol·o·gy *n.* the study of high-energy radiations, esp. their use in the treatment of disease

rad·ish *n.* an annual plant with a tuberous taproot esteemed for its pungent, crisp flesh ‖ this root

ra·di·um *n.* a metallic element which is radioactive

ra·di·us *pl.* **ra·di·i ra·di·us·es** *n.* a straight line drawn from the center of a circle to any point on its periphery ‖ the shorter of the two bones of the forearm in man

ra·don *n.* a radioactive gaseous element

raf·fish *adj.* somewhat disreputable, in a flashy way

raf·fle 1. *n.* a lottery **2.** **raf·fling raf·fled** *v.t.* to sell by raffle ‖ *v.i.* to take part in or conduct a raffle

raft 1. *n.* a floating platform used for transportation over water or moored as a diving platform **2.** *v.t.* to transport on a raft ‖ *v.i.* to go by raft

raf·ter *n.* one of the sloping beams forming the framework of a roof

raft·er *n.* a man who forms rafts out of logs

rag *n.* a torn, tattered scrap of cloth ‖ (*pl.*) shabby, tattered clothing ‖ cloth for cleaning or polishing

rag rag·ging ragged *v.t.* to tease ‖ to scold

rag·a·muf·fin *n.* a ragged person, esp. a street urchin

rage *n.* violent and uncontrolled anger ‖ intense emotion, passion ‖ an object of modish enthusiasm

rage *v.i.* **rag·ing raged** to utter with uncontrolled anger ‖ (of a storm) to be unchecked in its violence

rag·ged *adj.* torn or frayed ‖ having a broken, jagged outline or surface

ra·gout *n.* a dish of stewed meat and vegetables

rag·time *n.* a type of early jazz

rag·weed *n.* a genus of plants whose pollen may cause hay fever and asthma

raid 1. *n.* a swift, sudden military attack with a limited objective ‖ air raid ‖ a sudden swoop on suspected premises by law-enforcement officers to arrest criminals **2.** *v.* to make a raid

rail 1. *n.* a horizontal bar for a support in climbing stairs etc. or for a guard or barrier ‖ the fence on either side of a racetrack **by rail** by railroad train **2.** *v.t.* to separate from an adjoining or surrounding space by a rail

rail *v.i.* to utter curses ‖ to shout abuse

rail·ing *n.* a fence, barrier ‖ material for rails

rail·ler·y *n.* good-humored teasing

rail·road 1. *n.* a road or system of roads on which parallel rails are laid for trains to run on **2.** *v.t.* to rush through quickly ‖ to cause (someone) to be sent to prison on a false charge

rai·ment *n.* clothing, esp. of fine quality

rain *n.* a multitude of falling drops of water formed by the coalescing of droplets in a cloud

rain *v.i.* to fall as rain ‖ *v.t.* to cause to fall like pouring rain

rain·bow 1. *n.* an arc of concentric bands in the atmosphere in the colors **2.** *adj.* many colored

rain·fall *n.* a fall of rain ‖ the precipitation of a given period on a region as measured by the depth of the water in a rain gauge

raise 1. *v.t.* **rais·ing raised** to cause to rise or come to a vertical or standing position ‖ to rouse ‖ to incite ‖ to bring back to life ‖ to build up or construct ‖ to initiate ‖ to bring up ‖ to elevate ‖ to cause (the voice) to rise in pitch or strength ‖ to cause to rise in amount, size, value, price etc. ‖ to remove ‖ to bring up ‖ to breed ‖ to cause to grow 2. *n.* an increase in salary

rai·sin *n.* grape dried either in the sun or artificially

rai·son d'ê·tre *n.* the justifying reason for the existence of something

rake *n.* a hand tool for smoothing out loose soil or gravel, collecting fallen leaves etc.

rake *n.* a thoroughly dissolute man, esp. one in fashionable society

rake rak·ing raked *v.t.* to collect with a rake ‖ to gather ‖ to make clean, smooth, loosen ‖ to search minutely ‖ (usually with 'in') to take in a great deal of (money) ‖ *v.i.* to use a rake

rak·ish *adj.* jaunty

ral·ly 1. *v.* **ral·ly·ing ral·lied** *v.t.* to gather together ‖ to cause to regain vigor ‖ to summon together for a common purpose ‖ *v.i.* to come back to a state of order ‖ to regain strength ‖ (of stocks etc.) to rise again in price after a fall 2. *pl.* **ral·lies** *n.* *(tennis)* a sustained to-and-fro succession of strokes by opposing players

ram *n.* a male sheep ‖ a battering ram

ram ram·ming rammed *v.t.* to crash head-on into ‖ to stuff with tightly pressed material ‖ (of a ship) to attack with a ram ‖ *v.i.* to crash violently into an obstacle ‖ to pound earth **to ram something down someone's throat** to force someone to accept an unwelcome fact

ram·ble 1. *v.i.* **ram·bling ram·bled** to go for a long, unplanned walk purely for enjoyment ‖ to talk or write without any clear thread 2. *n.* the act of rambling **rám·bler** *n.* any of several climbing roses **rám·bling** *adj.* seeming to be constructed on no clear plan ‖ wandering, disconnected

ram·bunc·tious *adj.* boisterous ‖ difficult to control

ram·e·kin *n.* cheese dish ‖ a dish for baking this

ram·i·fi·ca·tion *n.* the process of branching ‖ a branch or offshoot ‖ a development or outgrowth of something which has expanded as though by branching

ram·i·fy ram·i·fy·ing ram·i·fied *v.t.* to cause to produce branches or subdivisions ‖ *v.i.* branching

ra·mose *adj.* composed of or having branches

ramp *n.* a sloping path joining different levels of a road etc. ‖ a passenger stairway for boarding an aircraft

ram·page 1. *v.i.* **ram·pag·ing ram·paged** to behave violently, be in a storm of anger 2. *n.* violent or uncontrolled behavior **ram·pá·geous** *adj.*

ramp·ant *adj.* *(heraldry,* of a lion) on the hind legs with forepaws menacingly or aggressively outstretched and the head in profile ‖ growing unchecked

ram·part *n.* a broad-topped embankment constructed for defense

ram·rod *n.* a rod of iron used to force the gunpowder and bullets down the barrel of a muzzle-loading gun ‖ a rod for cleaning a rifle or gun

ram·shack·le *adj.* disrepair

ranch 1. *n.* a farm for breeding and raising cattle, horses or sheep 2. *v.i.* to manage a ranch ‖ *v.t.* to raise (an animal) on a ranch **ránch·er** *n.* a person who owns or manages a ranch, or a ranch hand

ran·cid *adj.* smelling or tasting foul because of chemical change **ran·cid·i·ty** *n.*

ran·cor *n.* bitter, lasting hatred **rán·cor·ous** *adj.*

ran·dom 1. *n.* in an unplanned way, without any predetermined purpose or method 2. *adj.* haphazard

range *n.* a row, file or rank of things ‖ a group of mountain ‖ a cooking stove ‖ grazing land ‖ a maximum attainable distance ‖ field, scope ‖ a place for practicing shooting

range rang·ing ranged *v.t.* to place in a line or orderly pattern ‖ to pasture (cattle etc.) on a range ‖ *v.i.* to stretch in a line ‖ to be found over a specific region ‖ to vary within limits

rang·er *n.* an officer who patrols a public forest

rang·y rang·i·er rang·i·est loose-limbed

rank 1. *n.* a homogeneous line or row of persons or things ‖ a level of relative excellence ‖ position in a hierarchy ‖ high social position 2. *v.t.* to arrange in a rank or ranks ‖ to hold a higher rank than ‖ v.i. to form a rank or ranks ‖ to belong to a category in a hierarchy

rank adj. excessively luxuriant in growth ‖ gross, crude ‖ smelling like partly rotted vegetation ‖ utter

ran·kle ran·kling ran·kled v.t. to cause bitter feelings in

ran·sack v.t. to search thoroughly ‖ to steal everything valuable from

ran·som v.t. to secure the release of by paying a ransom

ransom n. money paid or demanded for the release of a person held captive

rant v.i. to use bombastic language ‖ to be noisily angry ‖ v.t. to utter with exaggerated emphasis

rap 1. n. a sharp, quick blow ‖ the sound of such an impact **to take the rap** to take blame or punishment **2.** v. **rap·ping rapped** v.t. to strike with a quick sharp blow ‖ to express (something) quickly and forcefully ‖ v.i. to knock sharply

ra·pa·cious adj. grasping, avid for wealth or gain ‖ ravenous

rape illicit sexual intercourse by force ‖ the doing of violence

rape rap·ing raped v.t. to commit rape on

rap·id 1. adj. occurring, done or acting with speed **2.** n. (esp. pl.) that part of a river where the water flows turbulently **ra·pid·i·ty** n. the state or quality of being rapid

ra·pi·er n. a light, straight, thin, two-edged sword

rap·ist n. a person who has committed rape

rap·port n. sympathetic connection, harmony

rap·proche·ment n. a renewal of friendly relations

rapt adj. carried away in imagination from the reality of one's environment

rap·to·ri·al adj. adapted for seizing prey

rap·ture n. an emotional state in which intense joy, love etc. possesses the mind to the exclusion of every other emotion or consideration **rap·tur·ous** adj. characterized by rapture

rare adj. infrequently found, seen or experienced ‖ unusually good ‖ intense, extreme

rare adj. cooked very lightly

rare·bit n. Welsh rabbit

rare·fy, rar·i·fy rare·fy·ing, rar·i·fy·ing rare·fied, rar·i·fied v.t. to refine, make more subtle

rare·ly adv. very infrequently

rar·ing adj. full of eagerness

rar·i·ty pl. rar·i·ties n. something which is rare

ras·cal 1. n. a rogue, trickster ‖ an endearingly mischievous person **2.** n. the quality of being a rascal or behaving like a rascal

rash adj. made or done hastily without considering the possible consequences or attendant risks

rash n. small red patches on the skin

rash·er n. a thin slice of bacon or ham

rasp v.t. to remove unevennesses etc. from by rubbing with a rasp ‖ v.i. to make a rough scraping sound ‖ to grate

rasp n. a type of coarse file with individual, hard, raised teeth set very close together ‖ a noise made as if by rasping ‖ a machine that grinds waste into a manageable material

rasp·ber·ry pl. rasp·ber·ries n. a genus of tall-growing shrubs bearing succulent red or black aggregate fruits ‖ the fruit of this shrub ‖ the color or flavor of the fruit of the red raspberry

rat 1. n. any of various omnivorous rodents ‖ a contemptible person, esp. one who betrays or deserts associates **2.** v. **rat·ting rat·ted** v.i. to desert or betray one's associates

rate 1. n. a fixed ratio between two things quantities etc. ‖ a fixed charge per unit of a commodity, service etc. ‖ a charge asked or paid for a service etc. **at any rate** at least, in any case **2.** v. **rat·ing rat·ed** v.t. to assess the quality or worth of ‖ to consider as something ‖ to deserve, merit

rate rat·ing rat·ed v.t. to scold severely

rath·er adv. preferably ‖ more truthfully, more exactly ‖ on the contrary

rat·i·fi·ca·tion n. a ratifying or being ratified

rat·i·fy rat·i·fy·ing rat·i·fied v.t. to confirm

rat·ing *n.* classification ‖ an estimate of achievement, status etc.

ra·ti·o *n.* the relation between two quantities

ra·tion 1. *n.* an amount (of food, time etc.) which one permits oneself or which one is permitted ‖ (*pl.*) provisions allotted **2.** *v.t.* to allow to consume only a certain amount of something

ra·tion·al *adj.* of or relating to reason ‖ well suited to its purpose ‖ sensible, sound-minded

ra·tion·ale *n.* the logical justifying grounds for something ‖ a statement of principles

ra·tion·al·ize   ra·tion·al·iz·ing ra·tion·al·ized *v.t.* to discover and express the reason for ‖ to put a natural explanation in place of a supernatural one for (something)

rat·tan, ra·tan *n.* any of various climbing palms growing in India and S.E. Asia ‖ a part of the long stem of this plant used for wickerwork

rat·tle 1. *v.* **rat·tling rat·tled** *v.i.* to emit a rapid succession of short, sharp sounds ‖ to move rapidly ‖ (often with 'on') to talk rapidly, incessantly **2.** *n.* the sound made by something which rattles ‖ a baby's toy designed to make this sound ‖ the horny rings on a rattlesnake's tail

rat·tle·snake *n.* genus of North American poisonous snakes

rau·cous *adj.* hoarse, grating, rough-sounding

raun·chy *adj.* bawdy — **raunchiness** *n.*

rav·age *n.* devastation ‖ (*pl.*) ill effects

rav·age rav·ag·ing rav·aged *v.t.* to lay waste to ‖ *v.i.* to do ruinous damage

rave 1. *v.i.* **rav·ing raved** to talk or act wildly or incoherently ‖ to express or feel exaggerated admiration **2.** *n.* the act of raving ‖ an excessively enthusiastic criticism

rav·el *v.* **rav·el·ing rav·eled** *v.t.* to separate the threads of ‖ to cause to fray ‖ *v.i.* to become tangled or confused ‖ to become untwisted ‖ to fray

ra·ven 1. *n.* a large, black, omnivorous and occasionally predatory bird about **2.** *adj.* glossy black

rav·en·ous *adj.* fiercely hungry ‖ devouring greedily

ra·vine *n.* a long, deep, narrow hollow

rav·ing 1. *adj.* talking wildly or incoherently **2.** *adv.* to the extent of raving **3.** *n.* incoherent talk

ra·vi·o·li *pl. n.* small cases of pasta filled with meat, spinach etc. cooked and served with a sauce

rav·ish *v.t.* to rape **ráv·ish·ing** *adj.* so beautiful as to cause rapture

raw 1. *adj.* uncooked ‖ untrained, inexperienced ‖ having the skin partly or wholly removed ‖ cold and damp ‖ indecent **2.** *n.* (in the phrase) **in the raw** in the original state ‖ naked

ray 1. *n.* a line of light that appears to radiate from some light-producing or light-reflecting objects ‖ a stream of particles ‖ a light manifestation, e.g. of hope or intelligence **2.** *v.i.* to issue in rays

ray *n.* a cartilaginous fish similar to the skate

ray·on *n.* a textile fiber ‖ any of various textiles made of such fibers

raze, rase raz·ing, ras·ing razed, rased *v.t.* to destroy completely

ra·zor *n.* an instrument with a very sharp rigid cutting edge used esp. to shave hair

razz *v.t.* to tease

re *prep.* in the matter of, as regards

re *n.* the note D in the fixed-do system of solmization

re- *prefix* again, another time

reach 1. *v.i.* to arrive at ‖ to extend ‖ to pass with the hand ‖ to get in touch with ‖ to touch the mind or feelings of ‖ *v.i.* to extend in dimension, scope etc. ‖ (of the voice, eye etc.) to carry, penetrate **2.** *n.* the act of stretching out or reaching ‖ intellectual or imaginative range

re·act *v.t.* to act again

re·act *v.i.* to act in response to a stimulus etc.

re·ac·tion *n.* a response to a stimulus ‖ the tendency to favor extremely conservative social or political policies ‖ a chemical change involving two or more substances

re·ác·tion·ar·y 1. *adj.* characterized by reaction, esp. in politics **2.** *n. pl.*

re·ác·tion·ar·ies a reactionary person
re·ac·ti·vate re·ac·ti·vat·ing re·ac·ti·vat·ed *v.t.* to cause to be active again ‖ *v.i.* to be active again
re·ac·tor *n.* a vessel or other piece of equipment in which a chemical reaction is carried out ‖ a device in which a fission chain reaction is initiated and controlled
read 1. *v.* **read·ing read** *v.t.* to understand the meaning of (symbols, signs, gestures etc.) ‖ to say aloud (written or printed material) ‖ to discover the meaning of by observation ‖ to predict ‖ to explain or interpret ‖ *v.i.* to be able to read books etc. ‖ to learn or study by reading **to read out into** to attach to (something) a meaning which is neither stated nor intended **2. read** *adj.* learned or informed through reading **réad·a·ble** *adj.* easy or pleasant to read ‖ legible
read·er *n.* a person able to read ‖ a book for children learning to read ‖ a book containing selections for reading for a beginner ‖ a person very fond of reading ‖ someone who reads and criticizes manuscripts for a publisher, literary agent etc. ‖ a proofreader **réad·er·ship** *n.* tthe collective body of readers of a newspaper or periodical
read·ing 1. *n.* the act of one who reads ‖ the material a person is reading ‖ a public entertainment at which passages from a book, stories, poems etc. are read aloud **2.** *adj.* of or for reading or readers
read·out *n.* **1.** information taken from storage for transcription and recording **2.** the processor output — **readout** *v.* to produce a readout — **read-out device** *n.* the device
read·y 1. *adj.* **read·i·er read·i·est** in a state for immediate action, use etc. ‖ immediately available ‖ willing ‖ quick and easy ‖ forward, prompt **2.** *n.* *v.t.* **read·y·ing read·ied** to prepare
read·y-made *adj.* made to a stock size, not to individual requirements
re·al 1. *adj.* existing ‖ natural, not artificial ‖ proper ‖ (used merely for emphasis) great ‖ relating to objective things in the physical world ‖ not imaginary ‖ (of wages) measured by their purchasing power **2.**

adv. really
real estate immovable property
re·al·ism *n.* an attitude based on facts and reality as opposed to emotions ‖ (in art, literature etc.) fidelity to life as perceived and experienced
re·al·i·ty *pl.* **re·al·i·ties** *n.* someone or something that is real or exists in fact ‖ the real world ‖ the true or actual nature of something **in reality** actually, in fact, really
re·al·i·za·tion *n.* a realizing or being realized ‖ that which is realized
re·al·ize re·al·iz·ing re·al·ized *v.t.* to be aware of the truth of ‖ to make real or actual (something imagined, hoped for etc.) ‖ to convert into money ‖ to acquire, gain
re·al·ly *adv.* in reality ‖ (emphatic) truly
realm *n.* kingdom ‖ province, domain
re·al·ty *n.* real estate
ream *n.* a unit of measurement for paper ‖ (usually *pl.*) a huge amount
ream *v.t.* to widen or shape with a reamer ‖ to extract (fruit juice) with a reamer **réam·er** *n.* a rotating tool with cutting edges ‖ a lemon squeezer
reap *v.t.* to gather (a acrop) ‖ to cut the crop of ‖ to receive as the result of one's own acts **réap·er** *n.* a machine for reaping grain
rear 1. *n.* the back of something ‖ the buttocks **2.** *adj.* located at or toward the rear
rear *v.t.* to erect ‖ to raise ‖ to bring up ‖ to breed ‖ *v.i.* (of a horse) to rise up on its hind legs
rea·son *n.* the ability to think logically, to understand, and to draw inferences ‖ sound thinking **to stand to reason** to be obviously true **within reason** within reasonable limits
reason *v.i.* to think or talk logically ‖ to argue persuasively with someone ‖ *v.t.* to analyze by reasoning
rea·son·a·ble *adj.* ready to listen to reason ‖ not expensive ‖ neither more nor less than reasonable **réa·son·a·bly** *adv.*
rea·son·ing *n.* the act of someone who reasons
re·as·sem·ble **re·as·sem·bling**

re·as·sem·bled *v.t.* to put together again

re·as·sure re·as·sur·ing re·as·sured *v.t.* to restore confidence to

re·bate *n.* a deduction from an amount to be paid

rebate re·bat·ing re·bat·ed *v.t.* to give a rebate to

reb·el 1. *n.* a person who resists authority 2. *adj.* rebellious of or pertaining to rebels

re·bel re·bel·ling re·belled *v.i.* to disobey ‖ to resist the lawful government by force ‖ to feel or show aversion

re·bel·lion *n.* an organized attempt to overthrow a lawful government by force of arms

re·bel·lious *adj.* defying authority or control

re·birth *n.* a renewal ‖ a renaissance

re·bound 1. *v.i.* to bounce back as if on impact 2. *n.* **on the rebound** in a state of hasty emotional reaction to some setback

re·buff *v.t.* to give a rebuff to

re·buff *n.* a curt rejection

re·buke 1. *v.t.* **re·buk·ing re·buked** to tell (someone) severely that his conduct or action is wrong or unsatisfactory 2. *n.* a rebuking or being rebuked

re·bus *n.* a word or series of words represented by pictures of objects, symbols etc. ‖ a puzzle

re·but re·but·ting re·but·ted *v.t.* to refute **re·but·tal** *n.*

re·cal·ci·trance *n.* the quality or state of being recalcitrant ‖ recalcitrant behavior

re·cal·ci·trant *adj.* refusing to submit to authority, rules etc.

re·call 1. *v.t.* to order to return ‖ to cause to return ‖ to recollect, remember 2. *n.* the act of recalling or an instance of this **beyond recall** impossible to undo, revoke, rescind etc.

re·cant *v.t.* to retract or renounce **re·can·ta·tion** *n.*

re·ca·pit·u·late *v.t.* **re·ca·pit·u·lat·ing re·ca·pit·u·lat·ed** to repeat or go over again briefly, summarize

re·cap·ture *v.t.* **re·cap·tur·ing re·cap·tured** to capture again

re·cede re·ced·ing re·ced·ed *v.i.* to draw back ‖ to become more distant ‖ to slope backwards ‖ to become less

re·ceipt *n.* the act of receiving ‖ a formal written acknowledgment that something has been received ‖ (esp. pl.) something received

re·ceiv·a·ble *adj.* that can be accepted or received, esp. as legal

re·ceive re·ceiv·ing re·ceived *v.t.* to be given, awarded or sent ‖ to accept ‖ to be subjected to ‖ to experience, undergo ‖ to welcome ‖ to admit into membership ‖ to accept and pay for ‖ to take (Communion) from the priest ‖ *v.i.* to be a recipient or receiver

re·ceiv·er *n.* a person who receives ‖ something that receives ‖ a person appointed by a court to administer property ‖ the earpiece of a telephone ‖ a television or radio receiving set

re·ceiv·er·ship *n.* the condition of being in the receiver's hands ‖ the position of being a receiver

re·cent *adj.* of or pertaining to a time not long before the present ‖ done or made during such a time

re·cep·ta·cle *n.* a container

re·cep·tion *n.* a receiving or being received ‖ a formal social gathering ‖ a welcoming or greeting in a specified manner ‖ the receiving of radio or television signals **re·cép·tion·ist** *n.*

re·cess 1. *n.* an alcove ‖ an interval of time during which an activity ceases ‖ a period between school classes ‖ sinus, cleft or hollow space 2. *v.i.* to go into recess

re·ces·sion *n.* a receding or withdrawing ‖ a temporary falling off of business activity

rec·i·pe *n.* a list of ingredients and set of cooking directions for a dish

re·cip·i·ent 1. *n.* someone who or something which receives 2. *adj.* receiving or able to receive

re·cip·ro·cal 1. *adj.* mutual ‖ corresponding, complementary 2. *n.* a thing that has a reciprocal relation to something else

re·cip·ro·cate re·cip·ro·cat·ing re·cip·ro·cat·ed *v.t.* to give in return ‖ to give and receive mutually ‖ *v.i.* to return in kind something done, given etc.

rec·i·proc·i·ty *n*. the state of being reciprocal

re·cit·al *n*. an enumerating or relating of facts, events etc. ‖ a performance given by one person or small group

rec·i·ta·tion *n*. an enumerating of facts, events etc. ‖ a reciting, esp. before an audience

re·cite re·cit·ing re·cit·ed *v.t.* to repeat aloud (something memorized) ‖ to enumerate

reck·less *adj*. careless ‖ indifferent to danger

reck·on *v.t.* to work out, calculate ‖ to think, suppose ‖ to estimate **to reckon with** to take into account

reck·on·ing *n*. the act of counting or calculating, or an instance of this ‖ a settling of accounts, differences etc., or an instance of this

re·claim *v.t.* to recover possession of

rec·la·ma·tion *n*. a reclaiming or being reclaimed

re·cline re·clin·ing re·clined *v.i.* to lie at ease ‖ to lean back comfortably

re·cluse *n*. someone who lives alone and avoids the company of others

rec·og·ni·tion *n*. a recognizing or being recognized ‖ acknowledgment

rec·og·nize rec·og·niz·ing rec·og·nized *v.t.* to identify ‖ to acknowledge ‖ to obligate ‖ *v.i.* to enter into a recognizance

re·coil 1. *v.t.* to start back in repugnance ‖ to shrink away ‖ to kick ‖ to retreat **2.** *n*. the sliding back or kick of a gun ‖ a physical or mental shrinking away

rec·ol·lect *v.t.* to call to mind, remember

rec·om·mend *v.t.* to write or speak in favor of (someone, something) to another person ‖ to advise

rec·om·men·da·tion *n*. the act of recommending a person or thing ‖ advice

rec·om·pense *n*. a gift or remuneration ‖ a payment or compensation

recompense   rec·om·pens·ing rec·om·pensed *v.t.* to give a recompense to

rec·on·cil·a·ble *adj*. able to be reconciled **rec·on·cil·a·bly** *adv*.

rec·on·cile rec·on·cil·ing rec·on·ciled *v.t.* to bring together again ‖ to induce (some-

one) to accept something disagreeable ‖ to make or show to be consistent ‖ to reach a compromise agreement **réc·on·cile·ment** *n*.

rec·on·cil·i·a·tion *n*. a reconciling or being reconciled

rec·on·dite *adj*. obscure, little known

re·con·di·tion *v.t.* to restore (something)

re·con·nais·sance *n*. a survey of an enemy-field area ‖ any preliminary survey

re·con·noi·ter 1. re·con·noi·ter·ing re·con·noitered *v.t.* to make a reconnaissance of **2.** *n*. a reconnaissance

re·con·sid·er *v.t.* to consider again, esp. with a view to changing one's opinion **re·con·sid·er·a·tion** *n*.

re·con·struct *v.t.* to rebuild ‖ to re-create mentally or in fact the known conditions

re·con·struc·tion *n*. something reconstructed

rec·ord 1. *n*. a recording or being recorded ‖ an account made in permanent form ‖ a minute or official text ‖ a public register ‖ a circular plate to which sound has been transferred, esp. electronically **off the record** private and not to be made publicly known **on record** publicly declared **2.** *adj*. of that which is the best so far officially recorded

re·cord *v.t.* to commit to writing as authentic evidence of ‖ to transcribe (sound) in some permanent form ‖ to register

re·count *v.t.* to relate, narrate in detail

re-count 1. *v.t.* to count again **2.** *n*. a second or additional counting, esp. of votes

re·coup *v.t.* get back the equivalent of (a loss) ‖ to compensate (oneself) for losses, expenses etc

re·course *n*. someone or something to which one turns for help

re·cov·er *v.t.* to get back possession of ‖ to regain the composure, control, balance etc. of (oneself) ‖ *v.i.* to return to normal health after illness

re-cov·er *v.t.* to provide with a new cover

re·cov·er·y pl. **re·cov·er·ies** *n*. the act or an instance of recovering ‖ a returning to normal health or prosperity ‖ a return to financial well-being after a depression ‖ the salvaging of useful material from waste products

rec·re·ant 1. *adj.* cowardly ‖ apostate, unfaithful **2.** *n.* a coward ‖ a deserter

rec·re·ate rec·re·at·ing rec·re·at·ed *v.t.* to put fresh life into

rec·re·a·tion *n.* a leisure-time activity engaged in for the sake of refreshment or entertainment ‖ a pastime

re·cre·a·tion *n.* that which is re-created

re·crim·i·nate re·crim·i·nat·ing re·crim·i·nat·ed *v.i.* to make counter accusations

re·cruit *v.* to enlist recruits ‖ to recuperate **re·crúit·ment** *n.*

recruit *n.* a newly enlisted member of the armed forces ‖ a new member or supporter of a society, cause etc.

rec·tal *adj.* of, relating to, or near the rectum

rec·tan·gle *n.* a plane quadrilateral figure with four right angles **rec·tan·gu·lar** *adj.* shaped like a rectangle ‖ right-angled **rec·tan·gu·lar·i·ty** *n.*

rec·ti·fi·a·ble *adj.* able to be rectified

rec·ti·fy rec·ti·fy·ing rec·ti·fied *v.t.* to put right

rec·ti·tude *n.* moral uprightness, integrity

rec·tor *n.* the head priest of a parish ‖ the head of some universities, colleges, schools or religious institutions **réc·tor·ate** *n.* **rec·tor·i·al** *adj.* **rec·tor·ship** *n.*

rec·to·ry *pl.* **rec·to·ries** *n.* a rector's house

rec·tum *pl.* **rec·tums, rec·ta** *n.* the portion of the large intestine nearest to the anus

re·cum·bent *adj.* lying down, reclining

re·cu·per·ate re·cu·per·at·ing re·cu·per·at·ed *v.t.* to regain (esp. one's health, one's losses)

re·cu·per·a·tion *n.* the restoration of health

re·cur re·cur·ring re·cur·red *v.i.* to occur again, esp. after some lapse of time

re·cur·rence *n.* the act or fact of recurring

re·cur·rent *adj.* recurring from time to time

re·cy·cle *v.* to process so that basic raw material may be used again **recycling** *n.*

red 1. red·der red·dest *adj.* ranging from orange to infrared, being the color e.g. of blood flowing from a vein **Red** of or pertaining to a Red or to a country, group

etc. of communist political persuasion **2.** *n.* a red color, pigment, fabric etc. **in (out of) the red** in (not in) debt **to see red** to be made suddenly very angry

red·cap *n.* a porter in a railroad station etc.

re·deem *v.t.* to get back full possession of, esp. by repaying the sum of money secured by the thing being recovered ‖ to fulfill ‖ to save from being a total failure **re·déem·a·ble** *adj.*

re·demp·tion *n.* a redeeming or being redeemed ‖ something which redeems

red-hand·ed *adj.* bearing clear signs of having just committed a crime

red herring a subject introduced into talk to divert attention from the truth or from the matter at issue

red-hot *adj.* so hot as to emit red light ‖ the very latest ‖ sensational

red-letter day a very fortunate day

red·o·lent *adj.* aromatic ‖ smelling, having a strong fragrance

re·doubt·a·ble *adj.* formidably hard to resist

re·dress *v.t.* to put right ‖ to make amends for

re·dress *n.* the reparation of a wrong

re·duce re·duc·ing re·duced *v.t.* to make smaller or less in size, weight, condition etc. ‖ to lower in rank ‖ to make physically weak ‖ *v.i.* to become reduced ‖ to lose weight by dieting **re·dúced** *adj.* decreased in size, cost etc.

re·duc·tion *n.* a reducing or being reduced ‖ the result of reducing, e.g. a lower price

re·dun·dance *n.* redundancy

re·dun·dan·cy *pl.* **re·dun·dan·cies** *n.* the state or quality of being redundant

re·dun·dant *adj.* unnecessarily repetitive or superfluous

red·wood *n.* a giant Californian conifer ‖ the hard reddish wood of this tree

reed *n.* any of several varieties of tall-growing, erect grasses ‖ a musical pipe made of one or more hollow reed stems ‖ a thin strip of cane or metal which vibrates when agitated by air pressure and thus emits sound

reef *n.* a line of rocks, sand, small stones etc., just above or near the surface of the water

reef·er *n.* **1.** a refrigerator **2.** a railroad freight car **3.** a thick, close-fitting, double-breasted jacket **4.** a cigarette containing marijuana

reek *n.* a very strong, unpleasant smell ‖ vapor

reek *v.i.* to give off an unpleasant smell

reel 1. *n.* a small revolving device attached to a fishing rod for winding in and letting out the line ‖ the quantity of line contained on it ‖ a spool **2.** *v.t.* to wind on a reel ‖ (with 'in') to bring in by reeling **to reel off** to recite easily without pause or interruption

reel 1. *v.i.* to sway unsteadily **2.** *n.* a reeling movement

reel 1. *n.* a lively Scottish dance ‖ the Virginia reel ‖ the music for these dances **2.** *v.i.* to dance a reel

re·fec·to·ry *pl.* **re·fec·to·ries** *n.* a room used for meals by a religious community

re·fer **re·fer·ring** **re·ferred** *v.i.* to speak or write of something in the course of dealing with some other or larger topic ‖ to relate ‖ *v.t.* to direct (someone) to a source of information etc. ‖ to assign to a specific place, period etc.

ref·er·ee 1. *n.* a person to whom something in dispute is referred for his opinion or decision ‖ a person appointed to make sure that a game is played or match fought according to the rules **2.** *v.i.* **ref·er·ee·ing** **ref·er·eed** to act as a referee ‖ *v.t.* to be the referee of

ref·er·ence 1. *n.* a referring or being referred or an instance of this ‖ an indication in a work of some other work to be consulted ‖ the work cited ‖ a written testimony as to the character, ability etc. of another person **in reference to** concerning **2.** *v.t.* **ref·er·enc·ing** **ref·er·enced** to furnish with references

ref·er·en·dum *pl.* **ref·er·en·da,** **ref·er·en·dums** *n.* the submission of a particular measure or question to the whole electorate ‖ such a vote

re·fine **re·fin·ing** **re·fined** *v.t.* to remove impurities or coarse elements from ‖ to make more subtle and efficient

re·fine·ment *n.*

re·fin·er·y *pl.* **re·fin·er·ies** *n.* a place or apaparatus for refining or for purifying

re·fit *v.* **re·fit·ting** **re·fit·ted** *v.t.* to supply with new equipment

re·flect *v.t.* to show as an image ‖ to be in accordance with and give an insight into ‖ *v.i.* to become reflected ‖ to act as a reflector ‖ to think back ‖ to ponder, meditate

re·flec·tion, **re·flex·ion** *n.* a reflecting or being reflected ‖ something reflected ‖ (often *pl.*) adverse criticism

re·flex 1. *n.* an automatic or involuntary response to a stimulus ‖ (*pl.*) the ability to respond in this way ‖ an automatic mental reaction **2.** *adj.* reflected, bent back ‖ of an automatic or involuntary response to a stimulus

re·flex·ive *adj.* denoting an action by the subject upon itself, e.g. of a verb whose subject and direct object are the same or of a pronoun which is the object of such a verb ‖ able to bend back

re·form *v.t.* to improve by removing faults and weaknesses ‖ to correct ‖ to persuade (a person) to change his ways for the better ‖ *v.i.* to become reformed

reform 1. *n.* a reforming ‖ a measure intended to reform something **2.** *adj.* of, pertaining to or advocating reform

re·form *v.t.* to form again ‖ *v.i.* to take form again

re·form·a·to·ry 1. *n. pl.* **re·form·a·to·ries** an institution to which young offenders may be sent for rehabilitation **2.** *adj.* reformative

re·fract *v.t.* to subject (waves of light, sound etc.) to refraction

re·frac·tion *n.* the change in direction of the path followed by electromagnetic waves (e.g. a ray of light) or other energy-bearing waves in passing obliquely from one medium to another in which its velocity is different

re·frac·to·ry 1. *adj.* resisting discipline ‖ not benefiting from treatament ‖ resisting high temperature **2.** *pl.* **re·frac·to·ries** *n.* any of various nonmetallic ceramic substances that resist great heat

re·frain *n.* a phrase or line in poetry or song

repeated at regular intervals

refrain *v.i.* to abstain from doing something

re·fresh *v.t.* to make (someone) feel restored aand freshened ‖ to recall to

re·frésh·er *n.* something that refreshes ‖ a refresher course

re·fresh·ment *n.* a refreshing or being refreshed ‖ something that refreshes ‖ (*pl.*) light food and drink

re·frig·er·ant 1. *adj.* cooling 2. *n.* a substance used in a refrigerating cycle or directly for cooling ‖ a medicine, ointment etc. used in reducing fever

re·frig·er·ate   re·frig·er·at·ing   re·frig·er·at·ed *v.t.* to cool, make or keep cold

re·frig·er·a·tion *n.* a refrigerating or being refrigerated

ref·uge *n.* shelter or protection ‖ a place offering this ‖ a person, thing, or course of action offering protection

ref·u·gee *n.* a person who flees, esp. to a foreign country, to escape persecution

re·ful·gent *adj.* shining brightly

re·fund 1. *v.t.* to pay back ‖ to reimburse 2. *n.* a repayment

re·fur·bish *v.t.* to renovate

re·fus·al *n.* the act of refusing

re·fuse   re·fus·ing   re·fused *v.t.* to decline to accept ‖ to decline (to do something) ‖ to make a refusal

re·fuse 1. *n.* remains having no value or use 2. *adj.* rejected as of no value or use

ref·u·tal *n.* a refutation

ref·u·ta·tion *n.* a refuting ‖ something which refutes

re·fute   re·fut·ing   re·fut·ed *v.t.* to prove (an assertion or argument) to be untrue or incorrect ‖ to prove (a person) wrong

re·gain *v.t.* to get back (something lost)

re·gal *adj.* befitting a king

re·gale   re·gal·ing   re·galed *v.t.* to entertain (someone) richly ‖ to feast (oneself) ‖ *v.i.* to feast

re·gard *n.* esteem ‖ consideration ‖ attention ‖ (*pl.*) a conventional expression of kindly feeling, esteem etc. **in** (or with **with**) **regard to** concerning

regard *v.t.* to concern ‖ to look closely at

re·gard·ful *adj.* heedful, mindful ‖ respectful

re·gard·ing *prep.* in or with regard to, concerning

re·gard·less 1. *adj.* paying no heed or attention 2. *adv.* without consideration of the situation, consequences etc.

re·gat·ta *n.* a series of rowing or sailing races

re·gen·er·ate   v.   re·gen·er·at·ing   re·gen·er·at·ed *v.t.* to give new life or vigor to ‖ to restore to moral or spiritual health ‖ to grow (a new part) to replace a lost or injured one

re·gen·er·a·tion *n.* a spiritual rebirth ‖ the regrowth or renewal of an organ, tissue or substance

re·gent 1. *adj.* acting aas regent 2. *n.* a person appointed to rule during the minority, absence or physical or mental disability of a monarch ‖ one of a governing board, esp. of a university

re·gime, ré·gime *n.* a system of rule or government ‖ any systematic organizational control ‖ a regimen

reg·i·men *n.* a regulated course of diet, exercise etc. for restoring strength and health or for keeping the body fit

reg·i·ment 1. *n.* an army unit ‖ a large number 2. *v.t.* to form into a regiment ‖ to assign to a regiment ‖ to subject to stultifying organization

re·gion *n.* a large part of space, land, sea or air which has certain distinctive characteristics ‖ the space or area surrounding a specified place ‖ an area which is a unit of administration **ré·gion·al** *adj.* **ré·gion·al·ism** *n.*

reg·is·ter *n.* an official or formal list ‖ a book in which a record is kept ‖ an automatic cash till ‖ the range of a voice or an instrument ‖ registration, registry ‖ *computer* a short-term storage of limited capacity used to facilitate operations

register *v.t.* to place on formal or official record ‖ to express or show (a feeling or emotion) ‖ to record ‖ to penetrate the mind ‖ to be in register, correspond exactly

reg·is·trar *n.* an official in charge of a register **rég·is·trar·ship** *n.*

reg·is·tra·tion *n.* a registering or being registered ‖ an entry in an official register

re·gress 1. *n.* a going back or returning ‖ a tendency to decline **2.** *v.i.* to move backwards

re·gres·sion *n.* a regressing ‖ a reversion to earlier stages of personality development or to objects of infantile attachment ‖ the return to an earlier or less complex form

re·gret *n.* the emotion arising from a wish that some matter or situation could be different from what it is ‖ *(pl.)* a conventional expression of disappointment, esp. at refusing an invitation

regret re·gret·ting re·gret·ted *v.t.* to feel or express regret for **re·gret·ful, re·gret·ta·ble** *adjs*

reg·u·lar 1. *adj.* conforming to a rule ‖ conforming to some standard pattern of proportion or symmetry ‖ customary ‖ disciplined ‖ real, complete ‖ having the normal type of inflection, formation etc. ‖ having equal sides and angles ‖ frequently received over a long period ‖ not varying **2. reg·u·lar·i·ty** *n.*

reg·u·late reg·u·lat·ing reg·u·lat·ed *v.t.* to control ‖ to adjust ‖ to arrange so as to adapt **reg·u·la·tion 1.** *n.* a regulating or being regulated ‖ a rule **2.** *adj.* correct, prescribed **reg·u·la·tive** *adj.* **reg·u·la·tor** *n.* a mechanical device controlling temperature, pressure, the admission of steam or water etc. **reg·u·la·to·ry** *adj.*

re·ha·bil·i·tate re·ha·bil·i·tat·ing re·ha·bil·i·tat·ed *v.t.* to restore to rank, privileges, rights etc. lost or forfeited ‖ to vindicate ‖ to restore **re·ha·bil·i·ta·tion** *n.*

re·hash 1. *v.t.* to serve up the same (food, arguments, ideas etc.) in a new guise **2.** *n.* the act or process of rehashing ‖ something which is the result of rehashing

re·hears·al *n.* a trial performance

re·hearse re·hears·ing re·hearsed *v.t.* to practice ‖ to enumerate

reign *n.* the power of a monarch ‖ the period during which a monarch reigns

reign *v.i.* to hold royal office, prevail

re·im·burse re·im·burs·ing re·im·bursed *v.t.* to compensate ‖ to repay **re·im·burse·ment** *n.*

rein 1. *n.* straps fastened to a horse's bit as a means of control ‖ *(pl.)* a means of control or restraint, or power to control **to give rein to** to allow to proceed without restraint **to keep a tight rein on** to keep under one's strict control **2.** *v.t.* to bring to a halt or to a slower gait

re·in·car·nate re·in·car·nat·ing re·in·car·nat·ed *v.t.* to cause to be reborn in a new body or a new form **2.** *adj.* born again in a new form **re·in·car·na·tion** *n.*

rein·deer *pl.* **rein·deer, rein·deers** *n.* any of several large subarctic deer

re·in·force re·in·forc·ing re·in·forced *v.t.* to strengthen by the addition of something

re·in·state re·in·stat·ing re·in·stat·ed *v.t.* to restore to a former position, state etc. **re·in·state·ment** *n.*

re·it·er·ate re·it·er·at·ing re·it·er·at·ed *v.t.* to repeat several times

re·it·er·a·tion *n.* a reiterating or being reiterated

re·ject 1. *v.t.* to refuse to accept ‖ to cast or set aside **2.** *n.* someone or something rejected

re·jec·tion *n.* a rejecting or being rejected ‖ something rejected

re·joice re·joic·ing re·joiced *v.i.* to feel joy ‖ *v.t.* to cause to feel joy **re·joic·ing** *n.* joyfulness

re·join *v.t.* to join again

re·join *v.t.* to reply, to retort

re·join·der *n.* a reply, retort **re·ju·ve·nate re·ju·ve·nat·ing re·ju·ve·nat·ed** *v.i.* to become as though young again **re·ju·ve·na·tion** *n.*

re·lapse 1. *v.i.* **re·laps·ing re·lapsed** to fall back into ill health, crime or heresy **2.** *n.* a relapsing or an instance of this

re·late re·lat·ing re·lat·ed *v.t.* to tell the story of, recount, narrate ‖ to show or establish a relation between ‖ *v.i.* to have or be in relation **re·lat·ed** *adj.* having or bearing a relationship ‖ in the same family

re·la·tion *n.* a recounting or narrating ‖ that which is recounted or narrated ‖ a relative ‖ the way in which one thing is associated with another ‖ *(pl.)* the terms on which one person has dealings with another person **in relation to** concerning

re·la·tion·ship n. the state of being related

rel·a·tive 1. adj. of something considered in reference to something else **2.** n. a person connected by birth or marriage with another person

rel·a·tiv·i·ty n. the state or quality of being relative ‖ a theory first formulated by Einstein (1905), and called the special theory of relativity

re·lax v.t. to loosen ‖ to make less strict ‖ to lower nervous tension ‖ to diminish

re·lax·a·tion n. a relaxing or being relaxed ‖ a recreation

re·lay n. a fresh supply of people, animals or materials ‖ a device which enables a current in one circuit to open or close another circuit to the flow of a current ‖ passing on ‖ a relay race

re·lay v.t. to pass on ‖ to transmit ‖ to control by using a relay ‖ to arrange in or supply with relays

re-lay re-lay·ing re-laid v.t. to lay again

re·lease n. a setting free or being set free from ‖ a putting of information or a new film before the public ‖ the surrender of a claim, right etc. to someone else ‖ the document containing this surrender ‖ something which releases

release re·leas·ing re·leased v.t. to free ‖ to surrender a right etc. to another

rel·e·gate rel·e·gat·ing rel·e·gat·ed v.t. to demote to some inferior or obscure place ‖ to pass to someone else ‖ to assign or refer to

rel·e·ga·tion n. a relegating or being relegated

re·lent v.i. to become less severe in one's attitude, intention, judgment etc. **re·lént·less** adj. unceasing

rel·e·vance n. the state or quality of being relevant **rél·e·van·cy** n.

re·li·a·bil·i·ty n. the state or quality of being reliable

re·li·a·ble adj. able to be relied on **re·lí·a·bly** adv.

re·li·ance n. readiness to believe in and depend on the good qualities of someone or something

rel·ic n. the material evidence of something which has ceased to exist ‖ the body or a

apart of the body of a saint or martyr

re·lief n. a freeing from or alleviating of oppression, danger, distress, pain etc. ‖ the sensation of being set free from emotional tension, anxiety, fear etc. ‖ a release from work or duty ‖ something, esp. money, food or clothing, given to alleviate privation

relief n. the extent to which, in a three-dimensional carving, sculpture, map etc., features are represented as raised above the general plane ‖ a carving etc. having this quality

re·lieve re·liev·ing re·lieved v.t. to alleviate ‖ to free (someone) from pain, distress, anxiety etc. ‖ (with 'of') to rob a ‖ to replace (someone on duty)

re·li·gion n. man's expression of his acknowledgment of the divine ‖ a system of beliefs and practices ‖ adherence to such a system

re·li·gious adj. of, pertaining to, or concerned with religion ‖ faithful in religion ‖ governed by principles adhered to as strictly as if they were those of a religion

re·lin·quish v.t. to give up, renounce **re·lín·quish·ment** n.

re·lish 1. v.t. to enjoy heartily **2.** n. keen enjoyment ‖ a savory embellishment to a dish

re·luc·tance n. an emotional or mental opposition to a course of action

re·luc·tant adj. marked by or showing reluctance

re·ly re·ly·ing re·lied v.i. to depend absolutely ‖ to place one's complete confidence in

re·main v.i. to stay behind ‖ to stay in the same place

re·main·der n. the portion which remains when part has been taken away ‖ the number remaining after subtraction or division ‖ a copy of a book withdrawn from normal sale and offered for sale at a reduced price

re·mains pl. n. the part which is left over ‖ (in funeral contexts) a dead human body

re·mand 1. v.t. to order back into custody ‖ to release on bail pending trial **2.** n. a remanding or being remanded

re·mark n. a brief spoken or written statement **to escape remark** to pass unnoticed

remark v.t. to make a remark

re·mark·a·ble adj. exceptional, unusual enough to arouse notice

re·me·di·al adj. of that which serves to remedy

rem·e·dy pl. **rem·e·dies** n. something which corrects a fault, error or evil ‖ a medicine ‖ legal redress

rem·e·dy rem·e·dy·ing rem·e·died v.t. to correct ‖ to heal or cure

re·mem·ber v.t. to bring back to mind ‖ to retain in the conscious mind ‖ to bear (a person) in mind ‖ to leave (a person) a legacy ‖ to give a gratuity to

re·mem·brance n. a remembering ‖ the condition of retaining in the conscious mind ‖ memory ‖ something which recalls a person, event etc. to the memory ‖ (pl.) greeting conveyed on one's behalf

re·mind v.t. to cause to remember **re·mind·er** n.

rem·i·nisce rem·i·nisc·ing rem·i·nisced v.t. to recall memories of past events

rem·i·nis·cence n. something which is remembered ‖ (pl.) personal memories of past events

re·miss adj. neglectful of doing one's duty or work efficiently ‖ marked by such negligence

re·mis·sion n. forgiveness ‖ a decrease in the magnitude of a force etc.

re·mit re·mit·ting re·mit·ted v.t. to return (a case) to a lower court ‖ to forgive ‖ to waive (a debt, fine, penalty etc.) ‖ to send (money) by mail or other means

re·mit·tance n. the sending of money ‖ the money sent

rem·nant n. a small remaining part, number, amount etc.

re·mod·el v.t. re·mod·el·ing re·mod·eled to give new shape or form to

re·mon·strance n. a remonstrating or an instance of this

re·mon·strate re·mon·strat·ing re·mon·strat·ed v.i. to express opposition or disapproval ‖ v.t. to say or urge in protest **re·mon·stra·tion** n. **re·mon·stra·tive** adj.

re·morse n. the emotion associated with painful recollection of something one would prefer not to have done or said **re·morse·ful** adj. **re·morse·less** adj.

re·mote adj. at a great distance in space or time ‖ (of an idea, intention, possibility etc.) very slight ‖ not closely related

re·mov·a·ble adj. able to be removed

re·mov·al n. a removing or being removed

re·move 1. re·mov·ing re·moved v.t. to move from a place ‖ to eliminate ‖ to take off ‖ to dismiss 2. n. (fig.) a degree of difference **re·móved** adj. distant by a specified number of degrees of relationship ‖ remote, distant **re·móv·er** n.

re·mu·ner·ate re·mu·ner·at·ing re·mu·ner·at·ed v.t. to pay money, or make a gift, to (someone) in return for his services ‖ to compensate for **re·mu·ner·á·tion** n. **re·mú·ner·a·tive** adj.

ren·ais·sance n. a revival or rebirth **Ren·ais·sance** 1. n. the artistic, literary and scientific revival which originated in Italy in the 14th c. 2. adj. of or relating to the Renaissance or its style in art, architecture, etc.

rend rend·ing rent v.t. to split or tear violently ‖ to cause emotional pain ‖ to become torn or split

ren·der 1. v.t. to give (what is due) ‖ to submit for payment ‖ to do (a service) ‖ to cause to become ‖ to clarify (a fat) by melting ‖ to translate ‖ to interpret, express artistically 2. n. first thin coat of plaster or cement applied to a wall **rénd·er·ing** n. the process of melting or extracting fat ‖ an artistic version or interpretation ‖ a translation ‖ an architect's perspective drawing for a building

ren·dez·vous 1. pl. **ren·dez·vous** n. a meeting at an aagreed time and place 2. v.i. to meet at an agreed time and place ‖ v.t. to assemble at an agreed time and place

ren·di·tion n. a translation ‖ an artist's interpretation of a dramatic part or piece of music

ren·e·gade n. someone who throws over authority or allegiance and gives himself to another allegiance

re·nege 1. v.i. re·neg·ing re·neged to go

back on a promise ‖ to revoke **2.** *n.* a revoke

re·new *v.t.* to revive, reawaken ‖ to make valid for a further period ‖ replenish ‖ *v.i.* to become new or as if new again **re·néw·al** *n.*

re·nounce *v.* **re·nounc·ing re·nounced** *v.t.* repudiate ‖ to give up ‖ to decline or abandon

ren·o·vate ren·o·vat·ing ren·o·vat·ed *v.t.* to make as good as new

ren·o·va·tion *n.* a renovating or being renovated

re·nown *n.* public recognition, fame

re·nowned *adj.* famous ‖ widely known

rent *n.* a payment made to an owner of land or property in return for the right to occupy or use it

rent *v.t.* to occupy or use (land or property) in return for payment

rent·al 1. *n.* a sum paid as rent ‖ a house etc. offered for rent ‖ a renting **2.** *adj.* pertaining to rent

re·nun·ci·a·tion *n.* a renouncing ‖ very strict self-denial **re·nun·ci·a·to·ry** *adj.*

re·pair 1. *v.t.* to make (something) good, strong, whole etc. after damage, injury etc. **2.** *n.* a repairing or being repaired ‖ a state of good condition

rep·a·ra·tion *n.* a righting of a wrong ‖ something done or paid as compensation for a wrong

rep·ar·tee *n.* quick, witty exchange between two speakers

re·past *n.* a meal ‖ the food eaten at a meal

re·pay re·pay·ing re·paid *v.t.* to pay back ‖ to recompense ‖ *v.i.* to make repayment **re·páy·a·ble** *adj.* **re·páy·ment** *n.*

re·peal *n.* a repealing or an instance of this

repeal *v.t.* to cancel, revoke

re·peat 1. *v.t.* to say again ‖ to do or make again ‖ to undergo again ‖ to cause or allow to recur **2.** *n.* repeating ‖ something repeated **re·péat·er** *n.* someone or something that repeats

re·pel re·pel·ling re·pelled *v.t.* to exert a force tending to move (a body) further away ‖ to drive back ‖ to repress ‖ to cause to feel aversion, to repulse

re·pel·lent 1. *adj.* repelling, driving back

‖ causing aversion **2.** *n.* a preparation for repelling

re·pent *v.i.* to grieve for sins committed or for things sinfully left undone ‖ to feel extreme regret ‖ to change one's mind and regret the original decision ‖ *v.t.* to do penance for

re·pent·ance *n.* the act of repenting

re·per·cus·sion *n.* a recoil ‖ a reverberation, echo ‖ a usually unanticipated and indirect reaction to some event

rep·er·toire *n.* an inventory of capabilities ‖ *(computer)* the operations that can be contained in a specific code

rep·e·ti·tion *n.* a repeating or being repeated ‖ something done or said again

rep·e·ti·tious *adj.* full of repetition, esp. boringly so

re·pet·i·tive *adj.* repeating or tending to repeat

re·place re·plac·ing re·placed *v.t.* to put back (something) in its original place ‖ to take the place of (someone or something) ‖ to fill the place of (someone or something) with another **re·pláce·ment** *n.* a replacing or being replaced

re·plen·ish *v.t.* to fill again ‖ to get a new supply of **re·plén·ish·ment** *n.*

re·plete *adj.* gorged ‖ richly supplied or imbued ‖ completely filled **re·plé·tion** *n.*

rep·li·ca *n.* an accurate copy ‖ someone or something very closely resembling someone or something else

re·ply 1. *v.t.* **re·ply·ing re·plied** *v.i.* to say or write something in return ‖ to act by way of a return **2.** *pl.* **re·plies** *n.* a replying ‖ something said, written or done in replying to a question, letter, action etc.

re·port *n.* something reported ‖ an unsubstantiated item of information or news ‖ a loud explosive noise a ‖ a periodic statement of a student's academic rating

report *v.t.* to give information about or relate ‖ to write an account of ‖ to tell about following inquiry, investigation etc. ‖ to give a formal statement of ‖ *v.i.* to make a report ‖ to work as a reporter ‖ to present oneself

re·port·er *n.* a person who writes accounts of events for publication

re·pose n. a state or condition of rest ‖ sleep ‖ a state of tranquility ‖ a restful attitude ‖ a restful effect

repose re·pos·ing re·posed v.t. to rest ‖ to lie in a restful position ‖ to have as a support or basis

repose re·pos·ing re·posed v.t. (usually with 'in') to place (trust, confidence etc.) in someone or something

re·pos·i·to·ry pl. **re·pos·i·to·ries** n. anything thought of as a place of storage

re·pos·sess v.t. to possess again ‖ to put in dispossession again **re·pos·ses·sion** n.

rep·re·hend v.t. to blame, be critical of

rep·re·hen·si·ble adj. (of an act or of conduct) that ought to be blamed or punished

rep·re·sent v.t. to present an image of ‖ to point out ‖ to act on behalf of ‖ to be a fair sample of ‖ to correspond to

re·pre·sent v.t. to present again

rep·re·sen·ta·tion n. a representing or being represented ‖ something which represents **rep·re·sen·tá·tion·al** adj.

rep·re·sen·ta·tive 1. adj. serving to represent **2.** n. someone or something regarded as characteristic or serving to exemplify ‖ a person who is appointed to act and speak for another person or for a country, company, group etc. ‖ a traveling salesman

re·press v.t. to put down ‖ to keep back ‖ to hinder the natural expression or development of

re·pres·sion n. a repressing or being repressed

re·prieve 1. v. **re·priev·ing re·prieved** v.t. to suspend the punishment of ‖ to a give temporary relief or respite to **2.** n. a reprieving or being reprieved ‖ a revoking or commuting of a punishment, esp. of a death sentence

rep·ri·mand n. a severe rebuke

reprimand v.t. to rebuke severely, esp. using authority

re·pris·al n. an injury inflicted in return for one suffered, or as vengence

re·proach v.t. to tell (someone) that he has acted wrongly

reproach n. a reproaching ‖ an expression of such reproaching ‖ something which merits reproaching

rep·ro·bate 1. adj. of someone who pursues evil in preference to good **2.** n. a reprobate person **3.** v.t. **rep·ro·bat·ing rep·ro·bat·ed** to condemn severely **rep·ro·ba·tion** n.

re·pro·duce re·pro·duc·ing re·pro·duced v.t. to repeat exactly or very closely ‖ to produce by sexual or asexual methods ‖ to re-create mentally ‖ to quote the exact text of in writing or printing ‖ to make a copy of, esp. by mechanical means

re·pro·duc·tion n. a reproducing or being reproduced

re·proof n. a reproving or an instance of this

re·prove re·prov·ing re·proved v.t. to rebuke (someone)

rep·tile 1. n. a member of a class of cold-blooded vertebrates incl. snakes, lizards, crocodiles and turtles etc. **2.** adj. of, like or having the characteristics of a reptile **rep·til·i·an** adj. and n.

re·pub·lic n. a form of government in which the sovereign power is widely vested in the people either directly or through elected representatives

res·o·nant adj. resounding ‖ (of a sound) loud and rich in overtones

re·sort v.t. to have recourse ‖ (often with 'to') to go

resort n. a place to which people go frequently or habitually for rest, pleasure etc. ‖ a person to whom or a thing to which one applies for aid

re·sound v.i. to sound loudly and with rich quality

re·source n. a source of supply or support ‖ something to which one resorts for comfort or help ‖ (pl.) assets, wealth **re·sóurce·ful** adj.

re·spect 1. n. the special esteem or consideration in which one holds another person or thing ‖ aspect, detail ‖ (pl.) conventional expressions of esteem, sympathy etc. **in respect of, with respect to** as regards, concerning **2.** v.t. to feel or show respect or consideration for

re·spect·a·bil·i·ty n. the state or quality of

being respectable

re·spect·a·ble *adj.* conforming to the standards of what one considers proper, socially acceptable etc. ‖ fairly large ‖ good **re·spéct·a·bly** *adv.*

re·spect·ful *adj.* showing respect

res·pi·ra·tion *n.* any of various processes by which an organism takes in air or dissolved gases and expels both the gaseous by-products and the unused part of the air or gas

res·pi·ra·tor *n.* a device for inducing artificial respiration

res·pi·ra·to·ry *adj.* of or relating to respiration ‖ serving for respiration

res·pite *n.* an interval of relief during a period of work, suffering etc.

re·splend·ent *adj.* brightly glowing with light or color

re·spond *v.i.* to reply ‖ to show an effect due to a force, influence or stimulus

re·sponse *n.* a reply ‖ something answered ‖ the reaction to a stimulus

re·spon·si·bil·i·ty pl. **re·spon·si·bil·i·ties** *n.* the state or quality of being responsible **to take responsibility for** to consider oneself answerable for

re·spon·si·ble *adj.* placed in control and having to give satisfaction ‖ (of a position) held by such a person or persons ‖ fit to be placed in control **re·spón·si·bly** *adv.*

re·spon·sive *adj.* giving a response, e.g a stimulus ‖ quick to respond

rest *n.* the state of being motionless ‖ the state of being inactive ‖ sleep ‖ something serving as a support for something else **to lay to rest** to bury (a dead person) **to set (someone's) mind at rest** to cause (someone) to be free of worries etc.

rest *v.i.* to be motionless ‖ to refrain from activity ‖ to be or become tranquil ‖ to be fixed or supported ‖ to remain in abeyance

rest *n.* the portion which remains after part has been taken away

res·tau·rant *n.* a place where meals are served

rest·ful *adj.* enabling a person to rest his body or mind ‖ having a calming effect

res·ti·tu·tion *n.* the act of giving back to a rightful owner ‖ a giving of something as

an equivalent for what has been lost, damaged etc.

res·tive *adj.* having too much energy to be willing to remain at rest or to submit to control ‖ (of a crowd, audience etc.) uneasy or beginning to show displeasure

rest·less *adj.* agitatedly moving about ‖ in continual motion ‖ constantly seeking change

res·to·ra·tion *n.* a restoring or being restored

re·store re·stor·ing re·stored *v.t.* to give back ‖ to make (something) look as it looked originally by repairing, retouching etc. ‖ to put back ‖ to put back into place **re·stór·er** *n.* someone who restores

re·strain *v.t.* to prevent from doing something ‖ to set limits to ‖ to repress ‖ to deprive of physical liberty

re·straint *n.* a restraining or being restrained ‖ something which restrains ‖ confinement **without restraint** freely, with no holding back

re·strict *v.t.* to keep within certain limits **re·stríct·ed** *adj.* limited

re·stric·tion *n.* a restricting or being restricted ‖ something which restricts

re·stric·tive *adj.* restricting or tending to restrict

re·sult 1. *v.i.* be the effect of something ‖ to have a specified effect 2. *n.* an effect ‖ a solution arrived at by calculation or reasoning ‖ the outcome of an examination, election or similar contest ‖ (pl., of sports) published or announced scores and winners etc.

re·sume re·sum·ing re·sumed *v.t.* to begin again ‖ to go back to using ‖ to sum up

ré·su·mé *n.* a summary ‖ a curriculum vitae

re·sump·tion *n.* the act or fact of beginning again

re·sur·face re·sur·fac·ing re·sur·faced *v.t.* to give a new surface to

re·sur·gence *n.* a rising again

re·sur·gent *adj.* rising or seeming to rise again

res·ur·rect *v.t.* to bring back to life ‖ to bring back to memory or into use ‖ *v.i.* to rise from the dead

res·ur·rec·tion *n.* the act of rising again

after death ‖ a bringing back into use, memory etc.

re·sus·ci·ta·tion *n.* a resuscitating or being resuscitated

re·sus·ci·tate re·sus·ci·tat·ing re·sus·ci·tat·ed *v.t.* to bring (someone unconscious or seemingly dead) to life or consciousness again ‖ to revive ‖ *v.i.* to come to life again **re·sús·ci·ta·tor** *n.* someone who or something that resuscitates

re·tail 1. *n.* the sale of goods in small quantities directly to consumers **2.** *adj.* of, relating to, or engaged in the sale of goods in this way **3.** *adv.* by retail sale **4.** *v.t.* to sell in small quantities

re·tain *v.t.* to keep in one's possession or control ‖ to keep available ‖ to keep in one's memory **re·táin·er** *n.* something which retains ‖ the engaging by a client of the services of an attorney ‖ a fee paid to an attorney to retain his services

re·tal·i·ate re·tal·i·at·ing re·tal·i·at·ed *v.i.* to return blow for blow, insult for insult, harm for harm **re·tal·i·á·tion** *n.* **re·tál·i·a·tive, re·tal·i·a·to·ry** adjs

re·tard *v.t.* to slow down the advance of, delay

re·tard·ed *adj.* physically or mentally backward

retch 1. *v.i.* to try to vomit but fail to do so **2.** *n.* the act of retching

re·ten·tion *n.* a retaining or being retained ‖ the capacity of retaining ‖ a remembering or a keeping in the memory

ret·i·cence *n.* an inclination to be reserved in speech or behavior ‖ an instance of this

ret·i·cent *adj.* characterized by reticence

re·tic·u·lar *adj.* netlike ‖ intricate

ret·i·na *pl.* **ret·i·nas, ret·i·nae** *n.* the membrane which forms the inner lining of the back wall of the vertebrate eye **rét·i·nal** *adj.* **ret·i·ni·tis** *n.* inflammation of the retina

ret·i·nue *n.* the persons following someone as attendants

re·tire re·tir·ing re·tired *v.i.* to give up active participation in a business or other occupation ‖ to draw back from an area of combat, danger etc. ‖ to seek privacy to go to bed ‖ *v.t.* to withdraw (money) from circulation ‖ to cause to fall back **re·tíred** *adj.* **re·tíre·ment** *n.* a retiring or being retired **re·tír·ing** *adj.* (of persons) reserved, preferring seclusion

re·tort *n.* a vessel of metal etc. used for distilling metals ‖ a vessel usually of glass with a long slanting tube, used in distillation

retort 1. *v.t.* to make a retort ‖ to retaliate ‖ *v.t.* to turn against the user **2.** *n.* a quick witty or sarcastic reply

re·touch 1. *v.t.* to improve by making small alterations in **2.** *n.* a retouching ‖ a detail which has been changed in retouching

re·tract *v.t.* to take back, withdraw ‖ *v.i.* to recant

re·trac·tion *n.* a retracting of something said

re·tread *v.t.* to supply (a tire) with a new tread

re·treat *n.* the withdrawal of troops ‖ a place to which one withdraws for peace, safety etc. ‖ a signal given by a bugle at sunset, announcing the ceremony of flag lowering ‖ a period during which a person withdraws from worldly activities to e.g. a monastery

re·trench *v.i.* to cut down expenses ‖ *v.t.* to curtail, economize **re·trénch·ment** *n.* a retrenching ‖ an inner line of defense to which troops can retreat

ret·ri·bu·tion *n.* merited punishment ‖ something given in recompense

re·trieve 1. re·triev·ing re·trieved *v.t.* to get back ‖ to win back ‖ to save ‖ to put right ‖ *v.i.* (of dogs) to bring back fallen game **2.** *n.* (games) the return of a difficult ball **re·tríev·er** *n.* a dog trained to recover fallen game

ret·ro·act *v.i.* to have effect as from a stipulated date in the past **ret·ro·ác·tion** *n.* **ret·ro·ác·tive** *adj.*

ret·ro·spect *n.* an instance of looking back on past events **in retrospect** the past being looked at afresh **ret·ro·spéc·tion** *n.* the act of reviewing the past **ret·ro·spéc·tive** *adj.*

re·turn 1. *n.* the act of returning to or from another place or condition ‖ something returned ‖ profit from business etc. ‖ *(pl.)* the results of balloting ‖ (fencing) a riposte ‖ (tennis) the act of returning a ball **in return** by way of reward or retaliation **2.** *adj.* given or done in return

return *v.i.* to go or come back to the same place ‖ to revert ‖ to occur again ‖ *v.t.* to give back by way of thanks or retaliation ‖ to repay ‖ to pronounce (a verdict) ‖ to yield (e.g. a profit)

re·un·ion *n.* a reuniting ‖ a meeting of former associates or of members of a family separated for a long time

re·u·nite re·u·nit·ing re·u·nit·ed *v.t.* to unite again after a period of separation

re·vamp *v.t.* to refurbish, revise and improve

re·veal *v.t.* to make known ‖ to expose to view ‖ to divulge

rev·eil·le *n.* a signal sounded esp. by a bugle, to wake members of the forces in the morning

revel rev·el·ing rev·eled *v.i.* to take intense pleasure

rev·e·la·tion *n.* a revealing ‖ something revealed

re·venge 1. *v.t.* **re·veng·ing re·venged** to inflict injury etc. in return for (injury etc.) ‖ to avenge **2.** *n.* a revenging ‖ (games) a chance to win after a previous defeat

rev·e·nue *n.* return from investments, property etc. ‖ *(pl.)* items of income collectively

re·ver·ber·ate re·ver·ber·at·ing re·ver·ber·at·ed *v.t.* to reflect ‖ to throw back (sound) ‖ *v.i.* to reecho ‖ to be reflected

re·ver·ber·a·tion *n.* a reechoing of sound ‖ a reflecting of light etc. ‖ a deflection of heat etc. ‖ something reverberated

re·vere re·ver·ing re·vered *v.t.* to regard with affectionate awe or veneration

rev·er·ence 1. *n.* a revering ‖ a bow or curtsy **2.** *v.t.* **rev·er·enc·ing rev·er·enced** to revere

rev·er·ent *adj.* feeling or showing due reverence

rev·er·ie *n.* dreamlike contemplation

re·vers *pl.* **re·vers** *n.* a lapel on jackets, coats etc.

re·ver·sal *n.* a reversing or being reversed

re·verse re·vers·ing re·versed *v.t.* to change the direction, arrangement, nature etc. of (something) to its opposite ‖ to turn inside out ‖ to turn upside adown ‖ to cause to move backwards ‖ to annul, make void (a decision etc.) ‖ *v.i.* to turn backwards

reverse 1. *adj.* opposite ‖ backward ‖ causing backward movement **2.** *n.* the opposite of something ‖ the back side of a coin, medal etc. ‖ a gear, for causing a motor etc. to run backwards

re·vers·i·ble *adj.* able to be reversed ‖ (of a garment) made so that either the inside or outside can be worn outermost **re·vers·i·bly** *adv.*

re·vert *v.i.* to return to a former belief, opinion, condition etc. **re·vert·i·ble** *adj.* subject to reversion

re·view 1. *n.* a looking over again ‖ a general consideration of past events ‖ a ceremonial inspection of troops etc. ‖ a critical evaluation of a book, concert, theatrical performance etc. ‖ a brushing up **re·view·er** *n.* a person who writes reviews of books, plays etc. **2.** *v.t.* to consider again ‖ to write a critical evaluation ‖ to brush up

re·vile re·vil·ing re·viled *v.i.* to speak abusively

re·vise 1. **re·vis·ing re·vised** *v.t.* to mend errors in (a text etc.) **2.** *n.* (printing) a proof of corrected type

re·vi·sion *n.* a revising ‖ a revised text **re·vi·sion·al** *adj.*

re·viv·al *n.* a reviving ‖ a coming back to health or consciousness ‖ an awakening of religious fervor ‖ an evangelistic meeting ‖ a restaging of a play **re·viv·al·ism, re·viv·al·ist** ns

re·vive re·viv·ing re·vived *v.i.* to come back to consciousness ‖ to recover strength ‖ *v.t.* to restore to consciousness, vigor etc. ‖ to produce again ‖ to make valid again ‖ to bring to mind again ‖ to bring back into fashion

re·voke re·vok·ing re·voked *v.t.* to cancel, withdraw

re·volt *n.* an opposing of authority, esp. by armed rebellion

revolt *v.i.* to rebel against other authority ‖ to feel disgust ‖ *v.t.* to disgust **re·vólt·ing** *adj.*

rev·o·lu·tion *n.* one complete turn in the action of revolving ‖ an unconstitutional overthrow of an established government ‖ a fundamental social change ‖ (of heavenly bodies) the action of going around in an orbit **rev·o·lú·tion·ar·y 1.** *adj.* relating to a political revolution **2.** *pl.* **rev·o·lu·tion·ar·ies** *n.* a revolutionist **rev·o·lu·tion·ize rev·o·lu·tion·iz·ing rev·o·lu·tion·ized** *v.t.* to change completely

re·volve re·vol·ving re·volved *v.t.* to cause to turn around an axis ‖ to ponder ‖ *v.i.* to move around an axis ‖ to recur

re·volv·er *n.* a pistol with a revolving feeding mechanism

re·vue *n.* a stage spectacle consisting of sketches, songs etc. in which parody and satire predominate

re·vul·sion *n.* a sudden, violent antipathy ‖ disgust

re·ward *n.* something given in recognition of service rendered

reward *v.t.* to give a reward to **re·wárd·ing** *adj.* giving personal satisfaction

rhap·so·dy *pl.* **rhap·so·dies** *n.* extravagant enthusiasm in speaking or writing ‖ a title given to some usually single-movement compositions

rhe·sus *n.* a small light brown Indian monkey

rhet·o·ric *n.* the art or science of communication in words ‖ overornate or ostentatious language **rhe·tor·i·cal** *adj.*

rhetorical question a question posed for rhetorical effect, emphasis etc. and not meant to be answered

rheu·mat·ic 1. *adj.* affected by or suffering from rheumatism **2.** *n.* someone afflicted with rheumatism

rheumatic fever a disease, often recurrent, which sometimes follows an infected throat, occurring mainly in children or young adults

rheu·ma·tism *n.* any of various conditions characterized by pain and swelling in and around the muscles and joints

rhine·stone *n.* an artificial gem cut to resemble a diamond

rhi·noc·er·os *pl.* **rhi·noc·er·os·es, rhi·noc·er·os** *n.* any of various herbivorous mammals weighing from 2 to 3½ tons and having either one or two horns curving up from the snout

rhom·bus *pl.* **rhom·bus·es, rhom·bi** *n.* an equilateral parallelogram other than a square

rhu·barb *n.* a genus of perennial, large-leaved plants. The fleshy, reddish stems are peeled and cooked and used in making pies, preserves etc.

rhyme *n.* identity or similarity in the sounds of word endings **without rhyme or reason** having no system or sense

rhyme rhym·ing rhymed *v.i.* to form a rhyme ‖ to write verse ‖ *v.t.* to use as a rhyme

rhythm *n.* (in language) the irregular alternation of stress, duration or pitch, tending with heightened emotion towards meter ‖ (in music) the pattern produced by the relative duration and stress of notes

rhyth·mic *adj.* having or using rhythm

rib 1. *n.* one of the paired, curved bones that form the bony cage which encloses and protects the thoaracic cavity of most vertebrates ‖ a raised molding on a ceiling ‖ (bot.) the principal vein of a leaf ‖ a cut of meat including a rib or ribs **2.** *v.t.* **rib·bing ribbed** to tease (someone)

rib·ald *adj.* wittily indecent or coarse **rib·ald·ry** *n.* ribald wit or language

rib·bon *n.* a narrow strip of satin, silk, velvet etc. used e.g. for tying the hair, or for trimming or decoration, etc. ‖ a colored strip of material indicating that the wearer has received a particular medal or decoration

rice *n.* an annual cereal grass cultivated for its seed

rich 1. *adj.* possessing great wealth ‖ having many natural resources ‖ abundant ‖ costly, precious ‖ abounding ‖ fertile ‖ containing a high proportion of fat ‖ vivid, deep and intense **2.** *n.* **the rich** rich people in general

rich·es *pl.n.* wealth, abundance

rick·ets pl. *n.* a disease characterized by a softening of bone structure

rick·et·y *adj.* suffering from rickets ‖ shaky, insecure

ric·o·chet 1. *n.* the glancing off at a tangent of a bullet or other missile after hitting a flat surface which it does not penetrate 2. *v.i.* **ric·o·chet·ing ric·o·cheted** to glance off, to rebound

rid *v.t.* **rid·ding rid, ridded** to free of a nuisance **to get rid of** to get free from **rid·dance** *n.* a ridding or being rid **good riddance!** an expression of satisfaction at getting rid of someone or something

rid·dle 1. *n.* a question phrased obscurely and posed to test the ingenuity of the person trying to find the answer ‖ a puzzling person or thing 2. *v.* **rid·dling rid·dled** to speak in riddles

riddle 1. *n.* a coarse sieve 2. *v.t.* **rid·dling rid·dled** to sieve through a riddle ‖ to fill with holes

ride 1. **rid·ing rode rid·den** *v.i.* to sit in a car, train etc. and be carried along ‖ to sit on and be carried along by a horse while controlling its movements ‖ (of a ship) to lie at anchor ‖ (of clothing, with 'up') to work upward out of place ‖ *v.t.* to sit on (an animal) or on or in (a vehicle) and be carried along while controlling its movements ‖ to move along on and be supported by ‖ to give a ride to ‖ to tease **to ride out** to come through safely 2. *n.* a journey made by riding **to take (someone) for a ride** to deceive or trick (someone)

rid·er *n.* someone who rides ‖ an additional clause or amendment added to a legislative bill, document etc.

ridge 1. *n.* the horizontal angle at the junction of two slopes ‖ a long, narrow elevation of land ‖ the raised earth thrown up between furrows 2. *v.* **ridg·ing ridged** to form into ridges

rid·i·cule 1. *n.* contemptuous laughter 2. *v.t.* **rid·i·cul·ing rid·i·culed** to treat with ridicule

ri·dic·u·lous *adj.* provoking derisive laughter ‖ unworthy of consideration, unreasonable

rife *adj.* widespread, prevalent

riff·raff *n.* people regarded as disreputable

rif·fle 1. *n.* a shallow in the bed of a stream across which the water flows rapidly, producing small choppy waves ‖ one of these waves ‖ the sound of cards being riffled 2. **rif·fling rif·fled** *v.t.* to form a riffle or riffles in (water) ‖ to leaf through (e.g. the pages of a book) rapidly, causing a slight rustling sound

ri·fle 1. *v.t.* **ri·fling ri·fled** to steal ‖ to carry off as booty 2. *n.* a gun having spiral grooves cut in the bore

rift *n.* a crack, fissure ‖ a clearing or opening ‖ a break

rig 1. *v.t.* **rig·ging rigged** to fit (a ship) with ropes, spars and all necessary tackle ‖ (esp. with 'out') to provide with clothes ‖ (esp. with 'up') to put together quickly as a temporary arrangement 2. *n.* the manner in which a ship's sails, masts etc. are arranged ‖ distinctive dress ‖ the equipment used in drilling an oil well

rig·ging *n.* all the ropes, chains etc. used for hoisting and lowering the sails

right 1. *adj.* obeying the moral law ‖ correct ‖ true, logically sound ‖ appropriate, opportune ‖ suitable ‖ on the side of the body away from the location of the heart ‖ (of a river bank) on this side of an observer facing downstream ‖ mentally sound **in one's right mind** in full possession of one's mental faculties 2. *n.* that to which one is morally or legally entitled ‖ the right side or direction

ridge 1. *n.* the horizontal angle at the junction of two slopes ‖ a long, narrow elevation of land ‖ the raised earth thrown up between furrows 2. *v.* **ridg·ing ridged** to form into ridges

rid·i·cule 1. *n.* contemptuous laughter 2. *v.t.* **rid·i·cul·ing rid·i·culed** to treat with ridicule

ri·dic·u·lous *adj.* provoking derisive laughter ‖ unworthy of consideration, unreasonable

rife *adj.* widespread, prevalent

riff·raff *n.* people regarded as disreputable

rif·fle 1. *n.* a shallow in the bed of a stream across which the water flows rapidly, producing small choppy waves ‖ one of these waves ‖ the sound of cards being riffled 2. **rif·fling rif·fled** *v.t.* to form a riffle or riffles in (water) ‖ to leaf through (e.g. the pages of a book) rapidly, causing a slight rustling sound

ri·fle 1. *v.t.* **ri·fling ri·fled** to steal ‖ to carry off as booty 2. *n.* a gun having spiral grooves cut in the bore

rift *n.* a crack, fissure ‖ a clearing or opening ‖ a break

rig 1. *v.t.* **rig·ging rigged** to fit (a ship) with ropes, spars and all necessary tackle ‖ (esp. with 'out') to provide with clothes ‖ (esp. with 'up') to put together quickly as a temporary arrangement 2. *n.* the manner in which a ship's sails, masts etc. are arranged ‖ distinctive dress ‖ the equipment used in drilling an oil well

rig·ging *n.* all the ropes, chains etc. used for hoisting and lowering the sails

right 1. *adj.* obeying the moral law ‖ correct ‖ true, logically sound ‖ appropriate, opportune ‖ suitable ‖ on the side of the body away from the location of the heart ‖ (of a river bank) on this side of an observer facing downstream ‖ mentally sound **in one's right mind** in full possession of one's mental faculties 2. *n.* that to which one is morally or legally entitled ‖ the right side or direction

right *adv.* in conformity with the moral law ‖ correctly, accurately ‖ directly **right away** immediately

right *v.t.* to restore to, or set in, the proper position ‖ to put (oneself) back into balance ‖ to redress (a wrong)

right·eous *adj.* conforming to moral law ‖ caused by outrage against injustice

right·ful *adj.* having a just claim ‖ proper

rig·id *adj.* stiffly set ‖ rigorous ‖ inflexible **ri·gid·i·ty** *n.*

rig·ma·role *n.* a disconnected narration ‖ a protracted, tiresome procedure or ceremonial

rig·or *n.* uncompromising firmness ‖ extreme harshness ‖ (*pl.*) hardships

rig·or mor·tis *n.* the stiffening of the muscles after death

rig·or·ous *adj.* characterized by rigor ‖ precise

rile ril·ing riled *v.t.* to arouse anger or resentfulness in ‖ to roil (a liquid)

rim 1. *n.* the outer edge of a circular, oval or otherwise curved object ‖ a curved frame, e.g. of a wheel or lens 2. *v.t.* **rim·ming rimmed** to furnish with a rim

rime 1. *n.* white hoarfrost 2. *v.t.* **rim·ing rimed** to cover with or as if with rime

ri·mose *adj.* having many clefts or fissures

rind *n.* peel ‖ a hard skin

ring 1. ring·ing rang rung *v.i.* to sound a bell as a summons ‖ *v.t.* to cause (a bell) to sound **to ring a bell** to evoke a vague memory **to ring false (true)** to sound false (true) 2. *n.* the sound of a bell ‖ a telephone call

ring 1. *n.* a circular band, usually of precious metal, worn on a finger as an ornament or symbol ‖ the rim of a circular object ‖ the circular arena in which the acts of a circus are performed ‖ the square enclosure in which boxing oaand wrestling matches are held ‖ a bullring ‖ a piston ‖ an annual ring ‖ a group of persons or things arranged in a circle ‖ a circular course ‖ a group of persons working together, often illicitly **to throw one's hat in the ring** to announce that one is a candidate in a political contest 2. *v.t.* to encircle ‖ to fit with a ring ‖ *v.i.* to form into a ring or rings

ring·er *n.* a person who, or thing which, rings a bell ‖ (often with 'dead') a person who strongly resembles another

ring·lead·er *n.* a leader of a group of people engaged in unlawful or objectionable acts

ring·let *n.* a long lock of curly hair

ring·mas·ter *n.* an official in charge of the various acts in a circus

ring·side *n.* the area immediately outside a boxing or circus ring where a good view is afforded

ring·worm *n.* any of various contagious diseases of hair, skin and nails caused by fungi

rink *n.* an area of natural or artificial ice used for ice-skating ‖ a wooden or asphalt floor used for roller-skating

rinse 1. *v.t.* **rins·ing rinsed** to remove the soap, dirt etc. with clear water 2. *n.* a solution that tints the hair temporarily

ri·ot n. a public tumult, often in defiance of authority and the law ‖ a very funny person or entertainment

riot v. i. to take part in a riot

ri·ot·ous adj. marked by rioting‖disorderly

rip 1. rip·ping ripped v.t. to break the fibers of (e.g. cloth) by a sudden pull, tear, cut etc. ‖ to split ‖ v.i. to be suddenly torn, cut, split etc. **2.** n. a tear or rent made by ripping

ri·par·i·an adj. of a riverbank ‖ located on a riverbank

ripe adj. ready to be harvested ‖ (of time) at a propitious juncture ‖ mature **rí·pen** v.i. to become ripe ‖ v.t. to cause to become ripe

rip·ple 1. rip·pling rip·pled v.i. (of water) to have the surface disturbed by ripples ‖ to make the sound of ripples ‖ (of fabric) to fall in ripplelike folds ‖ v.t. to give a wavy appearance to **2.** n. a small wave spreading outwards from a point where the surface of water is disturbed ‖ the sound or the action of the wind on waves ‖ a ripple mark

rise 1. ris·ing rose ris·en v.i. to come to a vertical position after sitting, kneeling, lying etc. ‖ to get up after sleeping ‖ to move upwards‖to appear above the horizon ‖ to increase in degree, quantity, volume, price etc. ‖ to swell, puff up ‖ to advance in rank ‖ to revolt ‖ to come into being ‖ to be in the process of being erected ‖ v. to cause (birds) to soar up from the ground ‖ to cause (fish) to come towards the surface of the water **2.** n. an upward-sloping piece of ground ‖ advancement in social status etc. ‖ the emergence and early growth of something ‖ an increase in price, rate, value, volume etc. ‖ (of a body of water) a coming to a higher level **rís·er** n. the vertical piece connecting two stair treads

ris·i·ble adj. exciting laughter ‖ easily disposed to laugh

risk 1. n. the possibility of danger, injury, loss etc. ‖ the possibility of loss in the case of goods covered by an insurance policy ‖ the probability of such loss ‖ hazard **to**

run or take a risk to expose oneself or be exposed to danger, injury, loss etc. **2.** v.t. to run or take the risk of

risk·y risk·i·er risk·i·est adj. involving risk

ris·qué adj. close to being indecent

rite n. a religious ceremony or formal act of worship

rit·u·al 1. adj. relating to rites **2.** n. a strictly ordered traditional method of conducting and performing an act of worship or other solemn ceremony

ri·val 1. n. a person in competition with another or others **2.** adj. competitive **3.** v.t. **ri·val·ing ri·valed** to be in competition with **rí·val·ry** pl. **ri·val·ries** n.

riv·er n. a stream of fresh water flowing into another body of water ‖ a voluminous flow of something

riv·et 1. n. a metal pin or bolt inserted into two or more metal plates hammered out flat to hold the plates firmly together **2.** v.t. **riv·et·ing, riv·et·ting riv·et·ed, riv·et·ted** to join with rivets ‖ (with 'on') to fix (the attention, eyes, gaze etc.)

riv·u·let n. a small stream

roach n. a cockroach

road n. a strip of smoothed, cleared land, usually provided with a hard surface, for the passage from place to place of vehicles, riders, pedestrians etc.

roam 1. v.i. to walk with no particular goal ‖ v.t. to wander **2.** n. a roaming, ramble

roar 1. v.i. to emit the loud, deep sound characteristic of some savage or enraged beasts ‖ to talk, sing or laugh boisterously ‖ (e.g. of flood water or the sea) to emit a loud, deep, confused, sometimes rumbling, noise ‖ v.t. to utter or express with a roar **2.** n. a roaring noise **róar·ing 3.** n. the sound made by someone who roars **4.** adj. that roars

roast 1. v.t. to cook (meat etc.) by exposing it to the radiant heat from a fire, or the dry heat of an oven ‖ to dry and partly scorch ‖ to heat excessively ‖ to criticize mercilessly ‖ v.i. to be roasted **2.** n. a cut of meat **róast·er** n. a chicken, pig, rabbit etc. suitable for roasting ‖ an oven for roasting

rob rob·bing robbed v.t. to take property

from (a person) illegally ‖ to deprive (a person) of something desired or due ‖ *v.i.* to engage in robbery .

rob·ber *n.* a person who robs

rob·ber·y *pl.* **rob·ber·ies** *n.* the act of robbing

robe 1. *n.* a long, loose outer garment **2. rob·ing robed** *v.t.* to put a robe on

rob·in *n.* a large thrush having an olive-gray back, a black throat streaked with gray, and a dull-red breast

ro·bot *n.* a mechanical device designed to do the work of human beings ‖ an efficient but unfeeling person

ro·bot·ics *n.* the science of automated devices

ro·bust *adj.* strong ‖ coarse ‖ hardy

rock an aggregate of particles composed of one or more minerals ‖ a large, usually jagged, mass of this material ‖ a piece broken off from such a mass ‖ a firm foundation or support

rock 1. *v.t.* to cause to shake, vibrate, sway etc. violently ‖ to disturb emotionally ‖ *v.i.* to move to and fro ‖ to sway violently **2.** *n.* the act of rocking

rock·er *n.* either of the curved pieces on which a rocking chair or cradle rocks ‖ a rocking chair

rock·et 1. *n.* a projectile **2.** *v.t.* to rise very rapidly

rock·et·ry *n.* the study of or use of rockets

rock·y rock·i·er rock·i·est *adj.* full of rocks ‖ made of rock ‖ hard as rock

rock·y rock·i·er rock·i·est *adj.* shaky or weak

ro·co·co 1. *n.* a highly ornamental style in architecture **2.** *adj.* relating to painting, music, literature etc. having similar ornately decorative characteristics

rod *n.* a slender, sometimes extensible, bar, shaft, pole, staff etc. in wood, cane, metal, glass etc. ‖ a stick used to measure with ‖ a measure of length equal to 5½ yds or 16½ ft ‖ a rod-shaped bacterium

ro·dent 1. *n.* a small gnawing mammal including rats, mice, squirrels, marmots etc. **2.** *adj.* of or relating to a rodent

ro·de·o *n.* a roundup ‖ a public exhibition of skill by cowboys, often in competition

roent·gen, ront·gen *n.* a unit of X-ray or gamma radiation

rogue *n.* a man who gets along in life by cheating, deceiving, and taking advantage of others ‖ a mischievous child or person ‖ any enraged, large animal which has left the herd

ro·guish *adj.* acting like a rogue ‖ mischievous

roil *v.t.* to stir up sediment in (a liquid) and make it turbid ‖ to irritate **róil·y roil·i·er roil·i·est** *adj.* turbid

roist·er *v.i.* to engage in noisy, drunken revelry

role, role *n.* the part in which an actor is cast in a play ‖ the part a person plays in a specific situation

roll *n.* a quantity of cloth, wrapping paper, wall paper etc., rolled up in the form of a cylinder ‖ any of variously shaped pieces of baked dough ‖ a scroll ‖ an official list of names

roll 1. *v.i.* (of a wheeled vehicle) to move ‖ to flow forward in undulations, streams, etc. ‖ (of a ship) to move with a heavy side-to-side motion ‖ (of a person) to walk in this manner ‖ (of the eyes) to turn from side to side ‖ *v.t.* to cause to move on wheels, rollers etc. ‖ to level, smooth, flatten etc. with a roller ‖ to beat a roll upon (a drum) ‖ to throw (dice) ‖ to rob (someone) while he is asleep, unconscious etc. **to roll out** to make flat or thin by using a roller **2.** *n.* a rolling movement, e.g. of a ship in heavy seas ‖ (of a person) a rolling walk ‖ a succession of rapid beats on a drum

rol·lick 1. *v.i.* to act with exuberant gaiety **2.** *n.* a burst of exuberant gaiety **ról·lick·ing** *adj.*

ro·ly-po·ly 1. *adj.* round and plump **2.** *pl.* **ro·ly-po·lys, ro·ly-po·lies** *n.* a roly-poly person or animal ‖ a weighted toy which, when pushed down, returns to an erect position

Ro·man Cath·o·lic 1. *adj.* of or pertaining to the Roman Catholic Church **2.** *n.* a member of this Church

ro·mance 1. *n.* a medieval literary dealing with deeds of chivalry or with historical or mythological events ‖ an imaginative story of idealized love ‖ the type of literature comprising such stories ‖ a love affair ‖ a pure exaggeration, falsehood **2. ro·manc·ing ro·manced** *v.i.* to indulge in highly exaggerated stories ‖ *v.t.* to give a made-up version of

Roman numerals letters of the Roman alphabet used as symbols for numbers until the 10th c. A.D.

ro·man·tic 1. *adj.* pertaining to romance ‖ susceptible to romance ‖ not based on fact, exaggerated ‖ not very practical **2.** *n.* a romantic person **ro·mán·ti·cal·ly** *adv.* **ro·mán·ti·cism** *n.* the quality of being romantic **ro·mán·ti·cist** *n.* **ro·mán·ti·cize ro·man·ti·ciz·ing ro·man·ti·cized** *v.t.* to interpret romantically

romp 1. *v.i.* to play bisterously **to romp home** to win easily **2.** *n.* the act of romping **rómp·ers** pl.*n.* a child's one-piece garment

rood *n.* a crucifix

roof 1. pl. **roofs** *n.* the structure which covers the top of a building ‖ a home or house as affording shelter and hospitality **to raise the roof** to create a noisy disturbance **2.** *v.t.* to furnish with a roof **roof·age** *n.* roofing

roof·ing *n.* the material used to surface a roof

rook 1. *n.* a crow ‖ a cheat **2.** *v.t.* to cheat

rook *n.* (chess) a castle-shaped piece

rook·ie *n.* a raw army recruit ‖ (baseball) a player in his first season with a major league team

room 1. *n.* a space within a building ‖ space regarded as available to contain something, or something more ‖ (*pl.*) a suite in a boarding house rented for a period **to make room for** to move so as to leave space for **2.** *v.i.* sharing accommodation **room·mate** *n.* someone with whom he shares a room

room·y room·i·er room·i·est *adj.* having plenty of room

roost 1. *n.* the perch of a bird or fowl ‖ the part of a hen house where fowls roost **2.** *v.i.* to be perched for the night **róost·er** *n.* a male domestic fowl

root 1. *n.* that part of a plant which in most species penetrates the earth. It absorbs moisture, stores food, and also serves as an anchor and support ‖ a fundamental or essential part ‖ the original cause of something ‖ that part of a word remaining after removal of prefixes, suffixes, inflectional endings etc. **2.** *v.i.* to grow roots ‖ to become firmly fixed by or as if by roots ‖ *v.t.* to cause to root ‖ to fix firmly

root *v.i.* to give moral support

rope 1. *n.* a thick cord made of twisted strands of hemp, flax, wire etc. ‖ a lasso **at the end of one's rope** at the limit of what one can bear **to know the ropes** to know what procedures to follow etc. **to give someone enough rope to hang himself** to allow someone to continue unchecked until he brings about his own downfall **2.** **rop·ing roped** *v.t.* to fasten or secure with a rope ‖ to lasso

ro·sa·ry pl. **ro·sa·ries** *n.* a rose garden ‖ a string of beads for keeping the count of the prayers of the Rosary

rose 1. *n.* a genus of erect, climbing or creeping shrubs, usually with prickles ‖ the flower of any of these shrubs ‖ the dark pinkish color characteristic of some of these flowers ‖ the card of the mariner's compass **2.** *adj.* scented or flavored with roses ‖ having a rose color

ro·se·ate *adj.* flushed pink

ro·sette *n.* a knot of ribbon or other small decoration in the shape of a rose ‖ a cluster of leaves arising in close circles from a central axis

Rosh Ha·sha·nah the Jewish New Year

ros·in 1. *n.* the resin obtained from the oleoresin of pine by the removal of the volatile turpentine **2.** *v.t.* to rub (esp. a violin bow) with rosin

ros·ter *n.* any itemized list or roll

ros·trum pl. **ros·trums, ros·tra** *n.* a platform from which a speaker addresses his audience

ros·y ros·i·er ros·i·est *adj.* like a rose ‖ having a healthy, rose-colored complexion ‖ promising ‖ optimistic

rot rot·ting rot·ted *v.i.* to decay ‖ to degenerate morally ‖ *v.t.* to cause to decay

rot n. a rotting or being rotten ‖ something rotting or rotten ‖ (pop.) rubbish, nonsense ‖ a process of decline

ro·ta·ry 1. adj. rotating, turning on an axis **2.** pl. **ro·ta·ries** n. a traffic circle

ro·tate ro·tat·ing ro·tat·ed v.i. to turn around an axis ‖ to turn on a pivot with a circular movement ‖ v.t. to cause to revolve ‖ to cause to recur in a cycle

ro·ta·tion n. a rotating ‖ a repetitive arrangement or occurrence **ro·ta·tion·al** adj.

ro·ti·fer n. a class of usually microscopic, many-celled aquatic animals

ro·to·gra·vure n. a process of photogravure using a rotary press ‖ a print reproduced by this method

ro·tor n. the rotary part of an electrical machine

rot·ten adj. decayed, decomposed ‖ morally corrupt ‖ completely unsatisfactory ‖ very unpleasant

rot·ter n. a person having no moral integrity

ro·tund adj. round, plump ‖ florid, rhetorical

ro·tun·da n. a circular building with a dome or cupola ‖ a large circular room

ro·tun·di·ty pl. **ro·tun·di·ties** n. the state or quality of being rotund ‖ a rotund phrase

rouge 1. n. a cosmetic for heightening the color of the cheeks **2. roug·ing rouged** v.i. to use rouge

rough 1. adj. having a surface which is uneven or marked by protuberances or other irregularities ‖ having a coarse texture ‖ turbulent ‖ harsh and rasping ‖ approximate ‖ unrefined ‖ characterized by violence ‖ crudely executed ‖ unpolished ‖ lacking luxuries, comfort etc. **2.** adj. roughly **3.** n. uneven, stony ground ‖ anything in a rough, unfinished state ‖ v.t. to make rough ‖ to treat roughly **to rough it** to live without the comforts and amenities of civilized life **rough·age** n. the rough or refuse part of grain etc.

rough·neck n. a tough, rowdy man or boy

rou·lette n. a gambling game ‖ a toothed wheel for making dots or incisions, e.g. in engraving ‖ a series of small slits separating rows of postage stamps

round 1. adj. having a circular shape ‖ having a spherical shape ‖ plump ‖ full-toned and even ‖ full, complete **2.** n. a route habitually taken ‖ a succession of events, actions etc. ‖ (boxing) one of the periods into which a match is divided ‖ a unit of play in which each player has a turn ‖ a drink of liquor served at the same time to each member of a group of people **3.** v. to make round ‖ to pronounce with rounded lips ‖ to pass esp. by making a circuit of ‖ to make full or plump ‖ to polish (phrases or style) **to round up** to drive (cattle) together ‖ to bring in for questioning **4.** adv. in a circle or in a circular course ‖ from beginning to end ‖ to everyone present ‖ so as to encircle ‖ so as to see the sights, inspect a property etc. **5.** prep. on every side of ‖ so as to encircle ‖ so as to revolve about ‖ near ‖ here and there in **round the clock** for 24 hours nonstop

round·a·bout adj. circuitous, indirect

round-up n. the collecting of scattered cattle ‖ a collecting of scattered people, esp. of criminals by police

rouse rous·ing roused v.t. to awaken from sleep ‖ to provoke

rous·ing adj. exciting ‖ very enthusiastic

roust·a·bout n. a deckhand ‖ an unskilled laborer

rout n. a disorderly flight **to put to rout** to defeat utterly

rout v.i. to rummage ‖ v.t. (with 'out') to search for and discover ‖ to dig out

route 1. n. a course of travel ‖ a regularly followed course **2.** v.t. **rout·ing rout·ed** to send by a certain route

rou·tine 1. n. a regularly repeated course of action or standard practice ‖ an act (feature in a show) **2.** adj. in accordance with a routine

rove rov·ing roved v.i. and t. to roam

row 1. v.t. to propel by using oars ‖ to compete against in a race ‖ to employ (a specified number of oars) ‖ to take (passengers) in an oar-propelled boat ‖ v.i. to use oars **2.** n. a journey in a rowboat

row n. an orderly line

row n. a quarrel or disturbance, esp. a noisy

one
row·dy 1. row·di·er row·di·est *adj.* noisy
2. pl. **row·dies** *n.* a disorderly person
rów·dy·ism *n.*

roy·al *adj.* relating to a king or queen ‖ very
imposing, splendid, majestic etc.

roy·al·ty pl. **roy·al·ties** *n.* a person having
royal rank ‖ royal persons collectively ‖ the
sum, e.g. a percentage of the sales figure,
paid to the owner of a literary etc. property by the person who exploits it
commercially

rub 1. rub·bing rubbed *v.t.* to clean or
polish with a pressing motion ‖ to chafe
‖ to move in contact causing friction ‖ *v.i.*
to be subjected to friction **to rub down** to
dry the sweat off (a horse) after exercise
or a race **to rub it in** to emphasize, and
continue to emphasize, a person's short-
comings, failures, mistakes etc. **to rub out**
to erase ‖ to become erased **to rub shoulders (elbows)** (esp. with 'with') to associate with someone whom one would not
noramally expect to associate with **to rub
(someone) the wrong way** to offend the
susceptibilities of (someone) and so irritate him 2. *n.* a rubbing

rub·ber *n.* an elastic substance obtained
from latex ‖ a low rubber overshoe worn
in wet weather

rubber *n.* three successive games of
bridge, or the first two only if the same
side wins both

rub·bish *n.* waste material, refuse ‖ worthless goods etc. ‖ nonsense **rub·bish·y** *adj.*

rub·ble *n.* pieces of broken brick, stone etc.

ru·bel·la *n.* German measles

ru·be·o·la *n.* measles

ru·bi·cund *adj.* (of complexions) ruddy

ru·bric *n.* the heading of a chapter or a
section so indicated ‖ a liturgical direction
in a prayer book **rú·bri·cal** *adj.*

ru·by 1. pl. **ru·bies** *n.* a precious stone of
red corundum 2. *adj.* of the color of ruby

ruck·us *n.* a noisy disturbance, argument
etc.

rud·der *n.* a flat piece of wood or metal
hinged vertically to a vessel's sternpost,
used for steering ‖ a similar device for
controlling the direction of an aircraft's

flight

rud·dy rud·di·er rud·di·est *adj.* red-tinted
‖ glowing healthily

rude rud·er rud·est *adj.* very impolite ‖
vulgar ‖ roughly put together ‖ crude ‖
uncivilized

ru·di·ment *n.* (esp. pl.) a basic principle
of a subject ‖ (esp. pl.) the merest beginning of something capable of being developed **ru·di·men·ta·ri·ly** *adv.*
ru·di·men·ta·ri·ness *n.* **ru·di·men·ta·ry**
adj. very elementary ‖ in an early or arrest-
ed stage of development ‖ vestigial

rue ru·ing rued *v.t.* to regret, to repent of
rúe·ful *adj.* regretful, sorrowful

ruff *n.* a natural growth of hair or feathers
around the neck of a bird or beast

ruff 1. *n.* (card games) the act of trumping
2. *v.* to trump

ruf·fi·an *n.* a man who is coarse, tough,
brutal ‖ a boisterous, rascally boy
rúf·fi·an·ism *n.* **rúf·fi·an·ly** *adj.*

ruf·fle 1. ruf·fling ruf·fled *v.t.* to destroy
the smoothness of ‖ to disturb the self-
possession of ‖ (of a bird) to stiffen and to
raise (the feathers) e.g. in fright ‖ to gather
(ribbon) into a ruffle ‖ *v.i.* to become
confused 2. *n.* an ornamental frill
attached to a garment

ruffle 1. *n.* a low throbbing drumbeat 2. *v.i.*
ruf·fling ruf·fled to beat a ruffle

rug *n.* a mat usually of thick wool used esp.
to cover part of a floor ‖ a thick blanket

rug·ged *adj.* (of country) wild and broken
‖ (of ground) very rough-surfaced ‖
irregular features ‖ lacking polish ‖ hard
and austere ‖ hardy

ru·in *n.* a state of advanced destruction or
decay ‖ *(pl.)* the remains of something
which has been destroyed ‖ financial
disaster

ruin *v.t.* to destroy ‖ to wreck financially
ru·in·a·tion *n.* a ruining ‖ a cause of ruin
ru·in·ous *adj.* likely to cause ruin ‖
dilapidated

rule *n.* control by authority ‖ the reign of
a monarch ‖ an accepted method of
behavior or procedure ‖ *(pl.)* the regulations setting forth the method of play in

a sport ‖ a ruler (strip of wood etc.) **as a rule** usually

rule rul·ing ruled *v.t.* to exercise authority or dominion over ‖ to decide or decree with authority ‖ to draw (a line) with a ruler ‖ *v.i.* to exercise authority or power ‖ to decide a point of law or lay down a formal ruling

ru·ler *n.* a sovereign ‖ a strip of wood, metal etc. used in drawing straight lines, measuring etc.

ru·ling 1. *adj.* exercising sovereignty ‖ predominant 2. *n.* the act of someone who rules ‖ the drawing of lines ‖ the lines drawn ‖ an authoritative decision

rum *n.* an alcoholic liquor prepared by fermenting molasses, sugarcane etc. and distilling it

rum·ble 1. **rum·bling rum·bled** *v.i.* to make a dull, rolling sound ‖ *v.t.* to utter in a deep, gruff voice 2. *n.* a rumbling sound

ru·mi·nant 1. *n.* any member of the order Artiodactyla, suborder Ruminantia, e.g. the sheep, cow, camel, llama, goat, giraffe, deer. These animals chew the cud 2. *adj.* of one of these animals ‖ meditative

ru·mi·nate ru·mi·nat·ing ru·mi·nat·ed *v.i.* to chew the cud ‖ to reflect at length ‖ *v.t.* to ponder over

ru·mi·na·tion *n.* the act or process of ruminating

rum·mage 1. **rum·mag·ing rum·maged** *v.i* to make a search, creating disorder ‖ *v.t.* to search through, ransack 2. *n.* odds and ends

rum·my *n.* a card game

ru·mor 1. *n.* an unauthenticated story or report put into circulation 2. *v.t.* to spread or report by rumor

rump *n.* the upper hindquarters of an animal ‖ a cut of beef between the loin and the round ‖ the buttocks

rum·ple 1. **rum·pling rum·pled** *v.t.* to make disorderly, wrinkled etc. ‖ *v.i.* to become wrinkled 2. *n.* a wrinkle in clothes etc.

rum·pus *n.* an uproar, disturbance, row

run 1. **run·ning ran run** *v.i.* to move rapidly with long, usually even, strides ‖ to escape ‖ to move about without restraint ‖ to compete in a race ‖ to be a candidate in an election ‖ to move with a smooth, gliding motion ‖ to go regularly between two places ‖ to circulate ‖ to flow rapidly ‖ to melt and flow ‖ to be operation ‖ to continue in effect ‖ (of liquids, e.g. ink) to spread on being applied to a surface ‖ (of colors in a fabric) to spread or become mixed together when washed or moistened ‖ (of a stocking etc.) to develop a vertical flaw ‖ *v.t.* to enter (a horse) in a race ‖ to enter (someone) as a candidate in an election ‖ to attempt to get through (a blockade etc.) ‖ to cause (a liquid) to flow ‖ to manage or control **to run across** to meet by chance **to run after** to chase **to run a temperature** to have a fever **to run away** to flee ‖ to elope **to run down** to run against and knock down ‖ (baseball) to tag out (a base runner) between bases **to run in** to arrest **to run into** to collide with ‖ to meet by accident ‖ to amount to **to run low** to become scarce **to run on** to continue **to run out** to come to an end **to run over** to drive over ‖ to flow over the edge of a container **to run short of** to have less than enough of 2. *n.* an act of running ‖ the distance covered in running ‖ the time spent in running ‖ (of a theatrical production) a continuous succession of performances ‖ a number of fish migrating together ‖ a vertical flaw in a stocking ‖ a rush of tidal water ‖ (printing) an edition size ‖ (baseball) the point scored by a player in completing a circuit of the bases ‖ a downward course, e.g. for skiing **in the long run** measured over a prolonged period of time **on the run** retreating in disorderly haste

run·a·way 1. *n.* a fugitive ‖ a horse running out of control 2. *adj.* escaping ‖ achieved by eloping ‖ easily won ‖ rising very rapidly

run·down *adj.* in poor health ‖ exhausted ‖ dilapidated **run-down** *n.* a summary

rune *n.* one of the characters of an ancient alphabet used for making inscriptions and magic signs

rung *n.* a crosspiece in a ladder ‖ a bar

joining the legs of a a chair ‖ a spoke in a wheel

run-in *n.* a minor altercation

run·ner *n.* a person who or animal which runs, esp. in a race ‖ a person who runs errands ‖ a smuggler ‖ a ship carrying smuggled goods ‖ the blade of an ice skate ‖ a long strip of carpet for a corridor, staircase etc. ‖ either of the pieces on which a sled or sledge slides ‖ a groove along which something (e.g. a drawer) slides

run·ning 1. *n.* the act of a person or thing that runs **in the running** having a good chance of winning a competition **2.** *adj.* moving at a run ‖ interrupted ‖ flowing ‖ operating ‖ discharging pus **3.** *adv.* sucessively

run·off *n.* a final contest, made necessary because a previous contest was drawn or without a result ‖ water drained from surface soil

run-of-the-mill *adj.* not outstanding, ordinary

runt *n.* the smallest in a litter

run·way *n.* a strip on an airfield for taking off or landing ‖ the trail made by animals in going to and from their regular feeding places

rup·ture 1. *n.* a drastic break in harmonious relations ‖ a hernia ‖ a breaking apart **2. rup·tur·ing rup·tured** *v.t.* to cause a break in ‖ *v.i.* to suffer a rupture

ru·ral *adj.* characteristic of the country

ruse *n.* a piece of cunning ‖ cunning

rush 1. *v.i.* to move with speed and violence ‖ to hasten ‖ to act swiftly with too little reflection ‖ *v.t.* to cause to move with great speed ‖ to court (a girl) assiduously **to rush at** to charge **2.** *n.* a violent forward movement or the sound of it ‖ feverish movement ‖ the state of being

busy and pressed for time ‖ (with 'on') a great demand for a commodity ‖ (movies, esp. *pl.*) the first print of a sequence of filming **3.** *adj.* characterized by enormous bustle and activity

rusk *n.* a slice of crisp, twice-baked bread

rus·set 1. *n.* a color between red and brown ‖ a variety of rough-skinned russet-colored eating apple **2.** *adj.* reddish-brown

rust 1. *n.* a hydrated oxide of iron, formed when iron is exposed to air and moisture ‖ the reddish-brown color of this substance ‖ any of several diseases of grasses and other plants **2.** *v.* to become coated with rust ‖ to deteriorate through lack of use

rus·tic 1. *adj.* characteristic of the countryside ‖ simple in workmanship ‖ made of untrimmed wood ‖ rural **2.** *n.* a person born and bred in the country and quite unsophisticated **rús·ti·cal·ly** *adv.*

rus·tle rus·tling rus·tled *v.i.* to make light sounds like those of stirring leaves etc. ‖ to move energetically ‖ to steal cattle ‖ *v.t.* to cause to make light sounds like those of stirring leaves ‖ to steal (cattle) **to rustle up** to get together by foraging **rús·tler** *n.* a cattle thief

rus·ty rus·ti·er rus·ti·est *adj.* coated with rust ‖ having the color of rust ‖ deteriorated by disuse ‖ stiff from age or neglect

rut 1. *n.* a groove made by wheels in soft ground **2.** *v.t.* **rut·ting rut·ted** to make ruts in

ru·ta·ba·ga *n.* a turnip having a large yellowish root

ruth·less *adj.* merciless

rye *n.* a tall-growing cereal ‖ its grain, used in making bread and for the distilling of rye whiskey

S, s the 19th letter of the English alphabet

sab·bath *n.* the seventh day of the Jewish week (from sundown on Friday until sundown on Saturday) ‖ Sunday, the first day of the Christian week ‖ a day of the week set apart regularly for worship

sab·bat·i·cal 1. *adj.* relating to the sabbath ‖ of an extended period available for special study given to teachers by some schools etc. **2.** *n.* such an extended period

sa·ber *n.* a heavy cavalry sword with a curved blade

sa·ble *n.* a small carnivorous mammal, highly valued for its lustrous dark brown fur ‖ the fur or pelt of this animal

sab·o·tage 1. *n.* deliberate damage done to property e.g. by enemy agents or by hostile employees **2. sab·o·tag·ing sab·o·taged** to commit sabotage upon

sab·o·teur *n.* a person who commits sabotage

sac a part shaped like a pouch in an animal or plant, often filled with a fluid

sac·cha·rin *n.* a white crystalline extremely sweet substance used as a sugar substitute **sac·cha·rine** *adj.* very sweet **sac·cha·rin·i·ty** *n.*

sa·chet *n.* a small bag containing perfumed dried herbs

sack 1. *n.* a large receptacle ‖ summary dismissal, esp. from employment **2.** *v.t.* to put into a sack ‖ to dismiss

sack 1. *n.* the violent plundering by soldiers of a captured town, city etc. **2.** *v.t.* to plunder and lay waste

sac·ra·ment *n.* any of certain Christian rites **the Sacrament** the Eucharist ‖ a solemn oath or pledge

sac·ra·men·tal 1. *adj.* of, relating to or having the nature of a sacrament **2.** *n.* a religious rite resembling a sacrament **sac·ra·mén·tal·ism, sac·ra·mén·tal·ist** *ns*

sa·cred *adj.* consecrated, holy ‖ hallowed ‖ having a religious, not a profane character ‖ to be held in reverence ‖ inviolate

sac·ri·fice 1. *n.* an offering made to a deity etc. as propitiation, thanksgiving etc. ‖ the act of depriving oneself of something

for the sake of attaining some goal or for the sake of someone else ‖ the thing given up in this way ‖ (baseball) a sacrifice bunt or fly which does not count as an official time at bat **2. sac·ri·fic·ing sac·ri·ficed** *v.t.* to offer as a sacrifice ‖ *v.i.* to make a sacrifice

sa·cri·fi·cial *adj.* of or pertaining to sacrifice

sac·ri·lege *n.* the violation of a sacred building, or stealing, misuse, destruction etc. of a sacred object

sac·ri·le·gious *adj.* guilty of sacrilege

sac·ro·sanct *adj.* most holy, inviolable **sac·ro·sánc·ti·ty** *n.*

sac·rum *pl.* **sac·ra sac·rums** *n.* a bone composed of fused vertebrae that forms the back of the pelvis

sad sad·der sad·dest *adj.* grieving ‖ depressed in spirits ‖ deplorable **sad·den** *v.t.* to make sad ‖ *v.i.* to become sad

sad·dle *n.* a seat for the rider of a horse, camel etc. ‖ an object resembling a riding saddle, esp. a ridge between two mountain peaks ‖ a cut of mutton or venison **saddle sad·dling sad·dled** *v.t.* to put a saddle on ‖ to place a burdensome duty, responsibility etc. on

sad·ism *n.* the deriving of pleasure from inflicting pain on another **sád·ist** *n.* **sa·dis·tic** *adj.* **sa·dís·ti·cal·ly** *adv.*

sa·fa·ri *pl.* **sa·fa·ris** *n.* a hunting expedition, esp. in E. Africa

safe saf·er saf·est *adj.* out of danger ‖ not presenting any risk ‖ uninjured ‖ **on the safe side** covered so as to reduce or avoid risk

safe *n.* a fireproof and burglarproof container for valuables

safe·guard 1. *n.* someone who or something that serves as protection **2.** *v.t.* to provide with a protection

safe·keep·ing *n.* the act of keeping safe ‖ custody

safe·ty *pl.* **safe·ties** *n.* the condition of being safe from risk or danger

sag 1. *v.i.* **sag·ging sagged** to bend, hang or sink in the center as a result of weight or pressure ‖ (of sales or market prices) to fall ‖ to cease to hold interest **2.** *n.* a sagging ‖ a depression

sa·ga n. a prose epic narrating the history of early heroes or families

sa·ga·cious adj. keen and perceptive

sa·gac·i·ty n. the quality of being sagacious

sage 1. sag·er sag·est adj. having or showing great wisdom and sound judgment **2.** n. a very wise man

sail n. a piece of canvas or other cloth suspended from the spars of a boat or ship to catch or deflect the wind and drive the vessel along ‖ a voyage by ship ‖ a fin, tentacle or wing **to set sail** to hoist a boat's sails ‖ to begin a sea voyage

sail v.i. to travel in a boat with sails ‖ to make or start a sea voyage ‖ to move or glide effortlessly in the air ‖ v.t. to manage (a boat or ship with sails)

sail·boat n. a boat propelled by sail

sail·or n. a member of a ship's crew below the rank of officer

sail·plane 1. n. a light glider **2.** v.i. **sail·plan·ing sail·planed** to glide in a sailplane

saint 1. n. a person whose holiness has been attested by miracles after his death and who has been officially recognized (canonized) by the Church as worthy of veneration ‖ a person of great charity, patience, purity and meekness **2.** v.t. to canonize

sa·ke, sa·ké, sa·ki n. a Japanese liquor made from fermented rice

sake n. (in phrases) **for the sake of (someone or something)** and **for (someone's or something's) sake** for the benefit of ‖ for the purpose of attaining, achieving etc.

sa·la·cious adj. lewd in character

sal·ad n. a cold dish of (esp. raw, green) vegetables etc., usually with a salad dressing ‖ lettuce

sal·a·man·der n. an order of amphibians superficially like lizards but with a soft, moist, brightly colored skin and no scales **sal·a·mán·dri·an** adj.

sa·la·mi n. a highly seasoned sausage of pork and beef

sal·a·ried adj. receiving a salary

sal·a·ry pl. **sal·a·ries** n. a payment made to workers

sale n. a selling ‖ the amount of goods sold ‖ a public selling by auction ‖ a selling at reduced prices

sa·li·ent 1. adj. being most prominent **2.** n. a part of a defense line which projects into enemy territory

sa·line 1. adj. of or containing salt ‖ relating to chemical salts **2.** n. a salina ‖ a salt spring ‖ a saline solution **sa·lin·i·ty** n.

sa·li·va n. a colorless viscous fluid secreted into the mouth from special glands

sal·i·var·y adj. pertaining to or secreting saliva

sal·low adj. (esp. of complexion) dull yellow

sal·ly 1. pl. **sal·lies** n. a brief and clever witticism ‖ a burst of activity or outburst expressing emotion ‖ a sudden attack made from a fortified position **2.** v.i. **sal·ly·ing sal·lied** make a sally

salm·on pl. **salm·on, salm·ons** n. a large game fish prized for its flesh as food ‖ the pink color of its flesh

sa·lon n. a drawing room in a French home ‖ a room in which hairdressers, dressmakers etc. receive their clients ‖ an exhibition of paintings etc.

sa·loon n. a public room or establishment where alcoholic drinks are served

salt 1. n. a white crystalline compound which occurs widely in nature both as a solid and in seawater (2.6%) **to take with a grain of salt** to have doubts about, regard as exaggerated **2.** adj. preserved in salt ‖ tasting of salt

salt v.t. to flavor, treat or preserve with salt

salt·y salt·i·er salt·i·est adj. containing or tasting of salt ‖ smelling like the sea ‖ pungent, piquant

sa·lu·bri·ous adj. good for the health ‖ wholesome

sal·u·tar‖**y** adj. beneficial, esp. to the health ‖ designed to effect improvement

sal·u·ta·tion n. the act of saluting ‖ something said in greeting

sa·lu·ta·to·ry adj. having the nature of a salutation

sa·lute sa·lut·ing sa·lut·ed v.t. to address with some spoken formula of greeting to make a prescribed gesture of respect to

sa·lute *n.* the gesture, position, act or form of saluting

sal·vage 1. *v.t.* **sal·vag·ing sal·vaged** to rescue from ruin, fire, shipwreck etc. **2.** *n.* things salvaged || the act of salvaging

sal·va·tion *n.* the act of saving from destruction, esp. the saving of the soul from sin or its consequences

salve *n.* a healing ointment || something that soothes

salve salv·ing salved *v.t.* to soothe or set at ease

sal·vo *pl.* **sal·vos, sal·voes** *n.* a simultaneous discharge of guns, explosion of bombs, or burst of cheers

same 1. *adj.* corresponding || not changing || being the one already mentioned **2.** *adv.* in the same way **all the same** nevertheless **just the same** exactly alike **3.** *pron.* the same person or thing

sam·o·var *n.* a Russian tea urn

sam·ple 1. *n.* an individual portion by which the quality of more of the same sort is to be judged **2.** *v.t.* **sam·pling sam·pled** to judge the quality etc. of (the whole) by examining a part

sam·pler *n.* a decorative piece of embroidery showing samples of different kinds of stitches || someone who tests quality by inspecting samples

sam·pling *n.* the act of selecting a sample || the sample selected

san·a·tar·i·um *pl.* **san·a·tar·i·ums, san·a·tar·i·a** *n.* a sanatorium

san·a·to·ri·um *pl.* **san·a·to·ri·ums, san·a·to·ri·a** *n.* a residential establishment for patients undergoing treatment, or one for convalescents

sanc·ti·fi·ca·tion *n.* a sanctifying or being sanctified

sanc·ti·fy sanc·ti·fy·ing sanc·ti·fied *v.t.* to make holy || to give authority to

sanc·ti·mo·ni·ous *adj.* making a pretense of holiness

sanc·ti·mo·ny *n.* the quality of being sanctimonious

sanc·tion 1. *n.* explicit permission given by someone in authority || a penalty for violation || ratification of a law by a supreme authority **2.** *v.t.* to permit || to give encouragement to || to ratify || to attach a penalty to the violating of (a law)

sanc·ti·ty *pl.* **sanc·ti·ties** *n.* holiness

sanc·tu·ar·y *pl.* **sanc·tu·ar·ies** *n.* a sacred place || a place set apart as a refuge

sand 1. *n.* small grains of quartz resulting from the breaking down of siliceous rocks || (often pl.) a stretch of this, e.g. on the seashore **2.** *v.t.* to abrade with sand or sandpaper

san·dal *n.* a sole attached to the foot by straps **sán·daled** *adj.* wearing sandals

sand·bag 1. *n.* a bag filled with sand or soil **2.** *v.t.* **sand·bag·ging sand·bagged** to stun with a sandbag || to put sandbags against, bank up with sandbags

sand·bank *n.* a raised portion of the bed of a sea or river, made of sand accumulated by waves or currents

sand·blast 1. *n.* a high-speed jet of sand **2.** *v.t.* to clean, polish, cut or engrave with a sandblast

sand·er *n.* a machine that sprinkles sand or abrades with sand || a person who cleans, polishes etc. by hand with sand or sandpaper

sand·hog *n.* a workman employed in underground or underwater construction projects which use pneumatic caissons

sand·stone *n.* a porous rock consisting of grains of sand cemented together by substances such as clay or silica which give it characteristic colors

sand·wich 1. *n.* two slices of buttered bread with meat, fish, etc. between them **2.** *v.t.* insert between two other things, places, persons etc.

sand·y sand·i·er sand·i·est *adj.* full of or covered with sand || like sand

sane san·er san·est *adj.* in full possession of the mental faculties || sound || sensible

sang-froid *n.* self-possession at a time of danger

san·gui·nar·y *adj.* accompanied by much bloodshed || murderous

san·guine *adj.* ruddy || cheerfully optimistic

san·i·tar·i·um *pl.* **san·i·tar·i·ums, san·i·tar·i·a** *n.* a sanatorium

san·i·tar·y *adj.* concerned with, promoting or conducive to the preservation of health

san·i·ta·tion *n.* the provision of means whereby health is protected, esp. the arrangements for the disposal of sewage

san·i·ty *n.* the quality or state of being sane

sans ser·if, san·ser·if *n.* a printing type with no serifs

sap 1. *n.* the solution of raw materials and organic products of metabolism which circulates in a plant or tree ‖ a stupid person easily fooled **2.** *v.t.* **sap·ping sapped** to drain (a tree) of its sap

sap sa·ping sapped *v.t.* to undermine (strength, energy etc.)

sa·pi·ent *adj.* wise, knowledgeable

sap·ling *n.* a young tree

sap·phire 1. *n.* a precious stone of transparent blue corundum ‖ the deep blue color of the true sapphire **2.** *adj.* of this blue color

sap·py sap·pi·er sap·pi·est *adj.* full of sap ‖ foolish

sar·casm *n.* a cruelly humorous statement or remark

sar·cas·tic *adj.* involving sarcasm **sar·cás·ti·cal·ly** *adv.*

sar·co·ma *pl.* **sar·co·mas, sar·co·ma·ta** *n.* a malignant tumor **sar·co·ma·tous** *adj.*

sar·coph·a·gus *pl.* **sar·coph·a·gi, sar·coph·a·gus·es** *n.* a stone coffin

sar·dine *pl.* **sar·dines, sar·dine** *n.* a young pilchard cured and preserved in oil

sar·don·ic *adj.* expressing bitterness **sar·dón·i·cal·ly** *adv.*

sa·ri *pl.* **sa·ris** *n.* the robe of a Hindu woman

sa·rong *n.* an ankle-length garment worn by men and women in the Malay Archipelago

sash *n.* a framework holding glass, in a window or greenhouse etc. ‖ a movable frame of a sash window

sash *n.* a ribbon worn as an adornment around the waist

sa·shay *v.i.* to walk nonchalantly ‖ to swagger about

sass 1. *n.* impudent talk **2.** *v.t.* to speak impudently to

sas·sy sas·si·er sas·si·est *adj.* impudent

Sa·tan *n.* the chief of the rebel angels, the Devil

sa·tan·ic *adj.* characteristic of Satan

satch·el *n.* a bag of leather or stout canvas, usually carried slung over the shoulder by strap

sate sat·ing sat·ed *v.t.* to satisfy totally

sat·el·lite *n.* a natural or man-made body moving in orbit around one of the planets etc. ‖ a state economically and politically dependent on another

sa·ti·ate sa·ti·at·ing sa·ti·at·ed *v.t.* to satisfy (a desire or someone), esp. so fully that desire gives place to a revulsion of feeling **sa·ti·a·tion** *n.*

sa·ti·e·ty *n.* the state of being sated

sat·in 1. *n.* a fabric of silk with a glossy surface on one side **2.** *adj.* made of satin ‖ smooth and glossy

sat·in·y *adj.* like satin in glossy smoothness

sat·ire *n.* a literary genre in which ridicule is thrown upon something by stressing its worst features, often by the use of irony ‖ a literary work in this genre

sa·tir·ic *adj.* of, containing or characterized by satire

sa·tir·i·cal *adj.* given to the use of irony or sarcasm

sat·i·rist *n.* a writer of satires

sat·i·rize sat·i·riz·ing sat·i·rized *v.t.* to treat in a satirical way

sat·is·fac·tion *n.* a satisfying or being satisfied ‖ a source of pleasure, fulfilment or gratification ‖ a payment for damage, injury etc.

sat·is·fac·to·ry *adj.* adequate ‖ giving satisfaction

sat·is·fy sat·is·fy·ing sat·is·fied *v.t.* to provide what is required by (a need, obligation, standard etc.) ‖ to pay (a creditor) ‖ to counter convincingly ‖ *v.i.* to give satisfaction

sat·u·rate sat·u·rat·ing sat·u·rat·ed *v.t.* to fill completely ‖ to cause (a substance) to become impregnated to the point where it can absorb no more **sát·u·rat·ed** *adj.*

sat·u·ra·tion *n.* a saturating or being saturated

Sat·ur·day *n.* the seventh and last day of the week

sat·ur·nine *adj.* gloomy, surly

sa·tyr *n.* a god often depicted with a goat's tail and a goat's legs and ears

sa·tyr·ic *adj.* of or like a satyr **sa·týr·i·cal** *adj.*

sause 1. *n.* a liquid added to food e.g. to make it more piquant ‖ impertinence **2.** *v.t.* **sauc·ing sauced** to add sauce to

sau·cer *n.* a small, shallow dish in which to place a cup

sau·ci·ness *n.* the quality of being saucy

sau·cy sau·ci·er sau·ci·est *adj.* impudent ‖ smart, gaily stylish

sau·er·kraut *n.* shredded cabbage fermented under pressure in its own juices

sau·na *n.* a Finnish steam bath

saun·ter 1. *v.i.* to walk in a leisurely manner, with no particular aim in view **2.** *n.* a leisurely walk

sau·sage *n.* a quantity of finely minced meat, forced into a thin-walled tube

sau·té 1. *adj.* fried quickly in a pan with a little hot butter or other fat **2.** *v.t.* **sau·tée·ing sau·téed** to fry in this way **3.** *n.* a dish prepared in this way

sav·age 1. *adj.* primitive, uncivilized ‖ wild and ferocious ‖ extremely cruel **2.** *n.* an uncivilized human being

sav·age·ry *pl.* **sav·age·ries** *n.* a savage act

sa·van·na, sa·van·nah *n.* tropical or subtropical grassland ‖ a treeless plain, esp. in the southeastern U.S.A.

sa·vant *n.* a man of great erudition

save sav·ing saved *v.t.* to keep alive, free, safe or in good condition ‖ to economize ‖ to reserve for future use **to save face** to avoid injury to one's pride or public disgrace

save 1. *prep.* except **2.** *conj.* (with 'that') except

sav·ing 1. *adj.* making an exception ‖ outweighing faults **2.** *n.* a desirable economy in time, money etc. ‖ (*pl.*) money saved

sav·ior *n.* someone who saves **the Sav·ior** Christ

sa·voir faire *n.* tact and assurance in social relationships

sa·vor *n.* tastiness ‖ a smell of cooking which promises well ‖ the characteristic quality of something

savor *v.t.* to have the distinctive taste of ‖ to take pleasure in the taste, smell or characteristic quality of

sa·vor·y *adj.* having a pleasant and piquant taste and smell

saw 1. *n.* a cutting tool with a toothed edge **2. saw·ing** past **sawed sawed, sawn** *v.t.* to cut with a saw ‖ *v.i.* to use a saw ‖ (of a saw) to cut

saw·tooth *pl.* **saw·teeth 1.** *n.* a tooth of a saw **2. sáw·toothed** *adj.*

sax·o·phone *n.* any of a family of instruments classified as woodwinds, having a long, usually curved metal body

say 1. say·ing said *v.t.* to utter ‖ to express vocally, in writing etc. ‖ to allege ‖ (imperative) to assume, suppose ‖ to declare, assert ‖ to recite ‖ *v.i.* to make a statement **2.** *n.* the opportunity to express one's ideas etc.

say-so *pl.* **say-sos** *n.* an unsupported assertion

scab 1. *n.* a tough crust formed over a sore or wound ‖ a worker who refuses to join the union **2.** *v.i.* **scab·bing scabbed** to become covered with a scab ‖ to work or act as a scab

scab·bard *n.* the sheath of a sword

scab·rous *adj.* salacious ‖ having a rough surface

scaf·fold *n.* a platform suspended by ropes, used by men building, repairing etc. at a height ‖ a platform constructed for the execution of criminals **scáf·fold·ing** *n.* the poles, planks and ties used in constructing a scaffold

scald 1. *v.t.* to burn ‖ to heat (liquid) almost to boiling **2.** *n.* the injury to the skin caused by scalding

scale 1. *n.* an arrangement of accurately spaced marks representing a series of numerical values, used in measuring lengths, angles, temperature etc. ‖ a series of notes **2. scal·ing scaled** *v.t.* to apply a scale to ‖ to ascend by a ladder

scale 1. *n.* a balance (instrument for measuring weight) **2.** *v.t.* **scal·ing scaled** to weigh on scales

scale 1. *n.* one of the thin, horny, bony or chitinous plates serving to protect the skin of fishes or reptiles ‖ a small, loosely adhering, hardened flake of skin **2. scal·ing scaled** *v.t.* to remove the scales from ‖ *v.i.* to form scales ‖ to shed scales

scal·lion *n.* the shallot ‖ the leek ‖ a green onion

scal·lop 1. *n.* any of several marine bivalve mollusks having a fan-shaped fluted shell with an undulating margin ‖ the edible adductor muscle of such a mollusk **2.** *v.t.* to ornament with an edging of scallops **scál·lop·ing** *n.* a scalloped edging

scalp 1. *n.* the skin on the top and back of the head **2.** *v.i.* to buy and sell stocks (or theater tickets etc.) in order to make quick returns

scal·pel *n.* a small very sharp knife used in surgery

scalp·er *n.* a person who buys up theater tickets and sells them for more than the established price

scal·y scal·i·er scal·i·est *adj.* covered with scales ‖ shedding flakes ‖ resembling scales

scam *n.* an illegal operation

scamp·er 1. *v.i.* to dart about with nimble movements, esp. playfully ‖ to make a dash **2.** *n.* a scampering

scan scan·ning scanned *v.t.* the path periodically followed by a radiation beam ‖ to examine a body by X-ray or other radioactive material ‖ to glance at hastily

scan·dal *n.* a serious breach of the moral or social code which becomes widely known ‖ malicious gossip

scan·dal·ize scan·dal·iz·ing scan·dal·ized *v.t.* to give offense by acting contrary to what is morally or socially right

scan·dal·ous *adj.* offensive and shocking

scan·ner *n.* someone who or something that scans

scant 1. *adj.* meager ‖ less than enough ‖ barely enough **2.** *v.t.* to be stinting in the supply of

scant·y scant·i·er scant·i·est *adj.* barely enough

scape·goat *n.* a person made to bear the blame which should fall on others

scar 1. *n.* a permanent mark on the skin or other tissue, formed where a wound, ulcer etc. heals **2. scar·ring scarred** *v.t.* to mark with a scar ‖ *v.i.* to form a scar

scarce scarc·er scarc·est *adj.* available in insufficient amount **scárce·ly** *adv.* barely, only just

scar·ci·ty pl. **scar·ci·ties** *n.* a limited supply

scare 1. scar·ing scared *v.t.* to arouse fear in ‖ *v.i.* to become afraid **2.** *n.* an instance of being scared ‖ a widespread panic

scare·crow *n.* a figure stuffed with straw and dressed in ragged old clothes, set up to scare birds away from the crops

scarf pl. **scarfs** *n.* a piece of material wrapped around the neck, head or shoulders for warmth ‖ a sash

scar·let 1. *n.* a brilliant red color **2.** *adj.* of the color scarlet

scar·y scar·i·er scar·i·est *adj.* alarming, causing fright

scathe scath·ing scathed *v.t.* to attack with bitterly severe criticism **scáth·ing** *adj.*

scat·o·log·i·cal *adj.* of scatology

sca·tol·o·gy *n.* preoccupation with excrement, defecation etc. ‖ the scientific study of animal droppings

scat·ter 1. *v.t.* to cause to break up and go in different directions ‖ to cause (shot) to spread ‖ *v.i.* to separate in different directions **2.** *n.* something scattered

scav·enge scav·eng·ing scav·enged *v.t.* (of animals) to seek out and devour (refuse or dead organic matter) ‖ to remove refuse or impurities from ‖ to search for usable refuse

scav·en·ger *n.* an animal which feeds on dead organic matter

scene *n.* the place where some event occurs ‖ the place where the action of a play, novel etc. is supposed to take place ‖ a division of an act in a play ‖ a display of strong emotion, e.g. of anger ‖ a view

scen·er·y pl. **scen·er·ies** *n.* the painted flats etc. used in a theater ‖ natural geographical features

sce·nic *adj.* of natural scenery ‖ beautiful

or picturesque **scé·ni·cal·ly** adv.

scent 1. v.t. to perceive by the sense of smell ‖ to begin to have an awareness or suspicion of **2.** n. a smell, usually pleasing

scep·ter n. a staff carried by a sovereign as symbol of authority **scép·tered** adj.

sched·ule 1. n. a written or printed list ‖ a timetable **2.** v.t. **sched·ul·ing sched·uled** to make a list of ‖ to work out a program or timetable for

scheme 1. n. a detailed plan ‖ a secret, dishonest or malicious plot **2.** v.i. **schem·ing schemed** to form plans or schemes **schém·er** n. someone who devises dishonest plans **schém·ing** adj. intriguing

schism n. a destruction of the unity of a Church through disagreement on doctrine ‖ a division of any party etc. into differing factions

schis·mat·ic 1. adj. causing schism **2.** n. a person who causes or fosters schism **schis·mát·i·cal** adj.

schiz·o·phre·ni·a n. a mental disease whose characteristics may include withdrawal from social relationships, delusions and hallucinations **schiz·o·phren·ic** adj. and n.

schol·ar n. a learned person

scho·las·tic adj. pertaining to school education

school 1. n. a community of those who teach and those who are taught ‖ the building itself ‖ formal education ‖ the conditions of gaining skill or knowledge **2.** v.t. to train or discipline

school n. a number of fish or aquatic mammals keeping together while feeding or migrating

school·ing n. school education ‖ disciplined training

schoon·er n. a vessel with two or more masts

sci·at·ic adj. pertaining to the hip

sci·at·i·ca n. pain due to irritation of the sciatic nerve

sci·ence n. knowledge acquired by careful observation, by deduction of the laws which govern changes and conditions,

and by testing these deductions by experiment

sci·en·tif·ic adj. pertaining to science ‖ using methods based upon well-established facts ‖ thorough and accurate **sci·en·tif·i·cal·ly** adv.

sci·en·tist n. a specialist in science

scim·i·tar n. a short, curved, Oriental sword

scin·til·late scin·til·lat·ing scin·til·lat·ed v.i. to sparkle or twinkle like a star ‖ to be brilliant **scin·til·lá·tion** n.

sci·on n. a shoot or branch used for grafting ‖ a young descendant of a family, esp. of a noble family

scis·sors pl. n. a cutting tool consisting of two sharp-edged beveled blades which are pivoted near two handles

scoff 1. v.i. to adopt a disbelieving or contemptuously mocking attitude towards something **2.** n. an expression of such mockery

scold v.t. to rebuke angrily ‖ v.i. to utter angry, noisy language or expressions

sconce n. a holder attached to a wall for a candle

scone n. a small, soft cake of wheat or barley flour

scoop 1. n. any implement for holding or removing liquids or loose solids ‖ a small concave holder with a handle for serving ice cream etc. ‖ a cutting or gouging instrument with a spoon-shaped blade ‖ a quantity gathered by using a scoop ‖ a piece of news published before it has been published by a rival **2.** v.t. to hollow out ‖ to empty out (water) by bailing

scoot v.i. to go quickly **scóot·er** n. a child's vehicle consisting of a low board fitted with a wheel at each end and a steering handle ‖ a low-powered motorcycle

scope n. the area covered by an activity ‖ limit of capacity

scorch 1. v.t. to apply such intense heat to (something) as to dry it up ‖ to burn (something) just enough to affect its color or taste ‖ to criticize very harshly ‖ v.i. to become dried up by intense heat **2.** n. a discoloration caused by scorching

scorch·er n. a very hot day ‖ a biting

criticism

score *n.* a notch cut in the surface of something‖the number of points gained by a player or team in a game ‖ (pl. **scores, score**) a set of twenty ‖ (*pl.*) a great number ‖ a copy of a piece of music ‖ a number symbolizing the degree of success in a test

score scor·ing scored *v.* to mark with cuts, lines, scratches etc. ‖ to arrange (a composition) for performance by certain instruments etc. ‖ to put down ‖ to disable

scorn *n.* a feeling of extreme contempt

scorn *v.t.* to reject with scorn ‖ to refuse

scorn·ful *adj.* feeling or showing scorn

scor·pi·on *n.* an order of carnivorous arachnids

Scotch 1. *adj.* Scottish **2.** *n.* (usually **scotch**) whiskey distilled in Scotland

scotch *v.t.* to put down, crush ‖ to disable

scot·free *adj.* not sentenced to any punishment ‖ unhurt

scoun·drel *n.* a man who acts with shameful lack of principle **scóun·drel·ly** *adj.*

scour 1. *v.t.* to clean by rubbing hard, esp. with an abrasive ‖ to remove (dirt etc.) in this way ‖ to purge ‖ to wear away by erosion etc. **2.** *n.* a scouring

scour *v.t.* to move rapidly, esp. in search of something

scourge *n.* a whip ‖ punishment

scourge scourg·ing scourged *v.t.* to whip ‖ to cause extreme misery to

scout 1. *n.* a soldier sent ahead to gain information ‖ anyone whose job is to search ‖ a person who reports on the abilities of players of rival teams ‖ the act of scouting **2.** *v.i.* to make a reconnaissance ‖ to make a search ‖ *v.t.* to reconnoiter

scow *n.* a flat-bottomed boat

scowl 1. *v.i.* to frown angrily or sullenly **2.** *n.* an angry or sullen frown

scrag·gly scrag·gli·er scrag·gli·est *adj.* unkempt ‖ rough and uneven

scrag·gy scrag·gi·er scrag·gi·est *adj.* scrawny ‖ rough and rugged

scram scram·ming scrammed *v.i.* to go away quickly

scram·ble 1. scram·bling scram·bled *v.i.* to climb or move about with hasty or

struggling movements, esp. on all fours ‖ struggle in order to obtain something ‖ *v.t.* to jumble ‖ to mix thoroughly together ‖ to cook (eggs) by beating them **2.** *n.* the act or an instance of scrambling **scrám·bler** *n.* someone who or something that scrambles

scrap 1. *n.* (*pl.*) paragraphs, pictures etc. cut out of a newspaper etc. as worth keeping or suitable for pasting into an album ‖ metal recovered from old ships, cars etc. ‖ a least bit ‖ (*pl.*) leavings, esp. leftovers of food **2.** *v.t.* **scrap·ping scrapped** to discard as useless

scrap *n.* a fight, struggle or quarrel

scrape 1. scrap·ing scraped *v.i.* to move against something roughly or graze it ‖ to clean or smooth something with an abrasive or sharp tool ‖ to make a harsh grating noise ‖ to make or save money in small amounts, with a struggle ‖ to succeed barely or proceed with difficulty **2.** *n.* the act or noise of scraping ‖ a scraped place, spot, hole etc. **scráp·er** *n.* a tool used to scrape

scrap·py scrap·pi·er scrap·pi·est *adj.* assembled from bits and pieces, disconnected and insubstantial

scrappy *adj.* fond of a scrap (fight or quarrel)

scratch 1. *v.i.* to dig with the nails or claws ‖ to draw the nails etc. lightly over the skin, e.g. to relieve itching ‖ to give out a scraping noise ‖ to withdraw from a race or contest **2.** *n.* a mark made by scratching ‖ the noise made when a surface is scratched ‖ a slight wound **to start from scratch** to begin from nothing with no advantage **3.** *adj.* assembled in a haphazard way

scratch·y scratch·i·er scratch·i·est *adj.* covered with scratches ‖ causing surface irritation or itching ‖ making a harsh, grating noise

scrawl 1. *v.* to write (something) with badly formed letters, esp. hurriedly **2.** *n.* a piece of scrawled writing **scráwl·y scrawl·i·er scrawl·i·est** *adj.*

scrawn·y scrawn·i·er scrawn·i·est *adj.* thin and rawboned or undernourished-looking

scream 1. *v.i.* to utter a sudden high-pitched, loud cry because of fear, pain or shock ‖ to make a similar sound in laughter etc. ‖ to speak in a shrill, loud manner, esp. in anger or hysteria **2.** *n.* the sound made in screaming ‖ someone who or something which is very funny **scréam·ing** *adj.*

screech 1. *v.i.* to give a short, shrill scream ‖ to make a noise like a scream **2.** *n.* the act or sound of screeching

screen 1. *n.* a movable partition ‖ a fixed structure of wood, metal etc. partly separating one room or section of a building from another ‖ anything giving protection, esp. from observation ‖ a transparency with very fine ruled lines used in halftone printing ‖ a white surface on which filmstrips, movies etc. are projected **2.** *v.t.* to shelter or conceal ‖ to sift with a coarse mesh ‖ to make (a story etc.) into a movie ‖ to subject (candidates) to exhaustive tests

screw 1. *n.* a device for fastening things **to have a screw loose** to be a little crazy **2.** *v.t.* to fasten, compress or tighten, using a screw or screws ‖ to twist ‖ to contort ‖ (pop.) to extract forcefully or with difficulty ‖ *v.i.* to be put together or taken apart with a screw or screws **to screw up one's courage** to brace oneself in order to face an ordeal, danger etc.

screw·ball *n.* (baseball) a pitched ball which breaks in the opposite way to a curve ‖ a person who is a little crazy in his behavior

screw·driv·er *n.* a tool for tightening or loosening screws

screw·y screw·i·er screw·i·est *adj.* crazy ‖ fantastically absurd

scrib·ble 1. *v.* **scrib·bling scrib·bled** to write hastily and carelessly **2.** *n.* a piece of hasty writing ‖ bad handwriting or literary composition

scrib·bler *n.* a person who writes rapidly and in great quantities

scribe *n.* a person skilled in handwriting ‖ a professional copyist

scrim·mage *n.* a confused struggle ‖ (football) the struggle for possession of the ball after it has been put into play by the center

scrimp *v.t.* to make too small, short etc. ‖ to treat stingily **scrimp·y scrimp·i·er scrimp·i·est** *adj.* excessively meager

script *n.* a handwriting as distinguished from print ‖ the printed or written text of a play, broadcast etc.

sculpture *n.* (often in pl.) the Bible ‖ a passage in the Bible ‖ the sacred writing or books of any religion

scroll *n.* a length of parchment or paper rolled into a cylinder ‖ anything, esp. an ornament, having the form of a partly opened scroll of paper, e.g. the head of a violin

scro·tum *pl.* **scro·ta scro·tums** *n.* the muscular sac containing the testicles

scrounge scroung·ing scrounged *v.t.* to get by hunting around for ‖ to pilfer

scrub *n.* thick undergrowth and stunted trees etc. ‖ land covered with such growth ‖ an undersized, insignificant person or animal

scrub 1. scrub·bing scrubbed *v.t.* to clean by rubbing hard, esp. with a brush, soap and water **2.** *n.* an act or instance of scrubbing **scrub·ber** *n.* a person or thing that scrubs

scrub·by scrub·bi·er scrub·bi·est *adj.* stunted ‖ covered with scrub ‖ inferior, shabby

scruff *n.* the nape of the neck

scruff·y scruff·i·er scruff·i·est *adj.* unkempt, grubby and neglected-looking ‖ (of terrain) dry, without vegetation

scrump·tious *adj.* delicious ‖ delightful

scru·ple 1. *n.* a feeling of uneasiness, doubt, objection or reluctance based on principle or propriety **2.** *v.i.* **scru·pling scru·pled** to hesitate

scru·pu·lous strictly honest and adhering to moral principles ‖ painstakingly thorough

scru·ti·nize scru·ti·niz·ing scru·ti·nized *v.t.* to examine with care and in detail

scru·ti·ny *pl.* **scru·ti·nies** *n.* close, searching examination

scu·ba *n.* a breathing apparatus for free-swimming divers

scuff 1. *v.i.* to walk by scraping or dragging the feet along the ground instead of lifting them ‖ to become worn, chipped etc. **2.** *n.* a scuffling or a scuffling sound ‖ a worn spot ‖ a soft, flat house slipper

scuf·fle 1. *v.i.* **scuf·fling scuf·fled** to struggle or scrap in a confused way at close quarters **2.** *n.* a confused struggle or scrap at close quarters

scull 1. *n.* one of a pair of short oars ‖ a single oar used at the stern in propelling a boat ‖ a sculler (boat) **2.** *v.t.* to propel (a boat) using sculls or a scull ‖ to convey (a person etc.) in a boat which one sculls **scúll·ern.** a person who sculls ‖ a boat designed for sculling

scul·ler·y *pl.* **scul·ler·ies** *n.* a room adjacent to a kitchen, used for washing and cleaning cooking utensils and preparing vegetables etc.

sculpt *v.i.* to make a sculpture or practice sculpture

sculp·tor *n.* a person who makes sculptures **sculp·tress** *n.* a female sculptor

sculp·ture 1. *n.* the making of three-dimensional works of art in stone, clay, metal, wood etc. ‖ one of these works ‖ such works collectively **2.** *v.t.* **sculp·tur·ing sculp·tured** to make sculpture out of (stone, clay, metal etc.)

scum *n.* impurities which rise to the surface of a liquid and collect on it ‖ people in a class one regards with profound contempt **scum·my scum·mi·er scum·mi·est** *adj.* of, like or covered with scum

scurf *n.* small flakes of dry skin, esp. on the scalp ‖ any scaly surface matter **scúrf·y scurf·i·er scurf·i·est** *adj.*

scur·ril·i·ty *pl.* **scur·ril·i·ties** *n.* the quality of being scurrilous ‖ scurrilous language

scur·ril·ous *adj.* expressed in or using language which is offensively or indecently abusive

scur·ry *v.i.* **scur·ry·ing scur·ried** to move along quickly

scur·vy 1. **scur·vi·er scur·vi·est** *adj.* meriting contempt, vile **2.** *n.* a disease by

a deficiency of vitamin C

scut·tle *n.* a small container holding coal, coke etc.

scuttle 1. *n.* a hole in the side or deck of a ship, furnished with a movable cover ‖ the cover itself **2.** *v.t.* **scut·tling scut·tled** to make or open holes in (a ship) below water level in order to sink it

scythe *n.* a long, curved blade with a sharp edge on the inner side of the curve, fitted to a long wooden handle, used to cut grass etc.

sea *n.* the continuous body of salt water covering most of the earth's surface ‖ a named portion of this body of water, smaller than an ocean, sometimes partly or wholly enclosed by land ‖ a heavy swell or wave ‖ a vast expanse, quantity or mass **to go to sea** to become a sailor

sea·board 1. *n.* the strip of land nearest to a seacoast **2.** *adj.* bordering on the sea

seal 1. *pl.* **seals, seal** *n.* any of several fish-eating mammals **2.** *v.i.* to hunt seals

seal *n.* a device having a design which can be impressed into a plastic material ‖ the design on this device ‖ the piece of plastic material thus impressed, attached to a document ‖ anything which serves to keep something secured or closed ‖ a sign or guarantee of authority, approval etc. **seal** *v.t.* to attach or mark with a seal ‖ to close up thoroughly ‖ to confirm the validity, authenticity etc. of

seal·ant *n.* *(dentistry)* liquid plastic filler

seal·er *n.* a person or vessel engaged in seal hunting

sealer *n.* someone who or something which seals

seam 1. *n.* a line of stitches where two pieces of cloth have been sewn together ‖ a thin layer of coal etc. between two strata of rock **2.** *v.t.* to join by a seam

sea·man *pl.* **sea·men** *n.* a sailor below the rank of officer **séa·man·like** *adj.* **séa·man·ship** *n.*

seam·stress *n.* a woman who makes her living by sewing

seam·y seam·i·er seam·i·est *adj.* having seams **the seamy side** the sordid aspect of something

se·ance *n.* a spiritualist meeting

sea·port *n.* a town on a seacoast, or connected by river with the coast, having a harbor, docks etc.

sear *v.t.* to wither by applying heat ‖ to burn or scorch ‖ to cauterize

search *n.* an investigation or scrutiny, in order to find something, gain information etc. **in search of** looking for

search *v.t.* to go or look into, over or through in order to find something, gain information etc. **search·ing** *adj.*

sea·shore *n.* the land adjacent to the sea

sea·sick *adj.* suffering from seasickness

sea·sick·ness *n.* nausea and vomiting caused by reaction to the motion of a vessel at sea

sea·son *n.* a period in the year regarded as having its own characteristic weather, length of days etc., esp. any of the four divisions of the year (spring, summer, autumn and winter) ‖ the period during which a specified activity is or may be engaged in **in season** (of fruit, vegetables, shellfish etc.) being harvested **out of season** not in season

season *v.t.* to dry out and harden (lumber) for use ‖ to make more suitable ‖ to add condiments or spices to (food)

sea·son·a·ble *adj.* suitable to the season ‖ opportune **sea·son·a·bly** *adv.*

sea·son·al *adj.* characteristic of a season or the seasons ‖ occurring at, determined by or active during a certain season or seasons

sea·son·ing *n.* something added to food to enhance the flavor ‖ something which seasons

seat **1.** *n.* anything on which one sits or may sit ‖ that part of a chair etc. which supports the weight of the person sitting ‖ the buttocks ‖ the part of a pair of pants or skirt which covers the buttocks ‖ a country mansion ‖ a center of some activity etc. **2.** *v.t.* to provide seats for **seat·ed** *adj.* sitting ‖ situated or established in a specified way or place **seat·er** *n.* (in compounds) something having a specified number of seats **seat·ing** *n.* the provision made for people to sit ‖ the

arrangement of seats ‖ a surface on which something is supported

sea·way *n.* a route over the sea ‖ a deep inland river up which an oceangoing vessel can sail

sea·weed *n.* any marine plant, esp. a marine alga

se·ba·ceous containing or secreting fatty oily matter

se·cede se·ced·ing se·ced·ed *v.i.* to withdraw formally from membership of some body

se·ces·sion *n.* the act of seceding

se·clude se·clud·ing se·clud·ed *v.t.* to keep (someone) apart from others, isolate **se·clud·ed** *adj.*

se·clu·sion *n.* a secluding or being secluded

sec·ond *n.* a unit of time ‖ a unit of angular measure ‖ an undefined very short time

second **1.** *adj.* being number two in a series **2.** *n.* the person or thing next after the first ‖ someone who attends a principal in a boxing match, duel etc. ‖ *(pl.)* substandard or inferior goods ‖ (pl.) a second helping of food **3.** *v.t.* to give formal support to (a motion) before it is open to general discussion ‖ to aid or encourage (someone's efforts) **4.** *adv.* in the second place

sec·ond·ar·y **1.** *adj.* being second in succession, rank, importance etc. ‖ immediately derived from what is primary **2.** *pl.* **sec·ond·ar·ies** *n.* a secondary person or thing

sec·ond-class *adj.* of or in a class next below the first ‖ of mediocre quality

second hand (in the phrase) **at second hand** (of getting information) through an intermediary **sec·ond·hand** **1.** *adj.* used by a previous owner or owners ‖ not original, derivative **2.** *adv.* after use by someone else ‖ indirectly

second hand the hand marking the seconds on a clock or watch

sec·ond-rate *adj.* inferior, of poor quality

se·cre·cy *pl.* **se·cre·cies** *n.* the state of being secret

se·cret **1.** *adj.* kept from the knowledge of others ‖ hidden **2.** *n.* something kept from the knowledge of others ‖ a hidden or not obvious explanation

sec·re·tar·i·al *adj*. of or relating to a secretary

sec·re·tar·y *pl*. **sec·re·tar·ies** *n*. a person responsible for dealing with the correspondence and records of an organization or individual employer ‖ (in titles) a minister in charge of a government department

se·crete se·cret·ing se·cret·ed *v.t*. to produce and emit (a secretion)

secrete se·cret·ing se·cret·ed *v.t*. to conceal

se·cre·tion *n*. a substance (e.g. saliva) elaborated by a gland or other organ or by a plant

secretion *n*. a hiding or concealing

se·cre·tive *adj*. fond of or given to having secrets ‖ unduly reticent

sect *n*. a body of people, sharing religious, philosophic or political opinions

sec·tar·i·an 1. *adj*. of or relating to a sect or sects ‖ narrow-minded **2.** *n*. a member of a sect ‖ a narrow-minded or bigoted adherent of a sect **sec·tár·i·an·ism** *n*.

sec·tion 1. *n*. a part cut off or separated by cutting, splitting etc. ‖ a division or part ‖ a division of written or printed matter ‖ a distinct part of a community ‖ a thin slice prepared for study through a microscope **2.** *v.t*. to cut into or arrange in sections

sec·tion·al *adj*. relating to or characteristic of a particular section of something **séc·tion·al·ism** *n*. exaggerated loyalty to a particular section of a community

sec·tor 1. *n*. the plane figure bounded by two radii of a circle and the intercepted arc ‖ a division or section **2.** *v.t*. to divide into sectors

sec·u·lar 1. *adj*. of or concerned with worldly matters ‖ profane **2.** *n*. a member of the secular clergy **séc·u·lar·ism** *n*. the belief that religious influence should be restricted **séc·u·lar·ist** *n*. **sec·u·lar·is·tic** *adj*.

sec·u·lar·i·za·tion *n*. a secularizing or being secularized

sec·u·lar·ize sec·u·lar·iz·ing sec·u·lar·ized *v.t*. to make secular

se·cure 1. *adj*. safe ‖ sure, certain ‖ fixed firmly **2. se·cur·ing se·cured** *v.t*. to make secure against injury, loss etc. ‖ to make firm ‖ to get possession of

se·cu·ri·ty *pl*. **se·cu·ri·ties** *n*. freedom from danger or anxiety ‖ something given or pledged as a guarantee ‖ something which guarantees or safeguards ‖ (esp. pl.) a bond, stock certificate etc.

se·dan *n*. an automobile with a large closed body, a hard roof, and no internal partitions

se·date *adj*. characterized by calm dignity, without any appearance of haste, excitement or confusion

se·da·tion *n*. a calming or being calmed

sed·a·tive 1. *adj*. soothing, reducing excitment or nervousness **2.** *n*. something that soothes in this way

sed·en·tar·y *adj*. involving a great deal of sitting ‖ accustomed, or compelled to sit for much of the time

sed·i·ment *n*. matter that sinks to the bottom of an undisturbed liquid with which it was previously mixed ‖ matter or a mass of matter deposited by wind, glaciers etc. **sed·i·men·ta·ry** *adj*.

sed·i·men·ta·tion *n*. the act or process of settling as a sediment

se·di·tion *n*. the inciting of hostility against the government

se·di·tious *adj*. of, tending toward or guilty of sedition

se·duce se·duc·ing se·duced *v.t*. to cause by persuasion or enticement to have sexual intercourse with one ‖ to persuade (a person) to act contrary to the principles by which he normally abides

se·duc·tion *n*. a seducing or being seduced

se·duc·tive *adj*. tempting

se·du·li·ty *n*. the quality of being sedulous

sed·u·lous *adj*. diligent, painstaking, assiduous

see *n*. a bishop's diocese, or his office

see see·ing saw seen *v.t*. to perceive with the eye ‖ to form a mental picture of ‖ to understand ‖ to find out ‖ to examine ‖ to call on, arrange to be received by (a person) ‖ to meet ‖ to have or obtain knowledge or experience of **to see after**

to attend to **to see into** to investigate ‖ to help (someone) to overcome a difficulty ‖ to finish

seed 1. *pl.* **seed, seeds** *n.* the fertilized ovule of a plant and its covering ‖ a spore ‖ semen ‖ a beginning or source ‖ descendants **2.** *v.t.* to take the seeds out of (fruit) ‖ to sow ‖ to sprinkle with seed ‖ to sprinkle chemicals in (clouds) in order to induce rain to fall ‖ *v.i.* to shed seed **3.** *adj.* (of a crop) grown for production of seed or set aside for use as seed

seed·i·ness *n.* the quality or state of being seedy

seed·ling *n.* a young plant grown from seed ‖ a young tree under 3 ft in height

seed·y seed·i·er seed·i·est *adj.* having abundant seeds ‖ shabby ‖ in rather poor health

see·ing 1. *n.* the power or faculty of vision **2.** *adj.* able to see **3.** *conj.* (usually with 'that') since, considering

seek seek·ing sought *v.t.* to try to find ‖ to ask for ‖ (with infin.) to try

seem *v.i.* an impression of something specified ‖ to have the appearance of being true **séem·ing 1.** *adj.* having the false appearance of being **2.** *n.* appearance, esp. false appearance **séem·ing·ly** *adv.* truly as far as can be judged

seem·li·ness *n.* the quality or state of being seemly

seem·ly seem·li·er seem·li·est *adj.* conforming to accepted standards of behavior or appearance

seep *v.i.* (of a fluid) to pass slowly through a porous body **séep·age** *n.* the act or an instance of seeping

se·er *n.* a wise man gifted with powers of divination

see·saw 1. *n.* a plank balanced in the center with its ends free to rise and fall alternately ‖ a back-and-forth or up-and-down movement ‖ any situation in which two factors alternately rise and fall **2.** *v.i.* to rise and fall alternately on or as if on a seesaw ‖ to cause to do this **3.** *adj.* moving up and down

seethe seeth·ing seethed *v.i.* to bubble violently as if boiling ‖ to be in a state of

rage or turmoil

seg·re·gate seg·re·gat·ing seg·re·gat·ed *v.t.* to separate ‖ *v.i.* to be or become segregated **ség·re·gat·ed** *adj.* conforming to a policy of racial segregation

seg·re·ga·tion *n.* a segregating or being segregated **seg·re·gá·tion·ist** *n.* a person who believes in racial segregation

seine 1. *n.* a large fishing net **2.** *v.t.* and *i.* **sein·ing seined** to fish with a seine

seis·mo·gram *n.* a record made by a seismograph

seis·mo·graph *n.* an instrument for recording the period, magnitude and direction of earth tremors **seis·mo·gráph·ic** *adj.* **seis·mog·ra·phy** *n.*

seis·mol·o·gy *n.* the scientific study of earthquakes

seize seiz·ing seized *v.t.* to take suddenly and hold firmly ‖ to take by force ‖ to overwhelm mentally

sei·zure *n.* a seizing or being seized ‖ a sudden attack of an illness, e.g. of epilepsy

sel·dom *adv.* not often, rarely

se·lect 1. *v.t.* to take (something or someone) from among a number **2.** *adj.* socially exclusive

se·lec·tion *n.* a selecting or being selected ‖ something selected

se·lec·tive *adj.* discriminating, tending to select

self 1. *adj.* of the same kind, material, color etc. as the rest **2.** *n. pl.* **selves** the individuality or nature of a person or thing ‖ a person with respect to his full mental or physical health ‖ personal advantage **3.** *pron.* myself, himself or herself

self-as·sur·ance *n.* self-confidence **sélf-as·sured** *adj.*

self-cen·tered *adj.* thinking primarily or solely of what concerns oneself

self-com·mand *n.* self-control

self-con·fi·dence *n.* reliance on one's capacities **sélf-cón·fi·dent** *adj.*

self-con·scious *adj.* thinking of one's own appearance or behavior as these may be assessed by others

self-con·trol *n.* the ability to exercise the

will so as to prevent oneself from acting impulsively

self-de·fense *n.* a defending of one's life, property or reputation **sélf-de·fén·sive** *adj.*

self-de·ter·mi·na·tion *n.* the right of a people to decide its own form of government or political status ‖ the free determining of one's own actions **sélf-de·tér·min·ing** *adj.*

self-ev·i·dent *adj.* needing no proof of its truth

self-ex·plan·a·to·ry *adj.* (of a statement) containing within itself all that is necessary for the understanding of it

self-ex·pres·sion *n.* expression of one's personality

self-gov·ern·ing *adj.* (of a state) administering its own government without interference from any other state **sélf-góv·ern·ment** *n.*

self-im·por·tance *n.* an exaggerated estimate of one's worth **sélf-im·pór·tant** *adj.*

self-in·dul·gence *n.* satisfying one's desires and appetites too readily **sélf-in·dúl·gent** *adj.*

sel·fish *adj.* concerned only to satisfy one's own desires

self·less *adj.* concerned for others and not for one's own advantage, pleasure, comfort etc.

self-made man a man who has materially succeeded in life by his own efforts and capacity

self-pit·y *n.* pity for oneself

self-pos·sessed *adj.* having or showing self-possession

self-pos·ses·sion *n.* self-control ‖ presence of mind

self-pres·er·va·tion *n.* the instinct to avoid being injured or killed

self-re·li·ance *n.* confidence in one's own abilities, power of judgment etc. **sélf-re·lí·ant** *adj.*

self-re·spect *n.* the proper esteem in which one holds oneself **sélf-re·spéct·ing** *adj.*

self-right·eous *adj.* regarding oneself as more virtuous than others, or revealing this attitude

self-serv·ice 1. *adj.* of a restaurant or shop where the customer takes what he wants from the counter or shelf, paying at the exit **2.** *n.* such a restaurant or shop

self-suf·fi·cien·cy *n.* the quality of being self-sufficient

self-suf·fi·cient *adj.* needing no outside help

self-will *n.* determination to follow one's own wishes **sélf-willed** *adj.*

sell 1. sell·ing sold *v.t.* to dispose of (goods, property or rights) to another or others in exchange for money ‖ to offer for sale ‖ to betray for a reward ‖ to persuade others to accept ‖ *v.i.* to offer something for sale **to sell out** to sell all the goods one has ‖ to betray (a cause, partners in crime etc.) **2.** *n.* salesmanship or sales appeal **séll·er** *n.* a person who sells ‖ a product with respect to its rate of sale

se·man·tic *adj.* of meaning in language

se·man·tics *n.* linguistic science which deals with the meanings of words and esp. with development and change

sem·blance *n.* just enough outward show to be plausible ‖ a wilfully deceptive appearance

se·men *n.* the fluid secreted by the male's testes and accessory glands, containing spermatozoa

se·mes·ter *n.* one of the two divisions of the academic year in some universities

semi- prefix half ‖ in part ‖ occurring twice within a specified period

sem·i·an·nu·al *adj.* occurring every half year

sem·i·cir·cle *n.* half a circle

sem·i·cir·cu·lar *adj.* having the shape of a semicircle

sem·i·co·lon *n.* a punctuation mark (;)

sem·i·con·duc·tor *n.* any of a group of materials (e.g. germanium, selenium, copper oxide, cadmium sulfide) having a electrical conductivity between that of metals and insulators. They are used in transistors, rectifiers, photoelectric cells and as thermometers

sem·i·con·scious *adj.* not fully conscious

sem·i·fi·nal *adj.* of a game or match played immediately before the final one of an eliminating series **se·mi·fi·na·list** n. a contestant in a semifinal

sem·i·month·ly adj. occurring, appearing, etc. twice a month

sem·i·nal adj. of seed or semen

sem·i·nar n. a group of advanced students working in association under the guidance of a teacher ‖ a course for or meeting of such a group

sem·i·nar·i·an n. a seminarist

sem·i·nar·y pl. **sem·i·nar·ies** n. a place where intending priests, ministers or rabbis are trained

sem·i·of·fi·cial adj. derived from official sources but not having official authority

sem·i·pre·cious adj. (of a gem) not having the commercial value of precious stones

Sem·ite n. a member of any of the peoples speaking Semitic languages

Se·mit·ic adj. of, like, or concerning the Semites **Se·mit·ics** n. the study of the Semitic languages, cultures etc. **Sem·i·tism** n. a Semitic characteristic

sem·i·trop·i·cal adj. subtropical

sem·i·week·ly 1. adj. occurring twice a week 2. pl. **sem·i·week·lies** n. a paper, magazine etc. issued twice a week 3. adv. twice a week

sen·ate n. the upper legislative assembly in the U.S.A. ‖ the governing body of certain U.S. universities

sen·a·tor n. a member of a senate

sen·a·to·ri·al adj. of, relating to, or befitting a senate or senator

send send·ing sent v.t. to cause (a person) to go to a specified place, in a specified direction or for a specified purpose ‖ to cause (a thing) to go or to be taken to another place ‖ to transmit ‖ v.i. to send a letter asking for something ‖ to send someone to fetch something **to send out** to emit ‖ to put forth ‖ to distribute, dispatch **to send packing** to dismiss without ceremony

send·er n. a person who sends something ‖ a transmitter

se·nes·cent adj. growing old

se·nile adj. arising from old age ‖ having the infirmities of old age **se·nil·i·ty** n.

sen·ior 1. adj. indicating the older of two

‖ of higher rank, longer service etc. 2. n. someone who is senior by age, rank, length of service etc. ‖ a student in the graduating class of a school

sen·ior·i·ty n. the quality or state of being senior

se·nor n. pl. **se·nors** , Span. **se·nor·es** n. a courtesy title for a Spanish man (the equivalent of 'Mr') and (without the surname) a term of address

se·nor·a pl. **se·nor·as** n. a courtesy title for a married Spanish woman (the equivalent of 'Mrs') and (without the surname) a term of address

se·nor·i·ta pl. **se·nor·i·tas** n. a courtesy title for an unmarried Spanish girl (the equivalent of 'Miss') and (without the surname) a term of address

sen·sa·tion n. the activity of the senses ‖ a state of emotional excitement ‖ the cause of such a state of emotional excitement **sen·sa·tion·al** adj. **sen·sa·tion·al·ism** n. the use of methods, e.g. in journalism, by which inordinate, foolish or harmful emotional responses are produced

sense 1. n. any of the bodily faculties hearing, sight, smell, taste or touch ‖ a meaning of a word ‖ (pl.) normal control of mental processes **in a sense** from one point of view **to make sense** to have a clear meaning or be rational 2. v.t. sens·ing sensed to perceive, esp. by intuition ‖ to read (computer data etc.) mechanically, electrically etc. **sense·less** adj. unconscious ‖ foolish, irrational

sen·si·bil·i·ty pl. **sen·si·bil·i·ties** n. the ability to respond to a sense stimulus ‖ emotional responsiveness ‖ extreme refinement of taste ‖ (pl.) feelings easily hurt

sen·si·ble adj. showing good sense, being reasonable, practical ‖ capable of being perceived

sen·si·bly adv. in a sensible way

sen·si·tive adj. able to respond to a stimulus ‖ able to respond to a very slight stimulus ‖ easily hurt emotionally ‖ (of a part of the body) liable to be painful

sen·si·tiv·i·ty pl. **sen·si·tiv·i·ties** n. the state or quality of being sensitive

sen·si·tize sen·si·tiz·ing sen·si·tized *v.t.* to render sensitive

sen·so·ry *adj.* of or relating to sensation

sen·su·al *adj.* pertaining to the body and the senses as distinct from the intellect ‖ pertaining to the satisfaction of bodily desires ‖ (of people) having great liking for bodily pleasure, esp. sexual pleasure

sén·su·al·ism *n.* the belief that the gratification of the senses is the highest good

sén·su·al·ist *n.* **sen·su·al·is·tic** *adj.*

sen·su·al·i·ty *n.* great liking for sensual pleasures

sen·su·ous *adj.* relating to, derived from, or affected by, the senses

sen·tence 1. *n.* a word or group of words which states, asks, commands or exclaims something ‖ the statement of a judicial decision to punish ‖ the penalty which forms a part of such a statement

sentence sen·tenc·ing sen·tenced *v.t.* to state the penalty to be paid by (a person)

sen·ten·tious *adj.* terse, pithy

sen·tient *adj.* capable of feeling, having the power of sense perception

sen·ti·ment *n.* a group of emotions and opinions associated with and aroused by an idea ‖ expression of emotional ideas in art, music or literature ‖ sentimentality **sen·ti·men·tal** *adj.* characterized by excessive emotional show ‖ influenced by feeling rather than reason **sen·ti·mén·tal·ism, sen·ti·mén·tal·ist, sen·ti·men·tal·i·ty** *ns* **sen·ti·mén·tal·ize sen·ti·men·tal·iz·ing sen·ti·men·tal·ized** *v.i.* and *t.*

sen·ti·nel *n.* someone who keeps watch

sen·try *pl.* **sen·tries** *n.* a soldier on guard duty

sep·a·ra·ble *adj.* capable of being separated

sep·a·rate 1. sep·a·rat·ing sep·a·rat·ed *v.t.* to form a boundary between ‖ *v.i.* to cease to be connected or associated ‖ (of man and wife) to cease to live together ‖ (with 'from') to withdraw ‖ to become disconnected **2.** *adj.* not joined to or mixed with something else ‖ isolated ‖ not shared **3.** *n.* an offprint ‖ (*pl.*) women's clothes (blouses, skirts etc.) meant for wearing either in combination with one another or with other alternatives

sep·a·ra·tion *n.* a separating or being separated

sep·a·ra·tist *n.* a member of a political or religious minority favoring secession

se·pi·a *n.* the black inky secretion of cuttlefish ‖ a dark brown pigment prepared from this ‖ a dark brown color

Sep·tem·ber *n.* the ninth month of the year

sep·tic *adj.* causing to putrefy ‖ due to putrefaction

se·pul·cher *n.* a burial vault

se·quel *n.* something which follows, a continuation ‖ a result or aftereffect

se·quence *n.* a succession of things which are connected in some way

se·quen·tial *adj.* characterized by or constituting a sequence ‖ occurring as a result

se·ques·ter *v.t.* to seize, confiscate ‖ to place apart **se·qués·tered** *adj.* withdrawn from social intercourse ‖ in rural isolation

se·quoi·a *n.* a genus of very large North American coniferous trees including the redwood

ser·aph *pl.* **ser·aphs, ser·a·phim** *n.* a member of the highest order of angels

ser·e·nade 1. *n.* a piece of music played or sung at night in the open air, esp. by a lover beneath his mistress' window **2. ser·e·nad·ing ser·e·nad·ed** *v.t.* to entertain with a serenade

ser·en·dip·i·ty *n.* the gift of being able to make delightful discoveries by pure accident

se·rene *adj.* (of the weather) fine, clear and calm ‖ (of a person) tranquil, at peace with himself

se·ren·i·ty *n.* calmness ‖ clearness

serf *n.* a feudal laborer bound to an estate **sérf·age, sérf·dom, sérf·hood** *ns*

ser·geant *n.* a noncommissioned officer ‖ a police officer

se·ri·al 1. *adj.* being, being arranged as, or forming a series ‖ appearing regularly in a series of parts **2.** *n.* a serial story, radio or television program etc. **sé·ri·al·ize** *v.t.* **se·ri·al·iz·ing se·ri·al·ized**

se·ries *pl.* **se·ries** *n.* a number of similar

things occurring one after another, in space or time, in an orderly way ‖ a number of successive events of the same kind ‖ (of stamps and coins) a complete set

ser·if *n.* a small terminal line across the top or bottom of a main stroke of a printed or written letter

se·ri·ous *adj.* of great importance ‖ grave and thoughtful ‖ scholarly and thought-provoking ‖ in earnest ‖ alarming, critical

ser·mon *n.* an address delivered by a priest or minister ‖ a serious reproof or exhortation expressed at tedious length **sér·mon·ize sér·mon·iz·ing ser·mon·ized** *v.t.* and i.

se·rous *adj.* of or like serum ‖ thin, watery

ser·pent *n.* a snake

ser·pen·tine 1. *adj.* of or like a serpent ‖ twisting, winding **2.** *n.* a hydrated magnesium silicate

ser·rate *adj.* having notches or teeth like the cutting edge of a saw **ser·rat·ed** *adj.* **ser·ra·tion** *n.*

se·rum *pl.* **se·rums, se·ra** *n.* the colorless liquid remaining after blood has clotted

serv·ant *n.* a person paid to wait on another or others ‖ an official

serve 1. serv·ing served *v.* to be a servant to ‖ to satisfy the needs or requirements of ‖ to render service to under arms ‖ to supply (customers) with goods ‖ to deliver (a writ, summons etc.) ‖ to bring (food etc.) to the table for distribution ‖ to undergo (a term of imprisonment) ‖ (tennis etc.) to hit (the ball) to an opponent to start play **to serve someone right** to be the punishment someone deserves **2.** *n.* (tennis etc.) a service **sér·ver** *n.*

serv·ice 1. *n.* the occupation of being a servant ‖ government employment ‖ the armed forces as a career ‖ the performance of military duties, esp. in war ‖ assistance ‖ use ‖ notification of legal action ‖ the act or manner of serving food ‖ maintenance, repairs ‖ the cups, plates, dishes etc. used in serving a particular meal, drink etc. ‖ the time and route of a bus, airplane etc. ‖ attendance on a client, esp. with respect to quality **2.** *adj.*

of or for servants or service ‖ providing services **3.** *v.t.* **serv·ic·ing serv·iced** to provide service for

serv·ice·a·bil·i·ty *n.* the quality of being serviceable

serv·ice·a·ble *adj.* able to be of use ‖ durable

serv·ice·man *pl.* **serv·ice·men** *n.* a member of the military forces ‖ a man who services machinery, equipment etc.

ser·vile *adj.* showing oneself to be in complete submission to another **ser·vil·i·ty** *n.*

serv·ing 1. *n.* the act of one who or that which serves ‖ a portion of food or drink **2.** *adj.* used in holding or passing out food or drink

ser·vi·tude *n.* slavery, bondage

ses·a·me *n.* a herbaceous tropical and subtropical plant with small flat seeds, yielding oil used in salads, margarine and soap and as a laxative

ses·sion *n.* the sitting of a court, parliament or other assembly ‖ a period of time spent in some activity

set 1. set·ting set *v.* to cause to occupy a certain position ‖ to put (one's jaw or shoulders) into a position showing determination ‖ to decorate, encrust e.g. with gems ‖ to fix in a desired position ‖ to bring together the parts of (a broken bone) ‖ to curl or wave (hair) ‖ to put (words) to music ‖ to put into type ‖ to lay (a table) ‖ to fix (e.g. one's mind, purpose or heart) firmly on something ‖ to fix (a time, date etc.) for something ‖ to furnish (a precedent or an example) ‖ to fix (an amount, price etc.) ‖ to place in some locality ‖ (of colors) to become fast ‖ (of the sun etc.) to appear to descend below the horizon **to set forth** to give an account of **to set out** to begin a journey **to set up** to start in business etc. ‖ to arrange (a machine etc.) in a state in which it can be used **2.** *adj.* located ‖ fixed ‖ determined ‖ routine, invariable ‖ rigid, immovable ‖ (of opinions) tenaciously held ‖ firm in consistency ‖ (of a topic) specified ‖ inflexible, unchanging ‖ stereotyped ‖ ready **3.** *n.* a number of things related to one another by similarity ‖ a number of people having similar interests, occupations etc. or the same friends ‖ a television or radio receiver ‖ a group of games counting as a unit toward a match ‖ the setting of hair ‖ a clutch of eggs ‖ the flats, drops, furniture, props etc. used in the theater or in film

set·back n. an unwelcome reversal of fortune

set·ter n. a large long-haired gundog

set·ting n. the frame in which a gem is set ‖ the background against which a person or thing is seen ‖ the local or historical background of a story ‖ a clutch of eggs

set·tle set·tling set·tled v. to cease to move around and come quietly or gently to rest ‖ to take up permanent residence ‖ (of a turbid liquid) to become clear when the suspension sinks to the bottom ‖ to come to a decision ‖ to end a dispute or difference ‖ to adjust accounts ‖ (of a fog etc.) to descend on the landscape ‖ (of a disease etc.) to become localized ‖ to pay what is owing or agree on a sum of money to be paid out ‖ (of the ground) to become firm ‖ to provide (a region) with settlers **to settle down** to adopt a quiet, regular way of life ‖ to become quiet and peaceful ‖ to apply oneself

set·tle·ment n. a settling or being settled ‖ a choice or decision made to end a controversy ‖ a small, isolated hamlet or village ‖ the conveyance of property etc. settled on a person, e.g. at marriage

set·tler n. a colonist

set-up n. all the arrangements, installations etc. that enable some activity to be carried on

se·ven adj. being one more than six

sev·en·teen adj. being one more than 16

sev·en·teenth adj. being number 17 in a series

seventh adj. being number seven in a series

sev·en·ty adj. being ten more than 60

sev·er v.t. to cut completely through ‖ to divide from the main part ‖ to break off, bring to an end ‖ v.i. to become divided or ended in this way **sév·er·a·ble** adj.

sev·er·al adj. being more than two but not

many ‖ separate, individual **sév·er·al·ly** adv. each by itself, apart from others, separately

se·vere adj. austere ‖ difficult to endure ‖ difficult and trying

se·ver·i·ty pl. **se·ver·i·ties** n. the state or quality of being severe ‖ an instance of being severe

sew sew·ing sewed sewn sewed v.t. to join or fasten by stitches ‖ v.i. to use a needle and thread **to sew up** to attend to all the details of (something, e.g. a contract) and finish it

sew·age n. the waste matter that is carried away through sewers

sew·er n. an underground tunnel that carries off the drainage and waste matter from a house or town

sex n. male or female as a classification ‖ sexual desires and instincts and their expression

sex·a·ge·nar·i·an 1. adj. in the age span 60 **2.** n. a sexagenarian person

sex·i·ness n. the state or quality of being sexy

sex·tant n. an instrument used in navigation

sex·tet, sex·tette n. a group of six

sex·tu·ple 1. adj. six times as much or as many ‖ having six beats in a bar **2. sex·tu·pling sex·tu·pled** v.t. to multiply by six

sex·u·al adj. pertaining to sex ‖ having sex **sex·u·al·i·ty** n. the quality of being sexual ‖ sexual desires and their gratification

sex·y sex·i·er sex·i·est adj. exciting sexual desire

shab·bi·ness n. the state or quality of being shabby

shab·by shab·bi·er shab·bi·est wearing badly worn clothing ‖ shameful or mean in a petty way ‖ poor in quality

shack n. a crudely made hut, esp. one to live in

shack·le 1. n. a chain or ring used to prevent the free movement of arms or legs ‖ any of certain fastening devices **2.** v.t. **shack·ling shack·led** to fasten with shackles ‖ to impede the freedom of action or expression of

shade 1. *n.* a place partly sheltered from the full light or heat of the sun ‖ a window blind ‖ comparative darkness ‖ a variation of individual depth or brightness of a color ‖ a slight degree **2. shad·ing shad·ed** *v.t.* to shelter from the full light or heat of the sun etc. ‖ to darken (parts of a drawing etc.)

shad·ing *n.* a provision of shade ‖ the representation of degrees of light or dark in a drawing

sha·dow *n.* a region of relative darkness ‖ the image of an opaque body projected on a surface elsewhere illuminated ‖ a mere semblance ‖ trace, hint ‖ an inseparable companion

shad·ow·y *adj.* full of shadows ‖ like a shadow, indistinct or fleeting ‖ shaded

shaft *n.* a long rod supporting a part of a machine or transmitting motion to a part of a machine ‖ the part of a column separating the capital and the base ‖ a long, more or less vertical, hollow space ‖ an arrow ‖ the straight, cylindrical part of a long bone ‖ a beam of light ‖ a bolt (of lightning)

shag·gi·ness *n.* the state or quality of being shaggy

shag·gy shag·gi·er shag·gi·est *adj.* (of hair) thick, dense and (often) unkempt ‖ having a rough surface

shake 1. shak·ing shook shak·en *v.t.* to move rapidly to and fro ‖ to vibrate or quiver **to shake hands** to give someone a handshake **to shake off** to get rid of (someone or something unwelcome) **to shake up** to shock, agitate ‖ to destroy the complacency of **2.** *n.* a shaking or being shaken ‖ a tremble or quiver ‖ a milkshake

shake·down *n.* an extorting of money

shak·i·ness *n.* the state or quality of being shaky

shak·y shak·i·er shak·i·est *adj.* unsteady, apt to shake ‖ trembling, infirm ‖ shaking ‖ wavering ‖ weak, not firmly based

shale *n.* a fine-grained sedimentary rock readily splitting into thin plates or layers

shall should auxiliary *v.* used to express futurity, or promise, intention or command

shal·lot *n.* a perennial producing clusters of small bulbs, resembling the common onion, used in cooking

shal·low *adj.* having little distance between the top and bottom or front and back surfaces ‖ superficial

sham 1. sham·ming shammed *v.t.* to simulate **2.** *n.* someone who pretends to be what he is not ‖ something pretended to be other than it is **3.** *adj.* having the appearance of being what it is not

sha·man *n.* a priest or witch doctor

sham·bles *pl.n.* a slaughterhouse ‖ a scene of great destruction ‖ extreme disorder

shame *n.* a painful emotion aroused by the recognition that one has failed to act, behave or think in accordance with the standards which one accepts as good ‖ utter disgrace ‖ something that causes disgrace ‖ something unfair ‖ something regrettable **to put (someone) to shame** to cause (someone) to feel inadequate

shame *v.t.* **sham·ing shamed** to cause (someone) to feel shame ‖ to bring shame or disgrace

shame·ful *adj.* causing shame ‖ offending one's sense of what is right or just

shame·less *adj.* lacking modesty ‖ imprudent

sham·poo 1. *v.t.* **sham·poo·ing sham·pooed** to wash (the hair) **2.** *n.* a washing of the hair or an instance of this ‖ a preparation for washing the hair

shang·hai *v.t.* to force (someone) by guile to do something

shank 1. *n.* the part of the leg between knee and ankle ‖ the back loop on a button ‖ the narrow part of a shoe sole under the instep

shan·ty *pl.* **shan·ties** *n.* a small shack of crude construction

shan·ty·town *n.* a town, or part of a town, consisting of shanties

shape *n.* the outward appearance of a person's body ‖ satisfactory arrangement ‖ state, condition ‖ a mold ‖ form, embodiment ‖ false appearance, semblance ‖ nature **to take shape** to develop

shape shap·ing shaped *v.t.* to cause to take

on a certain shape ‖ to produce by manipulating ‖ to make suitable or fit

shape·less adj. having no regular shape

shape·li·ness n. the state or quality of being shapely

shape·ly shape·li·er shape·li·est adj. well proportioned

shard n. a broken piece of brittle material

share n. one's portion ‖ capital stock division ‖ part v. **shared shar·ing** distribute in shares ‖ use jointly

shark n. any of several large, voracious, fishes ‖ a man who makes his living by swindles and trickery

sharp sharp·er sharp·est adj. well adapted to cut or pierce ‖ having a thin edge or a pointed shape ‖ making an acute or sudden angle ‖ piercing ‖ acid ‖ strong and shrill ‖ brisk, energetic ‖ hotly contested ‖ acute, keen ‖ clever, expert ‖ raised a semitone in pitch **1.** adv. to a sharp point or edge ‖ punctually ‖ at a sudden angle

sharp·shoot·er n. a person who is a good shot

shat·ter v.i. to break into fragments ‖ to become suddenly and totally destroyed

shave 1. shav·ing shaved shaved, shav·en v.t. to remove hair from (the skin) with a razor ‖ to remove thin slices from with a sharp tool ‖ to graze, rub against lightly **2.** n. shaving or being shaved ‖ a thin slice **sháv·er** n. an electric device for shaving **sháv·ing** the act of one who shaves ‖ a thin slice shaved off wood, metal etc.

shawl n. a square, oblong or triangular covering for the shoulders or head

she 1. pron., 3rd person sing., nominative case a female person, animal or personified thing already mentioned **2.** adj. (prefixed) female **3.** n. a female

sheaf 1. pl. **sheaves** n. cut stalks of grain bundled together in an orderly way ‖ a collection of things put together **2.** v.t. to make into a sheaf or sheaves

shear 1. v. **shear·ing sheared sheared, shorn** v.t. to cut or clip with shears ‖ v.i. to use shears **2.** n. something shorn off

sheath pl. **sheaths** n. a cover fitting closely over the blade of a weapon or tool ‖ a

protective covering, e.g. a membrane ‖ a close-fitting straight dress

sheathe sheath·ing sheathed v.t. to put into a sheath ‖ to protect in a case

shéath·ing n. a protective covering

shed 1. v. **shed·ding shed** v.t. to throw off ‖ to pour forth ‖ to cause (blood) to flow

shed n. a small hut, lean-to or light shelter

sheen n. brightness, shininess **shéen·y sheen·i·er sheen·i·est** adj.

sheep pl. **sheep** n. ruminant animals which have been domesticated for the their wool, flesh and skin ‖ a timid, easily led person

sheep·ish adj. shy and embarrassed

sheer adj. complete, utter ‖ perpendicular ‖ almost transparent

sheer v.i. to deviate from a course

sheet 1. n. a large rectangle of woven cotton, linen or silk etc. used esp. as bed linen ‖ piece of paper ‖ a large, thin, flat piece of metal, glass etc. **in sheets** (of printed matter) not folded or bound

sheet·ing n. the fabric in bulk from which sheets are made

sheikh, sheik n. an Arab chief, head of a family, or headman of a village **shéikh·dom, shéik·dom** n.

shelf pl. **shelves** n. a horizontal board, stone slab etc. mounted against a perpendicular surface, to put things on ‖ projecting, roughly horizontal, layer of rock

shell 1. n. the hard outer covering of an animal or fruit, or an organism, esp. the outer covering of a bird's egg ‖ a gutted building or one of which only the walls have been built ‖ a projectile ‖ a cartridge case ‖ a light racing boat ‖ the bottom crust of a pie **2.** v.t. to take out of the shell ‖ to separate the kernels of (wheat, corn etc.) from the ear

shel·lac, shel·lack 1. n. purified lac resin used in varnishes etc. **2. shel·lack·ing shel·lacked** v.t. to coat with shellac ‖ to defeat by a very large margin

shell·fish pl. **shell·fish, shell·fish·es** n. an aquatic invertebrate with a shell, e.g. a crab, lobster or oyster

shell shock combat fatigue **shéll-shocked** adj.

shel·ter 1. *n.* something providing protection from danger or injury, from rain and wind ‖ **2.** *v.t.* to protect from danger, injury, rain or wind ‖ shield

shelve shelv·ing shelved *v.t.* to put on a shelf ‖ to defer for the moment

she·nan·i·gans *pl. n.* trickery ‖ high jinks

shep·herd 1. *n.* a man whose occupation is tending sheep **2.** *v.t.* to act as shepherd

sher·bet *n.* a frozen dessert made of sugar, water, milk, egg white and fruit flavoring

sher·iff *n.* a usually elected officer responsible for law and order in his county

sher·ry *pl.* **sher·ries** *n.* a fortified wine

shield 1. *n.* a plate, screen etc. which serves to protect ‖ a protective body covering, e.g. the shell of a turtle ‖ a flat, three-sided area or surface on which a coat of arms is displayed ‖ someone or something thought of as serving to defend **2.** *v.t.* to protect with or as if with a shield

shift *n.* a change of position, direction or condition ‖ a substituting of one thing for another ‖ a tricky ruse ‖ a group of workers who work in turn with another group or other groups ‖ the period during which such a group works ‖ a woman's straight dress

shift *v.i.* to move from one position, place, direction or condition to another ‖ to change gears

shift·i·ness *n.* the state or quality of being shifty

shift·less *adj.* lazy and inefficient

shift·y shift·i·er shift·i·est *adj.* mean and untrustworthy, deceitful

shil·ly-shal·ly 1. *v.i.* **shil·ly-shal·ly·ing shil·ly-shal·lied** to waver continually between two opinions **2.** *pl.* **shil·ly-shal·lies** *n.* indecision

shim 1. *n.* a sliver of wood, metal etc., often tapered, used in adjusting levels or to take up wear in machinery **2.** *v.t.* **shim·ming shimmed** to fit or pack with this

shim·mer 1. *v.i.* to shine with glistening, tremulous light **2.** *n.* such a light **shim·mer·y** *adj.*

shin *n.* the lower part of the front of the leg

shin·dig *n.* a social gathering, esp. a very large one, on which no expense is spared

shine 1. *v.* **shin·ing shone shined** *v.i.* to emit or reflect light ‖ to glow ‖ to show great aptitude **2.** *n.* the quality of shining a ‖ a finish given by polishing **to otake a shine to** to take a liking to **shin·er** *n.* a black eye

shin·gle 1. *n.* a wedge-shaped tile used esp. in roofing **to hang out one's shin·gle** (esp. of a doctor or lawyer) to start a professional practice **2.** *v.t.* **shin·gling shin·gled** to cover (e.g. a roof) with shingles

shin·gles *n. Herpes zoster,* a painful but transient virus infection of a nerve

shin·ing *adj.* gleaming

shin·y shin·i·er shin·i·est *adj.* emitting or reflecting light ‖ polished ‖ smooth and glossy

ship 1. *n.* any large seagoing vessel ‖ an aircraft **when one's ship comes home** (or **in**) when one comes to have plenty of money **2.** *v.* **ship·ping shipped** *v.t.* to put in a ship ‖ to put in place ready to use ‖ to send (goods) by sea or by any means of transport ‖ *v.i.* to go by ship

-ship *suffix* indicating state or quality, as in 'friendship' ‖ indicating office, as in 'chancellorship' ‖ indicating ability, as in 'horsemanship'

ship·ment *n.* the loading of goods, esp. on a ship ‖ the goods so shipped

ship·per *n.* someone who ships goods, esp. as a profession

ship·ping *n.* the act of putting on board ship, going on board ship, or sending by ship or other means of transport

ship·shape *adj.* tidy, orderly

ship·wreck 1. *n.* destruction of a ship **2.** *v.t.* to cause to undergo shipwreck

ship·yard *n.* the premises where ships are built and repaired

shirk *v.t.* to avoid (e.g. work, responsibility or obligation), esp. out of indolence or selfishness

shirt *n.* a man's loose-fitting cloth garment covering the torso ‖ a woman's tailored blouse **to lose one's shirt** to lose virtually all one's money

shiv·er 1. *v.i.* to shake esp. with cold or

fear **2.** *n.* the act or sensation of shivering

shiver *n.* a small fragment resulting from the breakage of a brittle substance

shiv·er·y *adj.* feeling shivers ‖ causing shivers

shoal 1. *n.* a part of a river, sea, lake etc. where the water is very shallow ‖ a sandbank etc. causing such shallow water **2.** *adj.* (of water) shallow

shoal 1. *n.* a school of fish

shock *n.* a force of great magnitude applied suddenly ‖ a sudden condition of electric current through a person's body ‖ a temporary but dangerous condition caused by pain, strong emotion or loss of blood ‖ a sudden arousing of emotion or disturbance of mental stability by something unexpected, offensive or unwelcome ‖ something which causes this

shock *v.t.* to cause an emotional or mental shock to ‖ to give painful offense to ‖ to cause an electrical shock to ‖ to affect with physical shock

shock·er *n.* someone or something that shocks

shock·ing *adj.* causing shock ‖ very bad

shod·dy shod·di·er shod·di·est *adj.* made of poor material ‖ mean, shabby

shoe *n.* a foot covering of leather or other material ‖ a wooden block placed under a wheel to prevent or retard its motion ‖ part of a brake ‖ the sliding contact which picks up current from a live rail

shoe shoe·ing shod, shoed *v.t.* to supply or fit with shoes ‖ to attach a protective cover to the bottom or end

shoe·horn *n.* a narrow, curved instrument of e.g. horn or polished metal, inserted at the back of the shoe, to enable the foot to slide in easily

shoe·lace *n.* a lace or cord used to fasten the uppers of a shoe together over the instep

shoot 1. shoot·ing shot *v.t.* to fire (a gun etc.) ‖ to kill by doing this ‖ to go quickly through, under, over etc. ‖ to send (a letter, refuse etc.) down a chute ‖ to drive (a ball etc.) in the direction of a goal ‖ to detonate (a blast) ‖ (esp. *movies*) to photograph ‖ to play (dice) ‖ *v.i.* to go, arrive

or move with great speed like a moving projectile ‖ (of a plant) to begin to grow or put out young sprouts ‖ (of a gun etc.) to send forth a projectile ‖ (of a star, meteor etc.) to flash across the sky ‖ to dart painfully in or through a part or parts of the body **2.** *n.* a slope down which something can glide quickly, a chute ‖ a young outgrowth of a tree etc.

shooting star a meteor

shop 1. *n.* a store (building where retail trade is carried on) ‖ a workshop **to set up shop** to open a shop, business etc. **to talk shop** to discuss the techniques etc. of one's profession or trade **2.** *v.i.* **shop·ping shopped** to go to a shop or shops in order to buy goods

shop·keep·er *n.* a person who owns and manages a store

shop·lift·er *n.* someone who steals goods displayed for sale in a store **shop·lift·ing** *n.*

shop·per *n.* a person who buys in a store ‖ a person hired by a store to do this for others ‖ a person hired by a store to check prices, quality of goods etc. in a rival store or stores

shop·worn *adj.* (of goods) slightly damaged or dirty from long exposure for sale

shore *n.* the land forming the edge of a large expanse of water ‖ land as opposed to water

shore 1. *n.* a length of lumber or metal, resting firmly on the ground or other unyielding surface and adjusted usually at an angle with the vertical so as to support a structure above it **2.** *v.t.* **shor·ing shored** (with 'up') to support by using a shore

shore·line *n.* where the shore ends and the water begins

short 1. *adj.* not lasting a long time ‖ not tall ‖ easily aroused ‖ comparatively brief in duration ‖ (of memory) not retentive ‖ less than a correct or sufficient degree or amount ‖ not extending to or reaching a particular point or objective ‖ (of an alcoholic beverage) served in a small glass **2.** *adv.* unexpectedly and suddenly ‖ in a brusque, discourteous manner ‖ without actually owning the securities etc. sold **3.** *n. (movies)* a movie of one reel ‖ a short circuit ‖ *(pl.)* short pants covering the body from the waist to above the knees ‖ *(pl.)* underpants **4.** *v.t.* and *i.* to short-circuit

short·age *n.* the fact that there is less of something than is required

short·cake *n.* a dessert consisting of a crisp, short biscuit which is split, filled with fresh fruit and topped with more fruit and often cream ‖ this biscuit

short·change   short·chang·ing short·changed *v.t.* to give (a customer) less than the correct change

short·com·ing *n.* a failure to reach an expected or desired standard of conduct

short·cut *n.* a shorter, quicker way to a place or objective

short·en *v.t.* to make shorter **short·en·ing** *n.* the act of making or becoming shorter ‖ butter, fat etc. used to make pastry or cake crisper or flakier

short·hand 1. *n.* a rapid way of writing by using symbols to represent syllables or complete words or phrases **2.** *adj.* of, relating to or consisting of shorthand

short·hand·ed *adj.* having fewer persons available for work than is necessary or desirable

short-lived *adj.* not living or continuing long

short·ly *adv.* soon ‖ discourateously, brusquely

short-sight·ed *adj.* myopic ‖ not taking into account the probable results of one's behavior or actions

short-tem·pered *adj.* quick-tempered

short-wind·ed *adj.* out of breath

shot 1. *n.* an act of shooting ‖ a discharge of a firearm ‖ small spherical pieces of hardened lead ‖ an attempt ‖ a guess ‖ an opportunity to achieve or get something ‖ a marksman ‖ a photograph ‖ an injection of a drug ‖ a small quantity of liquor **2.** *v.t.* **shot·ting shot·ted** to load or weight with shot

shot *past and past part.* of SHOOT *adj.* worn out, broken ‖ ruined, in a useless state

shot·gun *n.* a short-range, smooth-bore firearm

shot put an athletic contesvt in which competitors put the shot ‖ a put of the shot in this contest

should *past* of SHALL *auxiliary v.* used to express moral obligation, necessity, probability, futurity

shoul·der 1. *n.* the joint connecting the arm with the body ‖ a part of something thought of as like a shoulder, esp. in the way it projects ‖ the flat top of the body of a type on which the bevel rises to the face ‖ either side of a road, off the roadway **shoulder to shoulder** standing side by side ‖ acting closely together **straight from the shoulder** direct and frank **2.** *v.t.* to take or carry on the shoulder ‖ to accept (a burden of responsibility)

shout 1. *n.* a loud, often wordless cry **2.** *v.i.* to utter this cry ‖ to speak very loudly **to shout (someone) down** to silence (a speaker) by shouting

shove 1. shov·ing shoved *v.t.* to push hard **to shove off** to push (a boat) away from shore ‖ to leave **2.** *n.* a hard push

shov·el 1. *n.* a tool consisting of a large shallow concave head attached to the end of a long handle ‖ the quantity it holds **2.** *v.t.* **shov·el·ing shov·eled** to lift and move with a shovel ‖ to dig

show 1. show·ing showed shown, showed *v.t.* to cause to be seen ‖ to put on view for entertainment ‖ to indicate, give to understand ‖ to point out ‖ to establish, prove ‖ to give evidence of ‖ *v.i.* to be visible ‖ to prove a point ‖ (of a movie) to be on view ‖ to finish third, esp. in a horse race **to show off** to make a show of one's virtues or skills **to show up** to put in an appearance **2.** *n.* a display ‖ a demonstration ‖ a public exhibition ‖ a public presentation of entertainment ‖ performance ‖ third place, esp. in a horse race **for show** in order merely to attract attention

show·down *n.* the last stage in a dispute

show·er 1. *n.* a brief fall of rain, hail or sleet ‖ a shower bath ‖ a festive gathering at which presents are given to a prospective bride or mother 2. *v.i.* to fall in or as if in a shower ‖ to take a shower bath

show·er·y *adj.* with rain falling briefly and frequently ‖ like a shower

show·ing *n.* the act of offering for public view ‖ an exhibition for display

show·man *pl.* **show·men** *n.* someone who has a flair for putting something before the public effectively **shów·man·ship** *n.*

show-off *n.* the act of showing off ‖ a person who shows off for admiration

show·y **show·i·er** **show·i·est** *adj.* ostentatious ‖ making attractive display

shrap·nel *n.* bullets and jagged pieces of metal sprayed by a bursting shell ‖ a projectile fired for this effect

shred *n.* a small piece torn or cut from something ‖ a small amount

shred **shred·ding** **shred·ded, shred** *v.t.* to tear or cut into shreds

shrew *n.* small, mouse-like, insectivorous, nocturnal animal ‖ a bad-tempered woman

shrewd *adj.* intelligent and worldly-wise ‖ clever and true or very near the truth

shrew·ish *adj.* bad-tempered, bullying

shriek 1. *v.i.* to utter a shrill, sharp cry ‖ to laugh in a shrill, high-pitched way 2. *n.* such a cry

shrill *adj.* high-pitched and piercing

shrimp 1. *pl.* **shrimps, shrimp** *n.* any of various members of small, edible crustaceans ‖ a tiny or undersized person 2. *v.i.* to fish for shrimps

shrine *n.* a box used to hold sacred relics ‖ a tomb or other place held sacred because it has special associations

shrink **shrink·ing** **shrank, shrunk shrunk,** (only in adj. uses) **shrunk·en** *v.i.* to become smaller ‖ to draw back in fear ‖ to lessen ‖ *v.t.* to cause to shrink **shrink·age** *n.* the act, process or extent of shrinking

shriv·el **shriv·el·ing** **shriv·eled** *v.i.* to become smaller and wrinkled

shroud 1. *n.* a sheet wound around a corpse ‖ something which conceals 2. *v.t.* to wind in a shroud ‖ to conceal

shrub *n.* a plant with several branching woody stems and no main trunk

shrúb·ber·y *pl.* **shrub·ber·ies** *n.* a number of shrubs growing close together **shrúb·by** **shrub·bi·er** **shrub·bi·est** *adj.* composed of shrubs

shrug 1. **shrug·ging** **shrugged** *v.t.* to lift (the shoulders) as a gesture expressing doubt, ignorance of the answer to a question etc. 2. *n.* this gesture

shud·der 1. *v.i.* to experience a sudden and forceful muscular contraction throughout the body 2. *n.* one of these muscular contractions

shuf·fle 1. **shuf·fling** **shuf·fled** *v.t.* to change, shift, push,.esp. in a clumsy way ‖ *v.i.* to move while dragging or sliding the feet instead of lifting them ‖ to get into or out of a position by shifty or evasive means ‖ to shuffle cards 2. *n.* a shuffling gait

shuf·fler *n.* a person who shuffles

shun **shun·ning** **shunned** *v.t.* to keep clear of, avoid

shunt *v.t.* to divert to a different direction ‖ to cause (someone) to divert his thoughts, interests, attention etc. in another direction ‖ a switch

shush 1. be silent! 2. *v.t.* to cause to be silent

shut **shut·ting** **shut** *v.t.* (often with 'up') to prevent exit from or entrance to ‖ (with 'up') to cause (someone) to stop talking ‖ *v.i.* to be or become shut ‖ (with 'up') to stop talking **to shut down** to cause to cease to work **to shut in** to surround **to shut off** to stop (machinery) from working by shutting off the power **to shut out** to prevent from entering ‖ (sports) to keep (an opponent or opposing team) from scoring

shut·ter 1. *n.* a cover used to secure a window against unlawful entry or to allow air but not sunlight to enter ‖ a mechanical device that acts to admit light into a camera during a specified time interval 2. *v.t.* to provide with a shutter

shut·tle 1. *n.* a device enclosing the bobbin which passes between the threads of the warp ‖ a passenger train, plane or bus which travels back and forth over a short route 2. **shut·tling** **shut·tled** *v.i.* to move back and forth

shy 1. shy·er, shi·er shy·est, shi·est adj. (of persons) finding it hard to overcome self consciousness ‖ (of animals) easily frightened ‖ showing timidity ‖ (with 'of') short of money **2.** v.i. **shy·ing shied** (of a horse etc.) to move suddenly to one side when startled

shy·ster n. a person, esp. a lawyer, who is unscrupulous in the practice of his profession

sib·ling n. a person in relation to someone having the same parents or having one parent in common

sick 1. adj. not healthy ‖ so consumed with passion as to have a feeling of illness ‖ likely to vomit ‖ feeling disgusted ‖ feeling weak and depressed ‖ (of humor, jokes) sadistic or suggesting heartlessness **2.** n. **the sick** people not in good health

sick·en v.i. to become ill ‖ v.t. to cause to feel sick **sick·en·ing** adj. nauseating, revolting ‖ distressing

sick·le n. a tool with a curved blade used for cutting long grass or trimming rough hedges etc.

sick·li·ness n. the state or quality of being sickly

sick·ly sick·li·er sick·li·est adj. weak in health ‖ caused by illness ‖ mildly nauseating

side 1. n. any one of the flat surfaces of an object ‖ one of the vertical surfaces of an object as distinguished from the top or bottom ‖ one of the lines bounding a figure ‖ the right or left part of a person's body ‖ one of two teams or sets of opponents in sport, war, politics etc. ‖ a line of descent traced through one parent **on the side** in addition to the main course of a meal **to take sides** to support one of the sides in a dispute **2.** adj. of, on, by, from or towards a side **3. sid·ing sid·ed** v.i. (with 'with' or 'against') to give sympathy to or support one party in a dispute

side·board n. a piece of furniture of a dining room used to store dishes etc.

side·burns pl.n. the short hair growing on a man's face in front of the ears when the beard is shaved off

side·kick n. someone who associates with another as a partner, assistant or companion

side·line n. goods sold in addition to one's regular stock ‖ a job done in addition to one's regular occupation ‖ a line marking the boundary at the side of a football field, tennis court etc.

side·split·ting adj. hilariously funny

side·step side·step·ping side·stepped v.t. to avoid by stepping sideways ‖ to be evasive about (an issue)

side·swipe 1. v.t. **side·swip·ing side·swiped** to strike with a glancing blow along the side **2.** n. a sideswiping

side·track 1. n. a siding **2.** v.t. to prevent action on (a matter) by diversionary tactics

side·walk n. a hard-surfaced pedestrian way

side·ward adv. and adj. toward one side **side·wards** adv. sideward

side·ways 1. adv. to the side ‖ from the side **2.** adj. to one side

sid·ing n. a short railroad track beside and connected with the main line ‖ boards forming the exposed surface of the outside walls of a frame building

si·dle 1. v.i. **si·dling si·dled** to go forward with a sideways motion ‖ to make a rather furtive approach **2.** n. the act or movement of sidling

siege n. the isolating of a fortified place by an attacking force in order to make it surrender ‖ a long, exhausting experience or period, esp. of ill health

si·er·ra n. a mountain chain with sharp peaks

si·es·ta n. a short rest taken in the hottest part of the day, esp. by Latin peoples

sieve 1. n. a utensil with a fine wire-mesh bottom used for straining substances **2.** v.t. **siev·ing sieved** to put through a sieve

sift v.t. (often with 'out') to separate or strain the finer from the coarser particles of (a material) by passing through a sieve ‖ to examine and evaluate **sift·er** n. a small cylindrical container with a fine wire mesh bottom through which flour, sugar etc. is passed

sigh 1. *v.i.* to expel a deep audible breath ‖ to make a sound like sighing ‖ *v.t.* to utter with a sigh **2.** *n.* the sound made in sighing

sight 1. *n.* the power of seeing ‖ range of vision ‖ *(pl.)* something worth seeing ‖ a device for guiding the eye when aiming a gun ‖ aim **at first sight** when first seen, before being examined closely **to know by sight** to know (someone) by appearance only, not to talk **2.** *v.t.* to get a sight of ‖ *v.i.* to take aim through a sight

sight·less *adj.* not having vision

sight·ly sight·li·er sight·li·est *adj.* of pleasing appearance

sight-see·ing *n.* the act of going around looking at places of interest **sight·se·er** *n.*

sign *v.t.* to mark with one's name ‖ (often with 'up' or 'on') to engage (esp. an athlete) by written agreement ‖ to intimate by gestures ‖ *v.i.* to write one's name **to sign off** to stop broadcasting **to sign up** to enlist in some organization

sign 1. *n.* a mark or gesture which conveys an idea or meaning ‖ something having symbolic character ‖ indication or evidence ‖ a notice or device advertising, admonishing, etc. ‖ a board, placard etc. bearing such a notice

sig·nal 1. *n.* a usually prearranged sign giving information **2. sig·nal·ing sig·naled** *v.t.* to order by signal ‖ to give information of by using a sign ‖ *v.i.* to make a signal

sig·nal·er *n.* someone responsible for communications

sig·na·ture *n.* a person's name written by himself

sig·nif·i·cance *n.* real or inner meaning ‖ importance

sig·nif·i·cant *adj.* important and influential ‖ expressive, heavy with implication

sig·ni·fi·ca·tion *n.* meaning or sense

sig·ni·fy sig·ni·fy·ing sig·ni·fied *v.t.* to make known, communicate ‖ *v.i.* to be significant, have meaning

si·lage *n.* green fodder packed in a silo

si·lence 1. *n.* a not speaking or making any noise ‖ taciturnity ‖ a not betraying of some confidence ‖ stillness, quiet ‖ oblivion **2.** *v.t.* **si·lenc·ing si·lenced** to quiet (fears, doubts, anxieties etc.) ‖ to compel to stop expressing an opinion **si·lenc·er** *n.* a device for muffling the noise of a gun

si·lent *adj.* making no sound ‖ free from sound ‖ taciturn ‖ withholding information ‖ (of a motion picture) without any sound track

sil·hou·ette 1. *n.* a portrait in profile, showing the outline only, and filled in with black, or cut out of black paper ‖ a person or object seen against the light **2.** *v.t.* **sil·hou·et·ting sil·hou·et·ted** to represent in silhouette

silk 1. *n.* a very fine, soft, lustrous fiber spun by the silkworm as its cocoon ‖ a thread or fabric made of this fiber ‖ the distinctively colored cap and jacket worn by a jockey **2.** *adj.* made of silk

silk·en *adj.* soft and lustrous ‖ smooth, suave ‖ made of silk

silk·worm *n.* the larva of any of various moths that spin cocoons of silk

silk·y silk·i·er silk·i·est *adj.* soft and glossy like silk

sill *n.* a ledge at the bottom of a window or a door

sil·li·ness *n.* the state of being silly ‖ a silly act

sil·ly sil·li·er sil·li·est *adj.* lacking common sense

si·lo 1. *pl.* **si·los** *n.* a pit or tall cylindrical structure used storing grain ‖ a subterranean shelter for guided missiles **2.** *v.t.* **si·lo·ing si·loed** to put or store in a silo

silt *n.* mud ‖ particles of minerals, soil etc. suspended in water, esp. in a river

sil·ver 1. *n.* a white, stable, malleable, ductile metallic element ‖ coins minted from this metal ‖ silverware ‖ a somewhat shiny whitish-gray color **2.** *adj.* like silver **3.** *v.t.* to coat with silver ‖ *v.i.* to take on the color of silver

silver plate a thin coating of silver **sil·ver-pláte sil·ver-plat·ing sil·ver-plat·ed** *v.t.* to apply a thin coating of silver to **sil·ver-plát·ed** *adj.*

sil·ver-tongued *adj.* wonderfully eloquent

sil·ver·ware *n.* tableware made of silver or silver plate

sil·ver·y *adj.* of silver ‖ clear in tone ‖ coated with silver

sim·i·an 1. *adj.* like an ape or monkey **2.** *n.* an ape or monkey

sim·i·lar *adj.* like ‖ having the same shape **sim·i·lar·i·ty** *pl.* **sim·i·lar·i·ties** *n.* a point of resemblance

sim·i·le *n.* a figure of speech in which one thing is likened to another

si·mil·i·tude *n.* resemblance ‖ semblance

sim·mer 1. *v.i.* to be just below boiling point ‖ *v.t.* to bring to, and cause to remain, just below boiling point **to simmer down** to become calm **2.** *n.* a state of simmering

sim·per 1. *v.* to smile foolishly and self-consciously **2.** *n.* an affected smile

sim·ple sim·pler sim·plest *adj.* consisting of only one kind, part etc. ‖ easy to deal with, understand etc. ‖ elementary ‖ without much ornamentation ‖ mere ‖ unpretentious ‖ guileless ‖ half-witted

sim·ple·ton *n.* a person who lacks common sense

sim·plic·i·ty *pl.* **sim·plic·i·ties** *n.* the quality or state of being simple ‖ a simple idea or fact

sim·pli·fi·ca·tion *n.* a simplifying or being simplified

sim·pli·fy sim·pli·fy·ing sim·pli·fied *v.t.* to make less complex ‖ to make easier to do or understand

sim·ply *adv.* in a simple way ‖ merely

sim·u·late sim·u·lat·ing sim·u·lat·ed *v.t.* to assume the appearance of falsely ‖ to reproduce a social or physical activity in computer terms to arrive at a solution

sim·u·la·tion *n.* a superficial resemblance ‖ a representation of a product in a different medium

si·mul·cast 1. *v.t.* **si·mul·cast·ing si·mul·cast** to broadcast by radio and television at the same time **2.** *n.* a simultaneous broadcast by radio and television

si·mul·ta·ne·i·ty *n.* the quality of being simultaneous

si·mul·ta·ne·ous *adj.* occurring at the same time

sin *n.* an action contrary to the law of God ‖ an offense against any widely accepted standard

sin sin·ning sinned *v.i.* to offend against any law

since 1. *adv.* at some time between a point in the past and now ‖ ago **2.** prep. during the time between a point in the past and now **3.** conj. during a period following a time when ‖ continuously ‖ because

sin·cere sin·cer·er sin·cer·est *adj.* honest and genuine

sin·cer·i·ty *pl.* **sin·cer·i·ties** *n.* the state of being sincere

si·ne·cure *n.* a position offering profit but carrying few duties

sin·ew *n.* a ligament ‖ physical strength **sin·ew·y** *adj.* like sinew ‖ muscular

sin·ful *adj.* marked by sin ‖ reprehensible

sing sing·ing sang sung *v.i.* to utter musical sounds with the voice ‖ (of birds, insects, brooks etc.) to produce sounds thought of as tuneful ‖ *v.t.* to utter (a song, musical note etc.)

singe 1. *v.t.* **singe·ing singed** to burn slightly on the surface **2.** *n.* a slight burn

sing·er *n.* someone who sings ‖ a bird that sings

sin·gle 1. *adj.* one and one only ‖ sole ‖ individual **2.** *n.* one individual person or thing ‖ (baseball) a hit by which the batter gets no farther than first base **3. sin·gling sin·gled** *v.t.* (with 'out') to choose (one) from many, esp. for special treatment

sin·gle-hand·ed *adj.* done without assistance

sin·gle-mind·ed *adj.* giving undivided effort to a single purpose ‖ without guile, utterly honest

sin·gly *adv.* separately, one at a time

sing·song 1. *n.* a monotonous chanting tone of voice **2.** *adj.* in monotonous rising and falling tone **3.** *v.t.* to utter in a singsong

sin·gu·lar 1. *adj.* denoting one person or thing ‖ very remarkable ‖ extraordinary **2.** the form of a word expressing one only ‖ the singular number

sin·gu·lar·i·ty *pl.* **sin·gu·lar·i·ties** *n.* the state of being unusual ‖ a peculiar characteristic

sin·is·ter *adj.* evil ‖ suggestive of misfortune

sink 1. sink·ing sank sunk , (only in *adj.* uses) **sunk·en** *v.i.* to move slowly down ‖ (of a heavenly body) to disappear below the horizon ‖ to move down through or under water, snow etc. ‖ to become lower in level ‖ (usually with 'in' or 'into') to penetrate ‖ (of sound) to drop to a lower tone or pitch ‖ to go down in value, amount etc. ‖ (of a sick person) to approach death ‖ *v.t.* to cause (e.g. a ship) to go to the bottom ‖ to cause to go down to lower level ‖ to invest (capital) **2.** *n.* a fixed basin of stone, stoneware or metal with a water supply and a drainpipe

sink·er *n.* a weight used to sink a fishing line or net etc.

sin·ner *n.* someone who sins

sin·u·os·i·ty *pl.* **sin·u·os·i·ties** *n.* the quality of winding

sin·u·ous *adj.* winding ‖ having many curves

si·nus *pl.* **si·nus·es** *n.* one of the air-filled cavities within the bones of the face and skull

sip 1. sip·ping sipped *v.t.* to drink by taking in a very slight quantity with the lips **2.** *n.* a small amount of liquid taken in by the lips

si·phon, sy·phon 1. *n.* a tube bent so that it has two roughly vertical and parallel legs of unequal length, used to transfer a liquid from a vessel placed at a higher level to a vessel at a lower level **2.** *v.t.* to cause to flow out through a siphon ‖ *v.i.* to flow through a siphon **si·phon·age** *n.*

sir *n.* a form of polite address to men

sire 1. *n.* the male parent of a quadruped ‖ a form of address to a king **2.** *v.t.* **sir·ing sired** to beget

si·ren 1. *n.* an instrument for producing a loud, penetrating sound as a warning ‖ an extremely seductive woman **2.** *adj.* of or relating to a siren

sir·loin *n.* the upper part of a loin of beef

sis·sy *pl.* **sis·sies** *n.* an effeminate boy or man

sis·ter *n.* a daughter in her relationship to

another child of the same parents ‖ a member of a religious community of women

sis·ter-in-law *pl.* **sis·ters-in-law** *n.* the sister of one's husband or wife, or the wife of one's brother

sis·ter·ly *adj.* of or like a sister

sit 1. sit·ting sat *v.i.* to rest the body on the buttocks ‖ (of birds) to stay covering eggs so as to hatch them ‖ to be situated ‖ to take up a position to be painted ‖ to be in session ‖ to remain in the same condition, esp. idle or unused ‖ *v.t.* to place (oneself) in a sitting posture ‖ to accommodate on chairs

sit-down strike a strike in which workers refuse to go away from their place of work

site 1. *n.* the geographical situation of a town or building ‖ the scene of a specified event **2.** *v.t.* **sit·ing sit·ed** to fix in a location

sit-in *n.* a group protest in which participants sit down in a public place and stay there until their demands are considered

sit·ter *n.* a baby-sitter ‖ a broody hen

sit·ting 1. *n.* a continuous period of time during which one sits over some occupation ‖ the act of posing for a portrait ‖ a meeting ‖ any of two or more consecutive eating sessions served in a dining room **2.** *adj.* being in office ‖ (of a hen) on eggs to hatch them

sit·u·ate sit·u·at·ing sit·u·at·ed *v.t.* to locate or site **sit·u·at·ed** *adj.* located or sited ‖ placed in particular circumstances

sit·u·a·tion *n.* the manner in which something is situated ‖ the circumstances in which someone is placed ‖ a paid occupation

six *adj.* being one more than five

six·teen *adj.* being one more than 15

six·teenth *adj.* being number 16 in a series

sixth *adj.* being number six in a series

six·ti·eth *adj.* being number 60 in a series

six·ty *adj.* being ten more than 50

siz·a·ble, size·a·ble *adj.* rather large

size 1. *n.* the length, area, volume or dimensions of something or someone ‖ one of a number of standards used for such comparison, size 9 shoes ‖ the total quantity ‖ magnitude ‖ (of things) scope ‖ true account **of a size** of equal size **2.** *v.t.* **siz·ing sized** to sort or arrange according to size **to size up** to estimate the character or qualities of (someone) ‖ to compare in respect to size

size 1. *n.* a thin gelatinous liquid used in glazing or for stiffening paper, textiles etc. **2.** *v.t.* **siz·ing sized** to apply this liquid to **siz·ing** *n.* liquid size

siz·zle 1. *v.i.* **siz·zling siz·zled** to make a hissing sound **2.** *n.* a noise so made **siz·zling** *adj.* very hot

skate pl. **skates, skate** *n.* a fish related to rays

skate 1. *n.* an ice skate ‖ a roller skate **2.** **skat·ing skat·ed** *v.i.* to move or glide along on skates

ske·dad·dle 1. *v.i.* **ske·dad·dling ske·dad·dled** to run off **2.** *n.* a hurried flight

skeet *n.* trapshooting at targets which simulate the speed and angle of flight of birds

skein *n.* a length of yarn, looped many times and then twisted ‖ a flock of wild geese in flight

skel·e·tal *adj.* like a skeleton

skel·e·ton *n.* a hard framework supporting or protecting the soft tissues and organs of a man, animal or plant ‖ a framework, e.g. of a building ‖ the essential nucleus of an organization

skep·sis *n.* philosophical skepticism

skep·tic *n.* a person who doubts the truth of anything **skep·ti·cal** *adj.*

skep·ti·cism *n.* an attitude of doubt

sketch 1. *n.* a quickly made drawing ‖ a drawing preliminary to more careful work ‖ a slight, short comedy **2.** *v.t.* to make a sketch of

sketch·i·ly *adv.* in a sketchy manner

sketch·i·ness *n.* the state or quality of being sketchy

sketch·y sketch·i·er sketch·i·est *adj.* lacking detail

skew 1. *v.t.* to cut or set slantingly ‖ to give a bias to ‖ *v.i.* to twist around **2.** *adj.* running at an angle, oblique **3.** *n.* a slant, oblique direction

skew·er 1. *n.* a metal or wooden pin for holding meat together while cooking **2.** *v.t.* to pierce with a skewer

ski 1. pl. **skis, ski** *n.* one of a pair of long, narrow, wooden, metal or plastic strips which curve up and taper to a point at the front end **2.** *v.i.* **ski·ing skied** to move on skis

skid 1. *n.* a sideways slip or slide of a wheel ‖ a block of wood or metal to prevent a wheel from turning ‖ one of a pair or set of bars etc. down which things can be slid or rolled **2.** *v.* **skid·ding skid·ded** *v.i.* to slide without gripping ‖ to slide sideways ‖ *v.t.* to cause to slip sideways

skiff *n.* a small rowing boat

skill *n.* ability to do something well **skilled** *adj.* having skill

skil·let *n.* a frying pan

skil·ful *adj.* having, showing or done with skill

skim 1. **skim·ming skimmed** *v.t.* to remove floating matter from the surface of (a liquid) ‖ to read superficially or hastily ‖ *v.i.* to go fast and smoothly on or just above some surface **2.** *n.* the act of skimming ‖ a thin covering

skim·mer *n.* an implement, esp. a perforated, flat ladle, used for skimming liquids

skimp 1. *v.t.* to keep in short supply ‖ *v.i.* to economize **skimp·i·ly** *adv.* **skimp·i·ness** *n.* **skimp·y skimp·i·er skimp·i·est** *adj.* unsatisfactory because of insufficiency

skin 1. *n.* the membrane which forms the outer covering of a human or animal body ‖ the outer covering of something, e.g. of a fruit, ship etc. **by the skin of one's teeth** with no margin to spare **to get under (someone's) skin** to have an irritating effect on (someone) **to save one's skin** to avoid capture, death, punishment or injury **2.** **skin·ning skinned** *v.t.* to remove the skin from ‖ to strip off ‖ to take all the money from

skin-deep *adj.* (of wounds) slight, affecting the skin only ‖ not affecting a person at all deeply

skin·flint *n.* a mean, miserly person

skin·ny skin·ni·er skin·ni·est *adj.* thin

skip 1. skip·ping skipped *v.i.* to move along with a series of short, quick hops ‖ to go over the top of with a single hop ‖ to read through a text hastily, omitting whole sections ‖ *v.t.* to go up faster than is normal in a ladder of promotion ‖ to cause (a stone) to bounce on the surface of water by skimming it ‖ to leave (town) quickly and secretly **2.** *n.* the act of skipping ‖ an omission

skip·per 1. *n.* the captain or master of any small vessel ‖ the chief pilot of an aircraft ‖ someone who leads or directs **2.** *v.t.* to act as skipper of

skir·mish *n.* a brief fight between soldiers ‖ a slight quarrel

skirt 1. *n.* a woman's outer garment hanging from the waist ‖ anything hanging like a skirt **2.** *v.i.* to be on or move around the edge

skit *n.* a short or satirical theatrical sketch

skit·tish *adj.* playful, esp. in a coy way ‖ (of a horse) nervous, restive and easily frightened

skul·dug·ger·y *n.* trickery, dishonest dealings

skulk *v.i.* to hang around in a sinister way

skull *n.* the cranium ‖ the mind of someone regarded as very obtuse

skunk 1. pl. **skunks, skunk** *n.* any of various North American omnivorous mammals ‖ the fur of any of these animals ‖ a contemptible person **2.** *v.t.* to defeat utterly

sky pl. **skies** *n.* (often pl.) the atmosphere above the earth, with or without clouds

sky·jack *v.* to assume control of an aircraft by force or threat of force **skyjacker** *n.* **skyjacking** *n.*

sky·lark 1. *n.* a European lark characterized by its high-pitched song uttered while soaring **2.** *v.i.* to be full of mischief and have fun

sky·light *n.* a window set into a flat roof as a dome etc.

sky·line *n.* the horizon ‖ objects seen against it

sky·rock·et 1. *n.* a fire work that consists of a rocket which explodes high in the air **2.** *v.i.* to rise very rapidly

sky·scrap·er *n.* a very tall building with many stories

slab 1. *n.* a thick, flat, oblong piece of something **2.** *v.t.* **slab·bing slabbed** to put on thickly

slack 1. *adj.* not under any tension ‖ lacking in diligence ‖ involving little work ‖ inactive ‖ (of tides, winds) slow-moving **2.** *v.i.* to be or become lazy ‖ to slacken **3.** *n.* the loose part of a rope ‖ a period of little trade ‖ any interval of inactivity ‖ (pl.) men's or women's long pants for casual wear **sláck·en** *v.t.* to make slower ‖ to make looser ‖ *v.i.* to become less energetic

slag 1. *n.* nonmetallic waste matter obtained when ore is smelted ‖ scoriaceous lava from a volcano **2.** *v.i.* **slag·ging slagged** to form as slag **slág·gy** *adj.*

slake slak·ing slaked *v.t.* to quench ‖ to satisfy ‖ to hydrate

sla·lom 1. *n.* a downhill race in which skiers zigzag between spaced markers **2.** *v.i.* to ski in such a race

slam 1. slam·ming slammed *v.t.* to shut noisily and violently ‖ to hit very hard ‖ to condemn in criticism ‖ *v.i.* to shut with a loud noise **2.** *n.* a loud bang ‖ a harshly critical notice

slan·der *n.* a statement which without due cause has the result of bringing its subject into disrepute

slander *v.t.* to write or say a slander against

slan·der·ous *adj.* having the quality of slander

slang *n.* widely used and understood language, consisting of new meanings attributed to existing words or of wholly new words ‖ a language that is peculiar to a group, profession or social class

slang·y slang·i·er slang·i·est *adj.* relating to slang

slant 1. *v.t.* to be at an angle with a given line or surface **2.** *n.* the angle made with the given line ‖ an aspect **3.** *adj.* slanting **slánt·ways, slánt·wise** *advs*

slap 1. slap·ping slapped *v.t.* to strike with the open hand **2.** *n.* a blow thus given ‖ the sound of such a blow ‖ an insult, affront ‖ a piece of sharp criticism **a slap on the back** congratulations

slap·stick *n.* fast, farcical comedy dominated by physical boisterousness

slash 1. *v.t.* to make a long cut in, esp. by striking violently and with wide sweeps ‖ to cut a slit in (a garment) ‖ to criticize severely ‖ to reduce (prices etc.) greatly **2.** *n.* a long cut made by slashing ‖ a slit in an article of clothing ‖ a great reduction in costs, prices, etc.

slash *n.* an area of soggy, esp. brush-covered swampland

slat slat·ting slat·ted *v.t.* (of sails) to flap noisily against

slat 1. *n.* a thin, narrow piece of wood, a lath **2.** *v.t.* **slat·ting slat·ted** to construct with slats

slate 1. *n.* a laminated rock which is readily split along parallel planes into large, thin pieces ‖ the blue-black or blue-gray color of slate ‖ a list of candidates drawn up by a political party **2.** *v.t.* **slat·ing slat·ed** to cover with slates ‖ to designate for an appointment

slat·tern *n.* a woman of unkempt appearance

slat·y slat·i·er slat·i·est *adj.* slate-colored

slaugh·ter 1. *n.* the killing of animals for food ‖ a massacre **2.** *v.t.* to kill mercilessly ‖ to kill in large numbers ‖ to kill (animals) for food

slave 1. *n.* a person who is the property of another ‖ a person dominated by some habit etc. **2.** *v.i.* **slav·ing slaved** to work like a slave

slav·er·y *n.* total subjection to a master ‖ slaveholding ‖ hard, grinding work ‖ addiction

slaw *n.* coleslaw

slay slay·ing slew slain to kill violently

slea·zi·ness *n.* the state or quality of being sleazy

slea·zy slea·zi·er slea·zi·est *adj.* lacking substance, of poor texture ‖ tawdry, vulgar ‖ squalid, shabby

sled 1. *n.* a vehicle mounted on runners for use on snow or ice **2.** *v.i.* **sled·ding sled·ded** to ride on a sled

sledge 1. *n.* a low sled used to transport usually heavy loads **2.** **sledg·ing sledged** *v.t.* to convey by sledge

sledge 1. *n.* a sledgehammer **2.** *v.i.* **sledg·ing sledged** to use a sledgehammer

sleek 1. *adj.* smooth, soft and shiny ‖ polished ‖ smoothly polite in a way that displeases **2.** *v.t.* to groom (hair) so that it is sleek

sleep sleep·ing slept *v.i.* to be in the natural and regular state of inactivity in which consciousness ceases and the bodily functions slow down or cease ‖ *v.t.* to slumber ‖ to spend (time) sleeping **to sleep in** to sleep at the place of work

sleep *n.* the state of sleeping ‖ a period of sleeping

sleep·er *n.* a railroad sleeping car ‖ a child's sleeping garment ‖ a book, racehorse etc. which achieves unexpected success

sleep·i·ly *adv.* in a sleepy manner

sleep·i·ness *n.* the state or quality of being sleepy

sleep·y sleep·i·er sleep·i·est *adj.* feeling ready to go to sleep ‖ without much activity Ua ‖ lacking alertness

sleet 1. *n.* partly frozen rain **2.** *v.i.* to shower in the form of sleet **sleet·y** *adj.*

sleeve 1. *n.* the part of a garment covering the arm ‖ a slipcase for a phonograph record **2.** *v.t.* **sleev·ing sleeved** to cover with a sleeve **sleeved** *adj.* provided with sleeves **sleeve·less** *adj.*

sleigh 1. *n.* a sled, drawn by a horse or horses and carrying passengers **2.** *v.i.* to ride in a sleigh

sleight of hand deft manual skill

slen·der *adj.* gracefully slim ‖ slight, small **slen·der·ize slen·der·iz·ing slen·der·ized** *v.t.* to make slender

sleuth 1. *n.* a detective **2.** *v.i.* to act as a sleuth ‖ *v.t.* to investigate the doings of or track (someone)

slice slic·ing sliced *v.t.* to cut into slices

slice *n.* a thin, flat piece, e.g. of bread or meat, cut from a larger piece ‖ a share of land, money etc.

slick 1. *adj.* clever and suave ‖ slippery

2. *adv.* smoothly ‖ smartly **3.** *v.t.* to make smooth **4.** *n.* an oil slick ‖ a tool for smoothing **slick·er** *n.* a swindler ‖ an oilskin or raincoat

slide slid·ing slid *v.i.* to move with continuous contact and little friction over a smooth surface ‖ to slip so as to nearly fall ‖ to move quietly and with great ease ‖ *v.t.* to cause to slide **1.** *n.* the act of sliding ‖ a smooth surface on which to slide ‖ a transparency ‖ the fall of a mass (e.g. of rock, snow) down a mountainside

slight 1. *adj.* very little ‖ lightly built and not very tall **2.** *v.t.* to treat as of very little importance ‖ to treat with calculated rudeness **3.** *n.* an instance of slighting **slight·ly** *adv.*

slim 1. slim·mer slim·mest *adj.* not thick ‖ not fat ‖ meager **2.** slim·ming slimmed *v.i.* to make oneself thinner, by dieting, exercises, drugs etc.

slime 1. *n.* fine, moist mud ‖ mucus **2.** slim·ing slimed *v.t.* to cover with slime ‖ *v.i.* to become slimy

slim·i·ness *n.* the state or quality of being slimy

slim·y slim·i·er slim·i·est *adj.* like slime ‖ covered with slime ‖ filthy, disgusting

sling 1. *v.t.* sling·ing slung to suspend by a sling **2.** *n.* a loop of leather, rope, chain etc. ‖ an instrument for casting missiles ‖ a large, triangular bandage hung around the neck to support an injured arm

slink slink·ing slunk *v.i.* to move stealthily in fear or shame **slink·y** slink·i·er slink·i·est *adj.* stealthy

slip slip·ping slipped *v.i.* to move in a sliding motion ‖ to lose one's balance by sliding on a slippery surface ‖ to slide from one's grasp and fall ‖ to move easily and rapidly, esp. without attracting attention ‖ to sink a little from a previous standard ‖ to make a mistake ‖ to put a garment on quickly ‖ to escape from one's memory **1.** *n.* a slipping ‖ a small unintentional mistake ‖ a dress-length undergarment

slip *n.* a long, narrow piece of wood, paper etc. ‖ a small person

slip·per *n.* light, comfortable indoor footwear

slip·per·i·ness *n.* the state or quality of being slippery

slip·per·y slip·per·i·er slip·per·i·est *adj.* offering little friction ‖ difficult to hold in one's grasp ‖ difficult to hold to an agreement ‖ requiring very tactful handling ‖ untrustworthy

slip·shod *adj.* negligent, careless

slip-up *n.* a slip, mistake

slit 1. *v.t.* slit·ting slit to cut or tear lengthwise ‖ to make a long, thin opening in **2.** *n.* a long cut or opening

slith·er 1. *v.i.* to slide ‖ to move with a smooth and slightly sinuous motion **2.** *n.* a slightly sinuous motion **slith·er·y** *adj.* slippery

sliv·er 1. *n.* a splinter of wood ‖ a very thin piece cut or torn off something **2.** *v.t.* to cut or tear into very thin pieces ‖ *v.i.* to slice or shred

slob *n.* a boorish, vulgar or slovenly person

slob·ber 1. *v.i.* to let saliva run from the mouth ‖ to gush sentimentally **2.** *n.* dribbling saliva ‖ feebly sentimental talk **slób·ber·y** *adj.*

slo·gan *n.* a catchword ‖ a pithy phrase

sloop *n.* a small vessel with one mast

slop 1. *n.* (*pl.*) dirty water ‖ (esp. pl.) swill fed to hogs **2.** slop·ping slopped *v.i.* to flow over the edge of a vessel ‖ *v.t.* to pour or splash

slope 1. *n.* a natural or artificial incline **2.** slop·ing sloped *v.i.* to be inclined at an angle with the horizontal

slop·pi·ness *n.* the state or quality of being sloppy

slop·py slop·pi·er slop·pi·est *adj.* wet with slopped-over liquid ‖ weakly sentimental ‖ slovenly ‖ careless

slot *n.* a groove or channel ‖ a narrow opening ‖ a slit in a machine for the insertion of a coin

sloth *n.* laziness ‖ spiritual apathy ‖ any of several tropical mammals

slouch 1. *n.* a bad posture or manner of walking ‖ a lazy or incompetent person **2.** *v.i.* to hold oneself or move with a drooping posture ‖ *v.t.* to cause (one's shoulders) to droop

slouch·i·ly *adv.* in a slouchy manner

slouch·y slouch·i·er slouch·i·est *adj.* slouching

slough 1. *n.* any part that an animal casts or molts **2.** *v.i.* to shed a skin etc.

slough *n.* a marshy, muddy place or swamp

slov·en *n.* a person who is untidy in appearance, slipshod in his work, and dirty in his habits

slov·en·ly slov·en·li·er slov·en·li·est *adj.* like a sloven

slow 1. *adj.* taking more time than is regarded as normal ‖ long drawn out ‖ not hasty ‖ dilatory ‖ (of business) not active, slack ‖ (of a timepiece) indicating a time behind the actual time **2.** *v.t.* to reduce the speed of production of ‖ *v.i.* to move at a reduced speed **3.** *adv.* slowly

slow·ness *n.* the state or quality of being slow

sludge *n.* the mud on a riverbed ‖ the treated, solid matter of sewage after drying, used as a fertilizer ‖ floating ice or snow **sludg·y** *adj.*

slue, slew *v.i.* **slu·ing, slew·ing slued, slewed** to swing or turn in an arc ‖ *v.t.* to cause to swing around

slug *n.* any roughly shaped piece of metal, esp. the head of a bullet ‖ (printing) a line of linotype type ‖ (printing) a strip of metal for spacing between lines ‖ a token for an automatic machine

slug *n.* a usually terrestrial gastropod mollusk

slug 1. *v.t.* **slug·ging slugged** to hit hard, esp. with the fist **2.** *n.* a heavy blow

slug·gish *adj.* slow to act ‖ few transactions taking place

sluice 1. *n.* an artificial waterway with a gate or other device to control the flow and level of the water ‖ the device itself **2. sluic·ing sluiced** *v.t.* to transport (logs etc.) by the stream of a sluice

slum 1. *n.* a heavily populated urban area of dilapidated buildings characterized by poverty and filth **2.** *v.i.* **slum·ming slummed** to visit a poor neighborhood in search of amusement

slum·ber 1. *n.* sleep ‖ a light sleep **2.** *v.i.* to sleep ‖ to sleep lightly **slum·ber·ous slum·brous** *adjs.*

slump 1. *v.i.* to fall suddenly ‖ to fall suddenly in value or activity **2.** *n.* a sudden or continued drop in price or stagnation in economic activity

slur 1. slur·ring slurred *v.i.* to speak indistinctly by running sounds together ‖ *v.t.* to speak of someone in such a way as to throw doubt on (his reputation) **2.** *n.* the act of slurring ‖ a remark which throws doubt on a reputation

slush *n.* watery mud ‖ melting snow ‖ sickly sentiment, gush

slush fund a fund for use in bribery or other corrupt practices in favor of a private interest

slush·y slush·i·er slush·i·est *adj.* of or having the character of slush ‖ covered with or full of slush

slut *n.* a dirty, slovenly woman ‖ a loose woman

sly sly·er, sli·er sly·est, sli·est *adj.* showing clever underhandedness ‖ crafty, mischievous **sly·ly, sli·ly** *adv.*

smack 1. *n.* a slight characteristic taste or flavor ‖ a very small quantity **2.** *v.i.* (with 'of') to have a taste or flavor ‖ to have a hint or suggestion

smack 1. *n.* a slap, a quick blow with the open hand or other flat surface ‖ the sound of such a blow ‖ a loud kiss **2.** *v.t.* to slap loudly ‖ to part (the lips) with a sharp sound

smack·er *n.* a loud kiss ‖ a heavy blow

small 1. *adj.* restricted in size ‖ more restricted in quality, amount, value, duration etc. ‖ of little importance ‖ of inferior rank or influence ‖ modest ‖ petty ‖ weak **to feel small** to feel humiliated **2.** *adv.* in small pieces **3.** *n.* the small, narrow part of something

small-mind·ed *adj.* narrow in outlook and sympathies ‖ petty

small·pox *n.* a severe and contagious virus disease

small-time *adj.* insignificant, petty

smart *adj.* sharp, severe ‖ brisk, lively ‖ clever in an impudent way ‖ intelligent ‖ shrewd ‖ fashionable ‖ well groomed and carefully dressed

smart 1. *v.i.* to cause a sharp, stinging

pain ‖ to feel such a pain 2. *n.* a sharp, stinging pain ‖ mental pain

smart·en *v.t.* to make smart ‖ *v.i.* (with 'up') to become smart, esp. in appearance

smart·ness *n.* the quality of being smart

smash 1. *v.t.* to break violently to pieces ‖ to hurt or damage very badly ‖ to hit or throw violently ‖ *v.i.* to come into violent collision ‖ to progress with violent effort so as to overcome obstacles 2. *n.* the act or noise of breaking into pieces ‖ a heavy blow with the fist ‖ complete financial failure 3. *adv.* smack **smash·ing** *adj.* crushing

smat·ter·ing *n.* (with 'of') a slight, superficial knowledge

smear *v.t.* to spread, daub (a greasy, oily or sticky substance) over an area ‖ to spread (e.g. wet ink or paint) beyond the proper outline by rubbing ‖ to soil or stain (something) in this manner ‖ to spoil the good reputation of (someone)

smear *n.* a mark on a surface made by smearing ‖ a preparation of a substance for microscopic examination ‖ something which casts a slur on someone's good reputation, esp. falsely

smell 1. **smel·ling smelled, smelt** *v.t.* to perceive or recognize by means of the nose and olfactory nerves ‖ to detect or discover as if by smell 2. *n.* the sense by which odor is perceived ‖ the act of smelling ‖ the characteristic odor of a substance ‖ an air or hint of something bad

smell·y smell·i·er smell·i·est *adj.* having an unpleasant smell

smelt *pl.* **smelts, smelt** *n.* a genus of small food fishes that resemble the salmon in structure

smelt *v.t.* to fuse (an ore) **smelt·er** *n.* someone who smelts ‖ the owner or operator of a smelting works **smelt·er·y** *pl.* **smelt·er·ies** *n.* a smelting works

smile 1. **smil·ing smiled** *v.i.* to make a facial expression which may show amusement, satisfaction, affection, irony or derision etc. ‖ (with 'at', 'on' or 'upon') to look with favor ‖ *v.t.* to express with a smile 2. *n.* the act of smiling ‖ the facial expression made in smiling

smirch 1. *v.t.* to smear (esp. a reputation) 2. *n.* something which smears, esp. a reputation

smirk 1. *v.t.* to smile in a conceited or affected way 2. *n.* such a smile

smite 1. *v.t.* **smit·ing smit·ten** to deliver a powerful, sudden blow to ‖ to arouse an intense emotion in ‖ to afflict with 2. *n.* a tremendous blow

smith·er·eens *pl.n.* small fragments

smock 1. *n.* a loose outer garment, resembling a long shirt 2. **smock·ing** *n.* decorative needlework used to gather cloth and make it hang in folds

smog *n.* heavy fog injurious to health because it contains smoke and gases produced by the partial combustion of fuels

smoke *n.* a suspension of solid particles in a gas ‖ any vapor resembling smoke ‖ the act of smoking tobacco ‖ something to smoke **to go up in smoke** to be pure waste

smoke smok·ing smoked *v.i.* to draw smoke into the mouth or lungs and exhale it ‖ to emit smoke ‖ to emit any vapor resembling smoke ‖ *v.t.* to cure (meat etc.) by exposure to smoke ‖ to fumigate

smok·er *n.* someone who or something which smokes

smoke·stack *n.* a chimney

smok·i·ly *adv.* in a smoky manner

smok·i·ness *n.* the state or quality of being smoky

smok·y smok·i·er smok·i·est *adj.* of or like smoke ‖ giving off smoke ‖ filled with smoke ‖ of the color or smell of smoke

smol·der, smoul·der *v.i.* to burn slowly at a low heat without flames ‖ to betray feelings one is trying hard to supress

smooth 1. *adj.* even, not rough ‖ a surface which offers little frictional resistance ‖ free from obstacles or difficulties ‖ free from hair, beard etc. ‖ suave, ingratiating ‖ not jolting ‖ not grating, rasping or loud 2. *v.t.* to make smooth ‖ to free from difficulty

smooth·en *v.t.* to make smooth

smor·gas·bord *n.* a buffet meal at which a great variety of dishes is offered

smoth·er *v.t.* to kill by depriving of air ‖ to suppress and hide ‖ to give to in profusion ‖ to cover thickly ‖ *v.i.* to die for lack of air

smudge 1. smudg·ing smudged *v.t.* to blur ‖ to soil by touching with something dirty ‖ *v.i.* to become smudged **2.** *n.* a mark made by smudging **smúdg·i·ly** *adv.* **smúdg·i·ness** *n.* **smúdg·y smudg·i·er smudg·i·est** *adj.*

smug smug·ger smug·gest *adj.* very self-satisfied

smug·gle smug·gling smug·gled *v.t.* to import or export without paying duty ‖ to convey secretly in defiance of the law **smúg·gler** *n.*

smut 1. *n.* a small piece of solid carried off from burning fuel ‖ the black mark made by a smut ‖ a disease of cereal or other plants ‖ indecent talk, pictures etc. **2. smut·ting smut·ted** *v.t.* to mark with smuts ‖ to blacken

smut·ti·ness *n.* the state or quality of being smutty

smut·ty smut·ti·er smut·ti·est *adj.* soiled with smut ‖ (of plantts) affected with smut ‖ indecent

snack *n.* a very slight, hurried meal, esp. between regular meals

snag 1. *n.* the roughly pointed piece left when a tree trunk, branch, tooth etc. is unevenly broken off ‖ a difficulty which emerges ‖ any sharp projection ‖ a small tear **2.** *v.t.* **snag·ging snagged** to catch on a snag

snail *n.* one of many species of gastropod mollusks with a spiral protective shell ‖ an irritatingly slow person

snake 1. *n.* a limbless reptile with epidermal scales ‖ a malevolent person **2. snak·ing snaked** *v.i.* to move like a snake

snak·y snak·i·er snak·i·est *adj.* resembling a snake ‖ having the qualities of a snake in the grass

snap 1. snap·ping snapped *v.t.* to close or open with a sudden rapid movement ‖ to seize with the jaws ‖ to break with a sharp sound ‖ to utter very fast, esp. in anger ‖ *v.i.* to break suddenly ‖ to speak sharply ‖ to take sharp quick bites ‖ to snatch

eagerly ‖ to make a sudden sharp sound **to snap out of it** to make an effort of the will and dominate one's lethargy, self-pity etc. **2.** *n.* the sound of snapping ‖ a snap fastener ‖ a snapshot ‖ an easy task giving sure promise of success **3.** *adj.* done quickly without deliberation ‖ simple, easy **4.** *adv.* with a snap

snap·per *pl.* **snap·per, snap·pers** *n.* any of various carnivorous food or game fishes ‖ a snapping turtle ‖ a click beetle

snap·pi·ly *adv.* in a snappy manner

snap·pi·ness *n.* the state or quality of being snappy

snap·pish *adj.* frequently cross, testy

snap·py snap·pi·er snap·pi·est *adj.* short-tempered ‖ lively ‖ fast and stylish

snap·shot *n.* a photograph taken with a very short exposure, usually of unposed subjects

snare 1. *n.* a device, usually a slip noose, used for catching birds and animals ‖ an artifice for deceiving somebody **2.** *v.t.* **snar·ing snared** to catch

snarl 1. *v.i.* to growl fiercely ‖ to show anger **2.** *n.* the sound of snarling

snarl 1. *n.* a tangle of threads, hair etc. ‖ an entanglement **2.** *v.t.* to entangle ‖ *v.i.* to become entangled

snatch 1. *v.t.* to seize suddenly, esp. without permission ‖ to remove suddenly **2.** *n.* a sudden grab ‖ a portion of talk of short duration

snatch·y *adj.* done in snatches

sneak 1. *v.i.* to move stealthily or furtively ‖ *v.t.* to do in a stealthy manner ‖ to steal **2.** *n.* someone who sneaks **3.** *adj.* happening without warning

sneak·ers *pl.n.* light, rubber-soled, canvas shoes

sneak·y sneak·i·er sneak·i·est *adj.* like a sneak

sneer 1. *v.i.* to make a contemptuous grimace ‖ to express derision ‖ *v.t.* to utter in a scornfully derisive way **2.** *n.* the act of sneering

sneeze 1. *v.i.* **sneez·ing sneezed** to expel air from the nose and mouth suddenly **2.** *n.* the act or sound of sneezing

snick·er 1. *v.i.* to laugh in a sly, half-suppressed manner **2.** *n.* this kind of laugh

snide *adj.* mean, cheap ‖ obliquely malicious

sniff 1. *v.i.* to inhale suddenly and so forcefully through the nose that the action is audible ‖ *v.t.* to draw forcibly into the nostrils ‖ to test the smell of by sniffing **2.** *n.* the sound or act of sniffing ‖ something sniffed

snif·fle 1. *v.i.* snif·fling snif·fled to sniff repeatedly because one's nose is blocked with catarrh or as a result of weeping **2.** *n.* the act or sound of sniffling **the sniffles** a slight head cold

snip 1. *v.t.* snip·ping snipped to cut with scissors or shears using quick short strokes **2.** *n.* a piece snipped off ‖ an impertinent person

snipe 1. *pl.* snipe, snipes *n.* a genus of long-billed brown marsh birds **2.** snip·ing sniped *v.i.* to fire single shots from cover at an enemy **snip·er** *n.*

snitch 1. *v.t.* to steal ‖ *v.i.* to give evidence against someone **2.** *n.* an informer

sniv·el sniv·el·ing sniv·eled 1. *v.i.* to have mucus running from the nose ‖ to breathe audibly ‖ to whine and make a pretense of weeping **2.** *n.* the act of sniveling

snob *n.* a socially exclusive person ‖ someone who likes to think of himself as belonging to the social class next above his own **snób·ber·y** *n.* **snób·bish** *adj.*

snoop 1. *v.i.* to pry in a sneaking or interfering way **2.** *n.* someone who snoops **snóop·er** *n.* a snoop

snoot·i·ness *n.* the state or quality of being snooty

snoot·y snoot·i·er snoot·i·est *adj.* snobbish ‖ supercilious

snooze 1. *v.i.* snooz·ing snoozed to sleep lightly for a short time **2.** *n.* a short, light sleep, esp. in the daytime

snore 1. *v.i.* snor·ing snored to breathe through the open mouth and the nose when asleep, producing a harsh noise **2.** *n.* the sound made by snoring

snor·kel *n.* an air tube enabling a swimmer to breathe under the surface of the water

snort 1. *v.i.* to expel air suddenly and loudly through the nostrils, expressing anger or contempt ‖ *v.t.* to express by or with a snort ‖ to inhale drugs **2.** *n.* the sound or act of snorting ‖ a small drink of liquor **snórt·er** *n.* a violent gale

snout *n.* the nose of various animals ‖ the human nose, esp. when large and ugly

snow 1. *n.* frozen water vapor which falls to the earth in soft, white crystalline flakes ‖ cocaine **2.** *v.i.* (*impers.*) to be forming a fall of snow, it is snowing **snowed under** overwhelmed (by correspondence, things to do etc.)

snow·ball 1. *n.* a handful of snow, pressed or rolled and shaped into a ball **2.** *v.i.* to grow rapidly larger, at an ever increasing rate ‖ to throw snowballs

snow·flake *n.* a single crystal of snow

snow·mo·bile *n.* motor vehicle for travel on snow

snow·y snow·i·er snow·i·est *adj.* covered by, or abounding in, snow ‖ as white as snow

snub 1. *v.t.* snub·bing snubbed to refuse to notice the presence of someone ‖ to stave (someone) off deliberately **2.** *n.* the act or an instance of snubbing

snuff 1. *v.t.* to inhale through the nose usually in order to smell, to sniff **2.** *n.* powdered tobacco inhaled into the nose

snug 1. snug·ger snug·gest *adj.* safe and comfortable ‖ small but comfortably arranged ‖ close-fitting ‖ trim and seaworthy

snug·gle snug·gling snug·gled *v.i.* to lie closely for warmth, protection, affection etc.

so 1. *adv.* in a certain way ‖ to a certain degree ‖ as a result ‖ also **and so on** et cetera **so as** in order to **2.** *conj.* in order that ‖ with the result that ‖ therefore **3.** *pron.* approximately that much **4.** *adj.* true **5.** *interj.* used to express surprise, understanding or indifference

soak *v.i.* to be or become thoroughly wet by lying immersed in fluid ‖ to penetrate the mind ‖ *v.t.* to make very wet ‖ to place (something) in a liquid in order to saturate it **sóak·age** *n.* the process of soaking

soap 1. *n.* a cleaning or emulsifying agent **2.** *v.t.* to treat with soap

soap·y soap·i·er soap·i·est *adj.* resembling, mixed or covered with soap ‖ (of a person) ingratiating, smooth

soar 1. *v.i.* to rise high into the air ‖ (of prices, profits etc.) to rise to a very high level ‖ (of hopes, thoughts etc.) to become more spiritual **2.** *n.* the act of soaring

sob 1. *v.* **sob·bing sobbed** *v.i.* to weep violently ‖ to make a sound like sobbing **2.** *n.* the sound of sobbing ‖ the convulsive catch of the breath in sobbing

so·ber 1. *adj.* not drunk ‖ temperate ‖ staid, sedate ‖ showing discretion and moderation ‖ not fanciful ‖ subdued **2.** *v.t.* to make sober ‖ *v.i.* to become sober

so·bri·e·ty *n.* the quality or state of being sober

so·bri·quet *n.* an epithet ‖ a nickname

so-called *adj.* popularly named

soc·cer *n.* a game developed in Britain 1863. It is played by two teams each of 11 men, with a round football, on a rectangular field

so·cia·bil·i·ty *pl.* **so·cia·bil·i·ties** *n.* the quality or state of being sociable

so·cia·ble *adj.* fond of the company of others ‖ friendly

so·cial 1. *adj.* relating to human society ‖ living in communities ‖ sociable ‖ relating to social activities **2.** *n.* gathering

so·cial·ism *n.* a political and economic theory advocating collective ownership of the means of production and control of distribution

so·cial·ist 1. *n.* a person who advocates socialism **2.** *adj.* of, relating to socialism

so·cial·is·tic *adj.*

so·cial·ite *n.* someone prominent in fashionable, society

so·cial·i·za·tion *n.* a socializing or being socialized

so·cial·ize so·cial·iz·ing so·cial·ized *v.t.* to bring under public ownership and control ‖ *v.i.* to be active in social affairs

so·cial·ly *adv.* in a social way

so·ci·e·ty *pl.* **so·ci·e·ties** *n.* the state of living in organized groups ‖ any number of people associated together geographi-

cally, racially or otherwise with collective interests ‖ a civil or business association organized under law ‖ that part of a community considered to be the élite by birth, wealth or culture etc.

so·ci·o·log·i·cal *adj.* of sociology ‖ of human society and its development and organization

so·ci·ol·o·gist *n.* a specialist in sociology

so·ci·ol·o·gy *n.* the study of the origin, the history and the structure of human society and its institutions

sock *n.* a wool, cotton or nylon etc. covering for the foot, ankle and lower part of the leg

sock 1. *v.t.* to hit hard with the fist or a heavy object **2.** *n.* such a blow

sock·et *n.* a hollow part or piece adapted or contrived to receive and hold something

sod 1. *n.* surface soil with grass growing on it **2.** *v.t.* **sod·ding sod·ded** to lay sods on (an area) in order to make it a lawn

so·da *n.* crystalline sodium carbonate ‖ soda water

so·dal·i·ty *pl.* **so·dal·i·ties** *n.* a fellowship, community or organized society

soda water water charged under pressure with carbonic acid gas

sod·den *adj.* saturated with moisture ‖ dulled and stupid from frequent drunkenness

so·di·um *n.* a metallic element of small desity

sodium bicarbonate a weakly basic salt

sodium chloride salt

sod·om·ite *n.* a person who practices sodomy

sod·om·y *n.* sexual intercourse between males or unnatural sexual intercourse between a man and a woman

so·fa *n.* a long, upholstered seat

soft *adj.* offering little resistance to pressure ‖ not hard ‖ mild ‖ not loud ‖ not sharp in outline ‖ feeble-minded ‖ foolishly sentimental ‖ smooth, insinuating ‖ weak ‖ nonalcoholic ‖ bland ‖ malleable

sof·ten *v.t.* to make soft or softer ‖ to wear down the opposition or resistance of ‖ *v.i.* to become soft or softer

soft-heart·ed *adj.* very ready to sympathize with others and act accordingly

soft-spo·ken *adj.* suave in speech

soft·ware *n.* *(electronics)* the system of general programs which simplifies and links the work of computer and user ‖ *(computer)* nonhardware properties, e.g., programs, languages, routines, instructions etc., utilized in operations

sog·gy sog·gi·er sog·gi·est *adj.* soft and heavy because impregnated with water

soil *n.* the uppermost stratum of the earth's crust ‖ land, country

soil *v.t.* to make dirty, to stain ‖ to tarnish or harm ‖ *v.i.* to become stained or dirty

soi·ree, soi·rée *n.* a formal evening party or gathering

so·ja bean a soybean

so·journ 1. *v.i.* to stay or dwell for a time in a place or among certain people **2.** *n.* a temporary stay

sol·ace 1. *n.* that which lessens disappointment or grief or loneliness **2.** *v.t.* **sol·ac·ing sol·aced** to lessen the disappointment, grief or loneliness

so·lar *adj.* of or relating to the sun

so·lar·i·um *pl.* **so·lar·i·ums, so·lar·i·a** *n.* a room or building so constructed as to be exposed to the radiant energy of the sun and to trap much of this energy

sol·der 1. *n.* a metallic alloy which, melted between clean metal surfaces, itself alloys with these and so bonds them together **2.** *v.t.* to join (metal surfaces) thus

sol·dier 1. *n.* a man serving in an army **2.** *v.i.* to serve as a soldier

sole *adj.* only ‖ unshared

sole 1. *n.* the undersurface of the foot ‖ part of a shoe ‖ the lower part or surface of something **2.** *v.t.* **sol·ing soled** to provide with a sole

sol·e·cism *n.* a grammatical or syntactical deviation from what is conventionally regarded as correct speech ‖ a deviation from what are regarded as good social manners

sole·ly *adv.* only, exclusively

sol·emn *adj.* serious or profound ‖ of grave significance ‖ earnest and gloomy

so·lem·ni·ty *pl.* **so·lem·ni·ties** *n.* solemn expression, behavior or character

so·lic·it *v.t.* to beg for, canvass, appeal for ‖ to importune ‖ to propose sexual intercourse to in return for money

so·lic·i·ta·tion *n.* the practice, or an act, of soliciting

so·lic·i·tor *n.* a professional canvasser for money for a fund, trade, support etc.

so·lic·i·tous *adj.* attentive, full of anxious concern ‖ (with infin.) eager

so·lic·i·tude *n.* anxious concern

sol·id 1. *adj.* nonfluid ‖ having three dimensions ‖ continuous ‖ without openings ‖ real, sound ‖ dense, thick ‖ not hollow ‖ firm and compact ‖ sound, serious ‖ full, complete ‖ unanimous ‖ dependable ‖ having no leads separating the lines of type **2.** *n.* a substance that has little or no tendency to flow ‖ a figure having three spatial dimensions ‖ *(pl.)* food which is not liquid

sol·i·dar·i·ty *pl.* **sol·i·dar·i·ties** *n.* common interest and active loyalty within a group

so·lid·i·ty *n.* moral or financial soundness

sol·id-state *adj.* of semiconducting material used to control flow of electricity

so·lil·o·quize so·lil·o·quiz·ing so·lil·o·quized *v.i.* to deliver a soliloquy

so·lil·o·quy *pl.* **so·lil·o·quies** *n.* the act of speaking one's thoughts aloud in solitude

sol·i·taire *n.* a single gem set alone ‖ any of certain card games, generally for a single player

sol·i·tar·y 1. *adj.* one alone, without others ‖ not gregarious ‖ lonely, without company ‖ unfrequented ‖ (of insects) not social **2.** *pl.* **sol·i·tar·ies** *n.* a recluse ‖ solitary confinement

sol·i·tude *n.* the state of being solitary ‖ loneliness ‖ isolation ‖ a lonely place

so·lo 1. *pl.* **so·los, so·li** *n.* a passage of music to be performed by one instrument or voice ‖ any performance by one person ‖ an airplane flight alone without passengers or instructor **2.** *adj.* alone, without accompaniment **3.** *v.i.* to fly an airplane alone

so·lo·ist *n.* a person who performs a solo

sol·stice *n.* either of the two points in the sun's apparent annual orbit in relation to the fixed stars at which it is furthest from the equator i.e. June 21-2, the summer solstice, Dec. 21-2, the winter solstice

sol·u·bil·i·ty *n.* the quality of being soluble

sol·u·ble *adj.* capable of being dissolved ‖ capable of being solved or explained

so·lu·tion *n.* a homogeneous mixture of two (or more) substances ‖ the answer to a problem ‖ the act, method or process by which such an answer is obtained

solve solv·ing solved *v.t.* to find the answer to, work out (e.g. a problem)

sol·ven·cy *n.* the state or quality of being solvent

sol·vent 1. *adj.* having enough money to pay all debts ‖ able to dissolve **2.** *n.* a substance, usually a liquid, capable of dissolving other substances

so·mat·ic *adj.* relating to the body as distinguished from the soul or mind

som·ber *adj.* depressingly dark and shadowy

som·bre·ro *pl.* **som·bre·ros** *n.* a large felt or straw hat with a wide and often upturned brim

some 1. *adj.* of a person or persons not known or specified ‖ being an unspecified amount or proportion of a whole or quantity ‖ a considerable amount ‖ remarkable, notable, striking **2.** *pron.* an indefinite quantity or indefinite number of people or things **3.** *adv.* (with a number) approximately

-some suffix used added to numbers to indicate a group, as in 'foursome'

some·bod·y 1. *pron.* an unspecified or unknown person **2.** *pl.* **some·bod·ies** *n.* a person of importance

some·day *adv.* at some distant, future time

some·how *adv.* (often with 'or other') by some means unknown or undefined ‖ for some unknown cause or reason

some·one *pron.* somebody

som·er·sault, sum·mer·sault 1. *n.* a head over heals revolution of the body **2.** *v.i.* to perform a somersault

some·thing 1. *pron.* a thing, act or quality undefined or unspecified ‖ (often with 'quite' or 'really') a thing which can be regarded as a minor achievement ‖ somewhat **2.** *adv.* in a limited degree

some·time 1. *adv.* at some indefinite time in the future or past **2.** *adj.* former

some·times *adv.* occasionally, now and then

some·way *adv.* somehow

some·what 1. *adj.* rather **2.** *pron.* some previously mentioned person or thing having to some degree the nature of something specified

some·where 1. *adv.* in or to some place unknown or unspecified

som·nam·bu·late som·nam·bu·lat·ing som·nam·bu·lat·ed *v.i.* to walk when asleep **som·nám·bu·lism, aoeaoesom·nám·bu·list** ns

som·no·lent *adj.* inclined to sleep, drowsy ‖ inducing sleep

son *n.* a male human being in relation to his parents ‖ (*pl.*) male descendants

so·nar *n.* an apparatus which locates a submerged object by emitting high-frequency sound waves and registering the vibrations reflected back from the object

sonde *n.* a device for testing atmospheric conditions at high altitudes

song *n.* the act or art of singing ‖ a short composition in which words and music together form a unity **for a song** for a disproportionately small amount of money

son·ic *adj.* of sound waves ‖ of or relating to the speed of sound in air

son-in-law *pl.* **sons-in-law** *n.* a daughter's husband

son·net *n.* a poem of 14 lines

so·no·rous *adj.* giving out sound ‖ impressive, lofty

soon *adv.* in a short time ‖ quickly ‖ early **as soon as** at the moment when **sooner or later** inevitably but with no certainty when

soot 1. *n.* black particles of carbon formed by the incomplete combustion **2.** *v.t.* to cover or treat with soot

soothe sooth·ing soothed *v.t.* to calm, reassure ‖ to smooth ‖ to alleviate

sóoth·ing *adj.*

sooth·say·er *n.* a person whose profession was telling the future

soot·y soot·i·er soot·i·est *adj.* having the color of soot ‖ covered with soot ‖ of or like soot

sop *n.* a piece of bread, cake etc. soaked in liquid before it is eaten ‖ something given to soothe

sop sop·ping sopped *v.t.* to soak ‖ (with 'up') to absorb

soph·ism *n.* a piece of plausible but false reasoning

so·phis·ti·cate so·phis·ti·cat·ing so·phis·ti·cat·ed *v.t.* to deprive of simplicity or sincerity ‖ to make complex **so·phis·ti·cat·ed** *adj.* having the worldly wisdom characteristic of fashionable life ‖ elaborated ‖ too affected or artificial, lacking in naiveté or naturalness **so·phis·ti·cá·tion** *n.*

soph·ist·ry *pl.* **soph·ist·ries** *n.* a piece of plausible but false reasoning, sophism

soph·o·more *n.* a second-year student at a college or secondary school

soph·o·mor·ic *adj.* of or relating to a sophomore

so·pran·o 1. *n.* the highest singing voice in women, boys or castrati ‖ a singer with such a voice **2.** *adj.* of or relating to a soprano

sor·cer·er *n.* a person who practices sorcery

sor·cer·ess *n.* a female sorcerer

sor·cer·y *pl.* **sor·cer·ies** *n.* the use of magic powers derived from evil spirits ‖ an instance of this

sor·did *adj.* dirty, squalid ‖ mean, contemptible

sore 1. sor·er sor·est *adj.* painful ‖ causing painful emotions ‖ feeling wounded in one's pride ‖ grievous, in sore need **2.** *n.* a sore place on the body

sore·ness *n.* the quality or state of being sore

so·ror·i·ty *pl.* **so·ror·i·ties** *n.* a private, often residential social club of female students

sor·row *v.i.* to grieve, to feel sorrow

sorrow *n.* grief, sadness **sór·row·ful** *adj.*

sor·ry sor·ri·er sor·ri·est *adj.* feeling pity ‖ feeling sympathy ‖ feeling regret ‖ arousing pity or contempt

sort 1. *n.* a group having its own special qualities ‖ someone having the qualities characteristic of a group **out of sorts** a little unwell ‖ cross, in a bad humor **2.** *v.t.* to separate into groups having special qualities ‖ (with 'out') to select (one, or some) of a particular kind

so·so 1. *adj.* neither good nor bad, middling **2.** *adv.* passably ‖ not very well

souf·flé *n.* a light, baked dish made by adding whipped egg whites to a sweet or savory mixture

soul 1. *n.* the immortal part of man, as distinguished from his body ‖ the vital principle which moves and animates all life ‖ a human being **2. sóul·ful** *adj.* expressing or appealing to the emotions, often with sentimentality **sóul·less** *adj.* lacking nobility of mind ‖ deadening

soul food traditional food of American blacks in the South (now nationwide)

sound *v.t.* to cause to emit sound ‖ to pronounce, give sound to, articulate ‖ *v.i.* to emit sound ‖ to convey a specified impression

sound *n.* the sensation experienced when the brain interprets vibrations within the structure of the ear caused by rapid variations of air pressure ‖ such a sensation ‖ mere noise

sound *n.* a narrow channel of water ‖ a long, rather broad ocean inlet ‖ a probe for investigating esp. cavities in the body

sound 1. *adj.* not diseased or injured ‖ firm and solid ‖ wise, reliable ‖ financially satisfactory ‖ valid, convincing **2.** *adv.* soundly

sound *v.t.* to measure the depth of (usually water) ‖ to examine (the ocean floor etc.) with a lead that brings up samples ‖ to investigate (feelings or ideas) ‖ to examine (a person's body) with a sound

sound·ing *adj.* resonant ‖ making a sound

sound·ing *n.* the act of someone who sounds ‖ a measurement or investigation made by sounding ‖ (*pl.*) the depth of water in the sea or a river measured by sounding

sound·ly *adv.* wisely, prudently ‖ thoroughly ‖ deeply

sound·ness *n.* the state or quality of being sound

sound·proof 1. *adj.* impenetrable to sound waves **2.** *v.t.* to make soundproof **sóund·proof·ing** *n.*

soup *n.* a liquid food made by stewing ingredients such as meat, vegetables, fish **from soup to nuts** everything included **in the soup** in a difficult position

sour 1. *adj.* tasting or smelling acid, sharp or biting ‖ changed, e.g. by fermentation ‖ embittered ‖ (of soil) acid in reaction **2.** *v.t.* to make sour ‖ *v.i.* to become sour

source *n.* the spring of a stream ‖ the place or thing from which something begins or arises ‖ a person, book, document etc. consulted for information

souse 1. *n.* pickled food ‖ a preparation used for pickling ‖ a soaking ‖ a drunkard **2.** *v.t.* **sous·ing soused** to pickle ‖ to soak **soused** *adj.*

south 1. *adv.* toward the south **2.** *n.* one of the four cardinal points of the compass **3.** *adj.* facing south

south·er·ly *adj.* and *adv.* in or toward the south ‖ (of winds) from that direction

south·ern *adj.* situated, facing, or moving toward the south

south·paw *n.* a left-handed person, esp. a pitcher in baseball

South Pole the southern end of the earth's axis

south·ward *adv.* and *adj.* toward the south

sou·ve·nir *n.* something that serves to recall the past

sov·er·eign 1. *adj.* of or relating to a sovereign ‖ unlimited, absolute **2.** *n.* a person supreme in a state

sov·er·eign·ty *pl.* **sov·er·eign·ties** *n.* the state or quality of being sovereign ‖ a sovereign state

so·vi·et *n.* an elected governing council in the U.S.S.R. **So·vi·et** *adj.* of or relating to the U.S.S.R.

sow *n.* an adult female hog

sow sow·ing sow·ed sown sowed *v.t.* to scatter or bury (seed) on or in the soil ‖

to implant or spread (unrest, discontent etc.)

soy *n.* an Oriental piquant sauce made from soybeans

soy·bean *n.* a plant now cultivated in many parts of the world. The edible, highly nourishing seeds are used as a source of oil, flour and meal

spa *n.* a resort where there is a spring of mineral water ‖ a spring of mineral water

space 1. *n.* (without the article) that which contains and surrounds all material bodies ‖ the distance between two points, objects etc. ‖ a time interval ‖ (without the article) the region outside the earth's atmosphere ‖ a limited extent or area for a specific purpose **2.** *v.t.* **spac·ing spaced** to arrange at regular or suitable distances or time intervals

space·craft *pl.* **space·craft** *n.* a vehicle designed to travel beyond the earth's atmosphere

space·man *pl.* **space·men** *n.* an astronaut

space·ship *n.* a spacecraft

spa·cious *adj.* roomy

spade 1. *n.* a long-handled tool with a broad, flat blade, used for digging **to call a spade a spade** to name bluntly what one might choose to refer to by a euphemism **2.** *v.t.* **spad·ing spad·ed** to dig or cut with a spade

spade *n.* one of the four suits of playing cards ‖ a card of this suit

spa·ghet·ti *n.* pasta in the form of very thin, long, solid rods, a little thicker than vermicelli

span 1. *n.* a pair of animals used together, esp. a matched pair of horses

span 1. span·ning spanned *v.t.* to extend from side to side of or over ‖ to form an arch across **2.** *n.* the distance between two extremities ‖ the interval between two points in time ‖ the distance between tips of the little finger and thumb when the hand is extended

span·gle 1. *n.* a tiny disk of glittering material, esp. one sewn onto a garment **2. span·gling span·gled** *v.i.* to glitter with or as if with spangles

spank *v.t.* to smack or slap (someone) on

the bottom

spank·ing *n.* a series of slaps on the bottom with the open hand, to punish a child etc.

spar *n.* a mast, yard or boom of a ship

spar *v.i.* **spar·ring sparred** (boxing) to fight practice rounds ‖ to try to score verbally in argument

spare 1. *v.t.* **spar·ring spared** to conserve (one's strengtth or energy) ‖ to leave unhurt or undamaged, let go free, let live ‖ to refrain from injuring or distressing or punishing ‖ to omit, exclude ‖ to part temporarily with ‖ to use frugally or economically **2.** *adj.* held in reserve for future use ‖ meager, frugal **3.** *n.* a duplicate kept in reserve ‖ a spare part, esp. of a machine

spare·ribs pl. *n.* pork ribs with little meat left on them because the fleshy part has been cut off for bacon

spar·ing *adj.* using little

spark 1. *n.* a particle e.g. thrown off from a burning log, which is so hot that it emits light as well as heat ‖ a discharge of static electricity ‖ such a discharge in the spark plug of an internal-combustion engine **2.** *v.i.* to emit sparks ‖ *v.t.* (with 'off') to initiate (a process) as if by using a spark

spar·kle 1. *v.i.* **spar·kling spar·kled** to give off flashes of reflected light ‖ to give off flashes of wit or gaiety ‖ (of eyes) to show animation, intelligence, wit, pleasure, mischief etc. ‖ to be brilliant **2.** *n.* a flash of reflected light ‖ brilliance ‖ animation **spár·kler** *n.* an indoor firework **spár·kling** *adj.* glittering ‖ lively, vivacious ‖ (of wine) effervescent

spar·row *n.* a member of Passer, fam. Fringillidae, esp. the house sparrow

sparse *adj.* occurring at widely separated places or times ‖ not thickly grown **spar·si·ty** *n.*

spasm *n.* a sudden involuntary muscular contraction

spas·mod·ic *adj.* relating to, spasms ‖ intermittent, not sustained **spas·mód·i·cal·ly** *adv.*

spas·tic 1. *adj.* relating to spasms ‖ of a long-standing paralysis of some muscles,

esp. caused by injury at birth **2.** *n.* someone who suffers from such paralysis **spás·ti·cal·ly** *adv.*

spat 1. *n.* a brief, trifling quarrel ‖ a little splash **2.** **spat·ting spat·ted** *v.i.* to engage in a trifling quarrel

spat·ter 1. *v.t.* to project (a fluid, mud etc.) in drops ‖ *v.i.* to fall in drops **2.** *n.* a short fall of rain etc.

spat·u·la *n.* an instrument with a broad, flexable, usually dull-edged blade

spawn 1. *n.* the mass of eggs deposited by fish, bivalve mollusks and some other aquatic animals **2.** *v.t.* to produce ‖ to produce in great numbers ‖ *v.i.* to deposit spawn

spay *v.t.* to remove the ovaries of (an animal)

speak speak·ing spoke spo·ken *v.i.* to utter words ‖ to talk ‖ to make a speech ‖ to discuss ‖ *v.t.* to express (an idea) by speaking ‖ to use (a language) in speaking ‖ to utter orally **so to speak** if the expression is admissible **to speak one's mind** to be completely frank

speak·er *n.* someone who speaks ‖ someone who makes a speech **Speak·er** the presiding officer of the U.S. House of Representatives

speak·ing 1. *adj.* (of a likeness) close ‖ seeming to speak **2.** *n.* the act of one who speaks **generally speaking** usually, in most cases

spear 1. *n.* a thrusting, hurling or stabbing weapon consisting of a long shaft with a pointed blade **2.** *v.t.* to pierce with a spear, or as if with one

spear·mint *n.* common garden mint

spe·cial 1. *adj.* particular in kind ‖ superior ‖ specialized ‖ (of friends) close **2.** *n.* a train run in addition to the scheduled trains ‖ a special edition ‖ something specially singled out and featured

spe·cial·ist *n.* someone who devotes himself to a particular branch of his profession

spe·cial·i·za·tion *n.* a specializing or being specialized

spe·cial·ize spe·cial·iz·ing spe·cial·ized *v.i.* to restrict one's studies to a particular branch or field ‖ to become specialized ‖ to adapt for a particular purpose ‖ *v.t.* to restrict, to limit

spe·cial·ly *adv.* with a special intention

spe·cial·ty pl. **spe·cial·ties** *n.* something in which one has special skill or special interest

spe·cies pl. **spe·cies** *n.* a group of individuals closely related in structure, capable of breeding within the group but not normally outside it

spe·cif·ic *adj.* clearly distinguished, stated or understood ‖ characteristic of something **spe·cif·i·cal·ly** *adv.*

spec·i·fi·ca·tion *n.* the act of specifying a detailed item, something specified ‖ (often pl.) a list of materials and work required for a project to be carried out

spec·i·fy spec·i·fy·ing spec·i·fied *v.t.* to name or mention explicitly ‖ to include in a specification

spec·i·men *n.* a part or individual taken to typify the whole or the class, a sample

spe·cious *adj.* apparently sound and reasonable, but fallacious

speck 1. *n.* a small bit, a particle ‖ a small spot or stain 2. *v.t.* to mark with specks

speck·le 1. *n.* a small spot or mark 2. *v.t.* **speck·ling speck·led** to mark with speckles

spec·ta·cle *n.* a display, usually on a large scale, which attracts attention ‖ (pl.) a pair of lenses, designed to correct certain defects of vision or to protect the eyes **spéc·ta·cled** *adj.* wearing spectacles

spec·tac·u·lar 1. *adj.* impressive to see ‖ of a kind to attract attention 2. *n.* a long, lavish television show

spec·ta·tor *n.* an onlooker

spec·ter *n.* the spirit of someone dead made visible ‖ a threatening vision of something to come

spec·trum pl. **spec·tra, spec·trums** *n.* an arrangement of the components of a beam, wave band or sound separated and displayed in order according to some varying factor ‖ the band of colors into which a beam of light is decomposed by a prism

spec·u·late spec·u·lat·ing spec·u·lat·ed *v.i.*

to consider possibilities and probabilities ‖ to undertake commercial transactions involving serious risk for the sake of possible large winnings

spec·u·la·tion *n.* theorizing, conjecture ‖ commercial activity involving serious risk in the hope of large profits

spec·u·la·tive *adj.* of or concerning speculation

spec·u·la·tor *n.* someone who speculates

speech *n.* the ability to speak ‖ the act of speaking, esp. an address to an audience ‖ manner of speaking

speech·less *adj.* without the ability to speak ‖ temporarily unable to speak ‖ silent

speed *n.* rate of motion ‖ velocity ‖ the rate at which something proceeds or is done

speed speed·ing sped speed·ed *v.i.* to move at a high speed ‖ to drive a vehicle more rapidly than is safe or legal ‖ *v.t.* to cause to move at a high speed **to speed up** to increase the speed of

speed (slang) a stimulant drug, esp. methamphetamine

speed·i·ly *adv.* with speed, quickly

speed·i·ness *n.* the state or quality of being speedy

speed·om·e·ter *n.* a device that shows the speed at which a vehicle is traveling

speed·up *n.* the act of speeding up

speed·y speed·i·er speed·i·est *adj.* swift ‖ prompt

spe·le·ol·o·gy *n.* the study of caves ‖ spelunking

spell 1. *v.t.* to relieve (a person) by taking a turn at work 2. *n.* a turn at work, a shift ‖ a short period ‖ a bout or period (of illness)

spell spell·ing spelled *v.t.* to name or write the letters of (a word) in order ‖ *v.i.* to form words by letters ‖ to explain in full detail

spell *n.* an incantation ‖ the power to charm

spell·bind spell·bind·ing spell·bound *v.t.* to put a spell upon ‖ to enchant **spéll·bind·er** *n.* a speaker who has strong power over an audience **spell·bound** *adj.* entranced

spell·ing *n.* orthography

spend spend·ing spent *v.t.* to pay out (money) for purchases ‖ to exhaust (oneself) ‖ to pass (time) ‖ *v.i.* to pay out

spend·thrift 1. *n.* someone who spends wastefully **2.** *adj.* spending too much

spent *adj.* exhausted ‖ devoid of further energy ‖ (of shells, cartridges etc.) exploded

sperm *n.* semen ‖ a spermatozoon

sper·ma·to·zo·on *pl.* **sper·ma·to·zo·a** *n.* a motile male reproductive haploid cell

spew *v.t.* to vomit ‖ to pour out with disgust

sphere the solid figure generated when a circle rotates about a diameter, every point on its surface being thus equidistant from the center of this circle ‖ a limited domain within which something is effective ‖ a range of knowledge

spher·ic *adj.* spherical **spher·i·cal** *adj.* shaped like a sphere ‖ relating to a sphere

sphinc·ter *n.* a ring-shaped muscle which is able to close or narrow an orifice **sphínc·ter·al** *adj.*

spice 1. *n.* any of many vegetable substances used to impart their strong and aromatic flavors to food ‖ something which stimulates agreeably **2.** *v.t.* **spic·ing spiced** to flavor by adding spice ‖ to make more interesting

spic·y spic·i·er spic·i·est *adj.* having the flavor of spices ‖ stimulating erotically

spi·der *n.* an animal having eight legs, a large unsegmented abdomen, usually four pairs of compound eyes, and spinnerets from which a very fine thread is drawn and woven into a web

spi·der·y *adj.* resembling the appearance of a spider

spig·ot *n.* a device which controls the flow of a fluid from a container ‖ a plug for the vent of a barrel

spike 1. *n.* a thin, sharp-pointed piece of metal, or other hard material ‖ a pointed nail set into the soles of climbing boots or running shoes ‖ a large nail used to fasten a rail to a railroad tie ‖ an eaear of grain, e.g. wheat **2.** **spik·ing spiked** *v.t.* to furnish, fasten or pierce with a spike ‖ to add liquor to (a nonalcoholic drink)

spill 1. *n.* **spill·ing spilled, spilt** *v.t.* to waste

(a fluid etc.) by permitting it to fall out of from its container ‖ to shed (blood) in violence ‖ to divulge ‖ *v.i.* to escape from a container and so be lost ‖ (with 'out') to overflow **2.** *n.* a fall from a saddle, vehicle

spin 1. **spin·ning spun** *v.i.* to turn rapidly about an internal axis ‖ to engage in the process of drawing out and twisting cotton, silk etc. into a long, continuous thread ‖ (of spiders and silkworms) to secrete a thread or threads ‖ to move very fast ‖ *v.t.* to cause to spin ‖ to draw out and twist into a long, continuous thread ‖ to tell (a story) at great length **2.** *n.* the act of spinning ‖ a rapid rotating movement

spin·ach *n.* a herbaceous annual. Its dark green, crisp leaves are cooked as a vegetable

spi·nal *adj.* pertaining to, or like the spinal column, spinal cord or spinal canal

spin·dle 1. *n.* a thin cylindrical rod which serves as an axis of rotation or itself rotates **2.** *v.i.* **spin·dling spin·dled** to grow long and thin ‖ *v.t.* to impale on a spindle

spin·dly spin·dli·er spin·dli·est *adj.* very long and thin

spine *n.* the spinal column ‖ a sharp-pointed outgrowth, e.g. from the stem or leaf of a athistle ‖ a similar protective outgrowth, e.g. one of the quills of a porcupine ‖ the back of a bound book

spined *adj.* having a spine or spines

spine·less *adj.* invertebrate ‖ having no spines or thorns ‖ without strength of character

spin·et *n.* a small stringed musical instrument resembling a harpsichord ‖ a small organ

spin·na·ker *n.* a large triangular sail, used when running before the wind

spi·nose *adj.* spinous (covered with spines)

spi·nous *adj.* full of spines ‖ having the form of a spine

spin·ster *n.* an unmarried woman **spín·ster·hood** *n.*

spin·y spin·i·er spin·i·est *adj.* covered with spines ‖ shaped like a spine or thorn

spi·ral 1. *adj.* of a curve which continuously changes its plane, and sometimes its curvature, in relation to a fixed axis ‖ curving in this way 2. *n.* a single coil or turn in something spiral ‖ a descent or an ascent in a spiral path 3. **spi·ral·ing spi·raled** *v.i.* to move, esp. to ascend or descend, in a spiral ‖ *v.t.* to cause to move in a spiral

spire *n.* a tall thin structure surmounting a tower, esp. of a church, and being of conical or pyramidal form

spir·it *n.* the intelligent or immaterial part of man as distinguished from the body ‖ a disembodied soul ‖ a supernatural being ‖ the emotional attitude or frame of mind characteristic of a group of people ‖ the essential character of something ‖ cheerful or assertive liveliness ‖ (often pl.) mood or temperamental state ‖ (esp. pl.) liquor of high alcoholic content 1. *adj.* of spirits or spiritualism 2. *v.t.* (with 'off', 'away') to cause (something) to be removed unseen, with mysterious rapidity **spir·it·ed** *adj.* lively

spir·it·ism *n.* spiritualism ‖ the belief that natural objects have indwelling spirits **spir·it·ist** *n.*

spir·it·less *adj.* having no animation ‖ lacking boldness

spir·it·u·al 1. *adj.* relating to the soul or spirit ‖ relating to religious or sacred matters 2. *n.* a religious song

spir·it·u·al·ism *n.* the doctrine that the spirit, surviving after the death of the body, can communicate with persons still living **spir·it·u·al·ist** *n.* a person who practices spiritualism

spir·it·u·al·ize spir·it·u·al·iz·ing spir·it·u·al·ized *v.t.* to make spiritual ‖ to give a spiritual meaning to

spit 1. **spit·ting spit, spat** *v.t.* to get rid of (saliva etc.) from the mouth ‖ to emit or eject as though spitting ‖ to express anger ‖ *v.i.* to eject saliva from the mouth 2. *n.* saliva

spit 1. *n.* a metal skewer on which meat to be roasted is impaled ‖ a shoal or reef 2. *v.t.* **spit·ting spit·ted** to fix (meat) on a spit

spite 1. *n.* animosity towards a person **in**

spite of regardless of 2. *v.t.* **spit·ing spit·ed** to injure out of spite **spite·ful** *adj.*

spit·fire *n.* someone very quick to become angry

spit·tle *n.* saliva, spit ‖ the secretion of some insects

spit·toon *n.* a flat vessel on the floor to receive spit

splash 1. *v.t.* to cause (liquid) to move through the air in separate drops ‖ to cause (something) to agitate and scatter a liquid ‖ to apply (paint etc.) in a careless or lavish way ‖ to make a display of (money, news) ‖ *v.i.* to agitate a liquid and scatter it 2. *n.* the sound of splashing ‖ the liquid which is splashed ‖ a bright patch of color **to make a splash** to make an ostentatious display

splash·down *n.* the landing of a spacecraft or missile on a body of water ‖ the moment of this landing

splash·y splash·i·er splash·i·est *adj.* causing splashes ‖ very showy

splat *n.* a single, broad, flat piece of wood

splat·ter 1. *v.t.* to spatter ‖ *v.i.* to become spattered 2. *n.* a spatter

splay 1. *n.* a sloping surface or bevel ‖ a spreading 2. *adj.* turned outwards, broad and flat 3. *v.t.* to spread ‖ to bevel ‖ *v.i.* to become splayed

spleen *n.* a soft fleshy organ chiefly concerned with the purification of blood **spleen·ful** *adj.*

splen·did *adj.* magnificent, gorgeous, sumptuous

splen·dor *n.* great brilliance ‖ display of magnificence

splice 1. *v.t.* **splic·ing spliced** to unite two parts of the same rope by interweaving the strands of one end into those of another part ‖ to join together the ends of (two pieces of wood) by making them overlap and fastening the overlaps together ‖ to join (film, tape etc.) at the ends 2. *n.* splicing

splint 1. *n.* a strip of wood etc. which, bound to a limb, keeps broken bones from moving apart 2. *v.t.* to secure with a splint

splin·ter 1. *n.* a thin, sharp piece of wood etc. broken or split off **2.** *v.t.* to break or split into thin, sharp pieces **3.** *adj.* (of a political or religious group) broken off from and independent of a larger organization

splin·ter·y *adj.* of or like a splinter

split 1. split·ting split *v.t.* to divide, separate, cleave, burst or force apart the layers of (a solid) ‖ to separate the two parts of (an infinitive) by an adverb, as in 'to carelessly write' ‖ to break (a molecule) into atoms ‖ (phys.) to produce nuclear fission in (an atom) ‖ *v.i.* to become divided, separated, cleft or forced apart ‖ to separate into groups holding opposing views ‖ to part **2.** *n.* the result of splitting ‖ a separation into groups holding different views **3.** *adj.* divided into layers ‖ separated ‖ torn by bursting

splotch 1. *n.* an irregular patch of paint, stain etc. **2.** *v.t.* to mark with splotches **splótch·y splotch·i·er splotch·i·est** *adj.*

splurge 1. *n.* a showy effect, lavish spending **2.** *v.i.* **splurg·ing splurged** to make a splurge

splut·ter 1. *v.i.* to speak rapidly with bad articulation ‖ (e.g. of a car engine) to make a sound resembling this manner of speaking ‖ to splash, spatter **2.** *n.* the sound of spluttering

spoil spoil·ing spoiled, spoilt *v.t.* to take away the pleasure from ‖ to damage or ruin ‖ to impair, detract from ‖ to injure (a child) by overindulgence or too much leniency ‖ to pamper ‖ *v.i.* to become unfit for use

spoil *n.* (esp. *pl.*) goods taken from a defeated enemy ‖ goods acquired by theft

spoil·age *n.* waste through decay ‖ goods spoiled

spoke 1. *n.* a radial rod transmitting stress from the rim to the hub of a wheel ‖ a rung of a ladder **2.** *v.t.* **spok·ing spoked** to furnish with spokes

spo·ken *adj.* oral as opposed to written

spokes·per·son *n.* one who speaks for another person, a group, or a cause, esp. for public consumption

sponge 1. *n.* the macerated, highly porous, elastic, spongin skeleton of a water dwelling animal ‖ a sterile cotton gauze used for sponging and wiping in surgical operations ‖ a heavy drinker ‖ someone who tries to live parasitically **2. spong·ing sponged** *v.t.* to moisten or wipe with a wet sponge ‖ to absorb with a sponge ‖ *v.i.* to prey on other people's good nature parasitically

spong·er *n.* a person who harvests sponges ‖ someone who lives parasitically

spong·i·ness *n.* the state or quality of being spongy

spong·y spong·i·er spong·i·est *adj.* having the porous, absorbent, elastic properties of a sponge

spon·sor 1. *n.* someone who accepts personal responsibility for another ‖ a godparent ‖ a firm paying for a broadcast during which time will be allowed to advertise **2.** *v.t.* to act as sponsor for **spon·so·ri·al** *adj.* **spón·sor·ship** *n.*

spon·ta·ne·i·ty *n.* the quality of being spontaneous

spon·ta·ne·ous *adj.* arising from impulse, not premeditated

spoof 1. *v.i.* to fool, pretend ‖ *v.t.* to deceive **2.** *n.* a hoax ‖ a light, but telling parody

spook *n.* a specter ‖ an intelligence agent **spóok·y spook·i·er spook·i·est** *adj.*

spool 1. *n.* a short cylinder on which thread or yarn is wound ‖ a reel **2.** *v.t.* to wind on a spool

spoon 1. *n.* a utensil consisting of a shallow bowl at the end of a handle, used for eating liquid food **2.** *v.t.* to gather up with a spoon

spoon-fed *adj.* indulged ‖ fed with a spoon

spoon·ful pl. **spoon·fuls** *n.* the amount a spoon will hold

spoor 1. *n.* the footprints and other signs of the passage of an animal **2.** *v.i.* to follow a spoor

spo·rad·ic *adj.* occurring at infrequent and irregular intervals **spo·rád·i·cal·ly** *adv.*

spore 1. *n.* a minute one-celled reproductive body produced usually by lower forms of plant life **2.** *v.i.* **spor·ing spored** to bear or develop spores

sport 1. *n.* the playing of games or participation in competitive pastimes involving physical exertion and skill ‖ any such game or pastime ‖ *(pl.)* athletics **2.** *v.i.* to play ‖ to joke ‖ to gambol, frolic **3.** *adj.* sports

sport·ing *adj.* pertaining to sport ‖ sportsmanlike in conduct

spor·tive *adj.* playful

sports·man *pl.* **sports·men** *n.* a person who practices a sport ‖ a person who behaves generously in defeat or victory

sports·man·ly *adj.*

sports·man·like *adj.* showing qualities of a sportsman

sports·man·ship *n.* generous behavior befitting a good sportsman

sport·y **sport·i·er** **sport·i·est** *adj.* sportsmanlike ‖ suitable for good sport

spot 1. *n.* a small disfiguring mark of dirt etc. ‖ a dark area on the face of the sun, moon or a planet ‖ a blemish on a good reputation ‖ a situation **in a spot** in a difficult situation **on the spot** at once ‖ on the site where something happened **2.** **spot·ting** **spot·ted** *v.t.* to look out for with the purpose of recording information ‖ to mark or discolor with spots ‖ to blemish ‖ to pick out beforehand ‖ to catch sight of ‖ *v.i.* to become stained or soiled ‖ to cause a spot **3.** *adj.* made at random

spot·less *adj.* irreproachable ‖ perfectly clean

spot·light *n.* a bright, narrow beam of light ‖ a lamp used to project such a beam ‖ public attention

spot·ted *adj.* marked with spots

spot·ti·ness *n.* the state or quality of being spotty

spot·ty **spot·ti·er** **spot·ti·est** *adj.* marked with spots ‖ occurring in spots ‖ irregular

spouse *n.* a husband or wife

spout 1. *v.t.* to force (a fluid) out of an aperture under pressure ‖ to utter volubly and at some length ‖ *v.i.* to gush **2.** *n.* a tubular projection for conducting e.g. rain off a roof, or pouring e.g. tea from a teapot ‖ a column of fluid ejected by pressure

sprain 1. *v.t.* to injure (a muscle or joint)

2. *n.* the injury thus caused

sprawl 1. *v.i.* to slump with the limbs stretched out in an ungainly way ‖ *v.t.* to stretch out (the limbs) in an ungainly and relaxed way **2.** *n.* the posture of sprawling

spray 1. *n.* liquid moving in the air in the form of fine drops ‖ the stream of fine drops ejected by an atomizer ‖ a device for ejecting such a stream **2.** *v.t.* to shoot out or apply in the form of spray

spray *n.* a small branch with attached leaves, flowers etc., used as a decoration

spread 1. **spread·ing** **spread** *v.t.* to open out more or less fully ‖ to display for sale ‖ (esp. with 'out') to cause to occupy more space by unfurling or smoothing out ‖ to distribute in a layer ‖ to distribute ‖ to extend, stretch (esp. limbs) ‖ to disseminate ‖ to make known (news etc.) ‖ to push apart ‖ *v.i.* to become widely distributed or scattered ‖ to increase esp. in growth or numbers **2.** *n.* the act of spreading or being spread ‖ a soft food for spreading on bread etc. ‖ a bedspread ‖ increase in girth ‖ wingspan ‖ two facing pages used for display

spread eagle the representation of an eagle with legs and wings outspread, e.g. the emblem of the U.S.A.

spread-ea·gle 1. *adj.* like a spread eagle **2.** *v.t.* **spread-ea·gling** **spread-ea·gled** to straddle or extend over or across (something) so as to have the arms and legs stretched out or sprawling

spree *n.* an outing involving lavish spending or drinking

sprig 1. *n.* a short or pretty little spray from a shrub or tree **2.** *v.t.* **sprig·ging** **sprigged** to adorn with sprigs

spright·li·ness *n.* the state or quality of being sprightly

spring 1. *n.* the action of springing ‖ the ability to spring ‖ an instance of springing ‖ the season of the year following winter and preceding summer ‖ a place where water or natural oil is forced out of the ground by its own pressure ‖ resilience ‖ a device of bent or coiled metal **2.** *adj.* supported on springs ‖ coming from a spring

spring spring·ing sprang sprung sprung
v.i. to come, appear or arise suddenly and
quickly ‖ to move as a result of elasticity
‖ to be descended ‖ to originate ‖ (of winds,
storms etc., with 'up') to begin to blow,
be felt or have effect ‖ to explode ‖ *v.t.* to
jump over or across ‖ to release the spring
of ‖ to develop (a leak) suddenly

spring·y spring·i·er spring·i·est *adj.* resil-
ient ‖ having many springs

sprin·kle 1. sprin·kling sprin·kled *v.t.* to
scatter in separate drops or particles ‖ to
place (esp. small quantities of something)
at wide intervals ‖ to vary or intersperse
‖ to rain slightly **2.** *n.* the act or result of
sprinkling

sprin·kling *n.* a small quantity or number
distributed here and there

sprint 1. *v.i.* to run for a short distance at
the greatest speed of which one is capable **2.** *n.* a run of this kind ‖ a short-
distance race

sprite *n.* a fairy, an elf

sprock·et *n.* a tooth on a wheel's rim,
engaging with the links of a chain

sprout 1. *v.t.* to put out young growth ‖ to
germinate ‖ *v.t.* to grow (something new)
‖ to let (e.g. a moustache) grow **2.** *n.* a
shoot on a plant ‖ *(pl.)* Brussels sprouts
‖ a new growth from a bud, seed etc.

spruce 1. *adj.* very neat, clean, tidy ‖ trim
2. *v.t.* **spruc·ing spruced** (with 'up') to
make very neat, tidy or trim ‖ neat and
trim

spruce *n.* a genus of quick-growing
conifers

spry spry·er, spri·er spry·est, spri·est
adj. (esp. of old people) quick in movement and in thought

spume 1. *n.* a mass of bubbles formed
from a liquid **2. spum·ing spumed** *v.i.*
to foam or discharge bubbles

spu·mous *adj.* of, like or covered with
spume

spum·y spum·i·er spum·i·est *adj.*
spumous

spunk *n.* spirited courage ‖ punk

spunk·y spunk·i·er spunk·i·est *adj.*
courageous, having spirit

spur 1. *n.* a device worn on the heel of a
riding boot for pressing into a horse's
flanks to force its pace ‖ a climbing iron
on the spur of the moment impulsively, without previous thought or plans **2.**
spur·ring spurred *v.t.* to use a spur on
(a horse) ‖ to cause to make a great effort

spu·ri·ous *adj.* having the appearance of
being genuine, but without being so ‖
illegitimate, bastard

spurn *v.t.* to reject with contempt

spurt, spirt 1. *v.i.* (of a fluid) to shoot out
suddenly in a jet ‖ (of a person) to make
sudden, violent effort, esp. in a race **2.**
n. a sudden shooting out of liquid in a jet
‖ a sudden short burst of activity or
energy

sput·ter 1. *v.i.* to splutter **2.** *n.* a sputtering ‖ the sound of sputtering ‖ rapid,
confused speech

spu·tum pl. **spu·ta, spu·tums** *n.* material expelled from the respiratory passages

spy pl. **spies** *n.* a person instructed to act
secretly in gathering information

spy spy·ing spied *v.t.* catch sight of ‖ to
make a secret investigation of ‖ *v.i.* to act
as a spy

spy·glass *n.* a portable terrestrial telescope

squab 1. *adj.* fat ‖ unfledged **2.** *n.* an
unfledged pigeon

squab·ble 1. *v.i.* **squab·bling squab·bled**
to engage in a noisy but not very serious
quarrel **2.** *n.* a not serious quarrel

squad *n.* a small number of men organized
to act together in a military maneuver ‖
an athletic team

squad·ron *n.* an air force unit

squal·id *adj.* filthy ‖ wretched, morally
degrading

squall 1. *v.i.* to cry loudly and discordant-
ly **2.** *n.* a sudden high wind ‖ a tearful
screaming etc. **squal·ly** *adj.* stormy

squal·or *n.* the state or quality of being
squalid

squan·der *v.t.* to use up unwisely

square squar·ing squared *v.t.* to make
square ‖ to cause to be at right angles
‖ to cause to conform, make consistent
(esp. with a 'off') to mark out in squares
‖ to pay (a bill) ‖ to multiply (a number

or quantity) by itself ‖ *v.i.* (with 'with') to agree or conform exactly ‖ to pay debts or bills

square 1. *adj.* having the shape of a square ‖ being at right angles ‖ leaving no balance ‖ arranged in good order **2.** *adv.* frankly, honestly ‖ directly

square *n.* a plane figure having four equal rectilinear sides, each adjacent pair forming a right angle ‖ a number which is the product of another number multiplied by itself ‖ a person who is ignorant of the latest in slang, styles, fads etc.

squash *n.* a genus of gourd plants grown for their fruit ‖ one of these fruits

squash 1. *v.t.* to press into a shapeless state ‖ to suppress **2.** *n.* a closely packed crowd ‖ a game for two or four players played with a special racket and soft ball ‖ a squashing **3.** *adv.* so as to squash

squash·y squash·i·er squash·i·est *adj.* easily squashed ‖ looking squashed ‖ mushy

squat 1. squat·ting squat·ted *v.i.* to lower the body into a sitting posture, supporting it by the thigh muscles only ‖ to settle on land or in premises without any legal right to do so ‖ *v.t.* refl. to cause (oneself) to assume a squatting position **2.** *adj.* short and thick ‖ being in a squatting position **3.** *n.* the posture of squatting

squat·ter *n.* a settler occupying government land in order to acquire legal title to it ‖ a person who occupies (esp. premises) without legal title

squaw *n.* a North American Indian woman or wife

squawk 1. *v.i.* to utter harsh, loud cries, expressing angry complaint **2.** *n.* the sound of squawking

squeak 1. *v.i.* (of mice etc.) to utter squeaks ‖ to get by with a narrow margin ‖ *v.t.* to utter with a squeak **2.** *n.* a high-pitched, short cry of little volume **squéak·i·ly** *adv.* **squéak·i·ness** *n.* **squéak·y squeak·i·er squeak·i·est** *adj.* squeaking

squeal 1. *n.* a prolonged, very shrill cry, uttered under intense stress, fear etc. **2.** *v.i.* to become an informer

squeam·ish *adj.* affected with nausea ‖ easily disgusted ‖ excessively scrupulous

squee·gee 1. *n.* a strip of rubber mounted at the end of a long handle, used to sweep a surface clear of water **2.** *v.t.* **squee·gee·ing squee·geed** to sweep, smooth out etc. with a squeegee

squeeze 1. squeez·ing squeezed *v.t.* to exert pressure on ‖ to force into a place by pressing ‖ to cause (people) to occupy less space than is comfortable ‖ to press (a fruit) so as to expel the juice ‖ to get by force or unfair means ‖ to hug ‖ *v.i.* to exert pressure ‖ to force one's way by compressing oneself **2.** *n.* a squeezing ‖ a hug ‖ a small quantity of something (e.g. juice) obtained by pressing

squelch 1. *v.t.* to tread heavily on (mud, wet snow etc.) ‖ to crush with a very firm refusal or rebuke etc. **2.** *n.* the sucking sound made when one walks over soft wet ground ‖ a silencing remark

squid *pl.* **squid, squids** *n.* a member of marine cephalopod mollusks having ten arms and an internal shell

squint 1. *v.i.* to be crosseyed ‖ to look out of the corner of the eye ‖ to look through almost closed eyelids **2.** *n.* strabismus ‖ a look out of the corner of the eye **3.** *adj.* affected with strabismus ‖ oblique

squirm 1. *v.i.* to contort the body in little writhing movements ‖ to have feelings of shame and discomfort **2.** *n.* the act of squirming **squírm·y** *adj.*

squir·rel *n.* a widely distributed rodent mammal, the red squirrel, the gray squirrel

squirt 1. *v.t.* to shoot a thin stream of (fluid) from a small orifice ‖ to wet ‖ *v.i.* to be forced out in this way **2.** *n.* the act or an instance of squirting ‖ a thin stream of fluid forced out under pressure ‖ a pretentious boy or man

stab 1. stab·bing stabbed *v.t.* to wound by piercing with a knife or other pointed weapon ‖ to inflict sharp emotional pain on **2.** *n.* a thrust made with or as if with a pointed weapon ‖ (usually with 'at') an attempt to do something ‖ a sudden sensation of pain, anguish, envy etc. **a stab in**

the back a treacherous attack

sta·bile 1. *adj.* stationary ‖ not fluctuating ‖ resisting decomposition **2.** *n.* an abstract sculpture

sta·bil·i·ty *pl.* **sta·bil·i·ties** *n.* the quality or state of being stable

sta·bi·li·za·tion *n.* a stabilizing or being stabilized

sta·bi·lize sta·bi·liz·ing sta·bi·lized *v.t.* to render stable ‖ to prevent from changing

stá·bi·liz·er *n.* something that stabilizes

sta·ble 1. *n.* (often *pl.*) a building in which horses are housed, or a similar building for cattle ‖ a group of racehorses belonging to a particular owner **2.** *v.t.* **sta·bling sta·bled** to put or keep in a stable

stable *adj.* remaining or able to remain unchanged in form, structure, character etc. ‖ permanent, enduring ‖ firm of purpose

stack 1. *n.* a man-made pile, usually conical or rectangular, of hay, straw etc. ‖ a more or less orderly pile of things ‖ a tall vertical pipe or chimney ‖ (often *pl.*) a large quantity **2.** *v.t.* to make a stack of ‖ to load with stacks of something ‖ *v.i.* to form a stack

sta·di·um *pl.* **sta·diums** *n.* an athletic field surrounded wholly or in part by a tiered structure seating spectators ‖ (*pl.*) **sta·di·a** a stage in development

staff 1. *pl.* **staffs, staves** *n.* a stick, pole etc. used as support in walking or climbing, or as a weapon ‖ (*pl.* **staffs**) a body of people working for a chief authority ‖ ((*pl.* **staffs**) the personnel of an organization ‖ a tall pole supporting a flag ‖ a set of five horizontal lines on or between which symbols of notes are written or printed **2.** *adj.* of or relating to a staff of people **3.** *v.t.* to furnish with a staff of people

stag 1. *n.* the adult male of certain deer ‖ a man who attends a social gathering unaccompanied by a woman **2.** *adj.* for men only **3.** *v.i.* **stag·ging stagged 4.** *adv.* as a stag (unaccompanied man)

stage 1. *n.* a large, raised platform on which plays etc. are performed before an audience ‖ a platform for holding the objects to be observed through a microscope ‖ a point, period or level in a progressive change or development ‖ a section of a rocket containing a rocket engine or engines ‖ a stagecoach **2.** *v.t.* **stag·ing staged** to put (a play) on the stage or organize (a similar entertainment) ‖ to conceive and carry out (something) in a surprising, dramatic way

stage·coach *n.* a horse-drawn coach carrying passengers and goods

stage·struck *adj.* fascinated with the stage

stag·ger 1. *v.i.* to walk with uncertain, uneven steps ‖ *v.t.* to cause to reel under a blow ‖ to arrange (things) in oblique or zigzag fashion **2.** *n.* a staggering movement ‖ a zigzag or oblique arrangement

stag·eing *n.* the act or manner of putting on a play on the stage ‖ scaffolding ‖ in-flight separation of the first stage of a missile

stag·nan·cy *n.* the quality or state of being stagnant

stag·nant *adj.* not in motion or flowing ‖ foul ‖ dull through lack of variety of activity

stag·nate stag·nat·ing stag·nat·ed *v.i.* (of a liquid or gas) to be motionless or cease to flow ‖ to become foul ‖ to become dull **stag·na·tion** *n.*

stag·y, stage·y stag·i·er stag·i·est *adj.* showily exaggerated

staid *adj.* set in steady habits, rather dull

stain 1. *v.t.* to make an unwanted spot on the surface of ‖ to color by using a pigment which soaks in ‖ to spoil, taint (a reputation etc.) **2.** *n.* the colored area resulting from staining ‖ a moral taint etc.

stair *n.* a constructed step or one of a set of such steps ‖ (*pl.*) such a set of steps

stair·case *n.* a flight of stairs together with its supporting and protecting structures

stair·way *n.* a flight or several flights of stairs

stake 1. *n.* a length of esp. wood, pointed at one end used as a marker, support etc. ‖ the post to which a person was bound for burning to death ‖ a share or interest in something jointly owned ‖ money deposited as a wager **at stake** being risked **1.** *v.t.* **stak·ing staked** to support, protect, mark out, secure ‖ to wager ‖ to back (someone or something) financially

sta·lac·tite *n.* a deposit of calcium carbonate resembling an icicle, formed when water has dripped very slowly from the roof of a limestone cave **stal·ac·tit·ic** *adj.*

sta·lag·mite *n.* a deposit of calcium carbonate somewhat like an inverted stalactite, standing on the floor of a limestone cave **stal·ag·mit·ic** *adj.*

stale 1. *adj.* impaired in texture, taste etc. through age ‖ no longer fresh ‖ (of bread) being a day or more old ‖ having lost novelty and interest ‖ (of an athlete etc.) in a deteriorated condition through too much or too little activity **2. stal·ing staled** *v.i.* to become stale ‖ *v.t.* to make stale

stale·mate *n.* (chess) a position in which one player not in check cannot move without putting his king in check ‖ a set of circumstances in which no progress can be made

stalk *n.* the main stem of a herbaceous plant

stalk 1. *v.i.* to walk stiffly, as wading birds do ‖ to pursue e.g. deer in such a way as not to be seen, heard or scented by them ‖ *v.t.* to pursue (deer etc.) by stalking **2.** *n.* a stiff gait ‖ the act of stalking deer etc.

stall 1. *n.* a compartment in a barn or stable, housing one animal ‖ a booth or table used for displaying goods on sale (e.g. in a market) ‖ a fixed seat in the choir of a church **2.** *v.t.* to put or keep (an animal) in a stall ‖ to cause (an engine) to stop because of overloading or insufficient fuel ‖ *v.i.* (of an engine or vehicle) to stop by being stalled ‖ to stick fast, e.g. in mud or snow

stall 1. *v.i.* to talk or act evasively in the hope of delaying something or putting someone off ‖ *v.t.* (esp. with 'off') to get rid of or delay by evasion **2.** *n.* a trick used to get out of making a decision

stal·lion *n.* an uncastrated male horse

stal·wart 1. *adj.* unshaken in determination or loyalty by risks or difficulties ‖ of strong, sturdy build **2.** *n.* a zealous supporter of a cause

sta·men *n.* the male organ of a flower

stam·i·na *n.* capacity for resisting fatigue or disease

stam·mer 1. *v.i.* to speak with difficulty, repeating sounds and syllables **2.** *n.* the affliction or habit of stammering

stamp *v.t.* to make (a mark) by pressure ‖ to affix postage stamps to ‖ to bring (one's foot) down heavily ‖ to mark out, identify ‖ to affect so deeply as to change permanently ‖ (with 'out') to crush, extinguish etc. **1.** *n.* the act of stamping ‖ a device used to impress a mark ‖ the mark made by such a device ‖ an official mark, seal etc. ‖ a postage stamp

stam·pede 1. *n.* a sudden flight of frightened animals ‖ any spontaneous mass action **2. stam·ped·ing stam·ped·ed** *v.i.* to move or take part in a stampede ‖ *v.t.* to cause to stampede

stance *n.* a way of standing

stanch *adj.* staunch

stanch *v.t.* to prevent or stop the flow of (blood) from a wound

stand 1. stand·ing stood *v.i.* to be or remain motionless and more or less vertical ‖ to rise to such a position ‖ to be or remain erect and supported on its base ‖ to maintain a position, resolve etc. ‖ to cease walking, halt ‖ to remain unchanged ‖ to remain valid or effective ‖ *v.t.* to place in an erect position ‖ to support without deformation ‖ to undergo ‖ to endure **to stand a chance** to have a possibility of succeeding, winning etc. **to stand for** to represent ‖ to tolerate **to stand on (or upon)** to insist on the observing or respecting of **to stand one's ground** to maintain one's position against opposition **to stand pat** to refuse to contemplate changes **to stand up for** to defend against opposition or from censure **to stand up to** to resist successfully **2.** *n.* a stopping of motion or progress ‖ a position, maintained with regard to some issue ‖ a piece of furniture for holding something specified ‖ a raised structure used to accommodate spectators, members of a

band etc. ‖ a temporary stall for exhibiting wares to be sold or looked at ‖ a place where public vehicles are parked while waiting for passengers ‖ a witness stand
stand·ard 1. *n.* a model to be followed or imitated ‖ a degree of quality, level of achievement etc. ‖ an established unit of weight or other measurement ‖ the basis of value in a monetary system ‖ the flag of a regiment ‖ a vertical supporting pillar, post etc. **2.** *adj.* accepted as a model to be followed or imitated ‖ of the ordinary type, without extra or unusual features
stand·ard·i·za·tion *n.* a standardizing or being standardized
stand·ard·ize **stand·ard·iz·ing** **stand·ard·ized** *v.t.* to make conform to a standard ‖ to test against a standard
stand·by 1. *n.* someone or something that can be relied on in an emergency **2.** *adj.* ready to utilize time or space that may become available
stand-in *n.* any person who is a substitute
stand·ing 1. *n.* reputation or status, esp. when high ‖ duration **2.** *adj.* established ‖ permanent, not occasional ‖ (of crops) not yet cut ‖ (of water) stagnant ‖ done from an erect position
stand·off·ish *adj.* reserved, aloof
stand·point *n.* a point of view
stand·still *n.* a ceasing of movement or activity
stan·za *n.* a group of lines of verse forming a structural division of a poem
stan·za·ic *adj.*
sta·pes pl. **sta·pes, sta·pe·des** *n.* the innermost of the three bones of the middle ear
staph·y·lo·coc·cus pl. **staph·y·lo·coc·ci** *n.* a genus of nonmotile bacteria living on the skin and mucous membranes
sta·ple 1. *n.* the principal commodity produced, grown or sold in a particular place ‖ a chief ingredient or constituent ‖ a raw material **2.** *adj.* of, relating to or having the nature of a staple (commodity)
staple 1. *n.* a small piece of wire in the form of a square bracket, used to fasten sheets of paper etc. together **2.** *v.t.* **sta·pling sta·pled** to fasten with a staple or staples

sta·pler *n.* a hand-operated device for stapling together sheets of paper etc.
star 1. *n.* any of a vast number of hot, usually luminous celestial bodies ‖ a conventional symbol for such a body, often having five projecting points or several lines radiating from a central point ‖ a leading performer in a play, film etc. ‖ an asterisk **star·ring starred** *v.i.* to be the most prominent person in a collective activity
star·board 1. *n.* the side of a ship or aircraft that is on the right of someone aboard facing forward
starch 1. *n.* a white granular polysaccharide synthesized by green plants ‖ starchy foods **2.** *v.t.* to stiffen (cloth etc.) with starch
starch·y starch·i·er starch·i·est *adj.* of or like starch ‖ containing starch ‖ stiffened with starch
stare 1. star·ing stared *v.i.* to look fixedly with wide eyes ‖ to have a blank, unseeing look **2.** *n.* a fixed gaze
star·fish pl. **star·fish·es, star·fish** *n.* a class of echinoderms possessing five radially symmetric arms
stark 1. *adj.* bare, bleak, sheer, utter **2.** *adv.* absolutely
star·let *n.* a young film actress who is being prepared for a career as a star
star·ry star·ri·er star·ri·est *adj.* full of stars ‖ shining like stars ‖ coming from the stars
star·ry-eyed *adj.* bemused with enchantment or wonder
start 1. *v.t.* to cause (something) to come into existence, operation or activity ‖ to perform (an action, course etc.) for the first time ‖ to establish ‖ to give the signal for the beginning of (a race) ‖ *v.i.* to come into existence, operation or activity ‖ (of a person, vehicle, ship etc.) to set forth on a journey ‖ to spring up or out suddenly from or as if from shock **2.** *n.* the starting of an action, journey, race or course of events ‖ a nervous jerk or jump due to surprise or shock **start·er** *n.* someone who gives the signal for the start of a race ‖ a person or animal that starts in a race

|| the self-starter of a motor

star·tle star·tling star·tled *v.t.* to cause to jump in alarm or surprise || *v.i.* to become alarmed **stár·tling** *adj.*

star·va·tion *n.* a starving or being starved

starve starv·ing starved *v.i.* to die for lack of food || to suffer acutely from lack of food || to feel very hungry

stash *v.t.* to hide or put (something) away for future use

state 1. *n.* a form or mode of being, a condition || a self-governing political community occupying its own territory || a partly autonomous member of a political federation || luxury and splendor **2.** *adj.* pertaining to a state || involving or calling for some display of ceremony **3.** *v.t.* **stat·ing stat·ed** to utter (a fact, opinion, principle etc.) or put it in writing etc.

stat·ed *adj.* fixed, declared || officially recognized || explicitly announced

state·ly state·li·er state·li·est *adj.* of dignified and impressive appearance or manner

state·ment *n.* the act of stating in speech, writing etc. || that which is stated || a financial accounting sheet

states·man *pl.* **states·men** *n.* a person having a large degree of responsibility in the government of a state **státes·man·like** *adj.* characteristic of a wise statesman **státes·man·ly** *adj.* **státes·man·ship** *n.*

stat·ic 1. *adj.* having no motion || being in equilibrium || not changing **2.** *n.* atmospherics **stát·i·cal** *adj.*

sta·tion 1. *n.* a place where someone or something stands || a building, post etc. where a body of people work together || a place along a route where trains or buses stop || the building or buildings connected with this place || rank, status in society **2.** *v.t.* to assign a position or post to

sta·tion·ar·y *adj.* not moving || not changing

sta·tion·er *n.* a seller of writing materials **sta·tion·er·y** *n.* writing materials

sta·tis·tic *n.* a statistical item

stat·is·ti·cian *n.* an expert in compiling statistics

sta·tis·tics *n.* the collection and study of numerical data, esp. as a branch of mathematics || *(pl.)* these data

stat·ue *n.* a three-dimensional representation of a person or animal

stat·u·esque *adj.* having the stateliness and grace associated with statues

stat·ure *n.* the height of a person || moral worth

sta·tus *n.* position, rank or social standing || prestige

status quo *n.* the existing state of affairs

stat·ute *n.* a law passed by a legislative body

staunch *v.t.* to stanch

staunch *adj.* firmly loyal || watertight || strongly made

stave 1. *n.* one of the strips of wood set edge to edge to form the sides of a barrel, tub etc. || the rung of a ladder **2.** *v.* **stav·ing staved, stove** *v.t.* to break a hole in || to supply with staves **to stave off** to ward off

stay 1. *v.i.* to be in the same place over a period || to reside for a while || to stop || *v.t.* to prevent or slow the progress of || to postpone || to have unflagging endurance **2.** *n.* a remaining in one place || *(law)* a postponement

stay 1. *v.t.* to support, prop up **2.** *n.* a prop, buttress etc.

stead *n.* **in someone's** (or **something's**) **stead** in someone's (or something's) place as a substitute **to stand (someone) in good stead** to be of service to (someone), esp. in a difficulty

stead·fast *adj.* adhering firmly to a cause etc. || fixed

stead·i·ly *adv.* in a steady manner

stead·i·ness *n.* the quality or state of being steady

stead·y 1. stead·i·er stead·i·est *adj.* not changing, constant, regular || well balanced and serious || not given to sudden changes of behavior etc. **2.** **stead·y·ing stead·ied** *v.t.* to make steady || *v.i.* to become steady

steak *n.* a beefsteak || any thick slice of meat or fish

steal 1. steal·ing stole sto·len *v.t.* to take

without its owner's consent, esp. secretly ‖ to obtain without asking permission *v.i.* to engage in stealing ‖ to go, come etc. without being noticed **2.** *n.* a real bargain

stealth *n* a way of taking action designed to escape notice

stealth·i·ly *adv.* in a stealthy way

stealth·y stealth·i·er stealth·i·est *adj.* characterized by stealth

steam *n.* the vapor into which water is converted when it boils ‖ energy, drive

steam *v.i.* to emit steam or vapor ‖ to be converted into steam ‖ *v.t.* to subject to the action of steam, in cooking etc.

steam·i·ness *n.* the quality or state of being steamy

steam·roll·er *n.* a steam-driven vehicle with a heavy roller used for flattening freshly laid road surfaces ‖ force that ruthlessly overrides any opposition

steam·ship *n.* a ship driven by steam

steam shovel a large, steam-operated digging machine

steam·y steam·i·er steam·i·est *adj.* full of steam ‖ of or like steam

steed a horse, esp. one full of mettle

steel 1. *n.* any of numerous alloys of iron and carbon **2.** *v.t.* to make resolute **3.** *adj.* like steel ‖ having the color of steel

steel·y steel·i·er steel·i·est *adj.* made of steel ‖ having great strength and hardness ‖ severe, cold ‖ of the gray-blue color of tempered steel

steep 1. *adj.* making a large angle ‖ (of a price etc.) excessive ‖ exaggerated **2.** *n.* a steep slope

steep 1. *v.t.* to soak thoroughly in a liquid ‖ to immerse ‖ *v.i.* to soak in a liquid to infuse **2.** *n.* a steeping

steep·en *v.t.* to make steeper ‖ *v.i.* to become steeper

stee·ple *n.* a church tower together with a spire

steer *n.* a young castrated bull

steer *v.t.* to direct the course of ‖ *v.i.* to respond to such directing **to steer clear of** to avoid

steer·age *n.* the part of some passenger ships allotted to passengers paying the smallest fare

stein *n.* a beer mug, usually with an attached lid

stel·lar *adj.* relating to a star ‖ principal

stem 1. *n.* the main aerial axis of a tree or plant ‖ the slender rod or tube supporting a wineglass or other vessel on its base ‖ the part of a word which remains unchanged by inflectional additions **2. stem·ming stemmed** *v.t.* (of a ship or navigator) to make headway against ‖ *v.i.* to be derived

stem 1. stem·ming stemmed *v.t.* to dam up ‖ to hold back

stench *n.* a powerful, offensive smell

sten·cil 1. *n.* a thin sheet of metal etc., perforated with lettering or a design which is reproduced on a paper or fabric when ink is forced through the apertures ‖ the pattern or lettering so produced **2.** *v.t.* **sten·cil·ing sten·ciled** to make (an impression) from a stencil

ste·nog·ra·pher *n.* a person employed, e.g. in an office, to take down and transcribe shorthand

sten·o·graph·ic *adj.* of or relating to stenography ‖ written in shorthand **sten·o·graph·i·cal** *adj.*

ste·nog·ra·phy *n.* the skill of making shorthand notes

sten·to·ri·an *adj.* (of the voice, etc.) very loud

step *n.* a single movement made by lifting up one foot and setting it down in a different position ‖ the distance covered by such a movement ‖ one of a series of movements in dancing ‖ (*pl.*) a course followed in walking ‖ pace, esp. in marching ‖ one unit in a flight of stairs or (*pl.*) a flight stairs ‖ the rung of a ladder ‖ one of a series of stages in a process, activity etc.

step step·ping stepped *v.i.* to move by performing a step ‖ to execute a step with the foot ‖ to put or press the foot on something specified **to step down** to give up a position of authority, retire **to step on it** to hurry **to step up** to increase

step·broth·er *n.* one's stepparent's son by a former marriage

step·child *pl.* **step·chil·dren** *n.* the child of one's husband or wife by a former marriage

step·daugh·ter *n.* a female stepchild

step·fath·er *n.* a male stepparent

step·lad·der *n.* a folding ladder having broad flat steps

step·moth·er *n.* a female stepparent

step·par·ent *n.* the husband or wife of one's mother or father by a remarriage

steppe *n.* a vast, treeless, usually level plain

step·sis·ter *n.* one's stepparent's daughter by a former marriage

step·son *n.* a male stepchild

step-up *n.* an increase in amount, size, power

ster·e·o·phon·ic *adj.* of sounds which appear to have their sources distributed in space

ster·e·o·type 1. *n.* a plate providing a solid printing surface cast from a mold taken from a body of movable type **2.** *v.t.* **ster·e·o·typing ster·e·o·typed** to amake (a plate) from movable type **stér·e·o·typed** *adj.* lacking originality

ster·ile *adj.* lacking the ability to produce offspring ‖ unproductive ‖ free from living microorganisms ‖ lacking in inspiration, ideas etc.

ster·il·i·ty *n.* the state or quality of being sterile

ster·i·li·za·tion *n.* a sterilizing or being sterilized

ster·i·lize ster·i·liz·ing ster·i·lized *v.t.* to render incapable of producing offspring ‖ to rid of living microorganisms

ster·ling 1. *n.* the legal currency of England ‖ sterling silver **2.** *adj.* relating to British sterling ‖ having an accepted standard of purity ‖ of excellent quality

stern *adj.* severe uncompromising ‖ forbidding

stern *n.* the rear end of a ship

ster·oid *n.* any of a class of compounds having a complex structure like the sterols, and that usually includes the sterols and numerous naturally occurring compounds, e.g. vitamin D, certain hormones and glucosides

ster·ol *n.* any of a large class of complex alcohols, some of which are highly active

physiologically

stet 1. *n.* the word used as an indication to a printer that an instruction to delete is to be ignored **2.** *v.t.* **stet·ting stet·ted** to write 'stet'

steth·o·scope *n.* an instrument which, placed on the thorax, conveys amplified sounds of the heartbeat or lung action **steth·o·scop·ic steth·o·scóp·i·cal** *adj.* steth·o·scóp·i·cal·ly *adv.* ste·thos·co·py *n.*

ste·ve·dore *n.* a man employed to store goods in a ship's hold, or to unload such goods

stew 1. *v.t.* to cook slowly *v.i.* to be cooked in this way ‖ to fret, be anxious **2.** *n.* stewed meat and vegetables

stew·ard *n.* a male attendant aboard ship ‖ an employee on an airplane, train etc. in charge of preparing and serving meals etc. **stéw·ard·ess** *n.* a woman steward

stick 1. *n.* a piece of wood cut or broken from a tree ‖ a walking stick ‖ a stiff, formal person **the sticks** the backwoods

stick stick·ing stuck *v.t.* to cause to adhere ‖ to paste or otherwise fasten ‖ (with 'in', 'into' or 'through') to thrust so as to penetrate or pierce ‖ *v.i.* to become embedded in something by means of a sharp point ‖ to adhere ‖ to become fixed ‖ to remain ‖ (with 'out', 'up', 'down' etc.) to protrude

stick·i·ness *n.* the state or quality of being sticky

stick·ler *n.* a person who insists on the observance of regulations etc. ‖ a puzzling problem

stick·up *n.* an armed robbery

stick·y stick·i·er stick·i·est *adj.* tending to stick ‖ covered with something adhesive ‖ difficult ‖ very ahumid

stiff 1. *adj.* resistant to bending ‖ sore and lacking in suppleness ‖ hard to move ‖ unyielding ‖ lacking grace ‖ difficult ‖ of high alcoholic content ‖ (of prices) very high **2.** *n.* a corpse **3.** *adv.* exceedingly **stíf·fen** *v.t.* to make stiff

sti·fle sti·fling sti·fled *v.t.* to keep (someone) from breathing ‖ to repress ‖ to suppress ‖ to silence ‖ *v.i.* to be stifled

sti·fling *adj.* almost unbearably hot and

stuffy

stig·ma *pl.* **stig·ma·ta, stig·mas** *n.* that part of the pistil which receives the pollen ‖ an arthropod spiracle ‖ a colored wing spot of certain insects ‖ a mark of social disgrace **stig·ma·ta** *pl. n.* marks appearing on the body which resemble the wounds of the crucified Christ

sti·let·to *pl.* **sti·let·tos, sti·let·toes** *n.* a small, thin dagger

still *n.* an apparatus used for distilling alcoholic liquors or preparing distilled water

still 1. *adj.* having no motion ‖ making or having no sound **2.** *n.* complete silence ‖ a static photograph **3.** *adv.* at a given time just as before it ‖ even now (even then) ‖ (with *comp.*) even ‖ without sound or movement, yet **4.** *conj.* nevertheless

still *v.t.* to quiet ‖ to make silent ‖ to satisfy ‖ *v.i.* to become motionless or silent

still·born *adj.* dead when born

still life *pl.* **still lifes, still lives** a painting or photograph of inanimate objects

stilt *n.* one of a pair of long poles, each of which has a footrest at some distance from its lower end, used to elevate the wearer ‖ one of a number of posts on which a house is supported to raise it above ground or water level **stilt·ed** *adj.* supported by stilts ‖ stiff and artificial

stim·u·lant *n.* something which stimulates a ‖ a drug

stim·u·late stim·u·lat·ing stim·u·lat·ed *v.t.* to rouse to greater effort ‖ to arouse ‖ *v.i.* to act as a stimulant

stim·u·la·tion *n.* a stimulating or being stimulated

stim·u·lus *pl.* **stim·u·li** *n.* something that stimulates physiological activity ‖ something that acts as a spur to mental processes

sting 1. sting·ing stung *v.t.* to wound with a sting ‖ to goad ‖ to cause emotional pain ‖ *v.i.* to cause or feel the pain of a sting **2.** *n.* the pain caused by a stinger ‖ a sudden, sharp pain ‖ the act of stinging ‖ a successful confidence game

sting·er *n.* a small sharp organ in some animals and plants, able to pierce the skin of a victim ‖ a painful blow or remark ‖ a cocktail made of brandy and liqueur

stin·gi·ness *n.* the state or quality of being stingy

stin·gy stin·gi·er stin·gi·est *adj.* refusing to give any more than a very small amount ‖ meager, inadequate

stink 1. stink·ing stank, stunk stunk *v.i.* to emit a strong and very unpleasant smell ‖ to be very low in quality ‖ *v.t.* to cause to stink **2.** *n.* a strong, foul smell

stint 1. *v.t.* to limit (someone) parsimoniously or with frugality ‖ *v.i.* to be sparing in giving **2.** *n.* limitation ‖ an allotment or period of work

sti·pend *n.* a fixed, usually moderate sum of money paid at regular intervals

stip·u·late stip·u·lat·ing stip·u·lat·ed *v.t.* to state as a condition for reaching an agreement ‖ to specify

stip·u·la·tion *n.* a stipulating ‖ something stipulated

stir 1. stir·ring stirred *v.t.* to give motion to (a fluid or semifluid), by a continued rotary motion ‖ (esp. with 'up') to cause to rise by stirring ‖ to cause to move ‖ to cause to act, feel or think ‖ to arouse strong emotions **2.** *n.* the act of stirring ‖ a slight movement ‖ a state of excitement

stir·ring *adj.* arousing strong emotions

stir·rup *n.* a footrest for a horseman

stitch 1. *n.* one in-and-out passage of a thread through a fabric in sewing or embroidering ‖ one turn of the wool etc. around the needle or hook in knitting, crocheting etc. ‖ a particular style of making such loops in sewing, embroidering, knitting or crocheting ‖ a sudden sharp pain in the side **in stitches** in helpless laughter **2.** *v.t.* to fasten, repair ‖ *v.i.* to sew

stock 1. *n.* an accumulation of things which is maintained as a constant source of supply ‖ ancestors, family ‖ shares of corporate capital or their certificates of ownership ‖ livestock ‖ the raw material from which a manufactured article, e.g. paper, is made ‖ the wooden part of a rifle by which the barrel is held ‖ liquid in which bones, meat, fish or vegetables have been simmered, used as a basis for soups, sauces etc. ‖ a theatrical stock company ‖ a hive of bees ‖ the trunk of a tree or stem of a plant 2. *v.t.* to furnish with a supply ‖ to furnish (a farm) with stock ‖ to accumulate a supply of ‖ *v.i.* to take in stocks esp. of manufactured goods 3. *adj.* always maintained in stock ‖ (of an argument, answer etc.) usually used, not original ‖ (of a farm) devoted to breeding

stock·ade 1. *n.* a fortification consisting of a fence of posts ‖ strong enclosure fenced in by posts 2. *v.t.* **stock·ad·ing stock·ad·ed** to furnish with a stockade

stock·brok·er *n.* someone who deals in stocks and shares **stóck·brok·ing** *n.* the business of a stockbroker

stock exchange a place where stocks are bought and sold

stock·hold·er *n.* a person who owns stock (shares of corporate capital)

stock·i·ness *n.* the state or quality of being stocky

stock·ing *n.* a close-fitting covering for the foot and leg

stock market a stock exchange ‖ the buying and selling of stocks and shares

stock·pile 1. *n.* essential matériel accumulated for use when the normal sources of supply are cut off 2. *v.* **stock·pil·ing stock·piled** *v.i.* to accumulate a stockpile

stock·y stock·i·er stock·i·est *adj.* short, sturdy and thickly built ‖ having sturdy, thick stems

stodge 1. **stodg·ing stodged** *v.t.* to cram with food, facts etc. ‖ *v.i.* to eat to excess 2. *n.* dull, heavy, filling food **stódg·i·ly** *adv.* in a stodgy way **stodg·i·ness** *n.* the quality of being stodgy **stódg·y stodg·i·er stodg·i·est** *adj.* heavy and filling ‖ dull, tedious

sto·ic 1. *n.* a person who endures hardship with fortitude 2. *adj.* able to bear adversity with fortitude **stó·i·cal** *adj.* **sto·i·cism** *n.* stoical behavior

stoke stok·ing stoked *v.t.* to add fuel to a (a fire, furnace etc.)

stok·er *n.* a man who a fire, furnace etc.

stole *n.* a long, wide length of material, fur etc. worn by women, draped over the shoulders

stol·id *adj.* difficult to arouse, either emotionally or mentally

sto·lid·i·ty *n.* the state or quality of being stolid

stom·ach 1. *n.* an enlarged portion of the alimentary canal of a vertebrate between the esophagus and the small intestine ‖ a digestive cavity, e.g. in invertebrates ‖ appetite, liking 2. *v.t.* to find palatable or digestible

stomp 1. *v.i.* to put one's feet down heavily 2. *n.* a jazz dance

stone 1. *n.* rock ‖ a grindstone, a tombstone ‖ a small piece of an ornamental and rare mineral, cut and polished ‖ calculus ‖ the hard case of the kernel in a fruit ‖ (*pl.* **stone**) a British unit of weight equal to 14 lbs avoirdupois **a stone's throw** a short distance **to leave no stone unturned** to use every possible means to achieve a purpose 2. *v.t.* **ston·ing stoned** to throw stones at ‖ to take the stones out of (fruit) 3. *adj.* made of stone

stonewalling *v.* obstructing an investigation, a vote

ston·i·ness *n.* the state or quality of being stony

ston·y ston·i·er ston·i·est *adj.* containing many stones ‖ as hard as stone ‖ lacking pity

stooge 1. *n.* someone who acts as a butt for a comedian ‖ a stool pigeon (informer) 2. *v.i.* **stoog·ing stooged** to act as a stooge

stool *n.* a backless and armless seat ‖ a footstool ‖ a decoy bird ‖ the evacuation of waste matter from the bowels ‖ the waste matter so evacuated

stoop 1. *v.i.* to bend the body forward and downward ‖ to lower one's dignity 2. *n.* a posture in which the shoulders are permanently bent forward and downward

stop 1. **stop·ping stopped** *v.t.* to discontinue, cease ‖ to prevent from moving or acting ‖ to cut off, withhold ‖ (often with 'up') to fill (a hole, crack etc.) ‖ to close, obstruct ‖ to plug ‖ to instruct one's bank to withhold payment of (a check etc.) ‖ *v.i.* to cease to do something ‖ to come to an end ‖ to become obstructed **to stop off** to make a brief stay at a place while on a journey **2.** *n.* a stopping ‖ a place where a bus, streetcar etc. picks up or deposits passengers

stop·gap *n.* a person or thing serving as a substitute or temporary expedient

stop·page *n.* a stopping or being stopped

stop·per *n.* a plug or other device which closes an opening

stor·age *n.* a storing ‖ space for storing

store *n.* something put aside for future use ‖ a room where retail sale is carried on ‖ any shop **in store** kept for future use

store storing stored *v.t.* to accumulate and keep for future use ‖ to put into storage

sto·rey, sto·ry *pl.* **sto·reys, sto·ries** *n.* one of the floor-to-ceiling portions of a building above aground level

sto·ried *adj.* celebrated in legend or history

sto·ried, storeyed *adj.* (in compounds, of a building) having a specified number of stories

stork *pl.* **storks** *n.* a wading birds with a long bill and long legs

storm 1. *n.* a very strong wind ‖ a heavy fall of rain, snow, hail or sleet ‖ any violent atmospheric disturbance in the air ‖ jealousy or rage ‖ any commotion or agitation ‖ an attack in force on a fortified place **2.** *v.i.* to rain, snow, hail etc. with violence ‖ to be in a passion of rage ‖ to rush angrily and violently

storm·y storm·i·er storm·i·est *adj.* having the characteristics of a storm ‖ characterized by violence

sto·ry *pl.* **sto·ries** *n.* an oral or written account of real or imagined events ‖ the plot of a literary work ‖ a news item in a newspaper ‖ a rumor circulating ‖ a lie

stout *adj.* having a heavy and rotund body ‖ strong ‖ brave ‖ resolute, firm

stout·heart·ed *adj.* courageous

stove *n.* a largely enclosed apparatus in which fuel is burned to provide heat for comfort or cooking

stow *v.t.* to pack away in an enclosed space ‖ to fill (a hold etc.) with cargo

stow·age *n.* a stowing ‖ goods stowed ‖ storage capacity

stow·a·way *n.* a person who hides on a ship, train etc.

strad·dle 1. strad·dling strad·dled *v.i.* to walk, or stand, with the legs wide apart ‖ to sit on a fence, wall etc. with one leg on either side of it ‖ to seem to favor both sides of an issue ‖ *v.t.* to spread (the legs) wide apart **2.** *n.* the position of straddling

strafe 1. *v.t.* **straf·ing strafed** to sweep with maachine-gun fire **2.** *n.* such an attack

strag·gle strag·gling strag·gled *v.i.* to lag behind, or stray **strág·gly strag·gli·er strag·gli·est** *adj.*

straight 1. *adj.* having an unchanging direction ‖ showing no deviation from the vertical or horizontal ‖ honest, trustworthy ‖ frank ‖ correctly stated or understood ‖ unmixed ‖ undiluted ‖ not curly **2.** *adv.* in a straight line ‖ directly, uniquivocally

straight·en *v.t.* to make straight ‖ *v.i.* to become straight

straight·for·ward 1. *adj.* honest and direct without hiding anything, frank ‖ clear-cut, unequivocal **2.** *adv.* straight ahead **straight·for·wards** *adv.*

strain *n.* a group of organisms possessing a particular physiological quality ‖ a line of descendents ‖ an inherited but not dominant quality ‖ a persistent trait of character

strain 1. *v.t.* to injure by overuse or misuse ‖ to force (oneself) to the utmost ‖ to cause mental tension ‖ to make excessive demands on ‖ to subject (a relationship) to a considerable degree of tension ‖ to pass (a liquid) throught a filter or sieve ‖ *v.i.* to make or exert great physical or mental effort ‖ to filter or sieve **2.** *n.* a straining ‖ a deformation of an elastic body under an applied force ‖ mental tension causing distress ‖ a great demand imposing hardship

strain·er *n.* a sieve or filter

strait *n.* a narrow stretch of water between two land masses ‖ severely restricting difficulties

strait·jack·et, straight·jack·et *n.* a garment used to restrain the movement of a violent, usually insane, person who could harm himself or others

strait·laced, straight·laced *adj.* exceedingly strict about matters of propriety

strand 1. *n.* the shore of a body of water **2.** *v.t.* to run (a boat) aground ‖ to cause (someone) to find himself accidentally held up on a journey without resources

strand *n.* any of the threads, strings, wires etc. which, when twisted together, form a rope ‖ a tress ‖ a single string of beads or pearls etc.

strange *adj.* not within one's previous experience ‖ unusual ‖ not accustomed

stran·ger *n.* a newcomer ‖ a person who is not known to one

stran·gle stran·gling stran·gled *v.t.* to kill by compressing the windpipe and so preventing breathing ‖ to suppress (e.g. criticism) ‖ *v.i.* to be strangled

stran·gle·hold *n.* an illegal hold in wrestling ‖ any force which prevents freedom of action

stran·gu·late   stran·gu·lat·ing stran·gu·lat·ed *v.t.* to stop the circulation of fluid or blood supply in (a tissue), e.g. in hernia **stran·gu·la·tion** *n.* the action or process of strangling

strap 1. *n.* a long strip of leather etc. used to fasten or bind ‖ a strip of metal used similarly ‖ a razor strop ‖ a shoulder strap ‖ a loop suspended from the ceiling of public vehicles for a standing passenger to hold as a support **2.** *v.t.* **strap·ping strapped** to fasten or bind with a strap ‖ to beat with a leather strap

strap·ping *adj.* very big and strong in build

strat·a·gem *n.* a subtle piece of planning designed to trick or gain an end ‖ a ruse

stra·te·gic *adj.* of or relating to strategy ‖ of material needed for war **stra·té·gi·cal** *adj.* **stra·té·gi·cal·ly** *adv.* **stra·té·gics** *n.* the science of strategy

strat·e·gist *n.* a person skilled in strategy

strat·e·gy *pl.* **strat·e·gies** *n.* the science and art of conducting a military campaign in its large-scale and long-term aspects ‖ skill in using stratagems

strat·i·fi·ca·tion *n.* the formation of strata ‖ the condition of being stratified ‖ arrangement in strata

strat·i·fy strat·i·fy·ing strat·i·fied *v.t.* to form in strata

strat·o·sphere *n.* a division of the earth's atmosphere extending about 30 miles

stra·tum *pl.* **stra·ta, stra·tums** *n.* a roughly horizontal layer of homogeneous material with its surfaces parallel to those of layers of material of different kinds on either side ‖ a level or division

straw 1. *n.* the stems of any of several cereals after cutting and threshing ‖ one of these stems ‖ a tube of plastic or paper used for drawing liquids into the mouth **a straw in the wind** a small sign, indicative of some coming event **2.** *adj.* made of straw ‖ resembling straw

straw·ber·ry *pl.* **straw·ber·ries** *n.* a genus of plants widely cultivated for their edible, juicy, sweet, red fruit ‖ the fruit of any of these plants

stray 1. *v.i.* to leave a proper place or course ‖ to deviate morally ‖ to roam **2.** *n.* something (esp. a domestic animal) which has strayed **3.** *adj.* having strayed ‖ out of place ‖ random

streak 1. *n.* a linear mark differing in color and/or texture from the background it appears on ‖ a trace ‖ a flash **2.** *v.t.* to mark with streaks ‖ *v.i.* to become streaky

streak·y streak·i·er streak·i·est *adj.* marked with streaks ‖ occurring in streaks

stream 1. *n.* a small body of fresh water in a channel ‖ a continuous procession of people or animals moving in one direction ‖ a continuous emission ‖ a swift oceanic current **2.** *v.i.* to flow as if in, a stream ‖ (of many people or things) to move in one direction ‖ *v.t.* to emit (fluid) in a stream **stréam·er** *n.* a festive decoration made of a long thin ribbon of colored paper ‖ a banner headline

stream·line 1. *n.* the contour given to a solid body so that it can move through a fluid with the minimum resistance **2.** *v.t.* **stream·lin·ing stream·lined** to shape (a solid body) in this way ‖ to render more efficient by modernizing **stréam·lined** *adj.* shaped so as to be able to move with minimum resistance ‖ modernized and speeded up

street *n.* a road in a town or village ‖ this road together with the houses etc. abutting it

street·car *n.* a passenger car for public transport running on rails laid in the street or roadway

street·walk·er *n.* a prostitute

strength *n.* capacity to exert force ‖ ability to resist attack ‖ physical, emotional or mental resources ‖ the potency of a drug or beverage ‖ soundness **strength·en** *v.t.* to make stronger ‖ *v.i.* to become stronger

stren·u·ous *adj.* requiring a great effort

strep·to·coc·cus *pl.* **strep·to·coc·ci** *n.* bacteria, usually occurring in chains of coccoid cells

stress 1. *n.* the state of an elastic body under conditions of strain ‖ a state in which a strong demand is made on the nervous system ‖ special emphasis given to something ‖ accent **2.** *v.t.* to give emphasis to ‖ to accent ‖ to impart mechanical stress to

stretch 1. *v.t.* to pull or otherwise exert force on (an elastic body) ‖ to pull or spread out fully ‖ to strain (a tendon) ‖ *(refl.,* often with 'out on') to cause (oneself) to lie full length ‖ to make (food etc.) appear to go further ‖ to knock (someone) flat ‖ to cause (e.g. the intelligence or imagination) to exceed previous limits ‖ *v.i.* (of an elastic body) to become enlarged in length and/or breadth ‖ to become permanently enlarged ‖ (often with 'out') to lie full length ‖ to reach out, esp. one's hand **to stretch a point** to go beyond what is justified **2.** *n.* a stretching or being stretched ‖ capacity for being stretched ‖ a period of imprisonment ‖ a usually straight section of racetrack **stretch·er** *n.* a length of canvas etc. used for carrying, esp. the sick or dead in a prone position

stretch·y stretch·i·er stretch·i·est *adj.* elastic

strew strew·ing strewed strewed, strewn *v.t.* to scatter ‖ to drop or throw about in a disorderly way

strick·en *alt. past part.* of STRIKE ‖ *adj.* afflicted by some overwhelming disaster, grief, disease etc. ‖ (in compounds) suddenly possessed by a specified emotion

strict *adj.* rigorous and often severe in imposing discipline ‖ adhering rigorously to rules or standards ‖ precise, exact, rigorously adhered **strict·ly** *adv.*

stric·ture *n.* an adverse criticism ‖ an abnormal contraction of a duct or channel of the body

stride 1. strid·ing strode strid·den *v.i.* to walk with long steps ‖ *v.t.* to pass over in one step **2.** *n.* a long walking step ‖ *(pl.)* rapid advances **to take in one's stride** to do (something), or adjust oneself to (something) easily or without fuss

stri·dent *adj.* (of a sound) loud, grating and harsh

strife *n.* a condition of enmity often arising out of rivalry ‖ discord

strike 1. strik·ing struck struck, strick·en *v.i.* to deal a blow or blows ‖ to attack ‖ to chime ‖ (of a match) to become ignited ‖ (of a fish) to grab at the bait ‖ (of a snake) to sink or try to sink its fangs into its prey ‖ (of a ship) to run aground ‖ to lower the flag, esp. as sign of surrender ‖ to stop working in order to put pressure on an employer **to strike home** (of a punch, blow etc.) to be very effective ‖ (of a remark) to produce a very pronounced effect **to strike off** to sever **to strike out on one's own** to start a new enterprise alone **to strike up** to begin (a friendship, a conversation) with someone met casually **2.** *n.* a blow ‖ a ceasing to work in order to put pressure on an employer ‖ the discovery of a deposit of oil etc. ‖ the horizontal direction of a stratum

strike·break·er *n.* a person engaged to do a striker's work

strik·er *n.* a worker on strike

strik·ing *adj.* remarkable, impressive, attracting attention ‖ on strike

string 1. *n.* a thin length of twisted fiber ‖ a length of e.g. silk or twine on which e.g. beads or fish can be threaded ‖ *(pl.)* the cords pulled to actuate a puppet ‖ a natural fiber, e.g. that along one edge of a bean pod ‖ a row of beads or other objects threaded on or as if on a string ‖ a number of things linked or tied together ‖ several homogeneous business concerns owned by one person or company ‖ a length of wire, gut etc. which produces sound when under tension and when made to vibrate by striking, plucking or bowing ‖ (pl.) the stringed instruments of an orchestra collectively ‖ a condition attached to something **to pull strings** to exert one's personal influence **2. string·ing strung** v.t. to furnish with a string or strings ‖ to thread on a string ‖ to fasten with a string ‖ to remove the stringy fibers from ‖ to form stringy fibers ‖ to stretch out in a long line **to string (someone) along** to fool (someone) **to string out** to prolong **to string up** to hang (execute)

strin·gen·cy pl. **strin·gen·cies** n. the state or quality, or an instance, of being stringent

strin·gent adj. strict, rigid ‖ tight, limiting ‖ convincing, closely argued

string·i·ness n. the state or quality of being stringy

string·y string·i·er string·i·est adj. consisting of fibers or strings ‖ fibrous, tough ‖ thin and wiry or scrawny

strip strip·ping stripped v.t. to remove (clothing) ‖ to deprive (something) of its covering ‖ to deprive (someone) of a possession etc. ‖ to remove (medals, decorations, honors etc. ‖ to make (something) bare by taking away removable parts ‖ to tear off

strip n. a long narrow piece of more or less uniform width ‖ a comic strip ‖ an airstrip

stripe 1. n. a narrow band usually of uniform width, distinguished by color or texture from its surroundings **2. strip·ing striped** to mark with a stripe or stripes **striped** adj.

strive striv·ing strove striv·en v.i. to make great efforts ‖ (with 'towards') to struggle or endeavor to attain some end

stroke 1. n. a blow ‖ a sudden manifestation (of e.g. genius, luck etc.) ‖ the sound of a bell or a striking clock ‖ a heartbeat ‖ an attack of apoplexy ‖ a single,

combined movement ‖ a single movement of a piston or similar thing ‖ a single movement of the hand in painting, drawing, writing etc. **2.** v.t. **strok·ing stroked** to be stroke for (a crew or boat)

stroke 1. v.t. **strok·ing stroked** to pass esp. the hand gently over once or repeatedly **2.** n. a stroking movement

stroll 1. v.i. to walk leisurely **2.** n. a short leisurely walk etc. ‖ n. a light wheeled chair for pushing a young child out in ‖ someone out for a stroll

strong 1. adj. having great physical strength ‖ able to resist considerable force ‖ morally powerful ‖ intellectually powerful ‖ especially proficient or well informed ‖ firmly grounded ‖ exerting great effect on one of the senses ‖ loyal and enthusiastic ‖ intense in degree or quality ‖ concentrated or having a high content of some specified or understood ingredient ‖ not squeamish ‖ (of wind) blowing forcefully ‖ (of lenses) having a high magnifying power **2.** adv. in a strong way

strong·hold n. a fortress ‖ a center of support for a cause or faction

strong-mind·ed adj. having firm and independent convictions ‖ able to resist temptation, resolute

strop 1. n. a leather strip on which a razor can be sharpened **2.** v.t. **strop·ping stropped** to sharpen with a strop

struc·tur·al adj. of or relating to structure

struc·ture 1. n. something (e.g. a building or an organism) made of parts fitted or joined together ‖ the essential supporting portion of this **2.** v.t. **struc·tur·ing struc·tured** to give a structure to

strug·gle 1. v.i. **strug·gling strug·gled** to make strenuous efforts ‖ (with 'with' or 'against') to contend physically with someone, or mentally with a problem etc. ‖ to make one's way with difficulty **2.** n. a great effort ‖ a strenuous contending with someone or something

strum strum·ming strummed v.i. to play a stringed musical instrument casually or without ability

strut 1. v.i. **strut·ting strut·ted** to walk esp. slowly, stiffly **2.** n. the characteristic walk of cocks, peacocks etc. or of a self-important person

strut 1. *n.* a piece of wood, metal etc. designed to resist stress **2.** *v.t.* **strut·ting strut·ted** to support with struts

strych·nine *n.* a highly poisonous crystalline alkaloid

stub 1. *n.* the short piece left when a pencil etc. is almost all used ‖ the butt of a cigarette ‖ the counterfoil of a check, a ticket or receipt etc. **2.** *v.t.* **stub·bing stubbed** to strike (a toe) against a hard obstacle ‖ (often with 'out') to put out (a cigarette) by crushing the lit end

stub·ble *n.* the short stalk of wheat etc. ‖ a rough, short growth, e.g. of beard **stúb·bly** *adj.*

stub·born *adj.* inflexibly declining to change a chosen position ‖ not responding to treatment ‖ (of problems etc.) hard to work out

stub·by stub·bi·er stub·bi·est *adj.* short and thick

stuc·co *n.* a mixture of cement, sand and lime applied to outside walls ‖ work done in stucco

stud 1. *n.* any male animal kept for breeding **2.** *adj.* of or pertaining to a stud ‖ kept for breeding

stud 1. *n.* a short, thick nail or rivet with a large head used mainly for decoration ‖ a shirt fastening ‖ a post to which the laths of a partition are nailed ‖ a dowel, pin or spindle in a mechanism **2.** *v.t.* **stud·ding stud·ded** to furnish with studs ‖ to set objects thickly on or as if on

stu·dent *n.* a person who attends a university, college or school for study

stud·ied *adj.* thought-out ‖ premeditated, calculated

stu·di·o *pl.* **stu·di·os** *n.* the workroom of an artist, musician, photographer etc. ‖ a place from which radio or television programs are transmitted ‖ a building or group of buildings in which movies are made

stu·di·ous *adj.* devoted or given to study ‖ carefully meditated, painstaking

stud·y *pl.* **stud·ies** *n.* the acquiring of knowledge ‖ (*pl.*) institutional education

‖ a preliminary painting or drawing for a work of art ‖ the learning of a part in a play ‖ something that can be scrutinized as though it were a book or a picture ‖ a room for studying in

study stud·y·ing stud·ied *v.t.* to seek knowledge of by study ‖ to observe very closely ‖ to memorize

stuff *n.* the material of which something is made ‖ the essence or basic quality of some esp. abstract thing ‖ personal belongings ‖ worthless ideas, opinions, writings etc.

stuff *v.t.* to force (some things or things) into a limited space by pressure ‖ to fill (a cushion, mattress etc.) with padding ‖ to fill the skin of (a dead animal, bird, fish etc.) in order to restore its natural shape ‖ to fill (something to be eaten) with esp. a savory mixture ‖ to plug or stop up ‖ to cram (something) esp. hastily and surreptitiously ‖ to put fraudulent votes into (a ballot box) ‖ *v.i.* to eat too much, gorge oneself

stuff·i·ness *n.* the state or quality of being stuffy

stuff·y stuff·i·er stuff·i·est *adj.* close and ill-ventilated and usually hot ‖ congested ‖ prim ‖ pompous and dull

stul·ti·fy stul·ti·fy·ing stul·ti·fied *v.t.* to render futile or useless ‖ to cause to be ridiculous

stum·ble 1. *v.i.* **stum·bling stum·bled** to have a partial fall or to lurch forward as a result of missing one's footing ‖ to hesitate and make a mistake in speaking, reading aloud etc. ‖ (with 'on', 'upon') to find, come upon by accident or chance **2.** *n.* the act of stumbling ‖ a slip (mistake)

stump 1. *n.* a short piece of the trunk of a tree ‖ the remaining part of an amputated limb ‖ the part of a broken, ground down or badly decayed tooth remaining in the gum ‖ a heavy, clumsy step ‖ the sound of such a step **2.** *v.i.* to walk stiffly and heavily ‖ to make speeches in a political cause ‖ to baffle

stump·y stump·i·er stump·i·est *adj.* (of people) stocky, thickset ‖ (of things) short and thick

stun 1. *v.t.* **stun·ning stunned** (of a person) to render unconscious or semiconscious ‖ to cause (someone) to be mentally or emotionally numbed **2.** *n.* the act or effect of stunning

stun·ning *adj.* very attractive ‖ causing admiring astonishment

stunt *v.t.* to check the growth or development of

stunt *n.* something done to show off skill or daring or ingenuity, for publicity, to attract custom etc.

stu·pe·fac·tion *n.* utter astonishment ‖ a state of profound drowsiness or stupor

stu·pe·fy stu·pe·fy·ing stu·pe·fied *v.t.* to put into a state of profound lethargy ‖ to cause utter consternation in

stu·pen·dous *adj.* amazing

stu·pid *adj.* (of persons) lacking intelligence ‖ (of actions) resulting from lack of intelligence ‖ (of persons or animals) foolish in speech or behavior

stu·pid·i·ty *pl.* **stu·pid·i·ties** *n.* a stupid act, remark etc.

stu·por *n.* a state of drowsiness or profound lethargy ‖ mental apathy **stú·por·ous** *adj.*

stur·di·ness *n.* the state or quality of being sturdy

stur·dy 1. **stur·di·er stur·di·est** *adj.* strongly built ‖ healthy and hardy ‖ resolute **2.** *n.* gid

stur·geon *n.* a genus of ganoid fishes

stut·ter 1. *v.i.* to keep repeating sounds or syllables in an effort to speak **2.** *n.* an act or instance of stuttering ‖ the affliction of having to stutter

sty, stye *pl.* **sties, styes** *n.* a small, inflamed swelling at the base of an eyelash

style 1. *n.* the distinguishing way in which something is done, written, made, executed etc. ‖ manner or tone assumed in speech or oratory ‖ preferred type ‖ the fashion, pattern and cut of clothing ‖ (without article) a mode of living or way of acting judged elegant or distinguished **2.** *v.t.* **styl·ing styled** to give (someone) his proper designation ‖ to fashion according to the current mode

styl·ish *adj.* in current fashion ‖ showing marked elegance in dress, bearing, etc.

sty·lus *pl.* **sty·li sty·lus·es** *n.* a pointed instrument for writing on waxed surfaces ‖ a needle point for cutting recordings or playing records ‖ an ancient instrument used for writing on parchment ‖ a device for punching dots in preparing Braille

sty·mie *v.t.* **sty·mie·ing sty·mied** to impede or hinder

styp·tic 1. *adj.* having an astringent effect ‖ tending to check bleeding **2.** *n.* a styptic substance

suave *adj.* bland, smooth and unctuous

suáv·i·ty *pl.* **suav·i·ties** *n.* the state or quality of being suave

sub- prefix under ‖ lower than or inferior to ‖ to a lesser degree than, not completely ‖ a smaller division

sub·a·tom·ic *adj.* of, relating to, or being any of the particles smaller than an atom

sub·con·scious 1. *adj.* not normally admitted to consciousness, or apparently forgotten **2.** *n.* the sum of such mental activity

sub·cu·ta·ne·ous *adj.* used, introduced, situated or occurring beneath the skin

sub·di·vide sub·di·vid·ing sub·di·vid·ed *v.t.* to divide again ‖ to divide up (a piece of land) into lots for selling

sub·di·vi·sion *n.* one of the parts resulting when something is subdivided

sub·due sub·du·ing sub·dued *v.t.* to control, discipline ‖ to make (sound, color etc.) less intense ‖ to reduce the vivacity of

sub·head *n.* a subheading **sub·head·ing** *n.* the title or heading of part of a chapter, essay etc. ‖ a subordinate heading of a title

sub·hu·man *adj.* less than human

sub·ject *v.t.* (with 'to') to cause to submit ‖ (with 'to') to cause to undergo ‖ (with 'to') to expose or lay open

sub·ject *adj.* (esp. with 'to') owing allegiance ‖ under external government or rule ‖ (with 'to') apt to prone ‖ (with 'to') exposed ‖ (with 'to') conditional

subject *n.* a member of a state in relation to his government ‖ something constituting or chosen as a matter for thought, discussion, action or study etc. ‖ theme ‖ someone or something experimented on ‖ the noun, or its equivalent, governing a verb

sub·jec·tion *n.* a subjecting or being subjected

sub·jec·tive *adj.* seen from the point of view of the thinking subject ‖ nominative **sub·jec·tív·i·ty** *n.*

sub·join *v.t.* to add (something) to the end of something stated or written

sub·ju·gate sub·ju·gat·ing sub·ju·gat·ed *v.t.* to conquer and hold in subjection

sub·ju·ga·tion *n.* a subjugating or being subjugated

sub·lease 1. *n.* the lease granted by a tenant to a subtenant of part or all of a property **2.** *v.t.* **sub·leas·ing sub·leased** to grant a sublease on

sub·let 1. *v.t.* **sub·let·ting sub·let** to rent out part or all of (a property rented or leased from the owner) **2.** *n.* a property obtained by or available for subletting

sub·li·mate 1. *v.t.* **sub·li·mat·ing sub·li·mat·ed** to purify ‖ to redirect ‖ *v.i.* to become sublimated **2.** *n.* a substance obtained by sublimating

sub·li·ma·tion *n.* a sublimating or being sublimated

sub·lime 1. *adj.* arousing the sensation of awe ‖ lofty, exalted ‖ outstanding ‖ (of muscles) lying near the surface **2.** *n.* **the sublime**

sub·lim·i·nal *adj.* not rising above the threshold of consciousness

sub·mar·gin·al *adj.* below the minimum necessary for

sub·ma·rine 1. *adj.* existing, operating etc. under water **2.** *n.* a vessel designed to operate submerged

sub·merge sub·merg·ing sub·merged *v.i.* to plunge beneath the surface of the water etc. **sub·mér·gence** *n.*

sub·merse sub·mers·ing sub·mersed *v.t.* to submerge **sub·mérsed** *adj.* growing entirely under water **sub·mers·i·ble** *adj.* capable of being submerged

sub·mer·sion *n.* a submerging or being submerged

sub·mis·sion *n.* the act of submitting ‖ the

state of being willing to submit

sub·mis·sive *adj.* willing to submit, humbly obedient

sub·mit sub·mit·ting sub·mit·ted *v.t.* to cause to undergo ‖ to offer for consideration, examination ‖ *v.i.* to cease to offer resistance ‖ to defer to another's wishes

sub·nor·mal *adj.* below, lower than, less than or smaller than normal **sub·nor·mál·i·ty** *n.*

sub·or·di·nate 1. *adj.* inferior in order, rank, importance etc. **2.** *n.* inferior in the official hierarchy **3.** *v.t.* **sub·or·di·nat·ing sub·or·di·nat·ed** to treat or consider as of secondary importance ‖ (with 'to') to make subject or subservient'

sub·or·di·na·tion *n.* a subordinating or being subordinated

sub·orn *v.t.* to incite (a person), usually by bribery, to commit perjury or other unlawful acts

sub·poe·na 1. *n.* a written order commanding a person to appear in a court of justice under penalty **2.** *v.t.* **sub·poe·na·ing sub·poe·naed** to serve with such an order

sub·scribe sub·scrib·ing sub·scribed *v.t.* to contribute or agree to contribute ‖ to add one's signature to ‖ *v.i.* to make a subscription ‖ to promise a subscription **to subscribe to** to take in regularly (a periodical, newspaper etc.) ‖ to express agreement with

sub·scrip·tion *n.* the act of subscribing ‖ a sum subscribed ‖ matter subscribed ‖ a signifying of assent or the assent itself ‖ the prepayment made to secure future issues of e.g. a periodical

sub·se·quence *n.* the act or state of being subsequent ‖ that which is subsequent

sub·se·quent *adj.* following, later

sub·ser·vi·ent *adj.* servile, obsequious

sub·side sub·sid·ing sub·sid·ed *v.i.* to sink in level or settle down into a lower position ‖ to return to a normal level ‖ to abate

sub·sid·ence *n.* the act or process of subsiding

sub·sid·i·ar·y 1. *adj.* auxiliary, supplementary **2.** *pl.* **sub·sid·i·ar·ies** *n.*

an assistant ‖ a subsidiary company

sub·si·dize sub·si·diz·ing sub·si·dized v.t. to pay a subsidy to ‖ to aid with public money

sub·si·dy pl. **sub·si·dies** n. a nonreturnable grant of money

sub·sist v.i. to keep oneself alive ‖ to exist or continue to exist

sub·sist·ence n. a means of providing oneself with the bare necessities

sub·son·ic adj. pertaining to speeds less than that of sound

sub·stance n. the matter, stuff, material of which a thing is made ‖ the main content ‖ solidity, correspondence with reality ‖ wealth

sub·stand·ard adj. falling short of a legally required or generally accepted standard

sub·stan·tial adj. having real existence, not imaginary ‖ firmly based ‖ relatively great in size, value or importance ‖ strong, made to last ‖ well-off, financially sound

sub·stan·ti·ate sub·stan·ti·at·ing sub·stan·ti·at·ed v.t. to establish, prove or make good **sub·stan·ti·á·tion** n.

sub·sti·tute 1. n. a person or thing taking the place of another person or thing **2. sub·sti·tut·ing sub·sti·tut·ed** v.t. to put in the place of another person or thing **sub·sti·tú·tion** n. **sub·sti·tú·tion·al, súb·sti·tu·tive** ,adjs.

sub·ter·fuge n. a deceptive stratagem enabling one to get out of a situation etc.

sub·ter·ra·ne·an adj. situated, existing, operating or functioning underground

sub·ti·tle 1. n. (esp. pl.) words projected on the screen to translate the dialogue of a foreign movie **2.** v.t. **sub·ti·tling sub·ti·tled** to give a subtitle or subtitles to

sub·tle adj. hard to grasp, elusive ‖ acute ‖ ingenious, cunning, clever ‖ working insidiously

sub·tle·ty pl. **sub·tle·ties** n. the quality or state of being subtle, esp. the making of fine distinctions

sub·tly adv. in a subtle manner

sub·tract v.t. (esp. with 'from') to take away (a number or quantity) from another number or quantity

sub·trac·tion n. the act or process of subtraction

sub·urb n. one of the residential or industrial districts on the edge of a big town or city **sub·úr·ban** adj. pertaining to the suburbs

sub·ver·sion n. a subverting or being subverted

sub·ver·sive 1. adj. tending to subvert **2.** n. a subversive person

sub·vert v.t. to cause the downfall or ruin of ‖ to corrupt

sub·way n. an underground passage or tunnel ‖ a city railroad system running entirely or mainly in tunnels under the ground

suc·ceed v.i. to be successful, to attain a desired end ‖ to ensure, to follow ‖ v.t. to be the successor to ‖ to come after

suc·cess n. accomplishment, achievement ‖ a person who or thing which succeeds **suc·céss·ful** adj.

suc·ces·sion n. a series of things in order ‖ the act or right of following one's predecessor in a post, position or title **in succession** one after another **suc·cés·sion·al** adj.

suc·ces·sive adj. consecutive

suc·ces·sor n. a person or thing that succeeds another

suc·cinct adj. clearly expressed in few words

suc·cor 1. v.t. to relieve the difficulty or distress of **2.** n. help given in time of need

suc·co·tash n. a side dish consisting of lima beans and corn kernels cooked together

suc·cu·lent 1. adj. juicy **2.** n. a plant with fleshy leaves or fleshy stems or both

suc·cumb v.t. to yield to superior strength ‖ to cease to offer resistance ‖ to die

such 1. adj. of a kind previously or about to be mentioned or implied ‖ of the same quality as something just mentioned ‖ of a degree or quantity stated or implicit ‖ similar, comparable **2.** pron. the same as something just mentioned ‖ this or that kind of person or thing **3.** adv. this or that degree of

suck 1. v.t. to draw (air) into the lungs by inflating them ‖ to draw up (moisture etc.)

by or as if by suction ‖ to hold (e.g. the thumb) in the mouth ‖ to allow (e.g. candy) to dissolve slowly in the mouth ‖ *v.i.* to draw something by or as if by producing a vacuum ‖ to make the sound of sucking **2.** *n.* the act of sucking ‖ the sound of sucking **súck·er** *n.* someone who, or something which, sucks ‖ someone who is easily taken in and gotten the better of

suck·le suck·ling suck·led *v.t.* to give milk from the teat

suc·tion *n.* the process of raising a fluid by reducing the pressure above it and so causing it to be forced upwards by the atmospheric pressure beneath it

sud·den 1. *adj.* unexpected **2.** *n.* (only in the phrase) **all of a sudden** unexpectedly

suds *pl. n.* frothy, soapy water or the froth itself **súds·y suds·i·er suds·i·est** *adj.* frothy

sue su·ing sued *v.t.* to bring a legal action against ‖ to make a petition or entreaty

suede *n.* leather having the flesh side napped

su·et *n.* the hard fat surrounding the kidneys and loins of cattle and sheep

suf·fer *v.t.* to be made to bear ‖ to be the victim of ‖ to put up with ‖ to undergo, be subjected to ‖ *v.i.* to experienbe made to bear ‖ to be the victim of ‖ to put up with ‖ to undergo, be subjected to ‖ *v.i.* to experience pain or injury

suf·fer·ance *n.* tacit consent

suf·fer·ing *n.* mental or physical pain ‖ the bearing of pain, distress, loss, damage etc.

suf·fice suf·fic·ing suf·ficed *v.* to be enough

suf·fi·cien·cy *pl.* **suf·fi·cien·cies** *n.* an adequate amount ‖ the state or quality of being sufficient

suf·fi·cient *adj.* enough, as much as is needed

suf·fix *n.* a sound, syllable or syllables added to the end of a word

suf·fo·cate suf·fo·cat·ing suf·fo·cat·ed *v.t.* to kill by stopping respiration ‖ to oppress, smother ‖ *v.i.* to die by being suffocated

suf·fo·ca·tion *n.* a suffocating or being suffocated

suf·frage *n.* the right to vote in political elections **suf·fra·gette** *n.* a female agitator for women's suffrage

suf·fuse suf·fus·ing suf·fused *v.t.* to spread or cover completely

suf·fu·sion *n.* a suffusing or being suffused

sug·ar 1. *n.* sucrose obtained chiefly by processing the juice from sugarcane or from sugar beets ‖ one of a class of simple carbohydrates soluble in water **2.** *v.t.* to sweeten with sugar ‖ to sprinkle with sugar ‖ *v.i.* to form sugar **to sugar the pill** to make something unpleasant acceptable

sug·gest *v.t.* to put forward ‖ bring to mind ‖ to propose ‖ to intimate ‖ prompt the doing of

sug·ges·tion *n.* a suggesting or being suggested ‖ that which is suggested ‖ a very slight amount

sug·ges·tive *adj.* stimulating ideas, emotions etc. ‖ tending to suggest something indecent

su·i·cid·al *adj.* involving or leading to suicide

su·i·cide *n.* the act of killing oneself intentionally ‖ an action for which one is responsible and which damages one's career or reputation irreparably

suit 1. *n.* a jacket and pants of the same material ‖ a jacket and skirt of the same material ‖ the act of suing in a court of law ‖ one of the four sets of cards in a deck ‖ an outfit adapted to a particular activity or circumstance **2.** *v.t.* to meet the needs or wishes of, be convenient for **to suit oneself** to satisfy one's own needs, convenience or wishes

suit·a·ble *adj.* meeting the requirements of a situation, purpose etc. ‖ unobjectionable **súit·a·bly** *adv.*

suit·case *n.* valise, luggage

suite *n.* a set of rooms, e.g. in a hotel ‖ a retinue, personal staff

suit·or *n.* a petitioner ‖ a man who courts a woman with a view to marriage

sul·fur, sul·phur *n.* a multivalent nonmetallic element found in crystalline or amorphous form

sulk 1. *v.i.* to make one's resentment or vexation felt by others by not talking to them, not cooperating etc. **2.** *n.* the state of sulking **súlk·i·ly** *adv.* **súlk·i·ness** *n.* **súlk·y 3. sulk·i·er sulk·i·est** *adj.* sulking or inclined to sulk **4.** *pl.* **sulk·ies** *n.* a light two-wheeled cart having one seat only and no body, esp. used for trotting races

sul·len *adj.* gloomy, ill-humored and unsociable ‖ dull, heavy ‖ sluggish

sul·ly sul·ly·ing sul·lied *v.t.* to soil

sul·try sul·tri·er sul·tri·est *adj.* hot and oppressive ‖ passionately sensual

sum 1. *n.* an amount of money ‖ gist, summary ‖ the result obtained by adding **in sum** in short **2.** *v.t.* **sum·ming summed** (often with 'up') to add together

sum·ma·ri·za·tion *n.* a summarizing or being summarized

sum·ma·rize   **sum·ma·riz·ing sum·ma·rized** *v.t.* to sum up, make a summary of ‖ to be a summary of

sum·ma·ry *adj.* giving the essentials briefly ‖ done quickly without formality ‖ marked by less than proper consideration

sum·ma·ry *pl.* **sum·ma·ries** *n.* a short statement of the essential points of a matter

sum·ma·tion *n.* the act of adding ‖ an aggregate ‖ a nerve impulse

sum·mer 1. *n.* the warmest season of the year **2.** *adj.* of summer ‖ done in the summer **3.** *v.i.* to pass the summer

sum·mer·y *adj.* of, relating to, or like summer

sum·mit *n.* the highest point ‖ a conference held by heads of state

sum·mon *v.t.* to order to appear ‖ to cite (a jury) ‖ to cite (an accused person or witness) to appear in court ‖ to call a meeting of

sum·mons 1. *pl.* **sum·mons·es** *n.* a request or order to appear, attend, perform some action etc. **2.** *v.t.* to serve with a summons

sump *n.* a drainage pit ‖ a cesspool

sump·tu·ous *adj.* lavish, luxurious

sun 1. *n.* the central controlling body of the solar system ‖ the light or heat received from the sun ‖ any heavenly body

that is the center of a solar system ‖ a source of splendor **2. sun·ning sunned** *v.i.* to sit or lie in direct sunlight

sun·bath *n.* a period of exposure of the body to the sun or to a sun lamp

sun·bathe sun·bath·ing sun·bathed *v.i.* to take a sunbath

sun·burn 1. reddening and blistering with consequent peeling of the skin through too sudden and too long exposure to the sun **2. sun·burn·ing sun·burned, sun·burnt** *v.i.* to become bronzed or blistered by exposure to the sun

sun·dae *n.* a portion of ice cream served with sauce, fruit, nuts, whipped cream etc.

Sun·day *n.* the first day of the week

sun·der *v.i.* to break apart, to separate

sun·down *n.* the part of day when the sun is setting

sun·dries *pl.n.* miscellaneous items, esp. items individually of small importance

sun·dry *adj.* various ‖ miscellaneous

sun·flow·er *n.* a genus of tall-growing plants with often very large yellow-rayed flowers

sun·glass·es *pl.n.* spectacles with lenses which are tinted to protect the eyes from glare

sunk·en alt.*adj.* below the surrounding level ‖ lying at the bottom of an ocean, river etc. ‖ appearing as if hollow

sun·lamp *n.* an electric lamp which produces ultraviolet radiation

sun·light *n.* the light emanating from the sun

sun·lit *adj.* shining in the light of the sun

sun·ny sun·ni·er sun·ni·est *adj.* made bright or warm by the sun ‖ cheerful

sun·rise *n.* the appearance of the sun above the horizon in the morning ‖ the time when this happens

sun·set *n.* the disappearance of the sun below the horizon at the end of the day

sun·shine *n.* the light received directly from the sun

sun·stroke *n.* heatstroke

super- prefix over, above ‖ higher ‖ greater in quality ‖ extra, additional

su·perb *adj.* of the highest quality ‖ magnificent to behold ‖ majestic in size, proportion etc.

su·per·charge   su·per·charg·ing   su·per·charged *v.t.* to force air and;or fuel under pressure into (an internal-combustion engine) to increase its power

su·per·cil·i·ous *adj.* showing patronizing disdain

su·per·fi·cial *adj.* not penetrating further than the surface ‖ apparent rather than real ‖ without depth of mind, feeling or imagination   **su·per·fi·ci·al·i·ty** *n.* **su·per·fí·cial·ly** *adv.*

su·per·fine *adj.* extremely fine

su·per·flu·ous *adj.* being more than is needed ‖ not needed, unnecessary

su·per·hu·man *adj.* beyond normal human capacity or power ‖ supernatural

su·per·im·pose   su·per·im·pos·ing   su·per·im·posed *v.t.* to lay (one thing) on or upon another **su·per·im·po·si·tion** *n.*

su·per·in·tend *v.t.* to direct ‖ to have charge of

su·per·in·tend·ent *n.* a person who superintends

su·pe·ri·or 1. *adj.* high or higher in position, rank, status etc. ‖ better in quality ‖ greater in value **2.** *n.* a person who is superior in rank or authority   **su·pe·ri·or·i·ty** *n.*

superiority complex a neurotic condition resulting from subconscious belief in one's superiority to others

su·per·la·tive 1. *adj.* of the highest quality, kind, degree etc. ‖ excessive **2.** *n.* the highest degree of something ‖ someone or something superlative ‖ the superlative degree of comparison

su·per·mar·ket *n.* a large self-service food and household goods store

su·per·nat·u·ral 1. *adj.* not able to be explained in terms of the known laws **2.** *n.* a supernatural being, force etc.   **su·per·nát·u·ral·ism** *n.* belief in the supernatural   **su·per·nát·u·ral·ist** *n.* **su·per·nat·u·ral·ís·tic** *adj.*

su·per·nu·mer·ar·y 1. *adj.* above the prescribed number, extra ‖ superfluous **2.**

pl. **su·per·nu·mer·ar·ies** *n.* a person employed for use as need directs

su·per·pow·er *n.* a nation which, by reason of its economic, political and military strength, influences the policies of less powerful nations

su·per·sede   su·per·sed·ing   su·per·sed·ed *v.t.* to outmode and take the place of ‖ to replace **su·per·se·dure** *n.*

su·per·son·ic *adj.* of waves of greater frequency than those to which the human ear responds ‖ of motion faster than the speed of sound waves in air ‖ moving at this speed **su·per·són·ics** *n.* the science dealing with supersonic phenomena

su·per·star *n.* **1.** a celestial body, emitting great energy, e.g. quasar **2.** a widely known personality of superior talent **superstardom** *n.*

su·per·sti·tion *n.* a belief or beliefs justified neither by reason nor evidence nor by any religious canon

su·per·sti·tious *adj.* of or relating to superstition

su·per·struc·ture *n.* the entire building above the main supporting level ‖ the structure of a ship above the main deck

su·per·vise   su·per·vis·ing   su·per·vised *v.t.* to superintend (work or the person doing it)

su·per·vi·sion *n.* a supervising or being supervised

su·per·vi·sor *n.* a person who supervises **su·per·vi·so·ry** *adj.*

su·pine *adj.* lying flat on the back ‖ listless

sup·per *n.* a meal taken in the evening

sup·plant *v.t.* to supersede ‖ to take the place of

sup·ple *adj.* easily bent ‖ readily changing to meet new situations

sup·ple·ment 1. *n.* something added **2.** *v.t.* to add to ‖ to supply a deficiency in **sup·ple·men·tal, sup·ple·mén·ta·ry** *adjs.*

sup·pli·cant 1. *n.* a suppliant **2.** *adj.* supplicating

sup·pli·cate   sup·pli·cat·ing   sup·pli·cat·ed *v.t.* to ask for in humble petition ‖ to entreat

sup·pli·ca·tion *n.* the act or process of

supplicating ‖ a humble request, prayer etc.

sup·pli·er *n.* someone who supplies

sup·ply 1. sup·ply·ing sup·plied *v.t.* to give ‖ to fill the needs of ‖ to satisfy (a need) ‖ to furnish **2.** *pl.* **sup·plies** *n.* stock or stores available for use ‖ the amount or quantity of goods available on the market for purchase

sup·port 1. *v.t.* to carry the weight of ‖ to prevent from falling, sinking etc. ‖ to be actively in favor of ‖ to assist or strengthen morally ‖ to bear, endure ‖ to give assistance to ‖ to second (a resolution) **2.** *n.* a supporting ‖ someone who or something which supports ‖ a means of sustenance **sup·pórt·a·ble** *adj.* **sup·pórt·er** *n.* a person who supports ‖ a partisan

sup·pose sup·pos·ing sup·posed *v.t.* to think likely ‖ to presume ‖ (used in the imperative) to imagine (something) ‖ to postulate **sup·posed** *adj.* thought, but not known, to be true ‖ imagined **sup·pos·ed·ly** *adv.* **sup·pos·ing** *conj.* on the supposition that, in the event that

sup·po·si·tion *n.* the act of supposing ‖ that which is supposed **sup·po·sí·tion·al** *adj.*

sup·press *v.t.* to subdue, put down by force ‖ to withhold ‖ to hold back ‖ to stop ‖ to dismiss from the conscious mind

sup·pres·sion *n.* a suppressing ‖ the conscious dismissing of an unacceptable idea, memory etc. from the mind

sup·pu·rate sup·pu·rat·ing sup·pu·rat·ed *v.i.* to discharge pus

sup·pu·ra·tion *n.* the discharging of pus

su·prem·a·cy *n.* the quality of being supreme ‖ the position of being superior to all others in something

su·preme *adj.* being the highest authority

sur·charge 1. *v.t.* **sur·charg·ing sur·charged** to overcharge ‖ to overload **2.** *n.* a charge or tax over and above what is standard ‖ an additional burden

sure 1. *adj.* accepted as the truth ‖ accepting something as true ‖ that can be relied upon **2.** *adv.* certainly

sure·ly *adv.* in a sure manner ‖ without a doubt

sure·ty *pl.* **sure·ties** *n.* the condition of being sure ‖ a person who makes himself a guarantor for another's actions ‖ something pledged as security

surf 1. *n.* the foam of waves breaking on the shore **2.** *v.i.* to ride a wave to shore on a surfboard

sur·face 1. *n.* the two-dimensional boundary of a material body ‖ the outward aspect of something **on the surface** so far as the eye can judge **2. sur·fac·ing sur·faced** *v.i.* to come to the surface of the water **3.** *adj.* of or at the surface ‖ superficial

sur·feit 1. *n.* an oversupply, excess ‖ overindulgence **2.** *v.t.* to oversupply ‖ to overfeed ‖ to satiate

surge 1. surg·ing surged *v.i.* (of the sea) to heave and swell in great force and agitation **2.** *n.* the heaving of waves ‖ a sudden access of interest ‖ a sudden abnormal rise of current followed by a drop

sur·geon *n.* a medical practitioner who performs surgery

sur·ger·y *pl.* **sur·ger·ies** *n.* the operating upon injuries, defects etc. ‖ the branch of medicine dealing with this ‖ the operating theater of a surgeon or hospital

sur·gi·cal *adj.* of surgeons or surgery ‖ used in surgery

sur·ly sur·li·er sur·li·est *adj.* uncivil, bad-tempered

sur·mise 1. *n.* a supposition based on slight evidence **2. sur·mis·ing sur·mised** *v.t.* to guess ‖ *v.i.* to suppose

sur·mount *v.t.* to overcome ‖ to climb over ‖ to surpass in height

sur·name *n.* a family name

sur·pass *v.t.* to excel ‖ to exceed **sur·páss·ing** *adj.*

sur·plus 1. *n.* excess in receipts over expenditure ‖ something left over **2.** *adj.* in excess of requirements

sur·prise 1. *n.* the emotion excited by something totally unexpected **to take by surprise** to come upon suddenly or unexpectedly ‖ to catch unprepared ‖ to astonish ‖ to capture by a sudden, unexpected attack 2. *v.t.* **sur·pris·ing sur·prised** to cause to experience unexpected emotion ‖ to attack suddenly and unexpectedly **sur·pris·ing** *adj.*

sur·re·al·ism *n.* a movement in art and literature

sur·ren·der 1. *v.t.* to give up ‖ to sign away one's rights under (an insurance policy) in return for an agreed sum ‖ *v.i.* to acknowledge defeat and by so doing put oneself into the power of an adversary 2. *n.* the act of surrendering

sur·rep·ti·tious *adj.* secretive, stealthy

sur·ro·gate 1. *v.t.* **sur·ro·gat·ing sur·ro·gat·ed** to appoint as a substitute for another 2. *n.* a substitute ‖ a judicial officer

surrogate mother a woman who bears a child for the convenience of another woman, conceiving such child by artificial insemination

sur·round 1. *v.t.* to encircle ‖ to cut off by enclosing with troops **sur·round·ing 2.** *adj.* which surrounds 3. *n.* (*pl.*) environment ‖ environs

sur·tax 1. *n.* an extra tax 2. *v.t.* to levy such an extra tax on

sur·veil·lance *n.* a close watch

sur·veil·lant *n.* a person who keeps a close watch over another ‖ a supervisor

sur·vey 1. *v.t.* to measure the extent, contours etc. of (a land area) ‖ to examine in detail ‖ to consider in general and in detail 2. *n.* a general inspection ‖ a careful examination ‖ the process of surveying an area of land

sur·vey·or *n.* a person whose profession is surveying land etc.

sur·viv·al *n.* the act, state or fact of surviving

sur·vive sur·viv·ing sur·vived *v.t.* to live or exist longer than ‖ to continue to live or exist in spite of **sur·vi·vor** *n.* a person who or thing which survives

survivor *n.* one who will not accept defeat

sus·cep·ti·bil·i·ty *pl.* **sus·cep·ti·bil·i·ties** *n.* the quality of being susceptible ‖ (*pl.*) sensibilities ‖ the quality of being liable or exposed or prone

sus·cep·ti·ble *adj.* affected or influenced

particularly easily **susceptible to** liable to ‖ able to be influenced by **sus·cép·ti·bly** *adv.*

sus·pect 1. *v.t.* to believe (someone) guilty of something without conclusive proof ‖ to presume (something) to be not what it seems ‖ to mistrust ‖ *v.i.* to be suspicious 2. *adj.* suspected 3. *n.* someone suspected, esp. of a crime

sus·pend *v.t.* to attach to some elevated point without support from below ‖ to debar from the exercise of an office ‖ to send (a student) away for a time as punishment

sus·pense *n.* the state of anxious expectancy or uncertainty while waiting for a decision, outcome etc. ‖ an effect of intense and prolonged expectancy

sus·pen·sion *n.* a being suspended ‖ an imposed temporary withdrawal of a right or privilege ‖ the stoppage of payment of debts

sus·pi·cion *n.* the act of suspecting ‖ the merest inkling **above suspicion** not to be suspected because held in such high reputation

sus·pi·cious *adj.* suspecting ‖ arousing suspicion

sus·tain *v.t.* to prevent from falling, collapsing or giving way ‖ to keep going ‖ to provide with nourishment etc. ‖ to support ‖ to endure ‖ to experience (a loss or injury)

sus·te·nance *n.* nourishment ‖ livelihood

su·ture 1. *n.* a line of union between bones ‖ the stitching up of a wound ‖ the thread or wire used in this operation 2. *v.t.* **su·tur·ing su·tured** to stitch (a wound)

svelte *adj.* slender, graceful

swab 1. *n.* a floor mop ‖ a twist of cotton etc. attached to a thin stick 2. *v.t.* **swab·bing swabbed** to clean with a swab

swag·ger 1. *v.i.* to walk in a way that betrays great conceit 2. *n.* a swaggering gait

swal·low *n.* a family of small migratory birds

swallow 1. *v.t.* to cause (food, drink etc.) to pass down the throat ‖ to engulf, envelop ‖ to accept without testing it for truth ‖ to hold back ‖ to retract (e.g. words said) **2.** *n.* the act of swallowing ‖ the amount swallowed in one gulp

swamp 1. *n.* spongy ground **2.** *v.t.* to fill with water ‖ to make very wet ‖ to submerge under too many demands ‖ to overwhelm **swámp·y swamp·i·er swamp·i·est** *adj.*

swan *n.* any of various large, stately, usually white, long necked aquatic birds

swank 1. *n.* ostentatious display, e.g. in dress or speech **2.** *v.i.* to show off **3.** *adj.* swanky **swánk·y swank·i·er swank·i·est** *adj.* showy ‖ stylish

swap, swop swap·ping, swop·ping swapped, swopped 1. *v.t.* to exchange by barter **2.** *n.* the act of bartering

swarm 1. *n.* a large number of honeybees migrating from a hive with their queen to establish a new colony ‖ any great moving throng **2.** *v.i.* (of bees) to emigrate in a body from a hive to form a new colony ‖ to move around in large numbers

swarth·y swarth·i·er swarth·i·est *adj.* dark-colored

swash·buck·ler *n.* a swaggering fighting man out for adventure **swásh·buck·ling** *adj.* characterized by bluster

swat, swot 1. *v.t.* **swat·ting, swot·ting swat·ted, swot·ted** to hit with a sharp blow **2.** *n.* a quick sharp blow

swatch *n.* a sample piece of fabric, leather etc.

swathe 1. *v.t.* **swath·ing swathed** to wrap, bind etc. with a swathe **2.** *n.* a wrapping or bandage

sway 1. *v.i.* to swing from side to side ‖ to go forward while moving in this way ‖ to incline to one side as a result of some force, e.g. wind **2.** *n.* a swaying

swear 1. *v.* **swear·ing swore sworn** *v.i.* to make a solemn oath ‖ to use sacred words irreverently ‖ *v.t.* to affirm by solemn oath ‖ to declare forcefully to be true ‖ to promise solemnly **to swear in** to induct into office by administering an oath to **2.** *n.* a swearword

sweat *n.* the usually colorless saline fluid secreted by the sweat glands ‖ moisture

exuded from, and forming beadlike drops on, a surface ‖ hard work ‖ a state of anxiety **sweat** *v.i.* to excrete moisture through the openings of the sweat glands ‖ (of rocks, glass etc.) to collect surface moisture from the air by condensation ‖ to toil laboriously ‖ to make wet with sweat **to sweat blood** to slave away at some task **sweat·er** *n.* a knitted garment, with or without sleeves

sweat·y sweat·i·er sweat·i·est *adj.* running with sweat ‖ smelling of sweat ‖ causing sweat

sweep 1. *v.* **sweep·ing swept** *v.i.* to spread rapidly ‖ to move with proud or dignified grace ‖ to use a broom in cleaning, clearing etc. ‖ *v.t.* to pass swiftly across ‖ to clean of dust, debris etc. ‖ to direct the gaze over in a wide arc ‖ to drag (e.g. the bottom of a river) **2.** *n.* the action of sweeping ‖ someone whose work is sweeping ‖ a long sweeping line or contour ‖ a wide expanse ‖ a length of cable used in dragging for obstructions, e.g. mines, in the sea **sweep·er** *n.*

sweep·ing 1. *n.* the action of a sweeper ‖ *(pl.)* refuse **2.** *adj.* on a very large scale ‖ too comprehensive to allow of distinctions ‖ moving in a wide curve

sweet 1. *adj.* having the characteristic taste of sugar ‖ containing sugar ‖ pleasing to the senses ‖ characterized by gentleness, kindliness etc. **2.** *n. pl.* sweet edible things

sweet·en 1. *v.t.* to make sweet to the taste ‖ to put into a kinder mood ‖ to make more attractive or more enjoyable ‖ *v.i.* to become sweet **sweet·en·ing** *n.* that which sweetens

sweet·heart *n.* a girl in relation to the boy in love with her, or a boy in relation to the girl in love with him ‖ a term of endearment

sweet potato a trailing vine grown for its sweet tubers ‖ the tuber, cooked and eaten as a vegetable

swell 1. **swell·ing swelled swol·len, swelled** *v.i.* to increase in volume ‖ to increase in number, degree, quantity etc.

|| to become louder || to rise above the normal level || to curve outward or upward **2.** *n.* the act of swelling || the state of being swollen || an increase in loudness || a succession of long, unbroken waves **3.** *adj.* excellent, marvelous etc.

swell·ing *n.* an increase or being increased in size, volume etc. || a swollen part of something

swel·ter 1. *v.i.* to be oppressively hot **2.** *n.* oppressive heat **swél·ter·ing** *adj.* sweltry **swél·try swel·tri·er swel·tri·est** *adj.* oppressively hot

swerve 1. *v.* **swerv·ing swerved** *v.i.* to change direction suddenly || to curve in flight || to deviate from an acceptable or right course of conduct, action etc. **2.** *n.* a sudden change of direction || a curve in flight of a ball

swift 1. *adj.* moving with great speed || rapid **2.** *n.* any of numerous small birds resembling swallows

swig 1. *v.* **swig·ging swigged** *v.t.* **2.** to drink in large gulps || *v.i.* to drink large quantities **3.** *n.* a drink taken in a long steady gulp

swill 1. *v.t.* to wash roughly || to cause (some liquid) to lap around inside a vessel by rotating it || to drink greedily **2.** *n.* hogs' liquid food || garbage || a swig

swim 1. *v.* **swim·ming swam swum** *v.i.* to move through or under the surface of water by movements of the limbs, strokes of fins, flippers, tail etc. || (of the head) to experience dizziness || *v.t.* to cross by propelling oneself through water **to swim against the stream** to go counter to the majority in one's ideas, policies etc. **2.** *n.* a period of swimming

swimming 1. *n.* the sport of swimming **2.** *adj.* adapted to swimming || afflicted with dizziness

swim·ming·ly *adv.* going along rapidly and easily

swin·dle 1. *v.* **swin·dling swin·dled** *v.t.* to trick || to get by fraud **2.** *n.* the act or process of swindling

swin·dler *n.* a person who practices swindling

swine *pl.* **swine** *n.* a hog

swing 1. swing·ing swung *v.i.* to sway freely to and fro || to aturn on a hinge, pivot etc. || to go back and forth in a swing or hammock || to move along in a rhythmic, swaying motion || to be executed by hanging || to dance to swing music **2.** *n.* the act of swinging || a seat suspended by ropes from a fixed support, in which one can swing to and fro || a free, easy motion, esp. in marching or walking **in full swing** operating with full vigor

swing·er *n.* **1.** one who has many sexual partners **2.** one who is up-to-date in modern fashions and activities

swipe 1. swip·ing swiped *v.t.* to steal || to hit with a swinging blow **2.** *n.* a powerful blow

swirl 1. *v.i.* to move in eddies and whirls || (of birds etc.) to move fast in a circular course || to have a whirling, dizzy sensation || *v.t.* to cause to whirl **2.** *n.* a whirling movement || a swirling mass of water etc.

swish 1. *v.i.* to cut through the air, e.g. with a whip, causing a sharp hissing or whistling sound || to rustle **2.** *n.* sharp, hissing sound or rustling sound **swish·y** *adj.*

Swiss chard *n.* a variety of beet eaten cooked or in salads

switch 1. *n.* a device for diverting a train from one line to another || a device for making or breaking an electric circuit || the act of switching || a thin, flexible stick, twig etc. || a complete change **2.** *v.t.* to beat with a switch || *v.i.* to move from one set of railroad tracks to another **to switch on (off)** to turn on (off) by using an electric switch

switch·board *n.* panel fitted with switches which control a number of electrical circuits

swiv·el 1. *n.* a mechanical device consisting of a pivot mounted in a ring so that the two parts of the device can revolve independently **2.** *v.i.* **swiv·el·ing swiv·eled** to turn on or as if on a swivel

swoon 1. *v.i.* to faint **2.** *n.* the action of fainting

swoop 1. *v.i.* to descend swiftly and

suddenly ‖ (esp. with 'down') to make a sudden attack **2.** *n.* a sudden attack

sword *n.* a weapon having a long, thin cutting bladed fitted into a hilt

syc·a·more *n.* a large, spreading tree

syc·o·phan·cy *n.* servile flattery

syc·o·phant *n.* a person who habitually uses flattery to gain personal advantage **syc·o·phan·tic** *adj.*

syl·lab·ic 1. *adj.* relating to syllables ‖ pronounced distinctly with stress on each syllable ‖ of a verse form arranged according to syllables per line **2.** *n.* a vocal speech sound capable by itself of forming a syllable **syl·láb·i·cal·ly** *adv.*

syl·lab·i·cate syl·lab·i·cat·ing syl·lab·i·cat·ed *v.t.* to syllabify

syl·lab·i·fi·ca·tion *n.* division into syllables

syl·lab·i·fy syl·lab·i·fy·ing syl·lab·i·fied *v.t.* to form or divide into syllables

syl·la·ble *n.* a word or part of a word pronounced with a single sounding of the voice

syl·la·bus *pl.* **syl·la·bus·es, syl·la·bi** *n.* a brief outline of lessons, lectures etc.

syl·lo·gism *n.* a logically consistent argument ‖ a branch of logic **syl·lo·gis·tic, syl·lo·gís·ti·cal** *adjs*

sylph *n.* a slender, graceful girl

syl·van, sil·van *adj.* of or situated in a wood ‖ wooded

sym·bi·o·sis *n.* the intimate association of two dissimilar organisms from which each organism benefits

sym·bol *n.* sign standing for some process, idea, quality etc. ‖ an object that represents a repressed unconscious drive, memory etc. **sym·bol·ic sym·ból·i·cal** *adjs* **sym·ból·i·cal·ly** *adv.*

sym·bol·ism *n.* representation by symbols

sym·bol·ize sym·bol·iz·ing sym·bol·ized *v.t.* to be a symbol of ‖ *v.i.* to use a symbols

sym·met·ric *adj.* symmetrical

sym·me·try *pl.* **sym·me·tries** *n.* the quality of possessing exactly corresponding parts on either side of an axis ‖ the quality of being well balanced or well proportioned

sym·pa·thet·ic *adj.* possessing sympathy ‖ exactly fitting in with one's mood ‖ favorably disposed ‖ of the sympathetic nervous system **sym·pa·thét·i·cal·ly** *adv.*

sym·pa·thize sym·pa·thiz·ing sym·pa·thized *v.i.* to feel sympathy ‖ to feel or express compassion ‖ to be favorably disposed

sym·pa·thy *pl.* **sym·pa·thies** *n.* a sharing in the emotions of others ‖ a mutual liking **to be in sympathy with** to be favorably disposed towards

sym·phon·ic *adj.* having the form of a symphony ‖ of or relating to harmony of sound

sym·pho·ny *pl.* **sym·pho·nies** *n.* musical composition for full orchestra ‖ a symphony orchestra

sym·po·si·um *pl.* **sym·po·si·a, sym·po·si·ums** *n.* a group discussion

symp·tom *n.* a condition in the body, noted by the patient, suggesting the presence of injury or disease

symp·to·mat·ic *adj.* of symptoms ‖ in accordance with symptoms **symp·to·mát·i·cal·ly** *adv.*

syn·a·gogue *n.* the building used by Jewish communities for worship

syn·chro·ni·za·tion *n.* a synchronizing

syn·chro·nize syn·chro·niz·ing syn·chro·nized *v.i.* to occur at the same time ‖ *v.t.* to regulate so as to agree in time ‖ *(movies)* to adjust (sounds) with the action

syn·co·pate syn·co·pat·ing syn·co·pat·ed *v.t.* to shorten (a word) ‖ to shift the regular accent to a normally unaccented beat **syn·co·pá·tion** *n.* a syncopated rhythm

syn·di·cate 1. *n.* a group of persons or firms authorized jointly to promote some common interest ‖ a chain of newspapers **2.** *v* **syn·di·cat·ing syn·di·cat·ed** *v.i.* to join together to form a syndicate ‖ *v.t.* to form into a syndicate **syn·di·cá·tion** *n.*

syn·od *n.* a consultative council of clergy

syn·o·nym *n.* a word having the same meaning as another word **syn·o·ným·ic** *adj.* **syn·o·nym·i·ty** *n.* **syn·on·y·mous** *adj.*

syn·op·sis *pl.* **syn·op·ses** *n.* an outline, summary

syn·tax *n.* the arrangement of words in a sentence showing their constructional relationship

syn·the·sis pl. **syn·the·ses** n. an exposition assembling the various parts into a whole ‖ the formation of a compound from elements or simpler compounds **sýn·the·sist** n. **syn·the·size** v.t. **syn·the·siz·ing syn·the·sized** to form into a whole by synthesis

syn·thet·ic 1. adj. produced by synthesis ‖ artificial, man-made **2.** n. a synthetic product **syn·thét·i·cal·ly** adv.

syph·i·lis n. a chronic, often congenital venereal disease **syph·i·lit·ic** n. and adj.

sy·ringe 1. n. a piston-fitted hand cylinder into which a liquid is sucked and then ejected in a stream **2.** v.t. **sy·ring·ing sy·ringed** to inject, cleanse etc. with a syringe

syr·up, sir·up n. a thick liquid consisting of a concentrated solution of sugar and water ‖ cloying sentimentality **sýr·up·y,** **sír·up·y** adj.

sys·tem n. an orderly, interconnected complex aarrangement of parts ‖ a set of principles linked to form a coherent doctrine ‖ a method of organization, administration or procedure ‖ a major division of rocks, formed during a period or era ‖ a group of bodily organs having the same or similar structure ‖ a method of classification

sys·tem·at·ic adj. constituting a system ‖ working in accordance with a system, methodical **sys·tem·át·i·cal·ly** adv. **sys·tem·at·ics** n. the science of classification

sys·tem·a·ti·za·tion n. a systematizing **sys·tem·a·tize** **sys·tem·a·tiz·ing** **sys·tem·a·tized** v.t. to make into a system

sys·to·le n. the regular contraction of an organ by which the blood is driven forward **sys·tol·ic** adj.

T

T, t the twentieth letter of the English alphabet

tab n. a small loop or flap attached to something ‖ an unpaid bill

tab·by pl. **tab·bies** n. a cat with brownish-gray fur marked with dark, wavy stripes ‖ a female cat

tab·er·nac·le n. a niche or recess having a canopy ‖ a Nonconformist place of worship

ta·ble 1. n. a piece of furniture having a flat, horizontal surface ‖ an orderly arrangement of facts set out for easy reference **to keep** or **set)a good (poor** etc.) **table** to serve good (poor etc.) food at one's table **to turn the tables on (someone)** to put (someone) who had the advantage over one at a disadvantage **2.** v.t. **ta·bling ta·bled** to postpone a decision

ta·ble·spoon n. a large spoon used for serving food from a dish to a plate **ta·ble·spoon·ful** pl. **ta·ble·spoon·fuls** n. as much as a tablespoon will hold

tab·let a medical pastille ‖ a pad of writing paper

ta·ble·ware n. dishes, cutlery etc. used in setting a table

tab·loid n. a small-format, heavily illustrated newspaper featuring news items of a sensational nature

ta·boo, ta·bu 1. n. anything which is prohibited by tradition or social usage **2.** adj. forbidden on grounds of tradition or social usage **3.** v.t. to condemn as not proper because of concentino etc.

tab·u·lar adj. set out in the form of a table ‖ computed from a table ‖ having a flat, tablelike surface, laminated

tab·u·late 1. v.t. **tab·u·lat·ing tab·u·lat·ed**

to arrange in tabular form **2.** *adj.* having tabulae **tab·u·lá·tion** *n.* **táb·u·la·tor** *n.* a business machine for tabulating data

tac·it *adj.* existing or implied but not stated

tac·i·turn *adj.* not given to saying much

tack 1. *n.* a short, sharp nail having a broad, usually flat, head ‖ the direction in which a vessel sails as the result of the position of her sails and helm ‖ the act of changing this direction by shifting the sails and helm ‖ a course of action **2.** *v.t.* to fasten with tacks ‖ to append as an addition ‖ *v.i.* to change the direction of a sailing ship ‖ to change one's course of action

tack·i·ness *n.* the state or quality of being tacky

tack·le 1. *n.* a ship's rigging ‖ a mechanism for lifting weights by ropes and pulleys ‖ equipment ‖ the harness for a horse **2. tack·ling tack·led** *v.t.* to come to grips with ‖ to apply oneself to a hard piece of work) ‖ to seize and stop or pull down

tack·y tack·i·er tack·i·est *adj.* still sticky to the touch

tacky tack·i·er tack·i·est *adj.* shabby, dowdy

tact *n.* an understanding of how to avoid giving offense **tact·ful** *adj.*

tac·tic *n.* tactics ‖ a detail of tactics

tac·ti·cal *adj.* astutely thought out so as to advance a purpose or gain an advantage

tac·tics *n.* (construed as *pl.*) carefully worked-out steps taken to achieve a purpose

tac·tile *adj.* perceived by the sense of touch **tac·til·i·ty** *n.*

tad·pole *n.* the tailed, legless, aquatic larva of the frog, toad or certain other amphibians

taf·fe·ta *n.* a thin, rather stiff glossy fabric of natural or artificial silk

tag 1. *n.* a label for identification, classification etc. ‖ a hanging, tatter bit of cloth **2. tag·ging tagged** *v.t.* to attach a tag to ‖ to attach as an addition ‖ *v.t.* (with 'along') to join up temporarily with someone else ‖ to drag oneself along

tag 1. *n.* a children's game in which a player chases other players until he manages to touch one **2.** *v.t.* **tag·ging tagged** to touch (a player) in this game

tail 1. *n.* the part of the body posterior to the anus in many vertebrates or this as a caudal appendage in prolongation of the vertebral column ‖ something resembling this in form or positon ‖ the last part of something ‖ (also *pl.*) the reverse side of a coin ‖ *pl.* full evening dress **with the tail between the legs** in a defeated or dejected way **2.** *v.t.* to follow (someone) so as to observe his actions ‖ to form the tail of (e.g. a procession) ‖ *v.i.* (with 'along' or 'behind') to tag along behind someone

tail gate the hinged board at the rear of a van

tail·gate tail·gat·ing tail·gat·ed *v.i.* to drive dangerously close behind another vehicle

tai·lor 1. *n.* a person whose occupation is making men's and women's coats, suits etc. **2.** *v.t.* to work as a tailor ‖ *v.t.* to make (garments) to measure ‖ to fashion to suit a particular need

tai·lor-made *adj.* made and fitted by a tailor ‖ fashioned specifically for the occasion or conditions

tail·spin *n.* a spiral dive, nose-foremost, by an aircraft

taint 1. *v.t.* to cause to rot, putrefy ‖ to corrupt morally ‖ to cause to be slightly spoiled by some undesirable quality **2.** *n.* a trace of infection or corruption

take 1. tak·ing took tak·en *v.t.* to get possession of by using force or superior strength ‖ to give or receive guidance ‖ to surprise, attack, catch or overcome, esp. suddenly ‖ to eat, drink or receive into the body in some other way ‖ to enter into a relationship with (someone) ‖ to steal or remove without right ‖ to assume (office, control etc.) ‖ to hire or rent ‖ to make use of ‖ to write down (notes, dictation) ‖ to study or have as a course of study ‖ to carry (something to someone ‖ to remove ‖ to subtract ‖ to react to ‖ to occupy ‖ *v.i.* to get or gain possession ‖ (with 'from') to detract **to take away** to carry off in one's possession ‖ to subtract **to take it** to submit to criticism, ridicule etc. with composure **to take it easy** to rest **to take**

it hard to be intensely hurt emotionally **to take it lying down** to be submissive **to take it on the chin** to endure punishment, suffering etc. bravely **to take out** to remove ‖ to acquire (insurance, a patent, a license) ‖ to escort to places of entertainment etc. **to take upon oneself** to begin to do something) without invitation, instruction or prompting **to take up with** to become friendly with **2.** *n.* the act of taking ‖ an amount taken or received in payment ‖ th eportion of one scene in the making of a film that is photographed at one time

take·off *n.* the act of leaving the ground, e.g. in beginning a flight ‖ the point at which this takes place ‖ the act of mimicking someone

take·o·ver *n.* the assuming of control, ownership or management of e.g. a corporation

tale *n.* an account of a real or imagined event ‖ a piece of gossip ‖ a lie

tal·ent *n.* innate artistic aptitude **tál·ent·ed** *adj.*

tal·is·man *n.* an object supposed to have magical protective qualities **tal·is·man·ic, tal·is·mán·i·cal** *adj.*

talk 1. *v.i.* to express ideas, thoughts etc. in speech ‖ to chatter idly ‖ to gossip ‖ to hold consultation ‖ *v.t.* to express in speech ‖ to discuss **to talk back** to answer rudely or impertinently **to talk big** to boast **2.** *n.* tha act of talking ‖ a speech ‖ a formal conference ‖ gossip ‖ idle chatter ‖ empty phrases

talk·a·tive *adj.* inclined to talk

tall *adj.* above average height ‖ difficult to believe, exaggerated ‖ (of a drink) served in a long, narrow glass

tal·low *n.* a mixture of hard animal fats **tál·low·y** *adj.*

tal·ly 1. *pl.* **tal·lies** *n.* a recorded score or recorded count of objects ‖ an identifying tag ‖ a card for recording a bridge player's score **tal·ly·ing tal·lied** *v.t.* to count ‖ to record on a tally ‖ *v.i.* to match or be consistent

tal·ly·ho 1. *n.* and *interj.* the cry of a huntsman upon sighting a fox **2.** *v.i.* to make this cry

Tal·mud *n.* the body of oral Jewish law

tal·on *n.* a claw, esp. of a bird of prey

tam *n.* a tam-o'shanter

ta·ma·le *n.* a Mexican dish of ground meat seasoned with chili pepper and rolled in cornmeal pastry

tam·bou·tinr *n.* a small drum consisting of a wooden hoop with parchment stretched across it at one end and loose metal disks set around the circumference

tame 1. *adj.* domesticated ‖ lacking liveliness **2.** *v.t.* **tam·ing tamed** to bring under control, make submissive

tam-o'shan·ter *n.* a woolen cap having a close-fitting headband and flat, round, very full crown, usually decorated with a pompon

tamp *v.t.* to ram down (the charge) in a pipe)

tam·per *v.i.* (only in) **to tamper with** to meddle with

tam·pon 1. *n.* a plug of cotton etc., to stop bleeding or to absorb secretions **2.** *v.t.* to pulg with a tampon

tan 1. *n.* the bark of oak or other trees containing tannic acid, used in tanning hides ‖ a color of the skin acquired by exposure to the sun and win ‖ a light brown color **2.** **tan·ner tan·nest** *adj.* light brown

tan tan·ning tanned *v.t.* to convert (hide) into leather ‖ to make brown by exposure to the sun or wind ‖ to thrash (someone) severely

tan·dem 1. *n.* a bicycle with two seats, one behind the other **2.** *adv.* one behind another

tang *n.* a sharp taste or smell ‖ (with 'of') a trace

tan·gent 1. *n.* a line or plane which meets a curve at a single point without intersecting it **to go (or fly) off on** or **at) a tangent** to change abruptly from the subject under consideration **2.** *adj.* touchinhg without intersecting **tan·gen·tial** *adj.* touching without intersecting **tan·gen·tial** *adj.* of, relating to or of the nature of a tangent

tan·ge·rine *n.* a variety of mandarin orange

tan·gi·bil·i·ty *n.* the state or quality of

being tangible

tan·gi·ble *adj.* able to be perceived by the sense of touch ‖ objective, definite **tán·gi·bly** *adv.*

tan·gle 1. *n.* a state of confusion **2. tan·gling tan·gled** *v.t.* to form into a tangle ‖ *v.i.* to become tangled **tán·gly tan·gli·er tan·gli·est** *adj.*

tan·go 1. *n.* a ballroom dance of Argentinian provenance **2.** *v.i.* to dance the tango

tang·y tang·i·er tang·i·est *adj.* having a tang

tank 1. *n.* a large container for liquids or gases ‖ armored combat vehicle **2.** *v.t.* to store in a tank

tank·ard *n.* a large drinking vessel with a handle

tank·er *n.* a ship built to carry liquids in bulk ‖ a heavy rail vehicle for transporting gasoline, milk etc.

tan·ta·lize tan·ta·liz·ing tan·ta·lized *v.t.* t otease by arousing expectations

tan·ta·mount *adj.* (with 'to') equivalent

tan·trum *n.* a fit of bad temper

tap *n.* a device which controls the flow of a fluid from a pipe **on tap** available when required ‖ on draft

tap 1. tap·ping tapped *v.t.* to strike lightly with a rapping sound ‖ (with 'out') to type or keyboard ‖ *v.i.* to walk lightly, making clicking sounds with the heels **2.** *n.* a light rap or blow ‖ a leather or metal reinforcement of the sole or heel of a shoe

tap tap·ping tapped *v.t.* to furnish (a cask etc.) with a tap ‖ to permit (liquid) to flow from a cask, tree etc. by opening a hole or vent ‖ to draw off a fluid from (an abscess etc.) ‖ to connect a listening device in order to intercept telephonic communications ‖ to draw on (resources)

tap dance an exhibition dance in which the rhythm of the music is tapped out by the feet of the dancer

tape 1. *n.* a narrow strip of cotton, silk, rayon, etc. for tying bundles etc. ‖ a narrow roll of thin adhesive paper or plastic ‖ a narrow roll of paper on which a teleprinter prints a message ‖ a tape recording ‖ a tape measure **2.** *v.t.* **tap·ing**

taped to furnish with tape ‖ to fasten with tape ‖ to record on magnetic tape

ta·per 1. *n.* a long, wax-covered wick used for lighting candles etc. **2.** *v.i.* to narrow gradually **to taper off** to become gradually less in number, amount etc. **3.** *adj.* regularly narrowing down to a point

tap·es·try *pl.* **tap·es·tries** *n.* a heavy, hand-worked fabric with pictures or designs used for hangings, chair seats, etc. ‖ a machine-made fabric imitating this

tape·worm *n.* a subclass of long, ribbon-shaped parasitic worms

tap·i·o·ca *n.* a cassava starch processed into grains, flakes etc. and used in puddings

ta·pir *pl.* **ta·pir, ta·pirs** *n.* any of several nonruminant, chiefly nocturnal ungulates

tap·root *n.* a primary root growing vertically downward and giving off small subsidiary roots

tar 1. *n.* a thick, black or dark brown viscous liquid obtained by the destructive distillation of wood, coal etc. **2.** *v.t.* **tar·ring tarred** to cover with tar ‖ to attach a moral stigma to

ta·ran·tu·la *n.* hairy, big spiders

tar·di·ly *adv.* in a tardy manner

tar·di·ness *n.* the quality or state of being tardy

tar·dy tar·di·er tar·di·est *adj.* coming late

tar·get *n.* a circular mat painted with five concentric circles, shot at in archery ‖ a sheet of cardboard or thin wood, similarly marked, aimed at in rifle shooting etc. ‖ any object at which a missile is aimed ‖ an object of attack, criticism etc.

tar·iff *n.* a scale of duties imposed by a government on goods imported or exported ‖ any scale of rates

tar·mac *n.* the hard, level surface of a road, airfield runway etc.

tar·nish 1. *v.t.* to dull brightness ‖ to sully ‖ *v.i.* to become tarnished **2.** *n.* the condition of being tarnished ‖ the film causing this ‖ the condition of being sullied

tar·pau·lin *n.* waterproof canvas or a sheet of this

tar·ry tar·ry·ing tar·ried *v.i.* to linger behind, delay

tart *n.* a piece of pastry containing jam, fruit etc.

tart *n.* a girl or woman of loose morals, esp. a prostitute

tar·tan *n.* a fabric, crossbarred with stripes in various widths and colors which form distinctive patterns

tar·tar *n.* a brownish-red deposit, chiefly of acid potassium tartrate, found in the juice of grapes ‖ a deposit on the teeth

task *n.* a definite amount of work set or undertaken ‖ any piece of work that has to be done

task·mas·ter *n.* (esp. in phrase **a hard taskmaster** a person who demands hard work from others, and who is difficult to satisfy

tas·sel 1. *n.* a tuft of threads or cords fastened at one end **2. tas·sel·ing tas·seled** *v.i.* (often with 'out') to put forth tassels

taste *n.* the sense which perceives and distinguishes between salt, bitter, sour and sweet substances ‖ the flavor detected through this sense ‖ a tasting ‖ discernment where beauty is concerned ‖ a liking, predilection

taste tast·ing tast·ed *v.t.* to examine (a substance) for its taste by putting some in one's mouth ‖ to distinguish the taste of ‖ to have a specified flavor

tast·y tast·i·er tast·i·est *adj.* having a very pleasant taste

tat·ter *n.* a torn piece of fabric, paper etc. ‖ (*pl.*) ragged clothing

tatter *v.t.* to tear into shreds, make ragged

tat·tered *adj.* in tatters ‖ wearing ragged clothing

tat·tle 1. *v.i.* **tat·tling tat·tled** to engage in idle talk ‖ to tell other people's secrets **2.** *n.* idle talk, gossip **tát·tler** a gossip

tat·too 1. *v.t.* to mark (the skin) with a permanent pattern by puncturing it and inserting a pigment **2.** *n.* the marks thus made

taunt 1. *v.t.* to jeer at ‖ to accuse in a jeering way of some contemptible crime ‖ to provoke by a taunt **2.** *n.* a jibe, a jeering accusation

taupe *n.* a soft, brownish-gray color

taut *adj.* under longitudinal tension ‖ tense **táut·en** *v.t.* to make taut ‖ *v.i.* to become taut

tav·ern *n.* an inn or bar

taw·dry taw·dri·er tas·dri·est *adj.* showy but of very poor quality

taw·ny taw·ni·er taw·ni·est *adj.* of a light reddish reddish-yellow brown color

tax 1. *n.* a charge made by a government to collect revenue ‖ a heavy demand made upon one's strnegth, patience, ets. **2.** *v.t.* to impose a tax ‖ to make a have demand on **tax·a·bíl·i·ty** *n.* **táx·a·ble** *adj.*

tax·a·tion *n.* the system by which taxes are imposed

tax·i 1. *n.* an automobile carrying passengers for a charge **2. tax·i·ing, tax·y·ing tax·ied** *v.i.* to ride in a taxi ‖ (of an aircraft) to move over the surface of the ground e.g. in parking

tax·i·cab *n.* a taxi

tea *n.* a shrub ‖ its dried and prepared leaves, used to make a beverage ‖ this beverage ‖ any of a number of plants used like tea ‖ a social gathering

tea bag a cloth or filter paper bag holding tea for infusion in boiling water

teach teach·ing taught *v.t.* to give instruction to, to train ‖ to cause to understand ‖ *v.i.* to be a teacher **téach·a·ble** *adj.* capable of being taught **téach·er** *n.* **téach·ing** *n.* the profession of a teacher

tea·cup *n.* a cup for drinking esp. tea

teak *n.* a large East Indian tree now also grown in W. Africa and tropical Amerkica for its wood

tea·ket·tle *n.* a utensil having a lid, spout and handle used to boil water in

teal *pl.* **teal, teals** *n.* a genis of freshwater ducks

team 1. *n.* two or more draft animals harnessed together ‖ a number of people working together on a common task ‖ a group forming one side in a game **2.** *v.i.* (often with 'up') to join in a common task

team·ster *n.* a person who drives a truck for a living

team·work *n.* the quality whereby individuals unselfishly subordinate their own part to the general effort of the group with whom they are working or playing

tea·pot *n.* a pot in which tea is brewed

tear *n.* a drop of the saline fluid secreted by the lachrymal gland ‖ (*pl.*) drops of this secretion that overflow the eyelids when certain strong emotions are aroused ‖ (*pl.*) the visible expressiono f grief ‖ something resembling a tear **in tears** weeping

tear 1. tear·ing tore torn *v.i.* to break by exerting a strong pull ‖ to remove by making an opening in this way ‖ to injure by lacerating ‖ to subject to intense or conflicting emotions ‖ to divide into opposing groups ‖ *v.i.* to give way under a strong pull ‖ (*pop.*) to move rapidly **2.** *n.* the act of tearing ‖ the line of brak resulting from tearing

tease 1. teas·ing teased *v.t.* to annoy by making irritating remarks ‖ to raise a nap on (cloth) with a teasel ‖ *v.i.* to indulge in teasing **2.** *n.* a teasing or being teased ‖ a person who teases

tea·sel, tea·zel *n.* a genus of thistlelike plants ‖ this flower head when dried, used to raise a nap ‖ a wire device used in place of this

tea·spoon *n.* a small spoon ‖ a teaspoonful **tea·spoon·ful** *pl.* **tea·spoon·fuls** *n.* as much as a teaspoon will hold

teat *n.* the protrusion of a mammal's breast or udder through which milk is drawn

tech·nic 1. *n.* technique ‖ (*pl.*) technology **téch·ni·cal** *adj.* pertaining to the mechanical, industrial or applied sciences ‖ arising from mechanical causes **tech·ni·cál·i·ty** *pl.* **tech·ni·cal·i·ties** *n.* the use of technical terms ‖ a detail of no particular importance ‖ the state or quality of being technical

tech·ni·cian *n.* a person skilled in the technical details and techniques of a subject

tech·nique *n.* the entire body of procedures and methocs of a science, art or craft ‖ skill in these procedures and methods

tech·no·log·i·cal *adj.* of, relating to or characterized by technology

tech·nol·o·gy *pl.* **tech·nol·o·gies** *n.* the science of technical processes

te·di·ous *adj.* boring, causing psychological fatigue

te·di·um *n.* the state or quality of being tedious

tee *n.* the letter T, t in the alphabet

tee 1. *n.* (*golf*) the area from which a person drives at the beginning of a hold ‖ a wooden or plastic peg on which the ball is placed for driving **2.** *v.t.* **tee·ing teed** to tee off ‖ (*golf*) to drive

teem *v.i.* (of rain etc.) to come down in torrents

teem *v.i.* to be full ‖ to pullulate

teen·age *adj.* of or relating to teenagers

teen·ag·er *n.* a person in his teens

tee·ter *v.i.* to move in a wobbly manner ‖ to show doubt, indecision etc. ‖ to seesaw

tee·ter-tot·ter *n.* a see saw

teethe teeth·ing teethed *v.i.* to develop teeth

tee·to·tal *adj.* completely abstaining from alcoholic drinks **tee·tó·tal·er** *n.*

tel·e·cast 1. tel·e·cast·ing tel·e·cast, tel·e·cast·ed *v.t.* and *i.* to televise **2.** *n.* a television broadcast

tel·e·gram *n.* a message transmitted, or received, by telegraphy

tel·e·graph 1. *n.* a method of transmitting messages over long distances ‖ *v.i.* to send a telegram **tel·e·gráph·ic** *adj.* **tel·e·gráph·i·cal·ly** *adv.* **te·leg·ra·phy** *n.* the act or process of sending by telegraph

te·lep·a·thy *n.* communication between the minds of different persons

tel·e·phone 1. *n.* a device for converting sounds into electrical impulses and reconverting them into sounds at the receiving end of the wire **2.** **tel·e·phon·ing tel·e·phoned** *v.t.* to transmit (a message) by means of a telephone

tel·e·prompt·er *n.* a prompting device for a speaker or actor on television

tel·e·scope 1. *n.* an optical device that focuses light from distant objects so that the image formed may be observed **2.** **tel·e·scop·ing tel·e·scoped** *v.t.* to cause to close up ‖ to shorten by condensing **tel·e·scop·ic** *adj.* **tel·e·scóp·i·cal·ly** *adv.* **tel·e·vise tel·e·vis·ing tel·e·vised** *v.t.* and *i.* to broadcast by television

tel·e·vi·sion *n.* the transmission of visual

images by means of electromagnetic waves

tell tell·ing told *v.t.* to make known ‖ to give an account of ‖ to inform (someone) of something ‖ to command ‖ to reveal by gestures, etc. ‖ to divulge ‖ to decide, choose ‖ *v.i.* (with 'of') to give a description, account, report etc. ‖ (with 'of) to give an indication ‖ to make known something which ought to be kept secret

tell·er *n.* a person who tells a story etc. ‖ a bank employee

tell·ing *adj.* effective, impressive

tell·tale 1. *n.* a person who informs, esp. about the small misdeeds of others

te·mer·i·ty *n.* recklessness

tem·per 1. *v.t.* to bring to a desired state of consistency, hardness etc. ‖ to make less harsh ‖ *v.i.* to be or become tempered 2. *n.* the state of a metal, alloy, clay etc. as regards its hardness, consistency, etc. ‖ anger, or the tendency to become angry ‖ the emotional state of a person or community

tem·per·a·ment *n.* the characteristic phsiological and emotional state of an individual **tem·per·a·men·tal** *adj.* liable to rapid and intense changes of mood

tem·per·ance *n.* the virtue which moderates desires and passions ‖ total abstinence from alcoholic drinks

tem·per·ate *adj.* moderate, avoiding both of two extremes ‖ (of climate) never very hot or very cold

tem·per·a·ture *n.* degree or intensity of heat or cold ‖ the internal heat of the body

tem·pest *n.* a very violent wind ‖ a very violent upsurge or expression of emotion

tem·pes·tu·ous *adj.* violent, turbulent

tem·plate, tem·plet *n.* a pattern, usually of thin sheet metal or wood, used when cutting, shaping etc.

tem·ple *n.* (esp. in ancient Greece, Rome of Egypt) a building used for the worship of a god

temple *n.* either of the flat portions of the head between the ear and the forehead

tem·po *pl.* **tem·pi, tem·pos** *n.* the speed at which a piece of music is played or is meant to be played ‖ rate of movement or of some activity

tem·po·ral *adj.* of ore relating to worldly matter ‖ of or relating to life in time ‖ of time

tem·po·rar·i·ly *adv.* for a time only

tem·po·rar·y *adj.* lasting only for a short time

tem·po·rize tem·po·riz·ing tem·po·rized *v.i.* to act so as to gain time in a difficult situation ‖ (with 'with') to come to terms

tempt *v.t.* to try to persuade (someone) to do i a sinful or wrongful act ‖ to be attractive, enticing etc. to

temp·ta·tion *n.* a tempting or being tempted ‖ something which tempts

ten *adj.* being one more than nine

ten·a·ble *adj.* able to be held ‖ able to be held against attack ‖ able to be maintained

te·na·cious *adj.* holding fast ‖ adhesive ‖ retentive ‖ persistent

te·nac·i·ty *n.* the state or quality of being tenacious ‖ tensile strength

ten·ant *n.* someone paying rent to the owner for the use of land or a building

tend *v.t.* to take care of, look after

tend *v.i.* to have a prevailing direction ‖ to be prone to act or think in a certain way ‖ to lead or be directed towards a condition or result

ten·den·cy *pl.* **ten·den·cies** *n.* the quality of tending towards something or of tending to do something

ten·der a small vessel for passing communications between shore and a larger ship ‖ a vehicle attached to a locomotive, carrying its fuel and water supply

tender 1. *v.y.* to offer (services etc.), offer for acceptance ‖ *v.i.* (often with 'for') to put in a competitive estimate for work to be done 2. *n.* an offer of a formal nature

tender *adj.* easily damaged ‖ easily chewed ‖ sore to the touch ‖ sensitive ‖ young and readily impressionable ‖ expressingor resulting from such emotions

ten·don *n.* a strong band of connective tissue

ten·dril *n.* a leafless organ in climbing plants, serving as a means of attachment

ten·e·ment *n.* any kind of permanent property, e.g. land or titles or rents, held by one person

ten·et *n.* a principle, belief or doctrine held by a person or a gruop

ten·nis *n.* lawn tennis ‖ court tennis

ten·or 1. *n.* the general, little varying course or overall direction ‖ intent or purpose ‖ a male voice between baritone and alto ‖ someone who sings with this voice 2. *adj.* of ore relating to a tenor

tense 1. *adj.* showing or undergoing emotional strain ‖ stretched tight 2. **tens·ing tensed** *v.t.* to make tense ‖ *v.i.* (often with 'up') to be or become tense

tense *n.* any of the forms of a verb expressing the time of the action or the state of being

ten·sion *n.* a tensing or being tensed ‖ the state of a conductor carrying an electric current ‖ a state of emotional stress ‖ a state of repressed hostility **tén·sion·al** *adj.*

tent 1. *n.* a shelter made of canvas, skins etc 2. *v.i.* to live in a tent

ten·ta·cle *n.* a slender flexible organ on the head of many invertebrate animals ‖ something that sems to reach out and have a grasp hard to evade **ten·tac·u·lar, ten·tac·u·late** *adjs.*

ten·ta·tive *adj.* provisional ‖ hesitating

ten·u·ous *adj.* flimsy, thin ‖ not dense ‖ so subtle as to be only vaguely apprehensible

ten·ure *n.* the act, manner or right of holding office or property ‖ the period of holding this

te·pee, tee·pee *n.* a conical tent made esp. of skins stretched over a framework of poles

tep·id *adj.* slightly warm ‖ unenthusiastic, without warmth **te·poid·i·ty** *n.*

term 1. *n.* a period of time, measured between its beginning and end ‖ a subdivision of the academic year ‖ the end of a period ‖ one of a set of words having exact limited meanings in certain uses ‖ *(logic)* a word or phrase ‖ the normal time for the end of pregnancy ‖ *(pl.)* requirements as to conditions, price etc. ‖ *(pl.)* language of a specified sort 2. *v.t.* to name or define by a term

ter·mi·nal 1. *adj.* of or forming the end ‖ considered likely to be fatal 2. *n.* an end, extremity ‖ a terminus (end of route, station, town or building) ‖ a device at the end of an electric wire etc. for facilitating connections ‖ *(computer)* the instrument, usu. a keyboard, enabling data to enter or leave a system

ter·mi·nate ter·mi·nat·ing ter·mi·nat·ed *v.t.* to bring to an end, to close ‖ *v.i.* to come to an end

ter·mi·nol·o·gy *pl.* **ter·mi·nol·o·gies** *n.* the terms proper to an art, sicence, profession etc.

ter·mi·nus *pl.* **ter·mi·ni ter·mi·nus·es** *n.* either end of a rail, air or bus route

ter·mite *n.* small, white, soft-bodied, social insects

tern *n.* a genus of slender, gull-like sea birds

ter·race *n.* a raised level cut into the side of a hill ‖ a level space adjoining a house etc. and used e.g. for sitting in the sun

terrace *v.t.* to form into a terrace or terraces ‖ to add a terrace to

ter·rain *n.* a stretch of land with respect to its features or condition

ter·res·tri·al 1. *adj.* earthly ‖ of the earth 2. *n.* an inhabitant of the earth

ter·ri·ble *adj.* arousing terror ‖ excessive, hard to bear ‖ very bad **tér·ri·bly** *adv.* very

ter·rif·ic *adj.* extreme, very great, very large, or in any way extraordinary ‖ very good indeed **ter·rif·i·cal·ly** *adv.*

ter·ri·to·ry *pl.* **ter·ri·to·ries** *n.* an area defended by a male bird or mammal as breeding and feeding ground ‖ an administrative division ‖ an area alotted to a travling salesman etc. to cover ‖ a very large tract of country ‖ a sphere or field of scholarship etc.

ter·ror *n.* great fear ‖ a person or thing htat causes great fear ‖ a person who is a dreadful nuisance

ter·ror·ism *n.* acts inspiring terror as a method of ruleing or of conducting political opposition

ter·ror·ist *n.* a person who practices terrorism

ter·ror·ize ter·ror·iz·ing ter·ror·ized *v.t.*

to fill with terror ‖ to dominate by inducing terror

terse *adj.* concise, sussinct

ter·ti·ary *adj.* third in order to rank

test 1. *n.* an examination of the nature or value of anything ‖ the method used in making such an examination ‖ a set of problems, questions etc. by which a person's knowledge, abilities, aptitudes or character are assessed ‖ a method or reaction for identifying a substance 2. *v.t.* to submit to a test

tes·ta·ment *n.* a will ‖ a solemn covenant

tes·tate 1. *adj.* having left a legally valid will 2. *n.* a deceased person who left such a will

tes·ta·tor *n.* a testate

tes·ti·cle *n.* one of the two male gonads

tes·ti·fy tes·ti·fy·ing ts·ti·fied *v.i.* to bear witness ‖ to give evidence

tes·ti·mo·ni·al 1. *n.* a written statement concerning the character of a person or value of a thing ‖ a gift made to show corporate appreciation of services rendered by an individual 2. *adj.* pertaining to or constituting a testimonial or testimony

tes·ti·mo·ny *pl.* **tes·ti·mo·nies** *n.* evidence ‖ an oral or written statement made under oath

tes·tis *pl.* **tes·tes** *n.* a testicle

tes·ty tes·ti·er tes·ti·est *adj.* irritable

tet·a·nus *n.* a disease marked by painful, tonic spasms of the vountary muscles esp. of the jaw

teth·er 1. *n.* a rope, chain etc. preventing an animal from moving away from a restricted locality 2. *v.t.* to attach a tether to

text *n* the sustained narrative, train of thought or argument etc. in a written or printed work ‖ th subject matter of a speech etcc. ‖ a short extract from the Scriptures ‖ libretto ‖ a textbook

text·book *n.* a book written and published for use by students as a basis for their studies

tex·tile 1. *adj.* woven ‖ suitable for ewearvng ‖ pertaining to weaving 2. *n.* a woven fabric

tex·ture *n.* the distinctive character of a fabric ‖ the parts of a whole thought of as woven like a textile fabric ‖ the structure of a rock, tissues etc

than *conj.* used after a comparative adjective or verb to connect the first to the second part of a comparison ‖ used ot express difference of kind, manner etc. ‖ when

thank 1. *v.t.* to express gratitude to ‖ to hold responsible for

thank·ful *adj.* feeling or expressing gratitude

thank·less *adj.* ungrateful ‖ unproductive, unprofitable

thanks *pl. n.* gratitude or expression of gratitude

thanks·giv·ing *n.* the act of expressing thanks

that 1. *pl.* **those** *adj.* designating the person to whom or thing to which attention is drawn ‖ designating one of two things which are acompared or contrasted ‖ designating the person or thing further away than another ‖ designating some well-known person or thing not described 2. *pl.* **those** *pron.* the person or thing indicated or understood ‖ the thing farther away ‖ one of two things which are compared or contrasted 3. *adv.* to such a degree 4. *conj.* introducing a noun clause **that's that** that's settled, finished

thatch 1. *v.t.* to cover with thatch 2. *n.* a covering, esp. for a roof, made of straw etc.

thaw *v.i.* to become liquid or soft due to the temperature rising above freezing point ‖ to melt ‖ to become less hard, less numb, less icy etc. ‖ to become more friendly, less stiff in manner

the 1. *adj.* the definite article used to denote a person or thing or persons or things being spoken of or already mentioned ‖ (equivalent to a possessive pronoun) used of something belonging to a person already mentioned ‖ preceding an adjective used substantivally 2. *adv.* (used before a comparative adjective or adverb) to that extent, in that degree **the. . .the** to what extent. . .to that extent, *the sooner the better*

the·a·ter, the·a·tre *n.* a building or open space where dramatic performances are given ‖ a place where dramatic events occur

the·at·ri·cal *adj.* of or pertaining to the theater

thee *pron.* objective case of THOU

theft *n.* the act of stealing something ‖ an instance of this

their *adj.* of, belonging to or done by them

theirs *pron.* that or those belonging to them

them *pron.* objective case of THEY

Theme *n.* the matter with which a speech, essay etc. is chiefly concerned ‖ a structurally important element of a composition ‖ a signature tune

them·selves *pl. pron.* refl. form of THEY ‖ emphatic form of THEY

then 1. *adv.* at that time ‖ at the time immediately following ‖ next in sequence, order etc. ‖ in addition ‖ consequently **2.** *adj.* being at an understood past time **3.** *n.* that time

thence *adv.* from that place or that time ‖ for that reason ‖ from that source

thence·forth *adv.* from that time onward

thence·for·ward *adv.* thenceforth

the·ol·o·gy *pl.* **the·ol·o·gies** *n.* the science which studies God and all that relates to him

the·o·rem *n.* a statement susceptible of logical proof when certain facts are accepted as true

the·o·ret·ic *adj.* theoretical

the·o·ret·i·cal *adj.* of, pertaining to or being theory

the·o·rize the·o·riz·ing the·o·rized *v.t.* to construct a theory of theories about

the·o·ry *pl.* **the·o·ries** *n.* an organized body of ideas as to the truth of something ‖ a general body of assumptions and principles ‖ a conjecture

ther·a·peu·tic *adj.* curative **ther·a·péu·ti·cal** *adj.*

there 1. *adv.* in or at that place ‖ to or towards that place ‖ then, at that point **2.** *pron.* used as an introductory work in impersonal constructions **3.** *n.* that place

there·af·ter *adv.* after that time or palce

there·by *adv.* thus, by that means

there·fore *adv.* thus, by this or that means

there·fore *adv.* for that reason

there·in *adv.* in that thing, place etc. ‖ in that respect

there·of *adv.* of the place, thing, event etc. just mentioned

there·on *adv.* on that thing just mentioned ‖ thereupon

there·u·pon *adv.* immediately after that ‖ as a result of that

there·with *adv.* immediately after that ‖ with this, that or it ‖ in addition to that

ther·mal *adj.* pertaining to heat or to a source of heat

ther·mo·dy·nam·ic *adj.* pertaining to thermodynamics **ther·mo·dy·nám·ics** *n.* the branch of physics dealing with the relation between heat and other forms of energy

ther·mom·e·ter any of several types of instrument used to measure temperature

ther·mo·nu·cle·ar *adj.* relating to nuclear fusion

ther·mo·stat *n.* a device used to maintain a constant temperature **ther·mo·stát·ic** *adj.* **ther·mo·stát·i·cal·ly** *adv.*

the·sau·rus *pl.* **the·sau·ri the·sau·rus·es** *n.* a book of synonyms and antonyms

the·sis *pl.* **the·ses** *·n.* a proposition ‖ a reasoned argument ‖ an affirmation

Thes·pi·an 1. *adj.* of dramatic art **2.** *n.* an actor

They *pron.*, *3rd person pl.*, *nominative case* two or more persons, animals or things already mentioned ‖ people or a group of people generally

thi·a·mine *n.* vitamin B_1

thick 1. *adj.* of relatively great depth ‖ large in diameter ‖ broad ‖ dense ‖ stuffy ‖ viscous ‖ hoarse and indistinct ‖ (of regional or foreign accent) strongly marked ‖ slow to understand ‖ intimately friendly **2.** *adv.* thickly **3.** *n.* the most intense, crowded part **thick·en** *v.t.* to make thick **thick·en·ing** *n.* the act of making or becoming thick ‖ an ingredient, e.g. flour, used to thicken

thick·et *·n.* a thick growth of small trees

and undergrowth

thick-skinned *adj.* insensitive

thief *pl.* **thieves** *n.* a person who steals

thieve thiev·ing thieved *v.t.* to take by theft ‖ to practice theft **thiev·er·y** *n.* theft

thigh *n.* the part of the human leg between the hip and the knee

thim·ble *n.* a cap of metal etc. worn on the fingertip in sewing

thin 1. *adj.* **thin·ner thin·nest** having little extent between opposite surfaces ‖ small in diameter ‖ of slender build ‖ not closely massed together ‖ of little strength or substance ‖ lacking plausibility **2.** *adv.* thinly

thin thin·ning thinned *v.t.* to make thin ‖ *v.i.* to become thin, or thinner

thine *possesive pron.* that or those belonging to thee

thing *n.* matter, object, not a living person or animal ‖ used in reference to a person, esp. in often condescending expressions of affection, pity etc. ‖ an action ‖ something not specifically named ‖ a uniquely personal activity ‖ something uttered or thought ‖ *(pl.)* affairs or concerns ‖ *(pl.)* belongings, clothes, utensils etc. ‖ *(pl.)* circumstances in general

think think·ing thought *v.i.* to turn something over in the mind ‖ (with 'of') to make provision ‖ (with 'of' or 'about') to have in mind as a provisional plan ‖ to consider ‖ to remember ‖ *v.t.* to conceive in the mind ‖ to work out by reasoning ‖ to determine by reflection ‖ to bring to a specified condition by mental activity **to think aloud** to speak one's ideas as they occur **th think nothing of** to take for granted **to think over** reconsider **to think twice** to reflect with special care before taking action

think·ing 1. *n.* the mental process of one who thinks ‖ an opinion or judgement ‖ a body of thought **2.** *adj.* that thinks or can think

thin-skinned *adj.* unusually sensitive to criticism

third *adj.* being number three in a series

thirst *n.* a desire for drink ‖ any keen desire

thirst *v.i.* to feel thirsty ‖ to have a keen desire

thirst·y thirst·i·er thirst·i·est *adj.* feeling thirst ‖ dry ‖ having a strong desire

thir·teen *adj.* being one more than 12

thir·teenth *ajd.* being number 13 in a series

thir·ti·eth *adj.* being number 30 in a series

thir·ty *adj.* being 10 more than 20

this 1. *pl.* **these** *adj.* of that which is here, or near, or just mentioned **2.** *pl.* **these** *pron.* the person just mentioned **3.** *adv.* to this extent or degree

this·tle *n.* any of several genera of tall, prickly plants

thith·er 1. *adv.* to or towards that place **2.** *adj.* on the more distant side

thong *n.* a leather strip used for fastening ‖ the leather lash of a whip

tho·rax *pl.* **tho·rax·es, tho·ra·ces** *n.* that part of the body between the neck and the abdomen

thorn *n.* the woody part of a leaf or stem modified to a stiff, sharp point ‖ any of various sharply pointed protuberances on an animal ‖ a source of sharp irritation

thorn·y thorn·i·er thorn·i·est *adj.* full of thorns or spines ‖ beset with difficulties or controversy

thor·ough *adj.* proceeding or done with great care or attention to detail, completeness etc

thor·ough·bred *n.* any horse, dog etc. of pure breed

thor·ough·fare *n.* a road or passage available to traffic and not closed at either end

thou *3rd pers. sing. personal pron.* now almost only used in prayer to God

though *conj.* used to introduce a statement of fact or a possibility which might prevent a second statement from being ture but does not in fact do so

thought *n.* the action or process of thinking ‖ the capacity to think ‖ an idea or pattern of ideas ‖ consideration ‖ intention

thought·ful *adj.* absorbed in the process of thinking ‖ showing consideration for others

thought·less *adj.* said or done without having given thought to a probable result ‖ showing lack of consideration for others

thou·sand 1. *n.* 10 times 100

thrash 1. *v.t.* to strike repeatedly with a cane or whip ‖ to thresh (wheat etc.) ‖ to defeat soundly ‖ *v.i.* to move the limbs or body violently **2.** *n.* the act of thrashing

thread 1. *n.* a fine cord used in sewing ‖ any of the fibers used in weaving material ‖ that which gives continuity to, or is continuous in, an argument, speech, story etc. ‖ the spiral groove of a screw, bolt etc. **2.** *v.t.* to pass a thread through the eye of (a needle) ‖ to furnish (e.g. a screw or tube) with a thread ‖ to feed film into (a movie camera or projector)

thread·bare *adj.* of a fabric from which the nap has been worn away ‖ wearing shabby clothes ‖ (of an excuse, plot etc.) obviously inadequate

threat *n.* a statement or other indication of intention to hurt, punish, destroy etc.

threat·en *v.t.* to utter or otherwise indicate a threat to (someone)

three *adj.* being one more than two

three-di·men·sion·al *adj.* (*abbr.* 3-D) having, or appearing to have, length, breadth and depth in space

thresh *v.t.* to separate the grain from the ear of ‖ *v.i.* to thresh grain ‖ to toss about, thrash **thrésh·er** *n.* a threshing machine

thresh·old *n.* the plank or stone at the bottom of a doorway ‖ a beginning

thrice *adv.* three times

thrift *n.* the practice of avoiding wasteful or avoidable expenditure

thrift·y thrift·i·er thrift·i·est *adj.* practicing thrift

thrill 1. *v.t.* to cause tense emotional excitement in **2.** *n.* a moment of excitement or intense emotion ‖ an unnatural vibration in the respiratory or circulatory systems

thrill·er *n.* a fictional work designed to thrill the audience or reader

thrive thriv·ing throve, thrived thrived, thriv·en *v.i.* to grow and function well ‖ to do well financially

throat *n.* the front part of the neck ‖ the upper part of the passage leading from the mouth to the stomach and lungs

throb 1. *v.i.* **throb·bing throbbed** to vibrate ‖ (of the pulse etc.) to beat strongly **2.** *n.* a pulsation of low frequency but large amplitude

throe *n.* a spasm of pain or anguish ‖ (*pl.*) a painful struggle, esp. of childbirth or of death

throm·bo·sis *n.* the formation of a clot inside a blood vessel

throne 1. *n.* a chair (usually decorated with carving, inlaid woods or jewels etc.) reversed for the use of a sovereign, bishop etc **2.** *v.t.* **thron·ing throned** to place on a throne ‖ to vest with the powers of sovereignty

throng 1. *n.* a great many people crowded together ‖ a great number of things crowded together **2.** *v.t.* to occupy (a space) by crowding into it

throt·tle 1. *v.t.* **throt·tling throt·tled** to choke **2.** *n.* a valve which regulates the supply of gasoline vapor and air to an engine

through 1. *prep.* from one end to the other end of ‖ in one side and outh the other side of ‖ during ‖ among ‖ by way of ‖ by means of ‖ up to and including **2.** *adv.* in one side and out the other ‖ from end to end ‖ all the way ‖ completely **3.** *adj.* not involving a change of ‖ finished ‖ having no further dealings

htrough·out 1. *adv.* continuously **2.** *prep.* in or during every part of

throw 1. *v.* **throw·ing threw thrown** *v.t.* to cause suddenly to move through the air by a muscular effort and fling of the arm ‖ to cause to fall to the floor or ground ‖ to cause to move rapidly ‖ to project ‖ to lose (a contest) by choise ‖ to give (a party) ‖ to cause (the blame) to fall on someone or something ‖ to place (an obstacle) in the way of someone ‖ *v.i.* to cast or hurl something **to throw away** to discard **to throw back** to reflect **to throw oneself into** to become wholeheartedly engaged in to **to throw out** to remove forcibly from a place ‖ to dismiss **to throw up** to vomit **2.** *n.* the action of one who throws ‖ an instance of throwing ‖ a light spread for a bed etc. ‖ the motion of a moving part

throw·back n. a reversion to ancestral type ‖ an instance of this ‖ soemone or something exhibiting this

thru adv. and adj. through

thrush n. any of various small or medium-sized songbirds

thrust 1. thrust·ing thrust v.t. to push suddenly and with force ‖ to force (a person) into a situation against his own or someone else's wishes ‖ to interpose (a question etc.) ‖ v.i. to make a sudden push ‖ to force one's way ‖ to surge powerfully upwards or press outwards 2. n. a sudden violent push ‖ the strong pressure of one part of a structure against another ‖ the driving force exerted throught a propeller shaft

thud 1. v.i. **thud·ding thud·ded** to fall with or make a dull heavy sound 2. n. a dull sound

thug n. any person who uses violence or brutality

thumb 1. n. the short thick digit of the hand which is opposable to the fingers **all thumbs** clumsy **under somenoe's thumb** completely dominated by someone 2. v.t. to handle or manipulate with the thumb

thump 1. v.t. to strike with a thump ‖ (with 'out') to play (a tune) in a loud unmusical way ‖ v.i. to deliver thumps ‖ to make the noise of a thump or thumps 2. n. a dull, heavy blow, or the sound of it **thump·ing** adj. very big

thun·der 1. n. the sounds accompanying an atmospheric electrical discharge ‖ loud sounds compared with this ‖ vehement rhetoric 2. v.i. to produce the sound of thunder ‖ to produce a very loud sound ‖ v.t. to utter in a thundering voice

thun·der·bolt n. a single, intense discharge of electricity, accompanied by the sound of thunder ‖ something or someone destructive or violent

thun·der·storm n. a storm of rain and wind accompanied by lightning and thunder

thun·der·struck adj. temporarily deprived of the power to speak or think by a sudden access of emotion, esp. astonishment

Thurs·day n. the fifth day of the week

thus adv. in this way ‖ for this reason ‖ to this degree

thwart 1. v.t. to prevent (a plan) from being carried out 2. adj. transverse 3. adv. transversely

thyme n. a genus of plants found chiefly in Mediterranean regions

thy·roid 1. n. an endocrine gland greatly influencing growth and development 2. adj. of the thyroid

ti·ar·a n. a coronet of usually precious metal worn by women ‖ the triple crown worn by the pope

tib·i·a pl. **tib·i·as** n. the inner of the two bones between the knee and the ankle

tic n. a recurrent twitch usually of the facial muscles

tick 1. n. one of the light sounds made by a clock ‖ any similar noise 2. v.i. to make the sound of a tick

tick n. any of various arachnids related to mites

tick·et 1. n. a tag showing the price of an article ‖ a piece of paper or cardboard authorizing the bearer to use a specified service ‖ the candidates of a particular political party ‖ a notice issued to someone who has violated a traffic regulation 2. v.t. to attach a ticket to

tick·le 1. tick·ling tick·led v.t. to touch (a part of the body) where the nerve ends are sensitive, and by so doing to cause laughter, spasmodic movement etc. ‖ to amuse ‖ v.i. to have a tingling sensation 2. n. a tickling **tick·lish** adj. sensitive to tickling ‖ sensitive, touchy

tid·al adj. pertaining to or affected by the tides

tidal wave an unusually large wave or very high water, esp. one caused by an earthquake

tid·bit n. a dainty or delicate morsel of food

tide 1. n. the alternate rising and falling of the seas ‖ soemthing thought of as ebbing and flowing like the tide 2. **tid·ing tid·ed** v.i. to use the tide in entering or leaving an estuary, harbor etc. ‖ to flow like the tide ‖ v.t. to carry with the tide

ti·dings pl. n. news

ti·dy 1. ti·di·er ti·di·est *adj.* in place, in order ‖ substantial **2.** *v.t.* **ti·dy·ing ti·died** to make tidy

tie 1. ty·ing tied *v.t.* to secure by a not ‖ to make (a knot) in a cord etc ‖ to fasten together or connect firmly ‖ to prevent the freedom of action of ‖ to be equal with in competition ‖ *v.i.* to be closed or fastened by means of a tie ‖ to be equal in a competition ‖ commit (e.g. capital) so as to leave one without freedom of action **to tie in** to link **2.** *n.* a cord, sltring etc. used for tying something ‖ something which restricts personal freedom ‖ a linking force between two or more things ‖ a competition or election that ends in a draw ‖ a necktie

tier 1. *n.* one or two or more parallel rows of seats at different levels **2.** *v.t.* to arrange in tiers

tiff *n.* a slight quarrel

ti·ger *pl.* **ti·gers, ti·ger** *n.* a large ferocious, carnivorous mammal native to Asia

tight 1. *adj.* closely packed ‖ allowing too little freedom of movement ‖ rigidly set ‖ so constructed that air, water etc. cannot pass through ‖ in short supply ‖ strict ‖ stingy **2.** *adv.* in a tight way **tight·en** *v.t.* to make tight ‖ *v.i.* to become tight

tight·rope *n.* a tautly stretched rope or wire, some height above the ground, on which an acrobat performs

tights *pl. n.* a skintight garment covering the body usually from the waist down

tile 1. *pl.* **tiles, tile** *n.* a thin piece of fired, unglazed clay used on roofs or walls ‖ a square piece of fired clay or other material (e.g. vinyl) used for flooring ‖ tiling **2.** *v.t.* **til·ing tiled** to cover with tiles **til·ing** *n.* the process of covering with tiles ‖ tiles collectively

till *n.* a money drawer ‖ a cash register

till 1. *pre.* up to the time of **2.** *conj.* up to the time when, until

till *v.t.* to work (the soil) for cultivation **till·age** *n.* the tilling of the soil

til·ler *n.* the lever by which the rudder is turned

tilt 1. *v.i.* to slant ‖ to joust ‖ *v.t.* to cause to slant **2.** *n.* a tilting **at full tilt** at full speed

tim·ber 1. *n.* wood suitable for construction ‖ one of the curved beams of wood forming the ribs of a ship **2.** *interj.* a shouted warning that a tree is falling

tim·bre *n.* the quality of a musical sound, depending on what overtones are present

time 1. *n.* the physical quantity measured by clocks ‖ finite duration as distinguished from infinity ‖ a duration ‖ a point in progress ‖ (often *pl.*) a period of history ‖ a period during which certain action is taken ‖ the period appropriate to the beginning or ending of a course of action ‖ the rjythm of a composition, the beat ‖ the tempo at which a composition is to be performed ‖ a period characterized by a general event ‖ rate of pay, esp. reckoned by the hour ‖ lifetime ‖ a period of imprisonment ‖ (*pl.*) following a number and used with a comparative adjective or adverb to indicate magnitude **at times** sometimes **behind the times** old-fashioned, not up-to-date **for the time being** for the present **from time to time** occasionally **in no time** very quickly **to pass the time of day** to stop for a little chat **2.** *v.t.* **tim·ing timed** to measure the duration ‖ to set the rhythm or tempo of **3.** *adj.* having to do with time ‖ regulated to explode etc. at a given time ‖ payable at a future date

time·less *adj.* not limited by time

time·ly time·li·er time·li·est *adj.* at a very suitable time, opportune

time·piece *n.* any instrument used for measuring time

time·ta·ble *n.* a tabulated list of the times at which certain events or activities are required to occur, or the order of occurrence ‖ a schedule of arrival and departure times

tim·id *adj.* very sensitive ‖ lacking self-confidence

ti·mid·i·ty *n.* the state or quality of being timid

tim·o·rous *adj.* timid, easily frightened

tin 1. *n.* a lustrous, silvery metallic element which is malleable ‖ tinplate **2.** *v.t.* **tin·ning tinned** to coat with tin

tinc·ture 1. *n.* a solution of a medical substance ‖ a slight coloration **2.** *v.t.* **tinc·tur·ing tinc·tured** to add a trace of color to

tin·der *n.* one of the pointed parts of an antler, fork etc.

tinge 1. *v.t.* **tinge·ing, ting·ing tinged** to impart a little color or a certain slight quality to **2.** *n.* the color, quality etc. imparted

tin·gle 1. tin·gling tin·gled *v.i.* to have a sensation as if the skin were being gently pricked or stung at innumerable points **2.** *n.* this sensation

tink·er 1. *n.* an itinerant tinsmith **2.** *v.t.* to mend ‖ *v.i.* to make an amateurish attempt to repair something

tin·kle 1. tin·kling tin·kled *v.i.* to make a succession of light metallic tings **2.** *n.* a tinkling sound

tin·sel 1. *n.* tin, brass or an alloy with a bright luster used in thin strips to give glittering decorative effects **2.** *ajd.* adorned with, tinsel ‖ superficially brilliant but worthless **3.** *v.t.* **tin·sel·ing tin·seled** to adorn with tinsel **tín·sel·ly** *adj.*

tint 1. *n.* any lighter or darker hue of the same color ‖ a small quantity of color **2.** *v.t.* to furnish with a tint

ti·ny ti·ni·er ti·ni·est *adj.* exceedingly small

tip 1. *n.* the pointed or tapering end of a long slim object **2.** *v.t.* **tip·ping tipped** to furnish with a tip ‖ to form the tip of

tip 1. tip·ping tipped *v.t.* to cause to incline ‖ to cause to overturn **2.** *n.* a tipping

tip 1. *v.t.* **tip·ping tipped** to impart information to in a confidential manner ‖ to forecast (something) as likely to bring in money ‖ to give a small gift of money to **2.** *n.* a suggestion privately given ‖ a small gift of money

tip·sy tip·si·er tip·si·est *adj.* somewhat intoxicated ‖ not steady, shaky

tip·toe 1. *v.i.* to proceed on the tips of one's toes **2.** *n.* **on tiptoe** on the tips of one's toes

tip-top 1. *adj.* of the highest quality **2.** *n.*

the highest point or part ‖ the best of all

ti·rade *n.* a long harangue full of vehement criticism

tire tir·ing tired *v.i.* to lose strength by exertion etc. ‖ to lose patience or interest **to tire out** to make very tired

tire 1. *n.* a solid rubber band, or a rubber casing makeing an airtight fit with a wheel rim **2.** *v.t.* **tir·ing tired** to fit with a tire

tired *adj.* weary ‖ hackneyed

tire·less *adj.* seemingly incapable of becoming tired

tire·some *adj.* tending to exhaust one's patience

tis·sue *n.* an aggregate of like cells of which animal and plant organs are composed ‖ a thin, semitransparent woven fabric ‖ a piece of tissue paper

ti·tan·ic *adj.* having great size or strength

tithe *n.* a tenth part of agricultural produce etc. paid as tax or as an offering to support a church

tit·il·late tit·il·lat·ing tit·il·lat·ed *v.t.* to stimulate pleasantly by or as if by tickling

ti·tle 1. *n.* a word, phrase or sentence used to designate a book, chapter, poem etc. ‖ a word or phrase attached to the name of a person in order to denote his office, social dignity or status ‖ a ground for a claim ‖ the legal right to the ownership of property **2.** *v.t.* **ti·tling ti·tled** to furnish with a title **ti·tled** *adj.* having a title of nobility

tit·ter 1. *v.i.* to laugh in a half-suppressed way **2.** *n.* such a laugh

tit·u·lar 1. *adj.* relating to a title **2.** a person having the title of an office without its duties

to 1. *prep.* in the direction of ‖ used to indicate someone or something reached ‖ into a condition of ‖ used to indicate a result ‖ in accompaniment with ‖ with respect to ‖ used to indicate degree or extent ‖ in conformity with ‖ in comparison with ‖ used to indicate the period before the hour, *5 to 7* ‖ until, *2 to 6* ‖ *adv.* to consciousness

toad *n.* a small, tailless, leaping amphibian with a warty skin having poison glands

toad·stool *n.* a posonous mushroom

toast 1. *v.t.* to brown the surface of by exposure to heat ‖ to propose or drink a toast to ‖ *v.i.* to become toasted ‖ to drink a toast **2.** *n.* bread browned by exposure to heat ‖ a drink in honor of a person

toast·master *n.* a person appointed to propose toasts, introduce speakers etc. **e.g. at a banquet**

to·bac·co *n.* a genus of plants with large ovate leaves and white or pink flowers ‖ the dried and cured leaves smoked, chewed or used as snuff

to·bog·gan 1. *n.* a long, narrow sled of flat boards, used for coasting downhill on ice or snow **2.** *v.i.* to ride on a toboggan ‖ to fall rapidly in value

to·day 1. *adv.* in or during this present day ‖ in the present time, nowadays **2.** *n.* the present time

tod·dle *v.i.* **tod·dling tod·dled** to walk with short, uncertain steps **tód·dler** *n.* a child beginning to walk

to-do *n.* a fuss, commotion

toe *n.* any of the five digits of the human foot **on one's toes** alert **to step on someone's toes** to offend someone, esp. by stealing his perogatives

toe·nail *n.* the nail growing on a toe ‖ a nail driven in obliquely

to·ga *n.* a man's loose outer garment, worn by a Roman citizen **to·gaed** *adj.* wearing a toga

to·geth·er *adv.* in contact or union ‖ at the same time ‖ with each other ‖ by combined action **together with** including **to go together** to accompany one another ‖ to be sweethearts **to·geth·er·ness** *n.* warm fellowship

toil *n.* hard effort ‖ task performed with such effort

toil *v.i.* to work very hard and for a long time

toi·let *n.* the process of dressing, washing etc. ‖ a lavatory ‖ a plumbing fixture

toi·let·ries *pl. n.* articles used in making one's toilet

to·ken 1. *n.* a symbol ‖ a keepsake ‖ a disk (usually metal) exchangeable under some

systems for transportation etc. **2.** *adj.* serving as a token ‖ merely symbolic

to·ken·ism *n.* policy or practice of fulfilling legal and/or moral obligations by a nominal conformity **tokenistic** *adj.*

tol·er·a·ble *adj.* able to be tolerated ‖ adequate or fairly good **tól·er·a·bly** *adv.*

tol·er·ant *adj.* willing to tolerate the beliefs of others

tol·er·ate tol·er·at·ing tol·er·at·ed *v.t.* to support (pain) with fortitude ‖ to permit ‖ to respect (the beliefs etc. of others) without sitting in judgment on them

toll *n.* a tax or charge levied on those who use a particular service ‖ a cost in life or limb

toll 1. *v.t.* to ring (a bell) usually as a solemn signal of death, disaster etc. **2.** *n.* a tolling

tom·a·hawk *n.* a light ax used by American Indians

to·ma·to *pl.* **to·ma·toes** *n.* a trailing herbaceous annual, widely cultivated for its fruit ‖ this fruit

tomb *n.* a burial chamber

tomb·stone *n.* a gravestone

tome *n.* a book, esp. one that is large and scholarly

to·mor·row 1. *n.* the day following today **2.** *adv.* on or during the day following today

ton *n.* a unit of volume for a ship's cargo ‖ a unit of volume for measuring the displacement of a ship ‖ any of various units of weight

ton·al *adj.* pertaining to tone or to tonality **to·nál·i·ty** *pl.* **to·nal·i·ties** *n.* the quality of having key ‖ the color relationships in a painting

tone 1. *n.* the quality of a sound ‖ a note ‖ an inflection or modulation of the voice denoting an emotion etc. ‖ a way of speaking or writing which denotes the person's sentiments, purpose etc. ‖ degree of luminosity ‖ *physiol.*) the proper condition of organs or tissues for healthy functioning **2. ton·ing toned** *v.t.* to give a certain tone of color or sound to ‖ *v.i.* to be harmonious

tongs *pl. n.* an implement constructed of two rods, pivoted together at or near the handle end, used to grasp and lift

tongue 1. *n.* a mobile, extensible structure of muscles which is attached to the floor of the mouth and to the hyoid bone ‖ a language or dialect ‖ the leather flap under the laces of a shoe ‖ a long, thin promontory of land or inlet of water **on the tipe of one's tongue** almost, but not quite, remembered 2. **tongu·ing tongued** *v.i.* project like a tongue

ton·ic 1. *adj.* mentally or morally invigorating ‖ based on a keynote 2. *n.* an invigorating medicine, meant to tone up the system ‖ the keynote of the scale ‖ an accented syllable

to·night 1. *adv.* during the present night ‖ on the coming night of the present day 2. *n.* the coming night

ton·nage, tun·nage *n.* the carrying capacity of a vessel measured in tons ‖ a duty based on the cargo capacity of a vessel

ton·sil *n.* one of a pair of lympatic organs situated on either side of the throat

ton·sil·lec·to·my *pl.* **ton·sil·lec·to·mies** *n.* removal of the tonsils by surgery

ton·sil·li·tis *n.* inflammation of the tonsils

ton·sure 1. *n* the shaving of a portion of the head on admission to the priesthood ‖ the part of the head left bare by such shaving 2. *v.t.* **ton·sur·ing ton·sured** to shave the head

too *adv.* excessively, more than is necessary ‖ very ‖ also

tool 1. *n.* anything which, held in the hands, assists a person to do manual work ‖ a machine tool ‖ a person who is made use of by another, e.g. for committing a crime 2. *v.t.* to shape with a tool ‖ *v.i.* to use a tool

tooth 1. *pl.* **teeth** *n.* one of the hard, bonelike processes set in the jaws of most vertebrates and some invertebrates ‖ a toothlike projection e.g. on the edge of a leaf or the rim of a cogwheel **armed to the teeth** very heavily armed **in the teeth of** facing, fully exposed to **to show one's teeth** to put on a threatening attitude 2. *v.t.* to furnish with teeth ‖ *v.i.* to interlock

as cogged wheels

tooth·ache *n.* a pain in or near the nerve of a tooth

tooth·brush *n.* a pain in or near the nerve of a tooth

tooth·brush *n.* a small brush for cleaning the teeth

tooth·some *adj.* with an appetizing taste, tasty

top 1. *n.* the highest peak of something ‖ the highest or best attainable position, rank, status, degree, pitch etc. ‖ a cover, esp. a lid ‖ the folding roof of a car or baby carriage 2. *v.t.* **top·ping topped** to be higher or more than ‖ to go over the top of ‖ the constitute the top of ‖ to do better than ‖ to be at the top of ‖ to furnish with a top 3. *adj.* on or at the top ‖ highest

top *n.* a toy shaped to spin on its tapered point

to·paz *n.* a mineral gemstone, the yellow topaz being the most precious

top·coat *n.* an overcoat ‖ a final coat of paint etc.

top·ic *n.* a subject of discussion, argument or writing **óp·i·cal** *adj.* arranged by topics

top·most *adj.* highest

top·notch *adj.* first-rate, of the highest

top·o·graph·ic *adj.* topographical

top·o·graph·i·cal *adj.* of or relating to topography

to·pog·ra·phy *pl.* **to·pog·ra·phies** *n.* a description of all the surface features, natural and artificial, of a particular region ‖ the science of drawing maps and/or diagrams which represent these features

top·ple top·pling top·pled *v.i.* to fall ‖ to be on the point of falling over ‖ *v.t.* to cause to topple ‖ to cause to fall from a position of power

tops 1. *adj.* first-rate in quality, performance etc. 2. *n.* **the tops** a person or thing one heartily approves of

top·sy-tur·vy 1. *adv.* upside down ‖ in or into a disorderly or muddled state 2. *adj.* in this condition

torch *n.* a portable light ‖ a very hot flame device, e.g. an oxyacetylene lamp for

welding **to carry a** (or **the**) **torch for**
(*pl.*) to be in love with

tor·e·a·dor *n.* (not used by Spaniards) a
bullfighter

tor·ment *n.* great pain of mind or body

tor·ment *v.t.* to cause torment to ‖ to vex
excessively

tor·men·tor *n.* someone who torments

tor·na·do *pl.* **tor·na·does, tor·na·dos** *n.*
a violent, whirling wind accompanied by
a funnel-shaped cloud

tor·pe·do 1. *pl.* **tor·pe·does** *n.* a long, self-
propelled missile, charged with an explo-
sive warhead and fired underwater or
from an aircraft to blow up ships **2.** *v.t.*
to destroy or attack with a torpedo

tor·pid *adj.* having ceased to move or feel
for a period, e.g. in hibernation ‖ lethar-
gic **tor·pid·i·ty** *n.*

tor·por *n.* suspended animation ‖ mental
or spiritual listlessness or apathy
tor·por·if·ic *adj.*

torque *n.* the agency that produces torsion

tor·rent *n.* a violently rushing stream ‖ a
great downpour ‖ a flood of violent
language **tor·ren·tial** *adj.*

tor·rid *adj.* very hot and dry or exposed
to great heat

tor·sion *n.* the state of being twisted
tór·sion·al *adj.*

tor·so *pl.* **tor·sos** *n.* the trunk of the human
body

tor·til·la *n.* a pancake, made of corn flour,
and eaten in Mexico as the equivalent of
bread

tor·toise *n.* any terrestrial species of turtle

tor·tu·ous *adj.* having many twists and
turns ‖ not frank or straightforward ‖ hard
to follow because involved

tor·ture 1. *n.* intense pain or suffering of
body or mind ‖ the infliction of such pain
or suffering **2.** *v.t.* **tor·tur·ing tor·tured**
to subject to torture

toss 1. *v.t.* to throw casually ‖ (of horned
animals) to throw up into the air with the
horns ‖ (of a horse etc.) to unseat (its
rider) ‖ to flick (a coin) into the air and
let it fall heads or tails ‖ to jerk (the head)
quickly upwards and backwards ‖ to mix
(food) gently so as to coat e.g. with a

dressing ‖ (with 'down') to swallow quickly, esp. in a single draft ‖ *v.i.* (of people
unable to sleep properly) to roll around
restlessly in bed **2.** *n.* a tossing

toss-up *n.* an even chance ‖ the tossing of
a coin

to·tal 1. *adj.* entire, the whole ‖ utter,
complete **2.** *n.* the sum of a number of
items ‖ a total wreck **3. to·tal·ing to·taled**
v.t. to amount to as a total ‖ to wreck a
motor vehicle beyond repair ‖ *v.i.* to add
up to, amount to

to·tal·i·tar·i·an *adj.* of a form of government or state in which the lives and
actions of every individual are controlled
by a dictator **to·tal·i·tár·i·an·ism** *n.*

to·tal·i·ty *pl.* **to·tal·i·ties** *n.* a whole ‖ the
phase during which an eclipse is total

to·tal·ly *adv.* completely

tote 1. tot·ing tot·ed *v.t.* to carry, esp. in
the arms or on the back **2.** *n.* a carrying
‖ something carried

to·tem *n.* something, esp. an animal,
which members of a totem group have as
their sign ‖ a fabricated, esp. a carved,
image of this

totem group a group of people united by
their relationship to a common totem

to·tem·ic *adj.* of a totem ‖ charactrized by
totemism

to·tem·ism *n.* religious beliefs based on
totems

to·tem·ist *n.* a person who practices totemism ‖ a specialist in the study of totemism **to·tem·is·tic** *adj.*

totem pole (only of Indians of N.W.
America) a column of cedarwood carved
with totemic symbols

tot·ter 1. *v.i.* to walk, or stand shakily, as
if about to overbalance **2.** *n.* an unsteady
gait **tót·ter·y** *adj.*

touch 1. *v.t.* to perceive, experience or
explore the nature of (something) that
there is no intervening space ‖ to exert
very slight force on ‖ to do physical harm
to, esp. by violence ‖ to relate to ‖ to arouse
a tender or sympathetic response in ‖ (in
negative constructions) to concern
oneself with, handle ‖ to apply something
lightly and briefly to ‖ *v.i.* (of two or more

things) to be or become so close to one another that there is no intervening space **to touch up** to work on (e.g. a painting) by adding some corrective strokes **2.** *n.* the manner of playing the keys or strings of a musical instrument, usually in relation to lightness or heaviness ‖ a distinctive trait etc. ‖ a gentle stroke, tap etc. ‖ a slight degree ‖ a mild attack ‖ person money is obtained from

touch·down *n.* a play in which a player grounds the ball on or past the opponent's goal line, or the score so made ‖ the moment when the landing gear to an aircraft touches the ground

tou·ché *interj.* *(fencing)* used to acknowledge a touch ‖ used to acknowledge that one has been scored off by a clever remark etc.

touch·y touch·i·er touch·i·est *adj.* apt to be easily offended ‖ apt to cause offense

tough 1. *adj.* difficult to cut, bite into or chew ‖ strong, difficult to tear or wear through ‖ able to endure hardship etc. ‖ difficult to do ‖ hard to bear ‖ apt to be aggressive and lawless ‖ hard to impress ‖ hard to learn, understand, solve **2.** *n.* someone apt to be aggressive and lawless **3.** *adv.* **to act tough** to behave in a menacing manner **tough·en** *v.t.* to make tough ‖ *v.i.* to become tough

tou·pee *n.* a small wig used to hide baldness

tour 1. *n.* a small wig used to hide baldness

tour 1. *n.* a journey made for sightseeing, business or education ‖ a series of performances by a theatrical company in a succession of theaters ‖ a tour of duty **2.** *v.i.* to make a tour ‖ *v.t.* to present (a play etc.) in a circuit of theaters

tour·ism *n.* the practice of touring for pleasure

tour·ist *n.* a person visiting a place on holiday

tour·na·ment *n.* a meeting at which a number of individual competitors or teams of competitors compete for championship in some particular game

tour·ni·quet *n.* a bandage for temporari-

ly stopping bleeding by compression

tou·sle 1. *v.t.* **tou·sling tou·sled** to make (hair etc.) wildly untidy **2.** *n.* a tousled mass

tow 1. *v.t.* to pull along with a rope **2.** *n.* a towing ‖ a towline ‖ something towed

to·ward *prep.* in the direction of ‖ with regard to, in relation to ‖ for the prupose of making possible etc. ‖ (of time) approaching, near ‖ facint

to·wards *prep.* toward

tow·el 1. *n.* a piece of absorbent material used to dry something **2. tow·el·ing tow·eled** *v.t.* to dry or rub down with a towel **tów·el·ing** *n.* the absorbent material of which towels are made

tow·er 1. *n.* a tall structure, high in proportion to its internal dimensions **2.** *v.i.* to rise high in the air ‖ (of emotions) very intense

town *n.* a place consisting of an agglomeration of houses, shops and other buildings, bigger than a village but usually smaller than a city ‖ a municipal corporation, simpler than a city, having powers of rural administration ‖ (without article) the business or shopping center of a town

town·ship *n.* a divison of a county with some administrative powers

tox·ic *adj.* poisonous, *toxic gas*

tox·in *n.* poison produced by certain bacteria

toy 1. *n.* a child's plaything **2.** *adj.* like a toy **3.** *v.i.* (with 'with')to give something not very serious consideration

trace *n.* a sign (e.g. a footprint) left by something moving over a surface ‖ the merest indication ‖ something traced or drawn

trace trac·ing traced *v.t.* to follow (a path, track etc.) ‖ to follow back the course or line of ‖ to discern (esp. by touch) by following the outlines of ‖ to copy by marking the lines on a transparent paper etc. laid over the original ‖ *v.i.* to have a traceable history, go back in time

tra·che·a *pl.* **tra·che·ae, tra·che·as** *n.* a tube through which air passes to and from the lungs

track 1. *n.* a path worn by the passage of

men or animals ‖ something, e.g. the ruts left by wheels, the scent of an animal or the wake of a ship ‖ (pl.) footprints ‖ the course followed by something ‖ any of various prepared courses on which contests or races are held ‖ the road with rails and ties on which a train or similar thing runs **2.** v.t. to hunt or pursue by following the tacks of ‖ to follow the course of (someone or something) by the traces left behind ‖ (with 'down') to follow the traces of and find ‖ (of wheels) to be in alignment**·to leave tracks all over a surface track·age** n. rails of railroad track

tract n. a short pamphlet or treatise

tract n. a wide expanse of land etc. without precise boundaries

trac·ta·ble adj. easily controlled ‖ malleable **trác·ta·bly** adv.

trac·tion n. pulling force ‖ the force of adhesive friction exerted by a body on the surface on which it moves **trác·tion·al** adj.

trac·tor n. a vehicle used for hauling or propelling

trade 1. n. the business of distribution, selling and exchange ‖ a deal, a purchase and sale ‖ an exchange ‖ a craft ‖ pl. trade winds **2. trad·ing trad·ed** v.i. to engage in trade, buy and sell as a business ‖ to be a customer ‖ v.t. to exchange or barter

trade·mark 1. n. the name or distinctive symbol attached to goods for sale as a warrant of their production by a particular firm **2.** v.t. to register a trademark

tra·di·tion n. a cultural continuity transmitted in the form of social attitudes, beliefs, principles and conventions of behavior etc. ‖ a convention established by constant practice **tra·di·tion·al** adj. **tra·di·tion·al·ism** n. fundamentalism **tra·di·tion·al·ist** n. **tra·di·tion·al·is·tic** adj. **tra·di·tion·al·ly** adv.

tra·duce tra·duc·ing tra·duced v.t. to misrepresent

traf·fic n. the passage to and fro of people and esp. of vehicles on a raod or street ‖ illicit or shady business dealings ‖ exchange by barter or by buying and selling

traffic traf·fick·ing traf·ficked v.i. to conduct traffic, esp. illicit traffic (in a commodity)

tra·ge·di·an n. an actor specializing in tragic roles

tra·ge·di·enne n. an actress specializing in tragic roles

trag·e·dy pl. **trag·e·dies** n. a drama portraying the conflict between the individual human will and fate or necessity ‖ a calamity, an event causing distress, sadness, anguish, shock etc.

trag·ic adj. causing grief, disappointment or horror and shock **trag·i·cal·ly** adv.

trail 1. v.t. to pull (something) along behind one ‖ to pursue (a person) by following up information about his movements ‖ to hunt (an animal) by following its tracks ‖ to shadow (someone) ‖ to lag behind ‖ v.i. to hang down or float loosely ‖ to walk slowly ‖ to fail to keep up with others **2.** n. the track or traces left by the passage of an animal or person ‖ a blazed or trodden path through a wild region

trail·er n. a short extract from a new film exhibited as advance publicity ‖ a wheeled vechicle designed to be towed by a car or truck

train n. a line of railroad cars coupled together ‖ a series of persons linked to one another ‖ the skirt of a woman's dress made to trail along the ground

train v.t. to cause to respond to discipline and instruction ‖ to make efficient by instruction and repeated practice ‖ (with 'on') to direct (a gun, cmera etc.)

traipse 1. v.i. **traips·ing traipsed** to trudge for a long distance **2.** n. a long, tiring walk

trait n. a distinguishing characteristic or feature

trai·tor n. a person who betrays a trust, esp. someone guilty of the crime of treason

tra·jec·to·ry pl. **tra·jec·to·ries** n. the path of a body in space, esp. of a projectile

tramp 1. v.i. to march or walk with a heavy tread ‖ to travel oin foot or go for long walks ‖ v.t. to trample ‖ to make (one's way) by tramping **2.** *n.* a cargo boat not traveling on a regular line ‖ a person without work who tramps the country ‖ a woman of loose morals

tram·ple 1. tram·pling tram·pled *v.t.* to crush or pack down by treading on ‖ *v.i.* to tread heavily **2.** *n.* the sound of trampling

trance *n.* a state of insensibility to external surroundings with partial, but unconscious, retention of function

tran·quil *adj.* free from agitation, peaceful

tran·quil·ize, tran·quil·ize tran·quil·izing, tran·quil·liz·ing tran·quil·ized, tran·quil·lized *v.t.* to make tranquil ‖ to reduce tension by trugs **tran·quil·iz·er, tran·quil·liz·er** *n.* a sedative drug

trans·act *v.t.* to perform, carry through (e.g. a business affair) ‖ *v.i.* to conduct business

trans·ac·tion *n.* the performance or management of business etc. ‖ a business deal

tran·scend *v.t.* to be or go beyond the limits or powers of ‖ to surpass, excel

tran·scend·ent *adj.* beyond normal limits, surpassing ‖ being above and independent of the limitations of the material universe

tran·scribe tran·scrib·ing tran·scribed *v.t.* to copy out in manuscript or type (notes, shorthand etc.) ‖ to arrange or adapt (a piece of musicf) ‖ *v.i.* to make a transcription

tran·script *n.* a copy written or typed

tran·scrip·tion something transcribed

tran·sect *v.t.* to cut across **tran·séc·tion** *n.*

trans·fer 1. *v.* **trans·fer·ring trans·ferred** *v.t.* to move from one place to another ‖ to redirect from one person or object to another ‖ to pass legal ownership to another person ‖ to convey (a design etc.) from one surface to another ‖ *v.i.* to get out of one bus and into another so as to continue a journey **2.** *n.* a being transferred ‖ something or someone transferred ‖ a design on paper etc. which can be transferred to another surface ‖ an act of conveyance of property from one person

to another ‖ a ticket entitling the bearer to change from one bus to another

trans·fer·ence *n.* a transferring

trans·fix *v.t.* to impale upon or pierce with a pointed instrument **trans·fix·ion** *n*

trans·form *v.t.* to change the form or appearance ‖ to change (an electric current) into one of different voltage

trans·for·ma·tion *n.* a transforming ‖ *(computer)* the change in composition or structure of data without any change in values or meanings

trans·form·er *n.* a device for converting a varying current from one voltage to another

trans·fuse trans·fus·ing trans·fused *v.t.* to communicate to ‖ to permeate ‖ to transfer (blood) from one person into the vein of another

trans·fu·sion *n.* a transfusing of blood, plasma or drugs into the veins of a patient

trans·gress *v.t.* to break (a rule, law etc.) ‖ *v.i.* to sin

trans·gres·sion *n.* a sin ‖ a transgressing

trans·gres·sor *n.* a person who transgresses

tran·sient 1. *adj.* brief, short-lived, impermanent **2.** *n.* a person who stays in a hotel etc. for only a short time ‖ a person who has no fixed abode or employment

tran·sis·tor *n.* any of several types of device incorporating an arrangement of semiconductor material and suitable contacts capable of performing many of the functions of thermionic and photoemissive tubes

trans·it *n.* a moving across, over, or from one plce to another ‖ conveyance of goods

tran·si·tion *n.* a change or passage from one place, action, mood, topic etc. to another **tran·si·tion·al** *adj.*

tran·si·tive 1. *adj.* *(gram.,* of certain verbs) expressing an action directed toward or performed on some person or thing **2.** *n.* a verb or construction which is transitive

tran·si·to·ry *adj.* passing, temporary, not lasting

trans·late trans·lat·ing trans·lat·ed *v.t.* to put (a word, text or language) into another language retaining the snese ‖ to put in different words in order to make clearer ‖ *v.i.* to make a translation

trans·la·tion *n.* a translating ‖ something translated

trans·lu·cent *adj.* of a medium through which light passes, but in such a way that a clear image cannot be formed of the object viewed through it

trans·mis·sion *n.* a transmitting ‖ something transmitted ‖ the mechanism by which power is transmitted from the engine to the axel of a car etc.

trams·mit trans·mit·ting trans·mit·ted *v.t.* to send from one place or person to another ‖ to pass on (an infection or disease) ‖ to convey from one mechanical part to another ‖ to send (a signal)? by radio waves or over a wire **trans·mit·ter** *n.* a person who or thing which transmits

trans·mu·ta·tion *n.* a transmuting ‖ the change of one element into another ‖ the change of one species into another

trans·mute trans·mut·ing trans·mut·ed *v.t.* to cause to change in form, nature or substance

tran·som *n.* a window above the lintel of esp. a door

trans·par·ent *adj.* of a medium through which objects can be viewed clearly ‖ easy to detect

tran·spire tran·spir·ing tran·spired *v.i.* to become known ‖ to happen ‖ *v.t.* to give off (water vapour, perspiration)

trans·plant 1. *v.t.* to remove and plant in another place ‖ to settle in another area ‖ to graft (living tissue or an organ) from one part of the body to another or from one person to another **2.** *n.* a transplanting **trans·plan·tá·tion** *n.*

trans·port 1. *v.t.* to carry (doods, people or animals) from one place to another **2.** *n.* the act of transporting ‖ a vessel or vehicle used to transport ‖ *(computer)* the mechanism that carries disk, tape, or paper past the sensing and recording heads **trans·por·tá·tion** *n.* a transporting ‖ a means of transporting

trans·pose trans·pos·ing trans·opsed *v.t.* to cause (two things) to change places

(esp. words in a sentence etc.) ‖ to write (a musical composition) in a key other than the original

trans·sex·u·al *n.* a person of one sex who undergoes surgery to become physically like the opposite sex **—transsexual** *adj.* **—transsexualism** *n.*

trans·verse 1. *adj.* crosswise **2. trans·vers·ing trans·versed** to lie across

trap 1. *n.* a devioe into which an animal may enter unawares, or be lured ‖ something devised to put an unsuspecting person in a situation which is to his disadvantage ‖ any hidden hazard ‖ a device, e.g. a water-filled bend, in a pipe, to prevent noxious gasses from passing ‖ a trapdoor **2. trap·ping trapped** *v.t.* to catch in a trap ‖ *v.i.* to set traps for game

tra·peze *n.* a short horizontal bar suspended by two parallel ropes or wires, used by acrobats

trap·pings *pl. n.* ornamental equipment ‖ a horse's ornamented cloth covering

trash *n.* rubbish ‖ meaningless talk or writing, nonsense ‖ worthless books etc. ‖ (without article) people considered as of no account

trash·y trash·i·er trash·i·est *adj.* like trash

trau·ma *pl.* **tram·ma·ta, trau·mas** *n.* a physical wound or injury ‖ a violent emotional blow ‖ a neurotic condition

trau·mat·ic *adj.* concerning, producing trauma

tra·vail 1. *n.* the pains of childbirth ‖ any intense pain or laborious work **2.** *v.i.* to suffer pains of childbirth ‖ to work hard

trav·el 1. brav·el·ing trav·eled *v.i.* to make a journey ‖ to proceed in a given direction or pass from one point to another ‖ to be tranmitted ‖ (of a piece of machinery) to move in a set path ‖ *v.t.* to journey over or through (a region etc.) ‖ to cover (a distance) **2.** *n.* the act of traveling ‖ journeys

trav·el·er *n.* a person who travels

tra·verse 1. *n.* the action of traversing ‖ something which lies or goes across·a sideways course **2.** *adj.* traverse

tra·verse tra·vers·ing tra·versed *v.t.* to move across or throught ‖ to extend across

‖ *v.i.* to go across, along, up and down etc. ‖ to pivot

trav·es·ty 1. *pl.* **trav·es·ties** *n.* a grotesque or crude imitation **2.** *v.t.* **trav·es·ty·ing trav·es·ties** to make a travesty of

trawl 1. *n.* a large bag net which is dragged along the bottom of the sea for fish by a boat **2.** *v.i.* to fish with a trawl **tráwl·er** *n.* a boat used to catch fish by using trawl nets

tray *n.* a flat piece of wood, metal, plastic etc., usually rimmed, for carrying small, light objects

treach·er·ous *adj.* all of the actions of a traitor ‖ unreliable

treach·er·y *pl.* **treach·er·ies** *n.* disloyalty, perfidy ‖ treason ‖ an act of disloyalty or treason

tread 1. treading trod trod *v.i.* to move on foot, to walk ‖ to proceed ‖ *v.t.* to wear away by walking on ‖ to crush with the foot **2.** *n.* the action, sound or way of treading ‖ the horizontal part of a step in a staircase ‖ the thickened, scored face of a tire

trea·dle 1. a foot-operated lever on a machine etc. **2.** *v.i.* **trea·dling trea·dled** to operate a treadle

tread·mill *n.* a mill worked by people treading on steps set in the circumference of the great mill wheel ‖ a mill driven by an animal treading on an endless belt ‖ any wearingly monotonous activity

trea·son *n.* an attempt to overthrow the government to which a person owes allegiance ‖ betrayal of trust, disloyalty **tréa·son·a·ble, tréa·son·ous** *adjs*

trea·sure 1. *n.* anything very valuable ‖ a person of rare excellence **2.** *v.t.* **treas·ur·ing treas·ured** to value highly

treas·ur·er *n.* an official in charge of the finances of a government, society etc.

treas·ur·y *pl.* **treas·ur·ies** *n.* a building used to store money, valuables etc. ‖ the funds of a society corporation, state etc. **Treas·ur·y** a government department responsible for the public revenue and expenditure

treat 1. *v.t.* to behave toward (someone or something) ‖ to pay for the food, drink etc.

of (another person) ‖ to give medical attention to (a patient) ‖ to coat with some preparation ‖ *v.i.* to pay for another's food, drink or entertainment etc. ‖ (with 'of') to offer an exposition **2.** *n.* something that gives special delight

trea·tise *n.* a written study of a particular subject

treat·ment *n.* the act of treating someone or something ‖ medical or surgical care

trea·ty *pl.* **trea·ties** *n.* a formal, signed and ratified agreement between states

tre·ble tre·bling tre·bled *v.i.* to become three times as much, as many or as great

tree *n.* any tall, perennial, woody plant usually with a single elongated stem (trunk) and having a head of branches and foliage, or foliage only

trek 1. *v.i.* **trek·king trekked** *(hist.)* to travel by ox wagon ‖ to make a long, hard or tedious journey **2.** *n.* a leg of a journey

trel·lis 1. *n.* a light frame of wooden or metal latticelike strips used as screen or for plants to climb on **2.** *v.t.* to furnish with a trellis

trem·ble 1. *v.i.* **trem·bling trem·bled** to shake involuntarily from fear, excitement etc. ‖ to vibrate **2.** *n.* a trembling **trém·bly trem·bli·er trem·bli·est** *adj.* shaky

tre·men·dous *adj.* enormous ‖ arousing awe

trem·or *n.* a trembling ‖ a vibration ‖ aquavering sound ‖ a shudder

trem·u·lous *adj.* trembling ‖ apprehensive ‖ quivering

trench *n.* a long, narrow and usually deep hollow cut in the ground

trench·ant *adj.* keen and effective, vigorous ‖ incisive

trend 1. *n.* a tendency, general direction ‖ a dominant movement **2.** *v.i.* to have a tendency

trep·i·da·tion *n.* a state of fear or apprehension

tres·pass 1. *n.* a trespassing **2.** *v.i.* to enter someone's property unlawfully ‖ to encroach or make an undue claim

tress *n.* supports on which planks, a tabletop etc. are laid ‖ a braced framework of wood for carrying a railroad over a depression

tri·ad *n.* a group of three

tri·al 1. *n.* a test by examination or experiment ‖ a hardship ‖ the state of being proved by endurance ‖ a judicial examination of inquiry and determination of a cause ‖ provisionally accepted 2. *adj.* used as a trial

tri·an·gle *n.* a plane figure bounded by three straight lines ‖ a percussion instrument ‖ a group of three people involved in some situation, esp. an eternal triangle

tri·an·gu·lar *adj.* shaped like a triangle ‖ involving three things, parts, persons etc. **tro·an·gu·lár·i·ty** *n.*

trib·al *adj.* like a tribe ‖ organized by tribes ‖ strong feeling for the tribe association of, and interbreeding between, a number of families

trib·u·la·tion *n.* suffering caused by adversity

tri·bu·nal *n.* a group of persons empowered to decide a specific issue according to the law

trib·u·tar·y 1. *pl.* **trib·u·tar·ies** *n.* a stream flowing into a larger stream 2. *adj.* contributory

trib·ute *n.* a payment in money or kind exacted from a state, by right of conquer or in return for protection ‖ a gift expressing gratitude or affection

trick (trik) 1. *n.* an act or action designed to deceive ‖ a dextrous feat ‖ a practical joke ‖ a knack ‖ the cards played and taken in one round 2. *adj.* of or relating to or intended as a trick 3. *v.t.* to deceive by a trick **trick·er·y** *n.*

trick·le 1. **trick·ling trick·led** *v.i.* (of a liquid) barely to flow ‖ to come or go as if in a thin, intermittent stream ‖ *v.t.* to give forth or cause to flow in a thin stream or in drops 2. *n.* a series of drops, a thin stream, or something compared to this

trick·y trick·i·er trick·i·est *adj.* difficult to understand or deal with ‖ deft, adroit

tri·cy·cle *n.* a light vehicle like a bicycle, but having a pair of wheels arranged side by side behind a single front wheel

tried *adj.* proved, tested reliable

tri·fle *n.* a valueless, insignificant fact or thing ‖ a small amount of money ‖ a dessert

trifle *n.* a valueless, insignificant fact or thing ‖ a small amount of money of money ‖ a dessert

trifle tri·fling tri·fled *v.i.* (with 'with') to talk or act lightly or insincerely ‖ *v.t.* (with 'away') to pass (time) idly or wastefully **tri·fling** *adj.* slight, insignificant

trig·ger 1. *n.* the steel catch which is pulled to fire a firearm, or similar catch used to actuate some other mechanism 2. *v.t.* to start, get going ‖ to release the trigger of

trig·o·nom·e·try *n.* the branch of mathematics concerned with the sides and angles of triangles

trill *n.* the warble of a bird ‖ a quick vibration of the tongue or uvula ‖ the letter or word pronounced in this way

tril·o·gy *pl.* **tril·o·gies** *n.* any set of three related novels, musical compositions etc.

trim 1. **trim·ming trimmed** *v.t.* to cut away unnecessary or unwanted parts from ‖ to make tidy ‖ to decorate 2. *n.* a state of proper fitness for work or action ‖ a light haircut ‖ a decorative addition to ‖ the lighter woodwork used in the finishing of a building 3. **trim·mer trim·mest** *adj.* neat, compact ‖ in good order

trin·i·ty *pl.* **trin·i·ties** *n.* a group of three **the TRIN·I·TY** Father, Son and Holy Ghost

trin·ket *n.* a small ornamental object

tri·o *pl.* **tri·os** *n.* a group of three ‖ a musical composition written for three performers

trip (trip) 1. **trip·ping tripped** *v.i.* to lose one's balance ‖ to make a mistake, blunder ‖ *v.t.* to expose (someone) as having told a lie ‖ to operate (a switch or other mechanism) by releasing a catch 2. *n.* a tripping up ‖ a short journey

tripe *n.* part of the first or second stomach of a ruminant used for food ‖ worthless matter

tri·ple 1. *adj.* having three parts ‖ repeated three times ‖ three times as much, as many or as great 2. *n.* a group of three ‖ an amount three times as much, as many or as great

triple tri·pling tri·pled *v.t.* to make three times as much, as many or as great

trip·let *n.* one of a set of three offspring born at one birth

trip·li·cate *adj.* made in three identical copies

tri·pod *n.* a stand with three legs for setting up a camera, theodolite etc. ‖ a cauldron etc. resting on three legs **trip·o·dal tri·pod·ic** *adjs*

tri·sect *v.t.* to divide into three equal parts **tri·séc·tion, tri·séc·tor** *ns*

trite *adj.* stale through too frequent repetition

trit·u·rate *v.t.* **trit·u·rat·ing trit·u·rat·ed** to grind to fine powder **trit·u·rá·tion, trit·u·ra·tor** *ns*

tri·umph *n.* a complete and thoroughly decisive victory

triumph *v.i.* to exult in victory ‖ (with 'over') to boast at the expense of the vanquished

tri·um·phal *adj.* pertaining to a triumph

tri·um·phant *adj.* victorious ‖ exultant

tri·um·vi·rate *n.* any group of three men in authority

triv·et *n.* a three-legged iron stand to put a knief etc. on by the fire ‖ a metal plate mounted on three short legs to hold a hot dish

triv·i·a *pl. n.* insignificant, unimportant matters or things

triv·i·al *adj.* of very little importance or value, trifling

triv·i·al·i·ty *pl.* **triv·i·al·ties** *n.* a trifle

troll 1. *v.t.* to sing in a loud, jolly, carefree way ‖ tofish in by drawing a line with a spoon attached behind a boat **2.** *n.* the act of trolling ‖ the spoon or spoon and line used in trolling

troll *n.* one of the supernatural beings, dwarfs, inhabiting caves, hills etc.

trol·ley, trol·ly *pl.* **trol·leys, trol·lies** *n.* a wheeled basket or carriage etc. that runs suspended from an overhead track ‖ a trolleybus ‖ a streetcar

trom·bone *n.* a brass wind instrument **trom·bón·ist** *n.*

troop 1. *n.* (*pl.*) soldiers, armed forces ‖

a scout unit ‖ a lot of people ‖ a herd or flock **2.** *v.i.* (often with 'off') to go in groups

troop·er *n.* a cavalry soldier ‖ a private in a state police ‖ a mounted policeman

tro·phy *pl.* **tro·phies** *n.* object won in a sporting contest ‖ any object cherished as a memento of a success won

trop·ic 1. *n.* either of two parallels of latitude on the globe passing through the most northerly and southerly points on the earth's surface **the Tropics** the region between the Tropics of Cancer and Capricorn **2.** *adj.* pertaining to the Tropics **tróp·i·cal** *adj.*

trot trot·ting trot·ted *v.i.* (of a horse etc.) to move at a steady pace, the action of the feet being in diagonal pairs and the rhythm duple (not quadruple) ‖ (of bipeds) to move at a pace between walking and running

trot *n.* the action of trotting ‖ a crib

trou·ba·dour *n.* one of a class of poets and poet musicians ‖ a strolling minstrel

trou·ble 1. trou·bling trou·bled *v.t.* to cause to worry ‖ to afflict ‖ to put to inconvenience **2.** *n.* worry ‖ misfortune ‖ a difficult situation ‖ effort, pains ‖ that which is wrong ‖ a physcial ailment not specifically named

trou·ble·some *adj.* giving trouble

trough *n.* a long open receptacle for animal food etc. ‖ a similar receptacle for kneading dough etc., ‖ a depression

troupe *n.* a company of entertainers etc. **tróup·er** *n.* a member of a troupe

trou·sers *pl. n.* an outer garment

trous·seau *pl.* **trous·seaux trous·seaus** *n.* a bride's personal clothing, together with the linen etc. for the household

trout *pl.* **trout, trouts** *n.* any of several food and game fishes

trow·el (tráuel) **1.** *n.* a short, flat-bladed tool for spreading mortar etc. **2.** *v.t.* **trow·el·ing trow·eled** to spread, smooth, shape etc. with a trowel

tru·an·cy *pl.* **tru·an·cies** *n.* an act or instance of plaing truant ‖ the state of being truant.

tru·ant 1. *n.* a pupil who stays away from

school without permission ‖ anyone who absents himself from work or duty without good reason 2. *adj.* of or pertaining to a truant

truce *n.* a temporary peace

truck 1. *n.* commodities suitable for exchange, barter or sale in small quantities ‖ *v.i.* to exchange or barter goods

truck 1. *n.* a strong vehicle used for road transport of heavy loads ‖ shelved frame work mounted on wheels 2. *v.t.* to transport in or on a truck

truc·u·lent *adj.* sharply self-assertive ‖ harsh and scathing

trudge (trad3) **1. trudg·ing trudged** *v.i.* to walk doggedly under fatiguing conditions

true 1. *adj.* in agreement with fact ‖ faithful to another or others, or to a cause or allegiance ‖ rightful ‖ genuine, sincere ‖ accurate, correct 2. *adv.* accurately

truf·fle *n.* the edible fruiting body of a genus of fungi

tru·ly *adv.* truthfully ‖ utterly, really ‖ accurately

trump 1. *n.* any card of a suit designated as having temporarily a higher rank than the other suits 2. *v.t.* to take (a card) with a trump card

trum·pet 1. *n.* a wind instrument fashioned from a long metal tube, with a curved, funnel-shaped free end ‖ something resembling this in shape 2. *v.t.* to play the trumpet

trun·cate *v.t.* **trun·cat·ing trun·cat·ed** to shorten by cutting off the top or end **trún·cat·ed** *adj.*

trun·dle 1. *n.* a small wheel or roller 2. **trun·dling trun·dled** *v.t.* to cause (esp. a heavy, awkward object) to roll along ‖ *v.i.* to roll awkwardly

trunk 1. *n.* the main stem of a tree ‖ the human or animal body excluding the head and limbs ‖ a proboscis, esp. of an elephant ‖ a large piece of heavy luggage ‖ the covered luggage container of an automobile ‖ *pl.* a man's bathing suit 2. *adj.* of a main line in a rail, road, telephone etc. system

truss *n.* a device used to support to support

a hernia ‖ a supporting framework

truss *v.t.* to tie up by binding fast ‖ to support

trust (trast)*n.* confidence in a person or thing because of the qualities one perceived ‖ acceptance of something as true ‖ a responsibility, charge, duty etc. ‖ faith in the future ‖ an equitable right or interest in a property held by one person on behalf of another ‖ the property so administered

trust *v.t.* to have faith in ‖ to rely on (someone) ‖ to believe ‖ to confide (someone or something) to a person's responsible care

trus·tee *n.* a person legally invested with property rights in the interests of another

trust·ful *adj.* ready to trust, not suspicious

trust·wor·thy *adj.* deserving trust

trust·y *adj.* **trust·i·er trust·i·est** trustworthy

truth *pl.* **truths** *n.* something which is true ‖ accuracy ‖ sincerity, integrity ‖ agreement with fact **trúth·ful** *adj.*

try 1. try·ing tried *v.t.* to attempt to do ‖ to test experimentally ‖ to submit judicial inquiry ‖ to bore, irritate ‖ to fatigue ‖ to strain (the eyes, someone's patience etc.) ‖ *v.i.* to make an effort to do something 2. *pl.* **tries** *n.* an effort

try·ing *adj.* causing impatience and annoyance ‖ causing worry or affliction

try·out *n.* a practical test of efficiency ‖ an opportunity to demonstrate qualifications

tryst *n.* an agreement between lovers to meet at a certain time and place ‖ that meeting

T square a drawing instrument shaped like a T

tub *n.* an open circular vessel with a flat bottom, made of staves held together by hoops ‖ a slow or clumsy ship ‖ a bathtub

tu·ba *n.* a long, narrow, hollow cylinder for holding or passing liquids, gases etc ‖ a small, flexible cylinder with a screw cap for holding toothpaste etc. ‖ an election tube ‖ (with 'the') *(slang)* television

tu·ber *n.* a modified underground stem (e.g. the potato), shortened, thickened and fleshy

tu·ber·cu·lo·sis *n.* a highly variable infectious disease

tuck 1. *v.t.* to push (something) into a little space, pocket etc., or under something, where it will be neatly held or conveniently hidden ‖ (with 'in') to cover (a person) with bedclothes ‖ **2.** *n.* the act or an instance of tucking ‖ a fold sewn into a garment

Tues·day *n.* the third day of the week

tuft 1. *n.* a bunch or cluster of feathers, hairs, etc. growing together at the base ‖ a small clump of plants ‖ a buttonlike cluster of loops **2.** *v.t.* to arrange in tuffs ‖ to provide with a tuft ‖ *v.y.* to grow in tufts **túft·ed** *adj.* (of birds) having a crest ‖ bearing flowers in dense clsters **túft·y tuft·i·er tuft·i·est** *adj.*

tug 1. tug·ging tugged *v.t.* to pull with force ‖ to pull by means of a tugboat ‖ *v.i.* to use force or violence in pulling **2.** *n.* a strong, violent pull ‖ a struggle ‖ the trace of a harness

tug·boat *n.* a small powerful steamer for towing

tu·i·tion *n.* the price charged for instruction ‖ teaching **tu·i·tion·al, tu·i·tion·ar·y** *adjs.*

tu·lip *n.* a genus of bulbous herbaceous plants ‖ the flower or the bulb of this plant

tum·ble 1. tum·bling tum·bled *v.i.* to drop in price at a rapidly increasing pace ‖ to toss or roll about ‖ (of words) to issue in a space without proper control ‖ to perform feats of acrobatic agility **2.** *n.* a fall ‖ a handspring, somersault etc.

tum·bler *n.* an acrobat ‖ an ordinary drinking glass without a foot or stem ‖ the movable part of a gear ‖ a moving part of the mechanism of a lock ‖ a roly-poly (weighted toy)

tu·mid *adj.* swollen ‖ bombastic, inflated **tu·mid·i·ty** *n.*

tu·mor *n.* an abnormal growth of tissue

tu·mult *n.* an uproar rioting ‖ noisy and violent disturbance **tu·mul·tu·ous**

tu·na *n.* highly prized game and food fish

tun·dra *n.* an often flat, treeless plain largely covered with mosses and lichens

tune 1. *n.* a succession of notes so related that they constitute a musical structure ‖ harmonious relationship **2. tun·ing tuned** *v.t.* to djust (an instrument) to correct musical pitch ‖ to adjust (a receiving apparatus) to the wavelength of a particular transmitter ‖ to adjust (a motor) so that it runs perfectly **tune·ful** *adj.* melodious **tun·er** *n.* a person whose job is to tune pianos, organs etc. ‖ a resonant circuit, or more than one, in a receiving set

tung·sten *n.* a metallic element akin to chromium having the highest melting point of all metals

tu·nic *n.* a loose, knee-length or longer, usually sleeveless, slip-on garment

tun·nel 1. *n.* a passageway cut through a hill or cliff side or under the ground, sea or a river ‖ a passage dug underground by an animal ‖ a wind tunnel **2. tun·nel·ing** *past* and **tun·neled** *v.i.* to make or use a tunnel

tur·ban *n.* a headdress, formed of a long piece of cloth wound around the head **tur·baned** *adj.*

tur·bid *adj.* thick, dense ‖ not clear, muddled **tur·bid·i·ty** *n.*

tur·bine *n.* an engine, actuated by the reaction, impulse, or both, of a current (water, steam or gas)

tur·bu·lence *n.* the state or quality of being turbulent **túr·bu·len·cy** *n.*

tur·bu·lent *adj.* in a state of commotion or stormy agitation ‖ violent by nature and hard to control

tu·reen *n.* a deep, covered dish for holding soup etc.

turf 1. *pl.* **turves, turfs** *n.* grass and the earth in which its matted roots are mangled ‖ (with 'the') horseracing **2.** *v.t.* to cover with turf

tur·gid *adj.* swollen ‖ bombastic, inflated **tur·gid·i·ty** *n.*

tur·key *pl.* **tur·keys** *n.* a large bird, raised mainly for its excellent flesh

tur·moil *n.* violent agitation or great confusion

turn 1. *v.* (sometimes with 'over') to put the other side of (a page) uppermost in order to read or write on it ‖ (with 'out') to expel, drive out ‖ to alter the course of (something) ‖ to proceed around (a corner) ‖ (with 'on') to direct, aim ‖ to change opinion or attitude ‖ to affect (a person) in a specified way ‖ to make sour, rancid, bad, curdled ‖ (with 'down') to fold back the sheets of (a bed) ‖ to move through an arc of a circle or about an axis or central point ‖ to use a lathe ‖ (esp. with 'toss and') to move about restlessly in bed ‖ (of the wind) to change quarter ‖ (of the tide) to start to ebb or flow ‖ (of the mind) to become deranged ‖ (of the eye, gaze etc.) to look ‖ (with 'from') to glance aside ‖ (with 'from') to face about so as not to see something ‖ to seem to go in a certain direction ‖ (of the stomach) to be upset ‖ (of the head) to seem to reel ‖ (with 'to') to take up something as a new interest, hobby etc. ‖ (with 'to') to change in nature ‖ (*impers.*, of the weather) to change in character in a specified way **2.** *n.* a turning through an arc of a circle or about an axis or central point ‖ the act of taking or changing a direction ‖ a bend or curve where a change of direction occurs ‖ a winding of rope or wire etc. around something ‖ a twisted condition ‖ one of alternating or successive opportunities or obligations ‖ a development in the progress of something ‖ a period of duty or activity **at every turn** constantly and in all directions **in turn** in proper sequence **out of turn** not in proper sequence ‖ tactlessly, without prudence

turn·a·round *adj.* of the time required to complete an operation and begin the next one

turn·coat *n.* a renegade

tur·nip *n.* a rough hairy-leaved biennial plant

turn·out *n.* a gathering of people for a demonstration, parade, meeting etc. ‖ the output of a product over a specified period

turn·over *n.* the cycle of purchase, sale and replacement of stock in a business ‖ the movement of people or things into and out of an establishment ‖ the number of workers leaving employment and being replaced within a given period ‖ a pie or pastry made by folding one half of the crust upon the other half to contain meat, fruit or jam

turn·pike *n.* (*hist.*) a tollgate ‖ a fast highway on which a toll is levied ‖ (*loosely*) any main road

turn·stile *n.* a gate, with four arms set at right angles, revolving on a central post

turn·ta·ble *n.* a circular revolving platform

tur·pen·tine *n.* an essential oil, chiefly pinene

tur·pi·tude *n.* inherent wickedness

tur·quoise *n.* an opaque skyblue or blue-green precious stone blue-green color

tur·ret *n.* a small tower projecting from the wall or a corner of a larger structure ‖ a revolving armored covering for a gun

tur·tle *pl.* **tur·tles, tur·tle** *n.* a reptile of the order *Testudinata* (or *Chelonia*)

tusk *n.* a long, sharp tooth, often curved, which projects beyond the closed mouth of certain animals **túsk·er** *n.* an elephant or wild boar with strongly developed tusks

tus·sle 1. *v.i.* **tus·sling tus·sled** to struggle in fight, sport or controversy **2.** *n.* a struggle

tu·te·lage *n.* guardianship ‖ instruction ‖ the state of being under a guardian or tutor

tu·tor 1. *n.* a private teacher **2.** *v.t.* to teach privately *v.i.* to earn a living by private or individual teaching **tú·tor·age** *n.*

tu·tor·i·al *adj.* of a tutor or tutors

tu·tu *n.* a ballet dancer's very short skirt of gauze frills

tux·e·do *pl.* **tux·e·does** *n.* a tailless dress coat

twang *n.* harsh, vibrating sound ‖ a sharp, nasal quality in the speaking voice

tweak 1. *v.t.* to pinch and pull with a quick twisting jerk **2.** *n.* a sharp pinch or pull

tweed *n.* a strong twilled woolen or wool and cotton cloth **twéed·y** *adj.*

tweez·ers *pl. n.* a small two-pronged instrument used to pick up or grip small objects, pull out hairs etc.

twelfth 1. *adj.* being number 12 in a series

twelve 1. *adj.* being one more than 11

twen·ti·eth 1. *adj.* being number 20 in a

series

twen·ty 1. adj. being one more than 19

twice adv. two times ‖ on two occasions ‖ doubly

twid·dle 1. twid·dling twid·dled v.t. to twirl idly ‖ v.i. to toy fussly **to twiddle one's thumbs** to have nothing better to do **2.** n. a slight twisting motion

twig n. a small shoot from a branch of a tree **twig·gy twig·gi·er twig·gi·est** adj. long and thin like a twig

twi·light 1. n. the dim light between total darkness and sunrise, or esp. between sunset and darkness ‖ the period when this light appears ‖ any dim light **2.** adj. of, pertaing to, like or appearing at twilight

twill 1. n. a textile fabric patterned with diagonal lines **2.** v.t. to weave so as to produce this pattern

twin adj. related as one of a pair of twins ‖ having identical characteristics with anothe rthing ‖ occuring in pairs **1.** n. either one of a pair of offspring produced in a single birth ‖ a person or thing very closely resembling another

twine 1. n. strong cord composed of two or more strands of e.g. Manila hemp twisted together ‖ a coil, twist **2. twin·ing twined** v.t. to twist (strands) so as to form something ‖ to interweave ‖ to interlace ‖ v.i. to coil ‖ wind so as to clasp

twinge 1. twing·ing twinged v.t. to affect with a sudden sharp pain ‖ v.i. to be affected in this way **2.** n. a sudden sharp physical pain ‖ a stab or mental pain

twin·kle 1. twin·kling twin·kled v.i. to emit intermittent gleams of light in rapid succession ‖ (of the eyes) to sparkle with fun, malice etc. **2.** n. a twinkling **twin·kling** n. a quick sparkling or flashing, esp. of a star or of eyes

twirl 1. v. to rotate rapidly ‖ to whirl ‖ to twiddle ‖ totwist so as to curl **2.** n. a arapid rotation ‖ a curl

twist 1. v. to cause to rotate ‖ to cause to spiral ‖ to wrench so as to cause to be out of shape or place ‖ to distort the meaning of ‖ to contort (the facial muscles) ‖ to turn about an axis ‖ to writhe, squirm

2. n. a twisting or being twisted ‖ a personal tendency, esp. an eccentric one ‖ an unexpected development in a situation or story ‖ a deliberate distortion or perversion of meaning ‖ a bad wrench ‖ a loaf of bread made in a twisted form ‖ strong cotton or silk yarn made by twisting ‖ a torque **twist·er** n. a tornado or cyclone ‖ a baffling problem etc. **twist·y twist·er twist·i·est** adj. not straightforward

twitch 1. v.t. to pull with a light jerk or jerks ‖ to move (a body part) nervously and jerkily **2.** n. a sudden involuntary jerk or contraction, e.g. of a muscle ‖ a quick light pull or tug

twit·ter 1. v.i. to utter a succession of thin chirps ‖ to be in a flurry and make agitated little noises ‖ to tremble and be very agitated **2.** n. the succession of chirping sounds made by birds ‖ a state of nervous agitation in people **twit·ter·y** adj.

two 1. adj. being one more than one

two-faced adj. having two surfaces ‖ hypocritically deceitful **two-fac·ed·ly** adv.

two·fold 1. adj. dual **2.** adv. two times as much or as many ‖ by two times

two-time two-tim·ing two-timed v.t. to deceive ‖ to double cross

two-way adj. moving or permitting movement, transmission etc. in each of two directions ‖ mutual ‖ involving two persons or groups

ty·coon n. a magnate, powerful financier

tyke, tike n. a mongrel dog ‖ a mischievous child

type 1. n. a kind or sort ‖ (biol.) the individual rgarded as most fully exemplifying the characteristics of a genus etc. ‖ a person, thing or event regarded as symbolic ‖ a piece of esp. metal having on its upper surface a character in relief which when inked and brought under pressure against apper leaves an impression of the character **2. typ·ing typed** v.t. to write using a typewriter ‖ to classify according to type ‖ for producing typelike writing ‖ to cast (an actor) over and over in the same kind of role ‖ v.i. to use a typewriter

type·wri·ter *n.* a machine operated by a keyboard

typhoid fever an acute infectious disease, producing a prolonged, debilitating fever and diarrhea

ty·phoon *n.* a violent cyclone in the China Sea

ty·phus *n.* any of several human infectious diseases conveyed by the bite of lice, fleas etc.

typ·i·cal *adj.* characteristic of an individual ‖ characteristic of a class

typ·i·fy typ·i·fy·ing typ·i·fied *v.t.* to be the representative symbol of ‖ to embody the essential characteristics of

typ·ist *n.* a person who operates a typewriter

ty·pog·ra·pher *n.* someone who lays out copy and sees to all the elements of printing design

ty·ran·nic *adj.* tyrannical **ty·rán·ni·cal** *adj.* acting like or characteristics of a tyrant **ty·rán·ni·cal·ly** *adv.*

tyr·an·nize tyr·an·niz·ing tyr·n·nized *v.t.* to treat tyrannically

tyr·an·ny *pl.* **tyr·an·nies** *n.* despotic rule ‖ the unjust and cruel exercise of power ‖ a tyrannical act

ty·rant *n.* a despot ‖ someone behaving like a despot

ty·ro *pl.* **ty·ros** *n.* a beginner

U

U, u the 21st letter of the English alphabet

u·biq·ui·tous *adj.* present everywhere at the same time

ud·der *n.* in cattle etc. the baggy organ containing two or more mammary glands, each having one teat or nipple

ug·li·ness *n.* the state or quality of being ugly

ugly ug·li·er ug·li·est *adj.* unsightly || morally offensive || quarrelsome || fraught with danger

u·ku·le, u·ke·le·le *n.* a small four-stringed musical instrument resembling the guitar

ul·cer *n.* an inflamed discontinuity in the skin or mucous membranes of the body || a source of corruption

ul·cer·ate ul·cer·at·ing ul·cer·at·ed *v.t.* to make ulcerous || *v.i.* to become ulcerous

ul·cer·a·tion *n.* a state of being ulcerated || an ulcer or several ulcers in a group

ul·cer·ous *adj.* having the nature of an ulcer

u·te·ri·or *adj.* further, more distant || beyond what is evident or professed

ul·ti·mate *adj.* farthest away in space or time || eventual || final

ul·ti·ma·tum *pl.* **u·ti·ma·tums, ul·ti·ma·ta** *n.* the final terms offered or demanded by one of the parties in diplomatic negotiations

ul·tra 1. *adj.* extreme 2. *n.* an extremist

ultra- *prefix* beyond || to an extreme degree

ul·tra·son·ic *adj.* supersonic **ul·tra·són·ics** *n.* supersonics

ul·tra·vi·o·let *adj.* (abbr. UV) relating to, producing or using ultraviolet radiation

um·ber 1. *n.* a dark brown earth rich in manganese and ferric oxides 2. *adj.* of the color of umber

um·bil·i·cal *adj.* of or relating to the navel

umbilical cord a cordlike structure joining the fetus to the placenta of the mother || the cable connecting an outside astronaut or aquanaut t his or her ship || a power supply line to a rocket or spacecraft preceding takeoff

um·bra *pl.* **um·brae** *n.* area of total shadow during an eclipse

um·brage *n.* resentment **to take (give) umbrage** to feel (cause to feel) pique

um·brel·la *n.* a portable device which, when opened, is used to keep rain off a person or to protect him from the sun

um·pire 1. *n.* someone chosen to enforce the rules of play || an arbitrator 2. **um·pir·ing um·pired** *v.i.* to act as umpire

ump·teen *adj.* very many

ump·ti·eth *adj.* numberless

un- *prefix* not, lack of, opposite

un- *prefix* added to verbs to indicate a reversal of the action of the verb, as in untie || added to nouns to indicate a release from the state expressed by the noun, as in 'undress'

un·a·ble *adj.* not able

un·a·bridged *adj.* not abridged

un·ac·count·a·ble *adj.* inexplicable || not accountable, not responsible **un·ac·cóunt·a·bly** *adv.*

un·ac·cus·tomed *adj.* unusual

un·af·fect·ed *adj.* without affection || not affected or influenced

u·na·nim·i·ty *n.* the state or quality of being unanimous

u·nan·i·mous *adj.* being of one mind, being in complete agreement

un·ap·proach·a·ble *adj.* not able to be approached || unrivaled

un·armed *adj.* having no weapons

un·as·sum·ing *adj.* modest, not pretentious

un·at·tached *adj.* not attached || not belonging to a particular gorup, organization etc.

un·a·void·a·ble *adj.* inevitable, not avoidable **un·avóid·a·bly** *adv.*

un·a·ware 1. *adj.* not aware 2. *adv.* unawares

un·a·wares *adv.* by surprise || unintentionally, without noticing

un·bal·anced *adj.* lacking balance || mentally unstable || (accounting) not balanced

un·be·com·ing *adj.* not becoming || unseemingly, not decent

un·be·liev·a·ble *adj.* true but astounding

un·be·liev·er *n.* a person how has no belief in matters of religion

un·bend un·bend·ing un·bent *v.t.* to make straight ‖ *v.i.* to become less distant or less stiff in manner

un·blush·ing *adj.* shameless ‖ not blushing

un·born *adj.* not yet born

un·bri·dled *adj.* unrestrained ‖ having no bridle on

un·bro·ken *adj.* intact, whole ‖ interrupted

un·called-for *adj.* unnecessary ‖ impertinent

un·can·ny un·can·ni·er un·can·ni·est *est.* inspiring feelings of apprehension ‖ almost superhuman

un·cer·e·mo·ni·ous *adj.* brusque, curt, abrupt ‖ without ceremony or formality

un·cer·tain *adj.* not certainly known ‖ not certain to occur ‖ not reliable ‖ variable **un ‖ cer ‖ tain ‖ ty** *pl.* **un·cer·tain·ties** *n.* the quality or state of being uncertain ‖ something uncertain

un·cle *n.* the brother of one's mother or father ‖ the husband of one's aunt

un·clean *adj.* impure ‖ dirty

un·com·fort·a·ble *adj.* causing discomfort ‖ feeling discomfort ‖ uneasy **un·cóm·fort·a·bly** *adv.*

un·com·mon *adj.* unusual

un·com·mu·ni·ca·tive *adj.* reticent, disinclined to talk or to give information

un·com·pro·mis·ing *adj.* making no concessions ‖ free of compromise

un·concern *n.* lack of concrn, indifference

un·con·cerned *adj.* not troubled, worried etc. ‖ not concerned **un·con·cern·ed·ly** *adv.*

un·con·di·tion·al *adj.* absloute, without qualifying conditions

un·con·scion·a·ble *adj.* unscrupulous ‖ immoderate, inordinate **un·cón·scion·a·bly** *adv.*

un·con·scious 1. *adj.* (with 'of') not consicious ‖ not intended ‖ of or relating to the unconscious **2.** *n.* the area of mental activity which escapes mental awareness

un·con·scious·ness *n.* lack of consciouness

un·con·sti·tu·tion·al *adj.* not in accordance with the constitution **un·con·sti·tu·tion·ál·i·ty** *n.*

un·cou·ple un·cou·pling un·cou·pled *v.t.* to disconnect

un·couth *adj.* awkward, rough

un·cov·er *v.t.* to remove the cover or covering from ‖ to reveal, disclose

unc·tion *n.* an anointing ‖ the oil used ‖ an ointment ‖ religious fervor

une·tu·ous *adj.* offusive ‖ made of or containing oil or fat ‖ (of soil) soft and rich ‖ (of clay) plastic

un·daunt·ed *adj.* fearless, not daunted

un·de·cid·ed *adj.* fearless, not daunted

un·de·cid·ed *adj.* that is not decided ‖ not having reached a decision

un·de·mon·stra·tive *adj.* not showing one's feelings

un·de·ni·a·ble *adj.* indisputable, certain, that cannot be denied **un·de·ni·a·bly** *adv.*

un·der 1. *pre.* in, at, or to a position lower than ‖ covered by ‖ lower in amount, quality, rank etc. than ‖ according to ‖ bound by ‖ subject to **2.** *adv.* in or to a lower position, beneat ‖ in or to a position of subordination, subjection etc. ‖ in or to a position of subordination, subjection etc. ‖ so as to be covered, concealed etc. ‖ less than a certain age, weight, length etc. **3.** *adj.* lower in amount, degree etc ‖ lower in authority, rank etc.

under- *prefix* in, at, to or from a lower position ‖ in a subordinate position, as in 'understyey' ‖ to a degree, amount etc. considered below standard

un·der·bid *v.t.* **un·der·bid·ding un·der·bid** to bid less than

un·der·brush *n.* undergrowth

un·der·class·man *pl.* **un·der·class·men** *n.* a freshman or sophomore

un·der·clothes *pl. n.* clothers worn under the outer garments

un·der·coat *n.* a layer of paint etc. applied as base for a top coat

un·der·cov·er *adj.* acting or carried out secretly

un·der·cur·rent *n.* a current below the

upper surface ‖ an underlying tendency

un·der·cut 1. *v.t.* **un·der·cut·ting un·der·cut** to undersell ‖ to work for lower wages than **2.** *n.* an underhand stroke, e.g. in tennis

un·der·dog *n.* someone who gets the worst of a struggle ‖ a victim of social injustice

un·der·em·ploy·ment *n.* **1.** employment that does not utilize one's best skills **2.** parttime employment

un·der·es·ti·mate *v.t.* **un·der·es·ti·mat·ing un·der·es·ti·mat·ed** to rate below true worth ‖ to quote too low a figure in giving an estimate **un·der·es·ti·má·tion** *n.*

un·der·foot *adv.* in the way

un·der·go un·der·go·ing du·der·went un·der·gone *v.t.* to endure, experience

un·der·grad·u·ate 1. *n.* a university student who has not yet obtained his forst (or bachelor's) degree **2.** *adj.* of undergraduates

un·der·ground 1. *adj.* being below the surface of the ground ‖ secret **2.** *n.* the **underground** a secret resistance movement **3.** *adv.* in hiding

un·der·hand 1. *adj.* decietful, sly ‖ performed with hand below the shoulder **2.** *adv.* in an underhand manner

un·der·hand·ed *adj.* secret, sly ‖ short-handed

un·der·lay 1. un·der·lay·ing un·der·laid *v.t.* to lay under, to support **2.** *n.* something laid under

un·der·line 1. un·der·lin·ing un·der·lined to draw a line under ‖ to emphasize **2.** *n.* a line drawn underneath a word

un·der·ling *n.* a subordinate

un·der·ly·ing *adj.* placed underneath ‖ being at the basis

un·der·mine un·der·min·ing un·der·mined *v.t.* to dig under so as to cause a fall ‖ (of water) to wash away the foundations of ‖ to injure by crafty, indirect methods

un·der·neath 1. *prep.* beneath, below **2.** *adj.* lower, under **3.** *n.* the bottom surface

un·der·pass *n.* a passageway passing under a railroad or highway

un·der·priv·i·leged *adj.* living below an acceptable level

un·der·rate un·der·rat·ing un·der·rat·ed *v.t.* to attribute less than full worth or importance to

un·der·score un·der·scor·ing un·der·scored *v.t.* to underline

un·der·shoot un·der·shoot·ing un·der·shot *v.t.* to shoot short of (the target) ‖ (of an aircraft) to fail to get onto (the runway) in coming into land

un·der·side *n.* the underneath

un·der·signed 1. *adj.* signed below **2.** *n.* the person having signed below

un·der·stand un·der·stand·ing un·der·stood *v.t.* to seize the meaning of ‖ to be thoroughly acquainted with ‖ to appreciate and sympathize with ‖ to gather, infer ‖ to accept as a fact, believe ‖ *v.i.* to have the power of forming reasoned judgments etc. ‖ to feel and show tolerance etc.

un·der·stand·ing 1. *n.* the ability to understand ‖ the power to form reasoned judgments ‖ an informal agreement ‖ a resolution of differences *adj.* feeling sympathy etc.

un·der·state un·der·stat·ing un·der·stat·ed 1. *v.t.* to represent as being less important etc. than is in fact the case **un·der·state·ment** *n.*

un·der·stood *adj.* agreed upon ‖ implied

un·der·stud·y 1. *pl.* **un·der·stud·ies** *n.* an actor who learns another actor's part in order to be able to replace him **2. un·der·stud·y·ing un·der·stud·ied** *v.t.* to be the understudy of

un·der·take un·der·tak·ing un·der·took un·der·tak·en *v.t.* to embark on ‖ to assume responsibility **ún·der·tak·er** *n.* a person whose trade is managing funerals **un·der·ták·ing** *n.* somethng undertaken ‖ a promise

un·der·tone *n.* a lower sound ‖ a subdued color

un·der·tow *n.* the undercurrent pulling

strongly seaward

un·der·wear *n.* underclothes

un·der·world *n.* the home of departed spirits ‖ the criminal section of society

un·der·write   un·der·writ·ing un·der·wrote un·der·writ·ten *v.t.* to execute (an insurance policy ‖ to undertake to meet the financial losses of ‖ to guarantee the purchase of (stocks, bonds etc.) issued for public subscription ‖ to assume liability to the sum of ‖ *v.i.* to be an underwriter in the insurance business **ún·der·writ·er** *n.*

un·do un·do·ing un·did un·done *v.t.* a bringing to ruin or destruction ‖ the destruction of something done **un·done** *adj.*

un·doubt·ed *adj.* not doubted or disputed, regarded as certain **un·doubt·ed·ly** *adv.* certainly

un·dress 1. *v.t.* to take off the clothes of ‖ **2.** *n.* comfortable, informal dress

un·due *adj.* excessive ‖ imporper, inappropriate

un·du·late un·du·lat·ing un·du·lat·ed *v.i.* to have a wavelike motion ‖ *v.t.* to cause to move in a wavy manner **ún·du·lat·ed** *v.i.* having a wavelike surface **un·du·lá·tion** *n.* a wavelike motion **un·du·la·to·ry** *adj.*

un·du·ly *adv.* excessively

un·earned *adj.* undeserved ‖ derived from investments

un·earth *v.t.* to dig up ‖ to bring to light

un·earth·ly *adj.* celestial, supernatural ‖ preposterous

un·eas·i·ly *adv.* in an uneasy manner

un·eas·i·ness *n.* the state or quality of being uneasy

un·eas·y un·eas·i·er un·eas·i·est *adj.* uncomfortable ‖ disturbed ‖ anxious ‖ ill at ease

un·em·ployed *adj.* not in paid empoyment ‖ not being used

un·em·ploy·ment *n.* the state of being unemployed

un·e·qual *adj.* not of the sami dimensions ‖ not uniform in quality, degree etc. ‖ not fit or adequate

un·e·qualed *adj.* without equal

un·e·quiv·o·cal *adj.* admitting of no doubt, not ambiduous

un·err·ing *adj.* certain, sure ‖ free from error

un·e·ven *adj.* not smooth ‖ not of the same size, length or quantity ‖ not consistently ‖ (of numbers) odd

un·faith·ful *adj.* failing one's trust, disloyal ‖ adulterous

un·fa·mil·iar *adj.* not well known, strange ‖ (with 'with') having little or no experience **un·fa·mil·i·ar·i·ty** *n.*

un·fa·vor·a·ble *adj.* not favorable, adverse

un·fin·ished *adj.* incomplete ‖ rough, unpolished

un·fit 1. *adj.* not suitable ‖ not well **2.** *v.t.* **un·fit·ting un·fit·ted** to render unsuitable

un·flinch·ing *adj.* resolute, not wavering

un·fold *v.t.* to open ‖ to cause to reveal itself gradually

un·for·tu·nate 1. *adj.* unlucky ‖ much to be regretted **2.** *n.* an unfortunate person

un·found·ed *adj.* having no foundation of fact

un·furl *v.t.* to unfold ‖ *v.i.* to become unfurled

un·gain·ly *adj.* clumsy, awkward

un·god·li·ness *n.* the state of being ungodly

un·god·ly *adj.* wicked ‖ unreasonable

un·gra·cious *adj.* lacking courtesy ‖ not attractive

un·guard *v.t.* to expose to attack **un·guard·ed** *adj.* without a guard ‖ marked by lack of caution

un·guent *n.* an ointment

un·hap·py un·hap·pi·er un·hap·pi·est *adj.* sad, in low spirits ‖ unlucky

un·health·y un·health·i·er un·health·i·est *adj.* not in good health ‖ not sound morally ‖ risky

un·heard-of *adj.* never met with, unprecedented

un·ho·ly un·ho·li·er un·ho·li·est *adj.* impious ‖ very bad

u·ni·cel·lu·lar *adj.* consisting of only one cell

u·ni·corn *n.* a legendary animal genrally

depicted as having the head and body of a horse and a long tapering horn growing from the middle of its forehead

u·ni·form 1. *adj.* being the same in form, character, degree etc. without variation ‖ consistent **2.** *n.* a costume worn by all of a certain category **ú·ni·formed** *adj.* wearing a uniform

u·ni·form·i·ty *n.* the state of being uniform

u·ni·fy u·ni·fy·ing u·ni·fied *v.i.* to become one

u·ni·lat·er·al *adj.* done by one side only ‖ affecting only one side of the body ‖ binding or affecting one party only

un·im·peach·a·ble *adj.* beyond reproach

un·ion *n.* something united ‖ a combination ‖ unity, harmony ‖ a marriage ‖ a grouping of states ‖ a trade union

un·ion·ize un·ion·iz·ing un·ion·ized *v.t.* to organize into a trade union

u·nique *adj.* being the only one of its kind ‖ incomparable ‖ rare, unusual

u·ni·sex *adj.* **1.** suitable for both men and women **—unisex** *n.* the trend

u·ni·son *n.* coincidence in pitch of two or more notes, voices etc. **in unison** in complete agreement

u·nit *n.* a fixed quantity adopted as a standard of measurement for other quanitites of the same kind ‖ a single thing, person or group that is a distinguishable element of a larger whole ‖ any subdivision (regiment, battalion etc.) of an army

u·nite u·nit·ing u·nit·ed *v.t.* to bring together so as to make one ‖ to cause to become attached ‖ to cooperate ‖ to become combined **u·nít·ed** *adj.* brought together ‖ harmonious

u·ni·ty *pl.* **u·ni·ties** *n.* the state of being one, singleness ‖ unification ‖ full agreement, harmony

u·ni·ver·sal *adj.* general, for everything or everybody ‖ of widest scope ‖ present everywhere

u·ni·ver·sal·i·ty *n.* the quality of being universal

u·ni·ver·sal·ize u·ni·ver·sal·iz·ing u·ni·ver·sal·ized *v.t.* to make universal

u·ni·verse *n.* the cosmos ‖ the earth and its inhabitants

u·ni·ver·si·ty *pl.* **u·ni·ver·si·ties** *n.* a group of faculties providing higher education ‖ the building and grounds

un·kempt *adj.* uncombed ‖ very untidy

un·kind *adj.* not kind ‖ harsh **un·kínd·ly** *adv.*

un·known 1. *adj.* not known **2.** *n.* an unknown quantity

un·learn·ed *adj.* possessing no learning

un·less 1. *conj.* if…not except that **2.** *prep.* except

un·let·tered *adj.* lacking education ‖ illiterate

un·like 1. *adj.* not alike, dissimilar **2.** *prep.* not like

un·like·ly 1. *adj.* improbable ‖ unpromising **2.** *adv.* improbably

un·lim·it·ed *adj.* without limits ‖ boundless, vast

un·laod *v.t.* to remove the goods from ‖ to remove the charge from (a gun) ‖ *v.i.* to discharge something, exp. a cargo

un·looked-for *adj.* not anticipated, not expected

un·luck·y un·luck·i·er un·luck·i·est *adj.* not lucky

un·mask *v.t.* to remove the mask from ‖ to expose the true nature or identity of

un·men·tion·a·ble *adj* not fit to be mentioned

un·mis·tak·a·ble *adj.* that cannot be mistaken, clear, obvious **un·mis·ták·a·bly** *adv.*

un·mit·i·gat·3d *adj.* not lessened abnormal ‖ absolute

un·nat·u·ral *adj.* not natural

un·nec·es·sar·y *adj.* not necessary, needless

un·or·gan·ized *adj.* not organized ‖ not having organic structure ‖ not belonging to a trade union

un·par·al·leled *adj.* having no equal

un·pleas·and *adj.* disagreeable **un·pléas·ant·ness** *n.* an unpleasant situation

un·pop·u·lar *adj.* not pupular, viewed with disfavor

un·prac·ticed *adj.* not skilled

un·prec·e·dent·ed *adj.* without precedent

un·prin·ci·pled *adj.* without moral principles

un·ques·tion·a·ble *adj.* not open to question **un·qués·tion·a·bly** *adv.*

un·ravel un·rav·el·ing un·rav·eled *v.t.* to untangle || to undo || to solve || *v.i.* to become unraveled

un·read *adj.* not read || not well-read

un·real *adj.* not real || existing only in the mind

un·rea·son·a·ble *adj.* not reasonable || immoderate **un·réa·son·a·bly** *adv.*

un·re·lent·ing *adj.* not weakening in determination

un·re·mit·ting *adj.* persevering

un·rest *n.* uneasiness || collective discontent

un·ri·valed *adj.* without a rival or equal

un·roll *v.t.* to open || to unfold to the view

un·ruf·fled *adj.* not ruffled || emotionally serene

un·ru·li·ness *n.* the state or quality of being unruly

un·ruly un·ru·li·er un·ru·li·est *adj.* undisciplined and causing trouble

un·sa·vor·y *adj.* tasteless, insipid || morally offensive

un·scathed *adj.* without being hurt

un·scru·pu·lous *adj.* unprincipled

un·seem·ly *adj.* unbecoming

un·set·tle un·set·tling un·set·tled *v.t.* to cause to be no longer stable || to cause to lose one's composure || to cause (the stomach) to be slightly upset **un·sét·tled** *adj.* (of an account) not paid || not stable || not populated || (of weather) changeable

un·sight·ly *adj.* unpleasant to see

un·skilled *adj.* not skilled || not requiring skill

un·so·cial *adj.* not sillingly associating with others

un·sound *adj.* not physically or morally sound || to open to logical attack || liable to collapse || (of sleep) fitful

un·spar·ing *adj.* without reserve in giving, striving etc. || without mercy

un·speak·a·ble *adj.* indescribably bad || inexpressibly delightful **un·spéak·a·bly** *adv.*

un·sta·ble *adj.* in a condition which may bery easily change || not to be depended on

un·stead·y un·stead·i·er un·stead·i·est *adj.* not firmly under control || changeable || lacking regularity

un·strung *adj.* emotionally distressed

un·sung *adj.* not given recognition

un·think·a·ble *adj.* inconceivable || out of the question

un·think·ing *adj.* lacking the power of thought

un·til 1. *prep.* till, to the time of || before **2.** *conj.* to the time when || to the degree that || before

un·time·ly 1. *adj.* **un·time·li·er un·time·li·est** premature || inopportune **2.** *adv.* too soon

un·told *adj.* not told || too many to count or measure

un·to·ward not favorable || unseemly

un·truth *pl.* **un·truths** a faslehood

un·truth·ful *adj.* untrue, false || inclined to tell lies

un·used *adj.* not currently in use || never having been used || (with 'to') unaccustomed

un·u·su·al *adj.* rare, different from others

un·ut·ter·a·ble *adj.* unspeakable

un·whole·some *aj.* not wholesome, not conducive to physical or mental health || morally harmful

un·wield·y un·wield·i·er un·wield·i·est *adj.* difficult to handle because of bulk || clumsy, ungainly

un·wil·ling *adj.* not willing, reluctant

un·wind un·wind·ing un·wound *v.t.* to undo, unroll || to sort out or straighten || *v.i.* to become unwound

un·wit·tine *adj.* unaware || not intentional

un·wont·ed *adj.* uncommon, rarely met with

un·world·ly un·world·li·er un·world·li·est *adj.* not concerned with worldly matters || spiritual

un·wor·thy un·wor·thi·er

un·wor·thi·est *adj.* lamentably below standard ‖ not deserving ‖ comtemptible

up 1. *adv.* from a lower towards a higher location ‖ towards a greater degree of intensity ‖ towards a higher rank ‖ to a higher amount ‖ from an earlier to a later period ‖ in or to a standing position ‖ out of bed ‖ into view ‖ ahead of an opponent with respect to points, strokes etc. **2.** *prep.* to, toward or at a higer point on or in ‖ to or towards a higher condition in or on ‖ at a point farther along ‖ toward the source of (a river) **up to** as far as ‖ as much as ‖ until **3.** *adj.* directed toward a position that is higher ‖ in a higher position ‖ above the horizon ‖ advanced in amount, degree etc. ‖ ina standing position ‖ out of bed ‖ (e.g. of the wind) in an active or agitated state ‖ at an end ‖ happening, being planned etc. **3.** *n.* **ups and downs** periods of good and bad fortune **4. up·ping upped** *v.t.* to increase ‖ to bet more than ‖ to move to a higher position

up·beat *n.* the beat before the main accented note

up·braid *v.t.* to scold, reproach

up·bring·ing *n.* the process of training and education

up·date up·dat·ing up·dat·ed *v.t.* to bring up to date

up·grade 1. *n.* a rising slope **on the upgrade** increasing **2.** *adv.* uphill **3.** *v.t.* **up·grad·ing up·grad·ed** to promote ‖ to raise the quality of

up·heav·al *n.* an upheaving ‖ a violent commotion

up·heave up·heav·ing up·heaved *v.i.* to rise upward with great force

up·hill 1. *adv.* in an ascending direction **2.** *adj.* ascending ‖ slow and difficult

up·hold up·hold·ing up·held *v.t.* to maintain or support ‖ to confirm, decide in favor of ‖ to life up

up ‖ **hol·ster** *v.t.* toprovide (furniture) with padding, springs, textile covering etc.

up·hol·ster·er *n.* a person whose trade is upholstery

up·hol·ster·y *n.* the craft and trade of upholstering

up·keep *n.* the maintenance of buildings, roads, equipment, etc. ‖ the cost of such maintenance

up·lift 1. *v.t.* to give encouragement to ‖ to push up **2.** *n.* spiritual encouragement ‖ the raising of a part of the earth's surface above the surrounding land

up·on *prep.* on ‖ up and on

up·per 1. *adj.* higher in position or place ‖ higher in status ‖ nearer the surface of the earth **2.** *n.* the part of a boot above the sole ‖ a stimulant drug

up·per·cut 1. *n.* a blow delivered at close quarters from below to the point of the chin **2. sp·per·cut·ting up·per·cut** *v.i.* to deliver such a blow

up·per·most 1. *adj.* highest in palce, rank, power, position etc. **2.** *adv.* in or into the most prominent position

up·raise up·rais·ing up·raised *v.t.* to lift up

up·right 1. *adj.* being in a vertical or erect position ‖ morally honorable **2.** *adv.* in a vertical position **3.** *n.* a vertical support for a structure ‖ (*pl.*) a goalpost

upright piano a piano with vertical strings

up·ris·ing *n.* an insurrection

up·roar *n.* a noisy tumult **up·roar·i·ous** *adj.* very noisy

up·root *v.t.* to tear up by the roots ‖ to eradicate

up·set 1. *n.* an upsetting ‖ a slight physical ailment ‖ an emotional disturbance ‖ a totally unexpected defeat **2. up·set·ting up·set** *v.t.* to tip over or capsize ‖ to cause distress to ‖ cause confusion in ‖ to defeat unexpectedly **3.** *adj.* distressed

up·shot *n.* outdome, final result

up·side down *adv.* in an inverted position with the top part underneath ‖ in great disorder **up·side-dówn** *adj.*

up·stage 1. *adv.* toward the back of the stage, away from the footlights **2.** *adj.* affecting superiority **3. up·stag·ing up·staged** to treat with ‖ to try to outdo

up·stairs 1. *adv.* on or towards an upper floor **2.** *adj.* of an upper floor **3.** *n.* that part of a house etc. that is above the ground floor

up·stand·ing *adj.* morally upright ‖ standing up straight

up·start *n.* a person who has risen swiftly from a humble position to wealth or power, and presumes on it by arrogant behavior

up·swing *n.* an upward trend, improvement

up·tight *adj.* not relaxed ‖ rigidly conservative

up-to-date *adj.* all information up to the present ‖ informed about current events ‖ currently fashionable

up·turn 1. *v.t.* to turn over ‖ to direct upward **2.** *n.* an upward trend

up·ward 1. *adv.* toward a higher position ‖ turned toward the sky ‖ indefinitely more **upward** (or **upwards) of** more than **2.** *adj.* directed toward a higher position ‖ showing improvement

up·wards *adv.* upward

u·ra·ni·um *n.* a radioactive white metallic element

U·ra·nus the seventh planet

ur·ban *adj.* of, relating to, belonging to or characteristic of a city or town

ur·bane *adj.* having sophisticated manners

ur·ban·i·ty *pl.* **ur·ban·i·ties** *n.* polished manners

ur·chin *n.* a mischeievous young boy ‖ a sea urchin

u·re·mi·a, u·rae·mi·a *n.* a serious toxic condition caused by an accumulation in the blood of waste products normally elimiated in the urine

urge 1. **urg·ing urged** *v.t.* to compel ‖ to attempt earnestly to persuade or encourage ‖ to advocate in a persistent way ‖ *v.i.* to make earnest recommendations **2.** *n.* a strong, instinctive desire

ur·gen·cy *pl.* **ur·gen·cies** *n.* the state of being urgent

ur·gent *adj.* of pressing importance

u·ri·nate u·ri·nat·ing u·ri·nat·ed *v.i.* to discharge urine

u·rine *n.* in mammals, a fluid formed in the kidneys and excreted throught the urinary organs

urn *n.* a closed metal vessel ‖ a vase or jar with a pedestal

us *pron., objective case of* WE

us·a·ble, use·a·ble *adj.* fit to be used

us·age *n.* the way in which someone or something is used or treated ‖ long established use or custom

use us·ing used *v.t.* to make (something) perform its function ‖ (often with 'up') to consume completely ‖ to exploit for some end ‖ (in the passive with 'to') to accustom ‖ *v.i.* (in the psat with an infinitive) to be accustomed

use *n.* the act of using ‖ the power to use ‖ usefulness ‖ the right, permission or privilege to use ‖ the opportunity to use ‖ function ‖ custom, habit, practice **to have no use for** to have no need of ‖ to dislike strongly

used *adj.* secondhand **used up** fully consumed

use·ful *adj.* likely to be of some practical value

use·less *adj.* of no practical value

ush·er 1. *n.* someone who escorts people to seat **2.** *v.t.* to conduct to a seat ‖ *v.i.* to act as an usher **to usher in** to mark the beginning of **ush·er·ette** *n.* a woman employed to show people to seats

u·su·al *adj.* normal **as usual** in his or its habitual way **u·su·al·ly** *adv.* customarily

u·su·rer *n.* someone who lends money at exorbitant interest

u·su·ri·ous *adj.* practicing usury

u·surp *v.t.* to seize and hold (a position) rightly belonging to another **u·sur·pá·tion** *n.*

u·su·ry lending money at an exorbitant interest

u·ten·sil *n.* any of various vessles or devices used in a kitchen ‖ any of various tools used by artisans, farmers etc.

u·ter·us *pl.* **u·ter·i** *n.* the organ in female mammals in which the embryo (fetus) develops

u·til·i·tar·i·an *adj.* of or relating to utiliy

u·til·i·ty *pl.* **u·til·i·ties** *n.* the quality or state of being useful ‖ a public utility

‖ a service provided by one of these ‖ *(pl.)* stock shares in public utility companies

u·ti·li·za·tion *n.* a utilizing or being utilized

u·ti·lize u·ti·liz·ing u·ti·lized *v.t.* to make use of

ut·most 1. *adj.* of the greatest degree **2.** *n.* the best of one's ability or power

u·to·pi·a *n.* any imaginary political and social system in which relationships between individuals and the state are perfectly adjusted

ut·ter *v.t.* to express vocally ‖ to emit (sounds) as if speaking

utter *adj.* with no qualification whatsoever

ut·ter·ance *n.* the act, power or manner of expresing vocally ‖ something utterd

ut·ter·ly *adv.* fully

ut·ter·most *adj.* and *n.* (used as an intensive) utmost

ux·o·ri·ous *adj.* excessively fond of one's wife ‖ showing such excessive fondness

V

V, v the 22nd letter of the English alphabet

va·can·cy *pl.* **va·can·cies** *n.* an empty place or space ‖ a post in employment which is not occupend

va·cant *adj.* empty, not filled ‖ (of a post or seat etc.) unoccupied ‖ untenanted

va·cate va·cat·ing va·cat·ed *v.t.* to go away and leave unoccupied ‖ to make vacant ‖ to annul, to make void

va·ca·tion 1. *n.* a holiday on vacation away from work, school etc. for a period of leisure **2.** *v.i.* to take a vacation **va·ca·tion·ist** *nx.*

vac·ci·nate vac·ci·nat·ing vac·ci·nat·ed *v.t.* to inoculate with a vaccine **va·ci·ná·tion** *n.*

vac·cine *n.* a preparation of microorganisms that are administered so as to produce (or increase) immunity to a particular disease

vac·il·late vac·il·lat·ing vac·il·lat·ed *v.i.* to change repeatedly from one opinion or intention to antoerh ‖ to sway to and fro **vac·il·lá·tion** *n.* **vac·il·la·to·ry** *adj.*

va·cu·i·ty *pl.* **va·cu·i·ties** *n.* something pointless

vac·u·ous *adj.* having or showing a lack of understanding or intelligence or serious purpose

vac·u·um 1. *pl.* **vac·u·ums, vac·u·a** *n.* a part of space in which no matter exists ‖ a space largely exhausted of air ‖ a void **2.** *v.t.* to clean with a vacuum cleaner

vag·a·bond 1. *adj.* wandering, not settled in a fixed home ‖ characteristic of a wandering way of life **2.** *n.* a tramp **vag·a·bond·age** *n.*

va·gar·y *pl.* **va·gar·ies** *n.* an irrational idea, passing fancy ‖ an odd or irrational action

va·gi·na *pl.* **va·gi·nae, va·gi·nas** *n.* a sheath or sheathlike tube, esp. the canal leading from the uterus to the vulva in female mammals **vag·i·nal** *adj.*

va·gran·cy *n.* vagabondage

va·grant 1. *adj.* wandering, esp. having no settled home ‖ living the life of a tramp ‖ random, stray **2.** *n.* someone who has no settled home, a vagabond ‖ a tramp

vague *adj.* not precise in expression ‖ not firmly determined ‖ hazy, not clearly perceived

vein *adj.* thinking too highly of one's appearance, attainments etc. ‖ failing to produce the desired result ‖ empth **in vain** without success ‖ to no purpose

val·ance *n.* short, decorative drapery

vale *n.* valley

val·e·dic·tion *n.* a farewell

val·e·dic·to·ri·an *n.* a student who delivers a valedictory

val·e·dic·to·ry 1. *adj.* spoken or done as a valediction **2.** *pl.* **val·e·dic·to·ries** *n.* a farewell oration

val·en·tine *n.* a sweetheart chosen on St. Valentine's Day ‖ letter or greeting card sent to someone of the opposite sex on this day

val·et *n.* a personal manservent ‖ a hotel attendant who looks after the clothes of patrons

val·iance *n.* bravery **val·ian·cy** *n.* valiance

val·iant *adj.* stouthearted, brave, heroic

val·id *adj.* in conformity with the law, and therefore binding ‖ based on sound principle

val·i·date val·i·dat·ing val·i·dat·ed *v.t.* to make valid or binding ‖ to confirm the validity of

val·i·da·tion *n.* a making or being made valid

va·lid·i·ty *pl.* **va·lid·i·ties** *n.* the state, fact or quality of being valid legally or in argument

va·lise *n.* a small traveling case

val·ley *pl.* **val·leys** *n.* a long depression in the earth's surface ‖ the land drained by a river

val·or *n.* personal courage, esp. in battle

val·or·ous *adj.* courageous ‖ showing valor

val·u·a·ble 1. *adj.* of great value ‖ very useful **2.** *n. (pl.)* precious possessions

val·u·a·tion *n.* an estimation of a thing's worth ‖ a personal view of one's own or somebody else's character or merits

val·ue 1. *n.* far return ‖ purchasing power ‖ the monetary equivalent of something ‖ the importance or rank accorded to a playing card, chessman etc. **2.** *v.t.* **val·u·ing val·ued** to estimate the value of ‖ to regard as having a high value

valve *n.* any of innumerable natural or man-made devices which control the direction or volume of flow of a fluid or of electricity

vamp *n.* a woman who uses her physical allure to attract and exploit men

vam·pire *n.* (in popular superstition) a ghost or evil spirit which leaves a grave at night to suck the blood of people asleep ‖ a person who exploits others ruthlessly

van *n.* a large covered vehicle

Van·dal *n.* a member of an E. Germanic tribe **vandal** someone who wantonly destroys natural or human works of beauty **ván·dal·ism** *n.*

vane *n.* a broad, thin, often curved surface fastened to a pivoted or rotating body

van·guard *n.* the soldiers who march at the front of an army, or this section of an army ‖ the forefront of a movement

va·nil·la *n.* a genus of climbing orchids ‖ a food flavoring extracted from pods

van·ish *v.i.* to become no longer able to be seen or felt

van·i·ty *pl.* **van·i·ties** *n.* the fact or quality of being vain ‖ something of no real worth ‖ a dressing table

van·quish *v.t.* to overcome, to conquer

van·tage *n.* a condition conferring superiority

va·pid *adj.* lacking zest or interest **va·píd·i·ty** *n.*

va·por 1. *n.* a substance in a gaseous state ‖ a liquid dispersed and suspended in the air in the form of very small drops **2.** *v.t.* to emit as vapor ‖ to reduce to vapor ‖ *v.i.* to rise as vapor

va·por·ize va·por·iz·ing va·por·ized *v.t.* to change into vapor ‖ *v.i.* to be changed into vapor

va·por·iz·er *n.* a device for converting a liquid into a vapor

va·por·ous *adj.* forming vapor ‖ like vapor

var·i·a·bil·i·ty *n.* a tendency to vary

var·i·a·ble 1. *adj.* apt to change ‖ able to be changed **2.** *n.* something variable

var·i·ance *n.* a sharp disagreement ‖ a variation, difference, change at variance in disagreement ‖ antagonistic

var·i·ant 1. *adj.* differing and alternative **2.** *n.* one of two or more alternatives of a form, reading, etc.

var·i·a·tion *n.* change as a process, condition or fact ‖ departure from a standard or norm, or an instance of this **var·i·á·tion·al** *adj.*

var·i·cose *adj.* swollen, distended, esp. of veins **var·i·co·sis, var·i·cos·i·ty** *ns*

var·ied *adj.* of different kinds, not all the same

var·ie·gate var·ie·gate var·ie·gat·ed *v.t.* to supply with various colors ‖ to diversify, to give variety to **vár·ie·gat·ed** *adj.* dappled or streaked with various colors ‖ varied, full of variety **var·ie·gá·tion** *n.*

va·ri·e·tal *adj.* of or pertaining to a variety

va·ri·e·ty *pl.* **va·ri·e·ties** *n.* the state or quality of not being always or everywhere the same ‖ a number or collection of things different in character ‖ one of a number of different forms or kinds of the same thing

var·i·ous *adj.* of different kinds ‖ characterized by variety ‖ several

var·nish 1. *n.* a liquid solution of resin, prepared in spirits or oil, applied to wood and metal surfaces to give a hard glossy transparent coating ‖ a superficial polish of manners and outward behavior **2.** *v.t.* to put a coat of varnish on

var·si·ty *pl.* **var·si·ties** *n.* a team that represents a university, school or club, in a game

var·y var·y·ing var·ied *v.t.* to introduce variety into *v.i.* to undergo change ‖ to differ ‖ (with 'from') to deviate from

vas·cu·lar *adj.* of, consisting of or containing vessels or ducts adapted for the transmission or circulation of blood, sap etc.

vase *n.* a glass, pottery or metal vessel used as a container for cut flowers or as an ornament

vas·sal *n.* a servant, bondman, slave

vast *adj.* immensely large in area ‖ very great

vat 1. *n.* a large open tub, tank etc. **2.** *v.t.* **vat·ting vat·ted** to place or treat in a vat

vaud·e·ville *n.* music-hall variety entertainment

vault 1. *v.i.* to project oneself through the air **2.** *n.* a leap or jump made with the help of the hands or a pole

vault 1. *n.* a usually arched room, usually underground, esp. a cellar or burial chamber ‖ the fireproof, burglarproof room of a bank **2.** *v.t.* to cover with a vault or arched roof structure **vault·ing** *n.* the art of building vaults

vaunt 1. *v.t.* to boast of, to brag about **2.** *n.* a boast

veal *n.* calf's flesh as food

vec·tor *n.* a quantity that is specified by magnitude, direction and sense

veer 1. *v.i.* to turn gradually or change direction ‖ (esp. of a mental attitude, opinion etc.) to change in direction **2.** *n.* a change of direction

veg·e·ta·ble 1. *n.* a plant (as distinguished from an animal or mineral) ‖ a human being who is nonfunctional **2.** *adj.* pertaining to, having the nature of, or made from, a plant

veg·e·tar·i·an 1. *n.* a person who abstains from eating meat **2.** *adj.* relating to vegetarians or vegetarianism ‖ consisting of vegetables **veg·e·tár·i·an·ism** *n.*

veg·e·tate veg·e·tat·ing veg·e·tat·ed *v.i.* to grow in the manner of a plant ‖ to live an inactive life

veg·e·ta·tion *n.* plant life in general

veg·e·ta·tive *adj.* of or concerned with vegetation ‖ of reproduction by bud formation, or by other asexual methods in plants or animals

ve·he·mence *n.* the state or quality of being vehement **vé·he·men·cy** *n.* vehemence

ve·he·ment *adj.* violent ‖ showing or arousing intense feeling

ve·hi·cle *n.* any kind of contrivance, on wheels or runners, used to carry people or goods from one place to another over land ‖ a fluid used as a medium for a suspension of a pigment ‖ any person or thing used as a medium to convey ideas, emotions etc.

ve·hic·u·lar *adj.* of or for vehicles

veil 1. *n.* a piece of light material draped over the face ‖ the headdress of a num ‖ a cover or curtain to hide or potect something ‖ a cloak, disguise, mask etc. **to take the veil** to become a num **2.** *v.t.* to cover or hide with a veil ‖ to conceal, disguise etc. **véil·ing** *n.*

vein *n.* one of the tubular vessels with moderately thin walls that carry blood to the hart in vertebrates ‖ a fissure in rock filled with ore ‖ a specified attitude or mood expressed in speech or writing ‖ a rib in a leaf or insect's wing **veined** *adj.* having veins **véin·ing** *n.* a pattern of veins

veld, veldt *n.* open grassland in S. Africa

vel·lum *n.* a fine parchment

ve·loc·i·ty *pl.* **ve·loc·i·ties** *n.* rate of motion

ve·lour, ve·lours *pl.* **ve·lours** *n.* a velvet-like woven fabric ‖ a fur felt used for hats

vel·vet 1. *n.* a closely woven fabric wholly or partly of silk, with a short, soft nap or pile on one side **2.** *adj.* made of or covered with velvet ‖ like velvet

vel·vet·een *n.* cotton material woven with a short pile

vel·vet·y *adj.* soft and smooth to the touch

ve·nal *adj.* soft and smooth to the touch

ve·nal *adj.* mercenary, esp. open to corruption

ve·nal·i·ty *n.* the state or quality of being venal

vend *v.t.* to sell, offer for sale

ven·det·ta *n.* a blood fued

ven·dor *n.* a person who sells, esp. one who hawks his goods in a public place

ve·neer 1. *v.t.* to cover (a surface of wood) with a thin coating of a finer wood **2.** *n.* a thin layer of fine wood laid over the surface of a cheaper wood ‖ any refined outer covering concealing a coarse structure **ve·neer·ing** *n.* the process of applying a veneer to wood

ven·er·a·bil·i·ty *n.* the state or quality of being venerable

ven·er·a·ble *adj.* deserving or evoking profound respect and veneration **vén·er·a·bly** *adv.*

ven·er·ate ven·er·at·ing ven·er·at·ed *v.t.* to regard with the deepest respect or reverence ‖ to worship as holy **ven·er·á·tion, vén·er·a·tor** *ns*

ve·ne·re·al *adj.* (of disease) contracted by sexual intercourse ‖ having or relating to venereal disease

venge·ance *n.* damage or harm done to another in retaliation for damage or harm to oneself

venge·ful *adj.* disposed to acts of vengeance ‖ vindictive

ven·i·son *n.* the flesh of deer as food

ven·om *n.* the poisonous fluid secreted by certain snakes, spiders, insects etc. ‖ spite, malice

ven·om·ous *adj.* poisonous ‖ malicious, spiteful

ve·nous *adj.* of a vein or veins

vent 1. *n.* a small aperture designed to provide an outlet from a confined space or an inlet into it **2.** *v.t.* to make an aperture in ‖ to relieve (one's feelings) in words or actions

vent *n.* a tailored slit, esp. one in the back of a coat

ven·ti·late ven·ti·lat·ing ven·ti·lat·ed *v.t.* to cause the passage of air into or through ‖ to expose to the air so as to freshen ‖ to give full and free expression to

ven·ti·la·tion *n.* a system for ensuring the circulation of fresh air

ven·ti·la·tor *n.* a contrivance for ensuring the free passage of air in an enclosed space

ven·tri·cle *n.* a cavity or chamber of the body, esp. in the heart

ven·tril·o·quism *n.* utterance which makes hearers think that the sound comes from a source other than the actual speaker

ven·tril·o·quist *n.* someone who practices the art of ventriloquism

ven·ture 1. *n.* something involving a risk which one decides to attempt **2. ven·tur·ing ven·tured** *v.t.* to risk, dare ‖ *v.i.* to take a risk **vén·ture·some** *adj.*

Ve·nus the second planet from the sun

ve·ra·cious *adj.* truthful, speaking the truth as a matter of course ‖ true, accurate

ve·rac·i·ty *pl.* **ve·rac·i·ties** *n.* the quality of telling the truth ‖ the quality of being true

ve·ran·da, ve·ran·dah *n.* an open, roofed portico or gallery extending along a side of a house

verb *n.* any of a class of words expressing an action performed or state suffered or experienced by a subject

ver·bal *adj.* relating to or consisting of words ‖ oral, spoken, not written ‖ (of translation) literal, word for word

ver·bal·ize ver·bal·iz·ing ver·bal·ized *v.i.* to be verbose ‖ *v.t.* to express in words

ver·bal·ly *adv.* in words, esp. in spoken words

ver·ba·tim *adv.* word for word, exactly as spoken

ver·bi·age *n.* the use of more words than are needed

ver·bose *adj.* employing or containing more words than are necessary

ver·bos·i·ty *n.* the state or quality of being verbose

ver·dan·cy *n.* very green or fresh

ver·dict *n.* a considered judgment after examination of evidence

ver·di·gris *n.* a green or greenish-blue crystalline substance formed on copper, brass or bronze

verge 1. *n.* a border, edge ‖ the imaginary line at which a new condition or action starts **2.** *v.i.* **verg·ing verged** (with 'on') to come near to being something specified

ver·i·fi·a·ble *adj.* able to be verified

ver·i·fi·ca·tion *n.* a verifying or being verified

ver·i·fy ver·i·fy·ing ver·i·fied *v.t.* to confirm, or test, the truth or accuracy of ‖ to substantiate by proofs

ver·i·si·mil·i·tude *n.* the quality, in a work of the imagination, of seeming to be true ‖ an apparent truth

ver·i·ta·ble *adj.* real, genuine, authentic **vér·i·ta·bly** *adv.*

ver·mi·cel·li *n.* very thin threads or tubes of rolled and dried pasta used esp. to give substance to soups

ver·mic·u·lar *adj.* wormlike

ver·mil·ion, ver·mil·lion 1 *n.* mercuric sulfide used as a pigment ‖ the brilliant red color produced by this pigment **2.** *adj.* of this color

ver·min *n.* animals (e.g. rats), insects (e.g. lice) harmful to crops, plants, human health or hygiene ‖ people thought of as resembling such creatures

ver·min·ous *adj.* infested with lice, rats, or other vermin ‖ of or consisting of vermin

ver·mouth *n.* a liquor used chiefly as an appetizer

ver·nac·u·lar 1. *adj.* of, using, or relating to the speech of a region or ethnic group **2.** *n.* the indigenous language or dialect of a region

ver·nal *adj.* belonging to, occurring in or associated with, the season of spring

ver·sant *n.* the general inclination of mountainous country

ver·sa·tile *adj.* possessing various skills

ver·sa·til·i·ty *n.* the state or quality of being versatile

verse *n.* poetry ‖ a stanza of a poem ‖ a numbered section of a chapter in the Bible

versed *adj.* (with 'in') skilled or knowledgeable

ver·sion *n.* a passage or work translated from one language into another ‖ an account or description of something from a particular point of view

ver·sus *prep.* (*abbr.* v. or vs.) against, opposed to

ver·te·bra *pl.* **ver·te·brae ver·te·bras** *n.* one of the bony segments composing the spinal column of a vertebrate

ver·te·brate *adj.* having a spinal column

ver·tex *pl.* **ver·tex·es, ver·ti·ces** *n.* the top,

highest point ‖ the zenith

ver·ti·cal 1. *adj.* perpendicular **2.** *n.* a perpendicular line, plane or circle

ver·ti·go *n.* a sensation of whirling

verve *n.* vivacity, liveliness, energy

ver·y 1. ver·i·er ver·i·est *adj.* same, precise ‖ actual ‖ complete, absolute **2.** *adv.* absolutely ‖ in a high degree, extremely

ves·i·cle *n.* a small cavity or sac, usually containing fluid ‖ a small cavity in a mineral or rock

ve·sic·u·lar *adj.* covered with vesicles ‖ resembling a vesicle in form or structure

ves·pers *pl. n.* the sixth of the seven canonical hours ‖ a public act of worship at this hour, evensong

ves·sel *n.* a container for liquids ‖ a boat or ship ‖ a tube or canal thorugh which a fluid can pass

vest *v.t.* to clothe with a ceremonial garment ‖ to grant authority, property, rights or privileges to (someone) ‖ *v.i.* to put on robes or vestments

vest *n.* a man's short, close-fitting, sleeve-less garment

ves·ti·bule *n.* an enclosed space between the outer and inner door or doors of a building ‖ the partly enclosed orch of a church etc

ves·tige *n.* faintly visible or otherwise discernible evidence of the former presence or existence of something whih is no longer present ‖ a very small amount **ves·tig·i·al** *adj.*

vest·ment *n.* a liturgical garment ‖ a ceremonial robe

ves·try *pl.* **ves·tries** *n.* a sacristy, a room in a church used to contain the vestments

vet·er·an 1. *adj.* of or pertaining to long service or experience in some form of activity **2.** *n.* (*abbr.* vet.) someone who has had long service or experience ‖ an ex-serviceman

vet·er·i·nar·y 1. *adj.* of the science of treating and preventing diseases of animals **2.** *pl.* **vet·er·i·nar·ies** *n.*

ve·to 1. *n. pl.* **ve·toes** a right, vested by law

in a person or constitutional body, to declare inoperative a decision made by others ‖ the exercise of this right 2. *v.t.* to refuse consent to by using the right of veto ‖ to forbid flatly

vex *v.t.* to annoy (someone)

vex·a·tion *n.* a vexing or being vexed ‖ **vex·a·tious** *adj.* causing vexation

vi·a *prep.* by way or means of

vi·a·bil·i·ty *n.* the state or quality of being viable

vi·a·ble *adj.* (of a fetus) able to maintain an independent life ‖ economically, politically or socially able to be independent ‖ sound, workable

vi·a·duct *n.* a bridge supported by many pillared arches, over which road or rail transport can pass

vi·al *n.* a small cylindrical container of glass

vi·and *n.* (usually *pl.,*) food

vibes or **vibrations** *n.* **1.** an aura or spirit emanating from a person or situation **2.** an instinctive sense of the nature of a person or a situation

vi·bran·cy *n.* the state or quality of being vibrant

vi·brant *adj.* vibrating ‖ full of life and energy ‖ resonant

vi·brate vi·brat·ing vi·brat·ed *v.i.* to move to and fro with simple periodic motion ‖ to seem to quiver ‖ *v.t.* to cause to vibrate

vi·bra·tion *n.* a vibrating or being vibrated ‖ the simple periodic to-and-fro motion of a body etc ‖ a single instance of this

vi·bra·tor *n.* a device which vibrates or causes vibration

vi·bra·to·ry *adj.* vibrating or capable of vibrating ‖ vibrant

vic·ar *n.* a priest

vic·ar·age *n.* the residence of a vicar ‖ his benefice

vi·car·i·ous *adj.* acting, or done, on behalf of someone else or in his place ‖ of someone else's experiences which one shares imaginatively

vice *n.* a habitual disposition to choose evil ‖ an evil practice

vi·ce *prep.* in place of

fice- *prefix* someone acting in the place of someone else

vice-pres·i·dent *n.* someone empowered to act for, or in the absence of, a president **vice-pres·i·den·tial** *adj.*

vi·ce ver·sa *adv.* similarly when the terms are reversed

vi·cin·i·ty *pl.* **vi·cin·i·ties** *n.* the immediate neighborhood **in the vicinity of** close to

vi·cious *adj.* characterized by vice ‖ seeking to injure ‖ spiteful, vindictive

vi·cis·si·tude *n.* (esp. *pl.*) a change in fortune or in a situation **vi·cis·si·tú·di·nous** *adj.*

vic·tim *n.* a person or thing made to suffer by a cause which is stated or implied ‖ someone who is cheated or made a dupe **vic·tim·i·zá·tion** *n.* **vic·tim·ize vic·tim·iz·ing vic·tim·ized** *v.t.* to cause to be a victim

vic·tor *n.* the winner

vic·to·ri·ous *adj.* having won a victory ‖ of or pertaining to victory

vic·to·ry *pl.* **vic·to·ries** *n.* the winning of a contest, esp. final success in battle or war

vict·ual *n.* (*pl.*) food provisions

victual vict·ual·ing vict·ualed *v.t.* to provision (e.g. a ship)

vid·e·o 1. *n.* the visual element of television ‖ television **2.** *adj.* of or pertaining to television

vid·e·o·disc *n.* a plastic disc containing a television recording

video tape a magnetic tape used to record a television program

vie vy·ing vied *v.i.* to compete

view 1. *n.* what one can see from where one is ‖ a wide spread of country as seen from a commanding position ‖ visual inspection ‖ a mental survey ‖ an opinion **on view** displayed for public inspection **2.** *v.t.* to inspect **view·er** *n.* member of a television audience ‖ a device for looking at color slides

view·point *n.* a point of view

vig·il *n.* the act of remaining awake at night ‖ the period of such wakefulness ‖ *(pl.)* evening prayers

vig·i·lance *n.* watchfulness

vig·i·lant *adj.* of someone who is tirelessly on the alert

vi·gnette 1. *n.* a portrait (engraving, photograph etc.) of head and shoulders which shades off into the background ‖ an ornament ‖ a brief but clear verbal description, esp. of a person **2.** *v.t.* **vi·gnet·ting vi·gnet·ted** to make a vignette portrait of

vig·or *n.* physical or intellectual power ‖ vitality, strength

vig·or·ous *adj.* of, having, calling for done with vigor

vile vil·er vil·est *adj.* morally hateful ‖ foul

vil·i·fi·ca·tion *n.* a filifiying or being vilified

vil·i·fy vil·i·fy·ing vil·i·fied *v.t.* to say abusive things about

vil·la a country house, esp. an imposing one

vil·lage *n.* the houses and other buildings of a community of between about a hundred and a few thousand people

vil·lag·er *n.* someone who lives and works in a village

vil·lain *n.* someone guilty or capable of vile deeds or wickedness **víl·lain·ous** *adj.*

vil·lain·y *pl.* **vil·lain·ies** *n.* villainous conduct

vim *n.* vigor, energy

vin·di·cate vin·di·cat·ing vin·di·cat·ed *v.t.* to prove the truth or virtue of, after this has been questioned or denied

vin·di·ca·tion *n.* a vindicating or being vindicated ‖ a fact which vindicates

vin·dic·tive *adj.* having the motive of revenge

vine *n.* a genus of slender, woody, climbing plants, with alternate, palmate-veined leaves

vin·e·gar *n.* a liquid containing up to 6% acetic acid used as a preservative in pickling and as a condiment **vín·e·gar·y** *adj.*

vine·yard *n.* a plot of land where grapevines are growing

vin·tage 1. *n.* grape harvest ‖ the yield of wine or grapes gathered in a particular district or year **2.** *adj.* venerable

vint·ner *n.* a wine merchant

vi·nyl *n.* a resin, plastic or synthetic fiber made from a vinyl compound

vi·o·la *n.* a stringed instrument

vi·o·late vi·o·lat·ing vi·o·lat·ed *v.t.* to break (a promise, law, principle etc.) by forceful opposition to it ‖ to rape ‖ to desecrate

vi·o·la·tion *n.* a violating or being violated

vi·o·la·tor *n.* a person who violates

vi·o·lence *n.* a use of physical force so as to damage or injure ‖ passion, fury ‖ distortion of meaning ‖ desecration

vi·o·lent *adj.* markedly intense ‖ furious ‖ caused by violence

vi·o·let 1. *n.* a small-flowered plant ‖ the bluish-purple color of the flowers **2.** *adj.* having a violet color

vi·o·lin *n.* a four-stringed treble musical instrument played with a bow

vi·o·lin·ist *n.* a violin player

vi·o·lon·cel·lo *n.* a cello

VIP *n.* a person of eminence or importance

vi·per *n.* an adder ‖ a person who behaves with great malice **vi·per·ous** *adj.* of, relating to or characteristic of a viper or vipers ‖ malicius

vir·gin 1. a person who has not had sexual intercourse **2.** *adj.* or or being a virgin

vir·gin·al *adj.* or or appropriate to a virgin

vir·ile *adj.* having the characteristics of a man as a male being ‖ capable of procreating

vi·ril·i·ty *n.* the state or quality of being virile

vir·tu·al *adj.* being something specified in essence or effect though not in name

vir·tue *n.* a quality held to be of great moral value ‖ moral excellence, goodness ‖ female chastity

vir·tu·os·i·ty *n.* great technical ability in a fine art, esp. in the playing of a musical instrument

vir·tu·o·so pl. **vir·tu·o·sos, vir·tu·o·si** n. someone very highly skilled in the technique of a fine art

vir·tu·ous adj. having moral virtue ‖ chaste

vir·u·lence n. the quality of being virulent **vir·u·len·cy** n.

vir·u·lent adj. characterized by severity, rapidity of course and malignancy ‖ extremely toxic or poisonous ‖ malignant, bitterly hostile

vi·rus pl. **vi·rus·es** n. a submicroscopic entity able to pass through bacteria-retaining fibers

vi·sa n. an official endorsement of a passport denoting that the owner has permission either to enter or cross a particular country

vis·age n. the face

vis·cer·a pl. n. the bodily organs occupying the great cavities, esp. the stomach, intestines etc. which occupy the trunk

vis·cer·al adj. of, like, or felt in the viscera

vis·cid adj. sitcky **vis·cíd·i·ty** n.

vis·cos·i·ty pl. **vis·cos·i·ties** n. the quality or property of a fluid that causes it to resist flow

vise n. a tool by which an object being worked is gripped between two jaws

vis·i·bil·i·ty n. the fact or state of being visible ‖ range of vision

vis·i·ble adj. able to be seen ‖ apparent to the mind **vís·i·bly** adv.

vi·sion 1. n. the act of seeing or the ability to see ‖ foresight ‖ a supernatural apparition **2. vision·al** adj. conjured up in the imagination without being related to facts

vis·it 1. v.t. to go or come to see (someone) socially, often for a short vacation ‖ to inspect as a sightseer ‖ to call on for professional advice ‖ (with 'with') to afflict with injury or trouble ‖ v.i. to make a visit **2.** n. a visiting or being visited

vis·i·tant n. a vantastic visitor ‖ a phantom

vis·it·ta·tion n. an official visit for inspection ‖ an instance of affliction or of blessing regarded as divine punishment

or reward

vis·i·tor n. someone who makes a visit

vi·sor, vi·zor n. a movable, perforated part of a helmet ‖ the peak of a cap, shielding the eyes from direct sunlight

vis·ta n. a view extending into the distance but bounded, e.g. by headlands or rows of trees

vis·u·al adj. of, pertaining to, or used in, seeing ‖ visible

vis·u·al·i·za·tion n. a mental picture

vis·u·al·ize vis·u·al·iz·ing vis·u·al·ized v.t. to from a mental picture of

vi·tal 1. adj. of concerned with or necessary to life ‖ full of life ‖ essential **2.** n. (pl.) those parts of the body without which life cannot continue

vi·tal·i·ty pl. **vi·tal·i·ties** n. the quality of being alive ‖ animation, energy, liveliness

vi·tal·ize vi·tal·iz·ing vi·tal·ized v.t. to give energy or vigor to, to animate

vi·ta·min n. any of a number of organic chemical substances present in various foods and essential in very small quantities to health

vi·ti·ate vi·ti·at·ing vi·ti·at·ed v.t. to spoil, make defective ‖ to currupt ‖ to invalidate **vi·ti·á·tion, ví·ti·a·tor** ns

vit·ro·ous adj. like glass, glassy

vit·ti·ol n. any of several metallic sulfates ‖ savage criticism

vit·ri·ol·ic adj. of, like or made from vitriol ‖ savage

vi·tu·per·ate vi·tu·per·at·ing vi·tu·per·at·ed v.t. to hurl abuse at

vi·tu·per·a·tion n. wordy and vehement abuse

vi·va·cious adj. full of life, spirited, animated

vi·vac·i·ty mental liveliness

viv·id adj. providing a very strong stimulus to the eye or to the imagination or memory

viv·i·fi·ca·tion n. a vivifying or being vivified

viv·i·fy viv·i·fy·ing viv·i·fied v.t. to enliven, animate

viv·i·sec·tion n. the performance of scientific experiments involving surgical operation on living animals **viv·i·séc·tion·al** *adj.* **viv·i·sec·tor** *n.* someone who vivisects

vix·en a she-fox ‖ a badtempered, spiteful or quarrelsome woman **víx·en·ish** *adj.*

vo·ca·ble *n.* a word, esp. one regarded phonologically

vo·cab·u·lar·y *pl.* **vo·cab·u·lar·ies** *n.* the stock of words at a person's command, or used in a particular work, branch of a subject, language etc.

vo·cal *adj.* of or pertaining to the voice ‖ spoken or sung ‖ inclined to express oneself or one's opinions freely ‖ voiced

vocal cords elastic folds of membrane inside the larynx which vibrate to produce voice sounds

vo·cal·ist *n.* a singer

vo·cal·ize vo·cal·iz·ing vo·cal·ized *v.t.* to form or utter with the voice, esp. to sing ‖ to voice

vo·cal·ly *adv.* in a vocal manner by singing

vo·ca·tion *n.* a conviction that one is called by God to do a particular kind of work ‖ any trade, profession or occupation **vo·cá·tion·al** *adj.*

vo·cif·er·ous *adj.* noisily clamorous

vod·ka *n.* liquor with a high percentage of alcohol, distilled from rye, wheat or potatoes ec.

vogue *n.* a prevalent or current fashion

voice 1. *n.* the sound uttered from the human mouth in speaking or singing etc. ‖ the faculty or power of human utterance ‖ a vote or opinion ‖ the medium by which something is expressed or represented **2.** *v.t.* **voic·ing voiced** to express, give utterance to

voiced *adj.* having a specific kind of voice

voice·less *adj.* having no voice ‖ having no vote

void 1. *v.t.* to annul, to invalidate **vóid·a·ble** *adj.*

voile *n.* a thin, semi-transparent material

vol·a·tile *adj.* evaporating quickly and easily at ordinary temperature ‖ changeable, fickle **vol·a·til·i·ty** *n.*

vol·can·ic *adj.* of, like, or produced by, a

volcano **vol·cán·i·cal·ly** *adv.*

vol·ca·no *pl.* **vol·ca·noes, vol·ca·nos** *n.* a rift or vent in the earth's crust through which molten material is erupted

vole *n.* a genus of rodents widely distributed in the northern hemisphere

vo·li·tion *n.* the exercise of one's will ‖ the ability to use one's will **vo·lí·tion·al** *adj.*

vol·ley 1. *pl.* **vol·leys** *n.* a discharge of many missiles at the same time ‖ *(tennis)* a return of the ball before it bounces **2. vol·ley·ing vol·leyed, vol·lied** *v.t.* to discharge, return, bowl, throw etc. in a volley

volt *n.* the practical unit of electromotive force

volt·age *n.* potential difference, expressed in volts

vol·u·bil·i·ty *n.* the quality or state of being voluble

vol·u·ble *adj.* characterized by or producing an unhesitating flow of words **vól·u·bly** *adv.*

vol·ume *n.* the amount of space occupied by, or contained in ‖ an amount, quantity etc. ‖ loudness or fullness of sound ‖ a book **to speak volumes for** to be abundant evidence of

vo·lu·mi·nous *adj.* consisting of many volumes ‖ of great size, bulky ‖ ample

vol·un·tar·i·ly *adv.* in a voluntary manner

vol·un·tar·y *adj.* acting, made or done freely, not under constraint or compulsion ‖ (of body parts or movements) controlled by or subject to the will

vol·un·teer 1. *n.* a person who undertakes some task or service of his own free will **2.** *adj.* voluntary ‖ made up of volunteers **3.** *v.t.* to offer willingly (one's services, a remark, an explanation etc.)

vo·lup·tu·ar·y 1. *pl.* **vo·lup·tu·ar·ies** *n.* someone who loves sensual pleasures **2.** *adj.* of sensual pleasures

vo·lup·tu·ous *adj.* full of sensual delight ‖ suggesting sensual pleasure

vom·it *v.t.* to throw up from the stomach through the mouth

vomit *n.* that which is vomited ‖ the act of

vomiting

voo·doo 1. *pl.* **voo·doos** *n.* an Animist religion accompanied by black magic ‖ the spell cast by a sorcerer **2.** to bewitch with voodoo **vóo·doo·ism, vóo·doo·ist** *ns*

vo·ra·cious *adj.* greedy for food, gluttonous

vo·rac·i·ty *n.* the state or quality of being voracious

vor·tex *pl.* **vor·ti·ces, vor·tex·ts** *n.* a mass of whirling fluid, esp. a whirlpool ‖ a whirlwind **vor·ti·cal** *adj.*

vote *n.* a decision to elect someone or to pass a law by voice, gesture or ballot ‖ the act of voting ‖ votes collectively

vote vot·ing vot·ed *v.i.* to use one's vote ‖ *v.t.* to decide by vote

vo·tive *adj.* offered in fulfillment of a vow

vouch *v.i.* to be guaranteed ‖ *v.t.* to testify

vouch·er *n.* a document, receipt etc.

vouch·safe vouch·saf·ing vouch·safed *v.t.* to condescend to grant, to give as a favor

vow *n.* a solemn promise or pledge **to take vows** to join a religious community

vow *v.t.* to promise solemnly ‖ *v.i.* to make a vow

vow·el *n.* a voiced speech sound ‖ a letter in the alphabet representing a vowel sound (a,e,i,o,u)

voy·age *n.* a long journey, esp. by sea

vo·yeur *n.* someone who finds sexual pleasure in looking at sex acts, genital organs etc. **vo·yéur·ism** *n.*

vul·can·i·za·tion the act or process of vulcanizing

vul·can·ize vul·can·iz·ing vul·can·ized *v.t.* to treat (rubber) with sulfer at a high temperature so as to increase its strength and elasticity

vul·gar *adj.* indecent ‖ offensive ‖ most common ‖ vernacular

vul·gar·ism vulgarity

vul·gar·i·ty *pl.* **vul·gar·iz·ing vul·gar·ized** *v.t.* to popularize ‖ to make coarse

vul·ner·a·bil·i·ty *n.* the state of being vulnerable

vul·ner·a·ble *adj.* open to attack, hurt or injury **vúl·ner·a·bly** *adv.*

vul·pine *adj.* of or like a fox ‖ crafty, cunning

vul·ture *n.* one of a group of large birds of prey

vul·va *n.* the orifice or external parts of the female genitals **vúl·var, vúl·vate** *adjs*

W

W, w the 23rd letter of the English alphabet

wack·y wack·i·er wack·i·est *adj.* crazy, absurdly silly

wad 1. *n.* a handy, compact lump of soft material ‖ a roll, esp. of paper money **2.** *v.t.* **wad·ding wad·ded** to plug with a wad ‖ to pad with soft material ‖ to press into a wad

wad·dle 1. *v.i.* **wad·dling wad·dled** to walk with short ungainly steps and moving slightly from side to side **2.** *n.* such a gait

wade 1. wad·ing wad·ed *v.i.* to walk through some depth of water ‖ *v.t.* to cross (a stream etc.) on foot **2.** *n.* an act of wading **wád·er** *n.* a wading bird

wa·fer *n.* a very thin, crisp cake, e.g. as eaten with ice cream

waf·fle *n.* a crisp batter cake baked on a waffle iron

waffle iron a utensil to make a waffle

waft 1. *v.t.* to carry gently across water by wave or wind, or through the air **2.** *n.* a puff, whiff, gentle gust or breath (of scent, wind, smoke etc.)

wag wag·ging wagged *v.t.* to shake quickly to and fro or up and down *v.i.* to move busily in idle chattering

wag *n.* someone with a reputation for making witticisms

wage *n.* a reward received in the form of a weekly payment

wage wag·ing waged *v.t.* to engage in, carry on (a war)

wa·ger 1. *n.* to bet ‖ an act of wagering **2.** *v.t.* to bet, gamble

wag·on *n.* a four-wheeled vehicle ‖ a patrol wagon

waif *n.* a stray or neglected child ‖ a stray animal

wail 1. *n.* a long drawn-out cry of pain or grief ‖ a sound like such a cry **2.** *v.i.* to utter a wail

waist *n.* the narrow part of the human body between ribs and hips ‖ the waistline ‖ the narrow middle part of an object

wait 1. *v.i.* to remain in a place or in a state of anticipation because of some event expected to happen or a person expected to arrive etc. ‖ to act as a waiter ‖ *v.t.* to await, wait for ‖ to delay **2.** *n.* an act or period of waiting

wait·er *n.* a man employed to serve food or drink in a restaurant ‖ a tray

wait·ress *n.* a woman or girl who waits on tables

waive waiv·ing waiv·ed *v.t.* to agree to forgo (a claim, right or privilege) **wáiv·er** *n.* the act of giving up some established claim ‖ a document making this effective

wake wak·ing woke, waked waked, wo·ken to become conscious after sleep or after being in a semiconscious state ‖ (often with 'up') to return to alertness ‖ *v.t.* to rouse, revive

wake *n.* a vigil over a corpse before burial

wake *n.* the track in the water behind a moving ship

wake·ful *adj.* watchful, alert ‖ unable to sleep

wak·en *v.t.* to arouse from sleep ‖ to stir into awareness, activity etc. ‖ to become awake

walk 1. *v.i.* to move in such a way that the legs support the body, one foot (in two-legged creatures) or two feet (in four-legged creatures) begin always on the ground ‖ to travel on foot **to walk out on** to abandon or desert without warning **to walk over** (or **all over**) to show complete disregard for the rights, wishes etc. of (someone) ‖ to defeat (one's opponent) overwhelmingly **2.** *n.* the route taken when walking ‖ a route pleasant to walk over ‖ a path ‖ a stroll taken on foot for pleasure or exercise ‖ a distance walked

walk·ie-talk·ie, walk·y-talk·y *n.* a portable battery-operated radio transmitter and receiver

walk·out *n.* a strike

walk·up *n.* an apartment house without an elevator

wall *n.* a vertical structure built to enclose, support, divide, protect, retain ‖ the upright part of the structure of a hollow vessel ‖ a layer of structural material bounding an organ, cavity, cell etc. ‖ a **barrier to drive** (or **push**) **to the wall** to force (someone) into a desperate or difficult position **to have one's back to the wall** to be hard pressed, be in a very difficult situation

wall *v.t.* to divide, separte etc. with a wall

wal·la·by *pl.* **wal·la·bies** *n.* small knagaroos

wall·board *n.* a large sheet of boarding used to like walls or ceilings

wal·let *n.* a small folding case for carrying paper money

wall·flow·er *n.* a perennial plant widely cultivated for its fragrant flowers ‖ a girl sitting out at a dance because she has not been asked to dance

wal·lop 1. *v.t.* to hit hard ‖ to thrash ‖ to defeat soundly **2.** *n.* a heavy blow **wál·lop·ing 3.** *adj.* huge, thumping, whopping **4.** *n.* a severe thrashing

wal·low 1. *v.i.* to roll about with pleasure (e.g. in mud) ‖ to revel with self-indulgence **2.** *n.* a mudhole where animals wallow

wall·pa·per 1. *n.* paper, usually decorative, for covering the walls of a room **2.** *v.t.* to cover with such paper

wal·nut *n.* a genus of tall-growing trees of temperate regions ‖ the eidble fruit of these trees

wal·rus *n.* Arctic, amrine, seal-like, carnivorous mammal

waltz 1. *n.* a smooth, graceful dance in triple time ‖ the music for this dance **2.** *v.i.* to dance a waltz

wam·pum *n.* beads made of shells and used by North American Indians as money or ornaments

wan wan·ner wan·nest *adj.* unhealthily pale ‖ barely perceptible ‖ faint, feeble

want *n.* a slender rod, esp. one carried by a fairy, magician etc

wan·der *v.i.* to travel around with no set goal ‖ to stray ‖ (of the mind) to be confused, incoherent or delirious ‖ to digress **wán·der·ing** *n.* a leisurely traveling around

wan·der·lust *n.* a strong desire to travel

wane 1. *v.i.* **wan·ing waned** to diminish in size and brilliance ‖ to ebb ‖ to decline or decrease **2.** *n.* the act or process of waning

wan·gle *v.t.* **wan·gling wan·gled** to get by cunning ‖ to falsify

want *n.* an insufficiency ‖ need ‖ privation because of poverty ‖ desires

want *v.t.* to wish fervently ‖ to possess less than the required amount ‖ *v.i.* (esp. with 'for') to suffer need

want·ing 1. *adj.* deficient **2.** *prep.* without, short of

wan·ton *adj.* lewd, licentious ‖ showing utter lack of moderation or justification ‖ luxuriant, uncontrolled

war 1. *n.* armed conflict between nations ‖ a concerted effort to put down, reduce or exterminate **2.** *v.i.* **warred** to be at war

war·ble 1. **war·bling war·bled** *v.i.* to sing with long trills **2.** *n.* the sound, or act, of warbling

ward *v.t.* (with 'off') to turn aside (a blow) ‖ to avert

ward *n.* a minor, under the care of a court or a legal guardian ‖ an electoral district ‖ a division of a prison or hospital

ward·en *n.* an official having special supervisory duties ‖ the official in charge or a prison

ward·robe *n.* a tall piece of furniture to keep clothes in ‖ a person's clothes

ware *n.* (*pl.*) goods for sale ‖ pottery

ware·house 1. *pl.* **ware·hous·es** *n.* a building where goods are stores **2.** *v.t.* **ware·hous·ing ware·housed** to put (goods etc.) in a warehouse

war·fare *n.* a state of war ‖ strife*n.*

war·head *n.* the explosive head of a missile

war·i·ly *n.* in a wary manner

war·i·ness *n.* the state or quality of being wary

warm 1. *adj.* having roughly the same temperature as the human body ‖ emitting heat, esp. in a comforting degree ‖ affectionate ‖ very cordial ‖ (of color) in the range yellow through orange to red **2.** v.i.to become warm ‖ v.t. to warm up ‖ to exercise before going into a game ‖ to reheat (cooked food)

warm·heart·ed *adj.* affectionate, sympathetic etc.

war·mon·ger *n.* a person who advocates war

warmth *n.* the state or quality of being warm

warn *v.t.* to draw the attention of (someone) to an impending danger ‖ to inform beforehand ‖ *v.i.* to give warning

wárn·ing 1. *n.* the act of someone who warns ‖ the fact of being warned

warp *n.* the lengthwise threads in a fabric or on a loom ‖ a twist or distortion ‖ a twist or distortion in the mind

warp *v.t.* to cause (wood) to become twisted ‖ to give a false account of ‖ *v.i.* to become twisted or distorted

war·rant *v.t.* to justify ‖ to guarantee **wár·rant·a·ble** *adj.* **wár·rant·a·bly** *adv.* **war·ran·tee** *n.* the person to whom a warranty is made **wár·rent·er, wár·rant·or** *ns* someone who gives a warrant or warranty

war·ran·ty *pl.* **war·ran·ties** *n.* an assurance given by the seller that the thing sold is exactly as represetned in the sale agreement ‖ a justification or authorization ‖ a guarantee

war·ren *n.* a rabbit burrow ‖ overcrowded tenement

wart *n.* a small hard excrescence on the skin

war·y war·i·er war·i·est *adj.* on one's guard, on the lookout for danger, trickery etc.

was *past* (lst and 3rd person sing.) of BE

wash 1. *v.t.* to clean with soap and water ‖ to cleanse ‖ to pass (a gas) through a liquid in order to remove soluble elements ‖ to sift (ore etc.) by the action of water ‖ (of the sea, a river, waves etc.) to flow over, against or past ‖ *v.i.* to cleanse oneself with soap and water ‖ to clean clothes etc. by soaping, rubbing etc. in water ‖ to serve as a cleansing

agent **to wash away** to remove or be removed by washing or by a rush of water **2.** *n.* the action or process of washing ‖ linen, clothes etc. washed or waiting to be washed ‖ a liquid used for a thin coat of color, esp. watercolor ‖ a wash drawing

wash·cloth wash·cloths *n.* a cloth for washing oneself

wash·ing *n.* the act of a person who or thing which washes ‖ clothes, linen etc. washed or to be washed ‖ *(pl.)* the metal etc. obtained by washing ore etc.

wash·out *n.* the washing away of earth in the bed of a road by a rainstorm, flood etc. ‖ a complete failure

wash·room *n.* a lavatory in a restaurant etc.

wash·y wash·ier wash·i·est *adj.* weak and watery ‖ feeble

wasp *n.* any of numerous winged insects of many different families **wásp·ish** *adj.* maliciously critical **wásp·ish** *adj.* maliciously critical **wásp·y wasp·i·er wasp·i·est** *adj.* waspish

WASP or **Wasp** *(acronym)* for white Anglo-Saxon Protestant —**Waspish** *adj.* **Wwaspishness** *n.* —**Waspdom** *n.* the milieu

Was·ser·mann test a test used to diagnose syphilis

wast·age avoidable loss due to wastefulness

waste 1. *n.* an expenditure of goods, material etc. without proportionate result ‖ needless and excessive consumption ‖ left over from a manufacturing process ‖ a region naturally barren and desolate ‖ superfluous matter, e.g. garbage, rubbish, human or animal excrement **to go to waste** to become spoiled and useless **2.** *adj.* (of land) desolate, uncultivated ‖ or or pertaining to refuse ‖ discarded as useless **to lay waste** to ravage

waste wast·ing wast·ed *v.t.* to spend to no purpose ‖ to enfeeble and emaciate ‖ to lay waste, to devastate

waste·land *n.* a tract of uncultivated country

wast·rel *n.* a waster

watch *n.* a small portable timepiece ‖ a period of time during which part of a ship's company is required to be on duty ‖ a person on duty, esp. at night, for purposes of guarding, protecting etc.

watch *v.t.* to observe attentively ‖ to be a spectator at ‖ to look after ‖ to pay attention to ‖ *v.i.* to be closely observant ‖ (with 'for') to keep a lookout

watch·ful *adj.* keenly observant or vigilant

watch·word *n.* a motto or slogan

wa·ter 1. *n.* the transparent, colorless liquid which falls from the sky as rain, issues from the ground in springs, and composes three-quarters of the earth's surface in the form of seas, rivers, lakes etc. ‖ any of various bodily fluids or secretions, e.g. tears, saliva, urine, amniotic fluid ‖ *(pl.)* natural mineral water **2.** *v.i.* to fill with tears ‖ to fill with saliva ‖ *v.t.* to soak or wet ‖ to give water to drink ‖ to dilute by adding water to

water bed a bed whose mattress is a vinyl bag filled with water, sometimes temperature controlled

wa·ter·col·or *n.* paint for which water, rather than oil, is the solvent ‖ a picture executed with this paint **wá·ter·col·or·ist** *n.*

wa·ter·cress *n.* a perennial cress living in running streams, eaten as salad, cooked in soup etc.

wa·ter·fall *n.* a steep descent of a river

wa·ter·fowl *pl.* **wa·ter·fowl** *n. (pl.)* swimming game birds

wa·ter·front *n.* the land abutting on a body of water

wa·ter·line *n.* lines on a ship up to which she may be submerged ‖ the surface level of a body of water

wa·ter·logged *adj.* soaked with water, saturated ‖ (of a ship or boat) so full of water that she hardly floats

water main the main pipe in a water supply system

wa·ter·mark 1. *n.* a mark showing the level to which water has risen ‖ a faint translucent design impressed on certain kinds of paper and visible only against the light **2.** *v.t.* to stamp (paper) with a watermark

wa·ter·mel·on *n.* a trailing vine widely cultivated ‖ its large round or elongated fruit, having a green rind and a red edible, very juicy, sweet pulp

water moccasin a pit viper

wa·ter·pow·er *n.* the energy of moving water converted into mechanical energy

wa·ter·proof *adj.* that will not let water in or through ‖ *v.t.* to make waterproof

wa·ter·shed *n.* a ridge, or other line of separation, between two river systems or drainage areas

wa·ter·spout *n.* a pipe etc. for clearing water off a roof ‖ a column of mist, spray and water caused by the meeting of a funnel-shaped cloud and a mass of spray thrown up from the sea by a whirling wind

wa·ter·tight *adj.* constructed so as to be impermeable to water ‖ not liable to doubt, thoroughly sound

wa·ter·way *n.* a navigable channel ‖ a traffic route by water

wa·ter·works *pl. n.* a system for the conservation and distribution of a water supply

wa·ter·y *adj.* containing too much water, overdiluted ‖ soggy ‖ moist

watt *n.* a unit of electric power

watt·age *n.* amount of electrical power

watt-hour *n.* a unit of energy

wat·tle *n.* a wrinkled, usually brightly colored flap of skin hanging from the throat of some birds

wave 1. *n.* a forward-moving swell on the surface of a liquid (e.g. of the ocean) ‖ something which has the shape of a wave, e.g. an undulation in hair or in a rippling flag ‖ a gesture of the hand or arm in a sweeping movement ‖ a social phenomenon resulting in a sudden increase **2. wav·ing wav·ed** *v.t.* to cause to move to and fro with a motion resembling that of a wave ‖ to call, order etc. with a waving motion of the hand or arm ‖ *v.i.* to move to and from or up and down with the motion of a wave ‖ to make a signal of farewell, welcome etc.

wa·ver 1. *v.i.* to hesitate ‖ to falter ‖ to move about unsteadily **2.** *n.* a wavering

wav·y wav·i·er wav·i·est *adj.* (of a line) having a form consisting of a succession of many little waves

wax 1. any of numerous mixtures that differ from fats in being harder and less greasy e.g. beeswax ‖ any of various natural or synthetic substances resembling wax ‖ sealing wax **2.** *v.t.* to apply wax to

wax *v.i.* (esp. of the moon) to increase in size and brilliance until full ‖ to grow

wax·en *n.* resembling wax ‖ made of wax

wax·work *n.* a figure modeled in wax, usually representing a famous or notorious person, living or dead

wax·y wax·i·er wax·i·est *adj.* resembling wax ‖ covered with wax

way *n.* the course taken in getting from one place to another, or the ground traveled over in taking such a course ‖ direction of movement ‖ a characteristic trait of behavior ‖ the procedures etc. involved in an activity **by the way** along or near the side of the road ‖ incidentally

way *adv.* to a great degree ‖ at a great distance

way·far·er *n.* a traveler, esp. on foot

way·lay way·lay·ing way·laid *v.t.* to wait for and attack in order to rob etc.

way·side 1. *n.* the side of a road etc. **2.** *adj.* situated on, at or near the side of a road etc.

way·ward *adj.* willfully turning away from what is right and proper, showing willfulness and heedlessness

we *pron.*, *1st person pl.*, *nominative case*

weak *adj.* having little physical strength ‖ lacking force ‖ low in intensity ‖ morally feble ‖ ineffective in the use of authority ‖ (of bodily organs) liable to collapse or not performing well **weak·en** *v.t.* to make weak ‖ *v.i.* to become weak

weak-kneed *adj.* lacking moral resolution

weak·ling *n.* a physically weak person or

animal ‖ a person without strength of character

weak·ly weak·li·er weak·li·est *adj.* delicate in health, lacking a strong constitution

weak·ness *n.* a defect ‖ self-indulgent fondness

wealth *n.* abundant worldly possessions ‖ an abundance of anything ‖ the natural resources of a country ‖ anything that can be exchanged for money or barter **wealth·i·ly** *adv.* **wealth·i·ness** *n.* **wealth·y wealth·i·er wealth·i·est** *adj.* characterized by abundance

wean *v.t.* to train (an infant or young animal) to accept food other than its mother's milk ‖ (with 'from') to induce to give up

wea·pon *n.* any instrument used for fighting or defending

wear 1. wear·ing worn *v.t.* to have (garments) on the body ‖ to arrange by prolonged use, abrasion etc. ‖ *v.i.* to diminish or deteriorate through use, friction etc. ‖ to resist dmange by use etc. **to wear out** to make or become unfit for further use ‖ to exhaust **2.** *n.* damage due to use ‖ the ability to resist damage due to use ‖ garments

wea·ri·ness *n.* the state or quality of being weary

wear·ing *adj.* of or pertaining to clothing ‖ very tiring

wea·ri·some *adj.* causing physical or mental fatigue

wea·ry 1. wea·ri·er wea·rid·est *adj.* tired and dispirited ‖ bored **2. wea·ry·ing wea·ried** *v.t.* to cause to be weary ‖ *v.i.* to become weary

wea·sel 1. *n.* a small carnivorous mammal **2.** *v.i.* to evade an obligation in a cunning manner

weath·er 1. *n.* the atmospheric conditions (heat, cold, wetness, dryness, clearness, cloudiness etc.) **2.** *v.t.* to expose (e.g. wood, stone) to changing atmospheric conditions ‖ to pass safely through a storm, a dangerous or difficult time etc. ‖ *v.i.* to undergo some change due to exposure to the weather

weath·er·beat·en adj. showing permanent signs of exposure to weather ‖ roughened, sunburned etc.

weath·er·man pl. **weath·er·men** n. a person who forecasts or reports on weather conditions

weath·er·proof 1. adj. able to resist exposure to the weather **2.** v.t. to treat (a material) so as to make it thus

weave 1. **weav·ing** **wo·ven**, **wove** v.t. to form (thread etc.) into a fabric by interlacing ‖ to make something by interlacing (rushes etc.) ‖ to construct (a narrative, plot, scheme etc.) ‖ v.i. to engage in weaving ‖ to move this way and that in order to avoid obstacles **2.** n. a manner or style of weaving **weav·er** n. a person who weaves

web 1. n. a piece of cloth in the process of being woven ‖ the fine network of threads spun by a spider ‖ something intended to create mystery, entangle etc. ‖ a membrane uniting the digits of certain aquatic birds, frogs etc. ‖ a thin flat piece connecting the more solid parts in a girder etc. **2.** v.t. **web·bing** **webbed** to cover or join with a web ‖ to snare with a web

we'd contr. of WE HAD, WE SHOULD, WE WOULD

wed **wed·ding** **wed·ded**, **wed** v.t. to marry ‖ to unite ‖ v.i. to get married **wed·ded** adj. married

wed·ding n. the ceremony of marriage with its accompanying festivities

wedge 1. n. a piece of wood or metal, thick at one end and narrowing down to a thin edge at the other, used for splitting wood, rock etc., for forcing something open, or for fixing into a crack to keep something in place etc. ‖ a golf club used for lofting **2.** v.t. **wedg·ing** **wedged** to fix tightly with a wedge ‖ to split open by driving in a wedge ‖ to cram into a small space

wed·lock n. the state of being married

Wednes·day n. the fourth day of the week

wee **we·er** **we·est** adj. very small

weed 1. n. any plant growing where it is not desired ‖ seaweed **2.** v.t. to remove weeds from ‖ to get rid of undesirable elements ‖ v.i. to remove weeds **weed·y** **weed·i·er** **weed·i·est** adj. full of weeds

week n. a period of seven day, beginning with Sunday ‖ the working days or hours of a seven-day period, a 40-hour week

week·day n. any day of the week except the sabbath

week·end the period from Friday night until Monday morning **1.** adj. on a weekend **2.** v.i. to pass the weekend

week·ly 1. adj. happening, produced, done every week **2.** adv. every week ‖ once a week **3.** pl. **week·lies** n. a publication produced every week

weep **weep·ing** **wept** v.i. to shed tears ‖ to mourn ‖ to exude some watery fluid ‖ v.t. to lament or cry for **weep·er** n. someone who weeps **weep·ing** adj. that weeps ‖ oozing moisture

wee·vil n. a group of small beetles having a long head prolonged into a snout

weigh v.t. to determine the weight of ‖ to consider the importance, relative truth or advantage of ‖ v.i. to have a certain weight ‖ (with 'on' or 'upon') to be a burden **to weigh one's words** to consider well the full implication of a statement before making it

weight 1. n. the force acting on a body in a gravitational field ‖ a known mass of metal used for comparing other weights ‖ the amount something or someone weighs ‖ a mass of metal used in a grandfather clock etc. to drive the mechanism ‖ importance **to carry weight** to be given serious consideration in the making of a decision **2.** v.t. to add weight to

weight·y **weight·i·er** **weight·i·est** adj. heavy ‖ burdensome, oppressive ‖ important

weird adj. uncanny, supernatural ‖ queer, odd

wel·come 1. v.t. **wel·com·ing** **wel·comed** to receive or greet with signs of pleasure **2.** n. a being welcomed **3.**

adj. received gladly ‖ permitted gladly

weld 1. *v.t.* to unite (surfaces) by softening them with heat and then hammering them together ‖ *v.i.* to become welded **2.** *n.* a welding ‖ a welded joint

wel·fare *n.* the state of being healthy, happy and free from want ‖ organized work to promote this state

well 1. bet·ter best *adv.* in a manner which gives satisfaction ‖ throughly ‖ fully, quite ‖ very likely ‖ properly, correctly ‖ intimately **as well** also **as well as** in addition to **2.** *adj.* in good health ‖ satisfactory ‖ pleasing **very well** expressing approval etc.

well *n.* a deep hole dug into the earth to reach a supply of water ‖ a shaft sunk into the earth to obtain oil, gas etc. ‖ the space running vertically through the floors of a building and containing the stairs or elevator ‖ a spring of water

well *v.i.* (of a liquid or tears) to rise up and pour out copiously

we'll *contr.* of WE SHALL, WE WILL

well-be·ing *n.* the state of being healthy, happy and free from want

well-bred *adj.* educated for polite society ‖ of good stock

well-dis·posed *adj.* feeling kindly or sympathetic

well-done *adj.* performed well ‖ thoroughly cooked

well-groomed *adj.* (of a person) impeccable in dress and appearance ‖ (of a horse etc.) well tended

well-ground·ed *adj.* well-founded ‖ well instructed in fundamental principles of some discipline

well-known *adj.* widely known ‖ intimately known

well-off *adj.* well-to-do ‖ well provided

well-read *adj.* having read a great deal

well-thought-of *adj.* of good reputation, esteemed

well-timed *adj.* arranged to occur at the right moment

well-to-do *adj.* having a comfortably large income

welt 1. an inflamed ridge raised on the skin ‖ a narrow strip of material sewn over the seam of a garment as reinforcement **2.** *v.t.* to provide with a welt

wel·ter 1. *v.i.* to wallow **2.** *n.* turmoil

wel·ter·weight *n.* a professional amateur boxer whose weight does not exceed 147 lbs

were *pl.* and *2nd pers. sing. past indicative* and *past subjunctive* of BE

we're *contr.* of WERE NOT

were·wolf *pl.* **were·wolves** *n.* (in supersititious elief) a human being changed into a wolf

west 1. *adv.* toward the west **2.** *n.* one of the four cardinal points of the compass ‖ in the direction of the setting sun **3.** *adj.* facing west

west·er·ly *adj. adj.* and *adv.* in or toward the west **1.** *pl.* **west·er·lies** *n.* a wind blowing from the west

west·ern *adj.* situated facing, coming from or moving toward the west **Wést·ern** *n.* a story, film etc. of life in the West of the U.S.A.

west·ern·ize west·ern·iz·ing west·ern·ized *v.t.* to cause to become Western in outlook, dress, character etc.

west·ward 1. *adv.* and *adj.* towards the west **2.** *n.* the westward direction or part **wést·wards** *adv.*

wet wet·ter wet·test *adj.* soaked in water ‖ characterized by much rain ‖ not yet dried

wet wet·ting·wet, wet·ted *v.t.* to make wet ‖ *v.i.* to become wet

wet blanket a person who discourages fun or conversation by his sober mood

we've *contr.* of WE HAVE

whack 1. *v.t.* to strike **2.** *n.* a resounding blow

whale 1. *n.* a member of any of many species of immense, fishlike marine mammals **a whale of** very large **2.** *v.i.* **whal·ing whaled** to hunt whales

whale whal·ing whaled *v.t.* to beat severely ‖ to defeat thoroughly

wharf 1. *pl.* **wharves wharfs** *n.* a landing stage to which barges and ships can be moored for loading and unloading **2.** *v.t.* to moor **whárf·age** *n*. the fee for using a wharf

what 1. *pron.* used interrogatively, requiring something to be identified ‖ that which ‖ how much **what about** an expression used to introduce a suggestion **what for?** for what reason or purpose? **what have you** et cetera **what's what** the true state of affairs **2.** *adj.* used interrogatively, referring to the nature, identity etc. of a person or thing ‖ (in exclamations) how great, ridiculous etc. **3.** to what extent, to what degree ‖ (in exclamations) used as an intensive, *what cold weather!* **4.** *interj.* an exclamation of surprise, anger etc.

what·ev·er 1. *pron.* anything that ‖ no matter what ‖ something of the sort **2.** *adj.* all the

what·not *n*. a piece of furniture consisting of a set of open shelves for displaying miscellaneous objects

what·so·ev·er *pron.* and *adj.* whatever

wheal *n*. a weal

whest *n*. an annual cereal grass ‖ the grain yielded from it

whee·dle whee·dling whee·dled *v.t.* to persuade by flattery, coaxing etc. ‖ to obtain in this way

wheel 1. *n*. a circular device, usually able to rotate about a central axle ‖ the control of a car, ship etc **to put one's shoulder to the wheel** to begin to use one's energies in accomplishing some taxk **to take the wheel** to assume control of a ship, car etc. **2.** *v.i.* to turn around on an axis ‖ to move on wheels ‖ *v.t.* to cause to move on wheels ‖ *v.t.* to cause to revolve or rotate

wheel·bar·row *n*. a shallow vehicle with one wheel in front and two legs and handles at the back

wheel·chair *n*. a chair on wheels for an invalid

wheeze 1. *v.i.* **wheez·ing wheezed** to breathe with difficulty, making a whistling sound ‖ *v.t.* to utter wheezily **2.** *n*. a wheezing sound **whéez·i·ly** *adv.*

whéez·i·ness *n*. **whéez·y wheez·i·est** *adj.*

whelp 1. *n*. a young lion, tiger, bear, wolf etc. ‖ a puppy **2.** *v.t.* (of animals) to give birth to

when 1. *adv.* at what time ‖ on which occasion **2.** *conj.* at, during or after the time that ‖ every time that ‖ in view of the fact that ‖ if, in the event that **3.** *pron.* what or which time **4.** *n*. the time of an event or an action

whence 1. *adv.* from where ‖ from what source or origin **2.** *conj.* from what place or source

when·e·ver *adv.* and *conj.* at whatever time, as often as ‖ (used emphatically) when

where 1. *adv.* in or at what place ‖ to or toward what place ‖ in what respect ‖ from what place or source **2.** *conj.* in or at what or which place ‖ insofar as **3.** *n*. a place, esp. a place in which something is or occurs

where·a·bouts 1. *adv.* (used interrogatively) near or at what place **2.** *conj.* in what place **3.** *n*. the place where someome or something is

where·as *conj.* while on the contrary ‖ since, considering that

where·by 1. *adv.* by which **2.** *conj.* by which

where·in 1. *adv.* in which place ‖ in what respect ‖ in which **2.** *conj.* in what or in which

where·of *adv.* and *conj.* of which, of what or of whom

where·to *adv.* to what place, purpose etc.

where·up·on 1. *conj.* after which, in consequence of which **2.** *adv.* upon which

where·ev·er 1. *conj.* after which, in consequence of which **2.** *adv.* upon which

where·ev·er 1. *conj.* at, in or to whatever place **2.** *adv.* where ‖ in any circumstance in which

where·with·al *n*. the means, what is necessary

whet 1. *v.t.* **whet·ting whet·ted** to sharpen ‖ to stimulate, arouse **2.** *n.* something that whets

wheth·er *conj.* (followed by 'or', 'or whether') introducing the first of two or more possibilities ‖ (introducing an indirect question) ‖ either

whey *n.* the watery part of milk left when curds have formed and separated

which 1. *pron.* what one or ones of several things, persons etc. pointed out, denoted, described etc. ‖ whichever one or ones **2.** *adj.* what one or ones

which·ev·er 1. *pron.* any one or ones of several **2.** *adj.* no matter which

whiff 1. *n.* a small volume of smoke, air etc. ‖ the smell of this **2.** *v.t.* to emit a small amount of (smoke, scent etc.)

while 1. *n.* a period of time **once in a while** on infrequent occasions **2.** *v.t.* **whil·ing whiled** (with 'away') to make (time) pass pleasantly

while *conj.* during the time that ‖ although

whim *n.* a freakish pattern of ideas

whim·per 1. *v.t.* to utter feeble little cries of fear or compaint or discontent **2.** *n.* a whimpering sound

whim·si·cal *adj.* full of whims ‖ subject to whims **whim·si·cal·i·ty** *pl.* **whimsi·cal·i·ties** *n.*

whim·sy, whim·sey *n.* feeble or sentimental fancy

whine 1. **whin·ing whined** *v.i.* to cry in or utter a high-pitched, long drawn-out, plaintive sound ‖ to complain in a querolous or childish way ‖ *v.t.* to utter whiningly **2.** *n.* a whining sound ‖ a complaint

whin·ny 1. whin·ny·ing whin·nied *v.t.* (of a horse) to neigh **2.** *pl.* **whin·nies** *n.*

whip *n.* a lash with a handle used for driving a horse or urging one on, or for punishing ‖ a whipping or thrashing motion ‖ a light dessert made with whipped ingredients ‖ *politics* an official appointed to maintain party discipline and esp. to enforce attendance in Congress etc.

whip whip·ping whipped *v.t.* to strike with a lash, rod etc. ‖ to beat to a froth ‖ to defeat by a good margin ‖ to wrap (a cord, twine etc.) around something ‖ *v.i.* to dart ‖ to flap with the noise made by the lash of a whip

whip·lash *n.* a whiplash injury

whiplash injury a neck injury

whip·per·snap·per *n.* a young, esp. undersized boy who behaves with more self-importance than is proper

whip·pet *n.* a dog of a fast-running breed

whir, whirr 1. *v.i.* **whir·ring whirr·ing whirred** to move, esp. through the air, with a sound resembling that of a bird's wings in rapid flight **2.** *n.* the sound itself

whirl 1. *v.i.* to revolve rapidly ‖ to rush with a great commotion ‖ *v.t.* to cause to whirl **2.** *n.* a whirling motion ‖ a feeling of giddiness or confusion

whirl·i·gig *n.* a pinwheel (child's toy)

whirl·pool *n.* a circular eddy or current in a river or the sea

whirl·wind *n.* a rotating windstorm

whisk 1. *n.* an instrument for beating eggs, cream etc. ‖ a quick, light movement **2.** *v.t.* to beat (eggs, cream etc.) into a froth ‖ to transport with speed ‖ to remove (something) with a quick, light motion ‖ *v.i.* to move quickly

whick broom a small, short-handled broom used esp. to brush clothes

whisk·er *n.* one of the long stiff bristles growing at either side of the mouth of some animals ‖ *(pl.)* the hairs growing in a beard or down the side of a man's cheeks **whísk·ered, whísk·er·y** *adjs*

whis·key *pl.* **whis·keys, whis·kies** *pl. n.* a strong alcoholic liquor

whis·per 1. *v.i.* to speak quietly ‖ to rustle ‖ *v.t.* to utter in a whisper ‖ to mention secretly, spread as a rumor **2.** *n.* a low soft utterance ‖ a rumor

whist *n.* a card game for four players

whis·tle 1. whis·tling whis·tled *v.i.* to make a shrill, piping sound by forcing the breath through pursed lips ‖ (of a bird) to make a sound resembling this **2.** *n.* a small instrument of wood, metal etc. blown to produce a shrill, piping sound ‖ the sound produced ‖ the piercing note of a bird ‖ something resembling this **whis·tler** *n.* someone who or something that whistles

whit *n.* the smallest possible amount

white 1. *adj.* of the color sensation stimulated by a combination of all the wavelengths of visible light ‖ (of hair) gray or silver ‖ (of hair) very blond ‖ (of vines) very pale yellow ‖ free from sin, pure ‖ pale ‖ of or relating to the Caucasian division of mankind ‖ blank, not printed **2.** a white pigment ‖ a member of the Caucasian division of mankind

white-col·lar *adj.* of, relating to or designating the salaried section of the working population

white elephant a rare, pale-colored elephant ‖ a property that is troublesome or expensive to keep

white lie a lie told for unmalicious reasons

whit·en *v.t.* to make white

white·wash 1. *n.* a liquid mixture of powdered lime or chalk and water, used for whitening walls, ceilings etc. ‖ an act or instance of covering up somenoe's faults **2.** *v.t.* to cover with whitewash ‖ to gloss over or cover p

whith·er 1. *adv.* to what place, where ‖ to what condition, result etc. **2.** *conj.* to what place

whit·ing *n.* a finely powdered chalk

whiting *n.* an edible marine fish

whit·tle whit·tling whit·tled *v.t.* to slice pieces from (wood) with a knife ‖ to reduce bit by bit ‖ *v.i.* to whittle wood

whiz, whizz whiz·zing, whizz·ing whizzed *v.i.* to make a whirring or hissing sound ‖ *v.t.* to cause to move with such a sound **1.** *n.* this sound

who *pron.* what or which person or persons ‖ that

who·ev·er *pron.* whatever person ‖ who

whole 1. *adj.* not lacking any part ‖ entire, undivided ‖ not broken or damaged **2.** *n.* something which lacks none of its parts ‖ all that there is of something

whole-heart·ed *adj.* with complete willingness

whole·sale 1. *n.* the sale of goods in relatively large quantities to be retailed by others **2.** *adj.* of or engaged in buying or selling in this way ‖ sold in this way **3.** *adv.* in a wholesale manner **4. whole·sal·ing whole·saled** *v.i.* to be sold wholesale ‖ *v.t.* to sell (goods) wholesale

whole·some *adj.* healthy ‖ morally sound

whole wheat *adj.* made of the pure meat of wheat, the whole grain being ground

whol·ly *adv.* entirely, totally ‖ solely, exclusively

whom *pron.* the objective case of *conj.* WHO

whoop 1. *n.* a loud cry of joy or excitement **2.** *v.i.* to utter a loud cry of joy or excitement

whop 1. *n.* a heavy thud ‖ a heavy blow **2.** *v.t.* **whop·ping whopped** to strike with a heavy blow **whóp·per** *n.* anything uncommonly large of its kind ‖ big lie **whóp·ping** *adj.* huge

whore 1. *n.* a woman who engages in sexual intercourse for money **2.** *v.i.* **whor·ing shored** to be a whore ‖ to fornicate with whores

whorl *n.* one of the spiral turns of a univalve shell ‖ a decorative motif resembling this **whorled** *adj.*

whose *pron.* the possesive case of WHO

who·so·ev·er *pron.* whoever

why 1. *adv.* for what reason ‖ with what intention ‖ for which **2.** *n.* the reason, the explanation

wick *n.* a piece or bundle of twisted fiber that supplies a lamp or candle flame with oil or melted grease

wick·ed *adj.* not good morally ‖ malicious ‖ trying ‖ vicious

wick·er 1. *n.* twigs or osiers plaited to make baskets, chairs, mats etc. **2.** *adj.* consisting of, or made of, wicker

wick·et *n.* a small door or gate ‖ a small window or opening

wide 1. *adj.* of relatively large extent from side to side, not narrow ‖ reaching over a fast area ‖ great in extent ‖ fully open ‖ lax ‖ of considerable scope **2.**

adv. fully, as much as possible

wide-a·wake *adj.* fully awake ‖ alert, keen

wid·en *v.t.* to make wide or wider

wide·spread *adj.* extended over a wide area

wid·ow 1. *n.* a woman who has not married again after her husband's death **2.** *v.t.* to make into a widow

wid·ow·er *n.* a man who has not married again after his wife's death

wid·ow·hood *n.* the state of time of being a widow

width *n.* measurement, distance or extent from side to side ‖ a piece of cloth etc. measured and cut

wield *v.t.* to use, exert (power, influence, authority etc.) ‖ to hold and use with the hands **wield·y** *adj.* nicely balanced for handling, although weighty

wie·ner *n.* a frankfurter

wife *pl.* **wives** *n.* the female partner in a marriage

wig *n.* an artificial head covering of hair

wig·gle 1. wig·gling wig·gled *v.t.* to cause to move in a small, rapid to-and-fro, side-to-side or up-and-down movement **2.** *n.* a wiggling movement

wig·wam *n.* a rounded or oval cabin or hut used as a dwelling by North American Indians

wild 1. *adj.* (of plants) propagated and growing without man's intervention ‖ (of animals) uncontrolled by man ‖ (of a region) uninhabited and uncultivated by man ‖ un civilized ‖ unrestrained ‖ out of control ‖ completely undisciplined ‖ (of dress or appearance) peculiar ‖ very angry ‖ very enthusiastic ‖ irrational **2.** *adv.* in a wild way **3.** *n.* **the wild** nature unspoiled by man

wild·cat 1. *n.* an undomesticated cat of Africa and S.W. Asia ‖ (*pl.* **wildcat**) any of several other species of small undomesticted cat, e.g. lynx, ocelot **2.** *adj.* risky, not to be relied upon ‖ (of a petroleum or gas well) drilled in an area where there is not clear evidence that oil exists

wil·der·ness *n.* an uninhabited and uncul-

tivated region

wild·fire *n.* a highly combustible material hurled onto the deck of an enemy vessel in naval warfare **to spread like wildfire** (of rumor, plague etc.) to spread exceedingly fast

wild!goose chase a futile search, esp. one deliberately instigated

wile 1. *n.* an artful method of persuasion ‖ a trick using guile so as to deceive or snare **2.** *v.t.* **wil·ing wiled** to subject to blandishments or to guile

will 1. *n.* the faculty of determining one's actions ‖ moral strength or energy ‖ determination ‖ a written statement of how one wishes one's property to be dealt with after one's death ‖ the legal document containing this statment **2.** *v.t.* to dispose of (property) by a will ‖ *v.i.* to exercise the will

will would *auxiliary v.* used to express futurity, usually implying determination, volition, necessity, obligation or acquiescence ‖ *v.i.* to wish ‖ *v.t.* to choose

will·ful, wil·ful *adj.* by intention **will·ful·ly** *adv.*

will·ing *adj.* working, helping etc. readily ‖ done, given etc. readily ‖ faborably disposed

wil·low *n.* a genus of trees or shrubs, comprising 300 species ‖ the wood of such a tree

wil·low·y *adj.* slender and graceful

will·pow·er *n.* the power of controlling one's actions and emotions by an effort of the will

wil·ly-nil·ly *adv.* whatever the will of the person involved may be

wilt *v.i.* (of plants) to become limp ‖ to lose strength or freshness ‖ *v.t.* to cause to wilt

wil·y wil·i·er wil·i·est *adj.* cunning

wimp *n.* one who is unimportant

win 1. win·ning won *v.t.* to achieve victory ‖ to obtain by effort ‖ (often with 'over') to persuade (another) to accept one's point of view, cause etc. ‖ to extract (a mineral) from the surrounding rocks

‖ to extract (a metal) from its ore **2.** *n.* a victory in a contest ‖ money etc. won, e.g. on a race

wince 1. *v.i.* **winc·ing winced** to draw suddenly back slightly and become more rigid, from pain or as if from pain **2.** *n.* a wincing

winch 1. *n.* windlass ‖ hoisting machine **2.** *v.t.* to haul with or as if with a winch

wind 1. wind·ing wound *v.i.* to go or move in a curved path ‖ to move in this way so as to encircle ‖ *v.t.* to cause to wind ‖ (often with 'up') to tighten the spring of by turning the screw or handle of (a clock, watch etc.) **to wind up** to conclude ‖ to come to an end, stop **2.** *n.* a winding or an instance of this

wind 1. *n.* a large body of air in rapid natural motion ‖ the wind instruments (brass and woodwind) of an orchestra ‖ breath, air drawn into or expelled from the lungs ‖ gas produced in the stomach and intestinal tract during digstion ‖ words spoken or written which have little significance **to get wind of** to receive information about (something secret) **to see how the wind blows** to find out the state of affairs **2.** *v.t.* to cause to breathe with difficulty, either by exertion or by a blow to the diaphragm ‖ to receive the scent of ‖ to allow to recover breath by giving a rest to

wind·chill factor the effect of wind velocity in raising or lowering discomfort caused by the temperature

wind·fall *n.* something of value received unexpectedly

wind·ing 1. *n.* the act of someone or something that winds ‖ one complete turn of something which is wound ‖ the way in shich something (e.g. a coil) is wound **2.** *adj.* which winds ‖ discursive, rambling

wind instrument a musical instrument which produces sound by the vibration of air in a pipe or tube

wind·lass *n.* a machine used for hauling and hoisting

wind·mill *n.* a mill worked by sails turned by the wind ‖ a pinwheel

win·dow *n.* an opening in the wall of a room, building etc. permitting light to enter ‖ the space directly behind such an opening used for displaying goods in a store etc. ‖ an opening resembling a window, e.g. that in a window envelope ‖ a time slot in cycles of celestial bodies when an atmospheric penetration is advantageous

win·dow·pane *n.* a sheet of glass forming part of a window

wind·pipe *n.* the trachea

wind·shield *n.* a sheet of glass in the front of a car or other vehicle to proted the driver

wind·up *n.* the act of winding up or ending **a swing of the arm before pitching**

wind·ward *n.* the direction from which a wind blows **1.** *adj.* in this direction **2.** *adv.* towards the source of the wind

wind·y wind·i·er wind·i·est *adj.* accompanied or characterized by wind ‖ wordy and without much significance

wine 1. *n.* a drink made of the fermented juice of grapes ‖ the dark, reddish-purple color of red wine **2.** *v.t.* **win·ing wined** to entertain with wine

wing 1. *n.* one of the specialized appendages used by a bird, bat, insect etc. in flying ‖ one of the structures, on either side of the fuselage of an aircraft ‖ a section of a buiding ‖ a faction within a an organization or political party ‖ (*soccer, hocket* etc.) a position in the forward line ‖ a subunit of an air force ‖ a sidepiece fitting into the back of an easy chair ‖ the area just offstage right or left ‖ *pl.* insignia of profiency worn by air force personnel **2.** *v.i.* to fly ‖ *v.t.* to equip with wings ‖ to wound in the wing

wink 1. *v.i.* to close an eye and then at once open it ‖ to blink ‖ (of a source of light) to shine momemtarily or intermittently **2.** *n.* an act of winking ‖ an instant of sleep ‖ a short or intermittent gleam

‖ a very short time

win·ner *n.* someone who or something that wins ‖ something extremely well done, made, thought out etc.

win·ning 1. *adj.* securing victory or gaining a contest ‖ attractive **2.** *n.* a securing of victory ‖ (*pl.*) money won from gambling, contests etc.

win·now *v.t.* to blow (grain) free of chaff ‖ to treat as though separating chaff from grain

win·some *adj.* charming, attractive

win·ter 1. *n.* the season of the year in latitudes outside the Tropics when the warmth due to the sun's radiation is least **2.** *adj.* of, for or adapted to the winter **3.** *v.i.* to live during the months of winter

win·ter·ize win·ter·iz·ing win·ter·ized *v.t.* to prepar (a ouse, automobile etc.) for the freezing conditions of winter

win·try win·tri·er win·tri·est *adj.* of or like winter ‖ quite unfriendly, chilling

wipe 1. *wip·ing wiped v.t.* to rub with a cloth etc. so as to free from surface moisture, dust etc. ‖ to clean by rubbing ‖ *v.i.* to dry dishes etc. **2.** *n.* a wiping ‖ a wiper **wip·er** *n.* soemone who or something that wipes, esp. a device for sweeping rain from the windshield of an automobile etc.

wire 1. *n.* metal drawn out into a thread-like form of uniform diameter ‖ a suspended length of this on which acrobats perform ‖ a telegram ‖ a snare for rabbits ‖ *pl.* the lines by which a puppet is controlled **2.** **wir·ing wired** *v.t.* to furnish with a wire or wires ‖ to bind or fasten with wire ‖ to provide with an electric circuit ‖ to telegraph ‖ *v.i.* to send a telegram

wire·tap 1. **wire·tap·ing wire·tapped** *v.i.* to listen clandestinely to telephone conversations by secretly making a connection with the telephone wire in use ‖ to obtain (information etc.) in this way **2.** *n.* this technique or an instance of it

wir·y wir·i·er wir·i·est *adj.* made of wire

‖ strong and flexible ‖ lean and sinewy ‖ (of hair) stiff

wis·dom *n.* the quality of being wise ‖ intelligence drawing on experience and governed by prodence ‖ a store of knowledge

wise *adj.* having the ability to ake a right decision or judgment ‖ (of a decision, judgment or action) resulting from the use of this ability ‖ possessing great knowledge and intelligence

wise·a·cre *n.* a man who foolishly pretends to great knowledge

wise·crack 1. *n.* a smart or flippant remark **2.** *v.i.* to make such remarks

wish 1. *v.t.* to feel or express good or ill will or a specified wish, greeting or invocation (to or fore someone) ‖ to require ‖ to foist off ‖ *v.i.* (with 'for') to hope **2.** *n.* a desire felt or expressed ‖ something wished for ‖ a request ‖ *pl.* greetings

whis·ful *adj.* having or manifesting a wish

wish·y-wash·y *adj.* weak, thin, watery ‖ (of a person) feeble and indecisive in character

wisp *n.* a small bunch ‖ a small amount or mre trace of something **wisp·y wisp·i·er wisp·i·est** *adj.*

wist·ful *adj.* desiring a little sadly what is not possible or easy to obtain

wit *n.* the association of apparently unrelated ideas in an unexpected, clever way, esp. with an effect of brilliance provoking laughter ‖ the ability to make such association ‖ a person with this ability ‖ *pl.* mental balance

witch 1. *n.* a woman practicing sorcery ‖ an ugly old woman **2.** *v.t.* to cast a spell on

witch·craft *n.* sorcery as practiced by a witch or witches

with *prep.* in the company of ‖ accompanied by ‖ by means of ‖ possessing, characterized by ‖ in regard to, concerning ‖ in the functioning of ‖ in the care or possession of ‖ at the time of ‖ in the same direction ‖ including

with·draw with·draw·ing with·drew

with·drawn *v.t.* to take away, remove ‖ to take back, to retract ‖ to draw back ‖ *v.i.* to leave, retire **with·dráw·al** *n.* a withdrawing **with·dráwn** *adj.* reserved, shy

with·er *v.i.* (of plants) to dry up and die ‖ (often with 'away') to lose vigor ‖ to cause to wither

with·hold with·hold·ing with·held *v.t.* to hold back, refuse to give

with·in 1. *prep.* not beyond the limits of ‖ in the scope of ‖ inside ‖ in the course of **2.** *adv.* inside ‖ in the mind or conscience

with·out 1. *prep.* free from ‖ refraining from, avoiding ‖ devoid **2.** *adv.* outside, outdoors

with·stand with·stand·ing with·stood *v.t.* to stand up against, to resist

wit·less *adj.* foolish

wit·ness 1. *n.* a person who has observed a certain event ‖ a person who testifies to this observation **2.** *v.t.* to observe (an event) ‖ to sign as a witness ‖ *v.i.* (esp. with 'to') to give as evidence ‖ to bear witness

wit·ti·cism *n.* a witty remark

wit·ting *adj.* deliberate, intentional ‖ conscious **wít·tng·ly** *adv.*

wit·ty wit·ti·er wit·ti·est *adj.* possessing or manifesting wit

wiz·ard *n.* a sorcerer, magician ‖ a person who seems to perform magic **wiz·ard·ry** *pl.*

wiz·ened *adj.* dried-up or shriveled

wob·ble 1. wob·bling wob·bled *v.i.* to be unsteady on its or one's legs ‖ (of a top etc.) to move unsteadily from side to side while revolving ‖ to change repeatedly from one opinion or intention to another ‖ to quaver ‖ to cause to wobble **2.** *n.* a wobbling movement or gait ‖ a quaver **wób·bly wob·bli·er wob·bli·est** *adj.*

woe 1. *n.* grief ‖ troubles, afflictions **2.** *interj.* alas

woe·be·gone *adj.* sorrowful, dismal

woe·ful *adj.* full of woe ‖ deplorable

wok *n.* a bowllike traditional Chinese cooking pot

wolf 1. *pl.* **wolves** *n.* a genus of large, fierce, doglike, carnivorous mammals ‖ a man who tries to pick up women and sduce them **2.** *v.t.* to eat greedily and quickly

wom·an 1. *pl.* **wom·en** *n.* an adult female human being **2.** *adj.* female

wom·an·hood *n.* the condition of being a woman ‖ women in general

wom·an·kind *n.* women in general

womb *n.* the mammalian uterus ‖ a place of origin and early development

women's rights the position of political and economic legal equality with men claimed for women

won·der *n.* (without article) a state of astonished admiration ‖ a fact or circumstance causing surprise ‖ *pl.* wonderfully good things ‖ a person whose skill or efficiency compels great admiration

wonder *v.i.* to feel wonder ‖ to ask oneself questions ‖ *v.i.* to feel curiosity about ‖ to be in a state of perplexity about

won·der·ful *adj.* arousing wonder ‖ unusually good

won·drous *adj.* wonderful

wont 1. *adj.* accustomed **2.** *n.* custom, habit

won't *contr.* of WILL NOT

woo *v.t.* to court ‖ to be assiduously attentive in seeking to win (something or someone)

wood 1. *n.* the hard fibrous substance comprising the largest part of the stems and branches of trees and shrubs ‖ (also *pl.*) a collection of growing trees ‖ firewood **out of the woods** out of danger or difficulty **2.** *adj.* made of wood

wood·craft *n.* skill in maintaining oneself in woods and forests

wood·cut *n.* a design cut on wood ‖ a print from such a block

wood·en *adj.* made of wood ‖ as if made of wood, lifeless, expressionless ‖ stiff, clumsy

wood·land 1. *n.* land largely given over to woods **2.** *adj.* living or growing in woodland

wood·peck·er *n.* an almost universally distributed chisel-billed, wood-boring bird

wood·pile *n.* a pile of wood, esp. firewood

wood·wind *n.* the section of the orchestra comprising instruments made of wood

wood·work *n.* objects made of wood, esp. parts of a building or interior fittings made of wood

wood·y wood·i·er wood·i·est *adj.* abounding in woods ‖ consisting of or like wood

wool *n.* the fibrous, usually crisped, growth on the skin of certain animals, esp. the sheep

wool·en 1. *adj.* made of wool **2.** *n.* a fabric made of wool ‖ *pl.* woolen goods

wool·gath·er·ing 1. *n.* the pursuit of stray thoughts when one should be concentrating **2.** *adj.* indulging in such stray thoughts

wool·ly, wool·y 1. wool·li·er, wool·i·er wool·li·est, wool·i·est *adj.* of or like wool ‖ lacking clearness of definition ‖ not thinking clearly **2.** *pl.* **wool·lies, wool·ies** *n.* a woolen undergarment

wooz·y wooz·i·er wooz·i·est *adj.* confused or muddled as the result of a blow, too much alcohol etc. ‖ physically weak

word 1. *n.* a speech sound or combination of sounds ‖ the written or printed symbol of one of these basic units of language ‖ *pl.* things said ‖ *pl.* the text (as distinct from the music) of a song, opera etc. **the last word** the final decision ‖ the last thing said, esp. in a dispute ‖ the most up-to-date model, example etc. **to take someone at his word** to believe that someone means what he says **2.** *v.t.* to phrase, put into words

word·i·ly *adv.* in a wordy way

word·i·ness *n.* the quality of being wordy

word·ing *n.* a putting into words ‖ the words used

word·less *adj.* not expressed or capable of being expressed in words

word·y word·i·er word·i·est *adj.* using many or too many words ‖ using words

work *n.* physical or mental activity undertaken to achieve a purpose and involving the expenditure of effort ‖ what one can achieve by such effort in a specified amount of time ‖ *pl.* the output of a writer, artist, composer etc. ‖ literary, artistic or musical output of a specified kind ‖ what one does n order to earn money ‖ a large engineering structure, e.g. a bridge ‖ *pl.* a factory or industrial plant ‖ *pl.* good deeds (as contrasted with faith) ‖ an example of the use of some skill or faculty

work work·ing worked *v.i.* to engage in activity requiring considerable effort ‖ to earn one's living ‖ to be effective, have the desired or intended effect ‖ (of yeast or a liquid) to ferment ‖ to progress with difficulty ‖ to apply oneself with effort ‖ (with 'on') to use persuasion ‖ (with 'out') to come to a satisfactory conclusion ‖ *v.t.* to bring aobut by labor ‖ to make (one's way) or cause (oneself) to advance by slow stages and with effort ‖ (with 'into') to excite or sitmulate the emotions of ‖ (with 'off') to repay (a debt) over a period ‖ (with 'in') to mix or blend, esp. by stirring ‖ (with 'off') to find an outlet for (rage, excess energy etc.) ‖ (with 'out') to find a solution or solve (a problem) **to work one's fingers to the bond** to exhaust oneself

work·a·ble *adj.* that will work, practicable

work·a·day *adj.* dull and commonplace

work·book *n.* a pupil's exercise book with printed problems etc. and space for answers ‖ a book of instructions for procedure and operation

worked up agitated, emotionally upset or tense

work·er *n.* an employee

work·ing *adj.* engaging in manual labor ‖ accurate enough to work by ‖ capable of being operated

working class the social and economic class of people who work for wages, esp. the industrial workers

work·man *pl.* **work·men** *n.* a working man ‖ a skilled laborer or craftsman

work·man·like adj. befitting a skilled workman **work·man·ship** n. the skill shown in a finished craft product

work·out n. a training session for a boxer, athlete etc.

work·shop n. a room in which work on a small scale is carried out ‖ an intensive seminar in some subject or study

world 1. n. the planet earth ‖ the universe ‖ human society ‖ any domain of existance, activity etc. **for the world** for any consideration whatever **out of this world** superb **to bring into this world** to give birth to

world·li·ness n. the quality of being worldly

world·ly world·li·er world·li·est adj. pertaining to the material world ‖ devoted to this life and its practical concerns rather than to spiritual concerns

world·wide adj. extending to all parts of the world

worm 1. n. any of various elongated creeping animals with soft, often segmented bodies ‖ any of certain larvae resembling these ‖ a mean, groveling or contemptible person 2. v.t. to work in a winding or insidious manner ‖ to elicit (information etc.) by devious ways ‖ v.i. to move like a worm ‖ to look for worms for bait

worm-eat·en adj. eaten into by worms, full of wormholes

worm part part. OF WEAR

worn-out adj. made useless by wear ‖ exhausted

wor·ri·some adj. causing worry ‖ easily worried

wor·ry 1. **wor·ry·ing wor·ried** v.t. to cause to feel disturbed or depressed, esp. through fear regarding some event, outcome etc. ‖ to give petty annoyance to ‖ v.i. to feel a nagging fear about something 2. pl. **wor·ries** n. a worrying ‖ something that causes worry

worse 1. adj. bad in greater degree ‖ in a less good state of health etc. 2. adv. more badly 3. n. something worse **wors·en** v.t. to make worse ‖ v.i. to become worse

wor·ship 1. n. reverence, homage or honor paid to God ‖ an utterly devoted admiration for a person 2. **wor·ship·ing wor·shiped** v.t. to pay religious devotion to ‖ to idolize, adore ‖ v.i. to be full of adoration ‖ to take part in religious ceremonies **wor·ship·er** n. someone who worships **wor·ship·ful** adj. adoring

worst 1. adj. most bad 2. adv. most badly 3. n. that which is worst **at worst** even on the least favorable reckoning **if worst comes to worst** if the worst happens 4. v.t. to defeat

wor·sted 1. n. fabric made from finely twisted wool yarn 2. adj. made of worsted fabric

worth 1. n. the amount of money etc. to which something is regarded as being equivalent, i.e. its monetary or material value ‖ the degree of excellence, importance etc. of someone or something ‖ a person's material wealth 2. prep. of the material worth of ‖ deserving **for what it is worth** without any guarantee as to accuracy, truthfulness etc.

wor·thi·ly adv. in a worthy way

wor·thi·ness n. the quality of being worthy

worth·less adj. of no worth

worth·while adj. meriting the time, effort etc. involved

wor·thy wor·thi·er wor·thi·est adj. having worth ‖ deserving ‖ (often with 'of') of a worth regarded as adequate

would past of WILL ‖ ausiliary v. used to express condition ‖ used to express the future in indirect speech ‖ used to express a wish

owuld-be adj. contr. of WOULD NOT

wound n. an injury to living tissues ‖ an injury to the feelings

wound v.i. to inflict a wound ‖ to hurt someone's feelings

wrack n. (esp. in phrase) **wrack and ruin** disaster, destruction

wraith n. an apparition ‖ a specter

wran·gled 1. **wran·gling wran·gled** v.i. to quarrel noisily ‖ to argue ‖ v.t. to herd or round up (horses or cattle) 2. n. a noisy quarrel **wrán·gler** *n.* someone who wrangles

wrap 1. wrap·ping wrapped *v.t.* (often with 'up') to cover ‖ to make a parcel of ‖ *v.i.* (with 'around' etc.) to twine ‖ (ith 'up') to put on extra clothes against the cold **wrapped up in** engrossed in **2.** *n.* something used to wrap oneself in **wráp·per** *n.* a book jacket ‖ anything that wraps ‖ a dressing gown **wráp·ping** *n.* anything with which something is wrapped

wrath *n.* intense anger or indignation

wreak *v.t.* to give full play to (one's anger etc.) ‖ to inflict (vengeance, harm etc.)

wreath *pl.* **wreaths** *n.* a circular band of flowers, leaves etc.

wreck 1. *n.* the ruins of a wrecked ship ‖ what is left of a building, vehicle etc., after destruction ‖ a person wasted by mental or physical sickness **2.** *v.t.* to cause the wreck of, destroy, ruin ‖ *v.i.* to suffer wreck **wréck·age** *n.* a person who wrecks ‖ soemone whose business is demolishing buildings

wren any of many small singing birds

wrench 1. *v.t.* to injure or hurt by twisting violently ‖ *v.i.* to twist or turn violently **2.** *n.* a violent twist ‖ an emotional pain ‖ a tool with adjustable jaws for gripping and turning nuts or bolts etc.

wrest to pull or force with a violent twist ‖ to arrive at (a meaning or interpretation) by distortion

wres·tle 1. wres·tling wres·tled *v.i.* to struggle with an opponent by grappling and trying to throw or trip him ‖ to struggle ‖ *v.t.* to throw (esp. a calf) for branding **2.** *n.* a wrestling bout ‖ a hard struggle **wrés·tler** *n.* **wrés·tling** *n.* a sport

wretch *n.* a person in great misfortune **wretch·ed** *adj.* miserably sad ‖ of exceedingly poor quality ‖ contemptible

wrig·gle 1. wrig·gling wrig·gled *v.i.* to twist and turn with short abrupt movements like those of a worm ‖ to act in an evasive, shifty way **2.** *n.* a wriggling movement

wring 1. wring·ing wrung *v.t.* to force out (water etc.) by squeezing and twisting ‖ to twist forcibly ‖ to extort by mental or bodily coercion ‖ to pain, distress **2.** *n.* a squeezing or twisting **wring·er** *n.* a machine for pressing water out of clothes **ring·ing** *adj.*

wrin·kle 1. *n.* a small furrow or ridge ‖ a novel technique **2. wrin·kling wrin·kled** *v.i.* to produce wrinkles in ‖ *v.i.* to acquire wrinkles

wrist *n.* the joint between the hand and the arm

wrist·watch *n.* a small watch worn around the wrist

writ *n.* a written command issued in the name of a sovereign, state, court of law etc.

write writ·ing wrote writ·ten *v.i.* to form letters, figures or symbols on paper ‖ to compose books or other literary matter ‖ to write a letter (personal communication) ‖ *v.t.* to set down (language, information etc.) in letters, words or symbols ‖ to compose as an author ‖ to communicate or state in writing or in print ‖ to undersrite ‖ to draw up in legal form **writ·er** *n.* a professional author of books

write-up *n.* an article in the press, esp. a favorable critical notice

writhe 1. writh·ing writhed *v.i.* to contort (one's body), esp. in pain or embarassment **2.** *n.* a writhing

writ·ing *n.* the act of someone who writes ‖ handwriting ‖ anything written, e.g. a literary compositon, book, article, inscription etc.

wrong 1. *adj.* not morally right ‖ not correct or accurate, false ‖ mistaken ‖ not suitable or proper ‖ amiss, out of order ‖ that which is morally wrong ‖ an act of injustice ‖ an invading of the rights of someone **in the wrong** mistaken ‖ morally responsible for an offense **to put (someone) in the wrong** to make (someone) appear to be the offender, affix blame to (someone) **3.** *adv.* incorrectly **4.** *v.t.* to treat unfairly or judge unjustly

wroth *adj*. angry, wrathful

wrought *adj*. worked, made, formed, fashioned ‖ (of metals) hammered and beated into shape

wrought iron *adj*. a very pure form of

commerical iron

wrought-up *adj*. nervously exited, agitated

wry wri·er wri·est *adj*. (of the neck or features) distorted ‖ bitter or ironic

X

X,x the 24th letter of the English alphabet

xan·thous *adj*. colored yellow

xen·o·pho·bi·a *n*. far or dislike of strangers or foreigners

Xmas *n*. Christmas

X ray an electromagnetic radiation ‖ a photograph made by exposure to X rays

X-ray 1. *v.t.* to examine or treat with X

rays **2.** *adj*. of or pertaining to X rays

xy·lem *n*. a complex lignified plant tissue

xy·lo·phone *n*. a percussion instrument consisting of a series of horizontal wooden bars and tuned in a chromatic scale **xy·loph·on·ist** *n*. a person who plays the xylophone

Y

Y, y the 25th letter of the English alphabet

yacht 1. *n.* any of various light, fast sailing or power-driven vessels used for pleasure cruises, racing etc. 2. *v.i.* to race or cruise in a yacht **yácht·ing** *n.* the sport of racing or cruising in a yacht

yachts·man *pl.* **yachts·men** *n.* someone who sails a yacht

yak *n.* a large, long-haired ox, domesticated in Tibet and the foothills of the Himalayas

yam *n.* the sweet potato

yank 1. *v.t.* and *v.i.* to jerk 2. *n.* a sharp pull

Yan·kee 1. *n.* an inhabitant of New England ‖ a native of any of the northern states of the U.S.A. ‖ a Union soldier in the American Civil War ‖ a citizen of the U.S.A. 2. *adj.* pertaining to Yankees

yap 1. *v.i.* **yap·ping yapped** to bark snappishly ‖ *(pl.)* to chatter 2. *n.* a sharp, shrill bark

yard *n.* *(abbr.* yd) a unit of length equal to 3 ft

yard·age *n.* length measured in yards

yard goods piece goods

yard·stick *n.* a measuring stick a yard long ‖ criterion

yarn 1. *n.* any spun thread (wool, flax, silk, cotton etc.) ‖ a long, often exaggerated tale of adventure ‖ to make up a rambling excuse 2. *v.i.* to tell a yarn

yaw 1. *v.i.* (of a ship or aircraft) to go off course 2. *n.* a temporary deviation ‖ a wobble in flight

yawl *n.* a ship's jolly boat with four or six oars ‖ a two-masted, fore-and-aft-rigged sailboat ‖ a fishing boat

yawn 1. *v.i.* to breathe in deeply, letting the mouth open wide, through sleepiness, weariness or boredom 2. *n.* the act of yawning ‖ a bore

yea 1. *adv.* yes ‖ indeed ‖ moreover 2. *n.* someone who votes in the affirmative

year *n.* the time taken by the earth to complete one orbit around the sun, 365.2425 days ‖ a period of 12 lunar months ‖ a period of 365 days (366 in a leap year) ‖ the period necessary for a planet to make one orbit around the

sun ‖ a solar year ‖ a lunar year **all year round** at all times during the year

year·ly 1. *adj.* occurring every year or once a year 2. *adv.* every year or once a year

yearn *v.i.* to be filled with longing **yéarn·ing** *n.* deep longing

yeast *n.* a substance used esp. in brewing and in bread making ‖ any of various fungi that produce alcohol and carbon dioxide from sugar **yéast·y** *adj.* containing yeast ‖ exuberant ‖ foamy ‖ frivolous, trivial

yell 1. *v.i.* to utter a loud, inarticulate cry or shout ‖ *v.t.* to utter or express with such a cry or shout 2. *n.* an instance of yelling

yel·low 1. *adj.* of the color between orange and green, the color of e.g. ripe lemons ‖ (of the Mongolian race etc.) having a skin somewhat of this color ‖ cowardly 2. *n.* a yellow color, pigment, fabric etc. ‖ the yolk of an egg ‖ *(pl.)* jaundice 3. *v.t.* to make yellow ‖ *v.i.* to become yellow

yellow jacket any of several varieties of bright yellow social wasps

yelp 1. *v.i.* (esp. of a dog) to make a sharp, high-pitched cry ‖ *v.t.* to utter with such a cry 2. *n.* such a cry

yen *n.* a persistent desire

yen *n.* the principal monetary unit of Japan

yeo·man *pl.* **yeo·men** *n.* a farmer who owns the freehold of his land ‖ *(U.S. Navy)* a petty officer who does clerical work

yes 1. *adv.* used to express agreement, consent, affirmation 2. *pl.* **yes·es yes·ses** *n.* an act or instance of expressing agreement, consent or affirmation, esp. by saying 'yes' ‖ an affirmative reply or vote

ye·shi·va *n.* a school for Talmudic study ‖ a Jewish day school which offers both secular and religious education

yes-man *pl.* **yes-men** *n.* a subordinate who always agrees with his superior

yes·ter·day 1. *n.* the day which preceded today ‖ recent time 2. *adv.* during a

yet 1. *adv.* up to and including the present ‖ at some future time ‖ before a specified time ‖ still at present ‖ even **2.** *conj.* nevertheless

yew *n.* any of several evergreen, coniferous shrubs or trees of the north temperate zone

yield 1. *v.t.* to have as a product or result ‖ to bring in as profit, interest, income etc. ‖ to surrender, give up ‖ to relinquish ‖ *v.i.* to be fruitful or profitable ‖ to admit defeat ‖ to give way to pressure, argument etc. **2.** *n.* a yielding ‖ the amount yielded **yield·ing** *adj.* giving in ‖ flexible, not rigid

Yip·pie *n.* a politically active radical group of hippies, from a member of the Youth International Party

yo·del 1. yo·del·ing yo·deled *v.i.* and *t.* to call or sing with repeated transitions to the falsetto **2.** *n.* a yodeled call **yó·del·er** *n.*

yo·ga *n.* a system of discipline and meditation widely practiced within Hinduism

yo·gi *n.* someone who practices yoga

yo·gurt yo·ghurt yo·ghourt *n.* a milk product prepared by partial evaporation and then fermentation

yoke 1. *n.* a wooden frame fitted across the necks of two draft animals, for joining them together as they pull a plow or vehicle ‖ a wooden bar shaped so that it rests across a person's shoulders for carrying balanced loads suspended at each end ‖ a shaped part of a garment at the shoulders or hips ‖ a bond, esp. of marriage **2.** *v.t.* **yok·ing yoked** to put under a yoke, join by a yoke ‖ to attach (e.g. an ox) to a cart etc. ‖ to unite

yo·kel *n.* a country bumpkin

yolk *n.* the yellow central part of the egg

Yom Kip·pur *n.* the annual day of fasting and repentance observed by Jews

yon·der 1. *adj.* at a distance but visible **2.** *adv.* at a somewhat distant yet visible place

yore *n.* (only in the archaic phrase) **of yore** long ago

you *pron.* 2nd person sing. and *pl. nominative* and *objective cases* the person or persons to whom one is speaking ‖ (in generalizing) a person, one

you'd *contr.* of YOU HAD, YOU WOULD

you'll *contr.* of YOU WILL, YOU SHALL

young 1. *adj.* in the early stages of development ‖ not far advanced ‖ having the vigor, resilience etc. associated with those who are young **2.** *n.* offspring **with young** (of an animal) pregnant

young·ster *n.* a child or adolescent

your *pass. pronominal adj.* of or belonging to you

yours *possessive pron.* that or those belonging to you

your·self *pl.* **your·selves** *pron.* refl. form of YOU ‖ emphatic form of YOU

youth *pl.* **youths** *n.* the period from childhood to maturity ‖ a young man ‖ young people of both sexes

youth·ful *adj.* pertaining to youth ‖ young

yowl 1. *v.i.* (esp. of an animal) to utter a long, loud, sad cry **2.** *n.* this cry

yo·yo *pl.* **yo·yos yo·yoes** *n.* a toy consisting of a double wooden disk, deeply grooved, which can be made to rise and fall on a string attached to its center and running in the groove ‖ a foolish person

yuc·ca *n.* a genus of American plants with thin, rigid, lance-shaped leaves ‖ the flower of any of these plants

yule *n.* the festival or season of Christmas

yule·tide *n.* the Christmas season

Z, z the last letter of the English alphabet

zap 1. *n.* a sudden hit **2.** *v.* to destroy suddenly

zeal *n.* persistent fervent devotion to a cause

zeal·ot *n.* someone who acts for a cause with excessive zeal **zéal·ot·ry** *n.* behavior etc. characteristic of a zealot

zeal·ous *adj.* full of zeal, showing zeal

ze·bra *n.* any of several swift-running equine mammals, covered with alternating black and white stripes

Zen *n.* a school of Mahayana Buddhism traditionally founded in China and widespread in Japan since the 12th c.

ze·nith *n.* the point in the sky vertically above the observer ‖ the highest point **zé·nith·al** *adj.* of, at or relating to the zenith

zeph·yr *n.* a gentle breeze ‖ any lightweight fabric or yarn, or an article of clothing made from this

Zep·pe·lin *n.* a rigid, cigar-shaped dirigible airship

ze·ro *n. pl.* **ze·ros ze·roes** the numerical symbol 0 denoting absence of value ‖ the beginning of a numerical scale (of distance, time, temperature etc.) ‖ the lowest point ‖ a nonentity **to zero in on** to adjust fire on (a target) ‖ to move in close to ‖ to concentrate on **1.** *adj.* having the value of zero

zero hour the time at which a military operation (or other project) is planned to begin

zest *n.* a piquant, enhancing quality ‖ enthusiastic enjoyment **zést·ful** *adj.*

zig·zag 1. *adj.* turning sharply left and right alternately as its course proceeds **2.** *n.* one of a series of sudden turns in a road, course etc. ‖ such a road or course ‖ a design etc. having a zigzag form **3.** *adv.* in a zigzag path **4.** **zig·zag·ging zig·zagged** *v.i.* to be or take a zigzag course ‖ *v.t.* to make (one's way or its way) in a zigzag course

zilch *n.* emphatically nothing — **zilch** *adj.*

zinc 1. *n.* a metallic element, hard and resisting corrosion **2.** *v.t.* **zinc·ing zinck·ing zinced zincked** to coat with zinc

zing 1. *n.* zest, energy ‖ a high-pitched humming noise **2.** *v.i.* to make a high-pitched humming noise

zin·ni·a *n.* a genus of half hardy annual plants, native to Mexico but widely cultivated

zip 1. *n.* a short, sharp sound like that made by a bullet traveling through the air ‖ vigor, snap **2.** **zip·ping zipped** *v.i.* to go with the sound of a bullet flying through the air ‖ to go very fast ‖ to be opened and closed with a zipper ‖ *v.t.* to fasten or unfasten with a zipper

ZIP code U.S. postal-delivery zone number code of five digits used in the addressing of mail [Zone Improvement Program] — **zip-code** *v.*

zip·per 1. *n.* a strip of interlocking metal or plastic teeth on tapes, used to fasten openings in garments, bags etc. **2.** *v.t.* and *i.* to fasten by means of a zipper

zip·py zip·pi·er zip·pi·est *adj.* full of vigor

zith·er *n.* a musical instrument consisting of 30 to 40 strings stretched over a flat sounding board, the strings being plucked with the fingers or with a plectrum

zo·di·ac *n.* an imaginary band on the celestial sphere which is divided into 12 equal parts, each named after a constellation ‖ a figure showing the 12 parts with their symbols and emblems

zo·di·a·cal *adj.* pertaining to or within the zodiac

zom·bi zom·bie *n.* a corpse revived by magic ‖ someone who looks macabre or who behaves as though half-dead **zóm·bi·ism** *n.*

zon·al *adj.* of, resembling, constituting or consisting of a zone or zones

zone 1. *n.* the area of the surface of a sphere bounded by two parallel planes which intersect the sphere ‖ one of the five climatic zones of the earth's surface ‖ a region of characteristic fauna or flora ‖ an area or region of the body ‖ an area within which a characteristic activity is carried on ‖ an area within which one rate of postage is charged or a city district having its individual number (postal delivery zone) **2.** *v.t.* **zon·ing zoned** to mark off into zones ‖ (residential, industrial etc.)

zoo *n.* a place where live animals are kept in captivity for the public to see

zo·o·log·i·cal *adj.* of or relating to zoology

zo·ol·o·gist *n.* a specialist in zoology

zo·ol·o·gy *n.* the branch of biology concerned with animal life

zoom 1. *v.i.* to climb at a steep angle ‖ to make a loud humming or buzzing noise ‖ (of a motion picture or television image) to seem to approach or recede from the viewer rapidly ‖ *v.t.* to cause (an aircraft) to climb at a steep angle **2.** *n.* a steep climb by a plane ‖ a loud, low hum or buzz ‖ a process by which a television or motion picture image is made to become quickly larger or smaller

zuc·chi·ni *pl.* **zuc·chi·ni zuc·chi·nis** *n.* a variety of summer squash with a dark green skin

zwie·back *n.* a rusk of toasted sweetened bread

zy·gote *n.* a cell formed by the union of two gametes, e.g. the fertilized ovum **zy·got·ic** *adj.*

NOTES